THE NEW
SOFTWARE
ENGINEERING

SUE A. CONGER

COURSE
TECHNOLOGY

ONE MAIN STREET, CAMBRIDGE, MA 02142

an International Thomson Publishing company I(T)P®

Cambridge • Albany • Bonn • Boston • Cincinnati • London • Madrid • Melbourne • Mexico City
New York • Paris • San Francisco • Singapore • Tokyo • Toronto • Washington

For Dave and Katie

MIS Editor: *Kathy Shields*
Editorial Assistant: *Tamara Huggins*
Production: *Greg Hubit Bookworks*
Designer: *John Edeen*
Print Buyer: *Barbara Britton*
Copy Editor: *Martha Ghent*
Cover: *Image House*
Compositor: *Alphatype*
Printer: *The Maple-Vail Book Manufacturing Group*

© 1994 by Course Technology – I⒯P®

I⒯P® The ITP logo is a trademark under license.

For more information contact:

Course Technology, Inc.
One Main Street
Cambridge, MA 02142

International Thomson Publishing Europe
Berkshire House 168-173
High Holborn
London WCIV 7AA
England

Thomas Nelson Australia
102 Dodds Street
South Melbourne, 3205
Victoria, Australia

Nelson Canada
1120 Birchmount Road
Scarborough, Ontario
Canada M1K 5G4

International Thomson Editores
Campos Eliseos 385, Piso 7
Col. Polanco
11560 Mexico D.F. Mexico

International Thomson Publishing GmbH
Kônigswinterer Strasse 418
53227 Bonn
Germany

International Thomson Publishing Asia
211 Henderson Road
#05-10 Henderson Building
Singapore 0315

International Thomson Publishing Japan
Hirakawacho Kyowa Building, 3F
2-2-1 Hirakawacho
Chiyoda-ku, Tokyo 102
Japan

10 9 8 7 6 5 4

ISBN 0-534-17143-5

Printed in the United States of America

THE NEW
SOFTWARE
ENGINEERING

CONTENTS

PART II
PROJECT INITIATION   111

PART III
ANALYSIS AND DESIGN   199

CHAPTER 7
PROCESS-ORIENTED
ANALYSIS   227

CHAPTER 9
DATA-ORIENTED ANALYSIS   328

CHAPTER 8
PROCESS-ORIENTED DESIGN   279

CHAPTER 10
DATA-ORIENTED DESIGN   391

PART IV
IMPLEMENTATION AND MAINTENANCE   637

PREFACE

As we move toward the 21st century, the techniques, tools, technologies, and subject matter of applications development are changing radically. Globalization of the work place is impacting IS development as well, by pressuring organizations to strive for competitive advantage through automation, among other methods. Strategic IS, reusable designs, downsizing, right-sizing, multimedia databases, and reusable code are all discussed in the same breath. Methodologies are being successfully coupled to computer-aided software engineering environments (CASE); yet object-oriented methodologies, which are being touted as the panacea for all problems, have not yet been fully automated . . . or even fully articulated. Few if any tools, methods or techniques address the needs of artificial intelligence and expert system development, which are currently driven by the program language being used for development. New technologies for true distribution of processing are maturing, and integration across hardware and software platforms is the major IS concern in multiple industries [*Computerworld*, 10/15/90].

IS professionals must be jacks-of-all-trades as never before, but there is also increased demand for domain experts who are intimately familiar with all aspects of a particular business area, such as money transfer in banking. It is difficult for any one person to be both expert and generalist. But there are many systems developers—I call them software engineers—who do possess these attributes. Today's ideal software engineer is familiar with the alternatives, trade-offs and pitfalls of methodologies (notice the plural form), technologies, domains, project life cycles, techniques, tools, CASE environments, hardware, operating systems, databases, data architectures, methods for user involvement in application development, software, design trade-offs for the problem domain, and project personnel skills. Few professionals acquire all these skills without years of experience including both continuing education and

variations in project assignments, company type, and problem type. This book attempts to discuss much of what should be the ideal software engineer's project-related knowledge and theoretical background in order to facilitate and speed the process by which novices become experts.

The goal of this book, then, is to discuss project planning, project life cycles, methodologies, technologies, techniques, tools, languages, testing, ancillary technologies (e.g., database), and computer-aided software engineering (CASE). For each topic, alternatives, benefits and disadvantages are discussed.

For methodologies, one major problem is that most writing on methods of development concentrates on *what* the analyst does. It is up to the individual instructor and/or student to develop the *how* knowledge. Yet, the what knowledge is easy and takes very little time to learn. If I say, "The first step in object-oriented methodology is to make a list of objects," that sounds like a simple step. I may understand *what* I'm to do, but not *how* to do it. This book is intended to shed some light on the *how* information. One technique used to facilitate the learning process is to develop the same case problem in each methodology, highlighting the similarities, differences, conceptual activities, decision processes, and physical representations. Another technique is to provide cases in the appendix that can be used throughout the text for many assignments, thus allowing the student to develop a detailed-problem understanding and an understanding of how the problem is expressed in different methodologies and using different techniques.

A related problem in software engineering texts is that little information is available on current research and future directions. Information systems development is a 30-year old activity that is beginning to show some signs of maturity, but is also constantly changing because the type of systems we automate is constantly changing. Research in every area of software development, from enterprise analysis through reengineering 20-year-old systems, is taking place at an unprecedented rate. Moreover, the landscape of system development will change radically in the next 20 years based on the research taking place today. This text attempts to highlight and synthesize current research to identify future directions.

Many software engineering texts never discuss problems attendant with methodologies. This text attempts to discuss methodologies in the context of their development and how they have evolved to keep pace with new knowledge about system development. Both useful and not-so-useful representation techniques will be identified. The book may be controversial in this regard, but at least the knowledge that there *are* problems with methods should remove some of the prevailing attitudes that there are right and wrong ways to complete everything. Unfortunately, *no* methodology is complete enough to guarantee the same results from two different analysts working independently, so interpretations differ. I try to identify my interpretations and generalizations throughout the text.

The book is case-oriented in several ways. First, a sample project is described, designed, and implemented using each of the techniques discussed. Second, cases for in-class development are provided. Third, cases for homework assignments are also provided. Research on learning has revealed that we learn best through practice, analysis of examples, and more practice. For each topic, an example of both acceptable and unacceptable deliverables is provided, with discussion of the relative merits and demerits of each. Through repeated use of different cases, students will learn both the IS topics and something about problem domains that will carry over into their professional lives.

Finally, this text has a bias toward planning, analysis, and design activities even though the entire life cycle is discussed. This bias is partly due to practical and space limitations; however, it is also because of the realities of changing software engineering work. CASE promises to remove much of the programming from business application development by automating the code generation process. Although languages are discussed, the discussion focuses on how *to choose* the correct language for an application based on language characteristics, rather than on how *to program* in the language.

The audience for this text includes business, computer information systems, and computer science students. The courses for which this text is appropriate include software engineering, advanced system analysis, advanced topics in information systems, and IS project development. Computer software engineering is moving away from a concentration on developing the perfect program to a realization that even perfect programs never work in isolation. Program *connections* are significantly more important than individual program code. Thus, even computer scientists are recognizing a need for methodologies, techniques for system representation, and language selection.

The text was originally planned to accommodate either quarter or semester classes. I have taught this material in both. While the written material is longer than anticipated, I believe the book can be covered in one quarter because there are usually more contact hours with students. One of my goals was a book that did not require much additional outside material to supplement the text; I hope this goal was met. Much of the bulk is explaining the *how* processes in Chapters 7–12, and these should be covered in class to discuss alternatives, possible flaws in my thinking, and so on. If programming is also included in the course, I suggest development of a two-quarter (or semester) sequence that includes software engineering through system design in the first course and the remaining subjects in the second course.

Every school seems to offer courses on "Advanced Topics in Systems Development" or Advanced Systems Analysis" or "IS Development Project" that frequently use no book because nothing covers all the desired topics. This book attempts to provide for these courses. Advanced systems analysis and development courses all tend to concentrate on alternatives during the design process from which decisions must be made. The typical systems analysis course might discuss one technique for each major topic area: enterprise modeling, data modeling, process modeling, program design. That alternatives are available is certainly mentioned, but there is simply not enough time to teach all topics, nor are students able to assimilate much information about alternatives without becoming hopelessly confused. Advanced courses try to broaden the knowledge base of students with discussions of alternatives in each area. Even in these courses, without a hands-on orientation and concrete examples to use for reference, the number of topics and alternatives is necessarily limited. The use of a single case throughout the text, together with cases for home/school work practice, should broaden the number of topic areas that can be covered adequately in a one-semester course.

ACKNOWLEDGMENTS

No textbook is published without the involvement of many people and I would like to acknowledge those who have helped bring this book to fruition. I am grateful, first, to my husband Dave and my daughter Katie, who have put up with haphazard meals and an absent-minded wife and mother for a long time. Baby-sitters were especially important when I commuted four hours a day. I thank Elaine Black, Lis Nielsen, Sarah Cropley, Louise Shipman, Jacquie Draycott, Ellen Crawford, and Angela Moore.

Also, I wish especially to thank Peter Keen for his unfailingly good advice and uplifting moral support. I have never before worked with someone so free with great ideas. Frank Ruggirello, who actually got me moving and enlisted the supportive and helpful reviewers, played a special part in the project. I want to thank the reviewers, who put up with my typos and grammar long enough to read about the ideas I am attempting to convey. Their comments have materially enhanced the final quality of this book. These reviewers include: Donald R. Chand, Bentley College; Dale D. Gust, Central Michigan University; Lavette Teague, California State Polytechnic University–Pomona; Jon A. Turner, New York University; Douglas Vogel, University of Arizona; Connie E. Wells, Georgia State University; J. Christopher Westland, University of Southern California; and Susan J. Wilkins, California Polytechnic University–Pomona. My thanks for the helpful and supportive comments.

Next, the Wadsworth "family" has been supportive throughout the work, including Kathy Shields, Rhonda Gray, Tamara Huggins, Peggy Mehan, Greg Hubit, and Janet Hansen. Martha Ghent, the copy editor, deserves special mention. Having never worked through the copy process before, I had no idea what was done. Martha was easy to work with and taught me how to improve both my writing and my punctuation.

Friends and colleagues, who have given me anecdotes, support, ideas, and comments, were invaluable. The friends who have materially contributed to this project include Peter Keen, Connie Wells, Judy Wynekoop, Irene Auerbach, Chung Pin Chuang, Karen Loch, Kuldeep Kumar, Scott Owen, Iris Vessey, Nancy Russo, Alex Heslin, Paul Haldeman, Marty Fraser, Eph McLean, Ross Gagliano, Jim Senn, Mike Palley, Dorothy Dologite, Ronnie Wilkes, Jong Kim, Seok Jung Yoon, Dennis Strouble, Mary Alexander, Ted Stohr, and the many student 'guinea pigs' (mine and others) from Georgia State University, Baruch College (CUNY), University of Texas–Arlington, University of Dallas, and New York University. Thank you all.

Finally, I would like to thank you, the reader, for buying this book and taking the trouble to read even a portion of it. If you should disagree with my reasoning or find errors or omissions that should be corrected, I would be grateful for suggestions and correspondence.

Sue Conger
Dallas, Texas

## CHAPTER 1

OVERVIEW OF SOFTWARE ENGINEERING

INTRODUCTION

Businesses around the world depend more and more on software in the very basics of their operations. U.S. firms alone have 100 billion lines of program code in use today. This code cost $2 *trillion* to create and costs $30 billion *a year* to maintain. The typical Fortune 1000 company maintains 35 million lines of code. Quality of software design and quality of business service are increasingly linked. We take for granted the everyday convenience we gain from reservation, telephone, automated teller, and credit card authorization applications. We can take these conveniences for granted until they 'crash' or have a 'bug.' Software engineers (SEs) developed those systems. The engineering skills they apply to developing applications go far beyond the writing of good programs. The skills SEs need are to deploy and manage the data, software, hardware, and communications business assets of a corporation. These computer-related assets now account for almost half of all U.S. business investment.

Software engineers are skilled professionals who can make a real difference to business profitability. The word *professional* is key here. Software development is notoriously difficult to manage; software projects are routinely over budget and behind schedule. Computer programmers are legendary for their lack of understanding of, or interest in, business. SEs who are professionals are more likely to manage and

deliver a quality project on time and within budget. One goal of this text is to challenge you to set high standards for personal excellence: to become a professional and to make a difference.

This chapter introduces you to the book and the topics to be covered in more detail in later chapters. The objectives of this chapter are to: (1) review what you might already know, (2) give you a vocabulary for discussing applications, and (3) introduce the topics of this text. Use this chapter to learn basic definitions and to begin building a mental picture of how different approaches to software engineering work. You will learn the details in later chapters.

Software engineering is the systematic development, operation, maintenance, and retirement of software. Software engineers (SEs) have a mental 'tool kit' of techniques to use in developing applications. As students of information systems, you know bits and pieces of the tool kit. This text will show you how to use the tools together, and will add to what you already know. For instance, you should already know data flow diagrams (DFDs). DFDs are one of many tools, including new diagrams such as process hierarchies, process dependencies, and object diagrams. No one tool is ideal or complete. The SE knows how to select the tools, understanding their strengths and weaknesses. Most of all, an SE is not limited to a single tool he or she tries to force-fit to all situations.

Software engineering is important because it gives you a foundation on which to develop a career as an information systems development professional. At the end of the course, you will understand a variety of approaches to analyzing, designing, programming, testing, and maintaining information systems in organizations. You will know the alternatives for developing applications, and you will know how and when to select from among them. You will be able to compare and contrast methodology differences and will know the major computer-aided software engineering (CASE) tools that support each methodology. Finally, you will have an appreciation of the roles of software engineers and how they work with project managers in application development.

In the next section, you will learn what it means to be a *software engineer*. Then, a framework for discussing applications will help you categorize characteristics, technologies, and types of *applications* in business organizations. The next several sections guide you through alternatives for overall management of the application development *process*. The last section briefly outlines the remaining chapters of the book. Along the way, major terms are highlighted in bold print and defined so you can begin to form a mental picture of the alternative approaches to software engineering work.

SOFTWARE ENGINEERING

This conversation might be overheard in a manager's office:

Consultant Manager: "All right, Mary, tomorrow you start work on the rental processing application we are developing for ABC's Video Company. Mary, you are the project manager. Are you ready?"

Mary: "Yes, our first job is to find out more about the application. Then, Sam and I will decide our approach to development and the documentation that is needed. ABC's manager, Vic, is willing to provide us with whatever we need. Then, we will complete a feasibility analysis and . . ."

Mary is describing the first steps used by a modern software engineer in the development of a computer-based application. **Software** is the sequences of instructions in one or more programming languages that comprise a computer application to automate some business function. **Engineering** is the use of tools and techniques in problem solving. Putting the two words together, **software engineering** is the systematic application of tools and techniques in the development of computer-based applications.

A **software engineer** is a person who applies a broad range of application development knowledge to the systematic development of application systems for organizations. Software engineers used to think of their job as conscientious development of well-structured computer programs. But, as the field evolved, systems analysis as a task appeared along with systems analysts, the people who perform that task. Now, there is a proliferation of techniques, tools, and technologies to develop applications. Software engineers' jobs have evolved to now include evaluation, selection, and use of specific systematic approaches to the development, operation, maintenance, and retirement of software. **Development** begins with the decision to develop a software product and ends when the product is delivered. **Operations** is the daily processing that takes place. **Maintenance** encompasses the changes made to the logic of the system and programs to fix errors, provide for business changes, or make the software more efficient. **Retirement** is the replacement of the current application with some other method of providing the work, usually a new application.

Fundamental skills of software engineers include

1. How to identify, evaluate, choose, and implement an appropriate methodology[1] and CASE tools
2. How and when to use prototyping
3. How and when to select hardware, software, and languages

---

1 Technically, the term *methodology* means 'the study of methods.' In information systems work, the term is colloquially accepted to mean a collection of tools and techniques used to represent an application's requirements. We use the Information Systems (IS) form of the term meaning 'collections of tools and techniques.' CASE software automates the use of the tools and techniques.

EXAMPLE 1-1

NEW YORK BANK

In 1970, NY Bank wanted to be first in the New York market with an automated teller machine (ATM) system. The bank contracted with a large computer vendor to build custom ATM software using the vendor's equipment. Because telecommunications technology was in its infancy at the time, and distributed processing did not exist when the system was installed in 1971, the two ATM locations used small, local computers to record transactions. The computers did not communicate with each other. Nor could they check customer balances to verify availability of funds for transactions.

Within one month of the opening of the ATMs, one customer had, in one 24-hour period, withdrawn $200,000 from the two machines. The customer's balance in his checking account was $50. One month, and one similar user later, NY Bank shut its ATM offices, canceled the contract with the vendor, and wrote off $30 million in development costs. Shortly after, NY Bank began another project to develop a "second-generation" ATM system in which balances were checked via communications with a centralized database application.

---

4. How to manage activities associated with configuration management, planning, and control of the development process
5. How to select computer languages and develop computer programs
6. How and which project testing techniques to apply
7. How to choose and use software maintenance techniques
8. How to evaluate and decide when to retire applications

The **goals of a software engineer** are to produce a high quality product and to enjoy a high quality development process. The *product* of a software engineering effort is a delivered, working computer system, some examples of which include:

- Accounts receivable processing
- Order processing
- Inventory monitoring and maintenance
- Decision support for overnight funds investment
- Collateralized mortgage obligation cost determination
- Insurance reimbursement processing
- Funds transfer processing
- Early warning system for problems with critical success factors

- Query processing for a customer information database

A quality **SE product** is

- on time
- within budget
- functional, i.e., does what it is supposed to do
- friendly to users
- error free
- flexible
- adaptable

In addition to a quality product, quality of process is desirable. The **software engineering process** describes the steps it takes to develop the system. We begin a development project with the notion that there is a problem to be solved via automation. The process is how you get from problem recognition to a working solution. A quality process is desirable because it is more likely to lead to a quality product. The process followed by a project team during the development life cycle of an application should be orderly, goal-oriented, enjoyable, and a learning experience.

That we try to apply engineering discipline to software development does not mean that we have all the answers about how to build applications. On

---

EXAMPLE 1-2

TUV INSURANCE COMPANY

In 1991, TUV Insurance Company began a restructuring project for an annuity premium processing application. The project team consisted of a manager who had been with the company 20 years and two analysts who were new hires in 1991. The two new people, Jacquie and Ted, both wanted to apply information engineering techniques to the work. They discussed the methodology with the project manager and clients who agreed to try a modified form of the new methodology.

During the first phase of development, an entity-relationship diagram was developed with accompanying data dictionary and process decomposition descriptions. The proj-

ect team and users were pleased with the results.

When the schedule for development was presented to the user, it was estimated that the entire project would take 18 months using information engineering. The client balked. He said, "The history of this company is that any project over one year never gets done. Therefore, I won't approve this. Just design me a file, like we have always done, and then add on the processing to create and maintain the file. When you revise the schedule to use this approach—file design and its processing—make sure it is under a year."

---

the contrary, we still build systems that are not useful and thus are not used. For example, New York Bank lost millions of dollars (see Example 1-1) because they used the wrong technology. Part of the reason for continuing problems in application development, like those of NY Bank, is that we are constantly trying to hit a moving target. Both the technology and the type of applications needed by businesses are constantly changing and becoming more complex. Our ability to develop and disseminate knowledge about how to successfully build systems for new technologies and new application types seriously lags behind technological and business changes. This book discusses where the field is now, and where it is likely to be in the 21st century. One thing is certain: The way we build systems in 10 years will be vastly different from the way we build systems today. The existing techniques that we expect to be using into the next century are discussed in this text. There will be other techniques yet to be developed, and you will have to learn to use them, too. One purpose of this text is to provide a foundation for learning to learn software engineering.

Another reason for continuing problems in application development is that we aren't always free to

apply the techniques we know work best. Why? you might ask. Organizations may *know* the right things to do, but it is hard to change habits and cultures from the *old way* of doing things, as well as get users to agree with a new sequence of events or an unfamiliar format for documentation. As Example 1-2 shows, compromise is possible. The example illustrates some problems with revolutionary change and how *revolution* can be pared down to *evolution* and made acceptable.

You might ask then, if many organizations don't use good software engineering practices, why should I bother learning them? There are two good answers to this question. First, if you never know the right thing to do, you have no chance of ever using it. Second, organizations will frequently accept evolutionary, small steps of change instead of revolutionary, massive change. You can learn individual techniques that can be applied without complete devotion to one way of developing systems. In this way, software engineers can speed change in their organizations by demonstrating how the tools and techniques enhance the quality of both the product and the process of building a system.

APPLICATIONS _____

Software engineering is the building of applications. An **application** is the set of programs[2] that automate some business task. Businesses are made up of functions such as marketing, accounting, manufacturing, and personnel. Each function can be divided into work processes for which it is responsible. For instance, marketing is responsible for sales, advertising, and new product development. Each process can be separated into its specific tasks. Sales, for instance, requires maintaining customer relations, order processing, and customer service. Applications could support each task individually. Conversely, one marketing application could perform all tasks, integrating the information they have in common.

All applications have some common and some unique features. One problem is that there is no agreed upon way to discuss these similarities and differences. In this book, we present three dimensions of applications to simplify and clarify this discussion. The dimensions of applications are characteristics, responsiveness, and type. **Characteristics** are common to all applications and include data, processes, constraints, and interfaces. The section on application characteristics is first and should be a review. **Responsiveness** defines the underlying time orientation of the application as batch, on-line, or real-time. By knowing the time orientation of an application, we can define minimal technology required to support the application. **Type** defines the business orientation of the application as transactional, query, decision, or intelligent.

Application Characteristics

This section is about shared characteristics of applications: data, processes, constraints, and interfaces (see Figure 1-1). All applications: (1) act on data and require data input, output, storage and retrieval; (2) imbed commands that transform data from one state to another state based on and constrained by

business rules; and (3) have some human interfaces and may have one or more computer interfaces. Application types vary in the extent to which these characteristics are known, defined, and understood. Each of the characteristics is discussed below. Since this is review, if you can define the terms in bold print, you might skip to the next section: Application Responsiveness.

Data

Data are the raw material (numbers and letters) that relate to each other to form fields (attributes), which define entities (see Figure 1-2). An entity is some definable class of people, concrete things, concepts, or events about which an application must maintain data. Examples of each entity type are customers, warehouses, departments, or orders, respectively. Data and entities can be described independently of their processing rules. Examples of data definition aids are entity relationship diagrams (see Figure 1-3) and third normal form linkage diagrams (see Figure 1-4).

Data requirements in applications include input, output, storage, and retrieval.

INPUT. Data **inputs** are data that are outside the computer and must be entered using some input device. Devices used for getting data into the computer include, for example, keyboard,[3] scanner, and transmission from another computer.

OUTPUT. **Output** is the opposite of input; that is, outputs are data generated to some media that is outside the computer. Common output devices include printers, video display screens, other computers, and microform equipment (e.g., microfiche, microfilm).

STORAGE AND RETRIEVAL. Data **storage** describes a physical, machine-readable data format for data, while data **retrieval** describes the means you use to access the data from its storage format. Storage and retrieval go together both conceptually and in software. Storage format and retrieval access

---

2 A program is composed of instructions that perform some well-defined task. Sometimes there are many tasks, composed of millions of instructions in an application. When there are many tasks, they are split into programs. This **decomposition** into subtasks which relate to programs is one topic in the chapters on application design.

---

3 Attached to video display or maybe some typewriter-like terminal, touch-tone phone, etc.

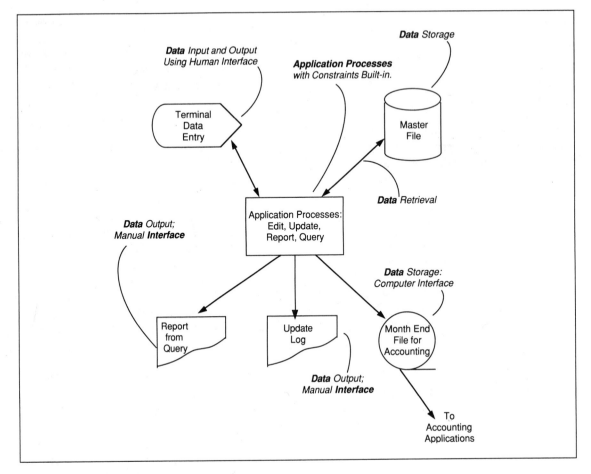

FIGURE 1-1   Application Characteristics

may be defined by your use of purchased software (such as a database management system's method, e.g., Oracle, DB2, or Adabas[4]), or may be defined by an access method provided by a hardware vendor (e.g., IBM's virtual sequential access method—VSAM).

Data storage require two types of data definition: logical and physical. The logical definition of data describes the way a user thinks about data, that is, the **logical data model**. These definitions might be

relational, hierarchic networked, or object-oriented. **Relational logical data models** are arranged in tables of rows and columns. **Hierarchic logical data models** define one-to-many relationships in a tree-shaped model that resembles an organization chart. **Network logical data models** define many-to-many relationships.

Object-oriented logical data models (OOLDMs) combine hierarchic and network logical models to form a lattice-structured hierarchy. OOLDMs are more specific in identifying classes and subclasses of objects in a hierarchy. **A class** is a set of data entities that share the defining characteristic. For instance, the class *customer* might have

4 Oracle is a trademark of the Oracle Corporation. DB2 is a trademark of the IBM Corporation. Adabas is a trademark of Software AG, Inc.

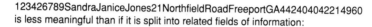

123426789SandraJaniceJones21NorthfieldRoadFreeportGA442404042214960
is less meaningful than if it is split into related fields of information:

ENTITY: Person

ATTRIBUTES: INSTANCE of Person

Social Security Number: 123-42-6789
                  Name: Sandra Janice Jones
          Address Line: 21 Northfield Road
                  City: Freeport
                 State: GA
              Zip Code: 44240
    (Area Code) Telephone: (404) 221-4960

FIGURE 1-2   Attribute-Entity Example

subclasses for *cash* and *credit* customers. The lattice network arrangement allows relationships to remain unconstrained by a data management software conceptualization.

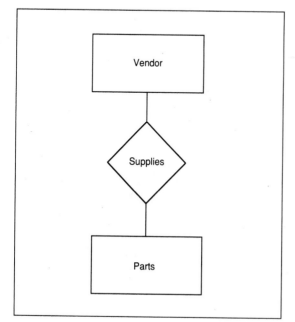

FIGURE 1-3   Entity-Relationship Example

Figures 1-5, 1-6, 1-7, and 1-8 show logical data structured in each of the four ways for vendor-parts information. Notice that the network and relational diagrams are somewhat similar. The relational model uses logical data connections to reflect relationships, while the network model uses physical address pointers imbedded in the data structure to maintain the relationships. For the hierarchic model, you must make a decision about which information is more important within the data context. If both vendors and parts are equally important, then complete redundancy with two hierarchies is required as shown in the diagram.

The physical definition of data, or **physical data model**, describes its layout for a particular hardware device. Physical layout is constrained by intended data use, access method, logical model, and storage device. External storage devices for data include magnetic disk, magnetic diskette, optical disk, compact disk, laser disk, digitally applied tape, and magnetic tape, to name a few. The major differences in devices are the number of times a device can be written to [e.g., as in write-once-read-many (WORM) technology], the cost, the amount of data that can be stored, the portability of devices, and the type of retrievals that can be done on data (e.g., magnetic tape requires front-to-back sequential processing versus direct accessibility to any data).

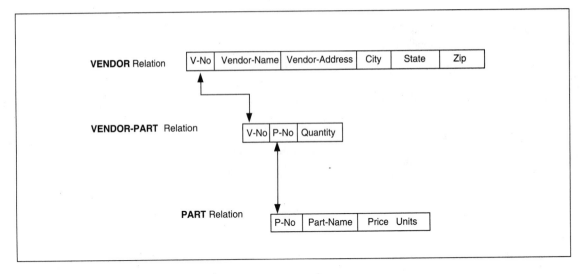

FIGURE 1-4   Third Normal Form Example

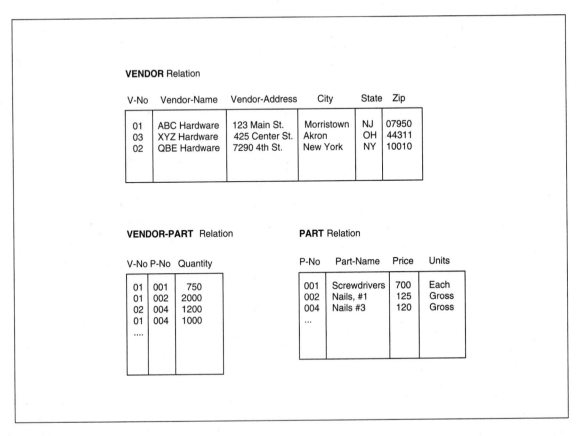

FIGURE 1-5   Relational Logical Data Model

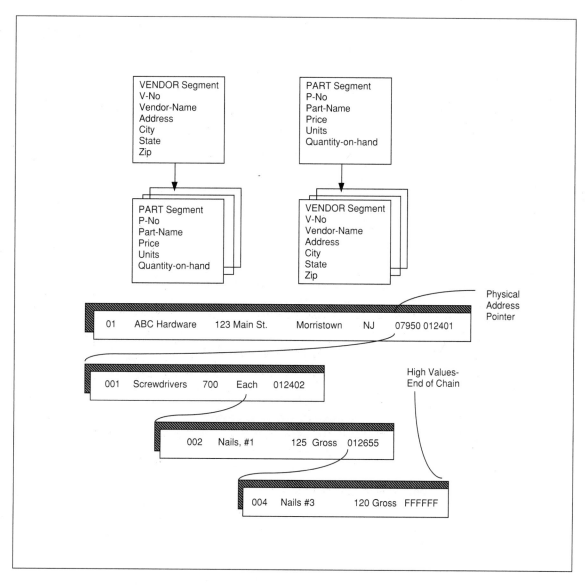

FIGURE 1-6   Hierarchic Logical Data Model

Processes

A **process** is the sequence of instructions or conjunction of events that operate on data. The results of processing include changes to data in a database, identification of data for display at a terminal or printing on paper, generated commands to equipment, generated program commands, or storage of new facts or rules inferred about a situation or entity.

Constraints

Processing is subject to **constraints,** which are limitations on the behavior and/or processing of entities.

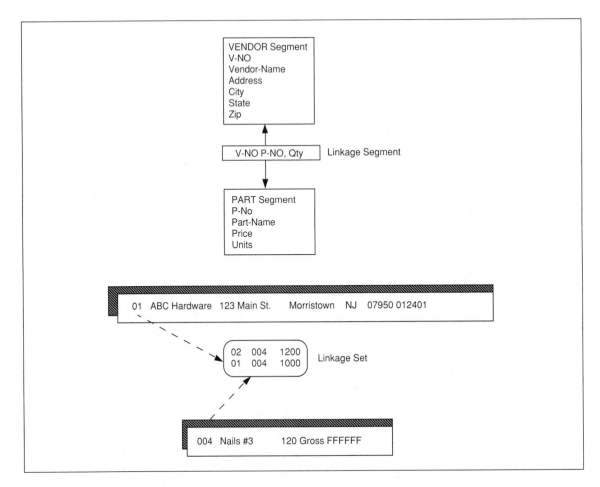

FIGURE 1-7   Network Logical Data Model

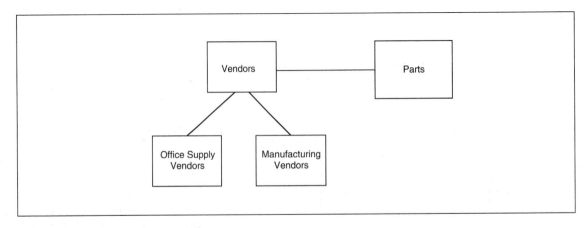

FIGURE 1-8   Object-Oriented Logical Data Model

If accounts receivable balance = zero
and prerequisite classes are taken
and course section is available   } *Prerequisites*
   then register student
else write appropriate message to
   student.

FIGURE 1-9   Prerequisite Constraint Example

1. Timing of processing, for instance, all money transfers in New York must be processed by 3 P.M. to meet the New York Federal Reserve Bank closing deadline.
2. Time allotted for a process, for instance, time-out of the database when remote site A's expected response is not received within ten seconds.
3. External time requirements, for instance, reports must be delivered to the Controller's office by noon.
4. Synchronous processing, for instance, locations A and B must both have completed their respective actions successfully for location C to perform action X.
5. Response time for external interface processing, for instance, the system must respond to the user terminal within two seconds after the enter key is pressed.

Constraint types are prerequisite, postrequisite, time, structure, control, or inferential.

PREREQUISITES.   **Prerequisite constraints** are preconditions that must be met for processing to occur. They usually take the form of 'if . . . then . . . else' logic in a program (see Figure 1-9).

POSTREQUISITES.   **Postrequisite constraints** are conditions that must be met for the process to complete successfully. They also take the form of 'if . . . then . . . else' logic, but the logic is applied *after* processing is supposedly complete.

TIME.   **Time constraints** may relate to one or more of the following:

STRUCTURE.   **Structural constraints** describe the relationships between data, meta-data (knowledge about data), knowledge and meta-knowledge (system generated knowledge) in applications (see Figure 1-10). Customers, for example, might have different processing if they pay by credit or cash. So, there would be a general *class* customer and two *subclasses,* credit-customer and cash-customer. Meta-data about customers includes, for example, the definition of the domain of allowable values for customer identification.

```
DATA :            CON100

META-DATA :       Field=Customer-ID
                  Size=6
                  Type=xxx999
                  Validation= Occurs once per customer

KNOWLEDGE:        CON001 must pay cash for sales

META-KNOWLEDGE:   If Customer-ID > ???050
                  and accounts receivable balance > 1000
                  cash sales only
                    else
                    OK credit sales up to 1000.
```

FIGURE 1-10   Structural Constraint Example

Structural constraints determine what type of inputs and outputs may be allowed, how processing is done, and the relationships of processes to each other.

CONTROL. **Control constraints** relate to automated maintenance of data relationships (e.g., the batch total must equal the sum of the transaction amounts).

INFERENCES. The word infer means to conclude by reasoning, or to derive from evidence. **Inferential constraints** are limits on the reasoning ability of the application and its ability to generate new facts from previous facts and relationships. These constraints come in several varieties. First, inferential constraints may relate to the application. For example, you might not want a medical expert system to build itself new knowledge based on new user information unless the "user" is an approved expert who understands what he or she is doing.

Second, inferential constraints may relate to the type of knowledge in the system and limits on that knowledge. For example, CASE tools cannot help you decide what information to actually enter into the system (yet). Rather, you as the user must already know what you want to describe and how to describe it when you use a CASE tool. What CASE *can* do is reason whether the information you entered conforms to its rules for how to represent information.

Third, inferential constraints may relate to the language in which the system is developed. For instance, you might be required to build an expert system in Prolog because that is the only language available. Prolog is a goal-oriented, declarative language with constructs for facts and rules that requires its knowledge (i.e., the data) to be imbedded in the program. Large programs in Prolog are hard to understand and may be ambiguous. Therefore, programmers write smaller, limited reasoning programs. If you have a large, complex knowledge base, you may want to separate the data from the program logic. But the language choice can constrain your ability to do such separation.

Interfaces

There are three types of interfaces: human, manual, and computerized. There are few guidelines in any methodologies for designing any of these interfaces. Each type of interface is discussed briefly in this section, and in more detail later in the text.

HUMAN. **Human interfaces** are the means by which an application communicates to its human users. Human interfaces are arguably the most important of the three types because they are the hardest to design and the most subject to new technologies and fads.

Most often, a human interface is via a video display which might have options for color, size of screen, windows, and so on. Many application developers are tempted to design elaborate screens with the assumption that more is better: more color, more information, and so forth. But a growing body of research combined with graphic design ideas show that this is not the case. Figure 1-11 shows the same information on a well designed screen and on a poorly designed screen. A screen should be organized to enhance readability, to facilitate understanding, and to minimize extraneous information. Few colors, standardized design of top and bottom lines, standardized use of programmable function keys, and easy access to help facilities are the keys to good screen design.

MANUAL. **Manual interfaces** are reports or other human-readable media that show information from the computer. You use manual interfaces whenever you pay electric, telephone, or water bills. Some simple standards for manual interfaces are to mirror screen designs when possible to enhance understanding, to fully identify the interface contents with headers, notes, and footers when needed, and to follow many of the same human interface "rules" for formatting information.

AUTOMATED. An **automated interface** is data that is maintained on computer-readable media for use by another application. Application interfaces tend to be nonstandardized and are defined by the data-sharing organizations. Guidelines for applica-

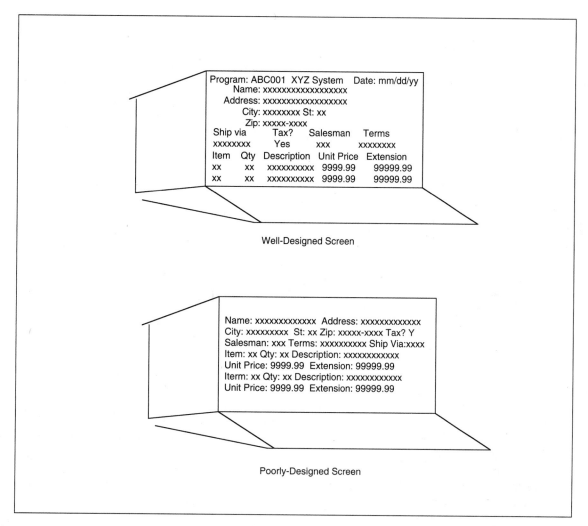

Well-Designed Screen

Poorly-Designed Screen

FIGURE 1-11   Good versus Bad Screen Design

tion file interfaces have evolved over the last fifty years to include, for instance, placement of identifying information first and placement of variable length information last. Other interfaces are governed by numerous formal standards, for instance, local area network interface standards are defined by the Institute of Electrical and Electronic Engineers (IEEE) and the open system interface (OSI) standard for inter-computer communication is governed by the International Standards Organization (ISO). Few such standards are currently relevant to an individual business application. Lack of standards, such as for graphics user interfaces (GUIs) slows business acceptance of new innovations. Uncertainty over which 'look' will become the standard, in the case of GUIs, leads to business caution in using new technology.

Application Responsiveness

In this book, application responsiveness is how long it takes the system to act on and respond to user

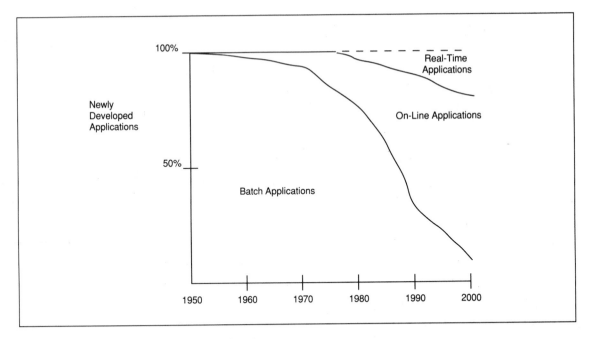

FIGURE 1-12   Application Type Transition

actions. Responsiveness of an application reflects the fundamental design approach as batch-oriented, on-line, or real-time. Each of these approaches is defined in this section. Of course, in the real world, any combination or permutation of these approaches are used in building applications. Most applications designed in the 1990s are on-line with some batch processing. In the 21st century, on-line applications will give way to more real-time applications. Figure 1-12 shows the transition from batch to on-line to real-time processing in the last half of this century. Table 1-1 compares application responsiveness on several categories.

Batch Applications

Batch applications are applications in which transactions are processed in groups. Transactions are gathered over time and stored together. At some predefined time, the batch is closed and processing on the complete batch is done. Transactions are processed in sequence one after the other. A system flow diagram of a typical batch application is shown in Figure 1-13. The *batch of transactions* is edited and applied to a *master file* to create a *new master file* and a printed *log of processing*. In batch applications the requirements relating to the average age and maximum possible age of the master file data determine the timing of processing.[5] In addition to processing transactions, other programs in batch applications use the master file as their major input and process in a specific fixed sequence.

On-Line Applications

On-line applications provide interactive processing with or without immediate file update. **Interactive processing** means there is a two-way dialogue between the user and the application that takes place during the processing. This definition of on-line differs somewhat from the use of on-line terminology in other texts which assume that on-line systems are

---

5 See Davis, G. and Olson, M., *Management Information Systems: Conceptual Foundations, Structure, and Development*, New York: McGraw-Hill, 1985, for a detailed discussion of batch systems.

TABLE 1-1   Comparison of Application Technologies

Category	Batch Applications	On-Line Applications	Real-Time Applications
Amount of data	Large	Small-Large	Medium
Visual review of inputs	No	Yes	Yes
Ratio of updates to stored data	High	Low-High	High
Inquiry	Batch	On-line	On-line
Reports	Long, formal	Short, informal	Short, informal
Backup/Recover	Copy files to tape	One or more of the following: Copy files to tape transaction log, preimage log, postimage log, mirror image files	One or more of the following: Copy files to tape transaction log, preimage log, postimage log, mirror image files
Cost to build*	Low	Medium	High
Cost to operate*	Low	Medium-High	High
Efficient use of	Computer resources	People time	People time
Difficulty to build*	Simple	Medium	Complex
Speed of processing all transactions	Fast	Slow	Medium
Speed of processing one transaction	Slow	Medium	Fast
Uses DBMS and data communications	May or may not	Probably	Yes
Function integration	Low	Medium	High

*Relative measure

also real-time (see the next section). In this text, on-line processing means that programs may be resident in memory and used sequentially by numerous transactions/events without reloading.

Figure 1-14 shows the difference between an on-line application and a batch application. In an on-line application, small modules perform the function and communicate directly *via data* passed between them. In the batch application, disjoint programs perform the function and indirectly communicate *via permanent changes to file contents* created by one program and interpreted by the next program(s). The on-line programs keep a log of transactions to provide recovery in case of error; this prevents re-entry of data.

On-line programs' dialogue with the user is to ensure entry of syntactically correct data. The error correction dialogue replaces the error portion of the update log. The remainder of the update log to document updates becomes optional and, instead, an acknowledgement of successful processing is displayed to the user.

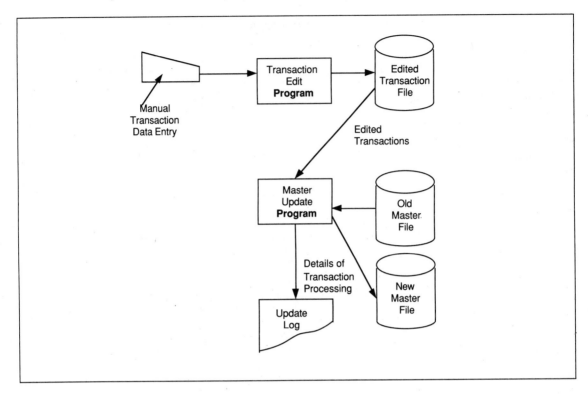

FIGURE 1-13   Batch Application System Flow Diagram

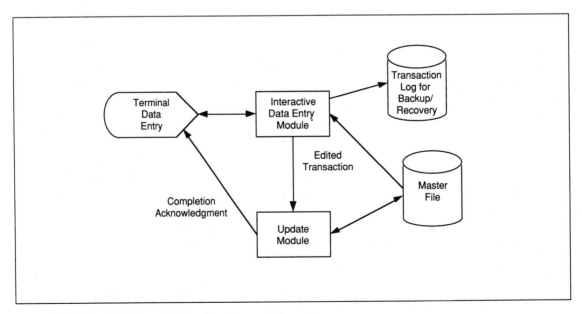

FIGURE 1-14   On-Line Application System Flow Diagram

Real-Time Applications

Real-time applications process transactions and/or events during the actual time that the related physical (real world) process takes place. The results of the computer operation are then available (in real time) to influence or control the physical process (see Figure 1-15). Changes resulting from a real-time process can be refreshed to users viewing prechange data when the change is completed. Real-time programs can process multiple transactions concurrently. In parallel processes, concurrency literally means that many transactions are being worked on at the same time. In sequential processes, concurrency means many transactions are *in process* but only one is actively executing at any one moment.

Database processing is more sophisticated in real-time systems. If an update to a data item takes place, all current users of the item *may* have their screens refreshed with the new data. Examples of real-time applications include automated teller machine

(ATM), stock market ticker, and airline reservation processing.

Types of Applications

There are four types of business applications: transaction, data analysis, decision support, and expert applications. Today, all four types are usually on-line although the application may use any (or all) of the responsiveness types, even on a single application. In addition, a fifth type of application: embedded, is defined briefly to distinguish computer science-software engineering from IS-software engineering.

Transaction-Oriented Applications

Transaction-oriented applications, also known as **transaction processing systems (TPS)**, support the day-to-day operation of a business and include order processing, inventory management, budgeting,

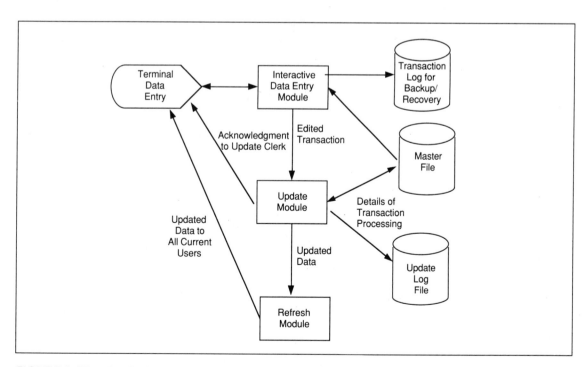

FIGURE 1-15   Real-Time Application System Flow Diagram

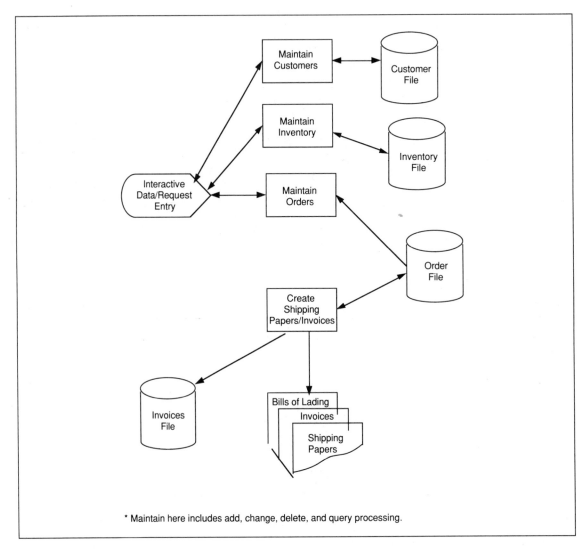

* Maintain here includes add, change, delete, and query processing.

FIGURE 1-16   Order Processing Applications

purchasing, payables, accounting, receivables, payroll, and personnel. They are characterized as applications for which the requirements, the data, and the processing are generally known and well-structured.[6] By known, we mean that the function is repetitive, familiar and unambiguous. By well-

structured, we mean that the problem is able to be defined completely and without ambiguity. The requirements are identifiable by a development team.

A transaction application example is order processing (see Figure 1-16). Order processing requires an order file, customer file, and inventory file. The contents of the files differ depending on the level of integration of order processing with accounts receivable, manufacturing, purchasing, and inventory processing. Processing of orders requires add, change,

---

6 An informative text on transaction processing systems is
On-line Business Computer Applications, 2nd ed., by
Alan Eliaison. Chicago: Science Research Associates,
Inc., 1987.

EXAMPLE 1-3

EFFECTIVE INSURANCE COMPANY

In the early 1980s, Effective Insurance realized they were generating 22 feet of paper each month in accounting reports that were sent to about 80 different parts of the organization. Yet, for all this paper, the number of legitimate requests for access to data was mushrooming and had reached about 200.

Rather than try to produce reports for each specific user, the company decided to automate the information and allow users to access their own data to generate their own reports. That way, paper could be reduced and each person would have the data they wanted, formatted the way they wanted it.

The company never anticipated the immense savings in time, money, and, more importantly, the increases in productivity and morale, that this move would produce. By 1989, there were over 2,000 users accessing some or all of the accounting information. Each user had his own terminal and the use of a fourth generation language,* to generate customized information interactively. Reports were created by each user as needed.

---

*A fourth-generation language is one in which a query language, statistical routines, and data base are integrated for application development by both IS and by non-IS professionals.

---

delete, and inquiry functions for all files, pricing of items, and creation of shipping papers and invoices. Inquiry functions should allow retrieval of information about orders by date, order number, customer ID, or customer name. The software engineer uses his or her understanding of general order processing to customize the application for a given organization and implementation environment.

Data Analysis Applications

Data analysis applications support problem solving using data that are accessible only in read-only mode. Data analysis applications are also known as **query applications**. A query is some question asked of the data. SQL, the standard query language for database access, poses questions in such a way that the user asks *what* is desired but need not know *how* to get it. The computer software figures out the optimal access and processing methods, and performs the operations it selects. An example of a query asking for the sum of all sales for customers in New York State for the first yearly quarter might look like the following:

```
SELECT CUST_NAME, CUST_ID, AND
SUM(CUST_SALES)
   FROM CUSTOMER
   WHERE CUST_STATE = 'NY' AND
   MONTH IN (1, 2, 3);
```

A language, such as SQL, is a **declarative language**, because you 'declare' *what* to do, not *how* to do it. Declarative languages are relatively easy to learn and use, and are designed for use by noninformation systems professionals.

Queries are one of three varieties:

1. Interactive, one-of-a-kind. These are assumed to be thrown away after use.
2. Stored and named for future modification and re-execution.
3. Stored and named for frequent unchanging execution.

The third type of query frequently replaces reports in transaction applications (see Example 1-3). The data for all query processing must be known in advance and tend to come from transaction applications. Query outputs may use program language formatting defaults (as in SQL), or may be formatted for formal visual presentation or fed into other software (e.g., graphical software) for summarizing.

Query applications support an evolving concept called **data warehouse**, a storage scheme based on the notion that most data should be retained on-line for query access. A warehouse stores past versions of major database entries, transaction logs, and historical records.

Decision Support Applications

Decision support applications (DSS) seek to identify and solve problems. The difference between decision support and query applications is that query applications are used by professionals and managers to select and summarize historical data like the example above, while DSSs are used by professionals and managers to perform what-if analysis, identify trends, or perform mathematical/statistical analysis of data to solve unstructured problems. Data for DSSs usually are generated by transaction applications.

Unstructured problems are ones for which not all information is known, and if it is known, the users may not know all of the relationships between data. An example of a structured problem is to answer the question: "What is the cost of a 5% salary increase?" An example of an unstructured problem is "What product mix should we manufacture next year?" The difference between these two kinds of questions is that the **structured problem** requires one query of known data to develop an estimate, while the product mix question requires economic, competitive, historical, and product development information to develop an estimate. Because the information may not all be known, DSS development uses an iterative problem-solving approach, applying mathematical and statistical modeling to the decision process. Corrected and/or supplemental data are fed back into the modeling processes to refine the analysis.

Executive information systems (EIS) are a spin-off from DSS. EIS applications support executive decision making and provide automated environmental scanning capabilities. Top executives deal with future-oriented, partial, inaccurate, and ambiguous information. They scan the economy, industry, and organizational environments to identify and monitor key indicators of business activity that affect their organization. EIS integrate information from external information databases and internal applications to provide an automated scanning and modeling capability. The major difference in EIS from DSS then, is the incompleteness, potential inaccuracy, and ambiguity of the data.

Group decision support systems (GDSS) are a special type of DSS applications. GDSS provide an historical memory of the decision process in support of groups of decision makers who might be geographically dispersed. GDSS focus more on the group interaction processes with little or no data modeling or statistical analyses. Data analysis software in GDSS tend to be less elaborate than DSS software, but may include a spreadsheet and routines to present summaries of participant votes on issues in either numerical or graphical formats. GDSS typically provide such functions as

1. Anonymous recording of ideas
2. Democratic selection of group leaders
3. Progressive rounds of discussion and voting to build group consensus

For all DSS, application development is more formal than query applications, and less formal than transaction applications. The development life cycle tends to be iterative with continuous identification of requirements. DSS software environments are sophisticated and typically include software tools for communications support, statistical modeling, knowledge-base maintenance, and decision process support.

Expert Systems

Expert systems applications (ES) are computer applications that automate the knowledge and reasoning capabilities of one or more experts in a specific domain. ESs analyze characteristics of a situation to give advice, recommend actions, or draw conclusions by following automated reasoning processes. The four major components of an ES are knowledge acquisition subsystem, the knowledge base, the inference engine (or rule base as it is sometimes called), and explanation subsystem. Each of these components are briefly explained here.

EXAMPLE 1-4

MEDICAL ES ETHICAL DILEMMA

A doctor who is not a specialist in rare diseases sees a patient in the emergency room who appears to be in respiratory distress. After a preliminary exam, he consults with an expert system that diagnoses many diseases and recommends a course of treatment. The ES requests all of the symptoms from the doctor who answers the questions to the best of his ability. The ES diagnoses the problem as advanced Legionnaires' disease with a probability of 80%. The ES suggests no other possible diseases. The doctor prescribes the ES's recommended treatment. The patient dies. On investigation, it turns out that the ES contains errors in its rules and that the correct diagnosis, following the exact same set of symptoms, would have led to a different diagnosis with different treatment.

There are ethical issues in every aspect of this problem. Who is responsible for ES accu-racy? Is the knowledge engineer who built the ES responsible for ensuring accuracy of information in the system? Or, does his or her responsibility only mean translating the reasoning processes correctly? What is the responsibility of the "expert" who supplies the information in ensuring it is correctly entered into an ES to supply correct reasoning? If a medical ES contains information on thousands of diseases, is it even possible to test it completely? How is consistency of diagnoses checked? What happens when symptoms are entered in different sequences? Is the doctor who uses the ES suggestion ethical? There is no consensus on answers to these questions at present. The lack of consensus highlights the need for discussion of ethical issues in IT applications.

The **knowledge acquisition subsystem** is the means by which the knowledge base is built. In general, the more knowledge, the 'smarter' the system can be. The knowledge acquisition subsystem must provide for initial loading of facts and heuristic rules of thumb, *and* be easy to use in adding knowledge to the knowledge base.

Frequently, we reason without knowing how we arrive at a solution. In fact, reflect how you yourself think when analyzing a problem to develop an application. How do you decide what the processes are? You follow an elaborate, highly internalized process that is difficult to talk about. You are not alone in having this difficulty. *Eliciting the information* about reasoning processes from experts is a major difficulty in building effective ES applications.

The **knowledge base** is the codified automated version of the expert user's knowledge and the rules of thumb (also called heuristics) for applying that knowledge. Designing the knowledge base is as difficult as eliciting the information because no matter how it is designed, it will be limited by the software

in which it is implemented. Therefore, special ES programming languages have been designed to allow the most flexibility in defining connections between pieces of information and the way the pieces are used in reasoning.

Just as people reason to develop a most probable outcome to a situation, ESs use reasoning and inference to develop multiple, probable outcomes for a given situation. Several solutions may be generated when there is incomplete information or partial reasoning. Probabilities of accuracy of the solution(s) are frequently developed to assist the human in judging the usefulness of a system-generated outcome. Ethical and moral issues may be more apparent in ESs than the other application types. Example 1-4 describes an ethical dilemma relating to a medical ES.

The last major component of ES is the ability to explain its reasoning to the user. The **explanation subsystem** provides the ability to trace the ES's reasoning. Tracing is important so the user can learn from the experience of using the system, and so he or she may determine his or her degree of confidence in the ES's results.

These four application types—transaction, query, DSS, and ES—will be referenced throughout the text to tie topics together and to discuss the usefulness of methodologies, languages and approaches to testing, quality assurance, and maintenance for each.

Embedded Systems

Embedded systems are applications that are part of a larger system. For example, a missile guidance application works in conjunction with sensors, explosives, and other equipment within a single missile unit. The application, by itself, is minor; its complexity derives from its analog interfaces, need for complete accuracy, and real-time properties within the missile's limited life span once it is released. Embedded applications development has been the province of computer science educated developers rather than information systems (IS) educated developers.

As business deploys ever more complex equipment in the context of computing environments, the need for embedded systems skills will increase. This implies that IS education must also address real-time, embedded system requirements, and that computer scientists will continue to move into business for application development.

Applications in Business

Applications are most successful when they match the organizations' needs for information. Most information in organizations is generated to allow the managers to control the activities of the organization to reach the company's goals. Goals may be short-term or long-term. Control of activities implies information evaluation and decision making. There are three levels of organizational decision making: operational, managerial, and strategic. Each level has different information needs and, therefore, different application needs.

At the operational level, the organization requires information about the conduct of its business. Deci-

sions deal with daily operations. For instance, the operational level in a retail organization is concerned with sales of products. The main operational level applications would be order processing, inventory control, and accounts receivable. In a manufacturing business, the operational level is concerned with sales and manufacturing. The main operational level applications would be manufacturing planning, manufacturing control, inventory management, order processing, and shipping.

The information at the operational level is current, accurate, detailed, available as generated, and relates to the business of the organization. Operational information is critical to the organization remaining in business. As a critical resource, the data requires careful management and maintenance. The types of applications that support operational level decisions and information are transaction processing applications (see Figure 1-17). Query applications for current operational data are other applications that support operational level decisions.

The information needs for managerial control are mostly internal information, can be detailed or summary, and should be accurate. Decisions made for managerial control concentrate on improving the existing ways of doing business, finding and solving problems, and take a medium-range (e.g., quarter or year) view of the company's business. The types of issues dealt with concern reduction of

- costs by comparing suppliers' prices
- the time to process a single order
- the errors in a process

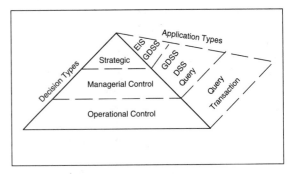

FIGURE 1-17   Application Types and Decision Types

- the number of manual interactions with an order, and so on

The types of applications that support these data needs are data analysis applications, DSS, and GDSS (see Figure 1-17). Each of these application types serves a different role in supporting managerial control decision needs. Data analysis applications can be used to find and solve problems. DSSs can be used to identify trends, analyze critical relationships, or compare different work processes for possible improvements. GDSSs facilitate meetings of people with different motivations and organizational goals, providing a means to reach consensus with a frank discussion of the issues.

At the strategic level, the types of decisions take a broad view of the business and ask, for instance, what businesses should we be in? What products should we produce? How can we improve market share? These questions require external information from many sources to reach a decision. The information is ambiguous, that is, able to be interpreted in many different ways. Because the information is future-oriented, it is likely to be incomplete and only able to be digested at a summary level.

The types of applications that support incomplete, ambiguous, external information needs best are executive information systems (EIS) (see Figure 1-17). EISs are specifically designed to accommodate incomplete, ambiguous information. GDSSs also might be used at the executive level to facilitate discussion of alternative courses for the organization.

PROJECT _____
LIFE CYCLES _____

There are several different ways to divide the work that takes place in the development of an application. The work breakdown in general comprises the project's life cycle. If you asked five SEs to describe the life cycle of a typical computer application, you would get five overlapping but different answers. Life cycles discussed here are the most common ones: sequential, iterative, and learn-as-you-go.[7]

Sequential Project Life Cycle

You should remember from systems analysis that a **sequential project life cycle (SPLC)** starts when a software product is conceived and ends when the product is no longer in use. Phases in a SPLC include

- initiation
- problem definition
- feasibility
- requirements analysis
- conceptual design
- design
- code/unit test
- testing
- installation and checkout
- operations and maintenance
- retirement

These SPLC phases are more appropriate to business than to military/government applications because, in the government, the first four phases (initiation, definition, feasibility, and functional requirements definition) are usually completed by a different organization than that of the implementers. Government projects are subject to congressional review, approval, and budgeting. So, a government project requiring congressional appropriation is usually defined as beginning at the conceptual design phase and ending with deployment of the system with operational status according to Department of Defense standard #2167a [DOD, 1985]. In contrast, business IS are typically initiated by a user department requesting that a system be built by an MIS department. The need for an IS is typically motivated by some business situation: a change in the method of business, in the legal environment, in the staffing/support environment, or in a strategic goal such as improving market competitiveness.

We call these SPLC phases a 'Waterfall' approach to applications because the output of each phase feeds into the next phase, while phases are modified via feedback produced during the verification and validation processes[8] (see Figure 1-18).

---

7 Future developments in life cycles are discussed in Chapter 18.

8 Boehm, Barry W., *Software Engineering Economics*. Englewood Cliffs, NJ: Prentice-Hall, 1981.

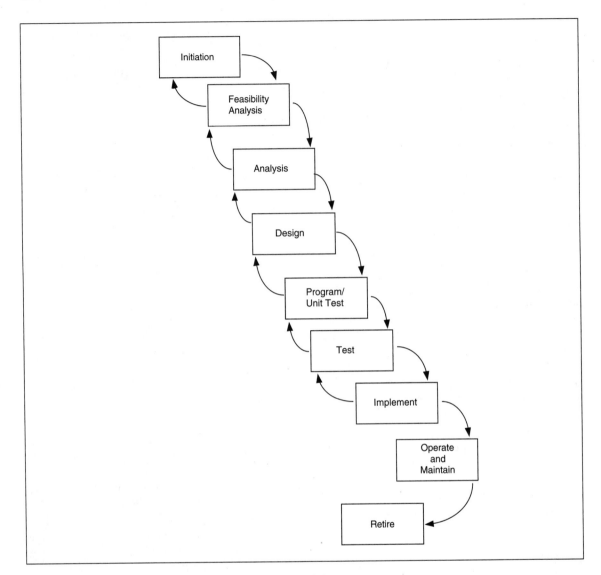

FIGURE 1-18   Sequential Project Life-Cycle Model

Phases in the waterfall definition are defined as discrete even though, in practice, the information is obtained in a nonlinear manner and the phase beginnings and endings are difficult to distinguish. To identify discrete beginnings and endings, most companies use the completion of the major product (i.e., program or document) produced during each phase as signaling the phase end. So, completion of a feasibility report, for instance, identifies the end of the feasibility analysis phase. In the following subsections, each phase of the project life cycle (SPLC) is defined,[9] with the main activities and documents identified.

9 This definition is adapted from work conducted during The Assessment and Development of Software Engineering Tools project sponsored by the U.S. Army Institute for Research in Management Information, Communications, and Computer Sciences (AIRMICS), contract DAKF11-89-C-0014.

SPLC Phases

INITIATION.   Project **initiation** is the period of time during which the need for an application is identified and the problem is sufficiently defined to assemble a team to begin problem evaluation. The people and organizations affected by the application, that is, the **stakeholders**, are identified. Participants from each stakeholder organization for the development team are solicited. The outcome of initiation is a memo or formal document requesting automation support and defining the problem and participants.

FEASIBILITY.   **Feasibility** is the analysis of risks, costs and benefits relating to economics, technology, and user organizations. The problem to be automated is analyzed in sufficient detail to ensure that all aspects of feasibility are evaluated.

Economic feasibility analysis elaborates costs of special hardware, software, personnel, office space, and so forth for each implementation alternative.

In **technical feasibility** analysis, alternatives for hardware, software, and general design approach are determined to be available, appropriate, and functional. The benefits and risks of alternatives are identified.

Organizational feasibility is an analysis of both the developing and using organizations' readiness for the application. Particular emphasis is placed on skills and training needed in both groups to ensure successful development and use of the application. The decision whether or not to use consultants and the type of role they would play during development is made during organizational feasibility analysis. Organizational decisions include effectiveness of the organization structure and definition of roles of individual jobs in the organization as they will be with the new application.

The feasibility report summarizes

- the problem
- the economic, technical and organizational feasibility
- risks and contingency plans related to the application

- preferred concept for the software product and an explanation of its superiority to alternative concepts
- training needs and tentative schedules
- estimates of project staffing by phase and level of expertise

After feasibility is established, the **Software Development Life Cycle (SDLC)**, a subcycle of the SPLC, begins. This subcycle typically includes phases for analysis, conceptual design, design, implementation, testing, and installation and checkout. SDLC end is signaled by delivery of an operational application.

ANALYSIS.   The **analysis** phase has many synonyms: Functional Analysis, Requirements Definition, and Software Requirements Analysis. All of these names represent the time during which the business requirements for a software product are defined and documented. Analysis activities define

1. Functional requirements—"what" the system is supposed to do. The format of the functional requirements definitions depends on the methodology followed during the analysis phase.
2. Performance requirements—terminal, message, or network response time, input/output volumes, process timing requirements (e.g., reports must be available by 10 A.M.).
3. Interface(s) requirements—what data come from and go to other using applications and organizations. The definition includes timing, media, and format of exchanged data.
4. Design requirements—information learned during analysis that may impact design activities. Examples of design requirements are data storage, hardware, testing constraints, conversion requirements, and human-machine interaction requirements (e.g., the application must use pull-down menus).
5. Development standards—the form, format, timing, and general contents of documentation to be produced during the development. Development standards include rules about allowable graphical representations,

documentation, tools, techniques, and aids such as computer-aided software engineering (CASE) tools, or project management scheduling software. Format information includes the content of a data dictionary/repository for design objects, project report contents, and other standards to be followed by the project team when reporting project accomplishments, problems, status and design.

6. The plan for application development is refined.

Analysis documentation summarizes the current method of work, details the proposed system, and how it meets the needs of the required functions. Requirements from the work activities are described in graphics, text, tables, structured English, or some other representation form prescribed by the methodology being used.

CONCEPTUAL DESIGN.   Once the proposed logical system is understood and agreed to by the user, conceptual design begins. Other names for conceptual design activity include preliminary design, logical design, external design, or software requirements specifications. The major activity of **conceptual design** is the detailed functional definition of all external elements of the application, including screens, reports, data entry messages, and/or forms. Both contents and layout are included at this level. In addition, the logical data model is transformed into a logical database schema and user views. If distribution or decentralization of the database is anticipated, the analysis and decision are made during conceptual design. The outputs of conceptual design include the detailed definition of the external items described above, plus the normalized and optimized logical database schema.

Not all organizations treat conceptual design separately. Outputs of conceptual design may be in a conceptual design document or might be part of the functional requirements document developed during analysis. Depending on the project manager's personal taste and experience, the conceptual design might be partially completed during logical design and fully completed during physical design. *In this text, the two phases, design and conceptual design, are treated as one.*

DESIGN.   **Design** maps "what" the system is supposed to do into "how" the system will do it in a particular hardware/software configuration.[10] The other terms used to describe design activities include detailed design, physical design, internal design, and/or product design.

During the design phase, the software engineering team creates, documents, and verifies:

1. Software architecture—identifies and defines programs, modules, functions, rules, objects, and their relationships. The exact nature of the software architecture depends on the methodology followed during the design phase.
2. Software components and modules—defines detailed contents and functions of software components, including, but not limited to, inputs, outputs, screens, reports, data, files, constraints, and processes.
3. Interfaces—details contents, timing, responsibilities, and design of data exchanged with other applications or organizations.
4. Testing—defines the strategy, responsibilities, and timing for each type of testing to be performed.
5. Data—physically maps "what" to "how" for data. In database terms, this is the definition of the physical layout of data on the devices used, and of the requirements, timing, and responsibility for distribution, replication, and/or duplication of data.

SUBSYSTEM/PROGRAM DESIGN.   **Subsystem** and/or **program designs** are sometimes treated as subphases of the design phase. Whether they are separate phases or not, the software engineering team creates, documents, and verifies the following:

1. Application control structure—defines how each program/module is activated and where it returns upon completion.

---

10 Anyone who has designed a system will tell you that you cannot perform the conceptual design without some knowledge and attention to the implementation environment. So, the "what" and "how" distinctions are generally, but not completely, accurate when described as discrete activities.

2. Data structure and physical implementation scheme—defines physical data layouts with device mapping and data access methods to be used. In a database environment, this activity may include definition of a centralized library of data definitions, calling routines, and buffer definitions for use with a particular DBMS.

3. Sizing—defines any programs and buffers which are expected to be memory-resident for on-line and/or real-time processes.

4. Key algorithms—specifies mathematically correct notation to allow independent verification of formula accuracy.

5. Program component (routine with approximately 100 source procedure instructions)—identifies, names, and lists assumptions of program component design and usage. Assumptions include expectations of, for instance, resident routines and/or data, other routines/modules to be called in the course of processing this module, size of queues, buffers, and so on required for processing.

CODE AND UNIT TEST.   During **coding**, the low-level program elements of the software product are created from design documentation and debugged. **Unit testing** is the verification that the program does what it is supposed to do and nothing more. In systems using reusable code, the code is customized for the current application, and checked to ensure that it works accurately in the current environment.

TEST.   During **testing**—sometimes called Computer Software Component (CSC) Integration and Testing[11]—the components of a software product are evaluated for correctness of integrated processing. Quality assurance testing may be conducted in the testing phase or may be treated as a separate activity. During **quality assurance** tests, the software product (i.e., software or documentation) is evaluated by a nonmember of the project team to determine whether or not the analysis requirements are satisfied.

IMPLEMENTATION.   Also called Installation and Checkout, **implementation** is that period of time during which a software product is integrated into its operational environment and is phased into production use. Implementation includes the completion of data conversion, installation, and training.

At this point in the project life cycle, the software development cycle ends, and the maintenance phase begins. Maintenance and operations continue until the project is retired.

OPERATIONS AND MAINTENANCE.   Operations and maintenance is the period in the software life cycle during which a software product is employed in its operational environment, monitored for satisfactory performance, and modified as necessary. Three types of maintenance[12] are

1. **Perfective**—to improve the performance of the application (e.g., make all table indexes binary to minimize translations, change an algorithm to make the software run faster, and so on.)

2. **Corrective**—to remove software defects (i.e., to fix *bugs*)

3. **Adaptive**—to incorporate any changes in the business or related laws in the system (e.g., changes for new IRS rules)

Each type of maintenance requires a mini-analysis and mini-design to determine social, technical, and functional aspects of the change. The current operational versions of software and documentation must be managed to allow identification of errors and to ensure that the correct copy of software is run. One aspect of change management specifically addresses *configuration management* of application programs in support of maintenance activities.

RETIREMENT.   Retirement is the period of time in the software life cycle during which support for a software product is terminated. Usually, the functions performed by the product are transferred to a successor system. Another name for this activity is phaseout.

---

11 This is a term used by DOD standard #2167a, 1985.

12 A detailed discussion of maintenance topics is presented in Lientz and Swanson, 1980.

UNIVERSAL ACTIVITIES. There are two universal activities which are performed during each life-cycle phase: verification and validation, and configuration management.

An integral part of *each life-cycle phase* is the verification and validation that the phase products satisfy their objectives. **Verification** establishes the correctness of correspondence between a software product and its specification. **Validation** establishes the fitness or quality of a software product for its operational purpose.

For instance, the individual code module specifications from design are verified to ensure that they contain accurate and complete information about the functions they perform. The modules are validated against the analysis phase specification to ensure that all required functions have corresponding designs that accurately reflect the requirements.

Configuration management refers to the management of change after an application is operational. A designated *project librarian* maintains the official version of each product. The project librarian is able at any time to provide a definitive version (or *baseline*) of a document or software module. These baselines allow the project manager to control both the software maintenance process and the software products.

History

The sequential life cycle was originally developed and documented in the 1960s to provide defense contractors a life-cycle documentation standard for Department of Defense (DOD) projects. The current DOD Standard #2167a lists all activities and details all documentation required for software development as fulfillment of military contracts. As industry recognized that their own application development projects were out of control, over budget, and unsatisfactory when complete, they modified the standard to eliminate defense/aerospace terminology and replace it with industry specific terminology. Organizations modified the standard to incorporate elements of methodologies, such as structured development, data flow diagrams, and walk-throughs, that were becoming known at the same time. In the late 1960s and early 1970s the waterfall and 2167 documentation standard were used throughout most Fortune 500 companies as cast-in-concrete requirements for building and documenting systems.

Problems

As nonnegotiable documentation requirements, projects frequently produced thousands of pages of documentation that no one except the authors ever read. Information about applications was rarely in any one person's head and communication overhead became a major problem to completing systems successfully. User/management approval to continue with each phase was not based on their knowledge of what the system would do, but on some other criteria. Published studies showed that the typical written application requirements document contained, on average, one-half to one error per page. The conclusion that paper prose is not a good medium for conveying the complex variety of application requirements led to the development of more graphical representation forms.

Eventually, IS managers realized that the waterfall, when applied too stringently, not only did *not* solve the problems of bad systems, it contributed to a new generation of overdocumented bad systems. The result has been a scaling back on required documentation. Standards have become 'guidelines' for experienced project managers to consider and to provide new project managers with review lists of activities whose relevance they should consider. Each project team customizes the documentation and development activities in addition to the tools and techniques they use.

Even with relaxation of required documentation, a sequential life cycle does not recognize the iterative, nonlinear nature of application development, and cannot easily accommodate overlap of phases. Many organizations now use a variant of the waterfall by performing the activities in an overlapped manner, sometimes called the 'pipeline' approach. Finally, the waterfall approach does not recognize that the level of detail necessary to adequately document application functions is significantly different with the use of automated tools, use of diagrams (e.g., DFDs) to replace text, and use of high level, fourth-generation languages (e.g., SQL).

Current Use

The sequential life cycle is still used but rarely in full detail, and mostly for transaction applications. The sequential life cycle and its terminology will be around for many decades to come, but two divergent trends will occur. On the one hand, demarcation of phases will be more relaxed. Three trends leading to phase relaxation are:

- increasing maturity of computer-aided software engineering (CASE) tools
- increasing use of high-level languages
- availability of reusable electronically stored application information

On the other hand, further alteration and customization to accommodate the need for more detail in systems using new, more complex, or otherwise novel hardware/software components will also take place. It is from these novel, groundbreaking applications that our industry frequently develops new techniques to better communicate application characteristics.

Iterative Project Life Cycle

Iterative PLC Description

An **iterative project life cycle** is a cyclic repetition of analysis and design events. Iterative PLC is sometimes called **prototyping** or a spiral approach to development.

Prototyping is the development of a system or system component in a short period of time without formal written specifications. Originally thought of as helpful for proving the usefulness of new technologies, prototyping caught on in the early 1970s as a way to circumvent the overload of documentation from the sequential life cycle. Frequently, prototyping was wrongfully used and led to bad systems. But, as experience with prototyping has grown, there are three specific uses for which prototyping can be very beneficial:

1. Complete iterative development of an application when requirements are not well-understood, e.g., DSS
2. Proof of utility, availability, or appropriateness for technology, software, or hardware

3. Rapid development of part of the system to ease a critical work situation for users, e.g., order entry without edit/validation to ease paper backlog

Some authors describe a completely different life cycle for prototyped applications. The notion that the lifecycle is completely different is not entirely correct. The life cycle depends on the nature of the prototype. If a complete application is built, then the model of the life cycle mirrors that of the waterfall with iteration between analysis-design-programming-testing-implementation as requirements become known (see Figure 1-19). The difference is the level of detail to which analysis and design are performed. Requirements of iteratively-developed applications are generally not well known or understood. They might be ambiguous or incomplete for some time. The prototype provides a base from which users and developers together discover the requirements for the application.

One use of prototyping tests proof of utility, availability, or appropriateness of the hardware, software, or design concept. The prototype development process is a subphase of development that may parallel either feasibility, analysis, or design. There is no significant testing of a 'proof' prototype because it is being used to verify that an activity can be automated in a certain way, or that hardware (or software) can be used as planned. An example of a proof-of-concept prototype is shown in Figure 1-20 as taking place at the same time as the feasibility study. By the end of feasibility analysis, the usefulness of the prototype is decided, and the feasibility report recommends that the tested product (or idea) be abandoned or used.

A third type of prototype is a partial application developed as a stopgap measure for a particular problem until the complete system is available. A partial prototype might be built with its complete life cycle paralleling one phase of the development life cycle as shown in Figure 1-21. The phases of the prototype development cycle mirror those of a normal development life cycle; they differ in that only a small portion of the entire application is developed. These prototypes can omit processing details. For instance, an on-line data entry might not fully validate data. Feedback to the design team would detail

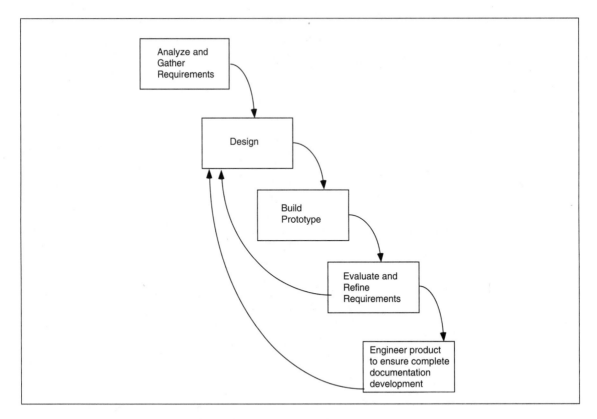

FIGURE 1-19   Full System Prototype Life Cycle

what is and is not in the prototype so that its design and development are completed during the regular application development.

Problems

There are two major problems with prototyping: misuse to circumvent proper analysis and design, and never completing prototypes as proper applications. Prototyping has been used as one way to circumvent rigidities in the sequential life cycle when it is treated as a set of nonnegotiable activities. In this misuse, some authors refer to 'quick analysis' and 'quick design' as if less work is done during those phases. In fact, if done properly, the activities and work are identical to those done in the life cycle, and the effort normally placed on documentation is diverted to building software.

The other major problem with development of a prototype is that the system might never get formalized. Details of processing, for instance, data validation and audit requirements, might be forgotten in the push to get a working prototype into production. While this problem is easily solved, it requires user and management commitment to a completed project. The problems with ensuring this commitment are political, not technical.

Current Use

Although still misused in the development of undocumented, incomplete applications, prototyping for the above intended purposes is also alive and healthy. All forms of query and DSS applications are candidates for iterative life cycles. Some languages (such as Focus, Rbase, Oracle) have easy to learn, short, very high-level programming languages that are naturally amenable to prototyping. A database can be defined, populated with data, and queried in

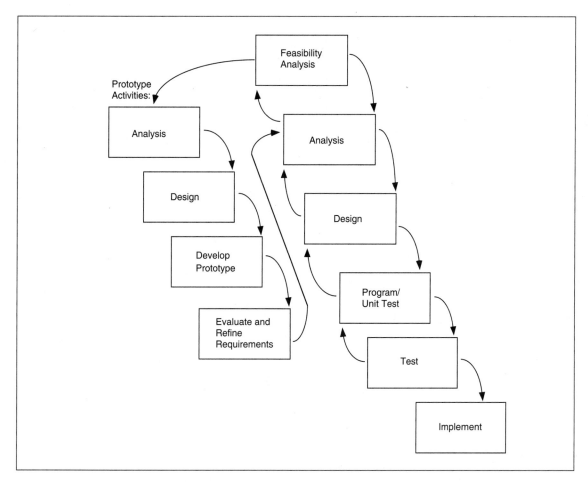

FIGURE 1-20   Proof of Concept Prototype Application Development Activities

under an hour to show capabilities of the languages or discuss requirements of a system. This kind of prototyping builds morale in the IS staff and confidence in the users, and is a great selling tool for in-house application development.

Future Use

Prototyping is appropriate to validate designs, to prove use of new hardware and/or software, or to quickly assist users while building a larger application. For these uses, prototyping is expected to be employed with increasing use of high-level languages to facilitate prototype development. Though there are few automated prototyping tools that also interface to CASE for full application definition, more such integrated tools are becoming available.

Learn-as-You-Go Project Life Cycle

Learn-as-You-Go PLC Description

With all the good news about developments in life cycles, there is a disturbing statistic that about 75% of all companies in the United States do not use any life cycle and/or methodology to guide their development work.[13] The title **learn-as-you-go** could equally well be called trial-and-error, or individual problem solving. The life cycle for the no-life cycle

---

13 Necco, Charles R., Carl L. Gordon, and Nancy W. Tsai, "Systems analysis and design: Current practices," *MIS Quarterly*, December 1987, pp. 461–476.

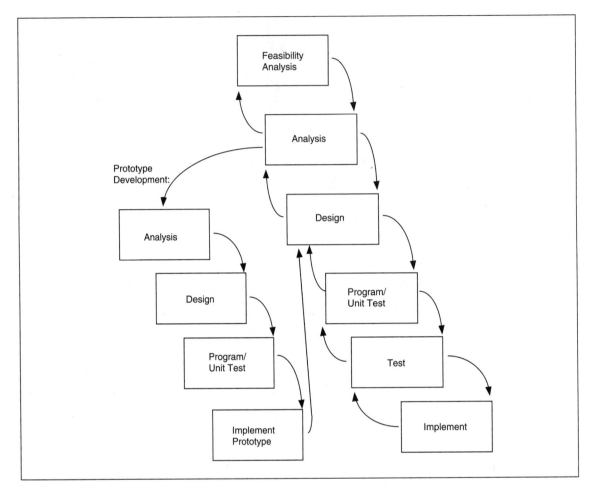

FIGURE 1-21   Partial System Prototype

approach is shown in Figure 1-22, which shows a generic life cycle. The problem is defined. The SE develops the application, which enters operation and maintenance. This approach is not suited to group work, so projects are limited to one person developing small applications. There are two different types of development groups that are in this category: developers of truly unique applications, and developers who do not want too much control or structure in their work.

The first developer view that the problem is unique and cannot easily be molded into a formal life cycle because of its nature is appropriate to applications using emerging technologies and techniques, such as expert systems and artificial intelli-

gence. There is no life cycle that describes building of expert systems, although with a feedback loop between maintenance and definition to indicate iteration, Figure 1-22 is appropriate to these systems. There is no methodology of knowledge engineering; rather, there are several techniques that one might use depending on the nature of the expertise, the personality of the expert, and the complexity of the problem domain. This life-cycle approach is appropriate for such emerging application domains as long as it is a disciplined experimentation loop that includes feedback and documentation.

The second view that all problems are unique, and if understood, do not require significant modeling, documentation, or sequences to the analysis and

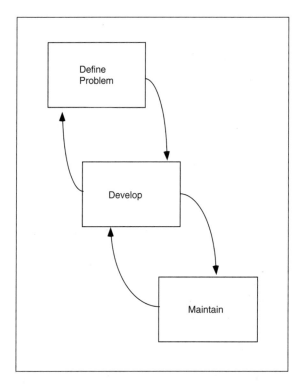

FIGURE 1-22   Generic View of Life-Cycle Development

development events. Since each problem is unique, there is no point in trying to repeat the analysis and design experience. Development is viewed as a *creative* activity that should be unconstrained. There should be no *formal* analysis, design, programming, or testing, even though each of these activities must be performed during the process. This approach denies the need for professional SEs or a profession of software engineering. In fact, it is frequently a cover for ignorance, or an excuse for laziness. This is a hacker's view of the world that is not appropriate to business organizations.

Problems

If building *small* systems (e.g., less than 2,000 lines of code in a 3GL, like Cobol, less than 400 lines of code in a 4GL), the developers, managers, and users may not have problems. Many financial analysis models and small systems in brokerage firms are

developed using no life cycle and no methodology. But anything other than small applications are unlikely to perform exactly as desired, may not be completely tested when placed into production, and cannot be integrated easily into existing applications.

A less obvious problem is that this technique relies on individual problem-solving capabilities and knowledge. Studies by IBM and others show individual programmer differences of as much as 16 times in productivity and more than that in accuracy. If the firm using this technique has only the best, top 5% of programmers on its staff, there is little risk. But how many firms actually have these people?

The view that we do not need a disciplined approach to developing applications implies that just anyone can design and build good applications. Yet daily we hear of users who have built complex spreadsheet DSSs only to leave a company with no documentation and no procedures for the next user. We also hear of users (and, regrettably, people with the title software engineer) who are leaders of projects that are canceled after spending millions of dollars, because the pieces just do not work together. For each type of application, there is a price with this view: DSSs without an architecture cannot be extended; ESs without a plan are unreliable and unmaintainable; TPSs without architectures and plans can only ever support one small piece of business; integration across subject data areas is impossible. Even though ES and AI problem solving both use the learn-as-you-go technique, both require a different *kind* of discipline and rigor.

Current Use

As related above, about 75% of all companies in the United States do not use any life cycle or methodology to guide their application development work. With this statistic, it is no wonder that most applications do not perform as intended, are delivered late, overrun the budget, and have unsatisfied users.

Future Use

For emerging technologies, techniques, or conceptualizations of applications, this approach *is* an effective way to nurture development of a field of knowledge. For these uses, it will remain. Unfortunately, it will also remain for companies who believe that discipline and order cost too much, and who will continue to suffer the risks involved with relying solely on one person's skill and integrity.

In summary, life cycles define a global breakdown of activities in the life of an application. No life cycle prescribes *how* to actually *do* the work within the phases of a PLC. For that definition, we turn to methodologies.

METHODOLOGIES _____

Methodologies are procedures, techniques, and processes used to direct the activities of each phase of a software life cycle. There are five classes of methodologies: process, data, object, semantic, or none. Each has its own unique view of an application that relates to its historical context, its own shortcomings, problems, and futures. In this section, a brief overview of the classes of methodologies is given with a general list of documents produced by the analysis phase, problems with the methodology, and short analysis of the methodology's current and future use. Much of this material should be review. If it is not review, don't panic. Use this material to learn the terminology for discussing the methods in detail later.

In addition to the methodologies prescribing how to do an analysis and design, a special class of methods advises how to bring users into the process. That class, sometimes called social methodologies, is the last part of this section.

Process Methodology

History

Process methodologies take a structured, top-down approach to evaluating problem processes and the data flows with which they are connected. Process methods developed during the 1970s in response to increasing complexity of application processing, increased complexity of operating system environments (e.g., the IBM 360 generation of hardware), and the introduction of disk file processing with sequential, indexed, and direct access methods. The

documentation produced by the process approach[14] includes, for example, context diagrams, data flow diagrams, data store definitions, and structured English process descriptions. In the course of a complete application development, many other types of analysis and design documentations are developed. These additional documents are discussed in the chapters on analysis and design.

Current Use

Individual techniques such as context and data flow diagrams are widely used and also supported in CASE environments. Other techniques have been replaced by newer methods, for example, paper-based data dictionaries have been replaced by CASE repositories or active data dictionaries, file design has been augmented by normalization, entity relationship diagramming, and so on.

Future Use

Process methods as attributed to DeMarco and others will fade as a distinguishable methodology with context and DFDs melded into a collection of techniques that will be used to support methodology customization.

Data Methodology

History

Data methodologies begin analysis activities by first evaluating data and their relationships to determine the underlying data architecture. When the data architecture is defined, outputs are mapped onto inputs to determine processing requirements. The most used data methodology is information engineering (IE) which was described by Finkelstein and Martin.[15] Documentation produced by the data

---

14 The architects of process methods were Yourdon and Constantine, 1978; DeMarco, 1979; Gane and Sarson, 1979.

15 See Martin, James, *Information Engineering, Book 1: Introduction, Book 2: Planning and Analysis, Book 3: Design and Implementation*, Englewood Cliffs, NJ: Prentice-Hall, 1990; and Finkelstein, C., *Information Engineering*, 1991.

approach discussed in this text is that of information engineering.

As the use of DBMS software became pervasive during the late 1970s and early 1980s, software engineers recognized a need for improved ways of designing data structures. Many methodologies were developed that concentrated strictly on the data aspects of applications with the processing added as an afterthought [cf. Warnier, 1981]. As an attempt to address the entire application development life cycle, Martin and Finkelstein borrowed techniques, packaged them in a new methodology, and integrated them to provide the first 'womb to tomb' methodology. Information engineering, the resulting methodology, begins with enterprise level analysis and proceeds through identification of applications and individual project life cycles. The methodology was not the work of one person; rather it integrates concepts that were thought of as the best at the time including entity-relationship modeling, normalization and other techniques relating to DB design. The enterprise level techniques are adapted and widely used in organizational reengineering.

An example of analysis documentation developed using information engineering includes entity relationship diagrams (ERD), entity hierarchy diagrams, process dependency diagrams, process hierarchy diagrams, and third normal form logical database definition.

Current Use

Information engineering is gaining acceptance in some of the largest U.S. corporations (e.g., Mobil, Texaco) and is used in Australia (where Finkelstein lives) but is not widely used otherwise. Other 'data' methods enjoy regional popularity.[16]

Future Use

Some of information engineering's appeal is its position as the only methodology that represents all levels of organizational analysis from enterprise

---

16 Michael Jackson's Jackson Structured Development (JSD) is used in England. Warnier-Orr techniques are used in companies such as AT&T. Chen's entity-relationship approach is used in isolation in many corporations but is also part of information engineering.

through application. IE *cannot* easily be altered, at this time, to accommodate object orientation or knowledge engineering. But it will be around for some time with parts of the methodology replaced in a customizing process. Individual techniques such as ERD will gain even more acceptance in the future as data administration increases.

Object-Oriented Methodology

History

Object-oriented methodology is an approach to system life-cycle development that takes a *top-down* view of data objects, their allowable actions, and the underlying communication requirement to define a system architecture. The data and action components are *encapsulated*, that is, they are combined together, to form abstract data types. Encapsulation means that if I know what data I want, I also know the allowable processes against that data. Data are designed as lattice hierarchies of relationships to ensure that top-down, hierarchic inheritance and sideways relationships are accommodated. Encapsulated objects are constrained only to communicate via messages. At a minimum, messages indicate the receiver and action requested. Messages may be more elaborate, including the sender and data to be acted upon.

Object orientation developed during the 1980s and 1990s as producing desirable software attributes (for instance, minimal coupling) espoused since the 1960s. Object-oriented designs can result in software with desirable properties: modularity, information hiding, functional cohesion, and minimal coupling. Like the other methodologies, bad designs lead to bad applications.

Object orientation appears able to support the abstract concepts needed to automate meta-data and meta-meta-data needed for expert, intelligent, and multimedia applications. **Meta-data** gives meaning to data and is information about data. For instance, a name or data type is information about the data in the example (see Figure 1-23). **Meta-meta-data** is information about the meta-data that describes its allowable use to the application. These types of definitions allow you to *plug-in* any hardware

Data	Cathrine Ratliff
Meta-Data	Name, Alpha, 16 Characters
Meta-Meta-Data	Type=Data Field, Logical Link = Process, Physical Link, Process, DBMS (EMPL DB)
Data	D01
Meta-Data	Drive Address, Alphanumeric, 3 Characters
Meta-Meta-Data	Type=Disk, Logical Link = I/O Driver Physical Link = SCSI Channel 0
Data	SC01
Meta-Data	Screen ID, 80x20 Alphanumeric Characters
Meta-Meta-Data	Type=3270 Black/White Terminal, Logical Link = I/O Driver, Process Physical Link = SCSI Channel 0

FIGURE 1-23   Object-Oriented Example

device, software, or data to *create* an application environment.

Object orientation is still an immature discipline, undergoing almost daily evolution and change. As such, the details presented for object orientation in this text may be considerably different in five years.

The documentation produced by one object approach for analysis/design includes, for example, a succinct paragraph describing the system, an object list, an object attribute list, an action list, an action attribute list, a message list, and several optional diagrams.

Current Use

Object orientation is the usual approach to developing applications in aerospace and defense organizations, and experiments with its use are occurring in most large companies. Object design appears to be the best suited method for real-time applications, and is useful for on-line applications. It is one of *the* IS buzzwords of the 1990s and appears often in every trade periodical, research journal, and booklist.

Future Use

Keeping in mind that it is neither a complete nor a mature methodology, the current high level of activity implies a future full of object-oriented applications, databases, and CASE tools. When done properly, object orientation appears capable of supporting many complex environments, including: intelligent applications, multimedia applications, and reusable code and reusable design objects. Look for object ori-entation to be around for a long time.

If you only learn one new methodology, this will be a profitable one to learn for the future.

Semantic Methodologies

History

Semantic methodologies are used in the automation of artificial intelligence (AI) applications. AI, like object orientation, is in its infancy. By definition, AI *methodologies* are also in their infancy.

AI applications cover a broad range of intellectual difficulty, ranging from recognizing to reasoning to learning (see Figure 1-24). Most AI applications in business are on the lower end of the AI spectrum, and provide limited reasoning in applications. Businesses are experimenting with more complex uses of AI.

This discussion is about AI applications that reason through problems to achieve expert level competence in a specific area of expertise. These applications are usually called knowledge-based systems (KBS) or expert systems (ES) applications. Most ES contain the reasoning processes of one or more human experts.

Semantic approaches to system life-cycle development automate the *meaning* of objects in the application. For example, a knowledge object might be composed of objects describing a 'legal' hardware configuration. The reasoning process in the ES first asks characteristics of hardware objects that are required for a system (e.g., speed of disk drive, size of disk drive). Then, using the required characteris-tics as constraints, the ES determines 'legal' configurations that meet the constraints.

At present, data and rules for evaluating data in semantic applications are defined together within the application and not separated as in traditional applications. There is no separation of analysis and design activities per se for semantic applications either. Rather, the task of knowledge engineering encompasses three general tasks: eliciting knowledge from an expert, analyzing it to define the heuristics and data, and automating the information in some logic-based language, such as Prolog.

Current Use

Knowledge-based systems are a growing segment of the applications portfolio in organizations today. This is another class of methodology, along with object orientation, that is in its infancy. Semantic methods are somewhat more well-defined for business use than object methods. But, the extent of special training and expertise required to implement intelligent applications make the knowledge inaccessible to most practicing SEs.

Future Use

There is a significant amount and diversity of research that will result in mature semantic methodologies over the next decade. One major activity in the future will be the addition of expert intelligence to current transaction, query, data analysis, and DSS systems. Semantic method use will continue to be a growth area in IS for the foreseeable future.

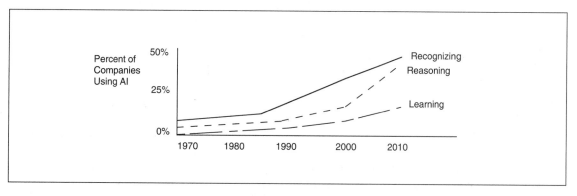

FIGURE 1-24   Range of Artificial Intelligence Applications

EXAMPLE 1-5

STOCK MARKET SELLERS, INC.

Stock Market Sellers, Inc. (SMSI) is a brokerage firm that had a reputation for slow, steady growth and low aggression relative to its industry. In 1988, SMSI embarked on a new, more aggressive position and began introducing new products practically overnight to keep up with its competition.

Automated support for SMSIs new products was the responsibility of Alec Ranier, a young Brit who was a whiz-kid programmer. Alec was promoted several times until, in 1991, he managed a staff of twenty programmers who developed applications to support new products.

When asked about his use of life cycles and methodologies, Alec said, "No, we don't use any of those methodologies or CASE technologies. We don't have time. A broker wants a new product or a new analysis the day after they ask for it, basically."

"Don't programmers have to talk to each other to coordinate their work?" I asked.

He replied, "Not usually. That's how we get away with being so informal."

"What happens when you *do* need to have programmers talk to each other?"

Alec answered, "It is a mess! (laughing) I'll grant that. We redesign, rewrite, and do a lot of code. Another side effect is we reinvent the wheel a lot. We probably have twenty programs that calculate collateralized mortgage obligations and their returns."

I was astonished. "How do you verify their accuracy?"

"Well, we don't because we can't. That is a problem. We're actually trying to design a few key modules to be reusable, but it's a problem because the potential-using programs are all going to need to be rewritten."

I asked, "Do you know any methodologies to help you do that design?"

Alec was honest. "Not really. I'm a good programmer who got promoted. Some day I might learn one but now I just want to 'get product out the door.' "

No Methodology

History

When you develop an application using no methodology, you rely on your own experience and problem-solving ability to automate a solution to a problem. The use of no methodology is implied by the discussion of the learn-as-you-go life cycle. There are no general activities because what is done and how it is done are left strictly to the individual.

Current Use

Most organizations in the United States currently use no methodology. Example 1-5 illustrates the box companies get themselves into when they do not use a methodology. As in the example, companies generally do not recognize any problems. On probing, they realize they have problems but have no idea for getting out of the situation short of rewriting all applications . . . a solution they consider too costly.

Future Use

There are two major reasons why use of no methodology will begin to disappear as a strategy for designing applications. First, trial-and-error is not a productive problem-solving strategy when the requirements for an application *can* be identified. Rather, a lack of methodology indicates laziness, shoddy work practices, and lack of rigor, usually where it is most needed. Hopefully in the future, more organizations will recognize the need for rigor in developing applications . . . their company's future might well depend on that recognition. Second, in order to use CASE tools and gain *any* of their productivity improvements, *some* methodology is required.

User Involvement in Application Development

Each of the previous methodology discussions approaches the problem of application development as if it were done only by technically oriented personnel. Where in this picture is the user of the application? Ultimately, users must supply information about the business functions and accompanying data that are being automated. In this section, we discuss user involvement in application development so you do *not* think SEs work only with each other. Although early applications *were* frequently built without discussions with users, isolation of SEs from users resulted in systems that might work technically, but often did not meet user needs, and frequently disrupted the workplace.

In the early 1960s, Scandinavians began to voice concerns over the social side effects of applications. Early systems frequently deskilled workers. Socially oriented methodologies of application development were created in response to the concerns about the effects of computerization. **Social methodologies** describe an approach to SDLC that attends to social and job-related needs of individuals who supply, receive, or use data from the application being built. Social methodologies are not really methodologies; rather, they are user involvement techniques. These techniques ignore technology completely and assume that some other approach to the technical aspects of application development is used along with user involvement.

The three main user-involvement techniques are joint application design (JAD), socio-technical systems (STS), and Ethics. The most practical and popular method is **joint application design** (JAD) which requires an off-site meeting of all involved users and systems people, who meet for five to ten days to develop a detailed functional description of application requirements. Daytime meetings are used for new analysis; nighttime meetings document daytime results for review and further refinement the next day.

There are many benefits from user involvement in application development. First, it builds commitment by users who automatically assume ownership of the system. Second, users, who are the real experts at the jobs being automated, are fully represented throughout development. Third, many tasks are performed by users, including design of screens, forms, and reports, development of user documentation, and development and conduct of acceptance tests.

We assume that user involvement is not only desirable, but *mandatory* to truly effective application development product and process. This does not imply that such design *will* result, only that it can. Using a social approach assumes that job enlargement is a desirable by-product of automation.

The most important aspect of user involvement is that it *must be meaningful*. The users must be decision makers and staff who fully understand the impact of their decisions, and who are interested in participating in the development process. Using low-level staff, or assigning 'expendable' managers is *not* the way to have users participate in developing applications. Neither is co-optation of users desired. Co-opting means that you get people to agree with the outcome because they 'participated' in the decision process even though the alternatives are all defined by the application developers.

The goal of user participation is for IS and non-IS people to work together as *business partners* rather than as adversaries. When users participate, *they* make all nontechnical decisions. The SEs explain and shepherd users to make semitechnical decisions, for instance, design of screens. The SEs explain both the impact and reasoning of major technical decisions. If this discussion implies that users call the shots, that is what is meant. User involvement means that users run the project, making the majority of decisions and having final say on *all* major decisions. The SEs and other Management Information Systems (MIS) staff act as service-oriented technicians, as they are.

In many organizations, the social aspects of work are specifically felt *not* to be within the scope of responsibility of software developers. If the development staff are only technical in their orientation, this is probably true. Then it is the responsibility of the project manager to educate user and IS management about the need to design the organization and jobs as well as the system.

In the United States, high levels of user involvement are still unlikely and usually at the discretion of the project manager. In many cases of 'user involvement', the reality is that users are not involved. Even in companies that have user project managers, IS staff can ignore user desires and build the systems *they* want to build.

SEs and users who have participated in user-involved application development tend to be fully committed to user involvement as a requirement in application development. Hopefully, the days of application development by technicians who never consult with users are gone, or soon will be. Future generations of computer-literate users will demand a say in how their systems are developed. The prognosis, then, is for user involvement to continue slow growth of use in the United States.

OVERVIEW OF THE BOOK

In this chapter so far, we have prefaced and introduced the major topics of the book. In addition to identifying specifically how the above topics will be used later in the book, there are many more topics that you will also learn that we briefly outline here.

Applications

Applications are the underlying topic of all we discuss in this text. You should already have a fairly good understanding of what an application is. We will not discuss that topic further.

What we will discuss throughout the text is how application types relate to each of the topics. You will get answers to questions such as: Which life cycles and methods are most appropriate to which application types? When do application characteristics and technologies affect the choice of life cycle and/or methodology?

Project Life Cycles

Project life cycles should also have been mostly review. PLCs, per se, are not mentioned again. Rather, the phases of feasibility, analysis, design, testing, language selection, and testing each have their own chapters. One difference between this text and most other texts is that multiple methodologies and deviations from the standard PLC are discussed in the context of each phase.

Part I: Preparation for Software Engineering

Part I prepares you for the tasks of developing and implementing an application. The chapters in this section introduce you to

- research on learning and software engineering to highlight an effective means of studying and practicing this work
- the ABC Video case used throughout the text
- the roles of project manager and software engineers
- methods of gathering information about the task to be automated
- proper behavior during application development

Part II: Project Initiation

After you know how to elicit information, we begin talking about project development. Part II first discusses organizational level re-engineering, a method to developing application plans. Then, feasibility analysis is detailed in the next chapter. These discussions are separated from those about the methodologies because these tasks are assumed by most methodologies. For each chapter, the theories underlying the concepts are introduced, a method of performing the tasks is described, and examples are provided from ABC to help make the information concrete.

Part III: Analysis and Design

Part III is devoted to analysis and design activities that each take about 20% of application development time. During analysis, the SE concentrates on defining *what* the application will do. During design, the requirements are translated to define *how* the application will operate in its specific hardware and software environment. One representative methodology from each broad class of methodologies is discussed in detail in Chapters 7 through 12. Chapters 7 and 8 discuss analysis and design, respectively, for process methodologies. Chapters 9 and 10 relate to data-oriented methodologies. Chapters 11 and 12 present object-oriented methodologies. Based on ABC's rental processing application, we will discuss what each methodology can and cannot do for you during logical definition of application requirements. For each methodology, the theories underlying its development are described and representative CASE tools available to support application development are provided.

At the conclusion of the methodology discussion, Chapter 13 recaps the graphical representations and thinking processes used in each methodology. The methodologies are compared and contrasted on several sets of criteria. In addition, future developments in technology and applications and their impact on methodologies are developed.

Some tasks are performed during analysis and design, but are not addressed by most methodologies. These forgotten activities are included in this section and discussed in Chapter 14.

Part IV: Implementation and Operations

Many tasks remain to complete an application development, including programming, testing, maintenance, and change management. Each of these topics is related to application and methodology types in Chapters 15 through 18. For every chapter,

applicable automated support tools are identified. Chapter 15 discusses the selection of a target language for an application. Code for applications will be increasingly generated by the CASE tool. As CASE use increases, the need to code, then, is replaced with a need to choose an appropriate language.

Similarly, many applications now use purchased software rather than customized code. Chapter 16 discusses the selection and purchasing of hardware, software, or consulting services for application development.

Testing is required of all applications developers at present whether a machine generates the code or not. Chapter 17 discusses different types of testing, testing techniques, and the development of test plans for an application.

Change is a way of life in application development. Chapter 18 deals with the management of change for documents and software. The section on software maintenance describes re-engineering as it applies to deciding whether or not to replace or maintain code. Several replacement options are presented.

Finally, the last chapter discusses careers in software engineering. Keeping current in a profession that constantly changes is a daunting task. In Chapter 19, you will receive tips on the type of reading you should do and the types of professional organizations you might join to enhance your ability to stay current. In addition, you will learn the types of jobs available to you as a novice software engineer and an approach for deciding on a starting job.

SUMMARY

This chapter prefaces and summarizes the contents of the text. Software engineering was defined as a systematic approach to the development, operation, maintenance, and retirement of software. A software engineer is a person who has a broad knowledge of methodologies, life cycles, languages, and all aspects of software development, and who applies that knowledge to the systematic development of application systems. The two main goals of software engineering are to build a quality *product* through a quality *process*.

Next we defined applications characteristics, responsiveness, and types. An application is a set of related programs that perform some business function. The characteristics that all applications have in common are data, processes, and constraints. Application responsiveness reflects whether the application is batch, on-line, or real-time. Finally, application types include transaction processing, query, DSS, and expert systems.

Project life cycle is the breakdown of work for initiation, development, maintenance, and retirement of an application. Alternative project life cycles include sequential, iterative, and the learn-as-you-go. The sequential life cycle includes a series of phases for initiation, feasibility, analysis, conceptual design, design, programming/unit testing, testing, implementation and checkout, maintenance, and retirement.

Methodologies are policies, techniques, and tools that guide the activities of each phase of a software project life cycle. The five classes of methodologies in this text are process, data, object, social, and semantic. Process and data methodologies are fairly mature guidelines for developing applications. Object and semantic are emerging methodologies that help us build systems using artificial intelligence and new technologies. Social methods are really techniques for involving users and assume the use of one of the other four methodology classes as well.

REFERENCES

Boehm, Barry W., *Software Engineering Economics*. Englewood Cliffs, NJ: Prentice-Hall, 1981.

Booch, Grady, *Software Engineering with Ada*, 2nd ed. Menlo Park, CA: Benjamin-Cummings, 1987.

Booch, Grady, *Object Oriented Design with Applications*. Redwood City, CA: Benjamin-Cummings, 1991.

Bostrom, Robert P., and J. Stephen Heinen, "MIS problems and failures: A socio-technical perspective," Part I, *MIS Quarterly*, September 1977, pp. 17–28.

Chen, P. P-S. "The entity-relationship model—Toward a unified view of data," *ACM Transactions on Data Structures*, Vol. 1, March 1976, pp. 9–36.

Davis, Gordon, and Margrethe Olson, *Management Information Systems: Conceptual Foundations, Structure and Development*, 2nd ed. New York: McGraw-Hill, 1985.

Department of Defense, *Standard for Application Development, Guideline #2167a*. Washington, DC: US Government Printing Office, 1985.

DeMarco, Tom, *Structured Analysis*. New York: Yourdon Press, 1979.

Eliason, Alan L., *Online Business Computer Applications*, 2nd ed. Chicago, IL: Science Research Associates, 1987.

Feigenbaum, E., P. McCorduck, and H. P. Nii, *The Rise of the Expert Company*. New York: Vintage Books, 1989.

Gane, C., and T. Sarson, *Structured Systems Analysis: Tools and Techniques*. Englewood Cliffs, NJ: Prentice-Hall, 1979.

Gane, Chris, *Computer-Aided Software Engineering: The Methodology, The Products and the Future*. Englewood Cliffs, NJ: Prentice-Hall, 1990.

IEEE, *IEEE Software Engineering Dictionary*. Piscataway, NJ: IEEE Press, 1983.

Lientz, B. P., and E. B. Swanson, *Software Maintenance Management: A Study of Maintenance of Computer Application Software in 487 Data Processing Organizations*. Reading, MA: Addison-Wesley, 1980.

McClure, Carma, *CASE is Software Automation*. Englewood Cliffs, NJ: Prentice-Hall, 1990.

Martin, James, *Information Engineering, Book 1: Introduction, Book 2: Planning and Analysis, Book 3: Design and Implementation*. Englewood Cliffs, NJ: Prentice-Hall, 1990.

Necco, Charles R., Carl L. Gordon, and Nancy W. Tsai, "Systems analysis and design: current practices," *MIS Quarterly*, December 1987, pp. 461–476.

Parnas, D. L., "On the criteria to be used in decomposing systems into modules," *Communications of the ACM*, Vol. 15, #12, 1972, pp. 1053–1058.

Sprague, Ralph H., Jr., and Hugh J. Watson, *Decision Support Systems: Putting Theory into Practice*. Englewood Cliffs, NJ: Prentice-Hall, 1986.

Swanson, E. B., *Information System Implementation: Bridging the Gap between Design and Utilization*. Homewood, IL: R. D. Irwin, 1988.

Turban, Efraim, *Decision Support and Expert Systems: Management Support Systems*. New York: Macmillan Publishing Company, 1990.

Yourdon, Edward, and Larry L. Constantine, *Structured Design*. New York: Yourdon Press, 1978.

KEY TERMS

adaptive maintenance
analysis
application characteristics
application
    responsiveness
application type
automated interface
batch applications
class
coding
computer-aided software
    engineering (CASE)
conceptual design
configuration
    management
constraint
control constraint
corrective maintenance
data
data analysis applications
data methodology
data warehouse
decision support
    applications
declarative language
design
development
economic feasibility
embedded system
    engineering
executive information
    system (EIS)
expert systems (ES)
feasibility
goals of SE
group decision support
    systems (GDSS)
hierarchic logical data
    model
human interface
implementation
inferential constraint
initiation
input
interactive processing
iterative project life cycle
joint application design
    (JAD)

knowledge acquisition
    subsystem
knowledge base
learn-as-you-go project
    life cycle
logical data model
maintenance
manual interface
meta-data
meta-meta-data
methodology
network logical data
    model
object-oriented logical
    data model
object-orientation
on-line application
operations
organizational
    feasibility
output
perfective maintenance
physical data model
postrequisite constraint
prerequisite constraint
process
process methodology
product
program design
prototyping
quality assurance
query application
real-time application
relational logical data
    model
retirement
retrieval
SE process
SE product
semantic methodology
sequential project life
    cycle
social methodology
software
Software Development
    Life Cycle (SDLC)
software engineer
software engineering

spiral application
    development
storage
structural constraint
structured problem
subsystem design
technical feasibility
testing
time constraint

transaction-oriented
    application
Transaction Processing
    System (TPS)
unit testing
unstructured problem
validation
verification

EXERCISES

1. Develop a table of application characteristics down the rows in the first column, and the application responsiveness levels across the columns. How does each application characteristic differ for each level of responsiveness?
2. Develop a table of application characteristics down the rows in the first column, and the methodology classes across the columns. Begin to develop a comparative table of the way each methodology prescribes documenting the requirements for each application characteristic. You will not be able to complete the table at this point.

STUDY QUESTIONS

1. Define the following terms:

application
    characteristics
batch application
constraint
data methodology
meta-data
object
on-line application

project life cycle
prototyping
real-time application
semantic methodology
time constraint
unstructured problem
validation

2. Define how each methodology's history is affected by technology.
3. What are the four application types and how do they differ?
4. What are the subtypes of decision support systems? How do they differ?
5. What is computer-aided software engineering?

6. What is an application?
7. How do real-time and on-line applications differ?
8. What is the range of artificial intelligence applications? What area do most expert systems cover today?
9. What is the starting point for analysis in a process methodology? for a data methodology?
10. Why is it important to know the orientation of a methodology?
11. If most companies do not use methodologies, why should you learn how to use them?
12. Is some methodology better than none? Is some life cycle better than none? Discuss the pros and cons of using and not using methodologies and life cycles.
13. What are the components of a feasibility study? What type of analysis is performed for each?
14. What are the phases of a sequential development life cycle? How do they vary when you use prototyping?
15. What are the five types of constraints? Give an example of each.
16. What are the four application types? Give an example of each.
17. How do on-line and real-time applications differ?
18. Draw a diagram showing the operation of a typical batch application. Then draw a diagram showing the operation of a typical on-line application. Discuss how they are similar and how they are different.

19. What is the difference between a semantic methodology and an object-oriented methodology?
20. What is quality assurance and when is it performed?
21. What is *meaningful* user involvement?
22. List the three uses of prototyping.
23. What are the dangers in using prototyping?
24. What is wrong with a learn-as-you-go life cycle?
25. What is dangerous about using no methodology and no life cycle?

★ EXTRA-CREDIT QUESTIONS

1. Develop the pros and cons of the ethical issues described in Example 1-5. What is your opinion? How can the open questions be resolved?
2. What can be done to further the involvement of users in applications development? Should this be done? How can it be done in an ethical way?
3. Are methodologies as you know them at this point culture free? How can culture get in the way of their use in a multinational organization?
4. Think beyond this text to the development of applications in a multinational organization. What are cultural and ethical issues in building applications that will be used in many countries of unequal computer resources?

PREPARATION FOR SOFTWARE ENGINEERING

The four chapters in this section prepare you for the actual work of software engineering. Chapter 2 serves two purposes: First, research on learning and software engineering are summarized to give you some ideas about how to organize the text's material. Good mental maps of the information ease your learning and help you keep the different methodologies distinct. Second, a case describing an application to be built is introduced: ABC Video rental processing. The application is developed in each of the methodologies we will discuss.

Project managers and software engineers perform different duties and are usually different individuals on a project team. In Chapter 3 you will learn the roles of project managers and software engineers and how they complement each other. The kinds of questions we will answer are: What does a project manager do? How does it differ from a software engineer? Why is knowledge of management important to a software engineer?

Last, in preparation for developing systems, Chapter 4 defines techniques for gathering the information you need to analyze and design a system. Then, we will discuss how you should act and how to evaluate what you are told during information gathering. Sample dialogues between ABC managers and the software engineering team illustrate the information presented in Chapter 2.

LEARNING APPLICATION DEVELOPMENT

INTRODUCTION

There is rarely one 'right' solution application in software engineering. Just as in Chapter 1, we said there is rarely one 'right' way of getting a solution for an application. Despite this ambiguity of the software engineering process and product, there *are* approaches to problem solving in software engineering that are more successful than others. Your gaining experience to know those approaches is one goal of this text. To assist you, this chapter discusses how we learn, how we evolve from novice to expert, and how you can apply this knowledge to mastering the material in this book. In the second section, the case study we follow throughout the text is introduced. The case is related to learning approaches suggested in the first section, and to the review in Chapter 1. First, let us turn to learning and the development of expertise.

HOW WE DEVELOP KNOWLEDGE AND EXPERTISE

Learning

There are two basic stages of skill development in learning that we call the declarative and procedural

knowledge development stages. In the **declarative**, or *what* stage, we learn basic skills, rules, and activity sequences. We learn declarative knowledge before process knowledge. During the **process**, or *how* stage, we imbed the *what* knowledge into a process. We learn *how* to perform the activity sequences, and *how* to integrate the different rules. In the last part of *how* learning, we internalize both the declarative and process knowledge so they become part of our automatic memory.[1]

The internalization of declarative and process knowledge occurs through

- experiencing real life
- doing classroom exercises
- reading cases and solutions
- developing practice problems with feedback
- studying both good and bad examples

Cognitive psychology and artificial intelligence research describe human thinking as case-based reasoning. **A case** is a predetermined representation of event sequences in a particular setting.[2] During

---

1 For a complete discussion of declarative and process knowledge, see Chi, Glaser, & Rees, 1982.

2 Kintsch & Mannes, 1987, discuss case-based reasoning. Schank & Abelson, 1977, also writing about artificial intelligence call case-based reasoning "script" based reasoning. The two terms—case and script—are essentially the same.

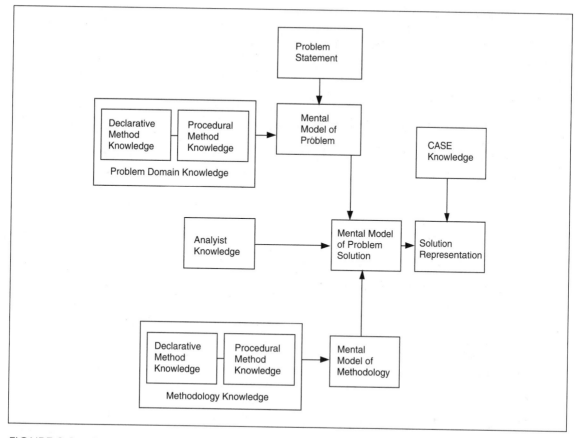

FIGURE 2-1   Interaction of Knowledge Types in Systems Analysis (adapted from Vessey & Conger, 1993)

learning, we recognize patterns of alternatives, expected actions, and decisions that work. After reaching a detailed level of understanding of the patterns, we internalize a *case*, imbedding the patterns, actions, and decisions into our knowledge structure.

In systems analysis, two different types of cases might be appropriate: analysis task and problem task. Figure 2-1 illustrates the information used in analysis and how they interact. The **analysis domain** case is the declarative and process knowledge of actions needed to do the analysis task. We can divide analysis tasks further into subjective and objective activities. Subjective analysis activities are subproblems in application development that accompany all methodologies. Some representative analyst knowledge includes knowing

- what life cycle is appropriate
- what data-gathering technique is likely to be most effective
- when data gathering is complete enough
- when we should iterate through earlier stages of the process

During objective analysis activities, we describe the functioning and design of a proposed application. We may further subdivide objective activities into techniques used, such as methodology or computer-aided software engineering (CASE) tools. When we do not follow a methodology, we rely on our own problem-solving ability and knowledge.

The second type of knowledge required to develop an application is problem task case knowledge. Problem task knowledge is the declarative and process knowledge of the **problem domain** being automated. For example, order entry–inventory control processing describes a general problem task domain. If we add that the system is for a retail business, it is less general. If we add that the system is for Sears and Roebuck, for instance, it is less general again. During the automation process, we apply our knowledge of how to do analysis to the problem domain. We use analysis knowledge both to describe the current system and to develop the functions of the new system.

Use of Learned Information

Case-based reasoning relies on our recall of past similar experiences, that is, analogous events. **Analogies** are similar experiences that we use to

- classify problems
- plan a course of action
- suggest explanations
- suggest means of recovery from failures

When the analogy matches the current situation, we use it to predict what will happen based on the analogous event. When the analogy *does not* fit, we look for similarities between current and past experiences from which we can generalize to build new analogies.

During the learning process, we build our own examples to help us learn new information. We recognize similarities between different episodes, compile the similar, generalized events, and form a new memory case. This **generalization** process *is* learning. Learning calls for failure of an analogous expectation to work for the current case, followed by explanation of the failure which we make sense of and fit into our own memory as a new case.

Why is the use of analogy so important? System analysis is work that requires judgment and adjustment. System analysis has nonoptimal solutions (i.e., relies on satisficing), and takes place within a bounded knowledge base. Analogical reasoning is better for systems analysis than reasoning by understanding because *analogical reasoning relies on experience* to generate cases while *understanding relies on experimental trial and error*. When analysts have applicable analogous experience, we try to fit that knowledge to the current situation to serve several purposes: understanding of situational dynamics, generating options, and calculating the chance of success of an application option.

In systems analysis tasks, there are frequently one or more aspects of a problem that are unfamiliar to the analyst. In unfamiliar situations, analysts first rely on aspects of the work with which we are familiar, then enlarge and broaden the applicability of our analogical knowledge. But what happens when we do not have the experience to use analogies or our analogies do not appear applicable? Then, we turn to expert/novice differences in problem solving for general tasks to see what happens.

Expert/Novice Differences in Problem Solving

The differences between experts and novices are difficult to pin down. **Expert** analysts are considered to have an extensive, internalized knowledge upon which they draw to apply analogous problem domains and problem-solving techniques to a current analysis task. They work quickly, knowing what they know and what they don't know, and are able to determine at least one workable solution quickly, sometimes within minutes. A **novice**, on the other hand, is slow and unsure, exhibiting some, but not all expert behaviors, and making mistakes throughout the process. Experts and novices differ considerably in their approaches to solving problems. For instance, novices

- develop **local mental models** of problem parts, that is, work on bits of small problems rather than on integrating the bits into a whole. For example, novices concentrate on adding customers instead of concentrating on customer maintenance, including add, change, delete, and retrieval processing.
- use **undirected search** in a trial and error manner (for example, to determine the utility of a new technology). The undirected way is to look through several magazines to see if

they have articles on the technology, instead of looking through a subject index at a library.

- analyze **surface features** (for example, think of control statuses and their allowable values instead of the implications for processing that relate to each value)
- simulate design entities in isolation (for example, simulate video rental processing without paying attention to how it works with return processing)
- misconceive actions (for example, never analyze the complete rental/return cycle)
- fail to integrate the chunked local models into a whole global problem solution (for example, fail to integrate history processing into the rental/return cycle)

Novice problem-solving strategies include satisficing and conservatism. **Satisficing** means to knowingly elect a nonoptimal solution.[3] Novices search for *any* solution; experts search for the *best* solution. **Conservatism** is minimal change of a solution; it means the problem solver takes the first solution rather than testing alternatives. Novices search for alternatives only when the existing method fails, but they cannot always tell that the existing method is failing. So, in becoming conservative, novices use their first conceptualization of a problem. In contrast, experts use optimizing and alternative evaluation in analysis and design. Because of conservatism, novices suffer **breakdowns**—errors in the problem-solving process. Since the process is both constrained and directed by a methodology, the breakdowns relate to the analyst's *mental model* of the problem and *use of a methodology* to develop a mental model of the solution.

Conversely, experts do

- **categorize** problems (for instance, ABC Video Rental processing is a simple form of an order entry problem)
- develop **global mental models** of the problem that they 'see' or visualize the entire problem solution

- use **directed searches** in problem expansion and identification of similar problems
- analyze **deep structures**, not just define terms but analyze their meaning, fit, and the political and technical implications
- use **goals** and **plans** to determine what steps to take in finding a solution
- perform skilled sequences of actions including mental simulation and top-down expansion of the problem

Experts use knowledge of the application development process to direct actions independently from the problem. For instance, regardless of the problem or methodology, you always begin with a definition of the scope of the activity. This abstract knowledge about structuring of a problem, procedures, and process uses internalized cases and plans, and relies on experience. Problem analysis and design involve decomposition of a problem into sub-problems, relying on substrategies of analogy and understanding to guide decomposition in a top-down manner. When the problem domain is new and the problem type is new, expansion progresses breadth-first. But, for problem solving in familiar domains, experts prioritize areas on which to focus, using a depth-first strategy for each new area.

With methodology training, practice, and feedback, novice software engineers can display many expert behaviors in a short time, i.e., after analyzing and designing as few as three case problems.[4] Methodologies sequence events, and constrain and direct the actual analytical process. Guidelines and heuristics about what to analyze and how to analyze it are supplied by the method with comments supplied by the text and instructor. Relationships are identified to link each deliverable within a method, associating the thought processes used to develop the deliverables. All of these directed activities speed and simplify both the development of expert behavior and the internalization of methodologies.

Research on whether there are differences between methodologies for facilitating expert

---

3 See Simon [1960] for a more complete discussion of satisficing and decision making.

4 See Vessey & Conger, 1993, for an example of this type of study.

behaviors is in its infancy. Several laboratory studies by the author and others identify process methods as easier to learn, with no noticeable difference between methodologies in the delivered quality of the resulting proposed logical system. One thing we *do* know is that not all methodologies work equally well for all problems. This information will be discussed in Chapter 13.

How to Ease Your Learning Process

In this text, we assume that you want to go beyond knowing the basics of systems analysis and design, but that you *do know* the basics. We assume you have a working knowledge of structured systems analysis and design, data base, and programming. Most systems analysis and design courses practice developing data flow diagrams. In this text, we will discuss DFDs and compare and contrast them with other methods, building on your current state of knowledge. If you don't feel confident about your ability to draw data flow diagrams, there are exercises at the end of Chapter 6 for practice. For database knowledge you should know and understand the value of normalization, and you should be familiar with SQL and at least one database package. For programming, you should have practice with some procedural language (e.g., Cobol) writing and debugging programs that read sequential files to generate reports. Knowledge of data structures, files, and a structured language, such as Pascal, is helpful but not necessary to using this book successfully.

Application development is essentially a problem-solving exercise which is unique because there is rarely one *right* or *best* answer to an automation problem. Practitioners and professors of application development will both tell you that the best way to learn software engineering is to "Do it!" A quote to support this idea comes from Confucius:

I see and I forget,
I hear and I remember,
I do and I understand.

In doing, you *will* make mistakes, get confused, and think you are completely wrong. Don't give up. Ask questions. Since we learn declarative knowledge first, try to remember as much of the procedural *what* knowledge as you can while you read the text.

Try to think like an expert. Try to develop a global picture of the problem, methodology, or other subject in your mind and develop a plan of attack for your work session. Try to categorize problems both that you are working on and that you are having with the work. Analyze your thought processes to develop a better understanding of your problem-solving approach. See if you can mentally simulate your application design, asking yourself how complete it is and how well it solves the problem. Attempt to analyze the 'deep structures' by asking what each term *means* and what it *implies*. Talk about all of these thought processes both with your instructor and with other students.

Practice your reasoning *process* by reviewing the example in the text, by working through problems at the end of each chapter, and by talking to other students about the reasoning you used to develop your representations. Try different ways of doing the same thing. When you find mistakes, try to learn *why* what you did was not the best, and *how* you could have reasoned to develop a better answer. Through these processes, you will learn valuable problem-solving skills that will be useful throughout your career in IS.

APPLICATION DEVELOPMENT CASE

Now, we are going to switch gears, away from the theoretical to the realistic. In this section, we present the case used throughout the text. The setting, a video store, is used for two reasons. First, it is a simple business that should allow you to build an accurate, complete mental model. A complete mental model is crucial to developing an accurate solution in *any* methodology. Second, most of us rent videos and have analogous knowledge that we can practice using. As you read the cases, try to apply the ideas discussed in the previous section. Ask yourself,

What is the 'big' picture? Do I understand this problem? Use analogies from your experiences as a video store customer (or clerk) to the way Vic wants to run his business.

The case—ABC Video Rental Processing—is representative of the class of order processing/inventory control problems. Through its processing, customer, inventory, and order files are maintained. In addition, ABC Video Rental Processing also is unique in that the video rental business is different from other businesses, and ABC's video rental processing is distinct from other video rental businesses.

ABC Video rental processing similarities and differences from other types of order processing applications highlight the importance of knowing how to learn. The similarities allow you to use analogy to determine the general requirements of the application. For instance, all order entry applications require *customer*, *order*, and *inventory* databases. Conversely, each company does its own detailed processing for order fulfillment. In ABC's case, it is a *rental* company, not a *sales* company, and rentals are not handled the same as sales. So even if you already know *order processing*, only a portion of the knowledge will be applicable to the rental situation. Keep this in mind when you discuss your own video store experiences. Each store has its own 'brand' of processing that might differ from ABC's. You must constantly evaluate the applicability of your past experience to the current situation, trying to use everything possible without forcing inappropriate past knowledge on the new client's application. Next, the context of the industry is described.

History of the Video Rental Business

The video rental industry experienced phenomenal growth during the 1980s. The cost of entry into the industry was low, every mom-and-pop store, supermarket, and small time entrepreneur entered the market. There was no stability in the market and competition was fierce. For instance, some businesses required "membership fees," others did not.

Some businesses charged one price for all rentals, usually about $2.00 per videotape per day. Some businesses offered promotions, such as "Two-Fer-Tuesdays," for which two tapes were the same price as one.

Soon businesses recognized that 80% of their videos were rented within 20 days of a tape's release into the market. With this recognition, video stores introduced a two-tiered pricing system, charging a *new-release* price and an *old-release* price. The market began to destabilize and small store owners, for whom the business was a sideline, were forced to decide if they wanted to devote the floor space to videos which soon became obsolete, or if they would abandon the business. They abandoned the business in droves and the video rental industry went through a period of consolidation.

The business today is stable, but is becoming monopolized by large chains: RKO and Blockbuster, for instance. ABC is an anomaly in this market because it is still a one-person, one-store operation. Vic, ABC's owner, would like to offer unique and useful services with a minimum of 'bureaucracy' in the process, and to eventually franchise his business expertise. With these goals in mind, we turn to his business requirements for defining the video order processing application Vic wants to build.

ABC Video Order Processing Task

ABC Video rents video cassettes to customers. Since this business is becoming more competitive, Vic, the owner, wants to automate rental processing, inventory maintenance, and an expert system to speed and simplify the rental process. Vic prepared information for the consulting team to begin work. Vic tried to separate what he wanted from what he needed. So, the application business requirements are listed. Then, Vic's 'vision' of the application is presented.

General Requirements (Excerpted from a memo from Vic to consultants)

. . . ABC Video currently owns two PC ATs and can get IBM compatible PCs cheaply. I would like all the machines hooked together somehow to share the information and have some equipment backup in case a PC breaks down. Each PC will have a printer for two-part forms. If the customer wants a copy of an order, he or she takes the top copy and signs the bottom. I need a signed copy to legally charge for unreturned tapes.

I want to minimize typing throughout all the processing. Bar code readers are cheap. Can we use that technology for keeping track of rentals?

There are three to six clerks doing rentals at any one time, sharing machines. Rental/return processing is about 90% of the business. Machines should be allowed to do any processing, but should stay set at rental/return processing once there. I want to be able to know where every tape in the store is—out on rental, on the shelf, or waiting reconditioning.

Business requirements relate to customer, videos, rentals, and history information. Each of these requirements are listed below.

Customer Requirements

Customers are people who desire to rent videos for one or more days.

1. All customers must be 'registered'. This means they must have an *easy to remember* identification code, plus their phone number, name, address, credit card number, credit card type, and credit card expiration date on record before they may rent videos.
2. All members of a household should be able to share the same identification number.
3. Customers are required to pay rentals in advance and settle late fees before any new rentals are allowed.
4. Customers can return tapes in three ways:

   - Drop off through a slot in the door
   - Drop off at the desk as they walk in to get new videos
   - Drop off as they take out new rentals

5. Customers who fail to return tapes or damage tapes are charged for the video on their credit cards. Their customer record must be marked 'bad credit risk' and they will not be allowed to rent videos.
6. Retrieval of customer information must be allowed by identification, phone, name, address, zip, or credit card number.

7. All fields must be allowed to be changed as required.
8. Reports on number of new customers by month, by year, 'bad credit risk' customers, late returning customers, expired credit card numbers must all be allowed.
9. Deleting of customers must be allowed by the manager (Vic) only.

Video Requirements

Videos are taped movies, sports, or music events that are rented to customers.

1. All videos received in the store must be 'registered' and tracked. Minimum information is identification number of copies, title, vendor, code, and date received. Video registration should use some technology (a bar code reader?) that does not require typing.
2. Individual copies of videos should be identifiable for rental/return processing.
3. All copies of a title must be identifiable to track rental trends.
4. Counts of the number of rentals by copy and by title should be available for reporting.
5. Retrieval of video information for reporting must be allowed on any single or multiple criteria. Common reports needed will be for maintenance (based on how many rentals), number of tapes and rentals by type (e.g., musical, horror, drama, comedy), and for tapes that have not rented in the last x days.
6. I don't know how hard or expensive this is, but I would like some history information, such as

   - rentals by copy by title
   - days rented by month by year by copy by title
   - rentals by customer so I can warn them when they try to re-rent a title

7. Future provisions should allow for

   - tracking the number of days of rentals by copy by title or by dates of rentals
   - multiple rental products (such as VCRs, camcorders, CDs, video games, Nintendo game sets, and so on)
   - automatic debit card or credit card payments
   - variable rental charges based on promotions, date of receipt, and so on

Rental Processing

1. First, NO BUREAUCRACY! Second, the process MUST BE EASY. The rental process must not require customers to carry a card, must not require clerks to type much, and must be easy to learn. Return processing must also be simple and flexible.
2. To take out tapes, customer ID and video IDs are entered. All other information should be pulled from the computer.
3. The system should compute total charges, include late fees, and compute change for money entered.
4. The computer must be hooked to a cash drawer or cash register that unlocks when the money is entered.
5. A printed copy of orders must be kept and signed by customers. These go to accounting and are reconciled at the end of the day.
6. End of day totals for the cash registers must show a total number of tapes out, cash paid, tapes in, on-time tapes, late tapes, late fees, and a total amount of money in for the day.

Vic's Vision of Rental/Return Processing

Customers choose videos for rental either by taking the empty box from a shelf in the store or by telling the clerk the video name(s). The clerk retrieves the tape(s), which are filed alphabetically by name. The clerk enters customer identification (could this be phone number?) into the system to retrieve the customer's record and to create an order. Any late fees from previous rentals must be settled before a new rental can occur.

The clerk uses a bar code reader (or other scanner) to scan the video identifier and enter videotape identification into the system. For each video bar code entered, the system completes the rental detail line on the screen with today's date, videotape identification, video name, and rental price. When bar code IDs for all videotapes to be rented have been entered, the system computes the total fee, automatically computing and adding in sales tax. Late fees may be added to the total if any are outstanding. The customer is told the total amount and the money is paid.

When the clerk enters the money amount into the system and puts the cash into the cash register, the system reduces the amount paid by the total fee amount to obtain the amount of change due to the customer. The amount due to ABC for the rental is reduced to

zero on the order. The customer signs a copy of the order form as it is printed on a printer and takes the video(s) home.

On return of tapes, the clerk scans the bar code IDs of the videos. The system should retrieve and display the order with the return date and any late fees added to the detail line. If either there are no late fees or late fees are settled upon return of the video, the order is deleted from the system and the history of use information for the tape is updated. Late fees, and the order information about tape(s) rented that caused the late fee(s), remain on file until they are paid.

Trend analysis should include query capabilities with statistics built in. This should be available on an ad hoc basis without having to anticipate all queries and/or types of analysis in advance. Part of the analysis is used to determine how many tapes of each film to purchase. Trends might be based on sequential nights of rental, number of nights rented within the first 20 days, number of nights rented within the second 20 days, and so on. Each individual tape, even though it might be the nth copy of m copies of the same film, should be identifiable for this analysis. These requirements are not included with the description of required file information above, because you should determine the best way to supply this information.

Discussion

Let's stop here a moment and think about the ABC Rental Processing case. First, get a global mental model of the problem. The problem is to automate rental/return, customer, and video inventory processing, including totaling of orders, computing change, monitoring of late returns, and creation of historical information. This sounds like a complete statement of problem scope, and it could be used for that purpose. In this case, the problem is small enough to hold most of the functions in mind at once.

Do you know enough to automate the problem? No, you do not, not if you want to do it properly. The processes, in terms of how a customer will interact with ABC personnel, are fairly simple. Rental processing has fairly well-defined data requirements and business requirements about how to do the process steps. The flow of processes for rentals still needs elaboration, but is complete enough for understanding the general problem.

What don't you know? The kinds of questions we will ask will be details of what we already know: How many? How often? What about variations on the process? Questions will also elaborate on constraints and determine if there are interfaces. Some examples of specific questions include: How many videos are there in the store? How many new ones arrive each month, week, day? How many customers are there? How many rentals per day? What kind of security is needed? Does Vic already have software in mind for this application?

There are many more questions we will ask as we move through the text, and the type of questions varies with the methodology. Even with many questions, we *do* know quite a bit about the overall process and Vic's ideas for how the process should work. We know much less about specific details of the operation that we need to fully understand the problem and devise a workable solution. We will get more details as we progress through the text.

In terms of the Chapter 1 discussion on types of applications, rental processing will be on-line with interactive processing. It is a transaction processing application with some query processing. The rental application transaction portion automates the paperwork of rentals, returns, and payments for rentals. The query and reporting part of the rental application uses predefined data in a read-only manner, and has predefined reporting requirements as well as ad hoc reporting requirements. The rental processing case is used throughout this text to reason through each methodology.

SUMMARY

In this chapter we explained the nature of learning and experience. Declarative knowledge is knowledge about *what* actions, procedures, or steps are taken to perform some task. Declarative knowledge is a required but incomplete learning. Process knowledge is knowledge about *how* to perform, reason, and integrate the steps we know from declarative learning. While we learn, we form analogies or cases that form patterns of experiences. When we match a pattern from experience with some current problem, we use analogical thinking. When a past experience does not match some current problem, we analyze the differences to develop a new case based on the new situation. The internalization of cases in our memory is learning.

Novices differ from experts in their problem-solving approach. Novices make mistakes because they do not have a global view of a problem, cannot mentally simulate a solution to the problem, and do not see connections and meaning in problem parts. Experts are able to analyze novel problems because they use analogies from their experience to develop a global view of the problem, can take a top-down view of what they know and do not know, can simulate their solutions mentally, and understand connections and meaning in problem parts. Several tips for practicing software engineering were provided to speed and simplify your learning.

The case company, ABC Video, and its role in the video rental business was described, rental-order processing details were developed.

REFERENCES

Adelson, B., and E. Soloway, "The Role of Domain Experience in Software Design," *IEEE Transactions on Software Engineering, SE-11*, Vol. 11, 1985, pp. 1351–1360.

Jeffries, R., A. A. Turner, P. G. Polson, and M. E. Atwood, "The Processes Involved in Designing Software," in *Cognitive Skills and Their Acquisition* (J. R. Anderson, ed.). Hillsdale, NJ: Lawrence Erlbaum Associates, 1987, pp. 255–283.

Kintsch, W., and S. M. Mannes, "Generating Scripts from Memory," in *Knowledge Aided Information Processing* (E. van der Meer and J. Hoffman, eds.). NY: Elsevier Science Publishing Co., Inc., 1987, pp. 61–80.

Klein, G. A., and R. Calderwood, "How do People Use Analogies to Make Decisions?," in *Proceedings of Case Based Reasoning Workshop* (J. Kolodner, ed.), DARPA/ISTO, Clearwater Beach, FL, May, 1988, pp. 209–218.

Littman, D. C., J. Pinto, S. Lechovsky, and E. Soloway, "Mental Models and Software Maintenance," in *Empirical Studies of Programmers—1st Workshop*

(E. Soloway and S. Iyengar, eds.). Norwood, NJ: Ablex Publishing Co., July 5–6, 1986, pp. 80–98.

Schank, R. C., and R. P. Abelson, *Scripts, Plans, Goals and Understanding*. Hillsdale, NJ: Lawrence Erlbaum Associates, 1977.

Schank, R. C., "Explanation: A First Pass," in *Experience, Memory and Reasoning*, (J. L. Kolodner and C. K. Riesbeck, eds.). Hillsdale, NJ: Lawrence Erlbaum Associates, 1986, pp. 139–166.

Shemer, I., "Systems analysis: A systemic analysis of a conceptual model," *Communication of the ACM*, Vol. 30, #6, June, 1987, pp. 506–512.

Simon, H., *The New Science of Management Decision*. NY: Harper and Row, 1960.

Vessey, I., and S. A. Conger, "Requirements specification: Learning object, process, and data methodologies," *Communications of the ACM*, accepted for publication, 1993.

Wand, Y., and R. Weber, "A unified model of software and data decomposition," in *Proceeding of the 12th International Conference on Information Systems* (J. I. DeGross, I. Benbasat, F. DeSanctis, and C. M. Beath, eds.). NY: SIGBDP, Association for Computing Machinery, 1991.

KEY TERMS

analogy	generalization
analysis domain	global mental model
breakdown	goal
case	local mental model
case-based reasoning	novice
categorize problems	plan
conservation	problem domain
declarative knowledge	process knowledge
deep structures	satisficing
directed search	surface features
expert	undirected search

EXERCISES

1. Develop pseudo-code for ABC Video's rental processing system. Identify and discuss what the essential portions of rental processing are. Discuss which procedures could be either included or omitted without changing the essence of the problem. (Note to Instructor: This is a useful exercise to ensure that all students have a good understanding of the problem.)

2. Describe a work situation you have experienced. Discuss the organization: the structure of the organization, its goals, its strategies for meeting its goals, its culture, its managers' style, the social life at work.

   A. Describe your job and how your job contributed to the organization's goals. Describe the computer applications, if any, you used in your job. Analyze what you did on your job and recommend computer applications that could have streamlined, enhanced, or broadened your job. Do you have the 'big picture' of the company and your job's role? If not, how would you go about developing a global view?

   B. Describe some area of the organization (you may or may not have worked there) that could use an application to speed its work, make its work more accurate, enhance jobs, provide better information to workers, or simplify work life. Describe the application and how it would meet its goals.

STUDY QUESTIONS

1. Define the following terms:

analogy	problem domain
conservatism	satisficing
declarative knowledge	surface features
global mental model	

2. Which comes first—declarative knowledge or process knowledge? Why? How does learning work?

3. Why and how do we use analogies?

4. Why are analogies better used in systems analysis and design than a trial-and-error method of problem solving?

5. Describe the details of what it means to rent a tape at ABC. How do the manual processes translate into computer processes? Use analogies from your own experience to discuss rentals.

6. Make a list of questions you have about ABC order processing that still need to be answered.

Use analogies from your own video rental experience to identify issues that still need to be resolved.

7. Describe the details of what it means to return a tape. How do the manual processes translate into computer processes? Identify subprocedures for which you have choices about when and how they are performed.

8. How do you *develop* a global mental model of some problem? How do you know *if you have* a global mental model of some problem? How do you validate your mental model?

9. What does it mean to create historical information? When does history get created? In the ABC case, is history created at video rental time? or at video return time? or at some other time? How do you know when you have the correct answer to this type of question?

★ EXTRA-CREDIT QUESTIONS

1. Write a one page analysis of some work experience you know about. Describe some function and how it contributed to the organization's goals. Describe the computer applications, if any, used in the function. Analyze the job and recommend computer applications that could streamline, enhance, or broaden the function. Make a list of questions you need answered to gain a complete understanding of the problem areas.

2. Draw a diagram or verbally describe (in pseudocode or your own words) how ABC Video performs order processing. Make a list of questions you have about ABC order processing that still need to be answered. Describe how your experience as a video store customer helps you understand what ABC is trying to do. Describe, from your experience as a video store customer, how you think a video store should be automated. How does it differ from Vic's desires? What should you do about those differences? What are Vic's goals for the application in addition to processing rental/returns? What features might you consider for the application to meet those goals? List three functions you can put in the system to help meet Vic's goal of "no bureaucracy."

## CHAPTER 3

PROJECT
MANAGEMENT

INTRODUCTION

The role of the software engineer (SE) differs from the project manager in that the SE provides technical expertise, while the project manager provides organizational expertise. Depending on the size of an organization and project team, one person might perform both roles. Small project teams (i.e., less than five people) and organizations with limited software development staff (i.e., less than 10 people) expect one person to assume both software engineer and project manager roles. The larger the organization, the more likely the functions are split and the more extensive each person's experience is expected to be.

The project manager and software engineer are responsible for tasks that include both complementary and supplementary skills. In general, the *software engineer* is solely responsible for management of the life cycle, including the following areas detailed in Chapters 4 through 14:

- Management and conduct of development process
- Development of all documentation
- Selection and use of computer-aided software engineering (CASE) tools
- Elicitation of user requirements
- Technical guidance of less skilled staff

- Assurance that representation techniques, such as data flow diagrams, are correct, consistent, and validated
- Oversight of technical decisions
- Assurance that constraints (e.g., two-second response time) are identified and planned as part of the application

Complementary activities are activities that are performed jointly but with different emphasis depending on the role. Complementary activities include planning the project, assigning staff to tasks, and selecting from among different application alternatives.

The project manager (PM) is solely responsible for organization liaison, project staff management, and project monitoring and control. These major responsibilities are discussed in this chapter.

When one person or another is identified as solely responsible for some activity, it does not mean that they alone *do* the work. The SE and PM are team leaders who work together in all aspects of development. The SE may have project management experience. Sole responsibility means that when a disagreement occurs, responsibility for the final decision rests with the responsible person. Different management styles determine how open a manager is to suggestion and discussion of alternatives.

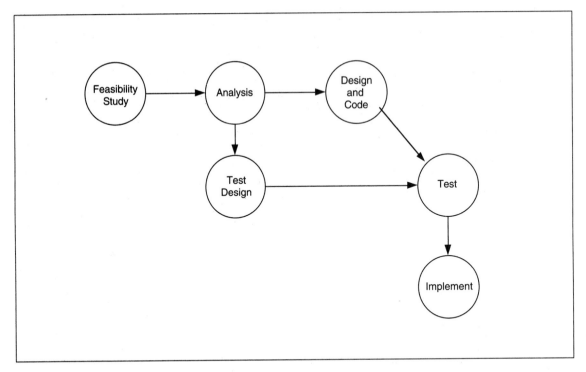

FIGURE 3-1   Example of Too General a Plan

A short discussion of appropriate behaviors for project managers is also included in this section. These behaviors are the project manager's responsibility toward the project.

First we discuss the joint SE and PM activities. Then we discuss activities for which the project manager is solely responsible. Management styles and a brief discussion of project manager responsibilities to the project team are included in the section on personnel management. The last section lists computer-aided support tools for project management.

COMPLEMENTARY ACTIVITIES

Joint activities of the software engineer and project manager include project planning and control, assigning staff to tasks, and selecting from among different alternatives for the application.

Project Planning

To plan the project, the project manager works with the SE to determine human, computer, and organizational resources required to develop the application. While a detailed discussion of planning is included in Chapter 6, the aspects of special interest to the project manager are in this section.

A **project plan** is a map of tasks, times, and their interrelationships. It can be very general (see Figure 3-1) or very specific (see Figure 3-2). Neither extreme of plan is very useful although some plan is better than none. A rule of thumb for level of detail is to define activities for which a weekly review of progress allows the SE and project manager to know whether the schedule is being met. Figure 3-3 shows an example of a well-defined plan.

The general methodology of planning is as follows:

1. List tasks. Include application development tasks, project specific tasks, interface organi-

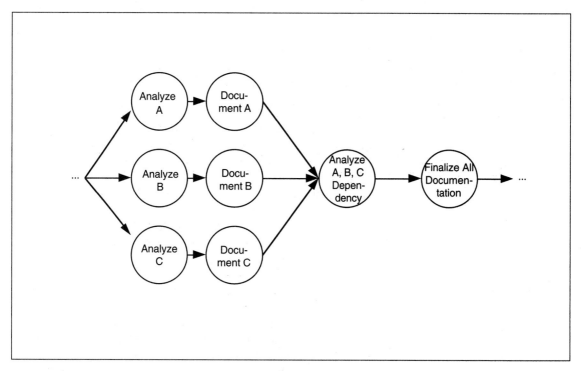

FIGURE 3-2   Example of Too Detailed a Plan

zation tasks, and review and approval tasks.

2. Identify dependencies between tasks.
3. Assign personnel either by name or by skill and experience level.
4. Assign completion times to tasks; compute the most likely time for each.
5. Identify the critical path.

The project manager and SE share responsibility for developing the plan. The *SE's responsibility* is to know all of the tasks relating to the application being developed; the *project manager's responsibility* is to ensure that all organizationally related tasks are included in the list. (The application tasks are discussed in Chapter 6.) Organization tasks include the following:

1. Review documents for completeness, content, consistency, and accuracy.
2. Negotiate, agree, and commit to start and end dates for work.

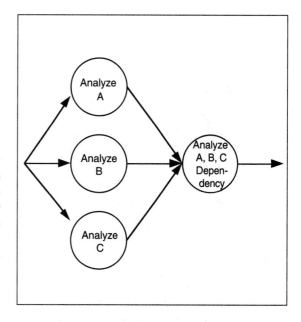

FIGURE 3-3   Example of Acceptable Level of Detail

3. Define necessary application interfaces; plan for detailed interface design work.

All documentation, plans, and design work of the project team is subject to review by at least the user/sponsor. Many other departments or organizations might also be required to review some or all of the work. These organizations might include managers of IS, users, quality assurance, legal, audit, operations, other application groups, government regulators, industry regulators, or others. Each organization applies its specialized knowledge to the application documents to assess their adequacy.

The second task is to obtain agreement and commitments from outside agencies or departments. Frequently, resources and work are provided by other departments. Clerical support, for example, might be from an Administrative Services Department. Operations departments supply support in terms of computer time, memory, disk space, terminals, log-on IDs, access to software environments, access to data bases, and so on as necessary to develop and test the application. Auditors frequently want to comment on auditing plans and change the design based on their findings. Quality assurance departments might review documents to find inconsistencies and errors that require correction. Vendors might need to install hardware, software, or related applications that need liaison from the project team and testing once installed. All of these activities need to be scheduled and planned. Since dates for commitments might not be known when the plan is developed, the plan contains the dates at which contact should be initiated and dates by which the commitment must be made in order not to impact the delivery date.

Third, the project manager obtains requirements for application interfaces from other application areas. An **interface** is data that is sent or received between applications. The interface application areas might be in the same company, but might also be an industry group or a government organization. The plan reflects dates by which contact should be initiated and by which the information is required.

If a make-or-buy decision will be made, the project manager and SE work together to develop the subplan for this decision. Subactivities relating to acquisitions include creating and submitting requests for a proposal (RFP), obtaining vendor quotes, evaluating vendor quotes, selecting and obtaining management approval for a vendor, negotiating contract and delivery dates, and planning and testing of the acquired item.

When all of the items are identified, they are related to each other. Tasks that are related are drawn on a **task dependency diagram** showing the sequences of dependencies. Sequences may be interdependent (see Figure 3-4). When all sequences of tasks are on the diagram, independent tasks are added. Milestones, such as the completion of a feasibility analysis document, are shown and are visually obvious because the preceding sets of tasks all feed into that task. Task sequencing can vary depending on the methodology used. (See Chapter 6 for more on this topic.)

Sequencing tasks is the first step to identifying the critical path of tasks for the application's development. The **critical path** is the sequence of dependent tasks that together take the most development time. If any of the tasks in the critical path are delayed, the project is also delayed. So, the critical path tasks are the greatest source of risk for project completion.

The next step is to estimate the amount of work. For this discussion, we assume the project manager and SE assign times to tasks based on their experience (i.e., reasoning by analogy). Other methods are discussed in Chapter 6. Times are assigned to each task based on its complexity and amount of work. Three times should be estimated: an optimistic time, a realistic time, and a pessimistic time. The formula used to compute the most likely time is shown in Figure 3-5. The figure weights the most likely, realistic time by a factor of two in relation to the other estimates.

While times are being assigned, the skill sets and experience levels of a person to do this task should be defined. The list of skill sets and experience levels is used to determine how many people and what type of people are required on the project for each phase. Other assumptions will surface, and a list of them should be kept, as shown in Table 3-1. The assumptions become part of the planning document.

When resource requirements and timing are complete, several activities take place. The SE develops

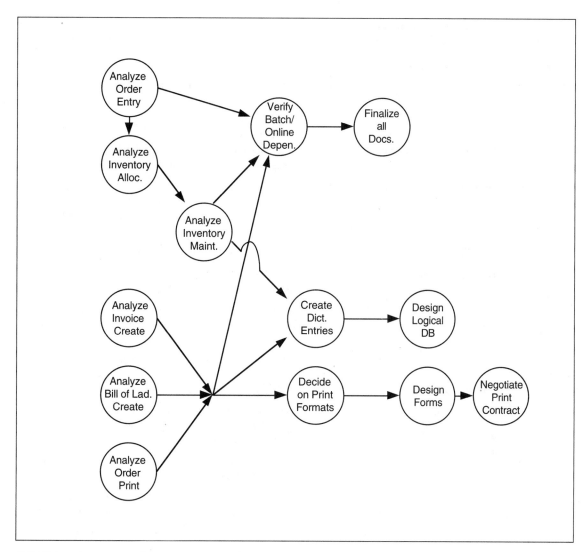

FIGURE 3-4   Example of Interdependent Sequences of Tasks

(O + 2R + P) / 4 = Most Likely Time Estimate

Legend:

O—Optimistic Time Estimate
R—Realistic Time Estimate
P—Pessimistic Time Estimate

FIGURE 3-5   Formula for Determining
Schedule Time

a schedule; the project manager develops a budget. They both identify the critical path and discuss it in terms of potential problems and how to minimize their likelihood. Task definitions are made more detailed for critical tasks, to allow more control and monitoring.

When complete, the plan, schedule and budget are submitted to the user and IS managers for comment and approval. Work begins, if it hasn't already, with the plan used to guide project work. The plan is used by the project team to see where their work

TABLE 3-1 Project Assumptions

Type Assumption	Example
Availability of configuration, component of mainframe, special hardware, programmer support equipment, tools, time	Programmers will gain access to IEW by September 10, 1994.
User time involvement. This may be expressed in time per day for a number of days, or may be in number of days.	A middle manager representative from Accounts Payable will be available in a Joint Application Design session scheduled for June 1–5, 1994.
Need for services from audit, law, vendors, quality assurance, or other support groups	The Audit Department will be able to review and comment on the adequacy of audit controls within 7 business days of receiving the review document.
Software performance	The Database Management Software will be able to process 10,000 transactions per day.
Test time, terminal time, or test shot availability	Batch programs can be tested simultaneously with on-line programs.
	Batch programs will be able to average three test runs per day with an average turnaround of less than 2.5 hours.
	Batch programs will be less than 160K and will require no more than two tape mounts each.
Disk space	Operations will make available 100 cylinders of IBM 3390 disk space for the project beginning 9/10/94. An additional 50 cyl. will be added for test databases by 10/30/94. An additional 250 cyl. will be added for production database conversion by 11/30/94.
Memory, CPU time, tape mounts, imaging access, or other mainframe resources	For testing, 30 CPU minutes per day plus 75 hours of terminal access time will be required beginning 10/30/94.
Personnel	Two senior programmer/analysts with 2–3 years of Focus experience and 2–3 years of on-line, multiuser, application development experience is required by 6/30/94.
	Four programmers with 1–2 years of Focus experience and one year of VM/CMS experience is required by 7/15/94.
Hardware/software availability	Imaging equipment will be available for application testing no later than 9/10/94.
	15 PCs or IBM 3279 terminals will be available for access and testing use no later than 9/10/94.

fits in the whole project, and it is used to monitor progress toward project completion.

The plan should *never* be cast in concrete. Plans should change when the tasks are wrong, times are underestimated, or there are changes in project scope that alter the activities performed in some way.

Assigning Staff to Tasks

Task assignment is fairly straightforward. The major tasks are to define the tasks and skills needed, list skills and availability of potential project members, and match people to tasks. The project manager and

SE actually begin discussing possible project staff when they are planning the project and tentatively assigning people to tasks. Then the project manager's real work begins.

The hard part of an assignment is the judgment required to match people whose skills are not an exact match for those needed; this is the usual case. For instance, you might want two programmer analysts with the following list of skills:

- design and programming experience on a similar application
- three to five years experience in the operational environment
- one to two years of experience with the database software
- managerial experience for two to four people
- known for high quality work
- known as an easy-going personality

Suppose your manager gives you a junior programmer right out of a training program, an analyst who does not program and who has no operational environment, database, or managerial experience, and a senior programmer who does no design, is known to be difficult, and sometimes does high quality work.

The good news is that you have three people instead of two. The bad news is no one of them has all of the qualifications you want. What do you do? This is what management is all about.

The project manager should get to know the team members well. This means assessing their position with the company, expectations on the project, specific role desired for the person, possible start and end dates for work, and personality or personal issues that might affect their work. Much of this information can be got from previous performance reviews. But nothing substitutes for discussing the information with the person.

The project manager has responsibilities to his or her manager, the client sponsor, and to the rest of the project team to get the best, most qualified people possible. In these capacities, the project manager honestly discusses previous problems with the person, any personal problems that might detract the person's attention from work, and any outside jobs, school, or other commitments that might also hinder their commitment. The person and the project

manager both should be given an opportunity to accept or reject the possibility of work. Even when there is no choice, it is also the responsibility of the project manager to make his or her expectations of quality and quantity of work clear. If the person will not report directly to the project manager, the person she or he will report to should also be at the meeting. In this way, everyone knows exactly what was said and what commitments were (or were not) made.

The answer to the task assignment problem above is to assign the tasks to best fit the skills. Assign the senior person responsibility for the work of the junior one, and provide motivation and incentives for quality work (see the following section on motivation). You also alter the schedule, if needed, to more closely mirror the actual skills of the team.

The **heuristics**, or rules of thumb, for personnel assignment are as follows:

1. Assign the best people to the most complex tasks from the critical path. Assign all critical path tasks. As the experience and skill levels of people decrease, assign less complex and smaller tasks. Do not give new, junior, or unqualified staff any tasks on the critical path. Assignment of senior people to critical tasks minimizes the risk of missing the target date.
2. Define a sequence of work for each person to stay on the project for as long as their skill set is needed. Try to assign tasks that provide each person some skill development.
3. Do not overcommit any person by assigning more tasks than they have time. Make sure each person will be busy, but allow time to finish one task before beginning another.
4. Allow some idle time (2–5%) as a contingency for each person. Do not allow more than eight sequential hours (i.e., one day) of idle time for any person.
5. Do not schedule any overtime. Scheduled overtime places unfair stress on people's professional and personal commitment and is a regular enough occurrence in development that it should not be scheduled at the outset.

The project manager is also responsible for coordinating movement from another assignment to the current development project. This coordination is done with the other project manager(s) involved and possibly the personnel department. New hires should be assigned a 'buddy' to help them get familiar with the company, its facilities, the computer environment, policies, and procedures. Senior staff should be assigned to mentor junior staff, encouraging the learning of new skills on the job.

Finally, the project manager must ensure that each person understands the expectations and duties assigned to him or her. All staff should have a copy of their job description. They should know the extent of their user interaction, extent of their intraproj-ect responsibility and communication, and policies about chain-of-command on who to go to with problems, project errors found, or problems with work assignments.

Ideally, the team should be given an overview of the application, a chance to review the schedule, and an opportunity to comment on their ability to meet the deadlines assigned. If they cannot meet the deadlines and have reasonable explanations, the plan, schedule, and budget should be changed. In addition, any training or learning on-the-job that is required should result in a lengthening of the schedule. If the team members agree to the schedule, then they are committed to getting the work done within the time

allowed and should be held accountable for that as part of their work assignment.

Selecting from Among Different Alternatives

Applications all have alternatives for implementation strategy, methodology, life cycle, and implementation environment. The project manager and SE together sort out the options, develop pros and cons, and decide the best strategies for the application.

Implementation Strategy

Implementation strategy is some mix of batch, on-line, and real-time programming. The decision is based on timing requirements of users for data accuracy, volume of transactions each day, and number of people working on the application at any one time. All of these numbers are estimates at the planning stage of an application, and are subject to change. The strategy decision might also change. In general, though, a decision can be made at the feasibility stage to provide some direction for data gathering.

As Table 3-2 shows, the timing of data accuracy drives the decision between batch and on-line. Keep

TABLE 3-2   Decision Table for Implementation Strategy Selection

Timing of Data Currency							
< 1 hour	N	N	N	N	Y	Y	Y
< 4 hours	N	Y	Y	Y	—	—	—
< 24 hours	Y	—	—	—	—	—	—

Peak Transaction Volume/Number of People Entering Data							
< 10	—	Y	—	—	Y	—	—
10–59	—	N	Y	—	N	Y	—
> 59	—	N	N	Y	N	N	Y

Options							
Batch application	X	X					
On-line application		X	X	X	X	X	
Real-time application			X	X		X	X

in mind that these are rules of thumb and need to be used in an organizational context. If data can be accurate as of some prior period, a batch application might be developed. If data must be accurate as of some time of the business day, either on-line or real-time strategies would be successful.

If the volume of transactions divided by the number of people is very high (over 60 per minute), then a high-performance application, with many concurrent processes, that is, a real-time application, might be warranted.

If the volume of transactions divided by the number of people is low (less than 25 per minute), but the timing requires on-line processing, an on-line application is best.

The gap in transactions per minute from 10 to 60 requires more information, specific to the project, for a decision. Answers to several questions are needed. For instance, how complex is a transaction? How was the number of workers arrived at, and can the number change? Is management willing to fund the difference in cost for a real-time application over an on-line one? Are there other factors (e.g., specific database software to be used) to consider in the decision? These questions are all context specific and the resulting decision would be determined by their answers.

Implementation Environment

The **implementation environment** includes the hardware, language, software, and computer-aided support tools to be used in developing and deploying the application. The decision is not final at the feasibility and planning stage, rather the alternatives and a potential decision are identified. The issues to be resolved for a final decision are then identified.

Frequently there is no choice of implementation environment. The organization has one environment and there are no alternatives; all development uses one mainframe and one language (for instance, COBOL). More often, as personal computers and local area networks become more prevalent, the alternatives are mainframe or network with PCs as the workstation in the chosen environment.

The decision is based frequently on the experience of the project manager, SE, and potential team members. People tend to use what they know and not use what they do not know. Ideally, the implemen-

TABLE 3-3   Decision Table for Implementation Environment

CPU Bound	N	N	Y	Y
I/O Bound	Y	Y	N	N
< 100,000 Trans/ Day	Y	—	Y	—
> 100,000 Trans/ Day	—	Y	—	Y
Hardware Mainframe	X	X	X	X
LAN	X			
LAN + Mainframe network		X	X	X

tation environment should be selected *to fit the application, not the skills of the developers*.

For instance, if a real-time application is being built for a Sun workstation environment under Unix operating system, C++ or Ada are probably the languages of choice. Certainly, Cobol is not a choice.

Guidance in implementation environment selection comes from the user. Do they have equipment they want to use? How is it configured? What other software or applications are on the equipment? How amenable is the user to changing the configuration to fit the new application?

Then, with this information, the decision table in Table 3-3 can be used as a guideline for selecting the implementation environment.

In general, whenever there is a specific requirement, it tends to drive the remaining decisions. Whenever there are general requirements, the decision can remain open for a longer time. Some direction—either toward a mainframe solution or a PC/LAN solution—should be tentatively decided during feasibility and planning. During this process, the project manager should identify the issues for further information needed in making a final decision.

Methodology and Project Life Cycle

The final issue to be tentatively decided is which methodology and how streamlined the life cycle

TABLE 3-4 Decision Table for Methodology and Life Cycle Selection

Source of Complexity								
Process	Y	—	—	—	Y	—	—	—
Data	—	Y	—	—	—	Y	—	—
Knowledge representation	—	—	Y	—	—	—	Y	—
Balanced	—	—	—	Y	—	—	—	Y
Novel problem	N	N	N	N	Y	Y	Y	Y
Methodology								
Process	X				X			
Data		X		X		X		X
Object	X			X	X	X	X	X
Semantic				X			X	

Read Vertically

will be. Frequently, there is no choice about these decisions, either. The organization supports one methodology and one life cycle and there is no discussion allowed. Equally frequently, enlightened managers know that not all projects are the same, therefore the development of the projects should also not be the same.

Methodology choices are process, data, object, social, semantic, or some hybrid of them (see Chapter 1). Life cycle choices are the sequential waterfall, iterative prototyping, or learn-as-you-go (see Chapter 1). These decisions are *not* completely separated from those of implementation environment in the previous section, because any fixed implementation requirements can alter both the methodology and the life cycle choices.

Assuming no special implementation requirements, the application itself should be the basis for deciding the methodology. In a business environment, the rule of thumb is to choose the methodology that addresses the complexity of the application best. If the complexity is procedural, a process method is best. If the complexity is data related, a data methodology is best. If the problem is easily

broken into a series of small problems, an object method might work best. If the project is to automate expert behavior or includes reasoning, a semantic methodology is best. A decision table summarizing heuristics on deciding methodology and life cycle is shown as Table 3-4.

Life cycle choice also requires some decision about what type and how much involvement there is of users. If some intensive, accelerated requirements or analysis technique is used [see joint requirements planning (JRP) and joint application design (JAD), Part II Introduction], either a streamlined sequential life cycle or an iterative approach can be used. Very large, complex applications with known requirements usually follow a sequential waterfall life cycle. If some portion of the application—requirements, software, language—is new and untested, prototyping should be used. Object orientation assumes prototyping and iteration. If the problem is a unique, one-of problem that has never been automated before, either a learn-as-you-go prototyping or an iterative life cycle would be appropriate.

In the next sections, the activities for which the project manager has sole responsibility are detailed.

These activities include liaison, personnel management, and project monitoring and reporting.

LIAISON

The project manager is a buffer between the technical staff and outside organizations. In this liaison role, the project manager communicates and negotiates with agents who are not part of the project team. A **liaison** is a person who provides communications between two departments. Examples of outside agents include the project sponsor (who may or may not be the user), IS managers, vendors, operations managers, other project managers, and other departments such as quality assurance (for validation and testing), law (for contracts), and administration (for clerical and secretarial support).

For each type of liaison, status reports are an important means of communication (see sample in Figure 3-6). Status reports document progress, identify problems and their resolution, and identify changes of plans to all interested parties. In addition, many other communications of different types are described for each type of liaison. The guidelines here are just that—guidelines. They are developed assuming that open communications between concerned parties is desired, but the guidelines require judgment and knowledge of the situation to separate a good action from a less good action.

Project Sponsor

The **sponsor** pays for the project and acts as its champion. A **champion** is one who actively supports and sells the goals of the application to others in the organization. A champion is the 'cheerleader' for the project.

The goals of liaison with the champion are to ensure that he or she knows the status of the project, understands and knows his or her role in dealing with politics relating to the project, and knows the major problems still requiring resolution.

The major duty of the champion is to deal with the political issues surrounding the project that the project manager cannot deal with. Politics are in every organization, and politics relate to organizational power. Power usually is defined as the ability of a person to influence some outcome. One source of power comes from controlling organizational resources, including money, people, information, manufacturing resources, or computer resources.

Political issues of application development do not relate to the project, but to what the project *represents*. Applications represent change. Changes can be to the organization, reporting structure, work flow, information flow, access to data, and extent of organizational understanding of its user constituency. When changes such as these occur, someone's status changes. When status changes, the people who perceive their status as decreasing will rebel.

The rebellion may be in the form of lies told to analysts, refusal to work with project members, complaints about the competence of the project team, or any number of ways that hinder the change. If the person causing trouble is successful, the project will fail and his or her status will, at worst, be unchanged. Politics, left unattended, will lower the chances of meeting the scheduled delivery date and raise the risk of implementing incorrect requirements. The project manager usually tries to deal with the political issues first, keeping the sponsor informed of the situation. If unsuccessful, the sponsor becomes involved to resolve the problem.

In some organizations, the project manager communicates to the sponsor only through his or her manager. In others, the project manager handles all project communications. In general, treat the sponsor like your boss. Tell him or her anything that will cause a problem, anything they should know, and anything that will cause the project delays.

User

The **user** is the person(s) responsible for providing the detailed information about procedures, processes, and data that are required during the analysis of the application. They also work with the SE and project manager in performing the feasibility analysis, developing the financial and organizational assessments of user departments for the feasibility study.

ICIA Industries—Interoffice Memo

DATE: October 10, 1994

TO: Ms. S. A. Cameron

FROM: J. B. Berns

SUBJECT: Order Entry and Inventory Control Project Status

Progress

We have resolved the testing problems between batch and on-line by going to a two-shift programming environment. The on-line programmers are working from 6 A.M. to 2 P.M. and the batch programmers are working from 2 P.M. to 10 P.M. This is not an ideal situation, but it is working at the moment.

We are still two weeks behind the schedule for programming progress, and we may not be able to make up the time, but we should not lose any more time.

The on-line screen navigation test began two days ago and is going smoothly. Several minor spelling problems have been found, but no logic problems have been found. George Lucas should complete the user acceptance of the screen navigation and screen designs within three days if no other problems surface.

Problems

The decode table for warehouse location, due 5/12/94 from George Lucas, is still not delivered yet. This is going to delay testing of the on-line inventory allocation programs beginning in ten days if we do not have it. Is there another person we can contact to get this information?

Operations found what appears to be a bug in one of the CICS modules. When a screen call is made, two bytes of the information are lost. We are double-checking all modules to ensure that it is not an application problem. Jim Connelly is calling IBM today to see if they have a fix for the problem. At the moment, this is not causing any delays to testing. But it will cause delays beginning next week if the problem is not resolved. The delays will be to all on-line modules calling screens and will amount to the time per module to code a workaround for the unresolved problem. This should be about one hour each for a total of 120 hours. We hope this delay can be avoided; everyone possible is working on the problem, including two experts from our company whom we called in last night as a free service to ICIA.

FIGURE 3-6   Sample Status Memo and Report

Project manager–user communication includes both planned and unplanned status meetings, written communications for status, analysis, interview results, documentation, and walk-throughs of application requirements as specified by the project team. Timing of user communications differs with the type of communication, but is most often daily until the application begins programming and testing. Then, a minimum of weekly personal contact should maintain the relationship.

In general, tell the user everything that might affect them, the project, or the schedule negatively; do not tell them anything else.

IS Management

IS managers, like most managers, want to know progress, problems *and* their solutions, warnings of lateness, and political issues. They do not want to handle all problems for their managers, nor do they appreciate finding out a project will be late the week before it is due. Tell your manager anything that might get him or her in trouble, that they need to know, or that might impact the project negatively. Always expect to propose solutions and argue if you think your solution is better than their's. Always accept their solution if it is mandated, unless it is unethical or illegal.

Technical Staff

Technical staff here means the project team. Always be open with them. Keep them current on progress, problems and resolutions, and any information that affects their ability to do their job. Praise quality work. Practice team building using common sense, like having small victory parties at the end of phases, sharing birthdays, or announcing promotions.

Operations

Operations affect the project differently depending on the phase. In early phases, word processing and PCs must be available for documentation. Computer-aided software engineering tool access might be required. Timing, type, and needs of access should be planned and negotiated well in advance. The kinds of problems a team might suffer from no access may delay documentation but does not delay the work of analysis. In the worst case, the work can be done manually.

During design, the database administrator must have access and resources allocated for the definition and population of a test database. This must also be negotiated well in advance.

During implementation, old data must be converted to the new format and environment, programs must be placed in production, and users begin using the application. At this time, the operations department assumes responsibility for running the application. This responsibility must also be planned and negotiated in advance.

When programming and testing begin, all project members need access to compilers, test database, editors, and, possibly, testing tools to work on their programs. Absence of resources at this time can severely delay project completion. For each day of person-time lost, there can be one day of project delivery time lost. Timing, type, and volume of access are all negotiated items. Advance negotiation should begin at least one month prior to the need. Most operations managers will tell you they want to know about a demand for their resources as soon as you can identify the demand and the date needed. Most operations managers will also tell you they want all requirements at once. So you should be prepared to discuss analysis, design, and implementation needs before much work takes place.

In general, operations managers need to know what the project needs from them and when. They also should be sent progress reports and told of any problems that affect the use of their resources.

Vendors

A **vendor** is any company, not your own, from which you obtain hardware, software, services, or information. If the application is installed in an existing environment, probably no vendor contacts are needed. If, however, acquisition of software, hardware, or both is planned, there are three types of contact with the vendor that take place. The first is proposal communication, the second is for negotiations, and the last is customer support.

A **Request for Proposal** (RFP) (see Chapter 16) is a document developed by the PM and SE to solicit bids from potential vendors. Vendors are asked to respond with an estimate of service and price within some number of days (e.g., 30). All bids received by the cut-off date are reviewed. Proposal communications are usually limited to information about the proposal. RFPs are accepted and responded to by vendor marketing staff with some technical assistance. Project manager contact is with the marketer.

Part of the RFP process is the development of a list of required features for the item being bid upon. This list should have priorities and weights assigned to it during the proposal stage for use during the analysis. Bids are rated on the requirements then compared to see which vendor most closely meets the needs of the application.

When a vendor is selected, a contract must be negotiated. Negotiation may be with the marketer, but might also be with a financial person or with the marketer's manager. Similarly, the project manager might do all or some of the negotiation with assistance from a financial person or his or her manager. Negotiations deal with price, time period of the contract, number of sites, number of users, type of license, guarantees in case the vendor goes out of business, warrantees, and so on. There is no one way to negotiate, and most often, all negotiations are turned over to legal staff for completion of contract terms. It is important never to commit to any terms until they are seen and approved by some manager in the organization. Frequently, contracts have far-reaching implications that an individual project manager may not know.

Other Project Teams and Departments

Other IS organizations that might need project communications include a database administration group, other project teams, and a quality assurance group. Other departments might include law, or audit. In all cases, the communication is similar. These groups need to know what their relationship to your project is, how soon and what type of support you need, who to contact for questions and information, and project status that might change any of these requirements.

In addition, you also have needs of these teams. If any of the organizations is performing work you need to complete your project, then you need the same things from them that they need from you. You need to know exactly what they will do for you and how it will be transmitted to your project, whom to contact, and task status that might affect your schedule.

To summarize, many other groups and departments in the organization need to have liaison activities with a project. It is the project manager's job to provide that liaison with communications tailored to the needs of the other organization.

PERSONNEL MANAGEMENT

For **personnel management**, the project manager hires, fires, coaches, motivates, plans, trains, and evaluates project team members.

Hiring

Hiring is usually coordinated through a personnel office that oversees all IS hiring, not just one project. Newspaper advertisements can be more cost-effective, general, and get a better response when coordinated for all projects. The personnel office receives the responses and filters obviously unqualified applications out from the pool of applicants. Then, working with the project manager, the personnel department screens the applicants and arranges project interviews.

As in most things, timing is important. Ads take from one to two weeks to get approved and placed. Receipt of resumes usually takes the same amount of time. Interviewing is time consuming and can take another one to two weeks for each hire. Then, offers are made and salary negotiations completed. The elapsed time to hire someone might be seven weeks or longer.

In addition, scheduling interviews may mean early-morning, evening, or lunch-time work. People searching for a job who already have one may not want to take vacation time for an interview. If the person appears qualified, the project manager is expected to shift his or her schedule to fit the needs of the applicant.

Firing

You may not agree, but keeping a person in a job for which they are unsuited does more damage to the manager, the person, and the project than you might think. Project managers are damaged because they think of little else and agonize over the decision much longer than necessary. People usually know if they are going to be terminated because they did not complete their specified tasks. They should have been told, in writing, before the termination date.

Prolonging a termination is damaging to the person being fired because it gives them a false sense of hope, makes them lose confidence in the person not following through on their described actions, and also allows them to influence other project members negatively.

Finally, procrastination on firing is damaging to the project because the longer the termination is delayed, the more likely the person being terminated will begin talking of his or her situation to other project members and disrupting work. As more people find out, more time is spent speculating on the situation. Less work gets done and the staff eventually loses confidence in the project manager.

No one gets into trouble overnight. Usually there is a period during which a problem is known, but it might be corrected before any real problems arise. It is at this time that the project manager should sit down with the person and talk about the situation. Legally, everyone in this situation is entitled to at least one warning letter which is also placed in their personnel file. This is followed by a letter of reprimand stating that performance is substandard with reasons for that judgment. The letter also states that the person is on probation and will be terminated by a specified date unless some actions are taken. The actions are then listed. If the person does the assigned work satisfactorily, they are off probation. All of these communications are in writing, monitored and approved by personnel and the IS manager, and

are the basis for any future legal action by the employee.

If the work is performed satisfactorily, probation ends. If not, the person is terminated. Termination from a project does not necessarily require termination from a company. If a person is ill-suited to a particular project, she or he might still be a valuable employee. A good project manager will first try to place the person somewhere else in the organization. If the person is terminated from the company, the company can try to help them find another job through an out-placement service or by providing company resources (a desk and phone away from the project) until a job is found. If the person is terminated for antisocial behavior, an addiction, or for some other nontechnical problem, the project manager might help them seek professional help.

Motivating

Motivation has personal and professional aspects. Professional motivation arises from a desire to do a good job. People are motivated to do a good job when they are treated like a professional and given meaningful, interesting work that includes some discretionary decision making and some creative design.

Personal motivation arises from a desire to improve one's position in life. Position in life is defined individually and may mean earning more money, buying a bigger house, becoming an analyst, or becoming a manager, and so on.

Project management style is the determining factor of personal motivation. A project manager who facilitates participation, fosters controlled risk-taking, and allows people to grow as individuals will gain undying loyalty from his or her staff. A project manager who treats the staff as stupid, lazy, and unmotivated might obtain desired behaviors from them, but it will be through intimidation and coercion.

The project manager needs to know the project team members individually in order to tailor reward systems and assignments to help them reach their goals. Project manager commitment to helping team members reach personal goals determines how professionally motivated the team members will be.

There are three aspects to motivation. First, the project work itself can be used to further professional goals that include doing novel work and advancing to new levels of seniority, experience, or responsibility. Second, the project manager must be careful to tailor reward and punishment systems to fit the tasks, being unbiased in terms of importance of individual contributions to the work. Third, the individual professional must make a commitment to doing something extra to gain the reward, either on-the-job or on his or her own time.

Take, for instance, a mainframe Cobol programmer who wants to move to a personal computer LAN environment using C++. The project has relaxed deadlines and the project manager might be able to help the person, but some commitment from the programmer is needed. The project manager recommends that the person find, attend, and pass a C++ course for which the company will pay. Then, the person will be assigned a task in the desired environment. If the task is successful, more tasks will follow. If the task is not successful, the situation will be reassessed.

Professional motivation might also come from fostering development of association ties outside of work. Meetings or user groups of vendors,[1] professional associations,[2] or other professional groups related to work duties might be paid for by the company to foster professional motivation.

Motivation also has a negative side. The actions that would be taken should the person fail to do their job competently must also be known. There should be company policies about quality and quantity of work that are also included as part of job descriptions. In the absence of company policy, the project manager should adopt rules, with the knowledge and consent of their manager, about punishments for failure to meet work requirements. These should also be made known to everyone on the project.

Career Path Planning

Motivating is an immediate activity of the project manager, but all employees and managers should be encouraged to develop longer range aspirations, as well. The project manager should help plan, with each individual, the tasks from this project that can be used to further his or her career.

The project manager should discuss goals and career paths at the beginning of the project and at least annually during performance reviews after that. The discussion should include a frank assessment of current perceptions of the individual's verbal, organizational, and professional skills, as well as helping the person plan courses, assignments, or opportunities to improve his or her performance. There should be direct ties from performance to rewards. Any time an individual does something significant enough to be mentioned on an appraisal, he or she should be told and either praised or counseled to change.

Training

The purpose of project training is to specifically address weaknesses of staff in techniques, technology, or tools used on the project. The SE and any project leaders are directly responsible for identifying training needs. The project manager is responsible for obtaining the training for the individual(s) who need it. A senior mentor for the trained skill should be assigned to monitor progress in the development of the skill, once training is complete.

Nonrelated training, as discussed above, may also be authorized by the project manager depending on employee need, rewards, and fit with employee goals.

Evaluating

Evaluations are annual assessments of the person from both professional and organizational perspectives. Evaluations are written and usually are signed

---

1 Guide and Share are IBM mainframe user groups with over 10,000 members each. DECus is the Digital Equipment users group. In these huge groups, there are subgroups with interests in every software package, language, and development environment offered by the vendor.

2 The Association for Computing Machinery (ACM) is one example.

by the reviewed person and the reviewer. Quality and quantity of work assignment are the professional assessments and are the most important aspects of junior level work. Junior staff, having no business experience, are monitored most closely for their ability to do their work. Competence for the assigned jobs is determined, and the more competent, the faster the person is promoted.

As people become more senior, quality and quantity of assigned work becomes assumed and organizing, motivating, communications, and interpersonal skills become more important. The nontask specific skills are viewed from an organizational perspective. More emphasis is placed on the ability to persuade, manage, motivate, and communicate with others, thus describing a good manager.

Promotion for most senior people is to the managerial ranks. In some companies, the importance of very senior, technical experts, is recognized. In those companies, equal emphasis is placed on the professional and organizational assessments. Technical staff can aspire to the senior technical positions without having to sacrifice their technical expertise in the bargain.

The usual performance evaluation contains sections for assignments, communications and interpersonal relations, absences, planning and organization, supervision, delegation, motivation, training, and special considerations. Each of these is described briefly.

The assignments section contains a brief description of four or five major assignments with expectations on quality and quantity of work for each as well as a brief paragraph assessing the extent to which the assignment was met. Quality and quantity of work are intangible and frequently subjective assessments, but there are always expectations of the amount of work a person should do, and of the extent to which reworking is needed. In addition, the individual's job description should give guidance on expectations for work quality and quantity. Finally, the extent to which the person needs to be monitored and assisted is an indicator of the extent to which they can work independently and competently at their job. The discussion of quality and quantity should be presented in terms of job description, manager expectations, and extent to which expectations are met. Specific examples are required to demonstrate very high and very low quality work.

Project managers evaluate communications and human relations. Assessments of both relating verbal and written communication skills are developed. Communication skills are related to specific project assignments and to other project activities, such as walk-throughs, that are not major assignments. Communication evaluation includes grammar, speed, persuasiveness, clarity, and brevity. The person's ability to develop and deliver a presentation, and actual experiences doing these are described.

Another area of assessment is interpersonal relationships with project manager, senior staff members, peers, others in the department, and users. Additional comments might discuss specific incidents that vary from the general assessment and that might highlight a need for improvement, or identify a particular skill. For instance, a person with good negotiating skills might be identified by their arbitration of a disagreement between two other project members.

Work absences are mentioned in terms of total days missed, number of absences, and type of absence. If there are company policies about absences and they are exceeded, a comment about the extent to which absences affected work might be added. The ability of the person to meet deadlines, maintain an accurate status of the project, and need special communications due to absences are all described. Extraordinary situations causing a long absence, such as emergency surgery, are included.

For planning and organization, accuracy, detail, independence of work, and cooperation with other affected groups are all assessed. In addition, the person's adherence to their own plans is discussed. Do they use it properly as a road map, or is it a rigid rule from which no straying is allowed, or is it ignored and treated as a task done for management?

Delegation is the extent to which the work is shifted from the manager to subordinates. Issues rated are how well work assignments match people's skills, allow monitoring to ensure completion, provide for personal and career improvement of subordinates.

Managerial style is assessed in terms of group motivation. Does the project manager obtain commitment from staff with enthusiasm, discomfort, unhappiness, or anger? Does the manager ask or command? How successful is the strategy and what must the manager do to change unsuccessful strategies? Are tactics altered to fit the person being managed, or is everyone treated the same way? Are people treated fairly or is favoritism prevalent?

Can the manager motivate others to learn new skills? To what extent does the manager provide needy staff with training, either formal or informal, on techniques, technology, and tools? If formal training is given by the person being rated, summaries of student ratings of quality and quantity of training should be presented. The person's ability to provide mentoring and quality of mentoring might be addressed.

Finally, there is usually a section for the project manager to recommend future assignments, training, or other professional activities for further development of the individual.

MONITOR AND CONTROL

Status Monitoring and Reporting

The rationale of the planned application development is that you monitor the plan to communicate activity status and interim checkpoints to clients. The overall goal—meeting the project installation date—is the end point of a lengthy complex set of processes. Without the plan, knowing whether or not the installation date will be met is difficult. **Status monitoring** is the comparison of planned and actual work to identify problems. **Project control** is the decisions and actions taken based on the project's status.

In a planned approach, project team members report time spent on each activity for some period. The sample time sheet (see Figure 3-7), allows breakdowns for several tasks listed across the top of the form and hours worked on the task reported by day of the month. Totals by day of the month and

by task over the period are tallied by row and column totals. This type of reporting allows the project manager to easily see for each person weekend work, how many hours are spent on each activity over a period, and how many effective work hours there are per day.

In addition, each person should write a short progress report. The report summarizes progress in qualitative terms, identifies problems, issues, errors, or other conflicts that might delay the work. If a task will be later than its schedule date, the reason for lateness must be explained. The project manager and SE both review the reports and time sheets to decide if problems need further action. A sample progress memo is shown as Figure 3-8.

The SE and project manager map actual progress of each person against the planned times. When progress looks slow, the project manager asks the person specifically if there are problems, if there are enough resources, for example, test shots, and if the person thinks they can meet the deadline. If the task appears to have been underestimated, the schedule is checked to see if changing the time allotted will cause completion delays. Similar tasks are checked to see if they are also underestimated. The cumulative effect of changes is checked to see if completion is in jeopardy. If it is, the project manager discusses the problem with his or her manager and they decide on the proper course of action.

The best policy is to address potential problems early, before they become big problems. If a person cannot finish work because of too many assignments, then reassign some of the work to another person. If they have not got enough testing time, arrange for more time. Active management prevents many problems.

Problem follow-up includes determining the severity and impact, planning an alternative course of action, modifying the plan as required, and continuing to monitor the problem until it is resolved or no longer has an impact on the delivery date.

Tell the client about problems that may not be solved so they are prepared for delays if they become inevitable. When changes become needed, tell the client about changes to planned dates even when they do not change the completion date.

Project: _____   Month: _____

Name: _____

Activities

Day of Month							Total for Day
1/16							
2/17							
3/18							
4/19							
5/20							
6/21							
7/22							
8/23							
9/24							
10/25							
11/26							
12/27							
13/28							
14/29							
15/30							
31							
Total							

FIGURE 3-7   Time Sheet

ICIA Industries—Interoffice Memo

DATE: October 10, 1994

TO: J. B. Berns

FROM: M. Vogt

SUBJECT: Order Entry and Status

Progress

We completed our screen design and navigation testing 10/7/94 and turned the modules over to George Lucas for user acceptance. He requested changes to several items:

1. The location of the total at the bottom of the screen is moved left five spaces.
2. The PF key assignment for PF3, which we were using to END any process. He would like END to be PF24. We explained that this is not a good design because the operator needs more key strokes (and hence is more likely to err) for PF24. Also, this is a very time-consuming change, about 10 hours, and that he should have mentioned his preference during the reviews. He decided to think about it and talk to some real operators before making a firm decision.

The other testing is progressing well. I am almost done testing the entire order process, except for inventory allocation. I need the warehouse codes from George by next week if I am to continue testing the programs.

Problems

The warehouse codes which were promised some months ago are getting to be on the critical path. If I do not have them by next week, I cannot continue to test the inventory allocation portion of the application. I can assign my own code scheme, then change it to the real one if I have to, but I would like to avoid the double work.

FIGURE 3-8   Sample Progress Report

The kinds of problems that occur and the activities the project manager monitors change over the course of the development. For instance, during the definition of the project scope, the project manager monitors the following:

Is the client cooperative?
Are all the stockholders identified and involved?

Are users being interviewed giving accurate, complete information?
Are users participating as expected?
Are there any apparent political issues to be addressed?
Does the scope look right? That is, does the current definition appear to include relevant activities?

By analysis, the project manager knows most users and how they work, should have identified potential political problems and dealt with them, and should be comfortable that the project scope is correct. The activities monitored turn toward the project team, and include the following:

Do all analysts know the scope of activity and work within it?

Is the analysts' work emphasis on what and not how?

Are users participating as expected?

Are all project members pulling their weight?

Is everyone interested and happy in their job?

Is there any friction between team members, or between team members and users?

Does everyone know what they and all others are doing?

Is there constant feedback-correction with users on interview results?

Are team members beginning to understand the users' business and situation? Are the team members objective and not trying to force their own ideas on the users?

Are walk-throughs finding errors and are they getting resolved?

Are documents created looking complete? Does the user agree?

Is the analysis accurately addressing the problems of the user? Are team members analyzing and describing exactly what is needed without embellishment?

Is typing turnaround, printing of word-processed documents, copying, or other clerical support acceptable?

Does communication between teams and between teams and users appear to be satisfactory?

Is the project on time? What is the status of critical path tasks? Has the critical path changed because of tasks that finished early?

Where are the biggest problems right now? How can we alleviate the problems?

What do we not know that might hurt us in design?

The functional requirements that result from analysis should describe what the application will do. The project manager is constantly vigilant that the requirements are the users. One problem many projects have is that the user wants a plain functional application but the analysts design a high-priced application with the user functions, but with many unnecessary features, or 'bells and whistles,' as well. This problem, if it occurs, must be dealt with before analysis ends or extraneous functions will be in the resulting application. When over-design problems surface, it is important to try to trace them to specific analysts for retraining in providing their services.

In design, the emphasis shifts to monitoring the rate, type, and scope of changes from the users. If the business is volatile, requirements change may become a constant problem. Change management procedures should be developed and used. At this point, the project manager's worries include the following:

Do the analysts know the application?

Is the translation to operational environment correct and complete?

Are walk-throughs finding errors? Are errors being resolved?

Are users participating as expected? Are users properly involved with screen design, test design, acceptance criteria definition?

Are all project members pulling their weight?

Is everyone interested and happy in their job? Is there any friction between team members, or between team members and users?

Does everyone know what they and all others are doing?

Are all team members aware of their changing responsibilities, and are they comfortable with and able to do design tasks?

Does communication between teams and between teams and users appear to be satisfactory?

Is the project on time? What is the status of critical path tasks? Has the critical path changed because of tasks that finished early?

Where are the biggest problems right now? How can we alleviate the problems?

What do we not know that might hurt us in programming? Is the implementation environment suitable for this application?

Can the database management software accommodate this application?

The number of project team members usually increases for programming to do parallel development as much as possible. The communication overhead necessary to know everyone's status and for them to know the project status increases. The problems in the programming and unit testing stage tend to focus on communications and programmer performance.

Does everyone understand how their work fits into the project? Does everyone know their critical-path status? Are all current project members pulling their weight? Does everyone know what they and all others are doing?

Is testing time sufficient? Is terminal access sufficient?

Does everyone know the technologies they are using sufficiently to perform independently?

Are junior staff paired with senior mentors?

Are users requesting further changes?

Are users participating as expected in test design, user documentation development, conversion, and training?

Is there constant feedback-correction with users on suspected errors?

Are prototypes being used as much as possible to demonstrate how the application will work?

Are walk-throughs productive, finding errors? Are errors getting resolved?

While programming and unit testing are proceeding, tests for integration and system level concerns are being developed. The database is being established and checked out. The operational environment is being prepared. Concern shifts from getting the application expressed in code to getting it working correctly. The kinds of questions a project manager might have are the following:

Are all current project members pulling their weight? Does everyone know what they and all others are doing?

Is testing time sufficient? Is terminal access sufficient?

Are users requesting further changes? Are users participating as expected in testing?

Is there constant feedback-correction with users on suspected errors?

Are walk-throughs productive, finding errors? Are errors getting resolved?

Does the system level test really prove that the functions are all accounted for?

Does the integration test verify all interconnections? How can it be leveraged to prove the reliability of the interconnections during the system test?

What do we not know about the operational environment that might hurt the project?

Is the database software working properly? Are back-up and recovery procedures adequate for testing?

How can we use the integration and system tests to develop a regression test package?

Is documentation being finalized? Is everyone working to capacity? Should we start letting programmers go to other projects? If we let a key person go, who can take their place when a problem occurs?

Finally, testing is complete, the application appears ready, and the user is ready to work. There should have been a plan for actually implementing the operational application that eases the user into use without too much trauma. The easing-in period gives the project team some time to fix errors found in production without excessive pressure. The issues now center on getting the application to work in its intended environment for its intended users. The questions include the following:

Is the site prepared adequately? Is air conditioning sufficient? Are lighting and ergonomic design sufficient?

Are users properly trained and ready to do work?

Are work cycles and evaluation of results identified sufficiently to allow implementation and verification of results?

When errors are found, are they getting resolved?

Are users taking charge as expected?

Are all current project members pulling their weight? Does everyone have enough work to do? Can people be freed to other projects?

Is communication between teams and between teams and users appearing satisfactory? Are users told whenever major problems occur? Are they participating in the decision making about error resolution?

Many of the questions above are technical in nature and would be referred to the SE to monitor. The project manager is like a mother hen and is supposed to worry about everything. Obviously, if the plan addresses the activities as it should, many of the answers to the above sets of questions are found in weekly progress reports of team members. Compiling the individual progress reports and project progress reports in a project log allows the manager and any of the staff to review decisions, problems and

their resolutions, and other issues as they occur during the development.

AUTOMATED _____ SUPPORT TOOLS _____ FOR PROJECT _____ MANAGEMENT _____

Project management support tools have increased in sophistication and performance since the mid-1980s when the first PC-based tools arrived. The tools in this section support project planning, task assignment and monitoring, estimation tools, and scheduling tools (see Table 3-5). Key tool capabilities

TABLE 3-5   Automated Support Tools for Project Management

Product	Company	Technique
CA-*products*	Computer Associates International, Inc. Islandia, NY	Project planning
DataEasy Project Management	Data Easy Software Foster City, CA	Task mapping
Demi-Plan	Demi Software Ridgefield, CT	Critical path project planning and tracking
Foundation	Arthur Anderson & Co. Chicago, IL	Project management Project planning
IEW, ADW (PS/2 Version)	Knowledgeware Atlanta, GA	Project planning
Life Cycle Manager	Nastec Southfield, MI	Project planning, task assignment, tracking
Life Cycle Project Manager	American Management Systems Fairfax, VA	Project planning, task assignment, tracking
Maestro	SoftLab San Francisco, CA	Problem tracking
microGANTT	Earth Data Corp. Richmond, VA	Project planning
Milestone	Digital Marketing Corp. Walnut Creek, CA	Critical path project planning and tracking
Multi-Cam	AGS Mgmt Systems King of Prussia, PA	Project planning and tracking

(Continued on next page)

TABLE 3-5   Automated Support Tools for Project Management   *(Continued)*

Product	Company	Technique
PMS II	North America MICA Inc. San Diego, CA	Project planning, task assignment, tracking Critical path PERT
Primavera Project Manager	Primavera Systems Inc. Bala Cynwyd, PA	Project planning, task assignment, tracking
Project	Microsoft Bellevue, WA	Project planning, task assignment, tracking
Project Workbench, Fast Project	Applied Business Technology NY, NY	Project planning, task assignment, tracking
System Architect	Popkin Software and Systems, Inc. NY, NY	Project planning
Teamwork	Cadre Technologies Inc. Providence, RI	Planned completion date tracking
vsDesigner	Visual Software, Inc. Santa Clara, CA	Project completion tracking Critical issues monitoring

not considered here include word processing, spreadsheets, calendars, or interfaces to electronic mail (these are considered useful for all organization members). Other tools that are used by a project manager but are discussed in other sections of the text are for configuration management, quality control, and metrics.

SUMMARY

The project manager role is frequently separate and distinct from that of the software engineer. The software engineer is generally responsible for technical aspects of project work. Some tasks are joint, complementary activities shared by project managers and software engineers. For these joint activities, the software engineer contributes technical skills, and the project manager contributes organizational skills.

The project manager is solely responsible for most people-related aspects of projects. The three main tasks of the project manager are organizational liaison, employee management, and project monitoring and control. Organizational liaison includes creating working relationships with other organizations and departments, resolving project-related problems regardless of their nature, and reconciling the project design with expectations of others. Employee management includes working with Personnel to hire, fire, and staff the project. Employee management also includes individual employee monitoring to help them evaluate, set, and attain career goals. Project monitoring and control is the other major project management activity. Monitoring means to trace the progress of project work and compare it to budgeted time and resources to maintain progress. Control includes deciding and implementing project changes when progress is not satisfactory. Project changes might include change of job assignments, introduction of training, or change to schedules, and plans.

REFERENCES

Abdel-Hamid, Tarek, and Stuart E. Madnick, *Software Project Dynamics: An Integrated Approach*. Englewood Cliffs, NJ: Prentice Hall, 1991.

Gilbreath, R. D., *Winning at Project Management: What Works, What Fails and Why*. NY: John Wiley and Sons, 1986.

Gildersleeve, Thomas R., *Data Processing Project Management*. New York: Van Nostrand Reinhold Company, 1974.

Glass, Robert L., *Software Conflict: Essays on the Art and Science of Software Engineering*. Englewood Cliffs, NJ: Prentice Hall, Yourdon Press, 1991.

Cleland, D. I., and William R. King, *Systems Analysis and Project Management*. NY: McGraw-Hill, 1983.

King, William R., and D. I. Cleland (eds.), *Project Management Handbook*, 2nd ed. NY: Van Nostrand Reinhold, 1988.

Pfeffer, Jeffrey, *Organizations and Organization Theory*. Boston: Pitman, 1982.

Rogerson, Simon, *Project Skills Handbook*. Lund, Sweden: Chartwell-Bratt, 1989.

KEY TERMS

champion	project control
complimentary activities	project plan
critical path	request for proposal
evaluations	(RFP)
heuristic	sponsor
implementation	status monitoring
environment	task dependency
implementation strategy	diagram
interface	user
liaison	vendor
personnel management	

EXERCISES

1. List and discuss three advantages and three disadvantages to project team members using time sheets to report work activities. What might some alternatives for reporting task progress and time spent be?

2. Write an honest appraisal of yourself for the work you have done in school toward your current degree. Give specific examples of good and, maybe, poor work. Rate your knowledge and skills gained in terms of a schedule that ends when you graduate.

3. Discuss the following comment: "It is important for a project manager to have been a programmer and an analyst. Otherwise, the manager has no feel for the problems and their severity."

STUDY QUESTIONS

1. Define the following terms:
   champion   critical path   heuristic
   liaison   project plan

2. When and why are the software engineer and project manager roles split?

3. Describe the project manager's role in planning.

4. Describe a general planning methodology.

5. What kinds of reviews are done on project documentation? Why are they necessary?

6. What are five types of operations resources that might be needed on a project?

7. What is the minimum lead time recommended for resource requests?

8. What is an RFP and when is it used?

9. What is the purpose of a task dependency chart?

10. What is a critical path and why is it important?

11. Should a plan be finalized and *cast in concrete*?

12. List four types of assumptions made during planning and describe why each is important.

13. Why should project team members submit time sheets?

14. Describe how to assign staff to tasks. Why is the process rarely this simple?

15. Describe the heuristics for assigning staff to projects.

16. Should planned overtime be in a schedule?

17. List five things every person should know about his or her job when working on an application development project.
18. What are the three alternatives for implementation strategy?
19. What are the heuristics for deciding implementation strategy?
20. List two choices for implementation environment.
21. Describe the heuristics for deciding implementation environment.
22. What are the choices for methodology and life cycle?
23. Describe the heuristics for deciding methodology.
24. Describe the heuristics for deciding life cycle.
25. What is a liaison? What project manager duties require liaison work?
26. List the contents of a project status report.
27. What is politics and how does it affect application development work?
28. Why are performance appraisals done?

EXTRA-CREDIT QUESTIONS

1. List and discuss types of assessment from a performance appraisal. How does a manager ensure the ratings are fair and objective? What should a manager do if he or she does not like the person being reviewed?
2. Develop a project plan for ABC Video based on the information in Chapter 2 only. Use the case and this chapter to decide the tasks. Use your experience, whatever it is, to decide the times for the tasks. Do not look at other information in this or other texts when planning the work. What assumptions do you have? How comfortable are you with your estimates? Keep this assignment and redo it at the end of Chapter 6.

## CHAPTER 4

DATA GATHERING FOR APPLICATION DEVELOPMENT

INTRODUCTION

Each phase of application development requires interaction between the developers and users to obtain information of interest at the time. Each phase seeks to answer broad questions about the application. For instance, in feasibility analysis, the questions are broad and general: What is the scope of the problem? What is the best way to automate? Can the company afford (not) to develop this application? Is the company able to support application development?

In analysis we seek *what* information about the application. For instance, What data are required? What processes should be performed and what are the details of their performance? What screen design should be used?

In design, we develop *how* information relating to the application. For example, How does the application translate into the specific hardware environment selected? How does the logical data design translate into a physical database design? How do the program modules fit together?

The kind of interaction that elicits answers to questions such as these differs by information type and phase. In this section we describe the alternatives for obtaining information to be used for application development. The alternative data gathering techniques are described, then related to application types. Then, ethical considerations in data collection and user relations are discussed.

DATA TYPES

Data differs on several important dimensions: time orientation, structure, completeness, ambiguity, semantics, and volume. Each of these dimensions is important in defining requirements of applications because they give guidance to the SE about how much and what type of information should be collected. Also, different data types are related to different application types and require different requirements elicitation techniques. Inattention to data dimensions will cause errors in analysis and design that are costly to fix. Error correction cost is an increasing function of the phase of development (see Table 4-1).

In addition to obtaining information, we also use the techniques for validating the information and interpretation in the proposed application. Use of validation techniques during each phase increases the likelihood that logic flaws and misinterpretations will be found early in the development.

TABLE 4-1   Cost of Error Correction by Phase of Development

Phase in Which Errors are Found	Cost Ratio to Fix the Error
Feasibility/Analysis	1
Design	3–6
Code/Unit Test	10
Development Test	14–40
Acceptance Test	30–70
Operation	40–1000

From Boehm, Barry, *Software Engineering Economics*. Englewood Cliffs, NJ: Prentice-Hall, 1981.

Time Orientation

Time orientation of data refers to past, present, or future requirements of a proposed application. Past data, for example, might describe how the job has changed over time, how politics have affected the task, its location in the organization, and the task. Past information is exact, complete (if maintained), and accurate. There is little guessing or uncertainty about historical records.

Current information is information about what is happening now, and its relevance in determining the future. For instance, current application information relates to operations of the company, the number of orders taken in a day, or the amount of goods produced. Current policies, procedures, business industry requirements, legal requirements, or other constraints on the task are also of interest in application development. Current information should be documented in some way that it can be read by the development team to increase their knowledge of the application and problem domains.

Future requirements relate to changes in the industry expected to take place. They are inexact and difficult to verify. Economic forecasts, sales trend projections, and business 'guru' prognostications are examples of future information. Future-oriented information might be used, for example, by managers in an executive information system (EIS).

Structure

Structure of information refers to the extent to which the information can be classified in some way. Structure can refer to function, environment, or form of data or processes. Information varies from unstructured to structured with interpretation and definition of structure left to the individual SE. The information structuring process is one in which the SE is giving a form and definition to data.

Structure is important because the wrong application will be developed without it. For instance, knowing that the user envisions the structure of the system to be one with 'no bureaucracy,' minimal user requirements, and no frills, gives you, the SE, a good sense that only required functions and data should be developed. In the absence of structuring information, technicians have a tendency to develop applications with all 'the bells and whistles' so the users can never complain that they don't have some function.

An example of structuring of data is shown in Figures 4-1 and 4-2. When you begin collecting information about employees for a personnel application, you might get information about the employees themselves, their dependents, skills the employees might have, job history information, company position history, salary history, and performance reviews.

The information comes to you in pieces that may not have an obvious structure, but you know that all of the data relates to an *employee* so there must be relationships somewhere. In Figure 4-2, we have structured the information to show how all of the information relates to an employee and each other in a hierarchic manner. Each employee has specific one-time information that applies only to them, for instance, name, address, social security number, employee ID, and so on. In addition, each employee might have zero to any number of the other types of information depending on how many other companies they have worked at, whether they have children, and how long they have worked at the company. The most complex part of the data structure is the relationship between position, salary, and reviews. If salary and performance reviews are disjoint, they would be as shown, related to a given

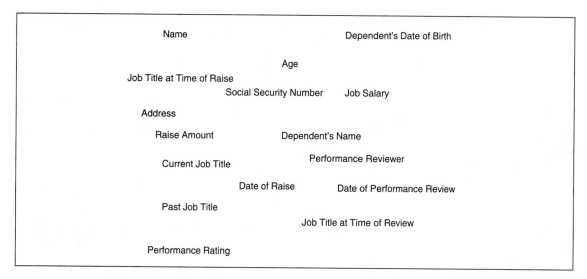

FIGURE 4-1   Unstructured Personnel Data

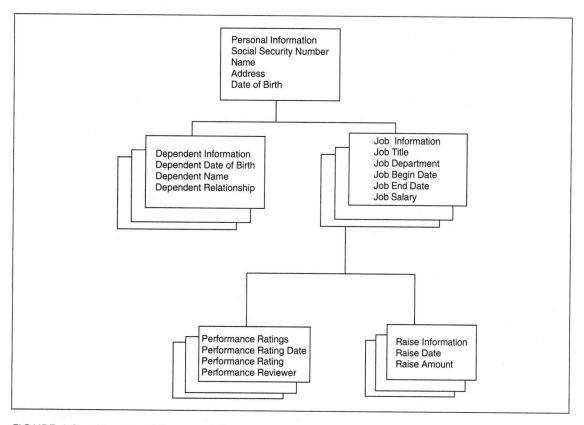

FIGURE 4-2   Structured Personnel Data

position the person held in the company (see Figure 4-2). The other option is that salary changes are dependent on performance reviews and the hierarchy would be extended another level.

Completeness

Information varies in **completeness**, the extent to which all desired information is present. Each application type has a requisite level of data completeness with which it deals. Transaction processing systems deal with complete and accurate information. GDSS and DSS deal with less complete information. EIS, expert systems, or other AI applications have the highest levels of incompleteness with which they must cope.

In applications dealing with incomplete information, the challenge to you is to decide when the information is *complete enough* to be useful. Sometimes this decision is made by the user, other times it is made within the application and there need to be rules defining *complete enough*.

Ambiguity

Ambiguity is a property of data such that it is vague in meaning or is subject to multiple meanings. Since ambiguity deals with meaning, it is closely related to semantics. An example of ambiguity is to ask the following query:

PRINT SALES FOR JULY IN NEW YORK

In this query, New York can mean New York State or New York City; both answers would be correct. Obvious problems will occur to a person who asks that request for one context (the state) and gets an answer for the other context (the city). Contextual cues help SEs to define the one correct interpretation of ambiguous items; further problems arise because of multiple semantic interpretations within a single context. For that reason, semantics is discussed next.

Semantics

Semantics is the study of development and change in the meaning of words. In business applications, **semantics** is the meaning attached to words. Meaning is a social construction; that is, the people in the organization have a collectively shared definition of how some term, policy, or action is really interpreted.

Semantics is important in applications development and in the applications themselves. If people use the same terms, but have different meanings for the terms, misunderstandings and miscommunications are assured. If embedded in an application, semantically ambiguous data can never be processed by a program without the user being aware of which 'meaning' is in the data. Applications that have semantically mixed data then rely on the training and longevity of employees for proper interpretation of the data. If these key employees leave, the ability to correctly interpret the meaning of the data is lost. Losing the meaning of information can be expensive to the company and can result in lawsuits due to improper handling of information.

An example of semantic problems can be seen in a large insurance company. The company uses the term 'institution' to refer to its major clients for retirement funds. The problem is that 'institution' means different things to different people in the company. In one meeting, specifically convened to define 'institution,' 17 definitions surfaced. The problem with semantic differences is not that 16 of the 17 definitions are wrong. The problem is that *all 17 definitions are right*, depending on the context of their use. It is the SEs job to unravel the spaghetti of such definitions to get at the real meaning of terms that are not well defined at the corporate level. Unraveling the meaning of the term 'institution' took about 20 person-months over a two-year period to get the user community to reach consensus on the *corporate* definition of the term 'institution.'

Volume

Volume is the number of business events the system must cope with in some period. The volume of new or changed customers is estimated on a monthly or annual basis whereas the volume of transactions for business operation is usually measured in volume per day or hour, and peak volume. **Peak volume** is the number of transactions or business events to be processed during the busiest period. The peak period might be annual and last several months, as with tax preparation. The peak might be measured in seconds and minutes, for example, to meet a Federal Reserve Bank closing deadline.

Volume of data is a source of complexity because the amount of time required to process a single transaction can become critical to having adequate response time when processing large volumes. Interactive, on-line applications can be simple or extremely complex simply because of volume. For instance, the ABC rental application will actually process less than 1,000 transactions per day. Contrast this volume with a credit card validation application that might service 50,000 credit check requests per *hour*. Credit card validation is simple processing; servicing 50,000 transactions per hour is complex.

Applications that mix on-line and batch processing using software that requires the two types of processes to be distinct, requires careful attention to the amount of time necessary to accommodate the volumes for both types of processing. For instance, the personnel application at a large oil company was designed for 20 hours of on-line processing with global access, and four hours of batch reporting. When the system went 'live,' the on-line processing worked like a charm because it had been tested, retested, and overtested. The batch portion, for which individual program tests had been conducted, required about *18 hours* because of the volume of processing. After several weeks, the users were fed up because printed reports had been defined as the means of distributing query results, and they had none. The solution required an additional expenditure of over $200,000 to redevelop all reports as pseudo-on-line tasks that could run while the interactive processes were running. Simple attention to the volume of work for batch processing would have identified this problem long before it cost $200,000 to fix.

DATA COLLECTION
TECHNIQUES

There are seven techniques we use for data gathering during application development. They are interviews, group meetings, observation, temporary job assignment, questionnaires, review of internal and outside documents, and review of software. Each has a use for which it is best served, and each has limitations to the amount and type of information that can be got from the technique. The technique strengths and weaknesses are summarized in Table 4-2, which is referenced throughout this section.

In general, you always want to validate the information received from any source through triangulation. **Triangulation** is obtaining the same information from multiple sources. You might ask the same question in several interviews, compare questionnaire responses to each item, or check in-house and external documents for similar information. When a discrepancy is found, you reverify it with the original and triangulated sources as much as possible. If the information is critical to the application being correctly developed, put the definitions, explanations, or other information in writing and have it approved by the users separately from the other documentation. Next, we discuss each data collection technique.

Single Interview

An **interview** is a gathering of a small number of people for a fixed period and with a specific purpose. Interviews with one or two users at a time are the most popular method of requirements elicitation. In an interview, questions are varied to obtain specific or general answers. You can get at people's feelings, motivations, and attitudes toward other departments, the management, the application, or any other entity of interest (see Table 4-2). Types of interviews are determined by the type of information desired.

Interviews should always be conducted such that both participants feel satisfied with the results. This means that there are steps that lead to good interviews, and that inattention to one or more steps is likely to result in a poor interview. The steps are summarized in Table 4-3. Meeting at the convenience of the interviewee sets a tone of cooperation. Being prepared means both knowing who you are interviewing so you don't make any embarrassing statements and having the first few questions prepared, even if you don't know all the questions.

TABLE 4-2   Summary of Data Collection Techniques

Interviews	
Strengths	Weaknesses
Get both qualitative and quantitative information	Takes some skill
Get both detail and summary information	May obtain biased results
Good method for surfacing requirements	Can result in misleading, inaccurate, or irrelevant information
	Requires triangulation to verify results
	Not useful with large numbers of people to be interviewed (e.g., over 50)

Group Meetings	
Strengths	Weaknesses
Decisions can be made	Decisions with large number of participants can take a long time
Can get both detail and summary information	Wastes time
Good for surfacing requirements	Interruptions divert attention of participants
Gets many users involved	Arguments about turf, politics, etc. can occur
	Wrong participants lead to low results

Observation	
Strengths	Weaknesses
Surface unarticulated procedures, decision criteria, reasoning processes	Might not be representative time period
Not biased by opinion	Behavior might be changed as a result of being observed
Observer gets good problem domain understanding	Time consuming

Review Software	
Strengths	Weaknesses
Good for learning current work procedures as constrained or guided by software design	May not be current
Good for identifying questions to ask users about functions—how they work and whether they should be kept	May be inaccurate
	Time consuming

TABLE 4-2   Summary of Data Collection Techniques (*Continued*)

Questionnaire

Strengths	Weaknesses
Anonymity for respondents	Recall may be imperfect
Attitudes and feelings might be more honestly expressed	Unanswered questions mean you cannot get the information
Large numbers of people can be surveyed easily	Questions might be misinterpreted
Best for limited response, closed-ended questions	Reliability or validity may be low
Good for multicultural companies to surface biases, or requirements and design features that should be customized to fit local conventions	Might not add useful information to what is already known

Temporary Assignment

Strengths	Weaknesses
Good to learn current context, terminology, procedures, problems	May not include representative work activities or time period
Bases for questions you might not otherwise ask	Time consuming
	May bias future design work

Review Internal Documents

Strengths	Weaknesses
Good for learning history and politics	May bias future design work
Explains current context	Saves interview/user time
Good for understanding current application	Not useful for obtaining attitudes or motivations

Review External Documents

Strengths	Weaknesses
Good for identifying industry trends, surveys, expert opinions, other companies' experiences, and technical information relating to the problem domain	May not be relevant
	Information may not be accurate
	May bias future design work

TABLE 4-3 Steps to Conducting a Successful Interview

1. Make an appointment that is at the convenience of the interviewee.
2. Prepare the interview; know the interviewee.
3. Be on time.
4. Have a planned beginning to the interview.
   a. Introduce yourself and your role on the project.
   b. Use open-ended general questions to begin the discussion.
   c. Be interested in all responses, pay attention.
5. Have a planned middle to the interview.
   a. Combine open-ended and closed-ended questions to obtain the information you want.
   b. Follow-up comments by probing for more detail.
   c. Provide feedback to the interviewee in the form of comments, such as, "Let me tell you what I think you mean, . . ."
   d. Limit your notetaking to avoid distracting the interviewee.
6. Have a planned closing to the interview.
   a. Summarize what you have heard. Ask for corrections as needed.
   b. Request feedback, note validation, or other actions of interviewee.

      ▪ Give him or her a date by which they will receive information for review.
      ▪ Ask him or her for a date by which the review should be complete.

   c. If a follow-up interview is scheduled, confirm the date and time.

A good interview has a beginning, middle, and end. In the beginning, you introduce yourself and put the interviewee at ease. Begin with general questions that are inoffensive and not likely to evoke an emotional response. Pay attention to answers both to get cues for other questions, and to get cues on the honesty and attitude of the interviewee. In the middle, be businesslike and stick to the subject. Get all the information you came for, using the techniques you chose in advance. If some interesting side information emerges, ask if you can talk about it later and then do that. In closing, summarize what you have heard and tell the interviewee what happens next. You may write notes and ask him or her to review

them for accuracy. If you do notes, try to get them back for review within 48 hours. Also, have the interviewee commit to the review by a specific date to aid in your time planning. If you say you will follow up with some activity, make sure you do.

Interviews use two types of questions: open-ended and closed-ended. An **open-ended question** is one that asks for a multisentence response. Open-ended questions are good for eliciting descriptions of current and proposed application functions, and for identifying feelings, opinions, and expectations about a proposed application. They can also be used to obtain any lengthy or explanatory answers. An example of open-ended question openings are: "Can you tell me about . . ." or "What do you think about . . ." or "Can you describe how you use . . .".

A **closed-ended question** is one which asks for a yes/no or specific answer. Closed-ended questions are good for eliciting factual information or forcing people to take a position on a sensitive issue. An example of a closed-ended question is: "Do you use the monthly report?" A 'yes' response might be followed by an open-ended question, "Can you explain how?"

The questions can be ordered in such a way that the interview might be structured or unstructured (see Table 4-4). A **structured interview** is one in which the interviewer has an agenda of items to cover, specific questions to ask, and specific information desired. A mix of open and closed questions is used to elicit details of interest. For instance, the interview might start with "Describe the current rental process." The respondent would describe the process, most often using general terms. The interviewer might then ask specific questions, such as, "What is the daily volume of rentals?" Each structured interview is basically the same because the same questions are asked in the same sequence. Tallying the responses is fairly easy because of the structure.

An **unstructured interview** is one in which the interview unfolds and is directed by responses of the interviewee. The questions tend to be mostly open-ended. There is no set agenda, so the interviewer, who knows the information desired, uses the responses from the open-ended questions to develop ever more specific questions about the topics. The

TABLE 4-4   Comparison of Structured and Unstructured Interviews

Strengths	
Structured	Unstructured
Uses uniform wording of questions for all respondents	Provides greater flexibility in question wording to suit respondent
Easy to administer and evaluate	Can be difficult to conduct because interviewer must listen carefully to develop questions about issues that arise spontaneously from answers to questions
More objective evaluation of respondents and answers to questions	May surface otherwise overlooked information
Requires little training	Requires practice
Results in shorter interviews	

Weaknesses	
Structured	Unstructured
Cost of preparation can be high	May waste respondent and interviewer time
Respondents do not always accept high level of structure and its mechanical posing of questions	Interviewer bias in questions or reporting of results is is more likely
High level of structure is not suited to all situations	Extraneous information must be culled through
Reduces spontaneity and ability of interviewer to follow up on comments of interviewee	Analysis and interpretation of results may be lengthy
	Takes more time to collect essential facts

same questions used above as examples for the structured interview might also be used in an unstructured interview; the difference is that above, they are determined as a 'script' in advance. In an unstructured situation, the questions flow from the conversation.

Structured interviews are most useful when you know the information desired in advance of the interview (see Table 4-4). Conversely, unstructured interviews are most useful when you cannot anticipate the topics or specific outcome. A typical series of interviews with a user client begins with unstructured interviews to give you an understanding of the problem domain. The interviews get progressively struc-

tured and focused as the information you need to complete the analysis also gets more specific.

User interview results should always be communicated back to the interviewee in a short period of time. The interviewee should be given a deadline for their review. If the person and/or information are critical to the application design being correct, you should ask for comments even after the deadline is missed. If the person is not key in the development, the deadline date signifies a period during which you will accept changes, after the date you continue work, assuming the information is correct.

It is good practice to develop diagram(s) as part of the interview documentation. At the beginning of the next interview session, you discuss the diagram(s) with the user and give him or her any written notes to verify at a later time. You get immediate feedback on the accuracy of the graphic and your understanding of the application. The benefits of this approach are both technical and psychological. From a technical perspective, you are constantly verifying what you have been told. By the time the analysis is complete, both you and the client have confidence that the depicted application processing is correct and complete. From a psychological perspective, you increase user confidence in your analytical ability by demonstrating your problem understanding. Each time you improve the diagram and deepen the analysis, you also increase user confidence that you will build an application that answers his or her need.

Interviews are useful for obtaining both qualitative and quantitative information (see Table 4-2). The types of qualitative information are opinions, beliefs, attitudes, policies, and narrative descriptions. The types of quantitative information include frequencies, numbers, and quantities of items to be tracked or used in the application.

Interviews, and other forms of data collection, can give you misleading, inaccurate, politically motivated, or irrelevant information (see Table 4-2). You need to learn to read the person's body language and behavior to decide on further needs for the same information. Table 4-5 lists respondent behaviors you might see in an interview and the actions you might take in dealing with the behaviors.

For instance, if you suspect the interviewee of lying or 'selectively remembering' information, try to cross-check the answers with other, more reliable sources. If the interview information is found to be false, ask the interviewee to please explain the differences between his or her answers and the other information. The session does not need to be a confrontation, rather, it is a simple request for explanation. Be careful not to accuse or condemn, simply try to get the correct information.

Persistence and triangulation are key to getting complete, accurate information. You are not required to become 'friends' with the application users, but interviews are smoother, yield more information for the time spent, and usually have less 'game-playing' if you are 'friendly' than if you are viewed as distant, overly-objective, or noninterested.

Meetings

Meetings are gatherings of three or more people for a fixed period to discuss a small number of topics and sometimes to reach consensus decisions. Meetings can both complement and replace interviews. They complement interviews by allowing a group verification of individual interview results. They can replace interviews by providing a forum for users to collectively work out the requirements and alternatives for an application. Thus, meetings can be useful for choosing between alternatives, verifying findings, and for soliciting application ideas and requirements.

Meetings can also be a colossal waste of time (see Table 4-2). In general, the larger the meeting, the fewer the decisions and the longer they take. Therefore, before having a meeting, a meeting plan should be developed. The agenda should be defined and circulated in advance to all participants. The number of topics should be kept to between one and five. The meeting should be for a fixed period with specific checkpoints for decisions required. In general, meetings should be no longer than two hours to maintain the attention of the participants. The agenda should be followed and the meeting moved along by the project manager or SE, whoever is running the meeting. Minutes should be generated and circulated to summarize the discussion and decisions. Any follow-up items should identify the responsible person(s) and a date by which the item should be resolved.

Meetings are useful for surfacing requirements, reaching consensus, and obtaining both detailed and summary information (see Table 4-2). If decisions are desired, it is important to ask the decision makers to attend and to tell them in advance of the goals for the meeting. If the wrong people participate, time is wasted and the decisions are not made at the meeting.

Joint application development (JAD) is a special form of meeting in which users and technicians meet continuously over several days to identify application requirements (see Figure 4-3). Before a

TABLE 4-5   Interviewee Behaviors and Interviewer Response

Interviewee Behavior	Interviewer Response
Guesses at answers rather than admit ignorance	After the interview, cross-check answers
Tries to tell interviewer what she or he wants to hear rather than correct facts	Avoid questions with implied answers. Cross-check answers
Gives irrelevant information	Be persistent in bringing the discussion to the desired topic
Stops talking when the interviewer takes notes	Do not take notes at this interview. Write notes as soon as the interview is done. Ask only the most important questions. Have more than one interview to get all information.
Rushes through the interview	Suggest coming back later
Wants no change because she or he likes the current work environment	Encourage elaboration of present work environment and good aspects. Use the information to define what gets kept from the current method.
Shows resentment; withholds information or answers guardedly	Begin the interview with personal chitchat on a topic of interest to the interviewee. After the person starts talking, work into the interview.
Is not cooperative, refusing to give information	Get the information elsewhere. Ask this person, "Would you mind verifying what someone else tells me about this topic?"
	If the answer is no, do not use this person as an information source.
Gripes about the job, pay, associates, supervisors, or treatment	Listen for clues. Be noncommittal in your comments. An example might be, "You seem to have lots of problems here; maybe the application proposed might solve some of the problems." Try to move the interview to the desired topic.
Acts like a techno-junkie, advocating state-of-the art everything	Listen for the information you are looking for. Do not become involved in a campaign for technology that does not fit the needs of the application.

JAD session, users are trained in the techniques used to document requirements, in particular, diagrams for data and processes are taught. Then, in preparation for the JAD session, the users document their own jobs using the techniques and collecting copies of all forms, inputs, reports, memos, faxes, and so forth used in performing their job.

A JAD session lasts from 3 to 8 days, and from 7 to 10 hours per day. The purpose of the sessions is to get all the interested parties in one place, to de-fine application requirements, and to accelerate the process of development. Several studies show that JAD can compress an analysis phase from three months into about three weeks, with comparable results. The advantage of such sessions is that users' commitment is concentrated into the short period of time. The disadvantage is that users might allow interruptions to divert their attendance at JAD meetings, thus not meeting the objective. JAD is discussed in more detail in the Introduction to Part II.

FIGURE 4-3   JAD Meeting

Observation

Observation is the manual or automated monitoring of one or more persons' work. In manual observation, a person sits with the individual(s) being observed and takes notes of the activities and steps performed during the work (see Table 4-2). In automated observation, a computer keeps track of software used, e-mail correspondence and partners, and actions performed using a computer. Computer log files are then analyzed to describe the work process based on the software and procedures used.

Observation is useful for obtaining information from users who cannot articulate what they do or how they do it (see Table 4-2). In particular, for expert systems, taking *protocols* of work is a useful form of observation. A **protocol** is a detailed minute-by-minute list of the actions performed by a person. Videotaping is sometimes used for continu-

ous tracking. The notes or tapes are analyzed for events, key verbal statements, or actions that indicate reasoning, work procedure, or other information about the work.

There are three disadvantages to observation (see Table 4-2). First, the time of observation might not be representative of the activities that take place normally, so the SE might get a distorted view of the work. Second, the idea that a person is being observed might lead them to change their behavior. This problem can be lessened somewhat by extensive observation during which time the person being observed loses their sensitivity to being watched. The last disadvantage of observation is that it can be time-consuming and may not yield any greater understanding than could be got in less time-consuming methods of data collection.

Advantages of observation are several. Little opinion is injected into the SE's view of the work.

The SE can gain a good understanding of the current work environment and work procedures through observation. The SE can focus on the issues of importance to him or her, without alienating or disturbing the individual being observed. Some barriers to working with the SEs that are needed for interviews and validation of findings might be overcome through the contact of observation.

Some ground rules for observation are necessary to prepare for the session. You should identify and define what is going to be observed. Be specific about the length of time the observation requires. Obtain both management approval and approval of the individual(s) to be observed before beginning. Explain to the individuals being observed what is being done with the information and why. It is unethical to observe someone without their knowledge or to mislead an individual about what will be done with the information gained during the observation session.

Temporary Job Assignment

There is no substitute for experience. With a temporary job assignment, you get a more complete appreciation for the tasks involved and the complexity of each than you ever could by simply talking about them. Also, you learn firsthand the terminology and the context of its use (see Table 4-2). The purpose, then, of temporary job assignment is to make the assignee more knowledgeable about the problem domain. Temporary assignments usually last two weeks to one month—long enough for you to become comfortable that most normal and exceptional situations have occurred, but not long enough to become truly expert at the job.

Temporary assignment gives you a basis for formulating questions about which functions of the current method of work should be kept and which should be discarded or modified.

The disadvantage of work assignments are that it is time-consuming and may not be a representative period (see Table 4-2). The choice of period can minimize this problem. The other disadvantage is that the SE taking the temporary assignment might become biased about the work process, content, or people in a way that affects future design work.

Questionnaire

A **questionnaire** is a paper-based or computer-based form of interview. Questionnaires are used to obtain information from a large number of people. The major advantage of a questionnaire is anonymity, thus leading to more honest answers than might be got through interviews. Also, standardized questions provide reliable data upon which decisions can be based.

Questionnaire items, like interviews, can be either open-ended or closed-ended. Recall that open-ended questions have no specific response intended. Open-ended questions are less reliable for obtaining complete information about factual information and are subject to recall difficulties, selective perception, and distortion by the person answering the question. Since the interviewer neither knows the specific respondent nor has contact with the respondent, open-ended questions that lead to other questions might go unanswered. An example of an open-ended question is: "List all new functions which you think the new application should do."

A closed-ended question is one which asks for a yes/no or graded specific answer. For example, "Do you agree with the need for a history file?" would obtain either a *yes* or *no* response.

Questionnaire construction is a learned skill that requires consideration of the reliability and validity of the instrument. **Reliability** is the extent to which a questionnaire is free of measurement errors. This means that if a reliable questionnaire were given to the same group several times, the same answers would be obtained. If a questionnaire is unreliable, repeated measurement would result in different answers every time. Questionnaires that try to measure mood, satisfaction, and other emotional characteristics of the respondent tend to be unreliable because they are influenced by how the person feels that day. You improve reliability by testing the questionnaire. When the responses are tallied, statistical techniques are used to verify the reliability of related sets of questions.

Validity is the extent to which the questionnaire measures what you think you are measuring. For instance, assume you want to know the extent to which a CASE tool is being used in both frequency of use and number of functions used. Asking the question, "How well do you use the CASE tool?" might obtain a subjective assessment based on the individual's self-perception. If they perceive themselves as skilled, they might answer that they are extensive users. If they perceive themselves as novices, they might answer that they do not use the tool extensively. A better set of questions would be "How often do you use the CASE tool?" and "How many functions of the tool do you use? Please list the functions you use." These questions specifically ask for numbers which are objective and not tied to an individual's self-perception. The list of functions verifies the numbers and provides the most specific answer possible.

Some guidelines for developing questionnaires are summarized in Table 4-6 and discussed here. First, determine the information to be collected, what facts are required, and what feelings, lists of items, or nonfactual information is desired. Group the items by type of information obtained, type of questions to be asked, or by topic area. Choose a grouping that makes sense for the specific project.

For each piece of information, choose the type of question that best obtains the desired response. Select open-ended questions for general, lists, and nonfactual information. Select closed-ended questions to elicit specific, factual information, or single answers.

Compose a question for each item. For a closed-ended question, develop a response scale. The five-response Likert-like scale is the most frequently used. The low and high ends of the scale indicate the poles of responses, for instance, *Totally Disagree* and *Totally Agree*. The middle response is usually neutral, for instance, *Neither Agree Nor Disagree*. Examine the question and ask yourself if it has any words that might not be interpreted as you mean them. What happens if the respondent does not know the answer to your question? Do you need a response that says, *I Don't Know*? Is a preferred response hidden in the question? Are the response choices complete and ordered properly? Does the question have the same meaning for every department and possible respondent? If the answers to any of these questions indicate a problem, reword the question to remove the problem.

If you have several questions that ask similar information, examine the possibility of eliminating

TABLE 4-6   Guidelines for Questionnaire Development

1. Determine what facts are desired and which people are best qualified to provide them.
2. For each fact, select either an open-ended or close-ended question. Write several questions and choose the one or two that most clearly ask for the information.
3. Group questions by topic area, type of question, or some context-specific criteria.
4. Examine the questionnaire for problems:

   - More than two questions asking the same information
   - Ambiguous questions
   - Questions for which respondents might not have the answer
   - Questions that bias the response
   - Questions that are open to interpretation by job function, level of organization, etc.
   - Responses that are not comprehensive of all possible answers
   - Confusing ordering of questions or responses

5. Fix any problems identified above.
6. Test the questionnaire on a small group of people (e.g., 5–10). Ask for both comments on the questions and answers to the questions.
7. Analyze the comments and fix wording ambiguities, biases, word problems, etc. as identified by the comments.
8. Analyze the responses to ensure that they are the type desired.
9. If the information is different than you expected, the questions might not be direct enough and need rewording. If you don't get useful information that you don't already know, reexamine the need for the questionnaire.
10. Make final edits, print in easy-to-read type. Prepare a cover letter.
11. Distribute the questionnaire, addressing the cover letter to the person by name. Include specific instructions about returning the questionnaire. Provide a self-addressed, stamped envelope if mailing is needed.

one or more items. If you are doing statistical analysis of the answers, you might want similar questions to see if the responses are also similar (i.e., are correlated). If you are simply tallying the responses and acting on the information, try to use one question for each piece of information needed. The minimalist approach keeps the questionnaire shorter and easier to tally.

Pretest the questionnaire on a small group of representative respondents. Ask them to give you feedback on all of the items that they don't understand, that they think are ambiguous, badly worded, or have responses that do not fit the item. Also ask them to complete the questionnaire. The answers of this group should highlight any unexpected responses that, whether the group identified a problem or not, mean that the question was not interpreted as intended. If the pretest responses do not provide you with new information needed to develop the project, the questionnaire might not be needed or might not ask the right questions. Reexamine the need for a questionnaire and revise it as needed. Finally, change the questionnaire based on the feedback from the test group. The pretest and revision activities increase the validity of the questionnaire.

Provide a cover letter for the questionnaire that briefly describes the purpose and type of information sought. Give the respondent a deadline for completing the questionnaire that is not too distant. For instance, three days is better than two weeks. The more distant the due date, the less likely the questionnaire will be completed. Include information about respondent confidentiality and voluntary questionnaire completion, if they are appropriate. Ideally, the questionnaire is anonymous and voluntary. To the extent possible, address the letter to the individual respondent.

Give the respondent directions about returning the completed questionnaire. If mailing is required, provide a stamped, self-addressed envelope. If interoffice mail is used, provide your mail stop address. If you will pick up responses, tell the person where and when to have the questionnaire ready for pickup.

Document Review

New applications rarely spring from nothing. There is almost always a current way of doing work that is guided by policies, procedures, or application systems. Study of the documentation used to teach new employees, to guide daily work, or to use an application can provide valuable insight into what work is done.

The term **documents** refers to written policy manuals, regulations, and standard operating procedures that organizations provide as a guide for managers and employees. Document types include those that describe organization structure, goals, and work. Examples of each document type follow:

Policies
Procedures
User manuals
Strategy and mission statements
Organization charts
Job descriptions
Performance standards
Delegation of authority
Chart of accounts
Budgets
Schedules
Forecasts
Any long- or short-range plans
Memos
Meeting minutes
Employee training documents
Employee manuals
Transaction files, e.g., time sheets, expense records
Legal documents, e.g., copyrights, patents, trademarks, etc.
Historical reports
Financial statements
Reference files, e.g., customers, employees, products, vendors

Documents are not always internal to a company. External documents that might be useful include technical publications, research reports, public surveys, and regulatory information. Examples of external documents follow:

Research reports on industry trends, technology trends, technological advances, etc.
Professional publications with salary surveys, marketing surveys, or product development information
IRS or American Institute of CPA reports on taxes, workmen's compensation, affirmative action, financial reporting, etc.

Economic trends by industry, region, country, etc.

Government stability analyses for developing countries in which the application might be placed

Any publications that might influence the goals, objectives, policies, or work procedures relating to the application

Documentation is particularly useful for SEs to learn about an area with which they have no previous experience. It can be useful for identifying issues or questions about work processes or work products for which users need a history. Documents provide objective information that usually does not discuss user perceptions, feelings, or motivations for work actions.

Documents are less useful for identifying attitudes or motivations. These topics might be important issues, but documents may not contain the desired information.

Software Review

Frequently, applications are replacing older software that supports the work of user departments. Study of the existing software provides you with information about the current work procedures and the extent to which they are constrained by the software design. This, in turn, gives you information about questions to raise with the users, for instance, how much do they *want* work constrained by the application? If they could remove the constraints, how would they do the work?

The weaknesses of getting information from software review are that documentation might not be accurate or current, code might not be readable, and the time might be wasted if the application is being discarded.

To summarize, the methods of collecting information relating to applications include interviews, group meetings, observation, questionnaires, temporary job assignment, document review, or software review. For obtaining information relating to requirements for applications, interviews and JAD meetings are the most common.

DATA COLLECTION AND APPLICATION TYPE

In this section, we identify the data gathering techniques most useful for each application type. Like most aspects of application development, the techniques can be used for all application types, but because of their strengths and weaknesses, they do not always result in the type of information that is needed most. In this section, we first match data collection techniques to the data types discussed in the first section. Then, the data types are matched to application types (from Chapter 1). Next, we match the data collection techniques to application types based on the data types they have in common.

Data Collection Technique and Data Type

Table 4-7 summarizes the discussion of the above sections. By matching technique for data collection to data type, we are more likely to identify information of interest than using other techniques. As the table shows, interviews and meetings are useful for eliciting all types of information. This is the reason they are most frequently used in application work.

Observation provides only crude numerical estimates of volumes, and is restricted to current time, varying ambiguity, and possibly variable semantics (see Table 4-7). Because the information from an observation is unstructured, some skill is required of the SE to impose a structure on it that fits the situation. Also, the information may be incomplete.

Questionnaires can ask structured questions about any time frame but only obtain complete answers for questions asked (see Table 4-7). If the questions are open-ended, the completeness might be quite low. Ambiguity in questionnaires should be low, but the question semantics might be misinterpreted by the respondents. Questions about volume at a department or organization level are usually inappropriate. Information about the volume of transactions or time for transaction processing for individual workers would get meaningful information.

TABLE 4-7   Data Collection Techniques and Data Type

Technique	Time	Structure	Completeness	Ambiguity	Semantics	Volume
Interview	All	All	All	All	Varies	All
Meeting	All	All	All	All	Varies	All
Observation	Current	Unstruct.	Incomplete	May vary	Varies	Crude measure
Questionnaire	All	Structured	Complete for questions asked	Low	Fixed but might be subject to interpretation	Individual volumes only
Temporary job assignment	Current	Unstruct.	Incomplete	Low-med.	Varies	For period of obser-vation but may not be represen-tative
Internal documents	Past-current	Unstruct.	Incomplete	Low-med.	Varies	Maybe
External documents	Mostly current-future	Unstruct.	Incomplete	Low-med.	Relatively fixed	N/A
Software review	Past-current	Structured	Complete for software	Low-med.	Fixed	Maybe

Temporary job assignments are similar to observation in having a high degree of uncertainty associated with the information obtained (see Table 4-7). The information tends to be current, unstructured, and incomplete depending on the period of work. Ambiguity varies from low to medium depending on how well-defined and structured the work is. Semantic content might vary depending on the shared definitions in the work group.

Documents provide unstructured, incomplete informations from which no relevant volume information is likely. The time orientation differs whether the documents are internal or external to the company (see Table 4-7). Internal documents are mostly oriented to the past or current situation. External documents are mostly oriented to current or future topics. The semantics of external documents on mature technologies or topics tend to be relatively fixed while that of internal documents might vary by department or division.

Software provides past, and possibly current, information that is structured because it is automated. The ambiguity should be low to medium, and semantics should be fixed since the application imbeds definitions of data and processes in code. Information on volumes may be present but should be cross-checked using other methods.

Data Type and Application Type

Application types are transaction processing (TPS), query, decision support (DSS), group decision support (GDSS), executive information (EIS), and expert systems (ES). Each of these has one or more predominate datatype characteristics that identifies its application. Table 4-8 shows all applications categorized for all data types. Here we discuss only

TABLE 4-8   Data Type by Application Type

Technique	Time	Structure	Completeness	Ambiguity	Semantics	Volume
TPS	Current	Structured	Complete	Low	Fixed	Any
Query	Past, current	Structured	Complete	Low	Fixed	Any
DSS	All	Structured	Varies	Low-med.	Varies	Med.-high
GDSS	Current-future	Unstruct.	Incomplete	Med.-high	Varies	Low
EIS	Future	Unstruct.	Incomplete	Med.-high	Varies	Low-med.
Expert system	Current based on past	Semi-structured	Incomplete	Med.-high	May vary	Low

the data types that differentiate between application types.

TPS contain predominantly known, current, structured, complete information (see Table 4-8). Recall that TPS are the operational applications of a company. To control and maintain records of current operations, you must have known, structured, current, and complete information.

Query applications have similar characteristics to TPS with the difference that they might concentrate on historical information in addition to current information (see Table 4-8). Queries are questions posed of data to find problems and solutions, and to analyze, summarize, and report on data. To perform summaries and reports with confidence, the data must be structured, complete, and interpreted consistently being both unambiguous and of fixed semantics.

DSS are statistical analysis tools that allow development of information that aids the decision process. The type of data that identifies DSS so that all time frames might be represented, may be incomplete, ambiguous, have variable semantics and medium to high volume (see Table 4-8). DSS might be used, for instance, in analyzing which of two variations on a given product might enjoy the larger market share. To do this analysis, past sales, current sales, and sales trends in the industry might all be analyzed and tied together to develop an answer.

GDSS are meeting facilitation tools for groups of people. GDSS tools operate in a structured manner working on data that is unstructured, current, and future-oriented. GDSS mostly deal with data that is incomplete and contains semantic and other ambiguities (see Table 4-8). The tools themselves are complete, unambiguous, and so forth, but the meeting information they process is not.

EIS are future-oriented applications that allow executives to scan the environment and identify trends, economic changes, or other industry activity that affect their governance of a company. EIS deal mostly with 'messy' data that is unstructured, incomplete, ambiguous, and contains variable semantics (see Table 4-8). Interpretation is always a problem with such data, which is why executives who excel at reading the environment are highly compensated.

Last, expert systems manage and reason through semistructured, incomplete, ambiguous, and variable semantic data (see Table 4-8). Experts and ESs take random, unstructured information and impose a structure on it. They reason through how to interpret the data to remove ambiguity and to fix the semantics. Therefore, even though the data coming into the application might have these fuzzy char-

TABLE 4-9   Data Collection Technique and Application Type

	TPS	Query	DSS	GDSS	EIS	ES
Interview	**X***	**X**	**X**	**X**	**X**	X
Meeting	X	X	X	**X**	X	X
Observation	X	X	X	Limited	Limited	**X**
Questionnaire	X	X	X			
Temporary job assignment	X	X	X			
Internal documents	X	X	X	Limited		
External documents	X	X	X	X	X	X
Software review	X	X	X	Limited	Limited	Limited

*Boldface identifies most frequently used method.

acteristics, the data processing is actually highly structured.

Data Collection Technique and Application Type

Finally, in discussing different data types, we desire to know which data collection techniques are best for each application type. By combining the information in Tables 4-7 and 4-8, we develop Table 4-9 to summarize data collection techniques for each application type. The table entry in boldface shows the principle method of data collection for each technique.

TPS and query applications can profit from the use of all techniques. Meetings and interviews predominate because they elicit the broadest range of responses in the shortest time (see Table 4-9). Observation and temporary job assignment are particularly useful in obtaining background information about the current problem domain, but need to be used with caution so as not to prejudice the design of the application. Questionnaires are useful when the number of people to be interviewed is over 50. Also, questionnaires are useful in identifying characteristics of users that determine, for instance, training required of users during organizational fea-

sibility analysis. Also, if the screen requires, for instance, colors or different types of screen arrangements, questionnaires might be useful for presenting a small set of alternatives from which the actual users choose.

DSS also are shown as having a use for all data collection techniques, but not all techniques are practical in all cases (see Table 4-9). DSS are generally developed for use by people in jobs with a significant amount of discretion in what they do and how they do it. Therefore, observing or working with one or two people as representative may result in a biased view of the application requirements for a general purpose DSS. Even for a custom DSS, observation and job assignments might both be impractical if the SE does not know enough about the job being supported to interpret what she or he observes. The same holds true of documents. Documents, such as statistical reports, might be useful for providing samples of the types of analyses desired in a DSS. Other documents, such as policies, procedures, and so on, are not likely to be relevant to the application. For general purpose DSS with a large number of users, questionnaires are a useful way to identify the range of problems and analysis techniques required in the DSS. This information might be followed by interviews or meetings to determine DSS details.

GDSS are usually custom-built suites of software packages that provide different types of support for automated meetings. As such, the SE working on a GDSS environment needs to know the types of issues, number of participants, as well as types of reasoning and group consensus techniques desired. GDSS components are neither common knowledge nor frequently used; you might build one GDSS in a career. Therefore, significant time would be spent finding out about the market, vendors, and GDSS components. External documents on vendor products are useful in developing questions that elicit the required information. After knowledge of the market is obtained, interviews and meetings are useful to determine the specific requirements and to review, with users, what the GDSS can and cannot do. Other methods might have some limited value. For instance, observation of an actual meeting that might be automated would be useful for the SE to gain insight about how a tool might work. Internal documents that provide information about meetings that the GDSS is expected to provide would also be useful. Both of these techniques, observation and document review, have a specific limited role in providing the information needed to build a GDSS. Any software review that is done would be review of other company's GDSS facilities or of vendor products, rather than review of in-house software.

EIS are similar to GDSS in the rarity and general lack of knowledge about what an EIS is. EIS are not standard applications with a screen for data entry of some type and reports that are displayed. EIS are information presentation facilities that can be structured with menus and selection tools, but may display document pages, newspaper articles, book abstracts, summary reports, and so on. EIS are usually built for a small number of users, which eliminates the use of questionnaires. EIS are custom and one-of-a-kind environments for which past documents or software will be of limited value. Observation is most likely limited because executives would be uncomfortable in being observed. Temporary job assignment is not possible because you cannot just 'be an executive' for a week or two. This leaves external documents, interviews, and meetings as the most likely techniques for data collection (see Table 4-9). As with GDSS, external documents will be mostly to identify the market, vendors, and products. Interviews are most likely to be used to determine executives' information needs and preferred delivery platforms.

Finally, SEs use interviews, observation, and external documents the most in developing expert systems (see Table 4-9). Experts frequently can talk about external aspects of their jobs, the physical cues they use as inputs, and the result of their reasoning and how it is applied to the business. They are just as frequently unable to discuss their reasoning processes and how they put the cues together to make sense of unstructured situations. Experts, by definition of the term expert, have so *internalized* their work that they just do it. They don't think *consciously* about *how* they are doing what they do. Therefore, observation, in particular, the use of protocol analysis, is useful in getting information the expert might not be able to articulate. Protocol analysis is time-consuming and indefinite because you, the SE, are inferring a reasoning process from actions taken. At best, the protocol analysis gives you questions to ask about the work that assist the experts in discussing aspects of work they ordinarily cannot. Thus, observation is interleaved with interviews to discuss what is observed. As the process continues, structure is imposed on both the data and the problems to begin to develop the ES. The process of obtaining an expert's reasoning processes is called **knowledge elicitation**. The process of structuring the unstructured data and reasoning information is called **knowledge engineering**. Knowledge engineering is an activity that is difficult to learn and requires training through an apprenticeship approach in which the trainee works with an expert knowledge engineer.

PROFESSIONALISM AND ETHICS

A **profession** is defined as a job requiring advanced training. Computer information systems development and any job dealing with information technologies qualify as professions. **Professionalism** is acting in accordance with the highest expectations of a professional group. Those expectations are codified in professional codes of ethics for various organizations. The organizations relating most closely to IS professions are the Association of Computing Machinery (ACM) and Data Processing Management Association (DPMA). Both organizations have ethical conduct codes and the codes are similar. The most widely publicized code for the Association for Computing Machinery [1990], follows:

1. The developer shall act with integrity at all times.
   a. The developer shall qualify an opinion outside his or her area of competence.
   b. The developer shall not falsify his or her qualifications.
   c. The developer shall not knowingly issue false statements about the present or expected status of a system.
   d. The developer shall not misuse confidential or proprietary information.
   e. The developer will remain sensitive to and will reveal potential conflicts of interest.
2. The developer should constantly strive to increase his or her competence in the profession.
   a. A developer will diligently attempt to develop systems that perform their intended functions and satisfy the organization's needs.
   b. A developer will help his or her colleagues develop professionally.
3. A developer shall accept only assignments for which there is reasonable expectation of meeting the goals of the system.
4. A developer should use his or her special knowledge to advance the health, privacy, and general welfare of the public and society.
   a. A developer should always consider the individual's right to privacy when working with data.
   b. A developer should refrain from participating in a project in which he or she feels there will be undesirable consequences for individuals, organization, or society as a whole.

If you read the ACM Code of Ethics carefully, note that it contains ethical topics and professionalism topics. To separate out what is professional conduct from what is ethical conduct, we first define

ethics terms and relate ethics to IS professions. Anything that is unethical is also unprofessional, but the reverse is not true. Professionalism is a broader subject than ethical behavior. In fact, the early name for codes of ethics was 'codes of professional behavior.' Ethics is in the section on data collection because many of the issues are concerned with user relations and are most evident in data collection activities.

So, what is ethics? **Ethics** is the branch of philosophy that studies moral judgment and reasoning. A **dilemma** is any situation requiring a choice between two unpleasant alternatives. Therefore, an **ethical dilemma** is any situation in which a decision results in unpleasant consequences requiring moral reasoning. The addition of information technologies to organizations presents novel, little understood opportunities for unethical behavior that are rarely discussed in texts.

Ethics is an issue of growing interest as it relates to information technologies. You, as users and developers of ITs, are sometimes in particular circumstances that subject you to dilemmas that need to be reasoned through to reach an ethical decision. One problem with ethics is that it is misunderstood as religious upbringing and the application of religious thought to real life situations. In fact, that is incorrect. Ethical decisions and reasoning are based on philosophies of rights, equity, and utility, that is, the greatest good for the greatest number of people. Ethics requires evaluation of alternatives, requiring only belief in the equality and dignity of man. Next, we discuss ethics as it relates to different aspects of data collection and user interactions in application development. Then, a procedure for reasoning that is likely to lead to ethical decisions is presented for your use.

Ethical Project Behavior

Confidentiality

Always be trustworthy of information told in confidence. In fact, assume that any interview information is in confidence, unless the person being interviewed is specifically told that it is 'on the record.' Besides being unethical, telling 'tales out of school' will eventually return to hurt your career.

If you think some information gained in privacy should be shared, ask if the interviewee minds if you discuss it. With permission, the bounds of confidentiality are removed and you are free to discuss the information.

The exception to this rule occurs when a person confides in you about an illegal act. You are legally bound to report any illegal activity to the managers, company authorities, and police, if no action is taken. By law, if you do not report illegal acts, you are an accessory to the act and are also libel to legal action.

Privacy

Experts have a right to know when their experience and knowledge are being used in an application. The basic rule is treat others as you would like to be treated. Would you like it if the company observed your use of computers and built systems based on it? Especially in building expert systems there are ethical issues about ownership of expertise. There should be no observation, in person or by computer, without permission. No one should be coerced into cooperation. Participation should be voluntary.

Ownership

Computers are now so much a part of corporate life that we tend to get confused about who owns the resources. On an intellectual level, most people recognize that the company that owns the computers also owns the computer time. But, in a given situation, most people feel that if the resource is not used it is wasted, and that computer time is like the *ether*, a free resource that is there for the taking. Most executives do not feel the same way, whether or not there is a policy about computer resource use.

Find out, in advance, the company policy or owner feelings about personal use of computing resources, then follow their guidance. Actions like running a program for a friend, doing personal finances, keeping track of the baseball team, and so on may or may not be ethical, depending on how the company feels about the use of its resources.

Who owns work and work-related products should be spelled out in detail so that if you feel

something is rightfully yours, so does the client/company and you can feel ethical about taking it. For instance, technical, user, or operational documentation, screen designs, data dictionary, program code, vendor literature, or other products that you develop or gather in the course of development are all subject to ownership confusion. If you work for a consulting company and develop a proprietary application, like ABC's rental system, you have no right to sell the processing to other companies. This right is *negotiable* and belongs only to the client unless that right is specifically itemized in the contract. Be clear about ownership and you are less likely to be fired or sued over ownership rights.

The expertise that you gain from working on a project is **intellectual property**. Expertise is yours unless you sign a contract to the contrary. However, it is unethical to use your company-specific knowledge for personal, noncompetitor, or competitor financial gain unless you have an agreement with your employer about such use. Usually employers ask that you not divulge proprietary information, but the definition of *proprietary* may be open to interpretation. Also, employers can bar you from using information for one to two years if they can prove that it might hurt their business. The best course of action is to get such issues in the open and decided in advance so no conflict occurs.

Politics

Try to never be mixed up in a political battle. This is easier than it sounds, especially if you are the SE or project manager. **Politics** is the science of management often driven by personal motivation. In organizations, most people have the company's interest in mind when they make decisions; everyone is also assumed to at least consider their personal situation in decisions, as well. Some people put personal improvement ahead of all other considerations, even to the detriment of the company. Extreme selfish motivation without regard to the outcome for others or the company is unethical.

In a political battle, the politician(s) try to manipulate the project results to improve their position in the company. Political maneuvering might take different forms: stalling, lying, artificial requirements, false cooperation, or different public and private statements. You, as the SE or PM, must become sensitive to such actions and learn how to diffuse them. The tactics are manifested in the discussion of interviewee actions and interviewer reactions in Table 4-5.

Courtesy

It is not necessary to tell every project problem to the user. You are ethically bound to discuss problems that might impact schedule, budget, or accuracy. *When* to tell a user about problems requires common sense. You should tell them early enough to warn them that the problem is coming, and late enough not to have been a whistleblower for nothing. Never wait until the last minute when nothing can be done to fix the problem, or all project participants lose credibility. Always solicit user assistance in problem resolution once they are told. The purpose of weekly status meetings is to provide status and identify problems and their anticipated resolution. These problems always foreshadow schedule and budget problems when they remain outstanding for a long period. A problem outstanding several months with no solution in sight will probably impact the schedule and budget. In keeping the user up-to-date on technical problems you indirectly apprise them of potential cost and budget overruns.

Personal Manner and Responsibility

When people work on a project with others, they sometimes lose sight of their contribution as standing on its own for quality review. Somehow the notions of 'on time, within budget, and accurate' have meaning to the project but not to the individual who is coding and testing a module. One role of the PM and SEs is to instill the sense of responsibility in every person. Each person should know their tasks, budget, expected resource use, and due date. Each person should be held accountable for meeting their deadlines and for having no errors in the code. Accountability is easy to displace in project work; who is responsible becomes diffuse. Some

people say the project manager is always accountable. Some say the analysts and SEs. Some say no one. The short answer is that *everyone* is responsible for and should be made accountable for his own work and its integration into the project whole.

Do not talk to your manager, client, or your employees about work problems that do not relate to project completion. This is just good business. Managers and clients want answers and solutions, not problems. Therefore, they should be informed of status and problems that might someday affect them, but should otherwise be left alone. A manager doesn't want to know how Suzie in the typing pool or Carl in the copy room butchered your work. You deal with it and forget it. If you have a problem with the quality of someone's work who does not report to you, mention it to that person, and if unresolved, talk to their manager. The less accusatory and more factual you can be, the less like a whiner and complainer you appear. Be sure you can back up any accusations you make.

Do not tell the client or your manager about your personal problems unless you have a personal relationship. Personal problems can always be blamed for everything that goes wrong, but that is neither adult nor ethical. Henry Ford's famous quote, "Never complain, never explain," comes to mind here. Your job at work is to work, so just do it.

Do not get emotionally involved with the user. If there is a budding relationship, it can wait until the project is complete. Emotional involvements are easy to fall into when you are together 10 to 15 hours a day for months at a time. They also are prone to collapse as soon as a new project begins and you and they both work with others 10 to 15 hours a day. Emotional attachments cloud judgment and do not belong in the office.

Never intentionally mislead. Never lie. Never give false impressions, false perceptions, or any information that might cause users to infer a better, bigger, more functional application than you plan to deliver. Users will form their opinions based on what you and their managers tell them. Don't oversell the application and what it can do for their job. Also, if a downsizing is taking place at the same time, don't falsely give people hope that their jobs will be saved when they might not. You don't raise alarms, but you don't give false hope either.

Ethical Reasoning

When you feel you are confronted with a problem that requires ethical reasoning, you need some way to identify all potential stakeholders, to evaluate the alternative courses of action, and to reason through the alternatives. One such method is presented here as a way to initiate reflection on your own thinking about the way you reason through tough problems. This is certainly not the only method of problem reasoning.

Identify Stakeholders

First, identify who might benefit or suffer from your decision. This action identifies **stakeholders**, people who have a stake in the outcome of your action. This is a difficult task, especially with computer use when you might not know the stakeholders personally. Stakeholders might be stockholders of a company, the company itself, your boss, you, the user community, the user/client for the application, society, or people subject to direct or indirect connection to the application. For instance, space shuttle astronauts, patients in a hospital, people who live near the plant in which the application will run, e-mail recipients, report users, governments, data entry clerks and their managers, all might be stakeholders.

Identify Actions Stakeholders Would Choose

Then, identify the action each stakeholder would prefer you to take and why. This task defines all possible actions. Begin with yourself. What do you want to do? Why do you think this is the best decision? Answer these questions from the perspective of each stakeholder group. Putting yourself in each stakeholder group's position requires objectivity and distance from the problem.

Eliminate Alternatives

Next, determine if there are any policies, procedures, laws, or other guidelines that make one or more

alternatives untenable. Cross them off the list. Once a type of conduct crosses over into governance by laws, it is no longer an ethical issue, but becomes a legal one. Always obey the laws of the country you are in and the country you represent. For instance, bribery is a way of life in many countries, but not in the United States. Therefore, you are legally bound not to use bribery in business when you work for an American firm.

Policies and procedures of companies are similar in codifying conduct, but do not hold the same stringency of penalty for their transgression. Violation of policies is usually a fireable offense, meaning you lose your job when you violate a policy. Procedures are less stringent, but are expected to be followed. You might receive a letter of reprimand for not following a procedure exactly.

Guidelines, such as the professional code of ethics listed above, also provide heuristics about conduct to help you in governing your work behavior. There is no direct penalty in not following a code of ethics. You might be sued or fired, but the punishment is not from the professional organization.

Reason Through Negative Outcome Alternatives

For the possible courses of action remaining on your list, reason through each by asking key negative questions. If the answer to any of these negative outcome questions is yes, remove the alternative action from the list.

Are the rights of any person or group violated by this action? Consider the right to privacy, ownership of information about individuals' buying habits, payment habits, income, tax status, and so on. Consider the rights to company privacy of customer, financial, personnel, medical, and other proprietary information. Ask if the lack of security and access controls, for instance, subject the database to casual browsing by system users. If such browsing could result in a violation of privacy to customers, it should be prevented.

Does taking this action result in inequitable treatment of a person or group? Equitable treatment requires judgment of equality. In multinational companies, inequity might be seen as a business decision. For instance, many US corporations initially got into international business by dumping their second rate quality goods in other markets. Was this ethical? The answer is in the manner in which it was done. If the goods were sold as second quality, there is no issue. If the goods were sold as first quality, the companies basically lied and were unethical.

Companies might be subject to inequity because of their internal staff quality, too. Does the company lose money because of the inefficiency of design? A manager, for instance, might insist on using a particular software because he knows it, even though it is not efficient for the task. The manager is making a trade-off of current knowledge versus cost and time for learning a new product, that can cross the line into unethical behavior when it costs the company tangible amounts of money. Using mainframes which rent for millions instead of networks that cost thousands could be construed as unethical when networks are not even considered because of a lack of expertise. In other words, making a business decision to stay with a significantly more expensive alternative after considering all alternatives, is ethical. Avoiding a comparison of alternatives or making a decision because of technical ignorance is not ethical.

Does taking this action have the potential of placing a person or company in jeopardy financially, physically, legally, or morally? Hospital applications that hook patients to computerized monitors, transportation industry applications that affect safety of planes and cars, power plant applications that deal with monitoring power-generation equipment, and so forth, are all potentially life-threatening. We need such applications, but their design and maintenance must be of the highest possible quality to pose the least risk to human life. If corners are cut on analysis, design, or testing, lives can be lost.

Reason Through Neutral and Positive Outcome Alternatives

For remaining actions, ask key positive outcome questions to select the best alternative. Does taking this action result in the best possible outcome for all stakeholders? What is the result of taking no action?

If only negative outcomes are possible, does taking this action result in the least harm to all stakeholders? If this is the case, who suffers and what type of injury? If the stakeholder is warned in advance, can the problem be averted?

Select a Course of Action

When all the pros and cons of each alternative have been identified, select the alternative that produces the greatest good for the greatest number of people, that does not violate anyone's rights, and that results in the most equitable decision, with all stakeholders' equity considered.

SUMMARY

Data gathering is done during every phase of application development, but serves different purposes in each phase. The types of data collected depends on the type application and phase of development.

Data types refer to the characteristics of data for time-orientation, structure, completeness, ambiguity, semantics, and volume. Attention to data types in selection of data collection technique is less likely to *cause* errors and more likely to *find* errors than inattention to data type. The cost of errors rises dramatically the later in the development process it is found. Time orientation of data refers to past, present, or future data requirements for an application. Data structure refers to the extent to which data can be classified. Data completeness is the extent to which desired information is present. Ambiguous data have unclear or multiple meanings; companies strive for unambiguous definitions for data. Data semantics are the meanings, we as organization employees, give to data. Volume is the numbers of each item of interest in an application. Volumes can have widely varying time orientations. SEs must attend to peak as well as average volume.

Several data collection techniques were discussed, including interviews, group meetings, questionnaires, observation, temporary job assignment, review of internal and external documents, and review of software. Interviews are meetings between two or three people for obtaining any type of information. Interviews can be structured or unstructured. Questions asked can be open-ended or closed-ended.

Group meetings include four or more people and can substitute for interviews or can be used to validate interview findings. Joint application development meetings are a special type of meeting specifically convened to develop application requirements. Special training and planning are required for JAD sessions. Both interviews and meetings require attention to an agenda and time period.

Observation is the monitoring of one or more persons' work. Observation is useful for learning a problem domain and is most often used in expert system development. A data analysis technique called protocol analysis is used to infer the reasoning processes of experts from detailed manuscripts of their actions during a period.

Temporary job assignment is an alternative means of gaining problem domain experience for nonmanagerial, nonexecutive jobs. Questionnaires are structured forms of interviews conducted on many people, usually more than 50. Statistical techniques are frequently used in analyzing questionnaire results. Reliability and validity of the questions are issues to be considered in questionnaire development.

Document review is useful in gaining background information about an application area. Documents can be internal or external to the company.

Software review is the analysis of programs and documentation to learn the details of a current application.

In developing the information about data collection technique related to application type, we also related data collection technique to data type and data type to application type. From these analyses, we find that interviews and meetings are most frequently used because they are the only techniques useful regardless of application type. The other techniques have specific purposes for each application type. For instance, software review for TPS, temporary job assignment, or observation are useful in gaining problem domain experience. Observation is most useful in expert system development. External documents are important in unique GDSS and EIS development. Questionnaires are most useful in DSS for general use in a company, for surveying user preferences for design options, or for obtaining detailed information about the application from a large number of people.

KEY TERMS

closed-ended question	meetings
data ambiguity	observation
data completeness	open-ended question
data semantics	peak volume
data structure	politics
data time-orientation	profession
data volume	professionalism
dilemma	protocol
document	questionnaire
ethical dilemma	reliability
ethics	semantics
intellectual property	stakeholder
interview	structured interview
joint application	triangulation
development (JAD)	unstructured interview
knowledge elicitation	validity
knowledge engineering	

REFERENCES

Flaaten, Per O., Donald J. McCubbrey, P. Declan O'Riordan, and Keith Burgess, *Foundations of Business Systems*, 2nd ed. Fort Worth, TX: Dryden Press, 1992.

Gause, Donald C., and Gerald M.Weinberg, *Exploring Requirements Quality Before Design*. NY: Dorset House Publishing, Inc., 1989.

Lucas, Henry C., Jr., *The Analysis, Design, and Implementation of Information Systems*, 4th ed. NY: McGraw-Hill, Inc., 1992.

Mockler, Robert J., and Dorothy G. Dologite, *Knowledge-based Systems: An Introduction to Expert Systems*. NY: Macmillan Publishing Co., 1992.

Zahedi, Fatemah, *Intelligent Systems for Business: Expert Systems with Neural Networks*. Belmont, CA: Wadsworth Publishing, 1993.

EXERCISES

1. Ethics is far from a settled issue, especially as it relates to use of information technologies. One issue, for instance, is that development of artificially intelligent applications might be unethical because we do not know how they will turn out. That means, we cannot predict if a person or company will get hurt. Debate this issue and develop conclusions for your class. Summarize the debate and send it to a trade magazine such as *Communications of ACM, Computerworld,* or *Datamation.*

2. For ABC Video, play the roles of Vic, Mary, and Sam. Either write or playact an interview to elicit requirements for the proposed rental application. Mix the use of open and closed questions to follow a chain of logic.

3. Develop a questionnaire that might be used with the user community of the Office Information System case in the Appendix.

STUDY QUESTIONS

1. Define the following terms:

ambiguity	professionalism
ethical dilemma	reliability
joint application	semantics
development	structure of data
professional	triangulation

2. Why are data types important? What happens when the wrong data collection techniques are used? How does data collection technique relate to costs in applications?

3. How do data types relate to applications?

4. Discuss the cost of fixing errors in applications.

5. How do ambiguity and semantics differ? Why are they both important?

6. When are temporary job assignments not a useful data collection technique?

7. What type of information can be got from temporary job assignments?

8. What is the use of reviewing documents? How do you choose whether to review internal or external documents?

9. Why would you ever review software? What are the pitfalls of software and software documentation review?

10. Compare and contrast individual interviews and meetings, listing two purposes that are the same for both techniques and two that are different.

11. Compare and contrast structured and unstructured interviews.

12. Compare and contrast open-ended questions and closed-ended questions.

13. Describe how an unstructured interview progresses. What types of questions are used as the opening? How does the interviewer know what types of questions to ask? What types of questions are used after the opening?

14. Which kinds of data can you best get from observation?

15. Which kinds of data can you best get from external document review?

16. Which kinds of data are you unlikely to get from a questionnaire?

17. Which data collection technique is most useful for obtaining expert reasoning processes? Why? Describe the use of the technique.

18. Which data collection technique is most useful for obtaining executive needs for an EIS?

19. Why are expert systems and EIS unique?

20. Which question types are used for factual, detailed explanations of work processes?

21. How do you select between structured and unstructured interviews?

22. What is the typical follow-up to an interview? Who does what and when?

23. Why are meetings a useful data collection technique? How do you plan a meeting to avoid wasting time?

24. Describe how to develop a questionnaire.

25. Describe protocol analysis. When is it used? What application type(s) is it most used for?

26. What type of data are most likely in a DSS?

27. Describe the time-orientation of EIS. What type of data is associated with EIS?

28. Describe knowledge engineering. When is it used and why?

29. What is the difference between professionalism and professional ethics?
30. Discuss three of the six areas of ethical conduct by IS professionals.
31. Describe an ethical dilemma you might face in application development work. How should it be dealt with?
32. Describe the reasoning process for developing an ethical solution to some issue.

★ EXTRA-CREDIT QUESTIONS

1. For ABC Video's rental application, we still do not know accurate counts for volumes of rentals, late returns, on-time returns, late fees, or customers. How would you go about finding this information? Be specific in identifying a data collection technique, the number of people involved, and the amount of time involved. At what stage of the development process should this information be got?

2. The ACM's Code of Ethics, number 2, discusses the need for developers to constantly increase competence in their profession and to help others to do likewise. Is this an ethical issue? Who are the stakeholders to the issue? Reason through the issues and develop your own thoughts on the subject. Compare them to classmates, arguing for your position.

3. List and define the data type for all data currently identified for ABC's rental application. Refer to Chapter 2 for the data definitions.

PROJECT
INITIATION

The two chapters in this section address the activities that take place before analysis of a specific project begins. Project initiation can take place in several different ways. First, it can be part of a larger enterprise reengineering effort. Second, a project might be initiated as part of an information systems planning effort. Third, a project might be initiated based on a user request for a specific project. All three methods of project initiation are equally feasible and equally useful in beginning an application development project.

Chapter 5 addresses the first two project initiation efforts. The main discussion is how to do a reengineering design of an organization and plan applications and technologies to support the redesign. Enterprise level planning, such as an information systems plan, is described as a subset of activities that focus on applications only and are an abbreviated reengineering study. Most researchers and industry experts, such as James Martin, recommend that at least an information systems plan (ISP) is a worthwhile planning activity in existing organizations. Both reengineering and ISPs result in plans for multiple applications which are prioritized for development.

Enterprise level planning exercises are costly, and some companies cannot afford to spend computer resources on such studies. In these companies, application development projects are initiated via a direct request from a user. Also, companies that do enterprise level plans might desire to reconfirm recommendations that might be two or three years old. For direct initiation and for reconfirmation of recommendations, a user memo to the Information Systems Manager or to an IS Steering Committee can initiate project assessment. Such an assessment is called a *feasibility study*.

Chapter 6 details the activities involved in a feasibility study. A feasibility study is performed to assess the financial, technological, and organizational readiness of the company for the application. Feasibility is an important analysis that is usually conducted on individual application projects rather than on a whole group of applications, such as might be identified in an ISP or organizational reengineering project. The feasibility analysis determines the extent to which new technologies, skills, or training are required by the user and developer staffs and assesses the ability of the company to pay for the development project.

Part of the technical feasibility is to define a direction for the application development through an evaluation of technical development alternatives. For instance, an application might be on-line or real-time; it might be on a standalone PC, on a PC connected to a local area network, or on terminals attached to a mainframe; it might use a 4GL database software such as Oracle™ or a full-service database such as IMS DB/DC.[1] Likely alternatives are evaluated to determine the extent to which functional requirements would be supported, and to determine any alternative-specific benefits that might be present. A recommendation for technical concepts is made and may (or may not) be accepted at the completion of the feasibility study. Even though the concept need not be cast in concrete at this time, it helps to have a sense of the operational environment for conducting the analysis phase of the project.

A risk assessment should be performed as part of feasibility analysis. The risk assessment identifies technical, personnel, and financial problems that could hinder the successful completion of the project. For each risk defined, two types of plans are developed. First, a contingency plan to deal with the problem if it should occur is defined. Second, immediate steps to minimize the probability of the risk's occurrence are planned and taken.

---

1 Oracle™ is a trademark of the Oracle Corporation. IMS DB/DC is a product of IBM Corporation.

## CHAPTER 5

ORGANIZATIONAL REENGINEERING AND ENTERPRISE PLANNING

INTRODUCTION

As the economy becomes more global and the business climate more competitive, companies need to reevaluate what they do and how they do it. Reengineering is the evaluation and redesign of business processes. The goal is to streamline the organization to include only the business functions that *should* be done rather than necessarily improve on what is done today. Reengineering can introduce radical change into organizations with information technologies as key to supporting new organizational forms and providing information delivery to its users.

When radical approaches are not necessary (or wanted), the techniques of reengineering can be scaled down to provide enterprise level plans for information systems. Enterprise level planning techniques originally were developed in response to managers' complaints that IS departments did not respond to their information needs and frequently built applications that the company did not need. Enterprise planning techniques match IS plans to organization plans and are also used within the context of reengineering. Techniques include stakeholder analysis, critical success factors, and infor-

mation systems planning (ISP). In this chapter, we first develop the conceptual basis and methodology for reengineering. Enterprise techniques are defined for use in reengineering analysis. Then, enterprise level IS planning, without organization design, is described. The last section identifies computer-aided software engineering (CASE) tools that support reengineering and enterprise level analysis techniques.

CONCEPTUAL FOUNDATIONS OF ENTERPRISE REENGINEERING

Organizational reengineering is the evaluation and redesign of business processes, data, and technology (see Figure 5-1). The goals of reengineering are to achieve *dramatic* improvements in quality, service, speed, use of capital, and reduced costs. The rationale for business reevaluation comes from need. The need may be to turn around a failing company, to increase competitiveness, to improve customer service, to increase product quality, or any combination of these. The philosophy of reengineering is

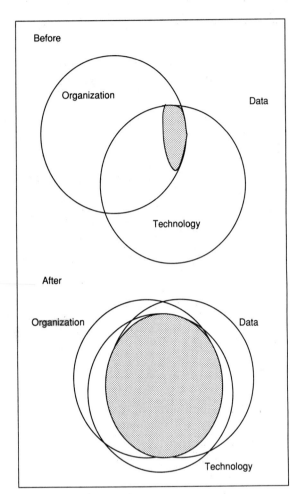

FIGURE 5-1   Reengineering Targets

evaluate the organization and its information requirements, how to reengineer both the organization *and* the technology, and how to plan for the implementation of radical change.

Reengineering theory comes from management and IS. Management theories about organization design, job design, and reskilling are all used in redesign of work and the organization structure.

First, good management practice dictates that only essential activities be done. To assure this, reengineering assumes an organization level plan for all functions, activities, and processes that accomplish the activities. It also assumes that the plan is actively managed to ensure that all processes directly relate to the organization's mission, goals, and objectives. Nonessential processes, departments, and layers of management are eliminated to streamline, speed, and lower the cost of process performance.

Second, in job redesign, a caseworker approach is preferred to an assembly line approach. **Caseworkers**[1] have increased control, decision making, authority, and discretion. Redesigned, enlarged jobs improve the quality of work life, thus, improving the quality of work.

To satisfy employees and customers, for instance, customer service departments might adapt a caseworker approach to work. In the caseworker approach, employees know the entire process from beginning to end and work independently to service their personal customers. In addition, the caseworker works closely with the marketing and sales force for those same customers. The consequences of caseworkers are great. The customer service agents have reskilled, enlarged jobs that are more interesting. Intrabusiness communications between, for instance, sales and customer service, are improved. External customer relations should also improve because customers have one consistent representative with whom they work.

Enlarged jobs are not a way to squeeze more work out of already overworked people. In the customer service example, initially a clerk does a small number of activities that present a partial view of a large number of customers. In a reengineered job,

that, when implemented alone, total quality programs, organization redesign, or information technology are inadequate for an organization to realize its potential. The main resources of organizations today are people and information. Both people and data, the raw material of information, have to be optimized to even *try* to meet the company's potential. Organization redesign optimizes the people resource; the interjection of quality improves both organization and data. Complete reevaluation of technology that provides the information infrastructure optimizes the data and delivery of data to the people who need it. This chapter discusses how to

---

1 Hackman [1990].

the clerk does a large number of related activities that present a complete view of a small number of customers. The move is away from an assembly line approach and toward self-sufficient workers or work groups.

The first reengineering improvement for case-workers comes from job redesign. If the 80–20 rule is applied to most businesses, 80% of the transactions in the business are the norm, and 20% are exceptions. Organizations are typically designed to handle exceptions well. The 80% of their work that is normal tends to take much longer than needed. One goal of reengineering is to increase handling speed and quality of handling for the 80% of normal transactions by an order of magnitude, for instance, by at least 10 times. A second goal is to decrease the number of exceptions to as close to zero as possible. For instance, at Ford, one way to prevent errors in the receipt of goods from vendors was to accept only complete, exact shipments. Any item that did not match an order item caused the entire order to be returned. Vendors got the message quickly that Ford would not accept their shoddy work practices any more and were forced to revise their procedures as well.

⋇ Empowerment of the caseworkers comes from job redesign, removal of errors from the process, *and* from the use of any and all information and technologies that assist them in performing their job. Information technologies *enable reengineering*. **Information technologies** (IT) are any technologies that support the storage, retrieval, organization, management, or processing of data. A technology plan and goals should be developed and managed at the organization level.

In addition, **data**, the raw material for information, requires recognition and organizational commitment as a corporate resource. As a corporate resource, data requires the same careful planning and ongoing management as cash-on-hand, office equipment, or personnel. Data must be managed at the corporate level as a key asset of the organization.

To manage and plan for the organization structure, its data, and its technology, enterprise level (i.e., the entire organization is the enterprise) plans must be devised. These plans, or **'architectures,'** provide a snapshot of the current organization. An

enterprise architecture is an abstract summary of some organizational component's design. The organizational strategy is the basis for deciding where the organization wants to be in three to five years. When matched to the organizational strategy, the architectures provide the foundation for deciding priorities for implementing the strategy.

The organization **process architecture** identifies the major functions of the organization, the activities that define the functions, and the processes that accomplish the activities. Examples of each of these levels are shown in Figure 5-2. It does not detail the procedures for how to do each task.

During reengineering analysis, the entire process architecture is reevaluated for its support in achieving organizational goals. For processes that survive the analysis, the organization is redesigned. Theories of interdependence, linking mechanisms, and organization design are applied to structuring work groups in the reengineered organization.[2] These theories are not new. Rather, theorists and practitioners have talked about them for years with little movement of theory into practice. Over the same years, information technologies matured sufficiently to support the integration and data sharing required of the *information organization*. In the early 1990s, a ground swell of changing companies became an avalanche, with many companies trying to implement the theories using information technologies to support the revised organization.

The second architecture, **data architecture**, identifies the enduring, stable data entities (people, places, organization, events, and applications) that are critical to the organization maintaining itself as a going concern. IS theories of information modeling and information systems planning are used in data analysis. In particular, entity-relationship modeling is used for documenting data and its relationships. Entity-process analysis is used to design subject area databases. Entity-application analysis and process-application analysis are used to define automation requirements. These analyses originated in IBM's

---

2 Interdependence theory is Thompson's [1967]. Galbraith [1976] and Galbraith and Nathansen [1979] propose linking mechanisms with some organization design. Other organization design work is listed in the references.

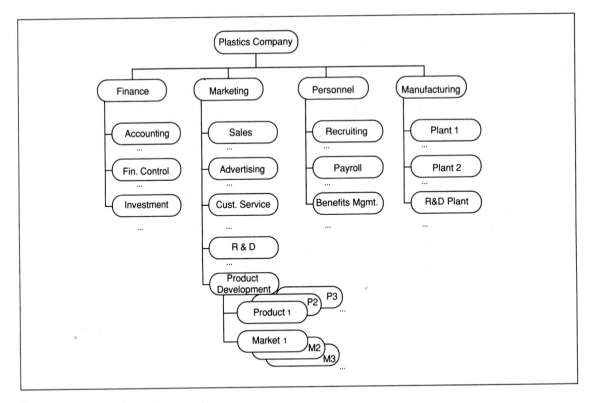

FIGURE 5-2   Sample Process Architecture

information systems planning (ISP) methodology and are expanded in reengineering.

The **network architecture** identifies all locations of work and their communications requirements. It is the basis for deciding telecommunications support.

Finally, the **technology architecture** contains information about platforms [e.g., mainframe, local area network (LAN), or personal computer (PC)], special-purpose technologies (e.g., multimedia, imaging, e-mail) and the locations of each. By mapping the network and technology architectures, organization level technology changes can be identified. New technologies, such as imaging, can be evaluated and positioned to provide the most leverage to the organization.

Successful reengineering is not assured. Necessary conditions, or *absolute prerequisites*, for reengineering include:

1. Management commitment, usually from the CEO or top manager of the organization.
2. Formally articulated organizational mission, goals, and objectives.
3. Full commitment of the reengineering team.
4. Training and support for the reengineering team.
5. The desire to change the organization and its culture.

In addition to the necessary conditions, reengineering assumes the following:

1. *Nothing escapes review.* The reengineering team has as its mission to evaluate the organization, including its structure, jobs, data, processes, and technology. Recommendations in any of the five areas of assessment may be made.

2. Enlarging jobs and empowering job holders as caseworkers rather than as assembly line workers is desirable.
3. Business and IS organizations must become *partners* in the redesign and technology empowerment.
4. In improving quality of processes, elimination of errors via elimination of functions and superfluous processes is desirable.
5. There are no technology constraints. Recommendations will be made without regard to current budgetary, organizational, or other constraints. Implementation planners, based on recommendations and manager's priorities, will attend to constraints.
6. Data shareability is desired. While normalizing data within an application environment minimizes redundancy in an application, *minimizing organizational data redundancy* via data administration and across applications is the *real* goal. Building subject area data bases and providing data access based on need rather than on organization structure is the means to achieving organizationally minimized data redundancy.

This assumption of no constraints may not be realistic in that politics and survival of participants can subvert the desired objectivity in a reengineering project. One of the management challenges in reengineering is to prevent politics from preventing the needed change.

Industry leaders and successful turnaround companies who now thrive provide the motivation for sweeping change. These companies are organized differently from their competition. Industry leaders today tend to have fewer departments, fewer layers of management, and fewer people doing analogous jobs than their competition. Their success is partly organizational and partly cultural. These successful companies succeed because they define their market in terms of what their customers want and demand, *then they exceed those expectations.* Because these companies do not have excess structure, they are flexible to continuously reevaluate what they are doing and how well they are doing it.

Ford Motor Company, for instance, turned around their losing company when introducing their 'Quality is number one' program. They compared their organization to others, including Japanese firms, and found they had many more people performing similar functions. In some cases, like the accounting area, the difference was more than 10 to 1 in numbers of people. Ford threw away the book about how accounting should be done, eliminated parochial interests about where decisions should be made, made data sharing from databases universal, and reduced their staff by over 60%. The result of the extensive changes is happier people with more skills used in a given job. Individual jobs are done faster and more cheaply with almost no errors.

The philosophy of reengineering is to define stakeholders' goals and then exceed them. The philosophy is based on the idea that change can be good. Companies must scan the business horizon and actively change the organization as needed to lower costs, and to improve, speed, and increase the quality of service(s) in meeting its mission. *They must be equally proactive about discontinuing* services, departments, applications, or technologies that no longer relate to organizational goals and objectives. In short, the organization must be proactive rather than reactive about all aspects of its operation.

PLANNING
REENGINEERING
PROJECTS

Schedules for reengineering projects can be based on several different scenarios. The goal of all scenarios is the same: redesign of organization, jobs, processes, data, and supporting technologies. A secondary goal is that all redesign planning be completed in a short period of time. The short period should be within four months from the time the team is formed until all recommendations are presented to the senior manager sponsor(s).

Reengineering projects can be completed faster or slower depending on several factors. First is the amount of actual time spent by each team member. Ideally, all team members should be relieved of their current duties and assigned full time to the reengineering effort. In reality, the best managers, who you want on the team, also are the most needed to run the current business. So, part-time or short duration full-time commitments might *have* to suffice.

In all cases, one to four senior IS staff (i.e., consultants, senior analysts, software engineers, or project managers) are assigned full time to the project. Much of the work performed during the reengineering project is identical to that performed as part of an information systems planning exercise. IS staff who already know ISP only need to learn several types of matrix analysis and organizational design to be fully capable of performing the reengineering work.

The second major factor in determining the amount of time is the size of the organization being analyzed. A 100-person, five-department organization can be analyzed easily within four months. A 10,000-person, 200-department with four hierarchic levels can also be analyzed within four months, but requires more people and more discipline to the team. A good rule of thumb is to have one person for every 10–15 departments or every 100 jobs.

Four months is the time most authors recommend for completion of the entire reengineering project, from inception to development of the implementation plan. The actual pilot testing and implementation of the changes might take several years to complete. There are several good reasons for a short time schedule. First, managers cannot suspend their work indefinitely and run a company, too. If several people are allocated full time it drains the management resource. Second, with a mentality oriented to quarterly results in the United States, most managers will not wait longer than that to prepare for change. Third, the project is bound to be known throughout the organization soon after it begins. When reorganizations are imminent, work is replaced by gossip and worry. The shorter the time of the reengineering study, the less lost work to the organization.

When the end date is mandated, the team does the amount of work they can accomplish within the time constraint. This approach to work is called 'level of effort.' With a **level of effort** approach, the team works at capacity up to the deadline and, what does not get done, does not get done. For large projects,

then, the level of effort approach assumes an incomplete analysis.

The assumption here is that error-prone and bottleneck processes are the targeted activities. While a high-level description of the entire enterprise is possible, only the problem activities are actually in the level-of-effort study.

Scenarios for three levels of user manager participation are provided in Figures 5-3 through 5-5. Figure 5-3 shows a short burst of participation, similar to a joint requirements planning (JRP).[3] In this scenario, users and analysts are trained and go off-site for an intensive 4–8 days (depending on the size of the organization) of requirements, data, process, and entity-process analysis. An alternative that minimizes the amount of time managers are absent from work is to hold the JRP meetings over one or two weekends. More than 90% of the data gathering can be completed using the JRP approach. In this scenario, most of the analyses are done by the full-time project staff, but are presented for review and decisions to the user-team participants. *In no case do the IS staff make the decisions and recommendations alone.*

The second scenario assumes constant part-time participation over time (see Figure 5-4). In this scenario, user managers are available for meetings, interviews, and analysis sessions 1–3 hours each day. They must be committed to participating and must not waver from participation, or the project will falter. Notice the dotted lines for all activities. The dotted lines imply a part-time, longer activity. The full-time IS staff actually do most of the legwork, interviews, and preparation for analyses. But, once again, the decisions are made by the user managers, not the IS staff.

The final scenario assumes full-time commitment for the duration of the project (see Figure 5-5). With full-time users and full-time IS staff, the length of the project can be as short as three weeks and, for large organizations (e.g., 1,000 people, 50 departments), as long as 16 weeks. Table 5-1 shows the major tasks and activities with expected percentages of effort for each task.

---

3 JRP is an innovation of IBM Corporation. It is fully discussed in the introduction to Part II.

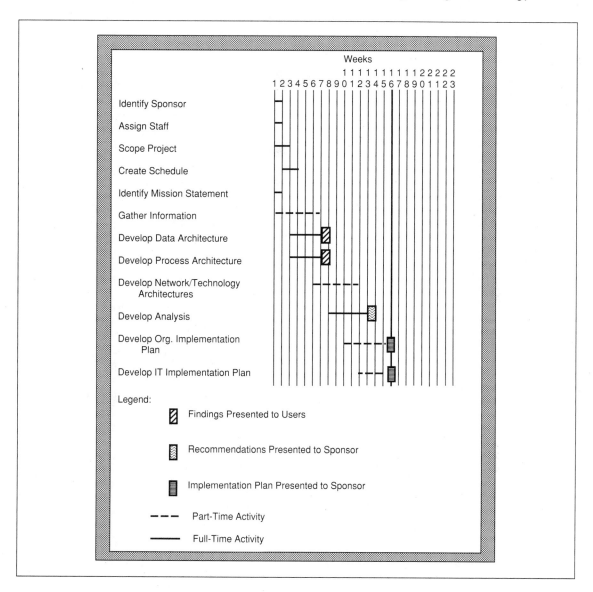

FIGURE 5-3   Reengineering with Part-Time Users

REENGINEERING

METHODOLOGY

Reengineering is most easily done within the scope of information system planning (ISP) projects. With a greater balance of process and data analysis, and several additional activities, reengineering uses the same information as the ISP. The major steps and

their results, type of questions asked, and analyses are listed in Table 5-1. The steps are summarized in Figure 5-6 which shows a significant amount of overlap between steps. The times allocated to the tasks are as individual stand-alone activities and do not reflect the amount of actual time spent on the step. For instance, the architectures are all allocated one week. But they are preceded by activities of four weeks during which they should also be developed.

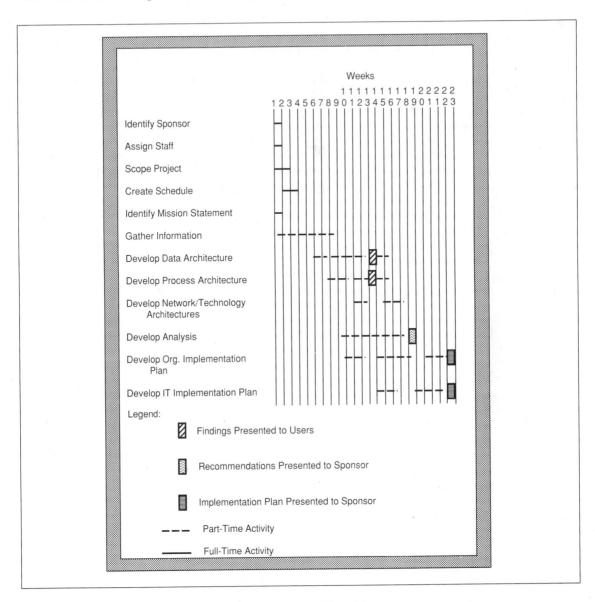

FIGURE 5-4   Reengineering with Continuous, Part-Time Users

All of those particular steps are iterative and require three to five weeks to complete. A detailed description of each reengineering step follows.

Identify Project Sponsor

The first step of reengineering is to enlist or be enlisted by the project sponsor. The **project sponsor** is a *senior* level manager who will pay for *and* champion the project. A **champion** is an individual with commitment, enthusiasm, credibility, and influence who can act as a 'cheerleader' for the project and its outcomes. The sponsor is the overall project manager for the reengineering project and must have the authority, fortitude, and desire to change the organization and its work, based on the recommendations from the reengineering analyses.

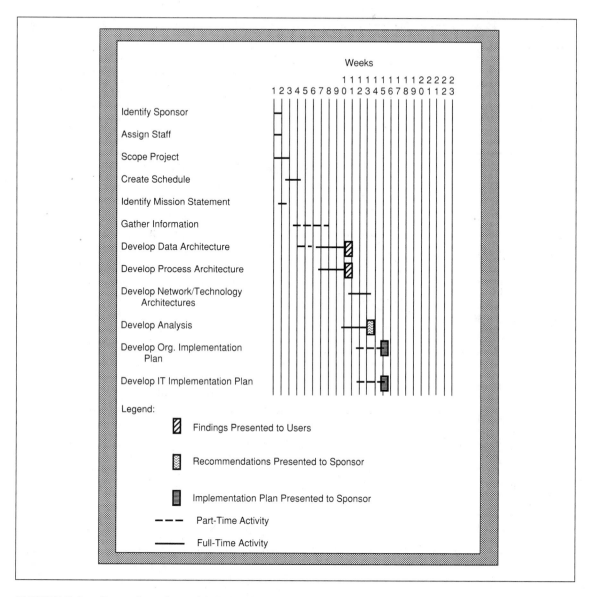

FIGURE 5-5   Reengineering with Full-Time Users

Assign Staff

Three or four user area, senior, or middle managers should be assigned to the reengineering project for a period not to exceed four months. At least one month of the initial commitment should be full time; the remainder of the work may require only part-time commitment. Two or three senior IS managers, or SEs, or data administrators, or consultants should be assigned to the project full time for its entire duration.

All team members should attend a reengineering workshop or class *together* to fully acquaint them with the techniques and goals of the activity. The individuals assigned must have commitment to this work. They *must* be senior enough and good enough at their own jobs to have instant credibility within their organization. Without both of these

TABLE 5-1   Percentage of Reengineering Effort by Task

Activity	% Effort
Obtain sponsor	N/A
Initiate project	N/A
Assign staff	N/A
Scope project (Concurrent with next two activities)	2–5% 2 Days
Develop schedule	2–5% 3–5 Days
Identify mission statement	2–5% 1 Day
Gather data	20–25% 3–4 Weeks
Develop process architecture	6–10% 3 Days–1 Week
Develop data architecture	6–15% 3 Days–1 Week
Develop and analyze entity/ process matrix	20–25% 3–4 Weeks
Develop implementation plan	20–25% 3–4 Weeks
Develop technology architecture	6–10% 3 Days–1 Week
Total duration	100% 12–17 Weeks

requirements, the target of four months for the total effort is doubtful.

Scope the Project

The key criteria for properly scoping a reengineering project are data self-sufficiency and user commitment. **Data self-sufficiency** is defined as 70% (or more) of data used in performing the business functions that must originate within the subject organization. The goal of **scoping** is to identify a group of departments that create their own information and are not dependent on other departments for data to do their work. Control over data creation equals data self-sufficiency.

The second criteria is user commitment. **User commitment** means that the managers participating in the reengineering project must be committed to changing the organization. This is not as difficult as it might sound. Few people enjoy their job when they know it is inefficient and hampered by ineffective organization or systems designs. When the best managers in an organization that needs change are assigned, they become enthusiastic about the prospect of designing the work groups to fit the work. Because their positions in the company are not at risk, there is little reluctance to participate.

Determining data self-sufficiency requires development of a quick entity-relationship diagram (ERD), process hierarchy, and entity/process matrix. The results should be about 80% complete and address the major entities and processes. The analysis of the matrix is to determine where data are created, nothing else. If data are not created within the organization, the amount of data and the creating (or originating) organization are identified and added to the study. In addition, the amount of data for all entities created within the organization must be identified to determine the percentage of data self-sufficiency. The percentage is derived from the formula shown as Figure 5-7.

The inputs to the formula (I) identify a count of transactions or other work items generated within the target reengineering organization. The outside work (O) represents a count of transactions or other work items coming into the department from elsewhere in the organization. Outside work is not subject to review or error reduction, and the goal is to keep it to a minimum in the study. In Figure 5-7, the target organization generates 75% of its own data and is, therefore, data self-sufficient enough to benefit from reengineering.

Less than 70% data sufficiency implies too narrow a scope because of too great a data dependency on outside organizations. Lack of data self-sufficiency artificially constrains (or may mask potential) elimination of errors, organizations, or levels of management that are not needed. If the scope is too narrow, the analysts present the information to the sponsor and request a broadened scope to include the information-creating organization(s).

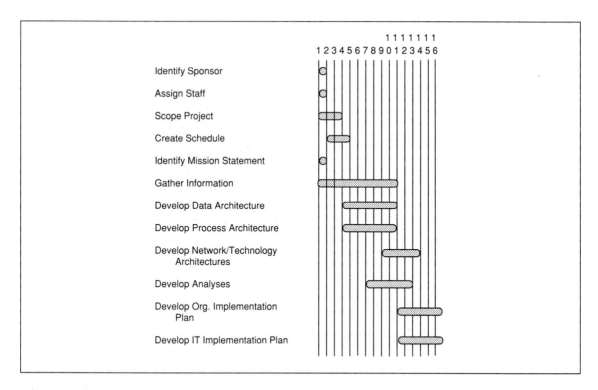

FIGURE 5-6   Overlap Between Reengineering Tasks

Formula:

$I / (I + O) * 100 = \% DS$

Example:

$I = 750,000$ records

$O = 250,000$ records

$750,000 / (750,000 + 250,000) * 100 = 75\%$

Legend:

I = Data generated inside the reengineered departments

O = Data generated outside the reengineered departments that is required for them to do their work.

DS = Data Self-sufficiency

FIGURE 5-7   Formula for Determining Data Self-Sufficiency

For instance, reengineering might target an accounting function. About 90% of the information in an accounting function originates from other organizations within the company. Without also including those functions in the reengineering study, changes that address, for instance, data accuracy or work location problems, are unlikely to be successful.

The scope might not be complete until the next several tasks are partially complete, due to a lack of information about data and responsibilities. Therefore, the initial scope should be reexamined before completion of the entity/process matrix analysis to reconfirm data self-sufficiency.

Create a Schedule

The team creates a schedule for the entire reengineering project not to exceed four calendar months. Each step has an estimated range of time that should be allotted as a percent of the project total shown in parentheses (see Table 5-1). Each task is assigned to a team member who is held accountable for the work.

Identify Mission Statement

Identify the mission statement for the organization with quantified goals for measurement. A **mission statement** is a short paragraph summarizing the overall purpose of the organization. The details of the document should include goals and objectives, along with determinants of success (i.e., critical success factors) for each, with required data for measuring the extent to which the goals are met (i.e., means-end analysis).

If the organization has no mission statement, or has no quantified goals and objectives, do not attempt to develop these for the organization. Disband the reengineering group and have the managers work on perfecting the mission, goals, and objectives before reconvening the reengineering effort.

Goals should have a three- to five-year horizon and should be specifically measurable (i.e., quantified) (see example in Figure 5-8). There should be at least one goal for each sentence in the mission statement. Goals relate to **stakeholders** who are people affected by the outcome. Some stakeholders

include customers, vendors, stockholders, owners, and boards of directors.

Identify critical success factors for determining that goals are met. A **critical success factor** (CSF) defines some essential process, data, event, or action that must be present for the outcome to be realized. For instance, if the goals in Figure 5-8 are desired, a CSF might be *Ensure that sales staff are fully trained in locating movie information.*

The last step of critical success factor analysis is to decide what information is required to measure goal success. In the example, goals relate to sales. The CSF also relates to 'training.' Success measures for sales and for sales staff knowledge of how to find movie information are required. Periodic evaluation with training for ill-informed sales staff is one way. Management needs to know evaluations that have taken place and misinformed staff who have been retrained. If the same person(s) are being retrained, management intervention might be warranted.

Intangible goal measurement is just as important as tangible goal measurement. An intangible goal might be increased customer satisfaction. To measure this, an outside polling company can canvass customers and ask different recall or direct questions about their satisfaction with the company's services. Recall-type questions are of the form: Which vendor that you work with has the best customer service? Direct questions are of the form: Rate the customer service of company *x*.

The next step is to link each CSF, critical information measure, and goal to functions, processes, technology and data in the organization. If this step cannot be completed yet, defer completion of this task until information gathering is complete. If new entities or processes are defined through CSF analysis, add them to the list for reengineering analysis.

Increase the number of new customers by 5% each year for five years.

Increase sales to existing customers by 8% per year for five years.

Increase number of rentals per store visit by providing an expert system to assist in selecting movies for rental.

Reduce sales support expenses by 10% in one year.

Reduce overhead expense by 10% each year for two years.

FIGURE 5-8   Example of Organization Goals for ABC Video

Gather Information

Gather information on processes, data, process problems, quality problems, data problems, accessibility to data, timing of work (e.g., lags that cause idle time), time constraints for performance, and problems related to timing. A sample list of questions are:

What are the major steps to accomplishing each process?

Which processes/procedures are required to accomplish the mission, goals, and objectives?

What data are used as input? Where does it come from? Who enters or creates data? uses or retrieves data? changes or updates data? deletes data?

How is the input transformed by the process to produce the results? That is, what do you do when you do your job?

What data are passed between processes? What is the current storage media for the data (e.g., computer, fax, paper, verbal, memo, etc.)?

Are the different types of data that you need for your job used sequentially or in parallel? Could you describe the procedure?

Where are time lags in your job during which you are waiting for someone else to give you work or information? How do you deal with these lags?

Where are quality problems? How do you deal with errors? What is the source of each type of problem? Where (in which process or outside organization) is each problem detected? Where are quality problems within the procedures you use to do your job? How do you try to guard against these problems?

What would you do differently if you could design your own job? How might computer technologies help you? Suppose you have all the new computer and other technologies available for your job's use. What technology would you use and how?

Information might come from forms, screens, reports, phone messages, fax messages, automated applications, policy and procedure books, and so on. The people actually doing the work provide this information.

Most information is obtained through an interview format. Interviews should be individual or in small groups (groups should have members who share common goals to minimize political conflicts). All middle and senior managers for the organization should be interviewed in addition to representative white-collar, blue-collar, or clerical staff. Treat the sessions as fact-finding, not fault-finding. Address all the topic areas for which information is required.

If you think you are getting incomplete or false information, cross-check, or triangulate, the information by asking the same questions of multiple sources. For instance, Manager A says his major problem is caused by erroneous data received from Manager B's area, and Manager B did not identify the problem in your first discussion. Return to Manager B and reinterview him or her, specifically discussing data quality as a problem identified by the other area.

To validate the complete findings, make a group presentation to all interviewees for final confirmation that the information is accurate and complete.

Summary of the Architectures

In this section, we expand Zachman's[4] **information systems architecture (ISA) framework** to describe how to express the reengineering information in terms of architectures. The four architectures of interest in reengineering are data, process, network, and technology. First, we define the framework and information presented at each level. Then, reengineering information is translated into the four architectures.

Conceptual Levels of the Architecture

The information systems architecture (ISA) describes distinct architectures relating business context to application context. The five levels are described in general terms below and are summarized in Figure 5-9. Only the first two levels, scoping and enterprise analysis, are used in reengineering.

Information systems application development and organizational redesign are complex engineering activities that are similar to constructing a building or an airplane. The ISA describes the intellectual levels of detail needed for complex engineering

---

4 John Zachman [1987]. Zachman's architecture discusses data, process, and network. ISA does not yet include a technology architecture. This idea is from reengineering consulting which requires a view of the technology as a basis for technology redesign.

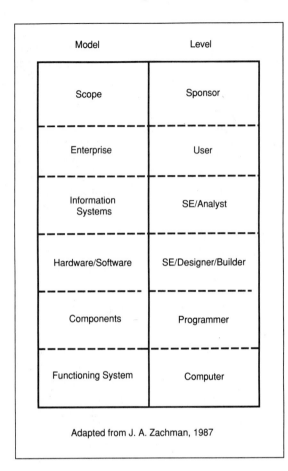

Model	Level
Scope	Sponsor
Enterprise	User
Information Systems	SE/Analyst
Hardware/Software	SE/Designer/Builder
Components	Programmer
Functioning System	Computer

Adapted from J. A. Zachman, 1987

FIGURE 5-9   Conceptual Levels of the Architecture

activities. Then, it links them to data, processes, networks, and technologies—the components of computer applications and reengineering.

In all three businesses—aerospace, architecture, and systems—we begin with a sponsor's idea of what the *item* being built should look like. This is the *scope of the reengineering project* that defines what is in and what is not in the problem. If the *item* is a house, for instance, users talk about a two-story colonial with four bedrooms, three bathrooms, and a fireplace in the family room. For reengineering, the sponsor targets departments doing order processing and customer assistance. In this case, the *item* is the order processing department.

The user talks to an expert to describe his or her view of the item, and the expert translates the user's idea into an enterprise level, logical description of the item. **A logical description** is one that lists *what* is done without saying *how*. The item begins to take more shape and be less specific. The description of the item is somewhat more abstract. For the house, we now have a family room of 13.5 feet by 16 feet with a cathedral ceiling that is open to the kitchen with entries to the foyer and living room. For reengineering, we have an order entry process that includes order receipt, order change, order inquiry, inventory allocation, creation of shipping papers, movement of goods, invoice creation, and an interface to accounts receivable. Both of these descriptions are significantly more detailed than the first. Neither description is complete. We still don't know the type of windows in each room, for instance. Nor do we know, for reengineering, whether the work is automated, how an order is processed, or whether any of the steps can be done together. In both cases, the details are unimportant *at this level*.

At the next level, the expert translates the logical, enterprise view of the item into terms and information that are useful to the analysts of the item. So, the expert (or different experts) translates the enterprise view into a logical information systems design. The logical design still describes *what* the item will do, but in more detail than before, and in terms understood by application developers. In reengineering, the logical design is very specific about the item, its parts, and how they fit with the other items and their parts. In our order processing example, we would know what data, what fields, what processes and their details, timing of processing, what applications and technology are currently used to support the work. Designers can review the detailed logical design and see *how* it can be automated.

In the next step, designers review the logical design and translate it to specific materials, thus creating a technology-based model. In reengineering studies, this translation takes redesigned work, work groups, departments, data, and technology as inputs. The inputs are translated into database schemas, applications' design specifications, network designs, and specific hardware/software platforms for supporting the redesigned work. In the order process-

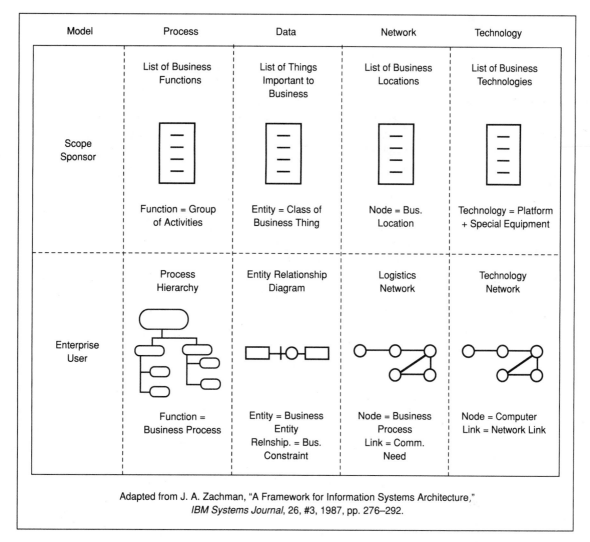

Model	Process	Data	Network	Technology
Scope Sponsor	List of Business Functions	List of Things Important to Business	List of Business Locations	List of Business Technologies
	Function = Group of Activities	Entity = Class of Business Thing	Node = Bus. Location	Technology = Platform + Special Equipment
Enterprise User	Process Hierarchy	Entity Relationship Diagram	Logistics Network	Technology Network
	Function = Business Process	Entity = Business Entity Relnship. = Bus. Constraint	Node = Business Process Link = Comm. Need	Node = Computer Link = Network Link

Adapted from J. A. Zachman, "A Framework for Information Systems Architecture," *IBM Systems Journal*, 26, #3, 1987, pp. 276–292.

FIGURE 5-10   Reengineering Levels and Architecture Domains

ing example, the requirements specification would be translated into program specifications for specific hardware, software, and language.

Finally, at the lowest component level, schemas, specifications, and technology plans are implemented and translated into working computer components.

Only the scope and enterprise models are discussed in this chapter; the other levels are too computer-oriented and not appropriate for reengineering.

Domains of the Architecture

The conceptual domains apply to four organizational domains: data, process, network, and technology. A **domain** is an area of interest. The **data domain** defines the entities of interest to the target organizations and the interrelationships between them. The **process domain** describes the functions, activities, and processes of the target organizations, without any identification of how they are accomplished. The

---

EXAMPLE 5-1

ABC VIDEO MISSION STATEMENT

The mission of ABC Video is to develop and maintain quality relationships with customers, vendors, and employees.

For customers, we provide a large selection of current and classic videos for rental at a fair price. We assist them in selecting videos with courtesy, service, and a minimum of bureaucracy.

For vendors, we order videos with reasonable lead times and timely payment of bills.

For employees, we provide a congenial atmosphere with comfortable, clean, and safe working conditions for a fair wage.

Process	Data	Network	Technology
Video Selection	Customer	Location = 1	None
Service Request (i.e., process rental)	Video Rental Vendor	(inferred)	
Order Creation	Order		
Accts. Payable	Video (= goods in inventory)		
Payroll	Employee		
Personnel			

---

network domain describes the organization from a geographic perspective. The **technology domain** describes the organization of work from a technology platform perspective.

Translating Information into Architecture

There are two levels of architecture we describe in this section for reengineering: the scope and the enterprise model.

Scope

In reengineering, we assume that the mission statement fully expresses the scope of the organization. The mission statement is translated into network technology, process, and data scopes to initiate the reengineering effort. Example 5-1 shows a mission statement for ABC Video and how it might be translated to identify the scope of the four domains. At the scope level, we should know the major entities of interest to the organization and the business functions and their activities.

The network and technology domains may or may not be mentioned in the mission statement. The sponsor or user participants define these when they are not in the mission statement. The **network scope** defines the location of work for each activity. The **technology scope** defines technology platform by location. Because ABC has only one location and no technology, it is a simple example. Another example here is for a plastics subsidiary of a large international company. Figure 5-11 shows existing hardware platforms listed by location. In Figure

Hardware Platform—Scope

Location 1
    Mid-Size Computer
    LAN 1—25 PCs
    LAN 2—15 PCs
    LAN 3—42 PCs
Location 2
    LAN 4—23 PCs
Location 3
    Mid-Size Computer
    5 Stand-alone PCs
    3 CAD/CAM Platforms
Location 4
    Mid-Size Process Control Computer
    LAN—25 PCs
    1 CAD/CAM Platform
Location 5
    Mainframe

FIGURE 5-11   Plastics Company Hardware Platform Scope

Activity by Location

Location 1
    Finance—3 products at this location
    Accounting—All products
    Customer Service—All products
    Product Management—3 products
    Personnel/Payroll
Location 2
    Finance—2 Products at this Location
    Product Management—2 Products
    General Manager
Location 3
    R & D
    Manufacturing Setup
Location 4
    Manufacturing Plant
Location 5
    Corporate Headquarters

FIGURE 5-12   Plastics Company Activity by Location

5-12, the activities from the process hierarchy are reused and identified by location.

At this point in reengineering, if the mission statement were suspect in its completeness, a stakeholder analysis might be developed to determine if all constituents of the organization are represented. If they are not, the mission statement would be redrafted to include missing constituencies. While this redrafting takes place, the reengineering study ceases operation. A stakeholder is any person who interfaces with, works for, or otherwise is impacted by an organization. Stakeholders include the owner, managers, employees, suppliers, customers, creditors, government, community, and competitors. Ideally, representative stakeholders from each group should review the strategy and offer suggestions for improvement.

When stakeholders are identified, the goals of each stakeholder are defined and related to the organization's functions and strategies. If a goal does not match a current function or strategy, management determines if the goal will, in fact, be met. The goals are translated into strategies which, in turn, are translated into work. The intention of stakeholder analysis is that rational, reasonable goals should have both strategic and organizational functions that relate to the attainment of goals. Even if goals are omitted from the final strategy, at least all stakeholders and their desires are identified and considered.

Enterprise Models

At the enterprise level, the user managers work with information systems (IS) project representatives to define business areas in logical terms. The principle business modeling activities include entity-relationship diagrams (ERD) for data, functional decomposition diagrams for work processes, a network diagram of process communication needs, and a technology network diagram

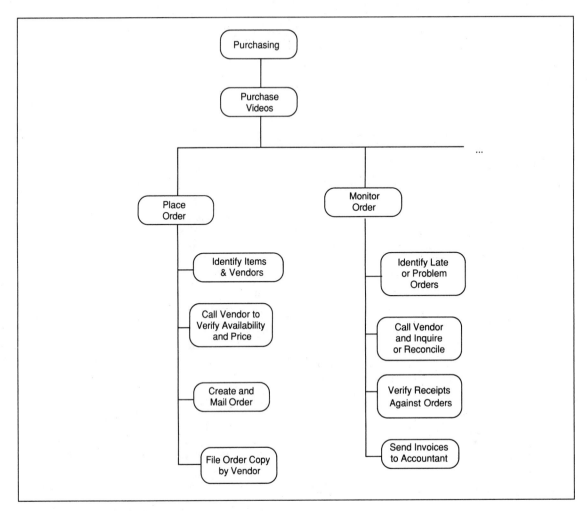

FIGURE 5-13   ABC Video Process Hierarchy

showing technology deployment. The ERD documents major data types and their interrelationships. The functional decomposition identifies business functions and their component activities and work processes. The network architecture shows the location of work and intraorganizational communication requirements. The technology architecture shows the hardware platforms by location and the telecommunication linkages between them. All four architectures are developed piecemeal as information becomes known. (ERD and functional decompositions are discussed in detail in Chapter 9 and are only summarized here.)

PROCESS ARCHITECTURE.   Process architecture development is concurrent with data gathering. The time recommended in Table 5-1 is for completion and validation of the information. The decomposition first identifies business functions, then the component activities and their processes. Figure 5-13 shows an example. A **business function** is a group of on-going activities that accomplish some complete job that is within the mission of the enterprise. Functions are general and fit most organizations. For instance, accounting and personnel are found in most organizations regardless of industry or business type. At the next level of detail, an **activity** defines one or more related procedures that accomplish some task. For accounting, for instance, activities might be monthly close, maintaining chart of accounts, or daily transaction processing. At the lowest level of detail for this diagram, a **business process** identifies the details of an activity, *fully defining* the steps taken to accomplish the activity. Business processes within an accounting monthly close might be gathering information, validating information, performing initial analysis, and so on.

The steps to developing a functional decomposition diagram include:

- Identifying the functions of the target organizations
- Interviewing the representatives from each area to identify the activities performed for each function
- Further identifying the processes for each activity

During the decomposition process, business problems are identified by the interviewees. The problems are prioritized by the users with the reengineering team in order of their significance to the organization's quality and function. Usually the number of major problems to be identified is fixed and between five and ten. Without a limit, the problem findings could overwhelm the analysts. Also, having the number of major problems fixed requires users to reach consensus about the seriousness and scope of problems.

DATA ARCHITECTURE.   This activity is concurrent with data gathering. One week of extra time is recommended to allow completion and validation of information. The data architecture is defined in an entity-relationship diagram. An entity is some person, object, concept, application, or event from the real world about which the organization maintains data. A relationship is a mutual association between entities.

For instance, a customer creates an order. *Customer* and *order* are entities; *create* is their mutual relationship. Figure 5-14 shows a basic ERD that summarizes this relationship. ERDs can be much more elaborate and include the number, or cardinality, of the relationship, and information about

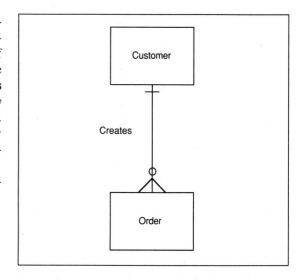

FIGURE 5-14   Sample Entity Relationship Diagram

whether or not the relationship is required. Cardinality identifies one-to-one, one-to-many, and many-to-many relationships. Each customer can have many orders; therefore, this is a one-to-many relationship. So in this ERD the cardinality is one-to-many. The *many* side of the relationship is shown with 'crow's feet' on the diagram. Orders don't come from thin air; there must be a customer to have an order. Conversely, customers are not *required* to always have orders. Therefore, *customer* is required, and *order* is optional in the relationship as signified on the diagram by the short bar and small oval, respectively.

The steps, then, to developing an ERD are:

- Identify data entities, including new entities required to attain and name organization goals
- Link entities to show their interrelationships
- Define relationship cardinality and the required/optional nature of relationships

NETWORK ARCHITECTURE.   The enterprise level of network architecture defines organization activities from the functional decomposition performed at each location and communications requirements between them. The architecture

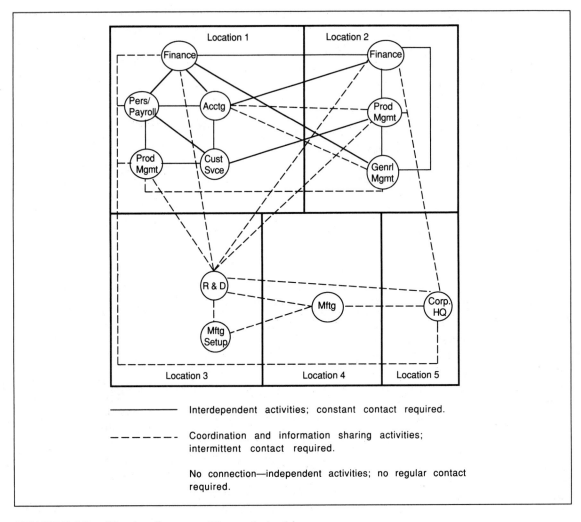

Interdependent activities; constant contact required.

Coordination and information sharing activities; intermittent contact required.

No connection—independent activities; no regular contact required.

FIGURE 5-15   Plastics Company Network Architecture

described in this section is of the current organization. During reengineering, if the changes recommended affect the locations of work or the activities of work, then the network architecture is redrawn to mirror the recommended organization. When the changes are presented to the sponsor for approval, the old network and recommended network architectures should be contrasted to highlight the changes.

The process hierarchy defined functions, activities, and processes. The network architecture *could*

define any of these levels. For ABC Video, we would choose the function level because there is only one work location. For the plastics company example (see Figure 5-15), the activity level is chosen because functions located in more than one place may not include the same activities at all locations. Using the activity level gives a further level of detail, and accuracy, to the work. If the company were very decentralized and diverse, the analysis *could* be at the process level.

For the architecture, each activity is placed in a

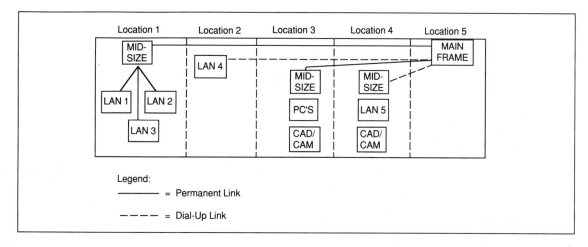

FIGURE 5-16   Plastics Company Technology Architecture

circle within a square identifying a location (see Figure 5-15). The circles are connected when the activities require communication to complete their work.

TECHNOLOGY ARCHITECTURE.   The technology architecture creates a network diagram of existing technology at each location using a network technique similar to the network architecture (see Figure 5-16). Then, the technology platforms are connected with lines to show telecommunications linkages between them. Dotted lines are used to show dial-up linkage. Solid lines are used to show permanent connections. At this level, other special hardware, such as imaging, CD-ROM, or technologies such as ISDN, are connected to the platform to which it is attached.

Like the network architecture this is a snapshot of the current technology deployed throughout the organization. If the recommendations for the redesigned organization eliminate or change locations, a second technology architecture is created to depict the new view of the organization.

At this point, the team is complete in their data gathering. The team conducts a group meeting with all previously interviewed individuals to summarize their findings and present the diagrams. The purpose and sole focus of the meeting is to verify the accuracy of the information presented. No further analysis, and no suggestions on the analysis, should be discussed at this meeting.

Architecture Analysis and Redesign

The analysis uses a series of matrices matching the architectures to redesign the organization, its data, applications, and technology infrastructures. The process and data architectures are the basis for the organization and data design. The current applications are mapped to the redesigned organization and data to recommend changes to the application environment. The technology and network architectures are analyzed to recommend telecommunications and technology infrastructure changes that best meet the enterprise's goals. These analyses are discussed here.

Organization and Data

A process called affinity analysis is used to analyze the data and processes. Think of this as normalizing data across the organization. **Affinity** means 'attraction' or 'closeness.' **Affinity analysis** clusters processes by the closeness of their functions on data

Entities =	Purchase Order	PO Item	Vendor Item	Inventory Item	Vendor
Processes =					
Identify Items & Vendors			R	R	CRU
Call Vendor to Verify Avail/Price			RU		RU
Create & Mail Order	CRUD	CRUD	CRU	R	R
File Order Copy by Vendor	R	R			
Identify Late & Problem Orders	R	R	R	R	RU
Call Vendor & Inquire on Order	RU	RU	RU	R	R
Verify Receipts against Order	RU	RU	RU		
Send Invoices to Accountant	RD	RD			

FIGURE 5-17   ABC Video Data/Process Matrix

entities they share in common. Because the average data/process matrix has about 400 entries, affinity analysis is best accomplished through an automated tool, such as ADW™.[5]

A matrix of processes from the process hierarchy diagram and data entities from the entity-relationship diagram is created. The processes are written in rows down the left side and data entities across the top (see Figure 5-17). Use the lowest level processes, such that all elemental processes for the organization and application area are present. When writing the process name, append a prefix to identify the activity and function from the hierarchy diagram.

In each cell, identify the functions each process is allowed to perform on data. Possible functions are create (C), retrieve (R), update (U), and delete (D). One or more of the letters, as defined by the current organizational responsibilities, are entered for each entity. This matrix gets its nickname from those functions; it is a **CRUD Matrix**.

Affinity analysis relates processes by their responsibility in *creating* shared entity information. The create responsibility for 80+% entities shared between processes shows high affinity. An affinity matrix is iteratively refined by affinity groups or processes with entity creation responsibility. In a typical 20 × 20 matrix with 400 cells, five to seven affinity clusters will emerge. Affinity clusters may contain processes from several current organizations; organizational location of responsibility is not of interest in this exercise.

Several clusters may overlap. This is normal and not a cause for worry. If only one cluster emerges, clustering continues with analysis of update responsibility, and, if necessary, delete and retrieval responsibility. When a reasonable number of clusters emerges, the next step begins. A reasonable number may be one to five clusters for a small organization, such as ABC, or six to nine for a large organization.

5 ADW is a trademark of Knowledgeware, Inc., Atlanta, Ga.

Figure 5-18 shows affinity clusters for ABC. A first analysis of create responsibility would place *Create & Mail Order* in a group and *Identify Items & Vendors* in a group without classifying the other entities. The final clusters shown in the figure emerge after also analyzing update, delete, and retrieval responsibility. The lines highlight the clusters and simplify diagram interpretation; they do not necessarily include all actions in the clusters. Notice that the *Call Vendor to Verify* . . . process overlaps both clusters. It is placed in the second cluster because it also updates *Vendor* information.

The next step is to analyze organizational adequacy. Each process is individually analyzed first to ensure process-goal correspondence. If the process is specifically tied to the organization goals, objectives, and mission, mark it for retention. If the process is *not* tied to the organization goals, objectives, and mission, either link it to goals or objectives, or mark it for elimination.

Next, for processes that are candidates for elimination, determine if they also create, update, or delete data. What is the relationship of this process to 'close' processes? Is it in a sequence with other processes? If so, can those processes take on its data responsibilities (thus enlarging the scope of the process)? If the eliminated process also stands alone, where else is the data used? If the answer is nowhere, mark the data for elimination. [Plan to return to the individual(s) who identified either the process or the data to confirm that you have not missed some information linking the process or data to the mission.] If data is created by the process marked for elimination, but updated and deleted elsewhere, can the other processes assimilate data creation? What other information will those processes now need in order to be able to create the entity? Ask similar questions for updating and deleting the data.

Next, analyze the current organization design. First, is each data entity created only in one process?

Entities =	Purchase Order	PO Item	Vendor Item	Inventory Item	Vendor
Processes =					
Create & Mail Order	CRUD	CRUD	CRU	R	R
Call Vendor & Inquire on Order	RU	RU	RU	R	R
Verify Receipts against Order	RU	RU	RU		R
Send Invoices to Accountant	RD	RD			
File Order Copy by Vendor	R	R			
Identify Late & Problem Orders	R	R	R	R	RU
Identify Items & Vendors			R	R	CRU
Call Vendor to Verify Avail/Price			RU		RU

FIGURE 5-18   *Affinity Clusters in ABC Data Process Matrix*

If not, is there some business reason why two processes are creating the same data? Or is there historically introduced redundancy? If the former, continue the analysis. If the latter, combine the processes and eventually redo the affinity analysis. Second, are the processes that cluster together in the same department? If so, the organization need not change. If not, then realign the organization boundaries to have all processes that create the same data reporting to the same manager. Expand the scope of the pro-cesses to include as much of the create-up-date-delete processing as possible. Needs for retrieval or access affect future plans rather than this decsion process.

When the process analysis is complete, the remaining processes are all critical to the organization mission. The next task is to tentatively redefine jobs within the context of the remaining processes. The goals of job redesign are to enlarge and enrich the jobs, and to eliminate interprocess dependencies through job design. Interprocess dependency is eliminated or reduced by the caseworker approach to job design and by expanding data access to all who use it.

To define a job, begin with the processes in a function. Add processes to the job until either the skill mix or activity served changes. Then, define another job until either the skill mix or activity changes. Continue to define jobs until all processes are assigned. There may be jobs that span activities but they should be exceptional.

After jobs are completely defined, map them to functions by their affinity, that is, in terms of their data creation and usage. Do not pay attention to the number or types of jobs reporting to functions at this point. Again, concentrate on eliminating errors, paper, and dependencies. When all jobs are mapped to activities, the first phase of organization redesign is complete. The next phase takes place during the implementation planning.

The second analysis and redesign that results from process/data analysis is for subject area databases and applications to support them. This is a more subjective analysis than job redesign because there is no theory of application development and how to size applications. The current thought is that applications that support well-defined subject areas will provide the best organizational support. The reason for this is that subject areas, data entities, and attributes are all fairly static. With well designed data, the processing can change without affecting the database.

First, use entity clusters to define subject area databases. Check that each entity is also linked to at least one goal or objective. If an entity is not linked, either establish the correspondence, or mark it for elimination. Conversely, analyze the processes which use the entity. If this is the only data used by the process, but the process is tied to some goal, determine the presence of data to measure progress toward the goal and, if needed, add a new entity to the list; otherwise, if the related process also stands alone, mark both the entity and the process for elimination.

The subject area databases defined by affinity analysis should be mapped to current, automated applications. If the subject areas are completely automated and the applications are integrated, no changes are needed. Rarely is this the case. Usually several applications process pieces of subject area data and both manual and automated usage of data is required. The only integration is through the experience of users who know where to go for information they need.

Redefine applications to support each subject area of data. Define application changes for process changes that reduce problems. Define ad hoc query facilities for all jobs requiring retrieval access to data. Assume on-line processing for most application work. Identify and recommend technologies that streamline and speed information storage and delivery. Based on the problems and solutions identified, determine the potential impact of applications for meeting goals. Prioritize applications for development to achieve the greatest impacts first.

Network/Technology Design

Before either the network or the technology designs are done, the receptiveness of the sponsor and managers to the changes in jobs and applications should be verified. If they support the work to date, the network and technology analyses can continue. If they do not support the job redesign or are reluctant about application suggestions, those aspects of the reengineering must be defined acceptably before this analysis.

There is no theory of network or technology design at the enterprise level. Rather, we have rules of thumb that must be evaluated in each business context. First, if the job redesign and process analysis substantially change the activities being performed in the organization, the enterprise network model should be recast in terms of the revisions. Next, if locations are significantly different, the technology model should be redrawn to reflect revised locations.

When the two network diagrams are acceptable, they are compared and analyzed to recommend new and changed technologies for supporting the new organization.

Using the technologies identified as needed to fully support jobs, develop an overview of the technology for the organization. Classify types of applications on mainframes, local area networks (LANs), and stand-alone personal computers. Classification should identify applications by size, 'corporateness' of data, data sharing requirements, specialized technology required, and number of users.

Across the organization, rationalize the use of technology resources, minimizing the overall cost to the organization. If new technologies are recommended, develop estimates of implementation costs and benefits, including average cost per expected user employee. If possible, identify incremental costs for expanding the user base once the technology is installed. Include training costs in the estimates. Identify and recommend possible uses for technologies to reduce incremental costs of use.

This activity is one in which the IS representatives have the most value added during reengineering. Being technology literate, IS representatives can work with their technology planners to determine possible technologies for consideration that have not been identified before. The IS people should take the lead in the rationalization of technologies. Deciding the type of applications that belong on various platforms for the organization requires the knowledge and guidance of the IS steering committee or the IS director (i.e., Chief Information Officer, MIS Manager, or some similar title). Explanations of the applications mapping to technology platforms should be in business terms but based on sound understanding of the technology involved.

An example of network/technology redesign for the plastics company example is provided. The plastics company architectures in Figures 5-15 and 5-16 are used to create the revised network in Figure 5-19. One obvious problem is that organizations that need to communicate for work are not electronically connected. This suggests a network change to interconnect all interdependent activities. This change means that the LANs that are only connected through a star configuration in *Location 1* might be connected via a backbone to the midsize computer. Backbones in each location with multiple LANs can be connected to provide intra-location communications, freeing the larger machines for inter-location connection and data processing. With this type of network design, everyone in the company can communicate with everyone else.

After this cursory analysis, we next look at the technologies used for subject databases and applications. First, the subject databases are added to the technology map. If pieces of databases are scattered, integrate them or determine distribution requirements. This type of recommendation should be coordinated with the applications recommendations which are probably similar. Recommendations about centralization, decentralization, federation, or distribution of both data and processes should be considered. Changes in all infrastructure software such as telecommunications monitors, database management software, terminal interfaces, and so forth should be considered for each activity at each location. Advantages and disadvantages of all technologies, current and proposed, should be developed and an estimated cost-benefit analysis developed.

In the plastics company example, software and applications are added to the network/technology analysis shown in Figure 5-20. Order information is only available at Location 1, even though all sales and product management organizations (Locations 1 and 2) require access. These data differences in what currently exists to what is required show the type of findings in network/technology analysis. To determine the best course of action, more information

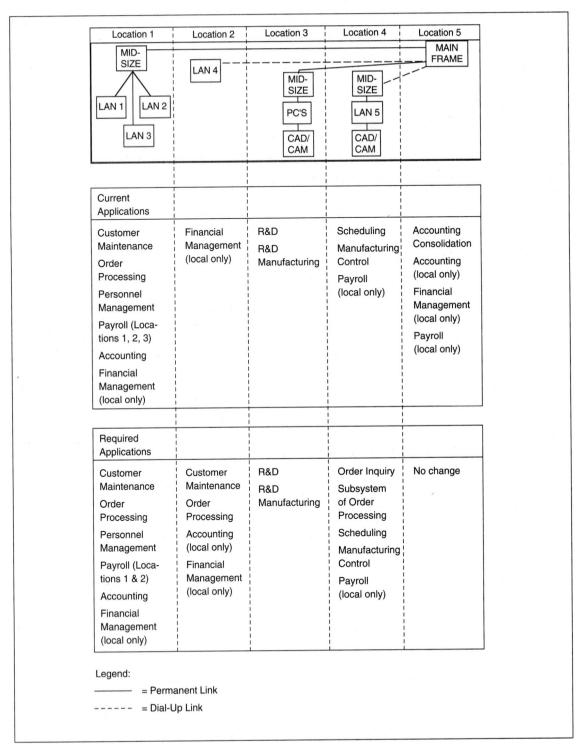

FIGURE 5-19   Plastics Company Network and Technology Analysis

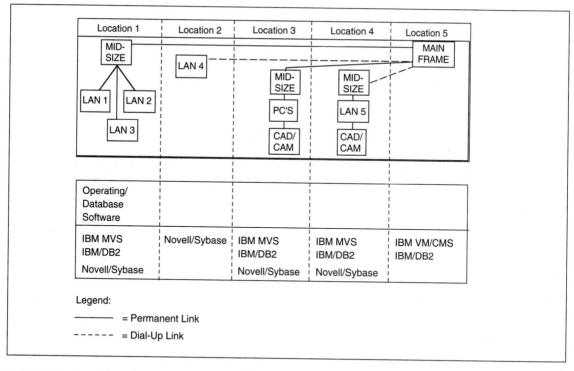

FIGURE 5-20   Plastics Company Technology and Software Details

might be requested of the locations. For instance, do they need up-to-the-minute information? Why or why not? The answer to this question determines the need to redevelop the applications as on-line rather than batch. If the locations need up-to-the-minute information, on-line applications are required. Let's say that the sales and product management information users need orders only as of the previous close of business and that customer service agents in Location 1 would like up-to-the-minute information because most changes are made the same day. This information about needs gives the reengineering team the details they need to make intelligent recommendations about application changes. In this case, either on-line order entry with retrieval, or the entire application as on-line might be acceptable alternatives.

Next, consider new technologies to manage paper and work flow. For instance, do using groups need facsimiles of the paper forms? In some industries, such as insurance, the answer would be yes. In plas-tics manufacturing, the answer is no. So, imaging or other micro-forms management hardware and software are not considered.

Specific operating environments should be considered next. If the networks are used to pass electronic mail and data files back and forth, the operating environments do not necessarily have to be the same. If, however, on-line query and file sharing across environments is desired, the network operating systems and database management software probably should be the same to simplify user access. This type of decision is aided by development of a cost-benefit analysis for data access using consistent software. What is cost of change? What is the risk and cost of not changing? How much added time is required, per request, to formulate and obtain information with no change, and with change? The answers to these questions are used to determine the redesigned operating environment.

In the plastics example, the current environment down-loads information nightly from Location 1 to

Locations 2 and 4. The managers at those locations would like access to interim data *if* the applications are moved to an on-line environment. In other words, they want the access if the data are more current. Customer service needs current information. We decide to move to the on-line environment and provide networkwide access to data and services on the net. If the network operating systems (NOS) and data bases are incompatible with this idea, they would need to be replaced and made compatible.

To summarize, the network and technology architectures are superimposed and compared to decide company changes. Then, technology requests and application and software recommendations are superimposed on the revised technology diagram. Evaluation of requests, suggested changes from IS, and recommendations from the organization design team takes place by analyzing each change. Change evaluation includes cost-benefit analysis, development of advantages and disadvantages of change, and issue analysis with information supplied by potential users.

Implementation Planning

Once the analysis and recommendations are complete and tentatively approved, a plan to prioritize and sequence the changes is developed. A reengineering study is of limited use if there is no road map for *how to attain* the recommendations based on where the organization is today. Implementation planning designs the map. The steps of this phase are:

1. Develop job descriptions.
2. Define the organization.
3. Plan information technology.
4. Plan training.
5. Plan implementation.

Define Job Descriptions

This is a first-cut at describing the new positions. The jobs still require human resources evaluation and refinement during the next stage: implementation. To develop jobs, we reanalyze the tentative job descriptions, attending to data needs for each job.

We define jobs as including related job skills for similar, related data. For each job, list the processes, data, and skills required of an incumbent. When the subject area database changes, create a new job, but keep as a goal that each job should do some 'whole thing,' have decision power, access to all needed data, and be self-contained. Keep in mind that constraints on job identification are data self-sufficiency, process self-sufficiency, and minimal coupling to other jobs and processes.

For each job, identify the processes and entities. Identify the technologies that would achieve the job objectives with the utmost speed and accuracy. Use suggestions (and return for more specific information if necessary) from interviewees about technology that might be used. At this point, do not worry about capital expenditures for technology. Keep technology information for the technology/network analysis.

Question all current methods of work and all process dependencies. For instance, do you need paper copies of orders? By law, you need records of orders, not *paper* orders. Devise schemes that eliminate paper, eliminate creation of paper, and eliminate any handling of paper. Replace paper with technology whenever the information must be retained for legal or governmental compliance.

Concentrate on implementing change to eliminate *all* identified problems. Relate each process and entity to one or more problems identified; determine how to improve quality of process and eliminate the errors. Finally, concentrate on eliminating dependencies between functions and between processes. Interfunctional dependency is minimized by eliminating physical interactions or replacing them with technology based interactions. For instance, eliminate shipping papers by providing the shipping department with access to the order database.

For each job within each process, write job descriptions to align job goals with the corporate goals and objectives. The outcome of this exercise is to give every individual the means—management structure, data, and technology—of meeting those goals. Give every individual, at every level, specific measurable responsibilities. Recommend changes to the compensation plans to relate compensation to meeting/exceeding of objectives and goals.

For each newly clustered, enlarged job, analyze its relationships with other jobs to minimize inter-job linkages. Reanalyze each job to ensure data and process self-sufficiency. Finally, define defect-free work procedures. If errors must be dealt with, describe where they might occur and their proper handling.

Define the Organization

A first-cut organization structure will have three layers: CEO, functional managers, and everyone else.

The implication is that self-directed work teams with either a limited hierarchy or a matrix management organization will result. Other organizational forms can result but are not specifically defined in any of the reengineering methodologies. The steps to developing a new organization design are: map jobs to functions, analyze relationships between jobs placing jobs in clusters or work groups, based on data self-sufficiency, process self-sufficiency and minimal coupling of clusters, and determine the location of work (in large organizations some jobs are centralized, some decentralized, and some centralized with replication in the remote locations). If the first-cut does not result in a completely irrational organization design, it might be accepted as it is for trial. If there are too many different clusters (use 5–7 as the rule) or too many different jobs in a cluster (use 5–15 as the rule), additional reevaluation might be required.

Grouping of jobs is based on their interdependence. There are three types of interdependence in organizations: pooled, sequential, and reciprocal. **Pooled interdependence** is a relatively independent, low level of interaction between departments or jobs. **Sequential interdependence** defines a serial relationship between departments or jobs. **Reciprocal interdependence** defines highly interrelated activities that are worked on jointly by multiple units requiring feedback and constant adjustment. For instance, a bank loan department might be viewed as relatively independent (i.e., pooled) from other parts of a bank in that they need customer information received from the customer for their decision with no other units involved. Purchasing, receiving, and payables are sequentially interdependent in that they all use purchase order data. Yet all these job types have different job skills; that is, they each make different decisions and perform different actions based on their access to the purchase order information. A reciprocally interdependent department is a hospital intensive care ward in which many specialists with different skills and knowledge all work toward the same goal of patient recovery.

To group jobs, three methods of organization design deal with the three types of interdependence. If the jobs relate to each other sequentially, cluster jobs with similar skills together. Affinity groupings of processes and entities are used to decide skill requirements. Clusters may be sequentially dependent with jobs within each cluster providing different skills. Plan to provide shared database access to link clusters; this minimizes paper movement and ensures data access.

For example, look at the bank loan department again. Bank loan department processes are sequentially related after the loan is made. Once the loan commences, records are established and payments are received, posted, and analyzed. In an assembly line approach, these processes are different jobs. In a caseworker approach, all of these processes are within one job. Caseworkers could conceivably monitor loans for any customer, but usually have a case 'load' that is defined by alphabetic groupings of last initial of loan-maker names or some similar scheme.

If the processes have pooled interdependence, then job clusters contain one job type. For pooled interdependence, use subject area data as the deciding factor on when to create a new job. Each job, cluster, or group should have its own data self-sufficiency.

If the jobs are reciprocally interdependent and pass work back and forth, or need discussion on details regularly during the performance of work, design work groups in the same way you designed jobs. That is, design work groups to include all skills needed to perform one activity or function. Find all of the jobs that reciprocally share information; then, define the set of different jobs that would comprise a work group. Try to keep groups small with under 12 different jobs represented. For instance, engineers, raw materials purchasing, manufacturing, and quality control may all need access to the same design drawings, specifications, and components lists. They may be able to identify alternatives, make decisions, and improve quality simply by sharing responsibility for finished products. These job types would be clustered in work groups (i.e., quality circles).

Plan Information Technology

The next step is to redefine the IS environment. The rationale for deciding priorities is to correct the major problems first, and/or meet the goals/objectives with the largest impact on net income. The steps to develop an IS redevelopment plan are:

1. Compile all subject area database and application changes, redevelopment, enhancement requirements.
2. Compile all technology and network infrastructure requirements.
3. Map technology and network needs to database and application needs.
4. Define software reengineering projects.
5. Define new application development projects.
6. Determine priorities for all projects.
7. Develop a plan for two years of development and reengineering work. Develop a tentative 3–5 year plan for the remaining projects.

To develop the technology plan, create three matrices: technology/process, process/entity, and an entity/technology matrix. The technologies are all those identified by interviewees and team members as potentially useful in the organization. Complete each matrix. In each cell of the process/technology matrix, enter whether the technology speeds delivery, improves accuracy, improves service, or lowers cost. Enter all improvements that apply. This matrix is used to determine priorities for change.

In the entity/technology matrix identify which data entities are already fully or partially automated and the type of automation. Types of automation include file, application database, or subject area database.

Using the original process/entity matrix, identify the extent and type of automation for each process/data cell. Types of automation for processes include full or partial, and batch, on-line, or real-time. These matrices may not be 100% complete, but are used to guide the implementation planning process by providing a summary of planned changes.

Plan Training

Develop a training plan to upgrade skill levels to meet new performance requirements, recommending how current jobs can be mapped onto the new jobs. This should be a skeleton plan defining sequencing of training and approaches—outside company, inside company, phased by department, phased over time, and so on. Actual training details cannot be complete until human resources' redefinition and formalization of job descriptions and levels, and estimates of number of people to be trained for each job are known. The plan should be sufficiently detailed to allow a pilot test of the training and new work approach before its complete deployment.

Plan Implementation

Develop an implementation plan that reflects some phased approach to changing the organization. The number of people in any one job type might be difficult to determine if the jobs are very different from the present. Moving from the assembly line to the caseworker or group work approaches changes the entire equation; more, rather than less, people might actually be needed. Human resources might be able to assist in this type of estimating. If estimates of numbers of people in caseworker jobs are too vague, a pilot study can be conducted to facilitate estimating of total personnel needs.

When the mapping is complete, summarize the recommended changes and determine how they can be implemented. The possible approaches are pilot organization, phased implementation (by function, location, business priority, or application), or total cut-over. Develop timing of changes. If the changes are expected to take more than six months, determine how the organization, processes, data, or technology can be streamlined, changed, added to, or eliminated *now* to provide immediate improvement and correction of some problem(s).

ENTERPRISE ANALYSIS WITHOUT ORGANIZATION DESIGN

Even without the extensive organization and technology redesign of reengineering, an enterprise analysis helps managers establish applications priorities and develop a plan for introducing new applications and technologies into their organizations.

The same analyses for entities and processes are performed. Current automation of the affinity clusters are summarized on the diagram. Recommended changes are mapped to organization goals and strategies to decide priorities for change. The changes from enterprise analysis are incremental and relate to applications and subject area databases. Sweeping technology and network reassessment are missing from this activity. Likewise, organization problems and finding obsolete functions are not goals of this analysis.

When organization problems are identified, they can be referred to the sponsor for consideration. One example of organization problems is identified from the entity/process matrix after affinity analysis is performed. Each process should have a prefix identifying its original function and activity relationships. If the function/activity prefix for each creating process for each entity is not the same, an anomaly is found in that multiple managers have responsibility for creating the same data. The idea is that processes which *do* share responsibility for creating some entity should report to the same manager. The same manager can minimize conflicts and maximize coordination and control over data creation.

A second type of organization problem is found in the process hierarchy diagram. Because the diagram is built to describe its information without regard to current organization, some overlap or duplication of activities may be found. When this occurs, an effective technique for showing duplication, for example, is to draw shadow boxes, behind the process (or activity or function) duplicated. Then, on each box, identify the organization having the responsibility, one box for each organization. This effectively communicates organizational overlap without a need for additional comment, and is less inflammatory than verbal or text descriptions because it is presenting organizational facts.

AUTOMATED SUPPORT TOOLS FOR ORGANIZATIONAL REENGINEERING AND ENTERPRISE ANALYSIS

The tools needed to support organization reengineering are similar to those for project planning, but include process hierarchy diagrams, entity-relationship diagrams, network architectures, and technology architectures. Many tools support one or more of these requirements. Few tools on the market currently support all of these requirements. The automated support tools are summarized in Table 5-2.

SUMMARY

Reengineering of an organization reevaluates data, processes, technologies, and communications needs to ensure that an enterprise meets its goals as stated in its mission statement. The activities of reengineering include the data collection, analysis, and development of recommendations to meet organizational goals through radical redesign of work.

Reengineering is intended to alter the shape and operations of an organization. Frequently, organizations and managers do not want sweeping change. When incremental change is desired, enterprise level

TABLE 5-2   Automated Support for Organizational Reengineering and Enterprise Analysis

Product	Company	Technique
Analyst/Designer Toolkit	Yourdon, Inc. New York, NY	Entity-relationship diagram (ERD)
Anatool, Blue/60 MacDesigner	Advanced Logical SW Beverly Hills, CA	ERD
Bachman	Bachman Info Systems Cambridge, MA	Bachman ERD
CA-*products*	Computer Associates International, Inc.	Data modeling Strategic planning
CorVision	Cortex Corp. Waltham, MA	ERD
Deft	Deft Ontario, Canada	ERD
ER-Designer	Chen & Assoc. Baton Rouge, LA	ERD
Excelerator	Index Tech. Cambridge, MA	ERD Structure chart
Foundation	Arthur Anderson & Co. Chicago, IL	ERD Project management Project planning
IEF	Texas Instruments Dallas, TX	ERD Enterprise analysis and planning Process hierarchy
IEW, ADW (PS/2 Version)	Knowledgeware Atlanta, GA	ERD Enterprise analysis and Planning Functional decomposition

analysis uses a subset of the analyses of reengineering to develop applications and subject area database development recommendations.

REFERENCES

Davenport, Thomas H., *Process Innovation: Reengineering Work through Information Technology.* Boston, MA: Harvard Business School Press, 1993.

Dunckel, Jacqueline, *Good Ethics, Good Business: Your Plan for Success.* North Vancouver, British Columbia: Self-Counsel Press, 1989.

French, W. L., and C. H. Bell, Jr., *Organization Development.* Englewood Cliffs, N.J.: Prentice-Hall, Inc., 1984.

Galbraith, Jay R., and Daniel A. Nathanson, *Strategy Implementation: The Role of Structure and Process.* St. Paul, MN: West Publishing Co., 1978.

Galbraith, J. R., *Organization Design.* Reading, MA: Addison-Wesley Publishing Co., 1977.

TABLE 5-2   Automated Support for Organizational Reengineering and
Enterprise Analysis (*Continued*)

Product	Company	Technique
MacAnalyst, MacDesigner	Excel Software Marshalltown, IA	Decision table Entity class hierarchy ERD
Maestro	SoftLab San Francisco, CA	ERD
Multi-Cam	AGS Mgmt Systems King of Prussia, PA	ERD Enterprise analysis and planning Project management
PacBase	CGI Systems, Inc. Pearl River, NY	Enterprise analysis and planning Process decomposition
ProKit Workbench	McDonnell Douglas St. Louis, MO	ERD
Silverrun	Computer Systems Advisers, Inc. Woodcliff Lake, NJ	ERD
SW Thru Pictures	Interactive Dev. Env. San Francisco, CA	ERD
System Architect	Popkin Software and Systems, Inc. NY, NY	ERD
System Engineer	LBMS Houston, TX	ERD
Teamwork	Cadre Technologies Inc Providence, RI	ERD
Telon, and other products	Pansophic Systems, Inc. Lisle, IL	ERD
The Developer	ASYST Technology, Inc. Napierville, IL	ERD Structure chart Organization chart

Greiner, L. E., and R. O. Metzger, *Consulting to Management*. Englewood Cliffs, NJ: Prentice-Hall, Inc., 1983.

Hage, J., and M. Aiken, *Social Change in Complex Organizations*. New York: Random House, 1970.

Hackman, J. R., ed., *Groups That Work (and Those That Don't): Creating Conditions for Effective Teamwork*. San Francisco, CA: Jossey-Bass, 1990.

Hackman, J. R., and G. R. Oldham, *Work Redesign*. Reading, MA: Addison-Wesley, 1980.

Hammer, M., "Reengineering work: Don't automate, obliterate," Harvard Business Review, July–August, 1990, pp. 104–112.

Hammer, M., "From cow paths to data paths," *Computerworld*, December 25, 1989–January 1, 1990, pp. 16–17.

IBM Corporation, *Business Systems Planning Information Systems Planning Guide*, IBM Document # GE 20-0527-1, Armonck, NY, 1978, pp. 1–92.

King, William R., "Strategy set transformation," *MIS Quarterly*, March, 1978.

King, W. R., and D. I. Cleland, eds., *Strategic Planning and Management Handbook*. NY: Van Nostrand Reinhold, 1988.

Huse, E. F., *Organization Development*. New York: West Publishing Co., 1980.

Kouzes, James M., and Barry Z. Posner, *The Leadership Challenge: How to Get Extraordinary Things Done in Organizations*. San Francisco, CA: Jossey-Bass, 1990.

Lindenfeld, F., and J. Rothschild-Whitt, eds., *Workplace Democracy and Social Change*. NY: Porter, Sargent, 1982.

Rockart, John, "Critical success factors," *Harvard Business Review*, March–April, 1979, pp. 81–91.

Singh, Arvind, Comments from A Business Reengineering Workshop given in NY to TIAA, Performance Development Corporation, Princeton, NJ, January, 1992.

Sowa, J. F., and J. A. Zachman, "Extending and formalizing the framework for information systems architecture," *IBM Systems Journal*, Vol. 31, #3, 1992, pp. 590–616.

Thompson, J. D., *Organizations in Action*. New York: McGraw-Hill, 1967.

Zachman, J. A., "A framework for information systems architecture," *IBM Systems Journal*, Vol. 26, #3, 1987, pp. 276–292.

KEY TERMS

affinity	level of effort
affinity analysis	logical description
architecture	mission statement
business activity	network architecture
business function	network domain
business process	network scope
caseworker	organizational
champion	reengineering
critical success factor (CSF)	pooled interdependence
CRUD matrix	process architecture
data	process domain
data architecture	project sponsor
data domain	reciprocal interdependence
data self-sufficiency	reengineering scope
domain	sequential interdependence
enterprise architecture	stakeholder
information systems	technology architecture
architecture (ISA)	technology domain
framework	technology scope
information technologies	user commitment

EXERCISES

1. Look at the questions suggested for data gathering on page 125. Think of other possible questions and why they might be good additions to those suggested. Discuss your suggestions with class members.

2. Describe how the information provided for the four architectures can be used in multiple ways as the basis for IS and organization redesign.

3. Discuss the differences in outcomes of an organizational reengineering project if one or more of the assumptions in the list on pages 116–117 are not met.

4. Try to develop process and data architectures for the Abacus Printing Co. case in the Appendix. Try to do an affinity analysis of the information. Develop a list of questions you need answered to do a complete analysis.

STUDY QUESTIONS

1. Define the following terms:

data architecture	organizational
enterprise analysis	reengineering
information	process architecture
technologies	technology
network architecture	architecture

2. What is the motivation for organizational reengineering?

3. What are the steps to organizational reengineering?

4. Why are caseworker or quality circle work groups preferred to the assembly line approach to work?

5. What is the 80–20 rule and how does it apply to reengineering?

6. What is an architecture and why is it important to reengineering?

7. What types of architectures are used in reengineering? What is the purpose of each architecture?

8. What is an entity and how is it used in the data architecture?

9. What is a platform and how is it used in the technology architecture?

10. List three prerequisites of reengineering. Why are they necessary conditions for a successful project?
11. What are four assumptions of reengineering?
12. Why are different scheduling scenarios necessary for the organization of reengineering projects?
13. What is a level-of-effort approach to work? Why is it used with reengineering?
14. Why is there overlap between reengineering tasks? Why is overlap necessary?
15. What is the role of the project sponsor?
16. List the types and roles of people who should be assigned to a reengineering project.
17. Why is data self-sufficiency the major criterion for scoping a reengineering project?
18. Describe a good mission statement. What makes the difference between a good mission statement and a bad one?
19. How are critical success factors used in reengineering?
20. List five information sources and the type of data that the team gets from each one.
21. Discuss the conceptual levels of Zachman's IS architecture. Which two relate to reengineering? Why are the others not used here?
22. What is the purpose of mapping the two levels of architecture into different domains? Why the domains chosen?
23. Who is a stakeholder? Why is a stakeholder important?
24. Describe a CRUD matrix and its use.
25. Why is affinity analysis important? What are the reengineering results that are based on affinity analysis?
26. List three rules of thumb for developing the network and technology recommendations.
27. Why is implementation planning important to a reengineering effort? When changes are

dramatic, what is a good approach to implementing change in the organization?
28. How does enterprise analysis differ from organizational reengineering? Are these differences significant? Why not do enterprise analysis only?
29. Which automated support tools provide all desired functionality for reengineering support?
30. What are the functions desired of an automated support tool for reengineering?
31. What are the key criteria for proper scoping of a reengineering project? Explain.

★ EXTRA-CREDIT QUESTIONS

1. You have been named to lead an organization reengineering effort for a small, one-location company. The company has functions for accounting, purchasing, inventory management, shipping, and sales. The business of the company is retail sales of furniture. The current computer system supports the billing, shipping, and invoicing process. No one but employees in the accounting department use or access the computer at present. Develop a plan and sample questions you might ask the employees and the owner for an organization reengineering project.
2. What are factors that can cause a reengineering project to complete faster or slower? Explain.
3. Imagine that you work in a company that has all types of computer hardware and networks: mainframes, mid-size, PCs, wide-area mainframe networks, and local area networks. What are the issues in defining what data and applications should be on each type of hardware? Develop and discuss possible guidelines for data and application location selection.

APPLICATION FEASIBILITY ANALYSIS AND PLANNING

INTRODUCTION

Feasibility is the first stage of application development. The purpose of the feasibility study is to ensure that the organization can accommodate the technology, organization changes, and cost of the new application. During feasibility analysis the major tasks are: define the scope and boundaries of the problem, generate technical alternatives, assess costs, benefits and risks, and recommend an application development strategy. The procedures described in this chapter are used for large, full life-cycle projects; selective and abbreviated forms of the analysis are used for iterative development and for small projects.

DEFINITION OF FEASIBILITY TERMS

The feasibility analysis tasks and the terminology of each are briefly described. The stages of work during feasibility are: gather information, develop alternatives, evaluate alternatives, and plan and document the recommended approach to development.

During the information gathering stage, the goal is to develop a request from a vague, general statement into a specific request with boundaries and scope completely defined. Key business and application leverage points are defined during the scoping activity. A **business leverage point** is some activity from which a competitive advantage can be gained. An **application leverage point** is some automated function that might provide a competitive advantage to the using business unit(s). Application leverage points frequently relate to improvements of *better*, *faster*, and *more* to work. Some business and application leverage points are:

Increase market share
Increase linkage to vendors or customers
Provide desired information that is not currently
    available.

Business and application leverage points are used as the starting point for developing the benefits that would result from a change in the current method of work. Benefits can be tangible or intangible. Both benefit types are important for management to decide whether or not to do the recommended changes. **Tangible benefits** are measurable improvements to a specific work product or process. For instance, reducing staff by 10 people and the resulting cost savings are tangible benefits. **Intangible benefits** are not directly measurable. For instance, improved customer service through integrated database access has tangible and intangible benefits:

Tangible Benefits

Decrease operating cost by 10% in first year
Increase market share by 5% per year for three years

Intangible Benefits

Improve company image
Increase customer satisfaction
Improve employee job satisfaction
Provide faster and more accurate information to customer services representatives

Another tangible benefit might be faster response time for inquiry requests from five minutes to 15 seconds. An intangible benefit from the same action might be improved customer satisfaction. More satisfied customers are less likely to go elsewhere for their products, but proving that customer satisfaction is improved is difficult to quantify, and is intangible.

Also in information gathering, the business environment, competitive environment, and current method of performing the work that would be revised are described in sufficient detail to allow determination of appropriate changes. The functions and procedures that are needed in the new application are identified, as are problems with current procedures and new functions that are not part of current procedures.

After the current problem domain is understood, alternative approaches to the problems are developed. **Alternative approaches** to an application are different configurations of work, hardware, firmware, or software. Alternatives can begin with non-automation alternatives, such as change in work flow, and progress to different platforms, software, and designs. Usually between two and five alternatives are considered. Alternative definitions include the technology, benefits, and risks of each approach. A **benefit**, as discussed above, is some improvement in the work product or process that results from a specific alternative. **Risks** are events that would prevent the completion of the alternative in the manner or time desired.

Risk assessment determines possible sources of events that might jeopardize completion of the application. In general, the goal is to develop the project on time, within budget, and without errors. Risk assessment and contingency planning help you meet this goal. **Contingency planning** is the identification of tasks designed to prevent risky events and tasks to deal with the events if they should occur. The goal is to minimize the possibility of the event occurring, but to also have a plan *just in case* the worst happens. Having a contingency plan prevents having to force decisions under pressure.

When the alternatives have been defined, they are evaluated. The number of requirements met by the approach is assessed, and the benefits and risks of each are weighed to identify the alternative with the least risk and most benefit. If an alternative exists that meets all required and optional requirements, meets all benefits, and has the least risk, it would be the recommended option. Most often, there is a mix of requirements met and risk incurred, that prevent selection of an alternative based on technical merits alone. Rather, several competing alternatives might be further evaluated to differentiate between them. To decide between the alternatives, development plans, costs, and financial analysis are developed.

A project plan is a schedule of tasks and estimated completion times for application development. A project plan includes tasks to be completed, tentative task assignments, staffing plans, and computer resources needed for the project. From the staff and resource estimates, costs of development are determined. If there are multiple alternatives, the costs of each are computed. The costs are used in the financial analysis which occurs next.

Several different types of financial analysis might be performed; the two most common ones are cost/benefit, and make/buy. **Cost/benefit analysis** is the computation of net present value for each alternative. **Net present value** (NPV) equalizes the cost estimates by accounting for the time value of money for multiperiod investments. A **make/buy analysis** chooses between alternatives for providing an item, such as a software application. The *make* analysis estimates the cost of building a customized application, while the *buy* analysis estimates the cost of purchasing a package.

Other financial analyses, such as internal rate of return and payback period, might also be computed. **Internal rate of return analysis** determines the interest rate which equates cash investment outflow with positive cash flow. **Payback period analysis** determines the number of years required to recover the cash outlays based on the projected monetary benefits.

After all the analyses are performed, a final recommended alternative is defined. Technical and monetary considerations are balanced and a recommendation is based on some mix of them. For instance, a recommendation might be based on the fastest payback coupled with most requirements met. Alternatively, the decision might be based on the lowest NPV and the extent to which leverage can be maximized. When the alternatives are virtually equal in comparison, multiple approaches to the application are presented and the user, IS managers, and project team decide together what approach is best. This is often the case.

Finally, a feasibility document is created to summarize the feasibility analysis and the recommendation. The document is a summary of all of the preceding steps and analyses taken during the feasibility phase. Next, we discuss each feasibility activity in detail.

FEASIBILITY _____
ACTIVITIES_____

Feasibility analysis is an activity that ranges from several days to several weeks in duration. In general, a feasibility should be completed in fewer than 12 weeks; after that point, one of two problems exists. Either the problem domain is too large and should be broken into smaller problem areas, or the feasibility team is going into too much detail and should summarize at a higher level. The information at the end of feasibility should be accurate enough to allow managers to decide on the worth of pursuing a project, but high level enough that an analysis phase to clarify details of requirements is

needed. The information is incomplete with about 95% confidence in the accuracy of the information. Similarly, a budget and project plan produced at this high level of abstraction should have about an 80% level of confidence attached to it. This means that the budget and time schedule are ±20% inaccurate, and implies budget adjustment later in the project. In this section, we detail the actions of feasibility analysis and project planning outlined in the previous section. For each topic, guidelines for completing the work are presented and followed by an example of the activity for ABC Video.

Gather Information

Guidelines for Gathering Information

The four major tasks during information gathering are:

1. Define the business and work environments
2. Describe current system of work
3. Identify key benefits and leverage points
4. Identify broad system requirements

The activities are done in parallel rather than sequentially. As information is collected, leverage points and requirements emerge from discussions on which old procedures to keep and what new technology, procedures, data, or interfaces are needed.

If an enterprise level plan exists, the data gathering begins with the architectures to obtain an overall view of the current data, processes, and technology of the target business area(s) (see Figure 6-1). The process decomposition is used to identify and match the affected jobs and tasks with those suggested by the requesting application sponsor. The data architecture is used to identify what data are involved and the extent to which the data are already automated. The technology architecture is checked to identify hardware, software, and applications supporting the work functions today, and to identify potential platforms as operational sites for the new application. For each job affected, the technology architecture matches jobs (from the process architecture) with applications capabilities.

The architectures, if present, are the basis for obtaining information from the user departments

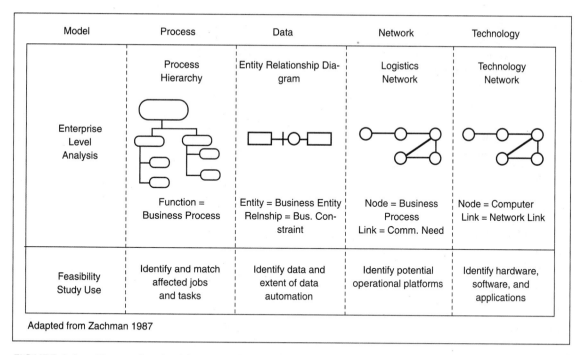

Model	Process	Data	Network	Technology
	Process Hierarchy	Entity Relationship Diagram	Logistics Network	Technology Network
Enterprise Level Analysis				
	Function = Business Process	Entity = Business Entity Relnship = Bus. Constraint	Node = Business Process Link = Comm. Need	Node = Computer Link = Network Link
Feasibility Study Use	Identify and match affected jobs and tasks	Identify data and extent of data automation	Identify potential operational platforms	Identify hardware, software, and applications

Adapted from Zachman 1987

FIGURE 6-1   Enterprise Architectures in Feasibility Study

involved. Recall that the methods of data gathering (from Chapter 4) might include interviewing, document review, observation, talking to other companies, temporary work assignment, and questionnaire surveys. During feasibility, interviews, document review, and other companies are the primary information sources. Although the other methods could be used, they take more time and elicit more detail than required for feasibility analysis.

Assume you are doing the information gathering using interviews. You might work in two-person teams for interviews so that the project has a built-in backup for every person, should someone get sick, called on jury duty, or be reassigned. One person asks the questions while the other person acts as scribe taking notes. This method of interviewing results in fewer misconceptions and errors from forgetting than interviews by one person. At the end of every session, follow-up steps should be identified for both you and the interviewee. For instance, you might document the interview and ask the interviewee to review and correct your documentation. You commit to having the material back by a specific

date and request the review within a set time. In this manner, you conclude the meeting with a commitment from the interviewee to do the review by a certain date.

During the writing of interview materials, graphical techniques for both data and processes can be used to synthesize the findings. The most common graphical techniques are entity-relationship diagrams (ERDs) for data, and process decomposition and process data flow diagrams for processes (PDFDs). Development of these diagrams is detailed in Chapter 9. An older variant of PDFDs called data flow diagrams (DFDs) are also used; they are detailed in Chapter 7. In general, ERDs capture information about the data entities that are within the scope of the study problem domain. An entity is any person, place, thing, or event about which the organization needs to keep data. The relationships between entities define some business-related association that is within the problem scope. The process decomposition diagram depicts the organization tasks that are being studied. The problem area is compared to the process hierarchy and ERD to ensure correct scoping. PDFDs summarize the processes of the problem and relate them to each other, the outside world, and to data entities.

In addition to diagrams which summarize the procedures and data of the target problem domain, you also create text documents that describe the current process, the aspects of the current process to be retained, and the changes and motivation for changes. In general, text should be minimized because it is easily misinterpreted. Diagrams and graphics are preferred to text. Lists of items are preferred to paragraph form text. Requirements for the new application should be as specific as possible. For instance, a requirement might be stated 'reduce turnaround time from receipt of an order through invoicing from 14 days to 2 days.' During the systems analysis phase, the actual details of functions to implement this requirement are developed.

As we said above, key business and application leverage points are defined during the data collection activity. Leverage points are context specific. What might be a leverage point in one company and industry might be standard procedure in another company and industry.

An example of leverage points is provided by examining imaging technology. **Imaging** technology automates facsimiles of business forms. Image files are databases of forms with indexes for retrieval and linkage to data databases. Applications can be developed to integrate data and image information for users at terminals. The technology provides both business and application leverage by improving work flow and allowing the management of paper flow through an organization.

The leverage provided by imaging is highest in organizations that are information and paper intensive, for instance, insurance and financial services. These paper intensive industries are required, by law, to provide original document search capabilities. Before imaging technology, these companies either used microforms or paper, both of which have only rudimentary indexing capabilities. Microforms require their own viewing equipment that is neither intelligent, nor capable of integration to an application. Paper, if kept, is so voluminous that whole buildings are dedicated to document storage. Trying to retrieve specific documents and files requires armies of clerks and dedication to accurate refiling. Simply applying imaging technology by itself buys marginal improvement to paper management. The big payoff is in integrating imaging with software to manage work.

Work flow management software is integrated with imaging technology to schedule work for clerks, monitor document locations, and monitor work progress through any number of departments (see Figure 6-2). All of these actions can be done without fear of losing the document because it is an electronic image. Printing of the image is possible if a paper copy is needed by a clerk for some reason.

Imaging and work flow management together can flatten hierarchies, reduce the number of clerks involved in image production, and eliminate the need for clerks to manage files. Staff reduction is a business leverage point and a benefit of the activity. For individual jobs, frustration is reduced because information can not be 'removed for use' from an image file. Clerks are more productive and their jobs can be upgraded because the emphasis now can be placed on understanding and interpreting the information rather than on simply collecting all the information correctly. Thus, an application leverage point is present in enhancing jobs of the people in the work flow.

Leverage points identify benefits of the proposed application. Other benefits might be present and should be identified; they may not have a direct strategic impact. For instance, in keeping with the idea that most proposed applications are to improve work, benefits about more, faster access, integrated, or improved quality data might be defined. Similarly, automation of more tasks, faster report generation, integration of processing, or improved timing of response might all be benefits. Conversely, the new application might be expected to reduce staff, linkages between departments, work errors, and so on. These benefits are all tangible and measurable and should be identified.

Intangible benefits are equally important, but are harder to quantify. Intangible benefits are indirect, unmeasurable benefits with a high degree of uncertainty. For instance, one benefit of personal work stations with access to software has been a rethinking,

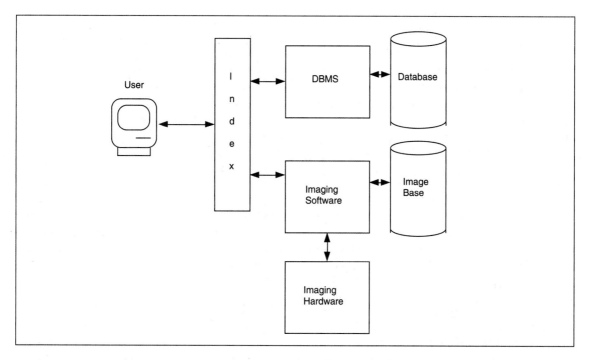

FIGURE 6-2   Logical View of Work Flow Management Software

by many people, of how they do their work. They now type their own documents directly and use secretarial support for changes and formatting. They do their own analyses and perform many different types of analysis that they could not do, and therefore never thought of doing, before they had desktop computer access. This type of change is an indirect benefit that increases the *effectiveness* of a person's work, while the tangible benefits deal mostly with *efficiency* improvements. Both types of benefits are important in application decisions.

The SE works with the users to define the tangible and intangible benefits relating to a project. Benefits identified are listed in the documentation of the proposed application, and a value is attached to each one. Tangible benefits are quantifiable by determining the change expected to result from the new application. Intangible benefits usually are listed with a possible range of benefit. In presenting this information to decision makers, you must be able to justify *why* intangible benefits exist. Managers will ask and expect the reasoning behind any expected financial gains, whether tangible or intangible.

Now let us turn to ABC Video to discuss how to perform the data collection activities.

ABC Video Information Gathering

Of the methods of data gathering available, several can be eliminated immediately. First, questionnaires for a total of six employees would be impractical. All employees are available for discussions during nonpeak times. Also, studying documentation is not possible because the manual methods are not documented. Observation and temporary work assignment can give some information about the current problems to be solved through automation, but are of limited value in actually designing the new application.

Talking to competitors is not feasible because they do not want to help the competition; however, to define benefits that might accrue for the ABC application, knowledge of competitor clerical assignments and computer systems is valuable. Observation of competitors is a good way to get some insight to the benefits Vic might get from automation. The remaining data collection method, interviews, should be used extensively for Vic and the clerks to determine the work flow, problems, and possibilities for the ABC application. To supplement the interviews, we should observe competitors by using their services for a period of time to get information about their work assignments and applications.

For ABC, we define the current environment, proposed environment, leverage points, and benefits. Through Vic's interviews we find that ABC operates in a highly competitive environment. Large chain video rental businesses are crowding small one-shop businesses, like ABC, out of the market. ABC must remain competitive to stay in business and to grow as Vic expects. Vic sees the future to be in services offered to customers. In terms of video rental processing, service translates into minimal bureaucracy with as many variations on service to customers as possible.

Currently, ABC uses a manual method of video rentals. The customer chooses a video and presents the video cover (or title) to a clerk. The clerk locates the video, locates a rental card for the customer, and writes the current rental on the card. Charges for late fees are computed from the card if any are owed, and the customer pays for the current and any late rentals. The customer signs the rental card which is filed by the clerk. During the peak business period, from 6 P.M. to 10 P.M., the rental cards are placed in a pile for later refiling. Frequently, cards are misplaced and the customer is then not charged late fees. If a tape is never returned and the accompanying card is lost, Vic has no way to trace who has what tape(s). This method is error prone and subject to whims of clerks who have been seen changing return dates for friends who return tapes late. Also, the time involved in locating a given customer's rental card ranges from 30 seconds to several minutes during nonrush time, and can be as high as 10 minutes during the peak rush time because clerks are waiting to access the card file.

Vic's requirement for the new application is to provide a fast, simple method of providing rental processing and accounting without introducing any new bureaucracy into the process. The system must be on-line, accommodate at least five clerks working simultaneously, provide for growth in video inventory, and expansion of the business to other related sale/rental items. At a summary level, the data entities in ABC rental processing are customers, video inventory, and rentals. Figure 6-3 is an ERD showing the relationships between these entities. Also at a summary level, the major processes of rental processing are customer maintenance, video maintenance, and rent/return processing. These processes are summarized in Figures 6-4 and 6-5.

Figure 6-4 is a hierarchic process decomposition diagram for the business, showing many more functions than just the rental processing. The rental processing area has bold lines to highlight it from the rest of the diagram. This diagram is developed at the enterprise level to ensure that the correct departments and processes are accounted for in an application development effort.

Figure 6-5 is a high level process data flow diagram for the rental activities only. The diagram shows the inputs, processes, and outputs of the rental activity. Inputs are rent/return requests, payments, process requests, new customer information, and new video information. Processes are maintenance, reporting, and rental/return. At the feasibility level, this is an acceptable level of detail for data and procedure knowledge and documentation.

To determine leverage points for ABC's application, we examine what the application does for ABC in the context of its industry and competitive environment. To do this we ask and answer several questions. First, can this application give ABC a competitive position in the industry? The answer to this question must be no. ABC is a one-shop organization that might grow to several branches but is not expected to grow to national prominence. Therefore, the application might give ABC a presence in the local market, but the application's strategic impact on the industry is zero.

Second, does the application give ABC competitive advantage in the local industry? All other things being equal, the application could give some local advantage over other video stores in Dunwoody, Georgia, the town where the company is located. The impact on the local industry, in terms of suburban Atlanta, is close to zero. The other 'things' that must be equal or better for ABC to obtain a local

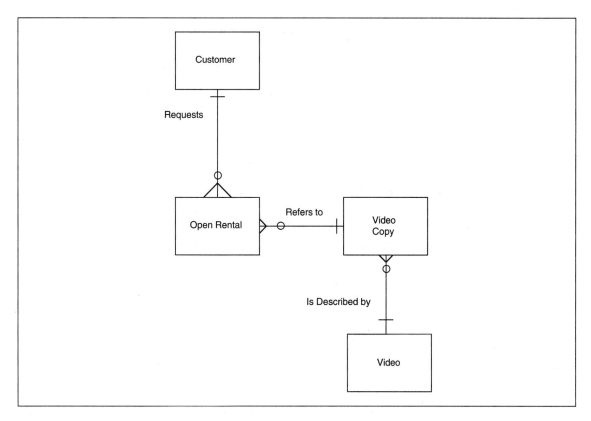

FIGURE 6-3   ABC Entity-Relationship Diagram

advantage include the number and variety of videos available, desirability of the location, and attitude of clerks to customers. For this discussion, we assume that location, attitude and variety of videos are at least equal.

Observation of the applications of the rival video stores is required to assess the potential impact of the subject application. There is a national chain store down the street, approximately .8 miles away. That store is evaluated since it is the closest competition. The chain store sells and rents Nintendo™, Sega Genesis™, and computer software as well as videos; plus, the chain store sells tickets to local rock concerts and events, and sells records, CDs, and audio tapes. Thus, the chain store is a recreational electronics store while ABC is simply a video rental store.

The fact that ABC is specialized and the chain store is general works in ABC's favor because of rel-

ative staffing levels. There are usually four clerks working in the chain store. Of the four clerks, two are at cash registers at which lines average three waiting patrons during peak periods. One of the other clerks roams the store assisting customers while the other clerk processes ticket orders. There are frequently lines at the ticket counter, especially when a famous rock group's tickets go on sale. Sometimes there are several hundred people on line. On average, there are 12 customers in the store at all times, with a peak average of 20. The peak times are the same as ABC's—6 P.M. to 11 P.M. Of the 20 customers during peak time, about 10 people actually rent or purchase something. The average age of a rental customer is about 19.

Contrast this situation with ABC. Five clerks work at ABC during the peak hours of 6 P.M. to 11 P.M. The remainder of the time, three clerks are on hand. The clerks, in general, do not roam the store

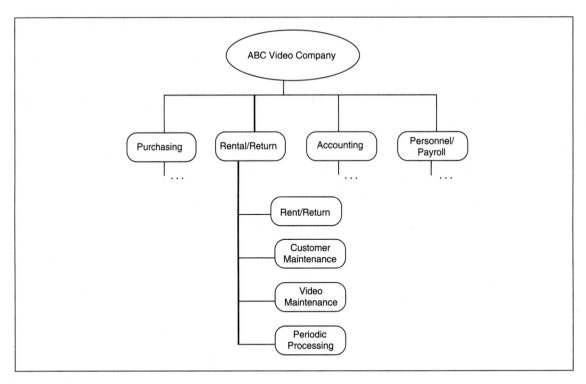

FIGURE 6-4   ABC Hierarchic Process Decomposition Diagram

assisting customers; they are all behind the counter doing payment processing for customer rentals. The lines, if any, form in the peak times and average two people per clerk. If a customer has a question, she or he waits until a clerk is free, then gets assistance and rental payment at the same time. On average, there are five people in the store at all times, with an average of 25 during the peak times. Of the 25 peak customers, 18 rent videos and seven leave empty-handed.

ABC's rental 'hit rate' of .72 (i.e., 18 of 25) is much higher than the industry average of .50.[1] Their single purpose may work against them for some customers who want full service electronic entertainment, and may work for them for other customers who only rent videos. The average age of an ABC rental customer is 22. Thus, the customer is slightly,

but not significantly, older than the chain store's customers.

So far, the company contrast neither favors nor disfavors ABC over the chain store. Next, we compare the company's procedures for rental processing. The chain store requires a *subscription* to their company's services that includes the presentation of a valid driver's license and credit card to establish an account. To use the account, each family member is assigned their own number and given his or her own ID card. The ID card is presented at the time of rental and payment of all current and past charges is required for a rental to take place. The presence of a family member ID allows parents who get stuck paying their children's fees to track the guilty party. If two family members make rentals in the same day, the clerk may or may not mention that a rental already exists to the later person. There is no procedure for clerks to help customers control the number of rentals in one day, nor is there a way for previous rentals to be known.

---

1 The industry average is located by doing library research on the industry.

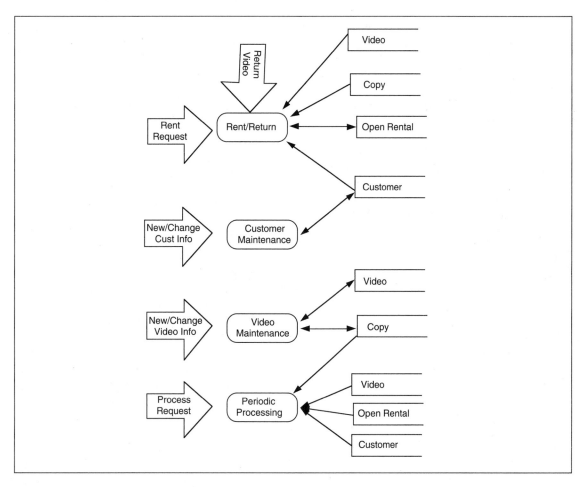

FIGURE 6-5   ABC Process Data Flow Diagram

ABC's expected rental processing is detailed in Chapter 2. Vic's vision of ABC's rental application does slightly favor ABC over the chain store. ABC will also assign family members their own IDs, but an ID card is not required of a customer. Rather, Vic envisions using the telephone number as the ID and asking the person for their name at the time of rental. A list will appear on the screen of all authorized renters for a given phone number with a sequential number the clerk selects beside each name. The procedures to accompany rental processing assume that customers *want to know* if a previous rental that day has occurred. Also, Vic envisions keeping track, electronically, of the previous rentals for a family

and giving them the chance to stop a rental transaction on a previously viewed video. Thus, Vic's scenario has less bureaucracy, more service, and more customer-oriented clerical procedures than the chain store. These three improvements are the leverage points for ABC in its local market.

Next, we define other noncompetitive benefits of the application. The application eliminates many of the errors that can happen in a manual system of work. For instance, clerks can no longer decide who pays late fees by changing return dates. Customer cards, which can be lost, are eliminated and replaced by automated file records which can only be deleted by Vic. Both videos and customers must be *on an automated file* to be eligible for rental processing.

The application will provide for automatic generation of end-of-day reports on receipts and transactions by clerk, by register, or by customer. If a discrepancy is found between receipts and money in the cash register, having a log of transactions that can be printed will assist the accountant in tracing errors. Both of these types of reports provide significant improvement over the current manual methods. Under the current method, receipts are tied to money in each register by sorting the paper copies of transactions and adding the totals. If there is an error, it is almost impossible to trace since no money is actually tied to an individual transaction. At the present, the accountant *writes off* errors.

Developing a list of the benefits for ABC's application is fairly easy because automation so improves a manual operation level task. Take the adjectives *faster, better, more* and, for each, define all the tasks or data that will be improved in some way relating to the adjective. For instance, processing an individual transaction will be faster because manual card lookup is gone, data entry is minimized to Customer ID and Video ID(s) with the computer retrieving and displaying all other information about each entity. Individual transactions will have improved data integrity by eliminating manual errors, such as writing the wrong amount, entering a wrong amount at the register, writing the wrong tape ID, retrieving the wrong customer card, and so forth. More information will be available for management use. For instance, end-of-day reports provide the accountant more information and Vic might develop ad hoc reports of all automated information. The benefits for ABC's rental application are summarized next.

Simplify customer IDs—Less bureaucracy than competition

Provide help to customers in finding tapes— More service than competition

Give customers information on previous rentals the same day and on videos they have previously rented—More customer-oriented clerical procedures than competition

Increase data accuracy for customers, videos, rentals

Allow tracking of late rentals

Allow accurate computation of late fees

Increase speed of customer and video information retrieval

Improve customer service

Provide accounting record of transactions

Allow tracking of transaction errors

Decrease time for individual transactions through minimal typing

Increase speed and accuracy of fee processing

Decrease file update time

Provide more accurate and timely end-of-day reports

Improve customer satisfaction with overall rental process through the above changes

After general benefits are identified, they are made specific and quantified for evaluation of costs. The benefits listed above are specific enough to quantify directly (see Table 6-1). Quantification, though, requires detailed knowledge of the business and expected benefits. Vic is the business expert and he participates in the quantification activity. For each benefit, he is asked how much revenue (or expense) is related to each item for one occurrence of each benefit. For each, Vic is also asked the degree of certainty for the benefit and his estimate. The numbers provided are multiplied for the total number of each benefit expected. The degree of certainty (ranging from 0.0 to 1.0) is then multiplied by each total amount to provide a range of estimates for each. In the example shown in Figure 6-6, the *benefit* of *more*

Total revenues	$500,000
Losses from inaccurate data	2% of revenues
Dollar loss from bad data	$10,000
Certainty factor	80%
Benefit of more accurate data	.8 * 10000 = $8,000–$10,000

FIGURE 6-6   Example of Benefit Computation

TABLE 6-1   ABC Quantified Benefits

Benefit	Expected Increase in Revenue
Simplify customer IDs—Less bureaucracy than competition	$1,000
Provide help to customers in finding tapes—More service than competition	$1,000
Give customers information on previous rentals the same day and on videos they have previously rented—More customer-oriented clerical procedures than competition	$ 500
Increase data accuracy for customers, videos, rentals	$8,000–10,000
Allow tracking of late rentals Allow accurate computation of late fees	$10,000–15,000
Increase speed of customer and video information retrieval	$1,000
Improve customer service	$1,000
Provide accounting record of transactions Allow tracking of transaction errors Provide more accurate and timely end-of-day reports	$3,000–5,000
Decrease time for individual transactions through minimal typing	$1,000
Increase speed and accuracy of fee processing	$1,500
Decrease file update time	$5,000
Improve customer satisfaction with overall rental process through the above changes	$2,500

accurate data entry, Vic figures his current losses at 2% of total revenues of $500,000, or $10,000. He feels the $10,000 estimate is about 80% accurate. Stated another way, by eliminating errors in data entry, Vic will gain $10,000 with 80% certainty. Thus, the benefit to be gained from more accurate data entry is $8,000–$10,000.

Table 6-1 shows the benefits from the list on p. 156 with dollar values associated with them. For the benefits resulting in $1,000 increases in revenue, Vic was unsure that there was much tangible outcome, but estimated about $3, or one rental, per day. For the higher dollar estimates, he worked through the estimates in the same way shown above for increased accuracy.

Develop Alternative Solutions

The activities in developing alternatives include definitions of technical alternatives, and benefits and risks of each alternative.

Define Technical Alternatives

There are no specific, theory-based guidelines for developing technical alternatives. Rather, the technical alternatives within a specific business are explored to determine what is possible and practical. First, define the application concept (see Table 6-2). How up-to-date does information maintained by the application need to be? If the answer is four

TABLE 6-2   Steps in Developing the Technical Alternatives

- Define the overall application concept
- Evaluate usefulness of existing hardware/software
- If new equipment or software is needed:
  - Determine data sharing requirements
  - Determine the criticality of data to the company
- If shared or critical data, select equipment (either LAN or mainframe) and software that allow centralized control over data.
- If noncritical and nonshared data, select the smallest equipment that allows necessary level of control. In multilocation settings, consider decentralizing or distributing the application by duplicating equipment, application, or data in several locations.
- Define special hardware requirements and ensure that the special hardware works with the selected hardware/software platform(s).

hours or more, a batch application is sufficient. If the answer is between two and four hours, interactive data entry with batch updates throughout the day might be acceptable. If the answer is in the range from seconds old to four hours, an on-line application is also sufficient. If the answer is that the system user must react to all transactions as they occur, a real-time application is needed. On-line is the most frequently selected option.

Next, for individual processes, determine the concept at the lower level of detail. For instance, for reporting, should answers be developed as a report request is entered or can they be run overnight? Some reports might need to be on-line, others might be run in batch mode. The volume of print, estimated time for processing, and urgency of data all are used to select the concept for individual processes. For instance, an ad hoc report that generates 10,000 lines of print should not be sent to a display screen; rather, it should be printed. Also, a long report might be created at the time of the request, but sent to a print queue for convenience of printing. *The decisions made during feasibility are not expected to be permanent at this point, rather, you are estimating the*

concept to help in the evaluation of complexity of design.

After the concept is developed, hardware and software are evaluated. If there is hardware and software already installed, investigate their use first. Can the application be developed for operation on the existing equipment? Can the existing software accommodate the application? Can the application coexist with other applications currently used? If the answers to these questions are "yes," the platform recommended is the existing equipment and software. If a "no" answer is given, then investigate new hardware or software as needed.

If no hardware or software are currently used, or the current equipment cannot be used to do the application, select the likely hardware platforms. First, determine whether the application users need to share information or not and how up-to-date the information must be. For instance, can copies of the application run in different locations with daily update of files, or must the users share all information throughout the day? Second, determine the 'corporateness' of the data. How critical to the organization is the application data? If the company depends on the data to stay in business, then a more centralized, controlled environment is required than if the data is not critical to the company.

The need for centralized control over data that is critical to the organization is one factor to consider in recommending a platform and environment for an application. The extent to which the company relies on application operability, the importance of data integrity, audit trails and security, and the ability of the environment to accommodate these needs are all assessed. Although there are no clear differences in application management between a LAN and a mainframe, software *does* make a difference. The levels of security, number of simultaneous users, size of database, locking of records for simultaneous update, and many other technical considerations differ widely across networks, operating systems, databases, and languages. When distribution is an alternative, the centralization issue becomes even more important to evaluate and resolve. Full discussion of the decision criteria for distributing data and applications are deferred until Chapter 10.

To determine hardware alternatives identify the smallest size computer possible that can accommodate the task, providing for data sharing and centralized control as needed. The cheapest and smallest platforms that meet the criteria are alternatives. For hardware we then ask if any other special purpose hardware is needed for this application. If other special purpose hardware is needed, enough research on the hardware should be done to determine what is required and whether or not it can be used with the identified alternatives.

From the hardware identification activity, the most likely platforms should be narrowed to two or three. The key factors in narrowing the selected platforms are reliability and flexibility. Portability might also be important, depending on the environment. **Reliability** is the extent to which the hardware, software, and application will be operational. **Flexibility** is the extent to which the hardware, software, or application can be modified easily. Hardware flexibility relates to the extent to which upgrades can be made, for example the number of additional boards, the maximum memory upgrade, the type bus, and type disk channel, to name a few. Software flexibility relates to package design and how often the vendor releases updates of new functions. Application flexibility relates to methodology, implementation language, and skill of the developers. Reliability and flexibility are important issues in, for example, selecting a PC workstation, because of the diversity and quantity of alternatives available. If you evaluate five different vendors of IBM PC-compatible equipment, you will have different reliabilities and flexibilities for each. But even more confusing is that five different configurations of a PC from *the same* vendor might also have five different reliabilities and flexibilities.

Portability is the extent to which the software can be moved to another hardware/operating system environment without change. The fewer changes when moving the application, the more portable it is. Portability is an issue when the application is developed in one environment (e.g., a LAN) and is ported or moved to another environment for operations (e.g., a mainframe). Portability is also important when an application is developed in one location and is implemented in multiple locations which may not

have the same configuration. Multiple locations with heterogeneous environments are the norm in distributed applications.

Hardware alone rarely determines the recommended alternative. In addition to picking hardware platforms that can accommodate the needs for multiple, simultaneous users, you also choose the software most likely to be used in each environment. Again, these selections might change as the design progresses, but their purpose during feasibility is to allow assessment of skills, training needs, cost, and application design complexity.

In choosing software, you identify a programming language, database environment, and any special software needed. Each alternative is developed to solve the entire problem, meeting all requirements and as many optional requests as possible. Only the best alternative(s) for a given environment is considered. Two sets of alternatives illustrate this statement.

The first set of alternatives is for a mainframe environment using different operating environments. The first alternative (see Figure 6-7a) identifies an IBM mainframe, running the MVS operating system, and using IBM's DB2 for database and IMS/DC for telecommunications control. The second alternative (see Figure 6-7b) identifies an IBM mainframe, running the conversational VM/CMS operating system, and using a Focus database. Telecommunications control is hidden from the

---

Figure 6-7a. Alternative 1

Hardware:	IBM Mainframe 309x
Operating System:	MVS
Database:	DB2
Telecomm Control:	IMS/DC

Figure 6-7b. Alternative 2

Hardware:	IBM Mainframe 309x
Operating System:	VM/CMS
Database:	Focus
Telecomm Control:	SNA through VM

FIGURE 6-7   Two Alternatives Using Different Software

Figure 6-8a. Alternative 1

Hardware:	IBM Mainframe 309x
Operating System:	VM/CMS
Database:	Focus
Telecomm Control:	SNA through VM

Figure 6-8b. Alternative 2

Hardware:	IBM PC-Compatible
Operating System:	MS/DOS, Windows
Database:	Focus
Telecomm Control:	Novell Ethernet

FIGURE 6-8   Alternatives Using Different Operating Environments

application and is through VM (i.e., using VTAM and SNA). Both of these scenarios might be proposed, with the deciding factors relating to time of development and expertise of staff, rather than to the desirability of one environment over the other.

The second set of scenarios is for a network version of an application (see Figure 6-8a) versus a mainframe version (see Figure 6-8b). Both environments would use a database which is already available in-house. In this case, the decision relates to environmental and cost factors since both alternatives use similar database software. Then, reliability, flexibility, and portability are issues.

Estimate Benefits of Recommended Alternatives

Two kinds of benefit estimates are developed. First, the general benefits defined are analyzed to determine that they are (or are not) met by each proposed alternative. Second, new benefits that relate to a specific proposed alternative are defined. Again, benefits are context specific, relating to a given alternative for a given company at a given time.

The first benefits estimate is a tally of the number of general application benefits met and, if it can be determined, the effectiveness of implementation within the proposed alternative. Effectiveness, for our purpose, is the extent to which an alternative will implement the application requirements *more*,

better, and *faster*. To measure the number of requirements met by each alternative, we simply count which are met in an implementation of each alternative.

To measure effectiveness, we need to determine the extent to which each requirement will be developed. This extent can only be defined in a specific context for a specific application. For instance, two requirements for ABC might be "Provide minimal data entry for customer and video identification" and "Use a scanner for data entry whenever possible" (see Figure 6-9). One alternative might assume the entry of scanned data only. A second alternative assumes the entry of scanned data while providing for keyboard entry in case of scanner hardware failure. A third alternative might assume the keyboarding of a minimal number of characters for each type of data. The first two alternatives meet both criteria. The third alternative does not meet the second requirement. Only the second alternative, however, provides both the requirement *and* a backup. The second alternative would be rated more *effective* in meeting the requirement than the others, while both the first and second alternatives meet the benefits. On a scale of one to three, the alternatives would be rated two, one, and three, respectively. In a different company with a different context, the same alternatives might be rated one, three, two respectively.

Define Risks

The purpose of risk assessment is to determine all the things that can go wrong. If you have heard of Murphy's Laws, you know they apply to applica-

Alternative 1:   Scan Data Entry

Alternative 2:   Scan Data Entry
or
Keyboard Data Entry with Minimal
Typing

Alternative 3:   Keyboard Data Entry with Minimal
Typing

FIGURE 6-9   Sample Evaluation of Alternative Effectiveness

TABLE 6-3   Sources of Risk

Source of Risk	Risks
Hardware	Not installed when needed
	Cannot do the job
	Does not work as advertised
	Installation not prepared in time
	Installation requirements (e.g., air-conditioning, room size, or electrical) insufficient
	Wiring not correct
	Hardware delivered incorrectly
	Hardware delivered with damage
Software	Not installed when needed
	Cannot do the job
	Does not work as advertised
	Contains 'undocumented features' that cause compromise on application requirements
	Vendor support inadequate
	Resource requirements are over budgeted, allocated amounts
Group	Key person(s) quit, are promoted elsewhere, go on jury duty, have long-term illness
	Skill levels inadequate
	Training not in time to benefit the project
Project management	Schedule not accurate
	Budget not sufficient
	Manager change
User	Quits, transfers, is replaced
	Not cooperative
	Not supportive
	Does not spend as much time as original commitment requested
Computer resources	Test time insufficient
	Test time not same as commitment
	Inadequate disk space
	Insufficient logon IDs
	Insufficient interactive time

tion development. The three most common of Murphy's Laws are:

1. If anything can go wrong, it will.
2. Things go wrong at the worst possible time.
3. Everything takes longer than it should.

Table 6-3 is a list of possible sources of risk. For each item on the list, you determine the likelihood of it occurring for this project. For instance, if you are using only existing equipment, you could skip the risks dealing with hardware installation problems. As sources of risk are identified, they should be placed in a separate table and rated for likelihood of occurrence for each alternative. In addition, other possible risks for the project might be added to the list. For instance, if revenue for current year drops 25%, the company might not be able to afford the project.

ABC Video Alternatives

First, technical alternatives for developing ABC's rental application are developed. Next, benefits and risks relating to each alternative are estimated.

To develop technical alternatives, the application requirements should be listed as follows:

1. Provide add, change, delete, inquiry functions for customer, video, and rental information
2. Automate processing of rental transactions, including

   - Interactive processing and data display for all outstanding video rentals, including fees owing
   - The maintenance of customer history of rentals, rental history for each video tape, creation and change of rental transaction records
   - Monitoring of outstanding rentals by customer
   - Computation of late fees owing from prior transactions
   - The ability to create new customers as part of rental processing
   - The ability to add new videos to the system as part of rental processing
   - Query of any rental related information

3. Minimize data entry in rental processing by using bar codes or similar technology
4. Provide interactive, on-line updating capabilities for all files
5. Provide transaction logging for database integrity
6. Do daily backup of all files and application programs
7. Provide ad hoc reporting capability for all files and legal combinations of files (e.g., customer with video rentals with customer rental history)
8. Provide end-of-day reports of activity by transaction with summaries by transaction type (i.e., rental, late fees, other fees)
9. Provide for future growth of 15% per year per file
10. Provide for future growth in number of system users to be one every 18 months for five years. A total of nine concurrent users should be supported.
11. Provide SQL compatibility for future growth and compatibility between software applications
12. Provide mean time between failures (MTBF) of 1 year for hardware selection and mean time to repair (MTTR) of 1 hour in hardware maintenance contracts
13. Provide on-line processing for all functions from 8 A.M. to 11 P.M. daily

ABC has specific requirements that imply an on-line application, significant ad hoc reporting, and interactive processing with immediate file update throughout the day. Batch processing should be feasible as a background task to on-line processing since the on-line portion of the day is so extensive and there might be a problem trying to staff the batch hours. Beginning with a hardware platform, then continuing to software and applications, the proposed alternatives are defined. Only alternatives that can meet all requirements should be identified; however, if that is not possible, any feasible alternatives are identified and evaluated later. In ABC's case, only alternatives that can meet all requirements are identified.

In a small business, the two most likely hardware platforms are multiuser minicomputers or client-server local area networks. These are considered here. The competing hardware platforms are an IBM AS/400 minicomputer versus a token ring local area network (LAN). Each of these decisions requires a minianalysis of the alternatives in their respective environments that are beyond the scope of this text. To specify the LAN, for instance, requires comparison of options and costs of probabilistic versus deterministic networks, cabling requirements, network operating systems (NOS), network interface card

TABLE 6-4   Hardware Platform Estimates[1]

Client/Server Alternative

Item	Cost
Workstation (6)	$ 4,800[1]
Server	$ 2,000
Software	$ 3,500
Cable—Shielded Twisted Pair (STP)	$ 1,900
Network Interface Cards (7)	$ 1,000
Network Operating System (Ethernet), 6–10 stations	$ 2,500
Total	$15,700

Minicomputer Alternative

Item	Cost
Workstation (6)	$ 4,800
Minicomputer	$15,000
Software	$ 5,000 Plus $200/ month
Cable—STP	$ 1,900
Total	$26,700 Plus $200/ month

[1]Keep in mind that these are estimates for the sake of discussion and *not* real dollar estimates.

(NIC), compatible software, and so on. Both hardware platforms can be implemented successfully in ABC's environment, can support the volume of transactions, and can support the expected company and applications growth.

Once the platforms are identified, the hardware cost of implementing the application on the alternative platforms is estimated (see Table 6-4). From these estimates, the most likely (e.g., the cheapest) two to three alternatives are selected. Also, if there is doubt about the economic feasibility of the application, the client/user can determine whether to continue with the analysis or not. As Table 6-4 shows, the client/server LAN is cheaper than the minicom-

puter hardware alternative. Both alternative definitions exclude software for rental processing which is estimated separately because the option to purchase software versus custom development of software should be evaluated.

The client/server alternative is recommended to Vic and he approves although he is concerned about the cost. As a small business person, his company nets under $1,000,000 per year and, in ABC's case, is closer to $500,000. A rule of thumb in automation expenditures is to spend under 10% of net income. Vic's concern is that the total cost may exceed $50,000 and his financial risk becomes a problem.

The remaining estimates use only the client/server solution to develop software application alternatives. The choices are between purchasing a software package and developing a customized package for rental processing. Mary researches available software packages and finds that the cheapest one is VidRent[2] which costs $7,500 plus $1,500 maintenance per year (see Table 6-5). VidRent will be compared to building a customized applications using either SQL Server[3] or Focus. SQL Server is selected as representing software specifically designed to

---

2 VidRent is a fictitious name.

3 SQL Server™ is a trademark of Sybase and Microsoft Corporations.

TABLE 6-5   Alternative Software Packages

Software	Initial Cost	Maintenance	Maximum Number of Users
SQL Server™	$17,500[a]	$1,800/year	Up to 20
LAN Focus™ with SQL	$12,000	$1,200/year	Up to eight
VidRent	$ 7,500	$1,500/year	Any number of users on one LAN

[a]Keep in mind that these are estimates for the sake of discussion and *not* real dollar estimates.

take advantage of client/server environments. Focus is selected as representing software with which Mary's team has extensive experience. The costs of each alternative are completely different and provide for different numbers of users. These factors are kept in mind, but the requirements must be analyzed to determine if one software should be favored functionally over the others.

The requirements are reevaluated and rated for each development alternative as shown in Table 6-6. First, consider the softwares' capabilities. VidRent provides neither query capabilities nor historical customer or video processing. It also cannot create new customer or video records as part of rental processing. VidRent also does not provide transaction logging. If this package were chosen, these requirements would go unmet. Through discussion with the vendor, Mary determines that query processing can be done by using any software that can access ASCII files. Thus, the addition of dBase™ or Oracle™ or some other single-user package to provide Vic with query capabilities is a cheap alternative that adds about $1,200 to the alternative. This alternative is still limited in that querying would be limited to an off-line function when the on-line application was not in operation. This requirement is caused by the record locking scheme in VidRent. Also, the software package could be modified by Mary's group to provide the history processing desired by Vic, without violating the vendor warranty. Thus, VidRent's cost increases, and it is capable of doing most requisite processing (see Table 6-7).

Both Focus and SQL Server are fully capable of supporting the application. Both require complete, custom development of the application, but both provide application generators and have built-in query capability. A quick estimate by Mary based on her experience and without a detailed project plan is that the total development work would take about six-person months. At $150 per day, for a 26-day month, the custom software development will be about $23,400 (i.e., 6 * 150 * 26). Except for cost, there is no advantage or disadvantage to either package based on application requirements. SQL Server's license allows 15 concurrent users which is more than Focus.

Next, consider the organizational impacts of each package. Mary's team requires training for either VidRent or SQL Server. Training for SQL Server, which is supplied by the vendor, would not be charged to Vic since the knowledge is useful to the team after the rental application is complete. VidRent training, also from the vendor, would be paid by Vic. Training costs must be added to its cost (see Table 6-7).

Next, consider vendor reputation and market stability. SyBase and Microsoft, the vendors of SQL Server, are both relatively young companies, with Microsoft the current leader in software for the PC market. Focus' company, Information Builders, Inc., is over 15 years old and has enjoyed steady growth. Therefore, both vendors are expected to remain viable market forces for the foreseeable future. VidRent's vendor, VidSoft, is 5 years old and still is run from the owner's home. The company has grown steadily by selling to the single video store firms such as ABC, but the owner, Mark Denton, does not publicize his earnings.

In summary, SQL Server and Focus both meet all software requirements of the application; VidRent could be made to provide most requirements. Cost favors the VidRent proposal with a total estimated software cost of $22,000. At this point, Vic must decide how much he wants the custom features of his application and whether the compromises on querying and ease of processing are worth $13,000.

Vic and Mary discuss the alternatives frankly. Mary recommends not going with VidRent because of the company size, lack of features, and need for customizing for any features not already in the package. Vic is staggered by the cost of custom software development and is inclined to purchase VidRent and forget his grand plans. Mary reminds him that if he does not develop his application as envisioned, the competitive advantages might disappear. Vic eventually decides that he does want the application as currently defined and that he is not willing to compromise his vision in any way. Therefore, only SQL Server and Focus alternatives are developed further to determine the benefits and risks of the softwares.

Only general benefits are evaluated for each alternative; there are no apparent benefits of one

TABLE 6-6   Rating Software Development Alternatives

Function	SQL Server	Focus	VidRent
Provide add, change, delete, inquiry functions for customer, video, and rental information	Yes	Yes	Yes
Interactive processing and data display for all outstanding video rentals, including fees owing	Yes	Yes	Yes
On-line processing from 8 A.M. to 11 P.M. daily	Yes	Yes	Yes
The maintenance of customer history of rentals, rental history for each video tape, creation, and change of rental transaction records	Yes	Yes	Yes
Monitoring of outstanding rentals by customer	On-line	On-line	Off-line
Computation of late fees owing from prior transactions	Yes	Yes	Yes
The ability to create new customers as part of rental processing	Yes	Yes	No
The ability to add new videos to the system as part of rental processing	Yes	Yes	No
Query of any rental-related information	On-line	On-line	Off-line
Minimize data entry in rental processing by using bar codes or similar technology	Yes	Yes	Yes
Provide immediate file update	Yes	Yes	Yes
Provide transaction logging for database integrity	Yes	Yes	No
Do daily backup of all files and application programs	Yes	Yes	Yes
Provide ad hoc reporting capability for all files and legal combinations of files	Yes	Yes	Only with another package
Provide end-of-day reports	Yes	Yes	Yes
Provide for growth of 15% per year per file	Yes	Yes	Yes
Provide for nine concurrent users	15	10	Any number
Provide SQL compatibility	Yes	Yes	For ASCII files
Total requirements met out of 18	18	18	15

software over the other. The benefits of the application identified in an earlier step are compared to each proposed software alternative. As you can see from Table 6-8, the benefits are identical for each implementation.

Finally, risks of the alternatives are defined. The list of possible risks is customized for the application and each risk is assessed for probability of occurrence with a specific alternative (see Table 6-9). The table of risks is repeated here with an analysis of the two language environments. Hardware risks apply equally to both alternatives. Software risks vary because of differences in product knowledge by the development team, product functionality, and expected cost, all of which favor Focus.

TABLE 6-7   Total Estimated Cost of Software Alternatives

Software	Initial Cost	Purpose
SQL Server™	$17,500[1] $23,400	License fee Custom software Total $37,900
LAN Focus™ with SQL	$12,000 $23,400	License fee Custom software Total $35,000
VidRent	$ 7,500 $ 2,500 $ 5,000 $ 7,000	License fee Database query software Training Customizing Total $22,000

[1]Keep in mind that these are estimates for the sake of discussion and *not* real dollar estimates.

TABLE 6-8   Benefits of SQL Server and Focus Alternatives

Benefits	SQL Server	Focus
Simplify customer IDs	Yes	Yes
Provide help to customers in finding tapes	Procedure	Procedure
Give customers information on previous rentals the same day and on videos they have previously rented	Yes	Yes
Provide data accuracy for customers, videos, rentals	Yes	Yes
Track and display late rentals	Yes	Yes
Compute and display late fees	Yes	Yes
Increase speed of customer and video information retrieval	Yes	Yes
Improve customer service	Yes	Yes
Provide accounting record of transactions	Yes	Yes
Allow tracking of transaction errors	Yes	Yes
Provide accurate and timely end-of-day reports	Yes	Yes
Decrease time for individual transactions through minimal typing	Yes	Yes
Increase speed and accuracy of fee processing	Yes	Yes
Decrease file update time	Yes	Yes
Improve customer satisfaction with overall rental process through the above changes	Yes	Yes
Total benefits met out of 15	15	15

TABLE 6-9   ABC Risks of Software Development Alternatives

Risks	SQL Server	Focus
Hardware not installed when needed	Low	Low
Hardware cannot do the job	Low	Low
Hardware does not work as advertised	Low	Low
Hardware installation not prepared in time	Low	Low
Hardware installation requirements (air conditioning or electrical) insufficient	Low	Low
Wiring not correct	Low–Medium	Low–Medium
Hardware delivered incorrectly	Low	Low
Hardware delivered with damage	Low	Low
Software not installed when needed	Low	Low
Software cannot do the job	Low	N/A
Software does not work as advertised	Low–Medium	N/A
Software contains 'undocumented features' that cause compromise on application requirements	Medium	N/A
Software vendor support inadequate	Low–Medium	N/A
Software resource requirements are over budgeted, allocated amounts	Low	N/A
Key person(s) quit, are promoted elsewhere, go on jury duty, have long-term illness	Low	Low
Group skill levels inadequate	Low–Medium	No
Training not in time to benefit the project	Low–Medium	N/A
Schedule not accurate	Low	Low
Budget not sufficient	Low	Low
Manager change	No	No
Vic quits, transfers, is replaced	No	No
Vic/clerks not cooperative	Low	Low
Vic/clerks not supportive	Low	Low
Vic does not spend as much time as original commitment requested	Low	Low
Test time insufficient	N/A	N/A
Test time not same as commitment	N/A	N/A
Inadequate disk space	N/A	N/A
Insufficient logon IDs	N/A	N/A
Insufficient interactive time	N/A	N/A

Once the benefits, risks, and alternatives are defined, they are evaluated to narrow the field to one (or two) proposed alternative(s).

Evaluate Alternative Solutions

The recommended alternatives are evaluated for technical adequacy, organizational feasibility, extent to which benefits are met, and severity of associated risks. In general, we select the alternative that meets the most requirements, yields the greatest benefit, and has the lowest associated risk. When these characteristics do not relate to the same technical alternative, one or two are selected for further analysis and the remaining alternatives are eliminated from consideration. In this section, we discuss technical, organization, benefit, and risk evaluations for narrowing the decision to one or two alternatives.

Evaluate Technical Feasibility

Technical feasibility assesses the technology, its maturity in the market, its availability to the company, and the likelihood of successful use. Technical feasibility is most important when using new technologies that are *leading edge*. You want to be *leading* the competition, not *bleeding*, when using new technologies!

The key questions used to evaluate technical feasibility are:

Is the technology in use elsewhere?
Is the technology used elsewhere for similar applications?
How mature is the technology?
How much industry experience is there with this technology?
Are staff with experience using this technology easy to find?
How does each alternative manage the application sources of complexity?
Does the proposed alternative require any compromise of application requirements? What type of compromise and which requirement(s)?

Each question is evaluated for each technical alternative proposed. Any issues about a technology's ability to perform as required for an application should be identified. Objective answers that may not be what managers want to hear are required to adequately assess technical feasibility. Maintaining objectivity is difficult when market pressure to develop an application exists and managers *want* to develop an application.

To perform technical feasibility analysis, the technical alternatives are listed and compared across alternatives. Then, the application requirements are listed and evaluated for number of requirements met across the alternatives. The alternative meeting the most requirements is favored during this analysis. If there is a difference in the extent to which a requirement would be met, that information is noted in the analysis.

Evaluate Organizational Feasibility

Organizational feasibility is the extent to which the organization is ready to implement the proposed application. First, using the questions below, organization structure is assessed to define organizational changes required.

Does the organization structure need to be changed?
Do all groups that create the same information report to the same manager?
Do user jobs require new procedures?
Do user jobs require new work organization? For instance, do they move from individual assembly line-type arrangement to work groups?
Do users have the required level of computer literacy?
Do users have the required level of typing skills?
Will users require training for the new application?
Can training be done by other users?
Are users involved in screen design, acceptance test design, and/or general application development?
Does the IS staff know the problem domain?
Does the IS staff know the software being used?
Does the IS staff know the operating environment being used?

Organization structure is evaluated to determine if the people who have creation authority for data all report to the same management and that all departments and jobs that will be needed in the new application are defined or currently exist. Second, expected users are evaluated to determine the extent to which training is required to implement the proposed application. For instance, some computer literacy and typing skills might be required. If users must know how to turn the machine on and activate an application, but do not currently use computers, you might need to do a short questionnaire or interview users to determine their level of computer literacy. Any needs identified are added to the implementation plan as a task (and cost) of the proposed application. The goal of this first type of organization analysis is to identify user department changes and user requirements for training, both of which must be satisfied before the organization can effectively use the proposed application.

A second type of organizational feasibility assesses the readiness of the IS organization to develop the proposed application. When a custom development is being done by consultants, you evaluate their skills with the technology and similar problems to determine their readiness. The assessment determines staff skill with the hardware, operating environment, programming language, database, and similar environments. As with the user organization, feasibility, level of expertise and training requirements are determined. Technical staff training requirements defined during this assessment are added to development plans for cost analysis.

The last type of feasibility assessment, financial feasibility, is performed after a plan for the recommended alternative(s) is developed. Financial feasibility is discussed in a following section.

Assess Benefits

Benefits defined for the application in general, and for specific implementation alternatives, are assessed to determine which proposed alternative yields the outcome with the highest reward to the organization.

Benefits are tallied for each alternative. First, a simple count of the benefits for each alternative is done. Then, for benefits assigned monetary values, the amounts of increased revenues or avoided expenses are summed to provide a single dollar-value benefit for each alternative. If there are no alternative-specific benefits, the number and value of benefits are the same for all alternatives. If there are alternative-specific benefits, then one or several alternatives might be preferred. These are identified by this analysis.

Assess Risks

Similar to the benefits analysis, the risks of each proposed alternative are assessed to determine the alternative with the least risk. First, a simple count of the risks for each alternative is done. Then, for alternative-specific risks, the extent to which they are likely to occur is assessed. If there are no alternative-specific risks, the risks are the same for all alternatives. When the risks are not the same, alternatives with lower, less likely risks are preferred to alternatives with a high likelihood of occurrence. If a dollar value of exposure is assigned to the risk, it is considered, with lower values of risk preferred to significant potential losses.

Propose New Application

Next, the recommended solution(s) are defined in sufficient detail to allow project planning and financial analysis. The development plans include hardware, software, operating environment, development concept, technical feasibility, organization feasibility, benefits, and risks.

The proposal of the new application might document the recommendations formally to begin to develop the feasibility report, or may still be an informal collection of information that supports the remaining analyses. The formality of this gathering of information is decided by the Project Manager and SE, based on their confidence in their decisions. If they are fairly confident that no major changes will take place, they might develop final versions of documentation and begin an informal review of their findings and recommendations with users.

ABC Video Evaluation of Alternatives

The alternatives first are assessed in terms of the technical and organizational feasibility. Then, the benefits and risks of each are assessed. Based on the differences between alternatives, a recommended solution is selected.

Both packages, SQL Server and Focus, appear capable of providing the complete application as envisioned by Vic. The implementation would probably be smoother with Focus given the high skill level of Mary and her staff with the product. SQL Server might have intangible benefits in that, if another store were opened, the software could easily communicate between stores, having been built specifically for distributed processing. This benefit is not immediate, however, and the current technical solution favored is Focus. Focus has a longer history, and is thus, a more mature product, has a large company backing it, provides all technical requirements for current and future plans; and is cheaper than SQL Server in the example.

From an organization perspective, neither product offers any distinct advantages or disadvantages. The staff at ABC would have to learn both products. Both vendors offer classes in the Atlanta area. The company does not need reorganization to accommodate the application regardless of software chosen. From the perspective of Mary's staff, Focus is preferred since they already have experience using it, but she feels confident that they could also build the application using SQL Server if desired.

The benefits analysis is simple in this case. The benefits do not favor either implementation scenario since they all apply to both. Thus, all benefits are expected to accrue from either implementation.

The risk analysis favors Focus over SQL Server slightly. The main difference in risk exposure is from the lack of usage experience of Mary's group with SQL Server. This lack of knowledge can only be partially removed by training. Experience in using the product is really required to develop knowledge of the 'undocumented features' and unanticipated limitations of the software. In this case, Focus is known to Mary's team and is therefore preferred.

In the example for ABC, both packages could probably be used with success in developing the ABC rental application. Both softwares appear capable of future growth and have apparent company stability. The cost differences favor a Focus solution, while the specific client/server orientation provides an as yet unneeded benefit to SQL Server. Vic

decides in favor of the Focus solution, but is clearly unhappy with the overall cost of $50,700. Vic wants to continue with the planning and financial analysis for the application, but is also interested in some way to reduce or defer the development costs of Mary's team services for customized software. In any case, the Focus, LAN solution will be planned and evaluated financially in detail. Before we continue with ABC's problem, we first talk about project planning.

Plan the Implementation

Estimating Techniques

Users are easy to deal with when they feel you understand their problem, when they think you can improve their situation through automation, you can estimate how long the job will take, and you can estimate their costs. These are not easy items to know or to develop. When users are comfortable that they can afford and use the proposed application within a reasonable amount of time, they become the champions of the project, fighting for its development in the political environment of the business. Research shows that a champion provides a major contribution to application development success. In this section, we discuss the last two important issues to making the user feel comfortable: planning and costing the project.[4]

Accurate estimates are important to

- allow cost-benefit and other financial analyses
- allow hardware/software trade-off analysis
- provide a basis for management evaluation of multiple projects
- act as the basis for schedule, staffing, project management, and structure definition
- avoid problems such as contract renegotiation, overtime, user cost increases, or project costs increases

At the feasibility level, estimates should be within 20% accurate. This means that the estimates might be overstated or understated by 20%. Planning

---

4 All the methods in this section are based on methods discussed in Barry Boehm's book, *Software Engineering Economics.* Englewood Cliffs, NJ: Prentice-Hall, 1981.

should be redone at the end of the analysis phase, at which time the estimates should be within 10%. Again, planning at the end of design should refine the estimates to within 5%. The redefinition of costs is one activity that meets with resistance from managers who tend to *cast in concrete* the first estimate they hear. Part of the Project Manager's role is to educate the managers and users involved to understand that as the degree of uncertainty about project activities decreases, the certainty of time estimates and costs increases. Therefore, the plans should be redone at the end of every major phase of activity.

The planning methods discussed in the next section are ways to generate time estimates for the person-days of project work. These are then converted into costs by allocating an amount of money for each person required. Ultimately, the Project Manager and SE rely on their knowledge of the organization and salaries of individuals. Additional costs are allocated for computer resources, acquisition of hardware, software, or consultants, and other supplies needed to complete the application.

There are many different approaches to planning which are discussed in the first section below. After that, we take a practical, experience-based approach to developing a critical path plan. The experience-based estimates are then *reality checked* against two sets of algorithmic planning formulae. The two planning methods used are function points and the CoCoMo model. Both have known flaws. By combining planning methods rather than using only one, you improve the likelihood of more accurate estimates.

Planning methods are usually classified into categories for algorithmic methods, expert judgment, analogy, Parkinson, price-to-win, top-down, bottom-up, or function points. These are defined here, and several methods are discussed in detail because they are the most frequently used. Advantages and disadvantages of each method are summarized in Table 6-10.

ALGORITHMIC METHODS.   An **algorithmic estimating** relies on one or more key formulae to develop an estimate of person-power required for project work. There are five types of algorithmic planning methods. The sequence in which they were developed and found to be inadequate is linear (see Figure 6-10), multiplicative (see Figure 6-11), analytic (see Figure 6-12), tabular (see Figure 6-13), and composite, which combines the others. All but the composite method are rarely used because they offer too simplistic a model of project work. The noncomposite methods do not support adjustment of the model for expertise of staff, tools used to aid development, or other factors that might alter the time and cost of development. All algorithmic methods suffer the same *fatal flaw* that they rely on some initial estimate that is difficult to guess and on which the accuracy of the entire estimate rests.

There are two key variables in the Composite Cost Model (CoCoMo): number of delivered source instructions and project *mode*. **Delivered source instructions** refers to lines of code used in a production version of an application and omits any modules or programs written to support the development effort. Since any sizable project has thousands of instructions, this term is expressed as thousands of delivered source instructions or **KDSI**. *Delivered* instructions are those that actually are in the finished product and excludes any code that is generated to facilitate project development. For instance, in a DBMS application, you frequently write programs to do a formatted print of the file that are not part of the finished application. These modules would be omitted from the estimate. The second important word is *source*. Source code means uncompiled, unlinked lines of code in whatever language is used. The implication is that some *compiled* language such as Cobol, Fortran, Pascal, or PL/1, is used. Control language code is omitted from KDSI, while the number of Cobol statements is reduced by a factor of .33 to compensate for the high percentage of nonexecutable code.

The model is based on three critical assumptions. First, it assumes that KDSI can be estimated with some accuracy. Second, it assumes that the waterfall life cycle approach is used. Third, the language of application development (Cobol, Pl/1, APL, and so on) is assumed to have no discernible impact on the amount of effort or staffing for a project. The latter two assumptions can be corrected for by the multipliers. The first assumption, that accurate estimates of KDSI are possible, is only true when projects are

TABLE 6-10   Advantages and Disadvantages of Estimating Techniques*

Method	Advantages	Disadvantages
Algorithmic	Objective, repeatable, efficient, analyzable formula Good for sensitivity analysis Objectively calibrated to experience	Subjective inputs Does not accommodate exceptional circumstances Assumes history predicts future applications
Expert Judgment	Assessment of representativeness, interactions, and exceptional circumstances can be factored into the judgment	No better than participants Biases, incomplete recall Representativeness of experience
Analogy	Based on experience	No better than participants Biases, incomplete recall Representativeness of experience
Parkinson	Might relate to experience	Reinforces poor practice
Price to Win	Often wins the contract	Produces large overruns Unethical misrepresentation of information
Top-Down	System level focus Efficient use of resources	Less detailed and stable than other methods Overlooks technical complexity
Bottom-Up	More detailed basis More stable than top-down Fosters individual commitment when individual estimates own work	May overlook system level complexity and costs Requires more effort than most other methods
Function Points	Objective, repeatable, objective inputs	Based on history Must be calibrated Focuses on application externals

*Adapted from Boehm, Barry W., *Software Engineering Economics*. Englewood Cliffs, NJ: Prentice-Hall, 1981, p. 342.

similar over time, and accurate statistics of past project KDSI are maintained.

Project mode refers to a combination of size, staff, and technology. The three main project modes are organic, semidetached, and embedded (see Table 6-11). An **organic project** is developed by in-house staff, is small to medium in size, and uses existing, familiar technology.

A **semidetached project** is one that is developed by in-house staff and contractors, is intermediate to large in size, and uses technology that is familiar to some of the project team.

An **embedded project** is one that is developed by contractors, is medium to very large in size, and uses state-of-the-art technology which is new and unfamiliar to all project members.

The five project sizes referenced by CoCoMo are small, intermediate, medium, large, and very large. Each size has an average number of thousands of source instructions to which it relates (see Table

Effort = $Ao + A1X1 + \ldots AnXn$

Where An = Weight
Xn = Source of Cost n (e.g., Personnel time)

Ex.:

Effort = -3.6

+9 (2)	High Uncertainty of Requirements
+10.7 (2)	Unstable Design
+55.7 (1)	Concurrent Hardware Development
+15 (1)	New Technology
+29.55 (1)	Multiple Target Hardware Platforms
+2.2 (.6)	Percent I/O
+.52 (.4)	Percent Match Instructions
= 137.58	Person Months

FIGURE 6-10   Linear Estimating Formula and Example

Effort = $Ao\, A1^{x1} A2^{x2} \ldots An^{xn}$

Where An = Source of Cost n (e.g., Personnel time)
xn = -1, 0 or 1 depending on presence of cost

Ex.:

Effort = $.6\ *$

$* .95^{1}$	High Uncertainty of Requirements
$* 1.7^{1}$	Unstable Design
$* 5.5^{1}$	Concurrent Hardware Development
$* 15^{0}$	New Technology
$* 2.55^{1}$	Multiple Target Hardware Platforms
$* 100^{1}$	Person Months Test Code
= 1359	Person Months

FIGURE 6-11   Multiplicative Estimating Formula and Example

$N1\,N2N \log 2N\, /\, 2SN2$

Where:

N1	=	Number of Program operators (e.g., Add)
N2	=	Number of Program operands (e.g., Data Fields)
N	=	N1 + N2
S	=	Approximately 18
N2	=	ΣN2 usage, i.e., the number of time the operands are used in instructions
N	=	ΣN1 + ΣN2 usage

Example: If

N1	=	30
N2	=	1000
N	=	N1 + N2 = 30 + 1000 = 1030
S	=	Approximately 18
N2	=	ΣN2 usage = 2500
N	=	ΣN1 + ΣN2 = 1000 + 2500 = 3500

then $N1\,N2N \log 2N\, /\, 2SN2$

	=	$30 * 2500 * 3500 \log_2 1030 / 2 * 18 * 1000$
	=	75000 * 4.5 / 36000
	=	9.1 Person Months

FIGURE 6-12   Analytic Estimating Formula and Example

Estimate number of functions by type.
Estimate number of LOC for each function.
Table lookup of productivity.
Sum all time.
Distribute according to table formula.

Type	MM/1000 LOC*
Math	6 MM
Report	8 MM
Logic	12 MM
Signal/Process Control	20 MM
Real-Time Control	40 MM

Example:

5	Math functions	=	2000 LOC
15	Reports	=	8000 LOC
25	Logic functions	=	5000 LOC
6	Signal control functions	=	1200 LOC
0	Real-time control	=	0 LOC

= (2*6) + (8*8) + (12*5) + (20*1.2)
= 12 + 64 + 60 + 24
= 160 MM

*MM = Person Months
LOC = Lines of Code

FIGURE 6-13 Tabular Estimating Formula and Example

TABLE 6-11 Three CoCoMo Project Modes

Organic	In-house developed
	Small–medium size
	Existing, familiar technology
Semidetached	Partially in-house and partially contractor developed
	Intermediate–large size
	Existing, familiar technology
Embedded	Contractor developed
	Medium–very large size
	State-of-the-art, unfamiliar technology

TABLE 6-12 Five CoCoMo Project Sizes

Size	Thousands of Lines of Source Code
Small	2
Intermediate	8
Medium	32
Large	128
Very Large	512+

From Boehm, Barry W., *Software Engineering Economics*. Englewood Cliffs, NJ: Prentice-Hall, Inc., 1981, p. 75.

6-12). Tables of the estimates, completed for each of the standard sizes, are provided in Boehm's book. These sizes provide a guide for calibrating nonstandard KDSI estimates.

To use CoCoMo, the mode is defined, KDSI are estimated, the formula for the matching project mode is computed. Table 6-13 shows the CoCoMo 'basic' formulae for each mode. The appeal of such a simple model is obvious. The model is reusable, objective, and simple to learn and use. The model's major source of uncertainty is in the need for an accurate estimate of KDSI. This difficulty of accurately estimating KDSI should not be minimized.

TABLE 6-13 CoCoMo Basic Formulae

Mode	Effort	Schedule
Organic	MM = $2.4(\text{KDSI}^{1.05})$	TDEV = $2.5(\text{MM}^{0.38})$
Semidetached	MM = $3.0(\text{KDSI}^{1.12})$	TDEV = $2.5(\text{MM}^{0.35})$
Embedded	MM = $3.6(\text{KDSI}^{1.20})$	TDEV = $2.5(\text{MM}^{0.32})$

MM = Person Months
TDEV = Time of Development

From Boehm, Barry W., *Software Engineering Economics*. Englewood Cliffs, NJ: Prentice-Hall, Inc., 1981, p. 75.

Next the multipliers are evaluated and used to modify the person-month estimate based on project specific factors (see Table 6-14). Risks, uncertainties, constraints, and staff experience are all evaluated to determine their potential impact on the schedule. The basic person-months estimate is multiplied by each relevant subjective multiplier to adjust for project contingencies.

Total months of effort is not very useful for a multiperson project unless there is also some way to know how much elapsed time the project should take and when to phase people onto and off of the project. CoCoMo provides these estimates. The second set of formulae are used to estimate total development time (TDEV) which accounts for multiple people working on the project. (Table 6-13 also shows the algorithms used to compute development effort.) To use these algorithms, you simply plug in the person-months value from the first formula into the TDEV formula matching the project mode.

Finally, the CoCoMo model includes a formula to estimate staffing levels over time in the shape of a Rayleigh (pronounced RAY-lee) curve. A Rayleigh curve (Figure 6-14) starts at some point above zero, increases to a high point, and gradually decreases to near zero. The formula for developing the number of people at any time requires an estimate of the time of the highest staffing level for the project (see Figure 6-14). This formula assumes a peak about one-third of the way into the elapsed time (TDEV).

TABLE 6-14   Sample CoCoMo Multipliers

Type Variance	Range of Multiplier
Product	
Reliability	.75–1.4
Data Base Size	.94–1.16
Software Complexity	.70–1.65
Computer	
Execution Time	1.00–1.66
Memory Constraints	1.00–1.56
OS Volatility	.87–1.3
Turnaround Time	.87–1.15
Project	
Modern	.82–1.24
Practice	
Use of Software Tools	.83–1.24
Schedule Constraints	1.10–1.23
Personnel	
Analyst Capability	.71–1.46
Programmer Capability	.70–1.42
Application Experience	.82–1.29
Operating System Experience	.90–1.21
Programming Language Experience	.95–1.14

Rate Each Cost Driver on a scale of 0 (Not applicable) to 5 (Highly applicable)

Multiply rating times multiplier to obtain final multiplier

Multiply MM Computation by final multiplier

From Boehm, Barry W., *Software Engineering Economics.* Englewood Cliffs, NJ: Prentice-Hall, Inc., 1981.

The advantages of any formula for estimating is that it is objective and repeatable (see Table 6-10). Further, they are easily understood and require little effort to use. The disadvantages are that the formulae all require some initial estimate that is *hard* to develop and frequently inaccurate. The formula might not fit the project and may be complicated to learn.

EXPERT JUDGMENT.   **Expert judgment estimating** is a technique by which the Project Manager and SE use their experience to guide the development of the time estimates. Each task is defined in terms of the program types likely to result from the task. Then, using their experience, the PM and SE assign times to each program, adding design time and analysis time.

For instance, assume there are 15 report programs. If a batch Cobol report interfacing with a DBMS averages one week to code and unit test, 3–5 days of design, and 2–4 days of analyses, then 15 reports will average 15 weeks for programming and one week is allocated per program. The other phase estimates are similar. A range of 30–60 days of analysis and of 45–75 days for design are allocated for the 15 reports. Similar estimates are made

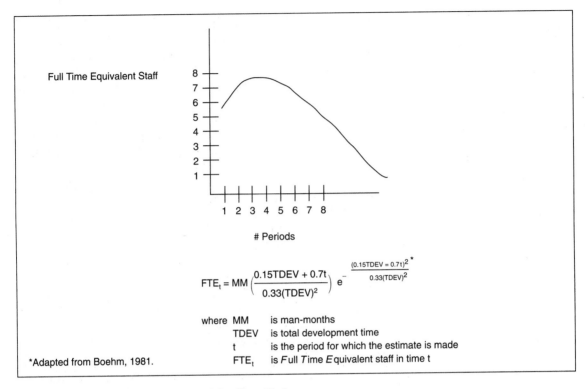

FIGURE 6-14   Rayleigh Curve of Staffing Estimates

for batch updates, on-line queries, on-line updates, and so forth.

When all program estimates are complete, the entire group is summarized to develop a project estimate. These are then presented as a range of estimates with the lowest number representing the optimistic schedule, the average number representing the most likely schedule, and the highest number representing a pessimistic schedule.

Costs are similarly assigned. Each program type is used to define the skill level of the desired programmer. For instance, a junior programmer might be assigned to batch reports, a senior programmer assigned to on-line processing, and a mid-level programmer to on-line reports. The times for each program type and programmer type are summed and multiplied by the cost of that level person. Similarly, the level of analyst or programmer-analyst needed for analysis and design of the tasks is estimated.

Finally, all costs are summed to develop a total cost for the project.

The advantages of expert judgment are the ability to factor experience into estimates, to tailor estimates to assigned personnel, and to develop estimates quickly and efficiently (see Table 6-10). The disadvantages are that the estimates are no better than the expertise of the PM and SE, they may be biased, are hard to rationalize, and not objectively repeatable. That is, the experience cannot be taught to others so two PM/SE teams estimating the same project will develop different estimates for the same problem. Finally, expert judgment is not useful in novel situations using new technology, methodology, or languages.

ANALOGY.   Analogical estimating is similar to applying experience. In **estimating** by **analogy**, a recently completed similar project is selected to act as a prototype baseline for developing cost estimates for a current proposed project. Costs are determined based on the match or mismatch of tasks and programs to the baseline. In other words, if a task is essentially the same, then the actual time of the task in the baseline project is used to estimate the actual time of the task for the proposed project. Analogy is applied to time, staff skill levels, and, eventually, resource, hardware, software, and other costs.

The advantage of analogy is that it is based on an actual, recent experience which can be studied for specific differences and only those differences require new cost estimates (see Table 6-10). The disadvantages of analogy are that the analogous project may not be representative of the proposed project, constraints, techniques, or functions. Some of the disadvantages can be reduced by matching project functions. This technique might work in large companies with many similar projects, but is not particularly useful in small companies, unique projects, or projects using new technology, methodology, or languages.

PARKINSON'S LAW.   **Parkinson's Law**[5] states that "Work expands to fill the available time." Based on this law, any time can be allocated and that is the time the project will take (see Table 6-10). For instance, there are 6 people available for 6 months, therefore the project will take 36 person-months. This is a cynical view of estimating that reinforces poor development practices by random assignment of time and people.

There are obvious flaws to Parkinson's Law. This method is likely to be grossly inaccurate in estimates generated (see Table 6-10). If people are allocated because they are available and not because they are needed, their skills are likely to be wasted and the project is more likely to be late. This method is *not* recommended.

PRICE-TO-WIN.   **Price-to-win** is a consultant strategy that uses a low estimate to obtain a job, with the implication that the time and cost will later be renegotiated. Like Parkinson's Law, this strategy is

not recommended. Price-to-win leads to forced user compromise on application requirements to try to meet a cost/time estimate, gives the consulting company bad public relations, always requires staff overtime, and most always results in cost overruns for both time and money.

You might ask, Why would anyone ever use a price-to-win strategy? Unfortunately, historical estimates by IS personnel are not very accurate unless combinations of modern techniques such as CoCoMo and function points are used *and* few problems occur on the project. Following this logic, people who use a price-to-win strategy usually believe any estimate is good as long as they get the job, since there is little relationship between real and estimated costs anyway. Frequently, in government projects especially, the lowest bid wins the job. This logic of choosing the lowest bid leads to price-to-win estimates. This has led to problems for several government entities.

TOP-DOWN.   Used with one or more of the other estimating techniques, **top-down estimates** use project properties to derive an estimate. Then total cost is split among the components. After a time estimate is derived, the 40-20-40 rule is applied to the estimate. According to the rule, 40% of project time is spent on analysis and design, 20% is spent on coding and unit testing, and 40% is spent on project testing.

The advantage of using a top-down approach is that, by focusing on global properties of the application, an estimate can be developed quickly—in a day or two. Using analogy to assess global properties, the proposed project is assumed similar to some other whole project. For instance, ABC's application is an on-line database application with create, change, delete, and query capabilities for all data, and an overall query facility for grouped data; system functions include start-up, shutdown, and monthly file maintenance processing.

The major disadvantage of a top-down approach is that the above description fits most on-line database applications (see Table 6-10). Such a high level focus cannot identify low level technical problems that drive up costs. For instance, in a complex database application, one particular data access need

---

5 Parkinson's Law was first published in 1957.

might require a month of design and prototyping time to prove that the concept works. This type of special process would be missed in a top-down estimate. Whole software components might be missed in the global assessment that, when developed, account for a disproportionate amount of time and cost. On balance, top-down estimates are less stable than more specific estimates.

BOTTOM-UP. The bottom-up approach takes the opposite view of an application from the top-down approach. Using a **bottom-up estimating** approach, each software component is identified and estimated, often by the person who would do the development. All individual component costs are summed to arrive at the estimated cost of the entire software product.

The bottom-up approach is as likely to miss components for development as the top-down approach (see Table 6-10). At the low level, integration work to combine modules and programs may not be estimated or is easily underestimated. Also, the bottom-up approach requires significantly more effort to develop because every module, program, screen, database interaction, and so on must be identified for estimating.

The advantages of the bottom-up approach are that the estimates are based on a more detailed understanding of the project than the other methods, and, when estimated by the person doing the work, the estimates are backed by a professional's commitment.

FUNCTION POINTS. The function point method takes an organizational history approach to estimating. **Function points** are a measure of complexity based on global application characteristics. A baseline developed by analyzing all previous applications is developed for each type application. The baseline number of function points is divided by the actual cost/time of development to get an estimate for one function point per application type (or language, or person-month). New applications are analyzed to determine an estimate of the number of function points in the project. Then, the base time and cost estimates for one function point are multiplied by the number of estimated function points for the proposed application to develop a total time and cost estimate.

Function point analysis rests on the ability of the project team to predict the inputs, outputs, queries, interfaces, and files. Figure 6-15 shows the counts and weights assigned for each type of I/O. Each item is counted and weighted for complexity. The weighted counts are summed.

Then a series of 14 questions to determine different types of application complexity are evaluated on a scale of zero to five to measure increasing importance of the item to the application (see Table 6-15). The answers to the 14 questions are also summed. The summed complexity weights and weighted counts are combined in one formula shown below to compute the total function points for a project.

Application Item	Count	Simple	Average	Complex	FP = Count * Weight
# Inputs (i.e., Trans Types)		3	4	6	
# Outputs (i.e., Reports, Screens)		4	5	7	
# Programmed Inquiries		3	4	6	
# Files / Relations		7	10	15	
# Application Interfaces		5	7	10	

From Pressman, Roger S., *Software Engineering: A Practitioner's Approach*, third edition. NY: McGraw-Hill, 1992, p. 49. Adapted with permission of McGraw-Hill.

FIGURE 6-15   Function Point Weighted Count Table

TABLE 6-15   Function Point Questions and Rating Scale*

Rating Scale from 0 (No influence) to 5 (Essential)

Factor Questions:

1. Is reliable backup and recovery required?
2. Are data communications required?
3. Are any functions distributed?
4. Is performance critical?
5. Is operational environment volume high?
6. Is on-line data entry required?
7. Does on-line data entry require multiple screens or operations?
8. Is on-line files update used?
9. Are queries, screens, reports, or files complex?
10. Is processing complex?
11. Is code design for reuse?
12. Does implementation include conversion and installation?
13. Are multiple installations and/or multiple organizations involved?
14. Does application design facilitate user changes? How integral is ease of use?

*From Pressman, Roger S., *Software Engineering: A Practitioner's Approach*, third edition. NY: McGraw-Hill, 1992, p. 50. Adapted with permission of McGraw-Hill.

$$FP = \text{Total weighted count} * (.65 + (0.1 * \Sigma(\text{complexity adjustments})))$$

Function points have become popular enough that several companies and software packages are available for developing function point estimates. In addition, tables of function points per number of lines of code are also available. For instance, 100 lines of Cobol is equal to 20 lines of Focus is equal to one function point. Translating function points into lines of code, then, requires a simple table lookup.

The appeal of function points is similar to that of CoCoMo. Any algorithmic method is likely to be easy to use, understand, and repeat (see Table 6-10). An algorithm gives the appearance of objectivity

that other methods do not. Of course, the function point estimate has flaws similar to those of CoCoMo, too. Function points must be calibrated for the organization based on its history of project development. It assumes that history predicts the future. Further, it assumes similar technology and skills across projects. The model assumes that methodology and CASE have no impact on project development time.

To summarize, there are several useful methods of project person-month or lines-of-code estimating. The most popular are expert judgment, analogy, CoCoMo, function points, top-down, and bottom-up. All of these methods have advantages and disadvantages. If a history of projects and function points is kept, that appears to be the most accurate estimating technique at the moment. If function points are not calibrated to the company's history, no one estimating technique is better than any other. Rather, the methods might be paired or used several at a time to develop estimates that are closer to reality than estimates developed using any one method alone.

Planning Guidelines

In the absence of calibrated function points for ABC, we will discuss the use of several methods in developing a plan for an application. By combining the methods, the schedule and plan developed should be better than using any one plan on its own.

Several variations for combining estimating techniques are feasible. They are:

1. Estimate inputs, outputs, interfaces, queries, and files according to function point directions.
2. Answer 14 questions and estimate project complexity.
3. Compute function points.
4. Lookup lines of code per function point (FP) in language table and compute total lines of code (LOC) for the project.
5. Decide the CoCoMo mode.
6. Using FP LOC as input to the CoCoMo model, compute person months of effort.
7. Analyze multipliers and adjust the estimate.
8. Compute total development time and project staffing estimates using the other CoCoMo formula.

If the company uses function point analysis for its baseline, function point planning is the first type performed. Then, the plan can be compared to the CoCoMo model estimates to verify its goodness of fit. Alternatively, the project manager can develop a top-down plan while the SE and any other project staff working on the feasibility develop a bottom-up plan by using the following steps:

1. PM and SE together estimate the development approach and all functions in the application.
2. PM uses top-down analysis to develop a list of activities to be performed and the times for each.
3. From this list, deliverable products and a schedule are developed.
4. The list is analyzed to determine task dependencies, and a first-cut critical path chart is developed.
5. Concurrently with steps two to four, the SE analyzes each function bottom-up to determine the complexity, possible problems, nondeliverable programs, and amount of effort to be assigned to each technical task.
6. Any new tasks identified by either the PM or SE are added to the plan and estimated. The SE and PM compare and adjust their time estimates until they agree.

Another alternative is to combine expert judgment, analogy, top-down, and bottom-up to develop a first set of estimates. Then, these estimates are compared to the standard function point estimate for a *reality check*. If the expert estimate is more than 15% lower than the function point estimate, then the plan should probably be revised upward. In this section, we use expert judgment and analogy, using a top-down approach to develop the estimate, then do a bottom-up analysis of each piece to ensure they are all present.

The steps to developing a plan are:

1. Decide the Development Life Cycle (DLC), approach, and methodology.
2. For each phase, list the deliverable products that mark completion of the phase.

3. Decide on information gathering technique(s) and use of JAD, prototyping, or other variants to DLC.
4. Decide which products the technical project team members will develop and which the users will develop.
5. Define dependencies and develop CPM chart.
6. Assign times to tasks and compute total project time.
7. Estimate inputs, outputs, interfaces, queries, and files according to function point directions.
8. Answer 14 questions and estimate project complexity.
9. Compute function points.
10. Lookup lines of code per function point (FP) in language table and compute total lines of code (LOC) for the project.
11. Estimate productivity in LOC/month.
12. Compare FP number of person months to the estimated total time.
13. Adjust time estimates, as required, and complete the CPM diagram by adding times.

For instance, assume the waterfall is followed and the phases include Feasibility, Analysis, Design, Program Design, Code/Unit Test, System Testing, Acceptance Testing, and Installation. Then, list deliverable products. Phases might have more than one deliverable product. Products usually coincide with the ending of life cycle phases. Products for these phases include a feasibility report, functional requirements specification, design specification, program specifications, plans for testing, conversion, training, and implementation, operational documentation, and user documentation.

From the choices in Chapter 4, decide the approach to information gathering. If you use JAD, for instance, the amount of time allocated to analysis is less than if you use interviews over time. Decide the overall system design approach. Is prototyping needed? How involved will users be in the development process? How extensive will user training be? Will CASE be used? Which tool? (Some tools add analysis and design time, some reduce it). How extensive are documents expected to be? Is on-line *help* software going to replace user manuals? Who is responsible for planning and executing the conversion? How much data *scrubbing* to remove errors from existing data is required? The answers to these questions increase or decrease the time allocated for each task.

Next decide which products the technical project team members will develop and which the users will develop. These tasks are estimated just as the technical team tasks are estimated, but they are also singled out for several reasons. First, the dependencies should clearly show the split of assignments for the technical team and users. Second, users should be allowed to comment on tasks for which they are responsible. The technical team usually takes responsibility for the tasks if the users will not take it.

Develop a list of tasks and define dependencies, developing a critical path chart for the project. Assign times to tasks. Compute function points. Using an estimate of LOC per month per person on the project, compute a total project time, and compare the FP estimate to your estimate. Adjust your estimate as required if it is more than 15% less than the FP estimate. In general, always use a higher estimate rather than a lower one. Project schedules have a way of losing time for meetings, nonproject responsibilities, and other legitimate, but nonproductive uses of time.

Now, let's go through each step to using combined techniques for estimating. To develop a critical path diagram, list the tasks on a sheet of paper. Begin with high level tasks, or tasks of a single phase, adding lower level tasks as they come to mind. Development of the task list requires some experience and is always done more easily by several people rather than one who is likely to forget some critical task. The task list, in critical path method terms, is called a **work breakdown**.

Define durations for each task. Durations may be an absolute number or a range of time. The critical path method recommends the identification of optimistic, likely, and pessimistic estimates. Then, the weighted formula ((Optimistic + 4(Likely) + Pessimistic) / 6) is applied to develop one number for use in financial analysis and software planning tools. Use either method for developing the time. Planning

software packages allow early, most likely, and latest possible dates to be entered. For some software you enter the project completion date and the software computes the early and late dates for tasks based on their durations.

Extend the times to develop dates at which each task is expected. A work breakdown shows the earliest start and end dates for each task, plus the latest start and end dates per task. The early dates assume that each preceding task took the minimum estimated number of days. The latest start and end dates assume that each preceding task took the maximum estimated number of days.

Next, create the CPM chart (see Figure 6-16). List all tasks on a piece of paper. Draw lines from later tasks to early tasks on which they are dependent. By dependent tasks, we mean those tasks that cannot be begun until information (or products or approvals) from the previous task are complete. The early task *feeds* the later one.

When the diagram is complete, compute the time to complete each *leg* of the diagram. The leg with the longest time is the critical path, that is, the tasks on which meeting the deadline for the project depends. If any one of the critical path tasks is late, the project will be late. When monitoring the project, the critical tasks get priority. When assigning staff to tasks, the critical tasks should be assigned the most experienced and skilled personnel.

Some sensitivity analysis on critical path and on task dependencies might be done, if using an automated tool for the analysis. Manual analysis is so time-consuming that it may not be worth the effort. The impact of different end dates is analyzed. For instance, if the user were to mandate a date two months earlier than the estimated end date, what is the impact on the project and tasks? Does the critical path change? Can other tasks, not fully analyzed, be made more parallel? Can any dependencies be removed by altering the plan or tasks? If the project suffers penalties (loss of revenue) from not meeting deadlines, the risks for each task might be reassessed to ensure that nothing is missed. The project manager continues this type of analysis until he or she is comfortable with the result.

After the critical path is identified, staff should be assigned to each task to complete project planning.

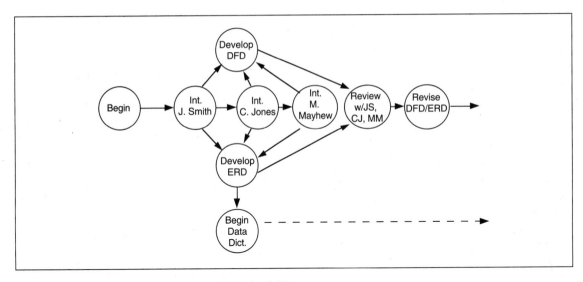

FIGURE 6-16   Sample Critical Path Method Chart

Assign people to minimize the amount of slack time for which they have no assignments, but allow some slack time in case problems arise. Assign the critical tasks first, allocating them to the best, most experienced people. A general rule of thumb is that, in absence of artificially short deadlines, people can be assigned to develop a whole *leg* of the critical path. The purpose for assigning sequential tasks in a leg are to leverage the knowledge gained from early tasks to later tasks, and to provide each individual a sense of contribution to the overall project by allowing them to take responsibility for a large *chunk* of work.

When the estimates are complete, develop a function point estimate, or have someone else do it in parallel. Weight the FP estimate by the answers to the 14 questions. Lookup the lines of code (LOC) per function point (FP) in a table (see Figure 6-17).[6] Estimate your productivity in LOC per month; for instance, 1000 LOC/Month for a 4GL is not uncommon. If your company keeps statistics, use its historical numbers for project type and language. Compute total person-months for the project using the formulae in Figure 6-18. Compare the FP estimate to your estimate and adjust as needed. Don't just blindly take the higher number. Rather, a difference means that information was interpreted dif-

---

6 Refer to Capers Jones' 1986 book, *Programming Productivity*, for extensive tables with this information.

Lines of Code/FP	Language
25	4 GL
25	SQL
100	Cobol

FIGURE 6-17   Example of LOC/FP for Different Languages

Number of Lines of Code per Function Point *
Number of Function Points = Total Lines of Code

Example   25 LOC/FP (4GL) * 100 = 2500 LOC

Total Lines of Code / Lines of Code per Month
= Number of Person Months

Example   2500 LOC / 1000 per Month = 2.5 Person
          Months

FIGURE 6-18   Function Point Computations for Total Person Months

ferently by the two methods of estimating. See if you can find what is different and which estimate is more realistic.

Use the 40-20-40 rule to check if the effort *looks* like it is reasonable across the phases. Analysis/design should be about 40% of effort if manual and 55% if using CASE. Code/unit test is about 20% effort if manual and 5% if a CASE tool generates code. System testing should be 30–40%. Testing estimates are usually low. If testing is the difference, ask if there is some reason to be optimistic, for instance, a skilled programmer. If the difference cannot be found, and the percentages are allocated about right, then changing your estimate is a judgment call.

For manual allocation of staff to a project, a list of tasks in CPM *legs* should be created and a person's name assigned to each task. This allows easy tracking of assignments and dates at which people rotate on and off the project. If using an automated tool, allocation of staff usually requires entry of the person's name and assignment of tasks by CPM ID. In either case, as people are assigned to tasks, note who they are and when they begin (and end) project work. Make sure you do not change the critical path by the assignment of personnel to overlapping or conflicting duration tasks.

Upon completion of task assignments, a Gantt Chart is developed to summarize the project. A **Gantt Chart** shows the entire set of project tasks, people assigned, and completion times estimated for the development effort (see Figure 6-19). A list of people and amount of time assigned to the project is created for use in the costing activity.

Scheduled Task	1	2	3	4	5	6	7	8	9	10	11	12	13	14	15	16	17	18	19
Interviews																			
J. Smith		SB	SB				S												
C. Jones				SB	SB		B												
M. Mayhew					SB	SB	S												
Develop DFDs		S –	– –	– –	– –	– –	S												
Define Data and ERD		B –	– –	– –	– –	– –	B												
Review and Revise DFD and ERD							SB	SB											
Begin Data Dict.		SB –	– –	– –	– –	– –	– –	– –	– –	– –	– –	– –	– –	– –	– –	– –	SB		
Define Problems w/Current System								SS											
Define Business Opportunities									BB										

Legend:

B = Barbara James, SE
S = Stan Smits, PM/SE

Where initials alternate, both Barbara and Stan participate in the activity.

FIGURE 6-19   Sample Gantt Chart

ABC Video Implementation Plan

ABC's rental application is a fairly average project with no obvious complexities, no state-of-the-art technologies, and a single, small organization. Mary, the PM, and Sam, the SE, decide to use a combination of analogy, top-down, and bottom-up and to check their estimate with function points based on the estimate of 25 LOC/FP for a 4GL. Before Mary and Sam begin, they first decide their approach and assumptions on which the estimates are based.

The project is expected to be implemented on a Novell ethernet LAN using PCs as workstations and a superserver (50 Mhz, 486-based machine). The software environment will be some SQL language with custom application software. There will be four main files, corresponding to the four main entities in the ERD. The main processing centers around

rental activity with standard maintenance procedures for the other files. Other files, which will be maintained during rental processing, include history and an end-of-day summary of transactions. The application will accommodate up to ten concurrent users for all processing.

If two people are estimating, as Sam and Mary are, a good approach is to split the two types of estimates between the individuals. Sam would do one and Mary the other. Then they compare and rationalize their work.

First, we develop a function point estimate for the work. The function point estimate (see Figure 6-20) shows that the project is not very complex in any of the key inputs or outputs. The weighting questions identify the on-line, interactive, and multiuser characteristics as contributing the greatest complexity to the application. The total function points are esti-

Application Item	Count	Simple	Average	Complex	FP = Count * Weight
# Inputs (i.e., Trans Types)	5	3	(4)	6	20
# Outputs (i.e., Reports, Screens)	6	4	(5)	7	30
# Programmed Inquiries	6	(3)	4	6	18
# Files / Relations	8	7	(10)	15	80
# Application Interfaces	(0)	5	7	10	0
				Total	148

Factor Questions	Score	
Reliable backup and recovery	4	
Data communications	0	
Distributed functions	0	
Critical performance	4	
High volume operations environment	4	
On-line data entry	5	
Multiple data entry screens or operations	5	
On-line file update	4	
Complex queries, screens, reports, or files	0	
Complex processing	4	
Reusable code design	0	FP = Total Weighted Count *
Conversion and installation	4	(.65 + (.01 * Σ(Complexity Adjustments)))
Multiple installations and/or multiple organizations	0	= 148 * (.65 + (.01 * 37))
User change; ease of use	3	= 148 * (.65 + .37)
Total	37	= 151 Function Points

FIGURE 6-20   ABC Function Point Estimate

mated at 151. Carrying the FP analysis through, at 25/LOC per function point, there are about 3775 LOC (i.e., 25 * 151) for the project. At a productivity rate of 2000 per month, the total number of person months for the project is about 1.9 months (i.e., 3775/2000). The estimate of 2,000 LOC/month is a company statistic based on the average productivity of each of the project participants.

Mary, in parallel, creates a task list which she converts into a work breakdown. The work breakdown identifies the tasks to complete the project, and the optimistic, likely, and pessimistic times for each task (see Table 6-16). The most likely time for each task is then computed and a total time for the project is estimated.

At this point, the two sets of estimates should be compared. The FP estimate suggests 1.9 person-months, while the work breakdown estimate of 172 hours translates into slightly under one month (25 days). The FP estimate is almost twice as high. Let's see where the differences might lie. At the end of Table 6-16, the total times for each phase are shown with percentages of the total computed for each number. The percentages do not follow the 40-20-40 rule closely. The realistic estimate shows 46% of time for analysis and design, 32% for coding and unit testing, and 22% for system testing. The estimate for system testing is low relative to the rule while the other estimates are somewhat inflated. Mary knows she and Sam are the only two people who are expected to work on the project and she based her estimates on their ability to debug and test quickly. But even she cannot defend this low number to Sam. Sam also points out that, if Vic wants much documentation, her estimates for all the tasks might be low. Mary has assumed that Vic, being a small company owner, will opt for less documentation to save on the expense.

On the other hand, Sam identified several complexities with which Mary takes issue, in particular with the difficulty of on-line update and the difficulty of interactive programming. Both of these were given a '5' rating of complexity. Mary feels that if the application were on a mainframe and using mainframe software and tools, the fives would be justified. Since the application platform is a LAN with which they have extensive experience, she feels

that the highest rating should be a four. This would then reduce the FP estimate. Both Mary and Sam discuss their estimates, defending their reasoning processes and subjecting them to criticism by their partner. In the end, they confirm with Vic that he does want only minimal documentation, and they decide to split the difference on their estimates adding a total of 90 hours to the project. Of that time, 18 hours (20%) is allocated to code/unit test and the remaining 72 hours (80%) to testing of the project. The final estimates would then show code/unit test time of 73 hours (28% of total) and testing time of 110 hours (42% of total). While these percentages are now slightly skewed away from analysis and design, which is now 30% of the total, these percentages are in line with the 4GL need to do less analysis and design. The total estimated project time used in the financial estimates will be 262 hours or 1.5 person-months.

The final work breakdown is converted into a CPM diagram to identify the critical path of work (see Figure 6-21 for the Analysis CPM). Based on the critical path, contingencies are planned to ensure meeting of the schedule. Figure 6-22 is a Gantt chart for analysis showing how Mary and Sam split their responsibilities.

If project planning software were used, the CPM is built first, then selection of an option converts the CPM into the work breakdown. To create either diagram, the tasks and durations must be known. Sophisticated software supports the insertion of a start date for the project and, based on the optimistic and pessimistic task durations, and on the dependencies from the CPM, the software computes all the dates for the project.

Evaluate Financial Feasibility

Financial Feasibility Analysis

Financial feasibility analysis evaluates the firm's ability to pay for a project, and compares recommended alternatives to determine which is more economically attractive. In general, projects are economically feasible when the sum of all IS projects plus the proposed project is less than 10% of firm net

TABLE 6-16   ABC Work Breakdown with Durations

Task: Analysis	Optimistic	Likely	Pessimistic	(O+4L+P)/6
Define Customer Maintenance Processing	2	3	4	3
Define Video Maintenance Processing	2	3	4	3
Define Rental Process	1	2	3	2
Define Return Process	1	2	3	2
Define How Intertwined	2	3	4	3
Define History	1	2	3	2
Define EODay, Audit, Trans Log	2	3	4	3
Define Cust Create, Video Create in Rental	1	2	3	2
Define Error Msgs, Abort Procedures	1	2	3	2
Define Screen Contents	2	4	6	4
Define Flow of Processing	1	2	3	2
Define Start-up/Shutdown	1	2	3	2
Define File Purge	.5	1	1.5	1
Define Backup/Recovery	.5	1	1.5	1
Define Conversion/Training	1	2	3	2
Analysis Total Time	**19**	**34**	**49**	**34**

Task: Design	Optimistic	Likely	Pessimistic	(O+4L+P)/6
Cust Maint Process	2	3	4	3
Video Maint Process	2	3	4	3
Rent/Return Includes: Display, Data entry, Retrieval, Payment, Accounting, File Update, History, EOD, Audit, Controls	7	11	21	12
Screens	10	14	16	15
Start-up/Shutdown	4	6	12	6
Backup/Recovery	1	1	1	1
Conversion, Training	2	5	8	5
Design Total Time	**28**	**43**	**66**	**45**

income. This uses industry averages as the guideline. To compare alternatives, several methods discussed in this section are used.

Cost-benefit analysis is the comparison of the financial gains and payments that would result from selection of some alternative. The analysis facilitates comparison of alternatives for one project or alternative projects.

Criteria used in alternative comparisons might be maximizing benefits, ratio of benefits to costs, net

TABLE 6-16   ABC Work Breakdown with Durations (*Continued*)

Task: Code/Unit Test	Optimistic	Likely	Pessimistic	(O+4L+P)/6
Cust Maint Process	2	4	6	4
Video Maint Process	2	4	6	4
Rent/Return Includes: Display, Data entry, Retrieval, Payment, Accounting, File Update, History, EOD, Audit, Controls	8	14	28	15
Screens	5	10	15	10
Start-up/Shutdown	8	10	12	10
Backup/Recovery	1	2	3	2
Conversion, Training	5	10	15	10
Code/Unit Test Total Time	**31**	**54**	**85**	**55**

Task: Testing	Optimistic	Likely	Pessimistic	(O+4L+P)/6
Scaffolding	2	4	5	4
Screen test	2	4	6	4
Subsystem Test	7	14	21	15
System Test	7	14	21	15
Testing Total Time	**18**	**36**	**53**	**38**

Project Totals by Phase	Optimistic	Likely	Pessimistic	(O+4L+P)/6
Analysis Total Time	19 19%	34 20%	49 19%	44 20%
Design Total Time	28 29%	43 26%	66 26%	45 26%
Code/Unit Test Total Time	31 32%	54 32%	85 34%	55 32%
Testing Total Time	18 19%	36 22%	53 21%	38 22%
Project Total Time	96 100%	167 100%	253 100%	172 100%

benefits, minimizing costs for given level of benefit, or maximizing project internal rate of return. The most popular criterion is maximizing net benefits, which requires analysis of the present value of benefits and costs.

Three types of costs are considered: acquisition, development, and operating costs are all considered in the development of the cost-benefit analysis. Several different sources of costs relate to each of these cost types:

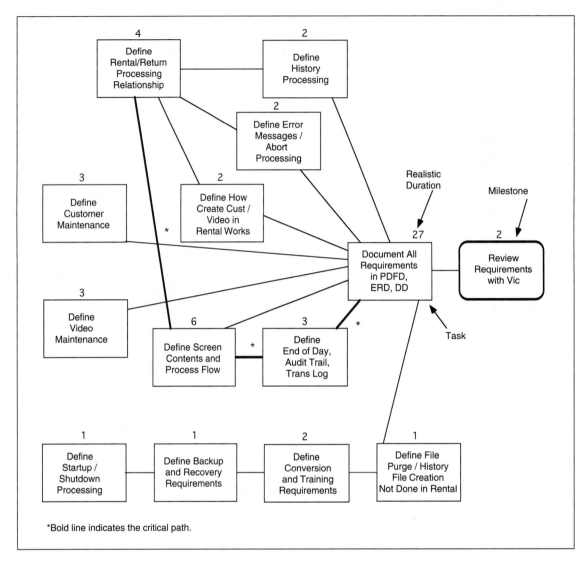

FIGURE 6-21   ABC CPM Chart for Analysis Activities

Acquisition Costs
   Consulting
   Equipment
   Software
   Site preparation
   Installation
   Capital
   Management staff assigned to acquisition
Development Costs
   Application development

Education of personnel
   Testing
   Conversion
   Losses relating to changeover, downtime,
     reruns
   Aggravation cost
Operating Costs
   Personnel allocated for maintenance
   Hardware operating expense (e.g., air
     conditioning, electricity, etc.)

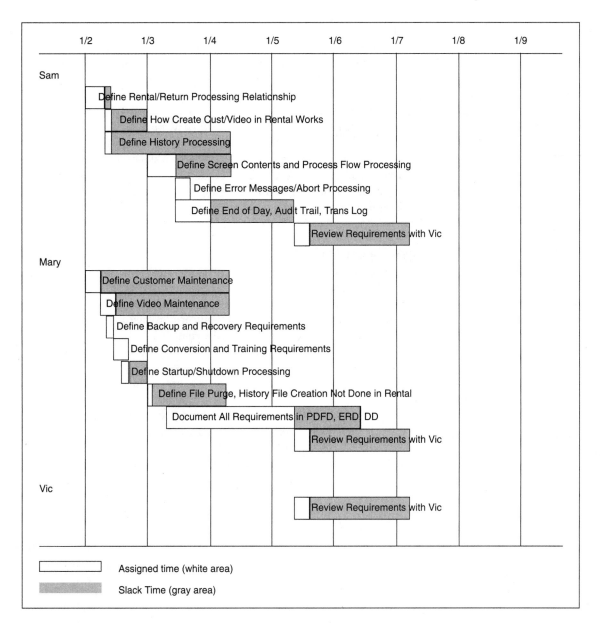

FIGURE 6-22   ABC Gantt Chart for Analysis Phase

Lease/rental costs
Depreciation on related capital acquisitions
Operating personnel overhead

In general, any time you spend money, a cost is generated. Whether the money is for salaries, personnel benefits, copy machine rental, PC acquisition, oper-

ating system acquisition, DBMS acquisition, and so forth, a cost is generated. The breakdown of costs into acquisition, development, and operating categories allows managers to do sensitivity analysis on alternatives. For instance, Alternative A might have a high acquisition cost relating to hardware site preparation and expense, whereas Alternative B has none. If the benefits are greater with Alternative A, we might ask if the acquisition of hardware is justified by the extra benefits relating to Alternative A.

All of the costs of each alternative are assembled according to type for the analysis. Depreciation schedules, leasing schedules, and any ancillary information relating to how costs are generated over time are also used in the analysis.

Similarly, all information about benefits expected from the application are assembled for the analysis. Benefits are identified as 'one time' or as continuous improvements. If a stream of revenues is generated over time by the application, these are identified as annual revenues.

The net present value formula is applied to the benefits and costs to develop a net present value for the application (see Figure 6-23). The formula accounts for the time value of money in computing the net benefits over costs. If inflation or fluctuating interest are expected, the interest rates might be changed for each time period to account for such fluctuations. Keep in mind that exactly the same analysis is required for all competing alternatives to ensure consistent NPVs. The example shown in Figure 6-23 shows a project for which the benefits outweigh the costs; such a project would be desirable.

The problems arise when a project does not generate a favorable NPV, but *numbers alone do not express project value*. Benefits may be insufficient to pay for the project. For instance, in complying with government regulations, there may be no specific benefits to the company. Similarly, when responding to a competitive need, the benefits might not outweigh the costs, but the cost of not doing the project might be the loss of the business. Start-up companies frequently build applications to support anticipated work; the applications might not be profitable until they are several years old. Benefits from such applications are difficult, if not impossible, to quantify because of the uncertainty associated with a new business. Finally, companies wishing to gain significant competitive advantage must frequently undertake a financially unjustifiable project to obtain their goals. American Airlines, for instance, in developing their $1 billion airline reservation system was betting that their ability to gain market share would outweigh their expenses. The financial analysis could not justify the project because of the high level of intangible benefits and the difficulty in estimating their worth. The risk paid off, but could just as easily have backfired. That is the nature of risk and why good managers develop skill in knowing when such a risky project is worth attempting.

Make/Buy and Other Types of Analysis

Other types of analysis that might be developed are make/buy, internal rate of return, and payback period. Each of these uses NPV as a starting point for determining the value of a project. Each develops a different analysis. Make versus buy decisions evaluate two types of development alternatives. First, make/buy compares the value of a customized application to the purchase of a software package. This sounds like a simple comparison, when in fact, it is not. Purchasing software for a complex application usually requires customizing and alteration. Packages are rarely used *off-the-shelf*. Consequently,

---

$NPV = \Sigma(\,(B_t - C_t)/(1 + d)^t\,)$

where: t is the time period, varying from 1 to n
        d is the discounted interest rate
        B is the value of period benefits
        C is the value of period costs

Example: $d = .08$

t	B_t	C_t	$(1 + d)^t$
1	0	50,000	1.0000
2	10,000	5,000	1.0800
3	30,000	5,000	1.1664
4	50,000	5,000	1.2597

$NPV = -(50,000/1)$
$+ \; 5,000/1.08$
$+ \; 25,000/1.1664$
$+ \; 45,000/1.2597$

$= -50,000 + 4,629 + 21,433 + 35,722$
$= \$11,784$

FIGURE 6-23   Net Present Value Formula and Computation

the analysis concentrates on the extent to which changes to the package are required and the cost of purchase plus changes versus the cost of custom development.

Second, make/buy is also used to compare the competitive value of building a software product internally versus development by a consulting firm. Occasionally companies which charge for in-house IS development services begin to overcharge their users. Users are then justified in obtaining competitive bids from consulting companies and using their services when the cost is less.

Internal rate of return (IRR) is a financial analysis of NPV such that positive cash flows (i.e., benefits) are equated to negative cash flows (i.e., costs). This means that the d, discount rate, in the NPV formula is found. This gives the true cost of funds for this particular project. When projects have similar NPVs, an IRR analysis identifies differences in cost of money based on when the cash flows are generated that might differentiate the alternatives.

Payback period is the number of years required to recover the investment (acquisition and development) costs from projected benefit cash flows. The payback period might decrease revenues for the time value of money or might use a simple analysis of payback. Payback analysis is popular because it is easily understood. It can discriminate against projects which have a long lead time to realizing benefits, but should not be the primary criterion for project selection decisions. In the example shown in Figure 6-23, the payback period would be 3 years and 2.4 months. This number is arrived at by identifying $10,000 in year 4 as contributing to the payback along with all benefits in years 2 and 3. 10,000 is 20% of 50,000, the fourth year's projected return. Therefore, 20% of 12 months is 2.4 months. The payback, rounded, is 3 years and 3 months.

Document the Recommendations

The documentation of the feasibility study pulls together all information relevant in developing the final recommendation. The purpose of the *summary* document is to provide managers a basis for decid-

ing whether or not to continue with the development effort. With this thought in mind, the feasibility document should contain mainly supporting diagrams, lists, and summary analyses. Text should be kept to a minimum to explain the attached diagrams and analyses. An outline of a feasibility document is provided in Table 6-17.

TABLE 6-17   Feasibility Report Outline

1.0 Management Summary

2.0 Current Environment

    2.1 Business Environment

    2.2 Work Procedures

    2.3 Evaluation of Strengths and Weaknesses of Current Procedures

3.0 Proposed Solution

    3.1 Scope of Proposed Solution

    3.2 Functional Requirements Overview

4.0 Technical Alternatives

    4.1 Alternative 1

        4.1.1 Description of Alternative

        4.1.2 Benefits of Alternative

        4.1.3 Risks of Alternative

    4.2 Alternative 2 . . .

    4.n Alternative n

5.0 Recommended Technical Solution

    5.1 Comparison of Alternatives

        5.1.1 Technical Comparison

        5.1.2 Benefits Comparison

        5.1.3 Risk Comparison

        5.1.4 Recommendation and Risk Contingency Plan

6.0 Project Plan

    6.1 Critical Path Chart

    6.2 Staffing Plan

7.0 Costs

    7.1 Cost of Recommended Alternative Hardware/Software

    7.2 Projected Staffing Cost

    7.3 Analysis of Alternatives (if necessary)

The Management Summary section is the most important because it is the only item read by most of the audience. Therefore, it should be brief, less than two pages, and should summarize the remainder of the document. In particular, the cost, NPV, other financial analyses, scope, purpose, technical recommendation, and importance of the project to the organization are highlighted in the summary section. All organizations involved in the development effort and the nature of their involvement should be highlighted.

The remaining sections summarize each of the main activities completed during the feasibility study. The current environment and proposed alternatives are described in sufficient detail to give the reader an understanding of the differences proposed. This section identifies hardware, operating environment, software, items for custom development, and requirements met by the alternative. Benefits and risks associated with each alternative are also listed and discussed to trace the reasoning leading to a selection.

The section on the recommended technical solution is more detailed than the alternatives discussion and discusses different topics. The tasks, key features, and development life cycle, methodology, and concept are highlighted in the proposed application section. In addition, the discussion lists constraints, assumptions, level of security, recovery, and auditability for the recommended solution. A contingency plan for minimizing the probability and for dealing with risks of the recommended alternative are detailed. Potential impediments to successful development, such as decisions or information not currently available, are identified. Ideally, the person responsible for resolving the outstanding issues is named and dates for resolution are identified.

The project plan section summarizes the planning effort. A critical path chart and staffing plan are presented with any attendant assumptions and requirements. Finally, the costs of the recommended alternative(s) and the financial analysis are detailed. Any assumptions, for instance, the discount rate for NPV, are listed. If sensitivity analysis was performed, the extent to which the estimates are sensitive and the source of sensitivity are identified. Sources of sensitivity might include, for instance, interest rates, economic fluctuation, or the presence of a key salesperson.

AUTOMATED SUPPORT TOOLS FOR FEASIBILITY ANALYSIS

There are two classes of tools that support the work performed during feasibility analysis: planning tools and analysis tools. Analysis tools can span any of the three methodologies covered in this text and are discussed in the respective methodology analysis section.

The planning tools might include project estimating products, project scheduling products, risk analysis products, or spreadsheets for financial analysis. Spreadsheets are general purpose and are not discussed here. Estimating products are based on an algorithmic method from those discussed above. Products based on CoCoMo estimating, Rayleigh curve, and function point techniques are included in the list. The tools assume that the underlying input information, for instance, KLOC, is known by some other, unspecified technique.

Planning products assume that a work breakdown with task duration assignment exists. The work breakdown planning tools support the definition of tasks, task interrelationships, assignment of staff, determination of early and late start dates, expected end dates, and cost of resources. From this information, the tool can generate Gantt Charts, critical path networks, cost summaries, and manpower planning guides. There are many good project management software products of both types on the market, several of which are listed in Table 6-18.

Two risk analysis products are included in the summary list. These products walk you through the assignment of risk types, probability of risk occurrence, and cost of the risk to develop a monetary value of risks related to the project. The cost of risk is factored into the financial analysis. More products of this type should be expected to be available as companies become more sophisticated in

TABLE 6-18   Automated Tools to Support Project Planning

Product	Company	Technique
DEC Plan	Digital Equipment Corp. Maynard, MA	CoCoMo Based Estimation Tool
ESTIMACS	Computer Associates, Inc. Long Island, New York	Function Point estimates extrapolated to include staffing, cost, risk, hardware configuration, and cost estimating
Harvard Project Manager	Harvard Graphics Corp. Boston, MA	Pert, CPM, and Gantt Charts Resource Allocation and Tracking
MacProject	Apple Computer Cupertino, CA	Pert, CPM, and Gantt Charts Resource Allocation and Tracking
ProMap V	LOG/AN, Inc.	Risk Analysis
RISNET	J. M. Cockerman Associates	Risk Analysis
SLIM	Quantitative Software Management	Costing Software based on Rayleigh curve and LOC
SPQR/20	Software Productivity Research, Inc. Cambridge, MA	Multiple choice approach to function point estimation
Time Line	Symantec Software Cupertino, CA	Pert, CPM, and Gantt Charts Resource Allocation and Tracking
WINGS	AGS, Inc. New York, NY	Pert, CPM, and Gantt Charts Resource Allocation and Tracking

their assessment of the risk associated with capital projects.

SUMMARY

Feasibility analysis is an important activity that gives a development project a scope and refined definition of application purpose, while providing information that allows the determination of technical, organizational, and financial readiness of the organization. The steps to performing feasibility analysis are: collect data, define scope and functions, define technical alternatives, define benefits and risks of each alternative, analyze organizational and technical feasibility, select technical alternative(s), define project plan, assess financial feasibility, and select final alternative. Data collection most frequently uses interviews or JAD-like sessions to define current work environment, problems, and desires for the new application. From the information collected, the team and user define the scope of the activity, including all departments involved. Then, the functions to be kept from the current work environment and functions to be added to provide the new functionality are defined at a high level.

Technical alternative definition begins with an assessment of the project's criticality to the organization and the need for different departments to share data. Based on that information, existing computer resources are analyzed to determine their usefulness for the proposed application. If existing resources are not adequate, new computer equipment, software, or packages are defined for acquisition. In general, the smallest size computer (or LAN) that can do the work and provide a migration path for growth is selected. Distributed resources might be identified as an option but are not fully analyzed at this time. Several technical alternatives are developed and analyzed to select one or two that meet the most requirements, provide for the greatest benefits, and pose the fewest risks.

The next activity is to define a project plan. There are many different estimating techniques for projecting time to complete a project: algorithmic, top-down, bottom-up, price-to-win, Parkinson's Law, expert judgment, function point analysis, and analogy. Of these, CoCoMo and function point are the most popular when a history of project development is maintained by a company. Function point analysis complements CoCoMo in developing an estimate of LOC. CoCoMo can use the LOC estimate as input to its formulae to develop total person-month, total development time, and project staffing estimates. Parkinson and price-to-win are *not* recommended. When other techniques are used, they are best used in combination. So, top-down, bottom-up, and expert judgment might be combined to develop best guesses of the time and effort involved in a development project. The project plan is used to develop personnel costs and computer resource usage. These and the other costs are factored into the financial feasibility assessment.

Financial feasibility techniques most commonly used include net present value analysis which accounts for the time value of money, internal rate of return which identifies the real interest rate of a project, and payback analysis which identifies the time at which net revenues equals net costs of project. Financial analysis also supports the comparison of make versus buy alternatives for a project. Two types of make/buy analysis can be developed. First, custom development of software versus purchase of a package can be evaluated. Second, in-house versus contractor development can be evaluated. Finally, alternative selection is based on financial value of the alternative(s) when more than one technical alternative for a project exists. Also, from the financial analysis, managers can evaluate several different projects using an objective method and can identify the project with the fastest, strongest returns.

REFERENCES

Albrecht, Albert J., and James E. Gaffney, "Software function, source lines of code and development effort prediction: A software science validation," *IEEE Transactions on Software Engineering*, November, 1983, pp. 639–648.

Boehm, Barry W., *Software Engineering Economics*. Englewood Cliffs, NJ: Prentice-Hall, 1981.

Charette, Robert N., *Software Engineering Risk Analysis and Management*. NY: McGraw-Hill, 1989.

Collins, Eliza G. C., and Mary Anne Devanna, eds., *The Portable MBA*. NY: John Wiley & Sons, 1990.

De Marco, Tom, "An algorithm for sizing software products," *Performance Evaluation Review*, ACM SIGMetrics Publication, Vol. 12, #2, Spring–Summer, 1984, pp. 13–22.

Gause, Donald C., and Gerald M. Weinberg, *Exploring Requirements Quality Before Design*. NY: Dorset House Publishing, 1989.

Jones, Capers, "Program Quality and Programmer Productivity: A Survey of the State of the Art," Presentation through Software Productivity Research, Inc., Boston, MA: March 15, 1989.

Jones, Capers, *Programming Productivity*. NY: McGraw-Hill, 1986.

Kendall, Ken E., and Julie E. Kendall, *Systems Analysis and Design*, 2nd Ed. Englewood Cliffs, NJ: Prentice-Hall, Inc. 1992.

King, John L., and Edward L. Schrems, "Cost-benefit analysis in information systems development and operation," *Computing Surveys*, Vol. 10, #1, March, 1978, pp. 20–34.

Rubin, Martin S., *Documentation Standards and Procedures for On-line Systems*. NY: Van Nostrand Reinhold Company, 1979.

KEY TERMS

algorithmic estimating
alternative approaches
analogical estimating
application leverage
   point
benefit
bottom up estimating
business leverage point
CoCoMo estimating
competitive environment
contingency planning
cost/benefit analysis
critical success factor
customer environment
delivered source
   instructions
Delphi method of
   estimating
discounted cash flow
embedded project
expert judgment
   estimating
feasibility
financial feasibility
flexibility
function point
function point analysis
Gantt Chart
goal
imaging

industry environment
intangible benefits
internal rate of return
   analysis
KDSI
leverage point
make/buy analysis
net present value (NPV)
objective
organic project
organizational feasibility
Parkinson's Law
payback period analysis
pert chart
platform
portability
price to win strategy
project mode
project plan
quick analysis
reliability
risk
risk assessment
semidetached project
tangible benefits
technical feasibility
top down estimating
vendor environment
work breakdown
work flow management

EXERCISES

1. Using Table 6-6 as a guide, develop a CPM for the design phase of ABC's project. While you do the diagram, reason through the dependencies. Assuming Sam and Mary do the project alone, how should the work be allocated between them to (a) allow Mary to do project management tasks, and (b) leverage the work they did during analysis?

2. Using Table 6-6 as a guide, develop a more detailed task list for some phase or portion of a phase (e.g., all rental/return processes, or conversion/training). Then, develop an estimate of the work based on your expertise and the idea

that you would perform the work. How does your estimate differ from Table 6-6? Why? Are the differences completely justifiable? Present your estimates to a group of classmates and provide your reasoning for the changes.

STUDY QUESTIONS

1. Define the following terms:
   Benefits   Function point
   Net present value   Leverage point
   Risk   Technical feasibility
2. Why is feasibility analysis performed?
3. What are the three main types of feasibility and why are they important?
4. List the steps to performing feasibility analysis.
5. What are the main data collection techniques used during feasibility analysis?
6. What is a leverage point?
7. How do business and application leverage points differ? How do they complement each other?
8. List five sources of benefits.
9. Discuss the differences between tangible and intangible benefits.
10. List five sources of risk and give an example of each.
11. Why is risk analysis performed? What do you do with the risks once they are identified?
12. How are technical alternatives generated?
13. Once technical alternatives are complete, how are they assessed? What is the basis for selecting one alternative as the preferred one?
14. Compare the advantages and disadvantages of algorithmic, function point, and combined top-down, bottom-up estimating.
15. What is the major weakness of CoCoMo estimating?
16. What is the major weakness of function point estimating?
17. Why do we have so many estimating techniques? Is one better than another?
18. What is the major financial analysis used to analyze project alternatives? Why is it the preferred method?

19. What is the purpose of make/buy analysis?
20. Describe the two types of make/buy analysis.

★ EXTRA-CREDIT QUESTION

1. The Office Information System described in the Appendix is an application that automates the support division of a large company. The units involved include a typing pool, copy center, print shop, and graphic arts department. Other projects are being developed in the IS Department that will cost approximately $2.4 million per year, and an additional $1.5 million in operating expenses.

The proposed budget for the OIS is $200,000 for a Cobol, mainframe application using a DBMS to store the data. Is this a reasonable amount? Develop one to three alternatives that are more financially attractive. One of the alternatives might be on the mainframe but can use different resources; at least one alternative should use different technology. Who should develop the application? Under what circumstances would you recommend to do/not do the application?

PART **III**

ANALYSIS
AND
DESIGN

INTRODUCTION

Analysis is the act of defining *what* an application will do. **Design** is the act of defining *how* the requirements defined during analysis will be implemented in a specific hardware/software environment. The next eight chapters define and describe functional analysis and design. Each set of analysis-design chapters uses major representation techniques from the methodology class it presents. In a traditional application development, there are many more analysis and design activities than we address here (see Tables III-1 and III-2). Most of these topics should already be part of your knowledge base from a systems analysis and design course. Many activities we *do* cover in this text are also in a systems analysis and design course. The difference is that here we develop three methodologies instead of one as in systems analysis. In this text, we concentrate on the activities which differ across the methodologies. Chapter 13 summarizes the similarities, differences, and automated support across the methodologies. It also discusses the future based on current research in methodologies. Chapter 14 discusses the forgotten activities in most methodology-related books and

many systems analysis texts. These activities include human interface design, input/output design, conversion design, and user documentation design.

At the end of the next eight chapters, you should be able to do the following:

1. Understand the conceptual foundations of the three classes of methodologies and how they are similar and how they differ.
2. Represent the functional requirements of an application using each of the three methodologies.
3. Be able to translate a functional requirements definition into a SQL-based design for an application using each of the three methodologies.
4. Compare the advantages, values and disadvantages of methodologies' uses for analysis.
5. Develop a critical understanding of the difficulties of translating what users want into representations that convey meaning.
6. Know some computer-aided and organizational supports for completing analysis and design work.

199

TABLE III-1   Representative Project Development Analysis Activities

Recurring activities/tasks
  Initiate phase
  Plan next phase
  Prepare report
  Review phase products

Analysis Phase Activities

Initiate hardware/software evaluation (as required)
Initiate prototype development (as required)

Define current system (as required)
  Document and files
  Data elements
  Compile data dictionary
  Processing
  Controls
  Volumes and timing
  Interfaces with other systems
  Responsibilities
  Work distribution
  Operating costs

Assess current system
  Review project objectives and scope
  Compare system in operation with recommended
    solution
  Identify opportunities for immediate improvements
  Assess organizational design appropriateness for
    application

Define proposed application's business requirements
  System concept and overview
    Major functions
    Scope
    User organizations involved
    Interface organizations
    Interface application systems
    Context diagram
    System concept—technology (i.e., DBMS, LAN,
      distribution plan, etc.)
    Major issues, unresolved problems that might hinder
      application development
    Schedule summary by phase
    Staffing summary by phase
  Assess proposed system requirements
    Identify alternatives for system design [e.g., data-
      base environment(s), hardware platform, software
      platform, special technology, packaged software,
      4GLs, user software (e.g., Lotus)]

Discuss and, as necessary, reassess technical, organizational, and economic feasibility as each relates to the alternatives identified

Define processing requirements
  DFD (or analogous graphic for the methodology)
  Steps (i.e., procedures to be followed; should match
    methodology)
  Required sequences of processing only
  Constraints (e.g., timing, memory, concurrency,
    other applications, etc.)
  Accuracy (e.g., to x decimal place, or timing as of
    y minutes)
  Formulae
  Performance criteria (e.g., volume, timing, response
    time)
  Inputs—name, source, frequency, volume, data
    elements, media
  Outputs—name, purpose, frequency, screen format,
    copies, elements, sequence, media
  Database—data requirements as expressed in
    methodology, relations, user views, organization,
    required reviews, access, security
  Reports—name, purpose, destination, frequency,
    form/screen, data elements, sequence
  User acceptance criteria

Define interface requirements
  Identification—name of interface, sending system/
    organization, receiving system/organization
  Responsibility/approvals
  Interface schedule—testing schedule and responsi-
    bilities, conversion schedule and responsibilities,
    delivery to production
  Requirements
    Inputs—name, purpose source, frequency, media,
      form #, components using each input, data ele-
      ments, data controls, data descriptions, formu-
      lae for computation
    Input layout—data direction, terminal devices,
      comm software, time outs, modem require-
      ments, line use, data characteristics, line
      characteristics, line protocol
    Output—name, purpose, frequency, format/screen
      #, copies, elements, sort sequence, media, com-
      ponent generating the output, source of data
      and name, data description, layout (transmitted
      output should have same information as input
      layout above)

TABLE III-1   Representative Project Development Analysis Activities (*Continued*)

Files—system name, system ID, file name, file ID, type of file (I/O), purpose, source, update cycle, sequence, frequency, volume, growth, media, usage (R, W, R/W), retention characteristics, security, blocking factor, file records types, components using file, file control characteristics

Record description—record name, file ID, record type (fixed, variable, spanned), record size, update cycle, form # for input, data elements and characteristics (definition, purpose, use in computation, formulae, precision, edit criteria, defaults, required/optional data, etc.)

Define control requirements
  Batch totals, item counts
  Hash totals, record counts
  Operation intervention and inquiry logs
  Exception reporting and responsibilities
  Processing controls—equipment failure
  Document control (e.g., for prenumbered checks)
  Transaction logging and on-line controls

Define security and backup requirements
  Recovery requirements data criticality, recovery plan in event of emergency
  Password and internal security checks

Define conversion requirements
  Data clean-up
  Clerical effort
  Systems effort—automated and manual files to be converted
  Volume and growth of files as it impacts conversion
  Alternatives for implementation
  Overall conversion timing requirements
  Conversion impact on user areas
  Conversion impact on operations
  Facilities alteration/site preparation
    Changes or additions to desks, tables, work spaces, cabinets, charts, etc.
    Forms, tapes, manuals, etc.
    Construction—walls, floors, ducts, etc.
    Cabling and electrical—outlets, switches, cables, lighting, other wiring, etc.
    Safety—extinguishers, alarms, first aid kits, etc.
    Security—badge-entry, guard service, etc.
    Environmental—air conditioning, humidification, dust, etc.

Maintenance—cleaning, equipment maintenance, etc.
Contingency—disaster plans, backup procedures, etc.

Define training
  Type of training, recipients, and details for all training, including but not limited to on-line data entry, remote location data input, native language manuals, general introduction to new system

Define system acceptance criteria
  Test data input by user
  Parallel runs
  Pilot runs
  Phased cutover
  Depending on acceptance criteria, include the following:
    Amount of test data to be entered, and number of clerks involved
    Size of pilot parallel (e.g., number of accounts, cycles, etc.)
    Length of time
    Performance criteria
    Impact on clerical staff
    Impact on operations

Define hardware
  Acceptable limits of downtime
  Average or maximum terminals down at the same time
  Inquiry response time
  Update response time
  Batch turnaround time
  Maximum percent of transmission errors
  Backup 'firedrills' plan and frequency
  Maintenance/reliability
  Peak and average time requirements
  Geographic constraints on terminal location
  Purchased hardware required cost/benefit analysis and RFP selection process
  List of hardware for this system, type, location, 'ownership,' system role, backup, criticality (This list should include terminals, PCs, controllers, modems, transmission lines, mini-computers, workstations, mainframes, peripherals, disks, CDs, tapes, etc.)

Define software/system/misc.
  Volume of each transaction type
  Growth
  Delivery time constraints

(*Continued on next page*)

TABLE III-1   Representative Project Development Analysis Activities (*Continued*)

Number of reruns
Backup 'firedrills' plan and frequency
Distribution of output messages
List of hardware for this system, type, location, 'ownership,' system on which it runs, backup, criticality [This list should include DBMS, operating system, LAN, communications, remote access (e.g., Carbon Copy), on-line help, etc.]
 	
Define initiate request for proposal (RFP)
  Determine criteria for decision
  List requirements for proposal
  Select vendors
  Prepare RFP report
	Define data requirements
	  Data dictionary should be an appendix to documentation if it is not automated. For automated application documentation, print the information from the dictionary. For manual applications, include the following for each data element:
	    Field name, alternative name, description, purpose, use in computation, use in determining conditions (with other fields), code reference, length, decimal positions, type, unit of measure, optional/required, allowable values (range, code structure, meaning of values), default value, external data source

In this section, we introduce the general characteristics of analysis and design that all methodologies have in common.

APPLICATION DEVELOPMENT AS A TRANSLATION ACTIVITY

The process of building applications is a series of translations. Historically, we first examine and translate the current physical system to develop an abstract, logical definition of the current system (see Figure III-1). Then, with the application users, we define the requirements of the new logical system which retains the aspects of the old system while incorporating the new requirements defined by users. The new logical system definition is the basis for translating to a working physical application.

This historical strategy is useful only sometimes. The strategy works when a new application will maintain 50% or more of the old application's functions. For example, we might redevelop an accounting application to move from batch to on-line, but to perform all the same functions. Another use of this strategy is when study of the old application can save time in providing code tables. For instance, state abbreviations, zip codes, and customer name

abbreviations all might be retained from an old application.

In many situations, however, the existing application is antiquated, full of obsolete design or riddled with errors. To study it is to learn erroneous design and procedures that must be unlearned. Why learn it in the first place? Rather, a frequently better approach is to begin analyzing the requirements of the new application. This is called 'essential' system analysis[1] and requires only that you, the analyst, attend to what relates to the new application. The old application or procedures may be studied for specific information, code tables, or crucial steps in the process; but in general, the old application and procedures are ignored.

The essential approach is used in this text. We ignore the details of the manual method of performing rental processing because the computerized method will completely replace the manual method. The major value of studying, for instance, what manual forms are filed and when they get retrieved, is to help get a sense of file processing in the new application. When the old procedures are being replaced, you may want to use the old methods as a way to confirm your thinking *after* you have developed the application concepts.

Whichever analysis method you use, translations performed during analysis all have the following five

---

1 See McMenamin and Palmer, 1984.

TABLE III-2   Representative Design Phase Activities

Recurring activities/tasks
  Initiate phase
  Plan next phase
  Prepare documentation
  Review phase products

Design Phase Activities

Initiate business system design

Design functional outline
  Review business functions
  Review interface requirements
  Develop alternative functional outlines
  Select best alternative
  Design data structure/database
    Normalize, optimize, then . . . denormalize as
      required
  Design interprogram flows and controls

Design input, output, and data
  Design output screens/documents
  Design input requirements/screens
  Design screen dialogue and system navigation

Design processing
  Design computer processing
  Design noncomputer processing

Design controls
  Describe business control procedures
  Define security and backup procedures

Design business system test plan
  Identify acceptance criteria
  Prepare tentative user acceptance strategy
  Identify critical resource requirements
  Prepare testing overview
  Develop system test plan

Complete business system design
  Complete data dictionary with elements, processes,
    messages, objects, modules, files/relations, data flows
  Define proposed organization
  Review conversion requirements
  Prepare operating schedule
  Perform program design as outlined below

Evaluate business system design
  Assure technical, operational, and economic feasibility
  Review risks

User procedures
Define manual procedures

Define user manual procedures
Define computer operations manual procedures
Prepare manual procedures test plan

Complete forms, documents, and screens
  Prototype forms, screens, reports
  Complete input documents/screens
  Complete output forms/screens
  Complete screen designs, error codes, screen inter-
    action process

Develop training
  Determine pedagogical training requirements
  Determine training methods
  Prepare training sessions and software
  Prepare training schedule
  Pilot test training

Prepare for installation
  Prepare and test user manual
  Verify readiness of user environment
  Train user personnel
  Test manual, backup, and disaster procedures

Design the physical database
  Define user views
  Define logical DB to DBMS
  Map logical DB to media, deciding specific access
    method, extra space allocation, algorithms, etc.
  Build and test a sample DB
  Work with test planners to build the test DB
    environment
  Work with conversion team to implement the produc-
    tion DB environment

Build conversion subsystem
  Work with user to translate and validate current data
  Specify, write, and test conversion programs
  Train conversion personnel
  Execute conversion plan to build permanent DB

Program design
Develop modular program structure
  Study data structure
  Develop logical program structure
    Complete methodology-related graphics
    Specify subprograms, modules, functions
  Document programs/modules individually and as a
    collection. Pay special attention to document inter-
    modular relationships and message passing between
    programs

(Continued on next page)

TABLE III-2   Representative Design Phase Activities (*Continued*)

Develop and unit test physical code Implement programs top-down using stubs Prototype as needed	Define development sequence Revise schedule and budget for programming phase

Plan program testing
  Prepare program test plan
  Create program test data
  Create test dialog for single user, multiple users,
    multiple functions
	Create source library members
	  Write record descriptions for source library (This is
	    not done if an active dictionary is used or if the dic-
	    tionary for the DBMS monitors all interactions to
	    the database. Instead, copy books or analogous code
	    are included to describe user views.)
	  Write standard program code to source library

Similar plans for subsystem, system, stress, multiuser,
  and acceptance testing are required and planned at this
  point. (If the application is on a tight deadline, testing
  and immediate conversion to production can be
  planned and implemented together.)
	Refine operational requirements
	  Revise computer run procedures
	  Produce tentative production control cards (JCL)

Define program development plan Determine development method	

common subactivities (the activities are summarized in Table III-3).

1. **Identification**—Find the focal *things* that belong. Identification, for instance, in the definition of the new logical system requires finding requirements. *Things* to be found include, for instance, entities, objects, relationships, functions, processes, and constraints.

2. **Elaboration**—Define the details of each *thing* identified. For instance, a requirement might be to provide consolidated customer account information for ad hoc reporting. During elaboration, you seek to answer questions like:

    What information should be consolidated about a user? Does it currently exist?
    What does ad hoc mean to the user?
    What type of queries do the users ask now?
    What types of questions do the users *want* to ask that they cannot ask now?
    What kinds of data analysis do users need?
    What form (for example, screen or paper) does output take?
    Where (geographically) are the users asking the questions?

    Where (centralized/distributed/decentralized) is the data? and where should it be?

3. **Synthesis**—Build a unified view of the application, reconciling any parts that do not fit and representing requirements in graphic form. The representation can be either manual (i.e., on paper) or automated, using computer-based tools.

4. **Review**—Perform quality control. At the end of the phase (either analysis or design), reanalyze feasibility, schedules, and staffing. Revise them as needed based on the more complete, current definition of the new application.

5. **Document**—Create useful documents from graphics and supporting text either manually or with computer-based tools.

Each of the three methodologies begins analysis by defining requirements, but each has a different starting (and ending) perspective for its analysis process. Similarly, for each of the other analysis activities, the results of the activity differ because the perspective at the start focuses your attention to different aspects of the application.

Keep in mind that even though we discuss these methodologies as fairly linear, sequential processes,

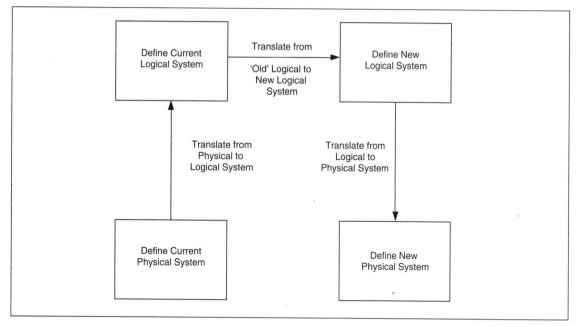

FIGURE III-1   Application Development Translations

they are not. You get application requirements in a nonlinear fashion, usually through interviews. Frequently, you get high-, low-, and medium-level information all at the same interview. Your job, as the SE, is to make sense of the information received. The sense-making activity is part of the process of building your mental model of the application domain. Since you receive information at different levels over time, your mental model of the domain gets fleshed out at different levels over time, too. You constantly have to reevaluate the information you currently have against new information to determine if adjustments to the current mental model are necessary.

A second point about the nonlinear aspect is that specification and implementation are never *really* separated completely in your thinking process. In systems analysis class you usually learn not to think about the language or implementation environment while you are performing analysis. You are told only to think about functional requirements. You must think of the implementation environment periodically in the real-world, however, because some desired function might not be able to be done (or done easily) in the planned environment. When

expensive or complex functions are requested, you must alert the user/sponsor to be sure they agree with the desired function. An expensive change is one that adds more than 10% to the cost of the application. A complex change is one that convolutes an otherwise simple process (see Example III-1).

Just as analysis is a translation activity, so too, is design. The goal of design is to map the functional requirements from analysis into a specific hardware and software environment. In design, the same five general subactivities are done, but they have different definitions.

1. **Identification**—Design is the act of mapping *how* logical requirements will work in the target computer environment. This means that we identify the system design structure (if not already decided). The system structure is the underlying design approach. Possible approaches include the following:

   ■ Batch, on-line (portions of complete), or real-time
   ■ Which functions are connected and how
   . . . how the application will work in the production environment

TABLE III-3   Summary of Analysis and Design General Activities

Activity	Analysis	Design
Identification	Find the focal *things* that are in the application. This includes, but is not limited to, entities, objects, relationships, functions, constraints, data elements, control, legal requirements, etc.	Refine the system concept and apply it to the functional requirements. Identify any compromises of requirements that might be necessary to work around implementation environment limitations. Define the general standards and rules for the implementation environment to which all remaining work must adhere.
Elaboration	Define the functional details of each *thing* identified. Users provide definitions for all terms and describe all procedures, formulae, and processing. This elaboration is independent of hardware, software, or location.	For each function, map the function to the hardware and software environment. Identify reusable modules. Finalize details of message processing and intermodule communications.
Synthesis	Develop a unified view of the application. Develop and document a representation of the application. Graphics, tables, and other techniques are preferred representations.	Develop a unified mapping of the application to the intended hardware and software environment. Determine geographic and package locations for all data and processes. Graphics, tables, and other techniques are preferred representations.
Review	Review and walk-through the analysis with peers and project members. Walk-through the analysis with users. Review and revise schedules and costs as necessary.	Review and walk-through design components, test plan, conversion plan, and DB design, with peers and project members, program specifications with the programmer and other peers, and screens with users. Review and revise schedules and costs as necessary.
Document	Develop 'final' forms of graphics and supporting text for *all* analysis activities.	Develop 'final' forms of graphics and supporting text for *all* design activities.

- General user interface as menu-driven, windows-icons-menus-pointers (WIMP), command-driven
- Mode of operation, that is, is user an expert, novice, or somewhere in between

2. **Elaboration**—Each requirement from the analysis phase is expanded into greater detail and mapped to hardware and software within the system design structure. Questions relate to:

How should the database be designed to provide, for instance, the best possible response time with the greatest efficiency?

EXAMPLE III-1

CARTER CORDUROY—YOU SHOULD HAVE ASKED AGAIN

Carter Corduroy, a $100 million company, wanted to install an integrated database application to perform order entry, inventory control, and manufacturing control. During the analysis of the application, George Dare was the user contact who approved all requirements, acted as liaison to the rest of the company, and provided many requirements.

The analysis phase of the project completed on time and all ten project team members felt they had a good understanding of the process required and what the resulting application would do. The two people preparing most of the documentation and all of the program specifications were Maria Martinez, SE/project manager for 10 years who had done two other such integrated order-inventory systems, and Charlie Chou, SE with 12 years of experience who had developed applications using all of the software involved.

During the middle of the analysis phase, the systems manager was replaced with a newly hired person, Robert Blake. Mr. Blake came from a larger fabric manufacturer and wanted to make a name for himself quickly in his new environment. He quickly forged a liaison with Harry Crater, the plants' manager. The application would be installed in his two finishing plants: one in Virginia and one in Arkansas.

Crater and Dare were political enemies. Dare had once worked for Crater and had not gotten along with him. Dare was young and highly proficient at his job and soon surpassed Crater. Crater now reported to Dare for purposes of developing the application—the biggest in the company's history.

These circumstances did not affect the application team until late in design, after programming had begun. Six weeks before the application was supposed to go into pro-

duction, Dare was on vacation. Crater had a validation meeting for reporting requirements with Martinez and Chou. At the meeting, he said that planned reports could not identify 'reworks,' goods that were defective and reentered into the finishing process a second time. He was adamant that he must have some way of knowing if a lot of goods were a 'first work' or a 'second work.' It was the first mention of anything other than one-time-through manufacturing. Maria said this constituted a major change to the requirements and a nontrivial change to all programs already begun. It was so significant that the end date of the project was in jeopardy. She decided to examine the specific impact, then talk to George about the change.

Mr. Blake heard of the meeting and, that afternoon, began pressuring Maria and Charlie to 'do what Crater wants.' After all, he was the real user.

Maria talked to the team and asked for an assessment of effort to change their programs to allow the same lot order to be processed more than once. She and Charlie then did their own assessment. The team was unanimous. The change would add four to six weeks time for programming and testing, all documentation would have to be modified, and all databases would be changed. In short, the change could add as much as $90,000 to the $225,000 contract—a 40% increase. Maria decided to speak to George before committing to the change.

Mr. Blake coerced the team, as their immediate boss no matter who the user of the application was, to begin work on the change. When George got back, he was immersed in another special project that was

(Continued on next page)

CARTER CORDUROY—YOU SHOULD HAVE ASKED AGAIN, *Continued*

taking most of his time. When Maria finally got to him, he said, "Yeah, if Blake approves and Crater insists, we probably need it." Still, Maria had doubts.

She put the changes with cost estimates in a memo to Blake. He never signed-off on the change, but verbally agreed again. The application was three weeks late when everyone at Carter exploded. Suddenly, no one remembered that the application would be late. No one remembered being warned that this one, small change would cause so many problems. Maria was to blame for a poor design that could not be made to work. Crater now said that he 'requested' the change but that it was not absolutely 'necessary.' Blake forgot the conversations, memo, and approvals. Dare was furious because his special project was now overbudget and late.

When the written memo and other documentation from the meetings held at the time were produced, Dare's comment to Maria was, "You are the expert, you should have asked again whether or not the change was necessary. You were the only one who knew how big it really was!"

In the end, the application was put into production with only one run through the finishing plant per work order. Reworks were assigned a new number and tracked as if it were the first time through the process. The costly change and insufficient whistle-blowing by the project manager led to unhappy clients, overworked project team members, and a less than optimal application. Could they have been avoided? Probably not. The client should have been made to realize the magnitude of the change, however. Maria and Charlie should have been more insistent on a detailed review of the request and sign-offs for this major change.

How should programs be packaged to fulfill processing constraints? Examples might be to provide five-second response time; to provide completion of reporting within a three-hour period daily; or to provide 24-hour access to information that is up-to-the-minute.

Other elaboration activities to be decided include common routines for commonly used processes. For instance, how will screen processing be performed? Will each programmer write his or her own version of screen interface or will there be common modules for screen interactions? The scope and details of system 'utility' programs to be used by all programmers are defined.

The last major elaboration activity is to examine the application constraints. We ensure that each constraint is considered in the design and that processing is within the prescribed limits.

3. **Synthesis**—Build a unified physical design of the application, reconciling any parts that do not fit and representing requirements in more detail. We may add functions to the application that are environment specific. For instance, in a mainframe IMS database environment, applications require user views, data base definitions (DBDs), data control blocks (DCBs), and data service blocks (DSBs). These control blocks are not required if using dBase IV on a PC. The representation can be either manual (i.e., on paper) or automated, using computer-based tools.

4. **Review**—Perform quality control. At the end of the phase, conduct a design walk-through, comparing design to logical requirements to validate completeness and correctness. Rean-

alyze schedule and staffing for coming stages of implementation, testing, conversion, training, and turnover, revising them as required.

5. **Document**—Create useful program specifications and an overall design document. The design document describes the database, application structure, constraints, and so on. Graphics and supporting text document the design. The program/module specifications include the details of processing, all interface designs, and any specific information required to develop the program.

As in analysis, these activities vary by methodology because the ending point of analysis, which provides the input to design, is different. However, the intention of all methodologies is to define the application such that programming and implementation can be started after the design is complete. Program/module specifications, in some form, are the desired output of the design phase.

Keep in mind that even though we discuss design as a straightforward mapping of 'what' to 'how,' it is not a one-to-one mapping. You might need to compromise analysis requirements during design. **Compromise of requirements** means that they may be rescoped, manipulated, dropped, or otherwise changed to fit the environment's limitations.

Prototyping is an important activity in design to minimize the amount of requirements compromise that takes place. Especially when you use a package or language for the first time, prototyping should be used because prototypes frequently find the language's limits. You must verify that the application structure and concept can be implemented using the software as planned. Frequently in a PC environment, you will find you are bumping into language/package limitations that cause you to rethink the design. Vendors call this process 'work around.' You are finding a way to **work around** the built-in limits of the language. Vendors will usually help find a work around if the application cannot be built in known ways. They also challenge users to find work arounds and broadcast them to others who have similar problems.

The linkage between analysis, design, and program design is looser or tighter depending on the methodology and implementation environment. For instance, data information required differs if we use dBASE IV[2] or if we use IMS DB/DC.[3] Level of requirements detail differs if we use the Focus[4] language or if we use C-language.[5] Where possible, we point out specific instances of these linkages.

You, as the SE, must constantly check your mental model of functional requirements when building a mental model of *how* they will be implemented. Do not be afraid to try different ways of thinking. Frequently the old way was not too good. We get trapped in our thought processes and don't even remember to do the **out of the box** thinking[6] that is necessary for innovative designs.

Before we discuss methodologies, some organization and automated supports that facilitate application development regardless of methodology are discussed.

ORGANIZATIONAL AND AUTOMATED SUPPORT

Organizational innovations that are useful with all methodologies are joint user-IS application development activities, user managed application

---

2 dBASE IV is a trademark product of Ashton-Tate, Inc.

3 IMS DB/DC is a trademarked mainframe product of the IBM Corporation. IMS, Information Management System, is a hierarchic database product. DB stands for *data*base; DC abbreviates *data communications.

4 Focus is a trademarked database, query, application generator, expert system product of Information Builders, Inc. Focus is thought of as a 4th-generation language because of its powerful query capabilities.

5 C-language is a trademark product of Bell Labs; C++ is a trademarked product of Borland International; and there are other versions of C-language.

6 Out of the box thinking means to rethink the entire process as if the current methods, procedures, and policies did not exist. Put yourself in the shoes of a caveman (or an intelligent child) who just walked into the company, and redesign the work as they might. Question everything. For instance, who says you need to keep a copy of an order? What is the *real*, i.e., legal requirement?

development, structured walk-throughs, and data administration. The goal of these organizational innovations is to speed the development process, foster user participation, and improve the quality of the resulting application. Automated support for structured analysis and design comes from computer-aided software engineering (CASE) tools. Each chapter will identify CASE tools that relate to the phase and activities. In this section we describe the characteristics of CASE tools and the ideal CASE environment.

Joint Application Development

Several techniques have been developed to describe the joint, intensive definition of application requirements—**Joint Requirements Planning (JRP)**, **Joint Application Design Development (JAD)**,[7] and **Fast-Track**.[8] They are all similar in that the goal is a collaborative, user-IS definition of application requirements. The planning and execution of a joint session are also similar. The differences are the level of participants, subject matter, and level of detail of the discussions. These are more fully described below.

JRP is an executive level user-IS activity to identify overall requirements at the enterprise level. Fast-Track and JAD both are designed to produce a functional requirements specification. If a JRP report exists, the Fast-Track/JAD uses the JRP report as constraining or defining the business environment within which the application is defined.

JRP, Fast-Track, and JAD activities are

- designed to shorten the application development process
- productivity tools
- structured to improve the quality of the application development deliverables.

These characteristics of the joint development activities can also provide opposite results if the sessions do not adhere to the guidelines defined by their

---

7 JRP and JAD are design techniques of the IBM Corporation.

8 Fast-Track is a design technique of the Boeing Computer Company.

developers. However, these techniques *do not substitute* for experience, good project management, or knowledge about the application! Even with user involvement in analysis and design, application developers *must* develop knowledge and shared mental models of both the application and problem domain. One purpose of the joint sessions is to be sure of a common mental model for all participants.

Requirements for a joint session relate to:

- the team
- the session
- joint structured process
- the meeting facility
- documentation tools.

The Team

The team is composed of client representatives, facilitator, systems representatives, and support personnel (see Table III-4). The clients must include decision makers at a high enough level to resolve conflicts and make decisions that affect the scope and content of the application. They must also be at a low enough level to be conversant and able to explain the daily functions and procedures. Finally, clients must represent *every* functional area affected by the application. You must also keep the number of client participants less than 15 and ideally between three to four people. The more people, the longer the process and the more difficult the decisions. Ideally, the whole session team is about seven people.

Systems representatives should include the project manager, an SE, and one to two analysts with technical expertise. The systems representatives must be able to assess feasibility of requested requirements and the expected complexity of implementing the requirements in the target environment. The main role of the system representatives is to learn the problem domain area during the sessions and ensure accurate problem restatement in system terms.

The facilitator is a specially trained individual who runs the session. The facilitator has several roles:

- Elicit information from participants
- Keep the meetings moving

TABLE III-4   Joint IS-User Team and Responsibilities

Role	Job Title	Responsibilities
Facilitator	Consultant IS Manager Senior SE Facilitator	Elicit information. Keep meeting moving. Minimize monopolization by one or few individuals. Identify and resolve conflicts. Maintain professional atmosphere.
User	Manager Professional Clerk	Make decisions about compromises, changes, or other aspects of the application requirements that require managerial approval. Participate in and contribute to discussions about requirements. Provide information, requirements ideas, and suggestions on the meeting topic. Maintain open, professional atmosphere. Interpret and explain application problem domain to IS personnel.
IS Representative	Project Manager Project Leader SE Systems Analyst	Learn the application problem domain. Assist in interpreting requirements into graphical representations. Determine technological capabilities and limitations as they relate to the application requirements. Interpret and explain technical IS domain to users.
Support	Secretary Systems Analyst	Take notes as requested. Plan for coffee, meals, etc. Act as liaison with outside world. Take notes as requested; assist in transcribing and documenting daytime work.

Keep the discussion from becoming monopolized by one individual
Identify and resolve conflicts
Keep the meeting on a business (rather than personal) level.

Frequently in joint sessions, organizational disagreements on goals and objectives arise. Such conflict is to be expected and is normal. The facilitator's job is to identify and ensure resolution of disagreements during the sessions. The conflicts are potentially explosive and can lead to personal conflicts.

The facilitator must recognize such situations and defuse them. Occasionally, defusing means asking for a participant to be replaced.

The facilitator is a cheerleader, meeting leader, and ring leader who keeps the session moving. Usually facilitators are senior staff from the information systems organization who already know how to develop application requirements, but who are specifically trained to facilitate joint user-IS sessions.

Finally, support personnel are individuals who take notes during the day and provide liaison with the outside world. The notes include data-related information and process-related information. Data information includes identification, naming and definitions of entities, elements, and entity relationships. Process information includes decision rationales, process identification, procedural details of processes, and policies that constrain processes. The actual results of the data and process discussions are reflected around the room (see the photo in Figure III-2) on flip-charts, blackboards, and other visual aids that are always accessible to the entire group.

A second kind of support is administrative assistance, which includes documenting the information during evening sessions, coordinating coffee and meals, and ferrying messages to and from work for participants.

Preparation

A meeting to prepare session attendees should be held for *all* participants. The primary purpose is to give participants a list of tasks to complete before they attend the joint session and to train participants in the completion of the tasks.

The meeting includes an orientation, document examples, data requirements, and training in development of graphical techniques being used to docu-

ment processing. The orientation discusses the expectations of the organization and normal results of such sessions. Then participants are given an overview of the joint structured process: what it is, how it is conducted, proper behavior, and decision-making necessity. The scope and purpose of the application are discussed and agreed upon again by all participants. If there is disagreement or problems with the scope, they are revised at this meeting so everyone has a shared understanding of what work functions and information are in, and what are not in, the application.

If data flow diagrams are the graphical technique being used, for example, the users are trained to develop a context diagram and first-cut data flow diagram of their current job. The list of tasks for data flow diagrams would include the following activities:

- Define the scope and functions of your position
- Document the 'what is' in a data flow diagram
- Try to draw a context diagram of all the departments, groups, and applications with whom you exchange information in your job
- Define all data used in your job

FIGURE III-2   Photo of Joint User-IS Session Room

- Collect statistics—how often, how much, when—for all data and processes
- Collect samples of all input and output documents.

Frequently these sessions are taught by an in-house facilitator, but they may be taught by a consultant who knows the techniques.

The Joint Structured Process

The ideal joint user-IS session is full-time, off-site, lasts three to five days, and has five to nine participants. All of these ideal characteristics can be loosened somewhat and still maintain the momentum that comes from intensive work sessions. The idea is to do the work intensively and quickly because no one has time to spend in months of meetings. Participants become very close and frequently become good friends as a result of working together. At best, the users and IS team realize they are business partners in the application development and that relationship prevails throughout the project's life.

Joint sessions are divided into mainly daytime and nighttime sessions. The word *mainly* is used because the activities can be done at any time. In general, daytime, when people are most alert, is devoted to creating new information; evening is devoted to documenting the new information.

During the day, activities are the following:

- Confirm business functions
- Identify and analyze specific requirements (processes by function, inputs and outputs for each process). For each process, identify what is done, how frequently, exception and error processing, periodic processing, problems with current procedures, policies that might need to be changed, and any new business requirements relating to the processes.
- Identify general requirements for the application. For data, how accessible and accurate does the information need to be? Can it be accurate as of close of business yesterday or must it be up to the minute? Can answers take one or two hours, or must the answer be within seconds?

Application constraints are a second type of general requirement. Constraints place limits on the application. For instance, upper bounds of cost and time are allocated for development, hardware, software, language, or DBMS. These constraints are general, but they place strict boundaries on how the application will be designed. They also identify, to the technical staff, activities that need to be further elaborated during the detailed design to accommodate the implementation environment. Constraints from the first chapter discussion also apply. They include time, pre- and postrequisites, structural, control, and inferential constraints.

- Identify the likelihood of requirements change over the next three to five years. If requirements are identified as changing within the expected implementation time of the project, then the expected requirements become the current requirements for the application.

For instance, users may currently need data up to the close of business yesterday. They discuss the industry as moving rapidly toward instant access of up-to-the-minute information and expect this requirement within 12–18 months, and the application will be implemented in 12 months. Build the new requirement into the application now to be an early leader and avoid costly redevelopment of the new application.

- Have the support staff record all processes, functions, data, outputs, data elements, terms of processing, names given to items, and so on.

Figure III-3 shows the first-cut data flow diagram developed by an accountant in a major company for a JAD/Fast-Track session. The *user*, after one training session, developed a DFD that was about 90% correct. Figures III-4 and III-5 show the related Level 0 and Level 1 diagrams, respectively, from the JAD which had minor changes during IS design. Figure III-6 shows the DFD level 2 as decomposed by the project team during design. Only one of the processes changed: General Ledger was elaborated to be Accounts Receivable and Accounts

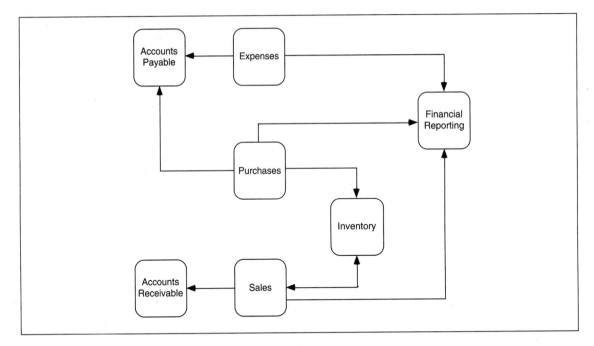

FIGURE III-3   User-Developed First-Cut DFD

Payable. The other changes were to files and external entities.

The evening sessions do the following:

Define all elements and terms
Document all processes
Draw formal DFDs
Document general application requirements and write an executive summary
Review documentation output of other mini-teams.

The group works together during the day to create information. In the evening, the group splits into mini-teams to perform one of the above activities. Documentation should be done using automated tools, including word processors, CASE tools, or other automated support tools that might be available. The goal is easily modifiable documents that can be formatted and printed.

When the mini-teams complete their work, they jointly review each others' work products. This review fosters the shared common view of the application and ends the participants' day with each having a clear sense of what was accomplished.

The Meeting Facility

The location should be at least 20 miles from the main work site of the participants to minimize interruptions and preclude people being pulled out of the sessions. The facility should provide above average meeting, sleeping, and eating arrangements in the same building. Phone access must be available but must be removed from the meeting room(s). The facility must provide computer accessibility. The location must be easily accessible for managers, who are not participants, to attend sessions for resolving conflicts. The facility must allow use of walls in the meeting room. The room should be equipped with flip-charts, overhead projector, markers, slide projector, and other meeting equipment as needed.

Documentation Tools

Documentation tools should include some word processing capability, dictionary support, and some graphical form support. All of these should ideally be in a computer-aided software engineering (CASE) tool. The CASE tool should allow customized reports of the information and should

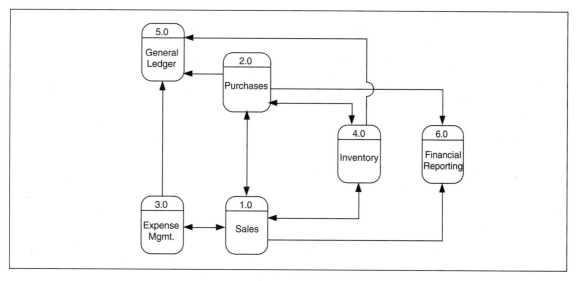

FIGURE III-4   JAD Team First-Cut and IS Final DFD Summary Level 0

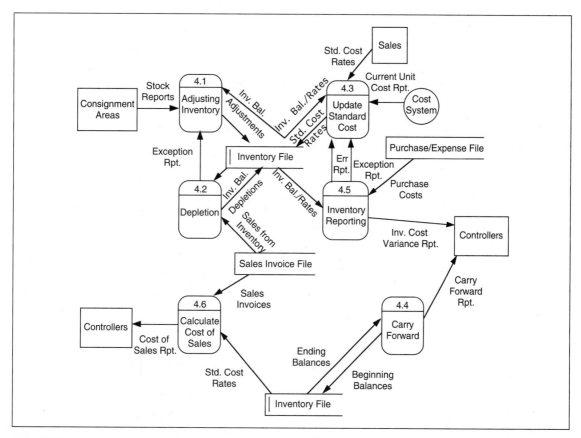

FIGURE III-5   JAD Team First-Cut and IS Final DFD Level 1

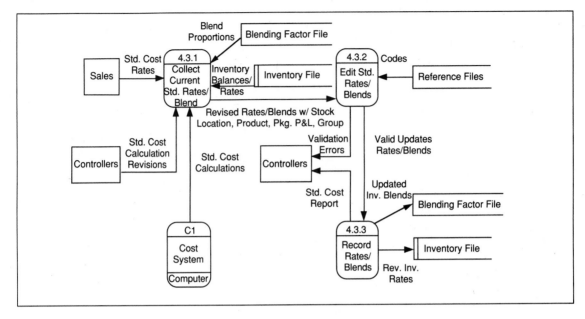

FIGURE III-6   IS Level 2 DFD for Updating Standard Costs

provide some intelligence on checking and cross-checking both completeness and accuracy of the information entered.

At a minimum, word processing should be provided via some tool such as WordPerfect,[9] Word Star,[10] MS Word,[11] and so on that allows graphics to be imbedded in text, creates tables easily, and does full text manipulation.

An **active data dictionary** is desirable for documenting the objects (e.g., entities, files, flows, objects) and object relationships defined during the sessions. An active dictionary is one that allows custom report development, provides intelligent assessment of completeness, and identifies potential duplicates based on name and definition. If a passive dictionary (i.e., has only vendor reports and no intelligence) is an option, you are better off using a word processor to document the information.

A graphical drawing tool is the third type of software needed. The tool should allow the type of drawing you are using with your methodology. An automated graphical tool is preferred to manual drawing because automated drawings are more easily changed and maintained. The joint groups frequently do several iterations of a drawing before they are satisfied with the result.

To summarize, joint user-IS sessions are a way to obtain quick results with a high degree of user participation in the development of requirements plans and application requirements. Joint sessions are intensive and require high commitment from participants. The rewards are a user-centered requirements document that frequently leads to more satisfied users and high user involvement throughout project development.

User-Managed Application Development

Joint sessions are designed to bring users and IS personnel together with the underlying understanding

---

9 WordPerfect is a trademark of WordPerfect, Inc.

10 Word Star is a trademark of Word Star, Inc.

11 MS Word is a trademark of Microsoft, Inc.

that users will always know more about their jobs than IS people. Joint sessions foster commitment to the IS development effort and give users a sense of participation. The user aspects of application development should not stop there. A **user manager** should be appointed for the application and should be the person ultimately responsible for the successful completion of both the application software and the organizational changes that accompany a new application.

The need for user-centered design seems obvious. **User-managed applications** foster a sense of business partnership; **IS-managed applications** foster a sense of them-and-us. User-managed applications provide a regular, natural communications line between the technicians and users; IS-managed applications provide a way for IS people to only talk among themselves. User-managed applications tend to require less IS involvement in application training, because users do their own training; IS training is notoriously condescending, inappropriate, and ineffective. Users 'own' the application and train their own staffs.

Not all is rosy with user managed applications. If the IS project manager is not used to working for a user, she or he will have to adjust some aspects of work. For instance, conversations will use business terms rather than technical terms. Variances in time and budget will require explanation and discussion. Rather than running the whole show, the project manager is clearly relegated to a supporting roll and only manages the actual software development.

User-managed development can also be subverted by unsupportive IS personnel. For instance, user teams can meet to develop functional requirements, but IS teams may not use them. IS groups have been notorious in ignoring user requirements. The comment heard is, "They can tell me anything, I'll give them what I want." The attitude is that mere users could never define as good a system as an IS person. How someone who does not know the business could make such a statement defies logic, but it is made. IS developers frequently need indoctrination that the business partnership aspect of application development *does* extend to the users.

Structured Walk-Throughs

Have you ever had a program bug that you spent hours trying to locate? You give up in frustration and turn to a friend for help. The friend takes a sideways glance and says, "Oh yeah, this period is out of place." Just like that, your hours have been a waste. That type of easily seen error is not a fluke. Your friend is not necessarily a genius, just as you are not necessarily stupid for not finding the error. The phenomenon at work is that you are too close to the problem to see the 'big picture.' At some point, we all reach this stage regardless of where on a project we work. Walk-throughs were designed to formalize the 'friendly review' described above.

A **walk-through** is a semiformal presentation of some work product for the sole purpose of finding errors. Work products might include all or part of the following:

- Functional requirements specification
- Project plan
- Design specification
- Logical or physical database design
- Program specification(s)
- Program code
- Test plan
- Test design.

This list is not complete. Its purpose is to give you an idea of the range of items that can be the subject of a walk-through. Virtually any work product, or piece of a work product, can be reviewed using the walk-through technique.

Ideally, a walk-through should not be scheduled for more than two hours at a time. If more time is needed, then additional walk-throughs are scheduled. Like all rules of thumb, this one is frequently broken. Participants who do not work on the development team sometimes have a difficult time walking-through application requirements in bursts. When they focus on the application, they like to see everything at once. So, occasionally you might have a marathon session that runs a whole day.

Walk-throughs are formalized in that there is preparation, a team with members having different responsibilities, and a process. Preparation for the session is as follows: The team is identified and approved by an SE or project manager. The day, place, and time are agreed upon. A memo of meeting details is sent to all participants several days in advance. *Attached to the memo is the work product to be reviewed.*

All participants are expected to review the work product, annotating questions and potential errors in the margins. They must come to the session already having some understanding of the work product.

Participants in a session include the facilitator, work producer, one or two peers who are on the same project, one or two outsiders, and a scribe. Ideally, the number of participants is between five and seven. The **facilitator** is much like a JAD facilitator. He or she keeps the meeting moving, makes sure no personal or blaming remarks are allowed, and maintains focus on the work product.

The producer presents his or her work. First, an overview focuses attention on the purpose of the product. Then, the work is reviewed in a page-by-page or line-by-line manner following the logic of the document. The peers and outsiders are there to question the correctness, completeness, efficiency, and effectiveness of the product. Questions, comments, or errors are discussed as the presentation is made. When an issue is raised and appears legitimate, the scribe notes the problem and its location (see Table III-5).

Possible 'outsiders' who might attend a walk-through include representatives from auditing, quality assurance, operations, or other project teams who need to approve or work with the final product.

After the session, the scribe types the notes and presents a memo to the author for resolution. The author then responds to each item (see Figure III-7). If an item is an error, the response details how and when it was fixed. If the item is an efficiency or effectiveness issue, the response describes what research was done and the resolution. Depending on the extent of problems or the importance of the product, another walk-through might be held. Usually, if the products are for analysis or design, two or three walk-throughs are held. If the product relates to program or test design, then the number of walk-throughs is determined by the number of errors. With

less than 10 errors, only one walk-through would be needed.

Data Administration

Data administration is the management of data to support and foster data sharing across multiple divisions, and to facilitate the development of database applications. The principle activity for the organization is the development of a **data architecture** which depicts the structure and relationships of major data entities, such as customer, vendors, and orders. A data architecture is similar to the frame of a building. Once the frame is constructed, the siding and façade are added. The frame provides the skeleton to which the other substructures, such as electrical wiring and plumbing, are added. In information systems, the data architecture defines automated and nonautomated data and how they are used in the organization. The architecture provides a 'frame' for defining new applications and documents all data uses and responsibilities for existing applications.

The other major organization level activity is defining, with users, data that is 'mission critical' for the organization. **Critical data** is defined as that data required to maintain the organization as a going concern. As such, critical data is subject to management and standards through the data administration function. Noncritical data is data that, while useful, is not required to maintain the organization in event of a disaster. Noncritical data does not require the same degree of management as critical data.

At a more detailed level, data administrators develop, administer, and maintain policies and standards regarding data definition, sharing, acquisition, integrity, and security for the corporation's data resource. Data administration provides guidance to project teams on storage, access, use, disposition, and standardization of data. Data administrators are responsible for maintaining corporate definitions in addition to the creation and maintenance of the data architecture representing the enterprise.

Historically, the motivation for data administration relates to a maturing organization. When DBMS software was installed in most organizations, a **database administration (DBA)** group was created to

TABLE III-5   Example of Errors Found in Walk-Throughs

Walk-Through Type	Representative Errors Found
Feasibility	1. One of organization, technical, or financial analyses is missing. 2. Financial analysis has mathematical errors. 3. Typos or poor English render the document (or some part) incomprehensible. 4. Analysis contains incorrect information.
Analysis	1. Data elements for data store, file, or other structure are incomplete. 2. Data items do not have formal names or names do not conform to standards. 3. Subsystem specification unclear. 4. Obvious 'holes' in the system as specified. 5. Graphical representations contain syntactical errors or confusing, ambiguous terms. 6. Nature of application interfaces not fully specified.
Logical Data Model	1. Logical data model (LDM) is not in third normal form (3NF). 2. Names do not conform to standards or are ambiguous.
Design	1. Mapping to implementation environment does not include all functional requirements. 2. Implementation as specified will be difficult to operate, maintain, or implement. 3. Design is incomplete . . . one or more screens are missing, screen dialog is incomplete, allowable navigation not provided, etc.
Physical Data Model	1. Physical mapping does not provide necessary user views and security simultaneously. 2. Numerous user views may be unwieldy in implemented environment. 3. Physical model does not provide growth anticipated.
Program Specification	1. Program specification does not clearly say what the program is to do. 2. Program specification does not map to design or functional requirements. 3. File requirements not specific . . . missing user view, copy lib name, JCL, etc. 4. Logic specification incomplete. 5. Faulty logic. 6. Access control for secure data not present.
Acceptance Test Plan (This could be any test plan)	1. Test plan does not test that all requirements are met. 2. Test case x data cannot perform as specified. 3. Missing/erroneous predicted results for reports, screens, file contents, or messages. 4. Missing on-line test dialog for single user functions. 5. Missing scenario and test dialogs for multiuser test. 6. Results predicted cannot be attained with current test design. 7. Test for breach of security missing. 8. Specific audit control tests missing/faulty.
Code	1. Logic error—missing, extra, or wrong logic. 2. Nonstructured format will make maintenance difficult and expensive. 3. Comments do not identify module linkages. 4. Comments on user view copy books do not clearly identify the database, user view, or JCL. 5. Access control for secure data not present. 6. Control totals for end of program counts missing. 7. Format error on report. 8. Misspelled word on screen, report, etc.

Consolidated NY Bank
InterOffice Memo

DATE: December 7, 1992

TO: Ms. Sandra Jones,
           Walk-Through Facilitator

FROM: Mr. John James,
           Producer

The following table includes all errors found during the Requirements Walk-Through on December 1 (see H. Hines, Scribe memo of 12/2). Each item has either been resolved or found not to be an error as indicated. One item, #5, identified an audit problem for which I am awaiting Audit Dept. resolution. They are supposed to respond by next Friday, December 11. Since we decided not to have another walk-through, I will proceed with finalizing the analysis phase.

Error #	Error Page	Description	Resolution
1	2	Overview inconsistent in treatment of errors for transactions.	Rewritten
2	10	System access code design not clear.	The lack of clarity was deliberate to prevent general access to security procedures. The group felt that the document should contain all of the information.
			Upon reviewing this request with Mr. Fields, Project Manager, we decided, for security reasons, not to include the information. Mr. Fields has a detailed description of security procedures and the document now refers individuals requesting the security information to him.
3	63	Test of screens is incomplete.	Missing information was added.
4	125	Security for accounting data not clear.	Same as #2.
5	127	Interface to accounting system has inadequate control counts and security.	Referred to the Audit Dept. for recommended action.

FIGURE III-7   Sample Walk-Through Error Resolution Memo

maintain and monitor the DBMS' use. There was no necessity for other data-related organizations because applications, for the most part, were isolated from one another and data sharing across organizational boundaries was low. Most industry followed this pattern of development.

In the normal process of maturation, companies realized that sharing and consolidation of databases across organization boundaries was desirable. The need to share data frequently accompanies the realization that individual division and work groups have their own vocabulary which often overlaps or conflicts with the vocabulary and terms used by other work groups. When divisions automate data, they incorporate local rules, policy, and definitions in their applications. Data, while having the same name, then, may have several different meanings, uses, formats, and connotations across an organization. Conversely, data may have different names but the same definitions. This lack of consensus about terminology and data characterizes predata administration organizations.

The lack of consensus about data definitions leads to the realization that data standards pertaining to definitions, usage, ownership, security, access, and maintenance are not only desirable, but mandatory, in large-scale development of shared databases. This need for standardization increases with the recognition of data as a shared resource of the organization.

A formal data administration function is needed to define and manage data company-wide. Data administration requires recognition and commitment to the notion that data is a resource of the corporation. As a critical corporate resource, data requires the same careful planning and on-going management as cash on hand, office equipment, or personnel.

Commitment to DA is sometimes difficult to develop because data are fundamentally different than other resources. Data are abstract and nonphysical, do not decay, and are easily replicated as the need arises. They are also subject to different confidentiality, accuracy, and access requirements. Data are all of these things. In service industries, especially, information is a primary product, and the quality of the data resource directly affects the company's bottom line and how customers perceive the quality of service delivered. Data administration consolidates information across the organization to simplify the development of applications to service customers.

Benefits of data administration outweigh the frustrations and difficulties of establishing the function. Some of the benefits include:

1. Creating and documenting a data architecture leads to formal recognition and agreement of business rules and relationships which are inherent in the data. This agreement improves communications and understanding of corporate data.
2. By defining and documenting data only once, efficiencies are realized throughout the system development life cycle. All subsequent

application—using previously defined data items—identify data required and obtain access to already automated data. The data design and documentation phases are shortened. Edit routines are reused, just like the data definitions, and ultimately the cost of program code is reduced.

3. Data administration leads to faster response to changing business conditions. The development of applications to support new products, for instance, can be speeded due to fully specified definition of data required to support a product.
4. Data administration provides a means for deciding what data must be controlled as part of the corporate data resource, and what data can be user-owned and controlled (including data that is off-loaded to PCs and LANs).
5. Data administration maintains definitions of *all* data in the corporation regardless of hardware platform or criticality. The central repository for this information, then, becomes the focal point of data-related activities.
6. By fostering data sharing, the cost of creating, sorting, updating, and backing up multiple copies of the same data items is reduced, if not eliminated. That is, we only introduce *planned data redundancy*. Just as DBMSs allow us to minimize intraapplication data redundancy, DA allows us to minimize interapplication data redundancy.

In summary, the creation of data administration is recommended to guarantee minimal redundancy, shared understanding of data item definitions, and a managed approach to providing for future database environments. Data administration should not be confused with DBA data management which includes physical DB design, disk space allocation, and day-to-day operations support for actual databases.

Data administration has numerous interfaces both within and outside of the IS area. Therefore, data administration interfaces occur at all levels of all divisions specifically to perform user liaison and application liaison.

User Liaison

The data administration function works with business areas to define the data which that area uses to perform its function. All data, whether it is under the control of a current information system or not, is subject to data administration review. Thus, all data on any hardware platform is subject to review. During the review, critical data entities and data items are defined, maintained, and managed by data administration. Applications with critical data will be required to comply with standards on data, access, and security.

The person performing user liaison must be able to understand and converse in business terminology, not technical jargon. He or she should have problem-solving and analytical skills but also should have excellent communication/negotiation skills, user orientation, and understanding of the role and functions of data administration. The individual must be able to translate user data, definitions, and rules into information in the corporate data repository.

Application Liaison

Data administration works with application project teams to define the data requirements of the application. The data administration analyst identifies what data is already automated and works with the project team to define logical descriptions of the data. The DA analyst, DBA, and project analyst together transform the logical database definition into a specific database's logical definition. The DA analyst down-loads the data definitions from the corporate central repository for use by the project team and DBA. DBA then works to develop a physical database definition of how best to store the data.

In project-oriented work, the project analyst and DA analyst reconcile all data requirements with existing information in the corporate repository. For instance, if a team needs a "plan" field, but their definition varies from that of the corporate definition, one of three actions is possible:

1. The corporate definition is changed to accommodate the new information.
2. The application redefines its use to be consistent with the corporate definition and usage.

3. A new data item is defined by the project analyst and DA; the new item is entered into the corporate central repository by the DA.

The skills, then, needed to perform application project liaison include analytical, communication, problem-solving, negotiation, data analysis, and modeling skills.

Where in the Organization is Data Administration

Ideally, the recommended organizational location of the DA function is independent of the corporate IS area, reporting to the president of the business entity it supports. DA affects and interacts with all departments and areas of the organization, including all of the application development groups as well as users, regardless of organizational position or hardware platform. The DA group could be part of an internal consulting/technology-related organization whose mission is to provide services across the entire organization. The DA group should be neutral about hardware, software, development, or management of applications as long as the data is not defined as critical.

CASE Tools

Computer-aided software engineering (CASE) is the automation of the software engineering discipline. You will find descriptions of ICASE, Upper CASE, and Lower CASE. These are variations on the theme with 'I' standing for 'integrated,' 'Upper' standing for conceptual or logical design only, and 'Lower' standing for programming support only. While these differences do exist, this text concentrates on CASE tools that support at least the analysis phase and may support others; they are all called 'CASE' here. We will identify which phases are now supported (of course, this might change by publication time).

The typical CASE environment includes a repository, graphic drawing tools, text definition software, repository interface software, evaluative software,

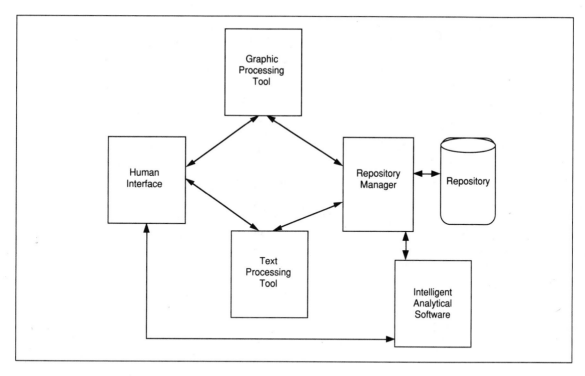

FIGURE III-8   CASE Architecture

and a human interface (see Figure III-8). A **reposi-tory** is an active data dictionary that supports the definition of different types of objects and the relationships between those objects. Graphic drawing tools support the development of diagram types and evaluates the completeness of the diagram based on predefined rules. Text software allows definition of names, contents, and details of items in the repository. The interface software is the interpreter which determines the form the data should take (either graphic or text). Evaluative software is the intelligence in CASE. Evaluative software analyzes the entries for a diagram or repository entry and determines if they are lexically complete (i.e., conforms to the definition of the item type), and if they are compatible with other existing objects in the application. The human interface provides screens and reports for interactive and off-line processing.

In this section, we discuss the characteristics of the ideal CASE environment. This is just an ideal

and is the author's own invention.[12] No commercially available products and no research prototypes are known to embody this ideal.

The ideal CASE should provide complete automated support for the entire project life cycle, beginning with enterprise level analysis and working through to maintenance and retirement. The ideal CASE then becomes the focal point for all work that takes place in software engineering, and the work of the SE concentrates on the logical aspects of design. The ideal CASE tool would provide for the technical, data, and process architectures of the organization, project planning and monitoring,

---

12 The ideal CASE in this section is partially the result of research done with Judy Wynekoop, UT San Antonio and Nancy Russo, U of Northern Illinois, published in Wynekoop and Conger [1991], Conger [1989], Conger and Russo [1990]. It also results from 10 years of frustration in using CASE tools and waiting for vendors and researchers to build decent products.

group work on applications, application and manual procedure definition, normalization of data, DB schema generation, generation of bug-free code in a user-selected language, automatic testing of generated code against the application logic, and intelligent assessment of completeness and correction along the way. Really advanced CASE would recognize components already in the repository for reusability of analyses, designs, and code.

The repository of CASE determines both what is supported and, to some extent, how much support can be provided. The repository is something of a *super dictionary* that captures and maintains meta-data. Meta-data is information about data (see Chapter 1). For example, a data element in an application is data, and its attributes constitute the meta-data that would be stored in the dictionary. Attributes of an element include, for instance, data type, size, volume, frequency of change, and edit criteria. A **CASE repository** acts as the DBMS for the engineering effort, provides the capability for expanded meta-data capture, and maintains all components and their interrelationships.

The ideal repository should allow customizing of the methodology supported and enforcement software that can evaluate the correctness of user-defined repository entries. To do this requires some decoupling of the repository from a specific methodology and an abstracting of methodology compliance rules within the repository. These are not trivial tasks! This decoupling would allow organizations to adopt and use the components of methodologies that work for them, and ignore those that don't. The initial sacrifice for this capability will be less intelligence. But, decoupling the intelligence from a specific methodology and type of repository entry will also allow customizing of evaluation software and enforcement of local rules.

Intelligence in CASE comes in two major forms: intelligence of the interface and intelligence of the CASE product itself. The interface should provide both novice and expert modes of operation. It should allow work to be saved and restarted as part of the functionality. The tool should be customizable by individual users. For instance, if I want yellow print on a blue background, and I call a data flow diagram

a DFD, I should be allowed to change the defaults to use my terms and formats.

Alternate forms of inputs should be reflected throughout the diagram sets. This means that if a user enters entities and attributes in a repository, when she or he moves to developing a graphical entity-relationship diagram, the information in the repository should be reflected on the diagram.

Intelligence of the CASE product includes analysis within and between both diagram types and repository entries. Ideally, application A's requirement that conflicts with enterprise goal Z, should be flagged for management consideration.

The ideal CASE should allow users to separate and integrate different applications easily. For instance, the company may want to document already operational applications and begin to manage them electronically. Users defining a new application may want to integrate it with an old application. They should be allowed to create an integrated third definition that highlights the overlaps, redundancies, inconsistencies, and other problems that the integrated pair have.

According to the 40-20-40 rule of systems development, 40% of project time is used for analysis and design, 20% is devoted to programming, and a full 40% is devoted to testing.[13] The current direction of vendors is to eliminate code, thereby cutting 20% off development time. But, the ideal CASE would cut the 40% devoted to testing as well. The urgency for CASE testing tools is low relative to other current concerns (like getting the products to work bug-free). At some point in the 1990s, vendors will begin to provide testing support in their CASE environments. Ideally, such support will include black- and white-box tests with human intervention allowed but not required. Black-box testing is for correctness of output based on inputs; white-box testing is for specific logic paths in a program. Intelligent software will analyze the type of process and determine the most appropriate testing strategy. Additional intelligent software will develop test data based on logical requirements, conduct the tests, and maintain test results. Test results will be integrated

---

13 Pressman [1987].

across test runs, phases of testing, versions of the software, and even hardware platform environments. When bugs are found, backtracking to find its source, possibly across modules, will be provided. Since the software built the bugs, it should be able to fix them; but, if the source is a logical, human specification, notice to the SEs will require correction of the errors.

Future products will eventually tackle the remaining 40% of project time by providing intelligence to identify reusable components of applications. Reusability of designs will have the most payback but is also the most difficult. Initially, reusable code modules will be enabled, then reusable designs, and finally, reusable logical analyses. Code reusability recognition should be available in CASE tools by the mid-1990s; the others will take until the turn of the century to surface.

This description of ideal CASE characteristics concentrates on what CASE should do rather than on what it currently does. For that, we discuss CASE as it supports each methodology and phase of development in the coming chapters. Although CASE and artificial intelligence (AI) are both in their infancy, the developments described above are currently feasible with current state-of-the-art technologies. The CASE repository will become the hub for all of the work that takes place in IS organizations. The limits to CASE intelligence that can be built are only due to human limitations.

SUMMARY

In this section preview, we identified the major activities of analysis and design. Analysis identifies *what* the application will do; design describes *how* the application will work in production. Both analysis and design have the same five generic activities: identification, elaboration, synthesis, review, and documentation. These activities are constrained and guided by a methodology. Each methodology takes a different perspective of an application leading to different phase-end results.

The organizational supports facilitate application development regardless of methodology. Organiza-

tional supports described in this chapter included joint requirements definition, joint application design, user-managed application development, data administration, and walk-throughs.

Software support that most facilitates application development is computer-aided software engineering (CASE). The ideal CASE environment has both expert and novice modes, can be customized for hybrid methodology use, and provides many additional intelligent functions beyond analyzing completeness of work. Future environments will identify reusable components of previous work to further reduce application development time.

The next six chapters discuss the analysis and design phases using the following example methodologies:

Process—Structured Analysis (Chapter 7) and Design (Chapter 8)
Data—Information Engineering—Business Area Analysis (Chapter 9) and Business System Design (Chapter 10)
Object—Object-Oriented Analysis (Chapter 11) and Object-Oriented Design (Chapter 12).

Chapter 13 summarizes and compares the methodologies and their CASE support. Chapter 14 discusses forgotten activities of systems analysis and design.

REFERENCES

Blum, B., *Software Engineering: A Holistic View*. NY: Oxford University Press, 1992.

Conger, S., "The active dictionary in a CASE environment," *Data Base Management*, #25-01-20, NY: Auerbach Publishers, 1989, pp. 1–12.

Conger, S., and N. Russo, "A Taxonomy of Applications: A Framework for Selecting and Designing Methodologies," Georgia State University Working Paper #90-0201, 1990.

Couger, J. D., M. A. Colter, and R. W. Knapp, *Advanced System Development/Feasibility Techniques*. NY: John Wiley & Sons, 1982.

McClure, C., *CASE is Software Automation*. Englewood Cliffs, NJ: Prentice-Hall, 1989.

McMenamin, S. M., and J. F. Palmer, *Essential Systems Analysis*. NY: Yourdon, Inc., 1984.

Pressman, R., *Software Engineering: A Practitioner's Approach*, 2nd ed. NY: McGraw-Hill, 1987.

Olle, T. W., J. Hagelstein, I. G. MacDonald, C. Rolland, H. G. Sol, F. J. M. Van Assche, and A. A. Verrijn-Stuart, *Information Systems Methodology: A Framework for Understanding*. Workingham, England: Addison-Wesley, 1988.

Swartout, W., and R. Balzer, "On the inevitable intertwining of specification and implementation," *Communications of the ACM*, Vol. 25, #7, July, 1982, pp. 438–440.

Wynekoop, J. L., and S. Conger [1991], "A review of computer-aided software engineering research methods," in *Information Systems Research: Contemporary Approaches and Emergent Traditions*, (H-E. Nissen, H. K. Klein, and R. Hirschheim, eds.). NY: North-Holland, 1991, pp. 301–326.

KEY TERMS

active data dictionary
analysis
CASE repository
compromise of
   requirements
computer-aided software
   engineering (CASE)
critical data
data administration (DA)
data architecture
database administration
   (DBA)
design
document
elaboration
facilitator

Fast-Track
identification
IS-managed application
joint application design
   (JAD)
joint requirements planning
   (JRP)
out of the box thinking
repository
review
synthesis
user-managed application
user manager
walk-through
work around

## CHAPTER 7

PROCESS-ORIENTED ANALYSIS

INTRODUCTION

In this chapter, we review process-oriented analysis using structured analysis following DeMarco [1979], Yourdon [1989], and McMenamin and Palmer [1985]. Structured analysis was the first well-documented, and well-understood method of describing application problems. While the techniques have changed as our understanding and application types have changed, the techniques will remain useful for many years to come. This material should be a review, and for that reason, you might want to skim or skip it altogether. You might rate your knowledge by tracing the development of the ABC Rental Processing case. If you understand *and can reproduce* the work, skip the chapter.

CONCEPTUAL FOUNDATIONS

Structured analysis (and design) follow the architectural notion that "form ever follows function."[1] Functions of an information system are the processes

that transform application data. Therefore, we emphasize processes and the flows of data into and out of those processes in **structured analysis**.

Structured analysis also is based on **systems theory** which assumes inputs are fed into processes to produce outputs. To complete the **systems model** (see Figure 7-1), there must be some sort of feedback to eliminate system entropy, that is, to keep the system from 'running down.'

To conceptually analyze complex systems as we have in IS, pieces of a problem are analyzed in isolation. We might look at inputs, outputs, and processes separately, then integrate them to produce a unified system. As system processing gets more complex, we study pieces of processes separately then integrate them. The pieces of the processes

---

1 Sullivan, Louis, "The Tall Office Building Artistically Considered," *Lippencott's Magazine*, March, 1896.

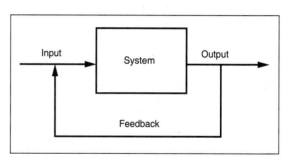

FIGURE 7-1   Systems Model

must themselves be self-contained, small systems. These smaller systems comprise a hierarchy of system components, such that a component at any level is itself a system of components. Each *system*, regardless of level, has its own inputs, processes, outputs, and feedback. At the lowest level of the hierarchy are the **elementary components** which can no longer be subdivided and retain their system characteristics.

Structured development provides heuristics, guidelines, and diagram sets for dividing an information system into a hierarchy of logical component parts.

SUMMARY OF STRUCTURED SYSTEMS ANALYSIS TERMS

Structured analysis begins with two assumptions. First, we assume that we are most interested in what the application is *to do*. That is, what are its functions or processes? A **function** or **process** is some activity that transforms an input data flow into an output data flow. Second, we assume that we will treat the problem in a top-down manner. In top-down analysis, we analyze the external interfaces of the application first, then high level functions, and finally, lower level functions.

At the highest level, we define the scope of project activity. The **scope** defines the boundaries of the project: what is *in* the project and what is *outside* of the project. We document the scope of the project in a context diagram. A **context** defines a setting or environment. In structured systems analysis, the **context diagram** defines the interactions of the application with the external world. External world interactions occur between external entities and the application via the data flows that pass between them. An **external entity** is a person, place, or thing with which the application interacts, such as

Accounts Receivable Application
Citibank
Customer

Customer Service Department
Medicaid Processing Application
Medicaid Administration
The Federal Reserve Bank
The Internet (or other public network)
U.S. Internal Revenue Service

A **data flow** is data or information that is *in transit*. A data flow might be a piece of paper, a report, a diskette, or a computer message. Data flows in a diagram are directed arrows that depict data movement from one place to another.

A context diagram depicts the scope of the project, using circles, squares, and arrows. A large circle designates the application (see Figure 7-2). Squares identify external entities with which the application must interact. Directed lines (i.e., with arrows) are the data flows which indicate movement of data between entities and the application.

At the next lower level of analysis, we look inside the circle representing the application to define the major functions and files. Again, the functions are the major transformations triggered by input data flows to create output data flows. **Files** or **data stores** are relatively permanent collections of data. *Data flows* are distinct from *data stores* in their time orientation. Data flows are temporary and cease to exist once they are acted upon by a process. Data stores are persistent and maintained over time. Data stores may represent one or more data structures.

A **data flow diagram (DFD)** (see Figure 7-3) is a graphic representation of the application's component parts. Notice in Figure 7-3 that the entities and data flows from the context are all present. Also notice that data flows may connect processes to other processes, data stores, or external entities. Data stores and external entities do not interact directly with each other. If we compare the context to the data flow, we can perform quality assurance for completeness and consistency. *Completeness* checking ensures that *all* data flows and entities are included. *Consistency* checking ensures that *only* expected data flows and entities are included and that they are in the correct locations in the diagram set.

We do several iterations of DFD process analysis. At the highest level of analysis, the DFD is said to

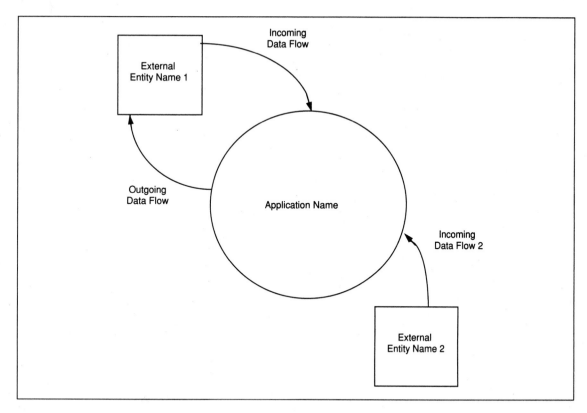

FIGURE 7-2   Sample Context Diagram

describe **Level 0** of the application. Each iteration is a *deeper* level of analysis to look into the processes from the previous level, analyzing the subprocesses, their constituent data flows, and their data stores. We link DFD levels through the process numbering scheme (see Figure 7-4). For example, process 1.0 from the level 0 diagram is decomposed into processes 1.1, 1.2, 1.3, and so on to describe the **Level 1** DFD. In Figure 7-4 Process 1.0 is decomposed into two subprocesses. Notice that a new file and an entity are other details added to the diagram. Level 1 DFDs may be further decomposed. To continue the example, process 1.1 might be decomposed into processes 1.1.1, 1.1.2, 1.1.3, and so on, until we reach the primitive, basic level. The **primitive level** is the level of each process at which no further decomposition can be done without fracturing the function. In other words, the decompositions at each level fully define the function, but may not

define all of the functional details. At the primitive level, all files, flows, entities, and individual functions have been defined. There is no *right* level of definition; level is usually related to the type of application and target implementation language. You may do only two or three levels of decomposition for a nonprocedural, fourth generation language; you may do six or seven levels of decomposition for assembler or low level procedural languages (e.g., COBOL or Pascal).

The **structured decomposition** technique is a mechanism for coping with application complexity through the principal of 'divide and conquer.' A large, complex application problem is divided into its parts for individual analysis. Each part is further divided and individually analyzed. Complexity is reduced by allowing us to analyze small parts of the problem in isolation. The difficulties in structured decomposition are in correctly identifying the

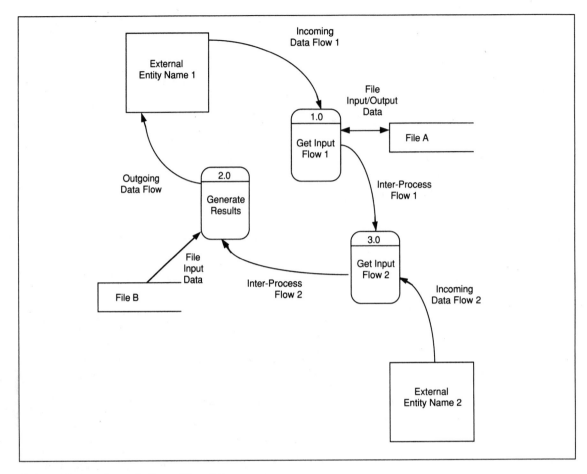

FIGURE 7-3   Sample Data Flow Diagram

isolated parts, and keeping the level of abstraction consistent.

After each analysis, the current level of DFDs is balanced with the previous level. **Balancing** is the act of checking entities, data flows, and processes across the levels of the diagram set. All entities and data flows from the higher level processes *must be* in every more detailed diagram. The names of entities and data flows must be consistent across the levels of the diagrams. We also balance processes. Lower level processes 'explain' or provide the details of higher level processes. Lower level processes are checked to be sure that they all relate to one, and only one, of the processes named at the higher level. They are then checked to be sure that they are in the

diagram set for their related higher level process. When complete, processing is fully documented in a **leveled set of DFDs**.

While a set of balanced DFDs is being created, the secondary documentation is also being created. The secondary documentation includes creation of a data dictionary and optional graphics for real-time applications called state-transition diagrams. The **data dictionary**[2] compiles detailed definitions for each element in a DFD (see Figure 7-5 for contents for each entry type). The dictionary entries for processes contain details of how to accomplish the

_____

2 See DeMarco [1979] and Yourdon [1989].

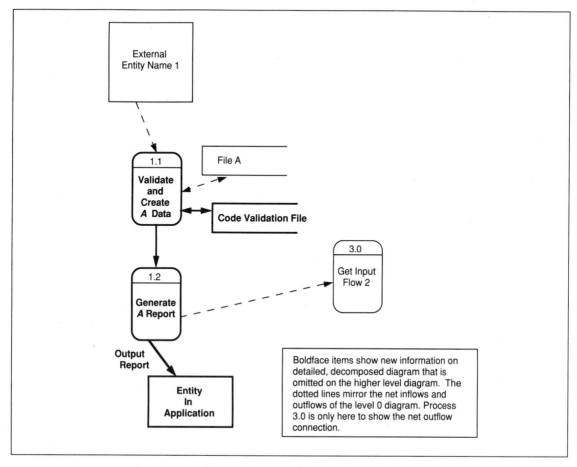

FIGURE 7-4   Example of Decomposed DFD

process. For instance, a process description for order creation might contain requirements for data entry, customer validation, item validation, order printing, and order filing. Since you get information on data piecemeal throughout the analysis (and design), it is easiest to document what you know as you go along. Surfacing assumptions, misconceptions, and data conflicts can be easier with this approach because the dictionary is always up to date with information and its source. If you collect pieces of paper and create the dictionary late in the analysis phase, identifying the source of conflicting information can be difficult.

Although not originally part of structured analysis, state-transition diagrams are frequently used to supplement DFDs in structured analysis for on-line

(and real-time) applications. A **state-transition diagram** shows the time ordering of processes and identifies relationships between processes. State-transition diagrams are an integral part of object-oriented analysis and are deferred until that discussion in Chapter 11.

STRUCTURED SYSTEMS ANALYSIS ACTIVITIES

The specific activities in structured systems analysis are:

1. Develop a context diagram
2. Develop a set of balanced data flow diagrams
3. Develop a data dictionary
4. Optionally, develop a state-transition diagram if building an on-line or real-time application.

Data File or Data Base	File/Database Name Aliases Primary Key Alternate Keys Size of Relations/Records Growth Percentage per Year Security Data Structure Organization

Data Field or Attribute	User Name
	System Name
	Aliases
	Definition, if needed
	Creating Process(es)
	Length
	Data Type
	Allowable Values and Meanings
	Validation Method (e.g., cross-
	    reference file, code
	    check, etc.)

Data Flow	Name
	Aliases
	Timing (e.g., daily, weekly, as
	    occurs, etc.)
	Contents
	Constraints (e.g., requires
	    5 second response; only oc-
	    curs for sales orders, etc.)

Process	Process Name
	Process Number
	Description
	Constraints (e.g., must be
	    complete within 20 seconds or
	    Process x times out.)

External Entity	Entity Name Aliases Definition Relationship to Application Contact (if entity is an organization)

FIGURE 7-5   Data Dictionary Contents by Type of Entry

Structured analysis can be likened to a video camera with a zoom lens. At a distance, with no zoom, the item being examined is abstract and fuzzy. It has shape but no details. We can tell the photo is a building but little else (see Figure 7-6). When we draw a context diagram, we are examining the abstract shape of the item, in our case an application. Next, we zoom in with the camera to identify a greater level of detail about the object. In the photo, colors are distinct and some features of objects stand out. Pieces of the structure, for instance, columns, can be discussed in isolation of other pieces. Internal photos might show position, size, and type decor of rooms. There are still details which remain indistinct. When we develop the Level 0 diagram, we zoom in a level to expose more details of the problem. At this level, we describe the major normal processes, data flows, and files, and how they interrelate with external entities from the context.

In the third photo, we see all of the details: loose tiles on a roof, a crack in a foundation. Internal photos at the same level might detail construction materials (e.g., hardwood or concrete floors), and windows and doors to the outside. We can describe the context and surroundings, as well as the photo item, in as much detail as needed to suit our purpose. Similarly, at each additional level of application problem decomposition, we are zooming in to examine ever more detailed layers of the item, until we arrive at the essential processes in the application. At the lowest level of decomposition, we analyze not just the normal processing but all exceptions, errors, and details of reporting that accompany the normal processes. From systems theory, we know we are finished decomposing when we can no longer identify *minisystems* as the components of subprocesses.

The problem with the photographic zoom analogy is that the activities in structured analysis are not strictly top-down. First, we do not think in a strictly top-down manner. We jump back and forth between levels of detail to 'test' how a higher level decision might look at a lower level, to get details of a new process so we are sure how it 'fits' with the other processes, and so on. When we are developing an application similar to something we have already done, we have a good understanding of familiar parts and little understanding of new parts. We spend time

FIGURE 7-6   Zoom Analogy to Structured Analysis

analyzing the new parts of the application to see how they fit with what we already know. We have to change our preconceptions based on the new information, and alter our 'mental model' at all levels of detail to accommodate the new information. We may go into great detail on a new aspect of the application, ignoring the known aspects temporarily. Then, when we understand the new parts, we can go back up to a high level of abstraction to document how the parts fit together.

Second, application analysis is iterative. We have already discussed planned iterations to move to lower levels of detail in documentation. We also reiterate through analysis when we find some unexpected, unknown, or changed requirement to ensure that it fits what we already know. To decide that fit, we must *walk-through* the entire process top to bottom. Recall that a **walk-through** is a formal review of analysis, design, program code, test design, or some other component of application development work. A walk-through can be used to determine

    where the new requirement fits
  what other processes, flows, stores, or entities
    are involved in the change

what are the ripple effects of the change through
    the set of DFDs.

Another analogy for structured analysis, as equally applicable as the photo zoom, is from geology (see Figure 7-7[3]). If we are trying to drill for oil, we might find a variety of different formations and even have different drilling results, depending on the depth and angle. So, too, in structured analysis our results depend on our approach and the information we obtain from interviews and information gathering. The information differs for each user because their perspective of the problem, their job goals, and their personal aspirations all distort their view. We require multiple approaches, multiple interviews with both the same and different people, and multiple perspectives of analyzing the information. Figure 7-6 shows unfocused probing. The pieces and views do not fit together. We know we are at the end of analysis when all users agree *and* all the disparate

---

3 This analogy is from Gary Moore, University of Calgary, who
  originally used it to describe research in information systems.
  It fits the application development context as well.

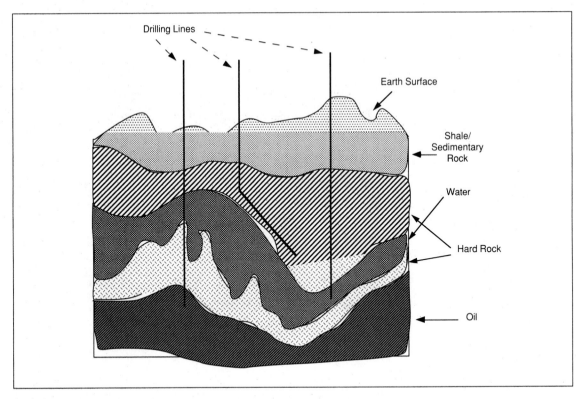

FIGURE 7-7   Geologic Analogy to Structured Analysis

views fit together coherently. Recall that triangulation is a data gathering technique comparing multiple verifying sources of all information. The purpose of triangulation is to ensure that *our* resulting view of an application accurately depicts the requirements of the work process it supports. So, we analyze top-down, sideways-out, bottom-up, *and* do them all more than once in the analysis process.

Now, we turn to the discussion of *how* to actually develop the documentation in structured analysis.

Develop Context Diagram

Rules for Developing Context Diagram

The context diagram summarizes the scope of the project. The rules for developing the context diagram are listed below for easy reference.

1. Define the boundaries (i.e., scope) of the application. Specifically, define what the application will do *and* what it will not do. Draw the circle identifying the application and write the application name in the center.
2. Using the application boundary as a starting point, identify all external entities with which the application must interact. For each entity, draw one square on the diagram and label the square.
3. For each entity, create a definition in the data dictionary.
4. For each external entity, identify the specific data flows that define the interface.
5. For each data flow, create a definition and list of tentative contents in the data dictionary.

Scoping may take place before analysis actually occurs and is usually part of the feasibility study as discussed in Chapter 6. Some organizations which might not perform feasibility analysis still require a bounding of the application. Review that portion of Chapter 6 if you do not remember the political and organizational issues involved. Here, we assume that boundaries are defined and that the application and its interfaces to external entities are reasonably well defined.

Definition of external entities is next. External entities are people, places, or things which interact with the application. Usually, we identify titles/roles (e.g., Customer), departments (e.g., Accounts Receivable), organizations (e.g., Medicare Administration), or applications (e.g., Accounts Receivable Application) as entities. The phrase 'interact with the application' has a very specific meaning. The entity is *outside* the control and/or processing being modeled for the current application. That is, external entity processing, procedures, and data are *not* subject to analysis or change. Relationships between external entities are *not* shown on the diagram(s) (i.e., external entities cannot connect to each other). For example, if you are modeling an order processing application that does not do inventory control, the warehouse would be on the context diagram. If inventory control and warehouse processing are within the scope of the application, the warehouse would not be on the context diagram.

After entities are identified and drawn on the diagram, they should be defined in the data dictionary. The entries for an entity include a name and definition (see sample Figure 7-8). This step is important for two reasons: to develop a common vocabulary, and to develop documentation as analysis proceeds. Frequently, individuals might believe they have a common vocabulary because they use the same words in their discussions. Only when they develop a common definition of the terms can they be sure that their shared terminology also means they share the meaning of the terms (see Example 7-1). Finally, in organizations having a data administration function, a dictionary (or repository) of 'corporate' data is an integral part of the organization's data architecture (see Chapters 9 and 10 for more on this topic). The name and definition of each entity (and, eventually, each attribute) should be matched against the organizational definitions to

Entity Name	Customer
Aliases	None
Definition	A company, government agency, nonprofit organization, or individual who orders goods and services from *X* Company
Relationship to Application	Order goods, return goods, receive invoice
Contact, if entity is an organization	None
Entity Name	Medicaid Administration
Aliases	Medicaid
Relationship to Application	Receives claims, sends claim reconciliation, payment
Contact, if entity is an organization	Mary Jones 202-445-0011, NY State Claims Adjustor Medicaid Administration 1401 Avenue C, NE Washington, D.C. 01010

FIGURE 7-8   Example of External Entity Description

ensure consistency with other uses of the same name, or uniqueness of the name if a new definition is developed.

There are several reasons for documenting definitions in the dictionary as work proceeds. First, the dictionary provides the basis for intraproject communication. Whenever a definition is developed and added to the dictionary, the more the team builds a shared view of the application reflecting the dictionary contents. Second, documentation is best done as the project progresses to ensure that it gets done. If documentation is delayed until after implementation, it rarely includes the wealth of detail and history of decisions that can be incorporated if done instream.

The next action in developing the context diagram is to define data flows between the application and each external entity. The questions you ask yourself to identify data flows are, "What *information* do I (as the application) need from this entity?" and "What *information* do I feedback or provide to this entity?" Frequently, but not always, input flows (to

---

EXAMPLE 7-1

A CASE OF NO SHARED MEANING

The XYZ Annuity Company was developing a new application to define the institutions which defined its customer base. The exercise was prompted partially by a lament from the head of marketing who claimed, "There are 6,400, 7,500, or 9,650 institutions, depending on who I ask and which application they are getting the numbers from. Can't I have *one* number of institutions?"

A newly founded Data Administration team decided that the first "corporate" definition they would tackle was institution. The data analyst assigned first asked *application developer* colleagues, "What is an institution?"

The replies were varied and generally, unsatisfactory:

> Anyone we do business with.
> An organization we do business with.
> Any legal entity we do business with.
> A school, research and development institution, not-for-profit foundation, or other organization which is approved by the IRS to contract for annuity business with XYZ Annuity.
> An organization that has a plan defining a group of annuity contracts.

Then the analyst asked the *users*, "What is an institution?"

> Some organization that remits annuity payments (a remittance clerk's definition)
> An organization with a plan defining a group of contracts (a accounting manager's attempt at a generic definition)
> An approved organization which may or may not have a contract plan (a marketing definition)

> An organization to whom annuity and pension product counseling is provided (a counselor's definition)
> A target audience for marketing and selling annuity products (a marketing definition)

The analyst then asked the *senior manager* in charge of institutional relations to please define an institution. His response was a three-page, single-spaced memo that defined six major variants and over 30 different situational definitions for an institution.

Two important ideas here are, first, *all of these definitions are correct*, and second, *each definition has some generally accepted component*. Definitions relate to perspective. A systems person defines an institution in relation to the application's use of the term. A user defines the term in relation to their job's use of the term. The manager tried to synthesize all perspectives and highlighted the variation and divergence that had evolved throughout the organization. Third, *all of these definitions have some element that appears important to defining "institution."*

When asked about the differences in the definitions, one user said, "Oh, yes, we know we don't all mean the same thing when we use the term institution. I even mean different things depending on the topic."

Resolution of the differences took over six months of part-time work, resulted in the definition of 20 new attributes of an institution, and required the approval of 72 managers in the process. Several applications under development that were using an institutional billing code as the primary key identifier underwent substantial redefinition as a result of the development of a shared term, 'institution.'

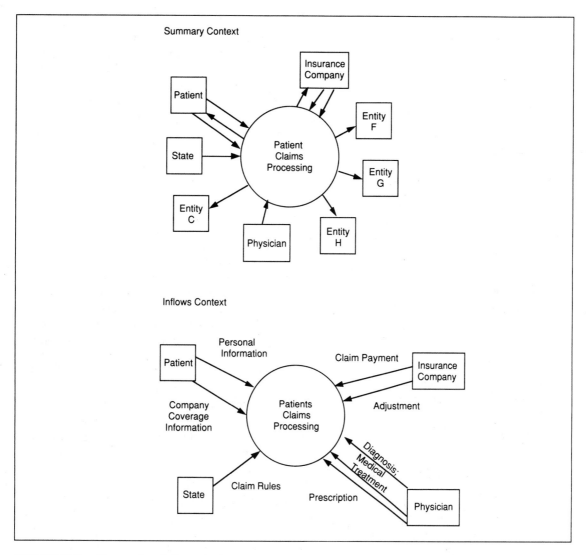

FIGURE 7-9   Example of Complex Context Diagram

the application) are matched with output flows to the same entity. For instance, customers place orders; the application sends an invoice (and goods) back to the customer. Check for reciprocating input-output flows such as these. When you identify single flows to/from an entity, you want to double check by asking, "How do I know they got this output?" or "Do I have to tell them I got this input?" As you define each data flow, draw the directed arrow on the context diagram, and label the flow. For a complex

application, you might need two levels of context diagrams (see Figure 7-9). One level summarizes *all entities* with directed arrows that are unlabeled. The other level shows *input flows* on one diagram, and *output flows* on the other diagram with labeled data flows on both diagrams.

Data flows are *information* about some business event being tracked by the application. They do not identify physical items. For example, an invoice is information about an order that would also have

Name	Order
Aliases	None
Timing	As Occurs

Contents	Customer Name
	+ [Address | Customer ID]
	+ Shipping Instructions
	+ 1{Item name
	  + (Item number)
	  + (Color)
	  + (Size)
	  + Quantity ordered}m

Constraints	80% must be billed and shipped within 24 hours 100% orders in by noon must be billed and shipped the same day

FIGURE 7-10   Example of Data Flow Dictionary Description

actual goods. A data flow to a customer shows the invoice but not the physical goods.

Last, for each data flow, create a definition in the data dictionary. The dictionary information provided for a data flow is its name, contents, and contents' source when it is not obvious (see Figure 7-10 for sample data flow description).

ABC Video Example Context Diagram

The scope of the project for ABC Rental Processing system is to provide rental/return processing for videos, including customer maintenance, video inventory maintenance, historical information maintenance, and reports to management. At the end of the day, accounting totals of sales information are generated, but there is no automated accounting interface. There is no purchase order processing in this application. The application's main function is rental processing, so we will call it 'ABC Rental Processing.' We draw the circle for the application in the context diagram and label it 'ABC Rental Processing.'[4]

---

4 The names of items from a diagram are in italics to set them off from the rest of the discussion and, hopefully, minimize your confusion.

Then we define the entities. Possible entities are customer, video vendor, ABC management, ABC accountants, and the Internal Revenue Service (IRS). The IRS is omitted because there is no tax-related processing performed in the application. *ABC accountants* are included because they receive an end-of-day report of receipts. How management and/or accountants use that information is beyond the scope of the application. ABC management could conceivably be on the diagram. Now, we ask ourselves, "Do we have control over what ABC management does with respect to the Order Processing application?" The answer, *in this case*, is yes, because ABC is so small. In other circumstances, the answer could be no. For instance, with a large application generating reports for many levels of management or for other departments' management, the answer might be no. Here, ABC management is not on the context diagram; in other companies or contexts it might be.

The entities left are Customers, Video Vendors, and video. *Customers* should be obviously correct. All rental and return processing relate to interactions of the application with customers. ABC has no control over customers' rental choices.

Vendors as an entity might be less obvious. Even though there is no automated purchase order process, the videos entered into the application come from somewhere, so video *vendors* should be identified as the source of video information.

Last, we deal with video. Is video an entity that the application interacts with? The answer is yes. Is video an entity that the application can control? The answer is again yes. Video is *not* on the context diagram because it is *in* the application. In effect, the video is *within the circle* that describes the ABC Rental Processing.

As a result of this analysis, we add three external entity squares to the context diagram labeled *Customer*, *Video*, *Vendor*, and *Accountant* (see Figure 7-11), and define the entities in the dictionary (see Figure 7-12).

Next, we define the data flows and document them in the dictionary. What happens in this application? When a customer selects a video, they first tell the clerk their phone number. The clerk uses the phone number to 'look up' the customer and validate their rentals. If the customer is new (i.e., not on file),

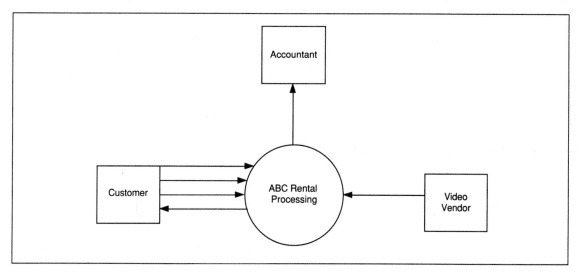

FIGURE 7-11   Skeleton ABC Rental Processing Context Diagram

the customer information is entered and stored. After phone number processing, the customer either gives the clerk the cardboard shell, or tells the clerk the video name (see Chapter 2). This sentence identifies

Entity Name	Customer
Aliases	None
Relationship to Application	Rents and Pays for Videos, Provides New Customer Information, Returns Videos
Contact	None
Entity Name	Video Vendor
Aliases	Vendor
Relationship to Application	Provides New Videos
Contact	None
Entity Name	Accountant
Aliases	None
Relationship to Application	Part-time employee receives end-of-day reports
Contact	None

FIGURE 7-12   ABC Rental Processing Data Definitions for External Entities

a data flow: *rental request*. After entering the information into the computer system, the clerk needs to provide some record with customer signature that the rental took place. This record accounts for the transaction and establishes customer liability for the rental property. This information identifies a reciprocating outward flow to the customer: *rental receipt*. When the tape is returned, the charges are computed based on the due date of the rental(s). This identifies another incoming data flow for a *video return*. So we have identified four data flows between the ABC Order processing application and customers:

- *New Customer* to store customer information
- *Rental request* (analogous to placing an order) from the customer to create a video rental and payments
- *Rental Receipt* from the application to confirm the rental
- *Video Return* to determine late charges, if any, and payment due.

For these four flows, there are four arrows between *customer* and ABC Rental Processing. Three arrows are *from customer* for *new customers, rental requests,* and *returns*. One arrow is *to customer* for the *rental receipt*.

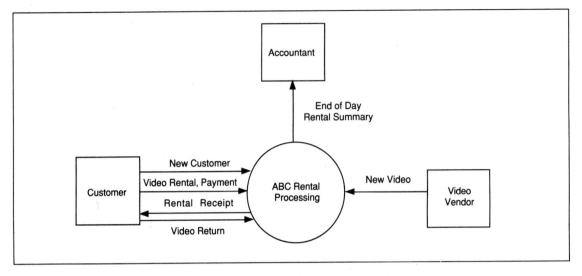

FIGURE 7-13   ABC Order Processing Context Diagram

The data flow relating to *vendors* is somewhat obscure, but is identified by the need to enter new video information. Since new video information comes from somewhere, its source must be identified as the entity. There is one data flow *from vendor* to ABC Rental Processing for *video information.* There are no data flows back *to vendor* because the scope does not include ordering videos from the vendor.

Last, we define the data flows to and from the accountant. The accountant does not feed any information into the application, and receives only an end-of-day rental summary. So, there is one data flow *to* accountant for the '*end-of-day rental summary.*' Next, we draw the data flows on the context diagram and label them (see Figure 7-13).

While we label the flows, we evaluate the names of the data flows to ensure their meaningfulness. *Rental request* implies a request for assistance in rental processing and is a weak name. Stronger, more meaningful names are '*Video rental*' or '*Video rental information.*' Either of these might be used. Here, we use *Video rental* since the word 'information' is not particularly meaningful. Also, rentals are always accompanied by payments which are added to the name to be more explicit.

Novice analysts frequently have trouble differentiating between the *thing*, and information *about the thing*. Keep in mind that what we document on DFDs is always information *about* the thing. So, when we name a data flow '*Video Rental*' we really mean *information about 'Video Rental.'* That is why the word 'information' is weak in the data flow name. The other names: *Rental Receipt, Video Return, New Customer, New Video (not* New Video Information), and *End-of-day Rental Summary* are all acceptable. Again, there are no 'right' or 'wrong' names for data flows. Some names are more descriptive than others, and, therefore, stronger. Many companies define their own conventions, or local rules, for naming data flows, entities, and processes.

Last, we define data flows in the dictionary (see Figure 7-14). Keep in mind that just because the information is in the dictionary does not mean it is cast in concrete. It is subject to review and change throughout the life of the project. The goal is to define the application at a level of detail so that changes can be made *before* they become costly, that is, during analysis.

Upon completion of the context diagram, you are ready to do the next level of analysis, opening up the circle, to define a data flow diagram.

Name	New Customer		
Aliases	None		
Timing	As Occurs		
Contents	Name + Address + Phone Number + Credit Card Type + Credit Card Number + Credit Card Expiration Date		
Constraints	None		

Name	Rental, Payment	Name	New Video
Aliases	None	Aliases	None
Timing	As Occurs	Timing	As Occurs
Contents	Phone Number + 1{Video ID}m + Total Amount of Order	Contents	Video ID + Video Name + Date + Rental Price
Constraints	None	Constraints	None

Name	Copy of Order	Name	End of Day Summary
Aliases	Printed Order	Aliases	EOD Rental Summary
Timing	One per rental transaction	Timing	Close of Business
Contents	Phone Number + Customer Name + Customer Address + 1{Video ID + Video Name + Rental Charge + Due Date}m + Total Amount + Total Amount Paid + Total Amount Due (should be zero)	Contents	Videos Rented + Total Fees Collected + Videos Returned + On-Time Returns + Late Returns + Total Late Days + Late Fees Collected
		Constraints	None
Constraints	Must be signed by customer. Optional that customer takes a copy.		

FIGURE 7-14   ABC Video Data Flow Definitions—Tentative

Develop Data Flow Diagram

Rules for Developing a Data Flow Diagram

To develop a data flow diagram, iterate through the following steps until a primitive level is reached:

1. Define the processes.
2. Define the files and other data flows required to support the processes.
3. Draw a Level 0 DFD. At level 0, ignore trivial error paths and data stores. If you define a validation process, you must eventually identify an error path. Define the error path at the primitive level. Similarly for data stores, define files when they are shared between processes. Introduce files that are only used within a given process at the level at which the file is shared between two or more subprocesses.
4. Balance the DFD with the context diagram. Compare the net inputs and outputs to external entities on the DFD to the net inputs and outputs on the context diagram. There should be a one-to-one correspondence between the diagrams.
5. Iterate through this procedure until the primitive level of DFD is reached for all processes.

Always balance the current level DFD's net inputs and outputs with those of the previous level.

First, we will discuss how to identify the Level 0 processes that are within the circle of the context diagram, without defining any data stores. The difficulty of this activity varies with your understanding of the problem domain and the scope of the project. One of the hardest parts of this activity is to decide the 'right' level of abstraction. What is right in one instance may not be right in another. For instance, if you have a multidepartmental, multiapplication environment you are trying to describe, the Level 0 diagram might link departments and the net data flows of the context diagram (see Figure 7-15). If you have a multidepartmental, single application environment, you might identify major functions and their relationships (see Figure 7-16). Or, if you have a single department, single function applica-

tion, such as ABC Rental Processing, you try to define the general functions to be performed. The approach in this text is to define the simple environment, discussing the common features for all levels of abstraction.

During the information gathering stage of the application, you discussed with users what they did and how they did it (see Chapter 4). The individual steps that each user performs in the tasks relating to the application are components of the applications' processes. There are a variety of ways to identify processes; some examples are:

1. **Direct identification:** If you have similar experience and either know the processes, or have articulate users who know the processes, identify them directly.
2. **Top-down:** Decompose the problem into its constituent parts. The functions at each level should completely define the problem and

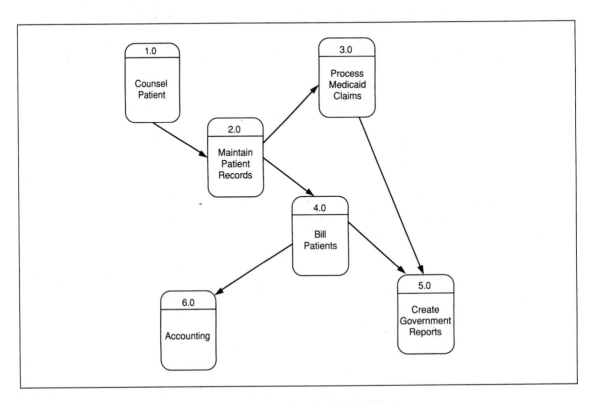

FIGURE 7-15   Multidepartment, Multiapplication Level 0 DFD

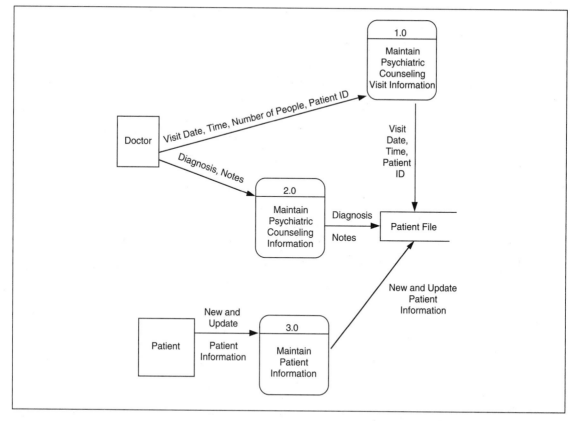

FIGURE 7-16   Multidepartment, Single-Application Level 0 DFD to Maintain Patient Records

should be as independent of each other as possible. The resulting independent functions can be analyzed in isolation of the other parts to develop each part's subprocesses. Decomposition continues until atomic levels of processing are identified.

3. **Bottom-up:** Do bottom-up analysis starting with the details of task steps and procedures described by users, synthesizing and combining the steps to define processes.

4. **Outward-in:** Use context diagram entities and data flows to identify 'boundary' processes with which they directly interact. Work outward-in to define what other transformations are required to link the input and output boundary processes.

5. **Functional sequence:** Examine the input data flows from external entities to identify

the 'first process' in a sequence of processes. From that first process, define the other transformations that are required to go through each function from beginning to end.

All of these approaches can work. None is more right than another. We all use one or more of these in performing analysis without thinking about how we actually do it. A good approach is to use two or three of the methods as a way of double-checking that all processes are defined and connected properly. For ABC, we will combine the last two approaches, using the information from the context diagram.

Once processes are identified, you draw them and connect them to the external entities via the named data flows. Other data flows and processes are identified to connect the initial ones defined until you feel the diagram completely describes the overall processing. Keep in mind while you are performing this activity that you do not pay attention to timing or sequencing of processes. You do not show start-up or shutdown activities on a data flow. If you have end of day, end of month, or other periodic processing, the DFD shows the processes without necessarily identifying the timing of the processing. As the processes are drawn, name each with a verb and the data they create, and number them. Numbering of processes is not meant to sequence them, even though we unconsciously tend to do this.

Also, at Level 0, ignore exception processing. You might have a data flow named '*Valid X*' without a matching '*Invalid X.*' The exception process is added at the next lower level. This avoids unnecessary clutter at the highest level.

After the processes are identified, next define file locations on the Level 0 data flow diagram. You could leave files for a lower level of analysis as many texts and companies do by convention. In that case, you are ready to draw the diagram. Here, we will develop the thoughts that are used to identify data stores.

To identify data stores, first consider each process. Can the process be completed without reading or writing to a data store? If your answer is yes, then you do not need a file at this level. If the answer is no, you need one data store for every required read action and every required write action. Many times, the reads and writes are to the same data store. Then, you have one data flow per input/output action. As these required reads and writes are identified, you add to the DFD to include the data store name and data flow(s). When you do this part of the drawing, make sure that each flow and store has a name.

Finally, when you have reviewed each process for determining whether to include data stores, review the diagram to make sure that its DFD syntax conforms to the rules. The first seven rules relate only to processes and their connectivity. Processes with connection errors are called 'pathological' processes because they do not follow the philosophy of DFDs that processes are connected via flows, files (data stores), or entities.

The next four rules check that all connections in the diagram are legal. The rule about no dangling

arrows[5] is our own. Work and teaching experience have proven that novices use dangling arrows to hide their lack of understanding of what they are doing. The final two rules deal with balancing, error handling, and the introduction of files.

The DFD syntax rules are:

1. *All* processes are *connected* to something else.
2. *All* process have *both inputs and outputs.*
3. *No* processes have only outputs or only inputs.
4. Processes may connect to anything: other processes, data stores, or entities.
5. All processes have a unique name and number.
6. Each process number is used once in the diagram set.
7. Only subprocesses of a process shall follow the numbering scheme of the parent process.
8. Entities and data stores may connect *only* to processes. Another way to state this is that each data flow must have at least one end connected to a process.
9. Data flows are the only legal type of connection between entities, processes, and data stores.
10. Make sure there are no dangling arrows.
11. The net data flows to and from context diagram external entities *must* balance, that is, be present, in each level of DFDs.
12. Trivial errors and exceptions are not handled until L1 or lower in the DFD set.
13. Trivial data stores show up in the diagram set the first time they are referenced by a process.

When the Level 0 DFD is complete, walk through the DFD with your peers, then review it with your user. Keep in mind that you are teaching the users

---

5 I realize that this is contrary to DeMarco, Yourdon, and many undergraduate texts. For novices, dangling arrows frequently mean you have no clue about what attaches at the other end. In addition, most companies want all terminators identified to ensure accuracy and to simplify quality assurance. Until you are proficient, draw the *entire* diagram!

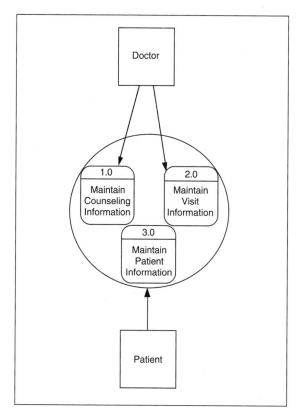

FIGURE 7-17   Context Expansion of Level 0
Processes: Maintain Patient Records

Do not expect to have agreement on the first, or even second, review. One benefit of data flow diagrams is focusing thoughts on the problem. Users will frequently 'see' what is missing when they look at a diagram that they could not 'see' when they discussed the topic verbally. When they begin a sentence, "Well, what about . . ." pay close attention; the subject is usually some variation, exception, or forgotten information that they did not discuss previously.

As you understand and users agree on the context and Level 0 processes (see Figure 7-18), begin work on the lower level DFDs. For each Level 0 process,

1. Draw the input and output flows and the icons to which they connect from the higher level diagram. This forms the skeleton of the diagram (see Figure 7-19). These are called the **net**[6] **inflows and outflows**.
2. Define the subprocesses by asking, "What are the steps required to *do* this process?" Then for each step, "Can I separate this from the other steps and do it in isolation?" For each *subprocess* you *isolate*, draw a process rectangle on the lower level diagram.
3. Identify whether data stores are required or not. Add them and, if they are new, name them.
4. Identify data flows to complete the diagram (see Figure 7-19). Make sure you provide *all and only* the information required to perform the process.
5. Review the diagram for unnecessary connections and, if found, remove them.
6. Update the data dictionary with all new information.

The goal of subprocess identification is to decompose the upper level processes into what will eventually be programmable modules. A good, that is, correct, design has certain characteristics that are

as well as having them review your work. If they do not understand what you are showing them, they cannot adequately comment on it. So, use a top-down approach to the presentation, too. First, show the users the context diagram. Define all of the items in the diagram. Once they agree on the external entities, show them a blowup of the context diagram that includes the inside of the circle: the major processes and the data flows connecting them to external entities (see Figure 7-17). Then, replace that diagram with a Level 0 DFD showing the entities and processes. Use overlays, adding the data stores and remaining data flows. Finally, review the detailed definitions from the data dictionary for each process, data flow, data store, and entity. If you take a step-by-step approach, users can more easily accept and assimilate the information.

---

6 Net, from accounting, means remaining after all necessary deductions. Here, net means remaining data flow and data store connections after the higher level process is removed. The net data flows in and out of a higher level process may connect to different subprocesses at the lower level.

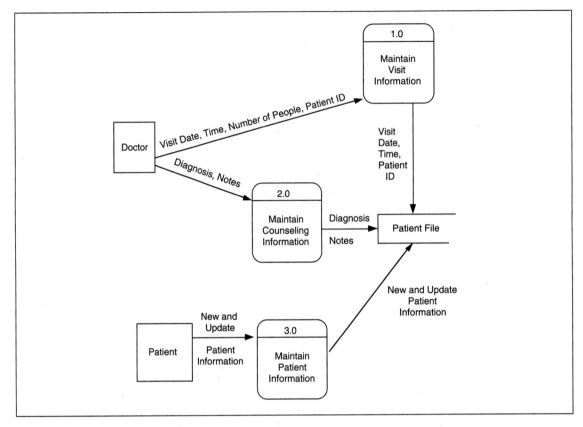

FIGURE 7-18   Completed Level 0 DFD to Maintain Patient Records

traceable back to a properly decomposed DFD. The two most important characteristics are maximal cohesion and minimal coupling. **Cohesion** measures the *internal* strength of a process (this is also called intraprocess strength). We want modules that result from process descriptions to have exactly the logic required to perform the task, and nothing more. Minimal **coupling** measures the *interprocess* connec-

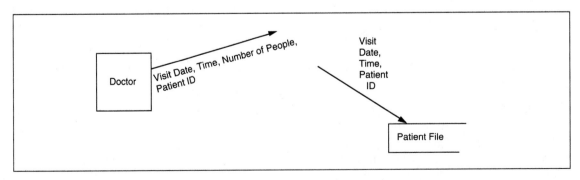

FIGURE 7-19   Skeleton Level 1 DFD with Net Inflows and Outflows for Process 1.0: Maintain Visit Information

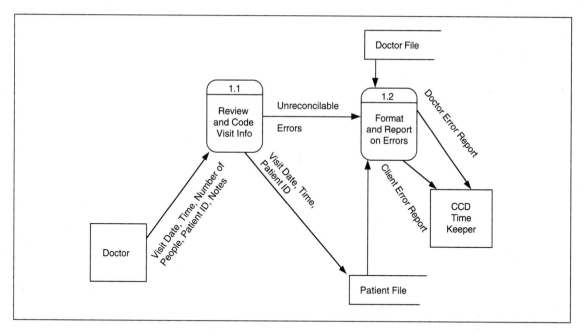

FIGURE 7-20   Completed Level 1 DFD: Maintain Visit Information

tions. Ideally, we want data flows and stores to contain exactly the information needed to trigger or perform each task, and nothing more. The questions and evaluation of processes in the decomposition process, if done properly, result in cohesive, minimally coupled processes.

Three types of quality checking are performed on the analysis results. First, **correctness checking** determines that the syntax and connections used in diagrams, charts, and so forth are accurately used. Next, **completeness checking** is performed with the users to validate the meanings of all terms and to verify the semantics used in all documentation. Last, **consistency checking** ensures consistency and correctness of all entries that span multiple diagrams, text, charts, and so on. Consistency checks evaluate the interitem syntax and semantics. These checks are first performed by the project team during walk-throughs or other quality assurance evaluations. Then, they may be reviewed by independent quality assurance analysts as an added check.

If you find data flows that are identical, with no transformations, going to many processes, reassess

the processes definitions (see Figure 7-21). On the other hand, if you have a transaction processing application in which each transaction has its own version of some process, this type of diagram is correct (see Chapter 8). If the processes all do different transformations *and* have either unique inputs or unique outputs, leave them separate. If the transformations have an if-then-else logic, they are at too low a level and should be combined (see Figure 7-22). If they all do different transformations to the incoming data, are the processes' outputs going to the same place? If so, you may have overdecomposed and should combine the processes. Figure 7-23 shows two possible corrections to the overdecomposition. Either correction may be acceptable depending on the 'Y.y' data complexity and their processing complexity. Semantic (i.e., interpreting problem *meaning*) DFD problems are discussed again in the next section.

At Level 0, we did not concern ourselves with exception processing. At the lower levels, when a data flow is named '*Valid X*,' you must balance that flow with another one called '*Invalid X*.' In other words, you *do* define errors and exceptions at the

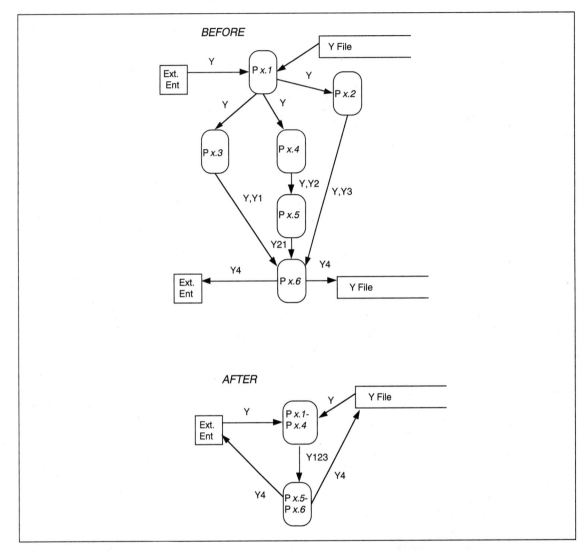

FIGURE 7-21   Example 1 of Excessively Detailed Processes

same level at which you define the split of valid and error/exception processing.

Let's examine how to apply these thoughts to develop a set of DFDs for ABC Rental Processing.

ABC Example Data Flow Diagram

We said above that in ABC Rental processing we are combining the analysis of context with analysis of the sequence of actions for each data flow. So, we

start with a customer placing a video rental request. Customer and video information trigger a 'Create rental' process. The first check in 'create rental' is to validate the *customer*; if the *customer* does not currently exist, we want to 'add new customer' to the company's files before rental processing. Here, we have a decision to make. We just described two input data flows to the *create rental* process. We need to decide if they are related or not. In this case, the issue is whether we can add new customers as a sub-

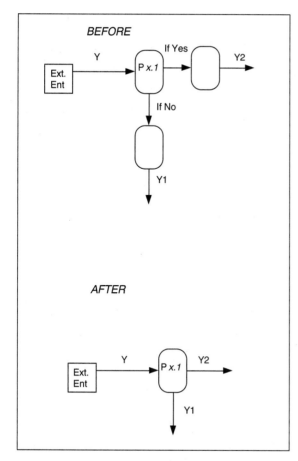

FIGURE 7-22   Example of If-then-else Logic in DFD

process of rental processing, or whether they are separate. If we separate the two, we have the two data flows we defined. If we combine them, we only have one data flow that optionally contains new customer information with rental information. If you do not know how the user wants the processing performed, you go back and ask. So, we will set this issue aside for the moment and finish defining what it means to 'create rental.'[7]

_____

7 Postponing decisions that are noncritical to the main logic is an important problem-solving behavior. Notice that we first identify alternatives and implications of the postponed item before setting it aside. If there are more side effects we have not identified, we are more likely to notice them with alternatives and implications than without.

After customer validation, we next have to validate the video and get a rental price. This requires reading some sort of video inventory file. Again, we ignore invalid video information for the moment. Once we have found the information on all the videos to be rented, we compute the total amount due. Again, we have a decision. At this point, how do we know whether late fees have been paid or not? Do we assume that people always return videos as they come into the store, and rent videos on their way out of the store? The rule is, _never assume anything_. If we know how to deal with this issue from the data gathering, we continue; otherwise, we add it to the list of questions for the user and continue.

After the rental amount is created (whatever it is and however it is computed), payment information is entered and customer change is computed. Then, the rental 'order' is written to a file and a paper copy is created for customer signing.

So, we have a process, 'Create rental,' and we have several subprocesses, 'Validate customer,' 'Validate video,' 'Compute rental total,' 'Process payment,' 'Write rental,' and 'Print rental.' We also have several questions and decisions that we deferred. We can create the Create rental process on the Level 0 diagram whether we deal with the deferred issues or not. But we cannot identify the other processes, with certainty, until the issues on new customers and late fees are decided. So, we review the interview information and go see Vic for the detailed answers.

Mary goes back to Vic and says: "We are talking about the options for entering rentals and we have several questions. The first question is about new customers. One option is to separate the functions, that is, add new customers in a separate process from rental processing. A second option is to allow adding a new customer as part of video rental processing. A third option is to allow both. Do you have a preference?"

Vic: "I don't know. What will the cost differences be?"

Mary: "No matter what, you want to be able to add, change, and delete customers. It seems desirable to do that without being tied to the rental process. However, rental processing is

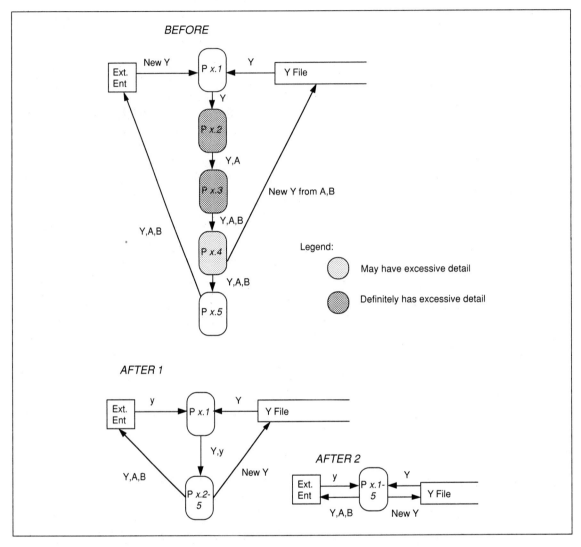

FIGURE 7-23   Example 2 of Excessively Detailed Processes

90% of your activity and you don't want to slow it down by having to leave that process to add a new customer. The slow-down for going from rental processing to add customer and back will range from 4 to 30 seconds depending on the PC's speed and the software we use. Unless you have a business reason for separating the two processes, I would suggest that you allow both. If we decide this direction now, there is no added cost. If we change direction in a few

weeks, there will be a cost, as high as several thousand dollars."

Vic: "OK, let's do both, then. It sounds more convenient this way anyway."

Mary: "OK, we will allow entry of new customers as a process to be run by itself, *or* as part of rental processing.[8] My second question

_____
8 Notice that Mary reconfirms the decision by repeating the agreed upon solution.

relates to video returns. When we collected our information, we observed people returning videos in several ways. First, they can put them into a slot and pay the fee the next time they rent a video. Second, they can return them and pay when they come in to get a new rental. Third, they can return them and rent a new video both at the same time. Do you want all of these options in the new system?"

Vic: "Yes, why wouldn't I?"

Mary: "It is easier for us if we have a somewhat fixed method of returns. But, if you want no changes, then we allow for all return methods. This may have a cost implication, but I can't tell right now. Should we talk about this again when I know what the cost of the options are?"

Vic was a little upset: "I told you at the beginning, NO bureaucracy and changes only if it improves convenience to my customers. If we don't allow them to return in all three of these ways, someone will get mad. Besides, don't customers pay when they rent? So, my only risk is on the 10% of customers who have late fees.

"Also, if I limit the ways they can return tapes, I lose my edge over Ajax Video's chain up the street. If there is a cost to allowing all of these things, why can't you tell now, and, if you can't tell now, when will you know?"

Mary tried to placate Vic somewhat but is still completely honest: "Usually, there is little incremental cost when all variations are known at this stage of the analysis. But I can't tell until we've proceeded a little further and have a sense of how many different programs will result from the most flexible design. I will know when we get to about two more levels of detail which will be in a few days. If there is no added cost, we will go for the flexibility. If there is an added cost, I will let you decide and give you an estimate for the different choices.

"Let me summarize: We will analyze for returns through the drop box, returns as a person coming in, or returns as part of rentals, and get back to you with cost implications, if any."

From the application perspective, maximum flexibility for both customer and return processing means, at least, that the rent and return screens and processing must be closely linked to each other. Now we need to guard against having the processes too closely coupled. Ideally, we want to accommodate Vic's wishes and still have processes separated as much as possible. To obtain this goal, we need to decide the minimum information needed to link customer and rental processing, and rental to return processing. Then, visualizing an implementation, we might be able to use, for example, windows for each process. We might open a new window to add a customer during rentals and maybe open another window to process returns during rentals. Also, with minimal coupling, we maintain separation even though the processes are interleaved.[9] This decision process is another example of how not top-down a top-down process is. We are going to an implementation level of detail to jump back up and define the data at the higher, more abstract level. Don't think this is the final answer. It is one way to reason through the problem and figure out how it might work at the computer level. Then, we back off to the logical level to describe that possible model.

We said before that the first step in *create rental* is to validate customer. If either the *phone number* or *customer name* is not retrieved, we know we have a new *customer* and can switch to that process. Once the *new customer information* is entered and saved, we can pass it back to rental processing as if it were in answer to an original request. Once we have the *customer information* in the *create rental process*, we can automatically check outstanding rentals. If there are any, we can ask if they want to return them or add the new *rentals* to the list. Our problem is solved unless Vic wants *late fees* processed whether or not the outstanding *rentals* have been physically returned. This decision, however, does not affect us until we try to define the details of processing. At the moment, we will assume *late fees* are only processed when the physical tape is returned.

---

9 Interleaving means weaving pieces of multiple processes together to give the *appearance* of parallel processing. Each process progresses a little. First, we switch to a process and do some of its function. Then we switch to another, then back to the first process, and so on.

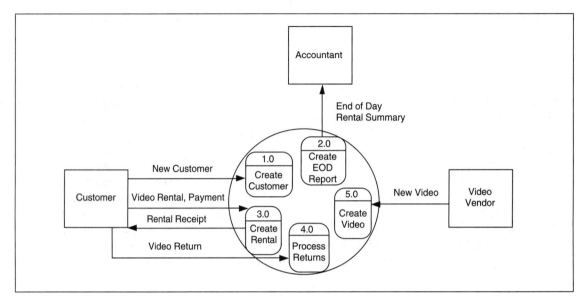

FIGURE 7-24   ABC Video Expanded Context Diagram

The result of this discussion so far is that we have three processes identified: *create rental*, *create customer*, and *process returns*. Each process could be initiated by the *create rental* process, or could be initiated by a customer action. We draw these processes (see Figure 7-24) and attach them to the correct data flows. Within the context circle expansion, do not show connections between processes. Processes still unaccounted for are '*create video*' and '*Create end of day report*' for summary totals. We know we have to get video information into the system, so we add that process and connect it to the data flow from video vendor. Since we must print an end-of-day summary for the accountant, we add the process to the diagram.

Figure 7-24 shows our high level processes of ABC Video Rental Processing, expanding the context diagram within the circle. The processes are shown in small circles or in rounded vertical rectangles, depending on local customs. This text uses rounded vertical rectangles. Notice that the data flows to/from each external entity are attached to a process, and all data flows are labeled and have a directional arrow showing which way the data is flowing. Also notice that the processes each have an

action name beginning with a verb, and each process has a numeric identifier.

The next step is to expand to a Level 0 DFD, defining the data stores[10] in the application and linking processes, as required (see Figure 7-25). Data store identification usually occurs naturally during the identification of processes and subprocesses. For instance, what actions are done to enter a rental? First, you would check to verify that the customer is, in fact, a customer. This means checking some permanent 'list' or file for presence of the customer. Then, you would ask for each video they want to rent and verify the description and its price. To retrieve the description and price, we need a permanent file of the video inventory. When the rental is complete, it is stored somewhere (in a rental file), completing the process. Following this logic, we need at least three files *at this level of analysis*: *customer file*, *video inventory file*, and *rental file*. At this stage, we don't concern ourselves too much with the file con-

---

10 Other names for data stores are files, relations, or databases. The term data store means data relating to this name and does *not* imply normalized form. Data stores can contain more than one data structure [Gane, 1990].

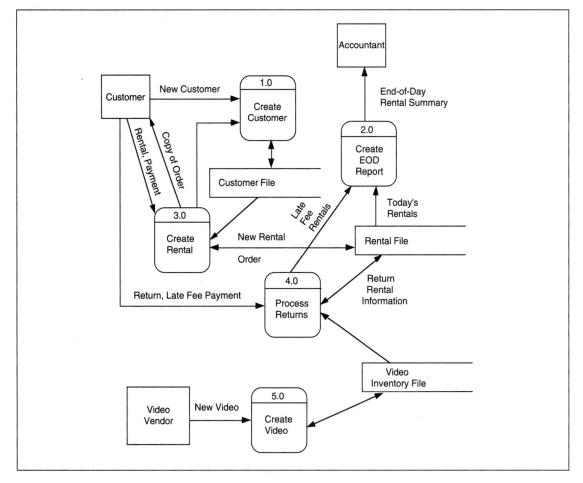

FIGURE 7-25   ABC Video First Cut Level 0 DFD

tents, although we identify the contents throughout analysis as they become known. As attributes, or fields, are discussed, it is a good practice to add to an attribute list for each file. The linkage between *create rental* and *create customer* is shown on the DFD as a data flow. The details of initiating *create customer* processing when a *customer* is not found are deferred to the next level of detail.

Before showing the DFD to Vic for his comments, we evaluate its level of abstraction and correctness (see Figure 7-25). Are *create customer*, *create rental, create video*, and *Process Returns* all on the same level of abstraction? The first clue that they are is that the first three processes all have the same verb. *Process returns* is the removal of rentals just as *create rental* is the creation of rentals; they are reciprocal processes. The reciprocal processes also appear to be at the same level. The name *process returns* is not the best we could choose to show reciprocity; *return rental* is a stronger name that does and we change the process name.

Next we evaluate correctness of the diagram. Are all the connections legal? Yes. Are there any pathological connections? No. Is there a *flow* through the application? Yes, the main flow is for rental and return processing.

Now, we could return to Vic and ask his opinion, giving him a verbal presentation of the details

TABLE 7-1 Decision Table for Decomposing Another Level of Detail

Conditions

Domain Knowledge	H	H	-	-	H	H	H	L	L	L	L
Language	4GL	3GL	3GL	3GL	2GL	2GL	2GL	4GL	4GL	3GL	2GL
Similar Experience	-	Y	N	N	Y	N	N	-	-	-	-
Simple Process/ Few Files or Complex Process or Many Files	-		S	C	-	S	C	S	C	-	-

Recommended Decomposition Levels

Level 0	X	X	X	X	X	X	X	X	X	X	X
Level 1	Opt.	X	X	X	X	X	X	Opt.	X	X	X
Level 2		Opt.	Opt.	X	Opt.	X	X	Opt.	X	X	X
Level 3 . . . n				X		Opt.	X		Opt.	X	X

Legend:

H	Extensive experience
L	Little experience
4GL	Fourth Generation Language, e.g., SQL
3GL	Third Generation Language, e.g., COBOL
2GL	Second Generation Language, e.g., Assembler
Y	Yes
N	No
S	Simple
C	Complex

underlying each of the processes, and in the details, getting verbal agreement to the next lower level of subprocesses.

At Level 1, we first decide which, if any, processes need decomposition. What happens when you create customer? A quick definition of fields and the type of validations required is necessary. According to the information (see Chapter 2), we need customer phone, customer name, customer address, and credit card ID, number, and expiration date. Validation for these fields is that the data are present and legal for the data type. For complex validation, you fre-

quently use extra **cross-reference files** to contain the legal codes and their meanings.

Do we also need to provide modify and delete processing for customers? Always is the answer, . . . and query processing as well. Now, we need to know the implementation language to decide whether or not to decompose further. The decision table shown in Table 7-1 summarizes the decision criteria and the most likely outcomes. Keep in mind that you can *always* go to another level of detail and can always get *some* benefit from the exercise. But, why do the work if you don't have to?

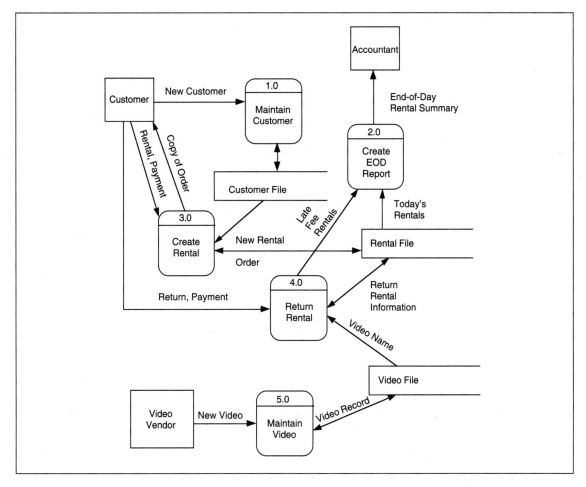

FIGURE 7-26   ABC Video Final Level 0 DFD

We are planning to build this application for a LAN environment, using a 4GL-nonprocedural language. For *create customer* there are no other data stores needed for validation. There will be add, change, delete, and query processing. The corresponding decision cell—4GL, simple process, one file—shows Level 1 to be optional. The decision depends on who is doing the programming. Is the person experienced with similar applications? Is the person involved in analysis fully knowledgeable about the requirements for this application? If the answer to either of these questions is 'no,' the next level of DFD should be developed with the details entered in the dictionary.

For ABC Rental Processing, we will opt not to discuss development of the Level 1 DFD for *create customer*. We will change the process name to '*maintain customer*' to denote the more general and expanded processing. The final Level 0 DFD is Figure 7-26; the Level 1 DFD is shown as Figure 7-27 for reference.

A similar set of arguments for Process 4.0, '*create video*,' is possible. We also rename that process '*maintain video*' to denote the expanded processing, and omit the level 1 DFD.

Both rental processing and return processing should be expanded regardless of the implementation language because they are fairly complex and

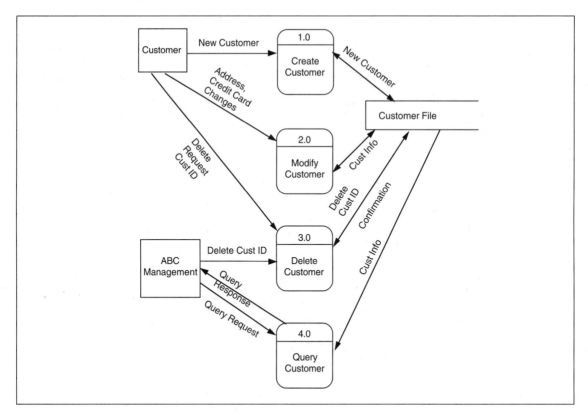

FIGURE 7-27 ABC Rental Level 1 DFD for Maintain Customer

we have not discovered how they work yet although we have described rental processing in some detail. First we examine the DFD from our knowledge so far, then expand it as required (see Figure 7-26). In the level 0 DFD, the create rental process interacts with customers twice and with all three data stores. To untangle and clarify the processing of these five interactions, we decompose the process further.

The first interaction is to get rental information from the customer. The 'rental information' includes *customer ID* (or name) and *video IDs* (or names). The *customer ID* is used to validate the customer and get the rest of the customer information for the rental. Similarly, the *video ID* is used to validate the video and get the rest of the video information for the rental. *Customer ID* is also used to check for late fees and to retrieve outstanding rentals. We also know that if the customer is not on file, we want to initiate process 3.0, *maintain customer*. When com-

bined, this processing is fairly complex and somewhat extensive. It is complete when the clerk does something to show that entry of rentals is complete. We can group these processes together and call them '*get valid rental*' (process 1.1) because once these actions are complete, the rental is ready for the next step of processing. The detailed steps we identified are either used to create another level of DFD or are documented in the dictionary for process 1.1.

A valid rental is totaled by adding all of the rental fees for the current set of entries and any late fees outstanding from past rentals. Once the total is displayed, the amount of money paid by the customer is entered into the system by the clerk. The total paid is subtracted from the total due to get the change due to the customer. When the change and total due amounts are both zero, the rental is complete and ready for the last part of the process. Because this stage is discrete, beginning with the successful vali-

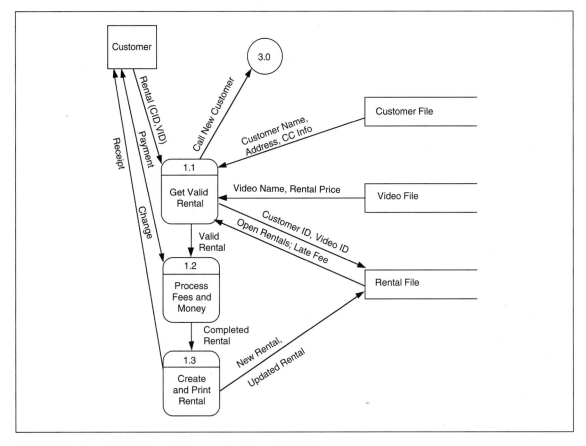

FIGURE 7-28   ABC Rental Processing Level 1 DFD

dation and ending when the change and total due are zero, we group these actions together and call them '*process fees and money*' (see Figure 7-28).

Finally, a rental is completed by saving all the information in the *rental file* and printing the *receipt* for customer signature. When these actions are complete, the *create and print rental* process is complete (see Figure 7-28).

Notice that we have decomposed the data flows as well as the processes. Where we group rental and payment on the level 0 diagram, we separate them on the level 1 diagram. We add *change* to the process because now we are dealing with the details. Similarly, the data flows connecting to the data stores are decomposed to show details of data passing back and forth. On a DFD, we assume all data can be passed when the data flows are not labeled, and it is okay to summarize on level 0. At level 1, we become specific and show the interface accurately and in detail.

When you are drawing the DFD, you have to guard against being too detailed. This is difficult, especially for novice analysts. If your drawing has these symptoms, you are too detailed and must combine processes to a higher level of abstraction. The semantic process problems to look for are listed with examples below. These problems violate one or more of the DFD Semantic Rules and Heuristics:

1. Processes that have only one data flow from the previous process as its input are probably overspecified. The solution is to

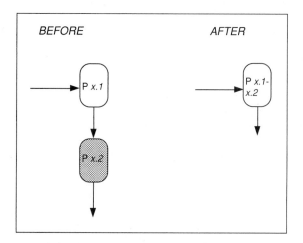

FIGURE 7-29   Example of Pathological Data Flow

combine the data flows (see Figure 7-29). Another solution may be the addition of a missing external entity (see Figure 7-30).

2. When several processes have interactions with the same external entity and at least one process has no other interactions, check that the data flows and transformations are different. If any two processes have the same outflow or are closely related, that is, passing one's input data to the next, they are probably overspecified. It may be possible to localize all external entity interactions in one process, and to perform all processing on the information obtained in the other process (see Figure 7-31).

3. When several processes have interactions with the same file and at least one process has no other interactions, check that the file contents read/written and transformations are different. One goal of all application is efficiency. If you read the same data more than once, it is inefficient. It is somewhat better to pass the data between processes. If you are identifying only logical processing and have the reading to show where data is used, make a note that during design you will need to redevelop the DFD to show

physical reads of the file. It may save time to redevelop the DFD at this stage rather than wait. Several solutions are possible (see Figure 7-32). In the first solution, all file interactions are localized in one process; in the other, inputting from the external entity and file are in one process and outputting is in the other. Both of these solutions require rethinking of the functional decomposition.

4. If several processes have more than one write to the same file, check that the processes are distinct and that the data must be written disjointly. Again, to have efficient file processing, minimal reading and writing is desired. The alternatives are to localize reading and writing as in the first solution (see Figure 7-33), or to combine

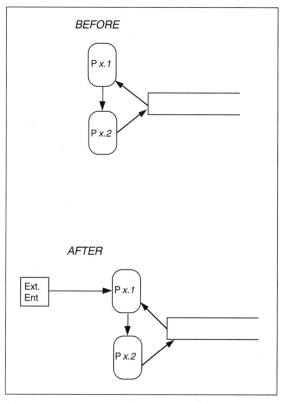

FIGURE 7-30   Example of Spontaneous Process

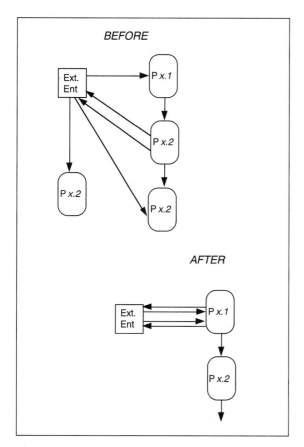

FIGURE 7-31   Example of Overspecified Entity Processes

information, do a credit status check, and identify outstanding late fees (see Figure 7-35). This example is an improvement because it is reading and validating all customer data only once.

7. Make sure that no physical entities, such as cash register or bar code reader, have sneaked into the DFD. Also make sure that no immediate users of the application are identified on the DFD. The solution to this problem is to remove all physical entities on any diagram in which they occur (see Figure 7-36).

8. Make sure that data flow names are field contents being passed or some group name for field contents that clearly identifies the information (see Figure 7-37). Unnamed data flows are frequently masking overspecified processes. If you cannot develop a unique, meaningful name, reevaluate the process they attach.

9. Data stores may show up on diagrams multiple times with the same name. To show that you know it is repeated, place a vertical bar down the left side of the file symbol.

10. Similarly, data flow names may show up multiple times with the same name. This condition is okay *if, and only if,* the contents are identical. This condition is rare, so when multiple data flows with the same name are present, there is frequently an error. Double check any data flows with the same name and give any unique data flows their own descriptive name (see Figure 7-38).

11. To simplify the design phase activities, make sure that process names include the transformation name and identify the data being transformed.

12. If data stores have only one input or one output, check that it is correct. This condition may be okay on the input side as long as maintenance is performed in some other application, or for files that are cross-reference tables only. The condition for output-only connections may be correct, for instance, for temporal databases in which

some of the processing but include writing in more than one process as in the second solution.

5. Any imbedded if-then-else logic that describes process interaction is wrong. Remove the logic by consolidating the processes. The logic belongs *inside* the process box, not outside; one solution is shown as Figure 7-34. If this problem occurs, make a note to include the control on the structure chart for the if-then-else logic, as required.

6. Processes that do only one very minor process, for instance, check customer number for validity, may be overspecified. A better process would check the customer

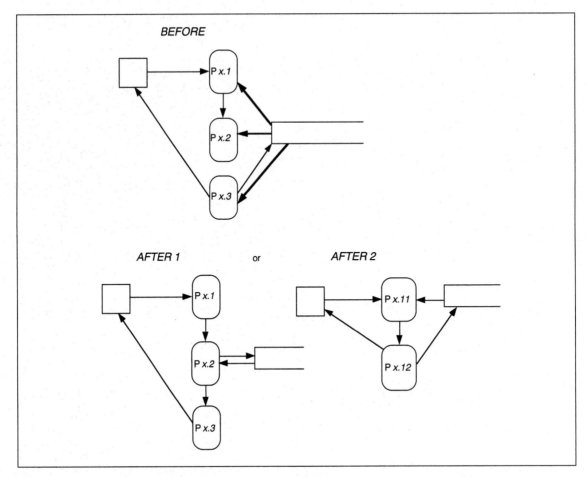

FIGURE 7-32   Example of Overspecified Read File Processing

nothing is thrown away. Check the business rules relating to the data and verify the processing.

For return processing, we need to walk-through the process to define if we need subprocesses. A *video ID* is entered and used to retrieve the rental. The system assigns today's date as the return date. *Late fees*, if any, are computed. The *total amount due* is computed. The *total amount due* is displayed, an amount of money received from the customer is entered, and *change* is computed. When both *total amount due* and *change* are zero, payment processing is complete. If no *late fees* are owing or payment

is complete, the *open rental record* is removed from the *open rental file* and *history information* is updated. If *late fees* are owed but not paid, the *open rental record* is rewritten with *return date* and *late fee* information. Return processing has several steps, but each is simple, requiring at most one file per step. There is little need for a Level 1 DFD for this process at this time.

Notice that the *process fees and money* is identical to the same process for rental processing. We can develop a common, reusable module for both rental and return processes. Also, notice that we introduce history here. If we decide to have a history file, it would show at this level of DFD.

At this point, we are ready to reevaluate the new DFDs and proceed to development of dictionary entries for all DFD information. Check the final DFDs for legal connections, similar levels of abstraction, and balanced net inflows and outflows between levels. Then, continue to the data dictionary.

Develop Data Dictionary

In this section we briefly discuss the contents and rules, if any, for each type of dictionary entry. Then, we will document the information from the ABC rental application. Since you have seen examples of each type of entry, this section is short.

Data Dictionary Contents and Rules—Entities

The contents of the dictionary for external entities are listed in Table 7-2. The most important are the name and the definition of the entity. In organizations with data administration functions, this information must conform to the 'corporate' dictionary definitions or must be reconciled with it to define new terms. The SEs work with users and data administrators to name and define the entities for the organization. IS personnel do *not* name and define the terms by themselves. Most external entities are people, job titles, organizations, or applications with

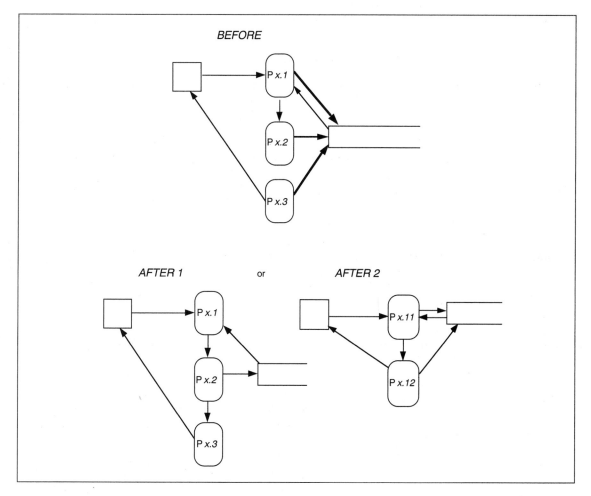

FIGURE 7-33   Example of Overspecified Write File Processing

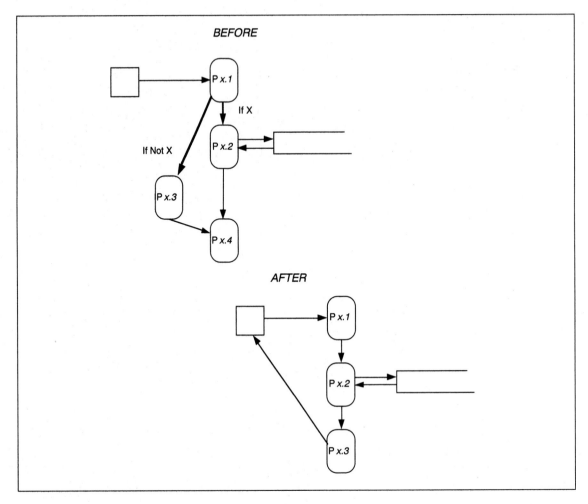

FIGURE 7-34   Example of If-then-else Logic in DFD

TABLE 7-2   Data Dictionary Entity
Contents

Entity name

Aliases

Definition

Relationship to application

Contact, if entity is an
organization

---

which the application under development interacts.
Choose a meaningful business name that describes
the entity accurately and completely. If you have a
data administration function, use their name. The
definition should be a business definition and should
be completely independent of *any* technology.

Make sure you include in the definition any
aliases or names used in your application that do not
conform to the corporate standard. Describe the
entity's relationship to the application in terms of
the nature and timing of the interaction. If the entity

is an organization, include the name, address, and phone number of the person most frequently contacted.

Figure 7-39 shows the notation to be used in describing the contents of an entity to a dictionary. Keep in mind that this convention works well if you are using a manual method. Automated tools have their own format and notation for repository contents. There is one notational structure for each type of entry: optional information, multiple repeating information, required information, selection between attributes, and primary keys.

ABC Example Data Dictionary—Entities

The external entities in ABC Rental are *customer*, *vendor*, and *accountant*. The entries for each of these are shown in Table 7-3. If the accountant is an

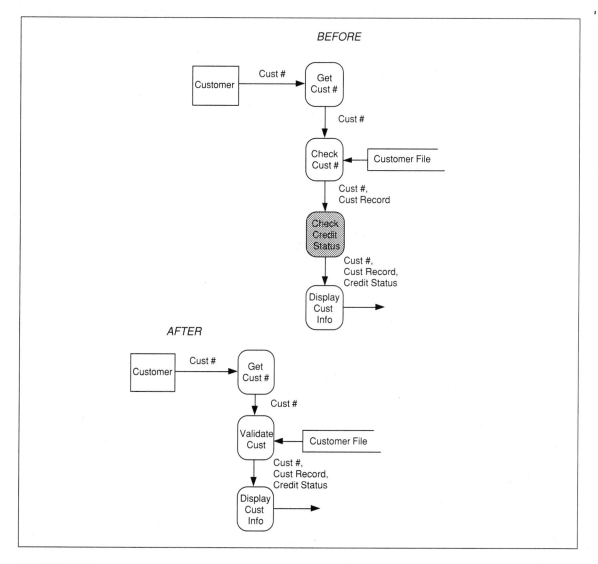

FIGURE 7-35   Example of Excessive DFD Detail

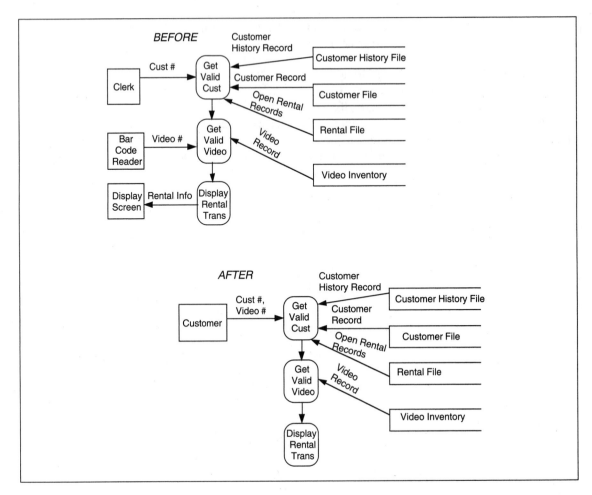

FIGURE 7-36   Example of Physical Entities

employee, you would not include his or her name in the dictionary. If the accountant is an outside firm, you *would* include the information.

Data Dictionary Contents and Rules—Processes

The contents of the dictionary for processes are listed in Table 7-4. For processes, we include the process number from the DFD to allow quality assurance, and to easily link back to the process model. In a computer-aided software engineering tool (CASE), if you used one, you usually have automatic linkage between the diagram and the

dictionary entries. The name of the process should be *exactly the same* as the process name used in the DFD.

The **process description** details the steps to complete the process and can take several forms. The most common are pseudo-code and structured English, supplemented by decision trees or decision tables as needed. **Pseudo-code** uses the syntax from a language in abbreviated form for easy translation into the target language. **Structured English** is a computer-language independent description of a process using only simple verbs and terms from the dictionary; no adjectives or adverbs are used. Structured English is used here.

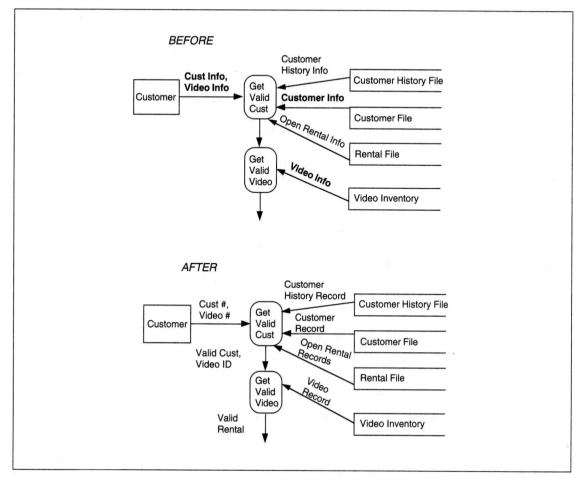

FIGURE 7-37   Example of Weak Data Flow Names

ABC Example Data Dictionary— Processes

The process entries for ABC are all included at the level 0 detail level (see Table 7-5). To document the entire application, you would create a data dictionary entry for each lower level process, then refer to that process in the higher level dictionary entries. In this way, the hierarchy of processing and linkages are documented.

Notice that there are some uneven levels of detail in the process entries. For instance, the *process fees and money* routine is fairly detailed, while the reference to *create history* in *return rental* is not

detailed at all. You document the information you have, replacing the high level abstract thoughts with the details as you come to know them. The dictionary is constantly evolving and changing as more information becomes known.

Data Dictionary Contents and Rules— Data Stores

The data store defines persistant data; contents of a data store dictionary entry are listed in Table 7-6. There is a significant amount of detail that is eventually documented. You begin completing the information as it becomes known and complete the rest

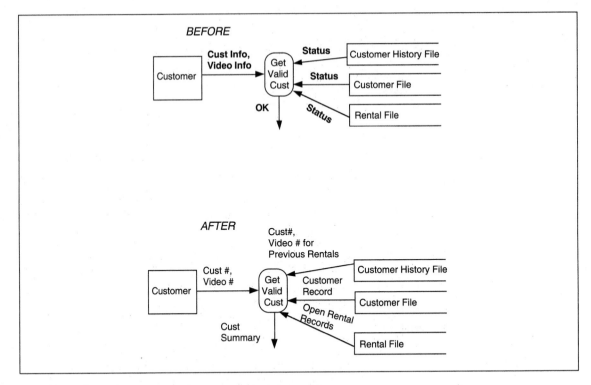

FIGURE 7-38   Example of Nonunique Data Flow Names

when it is available. Also, some of the information may not be relevant in your organization (for instance, if all projects always use DB2 relational files, you may not need detailed documents because the information already exists). The goal of the documentation is to present necessary information without much verbiage. Keeping that in mind, trim the dictionary entries to fit your situation.

ABC Example Data Dictionary— Data Stores

The dictionary entries for data stores are in Table 7-7. For now, we know very few of the details about, for instance, volume, growth, and security. Those entries are left blank.

Above, we said that you trim the contents of the dictionary entries to fit the project. In a consulting situation, such as Mary and Sam are in at ABC, the

likelihood of them also maintaining the application is unknown. So, the more detailed the documentation, the more you simplify future maintenance.

Data Dictionary Contents—Data Flows

Data flow contents are important pieces of documentation because they cause the creation and change of files and determine the data each process actually accesses. The data flow contents are shown in Table 7-8. Contents have a primary key to uniquely identify the data. The difference between primary key for a data flow and for a data store is one of time. What period of time is the flow 'alive'? Data flows usually have a short life which means that less data is required for a unique ID. For instance, the flow payment is a money amount which is acceptable here. At the implementation level, that field might also require a terminal ID or a transaction ID

Symbol	Definition
=	is composed of
+	and
( )	Parentheses show an optional entry which may or may not be present
n{ }m	Braces show iteration n is minimum entries m is maximum entries If no limit to entries, the maximum is shown as m.
[ ]	Square brackets identify selection from among alternatives
|	Vertical bar is a separator of alternative choices within square brackets
*	Comment
- - - - - -	Underline identifies a component of a primary key

*Adapted from Yourdon, Edward, *Modern Software Engineering*. Englewood Cliffs, NJ: Prentice-Hall, Yourdon Press, 1989, p. 191.

FIGURE 7-39   Data Dictionary Notation*

to be unique; implementation requirements are not dealt with in analysis. Data flow constraints are most often present in real-time applications or in applications with contingent processing of data. The source of the data flow is a cross-reference back to the entity, process, or file from which it flows.

ABC Example Data Dictionary— Data Flows

The data flows for ABC rental processing are shown in Table 7-9. There is nothing difficult about any of them. Keep in mind that these definitions are not cast in concrete; they can change whenever the need arises. It is important to keep this information up to date, because programmers use the dictionary to check that their modules are receiving the correct information.

TABLE 7-3   ABC Entity Dictionary Entries

Entity Name:	Customer
Aliases:	None
Definition:	A Customer is any individual, organization, or other entity authorized by ABC management to rent videos.
Relationship:	Rents and pays for videos
	Signs rental order
	Provides new customer information
	Returns videos
Contact:	N/A
Entity Name:	Video Vendor
Aliases:	Vendor
Definition:	A Video Vendor is any organization or individual from which ABC purchases or otherwise acquires videos.
Relationship:	Provides new video information
Contact:	N/A
Entity Name:	Accountant
Aliases:	None
Definition:	The employee providing accounting services for ABC video.
Relationship:	Gets end-of-day summary accounting reports
Contact:	N/A

TABLE 7-4   Data Dictionary Process Contents

Process ID Number
Process Name
Process Description
Constraints (e.g., concurrence, sequential with another process, time-out, etc.)

TABLE 7-5 ABC Process Dictionary Entries

Process Number:	1.0
Process Name:	Create Order
Description:	For each customer,

    Enter customer ID (or name)
    Read customer file using
        customer ID (or name)
        as key
    If NOT present display
      'Customer not currently on
      file, switching to create
      customer'
    Call New-customer
      routine.
Display all customer infor-
    mation.
Read Rental file using customer
    ID
    If rentals exists, display
      rentals
      If returns
        Call Return routine
      else
        continue
    else
    If late fees outstanding add
      late fees to total.

For each video,
    Read inventory file using
      video ID (or description)
      as key
      If NOT present display
        'Video not on file,
        switching to create
        video'
    Display video description
      (or number), price.

Add all extended price to total.
Perform process-money
    routine.

Write order to order-file.
Print order confirmation.
Return.

Process money routine
    Display total.
    Get amount.
    Subtract total from amount
      giving change.
    Display change.
    If change and total = zero,
      return,
    else go to process money.

Constraints:	None

Process Number:	2.0
Process Name:	Return Rental
Description:	For each video,

    Enter video ID
    Retrieve rental
      If NO rental,
        display error message and
        return.
    Use Customer ID to retrieve
      other rentals.
    Display entire rental.
Move to today's date to return
    date.
If return-date-rental-date > 2
    compute late charges
    display late charges
    add late charges to total.
Create history.
If new rentals,
    return
else
    call process money routine.

Constraints:	None

Data Dictionary Contents—Attributes

Attributes, or **fields**, are facts about an entity. Attribute definitions are tedious and tend to be over-documented unless you are using a CASE tool. As you can see from Table 7-10, there is a large amount of information about attributes that is needed to fully document them. In organizations with a data administration function, much of the information for the type of attributes used here would already be documented, and you would just copy that documentation.

TABLE 7-5   ABC Process Dictionary Entries (*Continued*)

Process Number:	3.0			retrieve video record
Process Name:	Maintain Customer			prompt "Are you sure you want to delete?"
Description:	If new			If yes,
	create new customer			delete video
	else			else
	If modify			else
	prompt customer ID			if query
	retrieve customer record			call query routine.
	get changes and verify			Return.
	rewrite customer			

Process Number: 3.0

Process Name: Maintain Customer

Description:
If new
   create new customer
else
If modify
   prompt customer ID
   retrieve customer record
   get changes and verify
   rewrite customer
else
if delete
   prompt customer ID
   retrieve customer record
   prompt "Are you sure you want
      to delete?"
   If yes,
      delete customer
   else
else
if query
   call query routine.
Return.

Constraints: None

Process Number: 4.0

Process Name: Maintain Video

Description:
If new
   create new video
else
If modify
   prompt video ID
   retrieve video record
   get changes and verify
   rewrite video
else
if delete
   prompt video ID

   retrieve video record
   prompt "Are you sure you want
      to delete?"
   If yes,
      delete video
   else
else
if query
   call query routine.
Return.

Constraints: None

Process Number: 5.0

Process Name: Create EOD Report

Description:
Read rental file
   count today's rentals
   total today's rental receipts
Read cash register
   count today's returns
   count today's late returns
   total today's late fees
   count today's rentals
   total today's rental receipts
Format and print end-of-day
   summary report.

Constraints: None

ABC Example Data Dictionary— Attributes

As the two examples provided in Table 7-11 show, the contents get quite long and take quite a bit of paper. In the interest of saving a few trees, and keeping the dictionary useable, when using a paper dictionary, capture only the essential information about attributes and put it in a short-form attribute table as shown in Table 7-12. Essential information is usually the user name, system name, data type, data length, and edit rules. If there is other

TABLE 7-6   Data Dictionary Data Store Contents

Data Store Name	Volume
Aliases	Percent change per cycle
Definition	Frequency of cycle (e.g., as occurs, daily, weekly, etc.)
Data Attributes (Contents in normalized form)	Growth percentage per year
Data Structure (e.g., relation, hierarchy)	Allowable actions (read, write, or read/write) by process
Organization (e.g., Vsam entry sequenced)	Security access restrictions
Sequence and sequence attributes	Backup/recovery requirements
Size of Relations/Records	Special processing considerations
Primary Key	If in a distributed environment, form of partitioning, schematic showing number/location of replications for each partition.
Alternate Keys	
Index Attributes	

information required, such as security restrictions or cross-reference file names, you would add it for that attribute but not all of the others. The short form is used in this text to document ABC's attributes.

AUTOMATED SUPPORT TOOLS

Structured analysis and process methods, in general, are the oldest and most widely used methods. Because they are most widely used, a large number of CASE tools to support structured analysis are available on the market. All of the tools support DFDs; all have a dictionary (although they are not all 'active'). A table of representative CASE tools supporting structured analysis is listed below in Table 7-13.

If you did not get the impression that CASE tools represent a 'buyer beware' situation, perhaps some comments from a recent survey will prove that it is. Data flow diagrams in 12 CASE environments were compared on DFD correctness checking.[11] The authors developed 19 rules by which automated DFDs might be evaluated. The most checked by any of the CASE tools evaluated was 13 (by two CASE tools); the least rules checked was three; the average was eight. The extent of intelligence in CASE obviously varies and is inconsistent with the collective wisdom about how DFDs should be developed and drawn.

Thus, there are many CASE tools available which 'support' structured analysis. The tools vary widely in the diagrams supported and in the extent to which rules about developing DFDs and other diagrams are enforced.

SUMMARY

Process-oriented structured analysis originated in the work of DeMarco, Gane and Sarson, and Yourdon. In structured analysis, we first define the application context then follow a top-down approach to progressively more detailed levels of process analysis. The application is documented

---

11 See Vessey, Jarvenpaa, & Tractinsky [1992].

(*Text continues on page 274*)

TABLE 7-7   ABC Data Store Contents

Data Store Name:	Customer File	Data Store Name:	Rental File
Aliases:	None	Aliases:	None
Definition:	A computer file of information about customers who are allowed to rent from ABC.	Definition:	A computer file of rental orders outstanding. When a rental is made, it is added to the file. When it is returned, if there are no late fees, it is removed. If there are late fees, the rental stays on file until the late fees are paid.
Data Attributes:	Customer Phone = [Area code + exchange + number] + Customer Last Name + Customer First Name + Customer Address line 1 + Customer Address line 2 + Customer City + Customer State + Customer Zip+4 + Credit Card Type + Credit Card Number + Credit Card Expiration Date + Date of entry	Data attributes:	Customer Phone + Customer Last Name + Customer First Name + Rental Date + Video ID + Video Title + Date Due + Date Returned + Rental Price + Late Fees
Data Structure:	Relational	Data Structure:	Relational
Organization:	Random	Organization:	Random
Sequence:	Entry	Sequence:	Entry
Sequence Attributes:	N/A	Sequence Attributes:	
Record Size:	198 Bytes decompressed	Size:	134
File Size:		Primary Key:	Customer Phone + Video ID
Primary Key:	Customer Phone	Alternate Keys:	
Alternate Keys:	Address line 1	Index Attributes:	Customer Last Name, Customer Phone, Video ID, Customer Phone+Video ID, Video Title
Index Attributes:	Customer last name, Customer zip, Credit Card Number, Address line 1		
Volume:		Volume:	
Percent Change:		Percent Change:	
Cycle Frequency:		Cycle Frequency:	
Growth:		Growth:	
Allowable actions by process:		Allowable actions by process:	Rental = Add, Change, Read Return = Change, Delete, Read
Security Access:		Security Access:	
Backup/Recovery:		Backup/Recovery:	
Special processing:		Special processing:	

TABLE 7-8 Data Dictionary Data Flow Contents

Data Flow Name

Aliases

Timing (e.g., as occurs, daily, weekly, etc.)

Contents

Constraints (e.g., requires 5-second response; only occurs for sales orders, etc.)

Source

TABLE 7-9 ABC Data Flow Dictionary Entries

Data Flow Name:	New Customer
Aliases:	None
Timing:	As occurs
Contents:	*Customer Phone* =
	[Area code + exchange + number]
	+ Customer Last Name
	+ Customer First Name
	+ Customer Address line 1
	+ Customer Address line 2
	+ Customer City
	+ Customer State
	+ Customer Zip+4
	+ Credit Card Type
	+ Credit Card Number
	+ Credit Card Expiration Date
	+ Date of entry
Constraints:	None
Source:	Customer

Data Flow Name:	Rental
Aliases:	Rental Information
Timing:	As Occurs
Contents:	[Customer Phone	Customer Name] + 1{[Video IS	Video Name]}m
Constraints:	None
Source:	Customer

Data Flow Name:	Payment
Aliases:	Money
Timing:	One per complete rental transaction
Contents:	Total Paid
Constraints:	None
Source:	Customer

Data Flow Name:	Copy of Order
Aliases:	Printed Rental Order
Timing:	One per complete rental transaction
Contents:	= Rental
Constraints:	None
Source:	System

Data Flow Name:	Return
Aliases:	Video Return
Timing:	As Occurs
Contents:	Video ID + (Customer Phone)
Constraints:	None
Source:	Customer

Data Flow Name:	Late Fee Payment
Aliases:	None
Timing:	As Occurs
Contents:	Total Late Fee
Constraints:	May be included within rental payment
Source:	Customer

TABLE 7-10   Data Dictionary Attribute Contents

Attribute User Name	Primary Data Store
System Name	Other files where stored
Aliases	Flows where used
Attribute Definition	Edit/Validation Rules
Data Type	Validation Method (e.g., cross-reference file, code check, etc.)
Data Length	
Allowable values and meanings	Security access restrictions
Creating Process(es)	Special processing considerations

TABLE 7-11   Sample ABC Attribute Dictionary Entries

User Name:	Customer Phone	User Name:	Video ID
System Name:	CPhone	System Name:	Video ID
Aliases:	None	Aliases:	None
Attribute Definition:	The customer's phone number	Attribute Definition:	The numeric identifier for a specific videotape. Uniquely identifies a copy of a group of tapes with the same title.
Data Type:	Numeric		
Data Length:	10, Area code (3), exchange (3), and number (4)	Data Type:	Numeric
		Data Length:	15
Allowable values and meanings:	Numeric	Allowable values and meanings:	Numeric
Creating Process(es):	Add custor	Creating Process(es):	4.1 Create video
Primary Data Store:	Customer	Primary Data Store:	Video File
Other Files:	Rental File	Other Files:	Rental File
Flows:	New rental order Customer record Rental Return rental information	Flows:	Video Information, Rental Information, Return rental information, New Rental Order
Edit/Validation:	Numeric	Edit/Validation:	Numeric
Validation Method:	Software check	Validation Method:	Software check
Security Access:	None	Security Access:	None
Special processing:	None	Special processing:	None

TABLE 7-12   ABC Attributes—Short Form Dictionary

User Name	System Name	Data Type	Length	Edit/Validation Rules
Customer Phone	CPhone	N	10	Must be present, Check for numeric
Customer Last Name	CLast	A	50	Must be present, Check for alpha
Customer First Name	CFirst	A	25	Must be present, Check for alpha
Customer Address Line 1	CLine1	A/N	50	Must be present
Customer Address Line 2	CLine2	A/N	50	None
Customer City	City	A	30	Must be present, Check for alpha
Customer State	State	A	2	Post Office Abbreviation
Customer Zip	Zip	N	10	Must be present, numeric
Credit Card Type	CCType	A	1	A=AmExpress V=Visa M=Mastercard
Credit Card Number	CCNo	N	17	Must be present, numeric
Credit Card Expiration Date	CCExp	N	8	Valid Date, Format YYYYMMDD
Date of Entry	EntryDate	N	8	Valid Date, Format YYYYMMDD
Credit Rating	CCredit	A	1	0 = OK, 1 = not OK

via graphical forms including a context diagram, leveled set of data flow diagrams, a data dictionary, and, optionally, a state-transition diagram. Diagram symbols and their meanings include (1) circle, entire application; (2) square, external entity; (3) rounded vertical rectangle, process; (4) open ended rectangle, data store, and (5) directed arrow, data flow. Each diagram symbol has a formal definition that is documented in a data dictionary. DFDs identify processes and the flow of data through those processes to achieve some business function. DFDs start at a high level of abstraction to summarize the processing taking place. At successively more detailed levels, procedural and data are added to describe the processing

in more detail. Graphical representation replaces much of the text, but does not completely replace text descriptions of individual processes. The data dictionary (or repository) is used to maintain definitions of all DFDs and other analysis information, including files, fields, flows, and external entities, in addition to processes.

The reasoning process for defining the application context and the detailed levels of data flow diagrams was presented. The definitions and contents of data dictionary entries were described. All diagrams and dictionary entries were developed using the ABC rental processing application to show variations and nuances in the thought processes.

TABLE 7-13   CASE Support for Structured Analysis

Product	Company	Technique
Analyst/Designer Toolkit	Yourdon, Inc. New York, NY	Context Diagram Data Flow Diagram (DFD) State-Transition Diagram
Anatool	Advanced Logical SW Beverly Hills, CA	DFD Structured English
Deft	Deft Ontario, Canada	DFD
Design/1	Arthur Anderson, Inc. Chicago, IL	DFD Warnier-Orr Diagram
The Developer	ASYST Technology, Inc. Napierville, IL	DFD Matrix Diagram (for decision tables and real-time systems)
Excelerator, Telon	Intersolv Cambridge, MA	DFD State-Transition Diagram Matrix graph (for real-time systems)
IEW	Knowledgeware Atlanta, GA	DFD Database diagram
MacAnalyst, MacDesigner	Excel Software Marshalltown, IA	DFD Decision Table State Transition Diagram Structured English
Maestro	SoftLab San Francisco, CA	DFD
MetaSystem Tool Set	Meta Systems Ann Arbor, MI	DFD

(*Continued on next page*)

TABLE 7-13 CASE Support for Structured Analysis, *Continued*

Product	Company	Technique
Multi-Cam	AGS Management Systems King of Prussia, PA	DFD State-Transition Diagram Matrix graph (for real-time systems)
PacBase	CGI Systems, Inc. Pearl River, NY	Context Diagram DFD
ProKit Workbench	McDonnell Douglas St. Louis, MO	DFD
ProMod	Promod, Inc. Lake Forest, CA	DFD State-Transition Diagram
Silverrun	Computer Systems Advisers, Inc. Woodcliff Lake, NJ	User-Controlled Modeling
SW Thru Pictures	Interactive Dev. Env. San Francisco, CA	Data Structure DFD State Transition Diagram
System Engineer	LBMS Houston, TX	DFD
Teamwork	CADRE Tech. Inc. Providence, RI	Decision Table DFD State Transition Diagram
Transform	Transform Logic Corp. Scottsdale, AZ	Uses ProKit, Excelerator
Visible Analyst	Visible Systems Corp. Newton, MA	DFD
vs Designer	Visual Software Inc Santa Clara, CA	DFD Ward-Mellor Diagram for real-time systems

REFERENCES

Curtis, B., M. I. Kellner, and J. Over, "Process modeling," *Communications of the ACM*, Vol. 35, #9, September 1992, pp. 75–90.

DeMarco, Tom, *Structured Analysis*. New York: Yourdon Press, 1979.

Frances, B., "A window into CASE," *Datamation*, March 1, 1992, pp. 43–44.

Gane, C., and T. Sarson, *Structured Systems Analysis: Tools and Techniques*. Englewood Cliffs, NJ: Prentice-Hall, 1979.

Gane, Chris, *Computer-Aided Software Engineering: The Methodology, The Products and the Future*. Englewood Cliffs, NJ: Prentice-Hall, 1990.

Krasner, J., J. Terrel, A. Lindhan, P. Arnold, and W. H. Ett, "Lessons learned from a software process modeling system," *Communications of the ACM*, Vol. 35, #9, September 1992, pp. 91–100.

Lee, T., "Bridging the CASE/OOP gap," *Datamation*, March 1, 1992, pp. 63–64.

Lindholm, E. "A world of CASE tools," *Datamation*, March 1, 1992, pp. 75–81.

Martin, James, *Systems Design from Provably Correct Constructs*. Englewood Cliffs, NJ: Prentice-Hall, 1985.

McClure, C., *The Three R's of Software Automation: Re-Engineering, Repository and Reusability*. Englewood Cliffs, NJ: Prentice-Hall, 1992.

McMenamin, Stephan M., and John F. Palmer, *Essential Systems Analysis*. NY: Yourdon Press, 1984.

Slater, D., "PacBase, IEF lead rising CASE satisfaction," *Computerworld*, August 3, 1992, p. 81.

Sullivan, Louis, "The tall building artistically considered," *Lippincott's Magazine*, March 1896.

Vessey, I., S. Jarvenpaa, and N. Tractinsky, "Evaluation of vendor products: CASE tools as methodology companions," *Communications of the ACM*, Vol. 35, #4, April 1992, pp. 90–105.

Yourdon, Edward, *Modern Structured Analysis*. Englewood Cliffs, NJ: Prentice-Hall, Yourdon Press, 1989.

KEY TERMS

attribute	bottom-up
balancing	cohesion
completeness checking	functional sequence
consistency checking	level 0 DFD
context	level 1 . . . n DFD
context diagram	leveled set of DFDs
correctness checking	net inflows and outflows
coupling	outward-in
cross reference file	primitive level
data attribute	process
data dictionary	process description
data flow	pseudo-code
data flow diagram (DFD)	quality assurance
data store	structured decomposition
direct identification	structured English
elementary components	structured systems analysis
external entity	systems model
field	systems theory
file	top-down
function	

EXERCISES

1. Complete the level 1 DFD for 2.0 Rental return process and discuss it in class. Compare several of the answers. Are they the same? Why, or why not?

2. Make a list of outstanding and deferred issues to discuss with Vic.

The next three questions have bothered my students for several years. For each question, identify and discuss the issues and ramifications of each decision, technical issues, user issues, legal or other issues.

3. How should customers be identified to the application? What are the security issues? What are the bureaucracy issues? Is there a way to 'minimize bureaucracy' and still have good security?

4. Should late fees relate to a person or a tape or a rental? What are the issues? How do you decide? Can Vic be helpful in deciding this issue?

5. Where should history get created—at tape rental time? or at tape return time? Can Vic be helpful in deciding this issue? How do you decide?

STUDY QUESTIONS

1. Define the following terms:

balancing	external entity
context	function
data flow	net inflow
data store	top-down
direct identification	

2. How do you define the scope of a project? Who should define the scope?
3. What is a leveled set of DFDs? How do you know you have that?
4. Why is the strategy of using net inflows and outflows from the previous level of DFD as a starting point for a new level of detail a good idea?
5. Is structured process analysis more like analyzing with a zoom feature on a set of photos or more like analyzing a geologic formation?
6. Define structured decomposition. Why do you use this technique?
7. What is the purpose of the data dictionary?
8. Discuss the reasoning process used in structured analysis. Does it guarantee that everyone will get the same analytical result? If not, why not?
9. How might the process of structured analysis be improved to be more rigorous, i.e., guarantee the same results regardless of who performs the analysis?
10. Evaluate the following diagram. What type of diagram is it? What is its purpose? Label errors and list all reasons why they are wrong. Redraw the diagram correctly.

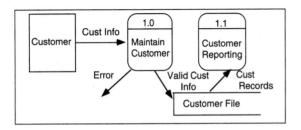

11. What are the major diagrams in the analysis phase? How are they derived?
12. List and briefly describe the five approaches to identifying processes.
13. Describe all data dictionary entries and give an example of each.
14. Why might CASE tools be useful in structured analysis?
15. Draw and identify five common DFD errors and their corrections.
16. Discuss the three types of quality checks done on DFDs.

★ EXTRA-CREDIT QUESTIONS

1. The example used in Figures 7-15 through 7-20 refers to a psychiatric clinic and processing performed for Medicaid claim processing. Perform a structured analysis of this problem as described in the Appendix Case: The Child Development Clinic. Refer to the figures in the text to help you if you get stuck.
2. Perform a structured analysis of any of the problems in the Appendix. Decide what information in the problem description is relevant to an automated application. Then, build a context diagram, a levels set of DFDs and a data dictionary.

## CHAPTER 8

PROCESS-ORIENTED DESIGN

INTRODUCTION

Structured design is the art of designing system components and the interrelationships between those components in the best possible way to solve some well specified problem. The main goal of design is to map the functional requirements of the application to a hardware and software environment. The results of structured design are programming specifications and plans for testing, conversion, training, and installation. In addition, the design may result in prototyping part or all of the application. This section discusses the mapping process and the development of program specifications. The other topics are discussed in Chapter 14.

The goals of structured design, as first documented by Yourdon and Constantine [1979], have not changed much over the years. They are to minimize cost of development and maintenance. We can minimize the cost of development by keeping parts manageably *small and separately solvable*. We can minimize the cost of maintenance by keeping parts manageably small and separately *correctable*. In design we determine the smallest solvable parts as a way of managing application complexity.

Conceptual Foundations

The concept 'form follows function' that informed analysis is again the basis for structured design. The application processes determine the form of the application. The divide and conquer principle guides the definition of the smallest solvable parts while keeping the general goals of maintainability and low cost in mind. Partitioning and functional decomposition are the basic activities used in dividing processes into modules. The basic input-process-output (IPO) model from the DFD results in a structure chart that adds a control component to the IPO model (see Figure 8-1).

Principles of good structured design are information hiding, modularity, coupling, and cohesion. **Information hiding** means that only data needed to perform a function is made available to that function. The idea is a sound one: You cannot mess up what you don't have access to. **Modularity** is the design principle that calls for design of small, self-contained units that should lead to maintainability. Following systems theory, each module should be a small, self-contained system itself. **Coupling** is a measure of intermodule connection with minimal

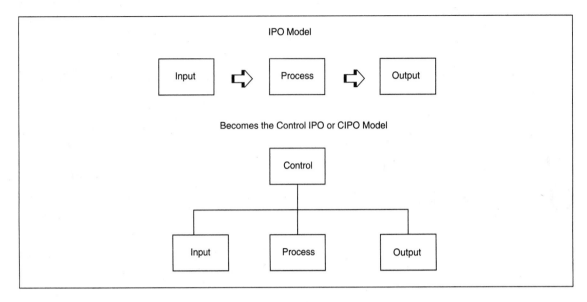

FIGURE 8-1   Input-Process-Output Model and Structure Chart

coupling the goal (i.e., less is best). **Cohesion** is a measure of internal strength of a module with the notion that maximal, or functional, cohesion is the goal. These principles are related to the process of design in the next section.

DEFINITION OF
STRUCTURED
DESIGN TERMS

The major activities of structured design are:

1. Transform or transaction analysis of DFD
2. Refine and complete structure chart
3. Identify load units and program packages
4. Define the physical database
5. Develop program specifications

The terms associated with each of these activities are defined in this section and summarized in Table 8-1.

In design we partition the application to divide subprocesses into codifiable program modules. **Partitioning** is the divide and conquer strategy by which we divide existing subprocesses from the DFD into groups for implementation. The two methods of partitioning used are transform analysis and transaction analysis.

DFD processes transform data from one form to another; these transformations will eventually be automated by programs each containing several modules. **Transform analysis** is the process of identifying the clusterings of subprocesses based on their major functions. The functions are either input, output, or transform-oriented. The input-oriented processes are called **afferent flows. Afferent** means bringing inward to a central part. Afferent processes read data and prepare it for processing. The output-oriented processes are called **efferent flows**, where **efferent** means moving away from the central part. Efferent processes write, display, and print data. The remaining processes are collectively called the **central transform**. The central transform processes have as their major function the change of information from its incoming state to some other state.

An example of a data flow diagram with its afferent and efferent flows and its central transform identified is shown in Figure 8-2. Notice that multiple afferent or efferent flow streams may be found.

TABLE 8-1   Structured Design Concept
Definitions

Term	Definition
Stepwise refinement	The process of defining functions that will accomplish a process; includes definition of modules, programs, and data
Program morphology	The shape of a program, including the extent of fan-out, fan-in, scope of control, and scope of effect
Data structure	The definition of data in an application includes logical data definition and physical data structure
Modularity	A property of programs meaning they are divided into several separate addressable elements
Abstraction	Attention to some level of generalization without regard to irrelevant low-level details
Information hiding	Design decisions in one module are hidden from other modules
Cohesion	A measure of the internal strength of a module
Coupling	A measure of the intermodule strength of a module

The streams are partitioned off from the rest of the diagram by drawing arcs showing where they end.

Examples of transform-centered applications include accounting, personnel, payroll, or order entry-inventory control. For these applications, getting data into and out of the system is secondary to the file handling and manipulation of numbers that keep track of the information. In accounting, for instance, balancing of debits and credits takes place at end-of-day, end-of-month, and end-of-year processing. These periodic process transfor-mations summarize and move data, erase some information, archive other information, and write data to the general ledger to summarize the details in the receivables and payables subledgers. All of these *transforms* process data that is already in the files.

These processes are the *heart* of accounting processing. Without these processes, the application would be doing something else.

Not all applications are transform-centered. Some applications do simple processing but have many different transaction types on which the simple processes are performed. These systems are called **transaction-centered**. **Transaction analysis** replaces transform analysis for transaction-centered applications with partitioning by transaction type, which may not be obvious from DFDs. Figure 8-3 shows an example of a partitioned DFD for a transaction-centered application. This detailed DFD looks like it contains redundancy because many of the same processes appear more than once. Look closely and you see that each set of processes relates to a different type of transaction.

When the high-level partitioning is done, the information is transferred to a first-cut structure chart. We will develop the structure chart from Figure 8-2. A **structure chart** is a hierarchic, input-process-output view of the application that reflects the DFD partitioning. The structure chart contains one rectangle for each lowest level process on the DFD. The rectangles are arranged in a hierarchy to show superior control and coordination modules. Individual process modules are the lowest in their hierarchy. The rectangles in the hierarchy are connected via undirected lines that are always read top-down and left to right. The lines imply transfer of processing from the top to the bottom of the hierarchy. Diamonds overlay the connection when a conditional execution of a module is possible using if-then-else logic. Reused modules are shown in one of two ways. Either they are repeated several times on the diagram and have a slash in the lower left corner to signify reuse, or they are connected to more than one superior module via the linking lines.

The identification of afferent flows, efferent flows, and transforms results in chains of processes, each its own 'net output.' If we look at Figure 8-2 again, we see the net afferent output is data flow *Good Input*. For the central transform, the net output is *Solution*. For the efferent flows, the net output is *Printed Solution*. These net outputs are used to determine the initial structure of the structure chart, using a process called factoring.

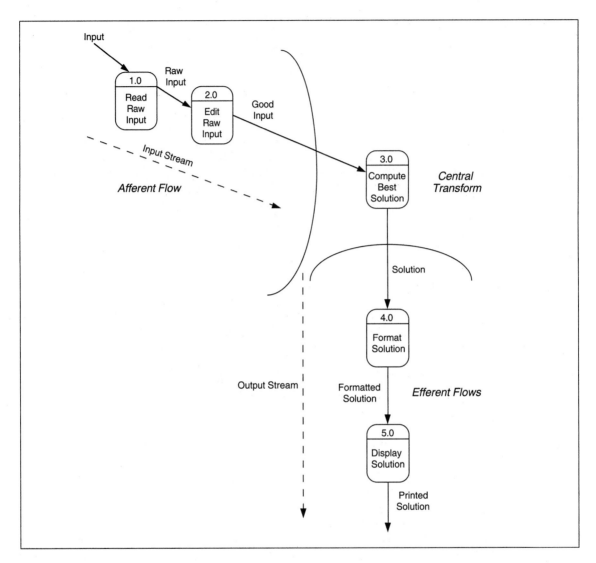

FIGURE 8-2   Transform-Centered DFD Partitioned

Factoring is the process of decomposing a DFD into a hierarchy of program components that will eventually be programmed modules, functions, or control structures. Each stream of processing is analyzed to determine its IPO structure. When the structure is identified, the processes are placed on the structure chart and named until all low-level DFD processes are on the structure chart (see Figure 8-4).

Next, data and control information are added to the structure chart. **Data couples** identify the flow of data into and out of modules and match the data flows on the DFD. Data couples are identified by a directed arrow with an open circle at the source end (see Figure 8-5). The arrowhead points in the direction the data moves.

Control couples identify the flow of control in the structure. Control couples are placed to show where the control data originates and which module(s) each couple affects. A control couple is usually a program switch whose value identifies how a module is activated. Control couples are drawn as

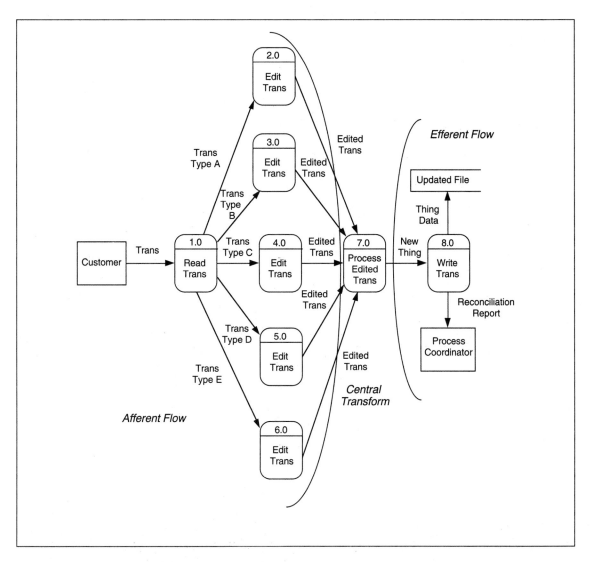

FIGURE 8-3   Transaction-Centered DFD Partitioned

directed arrows with a closed circle at the source end (see Figure 8-6). The arrowhead points in the direction the control travels. If a control couple is in, set and reset in the same module, it *is not* shown on the diagram. A control couple that is set and reset in one place, but used in another, is shown. If a control couple is set in one module and reset in another, it *is* shown as both input and output. Control is 'designed into' the application by you, the SE, based on the need for one module to control the processing of another module. The goal is to keep control to a min-

imum. Figure 8-4 shows the completed structure chart for the DFD in Figure 8-2.

Next, we evaluate and revise the structure chart to balance its morphology. **Morphology** means form or shape. The shape of the structure chart should be balanced to avoid processing bottlenecks. Balance is determined by analyzing the depth and width of the hierarchy, the skew of modules, the span of control, the scope of effect, and the levels of coupling and cohesion. When one portion of the structure chart is unbalanced in relation to the rest of the diagram, you

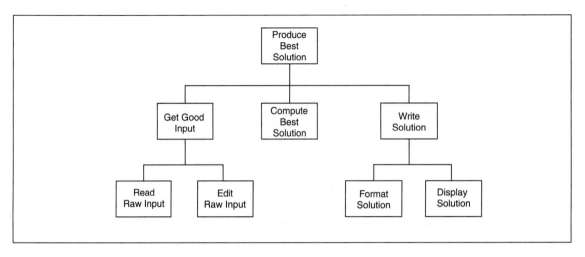

FIGURE 8-4 First-Cut Structure Chart

modify the structure to restore the balance, or pay closer attention to the unbalanced portion to ensure an efficient production environment.

The **depth of a hierarchy** is the number of levels in the diagram. Depth by itself is not a measure of good design nor is it a goal in itself. Rather, it can indicate the problem of too much communication overhead and not enough real work taking place (see Figure 8-7). Conversely, adding a level of depth can be a cure for too wide a hierarchy.

The **width of the hierarchy** is a count of the modules directly reporting to each superior, higher-level module (see Figure 8-8). **Span of control** is another term for the number of immediate subordinates and is a synonym for the width of the hierarchy. Width relates to two other terms: fan-out and fan-in. **Fan-out** is the number of immediate subordinate modules. Too much fan-out can identify a processing bottleneck because a superior module is controlling too much processing.

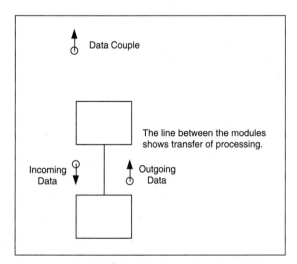

FIGURE 8-5 Data Couple Notation

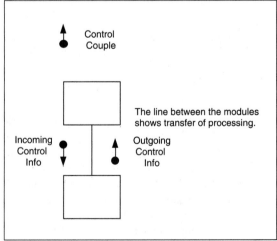

FIGURE 8-6 Control Couple Notation

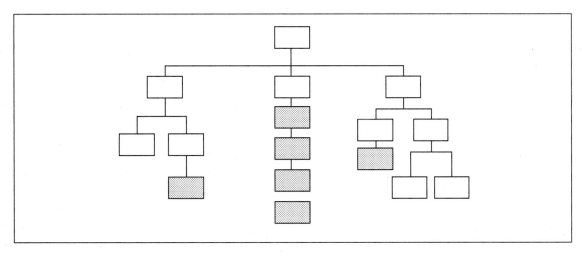

FIGURE 8-7   Excessive Depth of Hierarchy

While there is no one number that says 'how wide is too wide,' seven ±2 is the generally accepted guideline for number of fan-out modules. One solution to fan-out processes that are functionally related is to factor another level of processing that provides middle-level management of the low-level modules. Another solution to fan-out problems that are factored properly, but not functionally related, is to introduce a new control module at the IPO level.

Fan-in, on the other hand, is the number of superior modules (i.e., immediate bosses) which refer to some subordinate module (see Figure 8-9). Fan-in can be desirable when it identifies reusable components and reduces the total amount of code produced. The major tasks with fan-in modules are to ensure that they perform a whole task, are highly cohesive, and are minimally coupled.

Skew is a measure of balance or lopsidedness of the structure chart (see Figure 8-10). Skew occurs

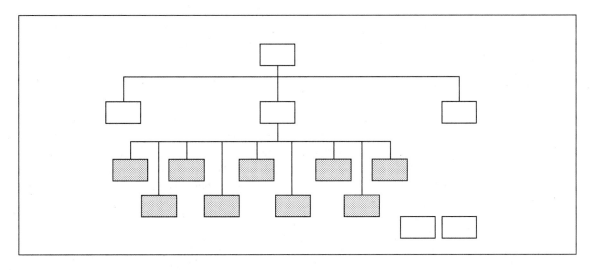

FIGURE 8-8   Excessive Width of Hierarchy

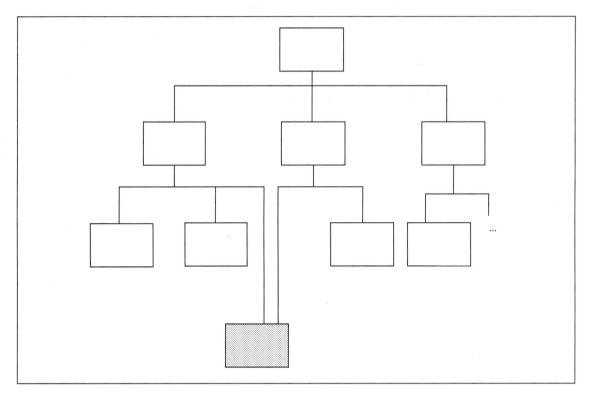

FIGURE 8-9   Example of Fan-In

when one high-level module has many subordinate levels and some or most of the other high-level modules have few subordinate levels. Skew can indicate incorrect factoring. If factoring is correct, then skew identifies a *driver* for the application that might require special consideration. If the skew is on the input side, we say the application is input driven or **input-bound**. Similarly, if the skew is on the output side, the application is **output-bound**. If the input and output are skewed with little transform processing, the application is **I/O-bound** (for input/output). Finally, if the application has little input or output, but lots of processing, the application is **process-bound**. The special considerations of each of these occurrences deal with ensuring correct language selection and meeting I/O and process time constraints.

The **scope of effect** of a module identifies the collection of modules that are conditionally processed based on decisions by that module (see Figure 8-11). The scope of effect can be identified by count-

ing the number of modules that are *directly* affected by the process results of another module. High scope of effect relates to fan-out, fan-in, and coupling in that it may identify potential problems with debugging and change management. Ideally, the scope of effect of any one module should be zero or one. That is, no more than one other module should be affected by any processing that takes place in any other module.

The last measures of structure morphology which are analyzed throughout the remainder of structure design are coupling and cohesion. Cohesion is a measure of the *intramodule* strength. Coupling is a measure of the *intermodule* linkage. Maximal, functional cohesion and minimal coupling are the ideal relationships. Coupling and cohesion are related inversely (see Figure 8-12). If cohesion is high, coupling is low, and vice versa; but, the relationship is not perfect. That means that if you have strong cohesion, you may still have strong coupling due to

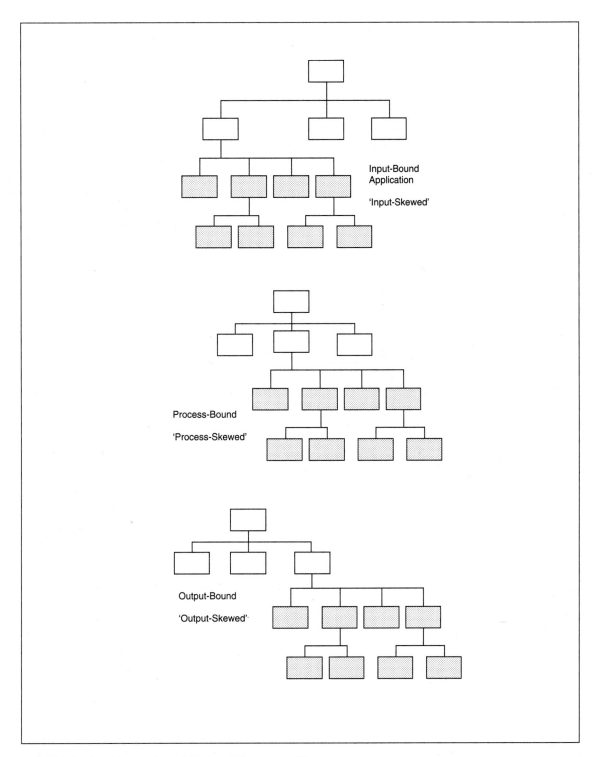

Input-Bound
Application

'Input-Skewed'

Process-Bound

'Process-Skewed'

Output-Bound

'Output-Skewed'

FIGURE 8-10   Examples of Skewed Structure Charts

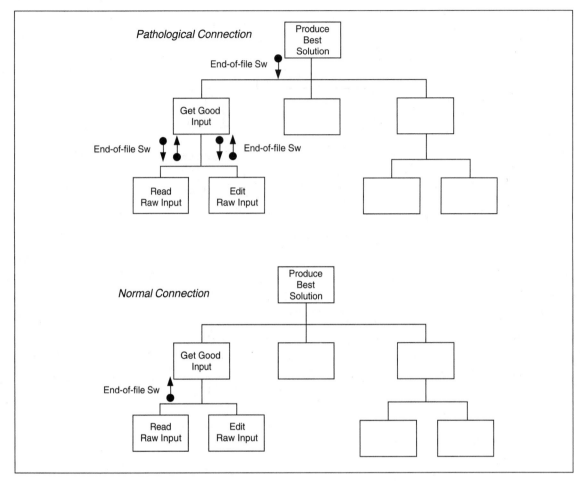

FIGURE 8-11   Example of Scope of Effect

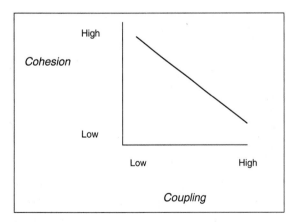

FIGURE 8-12   Relationship between
Coupling and Cohesion

poor design. So, attention to both coupling and cohesion are required.

Factoring and evaluation are followed by **functional decomposition**, which is the further division of processes into self-contained IPO subprocesses. Balanced structure chart subprocesses might be further decomposed to specify all of the functions required to accomplish each subprocess. Fan-out, span of control, and excessive depth are to be avoided during this process.[1] The decision whether

---

1 Some companies have as a local convention (a policy in their company) that a lower-level DFD is developed to describe programmable individual functions before partitioning. This is decomposition at the DFD level and has the same effect as decomposition here.

to decompose further or not relates to the details needed for the implementation language and how well the SEs understand the details.

Structure charts are only one of many methods and techniques for documenting structured design results. Most of the alternatives would replace, rather than supplement, structure charts. Each technique has its own slightly different way of thinking about the processes to finalize a design, even though the goals are the same. Several alternatives are IBM **Hierarchic input-process-output diagrams (HIPO)** (see Figure 8-13), **Warnier diagrams** (see Figure 8-14), **Nassi-Schneiderman diagrams** (see Figure 8-15), and flow charts (see Figure 8-16).

To complete design, program specifications (specifications is abbreviated to 'specs') must be developed, but before specs can be developed, several other major activities are required. First, the physical database must be designed. Then, program package units are decided. Several activities not discussed here (these are covered in Chapter 14) are performed, including verification of adequate design for inputs, outputs, screens, reports, conversion, controls, and recoverability.

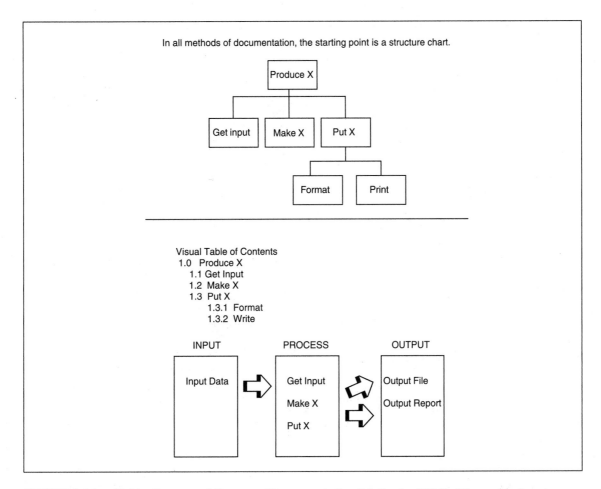

FIGURE 8-13   Other Structured Program Documentation Methods: IBM's Hierarchic Input-Process-Output (HIPO) Diagram Example

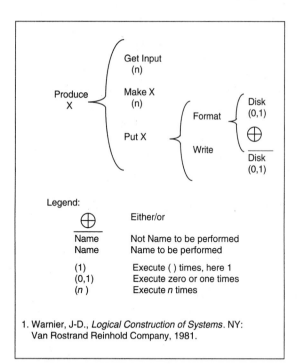

Legend:

⊕ (Name over Name)	Either/or
Name (over line)	Not Name to be performed
Name	Name to be performed
(1)	Execute ( ) times, here 1
(0,1)	Execute zero or one times
(n)	Execute n times

1. Warnier, J-D., *Logical Construction of Systems*. NY: Van Rostrand Reinhold Company, 1981.

FIGURE 8-14   Warnier Diagram[1]

Physical database design is concurrent with factoring and decomposition. Several common physical database design activities are:

- design user views (if this is not already done)
- select the access method
- map user views to the access method and storage media
- walk-through the database design
- prototype the database
- document and distribute access information to all team members
- train team members in access requirements
- develop a test database
- develop the production database

Keep in mind that many other activities may be involved in designing a physical database for a specific implementation environment.

While the details of physical database design and decomposition are being finalized, project team members are also thinking about how to package the modules into program units. A **program unit** or a **program package** is one or more called modules,

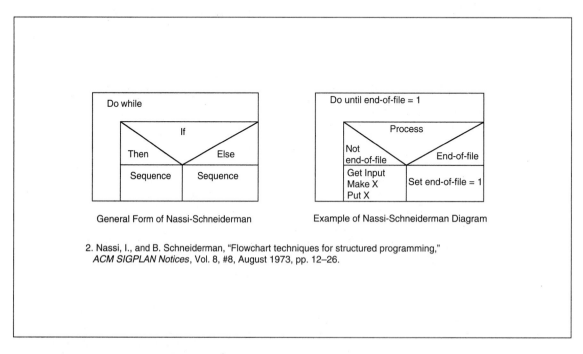

General Form of Nassi-Schneiderman

Example of Nassi-Schneiderman Diagram

2. Nassi, I., and B. Schneiderman, "Flowchart techniques for structured programming," *ACM SIGPLAN Notices*, Vol. 8, #8, August 1973, pp. 12–26.

FIGURE 8-15   Nassi-Schneiderman[2] Diagram Example

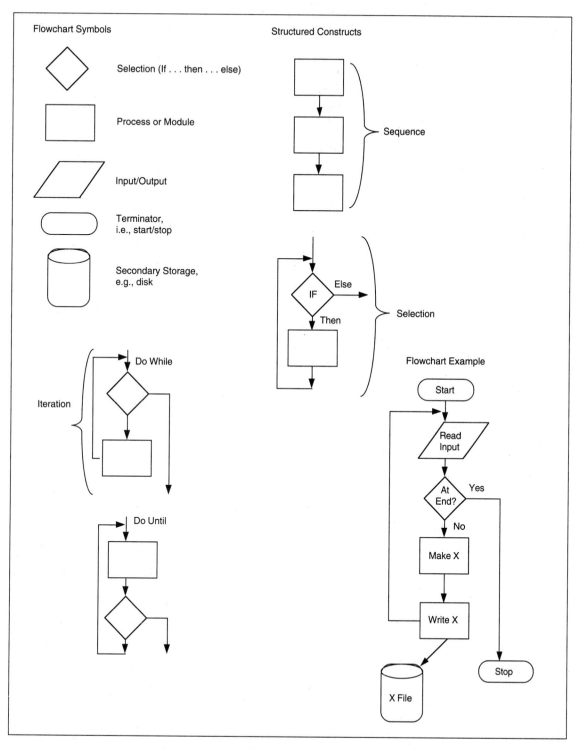

FIGURE 8-16   Flowchart Symbols, Structured Constructs, and Example

functions, and in-line code that will be an execute unit to perform some atomic process. In nonreal-time languages, an execute unit is a link-edited load module. In real-time languages, an execute unit identifies modules that can reside in memory at the same time and are closely related, usually by mutual communication. The guiding principles during these design activities are to minimize coupling and maximize cohesion (see Tables 8-2 and 8-3 for definition of the seven levels of coupling and cohesion).

An **atomic process** is a system process that cannot be further decomposed without losing its system-like qualities. An **execute unit** is a computer's unit of work (i.e., a task). A **module** is a 'small program' that is self-contained and may call other modules. Modules may be in-line, that is, in the actual program, or may be externally called modules. **In-line**

code is the structured program code that controls and sequences execution of modules and functions. For instance, a 'read' module might do all file access; a screen interaction module might do all screen processing and have submodules that perform screen input and screen output.

A **function** is an external 'small program' that is self-contained and performs a well-defined, limited procedure. For example, a function might compute a square root of a number. Functions usually do not call other modules but there is no rule against it. Even though the definitions of modules and functions are similar, they are different entities. Functions sometimes come with a language, for instance, the mathematical and statistical functions that are part of Fortran. Modules are usually user-defined and have a broader range of applicability, such as a

TABLE 8-2   Definition of Cohesion Levels

Type of Cohesion	Definition
Functional	Elements of a procedure are combined because they are all required to complete one specific function. This is the strongest type of cohesion and is the goal.
Sequential	Elements of a common procedure are combined because they are in the same procedure and *data* flows from one step to the next. That is, the output of one module, for example, is passed in sequence as input to the next module. This is a strong form of cohesion and is acceptable.
Communicational	Elements of a procedure are combined because they all use the same data type. Modules that all relate to customer maintenance—add, delete, update, query—are related through communication because they all use the Customer File.
Procedural	Elements of a common procedure are combined because they are in the same procedure and *control* flows from one step to the next. This is weak cohesion because passing of control does not mean functions in the procedure are related.
Temporal	Statements are together because they occur at the same time. This usually refers to program modules, for example, 'housekeeping' in COBOL programs to initialize variables, open files, and prepare for processing. Temporal cohesion is weak and should be avoided wherever practical.
Logical	The elements of a module are grouped by their type of function. For instance, all edits, all reads from files, or all input operations are grouped. This is undesirable cohesion and should be avoided.
Coincidental	This is the random or accidental placement of functions. This lowest level of cohesion occurs when there is no real relationship between elements of a module. This is undesirable cohesion and should be avoided.

TABLE 8-3   Definition of Coupling Levels

Level of Coupling	Definition
Indirect relationship	No coupling is possible when modules are independent of each other and have neither a need nor a way to communicate. This is desirable when modules are independent. An example of no direct relationship is a date translate routine and a net present value routine. There is no reason for them to be related, so they should not be related.
Data	Only necessary data are passed between two modules. There are no redundant parameters or data items. This is the desirable form of coupling for related modules.
Stamp	The module is given access to a complete data structure such as a physical data record when it only needs one or two items. The module becomes unnecessarily dependent on the format and arrangement of data items in the structure. Usually, stamp coupling implies external coupling. The presence of unneeded data violates the principal of 'information hiding' which says that only data needed to perform a task should be available to the task.
Control	Control 'flags' are shared across modules. Control coupling is normal if the setting and resetting of the flag are done by the same module. It is a pathological connection to be avoided if practical when one module sets the flag and the other module resets the flag.
External	Two modules reference the same data item or group of items such as a physical data record. In traditional batch applications, external coupling is unavoidable since data are passive and not directly relating to modules. External coupling is to be minimized as much as possible and avoided whenever practical. External coupling violates the principal of information hiding.
Common	Modules have access to data through global or common data areas. This is frequently a language construct problem but it can be avoided by passing parameters with only a small amount of additional work. Common coupling violates the principal of information hiding.
Content	One module directly references and/or changes the *insides* of another module or when normal linkage mechanisms are bypassed. This is the highest level of coupling and is to be avoided.

screen interaction module. Functions are usually reusable across applications without alteration; modules are not.

When program packages are decided, program specifications are developed. **Program specifications** document the program's purpose, process requirements, the logical and physical data definitions, input and output formats, screen layouts, constraints, and special processing considerations that might complicate the program. Keep in mind that the term *program* might also mean a module within a program or an externally called function. There are two parts to a program specification: one identifies interprogram (including programs in other applica-

tions) relationships and communication; the other documents intraprogram processing that takes place within the individual program. Another term for interprogram relationships is **interface**.

PROCESS _____
DESIGN _____
ACTIVITIES _____

The steps in process design are transform (or transaction) analysis, develop a structure chart, design the physical database, package program units, and write program specifications. Each of these steps is discussed in this section.

Since both transform and transaction analysis might be appropriate in a given system, the first activity is to identify all transactions and determine if they have any common processing. This activity can be done independently from the DFD and functional analysis, or it can be done as a side activity while you are doing functional analysis as the primary activity. If you cannot tell which is more appropriate, do a rough-cut structure chart using both methods and use the one which gives the best overall results in terms of coherence, understandability, and simplicity of design.

Transaction Analysis

Rules for Transaction Analysis

The basic steps in transaction analysis are to define transaction types and processing, develop a structure chart, and further define structure chart elements. A detailed list of transaction analysis activities follows.

1. Identify the transactions and their defining actions.
2. Note potential situations in which modules can be combined. For instance, the action is the same but the transaction is different—this identifies a reusable module.
3. Begin to draw the structure chart with a high-level coordination module as the top of the transaction hierarchy. The coordination module determines transaction type and dispatches processing to a lower level.
4. For each transaction, or cohesive collection of transactions, specify a transaction module to complete processing it.
5. For each transaction, decompose and create subordinate function module(s) to accomplish the function(s) of the transaction. If a transaction has only one unique function, then keep the unique action as part of the transaction module identified in the previous step.

6. For functions that are not unique, decompose them into common reusable modules. Make sure that the usage of the module is identical for all using transactions. Specifically identify which transactions use the module.
7. For each function module, specify subordinate detail module(s) to process whole detail steps as appropriate. If there is only one functional detail step, keep it as part of the function module defined in step 5.

A typical transaction application is money transfer for banks. Transactions for money transfer all have the same information: sending bank, receiving bank, sender, receiver, receiver account number, and amount. There might be other information, but this is required. What makes money transfer a transaction system is that transactions can come from phone, mail, TWX/Telex, fax, BankWire, FedWire, and private network sources. Each source of transaction has a different format. Phone, mail, and fax are all essentially manual so the application can require a person to parse the messages and enter them in one format. The other three are electronic messaging systems to be understood electronically. TWX/telex, which are electronic free-form messages, may have field identifiers but have no required order to the information. A summary DFD for a money transfer system might look like Figure 8-17, which shows a deceptively simple process. What makes the process difficult is that the data entry-parse-edit processes are different for each message type, having different edit criteria, formats, and acceptance parameters. The partitioning for the transaction DFD can be either a high-level summary or detailed. The summary partition (see Figure 8-17) shows afferent flows on the summary DFD, which is annotated that structuring is by transaction type. The detailed DFD (see Figure 8-18) shows each type of transaction with its own set of afferent and efferent flows.

To create a first-cut structure chart, one control module is defined for each transaction's afferent stream and efferent stream; there may be only one transform center. For each transaction, the afferent data flows are used to define data couples. The control couples relate to data passed between modules. When control is within a superior mod-

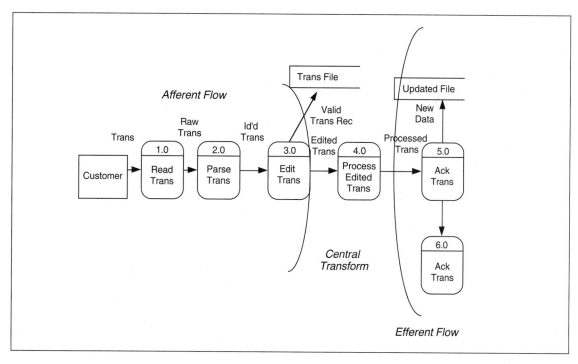

FIGURE 8-17   Summary Money Transfer DFD Partitioned

ule, it is shown via a diamond to indicate selection from among the transaction subprocesses (see Figure 8-19).

ABC Video Example Transaction Analysis

The first step to determining whether you have a transaction application or a transform centered application is to identify all sources of transactions and their types. Table 8-4 contains a list of transactions for ABC Video. As you can see from the list, there are maintenance transactions for customer and video information, there are rental and return transactions, and there are periodic transactions. The only common thread among the transactions is that they share some of the same data. The processing in which they are involved is different and there are no commonalities except reading and writing of files. Therefore, we conclude that ABC Video Rental processing is not a transaction-centered application and

move to transform analysis to complete the structure chart.

Transform Analysis

Rules for Transform Analysis

In transform analysis we identify the central transform and afferent and efferent flows, create a first-cut structure chart, refine the chart as needed at this high level, decompose the processes into functions, and refine again as needed. These rules are summarized as follows:

1. Identify the central transform
2. Produce a first-cut structure chart
3. *Based on the design strategy*, decompose the processes into their component activities
4. Complete the structure chart
5. Evaluate the structure chart and redesign as required.

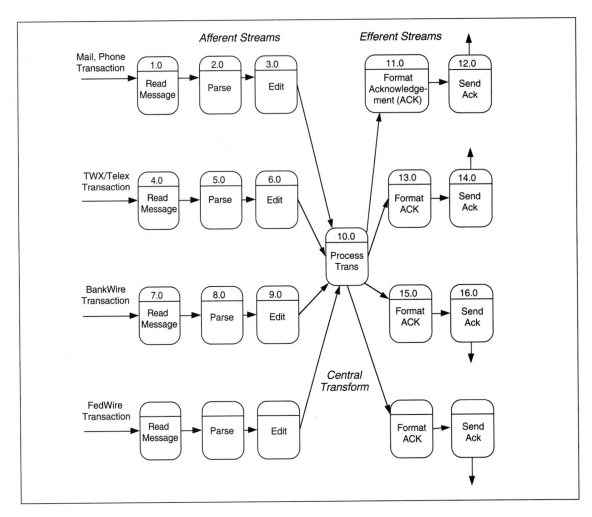

FIGURE 8-18   Detailed Money Transfer DFD Partitioned

To properly structure modules, their interrelationships and the nature of the application must be well understood. If a system concept has not yet been decided, design cannot be finalized until it is. The concept includes the timing of the application as batch, on-line or real-time for each process, and a definition of how the modules will work together in production. This activity may be concurrent with transform analysis, but should have been decided to structure and package processes for an efficient production environment. This activity is specific to the application and will be discussed again for ABC rental processing.

First, we identify the central transform and afferent and efferent flows. Look at the DFD and locate each stream of processing for each input. Trace each stream until you find the data flow that identifies valid, processable input that is the end of an afferent stream. The afferent and efferent arcs refer only to the processes in the diagram. During this part of the transform analysis, files and data flows are ignored except in determining afferent and efferent flows.

After identifying the afferent flows, trace backward from specific outputs (files or flows to entities) to identify the efferent flows. The net afferent and

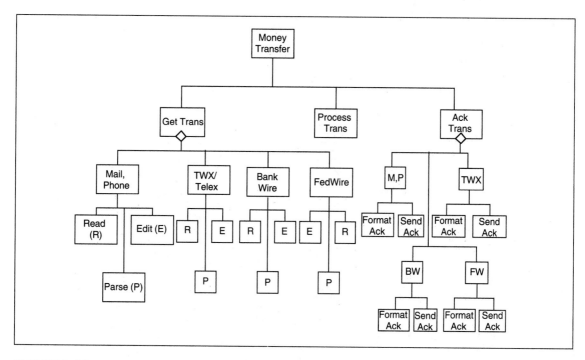

FIGURE 8-19   Sample Transaction Control Structure

TABLE 8-4   ABC Transaction List

Transaction	General Process	Data
Add Customer	Maintenance	Customer
Change Customer	Maintenance	Customer
Delete Customer	Maintenance	Customer
Query Customer	Periodic	Customer
Add Video	Maintenance	Video
Change Video	Maintenance	Video
Delete Video	Maintenance	Video
Query Video	Periodic	Video
Rent Video	Rent/Return	Video, Customer, History
Return Video	Rent/Return	Video, Customer, History
Assess special charges	Rent/Return	Customer
Query	Periodic	Video, Customer, History
Create History	Periodic	Video, Customer, History
Generate Reports	Periodic	Video, Customer, History

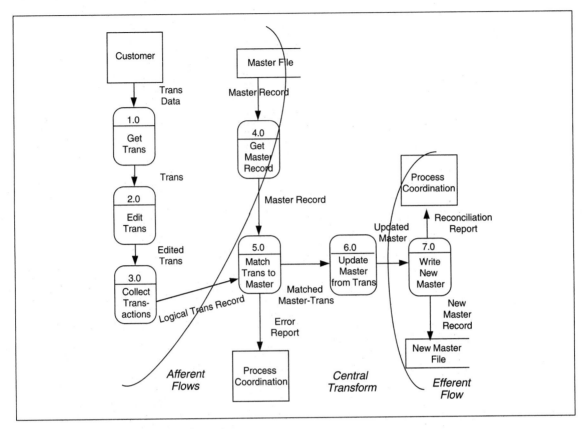

FIGURE 8-20   Master File Update DFD Partitioned

efferent outputs are used to determine the initial structure of the structure chart, using a process called factoring. **Factoring** is the act of placing each unbroken, single strand of processes into its own control structure, and of creating new control processes for split strands at the point of the split. The new control structure is placed under the input, process, or output controls as appropriate.

A master file update is shown as Figure 8-20 to trace the streams. In this diagram, we have two afferent data streams which come together at *Match Trans to Master*. The first input, *Trans Data* flows through process *Get Trans* and through *Edit Trans* to become *Edited Trans*. Successfully edited transaction parts flow through *Collect Transactions* to become *Logical Trans Record*.

The second input stream deals with the master file. The *Master Record* is input to *Get Master Record*; successfully read master records flow through the process. Once the *Logical Trans Record* and *Master Record* are both present, the input transformations are complete. These two afferent streams completely describe inputs, and the arc is drawn over the *Logical Trans Record* and *Master Record* data flows (see Figure 8-20).

The two streams of data are first processed together in *Match Trans to Master*. Information to be updated flows through *Update Master from Trans* to become *Updated Master*. The error report coming from the match process is considered a trivial output and does not change the essential transform nature of the process. The argument that *Match Trans to Master* is part of the afferent stream might be made. While it could be treated as such, the input data is ready to be processed; that is, transactions by themselves, master records by themselves, and transactions with master records might all be processed. Here, we interpret the first transformation as matching.

The data flow out of *Update Master from Trans* is a net outflow, and *Write New Master* is an efferent process. The efferent arc is drawn over the data flow *Updated Master*.

Next, we factor three basic structures that relate to input-process-output processing (see Figure 8-21). If there is more than one process in a stream, getting the net output data may require some interprocess coordination. The coordination activities are grouped and identified by a name that identifies the

net output data. So, in the example, the input stream is *Get Input*; the transform stream is *Process*; the output stream is *Write New Master*. Each stream represents the major elements of processing. Because the process and input streams both are compound, each has *at least* two streams beneath them—one for each sequential process stream to reach the net output data.

Notice that the DFD process names identify both data and transformation processes. Make sure that the lowest-level names on the structure chart are *identical* to the name on the data flow diagram to simplify completeness checking.

Notice also that there *is* transformation processing within the afferent and efferent streams. Modules frequently mix input/output and transform processing, and there is no absolute way to distinguish into

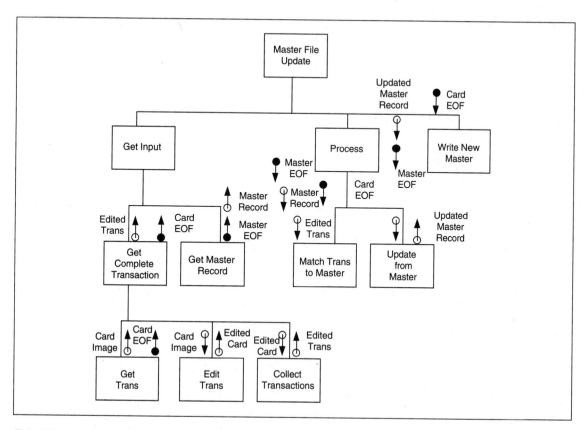

FIGURE 8-21   Master File Update Structure Diagram

which stream the module belongs. The rule of thumb is to place a module in the stream which *best describes* the majority of its processing.

Once the module is on the structure chart, we specifically evaluate it to ensure that it meets the principles of fan-out, span of control, maximal cohesion, and minimal coupling. If it violates even one principle, experiment with moving the module to the alternative streams and test if it better balances processing, without changing the processing. If so, leave it in the new location; otherwise note that the unbalanced part of the structure chart may need special design attention to avoid production bottlenecks.

Decompose the structure chart entries for each process. The three heuristics to guide the decomposition are:

- Is the decomposition also an IPO structure? If yes, continue; if no, do not decompose it.
- Does the control of the decomposed processing change? If yes, do not decompose it. If no, continue.
- Does the nature of the process change? That is, if the process is a date-validation, for instance, once it is decomposed is it still a date-validation? If no, continue. If yes, do not decompose it. In this example, I might try to decompose a date-validation into month-validate, day-validate, and year-validate. I would need to add a date-validate to check all three pieces together. Instead of a plain date-validate, I have (a) changed the nature of the process, and (b) added control logic that was not necessary.

The thought process in analyzing depth is similar to that used in analyzing the number of organizational levels in reengineering. We want only those levels that are required to control hierarchic complexity. Any extra levels of hierarchy should be omitted. Now let us turn to ABC rental processing to do transform analysis and develop the structure chart.

ABC Video Example Transform Analysis

The decisions about factoring are based on the principles of coupling and cohesion, but they also require a detailed understanding of the problem and a design approach that solves the whole problem. In ABC Video's case, we have to decide what the relationships of rent, return, history, and maintenance processing are to each other. If you have not done this yet, now is the time to do it. Before we continue with design of transform analysis, then, we first discuss the design approach and rationale.

DESIGN APPROACH AND RATIONALE. In Chapter 7, Table 7-5 identified the Structured English pseudo-code for ABC's rental processing and we did not discuss it in detail. Now, we want to examine it carefully to determine an efficient, cohesive, and minimally coupled decomposition of the process. When we partition the ABC Level 0 DFD from Figure 7-26, customer and video maintenance are afferent streams, reports are efferent, and rental and return are the central transforms (see Figure 8-22). We will attend only to create and return rentals since they are the essence and hardest portion of the application.

There is a design decision to have return processing as a subprocess of rental processing that needs some discussion. Then we will continue with the design. The overall design could be to separate rentals and returns as two different processes, but are they? Think in the context of the video store about how the interactions with customers takes place. Customers return tapes previously taken out. Then they select tapes for rental and pay all outstanding fees, including current and past returns that generate late fees. To have late fees, a tape must have been returned.[2] Rentals and returns are separated in time; they have separate actions taken on files. ABC has any combination of rentals with returns (with or without late fees) and open rentals. All open rentals are viewed during rental processing, but need not be during return processing. Adding a return date and late fees is a trivial addition. Returns could be

---

2 In a real video rental system, you would also have a delinquent or exceptional charges process to add fees for lost and damaged tapes. We do not consider that complexity here as it does not materially add to the discussion.

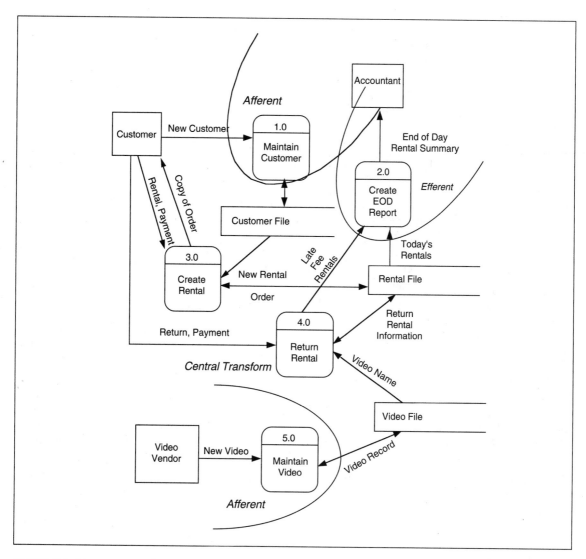

FIGURE 8-22   ABC Video Level 0 DFD Partitioned (same as Figure 7-26)

independent of rentals, so there are three design alternatives:

- Returns are separated from rentals.
- Rentals are a subset of returns.
- Returns are a subset of rentals.

If returns are separated from rentals, there would be two payment processes—one for the return and one for the rental. If a rental includes a return, this is not 'minimal bureaucracy' and is not desirable.

However, since returns can be done independently from rentals, the system should not require rental processing to do a return. This alternative is an acceptable *partial* solution, but the rest of the solution must be included.

The second alternative is to treat rentals as part of the return process. This reasoning recognizes that a rental precedes a return. All returns would need a rental/no rental indicator entry and assume that more than 50% of the time, rentals accompany returns.

Which happens more frequently—returns with rentals, or rentals without returns? Let's say Vic does not know and reason through the process. Since returns can be any of three ways, only one of which is with rentals, coupling them as rental-within-return *should* be less efficient than either of the other two choices.

Last, we can treat returns as part of the rental process. If returns are within rentals, we have some different issues. What information identifies the beginning of a rental? What identifies the beginning of a return? A customer number could be used to signify rental processing and a video number could signify a return. If we do this, we need to make sure the numbering schemes are distinct and nonoverlapping. We could have menu selection for both rental and return that determines the start of processing; then return processing also could be called a subprocess of rentals. Either of these choices would work if we choose this option. For both alternatives, the software needs to be reevaluated to maximize reusable modules because many actions on rentals are also taken on returns, including reading and display of open rentals and customer information.

Having identified the alternatives and issues, we conduct observations and collect data to justify a selection. The results show that 90% of returns, or about 180 tapes per day, are on time. Of those, 50% are returned through the drop box, and 50% (90 tapes) are returned in person with new rentals. The remaining 10% of returns also have about 50% (10 tapes) accompanying new rentals. So, about 100 tapes a day, or 50% of rentals are the return-then-rent type. These numbers justify having returns as a subprocess of rentals. They also justify having returns as a stand-alone process. We will allow both.

Deciding to support both separate and return-within-rental processing means that we must consciously decide on reusable modules for the activities the two functions both perform: reading and display of open rentals and customer information, payment processing, and writing of processing results to the open rental files. We will try to design with at least these functions as reusable modules.

DEVELOP AND DECOMPOSE THE STRUCTURE CHART. To begin transform analysis, we start with the last DFD created in the analysis phase, and the data dictionary entries that define the DFD details. Figure 7-28 is reproduced here as Figure 8-23, with a first-cut partitioning to identify the central transform.

First, we evaluate each process. We will use the pseudo-code that is in the data dictionary (see Figure 8-24). The DFD shows three rental subprocesses: *Get Valid Rental, Process Fees and Money*, and *Create and Print Rental*. Each of the subprocesses might be further divided into logical components. Try to split a routine into a subroutine for each function or data change. First, evaluate the potential split to make sure the subroutines are all still needed to do the routine. This double-checks that the original thinking was correct. Then, evaluate each potential split asking if adding the subroutine changes the control, nature, or processing of the routine. If yes, do not separate the routine from the rest of the logic; if no, abstract out the subroutine.

For ABC, *Get Valid Rental* is the most complex of the routines and is evaluated in detail. *Get Valid Rental* has three subroutines that we evaluate: *Get Valid Customer, Get Open Rentals*, and *Get Valid Video*. These splits are based on the different files that are read to obtain data for processing a rental. Without all three of these actions, we do not have a valid rental, so the original designation of *Get Valid Rental* appears correct. Figure 8-25 shows refined pseudo-code for ABC rental processing with clearer structure and only structured constructs. Subroutines are shown with their own headings.

If we are to accommodate returns during rental processing, we have to decide where and how rentals fit into the pseudo-code. We want to allow return dates to be added to open rentals. We also want to allow returns *before* rentals and returns *within* rentals. This implies that there are two places in the process where a rental *Video ID* might be entered: before or after the *Customer ID*. If the *Video ID* is entered first, the application would initiate in the *Return* process; from there, we need to allow additional rentals. If the *Customer ID* is entered first, the application would initiate rental; from there, we need to allow returns. To allow both of these actions to lead to rental and/or return processing, we need to add some control structure to the pseudo-code (see

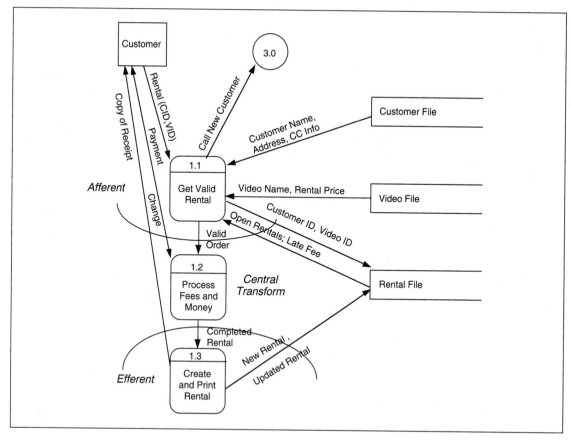

FIGURE 8-23   ABC Video Level 1 DFD Partitioned (same as Figure 7-28)

Figure 8-26). The control structure also changes the resulting structure chart somewhat even though the DFDs are not changed.

Next, we evaluate the refined pseudo-code and inspect each subroutine individually to determine if further decomposition is feasible (see Figure 8-27). For *Get Valid Customer*, does the processing stay the same? That is, are the detail lines of procedure information the same? By adding the subroutine we want to add a level of abstraction but not new logic. In this case, the answer is yes. Now look at the details of *Get Valid Customer*. The subprocesses are *Get Customer Number*—a screen input process, *Read and Test Customer File*—a disk input process with logic to test read success and determine credit worthiness, and *Display Customer Info*—a screen output process. Again, we have decomposed *Get*

Valid Customer without changing the logic or adding any new functions.

The results of the other evaluations are presented. Walk-through the same procedure and see if you develop the same subroutines. Here we used the pseudo-code to decompose, but we could have used text or only our knowledge of processing to describe this thinking. When the decomposition is complete for a particular process stream, it is translated to a structure chart.

Complete the Structure Chart

Rules for Completing the Structure Chart

Completion of the structure chart includes adding data and control couples and evaluating the diagram.

Get Valid Rental.
  For all customer
    Get customer #
    Read Customer File
    If not present,
      Cancel
    else
      Create customer
      Display Customer info.

  Read Open-Rentals
  For all Open Rentals,
    Compute late fees
    Add price to total price
    Display open rentals
    Display total price.

  For all video
    Read Video file
    If not present
      Cancel this video
    else

Create Video
Display Video
Add price to total price
Display total price.

Process Fees and Money.
  Get amount paid.
  Subtract total from about paid giving change.
  Display change.
  If change = zero and total = zero,
    mark all items paid
  else
    go to process fees and money.

Create and Print Rental.
  For all open rentals
    if item paid
      rewrite open rental.
  For all new rentals
    write new open rental.
  Print screen as rental confirmation.

FIGURE 8-24   ABC Rental Pseudo-code

Get Valid Rental.
  Get Valid Customer.
  For all customer
    Get customer #
    Read Customer File
    If not present,
      Cancel
    else
      Create customer
      Display Customer info.

  Get Open Rentals.
  Read Open-Rentals
  For all Open Rentals,
    Compute late fees
    Add price to total price
    Display open rentals
    Display total price.

  Get Valid Video.
  For all video
    Read Video file
    If not present
      Cancel this video
    else
      Call Create Video

Display Video
Add price to total price
Display total price, change.

Process Fees and Money.
  Get amount paid.
  Subtract total price from about paid giving change.
  Display total price, change.
  If change = zero and total = zero,
    mark all items paid
  else
    go to process fees and money.

Create and Print Rental.
  Update Open Rentals.
  For all open rentals
    if item paid
      rewrite open rental.

  Create New Rentals.
  For all new rentals
    write new open rental.
  Print screen as rental confirmation.

FIGURE 8-25   ABC Rental Pseudo-code Refined

Get Valid Rental.
Get entry.
If entry is Video
Call Return
else
Call Rental.

Rental.
  Get Valid Customer.
    For all customer
      Get customer #
      Read Customer File
      If not present,
        Cancel
      else
        Create customer
        Display Customer info.

  Get Open Rentals.
    Read Open-Rentals
    For all Open Rentals,
      Compute late fees
      Add late fees to total price
      Display open rentals
      Display total price.

  Get Valid Video.
    For all video
      Read Video file
      If not present
        Cancel this video

else
  Call Create Video
  Display Video
  Add price to total price
  Display total price, change.

Process Fees and Payment.
Create and Print Receipt.

Return.
  Get Open Rental.
    Read Open-Rentals
    Read Customer
    Display Customer
    Display Open Rental
    Add return date.
  Using customer ID, Read Open Rentals.
    For all Open Rentals
      Display open rentals.
      For all return request
        Add return date to rental.
        Compute late fees
        Add late fees to total price
        Display total price.
  If rental
    Call **Get Valid Video.**
  Call **Process Fees and Payment.**
  Call **Create and Print Receipt.**

FIGURE 8-26   Get Valid Rental Pseudo-code with Control Structure for Returns

Structure chart completion rules are:

1. For each data flow on the DFD add exactly one data couple. Use exactly the same data flow name for the data couple.
2. For each control module, decide how it will control its subs. If you need to refine the pseudo-code to decide control, do this. Add control couples to the diagram when they are required between modules.
3. For modules that select one of several paths for processing, show the selection logic with a diamond in the module with the logic attached to the task transfer line.

Rules of thumb for developing the structure chart are:

1. Evaluate the diagram for cohesion. Does each module do one thing and do it completely?
2. Evaluate the diagram for fan-out, fan-in, skew, and redesign as required, adding new levels of control. Note skewed processing for attention during program design.
3. Evaluate the diagram for minimal coupling. Is the same data used by many modules? Do control modules pass only data needed for processing? Do control modules minimize their scope of effect?

These are all discussed in this section.

First, the structure chart is drawn based on the decomposition exercises. Then data couples are added to the diagram for each data flow on the DFD. If the

Get Valid Rental.
Get entry.
If entry is Video
Call Return
else
Call Rental.

Rental.
Call **Get Valid Customer.**
Call **Get Open Rentals.**
Call **Get Valid Video.**

Return.
Call **Get First Return.**
Call **Get Open Rentals.**
If rental
Call **Get Valid Video.**

Process Fees and Money.

Create and Print Rental.
Update Open Rentals.
Create New Rentals.
Print receipt.

Get Valid Customer.
Get customer #
Read Customer File
If not present,
Create Customer.
If CCredit not zero, display CCredit
Display Customer info.

Get Open Rentals.
Read Open-Rentals
For all Open Rentals,
Compute late fees
Add late fees to total price
Display open rentals
Display total price, change.
For all return request
Call **Update Returns.**

Get Valid Video.
For all video
Read Video file
If not present
Cancel this video
else
Call Create Video
Display Video
Add price to total price
Display total price, change.

Get First Return.
Read Open-Rentals
Read Customer
Display Customer
Display Open Rental
Call **Update Returns.**

Update Returns.
Move return date to rental.
Update video history.
Compute late fees.
Add late fees to total price.
Display total price.

Process Fees and Money.
Get amount paid.
Subtract total price from about paid giving change.
Display total price, change.
If change = zero and total = zero,
mark all items paid
else
go to process fees and money.

Update Open Rentals.
For all open rentals
rewrite open rental.

Create New Rentals.
For all new rentals
write new open rental.

FIGURE 8-27   Complete Pseudo-code for Rentals and Returns

structure chart is at a lower level of detail, use the data flow as a starting point and define the specific data passed to and from each module. Show *all* data requirements for each module completely. Make sure that all names are *exactly* as they are in the dictionary.

Next, for each control module, decide *how* it will control its subprocesses and add the control couples to the diagram. Decide whether the logic will be in the control module or in the subprocess. If the logic is in the control module, the goal is for the controller to simply call the subordinate module, pass data to

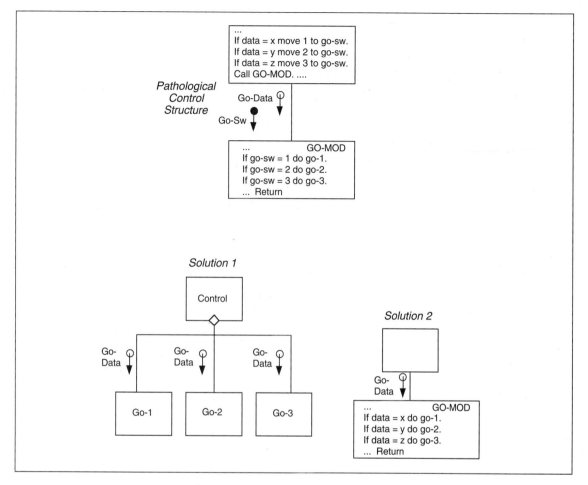

FIGURE 8-28   Pathological Control Structure and Two Solutions

transform, and receive the transform's data back. If any other processing takes place, rethink the control process because it is not minimally coupled.

A control couple might be sent to the subprocess for it to determine what to do. This may or may not be okay. Where is the control couple 'set' and 'reset'? If in the control module, this is acceptable. If somewhere else, rethink the control process and simplify it. Any time you *must* send a control couple for a module to decide which action to take, you identify a potential problem. The lower-level module may be doing too many things; otherwise it would not need to decide what to do, or the control may be in the wrong module.

An example of this problem and two solutions are illustrated in Figure 8-28. If the lower level is doing too many things, then decompose them to create several single-purpose modules. If the lower level is not doing multiple functions, then move control for the module into the module itself. In both cases, the goal of minimal coupling is attained.

Next, the diagram is evaluated for cohesion, coupling, hierarchy width, hierarchy depth, fan-out, fan-in, span of control, and skew. Evaluate the diagram for cohesion (see Table 8-2 for definition of cohesion types). Check that each module does one thing and does it completely. If several modules must be taken together to perform a whole function, the structure is excessively decomposed. Regroup the processes and restructure the diagram.

Evaluate the diagram for width, depth, fan-out, fan-in, and skew. These are visual checks to see if some portion of the structure is inconsistent with the rest of the structure. The inconsistency does not necessarily mean that the diagram is wrong, only that there may be production bottlenecks relating to the out-of-balance processes. For a wide structure, double check that the subprocesses really all relate to one and only one process. If not, add a new control module, else leave as is.

For deep structures, check to see if each level of depth is performing some function beyond control. Ask yourself why all the levels are needed. If there is no good reason, get rid of the level and move its functions either up or down in the hierarchy, preferably up. Ask yourself if fewer levels can accomplish the same process. If the answer suggests reducing the levels of hierarchy, restructure the diagram and keep only essential levels.

For fan-in modules, check that each using module has the same type of data being passed and expects the same type of results from the fan-in module. If there are *any* differences, then either make the using modules consistent, or add a new module to replace the fan-in module for the inconsistent user module.

Skewed diagrams identify a fundamental imbalance of the application that may have been hidden before: that it is input-bound, output-bound, I/O-bound, or process-bound. Skew is not necessarily a problem that results in restructuring a diagram. When skewed processing is identified, you should verify that it is not an artifact of your factoring. If it is, remove the skew from the diagram by restructuring the modules.

Skew is not always a problem. When a skewed application is being designed, the designers normally spend more time designing the code for the bound portion of the problem to ensure that it does not cause process inefficiencies. For instance, Fortran is notoriously inefficient at physical input/output (i.e., reading and writing files). For anything but a process-bound application, Fortran is not the best language used. For a process-bound Fortran application, with many I/Os, another language, such as

assembler or Cobol, might be used to make read/write processing efficient. The opposite is true of Cobol. Cobol is not good at high precision, scientific, mathematical processing. In a Cobol application, process-bound modules and their data would be designed either for another language, or to minimize the language effects.

Finally, evaluate the diagram for minimal coupling. First look at data couples. If you see the same data all over the diagram, there may be a problem. Either you are not specifying the data at the element level, or data coupling is the least coupling you will be able to attain. Make sure that only needed data is identified for passing to modules. Data coupling is not the best coupling, but it is tolerable.

Next look at control couples one last time. Make sure that they are set and reset in the same or directly-related modules, and make sure that, if passed, they are passed for a reason. If either of these conditions are violated, change the coupling.

To summarize so far, decide the system concept; partition the DFD; develop a first-cut structure chart; decompose the structure chart using pseudo-code of the functions as needed to guide the process; add data couples; add control couples; evaluate and revise as needed.

ABC Video Example Structure Chart

ABC's structure chart will begin with the Level 1 DFD factoring and progress to provide the detail for modules as expressed in the pseudo-code. There are three first level modules: *Get Valid Rental, Process Fees & Money*, and *Create and Print Rental* (see Figure 8-29). To get the next level of detail, we use the pseudo-code or decomposed structure charts. In our case, we use the pseudo-code. In Figure 8-27, the high level pseudo-code has only module names. We simply transfer those names to modules on the structure chart, attending to the control logic present in the diagram.

For each *if* statement, we need to decide whether that statement will result in a direct call (our choice, here) or whether it will result in a control couple being passed. Direct calls are preferred to minimize coupling. When a direct call is used, the module is executed in its entirety every time it is called.

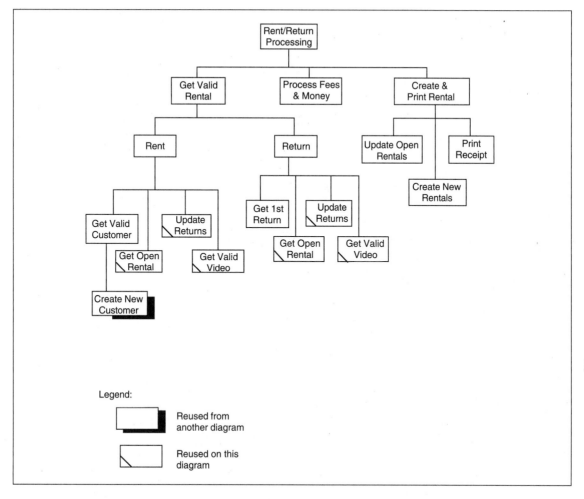

FIGURE 8-29   Rent/Return First-Cut Structure Chart

We identify reused modules by a slash in the lower left corner of the rectangles to show the complete morphology of the diagram. The first-cut structure chart shows that the processing is skewed toward input. Because there are three data stores affected by every process, there is no way to get rid of the skew without getting rid of the control level. Is the control level essential? If we omit the control level is the processing the same? Do we violate fan-out if we remove the control level? The answers are no, mostly, and no, respectively. If we remove the control level, its logic must go somewhere. The logic can move up a module and not violate fan-out. The

change may have a language impact, so we will not change it until we decide program packages.

We note it for attention during packaging and programming. There are no other obvious problems with the first-cut structure chart. Since we have developed it bottom-up, using the pseudo-code as the basis, it is as good as our pseudo-code.

Next, we add the data and control couples needed to manage processing. The final diagram is shown in Figure 8-30, which we evaluate next.

Each module appears to do only one thing. The diagram is input-skewed as already discussed. The span of control and fan-out seem reasonable.

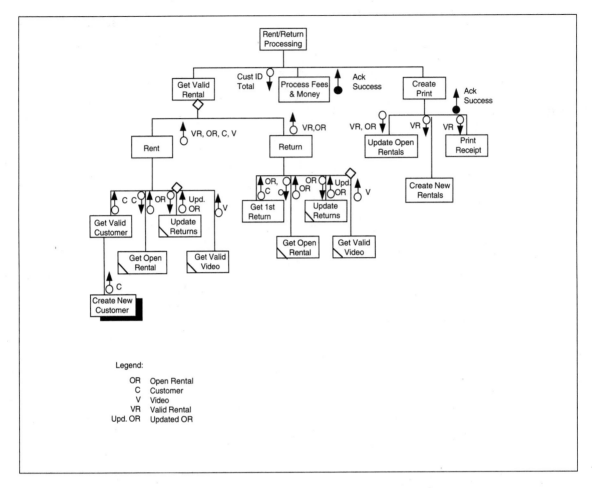

FIGURE 8-30   Completed Rent/Return Structure Chart

The reused modules each have the same input data. The hierarchy is not unnecessarily deep, although the control code for *Get Valid Rental, Rent,* and *Return* might be able to be combined depending on the language. Coupling is at the data level and is acceptable. Next, we turn to designing the physical database.

Design the Physical Database

Physical database design takes place concurrently with factoring and decomposition. A person with special skills, usually a database administrator (DBA), actually does physical database design. In companies without job specialization, a project team member acts as the DBA to design the physical database. Physical database design is a nontrivial task that may take several weeks or even months.

Rules for Designing the Physical Database

The general physical database design activities are summarized below. Keep in mind that many other activities may be involved in designing a physical database that relate to a specific implementation environment.

1. Define user views based on transaction types and data accessed for each transaction.

2. Identify access method if choices exist.
3. Map user views to access method and storage technology to optimize disk space and to minimize access time.
4. Build prototype and test, revising as indicated.
5. Develop database for application testing.
6. Document physical database design and distribute user view information to all project team members.
7. Work with conversion team to build production databases.

Designing user views means to analyze the transactions or inputs of each process to define which database items are required. In general, the data items processed together should be stored together. These logical design activities constrain the physical design and help the person mapping to hardware and software.

In selecting the access method, the physical data designer seeks to optimize matching available access methods to access requirements. Access method choices usually are data sequenced (i.e., indexed), entry sequenced (i.e., direct), inverted lists, or some type of b-tree processing. Each DBMS and operating system has its own access method(s) from which selection is made. The details of these access methods are beyond the scope of this text.[3]

User views are mapped to the access method and a specific media. Media mapping seeks to optimize access time for individual items and sets of items. It also seeks to minimize wasted space while providing for growth of the database. Since media have become one of the major expenses in the computing environment, there may be political issues involved with physical database design. At this point, a database walk-through reviews all database design before a prototype is built.

The DBA documents and trains team members in data access requirements. The DBA, working from the application specification, maps data requirements to user views to processes. Each process, then, has specific data items assigned. Every team member must know exactly what data items to access and how to access them. If a module or program accesses the wrong data item, an inconsistent database might result. Also, minimal data coupling requires that each process access only data that it requires. Incorrect use of access methods can lead to process bottlenecks or an inconsistent database. To assure that programs are using the data correctly, the DBA may participate in walk-throughs to monitor data access.

The DBA works with the test team to load the data needed for testing. The DBA also works with the conversion team to load the initial production database. These activities may be trivial or may require hiring of temporary clerks to input information to the database. The DBA and the two teams work together to verify the correctness of the data, to provide program test database access to the rest of the development team, and to provide easily accessed backup when the test database is compromised. After the test database is loaded, the backup and recovery procedures, transaction logic procedures, and other database integrity procedures are all finalized and tested.

To summarize, a person who intimately knows the technical production data environment acts as a DBA, mapping the database to a physical environment and building both test and production databases. The DBA provides training and guidance to the other team members for data access, and participates in data related walk-throughs.

ABC Video Example Physical Database Design

In order to do the physical database design, a DBMS must be selected. We will design as if some SQL engine were being used. SQL's physical design is closely tied to the logical design so the design activity becomes less DBMS software sensitive. In addition, SQL data definition is the same in both mainframe and micro environments so the design activity does not need to be hardware platform sensitive. The amount of storage space (i.e., number of tracks or cylinders) will vary, of course, since disks

---

3 For more on access methods and storage considerations, see references to Fabbri and Schwab [1992], Codd [1990], Bohl [1981], and Claybrook [1983] in the references.

on PCs do not yet hold as much information as mainframe disks.

Beginning with the logical design from Table 7-7, we define the relations and data items that are required to develop user views. Remember from database class, that the logical database design can map directly to the physical database. The relations defining the actual database may or may not be accessed by users. For security reasons, user views may be used to control access to data and only the DBA would even know the real relation names.

To define user views, we examine each process and identify the data requirements. List the requirements by process (see Table 8-5). Match similar data requirements across processes to identify shared user views. The problem is to balance the number of views against the number of processes. Ideally a handful of user views are defined; a heuristic for large applications is about 20 user views. Beyond that, more DBAs are required and database maintenance becomes difficult. In a large application, keeping the number of user views manageable may be difficult and require several design and walk-through iterations.

For ABC rental processing, we need a user view for each major data store: *Customer*, *Video Inventory*, and *Open Rentals*. We also need user views for the minor files: *Video History*, *Customer History*, and *End Of Day Totals*. If data coupling and memory usage are not an issue, using a SQL database, we can create one user view for each of *Customer*, *Video*, and *Open Rental*, and create one joined user view using the common fields to link them together. The individual views are used for processes that do not need all of the data together; the joined view can be used for query processing and for processes that need all of the data. The resulting data definitions for customer, video, open rentals, and the related user views are shown in Table 8-6. We also need separate user views for the history files and EOD totals. They are included in the table.

At this point, with SQL software, we are ready to prototype the database. If either access method selection or storage mapping is an issue, a prototype should be built. Otherwise, the next step is to map user views to access methods and storage media. This activity depends on the implementation environment and is beyond this text. The database may be walked through again at this point to verify processing requirements for the database. The database is then prototyped and documented. The information needed for each program is included in program specifications. Team members are usually given an overview of the database environment either as part of the last walk-through or as a separate training session. When the prototype appears complete and workable, test and production databases are developed.

Design Program Packages

Rules for Designing Program Packages

The activities for grouping modules into program packages are listed below; as you can see, they are general guidelines, not rules. There are no rules for packaging because it is an environment-dependent activity. Packages for firmware or an 8K micro computer are entirely different than packages for a mainframe. Also, the implementation language determines how and when some types of coupling are done. With these ideas in mind, the guidelines apply common sense to identifying program execute units.

1. Identify modules that perform functionally related activities, are part of iteration units, or which access the same data. The related modules identified should be considered for packaging together for execution.
2. Develop pseudo-code for the logic functions being performed. Use only structured programming constructs: iteration, selection, and sequence. Document complex logic using decision tables or decision trees.
3. Logically test the user views developed with the DBA to reevaluate their usefulness for each program package.
4. Design each module to have one entry and one exit.
5. Design each module such that its contents are unchanged from one execution to the next.
6. Design and document messages for called modules. Reevaluate the messages to minimize coupling.
7. Draw a diagram of the module and all other modules with which it interacts.

TABLE 8-5   ABC Data Requirements by Process

Process	Customer	Video Inventory	Open Rental	Other
Get Valid Customer	Customer Phone, Name, Address, Credit Rating			
Get Open Rentals			Customer Phone, Video ID, Copy ID, Video Name, Rent Date, Return Date, Late Days, Fees Owed	
Get Valid Video		Video ID, Copy ID, Video Name, Rental Price		
Get First Return			Customer Phone, Video ID, Copy ID, Video Name, Rent Date, Return Date, Late Days, Fees Owed	
Get Valid Video		Video ID, Copy ID, Video Name, Rental Price		
Update Rentals			Customer Phone, Video ID, Copy ID, Video Name, Rent Date, Return Date, Late Days, Fees Owed	
Process Fees and Money				End of Day Totals Total Price + Rental Information
Create Video history				Video History File: Year, month, Video ID, Copy ID
Create Customer history				Customer History File: Customer Phone, Video ID
Update Open Rentals			Customer Phone, Video ID, Copy ID, Video Name, Rent Date, Return Date Late Days, Fees Owed	
Create New Rentals			Customer Phone, Video ID, Copy ID, Video Name Rent Date, Return Date, Late Days, Fees Owed	
Print receipt				Customer Phone, Name, Address, For each Video: Video ID, Copy ID, Video Name, Rent Date, Return Date, Late Days, Fees Owed, Total Price

TABLE 8-6 SQL Data Definitions and User Views

Create Table Customer

(Cphone	Char(10)	Not null,
Clast	VarChar(50)	Not null,
Cfirst	VarChar(25)	Not null,
Cline1	VarChar(50)	Not null,
Cline2	VarChar(50)	Not null,
City	VarChar(530)	Not null,
State	Char(2)	Not null,
Zip	Char(10)	Not null,
CCtype	Char(1)	Not null,
Ccno	Char(17)	Not null,
Ccexp	Date	Not null,
CCredit	Char(1),	
Primary key	(Cphone));	

Create Table Video

(VideoID	Char(7)	Not null,
VideoNam	Varchar(50)	Not null,
VendorNo	Char(4)	
TotCopies	Smallint	Not null,
RentPrice	Decimal(1,2)	Not null,
Primary key	(videoID);	

Create Table Copy

(VideoID	Char(7)	Not null,
CopyID	(Char(2)	Not null,
DateRecd	Date	
Primary key	(VideoID, CopyID),	
Foreign Key	((VideoID) References Video);	

Create Table Rental

Cphone	Char(10)	Not null,
RentDate	Date	Not null,
VideoID	Char(7)	Not null,
CopyID	(Char(2)	Not null,
RentPaid	Decimal(2,2)	Not null,
FeesOwed	Decimal(2,2)	
Primary Key	(CPhone, VideoID, CopyID),	
Foreign Key	((VideoID) References Video)	
Foreign Key	((VideoID, CopyId) References Copy),	
Foreign Key	(CPhone) References Customer);	

Create view VidCrsRef
    as select VideoID, CopyID, VideoName, RentPric
      from Customer, Video, Copy
      where Video.VideoID = Copy.VideoID;

Create view RentRef
    as select Cphone, Clast, Cfirst, VideoID, CopyID, VideoNam,
    RentPaid, RentPric, FeesOwed
    from Customer, VidCrsRef, Rental
    where VidCrsRef.VideoID = Rental.VideoID
    and VidCrsRef.CopyID = Rental.CopyID
    and Customer.Cphone = Rental.Cphone;

A program package is a collection of called modules, called functions, and in-line code that does some atomic process, and that will become an execute unit. The hierarchy of criteria for designing packages is to package by function, by iteration clusters, or by need to access the same data. At all times, you must keep in mind any production environment constraints that must also be part of the design. For instance, if the application will be on a LAN, you may want to design packages to minimize the possibility of multiple users for a process.

Functional grouping is, by far, the most important. Functional grouping ensures high cohesion for the program. Any modules that are required to perform some whole function should be grouped together. The other two considerations frequently apply to functional groups as well.

If a group of activities repeat as part of an iterative sequence, all activities in the group should be together in the program package. Individual modules can be coded and unit tested alone, but they should be packaged for integration testing and implementation.

Grouping modules that access the same data minimizes physical reading and writing of files. The major goal is to read the same data record in any one pass of the processes no more than once. We want to minimize physical I/O because it is the slowest process the computer performs. Grouping modules by data accessed minimizes the frequency of reading. Real-time applications, especially, are vulnerable to multiple reads and writes of the same data, slowing down response time.

Grouping modules by data access is a form of data coupling that minimizes the chance of unexpected changes to data. If we do not package modules together, but only read and write data once, the major alternative to common packaging is to use global data areas in memory. Global data is not protected and is vulnerable to corruption.

When the packages are complete, develop Structured English pseudo-code for the logic functions being performed. Use only structured programming constructs—iteration, selection, sequence. Document complex logic using decision tables or decision trees. Include control structures and names for all modules. Pseudo-code may have been done as part of analysis, or earlier in design, as we did for ABC rental and return. Incidental activities, or less crucial activities, may have been overlooked or not refined. Pseudo-code is completed now and structured for use in program specifications.

Decision tables and trees might be used to document complex decisions. While a discussion of them is beyond this text, an example of each is shown in Figure 8-31.

As we design the program packages, we logically test the user views developed with the DBA to reevaluate their usefulness. The questions to ask are: Is all the needed data available? Is security adequate? Is extra data present? If any of these answers indicate a problem, discuss it with the DBA and determine his or her reasons for the design. If the design should change, the DBA is the person to do it.

Design each module to have one entry and one exit. Multiple entrances and exits to program modules imply problems because of selection and goto logic required to implement multiple exits and entrances. If each module is kept simple with one of each, there are fewer testing, debugging, and maintenance problems.

Ideally, each module should have its internal data contents the same before and after a given execution. That is, the state and contents of the module should be unchanged from one execution to the next. This does not mean that no changes take place during an execution, only that all traces of changes are removed when the execution is complete. When a module must maintain a 'memory' of its last actions, coupling is not minimized.

Design and document messages for called modules. Messages should contain, at most, calling/called module names, data needed for execution, control couples, and variable names for results of execution.

You might draw a diagram of the module and all other modules with which it interacts to facilitate visual understanding of the module and its role in the application.

ABC Video Example Program Package Design

Working with the final structure chart in Figure 8-30, our biggest decision is whether or not to package all of rental/return processing together, and how. Do we write one program with performed modules, one with called modules, or a combination of the two?

ABC is going to be in a SQL-compatible database environment, on a LAN, and requires access by PCs. The choice of language is not limited with these requirements, but packaging without knowing the language is not recommended. For this exercise, we will assume that Focus,[4] the 4GL, will be used.

Focus' application generator, called the "Dialogue Manager," allows both in-line and called modules to be used. Calling modules of nonFocus languages are allowed but can be tricky. The language has its own DBMS that is SQL-compatible, but it is not fully relational. It falls in the category of DBMSs called 'born again relational,' that is, the DBMS is hierarchic, networked, or relational at the DBA's discretion. Relationality is allowed but not required in Focus. Focus does not support the integrity rules. We will not redesign the database here since the SQL code above could be recoded without design changes in the Focus DBMS language.

At this point, we need to step back and decide how to package the entire application. What kind of 'glue' will hold customer maintenance, video

---

4 Focus is a trademark of Information Builders Inc., New York. Focus is representative of PC-based application generators, including Rbase, Dbase IV, Informix, etc.

Decision Table Format:

Conditions—Possible occurrences	Rules—Specific occurrences
Actions—Possible outcomes	Entries—Specific outcomes for rule combinations.

Decision Table Example:

Conditions

Customer	Old	Old	Old	Old	Old	Old	Old	Old	New	New
Open Rentals	Y	Y	Y	Y	N	N	N	N	—	—
Returns	Y	Y	N	N	Y	Y	N	N	—	—
New Rentals	Y	N	Y	N	Y	N	Y	N	Y	N

Actions

Create Customer	N	N	N	N	N	N	N	N	Y	Y
Check Late Fees	Y	Y	Y	Y	Y	Y	N	N	Y	N
Process Return	Y	Y	N	N	Y	Y	N	N	N	N
Process New Rental	Y	N	Y	N	Y	N	Y	N	Y	N
Process Fees and Money	Y	Y	Y	Y	Y	Y	Y	N	Y	N
Update Open Rental	Y	Y	Y	Y	Y	Y	N	N	N	N
Create Open Rental	Y	N	Y	N	Y	N	Y	N	Y	N
Print Receipt	Y	Y	Y	Y	Y	Y	Y	N	Y	N

Decision Tree Format: Tree structure showing conditions and actions.

Decision Tree Example:

FIGURE 8-31   Decision Table and Decision Tree

maintenance, end-of-day, and rental/return processing together. We do not discuss screen design here because it is not in the methodology (it is in Chapter 14), but we would finalize screens while these decisions are being made. We need all of the above functions to do this application, so all of the functions must be available in a unified environment. This means that all functions must be available for execution within the same run environment. Screens are the 'glue' that users see that unify application processing. The code behind the screens may or may not be unified depending on the design techniques and language. With Focus, unification is done through the Dialogue Manager.

4GL and PC-DBMS languages are deceptively simple. To perform trivial tasks is easy, but to build application requires expertise. Focus is no different. The complexities with Focus relate to when, where, and how often the databases are opened and processed, how the databases are related, and how many concurrent users are allowed. The concurrent environment increases DBA complexity but changes the answers to the questions about databases; it does not change the application code. So, we will assume one user at a time for processing.

Skeleton Focus code for the application is shown in Figure 8-32. Each DFD Level 0 process is accounted for at this level; we even have a query function that is new. Most applications require interactive file query and we have not talked about it at all as part of the rental return application. The trend in business today is for users to develop their own reports and queries using some 4GL. When the language has a built-in query facility, you can add it to the processing without any analysis or design work, as shown here with Focus. User developed queries allow users to 'stay in touch' with their data and remove a major design burden from IS personnel.

Now that the application is accommodated within one execute environment, we return to the problem of how to package rent/return processing. The ideal is to code and unit test each lowest level box on a structure chart as an independent module. Then, using the 'call' feature of the language, build a control structure, based on the design of the control and coordination boxes on the structure chart that calls modules as needed for execution. We will use this approach here as Figure 8-32 shows for the application, and Figure 8-33 shows for *rental* and *return* processing.

The alternative to called modules is in-line code that is 'performed' or executed as a pseudo-called module. This choice is selected with 3GL languages such as Cobol, Fortran, or PL/1 because it can be easier to code, test, and maintain.

Specify Programs

Rules for Specifying Programs

The specification documents all known information about programs. Program specifications document the program's purpose, process requirements, the logical and physical data definitions, input and output formats, screen layouts, constraints, and special processing considerations that might complicate the program. Keep in mind that the term *program* might also mean a module within a program or an externally called function, or even a code fragment (e.g., DB call). A program specification should include the items shown in Table 8-7. As with program packaging, there are no 'rules.' Rather there are items that should be included if they relate to the item being specified.

There are two parts to a program specification: one identifies interprogram relationships and communication, the other documents intraprogram processing that takes place within the individual program. Interfaces to other programs generally document who, what, when, where, and how communication takes place. *Who* identifies who initiates the communication and who, in the real world, is responsible for the interface. *What* identifies the message(s) content that is used for communication. *When* identifies the frequency and timing of the interface. *Where* locates the application and system in a hardware environment; where becomes complicated and is crucial to processing of distributed applications. *How* describes the nature of the interface—internal message, external diskette, and so forth.

Internal program processing information includes the data, processes, formats, controls, security, and constraints that define a particular program.

Focus Code	Explanation
-Set &&Globalvariables	Set variables needed for intermodule communication.
-Include Security	Check password in a security module.
-Run	Check password before any other processing.
-*	Comment indicator
-Mainline	A label identifying the main routine.
-Include Mainmenu	The call statement in Focus is 'INCLUDE.' Mainmenu is a module name.
-Run	Perform Mainmenu before any other processing.
-If &&Choice eq 'R' goto RentRet else	Interrogate the choices from Mainmenu to decide what to do
-If &&Choice eq 'V' goto Vidmain else	next.
-If &&Choice eq 'D' goto EndOfDay else	
-If &&Choice eq 'Q' goto Query else	
-If &&Choice eq 'S' goto StopSystem else	If in error, go back to the Mainmenu screen.
-Goto Mainmenu; -*	
-RentRet	RentReturn Label
-Include RentRet	Call Rent/Return processing.
-Run -Goto Mainline -*	When Rent/Ret is complete, return to the Mainmenu.
-Vidmain -Include Vidmain -Run -Goto Mainline -*	Video Maintenance Label and Processing
-Custmain -Include Custmain -Run -Goto Mainline -*	Customer Maintenance Label and Processing
Query -Include Tabltalk -Run -Goto Mainline -*	Query Label and Processing
-EndOfDay -Include Endofday -Run -Goto Mainline -*	End-of-Day Label and Processing
-StopSystem	Stop System Label
-End	End Processing

FIGURE 8-32   ABC Video Processing Focus Mainline

```
RentRet Focus Mainline Code

-Set &&Globalvariables
-*Rental and Return Processing

-Crtform Line 1
-"    ABC Video Rental Processing System <d.&date"
-"        Rentals and Returns"
-""
-""
-"        Scan or enter a card or video: <&&Entry"
-If &&entry like 't&' goto Return    else
-If &&entry like 'c&' goto Rental    else
-Include Entryerr;
-Run

-Return
-Include ValidCus
-Include OpenRent
-Include ValidVid
-Goto exit
-Run

-Rental
-Include FirstRet
-Include OpenRent
-Crtform Line 15
-"        Do you want to do rentals? <&&Rentresp/1"
-If &&Rentresp ne 'y' goto exit    else
-Include ValidVid
-Goto exit
-Run

-Exit
-End
```

FIGURE 8-33   ABC Rent/Return Focus Mainline

Frequently, program specifications also include a flowchart of the program logic, a system flowchart showing the system names of the files, and a detailed specification of timing and other constraints.

ABC Video Example Program Specification

The program specification for one program to perform *Get Valid Customer* is shown as an example (see Table 8-8). Since this is a compilation of already known information there is no discussion.

TABLE 8-7   Program Specification Contents

Identification

Purpose

Characteristics

Reference to Applicable Documents

DFD and Structure Chart (possibly also System Flowchart and Program Flowchart)

Narrative of procedures in Structured English, Decision Tables, Decision Trees

Automated Interface Definition

    Screen Interface

        Screen Design, Dialog Design, Error Messages

    Application Interface

        Communications Messages, Error Procedures Frequency, Format, Type, Responsible person

Input, Output, and System Files

    Logical data design

    User views, internal name, graphic of physical data structure

    List of physical data structures

Tables and Internal Data

    Internal name, graphic of physical data structure

    List of physical data structures

Reports

    Frequency, Format, Recipients, Special processing

AUTOMATED SUPPORT FOR PROCESS-ORIENTED DESIGN

Automated support in the form of CASE tools is also available, although fewer products support structured design than support structured analysis. Several entries provide *Lower CASE* support that begins

TABLE 8-8 ABC Example *Get Valid Customer* Program Specification

Identification:	*Get Valid Customer*, (ValidCus)
Purpose:	Retrieve Customer Record and verify credit worthiness
Characteristics:	Focus Included module
References:	See System Specification, Pseudo-code for CustMain
DFD:	Attached as Appendix 1
Structure Chart:	Attached as Appendix 2

Narrative:

```
    Accept CPhone
    Read Customer Using CPhone
    If read is successful
        If CCredit le '1'
            continue
        else
        Display "Customer has a credit problem; rating = <CCredit"
        Display "Override or cancel? : <&Custcredit"
        If &Custcredit eq 'C'
            include Cancel1
            Return
        else
        If &Custcredit eq 'O'
            continue
        else
        include crediterr
        return
    else
    Include CreatCus.
    Set &&ValidCus to 'Yes.'
    Set global customer data to values for all fields.
    Return.
```

Screen Interface

```
    Screen Design: None
    Dialog Design: None
    Error Messages:
        "Customer has a credit problem; rating = <CusCredit"
        "Override or cancel? : <&Custcredit"
```

Application Interface	None
Input:	Customer File
User views	Customer
Internal data names:	Customer Contents in Data Dictionary

Tables and Internal Data

Global fields correspond to all Customer File fields.
Set all fields to customer record values upon successful processing.

Reports:	None

TABLE 8-8   ABC Example *Get Valid Customer* Program Specification (*Continued*)

Appendix 1:   Data Flow Diagram

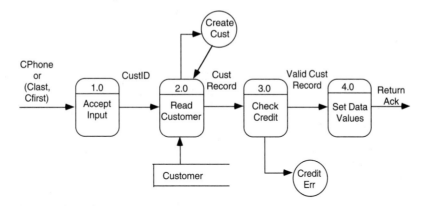

Appendix 2:   Structure Chart

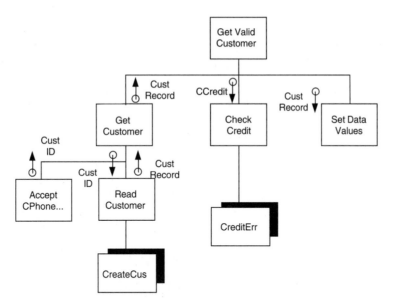

Appendix 3:   User View with Data Names

Table Customer

			State	Char(2)	Not null,
(Cphone	Char(10)	Not null,	Zip	Char(10)	Not null,
Clast	VarChar(50)	Not null,	CCtype	Char(1)	Not null,
Cfirst	VarChar(25)	Not null,	Ccno	Char(17)	Not null,
Cline1	VarChar(50)	Not null,	Ccexp	Date	Not null,
Cline2	VarChar(50)	Not null,	CCredit	Char(1),	
City	VarChar(530)	Not null,	Primary key	(Cphone));	

TABLE 8-9 CASE Tools for Structured Design

Product	Company	Technique
Analyst/Designer Toolkit	Yourdon, Inc. New York, NY	Structure Chart
Anatool, Blue/60, MacDesigner	Advanced Logical SW Beverly Hills, CA	Structure Charts Structured English
The Developer	ASYST Technology, Inc Napierville, IL	Structure Chart Operations Process Diagram Systems Flowchart
Excelerator	Index Tech. Cambridge, MA	Structure Chart Flowchart
IEW, ADW (PS/2 Version)	Knowledgeware Atlanta, GA	Structure Chart
Maestro	SoftLab San Francisco, CA	Nassi-Schneiderman Hierarchic input-process-output charts (HIPO) User Defined Functions
MacAnalyst, MacDesigner	Excel Software Marshalltown, IA	Decision Table Structured English Structure Chart
Multi-Cam	AGS Mgmt Systems King of Prussia, PA	Structure Chart

with program specification or code generation (see Table 8-9).

STRENGTHS AND WEAKNESSES OF PROCESS ANALYSIS AND DESIGN METHODOLOGIES

The objectives of structured analysis and design are reasonably clear; the manner of obtaining the objectives is much less clear. Structured methods rely on the individual SE's expertise to design the technical details of the application. For implementation specific details, that makes sense, but the heuristics for evaluation cannot be applied in every situation. Consequently, the SE must know what situations apply and don't apply. More than the other methods discussed in this book, you must know when to adhere to, bend, and break the rules of structured methods.

The methodology's ability to result in minimal coupling and maximal cohesion is low because of its reliance on the SE's ability. If coupling and cohesion are not optimal, maintenance will cost more than it should, and the application will be difficult to test. In 1972, D. Parnas wrote about maximal cohesion and minimal coupling as desirable characteristics of programs. In 1968, Dijkstra wrote about the problems with 'go to' statements in programs and proposed goto-less programming. In 1966, Böhm and Jacopini

TABLE 8-9   CASE Tools for Structured Design (*Continued*)

Product	Company	Technique
PacBase	CGI Systems, Inc. Pearl River, NY	Process Decomposition Structure Chart Flowchart
ProKit Workbench	McDonnell Douglas St. Louis, MO	Structure Chart
ProMod	Promod, Inc. Lake Forest, CA	Module Networks Function Networks Structure Chart
SW Thru Pictures	Interactive Dev. Env. San Francisco, CA	Control Flow Structure Chart
System Architect	Popkin Software and Systems, Inc. NY, NY	Flowchart Structure Chart
Teamwork	Cadre Technologies, Inc. Providence, RI	Control Flow Decision Table Structure Chart
Visible Analyst	Visible Systems Corp. Newton, MA	Structure Chart
Telon, and other products	Intersolv Cambridge, MA	Code Generation for Cobol- SQL, C and others
vs Designer	Visual Software, Inc. Santa Clara, CA	Structure Chart Warnier-Orr

proposed structured programming's minimalist contents as sequence, iteration (e.g., if . . . then . . . else) and selection (e.g., do while and do until). By the time structured analysis and design were documented in books, the notions of coupling and cohesion were understood fairly well; but how to obtain them was not.

General statements about keeping the pieces small and related to one part of the problem domain rely on the analyst to know what to do and when to start and stop doing it. Unfortunately, only experience can guide such vague suggestions. While novices can learn to rely on the methodology to guide their actions, they have no basis for evaluating the correctness or incorrectness of their work. Thus, the apprenticeship approach, with a junior person working with a more senior one to learn how to

evaluate designs, is required. The more complex the application, the more important having experienced senior analysts becomes.

Another problem is that structured design does not encompass enough of the activities to make it a complete methodology. We must have screen designs in order to develop a program specification. We must know the details of interfaces to other applications and messages to/from them to be able to develop program specifications. Structured methods do not pay any attention to either of these issues. To develop an application, the SE needs to analyze requirements and design for control, input, output, security, and recoverability. None of these are encompassed in the process-oriented methods. To summarize, process methods are useful in analyzing and designing applications that are procedural in nature;

but the methods omit a great many required analysis and design activities.

SUMMARY

In this chapter, structured design which follows structured analysis in development, was discussed. The results of structured analysis—a set of leveled data flow diagrams, data dictionary, and procedural requirements—are the inputs to the design process. The major results of structured design are program specifications which detail the mapping of functional requirements into the production hardware and software environment.

First, using either transaction or transform analysis, the DFD is partitioned into afferent, efferent, and central transform processes. The streams of processing are factored to develop a structure chart. The processes are further decomposed into system-like subprocesses until further decomposition would change the nature of the process. Data requirements are documented in data couples; control is documented in control couples. The chart is evaluated for fan-out, fan-in, skew, cohesion, coupling, scope of effect, and scope of control. The structure chart is revised and reevaluated as required.

The physical database is designed. Data needs for each data flow in the application are listed by process. Data similarities are matched and used to define user views. The access method and physical mapping are then decided. Physical database design walk-throughs may be held to validate the design. Test and production databases are created.

Program packages are decided based on the application concept and timing. The packages define which modules will communicate and how. Pseudo-code for processes is finalized and uses only structured programming constructs—iteration, sequence, and selection. Decision tables and trees are used, as necessary, to document complex decisions.

Finally, program specifications are written to document all known information about each module, function, or program. Specifications include data, process, interface, constraint, and production information needed for a programmer to code and unit test the work.

REFERENCES

Alexander, Christopher, *Notes on the Synthesis of Form*. Cambridge, MA: Harvard University Press, 1971.

Böhm, Corrado, and Guiseppe Jacopini, "Flow diagrams, Turing machines, and languages with only two formation rules," *Communications of the ACM*, Vol. 9, #5, May 1966, pp. 366–371.

Couger, J. D., M. A. Colter, and R. W. Knapp, *Advanced System Development/Feasibility Techniques*. NY: John Wiley & Sons, 1982.

Curtis, B., M. I. Kellner, and J. Over, "Process modeling," *Communications of the ACM*, Vol. 35, #9, September 1992, pp. 75–90.

DeMarco, T., *Structured Analysis and System Specification*. NY: Yourdon, Inc., 1978.

Dijkstra, Edsgar W., "Go to statement considered harmful," *Communications of the ACM*, Vol. 11, #3, March 1968, pp. 147–148.

Flaatten, P. O., D. J. McCubbrey, P. D. O'Riordan, and K. Burgess, *Foundations of Business Systems*, 2nd ed. NY: The Dryden Press, 1992.

Frances, B., "A window into CASE," *Datamation*, March 1, 1992, pp. 43–44.

Krasner, J., J. Terrel, A. Lindhan, P. Arnold, and W. H. Ett, "Lessons learned from a software process modeling system," *Communications of the ACM*, Vol. 35, #9, September 1992, pp. 91–100.

Lindholm, E., "A world of CASE tools," *Datamation*, March 1, 1992, pp. 75–81.

McClure, C., *The Three R's of Software Automation: Re-Engineering, Repository and Reusability*. Englewood Cliffs, NJ: Prentice-Hall, 1992.

McMenamin, S. M., and J. F. Palmer, *Essential Systems Analysis*. NY: Yourdon, Inc., 1984.

Olle, T. W., J. Hagelstein, I. G. MacDonald, C. Rolland, H. G. Sol, F. J. M. Van Assche, and A. A. Verrijn-Stuart, *Information Systems Methodology: A Framework for Understanding*. Workingham, England: Addison-Wesley, 1988.

Page-Jones, M., *The Practical Guide to Structured System Design*, 2nd ed. Englewood Cliffs, NJ: Prentice-Hall, 1988.

Parnas, David L., "One of the criteria to be used in decomposing systems into modules," *Communications of the ACM*, Vol. 15, #12, December 1972, pp. 1053–1058.

Swartout, W., and R. Balzer, "On the inevitable intertwining of specification and implementation," *Communications of the ACM*, Vol. 25, #7, July 1982, pp. 438–440.

Yourdon, E., and L. L. Constantine, *Structured Design: Fundamentals of a Discipline of Computer Program and Systems Design.* Englewood Cliffs, NJ: Prentice-Hall, 1979.

Yourdon, E., *Modern Structured Analysis.* Englewood Cliffs, NJ: Prentice-Hall, 1989.

BIBLIOGRAPHY

Bohl, M., *Introduction to IBM Direct Access Storage Devices.* Chicago, IL: SRA, 1981.
This booklet gives the clearest explanation of VSAM and the differences between data sequenced and entry sequenced storage options that I have seen.

Claybrook, B., *File Management Techniques.* NY: John Wiley & Sons, 1983.
This book provides a good general discussion of indexed, direct, and inverted list files.

Codd, E. F., *The Relational Model for Database Management, Version 2.* Reading, MA: Addison-Wesley Publishing Co., Inc., 1990.
Codd, the father of relationship database theory, argues the merits of an almost direct translation of the logical database to the physical database.

Fabbri, A. J. and A. R. Schwab, *Practical Database Management.* Boston, MA: PWS-Kent Publishing Co., 1992.
This book discusses physical mapping for relational databases and has some discussion of the issues involved for hierarchic and network databases.

KEY TERMS

afferent	external coupling
afferent flows	factoring
atomic process	fan-in
central transform	fan-out
cohesion	function
coincidental cohesion	functional cohesion
common coupling	functional decomposition
communicational	HIPO
cohesion	I/O-bound
content coupling	indirect coupling
control coupling	information hiding
coupling	in-line code
data coupling	input-bound
depth of hierarchy	interface
efferent	logical cohesion
efferent flows	modularity
executable unit	module
morphology	sequential cohesion
Nassi-Schneiderman	skew
diagrams	span of control
output-bound	stamp coupling
partitioning	structure chart
physical database design	structured design
procedural cohesion	temporal cohesion
process-bound	transaction analysis
program package	transaction-centered
program specification	transform analysis
program unit	Warnier Diagram
scope of effect	width of hierarchy

EXERCISES

1. Complete the design for the ancillary processes of ABC rental: customer maintenance, video maintenance, and end-of-day processing. Develop structure charts, including all of the required data and control couples. Evaluate the diagrams and revise as required. Refine the pseudo-code for these functions from Chapter 7. Develop program specifications and identify how the modules will be packaged. Make sure that you state your assumptions about the production environment clearly as part of the explanation of your decisions.

2. What is the linkage between structured analysis and structured design? How do you use the information and documentation from analysis to develop an application design? Do you think analysts and designers should be separate people? Why, or why not?

STUDY QUESTIONS

1. Define the following terms:

cohesion	morphology
coupling	partitioning
decomposition	program package
factor	program unit
function	transaction analysis
input-bound	transform analysis
module	

2. How does systems theory relate to structured design?

3. How do you know the difference between a transform centered application and a transaction-centered application?

4. What is the role cohesion plays in the partitioning process? in the decomposition process? in physical database design? in deciding program packages? in program specification?

5. What is the role coupling plays in the partitioning process? in the decomposition process? in physical database design? in deciding program packages? in program specification?

6. What are the major diagrams in the design phase? How are they derived? How do they relate to the work done in structured analysis?

7. What is the reasoning process for packaging program elements?

8. What is the purpose of Structured English? What are alternatives? For what are Structured English and its alternatives used? Why?

9. List the contents of a program specification.

10. Who usually does physical database design? Why would a specialist perform this task? Can SEs do physical database design as well? Why or why not?

11. Partition the following DFD and draw a structure chart. Identify potential afferent and efferent flows. (There are several alternatives for afferents.) Label the flows you decide best describe the processes you see. List other information you need to decide what the best partitioning should be.

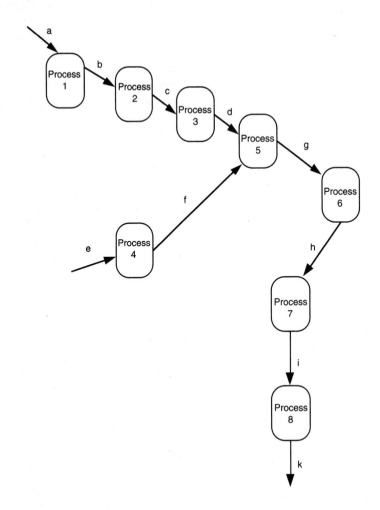

12. Evaluate the following structure chart. Describe the morphology. Is this diagram final or does it have problems? If so, what are the problems and how would you fix them?

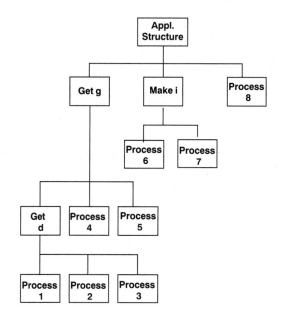

★ EXTRA-CREDIT QUESTION

1. Perform transform analysis on a case in Appendix A. Design the processing for the central transform from the high-level DFD. Develop lower level DFDs as required to assist your thinking. Factor and develop a first-cut structure chart. Develop pseudo-code for the processes you define. Refine the pseudo-code and finalize the structure chart, giving reasons for your design decisions. Develop program specifications and identify how the modules will be packaged. Make sure that you state your assumptions about the production environment clearly as part of the explanation of your decisions.

## CHAPTER 9

DATA-ORIENTED ANALYSIS

INTRODUCTION

Unlike process orientation, data-oriented analysis is not the result of the vision of a small set of people. Rather, it is the collective wisdom of many sources: computer vendors, MIS researchers, and consultants. The philosophy that underlies the data-oriented approach is that *data* are stable and more unchanging than *processes*. Processes can be revised with every reorganization. Data entities, on the other hand, rarely change in the lifetime of a business. Attributes of entities also rarely change. Even though the values of data do change constantly, the structure of the data does not. If data are stable, then they should be examined closely and first.

Data-oriented methodologies teach that data redundancy is to be minimized to best manage it in an organization. Database management software is assumed, but not required, in this approach. **Data administration**, that is, the conscious management of data as a resource of the business, is also assumed.

Information engineering (IE) is the methodology we use to discuss data-oriented analysis. IE teaches that to know *which* data should be the focus, we need architectures of data, business functions, and even organizational technology to guide the process. **Architectures** are conceptual descriptions of the items they define. Architectures are developed at the enterprise level (see Chapter 5). Data and functional architectures are defined further during business area analysis, then are divided into application areas and prioritized. Therefore, multiple application areas can result from one or more **business areas**.

IE methodology defines activities from the strategic organizational level through to implementation of individual applications. The major phases of information engineering are:

1. Enterprise Analysis
2. Business Area Analysis
3. Business System Design
4. Construction
5. Maintenance

In this chapter we discuss the Business Area Analysis (BAA) component of information engineering, which contains the activities that are most similar to analysis in other methodologies. IE analysis is called **Business Area Analysis** (BAA), rather than just *analysis*, because the focus is on *business* data and functions required to do the work. A departure from process-oriented analysis is that information engineering specifically ignores the current business organization, applications, and procedures. IE focuses on how the business *should* work, rather than on how it *does* work. Reengineering of the organization and its applications are common adjunct activities to information engineering (see Chapter 5). In the next section, we describe the conceptual foundations of data-oriented analysis. Then, the terminology of business area analysis is defined. This is followed by the rules and examples of how to conduct each activity.

CONCEPTUAL FOUNDATIONS

Data-oriented analysis is based mainly on theories about data. Process activities are based on the same systems theory which was the basis for the process development paradigm of Chapters 7 and 8.

The data-related theories are semantic information theory and relational database theory. Semantic information theory seeks to understand the meaning behind the data in applications and is most obvious in the depiction of meaning underlying entity relationship diagrams. By understanding the entities, or *things*, in the application, we know more about their domains—the allowable sets of values they may take. Eventually, rules about domain matching and entity integrity are applied to include domain processing along with data processing of the individual attributes of entities. Relationships between entities are as important as entities and domains. By knowing allowable business relationships, we can constrain processing naturally, by applying business rules, without regard to organizational design. Relationship cardinality, or number, is important to knowing how many of each related item should be evaluated. Cardinality prescribes either individual entity instances or sets of instances for processing. By knowing more about the meaning underlying the data in an application, constraints can be automated and made more general, thus, simplifying the application development process.

Relational database theory is based on mathematical set theory (or relational calculus) which describes allowable operations on sets of data items. Relational theory was developed to support provably correct processing of data items, something that *cannot* be guaranteed by either hierarchic or network database architectures. Set theory is the basis for relational theory which replaces the notion of 'record'

processing with 'set' processing. Record processing constrains languages and applications to one-at-a-time record read-manipulate-write processing actions even though most records receive identical treatment in programs. By specifying the rules for processing once and applying those rules to the *set* of data records, or *tuples* as they are called in relational theory, the individual program no longer does any read-write processing—it is performed by the DBMS. Applying set theory, the result of any operation is always a set. Thus, using mathematically based rules, the results of database processing can be known in advance and are provable.

Process activities performed are attributed to consulting practices that work and build on the systems theory underlying the process development paradigm. Some problems with DFDs are:

- DFDs do not accommodate time.
- DFDs have no implied sequence to processing.
- DFDs assign media to data early in analysis without any real deliberation.

These problems are eliminated in *process data flow diagrams (PDFDs)* that are built during IE analysis. Process methods of decomposition rely on analyst experience in process orientation. Data methods, such as information engineering (IE), provide a business-oriented approach to defining processes. Structured process constructs—selection, iteration, and sequence—are not consciously considered in process methods until structured design. Structured constructs are used in IE analysis to describe process relationships.

DEFINITION OF BUSINESS AREA ANALYSIS TERMS

The tasks performed during business area analysis (BAA) are:

1. Data modeling
2. Data analysis
3. Functional decomposition (i.e., process modeling)

4. Process dependency analysis
5. Process data flow diagramming
6. Process/data interaction mapping and analysis

Throughout the analysis, a data dictionary or repository is assumed to be used for documentation. The final step of BAA is completion of the repository for all information found during analysis.

For data modeling, the two major activities are the creation and refinement of an entity-relationship diagram (ERD) and entity structure analysis, along with an accompanying repository. When complete, the **ERD** describes the normalized data environment and data scope of the application. Each part of an ERD requires definition. An **entity type** (shortened to *entity* in this discussion)[1] is some person, object, concept, application, or event from the real world about which we want to maintain data (see Figure 9-1). There are three kinds of entities: fundamental, attributive, and associative. A **fundamental entity**, for instance, an order, is independent of all other entities and can be defined without thinking about other entities. An **attributive entity** is an entity whose existence *depends* on the presence of a fundamental entity. If *order* is the fundamental entity, then *order item* would be an attributive entity related to order (see Figure 9-2). Technically, you wouldn't have an order without any items, but you *cannot* have an order item without an order. Attributive entities contain repeating information relating to a fundamental entity. An **associative entity** is used to simplify and define complex relationships between entities. All entities are drawn on the entity relationship diagram (ERD) as rectangles.[2]

---

1 Technically, a customer is an entity who is uniquely described by a set of attributes. The set of all customers describes an entity type which is described by having the same attributes. A specific entity, e.g., customer 'Wells,' is an entity instance. In this text we use entity to be synonymous with entity type.

2 One method of diagramming is to show relationships with a diamond bisecting the line connecting entities. An associative entity, promoting a many-to-many relationship, is drawn as a rectangle with the diamond inside.

EXAMPLES			
Entity Type	**Insurance**	**ABC Video**	**Manufacturing**
Person	Policyholder	Customer	Customer
Object	Policy	Video	Bill of Lading
Concept	Policyholder Services	Accounting Department	Order
Event	Purchase of Policy	Rental of Video	Shipment of Goods
Organization	State Bureau of Insurance	Vendor	IRS, OSHA

FIGURE 9-1   Entity Type Examples

Entity	**ABC Video**	**Human Resources**	**Manufacturing**
Fundamental	Customer	Employee	Work Order
Attributive	Customer Rental History	Employee Work History	Work Order Detail Items
Associative	Vendor-Video	Employee-Job History	Work Order Item-Finished Part

FIGURE 9-2   Entity Examples

Number		Education Examples	Manufacturing Examples
One-to-One	1:1	Student to Transcript	Work Order Detail Item to Machine/Day/Time Operator
		Course Section to Room/Day/Time	
One-to-Many	1:N	Course to Section	Work Order to Work Order Detail Item
		Transcript to Course	
		Course to Room/Day/Time	Customer Order to Work Order
		Students to Major	Salesman to Customer
		Advisor to Student	
Many-to-Many	N:M	Student to Course	Part to Work Order Detail Item
		Professor to Course	Vendor to Inventory Part
		Professor to Section	

FIGURE 9-3   Relationship Cardinality Examples

A **relationship** is a mutual association between two or more entities. It is shown as a line connecting the entities. A relationship has **cardinality**, or the *number* of the relationship. Cardinalities may be one-to-one, one-to-many, or many-to-many (see Figure 9-3). Cardinality is shown on a diagram by crows' feet to indicate a 'many' relationship and a single line to indicate a singular relationship.

Refinement of the ERD has two activities: attributes are defined, and the ERD is normalized. **Attributes** are named properties or characteristics of an entity which take on values. We use the terms attribute, field, or data item, as synonyms. An **instance** is one occurrence of an attribute or relation. For example, an instance of the attribute customer-ID is the number 2922951.

Normalization is the refinement of data relationships to remove repeating information, partial key dependencies, and nonkey dependencies. Normalization can be directly applied to the ERD or can use a tabular method of data analysis. The **direct method** proceeds by examination of the relationship cardinalities and the attributes of entities. For $1:n$ relationships, and for entities with repetitive information in the entity, we create (or validate) attributive entities. For an $m:n$ relationship, the relationship is promoted to create an associative entity. A synonym for associative entity is **relationship entity**. The cardinalities of $m:n$ are reversed to create two $1:m$ relationships (see Figure 9-4).

The **tabular method** is recommended when data and relationships are not clearly specified. The tabular method forces explicit definition of all attributes and their relationships. When these dependencies are removed, each relation's data are fully, functionally dependent on the primary keys. An example is shown in Figure 9-5. By removing repeating information (first normal form), we create attributive entities (for $1:n$ relationships) and associative entities (for $m:n$ relationships). In Figure 9-5, we create the items from a purchase order as an attributive entity. By removing partial key (second normal form), and nonkey (third normal form) dependencies, we create new fundamental entities. In the example, the new fundamental entities relate to items and vendors.

Upon completion of data modeling, **entity structure analysis** is performed to determine whether a class structure applies. This analysis evaluates each entity to determine if the same processes and

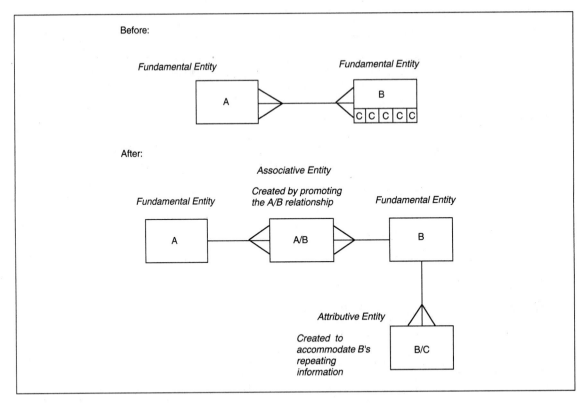

FIGURE 9-4   Direct Normalization of ERD

attributes apply to all entities of a given type. If contingent data usage applies, then classes are defined and a data hierarchy depicting the structure is developed.

Next, business functions are identified as a prelude to process modeling. A **business function** is a group of activities that accomplish some complete job that is within the mission of the enterprise. Business functions are ongoing and are not related to organization structure. Functions describe what is done in the organization from a high level of abstraction. Business function analysis is usually performed at the enterprise level, but can be the first activity of process modeling, if required. Representative or generic functions that may be present in a business are listed below. Some of the functions are specializations, for instance, public protection is usually a government function. Specialized functions

included are for banking, retail, governments, schools, and manufacturing. Other functions are general, like Finance, which every organization has.

Accounting
Alumni Affairs
Audit
Community Programs
Control and
    Measurement
Customer Relations
Data Administration
Distribution
Engineering Support
Facilities, Equipment,
    and Supplies
    Administration
Finance

Funds Management
Funds Transfer
Health and Hospitals
    Services
Human Resources
    Administration
Information Systems
Judicial Management
Legal Services
Management
Manufacturing
Marketing
Material Acquisition
    (Purchasing)

Unnormalized	First Normal Form	Second Normal Form	Third Normal Form	Relation Name*
Purchase Order				Purchase Order
(PO) *Number*	*PO Number*		*PO Number*	
PO Date	PO Date		PO Date	
PO Vendor ID	PO Vendor ID		PO Vendor ID	
PO Vendor Name	PO Vendor Name			
PO Vendor Address	PO Vendor Address	⟶		PO Vendor
PO Ship Terms	PO Ship Terms			
			PO Vendor ID	
PO Payment Terms	PO Payment Terms		PO Vendor Name	
*PO Item Number			PO Vendor Address	
POI Description		*PO Number*	PO Ship Terms	
POI Quantity	*PO Number*	*PO Item Number*	PO Payment Terms	
POI Price	*PO Item Number*	POI Quantity		
POI Extended	POI Description	POI Price		
Price	POI Quantity	POI Extended Price		
	POI Price			PO Item
			PO Number	
	POI Extended Price		*PO Item Number*	
			POI Quantity	
		Item Number	POI Price	
		Description	POI Extended Price	X
		Price		
			Item Number	Inventory Item
			Description	
			Price	

*X indicates deleted items or relations. Relations are deleted if they are duplicates, are consolidated if they have identical keys or are proper subsets, or are named. Attributes are deleted if they are derived by the application. POI Extended Price is derived by multiplying POI Quantity by POI Price.

FIGURE 9-5   Tabular Normalization Example

		Sample business functions for ABC Video are shown in Figure 9-6.
Operations	Public Service	
Planning	Research and	
Product Management	Development	
Product/Customer	Research	
Service	Sales	
Public Aid	Scheduling	
Public Facilities	Service Offering,	
Management	e.g., Instruction in	
Public Protection	a school	
Management	Student Management	
Public Relations		

Sample business functions for ABC Video are shown in Figure 9-6.

When the functions applicable to application development are identified, functional decomposition is performed. **Functional decomposition** starts at the business function level to identify the major activities of the function, and progresses to identify the processes and subprocesses for each function (see Figure 9-6). An **activity** is some procedure within a business function that can be identified by its input data and output data, which differ. The

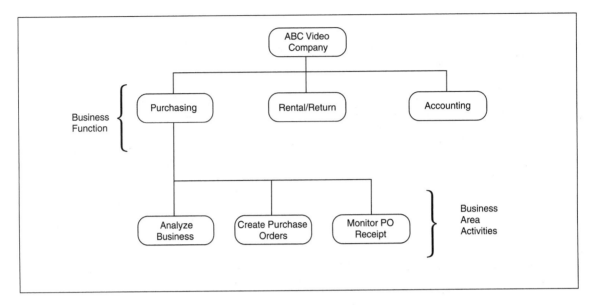

FIGURE 9-6   ABC Video Business Functions and Activities

activity level must *fully define* the function. That is, the activity level is complete when all possible procedures performed within the scope of the function are present in the diagram. Full definition is required to ensure complete data, process, impact, and organization design analysis.

Activity names are usually of the form *verb-object*, where the verb identifies the major transformation and the object identifies what is transformed. Exceptions to this rule are accepted when a name is conventionally called by a different form, for instance, *Cash Management* is more common usage than *Manage Cash*.

Activities are decomposed into their processes. A **business process** identifies the details of an activity, *fully defining* the steps taken to accomplish the activity. Again, full definition is required to ensure completeness of the ensuing analysis. Procedural steps named by processes are repeated and have definable beginnings and endings. Decomposition continues until the elementary, or atomic, level of each process is identified. An **elementary process** is a procedure that cannot be decomposed further without making the procedure lose its identity. Thus,

an elementary process is the smallest unit of work users identify.

Figure 9-7 is a sample decomposition showing processes that define the two purchasing activities within ABC Video. Don't forget that the business activities and processes in a decomposition *fully* define the scope of the parent business function.

Decomposition results are used to develop a process dependency diagram. A **process dependency diagram**, like an ERD for data, identifies the sequence and types of relationships between processes. **Process relationships** describe logical connections that include cardinality, sequence, iteration, and selection components (see Figure 9-8). Thus, the process dependency diagram shows the logic of sequence, iteration, and selection for each process. The process dependency diagram is then expanded to include entities and data stores to emulate a data flow diagram from process analysis. The result is a **process data flow diagram (PDFD)**.

Connections between procedural steps in a PDFD are due to data passing from one step to the next and causing it to activate. This type of connection is called a process data trigger. A **trigger** identifies the

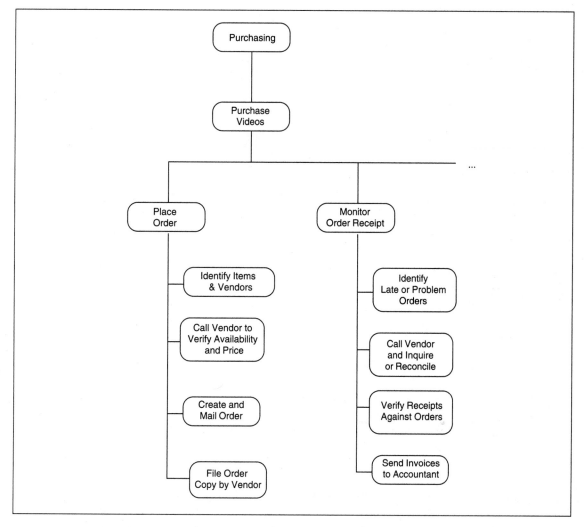

FIGURE 9-7   ABC Video Partial Functional Decomposition of Purchasing

arrival of some data that causes a business process to execute. **Process data triggers** (or just **data triggers**) identify data that flow from one process to another to start execution of the receiving process. In a PDFD, the directed lines between processes signify a data trigger. In addition, external events can cause a process to activate. An **event trigger** signifies data from some business transaction that causes processing to take place. Event triggers are drawn on the PDFD by large arrows with words inside the icons to name the events. For instance, the arrival of a new video releases list (see Figure 9-9) is an event that triggers the purchasing process.

Because the components of the process dependency diagram are different from those of a DFD, the PDFD that results from process dependency analysis is also different. Several key differences are important. First, there is a *sequence* to the process data flow. The directed arrows on Figure 9-9 indicate that some output from a process causes

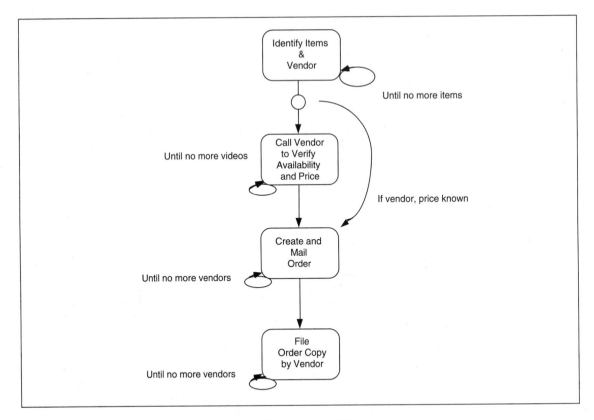

FIGURE 9-8   ABC Create Order Process Dependency Diagram

the execution of the next process. Variations in the directed arrow lines define variations in the sequence. Second, the *media* that connect processes are *not* implied as in a DFD.[3] The information that passes between processes *is* identified, but the form of the data is not. For example, the *Identify Items and Vendors* process in Figure 9-9 generates data that passes to later processes. The shared data might be mental, paper, an automated data flow, or a file. The decision of media, or *stored form*, of data is deferred until design unless it is fixed. Data files, such as *Vendor* and *Order* files on Figure 9-9, are identified because they are known. Third, data and event triggers *identify* the cause of execution of each process.

In a DFD, this information either is characterized as a data flow or is hidden within process logic.

The last step of BAA is the development and analysis of an entity/process matrix, also known as a **CRUD matrix**. If no enterprise level ERD exists first, then an ERD is created. The **entity/process matrix** lists entities across the top and business processes down the side (see Figure 9-10). Each cell of the matrix, then, points to a process-entity combination. For each cell, the systems engineers define Create (**C**), Retrieve (**R**), Update (**U**), Delete (**D**), or no (blank) responsibility of each process for each entity. Subject area databases are defined by analyzing logical groupings of processes and entities based on their affinity. **Affinity** means 'attraction' or 'closeness.' **Affinity analysis** clusters processes which share data creation authority for an entity.

---

3 Remember, DFDs require identification of either a *data flow* or a *data store* as the data linkages between processes.

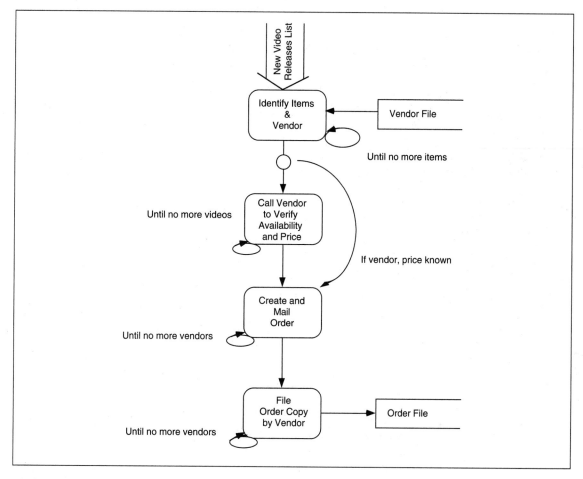

New Video Releases List

Identify Items & Vendor

Vendor File

Until no more items

Until no more videos

Call Vendor to Verify Availability and Price

If vendor, price known

Create and Mail Order

Until no more vendors

File Order Copy by Vendor

Order File

Until no more vendors

FIGURE 9-9   ABC Create Order Process Data Flow Diagram

These logical groupings become the basis for database design. In Figure 9-10, a partial example of *Create Order* and *Monitor Order Receipt* processes, and the entities they use, are analyzed in an entity/process matrix. The matrix shown is clustered by entity affinity and is ready for analysis. After analysis, the processes and entities are sorted to show affinity based on the actions taken on the same entities (see Figure 9-11).

Two sets of analysis are performed on the results of affinity analysis. The first analysis is to determine the adequacy of organization design based on who creates and has responsibility for data. Each cluster of processes is related back to the organization (in a similar matrix). Ideally, processes that share data responsibility should be in the same organization and report to the same manager. For instance, the ABC Purchasing processes show three potential groupings. If each process is evaluated with all of the data it uses, the three groupings meld into one based on the criteria that 70% or more of the data are commonly shared. If all of these processes report to one manager, the organization is probably adequate. If the three possible groupings all report to different managers, the organization should probably be redesigned.

Entities = Processes	Purchase Order	PO Item	Inventory Item	Vendor
Identity Items & Vendors			R	CRU
Call Vendor to Verify Avail/Price				RU
Create & Mail Order	CRUD	CRUD	R	R
File Order Copy by Vendor	R	R		
Identify Late & Problem Orders	R	R	R	RU
Call Vendor & Inquire on Order	RU	RU	R	R
Verify Receipts against Order	RU	RU		
Send Invoices to Accountant	RD	RD		

FIGURE 9-10   Create and Monitor Order Receipt Entity/Process Matrix

The second analysis looks at the data entities by process cluster to define subject area databases. A **subject area database** is normalized across the organization and provides shared support for one or more business functions. At the application level, one subject database is assumed. In the ex-ample in Figure 9-11, one database would support the purchasing function; the database would have at least two user views to package *Purchase Order* with *Purchase Order Item* and *Inventory Item* with *Vendor*. A fourth user view linking all entities might be used for retrieval processing.

At the organization level, if the process groupings are logical and useful, they are the basis for reaffirming the scope of applications. At the business area level, the groupings of processes should be consistent with the scope of the activities defined for the application. If they are not consistent, then management review and rescoping of the project are required.

The last step of BAA is to finalize all information found during the analysis in a data dictionary or CASE repository. Since dictionaries were discussed in detail in Chapter 7, in this chapter we will document the information found using the same format as in Chapter 7, but will not comment again on the format of entries.

To summarize, business area analysis begins with an entity-relationship diagram that is fully identified, normalized, and analyzed for class structure. Business functions are identified and decomposed to create process hierarchy, process dependency, and process data flow diagrams. The business processes from the decomposition are coupled to entities from the ERD. Data-related responsibilities are described for each process. Affinity analysis of the CRUD matrix is used to decide organizational and database groupings for further design and management action. Next, we turn to a detailed description of how to perform each activity, exemplified by the ABC Video Rental Processing application.

Entities = Processes	Purchase Order	PO Item	Inventory Item	Vendor
Create & Mail Order	CRUD	CRUD	R	R
Call Vendor & Inquire on Order	RU	RU	R	R
Verify Receipts against Order	RU	RU		R
Send Invoices to Accountant	RD	RD		
File Order Copy by Vendor	R	R		
Identify Late & Problem Orders	R	R	R	RU
Identity Items & Vendors			R	CRU
Call Vendor to Verify Avail/Price				RU

(Subject Area 1 spans Purchase Order and PO Item for the first five processes; Subject Area 2 spans Inventory Item and Vendor for the last three processes.)

FIGURE 9-11   ABC Purchasing Process Affinity Analysis

BUSINESS AREA ANALYSIS ACTIVITIES

Develop Entity-Relationship Diagram

Rules for Entity-Relationship Diagram

The steps to building an entity relationship diagram (ERD) are as follows:

1. Define fundamental entities and their primary keys.
2. Define the relationships between the fundamental entities.
3. Identify all attributes of entities, including primary keys.
4. Add attributive entities, where needed, to simplify one-to-many relationships.
5. Promote all many-to-many relationships to define associative entities.
6. Normalize the fundamental entities, analyzing if there are other entities which are hidden in the current definitions. Place new entities in the ERD. Define the new entities' attributes and primary keys.
7. Analyze the entities and their relationships to determine if a class structure is needed. If some instances of entities have identifiable differences in processing, data stored, or relationship participation, classes probably are needed.

The first step is to define fundamental entities and their primary keys. Identifying entities is a difficult process until you have done it several times. It is easy to talk about entities, but less easy to define them. Part of the difficulty is that entities are context related. An entity for one company/application may not be an entity in another company/

EXAMPLE 9-1

ENTITY DEFINITION IN XYZ ANNUITY

In Example 7-1, we discussed how at the annual meeting of the XYZ board of directors in 1991, the marketing director said that she had four different, irreconcilable counts of the number of institutions the company serviced. What was worse was that there was a defendable definition of each number.

The board thought that was terrible and ordered a redevelopment of the Institutional Processing application to resolve the problem. When Diane Smith, the software engineer, began work on the application, her first task was to develop an ERD for the information, without regard to the current files (12), applications (6), interfaces (4), procedures (28), or time relationships currently used in the organization. Just in sheer numbers, this was a significant amount of information to be ignored.

Twenty-two different people were interviewed, resulting in 22 different definitions of an institution. They included such descriptions as:

- an organization that pays in to a pension plan for its employees
- an organization that requires counseling about products and services provided by us
- an organization we target for marketing campaigns
- an organization that defines a pension plan
- an organization that is subject to a pension plan that may or may not be of its own definition
- an organization that is subject to legally defined pension plans by the state government in which it resides
- an organization that receives information about pension plans of the suborganizations for which it administers plans

Working with a data administrator, Diane and the key users unraveled the spaghetti of definitions to uniquely define major entities for

---

application. When in doubt, define more entities rather than less. You can always eliminate unnecessary entities when the information for deciding becomes clear.

It is important to define each entity using terms that apply for all of its uses in the company. Such definitions may not match current definitions of the entity in use in the organization. An example in defining the terms from an educational pension firm (see Example 9-1) shows the difficulty dealing with current thinking about entities and their definition. Current thinking is frequently imprecise, muddled, and even inconsistent as the example shows. Unraveling the spaghetti of definitions imbedded in the various terms used to describe institutions, colleges, campuses, plans, and their relationships took three people much of six months, working with 10 user departments for the information.

ERDs depict the *big picture*, capturing the organization and its constituent activities. For this diagram, we must constantly remember to ask: What processes and activities are legal *in the context of the business*? Not: What is legal based on *today's procedures* in our company?

In general, entities define some*thing* about which the business keeps information. An entity can be a person, object, application, concept, or event *about which the application maintains information*. For example, customer, order, and inventory are all entities. Entity names are usually nouns, however, NOT all nouns are entities. First, define a list of possible entities. Then, examine each entry and ask yourself the following:

1. Is this a noun? If yes, continue. If not, either rename it or strike it from the list.

EXAMPLE 9-1   (*Continued*)

the organization. The following definitions, which took six months to attain, fully explain all variations of XYZ Annuity's institutional processing.

XYZ Annuity Entity Definitions

State Optional Pension Plan (SOPP)—An optional pension plan(s) defined by law, governing institution(s) specified in the law. SOPP institutions must adhere only and completely to the legal requirements of the SOPP.

Institution—A legal entity that is governed by an SOPP or, if not, may define its own pension plan(s) subject to Internal Revenue Service limitations.

Campus—A legal entity that is a subunit of an institution. If an institution defines its own plan, one of the plan items specifies whether or not campuses are bound by its definition. If a campus is not bound by the institution plan, it may own its own plan(s).

Plan—A legal description of the product(s) offered, eligibility and waiting period requirements, and other pension plan provisions. Usually, and always after 1992, each plan defines the offering for one product.

Product—A pension service offered by Educational Pension Trust, including individual annuity, group annuity, supplemental retirement, or group supplemental retirement accounts. Each product defined requires definition of one or more investment types allowed.

Investment type—Annuity, Money Market, Educational Pension Trust Stock fund, and Educational Pension Trust Bond fund.

These six definitions sound simple enough to be obvious, but they began with a total of 120 different interpretations.

---

2. Is this *potential entity* (replace with the name of the *potential entity*) unique with a clearly defined purpose? If yes, continue. If no, either define the item uniquely from the context that led to its being on the list, or strike it from the list.

3. Can this *potential entity* take a value? If yes, it is an attribute; strike it from the list. If no, continue.

4. Does the business area need to keep information about this *potential entity*? If yes, continue. If no, ask why it is on the list. If it triggers processes, continue. If it is a different *form* of some other entity (for instance, an order report is a paper version of an order), strike it from the list. If it is unique but does not fit the other criteria, leave it on the list for now.

5. Give a formal name to the entity and define its primary key.

6. Draw one rectangle for each entity to begin developing the ERD.

Once you are comfortable with the entities, begin defining their relationships. Relationship names, describing entity associations, are usually verbs, however, NOT all verbs describe relationships. The goal is for all rules of association to be unambiguous. First, define possible relationships. In general, ask yourself how entities relate to each other. If I have *Entity A,* do I also have *Entity B*s? If so, how many are legal? Ask the question without regard to each entity's current usage in the company. As with entities, relationships should define what is legal within a business context. Sometimes, ignoring current definition is extremely difficult because we and users internalize such definitions and use them to narrow our focus and simplify the world.

Examine each possible relationship and ask yourself the following:

1. Is this a verb? If yes, continue. If not, either rename it or strike it from the list.
2. Is this verb an action? If no, continue. If yes, remind yourself that relationships do NOT describe processes or processing. If the verb is a process, strike it from the list.
3. Is this *potential relationship* (replace with the name of the *potential relationship*, e.g., place as in customers *place* orders) unique with a clearly defined purpose? If yes, continue. If no, either define the item uniquely from the context that led to its entry on the list, or strike it from the list.
4. Is this *potential relationship* needed to fully describe the business area's data? If yes, continue. If no, ask yourself why it is on the list. If it is not clear what the reason is, continue, leaving the relationship to be reevaluated when more information is known. If the reason is not related to the business area, strike it from the list.

Once you define a relationship, draw a line(s) to connect the entities participating in the relationship. Mark the diagram with a verb to describe each direction of the relationship. The convention is to read the relationship above the line from left-to-right, and the relationship below the line right-to-left. For instance, customer *places* order and order *is placed by* customer (see Figure 9-12). The words are placed differently depending on the placement of the entities on the diagram. By convention, the active verb (in this example, 'places') is positioned on top of the line with the acting entity ('customer' here) on the left of the diagram.

Next determine the number, or cardinality, of the relationship. The number of the relationship is one of three possibilities: one-to-one, one-to-many, or many-to-many. A **one-to-one relationship** defines a situation in which every entity *A* relates to one and only one entity *B*. In a **one-to-many relationship** every entity *A* relates to zero to *n*, that is, any number of entity *B*s. In a **many-to-many relationship** all *A*s can relate to any number of *B*s. Decide cardinality by asking the same questions of each side of the relationship: If I have one entity *A*, how many entity *B*s can I have associated with it *at any point in time*? Conversely, if I have one entity *B*, how many entity *A*s can I have associated with it at any point in time?

An example of the time issue relates to student registration and tracking. A student may take many classes in one semester; this describes a 1:*n* relationship. Over time, students take many courses and courses contain many students; this is an *m:n* relationship. Which is correct? The *m:n* relation that

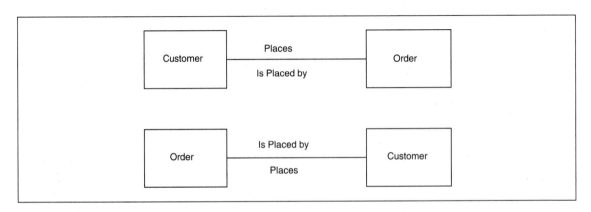

FIGURE 9-12   Placement of Words on Entity-Relationship Diagrams

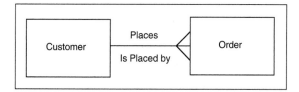

FIGURE 9-13   Relationship Cardinality and ERD Representation

describes the student-course relationship without *regard to time* is correct within the context of a student registration application.

Draw crows' feet to show cardinality of each relationship. Crows' feet are reverse arrow heads that indicate a 'many' numbered relationship.[4] The example in Figure 9-13 shows the relationship of customer to orders as one-to-many. That is, for any one customer, one to many orders may be associated with it. Conversely, the relationship of orders to customers is one-to-one. That is, for

_____

4 This is the IE convention. There are other techniques for drawing ERDs, such as Chen's [1976]. Chen uses multiple arrow heads for 'many' relationships and uses diamonds to identify relationships with only one verb. The logic of both approaches is identical. Martin's notation is used here because it is automated in CASE tools.

any given order, it is associated with one, and only one, customer.

Lastly, for each entity in a relationship, we decide whether the entity is required or optional in the relationship. In a **required relationship**, the entity must be present for the other entity to exist. In an **optional relationship**, the entity described may or may not exist when the other entity exists. Either an 'o' or a vertical bar, '|', shows each side of a relationship as optional (o) or required (|).

Returning to the order example, customers place orders at their discretion, so orders are optional. Customers are required to have been identified as customers to place orders, so customer is required (see Figure 9-14).

In the order-item relationship, orders do not exist if there are no items ordered, so order is required. The vertical bar ('|') bisects the relationship line close to the order entity. Examining the items, we have a similar relationship. For an order to exist, there must be at least one item, so item is also required. Both sides of the relationship line have a vertical bar (see Figure 9-14). 'Read' this entire relationship as follows:

Orders *contain* items. For each order, there are one or more order-items. For an order to exist, at least one order-item is required. An order-item *is contained in* order. For an order-item to exist, an order is required. For each order-item, there is one, and only one, order.

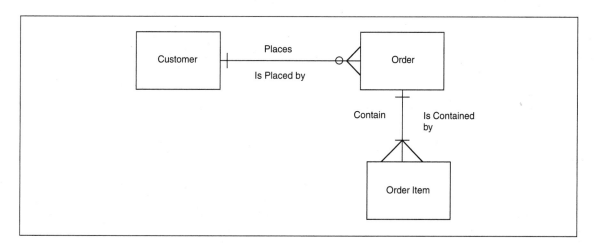

FIGURE 9-14   Required/Optional Relationship Representation

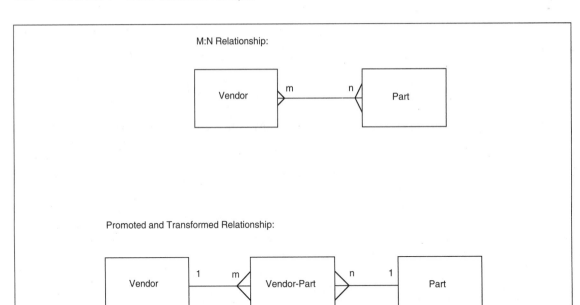

FIGURE 9-15   Many-to-Many Relationship Promotion and Transformation

Similarly, **associative entities** are created by promoting *m:n* relationships, joining the primary keys of each participating entity to identify the association. Other fields might also be needed to provide unique identification. The *m:n* relationship is converted into two 1:*m* relationships in the promotion process (see Figure 9-15).

After all known relationships are defined and entered on the diagram, we define attributes for the entities and normalize them (Steps 3–6 of list on p. 339). The goal of this part of the exercise is to define hidden attributive and associative entities. In the example above (see Figure 9-14), *Order* and *Customer* are fundamental entities. *Order-Item* is an attributive entity. If it had not already been identified, either normalization would identify it, or it would be identified by answering the question: Can any of the attributes relating to entity *Order* occur more than once? If the answer to this question is yes, there are attributive entities to be identified.

Direct normalization of ERDs is possible but requires detailed understanding of data. When you have an ERD but are less comfortable about your understanding of the data and their relationships,

tabular normalization can be used to complement, validate, or replace direct normalization. Tabular normalization requires complete definition of data and relationships, and results in *exactly the same* entities as direct normalization.

To use tabular normalization, first describe each entity and all entity attributes. Cluster attributes depending on whether they are singular or multiple occurrences. (Tabular normalization rules are summarized in Table 9-1.) Then, proceed to remove repeating groups. For each repeating group create a new relation. The key of the new relation is the key of the repeating group and the original key. To remove partial key dependencies, create new relations of any attributes and the part of the key to which they relate. The key of the new relation is the part of the original primary key that functionally defines the relationship. Finally, remove nonkey dependencies by creating new relations from the nonkey attributes that are related. The key to the new relation is the attribute(s) that define the functional relationship. In the tabular method, multivalued dependencies are treated as single attribute, repeating groups in the nonnormalized set-up stage.

TABLE 9-1 Normalization Rules

For Unnormalized Data

1. Identify all attributes that relate to an entity. Keep in mind that there are several types of attributes.

   - Nonrepeating, primary key attributes(s). A nonrepeating attribute is a single fact about an entity type. A **primary key** is a unique identifier for all attributes associated with an entity type.
   - Nonrepeating, nonkey attributes(s) are single facts about an entity type.
   - **Repeating attribute**(s) are facts that may have more than one occurrence for a specific value of an entity's primary key. Repeating attributes may be single repeating facts, such as the date of birth of offspring; or may be groups of repeating facts, such as date of birth and name of offspring. Repeating attributes are either repeating key attributes or repeating nonkey attributes. Repeating nonkey attributes are listed with their primary key identifier.

2. List all attributes that relate to an entity together. Indent repeating information. Skip a line or leave a space between entities and between repeating groups. Repeating groups might have only one attribute that repeats; this is also called a multivalued dependency. Place an asterisk at the first attribute of each repeating group to show its beginning.

3. Underline the primary key field(s) of the unnormalized relations, including keys of both singular groups and repeating groups.

4. Proceed to first normal form.

First Normal Form (1NF)—The Goal of 1NF Is to Remove Repeating Groups

1.1. Examine each relation. If the relation has no repeating groups, it is in 1NF. Draw an arrow from the unnormalized column to the normalized column to show that the analysis is complete, and continue.

1.2. If the relation has repeating groups, build a relation from the single nonrepeating fields. The key of the relation is the key of the original relation. Continue.

1.3. Next, for each repeating group, build a new relation of the repeating information. Append the key of the original relation to the repeating information. The key of this relation is the key of the original relation *plus* the key of the repeating group.

Second Normal Form (2NF)—The Goal of 2NF Is to Remove Partial Key Dependencies

2.1. Examine each relation independently. If the 1NF relation does *not* have a compound key, it is in 2NF. Draw an arrow from the relation through the 2NF column to show that it is complete, and continue.

2.2 If the 1NF relation has a compound key for each nonkey field, ask the following question: Do the data field relate to the *whole key*? In other words, do you need to know the whole key to know the values of the attribute, or do you only need part of the key to know the value of the attribute? If the answer is that you need the whole key for all fields, the relation is in 2NF. Draw an arrow from the relation through the 2NF column to show that it is complete, and continue.

2.3 If by knowing a *part* of the key we know the value of one or more data fields, then we will build two new types of relations. First, build a relation with the nonkey data field(s) that are wholly dependent on the compound key. The key of this relation is the key of the 1NF relation.

2.4 Second, build one new relation for each partial key identified. The new relation(s) include the nonkey data field(s) and the part of the original key on which they are fully dependent.

(Continued on next page)

TABLE 9-1   Normalization Rules (*Continued*)

Third Normal Form (3NF)—The Goal of 3NF Is to Remove Nonkey Dependencies

---

3.1   If the 2NF relation(s) have only one nonkey data field, it is in 3NF, go to optimization.

3.2   If all data fields in the relation(s) are dependent upon the key and nothing but the key, then the relation is in 3NF. The question here, is "Do nonkey fields relate to the key or do they really relate to each other?"

3.3   If a nonkey dependency exists, build one relation of the nonkey data field(s) that are dependent on the 2NF key (this include the nonkey field that is the key in the step below).

3.4   Build one new relation for each nonkey dependency identified. The new relation(s) include the nonkey data field(s) and the nonkey field on which they are dependent. The key of this relation is the nonkey field from the original relation on which the other field(s) is dependent.

   Now, check for anomalies . . . conditions that still will cause errors. This is one way of double-checking that your original relationships were correctly defined. Ask two questions.

1.   Given a value for a key(s) of a 3NF relation, is there *just one* possible value for the data? If the answer is NO, then multivalued dependencies exist. Check that the correct data relationships are defined, then treat the multi-valued single fact as a single-attribute repeating group and renormalize the data.

2.   All are attributes directly dependent upon their related key(s)? If the answer is NO, then transitive dependencies exist. Treat the transitive dependency like a nonkey dependency and renormalize the data.

   Finally, synthesize and integrate the relations.

1.   Remove any fields that are computed in the application. This does not mean that these attributes are not stored in the physical database; it means that they are not logically required to define the entity.

2.   If two or more relations have *exactly the same primary key*, combine them into one relation. Make sure that each attribute occurs only once.

At third normal form, synthesis of the resulting relations is performed to

- combine relations that have identical primary keys but different nonkey attributes
- eliminate relations which are exact duplicates, or proper subsets, of other relations
- combine relations for which the primary key of one is a proper subset of the primary key of another

After normalization and synthesis are complete, new entities (or relations) and their relationship to the fundamental entities are added to the diagram as needed to fully depict the information.

Next, the entities and relationships are analyzed to determine if a class structure is needed. The reasoning process is as follows:

1. Ask if this entity occurs in this, and only this, form (i.e., with all attributes) for *every* legal occurrence of the relationship being examined? If the answer is yes, continue. If the answer is no, you must define subclasses that describe the contingencies of existence for

the entity. This procedure is described in the next section.

2. Does this relationship hold for all occurrences of the entity? If yes, continue. If no, follow the reasoning below to determine the subclasses of the entity and their relationships.

3. Is this entity ever optional? If no, continue. If yes, follow the reasoning below to determine the subclasses of the entity and their relationships.

4. Can only a *subset* of occurrences of an entity participate in a given relationship? If no, continue. If yes, follow the reasoning below to determine the subclasses of the entity and their relationships.

5. Have several types, or kinds, or categories of an entity been identified? If no, continue. If yes, follow the reasoning below to determine the subclasses of the entity and their relationships.

6. Are words like "either, or, sometimes, usually, generally, in certain cases" ever used in describing entity behavior? If no, continue. If yes, follow the reasoning below to determine the subclasses of the entity and their relationships.

To determine subclasses, you must determine which information is kept (or which processing is done) for which type (or subclass) of orders. Ask questions about every possible variation of information and processing until 'if-then-else' logic surfaces. Use the alternative situations to define the subclasses. That is, one subclass for the *if* logic, another subclass for every other *else if* logic. Ask questions of each type of information about every entity. Don't stop just because you find one subclass; there may be others. When you have found all subclasses, verify them with the user and modify the diagram accordingly.

For instance, in an order fulfillment application, a legal entity relationship describes 'customers place orders' (see Figure 9-16), but that information may not be the same for all customers' orders. Does the time of day or time of month affect the relationship? Do the shipping address differences affect the relationship? Does the sold-to/ship-to arrangement affect the relationship? Does the type of goods ordered affect the relationship? Does the type of payment affect the relationship? In this example, we will say that *Cash Order* information kept includes *Customer ID* and *Total Amount*, where *Credit Order* information kept includes *Customer ID*, *Name*, *Sold-to/Ship-to addresses*, *Order Date*, *Shipping Terms*,

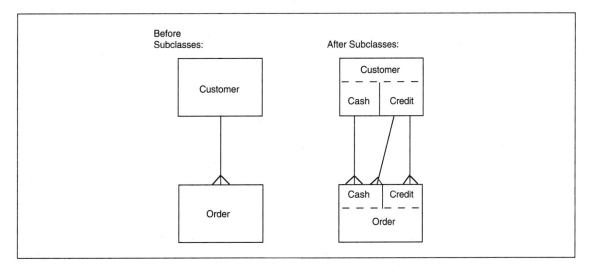

FIGURE 9-16   Examples of Subclasses in Customer-Order Relationship

for each item (*Item Number*, *Item Description*, *Quantity*, *Price*, *Extended Price*), *Sales Tax*, and *Total*. Here, we know there are subclasses because different sets of data are kept. The next issue is to decide the entity(s) to which the subclasses relate.

To decide which subclasses apply to orders, we ask if the entity *Order* is affected differently by cash and credit sales. If the answer is yes, different information is kept for each. In this example, there would be subclasses for *Cash Order* and *Credit Order*. Then, we ask if the entity *Customer* is affected differently for cash and credit customers. Are all customers either cash or credit? What are the rules for buying on credit? The common answer is applied here. Some customers are only cash, thus, creating a cash customer subclass. Some customers are qualified to buy on credit, but they are not *required* to buy on credit. That is, credit customers can pay either by cash or by credit. Therefore, knowing which type of order a customer will create is only possible if the customer is a cash customer. Depending on the application, these customer subclasses might be important. Here, we will say they are. The ERD is altered to show the subclasses of each entity class and how they now relate to each other. Notice that the simple before diagram in Figure 9-16 is more complex with subclass additions.

To summarize, first define entities, then relationships, then attributes. Promote the many-to-many relationships to associative entity status and modify the diagram to reflect the new entities. Add attributive entities as required for repeating information relating to entities. Identify all new attributes of all entities. If necessary, do tabular normalization of the relations. Analyze each entity to determine if subclasses are required and modify the diagram to describe them. These activities are best documented in a CASE tool with repository (or dictionary or encyclopedia) entries made as the work progresses. At the end of ERD creation, you have not only the ERD, but also the repository definitions for all items in the ERD.

ABC Video Example Entity-Relationship Diagram

The first step (refer to the list on p. 339) in developing the ERD is to identify fundamental entities. A first-cut definition of the potential fundamental entities in ABC rental processing includes: customer, video, rental, printed rental, clerk, and system. These entities are identified from the ABC Rental Processing requirements in Chapter 2. Next we analyze each potential entity to see if it really is in the business area and application.

Customer is a noun. It uniquely defines the people who rent and return videos. By itself, customer does not take on a value; rather, each customer is described by a set of attributes. The business must keep information about customers renting videos to do business with them. The formal name is *Customer*.

Video is a noun. It uniquely defines an item from inventory that is available for rent. By itself, video does not take on a value; it has descriptive attributes. The business must keep information about videos to conduct its business. The formal name is *Video*.

Rental is a noun that uniquely describes videos rented by customers for a specific period. By itself, *rental* does not take on a value; it combines attributes of *Customer* and *Video* with attributes of its own. The business must keep information about rentals to provide an audit trail for tax purposes. The formal name is *Rental*.

A Printed Rental is a noun that describes videos rented by customers for a specific time period. A printed rental is not unique since its definition mirrors that of rental. However, it is unique in that it shows the customer signature. If there is a legal dispute over charges, the business is required legally to provide documentation that rental took place, and the customer knowingly rented. The business does not keep information *about* a printed rental, though; the information is about a rental.[5] Printed rentals are another medium or form of *Rental*. Printed Rental is stricken from the list.

Clerk is a noun uniquely describing the person who initiates processing for the application. By itself, clerk does not take on a value. The business does not need to know who did the entry of information unless Vic changes the requirements of the

---

5 If customer signature was kept, or if we just left printed rental on the list, when the data were normalized we would find that the primary keys to the printed rental and the rental were identical. That would lead us to combine the fields in one relation called *Rental*.

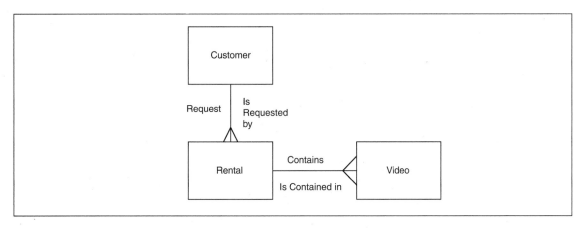

FIGURE 9-17   ABC Rental Processing—First-Cut Entity-Relationship Diagram

application. Since clerk is not required, we strike it from the list.

Similarly, system is a noun that uniquely describes the hardware/software environment that will do rental processing. The system has no personal values, and neither do we maintain information about the system. System is stricken from the list.

Next we draw a rectangle for each of the three entities that remain: *Customer*, *Video*, and *Rental*. Figure 9-17 shows the entities and relationship(s) between the fundamental entities. Customers *request* Rentals. Rentals *contain* Videos. The relationship names are unique verbs describing the interactions. The line connecting *Customer* and *Rental* contains crows' feet at the *Rental* side to show a one-to-many

relationship. That is, each *Customer* may place one or more *Rentals*. Each *Rental* is placed by one and only one *Customer*.

Similarly, each *Rental* contains one or more *Videos*; each *Video* can be rented by one and only one *Rental* at a time. We have a problem with the clause *at a time* in this definition. Relationships are supposed to be defined without regard to time. How do we account for this problem? We might defer a decision on how to deal with this until some later time, making a note of the need for 'date' as an identifier for the video-rental relationship. Or, we might remove time from the definition, creating the ERD in Figure 9-18 which shows a many-to-many relationship with rental and video. That is, each video may

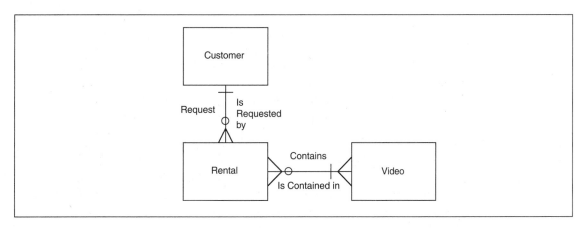

FIGURE 9-18   ABC Rental Processing—Second-Cut Entity-Relationship Diagram

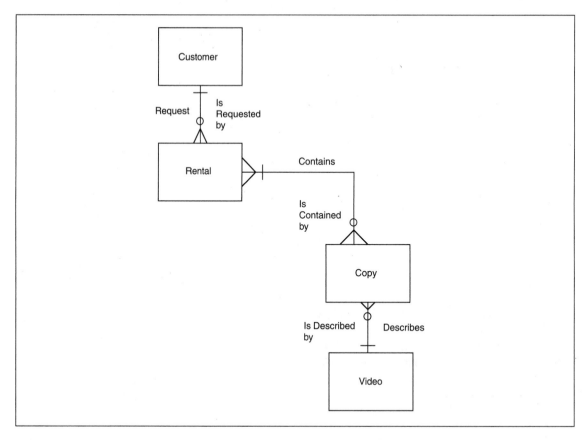

FIGURE 9-19   ABC Rental Processing—Third-Cut Entity-Relationship Diagram

be rented more than once, and each rental may contain more than one video. We take this option at the moment, knowing that it is an incomplete definition of the relationships which need to be refined.

Next we decide the nature of the relationships, whether they are required or optional. A *Customer* must exist to place *Rentals*. A *Video* must exist to be contained in a *Rental*. Does this make sense; must you have both a *Customer* and a *Video* to do a *Rental*? Yes, this makes sense. Now analyze the other side of the relationships. Are *Rentals* required for *Customers* to exist? No, *Customers* do not necessarily have rentals every day. Are *Rentals* required for a *Video* to exist? No, *Videos* can exist without being related to a *Rental*. Both relationships of *Rental* to the other entities are optional.

Identify attributes and associative entities. The *m:n* relationship of *Videos* and *Rentals* should be promoted to make an associative entity. The new entity relates to each physical tape being rented. Thus, we have a *Video* entity and a *Copy* entity. We reason through this creation in another way. Video information is not detailed enough to keep track of every physical tape in inventory because each video may have many copies. This leads us to add information about copies. Referring to the case in Chapter 2, we find that Vic wants to be able to track the status of any tape. The minimum copy information needed is *Video ID*, *Copy ID*, *Date Received*, and *Status*. Other information might be considered, for instance, current month rental counts, but we defer this for the moment. Figure 9-19 shows the ERD to this point.

Does the insertion of *Copy* take care of the many-to-many relationship? We can still have a *Copy* on many rentals over time and *Rentals* can contain many items, so the answer is no. Next we look at the Rental to further examine its details. Rentals are similar to orders. Just as an order has one or more items, each rental can have one or more rental items. There is a one-to-many relationship of *Rental* to *Rental-Item* which we add to the diagram. By itself, this does simplify the many-to-many relationship; a *Rental-Item* belongs to a specific *Rental* and relates to a specific inventory *Copy*. Now the entities and relationships look clean with all many-to-many relationships promoted, and all apparent one-to-many relationships explained (see Figure 9-20).

To confirm the original and promoted entities, we will normalize the data using the tabular method. For tabular normalization to proceed, first define the attributes of each entity. From the functional requirements in Chapter 2, list all attributes of each entity. The list is shown in Table 9-2, in unnormalized form, with the copy information identified as repeating within video information. Make a separate list for each entity. For each entity, list together attributes that occur only once. Indent repeating groups under the related entity, making sure that all information for each *group* is together. Underline primary keys for *both* nonrepeating and repeating information. Remember, the primary key *uniquely* identifies its information.

Next apply the rules in Table 9-1 to remove repeating groups, partial key dependencies, and non-key dependencies. Synthesize the 3NF results to ensure minimal redundancy. The result of ABC's

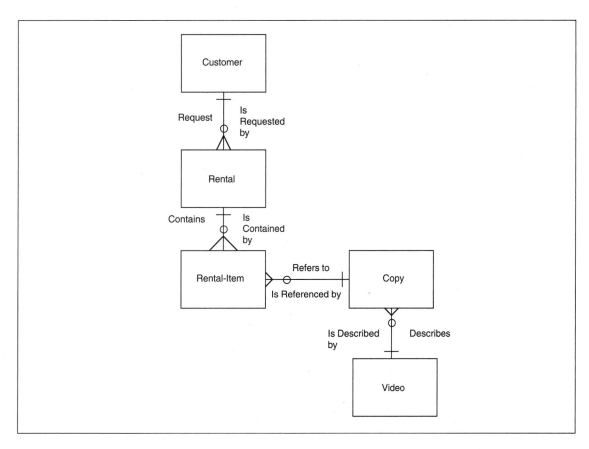

FIGURE 9-20   ABC Rental Processing Fourth-Cut Entity-Relationship Diagram

TABLE 9-2   List of ABC Video Entity Attributes

Unnormalized Form— Repeating Groups, All Primary Keys Identified	First Normal Form (1NF)—Repeating Groups	Second Normal Form (2NF)—Partial Key Dependencies	Third Normal Form (3NF)—Nonkey Dependencies	Dele

Customer Phone
Customer Name
Customer Address
Customer City
Customer State
Customer Zip
Customer Credit
Card Number
Credit Card Type
Credit Card
Expiration Date
 	
Customer Phone
All Customer Info
   from Above
Rental Date
Total Rental Fees
  *Video ID
   Copy ID
   Video Name
   Rental Date
   Return Date
   Rental Rate
   Late Fee Due
   Fees Due
 	
Video ID
Video Name
Entry Date
Rental Rate
  Copy ID
  Date Received
  Status				

normalization is shown in Table 9-3. Now we have six relations to be synthesized and evaluated.

In the synthesis step, several pieces of information are deleted. 'All Customer information' is not required to maintain rental information; only a *Customer Phone* or *ID* is required as a cross reference, or foreign key, to the *Customer* relation. *Total Rental Fees* are calculated and, therefore, not required. The

entire relation containing *Video ID*, *Video Name*, and *Rental Rate* is deleted because it *exactly* duplicates information already in the next relation which has more attributes.

To reconcile the 3NF results to the ERD, we look at the *Rental* relationships again, and use some 'out of the box' thinking. The relationship we identified for *Rental* to *Rental-Item* is similar for many busi-

TABLE 9-3   ABC Video Normalization Results

Unnormalized Form—Repeating Groups, All Primary Keys Identified	First Normal Form (1NF)—Repeating Groups	Second Normal Form (2NF)—Partial Key Dependencies	Third Normal Form (3NF)—Nonkey Dependencies	D e l e
Customer Phone Customer Name Customer Address Customer City Customer State Customer Zip Customer Credit Card Number Credit Card Type Credit Card Expiration Date	⟶	⟶	⟶	
Customer Phone All Customer Info from Above Rental Date Total Rental Fees	Customer Phone All Customer Info from Above Rental Date Total Rental Fees	⟶	⟶	X X
*Video ID Copy ID Video Name Rental Date Return Date Rental Rate Late Fee Due Fees Due	Customer Phone Video ID Copy ID Video Name Rental Date Return Date Rental Rate Late Fee Due Fees Due	Customer Phone Video ID Copy ID Rental Date Return Date Late Fee Due Fees Due Video ID Video Name Rental Date	⟶	
Video ID Video Name Entry Date Rental Rate	Video ID Video Name Entry Date Rental Rate	⟶	⟶	
Copy ID Date Received Status	Video ID Copy ID Date Received Status	⟶	⟶	

ness transactions: orders, confirmations, shipping papers, back-orders, and invoices. The question here is: Do we *need* both entities? We require the *Rental-Item* entity information because it documents the business transaction. The question then is: Do we need the *Rental* information separated? Is it uniquely different? *Customer Phone* is also in *Rental-Item*; *Rental Date* is also related to each video the

Customer:	xxxxxxxxxxxxxxxxxxxx, xxxxxxxxxxxx
	xxxxxxxxxxxxxxxxxxxxxxxxxxxxxxxxxx
	xxxxxxxxxxxxxxxxxxx, xx xxxxx
	(xxx) xxx-xxxx

Open Rentals:

Video	Copy	Description	Rental	Pd	Late	Pd	Other	Pd
xxxxx	xx	xxxxxxxxxxxxxxxxxxxxxxxxxxx	9.99	x	9.99	x	999.99	x
xxxxx	xx	xxxxxxxxxxxxxxxxxxxxxxxxxxx	9.99	x	9.99	x	999.99	x
xxxxx	xx	xxxxxxxxxxxxxxxxxxxxxxxxxxx	9.99	x	9.99	x	999.99	x
xxxxx	xx	xxxxxxxxxxxxxxxxxxxxxxxxxxx	9.99	x	9.99	x	999.99	x

New Rentals

xxxxx	xx	xxxxxxxxxxxxxxxxxxxxxxxxxxx	9.99	x				
xxxxx	xx	xxxxxxxxxxxxxxxxxxxxxxxxxxx	9.99	x				
xxxxx	xx	xxxxxxxxxxxxxxxxxxxxxxxxxxx	9.99	x				
xxxxx	xx	xxxxxxxxxxxxxxxxxxxxxxxxxxx	9.99	x				
xxxxx	xx	xxxxxxxxxxxxxxxxxxxxxxxxxxx	9.99	x				

		Total	99.99		99.99		9,999.99	
		Total Amount Due					9,999.99	
		Amount Paid					9,999.99	
		Balance					9,999.99	

FIGURE 9-21   Partial Rental Screen

customer has. We eliminate *Total Rental Fees* as a computed field but we need to redecide if we will ever need this information stored in a file.

Continuing this reasoning, think of the processing to be done. When a customer requests a video, the system should display all open rentals regardless of when they were rented. The *Rental-Item* information will be listed down the screen in rows, one row per video (see Figure 9-21).[6] A total of all open rental fees plus any new fees will be near the bottom. From where will customer information come? If we *keep* the *Rental* relation/entity, we either *choose one* from potentially several for display, or, if Customer Phone is entered first, we *ignore them all*. This sounds like

a kludge, that is, a mess! If we delete this entity/relation, can we get the information another way? That is, can we recreate this relationship if we need to for any reason? The answer *in this case* is, yes. *Rental-Items* all have *Customer Phone* and the first one accessed can be used to retrieve customer information. We conclude that we can eliminate the 'Rental' entity entirely. The completed, revised ERD is shown as Figure 9-22. *Rental-Item* is renamed to *Open Rental* to avoid confusion about its contents.

After removing the *Rental* entity, the relationships and entities now appear minimal. That is, we must keep all of these entities. If we remove any one of these entities, we *cannot* recreate the desired information for the removed entity, nor can we completely describe all data relationships. With these entities, we can represent the entire problem data

---

6 This is another example of the jumping between levels of detail required to complete each logical step in the process.

space, and we can accommodate all the processing required in the application. The ERD now appears complete. Keep in mind that complete does not mean cast in concrete; the ERD can be modified as required to accommodate new information.

The reasoning process we used to eliminate the rental entity can be used on any similar entities, for instance, orders. In other applications the higher level entity analogous to the *Rental* entity here might be required. You *cannot* eliminate an entity when any of the following conditions is true:

- The entity has unique information of its own.
- The entity, or its attributes, cannot be recreated through combining other entities.
- The entity is required for legal purposes.

An accurate and complete ERD is crucial to developing an application that solves a real-world problem. During development of the ERD, pay particular attention to entity definitions, making sure they are distinct, simple, and precise. Analyze each entity for selectivity in processing, data, or timing to determine if a class structure is warranted. Also analyze each entity for its actual need. If an entity can be recreated from other information, has no unique attributes of its own, and is not required for legal purposes, omit it. Analyze every possible relationship to determine relationship existence. When defining relationship cardinality and required/ optional status, make sure time and current procedures are ignored. Do pay attention to legal requirements and business requirements in defining cardinality and required status.

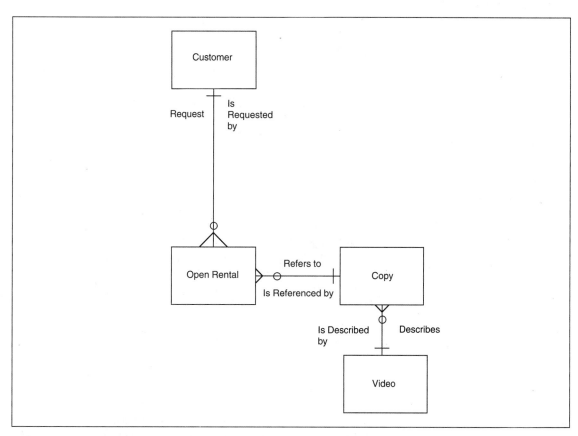

FIGURE 9-22   ABC Revised, Complete Entity-Relationship Diagram

Decompose Business Functions

Rules for Decomposing Business Functions

If a functional decomposition was not yet developed at the enterprise level, it is created now. If a decomposition was developed at the organization level, it is further decomposed here to define details of processes. In either case, decomposition is independent of the ERD; it can be done before, during, or after the ERD. IE recommends the ERD first, but while you gather data for the ERD, you invariably get process information. Many practitioners concentrate on data first, but begin to build the decomposition simultaneously. The steps to functional decomposition are:

1. Define the enterprise for which the diagram is being developed. Place the enterprise name in a rounded rectangle at the top of the diagram.
2. Define business functions of the enterprise. Using consistent parts of speech for each name, place the functions in rounded rectangles on the second row of the diagram. Do not pay attention to current organization, policy, or procedures in defining functions. Use current business practices in the industry to guide the definition and placement of functions (and activities and processes).
3. Define the activities that fully define each function. Name them using consistent parts of speech, usually of the form verb-noun. For each function, create a separate diagram with a row depicting the activities of the function.
4. For each activity, fully define the processes that describe work performed for each activity. Name each process using the form verb-noun. Add processes under their respective activities on the diagram in the sequence in which they are performed.
5. Continue to decompose the processes and add them to diagrams depicting successive levels of detail until the definitions are atomic.
6. Verify all diagrams with the user.

7. Define the detailed procedures for accomplishing each process and document functions, activities, processes, and procedures in the repository.

First, identify (or verify) the functions applicable to the BAA activity. An easy way to check functions is to review the list of generic functions on p. 332 and, for each, determine its applicability to the situation. Name each function so it relates to the business context of the BAA. For example, if the function deals with finance, but in the client context finance includes both Finance and Accounting, use the latter function name. Name each function with a noun, preferably a nonqualified noun. For example, Finance is preferred to *Corporate* Finance. If users have not participated in this activity, verify the list with a user. Place each function on the decomposition under the enterprise identifier in rounded rectangles (see Figure 9-23).

Next, for each function, define the major activities and place them under the function they describe. The diagram resembles an organization chart. When complete, the activities should *fully describe* each function. *Do not* pay attention to organizational boundaries or current organization policies and procedures. *Do* pay attention to legally required actions, actions that specifically relate to goals of the organization, and industry practices that are required. *Do* identify timing, cardinality, or current business practices for each activity.

Activity names do not have a specific form, but should be consistent in the part of speech used for all names. In the example above, the function *Finance* might include several activities, such as Corporate Finance, Regional (or *Subsidiary-name*) Finance, International Finance, Analysis and Reporting, Planning, Budgeting, and Funds Management. In this example, Funds Management might have been called Manage Funds, but the inconsistent part of speech makes this a weak name.

Next, for each activity, decompose the activity to define the processes that *fully describe* the activity. Processes may have their own subprocesses. Continue decomposing until the elementary, or atomic level, of process is identified. Recall that an elementary process is the smallest *unit of work* users can

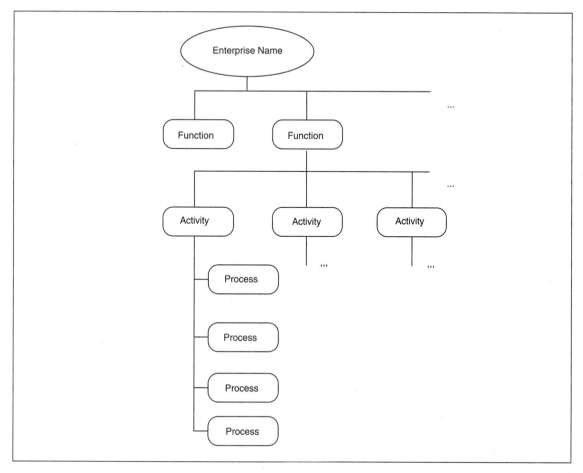

FIGURE 9-23   Placement of Functions, Activities, and Processes on a Functional
Decomposition Diagram

identify. Name each process with a verb-object name. Within Funds Management, for example, processes might include: Manage Overnight Funds, Manage Cash, Manage Payroll Accounts, and Manage Savings Accounts. Each of these processes can be further decomposed to identify the details of the procedure used to perform this process. Continuing with this example, Manage Overnight Funds might include: Identify Funds, Identify Options, Analyze Options, Place Funds, Complete Accounting Entries. Each of these is a process, too, but these processes cannot be further decomposed without requiring interrogation of multiple processes to locate all of its

component parts. Therefore, these processes are atomic, or elementary. That is, each can be performed as a unit, but cannot be further decomposed without losing its unit identity.

The difficulties of process decomposition lie in achieving parallel levels of abstraction and completeness. The goal is to maintain consistency within a level of process decomposition. The SE and user *must* work together during this definition because the levels of detail are beyond IS knowledge. Only job incumbents know exactly what they do and how they do it. The user is the main person defining the decomposition, but the SE is the person who actually abstracts the diagram and systems information from the user-supplied information. The user relates each process to all of the other processes, describing each in detail.

Some clues to consistency of abstraction are amount of work, user comfort, same type of inputs and outputs, and timing. If all processes appear to do similar amounts of work, they are probably at a similar level of abstraction. If the user feels comfortable that the information is similar, it probably is.

If the processes have similar types of inputs and outputs, that is, they have no error processing and no exception processing *at the same level*, then they are probably at a comparable level of abstraction. Similarly, if one process has error and exception processing, the others also should have error and exception processing *at the same level.*

For concurrent processes, each process must be performed completely independently of all other concurrent processes. If concurrent processes are independent, then the abstraction level is probably okay. If concurrent processes have dependencies, then determine the relationship between the processes. Either the dependent process is, in fact, a subprocess, or the processes are not concurrent.

During process identification and definition, mark the diagram for processes that are used in more than one place. This identifies both potential reusable processes for the design activity and possible job consolidation for organizational analysis. Make sure that the names assigned to reusable processes are exactly the same and actually perform the same work.

The larger the organization, the more likely you will need more than one level of process decomposition to describe fully the processes of each activity. Continue to decompose levels of subprocesses until you reach processes that can no longer be described as performing some *whole action*.

ABC Video Example Process Decomposition

To begin, we ask ourselves what are the functions of ABC that relate to this BAA. The functions of ABC are Purchasing, Rental Processing, Accounting and Personnel/Payroll as shown in Figure 9-6. This application is concerned only with Rental Processing, so we decompose only the Rental Processing function.

First, we define the activities of Rental Processing and place them on the diagram in rounded rectangles. Return to the case in Chapter 2 and outline the major activities. If you have difficulty finding activities, look at the entities and define the actions taken for each entity. Obvious activities relate to customer and video maintenance and actual rent/return processing. Can you identify any others? If not, add these to the diagram and decompose them. Activity identification is not a one-time activity; it is ongoing and other activities might become obvious as you work through the processes. Keep in mind that when you identify activities with a user, it is from their experience and not from written text, so it is somewhat more direct.

Both maintenance activities are decomposed into create, read, update, and delete processes (CRUD). Notice that the activity names are of the form *verb-object*. The resulting additions to the decomposition are shown in Figure 9-24.

Next, we must decide if rent and return are one activity or two. This is the same issue we dealt with in *process design* (in Chapter 8); here we will have slightly different results because the reasoning process is different. The questions here are: Can we define rental without reference to return? Can we also define return without reference to rental? And, does this completely define rent/return processing? The first two answers are yes, the third is no. Both rentals and returns must accommodate the other process as a subprocess for completeness. Therefore, rent and return processing must be combined as one activity.

An easy way to decompose these processes and be reasonably sure we are complete and correct is to decompose the four options separately. The options are rent without return, return without rent, rent with return, and return with rent. A table listing the four options and their subprocesses is shown as Table 9-4. Several issues can be identified for discussion. First, is *Check for Late Fees* the same level of abstraction as the other processes? Second, is *Print Receipt* the same type of process and does it belong on the table? Third, does this look complete? For

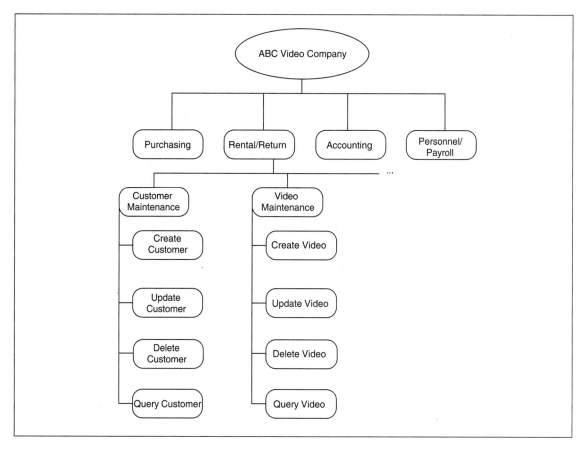

FIGURE 9-24   Decomposition for Customer and Video Maintenance

instance, where are *Create Customer* and *Create Video* when the items are not found in a database? Last, can we consolidate these four lists to develop one list for the decomposition diagram?

First, *Check for Late Fees* appears to be at a lower level of detail than the other processes. To check this, walk-through the process. To check for late fees, data from an open rental must be in memory.

> If the *Return Date* is not equal to zero, subtract *Rental Date* from *Return Date* to get *Number Of Days Rented.*
>
> If *Number Of Days Rented* is greater than the allowed amount (here we use two), multiply (*Number Of Days Rented* − 2) by $2.00 (the late charge) to get *Late Fees.*
>
> If *Late Fees* are greater than zero, display *Late Fees* and add *Late Fees* to *Total Amount Due.*

This is all logic; there is no reading or writing to files. Thus, this is a simple process that borders on being too small to be called a process. This logic could be included in another process if and only if the other process has the same execution pattern for each pass of the logic. This means we next look at how often Check for Late Fees is executed. Check for Late Fees is in every list, but is it executed for every rental and return? The answer is that for all open rentals, this process would execute to check for fees owed whether there are current returns or not. Also, for all returns, after the return date is added, the process Check for Late Fees should be executed.

Next we review the logic to see if exactly the same procedure is followed in both cases. The answer to this issue depends on *when* late fees are considered. So far, we have talked about late fees for

TABLE 9-4 Decomposition of Rental Options

Rental Without Return	Return Without Rental	Rental With Return	Return With Rental
Get Customer ID	Get Return Video IDs	Get Customer ID	Get Return Video IDs
Get Valid Customer	Get Open Rentals	Get Valid Customer	Get Open Rentals
Get Open Rentals	Get Valid Customer	Get Open Rentals	Get Valid Customer
Check for Late Fees	Add Return Date	Get Return Video IDs	Add Return Date
Get Valid Videos	Check Late Fees	Add Return Date	Check Late Fees
Process Payment and Make Change	Update Open Rentals	Check for Late Fees	Get Valid Videos
Create Open Rental	Update/Create History	Get Valid Videos	Process Payment and Make Change
Print Receipt	Process Payment and Make Change	Process Payment and Make Change	Create Open Rental
	Print Receipt	Create Open Rental	Update Open Rental
		Update Open Rental	Update/Create History
		Update/Create History	Print Receipt
		Print Receipt	

tapes with return dates only. You may be tempted to charge fees every day as they accrue, whether the tape is returned or not. If you do this, you need *very* complex logic to identify what fees are accrued, what fees are paid, and what fees are still owed. Complex logic is frequently wrong and is always error prone. If possible, use the KISS (Keep It Simple, Stupid) method and charge fees only when a return date is present. To continue this thinking, what rental attributes do we need to deal with late fees? Do we need a late fees field? A flag when late fees have been paid? The case does not tell us what Vic wants; so we need to talk to him about this.

In this case, Vic and the accountant decide that, for accounting purposes, they want to know all charges applied to a rental. Information to be kept includes: regular fees, regular fees payment, late fees, late fee payment, any extraordinary fees, and extraordinary fee payment. Notice they do not care about payment *dates*. We have two choices for dealing with late fee data. First, we can compute fees and add them to the file when paid or second, keep two

sets of fields, one for the fee and a flag for fee payment. The data and processing for the first option are simpler, but this now makes the processes creating and updating open rentals dependent on successful *Process Payment and Make Change*. This is not only an acceptable tradeoff, but a better business practice since we do not want to update with unsuccessful payment processing. We note the new attributes and add them to the repository.

The second issue deals with *Print Receipt*. Is *Print Receipt* the same type of process and does it belong on the table? The printed rental orders could be considered an output data flow of *Process Payment and Make Change* rather than requiring its own process. Since ABC defines printing of orders as a separate process required of the application, we could leave it on the list. Unfortunately, the methodology does not give guidance in the issue of whether to include or omit data printing processes. In general, if the printing is incidental to another process, that is, it is a record of the processing, then it is not separate. A print process should be distinct if it fulfills legal obligations, or is independent of all other processes, or is contingent on other processing. On the job, the SE, with the analysis team, decides which method of defining inputs and outputs will be used, then is consistent in their definitions. A related issue is the relationship of *Print Receipt* to the other processes. Does it follow payment processing, does it follow and confirm file creation and updating, or is it independent? At the moment, printing appears related to payment processing only, but here again is something we need to ask Vic. A similar problem arises with data entry procedures that we will discuss later.

Here is a sample dialogue between Mary and Vic to resolve the relationship issue.

Mary: "We are trying to decide about when to print receipts and how receipts relate to the rest of the process. Can you tell me the legal requirements and if you have any other business requirements?"

Vic: "Hm, now, we write down all the customer numbers, video numbers, amount paid, and reasons for each transaction. We don't really give customers a receipt in the manual system. I'm not sure what the legal requirements are; I'll get the accountant in here, too."

The accountant comes in and is asked the same question. She says, "It would be nice to have a paper copy of each transaction in which money is processed so I can locate errors when I do the bookkeeping. Trying to find an error by querying the computer might be longer than just adding up the days' receipts in different categories. It would also provide IRS documentation if you don't plan to do that on the computer. Do you?"

This leads to a discussion of the tax processing possible and the potential costs to the project, which are negligible at this stage. The final decision is to require receipts not only for transactions in which money is processed, but to offer a receipt as an option to the customer for nonmoney transactions.

The discussion then digresses into the issue of how long records must be kept on the rental file. If all money-related transactions are printed, records of paid transactions could be deleted. Vic wants access to transaction data for historical analysis but thinks

the history files will answer most of his questions. In his manual system, Vic purges the files once a year at tax time, but he says there is too much paper to look at any paper records unless a customer actually disputes a charge. In any case, Vic, the accountant, and Mary jointly decide to purge the transaction files monthly and move deleted records to an off-line archive file. This discussion causes a new activity to be added to the decomposition under *Periodic Processing*.

Next, Mary broaches the subject of keeping track of file updates and printing the receipt only when the file updates (or creates) are successful. Vic has two concerns. He needs the ability to fix a file problem if one occurs, and he wants the ability independently of the *rental* process. Second, he is leery about using the receipt as notification of a problem. "If users think there is a problem with the computer system, they might not trust the information we give them about late fees and other charges." Vic decides that printing is independent of file updates and that an operator message should be displayed for errors in writing to files.

The third issue is to evaluate the completeness of the processing defined. In particular, where are *Create Customer* and *Create Video* when the 'valid' items are not found in a database? From a simple evaluation of process names, the processing appears complete. To resolve the issue about the two create processes, we look specifically at those processes. Again, there are two options for dealing with the need to create customers and videos: It can be a separate process or it can be a subprocess to the associated *Get Valid . . .* process. The question to answer is: How important, in the rent/return activity, are create customer and video? The answer is that they are not very important. They are performed on an exception basis to allow processing continuity. Both processes are important to the related file maintenance activity. A related issue is the name given to the processes—*Get Valid Customer* and *Get Valid Video*. The implication from these names is that both valid and invalid conditions are dealt with *within* the procedure; only valid customers and videos will be passed for further processing. A missing condition would lead to the initiation of the create procedure. The resolution, then, is to leave the process

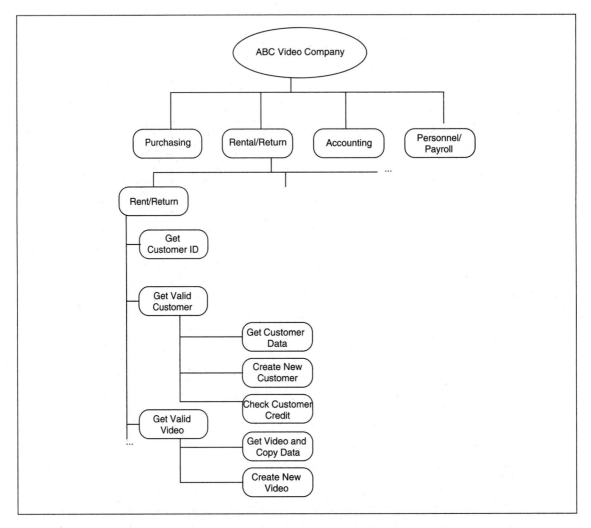

FIGURE 9-25   Partial Decomposition with Details of Get Valid Processing

definitions as they are and to treat the *Create*s as sub-processes under the associated *Get Valid* process. Figure 9-25 shows the details of the two get valid processes for the next level of decomposition.

The final issue is to consolidate these four lists to develop one list, completing the decomposition diagram. The consolidated list is shown, with sequence implied but without selection, in Figure 9-26, the final decomposition diagram. The fourth activity, *Periodic Processing*, has been added. At the moment, this activity includes archival, end-of-day, and query processing. Other processes may be added as we continue through analysis and design. We will use the separate lists of processes again in the next activity, developing the process dependency diagram.

To summarize, process decomposition can be performed independently of ERD development. This step concentrates on activities, processes, and sub-processes of all functions in the BAA. First, all activities are defined, then the processes for each activity are identified and defined. Both activities and processes are defined without regard for current organization, timing of processing, or current procedure. Emphasis is on processes and procedures that are required to fulfill business obligations. The

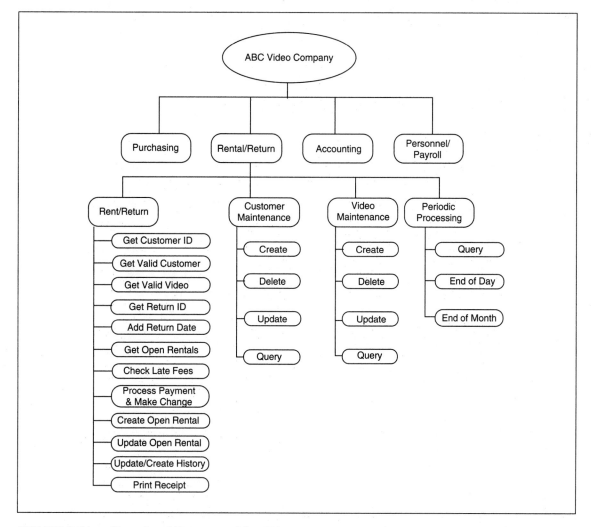

FIGURE 9-26   Completed Decomposition Diagram

final decomposition should be validated through user review.

Develop Process Dependency Diagram

Rules for Developing Process Dependency Diagram

Process dependency relates processes and shows cyclical, logical, and data connections between processes. For each activity and level of processes

decomposed, we examine the processes and sequence them by order of occurrence: what happens first, then second, and so on. A diagram using rounded rectangles for each process and arrows to connect them shows the sequencing of the processes. Processes that are independent of other processes are placed on the diagram but not connected to anything. *One diagram is created for each activity.* The steps for creating the process dependency diagram (PDD) are as follows:

1. For each activity, draw the processes on a sheet of paper.

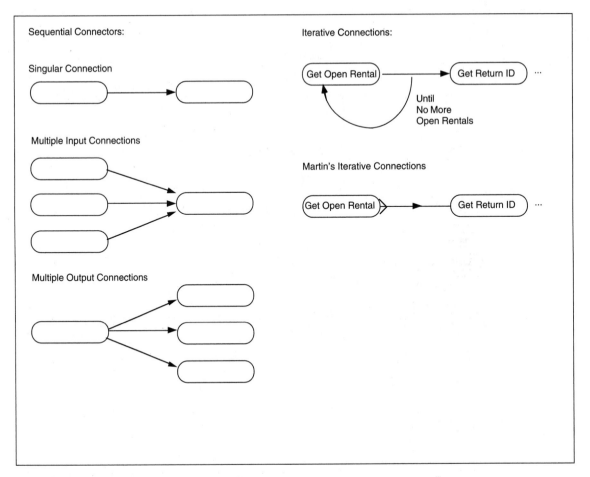

FIGURE 9-27   Types of Process Dependency Connections

2. Examine each process to determine how it is initiated. For processes that pass data to begin work, connect the process to its data receivers. These connections depict the *sequence* of processing.

3. For all connected processes, examine each to determine the cardinality of execution. Define *iterative* processing and document it on the diagram. Be careful to uncouple to the maximum extent possible based on business requirements.

4. For all connected processes, examine each to determine *selection* in processing. For mutually exclusive processes, alter the diagram to depict exclusivity. For all selected processes, add the selection conditions under which processing takes place.

5. For all connected processes, examine each to determine *Boolean* connections. Alter the diagram to include required Boolean logic.

6. Review all connections with the users to verify correctness.

The types of connections between processes in a process dependency diagram differ from those of data flow diagrams discussed in Chapter 7. In process dependency, four types of connections are allowed: sequence, iteration, selection, and Boolean (see Figure 9-27). All connections identify the data

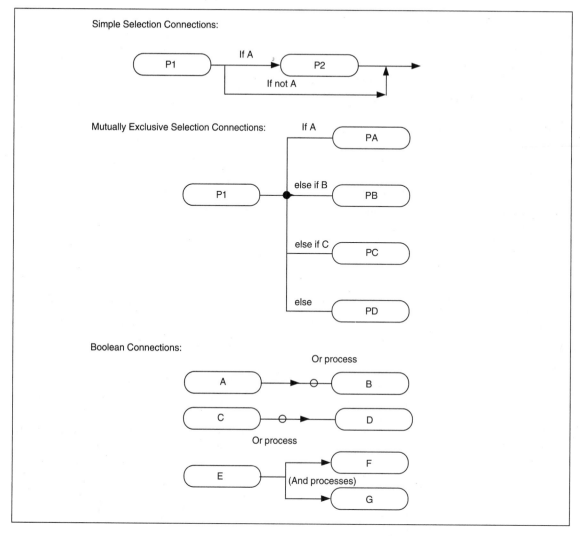

Simple Selection Connections:

Mutually Exclusive Selection Connections:

Boolean Connections:

FIGURE 9-27   Types of Process Dependency Connections (*Continued*)

passing between processes by writing its name, when known, above the line.

Sequential connections may be singular or multiple, with many processes feeding another process, possibly feeding the same data (as in reusable processes) (see Figure 9-27). Multiple entries into (or exits from) a single process do not imply any relationship between the multiple processes. That is, no control structure is required to ensure correct order of execution of the processes. In fact, multiple processes could be concurrent, if needed.

Iterative connections between processes are shown with feedback loops, with an indication of how many iterations are performed. A popular alternative is Martin's notation of iteration which uses cardinality indicators, i.e., crows' feet. This notation implies a coupling between processes that may not exist, so the decoupled, more standard iteration loop is used in this text. Both Martin's notation and the decoupled notation are in Figure 9-27.

Selection, or conditional, connections show the alternative choices connected by a solid circle to differentiate Boolean processes. The *if-then-else* logic conditions are written on each line.

Boolean connections identify 'and' or 'or' types of connections. Boolean connectors use connected lines with an open circle at the junction for optional (or) processes. Simple connected lines which join (or split) to show multiple ('anded') entry (or exit) from processes. That is, any processes not identified as optional or selected are assumed to be executed following the preceding process.

A comment about multiple required process connections is required. Two options for multiple processes, one using multiple directed lines, and one using multiple lines joining or splitting into one line, are discussed. These notations have specifically different connotations. The first, multiple directed lines, shows that any or all of the multiple processes can be executed *and* that control over that execution is imbedded in the processes. The second, multiple lines joining or splitting into one line, specifically identifies 'anded' processes and may require logic to ensure that all are executed.

In addition to showing the logical connections between processes, the lines connecting processes identify process data triggers, that is, data flows from a process to its dependent processes. The last step to the dependency diagram is to identify, as much as possible at this stage, the data that triggers the dependent processes. Attribute names, relation names, or other identifier names are written on the connective lines.

ABC Video Example Process Dependency Diagram

The dependency diagrams for ABC vary in their complexity. The maintenance diagrams are simple because all processes are independent (Figure 9-28). Similarly, the periodic processes are also unrelated (see Figure 9-29). The processes of rental and return are complex and are discussed in detail.

The discussion in the preceding sections identified a dependency of processes in rental/return processing that we need to carry forward: *Print Receipt* is dependent on *Process Payment and Make Change*.

There are other dependencies as well. To show the logic behind the final diagram, we show the

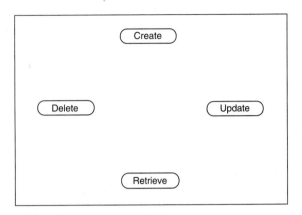

FIGURE 9-28   Maintenance Process Dependency Diagram

process dependencies for each process alternative as we did above. The four choices, again, are rentals with and without returns, and returns with and without rentals.

The first diagram lists the processes for rentals without returns and, *informally*, draws connections between them. We draw the informal diagram because changes are expected and changing an informal diagram is easier than changing a formal one.

When you start considering the processes, two apparent features are: first, they are not all sequential and second, they are not all done only once. Repetitive processes are *Get Open Rentals* (with *Check for Late Fees* in an iterative loop), and *Get Valid Videos*. Both of these are performed until there are no more

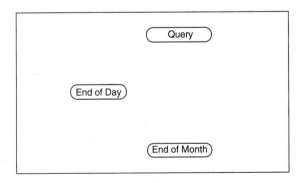

FIGURE 9-29   Periodic Process Dependency Diagram

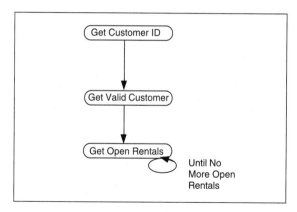

FIGURE 9-30   Get Customer ID and Get Valid Customer Process Dependency Diagram

of the items being got. Draw a circular line from the process to itself to show iteration. Is there any data passed from one iteration to the next? No specific data except an indicator to keep going and, maybe, a memory address at which to store the next data, but this is an implementation detail. We do not identify it now.

Next, walk-through the processing to identify dependencies, drawing the appropriate connections as you proceed. *Get Customer ID* provides the external display and entry processing and passes a *Customer ID* to *Get Valid Customer* (see Figure 9-30). We cannot go directly to any other process because we only want to process valid customers. Consequently, the only dependency is *Get Valid Customer*. *Get Valid Customer* retrieves a customer record, creating a new one if required, checks credit status, and passes a valid customer record to the next process: *Get Open Rentals* (see Figure 9-30). We already said *Get Open Rentals* iterates until there are no more open rentals, and it proceeds to *Get Valid Videos* after it is complete (see Figure 9-31). Could we go directly from *Get Valid Customer* to *Get Valid Videos*? That is, could *Get Valid Videos* and *Get Open Rentals* be concurrent? We need to jump into implementation details again to decide, since there is no business reason why these processes cannot be concurrent. What do we do *in* these processes? The open rentals procedure reads a file, checks late fees, composes and displays a line, and adds to a total

field, as required. The video process gets *Video IDs*, reads the Video and Copy relations, composes and displays lines, and adds to a total field. Both processes need access to the screen. So, we need a protocol, or set of rules, to govern where and when a process can display information. They cannot both try to use the same line. The easy method is to force one process to be first and to create an artificial dependency. This is what we will do: *Get Open Rentals* will be first, because we can also have the clerk verify late fees with the customer. So *Get Valid Videos* will be dependent for screen location information (and memory location information, too) on *Get Open Rentals*.

To continue, *Get Valid Videos* iterates until there are no more videos to be rented, then proceeds to *Process Payment and Make Change* (see Figure 9-32). We decided above that both *Create Open Rental* and *Print Receipt* are dependent on payment processing but independent of each other, so we draw two lines from *Process Payment* to each of these processes (see Figure 9-33). Putting all of these dependencies together, we arrive at Figure 9-34.

It is important to practice walking through the diagrams one step at a time to identify dependencies, considering each process alone and as possibly

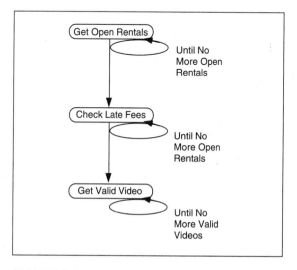

FIGURE 9-31   Get Open Rental and Check for Late Fees Dependent Processes

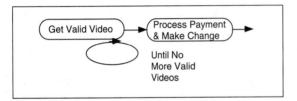

FIGURE 9-32   Get Valid Videos Dependent Processes

connected to all other processes. Ask if all of these processes get done once, or are some iterated? Can groups of processes that iterate together be identified?

Draw each connection as you consider it so it is translated properly. Finally, identify the data triggers when they are known so that you know *what you don't know* when your diagram is 'complete,' meaning it contains all known information.

Figure 9-34 shows the dependency diagram for Rentals Without Returns. Try to develop the process dependency diagram for each of the options on your own, without looking at the answers. The other process option dependency diagrams are shown as Figures 9-35–9-37. Keep in mind that iteration and sequencing required for each alternative way of processing are important because we eventually must

consolidate into one diagram—that is, a composite of the individual diagrams. We only discuss the difficult connections and connections that change the way we think about the rent/return process (i.e., may alter our mental model).

In Figure 9-35, we have several differences from the first dependency diagram (Figure 9-34). First, *Get Valid Customer* is only done for the first return, so we need a selection connector. If the Video ID (or Open Rental) is not the first, we proceed to *Add Return Date* and *Check for Late Fees*. We have two choices on the iteration grouping shown (see Figure 9-38). The first strategy shows coupled logic with the loop encompassing *Get Request, Get Open Rentals, Get Valid Customer, Add Return Date*, and *Check for Late Fees*. The second strategy shows several loops that may look more awkward, but reflect *required* coupling for the processes. This logic is uncoupled and shows three iterative loops, all iterating for all returns. The first loop is *Get Open Rentals*. The second loop is *Add Return Date*; the third is *Check for Late Fees*. Both of these alternatives would be acceptable in program specifications and selection for one over the other might be based on the common iteration pattern. At the logical requirement level, however, the preferred method is the more loosely coupled one because the iteration cycles may change when we consolidate the dia-

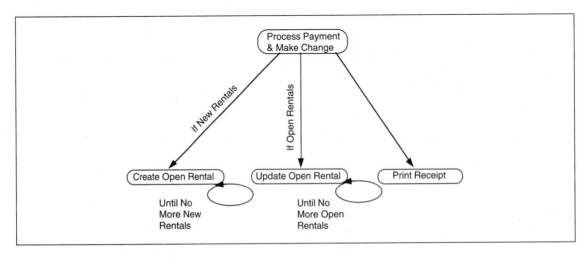

FIGURE 9-33   Process Payment and Make Change Dependent Processes

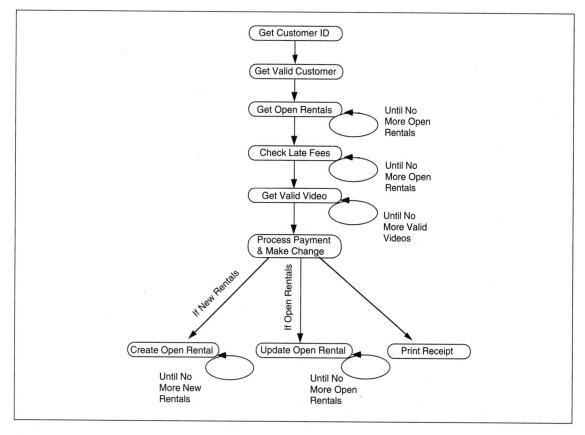

FIGURE 9-34   Rentals without Returns Dependency Diagrams

grams. If the diagrams were already consolidated, we could go to the program design level of detail to choose the iteration grouping. The more uncoupled dependency is shown in the completed diagram, Figure 9-35. The decisions about preferred looping are deferred until design.

The second difference in Figure 9-35 is that a receipt has selection criteria applied to its creation. A receipt *must* be printed whenever a payment is made, and *may* be printed upon request of a customer with returns but no payments. This selection is shown on the diagram.

Figure 9-36 shows rentals with returns. In this procedure, we have two iterative cycles: one for return processing and one for new rental-item processing. These, in effect, consolidate the previous two diagrams. Notice here that the initial input is

from *Get Customer ID* so returns do not include the selective execution of *Get Valid Customer*. Also notice that we again have coupling options for return processing (the coupling options for return processing are shown in Figure 9-38). In the selected option we have three iteration cycles. *Get Open Rentals* is performed for *all* open rentals. *Get Return ID*s and *Add Return Date* are performed together for all returns which may be a subset of open rentals. *Check for Late Fees* is performed for all open rentals whether or not returned today. The final difference is for history processing which is selected for open rentals with *Return Date* equal to today's date.

The last procedure is for returns with rentals (see Figure 9-37) which is similar to Figure 9-36 except for the initial entry of information. If a return is first,

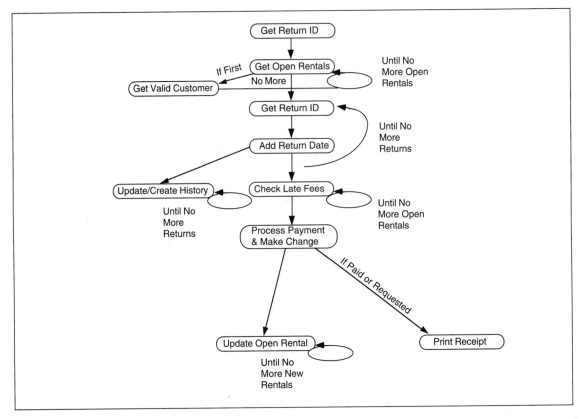

FIGURE 9-35   Returns Without Rentals Dependent Processes

Get Return ID is the first process and we need the selective execution of *Get Valid Customer*.

Now, we are ready to consolidate the diagrams into one (see Figure 9-39). The obvious complexity is in dealing with all of the return options, so they will be done first. If we look at the first step of each procedure, the differences are that for returns, *Video IDs* are entered first and for rentals, *Customer IDs* are entered first. If these are separate processes, we have a problem knowing which is, in fact, being executed. If we consolidate these processes, we can use program logic to figure out which numbers are for videos and which for customers. This means that *Get Return ID* and *Get Customer ID* are replaced with one process we will call *Get Request*. This process will select either *Get Valid Customer* or *Get Open Rentals* depending on the data entered. This

change is reflected back to the decomposition diagram also.

Next, for returns, we need selective execution of *Get Valid Customer*. To consolidate, we need to know whether we are processing a rental or a return. Two changes are required. *Get Request* must call either *Get Valid Customer* or *Get Open Rental*, depending on the type of entry. This is indicated by the selection logic in Figure 9-39. Second, *Get Request* has to pass some indicator to *Get Open Rentals* that it is the caller; this means data is triggering the process.

The last return issue is what to do with *Check for Late Fees*. There are three options. First, include it in *both Get Open Rentals* and *Add Return Date* to ensure complete processing of late fees for old and new returns. Second, leave it separate and execute it

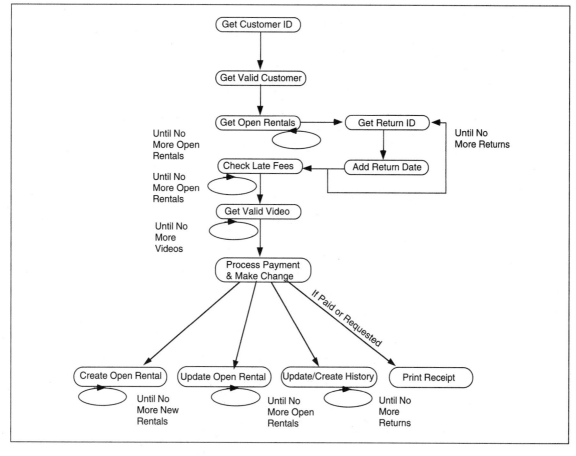

FIGURE 9-36   Rentals with Returns Dependency Diagrams

for all open rentals, including those returned today, as a separately iterated process. The first option guarantees double processing for all returns when rentals are also done. The second option requires somewhat complex logic for memory loop processing. Both options are acceptable technically and from a business perspective. The last option is to defer a decision. Since we have *no business basis* for a decision, we leave the process on the diagram and defer any decision about grouping until design. The final dependency diagram is shown in Figure 9-39 and reflects all of the decisions discussed above.

The dependency diagram for periodic activities is in Figure 9-40. The diagram is somewhat strange because there is no necessary connection between any of the processes. It reflects the independence of the processes, and is the basis for the PDFD which completes the dependency diagram. This type of independence also identifies possible concurrent processes and is considered a normal diagram. Notice that even though these processes would be connected on a menu for processing, no menu selection options are shown at this logical level. The reason is that the *business* requires no menu.

To summarize, to develop the dependency diagram list the processes for an activity, in sequence. Then, examine each process to determine its relation to all other processes. If complex processing is involved, as we have here, separate out the options

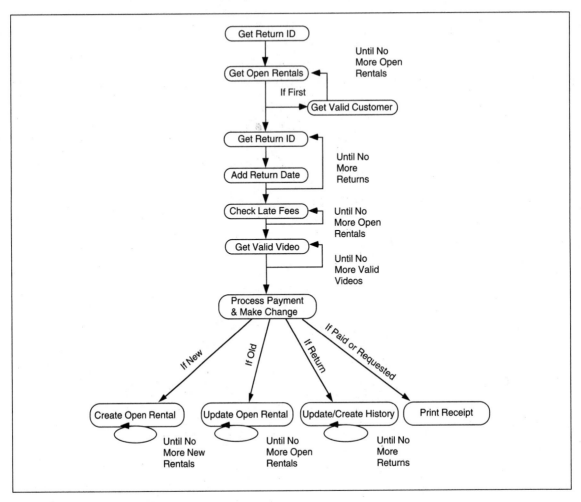

FIGURE 9-37   Returns With Rentals Dependent Processes

and develop dependency diagrams for each option. Be careful to couple processes based on business requirements rather than on convenience. Convenience is decided in design. Consolidate any options and only change processes if required to support integrated process interactions.

Notice also that in going back to the client for information during this procedure, we obtained information we would otherwise not have about the need for periodic purging of the file and requirements for IRS documentation.

Develop Process Data Flow Diagram

Rules for Developing Process Data Flow Diagram

This is a three step process:

1. For each process dependency diagram, examine every process to determine if external events provide information used in the execu-

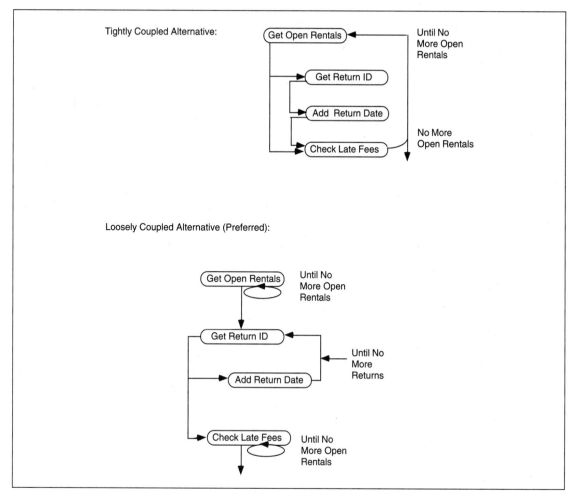

FIGURE 9-38   Alternative Coupling Strategies in Return Processing

tion of the work. For each external event, add an event trigger and identify the event (or the data it provides).

2. For entities from the ERD, examine their use by processes in each diagram. For known connections, add one file for each entity to the diagram and connect them to processes with arrows depicting the direction of data flow. For all files, when a relation is not the unit of data retrieved, list the attributes that make up the data flow.

3. Review the triggers and files with the user to verify correctness.

Using the process dependency diagram, first add the information about triggers, that is, the data or events that trigger each process. If arrival of information from another process is the trigger, identify the data on the lines connecting the rectangles. Use large arrow outlines for event triggers. Use single-directed lines for data triggers (see Figure 9-41).

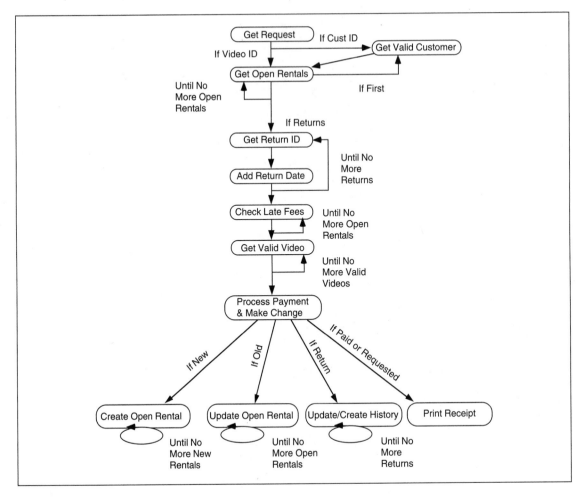

FIGURE 9-39   Consolidated Process Dependency Diagram

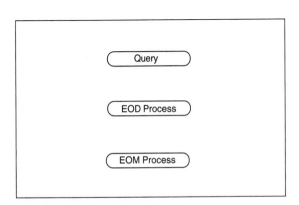

FIGURE 9-40   Periodic Activitied
Dependency Diagram

Each process *must* be triggered, or initiated, by either an event or arrival of data. If you have a process without either data or event as input, then you have missed information during data gathering and should return to the user to obtain the information.

Identifiers for both data and events should link directly to some entity. The trigger may be the arrival of some entity or may be some partial data from an entity. If the identified data does not map directly to an entity from the ERD, you are also missing information and should return to the user to obtain the information.

Next, data files are identified, if they are known. Not all files are necessarily identified at this point of

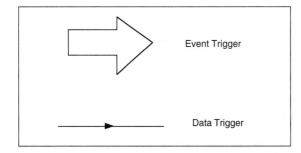

FIGURE 9-41   Trigger Identification on
Process Data Flow Diagram

the analysis. However, most information that is required in persistent files will have been identified as entities on the ERD. The files are connected to processes with the appropriate arrow signifying the direction of data flow. If a unit of data other than a logical relation is required, the lines connecting files should be labeled with their contents.

PDFD validation is performed last to guarantee that all functional requirements are satisfied by the processes depicted. The validation walk-through uses both the original text or functional specification, plus the decomposition from the specification, plus any additional user requirements or information obtained throughout the analysis activities.

ABC Video Example Process Data Flow Diagram

To complete the ABC PDFD, begin with the final process dependency diagram. We examine each process sequentially, adding events and data files as needed to complete the logical processing. For each process, ask: How does this process know to execute? What information does it need? Where does the information come from? Ask these questions without paying attention to current connections from other processes. For each process, when you have the answers, look at the current connections and decide if they completely define the required list of information. If not, define the external 'triggers'— either data or events—that initiate the processing. The individual chunks of the diagram on which we are working are shown with the discussion. They

are integrated into one diagram at the end of the discussion.

The first process, *Get Request*, requires input of either a phone number or a video ID to begin execution. The information is provided by the customer and entered into the computer (either by scanning or typing) by the clerk. Since the information is externally generated by a rental or return request, the data being entered is an event. That is, arrival of a *Customer ID* or *Video ID* into the computer triggers the *Get Request* process which begins the sequence of processes for rental/return processing. The hollow arrow is added to the diagram to show the arrival of the *Request* event (see Figure 9-42).

After the request is entered, the process determines which data were entered and passes control to the appropriate process. If the *Customer ID* was entered, the *Get Valid Customer* process would be triggered. For that process, customer information from storage is required for validation and credit checking. A file symbol for a customer information file with a line indicating data *into* the process is added to the diagram (see Figure 9-42). Since there is a possibility that the customer is new, an arrow going *to* the *Customer File* is also shown.

Next in rental processing, the *Open Rentals File* should be read to retrieve all information about *Open Rentals* relating to the present customer. These are formatted and displayed. The file is added as input to the *Get Open Rentals* process (see Figure 9-42).

If the request entered had been a *Video ID*, the *Get Open Rental* process followed by the *Get Valid Customer* process would have been triggered. The control of these processes is shown by the selection arrows from the dependency diagram. The data and trigger requirements do not change. We might make a note that, in this execution of *Get Valid Customer*, we do not allow new customers to be added. That is, it should be logically impossible for a new customer to have a return.

Return processing takes place next with two possible variations. First, if the first *Request* was a *Video ID*, there already *is* a return *Video ID* in memory and no *Get Return ID* is triggered. Instead, *Add Return Date/Late Fees* is triggered. The second variation is in the rental process; returns are entered after open rentals are displayed. The *Get Return ID* process is

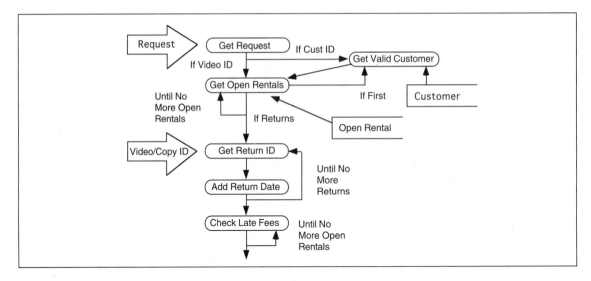

FIGURE 9-42   Process Request 'Chunk' of PDFD

triggered but it now needs the *Video ID*, external information, to process. The event trigger added to the process, then, contains *Video ID*s (see Figure 9-42). The data is made available to the *Add Return Date* process. *Get Return ID* and *Add Return Date* iterate until the *Return ID* is ended (exactly how is decided during design). Then all *Open Rentals* (and returns) are *Checked for Late Fees*.

Next, the *Get Valid Video* process executes to identify videos requested for rental. The information needed for this process comes from an external trigger, the customer-supplied *Video ID*. The ID is validated by reading the *Video File* and a *Copy File*. For rental/return processing, the *Video* and *Copy* files are always used together, so they are shown in one file symbol. By doing this, we are reminded that we need a user view that connects the two relations for rental processing. Customers are to be reminded when they have already rented a particular video, therefore, *Customer History File* is also read during this process. Its file symbol is added to the diagram.

The *Total Amount Due* is passed to trigger *Process Payment and Make Change*. The *Total Amount Due* is displayed from the previous process and awaits the external entry of *Customer Payment Amount* to compute change. This requires an event trigger for *Customer Payment Amount* (see Figure

9-43). The formula used is *Total Amount Due – Customer Payment Amount = Balance*. When the *Balance* is zero, the rental/return process is complete and all files may be updated as required. Each *line* of the rental/return, signifying either an existing *Open Rental* with/without *Return Date* or a new *Open Rental* is processed separately to determine the next process to execute. This represents the *normal* process; now we must also think about exceptions: What if the balance does *not* go to zero? Can a customer ever overpay and leave so fast that they are owed change? Can a customer ever owe money and leave without paying? If the answer to either of these questions is yes, we also need an optional event trigger *End of Payment* that forces completion of the *Process Payment* process and shows that the customer is owed money. For the present, we assume that we iterate through *Process Payment* until *Balance* equals zero. Finally, process payment needs to provide information for *End of Day* totals. A file for EOD data will be created from this process. Notice that this file is not on the ERD, but should it be? It does not represent an entity that the company keeps information about, or does it? When the ERD was developed, we focused on the rent/return processes only and ignored nonrental activities. By ignoring accounting and its needs for rent/return data, we

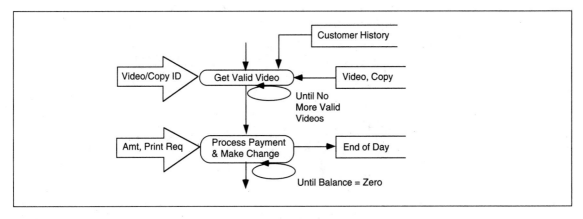

FIGURE 9-43   Rental and Payment 'Chunk' of PDFD

missed the entity for financial information relating to rent/return. We should recheck with the accountant, but it appears that the *EOD Accounting Information* should be an entity that is added to the ERD, connected to the *Open Rental* entity.

The last 'chunk' of the PDFD is for file update and print processes. For each new rental, *Create Open Rental* writes the new rental to the *Open Rental File* (see Figure 9-44). For each unpaid return (i.e., existing *Open Rental* with *Return Date* not null), the *Open Rental* is rewritten to the file (see Figure 9-44). For each paid returned video, some logical delete indicator must be set and the *Open Rental* is then rewritten to the file. If an existing *Open Rental* had no processing, no action is required, but it might be easier, and more consistent, to only look at return and paid criteria to determine correct writing. No business criteria exist for this option, therefore, this is a design decision not made here.

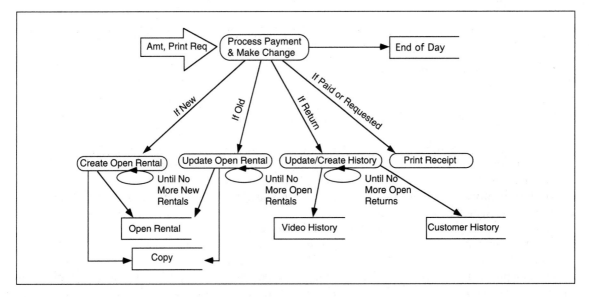

FIGURE 9-44   File and Update 'Chunk' of PDFD

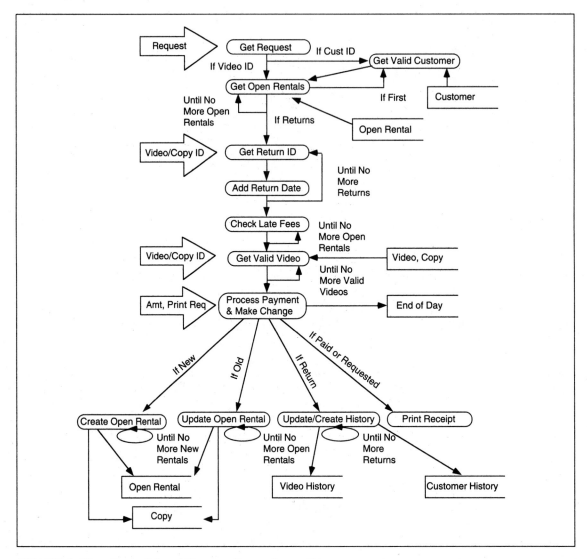

FIGURE 9-45   Consolidated Process Dependency Diagram

Next, history file processing updates both *Video History* and *Customer History*. Notice that the details of history processing require another level of decomposition, which is left as a student exercise. Last, the receipt is printed. The data trigger from *Process Payment* initiates this process; the physical output is not on the PDFD.

The composite PDFD with all of the chunks integrated is shown as Figure 9-45. Before you look at the other diagrams, try to develop one or all of them yourself. The remaining PDFDs are shown as Figure 9-46, for query processing, and Figure 9-47 for customer maintenance processing. The PDFDs for *Video Maintenance* processing are a practice exercise at the end of the chapter.

Next we evaluate the PDFD for completeness based on the decomposition information from the client and the original statement of the problem (Chapter 2).

Errors to watch for are:

1. Processes on the decomposition that are not self-contained are not processes. For instance, 'end process' is a system action, not a business process. You do not need a process to which all other processes feed to show a termination point on a PDFD (see Figure 9-48).
2. Processes on the PDFD that are not *identical* to the processes on the decomposition (see Figure 9-49).
3. If process data trigger contents cannot be identified, there may be no dependency. Reevaluate the relationship, talking to the user if necessary, to determine what data are required for the dependent process.
4. If a process data trigger exists in a different time, the connection is probably wrong. For instance, you might be tempted to connect query processing to rental/return in some way (see Figure 9-50). These are disjoint activities and the only connection is through the database.
5. For query processing, do not try to simulate a menu selection process in the PDFD (see Figure 9-51). Each type of query has its own event trigger requesting information. Each

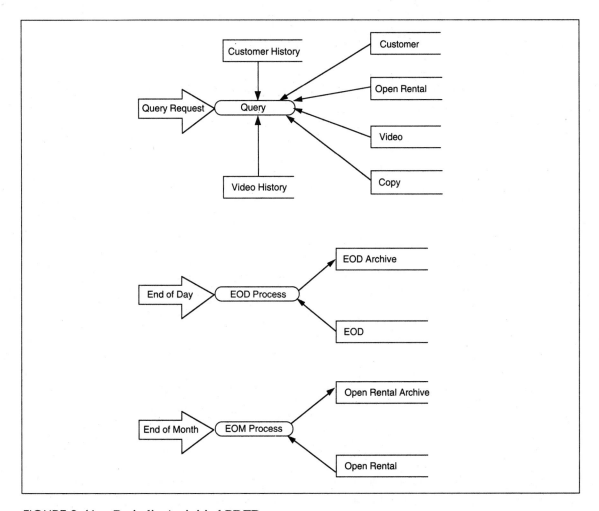

FIGURE 9-46   Periodic Activitied PDFD

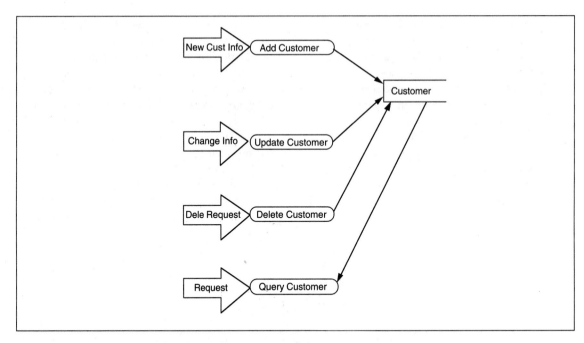

FIGURE 9-47   ABC Customer Maintenance PDFD

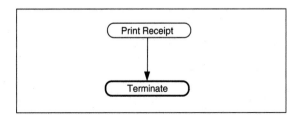

FIGURE 9-48   Nonprocess Problem

type of query is distinct and separate from all other queries. The queries may share files.

6. When more than one activity is shown on a PDFD, problems are encouraged and the diagram no longer clearly delineates any process (see Figure 9-52). Place *at most* one activity decomposition on a page. Use one side of the paper only. Keep in mind that most of the time, the information will be on a CASE tool until printed for documentation, so there is not really much wasted paper.

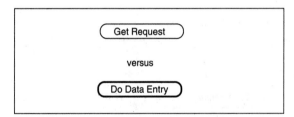

FIGURE 9-49   Name Names Do Not Match Decomposition

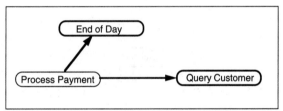

FIGURE 9-50   Data Trigger Timing Problem

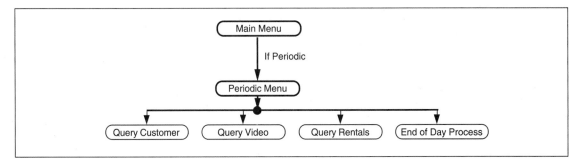

FIGURE 9-51   Simulated Menu Problem

Develop and Analyze Entity/Process Matrix

Rules for Developing and Analyzing an Entity/Process Matrix

This matrix is composed of the results from the ERD and process decompositions; it requires neither the process dependency nor the PDFD for completion. Along the left margin, list each lowest-level process from the process decomposition diagram. Use the lowest-level processes, such that all elemental processes for the organization and application area are present. Along the top, list the normalized entities from the ERD, with one entity in each column.

Completely identify which processes are allowed to Create, Retrieve, Update, and Delete (CRUD) each entity. Enter one or more of the letters as allowed by the current organization's policies and procedures for each entity.

When the matrix is complete, entities are grouped by their affinity, or closeness, in processing entities. If you do this step manually, group processes that share create responsibility first. If the number of clusters is reasonable for the size of the project, stop. When you have analyzed the entire matrix, rearrange the matrix by its clusters. You may have several clusters that overlap. That is normal and not a cause for worry. If you have only one cluster, reanalyze as necessary using first update processing, then delete processing, then retrieval, as the clustering criteria. When you obtain a reasonable number of clusters, go to the next step of the analysis. A reasonable number

may be one to five for a small application, such as ABC, or seven or more for a large application.

To perform manual affinity analysis, perform the following procedure (here we do create affinity only). Keep in mind that you are 'normalizing' process-entity relationships. Look at each process and its entities. For an entity/process cell, look down the column and identify other cells in which create processing is done (C). Make an erasable, colored mark in those cells. Do this for all entities for each process.

Even though it is an extra step, and quite a bit of work, create an interim matrix for each potential cluster. This interim matrix makes your visual inspection of relationships easier and actually speeds the affinity analysis. Iterating, build the interim matrix, analyze it as described below, and add the resulting cluster(s) to the new process/entity matrix. Iteration is required because the interim clusters may change as the relationships of each potential cluster are analyzed.

To analyze a potential cluster, start at the first process and look at the data it shares with the next process in the list. Do these two processes share 80%[7] or more of their data creation (or update, delete) responsibility? If yes, mark the original matrix to show they are together and add the processes and their entities to the interim matrix. If the percentage is less than 80%, circle the second

---

7 80% is not a hard number. You adjust the percentage affinity needed to find multiple clusters. If all processes share all responsibilities, the organizational processes must first be redesigned, then this analysis is repeated.

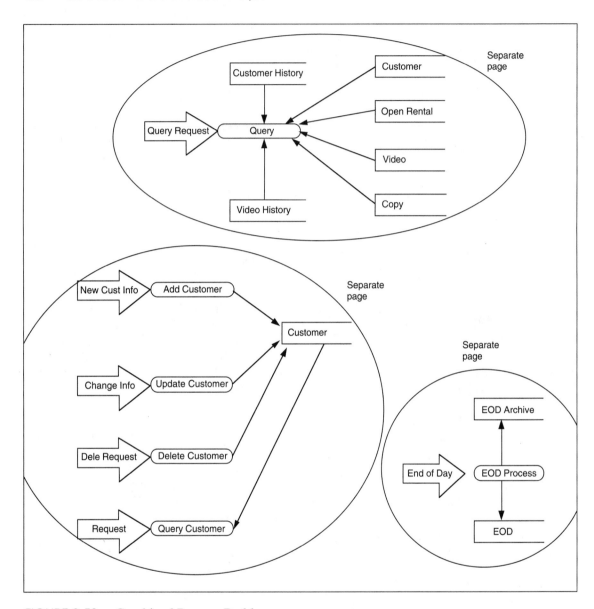

FIGURE 9-52   Combined Process Problem

process for potential deletion from this cluster. If the percentage affinity is between 50–80%, look at the next process that might be related. Do either of the two first processes share more than 80% of their data with the third process? If all three share, cluster them all. If the third strongly relates to the second process but not the first, or the third relates to the first but not the second, still cluster all of them for the moment. Continue to do this type of stepwise comparison of processes using entity affiliation to determine process affinity. Each successive process's functions on the entity are compared to all previous processes, not just the first. If a new process is strongly related to all of them, the cluster remains intact. If the new process strongly relates to some subset of processes, keep it. If the new process strongly relates to only one process, consider those two processes as a second cluster and set them aside (i.e., create a new interim matrix) with their data for analysis of that cluster. As you complete analysis of a cluster, add it to the new process/entity matrix. Return to the original matrix and draw a line through each process that has been added to a cluster, to ensure that there is no replication of a process and to ensure that processes that are not currently in a cluster are added to a cluster eventually.

As you create the new process/entity matrix, leave several lines and columns of space between each cluster. At the end of the analysis, reanalyze processes that have not been assigned to any cluster. Look at the interim matrices to which each odd process was compared. Find the cluster to which it has the *most* affinity, and add the process to that cluster. If there is no affinity, leave the entity separate.

When affinity analysis is complete, the clustered processes are ready for analysis to determine if they can be in the same execution unit, and the data shared by a cluster should be analyzed to determine the physical design of the database and the needed user views of data. These activities are done during the design phase.

ABC Video Example Entity/Process Matrix

To develop the entity/process matrix, list the lowest level processes from the decomposition diagram down the left column. Then, list the entities across the top, one per column. For each process, add which functions it has for each entity. Possible functions are create, retrieval, update, or delete (CRUD, respectively). The ABC process-entity matrix is shown as first completed in Table 9-5. In completing the table refer back to the PDFD. Use the arrows and names of the processes to identify the type of processing. For entities with arrows only going *into* a process, the correct code is 'R,' for retrieval. For entities with arrows only going *out* of a process, the correct codes are 'C,' 'U,' or 'D,' for create, update, or delete, depending on the processing to take place. For example, *Create Video* has a 'C' under *Copy* and a 'C' under *Video* because it creates both.

First, we check each entity to see if all possible processing is accounted for. *Customer*, *Copy*, and *Video* all have CRUD processing and appear complete. *Open Rental* has CRUD processing during rent/return and R processing as part of *Query*. *Open Rental*, too, looks complete.

EOD Financial Information is created but not ever deleted, which is wrong. It should be archived or deleted at the end of the processing day. We will assume archival at the moment and add both process and data changes back to all other diagrams as needed. We can further assume that the delete process and create process follow. This is an example of what happens with late identified entities. The processing is not as thoroughly analyzed and some information could 'fall through the cracks.' The entity/process matrix helps assure that processing is completely defined.

Finally, history is only created and retrieved. We have not yet defined history, so the decision may not be final. In general, history files *are* only created and retrieved. They are permanent records of past transactions or business states, so they can not be updated or deleted and still be known as 'history.'

When the matrix is complete, we cluster the processes by their entity affinity (see Table 9-6). There are five possible clusters, but most of the data are used by many of the processes. So, the clustering shown is to give an example of how, at the application level, affinity analysis can be used to determine user views for DBMS access. For ABC, because of the extensive retrieval activities, one subject database would be defined. *EOD* data are kept separate from all other data. *Customer*, *Video*, *Copy*, and *Open Rental* data are all used to create individual relations and joint user views.

First we analyze organizational sufficiency as it relates to processes. Is each entity created by one process only? The answer here is yes. Do all processes creating, updating, and deleting an entity report to the same manager? Here the answer is again, yes. So the organization is sufficient.

Next we look at the entities and their usage to determine subject area databases. Again, ABC is a small company, so the data are mostly in one

(Text continues on page 386)

TABLE 9-5   ABC Video Process/Entity Matrix

Entities = Processes	Customer	Video	Copy	Open Rental	Customer History	Video History	Rental Archive	EOD
Get Request	R							
Get Valid Customer	R							
Get Open Rentals		R	R	R				
Add Return Date								
Check for Late Fees								
Get Valid Videos		R	R			R		
Process Payment and Make Change								U
Create Open Rental				C				
Update Open Rental				U				
Update/Create History						CU		
Print Receipt								
Query Customer	R			R	R			
Query Rental	R	R	R	R			R	
Query Video		R	R	R		R		
Query History	R	R	R	R	R	R	R	
Query EOD								R
EOD Processing								CRD
Rental Archive Processing				D			C	
Create Customer	C							
Update Customer	U							
Delete Customer	D							
Create Video/Copy		C	C					
Update Video/Copy		U	U					
Delete Video/Copy		D	D					

TABLE 9-6   ABC Video Process/Entity Matrix Affinity Clusters

Entities = Processes	Customer	Video	Copy	Open Rental	Customer History	Video History	Rental Archive	EOD
Create Customer	C							
Delete Customer	D							
Get Valid Customer	R							
Query Customer	R			R	R			
Update Customer	U							
Create Video/Copy		C	C					
Update Video/Copy		U	U					
Delete Video/Copy		D	D					
Get Open Rentals		R	R	R				
Get Valid Videos		R	R			R		
Query History	R	R	R	R	R	R	R	
Query Video		R	R	R		R		
Create Open Rental				C				
Update Open Rental				U				
Query Rental	R	R	R	R			R	
Rental Archive Processing				D			C	
Update/Create History					CU	CU		
Process Payment and Make Change								U
EOD Processing								CRD
Query EOD								R
Add Return Date								
Check for Late Fees								
Get Request								
Print Receipt								

Data Entities and Final Attributes		Activities for Rental/Return and All Processes	
Entity	**Attributes (Key underlined)**	**Activity**	**Processes**
Customer	Customer Phone ID	Rent/Return	Get Request
	Customer Name		Get Valid Customer
	Customer Address		Get Open Rentals
	Customer City		Add Return Date
	Customer State		Check for Late Fees
	Customer Zip		Get Valid Videos
	Customer Credit Card		Process Payment and Make
	Number		Change
	Credit Card Type		Create Open Rental
	Credit Card Expiration Date		Update Open Rental
Open Rental	Customer Phone ID		Update/Create History
	Video ID		Print Receipt
	Copy ID	Periodic Processing	Query Customer
	Rental Date		Query Rental
	Return Date		Query Video
	Late Fee Due		Query History
	LF Paid		Query EOD
	Rental Fees Due		EOD Processing
	RF Pd		Rental Archive Processing
	Other Fees Due	Customer Maintenance	Create Customer
	OF Paid		Update Customer
Video	Video ID		Delete Customer
	Video Name		
	Entry Date	Video Maintenance	Create Video/Copy
	Rental Rate		Update Video/Copy
Copy	Video ID		Delete Video/Copy
	Copy ID		
	Date Received	**Deferred Items for Decision During Design**	
	Status		
Customer History	To Be Defined	**Item**	**Decision**
Video History	To Be Defined	Check for Late Fees	Separate or Consolidated
EOD	To Be Defined		with either/or both
Rental Archive	To Be Defined		*Get Open Rentals*
			Add Return Date
		History	Is video history updating going to be done to a history file or to the current *Copy* relations? This requires monthly update. The history file requires further decisions about what is on the file.

FIGURE 9-53   Summary Repository Entries

database. *Video, Customer, Open Rental,* and *End of Day* information will be stored together. *Video* and *Customer* are separate from the other entities because they are only modified by one process. His-

torical information could be stored in a separate database or set of files. In most companies and applications, history files *are* kept separate from the other databases and files. For applications with huge amounts of data, history is even on a different storage medium. History is frequently kept on tape and the current databases are on disk. Depending on volume, we would consider tape storage for history here, too.

The entity/process matrix analysis completes the BAA. At this time, all entities, processes, attributes, and their interrelationships should be known based on business requirements. All information is documented in a repository for use in the next phase. The repository entries, without details, are presented in Figure 9-53.

SOFTWARE SUPPORT FOR DATA-ORIENTED ANALYSIS

There are many CASE tools that support data modeling and other data-oriented analysis tasks. Tools that also support Information Engineering are integrated toolsets that cover the complete development life cycle. CASE support for Information Engineering is the best of any methodology. Two CASE environments support the entire IE life cycle from enterprise analysis through maintenance. The two tools are IEF™[8] and ADW. The CASE tools are by no means perfect, however; interphase linkages are weak; numerous bugs plague new releases of ADW; and old releases of IEF were designed so rigidly that all graphical and definitional forms were required to use the tool effectively. The positive aspect of both tools is that they can feed code generators that can automate development of as much as 70% of the necessary program code. Both ADW and IEF support all of the graphical and definitional forms discussed in this chapter. The list in Table 9-7 includes many other CASE tools that support some, but not all, graphical, documentation, or mental models of IE and data-oriented analysis.

---

8 IEF™ is a trademark of the Texas Instruments Co., Dallas, TX. ADW™ is a trademark of Knowledgeware, Inc., Atlanta, GA.

SUMMARY

Data-oriented methodologies are based on the notion that data are more stable than processes in business. Organizations and procedures change regularly; the data on which they work does not. Data-oriented methodologies, then, concentrate on data as the initial focus of study. The theory underlying data methods applies semantic modeling to data and system theory to business functions.

Information Engineering's business area analysis (BAA) is the example of data-oriented methodology described here. BAAs begin with an entity-relationship diagram that is fully identified and normalized. Business functions are decomposed to create process decomposition, process dependency, and process data flow diagrams.

Business processes from the decomposition are coupled to the entities from the ERD to form an entity/process matrix, also called a CRUD matrix (for create-retrieve-update-delete). The CRUD matrix defines responsibility for actions on each entity for each process. Affinity analysis of the CRUD matrix clusters processes and data into groups. The affinity groupings are used to decide the need for additional project scoping, future applications, and alternatives for subject database design. All information from the BAA is documented in a repository.

REFERENCES

Date, C. J., *An Introduction to Database Systems*, Vol. 1, 5th edition. Reading, MA: Addison-Wesley, 1990.

Finkelstein, Clive, *An Introduction to Information Engineering: From Strategic Planning to Information Systems*. Reading, MA: Addison-Wesley, 1989.

Knowledgeware, Inc., *Information Engineering Workbench™/Analysis Workstation, ESP Release 4.0*. Atlanta, GA: Knowledgeware, Inc., 1987.

Loucopoulos, Pericles, and Roberto Zicari, *Conceptual Modeling, Databases and CASE: An Integrated View of IS Development*. NY: John Wiley & Sons, 1992.

Martin, James, *Information Engineering: Book 2, Planning and Analysis*. Englewood Cliffs, NJ: Prentice-Hall, Inc., 1991.

Martin, James, and Carma McClure, *Diagramming Techniques for Analysts and Programmers*. Englewood Cliffs, NJ: Prentice-Hall, Inc., 1985.

TABLE 9-7   Data-Oriented Analysis CASE Support

Product	Company	Technique
Analyst/Designer Toolkit	Yourdon, Inc. New York, NY	Entity-Relationship Diagram (ERD)
Anatool	Advanced Logical SW Beverly Hills, CA	ERD
Bachman	Bachman Info Systems Cambridge, MA	Bachman ERD
CorVision	Cortex Corp. Waltham, MA	ERD
Deft	Deft Ontario, Canada	ERD
Design/1	Arthur Anderson, Inc. Chicago, IL	ERD
ER-Designer	Chen & Assoc. Baton Rouge, LA	ERD
Excelerator	Index Tech. Cambridge, MA	ERD
IEF	Texas Instruments Dallas, TX	Functional Decomposition ERD Entity Hierarchy Process Hierarchy Process Dependency Process Data Flow Diagram Entity/Process Matrix
IEW, ADW	Knowledgeware Atlanta, GA	Functional Decomposition ERD Entity/Process Matrix

Texas Instruments, *A Guide to Information Engineering Using the IEF*. Dallas, TX: Texas Instruments, 1988.

KEY TERMS

activity
affinity
affinity analysis
architectures
associative entity
attribute
attributive entity
business area analysis
   (BAA)

business function
business process
business redesign
cardinality
CRUD matrix
data administration
data trigger
direct method of
   normalization

elementary process
entity
entity-relationship diagram
   (ERD)
entity type
entity/process matrix
entity structure analysis
event trigger
functional decomposition
fundamental entity
instance
many-to-many relationship
normalization
one-to-many relationship
one-to-one relationship

optional relationship
process data flow diagram
   (PDFD)
process data trigger
process dependency
   diagram
process relationship
relational database theory
relationship
relationship entity
required relationship
subject area database
tabular method of
   normalization
trigger

TABLE 9-7   Data-Oriented Analysis CASE Support (*Continued*)

Product	Company	Technique
Maestro	SoftLab San Francisco, CA	ERD
Multi-Cam	AGS Mgmt Systems King of Prussia, PA	ERD
ProKit Workbench	McDonnell Douglas St. Louis, MO	ERD
SW Thru Pictures	Interactive Development Environments San Francisco, CA	ERD
System Engineer	LBMS Houston, TX	ERD Entity Life History Diagram
Teamwork	CADRE Tech., Inc. Providence, RI	ERD
Telon	Pansophic Systems, Inc. Lisle, IL	ERD
The Developer	ASYST Technology, Inc. Naperville, IL	ERD Organization Chart Operations Process Diagram Matrix Diagram
vs Designer	Visual Software Inc Santa Clara, CA	Process Flow Diagram

EXERCISES

1. Complete the PDFD for Video Maintenance.
2. The *Get Valid Video* process has as its sub-processes: *Get Video Data, Create Video File*, and feeds into the *Check Previous Rental* process. Do a process dependency diagram for these subprocesses. Then add event triggers and data files to complete the PDFD.

STUDY QUESTIONS

1. Define the following terms:

affinity
attributive entity
associative entity
CRUD matrix
elementary process
entity
entity-relationship
   diagram
functional
   decomposition
m:n relationship
normalization
possible *number* of
   entity relationships
possible *nature* of
   entity relationships
promoted relationship
trigger

2. Compare data flow diagrams from Chapter 7 to process data flow diagrams in this chapter. List five similarities and five differences between them.
3. Find a small company and develop an entity-relationship diagram of their data. For each

entity, develop an attribute list and normalize the data. Discuss the problems you have in developing the answer with your class.

4. What is a 'promoted relationship' in an ERD and what is the result of the promotion?

5. Normalization assumes that you know the relationships of data within and between entities. What happens if you do not have the data relationships correctly specified in normalization?

6. What does normalization, as performed during analysis, define? What does it *not* define?

7. What is the purpose of an entity/process matrix?

8. Describe the analysis of an entity/process matrix.

9. What is the significance of subject area databases? What do subject area databases have in common with normalization?

10. What is the importance of an organizational ERD? What problems might arise when you begin the ERD definition for an application during the business area analysis?

11. Describe the relationships between the diagrams developed throughout IE-BAA. That is, how is each diagram used in the creation of successor diagrams?

12. What is the purpose of functional decomposition?

13. What are the three conditions under which you cannot eliminate an entity?

14. On a process dependency diagram, what is the significance of directed lines connecting two processes? Does this meaning change when the processes are connected on a PDFD? If so, how?

15. When should printed items be included on a PDFD?

16. What is a functional decomposition in IE? Define the diagram and the contents at each level of detail. How do you know when the decomposition is complete, i.e., when to stop?

17. What are the steps to developing a PDFD?

18. Define the allowable inputs to a process on a PDFD.

19. What is a CRUD matrix? How is it used?

20. What are the allowable connections on a process dependency diagram?

21. What are the allowable connections on a process data flow diagram?

22. List four problems and their solutions when developing a PDFD.

★ EXTRA-CREDIT QUESTIONS

1. Develop an IE analysis for the accounting (or purchasing) function at ABC Video. Refer to other books to obtain details about accounting applications. One such book is *Online Business Computer Applications*, 3rd edition, Alan L. Eliason, NY: MacMillan, 1991.

2. Compare IE to process analysis. What are the similarities? What are the differences? How are the same terms used differently? Which method has the least ambiguity? Which method results in a more complete analysis?

3. Do an entity-relationship diagram for the AOS Tracking System problem in the Appendix. Normalize the data. Compile a list of issues for future resolution dealing with the data. The issues should relate to how many relations are needed, how the data will be used, and how to minimize the number of relations without having many unused attributes in each relation.

4. Do a process decomposition diagram and a PDFD for the AOS Tracking System described in the Appendix.

5. What do you *not* know after BAA is complete?

CHAPTER **10**

DATA-
ORIENTED
DESIGN

INTRODUCTION

Data-oriented design uses data as the basis for clustering processes, building databases, and identifying potential distribution of the application. In this chapter, we continue the discussion of Information Engineering as the example of data-oriented methodology. Since IE has several 'incarnations' that differ slightly, it is important to note that IE in this chapter is consistent with the Martin [1992], Texas Instruments [1988], and Knowledgeware™[1] versions.

CONCEPTUAL FOUNDATIONS

Information Engineering is the closest to a complete methodology of the methods in common use. It borrows from research and practice to build a complete view of the application and its environment. Structured programming tenets describe the importance of limiting program structure, as much as possible, to selection, iteration, and instruction sequence components. 'Go to' statements should be minimized. Modules should have one entry and one exit. In IE

design, these tenets are practiced in structuring the application as well as the program modules.

Subject area database design is based on theories of relational database and practice of data design. Data should be clustered with processes which create the data. Those processes determine 'subject areas' of data. Subject databases are stored in the same database environment and their processes are in integrated applications. These topics were discussed in Chapter 5 and are not repeated here. During analysis, the data entities are normalized and relations are identified (Chapter 9). Normalized data is the starting point for physical database design. Physical database design may automate the normalized relations directly or may denormalize for performance purposes. Also, in organizations with many using locations and potential for distribution of data and processes, a strategy for distribution is defined. These two activities, potential denormalization and distribution, are based on practical guidelines rather than theory.

From practice, we know that there is more to implementing an application than designing program specifications and a database. We need to design screens, a screen dialogue, provide for unauthorized and unwanted damage to the data, provide for conversion from the old to the new method of data storage, design and plan application implementation, install hardware, design and plan application tests,

---

1 Knowledgeware™ is a product of Knowledgeware, Inc., Atlanta, Ga.

and develop training programs for users. While all of these tasks are discussed in some books on IE, these activities are done regardless of methodology, and to discuss them as pertaining only to IE would be misleading. For this reason, the topics in this chapter include screen dialogue design, hardware planning, and providing for data security, recovery, and audit controls, in addition to procedure and database design. Human interface design, conversion, and training are discussed in Chapter 14; testing is the subject of Chapter 17.

DEFINITION OF INFORMATION ENGINEERING DESIGN TERMS

A full list of the activities in IE design is given here; included are references to chapters in which some topics are discussed.

1. Design security, recoverability, and audit controls
2. Design human interface structure

   ■ Develop menu structure
   ■ Define screen dialogue flow

3. Data analysis

   ■ Reconfirm subject area database definition
   ■ Denormalize to create physical database design
   ■ Conduct distribution analysis and recommend production data distribution strategy

4. Develop an action diagram and conduct reusability analysis
5. Plan hardware and software installation and testing
6. Design conversion from the old to the new method of data storage (Chapter 14)
7. Design and plan application tests (Chapter 17)
8. Design and plan implementation (Chapter 14)

9. Develop, schedule, and conduct training programs for users (Chapter 14)

The topics in this chapter are design of data usage, action diagrams (which are program specs), screen dialogues, security, recovery, audit controls, and installation planning. They are discussed in this section in the order above, by the amount of work involved, and their importance to the application.

The first activity in IE design is to confirm design of the database and determine the optimal data location. Invariably, when the details of processing are mapped to specifications, data usage changes from that originally envisioned. To confirm database design, the data is mapped to application processes in an entity/process (CRUD) matrix and the matrix is reanalyzed. (See Chapter 9 for a more complete discussion of entity/process matrices.) The entity/process matrix (see Figure 10-1) clusters data together based on processes with data creation authority. The subject area databases defined by the clusters are stored in the same database environment.

The second step of database design is to determine a need to denormalize the data. Recall that **normalization** is the process of removing anomalies that would cause unwanted data corruption. **Denormalizing** is the process of designing storage items of data to achieve performance efficiency (see Figure 10-2). Having normalized the data, you know where the anomalies are and can design measures to prevent the problems.

The next activity in data analysis is to determine the location of data when choices are present. A series of objective matrices are developed and analyzed. The matrices identify process by location and data by location and transaction volume. These are used to develop potential designs for distribution of data. The application processes and data are both mapped to locations. Cells of the **process/location matrix** contain responsibility information, identifying locations with major and minor involvement (see Figure 10-3). This information is used to determine which software would also be required to be distributed, if distribution is selected.

Two data/location matrices are developed. The first data/location matrix identifies data function as either update (i.e., add, change, or delete) or retrieval

Definition of Information Engineering Design Terms **393**

Entities = Processes	Purchase Order	PO Item	Vendor-Item	Inventory Item	Vendor
Create & Mail Order	CRUD	CRUD	CRU	R	R
Call Vendor & Inquire on Order	RU	RU	RU	R	R
Verify Receipts against Order	RU	RU	RU		R
Send Invoices to Accountant	RD	RD			
File Order Copy by Vendor	R	R			
Identify Late & Problem Orders	R	R	R	R	RU
Identify Items & Vendors			R	R	CRU
Call Vendor to Verify Avail/Price			RU		RU

FIGURE 10-1   Example of Entity/Process Matrix

by location (see Figure 10-4a). The second defines options for data in each location (Figure 10-4b). Together these matrices identify options for distributing data. The options for distributed data are replication, partitioning, subset partitioning, or federation (see Figure 10-5). **Replication** is the copying of the entire database in two or more locations. **Vertical partitioning** is the storage of all data for a subset of the tuples (or records) of a database. **Subset partitioning** is the storage of a partial set of attributes for the entire database. **Federation** is the storage of different types of data in each location, some of which might be accessible to network users. The selection of distribution type is determined by the usage of data at each location.

Then, a **transaction volume matrix** is developed to identify volume of transaction traffic by location. Cells of this matrix contain average number of transactions for each data relation/process per day (see Figure 10-6). In an active application, hourly or peak activity period estimates of volume might be provided. During matrix analysis, the data and processes are clustered to minimize transmission traffic. Then formulae are applied to the information to determine whether the traffic warrants further consideration of distribution.

Finally, subjective reasons for centralizing or for distributing the application are developed. The subjective arguments ensure that political, organizational, and nonobjective issues are identified and considered. Examples of subjective motivations for centralization/distribution relating to Figures 10-4, 10-5, and 10-6 are in Table 10-1. Recommendations on what, how, and why to distribute (or centralize) data are then developed from the matrices and subjective analysis. The recommendations and reasoning are presented to user and IS managers to accept or modify.

After data are designed, the design of the human interface can begin with a definition of interface requirements. The hierarchy diagram is used to determine the structure of selections needed by the application. A **menu structure** is a structured diagram translating process alternatives into a hierarchy

Unnormalized	First Normal Form	Second Normal Form	Third Normal Form	DeRelation
Order Number	Order Number		Order Number	Order
Order Date	Order Date		Order Date	
Order Ship Terms	Order Ship Terms		Order Ship Terms	
Order Payment	Order Payment		Order Payment	
Terms	Terms	⟶	Terms	
Customer Number	Customer Number		Customer Number	
Customer Name	Customer Name			
Customer Address	Customer Address			Customer
			Customer Number	
			Customer Name	
*Item Number			Customer Address	
Item Description				
Item Quantity	Order Number	Order Number		Order Item
Item Price	Item Number	Item Number		
Item Extended Price	Item Description	Item Description	⟶	
	Item Quantity	Item Quantity		
	Item Price	Item Extended Price		X
	Item Extended Price			
		Item Number	⟶	Inv. Item
		Description		
		Price		

Denormalized Design for Order

ORDER	Order Number
	Order Date
	Order Ship Terms
	Order Payment Terms
	Customer Number
	Customer Name
	Customer Address
Order Item	Order Number
	Item Number
	Customer Number
	Customer Name
	Item Description
	Item Quantity
	Item Price
	Item Extended Price

FIGURE 10-2   Example of Denormalized Data for an Order

Function	Location A	Location B	Location C	Location D	Location E
Purchasing	\	X			
Marketing	X	X	\		
Customer Service		X	\		
Sales	X	X	\		
Product Development	X	X	\	\	
Research & Dev.			X	X	\
Manufacturing				\	X

Legend:

X—Major Involvement

\—Minor Involvement

FIGURE 10-3   Example of Process/Location Matrix

of options for the automated application (see Figure 10-7). In general, we plan one menu entry for each process hierarchy diagram entry between the top and bottom levels. One level of menus corresponds to one level in the process hierarchy diagram. At the lowest level of the process hierarchy, a process corresponds to either a program or module. Screens at the lowest level are determined by estimating execute units. These functional screens may not be final in menu structure definition because execute

Data Usage by Location Matrix

Subject Data	Location A	Location B	Location C	Location D	Location E
Prospects	All—UR	All—UR			
Customer	All—UR	All—UR			
Customer Orders	All—UR	Subset—Own Products—UR		All—R	All—R
Customer Order History	All—R	All—R	All—R	All—R	
Manufacturing Plans	Subset— own products—R	Subset— own products—R		Subset— own site—UR	All—UR
Manufacturing Goods in Process	Subset— own products—R	Subset— own products—R		Subset— own site—UR	All—UR
Manufacturing Inventory	Subset— own products—R	Subset— own products—R	All—R	Subset— own site—UR	All—UR

U = Update, R = Retrieve

FIGURE 10-4a   Example of Data Matrices by Location

Distribution Alternatives by Location

Subject Data	Location A	Location B	Location C	Location D	Location E
Prospects	Replicate—Central Copy	Replicate			
Customer	Replicate—Central Copy	Replicate			
Customer Orders	Central Copy—A data	Vertical Partition by Product		Access central copy with delay	Access central copy with delay
Customer Order History	Replicate Central Copy	Replicate or access central copy with delay		Access central copy with delay	
Manufacturing Plans	Replicate or access central copies with delay	Replicate or access central copies with delay		Subset—own site	Subset—own site with delayed access to D
Manufacturing Goods in Process	Access D and E Databases	Access D and E Databases		Subset—own site	Subset—own site with delayed access to D
Manufacturing Inventory	Access D and E Databases	Access D and E Databases		Subset—own site	Subset—own site with delayed access to D

FIGURE 10-4b   Example of Data Matrices by Location

unit design is usually a later activity. Once the menu structure is defined, it is given to the human interface designer(s) for use during screen design (Chapter 14).

The structure is then analyzed further to determine the allowable movement between the options on the menu structure. The **dialogue flow diagram** documents allowable movement between entries on the menu structure diagram (see Figure 10-8). On the diagram, rows correspond to screens and columns correspond to allowable movements. For instance, in the menu structure example (Figure 10-7), *Customer Maintenance* has four subprocesses. A dialogue flow diagram shows how *Customer Maintenance* is activated from the main menu (or elsewhere) and the

options for movement from that level. From the *Customer Maintenance* menu, the options are to move to the main menu or to one of the four subprocesses. The dialogue flow diagram is used by the designers in developing program specifications, by the human interface designer(s) in defining screens, and by testers in developing interactive test dialogues.

Next, procedure design begins with analysis of the process hierarchy and process data flow diagrams developed during IE analysis (Chapter 9). Remember, in analysis, we developed one process data flow diagram (PDFD) for each activity. Now each PDFD is converted into an action diagram. An **action diagram** shows procedural structure and processing details suitable for automated code genera-

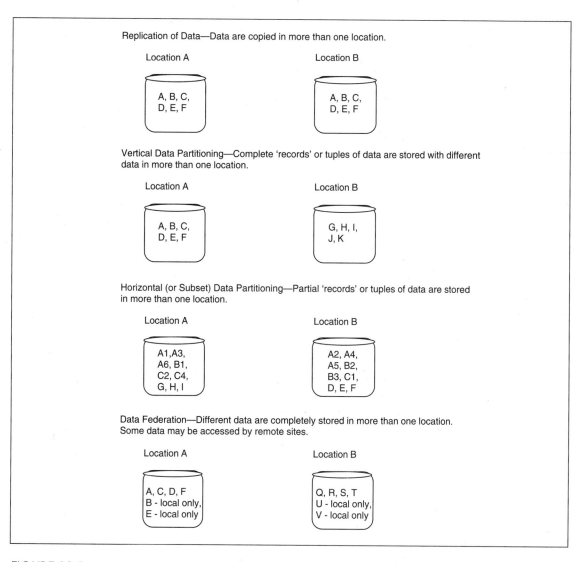

Replication of Data—Data are copied in more than one location.

Location A   Location B

A, B, C,   A, B, C,
D, E, F   D, E, F

Vertical Data Partitioning—Complete 'records' or tuples of data are stored with different data in more than one location.

Location A   Location B

A, B, C,   G, H, I,
D, E, F   J, K

Horizontal (or Subset) Data Partitioning—Partial 'records' or tuples of data are stored in more than one location.

Location A   Location B

A1, A3,   A2, A4,
A6, B1,   A5, B2,
C2, C4,   B3, C1,
G, H, I   D, E, F

Data Federation—Different data are completely stored in more than one location. Some data may be accessed by remote sites.

Location A   Location B

A, C, D, F   Q, R, S, T
B - local only,   U - local only,
E - local only   V - local only

FIGURE 10-5   Data Distribution Alternatives

tion. An action diagram is drawn with different types of bracket structures to show the hierarchy, relationships, and structured code components of all processes.

The first-cut action diagram translates the PDFD into gross procedural structures (see Figure 10-9). Then, using detailed knowledge obtained during the information gathering process, the details of each procedure are added to the diagram to develop program specifications (see Figure 10-10). These pro-

gram specifications may then be packaged into modules that perform one function. Data entities are added to the diagram at the level they are accessed (see Figure 10-11). Progressively more detail about data usage is provided about data attributes. Arrows are attached to show reading and writing of data (see Figure 10-12).

When the details are completely specified, the action diagram is mapped to procedural templates to determine the extent to which reusable modules

Location/Function	Subject Database						
	Prospect	Customer	Customer Order	Customer History	Mftg. Plan	Mftg. WIP	Mftg. Inven.
A							
Customer Service		100 R 20 U	250 R 400 U	5 R	2 R	2 R	
Sales	50 R 20 U	50 R 30 U	150 R 50 U	50 R	2 R	2 R	15 R
Marketing	15 R	5 R	10 R	50 R	2 R		1 R
B							
Customer Service		250 R 50 U	250 R 400 U	50 R	250 R	250 R	250 R
Sales	25 R 20 U	25 R 5 U	10 R 100 U	70 R	2 R	2 R	15 R
Marketing	20 R	10 R	10 R	50 R		2 R	5 R
D							
Manufacturing					50 R 5 U	50 R 250 U	500 R 2,000 U
E							
Manufacturing					100 R 15 U	200 R 2,500 U	500 R 25,000 U

Legend: U = Create, Update or Delete; R = Retrieve

FIGURE 10-6   Example of Transaction Volume Matrix

can be used in the application, and the changes to the action diagrams required to define modules for reuse. A **procedural template** is a general, fill-in-the-blanks guide for completing a frequently performed process. For instance, error processing and screen processing can be defined as reusable templates (see Figure 10-13). A data template is a partial definition of an ERD or database that is consistent within a user community. For example, the insurance industry has common data requirements for policy holders, third party insurance carriers, and policy information; most companies have similar accounting data needs, and so on. To be a **candidate for template** definition, a process must do exactly the same actions whenever it is invoked, and data must be consistent across users.

After reusability analysis, the action diagram set is finalized and used to generate code. If the appli-cation is specified manually, the action diagrams are given as program specifications to programmers who begin coding. If the application uses a CASE tool, automatic code generation is possible. A **code generator** is a program that reads specifications and creates code in some target language, such as Cobol or C. If the application uses a code generator, the action diagram contains the symbols and procedural detail specific to the code generation software. If the application uses a 4GL, the action diagram might contain actual code. If manual programming uses a 3GL or lower, the action diagram contains pseudo-code consisting of structured programming constructs.

The next activity in IE design is to develop security plans, recovery procedures, and audit controls for the application. Each of these designs restrict the application to performing its activities in prescribed ways. The goal of **security plans** is to

TABLE 10-1   Example of Subjective Reasons for Centralization and Distribution

General Measure—Argument	
D	Geographic distribution by function by product makes centralization difficult
D	Centralized mainframe in a sixth location is not close to distributed sites, nor interested in serving their needs
d	Little product overlap between sites A and B

Location A Measure—Argument	
d	General Manager in Location A—smallest needs
d	GM wants 'what is best' for division
C	Little technical expertise in the location; would increase travel expense required to support hardware/software

Location B Measure—Argument	
C	Customer service needs fast response to fulfill corporate objectives (90% of requests serviced within one phone call, less than three minutes)
C	Most application expertise in division is located here
C	IS manager, located here, wants the applications and data under his control

Location C Measure—Argument	
d	Actions mostly independent of other sites
d	Delays in retrieval of information could be tolerated

Location D Measure—Argument	
d	Historically, location controls its own hardware/software
d	Hardware/software not currently compatible with A, B, or C

Location E Measure—Argument	
d	Historically, location controls its own hardware/software
d	Historically, software has been successfully developed/bought as joint activity with IS group in Site B

Legend:
D/C = Strong argument for *D*istribution/*C*entralization
d/c = Weak argument for *d*istribution/*c*entralization

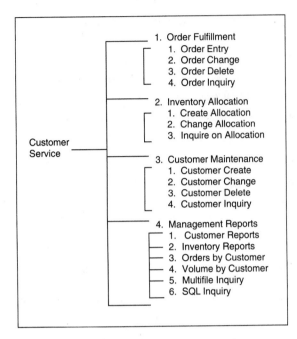

FIGURE 10-7   Menu Structure Example

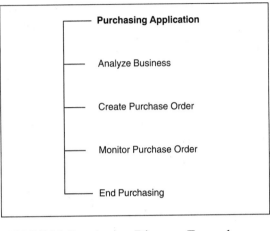

FIGURE 10-9   Action Diagram Example

protect corporate IT assets against corruption, illegal or unwanted access, damage, or theft. Security plans can address physical plant, data, or application assets, all by restricting access in some way. **Physical security** deals with access to computers, LAN servers, PCs, disk drives, cables, and other compo-nents of the network tying computer devices to-gether. **Data security** restricts access to and func-tions against data (e.g., read, write, or read/write). **Application security** restricts program code from access and modification by unauthorized users. Examples of the results of security precautions are locking of equipment, requirement of user pass-words, or assignment of a software librarian for pro-gram changes.

Recovery procedures define the method of restoring prior versions of a database or application software after a problem has destroyed some or all of

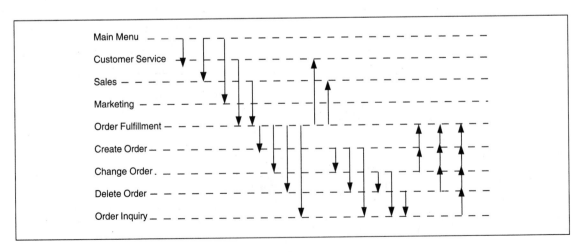

FIGURE 10-8   Dialogue Flow Diagram Example

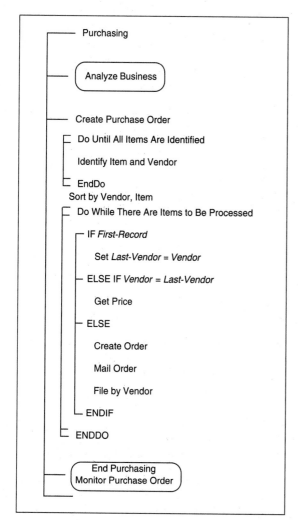

FIGURE 10-10   Action Diagram with Create Purchase Order Process Detail

it. Recovery is from a copy of the item. **Backup** is the process of making extra copies of data to ensure recoverability. Disasters considered in the plan include user error, hacker change, software failure, DBMS failure, hardware failure, and location failure. **Recovery** is the process of restoring a previous version of data (or software) from a backup copy to active use following some damage to, or loss of, the previously active copy. The backup/recovery strategy should be designed to provide for the six types of errors above. Several backup options add require-

ments to program design that need to be accommodated.

Next, **audit controls** are designed to prove transaction processing in compliance with legal, fiduciary, or stakeholder responsibilities. Audit controls usually entail the recording of day, time, person, and function for all access and modification to data in the application. In addition, special totals, transaction traces, or other special requirements might be applied to provide process audit controls.

Last, hardware installation is planned and implemented, if required for the application. Again, there is no theory or research about hardware installation, but long practice has given us guidelines on the activities and their timing.

INFORMATION ENGINEERING DESIGN

In this section, we discuss each activity in IE design in detail, and relate them to the ABC Video rental application. IE design topics in this section, in order of their occurrence in the application development process, include development of the following:

- data use and distribution analysis
- security, recovery, and audit controls
- action diagrams
- menu structure and dialogue flow
- hardware and software installation and testing plans

Analyze Data Use and Distribution

Guidelines for Data Use and Distribution Analysis

The two activities in this section precede physical database design which is assumed to be performed by a DBA. First, data usage analysis is performed to confirm the logical database design. Then the potential for distributing data throughout the organization is analyzed. The result is a strategy

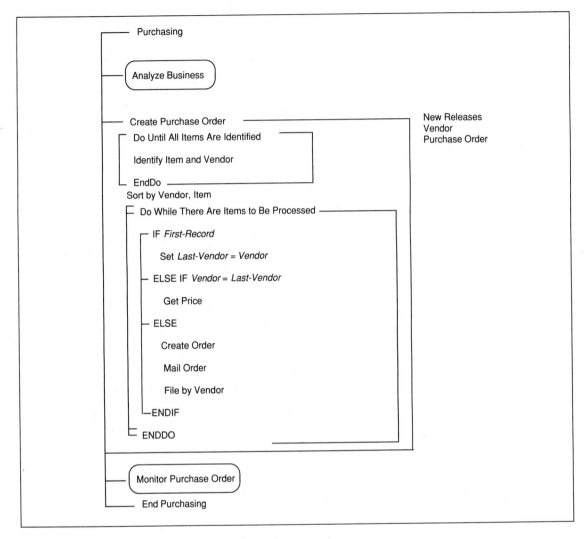

FIGURE 10-11   Action Diagram with Entities

for data and software location that best fits user needs.

The entity/process (CRUD) matrix from IE analysis is reanalyzed and mapped to the completed action diagram. Each process is identified on the action diagram with its associated data items and the related entity. Recall that the clustering of entities and processes on the matrix is primarily based on which processes have create responsibility for the data. The entities and processes are arranged into a

new entity/process matrix which is compared to the one developed during analysis. If the definition of subject area databases does not change, the distribution analysis can begin. If the definition of subject area databases does change, the logical definition of the databases is redone as discussed in Chapter 9.

The second step to data analysis is to determine the potential for data distribution. Distribution analysis uses three matrices as the objective basis for determining whether data should be distributed.

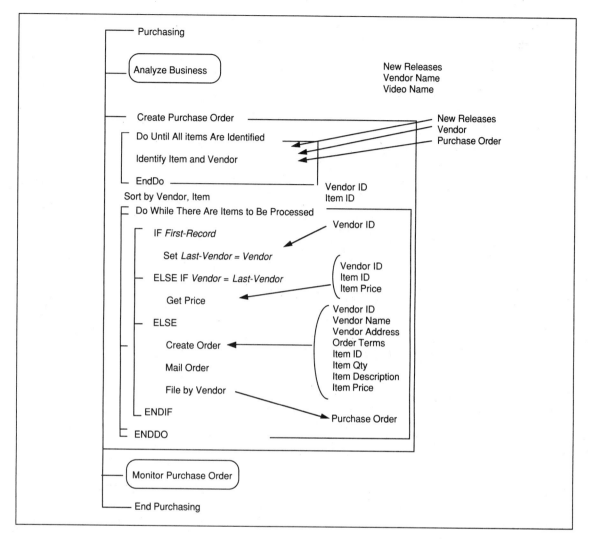

FIGURE 10-12   Action Diagram with Data Detail

First, a location/process matrix is developed to identify major and minor performance of processes in the application (see Figure 10-14). This location/process matrix determines which software is needed at each location to support the functions. The information needed to complete the matrix is provided by the users.

Next, a **data distribution by location matrix** is developed to show creation and retrieval needs by location (see Figure 10-15). This data/location matrix is used to determine the potential *age* of data required by each location. For instance, retrieval data might be down-loaded from a centralized location each day at the close of business, rather than maintained at the remote sites. Created data must be available for creation, and therefore, up-to-date at the creating sites. The information needed to complete the matrix is provided partly from the entity/process matrix from the first data analysis, and partly by the users.

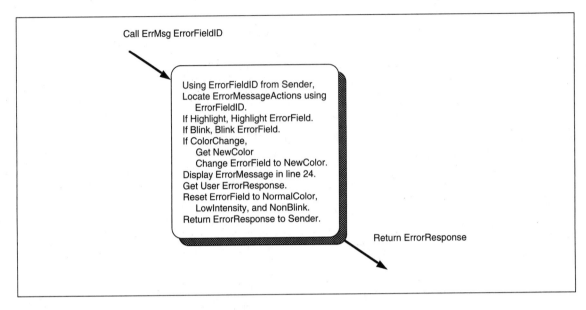

Call ErrMsg ErrorFieldID

Using ErrorFieldID from Sender,
Locate ErrorMessageActions using
    ErrorFieldID.
If Highlight, Highlight ErrorField.
If Blink, Blink ErrorField.
If ColorChange,
    Get NewColor
    Change ErrorField to NewColor.
Display ErrorMessage in line 24.
Get User ErrorResponse.
Reset ErrorField to NormalColor,
    LowIntensity, and NonBlink.
Return ErrorResponse to Sender.

Return ErrorResponse

FIGURE 10-13   Procedure Template for Error Message Processing

The next matrix shows **data usage by location** (see Figure 10-16). Recall from above that data can be centralized, vertically or horizontally partitioned, or federated. For instance, a bank branch might create data about customers, but it only accesses information about its own customers on a regular basis. So, for most processing, a vertical partition of the customer database, the branch's customers, could be accessible locally in the branch to speed processing.

The last objective matrix summarizes transaction volume by process by location (from the process/

Function	Location A	Location B	Location C	Location D	Location E
Purchasing	\	X			
Marketing	X	X	\		
Customer Service		X	\		
Sales	X	X	\		
Product Development	X	X	\	\	
Research & Dev.			X	X	\
Manufacturing				\	X

Legend:

X—Major Involvement

\—Minor Involvement

FIGURE 10-14   Process by Location Matrix Example

Subject Data	Location A	Location B	Location C	Location D	Location E
Prospects	All—UR	All—UR			
Customer	All—UR	All—UR			
Customer Orders	All—UR	Subset—Own Products—UR		All—R	All—R
Customer Order History	All—R	All—R	All—R	All—R	
Manufacturing Plans	Subset— own products—R	Subset— own products—R		Subset— own site—UR	All—UR
Manufacturing Goods in Process	Subset— own products—R	Subset— own products—R		Subset— own site—UR	All—UR
Manufacturing Inventory	Subset— own products—R	Subset— own products—R	All—R	Subset— own site—UR	All—UR

U = Update, R = Retrieve

FIGURE 10-15   Data Usage by Location Matrix Example

location table) against each subject database from the data analysis. Two daily transaction volume estimates for each process and location are developed (see Figure 10-17). The first estimate is for transactions that create or update the database. The second estimate is for read-only retrieval processing. Also notice that if no database access is performed by a process, no entry is made. This increases the readability of each matrix.

The analysis of this data is to first identify the location with the highest total transaction count for each database. The example shows a thick box around each such location (see Figure 10-18). If the application were distributed, with centralization of subject databases in one location, the boxes would identify the most likely location for each database. All other transactions, outside the boxes, represent transmission traffic. When the transmission traffic is a high percentage of the total traffic, say over 40%, different types of replication, federation, and partitioning are tried. To analyze the data, first box the transaction numbers for the site(s) representing 50% or more of the total processing. If there is one site boxed in a column, that identifies a centralized database at the location corresponding to the box. We have two of these in the example (Figure 10-18)—

the Work in Process and Inventory databases at location E. The initial recommendation would be to centralize this data at E. Even though D's volume is significantly less than E's, the data usage table shows that each site accesses only its own data, so the option to vertically partition data and provide 'home ownership' could be used to support the business needs.

The other databases all have access competition from two sites (Figure 10-18). Two locations, A and B, have fairly even usage of the *Prospect* and *Customer*, *Customer Order*, and *Customer History* data. The options from the Data Usage table show that Replication would be the distributed recommendation since the sites both access all data. Customer History processing differs from the other databases in that it is all read-only and it has a much lower volume than the others. Therefore, it could be centralized at either site with an access delay at the other site for retrievals. This option might be chosen if there are hardware configuration differences that favor centralization.

Locations B and E compete for the *Manufacturing Plan* data (Figure 10-18). Location B only retrieves the data, while the location E volume of updates is low. The database could either be

Subject Data	Location A	Location B	Location C	Location D	Location E
Prospects	Replicate or Central Copy	Replicate			
Customer	Replicate or Central Copy	Replicate			
Customer Orders	Replicate or Central Copy	Horizontal Partition by Product		Access central copy with delay	Access central copy with delay
Customer Order History	Replicate or Central Copy	Replicate or access central copy with delay		Access central copy with delay	
Manufacturing Plans	Replicate or access central copies with delay	Replicate or access central copies with delay		Subset— own site	Central Copy or Subset— own site with delayed access to D
Manufacturing Goods in Process	Access D and E Databases	Access D and E Databases		Subset— own site	Subset— own site with delayed access to D
Manufacturing Inventory	Access D and E Databases	Access D and E Databases		Subset— own site	Subset— own site with delayed access to D

FIGURE 10-16   Data Distribution by Location Matrix

centralized at B to provide fast query access, with delayed access by E, or, if politics are involved, the data could be centralized at site E, the owner, with delayed retrieval by B.

The second part of the analysis is to compute the ratio of data retrieval transactions (D_R) to data update transactions (D_U). If the ratio is greater than one less than the number of locations (L) (or nodes in the network), distribution should be considered (see Table 10-2). In the example, the ratio clearly favors centralization of data (Table 10-2). Keep in mind that centralization here means that each database is stored at *one* location. It does not mean that the databases are all at the *same* location.

If a delay can be introduced for retrieval processing, then the ratio changes. It becomes much easier to argue for distribution. Distribution should be considered when *retrieval* volume is less than the ratio of locations to the delay (D). The delay is for update transactions which are now transmitted in bulk once per period to each other location. In the example, with even a 15-minute delay, the numbers overwhelmingly favor distribution. The rationale for these ratios is given in Table 10-3.

This discussion about distribution is important because it highlights an ethical problem in software engineering. The numbers can be made to argue for distribution regardless of transaction activity. If the transaction ratio of retrievals to updates is large, then the no-delay argument is more likely to favor distribution. If the retrieval to update ratio is less than one, the delay argument is likely to favor centralization.

As an ethical person, you are bound to tell the client about all computations and how the formulae can make either argument.

Last, a subjective list of reasons for and against centralization and distribution is developed for the organization. The exact topic headings for this list are tailored to the company and application environment.

Critical data should be managed centrally
Data is/is not critical to corporation/business unit
Most data can/cannot be stored locally/ centrally

Needs/does not need specific DBMS
Requires/does not require larger machine than local sites have
Data ownership is/is not an issue
Data replication needed in one/many locations
Unique data/application in one location
Data affects/does not affect central corporate management
Fast response time important/not important
High availability important/not important
Local staff skilled/unskilled with computers
Application/data security is/is not vital to organization/business unit
Centralized operations is/is not at capacity

Location/Function	Subject Database						
	Prospect	Customer	Customer Order	Customer History	Mftg. Plan	Mftg. WIP	Mftg. Inven.
A							
Customer Service		100 R 20 U	250 R 400 U	5 R	2 R	2 R	
Sales	50 R 20 U	50 R 30 U	150 R 50 U	50 R	2 R	2 R	15 R
Marketing	15 R	5 R	10 R	50 R	2 R		1 R
B							
Customer Service		250 R 50 U	250 R 400 U	50 R	250 R	250 R	250 R
Sales	25 R 20 U	25 R 5 U	10 R 100 U	70 R	2 R	2 R	15 R
Marketing	20 R	10 R	10 R	50 R		2 R	5 R
D							
Manufacturing					50 R 5 U	50 R 250 U	500 R 2,000 U
E							
Manufacturing					100 R 15 U	200 R 2,500 U	500 R 25,000 U

Legend:

U = Create, Update or Delete

R = Retrieve

FIGURE 10-17   Summary Transaction Volume Matrix

			Subject Database				
Location/Function	Prospect	Customer	Customer Order	Customer History	Mftg. Plan	Mftg. WIP	Mftg. Inven.
A							
Customer Service		100 R 20 U	250 R 400 U	5 R	2 R	2 R	
Sales	50 R 20 U	50 R 30 U	150 R 50 U	50 R	2 R	2 R	15 R
Marketing	15 R	5 R	10 R	50 R	2 R		1 R
B							
Customer Service		250 R 50 U	250 R 400 U	50 R	250 R	250 R	250 R
Sales	25 R 20 U	25 R 5 U	10 R 100 U	70 R	2 R	2 R	15 R
Marketing	20 R	10 R	10 R	50 R		2 R	5 R
D							
Manufacturing					50 R 5 U	50 R 250 U	500 R 2,000 U
E							
Manufacturing					100 R 15 U	200 R 2,500 U	500 R 25,000 U

Legend:

U = Create, Update, or Delete

R = Retrieve

FIGURE 10-18   Analysis of Summary Transaction Volume Matrix

Down-loading of yesterday's data would/would not work in local sites

Updates with delay would/would not work in this application environment

Partitioning of data would/would not work in supporting this application

Replication of data would/would not work in supporting this application

Data integrity is/is not paramount to the application

Disaster recovery protection is/is not vital to the application

Operators are/are not at remote sites

Each reason is rated as weak or strong justification of its position. The purpose of list creation is to surface and attempt to objectify objections and arguments from each stakeholder viewpoint regarding distribution of data in the application. An easy analysis is to count the capital and small letters of each type, and compare them. A more elaborate analysis might entail giving a weight to each item and developing a weighted ranking of the central/distributed positions. If the results of this analysis support the objective measures and results, a compelling justification for the result can be developed and presented to user management for approval. If the subjective

TABLE 10-2   Distribution Ratio Formulae

The breakeven point for distribution occurs when

$$D_R/D_U > N - 1.$$

If the transaction ratio is greater than $N - 1$, distribute data.

An alternative is to allow a time delay for update transactions with all data replicated at all locations in a network. Then only updates generate network traffic. The breakeven point for distribution occurs with this scenario when

$$D_U < N/\text{TimeDelay} \quad \text{or} \quad D_U * \text{TimeDelay} < N$$

If the number of changes is less than the number of nodes divided by the time delay, distribution is favored.

Legend:

D_R = Number of data retrieval transactions

D_U = Number of data update transactions

N = Number of network nodes

D = Total number of data transactions ($D_R + D_U$)

Adapted from Martin (1990), p. 360.

analysis contradicts the objective measures, the user manager/champion might have to do some political maneuvering to obtain the desired result. Of course, if the champion is against the recommendation, the numbers in the traffic table still are useful in determining the size and speed of the machine and telecommunications lines required to service the application's data needs.

ABC Video Example Data Use Distribution and Analysis

ABC's one location simplifies the choices for this analysis. Centralization of data and processes is the only possible choice. For the record, a table of transaction volumes is presented in Figure 10-19.

A secondary issue, if not already decided, is hardware selection. ABC could use a multiuser mini-computer or a LAN. This analysis, too, is simple because ABC is a small company without a high volume of processing. A LAN is cheaper, more easily

maintained, more easily staffed, and less costly for incremental upgrades. Therefore, a LAN is the choice. Most multiuser mini-computers allow eight units without major expenditures for an additional I/O controller board. Mini-computers tend to have proprietary operating systems and use packages that tie the user to a given vendor. The strength of

TABLE 10-3   Rationale for Distribution Ratios

If T is the number of traffic units per hour (i.e., transactions), and if all data is centralized at one location (not necessarily the same), then the total traffic units per hours is

$$T_{\text{centralized}} = (D_R + D_U) * (N - 1)/N$$

Then, if all data is decentralized (i.e., fully replicated at all user locations), only update transactions generate network traffic, and

$$T_{\text{distributed}} = D_U * (N - 1)$$

Fully replicated, decentralized data generates less traffic than centralization if

$$T_{\text{centralized}} > T_{\text{distributed}}, \text{ or}$$

$$(D_R + D_U) * (N - 1)/N > D_U * (N - 1)$$

This reduces to $D_R / D_U > N - 1$. This formula means that when the ratio of retrievals to changes ($D_R / D_U = N - 1$) is greater than $N - 1$, favor distribution. When the ratio is equal to $N - 1$, either choice is acceptable from a network point of view. When the ratio is less than $N - 1$, favor centralization.

If changes can be applied with a delay, the equations change. Then the breakeven point occurs when

$$D_R < N/\text{TimeDelay}$$

The greater the delay, the more desirable a distributed strategy can be made to appear.

Legend:

D_R = Number of data retrieval transactions

D_U = Number of data update transactions

N = Number of network nodes

D = Total number of data transactions ($D_R + D_U$)

Adapted from Martin (1990), pp. 360–361.

Location/Function	Subject Database						
	Customer	Video	Item	Customer History	Video History	EOD	Archive
Dunwoody Village Rent/Return	500 R 15 U	500 R 5 U	250 R 400 U	500 R 500 U	500 R 500 U		
Video Maintenance		20 R 5 U	150 R 50 U				
Customer Maintenance	5 R 5 U						
Other						15,000 U/ Once/Mo	1,000 U	15,000 U/ Once/Mo

FIGURE 10-19   ABC Transaction Volume Matrix

multiuser minis is in their added horsepower that allows them to support applications with a high volume of transactions (in the millions per day). A multiuser mini is not recommended here because, for the money, it would be analogous to buying a new Porsche 911 Targa when a used Hyundai would do just fine. To discuss configuration of the LAN, we move to the next section on hardware and software installation.

Define Security, Recovery, and Audit Controls

Guidelines for Security, Recovery, and Audit Control Planning

The three issues in this section—security, recovery, and controls—all are increasingly important in software engineering. The threat of data compromise from casual, illegal acts, such as viruses, are real and growing. These topics each address a different perspective of data integrity to provide a total solution for a given application. Security is preventive, recovery is curative, and controls prove the other two. Having one set of plans, say for security, without the other two is not sufficient to guard against compromise of data or programs. Trusting individuals' ethical senses to guide them in not hurting your company's applications simply ignores the reality of today's world. Morally, *not* having planned for attempts to compromise data and programs, you, the SE, are guilty of ethical passivity that implicitly warrants the compromiser's actions. Therefore, design of security, recovery, and controls should become an integral activity of the design of any application.

The major argument against security, recovery, and audit controls is cost, which factors in all decisions about these issues. The constant trade-off is between the probability of an event and the cost of minimizing its probability. With unlimited funds, most computer systems, wherever they are located, can be made reasonably secure. However, most companies do not have, nor do they want to spend, unlimited money on probabilities. The trade-off becomes one of proactive security and prevention versus reactive recovery and audit controls. Audit controls, if developed as part of analysis and design, have a minimal cost. Recoverability has on-going costs of making copies and of off-site storage. Each type of security has a cost associated with it. Keep the cost issues in mind during this discussion, and try to weigh how you might balance the three methods of providing for ABC's application integrity.

Security plans define guidelines for who should have access to what data and for what purpose. Access can be restricted to hardware, software, and data. There are few specific guidelines for limiting access since each application and its context are different. Those guidelines are listed here:

1. Determine the vulnerability of the physical facility to fire. Review combustibility of construction. Determine adjacent, overhead, and underfloor fire hazards. Determine the status of current fire detection devices, alarms, suppression equipment, emergency power switches, extinguishers, sprinklers, and smoke detectors. Determine the extent of fire-related training. If the facility is shared, evaluate the risk of fire from other tenants.

   Plan for fire prevention and minimize fire threats by using overhead sprinklers, CO_2, or halon. Develop fire drills and fire contingency plans. If no emergency fire plans exist, develop one, reviewing it with the local fire department, and practicing the procedures.

2. Consider electrical/power facilities. Review electrical routing and distribution of power. Review the means of measuring voltage and frequency on a steady-state or transient basis. Determine whether operators know how to measure electrical power and can determine both normal and abnormal states. Define electrical and power requirements for the new application hardware and software. Determine power sufficiency for the computing environment envisioned.

   Correct any deficiencies before any equipment is delivered. For instance, install a universal power supply (UPS) if warranted by frequent power fluctuations or other vulnerabilities.

3. Review air-conditioning systems and determine environmental monitoring and control mechanisms. Evaluate the 'housekeeping' functions of the maintenance staff.

   Correct any deficiencies before any equipment is delivered. For instance, make sure the maintenance staff cleans stairwells and closets, uses fireproof waste containers, and does not use chemicals near computer equipment.

4. Determine the capability of the facility to withstand natural hazards such as earthquakes, high winds, and storms. Evaluate the facility's water damage protection and the facility's bomb threat reaction procedures.

   Design the facility without external windows and with construction to withstand most threats. To minimize bomb and terrorist threats, remove identifying signs, place equipment in rooms without windows, and do not share facilities. To minimize possible storm damage, do not place the facility in a flood zone or on a fault line.

5. Evaluate external perimeter access controls in terms of varied requirements for different times of day, week, and year. Determine controls over incoming and outgoing materials. Evaluate access authorization rules, identification criteria, and physical access controls.

   Plan the security system to include perimeter lights, authorization cards, physical security access, etc. as required to minimize the potential from these threats. Establish procedures for accepting, shipping, and disposing of goods and materials. For instance, shred confidential reports before disposal. Only accept goods for which a purchase order is available.

6. Evaluate the reliability and potential damage from everyday use of terminals and remote equipment from unauthorized employees.

   Plan physical locking of equipment, backup copies of data, reports, etc. to minimize potential threats. Design remote equipment to minimize the threat of down-loaded data from the central database except by authorized users. Usually this is done by having PCs without any disk drives as terminal devices.

7. Evaluate the potential damage from unauthorized access to data and programs.

   Protect programs and data against unauthorized alteration and access.

8. Evaluate the potential damage to the database from unwitting errors of authorized employees.

   Design the application to minimize accidental errors and to be fault tolerant (i.e., recovers from any casual errors).

In general, we consider internal and external physical environment, plus adequacy of data and program access controls. Security evaluation is a common enough event in many organizations that checklists of items for security review are available.[3] An example of general topics in such checklists follows:

Physical Environment
    Fire fighting procedures
    Housekeeping and construction
    Emergency exits
    Portable fire extinguisher location and
       accessibility
    Smoke detectors located above, under, and in
       middle of floor areas
    Automatic fire suppression system
Electrical Power
    Power adequacy and monitoring
    Inspection, maintenance, safety
    Redundancy and backup
    Uninterruptible power supply
    Personnel training
Environment
    Air-conditioning and humidity control
       systems
    Lighting
    Monitoring and control
    Housekeeping
Computer Facility Protection
    Building construction and location
    Water damage exposure
    Protection from damage or tampering with
       building support facilities
    Building aperture protection
    Bomb threat and civil disorder

Physical Access
    Asset vulnerability
    Controls addressing accessibility
       Perimeter
       Building
       Sensitive offices
       Media storage
       Computer area
       Computer terminal equipment
       Computer and telecommunications
         cable

An example of a detailed checklist for building access is provided next.

Facility type: Mainframe, LAN, PC, RJE, Remote, Communications

1. Are entrances controlled by
   _____ locking devices
   _____ guard force
   _____ automated card-key system
   _____ anti-intrusion devices
   _____ sign-in/out logs
   _____ photo badge system
   _____ closed circuit TV
   _____ other _____
2. Are controls in effect 24 hours per day? If not, why?

   _____
3. Are unguarded doors
   _____ kept locked (Good)
   _____ key-controlled (Better with above)
   _____ alarmed (Best with both of above)
4. If guard force, is it
   _____ trained (Good)
   _____ exercised (Better)
   _____ armed
5. Are visitors required to
   _____ sign in and out
   _____ be escorted
   _____ wear distinctive badges
   _____ undergo package inspection
6. If building is shared, has security been
   _____ discussed (Good)
   _____ coordinated (Better)
   _____ formalized (Best)
7. Sensitive office areas, media storage, and computer areas

---

3 Two IBM-user organizations, GUIDE and SHARE, both have active disaster recovery and security control groups that issue guidelines, checklists, and tutorials on the topic.

_____ Does access authority for each area require management review?

Is access controlled by

_____ locking devices
_____ guard force
_____ automated card-key system
_____ anti-intrusion devices
_____ sign-in/out logs
_____ photo badge system
_____ closed circuit TV
_____ other _____
_____ Are unique badges required?
_____ Do employees challenge unidentified strangers?

8. Control Mechanisms

_____ Do signs designate control/restricted areas?

If locks are used

_____ is key issuance controlled?
_____ are keys changed periodically?

9. Administration

_____ Does management insist on strict adherence to access procedures?

Are individuals designated responsibility for

_____ access control at various control points
_____ authorizing visitor entry
_____ establishing and maintaining policy, procedures, and authorization lists
_____ compliance auditing
_____ follow-up on violations

The probability of total hardware and software loss is low in a normal environment. In fact, the probability of occurrence of a destructive event is inversely related to the magnitude of the event. That is, the threat from terrorist attack might be miniscule, but the damage from one might be total. Each type of threat should be considered and assigned a current probability of occurrence. High probability threats are used to define a plan to minimize the probability. If the company business is vulnerable to bomb threats, for instance, buildings without external glass and without company signs are more anonymous and less vulnerable. Having all facilities locked at all times, with a specific security system for authorizing employees and screening visitors, reduces vulnerability even further.

The major vulnerability is not related to the physical plant in most cases; it is from connections to computer networks. The only guaranteed security against telecommunications invasion is to have all computers as stand-alone or as a closed network with no outside access capability. As soon as _any_ computer, or network, allows external access, it is vulnerable to invasion. There are no exceptions, contrary to what the local press might have you believe. Data and program access security protection reduce the risk of a casual break-in to an application. Monitoring all accesses by date, time, and person further reduces the risk because it enables detection of intruders. Encrypting password files, data files, and program code files further reduces the risks; it also makes authorized user access more complex and takes valuable CPU cycles.

The most common security in an application is to protect against unwanted data and program access. Data access can be limited to an entire physical file, logical records, or even individual data items. Possible functions against data are read only, read/write, or write only. Users and IS developers consider each function and the data being manipulated to define classes of users and their allowable actions. Allowable actions are to create, update, delete, and retrieve data. A hierarchy of access rights is built to identify, by data item, which actions are allowed by which class of users. A scheme for implementing the access restrictions is designed for the application.

Backup and recovery go hand-in-hand to provide correction of errors because of security inadequacies. A backup is an extra copy of some or all of the data and software, made specifically to provide recovery in event of some disaster. Recovery is the process of restoring a previous version of data or application software to active use following some damage or loss of the previously active copy.

Research by IBM and others has shown that companies go out of business within six months of a disaster when no backup copies of computer data and programs are kept. In providing for major disasters, such as tornados, **off-site storage**, the storing of backup copies at a distant site, is an integral part of guaranteeing recoverability. Off-site storage is usually 200+ miles away from the computer site, far enough to minimize the possibility of the off-site facility also being damaged. Old salt mines and other clean, underground, environmentally stable facilities are frequently used for off-site storage.

The disasters of concern in recovery design are user error, unauthorized change of data, software bugs, DBMS failure, hardware failure, or loss of facility. All these problems compromise the integrity of the data. The most difficult aspect of recovery from the first three errors is error detection. If a data change is wrong but contains legal characters, such as $10,000 instead of $1,000 as a deposit, the only detection will come from audit controls. If a data change is wrong because it contains illegal characters, the application must be programmed to detect the error and allow the user to fix it. Some types of errors, such as alteration of a deposit to a bank account or alteration of a payment to a customer, should also have some special printout or supervisory approval required as part of the application design to assist the user in detecting problems and in monitoring the correction process. DBMS software frequently allows transaction logging, logging of before and after images of database changes and assisted recovery from the logs for *detected* errors.

DBMS failure should be detected by the DBMS and the bad transaction should automatically be 'rolled-back' to the original state. If a DBMS does not have a 'commit/roll-back' capability, it should not be used for any critical applications or applications that provide legal, fiduciary, or financial processing compliance. *Commit* management software monitors the execution of all database actions relating to a user transaction. If the database actions are all successful, the transaction is 'committed' and considered complete. If the database actions are not all successful, the commit manager issues a *roll-back* request which restores the database to its previous state before the transaction began, and the transaction is aborted. Without commit and roll-back capabilities, partial transactions might compromise database integrity.

Other data and software backup procedures are either full or incremental. A **full backup** is a copy of the entire database or software library. An **incremental backup** is a copy of only changed portions of the database or library. A week's worth of backups are maintained and rotated into reuse after, for example, the fifth day. To minimize the time and money allocated to backup, incremental procedures are most common. A full backup is taken once each week with incremental backups taken daily. An active database would be completely backed-up daily with one copy on-site for immediate use in event of a problem. Regardless of backup strategy, an extra copy of the database is created at least once a week for off-site storage.

The extensiveness of backup (and recoverability) is determined by assessing the risk of not having the data or software for different periods (see Table 10-4). The less the tolerance for loss of access, the more money and more elaborate the design of the backup procedures should be. The severity of lost access time varies, depending on the availability of human experts to do work manually and the criticality of the application. In general, the longer a work area has been automated, the less likely manual procedures can be used to replace an application, and the less time the application can be lost without

TABLE 10-4   Backup Design Guidelines for Different Periods of Loss

Length of Loss	Type of Backup
1 Week or longer	Weekly Full with Off-site storage
1 Day	Above + Daily Incremental/Full
1 Hour	Above + 1 or more types of DBMS Logging
15 Minutes or less	Above + All DBMS Logging Capabilities: Transaction, Pre-Update and Post-Update Logs

severe consequences. The less important an application is to the continuance of an organization as an on-going business, the less critical the application is for recovery design. An application for ordering food for a cafeteria, for instance, is not critical if the company is an oil company but is critical if the company is a restaurant.

To define backup requirements, then, you first define the criticality of the application to the organization, and the length of time before lost access becomes intolerable. Based on those estimates, a backup strategy is selected. If the delay until recovery can be a week or more, only weekly full backups with off-site storage are required. If the delay until recovery can be one day or less, then, in addition to weekly backups, daily backups should be done. If the recovery delay can be only an hour, the two previous methods should be supplemented with one or more types of DBMS logging scheme. Finally, if a 15-minute recovery delay is desired, all types of DBMS logging, plus daily and weekly backups should be done.

Last, we consider audit controls which provide a record of access and modification, and prove transaction processing for legal, fiduciary responsibility, or stakeholder responsibility reasons. Audit controls allow detection and correction of error conditions for data or processing. As new technologies, greater dependence on ITs, and interrelated systems that are vulnerable to telecommunications attacks all increase, business emphasis on controls also increases. In manual systems of work, control points are easily identified; procedures are observable, errors can be reconstructed, and controls applied by humans. In automated applications, the application *is* the solution, nothing is directly observable, and complexity of functions makes identification of control points increasingly complex.

A **control point** is a location (logical or physical) in a procedure (automated or manual) where the possibility of errors exists. Errors might be lack of proper authorization, misrecording of a transaction, illegal access to assets, or differences between actual and recorded data. Control points are identified during design because the entire application's requirements should be known in order to define the most

appropriate control points. Controls are specified by designers in the form of requirements for program validation. For instance, controls for the validity of expense checks might be as follows:

1. Only valid, preauthorized checks can be written.
2. Check amounts may not exceed authorized dollar amounts.
3. Checks may not exceed the expense report total amount.

Application audit controls address the completeness of data, accuracy of data, authorization of data, and adequacy of the audit trail. Detection of processing errors is either through edit and validation checks in programs, or through processing of redundant data. Examples of **controlled redundancy** of data include double entry bookkeeping, cross footing totals and numbers, dual departmental custody of replicated critical data, transaction numbering, and primary key verification. Edit and validation rules are designed to identify all logical inconsistencies as early in the process as possible, before they are entered into the database.

ABC Video Example Security, Backup/Recovery, and Audit Plans

To design ABC's security, we first review the physical plant and recommend changes to the planned computer site to provide security. The six threats are considered, but the byword from Vic in discussing the possibility of changes is "be reasonable." So, if there is a 'reasonable' chance that a problem will occur, we will recommend a reasonable, and low cost, solution to the problem.

Moving from most to least serious, we consider the six types of threats to application security: location failure, hardware failure, DBMS failure, software failure, hacker change, and user error. For each threat, we consider the potential of occurrence for ABC, then devise a plan to minimize the potential damage. All threats and responses are summarized in Figure 10-21.

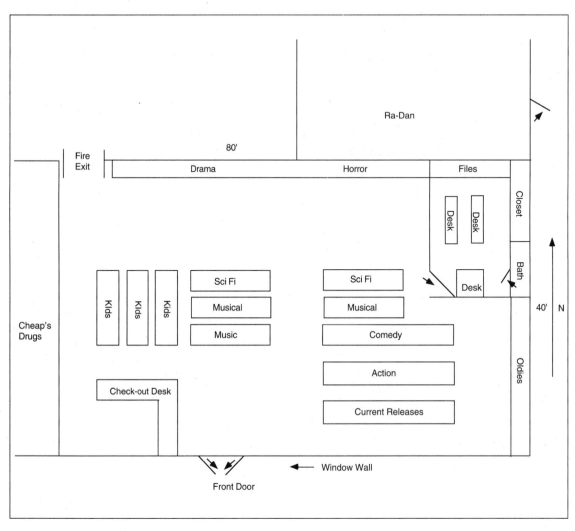

FIGURE 10-20   ABC Current Physical Plant

First, we review the physical plant and relate it to location and hardware failures. ABC Video is located in suburban Atlanta, Georgia, 300 miles from the ocean and 25 miles from the nearest large lake. The company is located in a mall, the Dunwoody Village, a clustering of small shops and offices in open-square buildings containing a plaza in the middle of the square. The company occupies 3200 square feet of 80' × 40' space in the southeast corner of Building A. The adjoining spaces are occupied by Cheap's Drugs and Ra-Dan Hair Salon. A schematic of the space is shown in Figure 10-20.

The northeast corner of the area (abutting Ra-Dan's) contains a 12' × 16' office which contains two desks, one supply closet, and a bathroom. The office has no windows and can be locked, although it is frequently empty and unlocked. The supply closet has double doors which do not currently have a lock.

The clerk's checkout counter is near the customer doors on the south side of the building in the western corner. The counter is an 'L' shape with the entry on the short side. A fire door, equipped with an alarm bar, is located in the northwest corner of the area and opens on a short alley behind the building.

Location failure usually results from violent weather, terrorist attacks, or government takeover. The chance of violent weather is the only potential major problem in the area. Tornadoes occur in the area regularly. The expectation is that there is a 20% chance of tornado damage some time in the next 10 years (see Figure 10-21). Tornadoes also imply strong thunderstorms which are common to the area. The chance of damage from a storm is about 30% within five years to the windows, and about 65% within two years for lightning to cause electrical spikes.

The response to location threats is to provide off-site backup of all information, with the site far enough away that it is unlikely to be affected by the same storm (see Figure 10-21). Vic should investigate the possibility of closing in the window wall in the southeast side of the building to minimize storm damage. He can also install lightning rods on the roof of the building to dissipate lightning when it hits.

The next category of problems relate to the hardware selected for the rental/return application. Vendor-cited reliability is 99 years mean time between failure (MTBF) for individual components. When the components are considered as a whole, the probability of component failure is once in two years (see Figure 10-21). The current plan is to have an extra PC in the office that could be moved to the front desk if needed. A hardware service contract with a local company to provide response within 24 hours is recommended.

The planned server location is near the bathroom in the northeast corner of the area. The toilet has a history of overflows during wet spring months. Because of the way the office was constructed, the water is confined to a small area but almost always runs into the supply closet and has been as high as one foot. The probability of component failure to file server and/or disks from water due to toilet overflow is 50% in two years. The answer to this problem is simple, but expensive: Build a new area, specifically for the computer, away from the toilet area to reduce this probability to near zero. Ideally, if the windows are closed in, the office could be moved to the front of the building and the old office removed. A new enclosure for the toilet facilities could be added or the toilet could also be rebuilt in the new location with whatever precautions are needed to preclude the spring overruns.

There is another problem with the planned server location. The planned location—the supply closet—has no ventilation. If the closet doors are open, ventilation for the office is sufficient for the planned equipment, but, ideally, the server closet doors should be locked. If the doors were locked, the probability of server failure due to lack of ventilation is 50% in two years. The solutions possible are to build a new area for the server equipment, or to add ventilation to the planned area to reduce this probability to near zero. Both solutions should be presented to Vic for his decision.

Less serious problems stem from the building location. Glass windows that run along 60' of external front wall and the drop ceiling are accessible from neighboring companies. Theft and break-ins are somewhat common in the area, but the probability of a break-in is 50% in 10 years. Most burglars are looking for money, but some might maliciously tamper with the computer equipment. Therefore, the probability of computer damage during a break-in is 60% according to police estimates.

The recommendations to minimize theft have to address the easy access to the company through windows and ceiling. If the office remains in its current location, a security system with movement sensors in the ceiling and glass-breakage sensors on all windows should be added (whether or not the computer is installed). Long-term, Vic should investigate the possibility of closing-in some or all windows to improve security of the company.

Next, because of the location of the checkout desk at the front of the building, the ability of clerks to monitor approaches to the office is low due to limited visibility. Further, theft of tapes is possible because clerks cannot see down all aisles without moving away from the desk area. For application security, we are concerned with office access; but, as professionals, we can make recommendations that will improve Vic's ability to reduce general theft as well. An easy, but somewhat expensive solution is to move the checkout desk to the center of the floor and assign surveillance duties to clerks. Even if the desk is not moved, mirrors installed in the corners of the

Finding	Recommendation
Location failure—Probability of tornadoes 10% in 10 years. Probability of strong storms causing damage to windows is about 15% within two years. Probability of lightning causing electrical spikes is 15% within two years.	Select off-site storage facility no closer than 200 miles. Investigate closing in the front windows, at least the contiguous 40 feet of windows on the southeast corner. Install lightning rods on the roof.
Hardware failure—Vendor-cited reliability is 99 years MTBF for each component. The probability of component failure is once in two years for some network component.	Move the extra PC in the office to the front desk if needed. A hardware service contract with a local company to provide response within 24 hours is recommended.
Hardware failure from external reasons—Planned server location is near bathroom with history of periodic overflows. Probability of component failure to file server and/or disk is 50% in two years.	Build a new area to reduce this probability to near zero.
Hardware failure from external reasons—Planned server location is a closet in the office area without any ventilation. Probability of server failure is 50% in two years.	Build a new area or add ventilation to the planned area to reduce this probability to near zero.
Hardware failure from external reasons—Current location has glass windows along 60' of external front wall and a drop ceiling accessible from neighboring companies. Probability of break-in is 30% in 10 years; probability of computer damage during a break-in is 60%.	If the office remains in its current location, add security system with movement sensors in the ceiling and glass-breakage sensors on all windows. Long-term, investigate the possibility of closing-in some or all windows, moving the office to the front of the building (away from plumbing).
Physical location vulnerabilities—Ability of clerks to monitor approaches to the office is low because of desk location and limited visibility.	Move the clerks' desk to the center of the floor and assign surveillance duties to clerks. Install mirrors in corners of room to allow monitoring of customers' actions.
DBMS failure—Vendor-stated reliability is two years MTBF. This is one of the best on the market, but each new release is unstable for at least six months.	Do not install latest releases until thoroughly tested using regression test package. Negotiate with vendor for data access software in event of DBMS failure. Include this software access in the vendor contract.
DBMS failure—Other reasons (e.g., electrical spike). Probability is 100% that electrical surges will occur, since they are common in the summer months.	Install a surge protector on the entire ABC electrical system to accommodate spikes (cost is about $100).
Probability of brownouts with reduced power are 30% in two years.	Install surge protectors on each individual outlet used by computer equipment to further protect the equipment since whole system protectors do not guarantee integrated chip safety in any devices. Install a limited, inexpensive, UPS to provide emergency power in event of electrical failure and for limited use during brownouts (cost about $1,000).

FIGURE 10-21   Security Review Findings and Recommendations

Finding	Recommendation
Software failure—Application failure due to software defects should be less than once in 15 years after the first three months. During the first three months of operation, the probability of application failure is about 75%; no more than one is expected.	The application is designed for 15-minute recovery of all data and programs. Loss of transactions in process will always occur with any failure; they will have to be reentered. Program problems will be fixed within one business day. Any lost transactions will be reentered free of charge by Software Engineers Unlimited.
Hacker change—Outside user access to the system should be zero since no telecommunications capabilities are planned. However, the untended server and occasional lack of clerks at the desk area may provide a local hacker enough time to access and modify the system.	Install security precautions listed above: security mirrors, move desk, assign clerks monitoring responsibility. *Always* lock office door; *always* lock file server door.
User error—The use of computer novices as clerks guarantees user error. Probability is 100% within one week of system operation.	Restrict data and process access to those required to perform each job. Design application to withstand any casual error—hitting any key on keyboard, scanning any bar code type, etc. A report of such errors can be created and printed on demand by Vic to allow retraining (or other action) for repeated errors by one user. Application design also includes validation of all fields such that only valid data can be in the database. On-demand reports of new customer and video entries will allow Vic to monitor the typing skills of employees. New-hire orientation and new-hire mentors should be used to stress the importance of data accuracy.

FIGURE 10-21   Security Review Findings and Recommendations (*Continued*)

room would allow clerks to monitor customers' actions. Both recommendations are made with the understanding that the mirrors should be installed whether or not the desk is moved.

After physical issues are evaluated, we next look at software security and reliability. Vendor-stated reliability for the planned DBMS is two years MTBF. This SQL software is one of the best on the market, but each new release is unstable for at least six months, and those instability figures are not in the MTBF estimates. The company routinely disclaims any responsibility for new release errors and loss of data or processing to using companies. The DBMS does stabilize and is usually reliable after a six-month trial period for each new release. The

simple solution to this problem is that unless a feature of a new release is needed, no change from the current stable version should be made. In addition, no software, whether vendor package or customer designed, should be allowed into production use until it is thoroughly tested using the application regression test package that will accompany the system.

A secondary problem with DBMS errors is that, if the DBMS fails, there is no other way to access the data. Part of the contract negotiation should include discussion of such software for the vendor to provide in event of DBMS failure. Other companies have successfully received such commitments from this vendor, although it is not volunteered. Such data access software should be included in the vendor contract.

Additional problems that might cause DBMS failure are electrical surges and brownouts due to uneven service in the area. Surges generally occur during the summer months when equipment comes on-line to service air-conditioning in the area. The probability of surges is 100% based on local electrical company history. The probability of brownouts with reduced power is 30% within two years, also using electrical history as the basis for the estimate. Problems from both causes can be minimized by a surge protector on the entire ABC electrical system which shuts down power if a particularly large surge is experienced. In addition, one surge protector for each outlet should be installed to further protect the equipment since whole system protectors do not guarantee integrated chip safety. Finally, a limited, inexpensive, uninterrupted power supply (UPS) should be installed to provide emergency power in the event of electrical failure and for limited use during brownouts to supplement reduced electricity from the local provider.

We consider application software failures next. Failure due to software defects should be less than once in 15 years after the first three months of operational use. During the first three months of operation, the probability of application failure is about 75%; no more than one is expected. The application is designed for 15-minute recovery of all data and programs. Loss of partial transactions will always occur with any failure; they will have to be reentered. Program problems will be fixed within one business day. Any lost transactions will be reentered free of charge by Software Engineers Unlimited (Mary's company).

Outside user access to the system should be zero since no telecommunications capabilities are planned. However, the untended server and occasional lack of clerks at the desk area may provide a local hacker enough time to access and modify the system. If the physical security precautions recommended above are provided, such hacker break-ins would be nearly impossible. Therefore, at a minimum the precautions for security mirrors, assigning clerks monitoring responsibility, and locking the office and file server doors should be implemented (see Figure 10-21).

Finally, the use of computer novices as clerks guarantees user errors. The probability of user errors is 100% within one week of system operation. To prevent any application or DBMS damage from user errors (inadvertent or otherwise), the first line of defense is to restrict what users may do and the data they may access as a way to prevent errors. Each job should be defined and a security access scheme developed to allow access to all processes and data required for the job, *and nothing more*.

Second, the application should withstand any casual error—hitting any key on keyboard, scanning any bar code type, and so on. If required, a report of such errors can be created and printed on demand by Vic to allow retraining (or other action) for repeated errors by one user. Application design also includes validation of all fields such that only valid data can be in the database. Such checks are not possible for alphanumeric data, however, so on-demand reports of new customer and video entries will allow Vic to monitor the typing skills of employees.

Application training will use computer-based training (CBT) in entering application data. The CBT will use simulated transactions and should minimize the user errors if taken seriously by clerks. New-hire orientation should include discussion of the importance of accuracy of work, especially with the computer. Further, new hires should be assigned a more senior 'mentor' for learning the application after training.

After disaster recovery is planned, application security must be developed. From the recovery plan, we know that each job should be evaluated to determine the data and processing requirements of the position. ABC jobs evaluated include clerks, owner, and accountant. The owner should be allowed to do any functions on the application and system that he desires. However, many owners do not *want* to become the chief user of the computer. When asked, Vic's reaction is, "Does this mean I can never take a vacation? Do I have to be here in the morning and at night? If so, define a new position that can do most of my functions, just not delete data!" So the position of chief clerk is also considered.

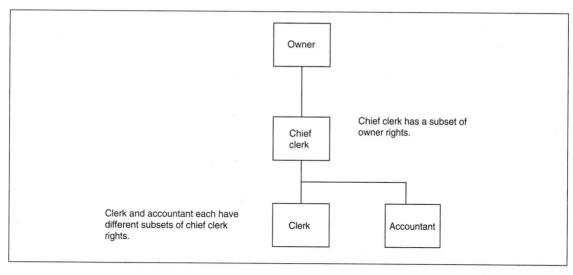

FIGURE 10-22   ABC Data Security Hierarchy of Access Rights

The owner should be the lead person and still be allowed to perform all functions, access all data, and provide security password changes, and so on (see Figure 10-22). The chief clerk, according to Vic's wishes, has all of those functions except deleting information (see Table 10-5). If there were sensitive data in the system, more discussion of the chief clerk's duties and access rights might take place. The clerks have access rights to rent and return videos, and to create and update customers and videos. Finally, the accountant has limited read-only access to several files.

Backup and recovery are considered next. First we decide the maximum tolerable time loss for a computer outage, then select the backup scheme that best fits the time loss maximum. The rental/return application is critical to ABC's ability to conduct business. Vic knows that when he moves all production work to the computer that the clerks will quickly forget the manual way of conducting business. Also, we know that if the databases are not kept up to date, the system is next to useless because the clerks won't know whether to look at manual or automated files for returns, fees, and so on. Therefore, the maximum outage should be less than 15 minutes with recovery of all fully complete transactions. Even at

15 minutes, if an outage were to occur during a peak time, as many as four transactions could need to be reentered and as many as 15–20 transactions would be queued for entry upon system return to production. Ideally, the system should be functional during all business hours.

The recovery requirements imply the most backup protection possible. From Table 10-4, a 15-minute recovery requirement means the use of weekly full backups with off-site storage, daily backups, and logging for transactions, preupdate data items and postupdate data items. Therefore, these are the backup and recovery requirements.

Requirements: Application and system availability during all store open hours, with no more than 15 minutes of down-time from failures of any type.

Backups: Transaction, preupdate, and postupdate logs

Transaction logs maintained one week until weekly backups are verified. Pre- and postupdate logs maintained for 72 hours.

Daily complete database backups with onsite copy plus off-site storage at owner's home.

TABLE 9-5   ABC User Classes and Access Rights

File/Function	Owner	Chief Clerk	Clerk	Accountant
Customer				
Create	X	X	X	
Retrieve	X	X	X	X
Update	X	X	X	
Delete	X			
Video				
Create	X	X	X	
Retrieve	X	X	X	X
Update	X	X	X	
Delete	X	X		
Open Rentals				
Create	X	X	X	
Retrieve	X	X	X	X
Update	X	X	X	
Delete	X			
Video History				
Create				
Retrieve	X	X	X	X
Update	X			
Customer History				
Create				
Retrieve	X	X	X	X
Update	X	X		
Startup	X	X		
Shutdown	X	X		
End Of Day				
Create	X	X		
Retrieve	X	X		X
Delete	X	X		
Initiate End of Month Process	X	X		

Paper copy of transactions maintained for one calendar year in accountant's office.

Weekly complete disk backups with on-site copy plus off-site storage at owner's home and a third copy at

Disaster Prevention Storage
321 Maple Ave.
Somewhere, OK
(618) 123-1234

If ABC's application processed millions of transactions each day, we would do further analysis of the cost of backup and recovery, but here that is not necessary.

Finally, we need to decide about audit controls as summarized here:

Data accuracy and completeness—All edit checks possible will be used as data are entered to prevent errors from entering the system. Sight verification by clerks and customers will be used to verify alphanumeric information.

Rental transaction accuracy can be verified by customers' signing for all monetary transactions. In case of discrepancy, transaction logs and historical paper copies of transactions can be consulted.

Data authorization—Security controls will provide sufficient authorization for data processing. Only the owner is authorized to perform any delete functions on customer, video, and open rental data. No delete functions for history records are provided.

User ID, date, and time of user to last change data will be maintained in Customer, Video, and Open Rental databases.

Audit trail—A paper trail of receipts should be maintained by the accountant for each calendar year. This is a sufficient trail since ABC is a cash business without any accruals.

Nonmonetary transactions (e.g., return of on-time tapes), have no paper audit trail. If a question about a tape return arises, the database can be checked to verify the information.

All edit checks possible should be used as data are entered to prevent errors from entering the system. To ensure complete editing, we review the data dictionary to check that all nonalphanumeric fields have edit and validation criteria.

On names, addresses, and other alphanumeric fields, little verification can be performed automatically. What cannot be done automatically should be done manually. Procedures for operators should be developed to document clerical 'sight verification' and customer verification standards. An example of such a procedure that would be part of the user manual is shown as Figure 10-23. **Sight verification** means that the person entering information into the computer reads the monitor to verify the accuracy of the information he or she entered. The user, then,

---

These paragraphs would be part of the user procedures:

Customer Maintenance

. . .

When customers are being added to the system, the clerk should read back all information as shown on the screen to verify its accuracy, as the computer cannot verify mixed alphabetic and numeric information.

. . .

Video Maintenance

. . .

When videos are being added to the system, the clerk should compare all information shown on the screen with the original printed information to verify its accuracy, as the computer cannot verify mixed alphabetic and numeric information.

. . .

Rent/Return Processing

. . .

Users should be encouraged to check the information on the printed rental before they sign it to verify that it is correct.

. . .

FIGURE 10-23   User Sight Verification Procedure

is responsible for data integrity of items that cannot be **computer verified**.

Rental transaction accuracy will be verified by customers' signing for all monetary transactions. In case of discrepancy, transaction logs and historical paper copies of transactions can be consulted. If many discrepancies persist (more than one per week), a special history file of transactions can be added to the application to speed the transaction look-up process.

Security controls can be designed to provide sufficient authorization for data processing. The security scheme should be developed to serve two goals: to provide data access and to provide function access to those who need it. To require several layers of security checking for a simple application does not make sense and wastes clerical time. So, once again the KISS (Keep It Simple, Stupid) method of one security access scheme is best. User ID, date, and time of user to last change data will be maintained in Customer, Video, and Open Rental databases. These attributes are added to affected database relations.

To minimize the extent to which damage can be done to data, only ABC's owner should be authorized to perform any delete functions on customer, video, and open rental data. No automated delete functions for history records are provided without circumventing the application completely. Changes to files will always be somewhat traceable because the historical record will reflect activity. If unauthorized file changes are thought to be a problem, Vic can always request a browsing capability for any of the transaction logs to check on problems.

A manual audit trail should be used for ABC to conserve computer resources. All monetary transactions can be reconstructed through a paper trail of receipts maintained by the accountant. The receipt form is a two-ply preprinted form on which all monetary transactions are printed. For rentals, customers sign the form as proof of rental responsibility. Paper records should be maintained for one calendar year in the accountant's office; this is sufficient since ABC is a cash business without any accruals. If a tape audit trail were to be necessary at some time in the future, it can be added to the system easily.

Nonmonetary transactions (e.g., return of on-time tapes), have no paper audit trail. If a question about a tape return arises, the user ID, date, and time of the return will be on the database and can be checked to verify the information.

Develop Action Diagram

Guidelines for Developing an Action Diagram

An action diagram is a diagram that shows procedural structure and processing details for an application. It is built from the process hierarchy and process data flow diagram developed during IE analysis (see Figure 9-45 for ABC's PDFD). The diagram uses only structured programming constructs to convert the PDFD into a hierarchy of processes that can be divided into programs and modules. First we discuss the components of the diagram, then we discuss how to build an action diagram from the process hierarchy and PDFD.

Action diagrams use different bracket structures to depict the code elements in an application. Basic structured programming tenets—iteration, selection, and sequence—are all accommodated with several variations provided. As Figure 10-24 shows, a **sequence bracket** is a simple bracket. It is optionally identified with a process name and ended with the term ENDPROC to represent a program module consisting of a sequence of instructions.

When a module is designed and detailed in another document or diagram, a rounded rectangle containing the module name is drawn between the brackets (see Figure 10-25). When the module is not yet defined in detail, a rounded rectangle with question marks down the right side is shown. Reusable

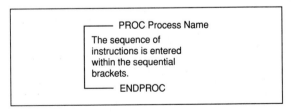

FIGURE 10-24   Simple Sequence Bracket Format

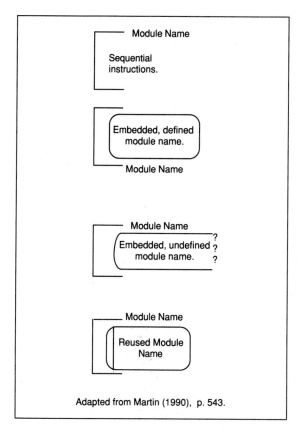

Adapted from Martin (1990), p. 543.

FIGURE 10-25   Module Designation Format

modules are drawn with a vertical bar to represent reuse.

Selection of modules from the PDFD is shown by a **selection bracket** (also called a **condition bracket**) which begins with an *IF* condition and ends with the term *ENDIF* (see Figure 10-26a). If the conditional statement has multiple conditions, two other options are allowed. The condition can be stated as an *IF* statement with one or more *ELSE* conditions (see Figure 10-26b), or a condition can be stated as a mutually exclusive selection list as in Figure 10-26c; this selection list is eventually translated into an *IF* statement.

Repetition is shown with a double bracketed figure. The **repetition bracket** name begins with either *DO* or *DO WHILE* + *condition* (see Figure 10-27). The bracket ends with either an *UNTIL* + *condition*

(Figure 10-27a), or *ENDDO* (Figure 10-27b). *DO WHILE* implies that the condition is checked *before* the conditional statements are executed. Do while processing may occur zero times. Conversely, *DO UNTIL* implies that the condition is checked *after* the lower statements are executed. Do until processes occur at least once.

Miscellaneous items include *goto*, *exit*, and concurrency identification. A *goto* is shown by an arrow leaving one level and pointing to the line for the destination level with a goto statement and destination at the right of the arrow (Figure 28a).

An *exit* is shown as an arrow leaving one level and pointing to the line for the destination level with the word *exit* at the right of the arrow (Figure 28b). Unless an exit destination is named with the exit, exit *always* means that the calling module is the exit destination. For example, if *Rent/Return* calls *CustomerAdd*, the exit from *CustomerAdd* returns to *Rent/Return*. Further, if *CustomerMaint* calls *CustomerAdd*, the exit from *CustomerAdd* returns to *CustomerMaint*. That is, the calling module, regardless of what it is, is the return module.

Processes can be sequential or concurrent. **Concurrent processes** execute at the same time. There are two types of concurrent processes: independent and dependent. **Independent concurrent processes** are those which execute at the same time but do not synchronize their process completion. For example, when *Process Payment and Compute Change* is complete in ABC's application, printing and file updates of several types could all be concurrent. If there is no checking on the success of their completions with subsequent action for any failures, these processes are independent. Independent concurrency is shown on the diagram by an arc which connects the module brackets (Figure 10-28). **Dependent concurrent processes** are those which must be synchronized to coordinate further application actions. Dependent concurrency is shown on the diagram by an asterisk (or some other special character) on the arc connecting the modules (Figure 10-28d). Dependent concurrent processes require the development of a synchronization module, if not already in the application, to ensure complete, accurate processing.

Now that you know the bracket symbols used to define action diagrams, we move to discuss the steps

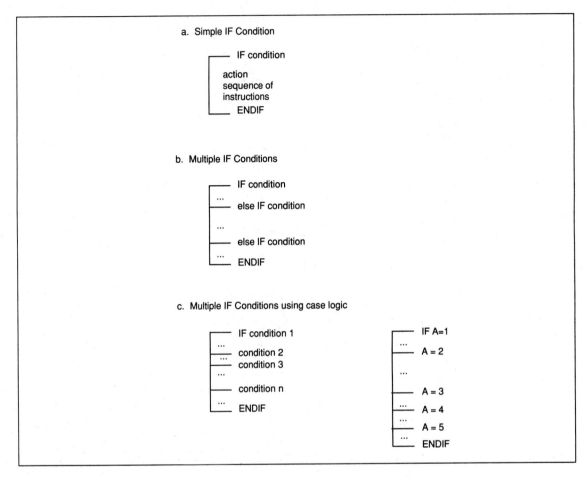

FIGURE 10-26   Conditional Bracket Design Formats

to developing one. The steps to define an action diagram are to translate processes into levels of action using structured constructs, design modules, perform reusability analysis, decide module timing, add data to the diagram, and optionally, add screens to the diagram.

The first step is to translate processes into levels of action. The first-level diagram is developed from the process hierarchy diagram to identify the major activities being performed by the application. The activities themselves are added to the diagram as they are written on the hierarchy diagram. The structured constructs should identify sequence and any selection or conditional processing relating to the activities. Most often, when the diagram is begun at

the activity level, the alternative processes are mutually exclusive. When the diagram starts at the process level (Figure 10-29), any construct might apply. The example shows a mutually exclusive selection from among the three alternatives.

Now we shift to the process data flow diagram (Figure 10-30) to add process details to the action diagram. Remember that the processes on the PDFD must match exactly the processes on the hierarchic decomposition diagram. We use the PDFD to translate the structural relationships between the processes correctly. The **structural relationships** are on the PDFD and not on the decomposition; they refer to the sequential, conditional, and repetitive relationships between processes.

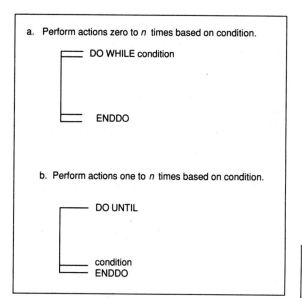

a. Perform actions zero to *n* times based on condition.

        DO WHILE condition

        ENDDO

b. Perform actions one to *n* times based on condition.

        DO UNTIL

        condition
        ENDDO

FIGURE 10-27   Repetition Bracket Design Formats

In developing the second-level action diagram, we first add the processes, in sequence, from the PDFD. Then the brackets are drawn to reflect the sequential, conditional, and repetitive structural relationships. In the example (Figure 10-31), the main processes are *Identify Item and Vendor*, *Sort by Vendor and Item*, *Get Price*, *Create Order*, and *Mail Order*. Between these processes, there are two repetitive blocks: one based on *New Releases*, and the other based on *Vendors* (see Figure 10-32). We identify the repetitive blocks by looking at the circular loops and the conditions for repeating the process(es). Notice that the *Sort* is not included in either loop.

Next, evaluate each process grouping. *Identify Item* is alone within its loop. *Sort* is also alone. The last three processes are together and are analyzed. The processes are sequential but according to the PDFD, they are not all processed in sequence. If the vendor has not changed from the previous item, we *Get Price* and *Create Order*. When the *Vendor* changes, we *File* and *Mail* the order. These statements from the PDFD translate into the *IF* conditional statement in the action diagram as shown in Figure 10-33.

The diagram is correct in interpreting the PDFD, but it is incomplete as a program specification. First we need to deal with the *First Vendor*. The *First Vendor* will *not* equal *Last Vendor*, and to file an order for a nonexistent vendor is wrong. Second, think about what an order looks like (Figure 10-34). There are one-time *Vendor* information and variable lines of *Item* information. Where the PDFD says *Create Order*, it really means *Add Item to Order*. When the *Vendor* changes and an order is complete, we want to format *Vendor information* for the new order. Figure 10-35 reflects these details and is ready for the next step. The purpose of this example is to show

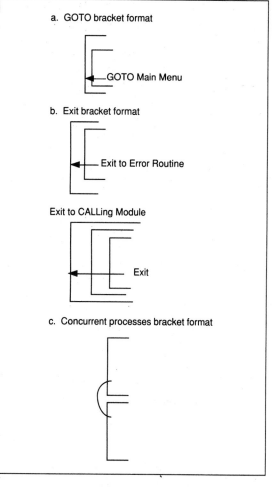

a. GOTO bracket format

                GOTO Main Menu

b. Exit bracket format

                Exit to Error Routine

Exit to CALLing Module

                Exit

c. Concurrent processes bracket format

FIGURE 10-28   Miscellaneous Bracket Design Formats

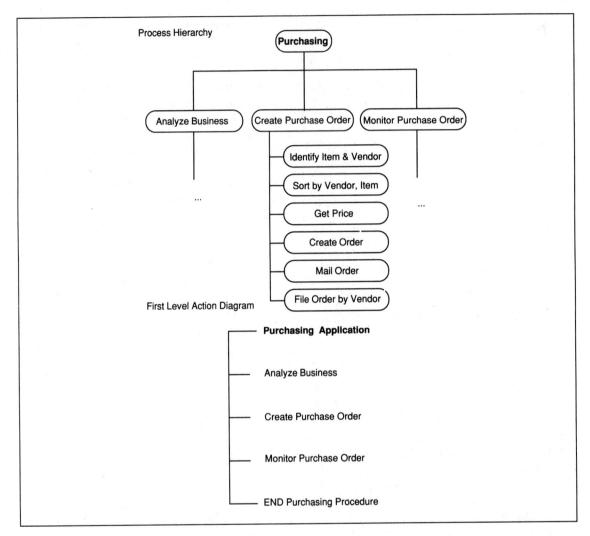

FIGURE 10-29   Process Hierarchy and First-Level Action Diagram

how a correct PDFD may need elaboration to translate into program specifications.

Using the action diagram, modules are defined. There are few guidelines on this aspect of Information Engineering. In general, you should try to define modules that perform one well-defined process and nothing else. The guidelines presented in Chapter 8 for module definition can be applied here. For the example in Figure 10-35, the *IF . . . ELSE IF . . . ELSE* processing is the module's control flow.

Within the control flow we have stand-alone processes that conveniently define modules. Figure 10-36 shows the module names, each enclosed in its own rounded rectangular box to indicate that there are more details for each module. The submodules are each further diagrammed or, if fully documented in a data dictionary, refer to the dictionary entry in the module box.

For *Create Purchase Order* processing, then, we have a main module and submodules for *Create Ven-*

dor Info, Get Price, Create Order Item, File Order, and Mail Order. Notice that Create Vendor Info is used twice.

Next, the action diagram modules are compared to templates already in use to determine whether reuse of existing modules is possible. As reusable modules are identified, the process details are removed from the action diagram and replaced with a call statement. The called module name should indicate whether the reused module is customized for this application or not. The conventional way to identify customized reused modules is by a prefix or suffix on the name. For example, a date compare

routine might be used to determine lateness. If not modified, the name of the routine might be Date-Compare. If customized, the name of the routine might be RentDateCompare or LateReturnDate-Compare. In the example in Figure 10-36, Sort uses a utility program, a special class of reusable module. The Sort statement is removed from the diagram and replaced with a call statement (Figure 10-37). No other modules in this example are general enough for reuse.

When reusability analysis is complete, the action diagram should show the mainline logic of the application with modules for the processes and

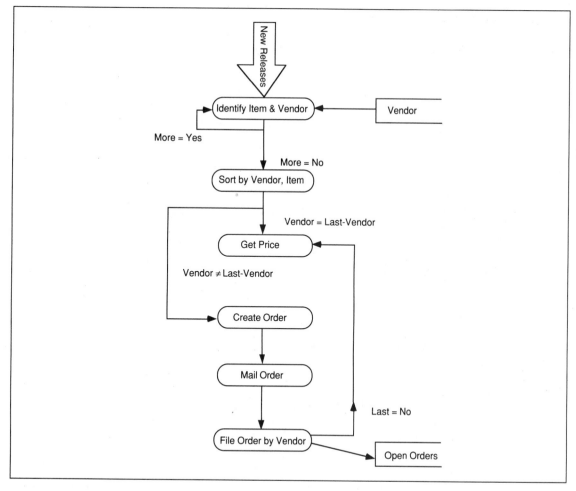

FIGURE 10-30   Sample Process Data Flow Diagram

FIGURE 10-31   Second-Level Action Diagram

sequential modules are evaluated at first. Then the groups themselves are evaluated for possible concurrency. In Figure 10-36, two groups of two or more modules are present. The first is *Get Price* with *Create Order Item*. The second group is *File Order*, *Mail Order*, and *Create Vendor Information on Order*. Working backward, we ask if the modules are dependent on each other. Could we create an order item without knowing the price? In this case, the answer is no, we must know the price. Therefore, the modules are dependent and cannot be concurrent. In the second group, we might perform *File* and *Mail*

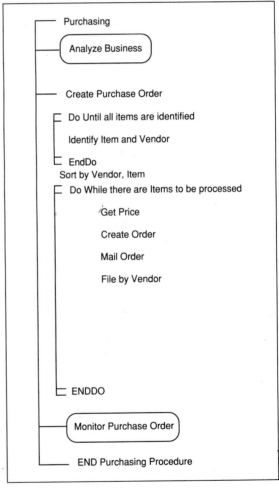

FIGURE 10-32   Repetitive Blocks on Second-Level Action Diagram

subprocesses. At this point, timing of processes is decided and added to the diagram. Recall that processes can be sequential or concurrent, and that concurrent processes can be either independent or dependent. Frequently, user requirements will identify required concurrency. If no user requirements identify concurrent operations, a design decision to offer or not offer concurrency is made by the SEs. Concurrency is expensive and adds a level of maintenance complexity to the application that the user might not want.

Optional concurrency is determined by evaluating module interrelationships again. Only groups of

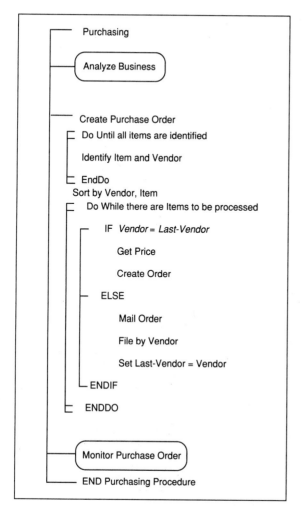

FIGURE 10-33   Conditional Statements on Second-Level Action Diagram

FIGURE 10-34   Order Example

Order at the same time, **IF** success of the file operation is not an issue. *Create Vendor* cannot be done until the last order is fully processed. To decide on concurrency, we need to know the details of error handling. In this case, we find that errors are checked and handled in the module in which they can occur. If a fatal error occurs, the application does no other processing on this order. This process definition *implies* sequence to the processes. If the processes were concurrent and a fatal error occurred, some undesired processing would occur. Therefore, in this example, concurrency is not an option.

Next, the entities and data elements used by the processes are added to the diagram(s). By the time this action is complete, every attribute of every relation must, at least, have been identified for creation and deletion (Figure 10-37). Any attributes not included in the processing should be reconsidered for elimination from the application. These process definitions should include attributes added to the relations as a result of design activities.

If the action diagrams are developed manually, screen identifiers can be added to the diagram with entities and attributes linked to screens (see Figure 10-38). The diagram then links data sources and destinations to both processes and screens. This type of diagram does manually what linkages in a CASE tool automate.

ABC Video Example Action Diagram

The steps to developing the action diagram are to develop the levels of action using structured constructs, perform reusability analysis, design modules, decide module timing, add data to the diagram, and optionally, add screens to the diagram (refer to p. 434). Only the first-level action diagram includes all of the processes. The lower-level diagrams consider Rent/Return processing and Video Maintenance only. The other processes are left as an exercise.

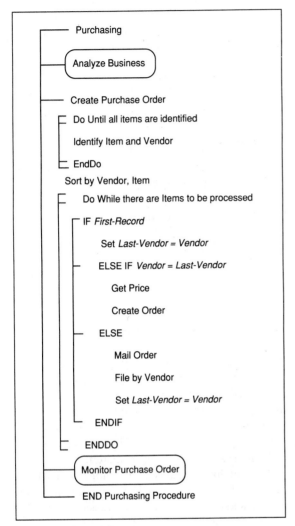

FIGURE 10-35   Order Format Details on Action Diagram

The first-level action diagram is based on the process hierarchy (Figure 10-39). First we draw the general bracket and add the module names, indicating the structural relationships between the modules by the bracket type (Figure 10-40). In the ABC diagram, the processes are all mutually exclusive.

Then, using the PDFD as reference (Figure 10-41), we develop the next level of procedural detail. The subprocess names are added to the diagram as shown in the PDFD (and process hierarchy). For each subprocess, the structural brackets indicating modular control are added.

The subprocesses for *Video Maintenance* are for create, retrieval, update, and delete processing. These processes are all mutually exclusive, so the diagram is simple (Figure 10-42). At the lowest level, we identify modules that refer to the dictionary for process details.

Rent/Return has all of the complexity in the application. Each cluster of modules is discussed separately. First, *Get Request* is always executed whenever *Rent/Return* is invoked (Figure 10-43).

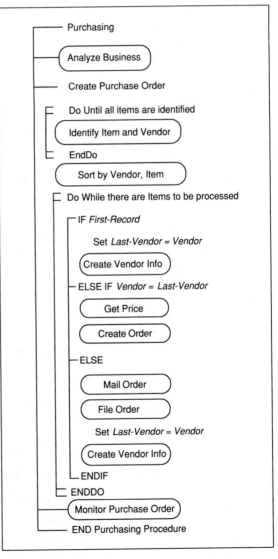

FIGURE 10-36   Module Boxes on Action Diagram

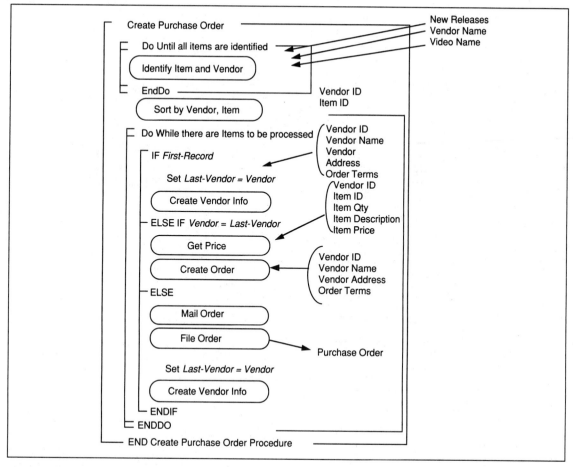

FIGURE 10-37   Data Addition to High-Level Action Diagram

Then the conditional statement for determining the type of request is added (Figure 10-43). The two options are *If Customer* and *If Video ID*, and each has its own processes.

Next, *Open Rentals* are read and displayed until all *Open Rentals* for this customer are in memory (Figure 10-44). The *Open Rental* loop is a simple *Do While* process.

Then video returns are processed using a repetition with a conditional structure (Figure 10-45). Late fees are checked in a repetitive loop for all *Open Rentals* (Figure 10-46). New rental *Video ID*s are entered for all new rentals (Figure 10-47). *Process Payment and Make Change* is a stand-alone module. Then, for all open and new rentals, the *Open Rentals* file is updated; for all of today's returns, history is updated; and if payment is made or a user

requests, a receipt is printed (Figure 10-48). The consolidated action diagram is shown in Figure 10-49.

Next, evaluate the diagram to identify program modules. As in the example above, we have naturally identified modules as part of process definition. For instance, *Get Valid Customer* is a small, self-contained module that does one thing only. The module uses a Customer ID to access the Customer relation. If the entry is present, the credit is checked. The name, address, and credit status are returned. The remaining modules, that we originally defined as business processes doing one thing, should each be reviewed to ensure that they are, in fact, single purpose. This is left as a class activity.

In addition, we can now resolve the issue held over from analysis about whether to keep separate or

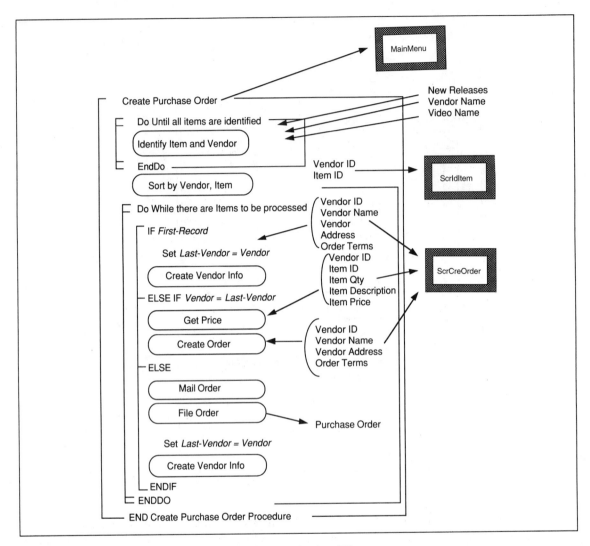

FIGURE 10-38   Optional Screen Processing on Action Diagram

consolidate *Get Open Rentals*, *Add Return Date* and *Check for Late Fees*. Individually, each of these processes is singular (i.e., does one thing). If they are consolidated, they would remain singular but be placed within the same repetition loop. The issue here, then, is which method is easier to program and implement in the intended language, and which provides the better user interface. We need to visualize the user interface and memory processing for each alternative.

If the modules are kept *separate*, all *Open Rentals* are read first and displayed. Then the clerk can be

prompted for new videos or for returns. If we prompt for returns every time, many wasted entries to deny return processing will be made. If we prompt for either new or return *Video ID*s, we need a method of knowing which is entered. Assuming we figure that out, we then get all returns and enter today's date for returned videos. Then all entries on the screen are scanned to determine new late fees.

If the modules are *consolidated*, as each *Open Rental* is read, *Late Fees* are computed for tapes with return dates and no late fees (see Figure 10-50). There are two options for this process. Either we

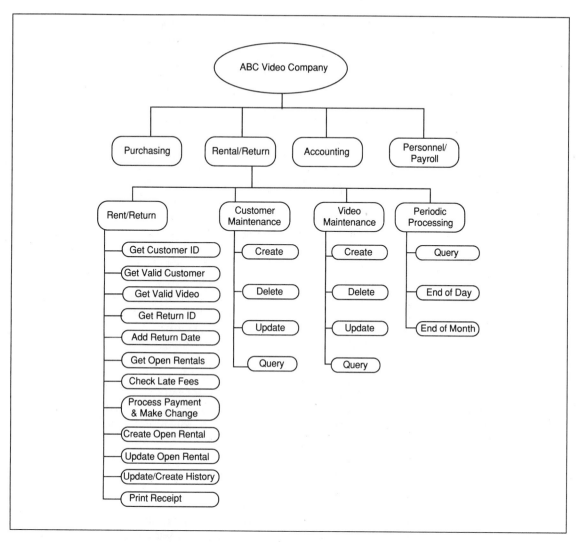

FIGURE 10-39   ABC Video Process Hierarchy Diagram

assume there are no more returns or the clerk must respond to each *Open Rental*. With the first option, the clerk would have a selectable option for more return processing. When chosen, each return *Video ID* is entered and *Late Fees* are computed for that video.

Notice that *both* alternatives have problems. The separation alternative has a problem in dealing with returns, and there will be a slight delay for *Late Fee* processing. The consolidation option actually modifies the processes from the PDFD somewhat for *Late Fee* processing.

Data storage for a rental in memory is the same for both alternatives. We need a location for customer information, a table for open rentals, a table for new rentals, and locations for payment information. We will have three iterations through the table for *Open Rentals* in the separate alternative, and one, or two if returns are present, iteration(s) in the consolidated alternative.

The alternatives are approximately the same in implementation complexity, although three iterations are more likely to contain bugs than one. The human interface design is the same for both alterna-

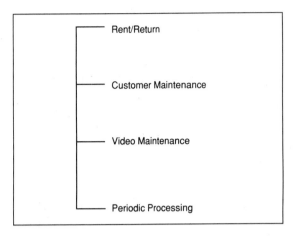

FIGURE 10-40   ABC First-Level Action Diagram

tives. The difference in the human interfaces is the speed and timing for data to appear on the *Open Rentals* lines. In this case the consolidated alternative is slightly faster. The difference in memory processing is the number of iterations through *Open Rental* data. Again, the consolidated alternative is preferred somewhat because it is less likely to contain bugs. With no overwhelming evidence for or against either alternative, this amounts to a judgment call. We will choose the consolidated alternative to minimize the probability of errors and the number of iterations through the data. The action diagram, reflecting consolidated open rental processing, is in Figure 10-50.

The next activity is reusability analysis. ABC has no library of reusable modules to consider since it currently has no computer processing. The types of modules the consultants are likely to have might be relevant to error processing or to screen interactions. For our purposes, we assume no reusable modules.

To assess module timing, we analyze the module clusters. The only modules that could be concurrent are those in the last cluster to update files and print a receipt. Before deciding concurrency, we must decide the details of history processing that were deferred from analysis. We have two types of history files: *Customer* and *Video*. *Customer History* is a separate file that contains the *Customer ID* and all *Video ID*s rented by that customer. No counts, dates, or copy information are anticipated. This description complies with the case requirements in Chapter 2.

Video History contains *Video ID*, *Copy ID*, *Year*, *Month*, *Number of Rentals*, and *Days of Rental* for each entry. This data description also complies with the case requirements in Chapter 2. The issue to be decided is whether or not *Video History* is maintained during on-line processing, or if the current month's activity is kept with *Copy* information. If the second alternative is chosen, we need a monthly process to update the Video History and reinitialize the counts in the *Copy* relation. If the first alternative is chosen, we have two more alternatives. First, we might need update and create processing because, for any one copy, we would not know in advance whether it has a historical entry or not. This alternative requires bug-prone processing that is more complex than keeping counts in the current *Copy* relation. Second, we could create an empty entry for every tape at the beginning of every month. This alternative is not attractive because it generates many empty records on history. Both of these alternatives would require history to be on-line. Keeping current counts with *Copy* relations does not require history to be on-line. The final argument for keeping the counts in *Copy* information is that, to maintain status of a given tape, *Copy* information must be updated upon video return anyway. As long as the tuple is being read, updating it with count information requires adding lines of code rather than a new module. From this discussion, it should be clear that keeping current counts in the *Copy* relation is the preferred alternative. We document this and the other changes in the Data Dictionary.

Now we can discuss module timing for the last group of modules. In this group we create and/or update *Open Rentals*, update *Copy*, and *Print Receipt*. Recall from analysis that Vic does not want file update success to be known to the customers. The receipt should be printed regardless of updating success. This implies that printing could be concurrent with the file processes. The file updates cannot be concurrent because they will all be on the same device. Since there is already contention for the file

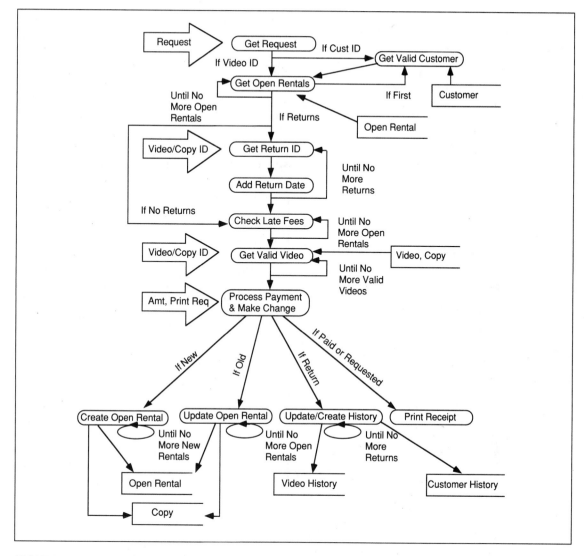

FIGURE 10-41   ABC Video Process Dependency Diagram

among the users, it is unlikely that we would want to increase contention by having the updates concurrent. If printing is the only concurrent process, it is not worth the cost to provide concurrency. Therefore, the processes will be made sequential for production operation. Figure 10-50 is not changed at this point.

The entities and data attributes are added to the diagram next to show input and output processing. Two entities, *EOD* and *Rental Archive*, are still undefined, having been deferred in analysis. These are left as an exercise. The entities referenced in *Rental/Return* processing, *Customer, Open Rental, Video, Copy, Customer History*, and *EOD* are all shown in Figure 10-51. When an action diagram arrow is from an entity to a process, it means that the entire tuple is accessed. The final action is to add screens to the action diagram, but they are not yet defined, so this activity will be left as a future exercise.

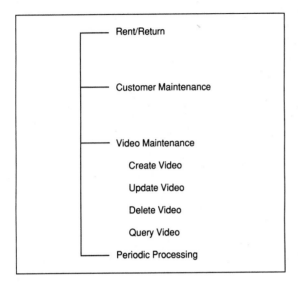

FIGURE 10-42 ABC *Video Maintenance* Second-Level Action Diagram

Define Menu Structure and Dialogue Flow

Guidelines for Defining the Menu Structure and Dialogue Flow

The interface structure includes design of a menu structure and design of dialogue flow within the menu structure. Both designs are based on the PDFD and process hierarchy diagram developed during IE analysis.

First, the menu structure is developed. Recall that the menu structure is a structured diagram translating process alternatives into a hierarchy of options for the automated application. The task hierarchy is analyzed to define the individual processing screens required to perform whole activities, and to identify the other processes and activities in the hierarchy which must be selected to get to the processing screens.

Let's walk through the development of the sample menu structure shown in Figure 10-7. The related process hierarchy diagram is shown as Figure 10-52 with the individual processing screens, selection alternatives, and hierarchy levels identified. For each level in the hierarchy, we identify a level of menu

processing. Using simple bracket structures to translate from the top to the bottom of the hierarchy, we first define the options for the first level menu (see Figure 10-53). Next, the menu options for the first process level of the hierarchy are shown in Figure 10-54. Finally, the remaining detailed processes are added to the diagram (see Figure 10-55).

If, for any reason, the hierarchy or lower-level processes are in doubt, review the proposed menu structure with the users before proceeding. If the

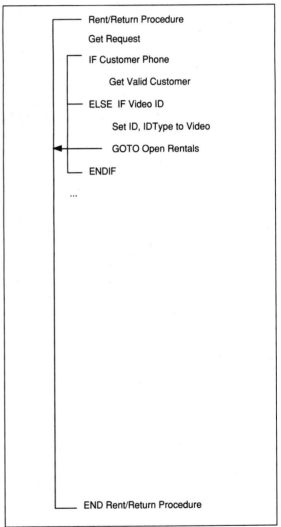

FIGURE 10-43 Request Processing Action Diagram Constructs

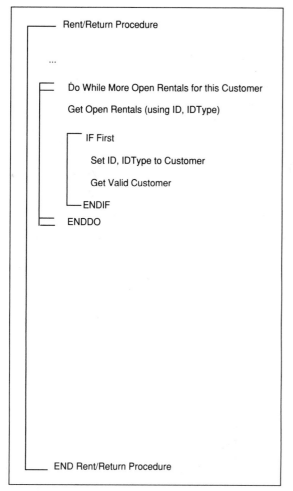

```
    ┌─── Rent/Return Procedure

  ...

    ┌─── Do While More Open Rentals for this Customer

        Get Open Rentals (using ID, IDType)

        ┌─── IF First

            Set ID, IDType to Customer

            Get Valid Customer

        └── ENDIF
    └─ ENDDO


    └─── END Rent/Return Procedure
```

FIGURE 10-44   *Open Rental* Action Diagram
Constructs

```
    ┌─── Rent/Return Procedure

  ...

    ┌─── IF Returns
    ┌─ DO Until no more returns

        Get Return ID

        Add Return Date

    └─ ENDDO
    └─── ENDIF

  ...



    └─── END Rent/Return Procedure
```

FIGURE 10-45   *Video Returns* Action
Diagram Constructs

process hierarchy diagram is accepted as correctly mirroring the desired functions in the application, proceed to the next step, defining the movements between menu items.

Traditionally, applications were constrained to moving top-to-bottom-to-top with no deviation. Anyone who uses such an interface for long knows it is irritating to wait for some menu that is unwanted and to enter choices purely for system design reasons. The decisions should relate to application requirements as much as possible. For instance, security access control requirements can be partially

met by restricting movement to functions as part of dialogue flow. The decisions about legal movement should be made by the users based on recommendations by the designers; although frequently, dialogue flow decisions are made by the SEs. In general, if the users are functional experts, an open design that allows free movement should be used. If users are novices or not computer literate, a more restrictive design should be used to minimize the amount of their potential confusion.

Figure 10-56 shows types of arrows used to depict movement between levels of a menu structure.

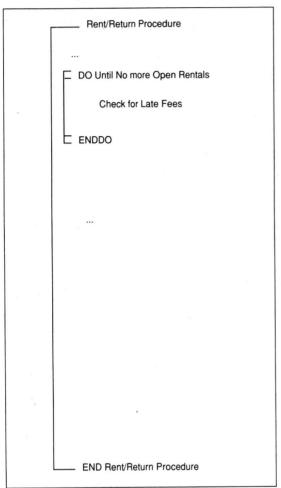

FIGURE 10-46   *Late Fee* Action Diagram
Constructs

FIGURE 10-47   *New Rentals* Action Diagram
Constructs

In a small diagram, with less than ten screens, only single-headed arrows are used, and at least two arrows are drawn for each entry: one entering and one leaving (Figure 10-56a). In a large diagram, with over ten screens, the triple-headed arrows can be added to the diagrams to depict call-return processing (Figures 10-56b and 10-56c).

An example of restricted screen movement that might be designed for novice users is shown in Figure 10-57a. In the diagram, all movement is to or from a menu. The diagram in Figure 10-57b shows that any level of upper menu might be reached from

the lower levels. This speeds processing through menus and is preferred to the design shown in Figure 10-57a which only allows a process to return to the menu level from which it was activated. Restrictive dialogue flow (Figure 10-57a) is the type of design that is most likely to waste user time and become annoying.

Experts and frequent users usually are provided more alternatives for interscreen movement because they become proficient with the application. Unrestricted screen movement is desirable for these users. An example of unrestricted movement in screen

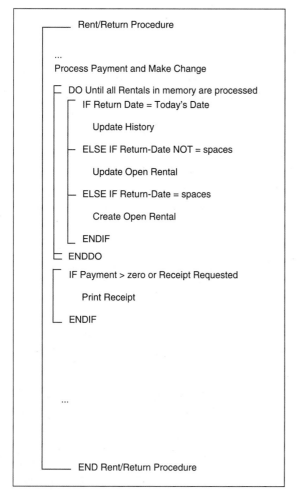

FIGURE 10-48   Payments, File Update and
Printing Action Diagram Constructs

control structure that must accompany an open
movement design. The added errors are from a need
to provide a specific location on the screen for
entry of the expert's direct screen requests. Each
request must be checked for access control and
legality, plus the current context (i.e., screen and
memory information) might need to be saved for
return processing.

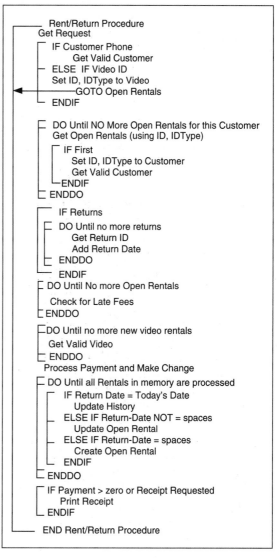

FIGURE 10-49   ABC Consolidated Action
Diagram

design is shown in Figure 10-57c. In the example,
the user begins at the main menu and may move
down the hierarchy in the same manner as a novice,
or may move directly to a process screen, at the
user's option. Unrestricted movement requires the
design and implementation of a command language
or sophisticated menu selection structure that is consistent with the basic novice menu selections, but
adds the expert mode.

Unrestricted movement can be costly and error-
prone, which are the main reasons why it is not
prevalent. The added cost is due to increased access

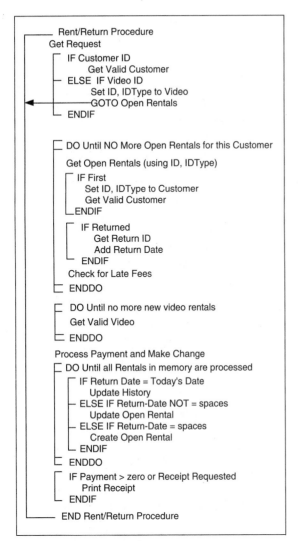

FIGURE 10-50   ABC Action Diagram with Consolidated Open Rental Processing

Upon completion, the menu structure and dialogue flow diagrams are given to the human interface designers to use in developing the screen interface (see Chapter 14). The dialogue flow diagram is also used by designers in developing program specifications. Before we move on, note that even though the menu structure is identified, the human interface may or may not be structured exactly as defined in the menu structure diagram. The human interface designers use the menu structure information to understand the dependencies and relationships between business functions, entities, and processes; they may alter the structure to fit the actual human interface technique used. If a traditional menu interface is designed, it could follow the menu structure diagram.

ABC Video Example Menu Structure and Dialogue Flow

The menu structure is derived from the process hierarchy diagram in Figure 10-58 (reprint of Figure 9-26). First, the activities from the decomposition form the main menu options (see Figure 10-59). The processes are used to develop submenu options. Then, the lowest level of processing completes the simple structure (Figure 10-60).

Notice that all Rent/Return processing is expressed in the first menu option even though we have many subprocesses in the hierarchy. Rental/return has many subprocesses performed as part of the hierarchy diagram. Unlike the other subprocesses, rental/return does not have individual menus and screens for each subprocess. Rather, rental/return requires a complex, multifunction screen with data from several relations and processing that varies by portion of the screen. The subprocesses for rental/return, then, describe actions on portions of the screen. You cannot tell from the decomposition diagram that rental/return has this requirement; rather, you know from application requirements (and experience) what type of screen(s) are needed. An incorrect rendering of the menu structure, such as the one in Figure 10-61, would look weird and should make you feel uncomfortable about its correctness.

Second, notice that we do not indicate access rights for any of the processing options on the diagram. The security access definition is superimposed on the menu structure by the interface designers to double-check the design thinking of the process designers. If there is an inconsistency, the two groups reconcile the problems.

Next we develop a dialogue flow diagram from the menu structure diagram. The rows of the dialogue flow diagram correspond to the entries in the menu structure (Figure 10-62). Rows are entered by level of the hierarchy by convention.

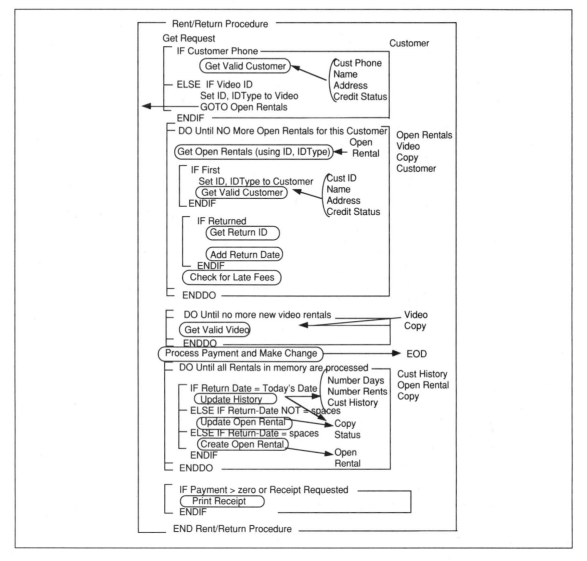

FIGURE 10-51   ABC Action Diagram with Data Entities and Attributes

We need to decide how much flexibility to give users, keeping in mind the security access requirements and the users' computer and functional skills. Users are mostly novices with little computer experience. The average job tenure is less than six months. Data and function access for clerks are unrestricted for customer, video, and open rentals add, change, and retrieve functions. Other options are more restricted in terms of which user class can perform each function.

First we define the options. We could define flexible movement between those options only, and restrict movement to other options through the hierarchy. Top-down hierarchic access is possible. We could allow hierarchic access combined with flexible 'expert' mode movement throughout the hierarchy, constrained by access restrictions.

For each option, ask the following questions. Does Vic have a preference? Which best fits the user profile? Which is the *cleanest*

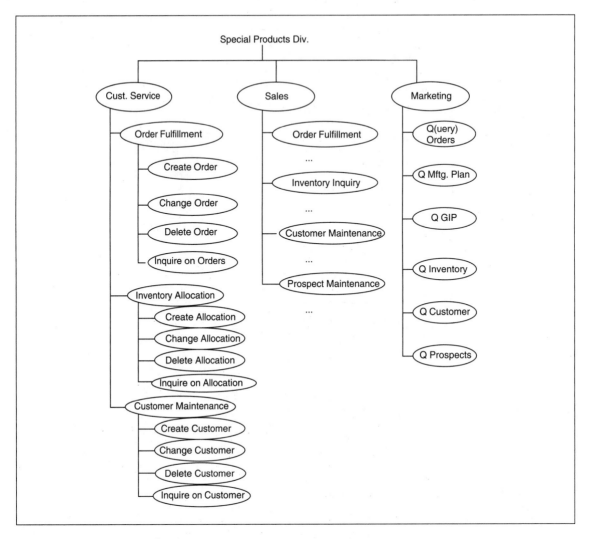

FIGURE 10-52   Example of Process Hierarchy Diagram

implementation, least likely to cause testing and user problems?

Vic, in this case, has no preference. Having never used computers, he has no background that allows him to make a decision. He says, "Do whatever is best for us. I let that up to you. But I would like to see whatever you decide before it is final." This statement implies interface prototyping, which should always be done to allow users to see the screens while they are easily changed.

Most of Vic's employees work there for $1\frac{1}{2}$ years and have little or no computer experience. Therefore, screen processing that is least confusing to new users should be preferred. Usually, novices prefer hierarchic menus, providing the number of levels do not become a source of confusion. Also, the simplest implementation is always preferred; that is, the hierarchic menu option.

Based on the answers to the questions, we should design a restrictive, hierarchic flow. As Figure 10-63

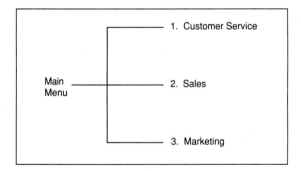

FIGURE 10-53   First-Level Menu Structure

shows, this design is simple and easy to understand. The dialogue flow and screens should be prototyped and reviewed with Vic at the earliest possible time to check that he does not want an expert mode of operation.

You might question whether the movement from rent/return to customer add and video add should be on the dialogue flow diagram. This is a reasonable concern since the process of rent/return does allow adding of both customers and videos within its process. The issue is resolved by local custom. In general, given the option, such flexibility should be shown on the diagram for clarity and completeness. Sometimes, local convention or a specific CASE tool requirement do not allow such completeness.

Plan Hardware and Software Installation and Testing

Guidelines for Hardware/Software Installation Plan

The guidelines for hardware and software installation planning are developed from practice and identify what work is required, environmental planning issues, responsibility for the work, timing of materials and labor, and scheduling of tasks.

Installation requirements should always be defined as far in advance of the needs as possible and documented in a **hardware installation plan**. Installation planning tasks are:

1. Define required work
   Define hardware/software/network
      configuration
   Assess physical environment needs
   Identify all items to be obtained
   Order all equipment, software, and services
   Define installation and testing tasks
2. Assign responsibility for each task
3. Create a schedule of work

If the SE team has no experience with configuring installations, their work definition should always be checked by someone who has experience. In general,

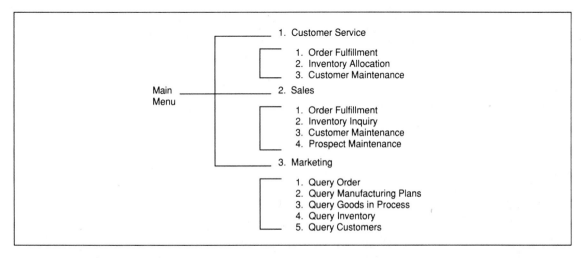

FIGURE 10-54   Second-Level Menu Structure

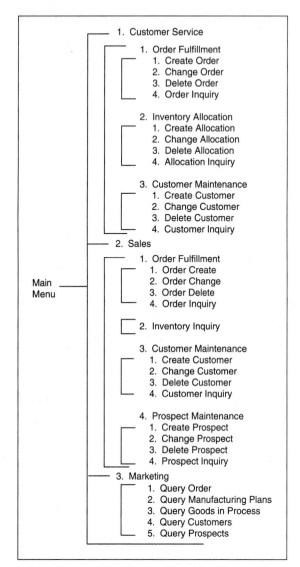

FIGURE 10-55   Final Menu Structure

you define the complete hardware, software, and network configuration needed, match the application configuration requirements to the current installation, get approval for all incremental expenditures, order all equipment and software, and install and test all equipment and software. In a mainframe environment, this task is simplified because the first step, configuration definition, can be abbreviated and done with help from an operations support group.

The operations support group also would install and test hardware and install software.

When the configuration is defined, it is matched to the current installation to determine what items need to be purchased. In new installations, the physical installation environment is as important as the equipment. Building, cooling, heating, humidity control, ventilation, electrical cable, and communications cable needs should all be assessed. If you have no experience performing these analyses, hire someone who does. Do not guess. You only do the client a disservice, and chances of making a costly mistake are high.

Once needed items are identified, they should be ordered with delivery dates requested on the orders. The delivery dates should conform to the expected installation schedule which is discussed below. The goal is to have all equipment and parts when they are needed and not before. For capital expenditures, this delays the expense until it is needed. Planning for large capital expenditures should be done with the client and accountant to stagger charges that might be a financial burden.

As items to be installed are identified and ordered, responsibility for installation and testing should be identified. The alternatives for who should do hardware and software installation are varied. Choices include consultants, unions, contractors, subcontractors, or current personnel. In many cases, there are three types of installations being made: software, hardware, and the network, and each has its own installation responsibility.

Software should be installed by system programmers in an operations support group in a mainframe installation, and by the software builders for a PC installation. Contracts, whether formal or informal, should state what work is to be done, timing of work, penalties for failure to meet the time requirements, and price. Other items such as number of hours and dates of access to the site might also be included.

Hardware, in a mainframe environment, is managed, ordered, and installed through an operations department. You, as an SE needing equipment, must know what you need, but must trust the operations department to obtain, install, and test the equipment. Most PC computer equipment is simplified enough that special assistance is not usually required. If

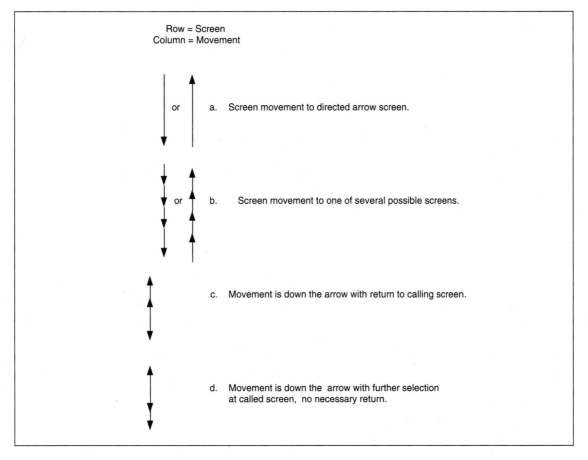

FIGURE 10-56   Dialogue Flow Movement Alternatives

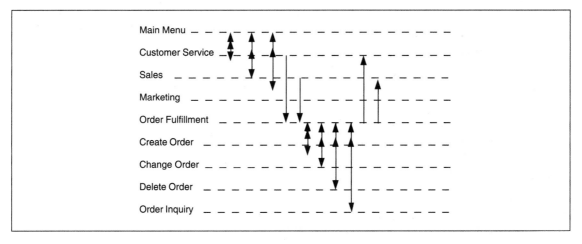

FIGURE 10-57a   Example of Restrictive Screen Movement

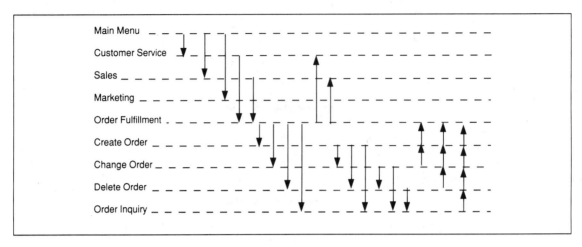

FIGURE 10-57b   Example of Less Restrictive Screen Movement

desired, you can usually negotiate with a hardware vendor to *burn-in* equipment and set it up for a small fee. **Burn-in** means to configure the hardware and run it for some period of time, usually 24–72 hours. If there are faulty chips in the machine, 90% of the time they fail during the burn-in period.

At least two terminals or PCs should be configured during installation of network cable for testing the cable. For LAN installation, *hire a consultant if you've never done this before*. The consultant helps you

- define what is to be done
- define required equipment (e.g., cabling, connectors, etc.)
- get permits from the government and building owners
- obtain zoning variances
- identify and hire subcontractors
- supervise and guarantee the work.

As the user's representative, you can prepare the installation for the work to be done. Mark walls

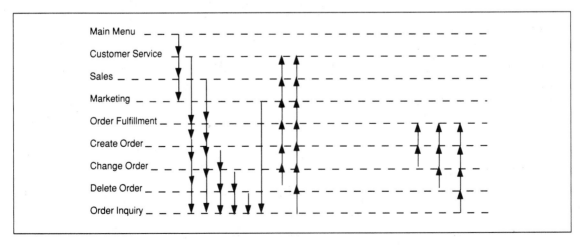

FIGURE 10-57c   Example of Less Restrictive Screen Movement

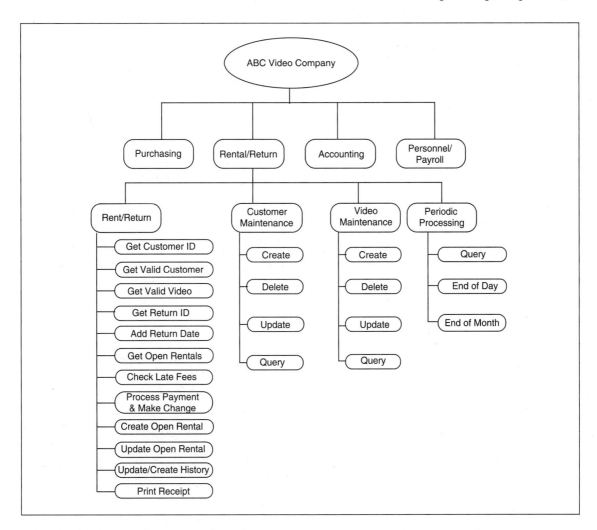

FIGURE 10-58   ABC Process Hierarchy

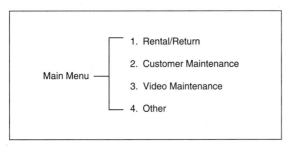

FIGURE 10-59   ABC First-Level Menu
Hierarchy

where all wires should be, using colored dots. For instance, you can use blue dots for phone lines, red dots for LAN cable, and green dots for electrical outlets. Number all outlets for identification of wires at the server end. Colored tape shows where cable runs should be placed in false ceilings and walls. Configure one PC, with the network operating system installed, in the location of the file server. As cabling is complete, move the second PC to each wired location, start-up the network, and send messages. Make sure the location is as expected and that

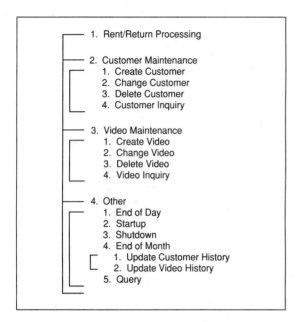

FIGURE 10-60   ABC Menu Structure

the wiring works. Test all wires because *they will be wrong*. Make sure all wiring is correct *before* the electrical contractor is paid and leaves.

The important issue is *to make a choice* of who will do what work long before the work is needed, and plan for what is to be done. Use a lawyer to write all contracts using information provided by you, as the client's representative, and the client.

Timing of installations can be crucial to implementation success. When different types of work are needed, such as air-conditioning and electrical cabling, the work should be sequenced so the contractors are not in each other's way, and in order of need. For instance, a typical sequence might be building frame, building shell, false floor/ceiling framing, electrical wiring, plumbing, air-conditioning, communications cabling, false floor/ceiling finishing, finishing walls, painting, and decorating. Any sequences of work should be checked with the people actually performing the work to guarantee that they agree to the work and schedule.

In general, you want to end testing of all equipment to be available for the beginning of design *at the latest*. This implies that all previous analysis work is manual. If CASE is to be used, the latest pos-

sible date for equipment and software availability is the beginning of project work.

Cabling is needed before equipment. Equipment is needed before software. Software is needed before application use. Some minimal slack time should be left as a cushion between dates in case there is a problem with the installation or the item being installed. Leave as big a cushion between installation and usage as possible, with the major constraint being payment strains on a small company.

ABC Video Example Hardware/Software Installation Plan

For ABC, a local area network is to be used. A file server with one laser printer, three impact printers, and five PCs are planned. The LAN will be a

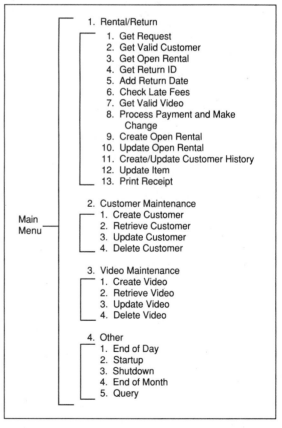

FIGURE 10-61   Incorrect Rental/Return Menu Structure

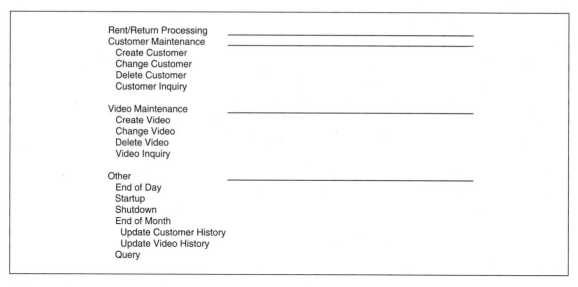

FIGURE 10-62   ABC Dialogue Flow Diagram Menu Structure Entries

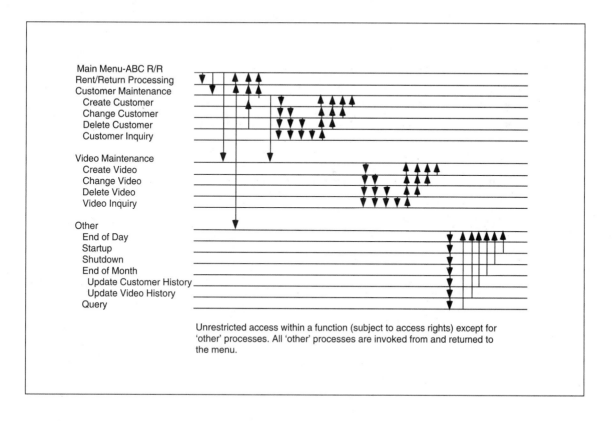

Unrestricted access within a function (subject to access rights) except for 'other' processes. All 'other' processes are invoked from and returned to the menu.

FIGURE 10-63   ABC Dialogue Flow Diagram

Novell ethernet with SQL-compatible DBMS software, Carbon Copy, Word Perfect, Lotus, Norton Utilities, Fastback, and Symantek Virus software. The goal is for all hardware to last at least five years if no other business functions are added to the system. The configuration details are shown in Figures 10-64 and 10-65. There should be adequate capacity to add accounting and order processing software if needed. The current average daily rentals of 600 is expected to double in five years. The current number of customers is 450, and is expected to be 1,000 in five years.

To develop a plan, assume that the current date is January 1, and that the application installation is scheduled for August 1. Design has just begun. The PCs and laser printer were installed five months ago for availability during planning, feasibility, and analysis. The currently installed software includes a CASE tool on two machines, Word Perfect, Norton Utilities, Fastback, the SQL DBMS, and SAM Virus software. The remainder of the software and hardware must be ordered, installed, and tested as part of this plan.

First we determine what we need. A comparison of currently installed items to the list of required items shows the following items need to be planned:

Network cable and connecters
File Server
Novell Software
Network Interface Cards (NICs, i.e., ethernet
    boards)
Impact printers
Bar Code Reader and Imprinter
Carbon Copy (network version)
Word Perfect (network version)
Norton Utilities (network version)
Fastback
SQL DBMS (network version)
SAM (network version)
Lotus (network version)

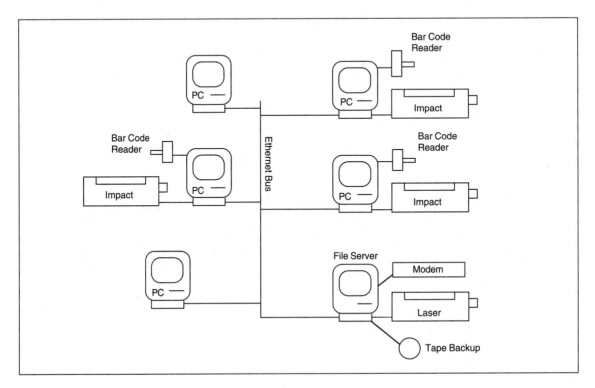

FIGURE 10-64   ABC Configuration Schematic

```
Hardware Characteristics:

File server        12 Mb Memory
                   800 Mb Disk
                   Super 486, SCSI Channel
                   Color monitor

1 Laser printer    8 Page/Minute

3 Impact printers for two-part forms (or 4 cheap lasers
with tear-apart forms)

5 PCs              2 Mb Memory
                   1.4 Mb Floppy disk for startup
                   No hard disk
                   Local printer (see above)

1 2400 Baud Modem for long distance troubleshooting

1 Streaming tape backup 100 Mb/Minute
```

FIGURE 10-65   ABC Hardware and Software Details

Everything should be ordered as soon as possible to ensure availability. Equipment and software ordering is the first item on the plan.

The group has installed network software before, but not the cable, so they obtain approval from Vic to engage another consultant, Max Levine, from their company to perform that work. Max has been installing mainframe and PC networks for over 20 years and knows everything about their installations and problems. He immediately takes over the network planning tasks. He first obtains a rough idea of the planned locations for equipment, computes cable requirements, and orders cable and connectors. Then, for the plan, he adds tasks for mapping specific cable locations for the installers, for installing and testing the file server, and for installing and testing the cable (see Table 10-6).

At the same time, Mary and Sam work at planning the remaining tasks. Each software package must be installed and tested. These tasks are planned for Sam and one junior person. The tests for all but the SQL package are to use the tool and verify that it works. For the SQL package, Sam and a DBA will install a small, multiuser application to test that the single and multiuser functions are working as expected. Of all the software being used, it is the

one with which they are least familiar, so they use the installation test as a means of gaining more experience.

All tasks relating to new equipment and software are scheduled to take place during a six-week period in January and February. This allows several months of cushion for any problems to be resolved; it also allows disruptive installations (e.g., cable) to be scheduled around peek hours and days. The schedule does not show elapsed time, but other work is taking place beside the installations. For instance, design work is progressing at the same time. As the application is implemented and the users have need for the equipment, the PCs and printers are moved to their permanent locations. This occurs in late spring for data conversion. The last stand-alone PCs are scheduled to be added to the network in late July, long before the application implementation date of August 15.

AUTOMATED TOOL SUPPORT FOR DATA-ORIENTED DESIGN

Many CASE tools support aspects of data oriented design (see Table 10-7). Two specifically support IE as discussed in this chapter. The IE CASE tools are Information Engineering Workbench[4] (IEW) by Knowledgeware, Inc., and Information Engineering Facility (IEF) by Texas Instruments, Inc. Both products receive high marks of approval and satisfaction from the user communities. Because of their cost, both products are used by mostly large companies. The products offer enterprise analysis in addition to application analysis, design, and construction (i.e., coding). Both IEF and IEW work on PCs, networks, and mainframes.

A typical IEF installation could include a mainframe version with the centralized repository. Users check out portions of a repository to work with on a PC. Then, when the work is complete and checked on the PC, it is merged with the mainframe reposi-

---

4 IEW for a OS/2 environment is called the Advanced Development Workbench (ADW).

TABLE 10-6   Installation Plan Items

Due Date	Responsible	Item
1/10	Mary/Sam	Order equipment and software
1/10	Mary/Sam	Order cable and connectors
1/15	ML	Plan cable, printer, PC, server locations
2/1	ML	Install and test file server and one PC
2/1	Sam, Jr. Pgmr.	Install and test impact printers
2/1	Sam, Jr. Pgmr.	Install and test bar code reader and printer
2/5	Sam, Jr. Pgmr.	Install and test Carbon Copy (network version)
2/5	Sam, Jr. Pgmr.	Install and test Word Perfect (network version?)
2/5	Sam, Jr. Pgmr.	Install and test Norton Utilities (network version)
2/5	Sam, Jr. Pgmr.	Install and test Fastback
2/5	Sam, Jr. Pgmr.	Install and test Lotus (network version)
2/5	Sam, Jr. Pgmr.	Install and test SAM (network version)
2/5	DBA, Sam	Install and test SQL DBMS (network version)
2/10	ML, Union Contractor	Install and test cable
2/15	DBA, Sam	Install test application and verify SQL DBMS
5/15	Sam, Vic's LAN Administrator	Move 2 PCs, bar code reader, and 3 printers to permanent locations and test
7/30	LAN Administrator	Move remaining three PCs to permanent locations and test
8/30	Mary, Sam	Remove CASE tools from PCs, remove single user software from PCs and file server

tory for official storage. When the merge takes place, the checked-out items are revalidated for consistency with all mainframe repository definitions. Both products offer automatic SQL schema generation for data. IEF offers automatic code generation for Cobol with imbedded SQL, and can interface to generators for other languages.

IEW and IEF differ in important ways. IEW is more flexible in that it does not require the completion of any matrices or diagrams. However, to take advantage of the interdiagram evaluation software that assesses completeness and syntactic consistency, all matrices and diagrams are required during a given phase. This means that you might not have the diagrams or analyses from planning, but you still can create levels of ERDs within the analysis tool. Similarly, you might not have the analysis tool, so action diagrams can be created directly within the design tool. IEF's strength is that its rigorous adherence to Information Engineering has led to substantive intelligence checking within the software. Both tools easily manage and sort large matrices that result from several of the analyses.

The weakness of the tools differs for each tool. IEW is primarily a PC-based product that can be unstable when used for large projects. IEW also provides DFDs, not PDFDs, and is not a *pure* data methodology tool. A strength of IEW is that Knowledgeware was an IBM partner in its repository definition; as a result, IEW is compatible with AD-cycle software from IBM.

IEF's strength is also its biggest weakness. IEF requires completion of every table, matrix, and diagram *at this time.*[5] The level of intelligent checking that can be performed is higher than with most other

CASE products, but the requirement to complete every table, and so on does not make sense for all projects. TI has recognized the severity of this shortcoming and is increasing the flexibility of the product without compromising its capabilities. The mainframe version of IEF uses DB/2 for repository management and can generate C, Cobol, DB/2, SQL, and other languages' codes.

---

5 1993

TABLE 10-7   Automated Tool Support for Data-Oriented Methodologies

Product	Company	Technique
Analyst/Designer Toolkit	Yourdon, Inc. New York, NY	Entity-Relationship Diagram (ERD)
Bachman	Bachman Info Systems Cambridge, MA	Bachman ERD Bachman IDMS Schema Bachman DB2 Relational Schema and Physical Diagram
CorVision	Cortex Corp. Waltham, MA	Action Diagram Dataview ERD Menu Designer
Deft	Deft Ontario, Canada	ERD Form/Report Painters Jackson Structured Design (JSD)—Initial Model
Design/1	Arthur Anderson, Inc. Chicago, IL	ERD
ER-Designer	Chen & Assoc. Baton Rouge, LA	ERD Normalization Schema generation
IEF	Texas Instruments Dallas, TX	Action Diagram Code Generation Data Structure Diagram Dialog Flow Diagram Entity Hierarchy ERD Process Data Flow Diagram Process Hierarchy Screen Painter

(Continued on next page)

TABLE 10-7   Automated Tool Support for Data-Oriented Methodologies (*Continued*)

Product	Company	Technique
IEW, ADW (PS/2 Version)	Knowledgeware Atlanta, GA	Action diagram Code generation Database diagram ERD Normalization Schema Generation Screen layout
System Engineer	LBMS Houston, TX	ERD DFD Menu Dialog Transaction Dialog Entity Life History Module Sequence DB2, ADABAS, IDMS, Oracle Table Diagram
Teamwork	CADRE Tech. Inc. Providence, RI	Control Flow Code Generation ERD Process Activation table Program Design Tools Testing Software
vs Designer	Visual Software Inc. Santa Clara, CA	Process flow diagram Action Diagram

SUMMARY

Data-oriented methods assume that, since data are stable and processes are not, data should be the main focus of activities. First, design focuses on the usage of data to develop a strategy for distributing or centralizing applications. Several matrices summarize process responsibility, data usage, type of data used, transaction volumes, and subjective reasons for centralizing or distributing data.

Next, processes from a process hierarchy diagram are restructured into action diagrams in design. The details of process interrelationships are identified from the PDFD and placed on the action diagram. Each process is fully defined either in a diagram or in the data dictionary. Process details are grouped into modules and compared to existing modules to determine module reusability. Modules are analyzed from a different perspective to reflect concurrency

opportunities or requirements on the action diagram. Entities are added to the diagram and related to processes. Lines connect individual processes to attributes to complete the action diagram specification of each application module. For manually drawn diagrams, an optional activity is to identify screens and link them to attributes and processes, to give a complete pictorial representation of the on-line portion of the application.

Data-oriented design focuses on the needs for security, recovery, and audit controls, relating each topic to the data and processes in the application.

The menu structure and dialogue flow for the application are defined next. The menu structure is constructed from the process hierarchy diagram to link activities, processes, and subprocesses for menu design. The structure can be used to facilitate interface designers' application understanding. The dialogue flow documents the flexibility or restrictiveness of the interface by defining the allowable movements from each menu level (from the menu structure) to other levels of menus and processing.

Finally, installation plans for all hardware and software are developed. A list of tasks is defined, responsibilities are assigned, and due dates are allocated to the tasks.

There are two fully functional CASE tools that support data-oriented methodology as discussed in this chapter, IEW and IEF. They are popular in companies that use data-oriented methods.

full backup	recovery
hardware installation plan	recovery procedures
horizontal data partitioning	repetition bracket
incremental backup	replication
independent concurrent	security plan
processes	selection bracket
menu structure	sequence bracket
normalization	sight verification
off-site storage	subset partitioning
physical security	structural relationships
procedural template	transaction volume matrix
process/location matrix	vertical partitioning

REFERENCES

Date, C. J., *An Introduction to Database Systems*, Vol. 1, 5th edition. Reading, MA: Addison-Wesley, 1990.

Finkelstein, Clive, *An Introduction to Information Engineering: From Strategic Planning to Information Systems*. Reading, MA: Addison-Wesley, 1989.

Knowledgeware, Inc., *Information Engineering Workbench™/Analysis Workstation, ESP Release 4.0.* Atlanta, GA: Knowledgeware, Inc., 1987.

Loucopoulos, Pericles, and Roberto Zicari, *Conceptual Modeling, Databases and CASE: An Integrated View of IS Development*. NY: John Wiley & Sons, 1992.

Martin, James, *Information Engineering, Vol. 3: Design and Construction*. Englewood Cliffs, NJ: Prentice-Hall, Inc., 1990.

Martin, James, and Carma McClure, *Diagramming Techniques for Analysts and Programmers*. Englewood Cliffs, NJ: Prentice-Hall, Inc., 1985.

Texas Instruments, *A Guide to Information Engineering Using the IEF*. Dallas, TX: Texas Instruments, 1988.

KEY TERMS

action diagram	data distribution by
application security	location matrix
audit control	data security
backup	data usage by location
burn-in	matrix
candidate for template	denormalization
code generator	dependent concurrent
computer verification	processes
concurrent processes	dialogue flow diagram
condition bracket	$D_R/D_C > N - 1$
control point	$D_R < N/D$
controlled redundancy	federation

EXERCISES

1. Analyze Figures 10-8 to 10-11 and Table 10-1. Develop and present a recommendation for centralization or distribution. Define all recommended data and software locations. Explain your reasoning for each choice.
2. Complete the action diagram for miscellaneous processing. Define the contents of the *EOD* File.
3. Go visit a local small business such as a video store, restaurant, or supermarket. Assess their security and physical layout. Develop a list of recommendations you would make if installing a computer system for this company. Present your findings to the class and the reasons for your recommendations.

STUDY QUESTIONS

1. Define the following terms:

action diagram	repetition bracket
code generator	replication
control point	security
controlled	transaction volume
redundancy	matrix
recovery	vertical data partitioning

2. What are structured programming tenets and why are they important in IE design?
3. What is the purpose of an action diagram?
4. Discuss this assertion: "Normalization to the third normal form and higher is always desirable for a physical database."

5. Define the four types of database distribution.

6. Describe how security, recovery, and audit controls complement each other.

7. There are six types of disasters considered in recovery planning. What are they and what data/application problems do they cause?

8. What are common methods of securing data against unwanted access?

9. What is the purpose of off-site storage? How off-site should off-site storage be?

10. What are the trade-offs in security and recovery design? Why not build a fortress to secure everything?

11. Discuss the differences between full and incremental backup.

12. What features of computers make audit controls difficult?

13. How is a menu structure diagram constructed? What is its purpose?

14. How can dialogue flow diagrams be used to partially provide for access control?

15. What are the structural relationships on an action diagram? Where do they come from?

16. List the steps in developing an action diagram.

17. For what types of applications does concurrency analysis become important?

18. What is reusability analysis? Why is it important?

19. Why, when developing an action diagram, must the processes sometimes change from what is on the PDFD?

20. Describe the matrices and formulae used to determine centralization or distribution of data. In the absence of subjective reasoning, would the matrices and formulae lead to a rational decision? Why or why not?

21. Why is an installation plan important? How can installation be used as a teaching exercise for junior people?

22. What aspects of physical environment should be considered in an installation plan for new equipment?

23. Describe the diagram interrelationships for data and processes from enterprise analysis to analysis to design.

EXTRA-CREDIT QUESTION

1. Analyze the Advanced Office System (AOS) case in the Appendix. Develop all of the distribution matrices and subjective reasoning for/against distribution. Develop recommendations and explain your reasoning for each choice.

OBJECT-ORIENTED ANALYSIS

INTRODUCTION

In this chapter, we reanalyze the requirements for the ABC Video's rental processing application using an object-oriented approach. This approach requires the definition of many new terms and a fundamentally different way of thinking about applications and their components. Keep in mind that object orientation is very much an immature methodology class that is still evolving.

Several distinct schools of thought have emerged on how best to represent object thinking. Since they discuss the same topics, the schools have considerable conceptual overlap. The first school is object orientation that uses many graphical forms paralleling those of other methodologies. Authors using this approach are Coad and Yourdon and Rumbaugh et al. (see References at the end of the chapter). The second school of object orientation is tabular, using mainly tables to list and define objects and their parts. This approach is used by Booch and Berrard. The graphical methodologies lack the reasoning processes of Booch's approach, while the tabular method is not easily communicated because of the extensive detail generated. Therefore, the Booch and Coad and Yourdon approaches are both modified and integrated throughout this discussion. Since few people dispute the need for analytical rigor and graphical richness, this type of object methodology is preferable to either one or the other approach used singly.

CONCEPTUAL FOUNDATIONS OF OBJECT-ORIENTED ANALYSIS

Two key concepts define object orientation: encapsulation and inheritance. **Encapsulation** is a property of programs that describes the complete integration of data with legal processes relating to the data. In addition, encapsulated objects have public and private *selves* (see Figure 11-1). The **public part** of an object defines what data are available in the object and the allowable actions of the object. The **private part** of an object defines local, object-only data and the specific procedures each action takes.

The second major property of object orientation is inheritance. **Inheritance** is a property that allows the generic description of objects which are then reused by *related* objects. Objects are grouped into **classes** that are defined as like objects that have *exactly* the same properties, attributes, and processes. Object **classes** are arranged in **hierarchies** of relationships. Within a hierarchy, objects at lower

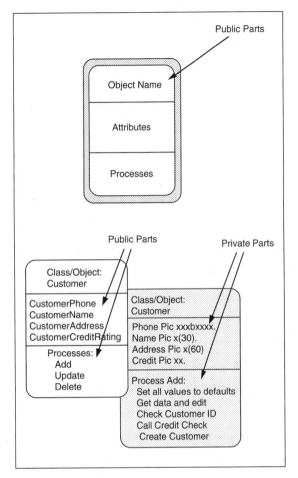

FIGURE 11-1 Encapsulated Object: Public and Private Parts

management committee subclass is said to have **multiple inheritance** because it inherits the properties, attributes, and processes of employees *and* managers as well as having its own.

Object orientation is an approach to thinking about problems that, when properly applied, represents a substantive improvement in the resulting analysis, design, and code modules. For 30 years, we have known that the key goal of software engineering is to manage the complexity of the problems we automate. We have also known that the best way to manage complexity is to decompose the larger problems into intellectually manageable, small tasks, that hide their internal workings from other modules, and that are coupled only by communicating messages.[1] These are the goals of analysis and design that lead to well-structured and well-formulated programs and modules. Object orientation, when properly applied, appears to come closer to automatically resulting in these desirable outcomes than other ways of thinking.

Thinking in objects requires a paradigm shift. A paradigm is a generally agreed upon way of thinking about a situation. In the process methods we concentrate on *functional* thinking, or the steps taken to perform some procedure. In data methods, we concentrate on *entity* thinking, or the data objects and their interrelationships that dictate much processing. Entity thinking is a difference in degree rather than a difference in kind—a foreground/background shift. We move from processes that change data to emphasizing data that require processing (see Figure 11-3).

levels inherit the data and processes of the superior classes. Hierarchies can also be linked to form lattice-like networks of hierarchies of objects.

An example of an object class is *employees* (see Figure 11-2). Each employee has a name, address, social security number, and so forth. Some employees are also managers. Managers are a subclass of the employee class. By subclass, we mean that managers have the same properties as employees (because they *are* employees), and that, in addition, they have additional properties that only managers have. Managers might have an additional subclass of managers who are on a management committee. The

1 See the works of CAR Hoare, David Parnas, Nicklaus Wirth, and Edsger Dijkstra. In particular, the discussions are summarized in the following references: Hoare, C. A. R., "The Emperor's Old Clothes," Dijkstra, Edsger, "The Humble Programmer," both in AMC Turing Lecture Awards, NY: ACM Press and Addison-Wesley, 1987, and Parnas, David, "A Technique for Software Module Specification with Examples," *Communications of the ACM*, Vol. 15, #5, May, 1972, pp. 330–336; Parnas, David, "On the Criteria to be Used in Decomposing Systems into Modules," *Communications of the ACM*, Vol. 15, #12, December 1972, pp. 1053–1058; and Wirth, Nicklaus, "Program Development by Stepwise Refinement," *Communications of the ACM*, Vol. 14, #4, April 1971, pp. 221–227.

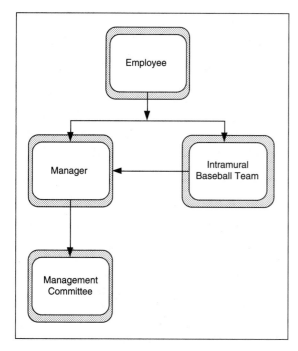

FIGURE 11-2   Example Object Class Hierarchy

In *object* thinking, we can identify data and processes somewhat independently, but they are *married* early on and must be thought of together, forever after, to reason properly about their behavior and contents. The paradigm shift to object thinking is from thinking of data and processes as separate to thinking of data and processes as one.

Several times in this discussion, we have mentioned the term "if properly applied." Object orientation is no different than any other methodology in that it requires consistency and correct reasoning to result in the desirable properties described. When improperly applied, object orientation results in a badly designed application that might actually be less efficient than the same application designed poorly using some other methodology.

DEFINITION OF _____
OBJECT-ORIENTED _____
TERMS_____

Object orientation is based on the notion of objects which encapsulate both data and processes on that

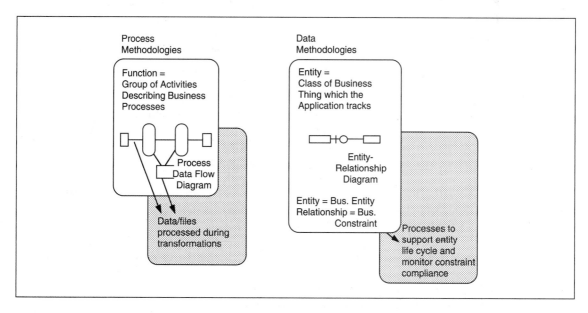

FIGURE 11-3   Process and Data Methodologies as Flip Sides of the Same Paradigm

data. An **object** is an entity from the real world whose processes and attributes (that is, the data) are modeled in a computerized application.

Processes are variously called functions, actions, services, programs, methods, properties, or modules; these terms may or may not have the same meaning to the people using them. For that reason, we stick to the term *process* to mean the transformational program language code that acts on its object data.

An **abstract data type (ADT)** is the name used in some languages (e.g., C) for the new, user-defined data type that *encapsulates* definitions of object data plus legal processes for that data. In this text, we use the terms encapsulated object, object, and abstract data type interchangeably.

The major analysis activities focus on defining objects, classes, and processes. Class/objects are the lowest level of logical design entity. **Class/objects** define a set of items which share the same attributes and processes, and manage the instances of the collection. The **class** defines the attributes and processes; the objects are the instances of the class definition.

There are different types of class-object relationships. First, classes can occur without having any real data associated with them. Classes whose instances are other classes are called **meta-classes**. For instance, we might define a class *Customer* with subclasses for *CashCustomer* and *CreditCustomer*. The class is a meta-class; the subclasses are class/objects which manage the data of *Customer*.

Classes can be composed of class/objects to describe a composition relationship of *whole* and *part*. A **whole class** defines the composed object type. The **part class** defines all the components of the whole class. For instance, a car, as a whole class, contains parts that include motor, wheels, doors, seats, and so on.

Classes can also be defined to allow specialized versions of an item. The meta-class is called a *generalization class*, or gen class for short. The subclasses are called *specialization*, or spec, *classes*. A **generalization class** defines a group of similar objects. For instance, vehicle is a generalization on car. The **specialization class** is a subclass that reflects an *is-a* relationship, defining a more detailed description of the gen class. For instance, a car, truck, or tank are all specializations of the general class vehicle. These could be further specialized themselves. For instance, car could have specializations by type car: full-size, mid-size, or economy.

Each type of class and its subclasses form a hierarchic, lattice-like arrangement of relationships. Through the relationships, the lower-level classes inherit the data and processes of the related higher-level classes. Thus, if we were to refer to an *economyCar* object, we would have information and processing for vehicles, cars, and economy cars all available.

Messages are the only legal means of communications between encapsulated objects. Messages are clear in their intention but not clear in their implementation, which is completely determined by the language (see message types in Figure 11-4). For instance, at the moment Ada does not implement message communication. In this text, a **message** is the unit of communication between two objects. Messages contain an addressee (that is, the object providing the process, also called a service object), and some identification of the requested process.

A major difference between object orientation and other methodologies is the shifting of responsibility for defining the data type of legal processes from supplier (or called) objects to client (or calling) objects. This shift, along with the notions of inheritance and dynamic binding, support the use of **polymorphism**, which is the ability to have the same process take different forms when associated with different objects. Dynamic binding is a language property that selects actual modules to execute during application operation. The concept is completely described in Chapter 12.

A **supplier object** is one that performs a requested process. A **client object** is one that requests a process from a supplier. For instance, I might need to have a date translated from month-day-year format to year-month-day format. As a client object, I request the translation of the supplier object and pass the date to translate. If the language supports polymorphism, I also pass the data type of the date to be translated.

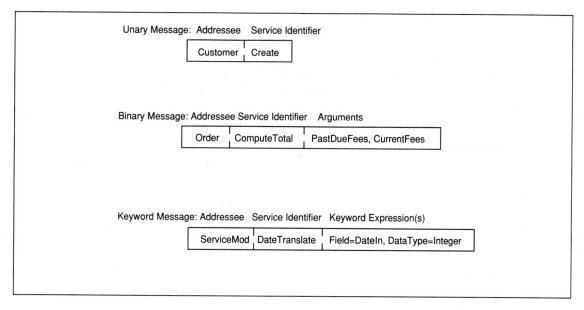

FIGURE 11-4   Example of Message Types

An example of polymorphism is, for instance, a process to perform comparison of two items to identify the 'larger' of the two. One object might be alphabetic, requiring a logical comparison; another object might be decimal numeric, requiring a numerical comparison; a third object might be an array, requiring numerical array comparisons. This polymorphic object has three implementations of its process to *compare and determine the larger of two items*. The client object requests a specific comparison process, here either alpha, numeric, or array.

To summarize the terms, objects are encapsulations of data and processes that have both public and private parts. Objects can communicate via messages which differ by language. Objects are arranged into classes of similar objects, and can belong to more than one class. By the property of inheritance, an object exhibits the attributes and provides the services of the classes of which it is a part. Polymorphism is a desirable property of objects but requires a client-server view of objects along with dynamic binding capabilities.

OBJECT-ORIENTED ANALYSIS ACTIVITIES

The documentation for object-oriented analysis[2] includes a series of tables and graphics (Figure 11-5). The tables are lists that document individual components of the analysis—objects, processes (and their assignment to objects), attributes, and classes. The graphics show relationships between objects and object classes, state transitions of intraobject changes in the application, and time-ordering interobject–event processing. Each documentation representation is elaborated by tracing the object-oriented analysis of ABC Video's rental processing system.

---

2 The analysis documentation builds primarily on the work of Booch [1983, 1991] and Berrard [1985]. The Class diagrams, subject summary, gen-spec and whole-part diagrams are all from Coad and Yourdon, 2nd ed. [1990].

Summary Paragraph	Provides a brief summary of all major functions to be performed.
Tables/Lists	
Object List	Contains potential objects (nouns) from the paragraph. Each entry is evaluated to determine that it is an object, to classify it as solution space or problem space related, and to assign it a unique, formal name.
Process List	Contains potential processes (verbs) from the paragraph. Each is evaluated to determine that it is a process, to classify it as solution space or problem space related, and to assign it a unique, formal name. All solution space class/objects are tentatively related to processes and the relationships are evaluated.
Object-Attribute List	Contains field name attributes with each object they describe. Each class/object's entries are normalized and other class/objects are created as needed.
Process-Attribute List	Contains formulae, constraints on processing, and state/status changes for each process as required; some processes have no attributes.
Diagrams	
Object Relationship Diagram	Identifies objects with connecting lines showing different types of interobject relationships.
Class Hierarchy Diagram	Shows objects arranged in one or more lattice hierarchies to link shared data/processes and to depict inheritance of those data/processes.
Generalization/Specialization Structure Diagrams	Depicts objects which express *is-a* relationships. This diagram is optional.
Whole/Part Structure Diagrams	Depicts objects which are compositions for which the *whole* class is composed of one or more of the *part* subclasses. This diagram is optional.
Subject Summary Diagram	The highest level of independent classes or class/objects in each leg of a hierarchy are promoted to *subjects* for inclusion in this diagram which provides a summary of the classes in the application. This diagram is optional.
State Transition Diagram	Contains system states (i.e., statuses) and the events (process outcomes) that cause those states to exist.

FIGURE 11-5   Summary of Object-Oriented Analysis Documentation

Develop Summary Paragraph

Rules for Summary Paragraph

The first, and most important, step of object-oriented analysis is to develop a single summary paragraph describing the problem. The purpose of the paragraph is to focus your attention on the most concrete, yet high-level description of the problem. Hidden within a good summary are the main class/objects and the main processes to be provided by the application. In a large application, development will be iterative with a series of more detailed summary paragraphs developed to elaborate the individual sentences from a summary. In a smaller problem, like ABC Video's, we only need one level of summary.

The guidelines for writing the paragraph are as follows:

1. Write only declarative sentences of the form:
   Noun–Verb
   Noun–Verb–Object
   Verb–Object
2. For ease of quality assurance, write each sentence on its own line.

3. Review the paragraph carefully to ensure:

- All desired functions are represented.
- All major information and processes are identified.
- All sentences are at the same level of abstraction, detail, and importance.

These are guidelines because the development of the paragraph is an individual activity performed by the SE with the user, and specific to each application. It is one result of interviews and other data collections that take place before and during analysis. Object orientation assumes that you have the requirements for the application in hand and understand what the application is supposed to do.[3] There are no graphical representations for paragraph information.

ABC Video Example Paragraph

Refer back to Chapter 2 for the description of ABC Video's rental processing requirements. The initial paragraph reads:

> Customers select one to n videos for rental. Customer phone number is entered to retrieve customer data and create an order. Bar code IDs for each tape are entered and video information from inventory is displayed. The video inventory file is updated (decrease the count of available copies by one). When all tape IDs are entered, the system computes the total. Money is collected and the amount is entered into the system. Change is computed and displayed. The rental is created, printed, and stored. The customer signs the rental form, takes the tape(s), and leaves. To return a tape, the video Bar Code ID is entered into the system. The rental is displayed and the tape is marked with the date of return. If past-due amounts are owed, they can be paid at this time; or the clerk can select an option which updates the rental with the return date and calculates past-due fees. Any outstanding video rentals are displayed with the amount due on each tape and a total amount due. The past-due amount must be reduced to zero when new tapes are taken out.

---

3 Lorenz [1993] recommends the development of 'use cases' which track all variations of each transaction through its processing. This is, in essence, what you do in interviews with users during a normal data collection activity.

1. Customers select one to n videos for rental.
2. Customer phone number is entered to retrieve customer data and create an order.
3. Bar code IDs for each tape are entered and video information from inventory is displayed.
4. The video inventory file is updated (decrease the count of available copies by one).
5. When all tape IDs are entered, the system computes the total.
6. Money is collected and the amount is entered into the system.
7. Change is computed and displayed.
8. The rental is created, printed, and stored.
9. The customer signs the order form, takes the tape(s), and leaves.
10. To return a tape, the video Bar Code ID is entered into the system.
11. The rental is displayed and the tape is marked with the date of return.
12. If past-due amounts are owed, they can be paid at this time; or the clerk can select an option which updates the rental with the return date and calculates past-due fees.
13. Any outstanding video rentals are displayed with the amount due on each tape and a total amount due.
14. The past-due amount must be reduced to zero when new tapes are taken out.
15. For new customers, the customer information is entered into the system and added to the customers.
16. For new videos, the video information is entered into the system and added to inventory.

FIGURE 11-6   Initial Paragraph in Numbered Sentence Format

For new customers, the customer information is entered into the system and added to the customers. For new videos, the video information is entered into the system and added to inventory.

The paragraph is reformatted as a numbered list of sentences (see Figure 11-6). This numbered sentence format is recommended because it simplifies discussion, quality assurance, and reviews.

Once the paragraph is drafted, you examine each sentence carefully to make sure all the pertinent information is present and clearly stated. In this paragraph, there is confusion about a 'new order' in sentence 2 and an 'outstanding video rental' in sentence 13. You ask yourself, What do we mean by an 'order'? If you do not know, you may need to ask the client what he means by an order.

Vic wants an order to have information that is linked to video information whenever customers have any videos out on rent, that is, they are an 'active' customer. An order should contain information about all current rentals, dates returned, and late fees. Any other fees owed, for instance, penalties assessed for late payment, should also be present until they are paid. In other words, Vic uses the word *order* to describe what we have termed a *rental*. This confusion is cleared up immediately because different words for the same items always cause confusion. Vic does not mind changing the term *order* to *rental*. He uses the term *order* because he thinks his business is similar to order-entry processing which he managed in an old job. The major differences between these two activities is that Vic has a cash business and order-entry applications are usually used in accrual accounting businesses that link to accounts receivable accounting. Vic is correct; there is similarity between rentals and order processing, but the term rental fits this particular business and will be used.

To be consistent in the use of terms, we modify sentence 2 to read:

2. Customer phone number is entered to retrieve customer data either to create a rental or to retrieve active rentals.

This change also implies a status for *rentals* of *'active'* or *'inactive'* which we will need to further clarify.

The term *video information from inventory* in sentence 3 should be more specific. Knowing the actual fields to be displayed will be helpful in the class analysis and in attribute definition. Upon further conversation with Vic, you change the information to read:

3. Bar code IDs for each tape are entered.
3a. Video name and rental price from inventory are displayed.

The next unclear issue is: When is money collected for new rentals? Can a customer rent a video, pay past-due fees, and pay for the current video rental upon its return? Again, we go back to Vic, the client, and ask him what he wants.

Vic says, "I would like as little bureaucracy as possible in this system. Since 80% of videos are returned on time, I want new rentals paid in advance—when they are rented. About 90% of my customers return their videos through a slot in the door during nonworking hours. Any videos that have late fees are checked in, and a note of past-due fees must be made.

"For legal reasons, I must be able to prove how past-due fees are derived. To meet this obligation, the past-due fee amount, rental date and return date must all be maintained.

"Also, I do not want to encourage 'deadbeats' who do not pay for their rentals, so I insist that any outstanding fees be paid before any new rentals."

With the above information supplied by Vic, we evaluate the sentences dealing with payments. Although they remain somewhat ambiguous, they would be sufficient if we chose not to change them. The information is clearer if sentences 13 and 14 are moved between sentences 2 and 3 and are renumbered 2a and 2b for the present.

One remaining ambiguity might be computations for the *'total'* and *'change.'* If the computations are understood, they are not required in the paragraph. We do not *need* the computations for the paragraph, but we do need it soon. So, if the computations are not understood, you again go back to Vic and ask how the computations are performed.

Vic: "There are two basic totals: one for settling past-due fees and one for the current rental. They may be computed together as the rental total equal to the sum of all past-due items, fees, taxes, and current rentals. Change is computed as the rental-total less amount paid."

Vic's definition of the rental-total raises a new question about the paying of late fees and sentence 2b. If past-due fees must be settled before any current rentals are allowed, how can you add the information together to create the rental-total?

Old #	New #	Sentence
2.	2.	Customer phone number is entered to retrieve customer data either to create a rental or to retrieve an active rental.
2a.	3.	Any outstanding video rentals are displayed with the amount due on each tape and a total amount due.
2b	Note	The past-due amount must be reduced to zero when new rentals are made.
3.	4.	Bar code IDs for each tape are entered.
3a.	5.	Video name and rental price from inventory are displayed.
5.	6.	When all tape IDs are entered, the system computes the total (= Σ past-due fees + Σ other fees + Σ current video rental fees).
6.	7.	Money is collected and the amount is entered into the system.
7.	8.	Change is computed (= amount entered—order-total) and displayed.
	9.	If the change amount is negative, that is, the customer did not pay for all fees, the clerk asks for more money.
	10.	If the customer gives the clerk more money, return to step 7, else, when the clerk presses an order complete key, the system 'pays-off' the fees on a first-in-first-paid order until the amount entered is used up. The rental is redisplayed. Past-due items 'paid-off' are marked paid and the status of the current video rentals are either paid or due.
	11.	If the amount entered paid for one or more current rentals, they are updated as paid and the videos are given to the customer; else when the clerk presses the rental complete key again, the current rentals not paid for are removed and placed back in stock.
4.	12.	When the clerk presses a rental complete key (to be defined by the system), this order is complete and the video inventory file is updated (decrease the count of available copies by one).
8.	13.	The rental is stored and printed.

FIGURE 11-7   Partially Renumbered Paragraph

"Oh," says Vic, "I meant that the clerk should not give the customer the video tapes until all of the past-due fees plus current rental fees are paid. They can still process the current rentals on the computer at the same time. Remember, my motto is no bureaucracy."

This new information does change at least the order of sentences 2 through 8 (see Figure 11-7). At the end of the paragraph, add the following so the information is not lost.

2b. NOTE: The amount paid less change must be equal to the rental-total or the clerk should politely refuse to give the customer the current tapes.

The new sentences 9, 10, and 11 add needed information to our understanding of the problem, but now they are at a different level of detail from the other sentences. They constitute *processing* that accompanies *change*. So, to keep the level of abstraction consistent, they should be removed from this paragraph and kept for use during the next iteration of *change processing*. To indicate that other steps are needed to process change, modify sentence 8 to read:

8. Change is computed (= amount-entered—rental-total), displayed, and further processed by the clerk as required.

At the moment, the final paragraph for ABC Video's rental processing system should read like the one in Figure 11-8. All major functions, data entities, information sources, and destinations are identified. All sentences are at the same level of abstraction, detail, and importance.

Identify Objects of Interest

Rules for Identifying Class/Objects

The next step is to identify and analyze all of the class/objects of interest. The items are called class/objects because they identify a collection (class) of like instances (objects). The rules are summarized here:

1. Underline all nouns in the summary paragraph.
2. List the underlined verbs on a separate sheet of paper, using the exact same sequence and spelling as in the paragraph.
3. Evaluate each noun to make sure it *is* an object. (Common errors are to include attributes objects, that are not of interest to the solution of *this* problem, or physical objects we do *not* keep information about).
4. Determine whether the object is in the *solution space* (must be present both to describe the problem *and* to develop a solution) or the *problem space* (must be present to describe the problem).
5. Name each unique object in the solution space. Ignore the processes in the problem space. Use the convention '*=name*' to identify duplicates of already named objects and to show that you know it is a duplicate.

The mechanics of the identification are to underline the nouns in the paragraph. Once the underlining is done, make a list of the nouns on a separate sheet of paper. When making the list, keep the nouns in exactly the same sequence as they occurred in the paragraph and use exactly the same spelling as occurred in the paragraph!

Next, evaluate each noun to make sure it *is* an object. Evaluate similar criteria for identifying entities in the data methodology: people, places, events, applications, organizations, or other abstractions about which the application must keep information

---

To rent tapes,

1. Customers select one to *n* videos for rental.
2. Customer phone number is entered to retrieve customer data either to create a rental or to retrieve an active rental.
3. Any outstanding video rentals are displayed with the amount due on each tape and a total amount due.
4. Bar code IDs for each tape are entered.
5. Video name and rental price from inventory are displayed.
6. When all tape IDs are entered, the system computes the total (= Σ past-due fees + Σ other fees + Σ current video rental fees).
7. Money is collected and the amount is entered into the system.
8. Change is computed (= amount entered − order-total), displayed, and further processed by the clerk as required.
9. When the clerk presses an 'order-complete' option key (to be defined by the system), this rental is complete and the video inventory file is updated (decrease the count of available copies by one).
10. The rental is stored and printed.
11. The customer signs the order form, takes the tape, and leaves.

To return a tape,

12. The video bar code ID is entered into the system.
13. The rental is displayed and the tape is marked with the date of return.
14. If past-due amounts are owed, they can be paid at this time; or the clerk can select the 'order-complete' option which updates the rental with the return date and calculates past-due fees.

To add a customer:

15. Enter customer information.
16. Create customer.

To add a new video:

17. Enter video information.
18. Create video inventory.

NOTE: The entire amount owed must be paid before any rentals are allowed. That is, the amount paid less change must be equal to the rental total or the clerk should politely refuse to give the customer the current tapes.

FIGURE 11-8   Final Paragraph for ABC Order Processing

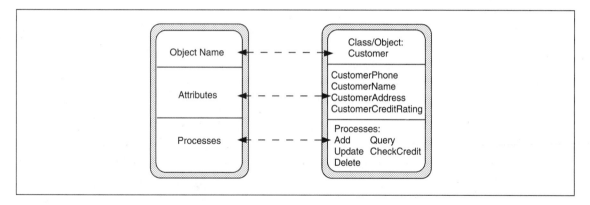

FIGURE 11-9   Class/Object Diagram Format

or for which processing is required. If the items in the list fit any of these criteria and pass the other tests, keep them on the list.

There are no hard and fast rules for this process, only heuristics or rules of thumb. Ask yourself the following sets of questions. Does the noun identify something from the real world you want to store information about? If so, keep going. If not, it is not an object in this system, so cross it off.

Does the noun identify something that takes on values itself, for instance, a social security number, balance, or rental total? If so, these are attributes (or fields) describing an object. Cross them off this list and put them on a list of attributes somewhere. If not, then keep going.

Does this name uniquely identify a set of things with the same attributes? If so, keep going. If not, if it identifies one unique thing, it may still be an object but you should look for commonalities and combine with some other class/object.

Once you have crossed off all nonobjects in this application, you are ready for the next analysis on objects: Determine if it is in the problem space or in the solution space. The **problem space** includes objects that are required to describe the problem but are not required to describe the solution. For instance, you might need to know something about IRS reporting requirements to properly define the length of time you need to keep an accounting file of transactions. But the IRS does not factor into the solution, nor do you keep any information about the

IRS in the application. In this example, the IRS would be a problem space object.

The **solution space** includes objects that are required both to describe the problem *and* to develop a solution. In ABC Video, 'customer' is necessary to both the problem definition and to the automated application solution. So, it is in the solution space.

When you are done evaluating all entries in the list, the solution space objects are given a class/object name by which they are known for the life of the application. During this step, we eliminate duplicates of each object. By convention, the name in the list is entered as either *ObjectName* or *=ObjectName*. The format *ObjectName* identifies a unique class/object. The format *=ObjectName* identifies a synonym of a class/object. The *=ObjectName* ensures quality assurance reviewers that you have accounted for all objects and have considered every entry on the list.

Finally, a class/object diagram is begun. A class/object is a collection of like *things* in a class; the objects are the individual *instances* of the *things* in the class. Class/objects are drawn as a rounded vertical rectangle with a shadow rectangle. The class/object is divided into three parts to depict the name, attributes, and processes (see Figure 11-9). The three areas identify public information relating to the class/object. Eventually other details are added for private information during design. Now, let us return to ABC's application to develop the object list.

ABC Video Example Object List

First, we underline the nouns from the paragraph (see Figure 11-10). Objects represent people, organizations, events, applications, or other abstractions from the real world about which we need to keep information. These are all identified by *nouns*. The underlined nouns represent all of the *potential* objects from the paragraph. If the paragraph is complete, this action should result in the identification of all major objects relating to the application.

Next, list the objects *exactly* as they are spelled and ordered in the paragraph. The first-cut object list is shown in Figure 11-11. The dispositions for each object are discussed here.

The first analysis is to eliminate attributes from the list. In the first-cut object list, attributes are crossed out and their respective objects are listed. Attributes change value for each related object instance. To identify an attribute, we ask, Can this *name* take on a value? If the answer is yes, it is an attribute. Attributes are set aside for use in a future step.

Figure 11-11 shows Rental attributes including *AmountDue, TotalAmountDue, RentalTotal, Amount,* and *Change.* Attributes of Videos on Rentals include *RentalPrice, ReturnDate,* and *Past-DueFees.* Video attributes include *BarCodeId* and *VideoName.* Finally, *PhoneNumber* is an attribute of Customer.

Next, we evaluate remaining nouns to determine if they are objects. The nouns that are clearly objects are the following:

customers
videos
rental (4 times)
tape (4 times)
money
clerk (3 times)
video inventory file
rental form
system

The objects in the above list do not take on values of their own. They are material and distinct, and they are of interest to the application. Therefore, they are objects.

To rent tapes,

1. Customers select one to *n* videos for rental.
2. Customer phone number is entered to retrieve customer data either to create a rental or to retrieve an active rental.
3. Any outstanding video rentals are displayed with the amount due on each tape and a total amount due.
4. Bar code IDs for each tape are entered.
5. Video name and rental price from inventory are displayed.
6. When all tape IDs are entered, the system computes the rental total (= Σ past-due fees + Σ other fees + Σ current video rental fees).
7. Money is collected and the amount is entered into the system.
8. Change is computed (= amount entered − order-total), displayed, and further processed by the clerk as required.
9. When the clerk presses a 'rental-complete' option key (to be defined by the system), this rental is complete and the video inventory file is updated (decrease the count of available copies by one).
10. The rental is stored and printed.
11. The customer signs the rental form, takes the tape, and leaves.

To return a tape,

12. The video bar code ID is entered into the system.
13. The rental is displayed and the tape is marked with the date of return.
14. If past-due amounts are owed, they can be paid at this time, or the clerk can select the 'rental-complete' option which updates the rental with the return date and calculates past-due fees.

For new customers,

15. Enter customer information.
16. Create customer.

For new videos,

17. Enter video information.
18. Create video.

FIGURE 11-10   Underlined Nouns

At this point we are not concerned that there are duplicates on this list, or that we will not keep automated information about all entries on this list. The less obvious, remaining entries we need to evaluate are:

Noun from Paragraph	Disposition	Noun from Paragraph	Disposition
Customers	Object	rental	Object
videos	Object	customer	Object
~~Customer phone number~~	Attribute of Customer, Rental	rental form	Object
customer data	Object	tape	Object
rental	Object	~~video Bar Code ID~~	Attribute of Video, VOR
active rental	Object	~~system~~	What we are creating
outstanding video rentals	Object	rental	Object
tape	Object	tape	Object
~~total amount due~~	Attribute of Rental	~~date of return~~	Attribute of Video on Rental
~~Bar code IDs~~	Attribute of Video, VideoOnRental (VOR)	~~past due amounts~~	Attribute of Rental, VOR
tape	Object	~~they~~ (meaning past due amount)	Attribute of Rental
~~Video name~~	Attribute of Video	clerk	Object
~~rental price~~	Attribute of Video, VOR	~~'rental complete' option~~	Event trigger
~~tape IDs~~	Attribute of Video, VOR	rental	Object
system	Object	~~return date~~	Attribute of Video on Rental
~~rental total~~	Attribute of Rental	~~past due fees.~~	Attribute of Video on Rental
Money	Object	~~customer information~~	All attributes of customer
~~amount~~	Attribute of Rental	customer	Object
~~system.~~	What we are creating	~~video information~~	All attributes of video
~~Change~~	Attribute of Rental	Video	Object
clerk	Object		
clerk	Object		
~~'rental complete' option key~~	Event trigger		
rental	Object		
video inventory file	Object		

FIGURE 11-11   Initial Object List for ABC Rental Processing

active rental
outstanding video rentals
'rental complete' option key (2 times)
customer information
video information

'Active' is an adjective describing a state of a rental. As soon as we say *describing* we know this is an attribute of some sort. The allowable states most probably are 'active' and 'inactive,' in which case this is the status of a rental, an attribute. We may want to reevaluate what an active/inactive rental is to make sure this is correct. Active, in the sense used here, appears to mean *open rental with rentals*, based on the paragraph. Then inactive would imply *no rentals outstanding*. If this

status were to remain in the application, it would be appropriate to change the wording to be more precise to open/closed rental. At some point, the analysis should be reviewed with Vic. So, for the active rental issue, for instance, we might ask Vic the following:

We have talked about active rentals. Does *active* really mean an open rental? If not, what other kinds of rentals are there? If yes, do we need to keep that status separate or is it implicit? For instance, is an open rental any for which a rental is not returned or is returned with late fees owed?

The next action on active rentals is based on the answers to these questions. Vic decides that *active* does mean *open rentals* and that a specific status is not required as long as he has access to *open rental information.*

Outstanding video rentals is also an adjectival description of videos on a rental that appears to be a status. Other statuses of videos on rentals that we might identify so far are combinations of:

outstanding/returned
on-time/late
paid/not paid.

We note these for the attribute list and eliminate them from further discussion here.

Last is the *rental complete option key*. This is a noun phrase describing an implementation detail—a key on the keyboard to be pressed to indicate the end of rental processing. It is not an object because it has no attributes, and we do not keep data about it in the application. It is an event trigger that will initiate some processing, but it does not enter into this level of analysis so it is eliminated from the object list.

Last are *customer information* and *video information.* These two items are similar in that they both reference a collection of attributes describing two entities. As such we could either list their attributes (then omit them from the list because they are attributes) or call them objects. We opt for calling them 'collections of attributes' and eliminating them from the object list.

Now we return to the objects we did find to decide if they are in the problem space or the solution space. Problem space objects are required to describe the task domain but not to develop an automated solution. Solution space objects are required to describe both the task domain and the automated solution. Once problem space objects are identified, they drop out of the remaining analysis. We decide which space each object describes (see Figure 11-12).

The last stages are to name each object with a unique name by which it will be known in the system and to eliminate duplicate names for the same object. When we find a duplicate, we indicate the name by an equal sign ('=') appended to the front of the name to signify that the name already appeared once.

During this exercise, we have two options for dealing with repeating information and relationship objects which describe one-to-many relationships. We can define them for later normalization or we can define them as fully as possible now. We opt for more completeness now because it usually means

Object	Space	Justification
Customers	S	Need automated customer information
Video	S	Need automated video information
Rental	S	Need automated rental information
Tape	3 S, 1P	Three references are tape information to be maintained in the system. One reference is to the tape taken home by customers; this reference is in the problem domain.
Money	P	Real money is outside of the system. We are concerned with the amount which is data entered into the system and related to rental.
Clerk	P	We do not keep statistics or other information on clerks in the system.
Video Inventory File	S	Need automated video information.
Rental Form	P	Just a different media than 'rental' . . . not relevant by itself to the solution.
System	P	This is irrelevant because 'system' is what we are building.

FIGURE 11-12   Object Space Justification

Noun from Paragraph	Solution or Problem Space	Object_Name
Customers	S	Customer
videos	S	VideoInventory
rental	S	Rental
active rental	S	=Rental
outstanding video rentals	S	VideoOnRental
tape	S	=VideoOnRental
tape	S	=VideoOnRental
rental	S	=Rental
video inventory file	S	=VideoInventory
rental	S	=Rental
rental	S	=Rental
tape	S	=VideoOnRental
rental	S	=Rental
customer	S	=Customer
video	S	=VideoInventory

FIGURE 11-13   Object List for ABC Rental Processing

less reworking later. For example, a rental has one or more related videos. We could define both of these as 'rental,' or we could define *Rental* and *VideoOnRental* separately. We opt for the normalized form because it results in a more complete analysis. This results in four class/objects: *Customer*, *Rental*, *VideoOnRental*, and *VideoInventory*.

Figure 11-13 shows the class/objects from this analysis in their final form (for this step). Notice the objects are still in order by their sequence in the paragraph, all have a space designation, and all solution space objects are named.

Finally, we depict class/objects from this list. We switch from the term object to the term *class/object* to acknowledge both the shared attributes and processes *and* the instantiation of them. ABC has four class/objects corresponding to *Customer*, *VideoOn-*

Rental, *Rental*, and *VideoInventory*. The four class/objects are depicted in Figure 11-14 for further elaboration in future steps. Information that we know at this point is also in the diagram.

Identify Processes

Rules for Identifying Processes

The next step is to identify processes. The rules for identifying processes are summarized as follows:

1. Circle all verbs in the summary paragraph.
2. List the circled verbs on a separate sheet of paper, using the *exact* same *sequence* and *spelling* as in the paragraph.
3. Evaluate each verb to make sure it *is* a process. (Common errors are to include status, physical actions, or comments.)
4. Determine whether the process is in the *solution space* or the *problem space*.
5. Name each unique process in the solution space. Ignore those processes in the problem space. Use the convention '=*name*' to identify duplicates of already named processess and show that you know it is a duplicate.
6. Assign objects to verbs if the object is transformed by the process or if the object data is read by the process.
7. Evaluate the object assignments:

   If there is only one object assigned to a process, continue.

   If all objects are read-only, continue.

   For processes with more than one object transformation, evaluate the transformation process:

   If all processes are exactly the same, and all data types acted on are exactly the same, then mark the process for creation of a reusable module.

   If all processes are exactly the same, but all data types are not the same, mark the process for polymorphic module creation.

   If all processes are not exactly the same, redevelop the paragraph to more specifically define the processing.

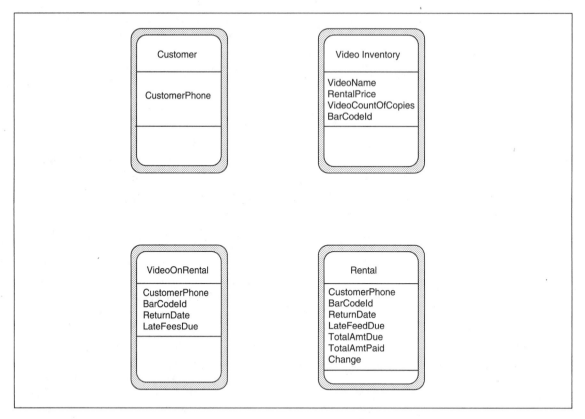

FIGURE 11-14   ABC Class/Objects

Processes are actions described by verbs. We identify the verbs in the summary paragraph, circling them to distinguish them from the nouns. Once the circling is done, make a list on a separate sheet of paper of the verbs. When making the list, keep the verbs in exactly the same sequence and use exactly the same spelling as occurred in the paragraph!

Then, evaluate each verb to make sure it *is* a process. Ask yourself if the verb is a process that the *application* must provide. If yes, keep going; if not, cross the verb off. For instance, if the paragraph said "The clerk enters the customer's phone number into the system," the clerk has been removed as a problem space object. But, the verb *enters* as applied to the customer's phone number *is* required data entry to begin the rental entry process. So, *enters* remains in the system. If we had included the terms *To rent a tape* or *To return a tape* in the list, these are summary descriptions of entire procedures

and the verbs *rent* and *return* would be excluded as nonprocesses.

After the first evaluation, review each verb again to determine if it is in the solution space or the problem space. The meanings of solution and problem space are the same as for class/objects. Problem space means the process is required to define the problem but not the automated solution. Solution space processes are required both to define the problem and to define the solution.

Next, review each verb carefully and give it a meaningful name. Try to define meaningful process names that indicate *both* the process and the class/object on which it acts. So, for *enter a customer phone number*, the process name might be *enterCustPhone.*

For any processes that use the same verb descriptor, or that you think are *exactly* the same, mark with an asterisk for further evaluation in the design phase.

Include an asterisk on processes that work on objects with different data types. Name them the same verb appending a unique identifier for each instance. These unique names make recognizing these processes in the next step easier. One possible naming convention[4] is to describe the situation, such as *enterTapeIdRental*, *enterTapeIdReturn*, and *enterTapeIdRenew*. The idea is to assign names that you can live with for the entire life of the object and its processes. In design, if these processes are all defined as the same, we simply truncate the names to *enterTapeId*.

The last step in identifying processes is to assign class/objects to operations. List each object with all processes that *use* or *transform* it. When this identification is done, reevaluate all processes with more than one object assignment.

The three questions you ask in this evaluation are summarized in Figure 11-15. First, ask if only one object is actually transformed by this process. If the answer is yes, go to the next process to be evaluated. If the answer is no, then continue with the evaluation.

Next, for the processes being transformed, does the *exact* same processing occur to each object? That is, are the data types *and* the process steps identical? If the answers to these questions are all yes, no further analysis is required. You have identified a candidate for development as a reusable module. If the answer is no, then you must identify the specific differences with the next set of questions.

Third, are the data types different or identical? Are the processes different or identical? If the data types are different and the process is the same, these process-object combinations are candidates for polymorphic module creation and should be noted with an asterisk. If the processes are different, then you must refine your paragraph to define the specific processes for each object, and redo this part of the analysis from the beginning.

When you have evaluated all of the multiobject processes and resolved any inconsistencies, you are ready to perform the next step. Next, we identify the processes for ABC Video's rental application.

---

4 A convention is a locally agreed upon way to do some activity.

1. Is only one object actually transformed by this process?

    If yes, this process is complete.

    If no, continue.

2. Does the exact same processing occur for each object? This means the same steps and the same transformations.

    If no, go to step 3.

    If yes, are all object data types the same?

    If yes, this process is complete; create one reusable module for this process.

    If no, mark for polymorphic module creation.

3. Redefine the sentence(s) to identify the specific processing of each object. Then, reevaluate the processes beginning at step 1.

FIGURE 11-15   Multiobject Process Evaluation

ABC Video Example Process List

The steps we follow here are to circle the verbs, evaluate them as processes of interest, define solution and problem space processes, assign class/objects to processes and evaluate those object assignments (refer to the summary list on p. 473).

The first step is to return to the paragraph and circle the verbs. Analyze each verb to ensure that it *is* a process. For instance, if you include in your list the terms 'To rent tapes' and 'To return a tape,' the verbs 'to rent' and 'to return' are omitted from the list because they are identifying the entire process, but are not processes in the system. All verbs in the paragraph are processes. Figure 11-16 shows the verbs circled in the final paragraph.

Next, list verbs and identify their *space*. Remember, problem space identifies processes needed to describe the problem but *not* the solution; solution space processes are needed to describe both the problem and the solution. Figure 11-17 identifies the space of each process listing a reason for exclusion of problem space items. The problem space processes all refer to physical actions which are not tracked by the application. The verb *is complete* is the only nonprocess in the list. *Is complete* refers to

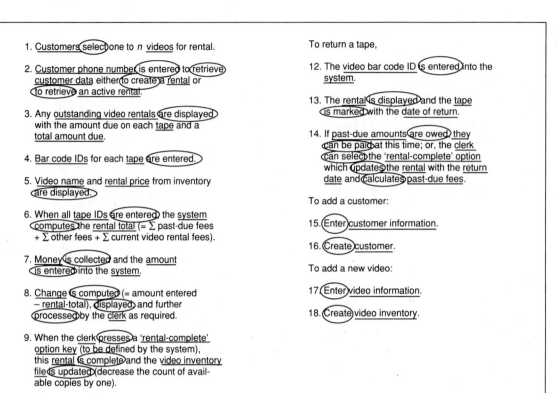

FIGURE 11-16   Paragraph with Verbs Circled for ABC Rental Processing

a rental status in the procedure which signals different processing. This status is an attribute of the process that we will deal with in the next step.

Next we name solution space processes, eliminating duplicates. Figure 11-18 shows the list of solution processes with names. The duplicate actions are *EnterBarCode, DisplayRental, DisplayVideoOn-Rental, RetrieveRental, RetrieveVideoOnRental,* and *WriteRental.*

Several actions deserve further comment. Sentence 5 for tape rental says, 'Video name and rental price from inventory are displayed.' This sentence implies that name and prices are retrieved from inventory, so the sentence should be modified to reflect this action. Sentence 13 for tape return is sim-

ilar in saying 'The rental is displayed. . . .' The rental cannot be displayed until it is retrieved. The word 'tape' in the same sentence is ambiguous. Does this refer to the *VideoOnRental* or to *VideoInventory*? In fact, both are affected by this action. The *VideoOn-Rental* is updated with the return date and the *Video-Inventory* is updated to add one to a count of available tapes (the opposite of the action in sentence 9). The sentence should be rewritten to reflect these differences. The new sentence now reads:

13. The rental, related video(s) on the rental, and video(s) in inventory are retrieved and displayed. The return date is added to the video(s) on the rental. One is added to the count of available tapes in inventory. Inventory is updated.

Verb from Paragraph	Disposition	Verb from Paragraph	Disposition
select	P—Customer physical action—delete	printed	S—process
is entered	P—process (could be more meaningful if called, e.g., read-from-terminal)	signs	P—Customer physical action—delete
to retrieve	S—process	takes	P—Customer physical action—delete
to create	S—process	leaves	P—Customer physical action—delete
to retrieve	S—process	is entered	S—process
are displayed	S—process	is displayed	S—process
are entered	S—process	is marked	S—process
are displayed	S—process	are owed	Rental status—attribute
are entered	status-attribute	can be paid	P—optional physical action—delete
computes	S—process	can select	P—Clerk physical action—delete
is collected	P—Clerk physical action—delete		
is entered	S—process	updates	S—process
is computed	S—process	calculates	S—process
displayed	S—process	enter	S—process
processed	P—Clerk physical action—delete	create	S—process
presses	P—Clerk physical action—delete	enter	S—process
is complete	status—attribute	create	S—process
is updated	S—process		
is stored	S—process		

FIGURE 11-17   Process Dispositions for ABC Rental Processing

A similar ambiguity is present in sentence 14 which states that 'amounts . . . owed . . . can be paid.' This process, can be paid, refers to sentences 6–8 in the tape rental process. Because these processes are present, we do not need to change the paragraph, but we must reference those sentences so the actions are clear. Sentence 14 now reads:

14. If past-due amounts can be paid at this time (repeat sentences 6–8 above); else the past-due fees are calculated and the rental is updated.

This new sentence omits the extraneous information previously present. Both the object list and the process list are reevaluated to reflect these changes. The verbs in sentences 6–8 are also reviewed to ensure identical processing and are added in the proper sequence to the process list. The old verbs are replaced with 'are calculated' and 'is updated.' We review that the nouns from sentences 6–8 and 14 are accounted for in the object list.

The last step is to review the sentences once more, using the object list as reference to assign objects to processes. Figure 11-19 shows the result of this activity. The rule for performing this activity is that any object that is read or acted on by this process is identified.

All processes relating to multiple objects are reanalyzed to determine if they are the same processes. *RetrieveRentalVOR* is identified in the figure as requiring two actions which we discuss here. The processes dealing with *Rental* and *VOR* take information that is separate and process it as if it were integrated. The *Rental* information identifies the customer and the *VOR* describes a video. There is one *Rental* per transaction and one *VOR* per video. The question then becomes one of definition: Is it necessary to maintain this *Rental*, or can it be added to each *VOR* and eliminated?

As in the other methodologies, the *Rental* information and the *Customer* information are essentially

Verb from Paragraph	Space	Process Name	Object Assignment
is entered	S	EnterCustPhone	
to retrieve	S	ReadCust	
to create	S	CreateRental	
to retrieve	S	RetrieveRentalVOR	
are displayed	S	DisplayRentalVOR	
are entered	S	EnterBarCode	
are retrieve	S	RetrieveInventory	
are displayed	S	DisplayInventory	
computes	S	ComputeRentalTotal	
is entered	S	EnterPayAmt	
is computed	S	ComputeChange	
displayed	S	DisplayChange	
is updated	S	UpdateInventory	
is stored	S	WriteRental	
printed	S	PrintRental	

FIGURE 11-18   Named Process List for ABC Video

duplicates. If the company operates on a cash basis and simply needs to know videos outstanding for a customer, then we do *not* need *Rental*. If the company operates on an accrual basis and needs to be able to exactly reconstruct individual transactions, then we need *Rental*. Video rental is a cash basis business; therefore, we do not need *Rental* but we do need to carry its information in *VOR*.

Next, we consider Vic's potential need to differentiate between rentals for a customer or to maintain information beyond the rental's life. Once again, the software engineers return to Vic to find the answer.

Vic: "I have customers sign a copy of a rental and I keep those. I use them to resolve disputes, to find errors, and to provide accounting records. I don't care how you identify rentals because I don't have a need, at the moment, for any

analysis. I would like to add trend analysis in the future."

From this discussion, we know there is no business requirement to separate the two objects. A side issue to the decision is whether separation or joining of the objects impacts processing time. For ABC, there is no process time impact. If there were an impact, we would probably opt for the faster solution. We could choose consolidation of *VOR* and *Rental* to simplify processing. In this case, *Rental* would be removed from the list and declared in the object list as =*VOR*. Another option is to leave it as it is. A third option is to think about *Rental* as *Transaction* since attributes, such as *TotalAmountDue*, apply to a specific grouping of videos for a customer at a point in time. There is no 'right' answer to this question, and we do not have enough information to make a final decision although transaction sounds like an idea we will need in design. For now, we will

Verb from Paragraph	Space	Process Name	Object Assignment
is entered	S	EnterBarCode	
is retrieved	S	RetrieveRentalVOR	
is displayed	S	DisplayRental VOR	
is added	S	AddRetDateVOR	
is added	S	Add1toVInv	
is updated	S	UpdateInventory	
can be paid	S	=ComputeRentalTotal	
		=EnterPayAmt	
		=ComputeChange	
		=DisplayChange	
are calculated	S	ComputeLateFees	
is updated	S	WriteRentalVOR	
enter	S	EnterCustomer	
create	S	CreateCustomer	
enter	S	EnterVideoInventory	
create	S	CreateVideoInventory	

FIGURE 11-18   Named Process List for ABC Video (*Continued*)

change the name of *Rental* to *TempTrans* to reflex this thinking and will revisit the need for this class/object again during design. There are no other multiobject processes. The final process list is Figure 11-20.

Define Attributes of Objects

Rules for Defining Object Attributes

An **attribute** is a named field or property that describes a class/object or a process. Each object is a collection of attributes which take on values. A set of specific attribute values describes an object or **instance**. Each object is identified by a **primary key** which is a unique set of values comprised of one or more attributes. A primary key in object-orientation may not actually be used to identify stored objects; physical addresses are most often used.

To define the attributes of an object, we identify all of the information *about* objects. First, attributes that were set aside during object definition are now assigned to a class/object. All items from the original object list that we deleted because they were attributes are now listed with the class/objects they describe.

The original description of the project is rechecked to identify any adjectives or adjectival phrases describing nouns that are now objects in the solution space. In our case, we reread Chapter 2's description of the case and rewrite any attributes identified there that are missing from the object list. These attributes are added to the list.

Next, evaluate the rewritten paragraph to find any data requirements underlying what is stated in the paragraph but not already known. For instance, a status is implied in the statement 'Retrieve all open rentals.' The adjective 'open' implies a status of open/closed. Any *qualified* class/objects should be

Verb from Paragraph	Space	Process Name	Object Assignment—Action
			Actions are (R)ead, (W)rite, Data Entry (DE), (D)isplay (P)rocess in memory, (PR)int
is entered	S	EnterCustPhone	Customer (DE)
to retrieve	S	ReadCust	Customer
to create	S	CreateRental	Rental (R)
to retrieve	S	RetrieveRentalVOR	Rental (R), VideoOnRental (VOR, R), (NOTE: This requires two *different* actions because the primary keys and read processes are different. We are keeping these together for now for simplicity. All processes marked . . . Rental VOR fit this requirement.)
are displayed	S	DisplayRentalVOR	Rental, VOR (D)
are entered	S	EnterBarCode	VOR (DE)
are retrieved	S	RetrieveInventory	VideoInventory (R)
are displayed	S	DisplayInventory	VideoInventory (D)
computes	S	ComputeRentalTotal	Rental (Process)
is entered	S	EnterPayAmt	Rental (DE)
is computed	S	ComputeChange	Rental (P)
displayed	S	DisplayChange	Rental (D)

FIGURE 11-19   Class/Object Assignments to Processes for ABC Video Processing

evaluated to determine if the qualification is identifying an attribute. When evaluating the paragraph, ask what information is needed to perform, document, or track each action taken. When you identify new information, create attributes for each piece of information.

Next, normalize each set of attributes to third normal form (3NF).[5] For any newly normalized sets of objects, any process-object encapsulations should be reexamined to determine that they encompass both the original object and new objects resulting from the normalization process.

When all attributes are listed with an object, identify a primary key identifier. A primary key provides a unique identification for the object and is composed of one or more attributes. Compare objects to determine if any have identical primary keys. If the answer is yes, consolidate the objects, or change the object with the incorrect primary key. Now, let us walk through attribute identification for ABC.

ABC Video Example Object Attribute List

All items from the original object list that we deleted because they were attributes are first listed with the

---

5 Recall that normalization includes the following:
  1NF—Removal of repeating groups of information
  2NF—Removal of partial key dependencies
  3NF—Removal of nonkey dependencies.
  If you have problems with this activity, refer to Chapter 9 to refresh yourself on this activity.

Verb from Paragraph	Space	Process Name	Object Assignment—Action
is updated	S	UpdateInventory	VideoInventory (P)
is stored	S	WriteRental	Rental, VOR (W)
printed	S	PrintRental	Rental, VOR (PR)
is entered	S	EnterBarCode	VOR (DE)
is retrieved	S	RetrieveRentalVOR	Rental (R), VOR (R)
is displayed	S	DisplayRental VOR	Rental (D), VOR (D)
is added	S	AddRetDateVOR	VOR (P)
is added	S	Add1toVInv	VideoInventory (P)
is updated	S	UpdateInventory	VideoInventory (W)
can be paid	S	=ComputeRentalTotal =EnterPayAmt =ComputeChange =DisplayChange	
are calculated	S	ComputeLateFees	Rental (P), VOR (P)
is updated	S	WriteRentalVOR	Rental (W), VOR (W)
enter	S	EnterCustomer	Customer (DE)
create	S	CreateCustomer	Customer (W)
enter	S	EnterVideoInventory	VideoInventory (DE)
create	S	CreateVideoInventory	VideoInventory (W)

FIGURE 11-19   Class/Object Assignments to Processes for ABC Video Processing (*Continued*)

class/objects they describe. We refer to Figure 11-14 to find those items. A partial list of the attributes from our paragraph is shown in Figure 11-21.

Next, we review the Chapter 2 description of the case and rewrite any attributes identified there that are missing from the object list. These attributes are added to the list as shown in Figure 11-22.

Next, we reconsider our paragraph to find any hidden attributes that are implied by other information such as statuses. We have open and closed rentals, but we might not require a specific attribute for the status. We know a rental is open when it has a *RentalDate* without a *ReturnDate*, or when it has late fees owing. We can check those attributes in lieu of carrying a specific *RentalStatus* attribute. Keeping this attribute requires a judgment call. If junior peo-

ple are doing the programming, a *RentalStatus* attribute is simpler. If senior people are doing the programming, either method is acceptable. As a matter of choice, we will carry the *RentalStatus* to make sure that future maintenance programmers can also easily understand the processing.

Figure 11-23 shows the initial attribute list for each object. We evaluate each, in turn, to determine its completeness and primary key.

Customer[6] appears complete in its information required to perform rental processing. *VideoOnRental* is considered next. We know we need a

---

6 Note that if *Rental* had been retained, it would have had the same primary key as Order and would have been eliminated in this step rather than the earlier one.

Verb from Paragraph	Space	Process Name	Object Assignment—Action
			Actions are (R)ead, (W)rite, Data Entry (DE), (D)isplay (P)rocess in memory, (PR)int
is entered	S	EnterCustPhone	Customer, Data entry (DE)
to retrieve	S	ReadCust	Customer
to create	S	CreateRental	TempTrans (R)
to retrieve	S	RetrieveRentalVOR	TempTrans(R), VideoOnRental (VOR, R)
are displayed	S	DisplayRentalVOR	TempTrans (D)
are entered	S	EnterBarCode	TempTrans (DE)
are retrieved	S	RetrieveInventory	VideoInventory (R)
are displayed	S	DisplayInventory	VideoInventory (D)
computes	S	ComputeTempTransTotal	TempTrans (Process)
is entered	S	EnterPayAmt	TempTrans (DE)
is computed	S	ComputeChange	TempTrans (P)
displayed	S	DisplayChange	TempTrans (D)
is updated	S	UpdateInventory	VideoInventory (P)
is stored	S	WriteVOR	VOR (W)

FIGURE 11-20   ABC Final Process List

Customer Phone to tie rentals to customers and a *Video ID* to tie rentals to inventory. From Chapter 2, we also need rental and return dates. The question is how much fee information we need. Vic supplies the information that he needs to know that regular fees, late fees, or other fees have been paid and the amount of the fee. Therefore, we add those attributes to the list and it also appears to be complete.

The *VideoInventory* is not normalized. While we are normalizing, we can also evaluate the impact of Vic's nebulous desire for promotions on inventory objects. Refer to Figure 11-23's list of the fields and definitions relating to videos in inventory. Repeating information is indented. Primary keys of each part of the information are underlined. The 3NF result of normalization is four relations (see Figure 11-24): *VideoInventory, BarCodeVideo, VideoPromo*, and *PromoVideo*.

The distinct definition of *VideoPromo* means we can omit it after this analysis because promotions are a future requirement. The separation of *BarCode-Video* from *VideoInventory* means we need to reevaluate the object and process lists to define related changes. Since *VideoInventory* and *BarCodeVideo* are always accessed together, we can just add *Bar-CodeVideo* to the lists anytime *VideoInventory* is present. We may want to consolidate the two objects later in the design, for convenience of processing, if we can accommodate repeating information.

The final object attribute list is shown in Figure 11-25 and omits the *VideoPromo* Promo Type objects as discussed above. The attribute list shows the class/objects with their attributes. The process-object figure is corrected to reflect the new *Bar-CodeVideo* class/object. The objects are all 3NF and appear complete for ABC rental processing.

Verb from Paragraph	Space	Process Name	Object Assignment—Action
printed	S	PrintTempTrans	TempTrans (PR)
is entered	S	EnterBarCode	TempTrans (DE)
is retrieved	S	RetrieveVOR	TempTrans, VOR (R) VideoInventory (R)
is displayed	S	DisplayTempTrans	TempTrans (D)
is added	S	AddRetDateTempTransVOR	TempTrans (P), VOR (P)
is added	S	Add1toVInv	VideoInventory (P)
is updated	S	UpdateInventory	VideoInventory (W)
can be paid	S	=ComputeTempTransTotal =EnterPayAmt =ComputeChange =DisplayChange	
are calculated	S	ComputeLateFees	TempTrans (P), VOR (P)
is updated	S	WriteVOR	TempTrans, VOR (W)
enter	S	EnterCustomer	Customer (DE)
create	S	CreateCustomer	Customer (W)
enter	S	EnterVideoInventory	VideoInventory (DE)
create	S	CreateVideoInventory	VideoInventory (W)

FIGURE 11-20   ABC Final Process List (*Continued*)

Define Attributes of Processes

Rules for Defining Process Attributes

Attributes of processes define formulae, constraints, or status processing performed by or on processes in the application being developed. In particular, **process attributes** define:

- how the process is performed in the system (that is, formulae performed by the process, for example, the formula computing change for a video rental)
- status changes resulting from the process execution (for example, a customer changes from an overdue status to a current status when late fees are paid)
- constraints on the process (that is, prerequisite, postrequisite, time, structure, control, and

inference limitations; for example, a prerequisite of video rental is that all late fees must be paid).

The steps to define process attributes are similar to those for object attributes.

1. Assign attributes which were set aside during object or process definition to a class/object.
2. Review the original problem description and any notes from data collection to find attributes.
3. Review the summary paragraph to find implied attributes, such as statuses a process can take.

We use the original description of the problem and the paragraph to determine process attributes.

Object Name	Attribute Name
Customer	CustomerPhone
TempTrans	CustomerPhone
	BarCodeId
	ReturnDate
	LateFeesDue
	TotalAmtDue
	TotalAmtPaid
	Change
VideoOnRental	CustomerPhone
	BarCodeId
	ReturnDate
	LateFeesDue
VideoInventory	VideoName
	RentalPrice
	VideoCountOfCopies
	BarCodeID

FIGURE 11-21   A Partial List of Attributes from the Paragraph

Status attributes identify state changes due to a process's successful completion. The status attributes will, during design, be assigned to a class/object. The purpose of identifying them with processes is that they are more obvious and less likely to get lost.

The constraints are identified to ensure that the procedural code generated during design includes the constraints. The formulae are included as process attributes because they provide some of the logic detail that is also included in the process design.

One inadvertent consequence of process attribute identification can be the definition of artificial constraints on processes. For instance, in the ABC Video rental process, we know that customers must return and pay for prior rentals before taking out new rentals. But consider this situation:

A customer has several tapes on loan. The customer returns all but one video and wants to rent two others. The customer could pay for all past rentals, the new rentals, and late fees up to the current date for the tape still on loan.

Or the customer could pay for all past rentals and the new rentals. The remaining tape, because it is not returned, is left unchanged.

Both of these solutions might be acceptable, but the first places the prerequisite that 'all rental fees be up-to-date' on the customers. This requirement is slightly different than 'all late fees must be paid before new rentals.' The difference is in how late fees are defined; that is, do customers incur late fees when the due date is past the current date or when a video is returned and it has been kept out past the expected return date? In keeping with Vic's edict of the least bureaucracy placed on the customer, the latter definition would be preferred, and he verifies this preference. With this discussion, let us turn to defining the attributes for ABC Video.

Object Name	Attribute Name
Customer	CustomerPhone
	CustomerLastName
	CustomerFirstName
	CustomerAddress
	CustomerCity
	CustomerState
	CustomerZip
	CustomerCreditCardType
	CustomerCCNumber
	CustomerCCExpDate
	CreditRating
	CustEnrollDate
TempTrans	CustomerPhone
	BarCodeId
	ReturnDate
	LateFeesDue
	TotalAmtDue
	TotalAmtPaid
	Change
VideoOnRental	CustomerPhone
	BarCodeId
	ReturnDate
	LateFeesDue
VideoInventory	VideoName
	RentalPrice
	VideoCountOfCopies
	BarCodeId
	TypeVideo
	Vendor
	DateReceived

FIGURE 11-22   Additional Attributes from Chapter 2

Object Name	Attribute Name (Primary key is underlined, Repeating information is indented.)	Object Name	Attribute Name
		VideoOnRental	CustomerPhone
			BarCodeId
			RentalDate
			FeesPaid
Customer	CustomerPhone		ReturnDate
	CustomerLastName		LateFeesDue
	CustomerFirstName		LateFeesPaid
	CustomerAddress		FeesDue
	CustomerCity		FeesPaid
	CustomerState		
	CustomerZip	VideoInventory	VideoName
	CustomerCreditCardType		RentalPrice
	CustomerCCNumber		VideoReleaseDate
	CustomerCCExpDate		VideoCountOfCopies
	CreditRating		TypeVideo
	CustEnrollDate		Vendor
			DateReceived
TempTrans	CustomerPhone		PromotionType
	TotalAmtDue		PromoOnDate
	TotalAmtPaid		PromoOffDate
	Change		PromoPrice
	BarCodeId		
	RentalDate		BarCodeId
	FeesPaid		BarCodeRentalCount
	ReturnDate		BarCodeRentalDays
	LateFeesDue		
	LateFeesPaid		
	FeesDue		
	FeesPaid		

FIGURE 11-23   Initial Object Attribute List for ABC Rental Processing

ABC Video Example Process Attribute List

First, we list all processes down the left margin of a page (see Figure 11-26). Then, we examine each process to determine whether it is constrained in any way. To identify constraints we return to the original description of the problem and the final paragraph to determine processing formulae, constraints, and statuses.

The obvious process attributes are the formulae used to compute rental total and to compute change. Each of these are entered in the table (see Figure 11-26). To ensure proper payment processing, a postrequisite that Change be greater or equal to zero is defined. If this postrequisite is not met, payment processing is performed again.

The first entry in the table for *RetrieveRental-VOR* is a prerequisite that the *Customer* information must be retrieved and a *Rental* able to be developed. If this process is not successful, it is due to a new customer and the *EnterCustomer* process is initiated.

Several status attributes which were set aside during process identification are defined here. Two statuses were identified for knowing when all video data entry is complete and when all transaction processing is complete. Both of these prerequisite statuses are listed with related processes in Figure 11-26. Notice that for the constrained processes, we listed the type of constraint and the details of processing relating to the constraint. Also, notice that many processes have no specific attributes.

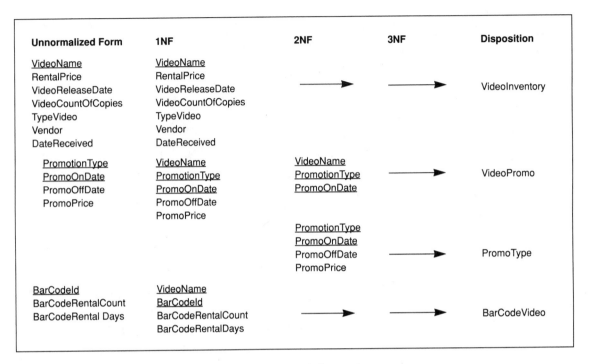

FIGURE 11-24   Normalization of ABC Inventory Information

Perform Class Analysis

Rules for Analyzing Classes

This step is conceptually one of the more difficult steps in object-oriented analysis. It is also crucial to defining the class relationships properly. You have already learned to define entities, relationships, and class hierarchies in Information Engineering, so many of the ideas are not new. What is new is the notion that not just data is inherited: Both data and processes are inherited and considered in this analysis.

The goal is to define classes of class/objects and their relationships. A class defines the attributes and processes that are shared by one or more class/objects. All objects are members of at least one class. When multiple objects share attributes, or share processes, we extract the attributes and processes in common, and create a **superset** class. The important issue is to ensure that the class does, in fact, relate in exactly the same way to all of the mul-

tiple class/objects. The class has no objects of its own; it is simply identifying shared data and processes.

Classes are similarly evaluated for commonly shared attributes and processes to create layers of classes. The notation for such a relationship is similar to that of an entity-relationship diagram with directed arrows indicating the direction of the relationship and small numbers indicating the cardinality (i.e., number) of the relationship (see Figure 11-27). Recall that cardinality can be one-to-one (1:1), one-to-many (1:*m*), or many-to-many (*m:n*).

To **instantiate** means to define the values of a specific occurrence of an object. (Keep in mind that processes are the same for all instances.) For example, the class/object *Customer* has one instance object for each customer. At the analysis level, an instance is analogous to a tuple in a relation or a record in a file. In an order entry example, illustrated in Figure 11-28, *Customer* class has no specific data; it is an abstract class. The *Cust* class/object instantiates, that is, defines the data values for the customer class. The *Order* class/object inherits the data and processes in the *Customer* class.

Inheritance relationships identify shared data and processes. The object at the arrow-headed end shares or inherits from the other object. Inheritance relationships identify hierarchical networks of relationships.

Booch [1991] also recommends the design of classes for class/objects whose data or processes are used by another class/object. For instance, an order *uses* information about inventory items. Therefore, another class would be created shared inventory information (see Figure 11-29). This notation is the same as for general classes.

A fifth type of class, a meta-class, can also be defined, but is usually developed during design. The

meta-class relationship defines a class whose instances are themselves classes. For instance, customers contain *CustomerName* which defines a subclass 'character string,' which defines a subclass 'character.' Customer is a meta-class representing its character string contents. In general, *all* classes and class/objects from analysis are meta-classes that are elaborated during design.

Coad and Yourdon [1990] recommend looking for classes by evaluating each class/object for special cases and creating *generalization* classes for *specialization* class/objects. For example, cash and credit customers might be specialized class/objects of the general class *customer* (see Figure 11-30). Coad and Yourdon customize their notation for generalization-specialization relationships, although

Object Name	Attribute Name (Primary key is underlined, Repeating information is indented.)	Object Name	Attribute Name
		VideoOnRental	CustomerPhone
			BarCodeId
			RentalDate
Customer	CustomerPhone		FeesPaid
	CustomerLastName		ReturnDate
	CustomerFirstName		LateFeesDue
	CustomerAddress		LateFeesPaid
	CustomerCity		FeesDue
	CustomerState		FeesPaid
	CustomerZip	VideoInventory	VideoName
	CustomerCreditCardType		RentalPrice
	CustomerCCNumber		VideoReleaseDate
	CustomerCCExpDate		VideoCountOfCopies
	CreditRating		TypeVideo
	CustEnrollDate		Vendor
TempTrans	CustomerPhone		DateReceived
	TotalAmtDue		
	TotalAmtPaid	BarCodeVideo	VideoName
	Change		BarCodeId
TempTransDetail	CustomerPhone		BarCodeRentalCount
	BarCodeId		BarCodeRentalDays
	RentalDate		
	FeesPaid		
	ReturnDate		
	LateFeesDue		
	LateFeesPaid		
	FeesDue		
	FeesPaid		

FIGURE 11-25   Final Object Attribute List for ABC Rental Processing

Process	Attribute
EnterCustPhone	
CreateTempTrans	
RetrieveRentalVOR	Prerequisite: CreateTempTrans process must be successful to continue rental processing. If not successful, goto EnterCustomer process.
DisplayTempTransVOR	
EnterBarCode	Status: Bar code entry finished.
RetrieveInventory	
DisplayInventory	Postrequisite: All rentals are entered.
ComputeRentalTotal	Formula = ΣLateFeesDue + ΣVideoPrice by CustomerPhone
EnterPayAmt	
ComputeChange	Formula = TotalAmountDue − Total Amt Pd by CustomerPhone
	Postrequisite: Change must be $\geq$ zero to successfully complete this process. If change < zero repeat payment process.
DisplayChange	
UpdateInventory	Prerequisite: TotalAmountDue=zero, and processing is complete.
WriteRental	Prerequisite: TotalAmountDue=zero, and processing is complete.
PrintTempTrans	Prerequisite: TotalAmountDue=zero, and processing is complete.
EnterBarCode	Status: Bar code entry finished.
RetrieveRentalVOR	
DisplayTremTransVOR	
AddDateToVOR	
UpdateInventory =ComputeTempTransTotal =EnterPayAmt =ComputeChange =DisplayChange	
Write Rental	
ComputerLateFees	Formula = Σ LateFees by CustomerPhone
EnterCustomer	
CreateCustomer	
EnterVideoInventory	
CreateVideoInventory	

FIGURE 11-26   Process Attribute List for ABC Rental Processing

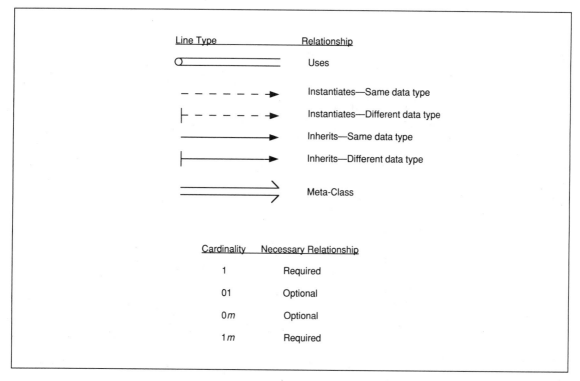

FIGURE 11-27   Relationship Types and Cardinality for Object Class Diagram

it is not necessary to do so unless using their CASE tool. Figure 11-30 shows two alternative *generalization-specialization* notations.

Coad and Yourdon also recommend that classes be created to express *whole-part* relationships. For example, in manufacturing, finished goods are assemblies of other goods; the *whole* class might be for the finished product, while the *part* class/objects define each component (see Figure 11-31). Again, Figure 11-31 shows two notations, a customized version of whole-part as expressed by Coad and Yourdon, and the more general notation used in manual drawings and other CASE tools.

To summarize, we have five types of relationships that we evaluate for specifically. First, we look for shared attributes and processes across class/objects to define inheritance classes. Then we evaluate the class/objects for specialization and for component part relationships. Next, class/objects which *use* the

attributes or processes of another class/object are identified to create a class for the common class/object items. Finally, we define meta-classes as abstract classes whose instances are themselves classes.

To create less cluttered diagrams, elevate the highest independent class or class/object on each diagram to define *subjects*. A **subject** is the most abstract class represented in an application. The purpose of subjects is to provide a summary identifier that represents the cluster of subordinate relationships which inherit from the class (see Figure 11-32).

Finally, we reevaluate and, as necessary, redefine both process-object assignments, class, and class/object definitions again. We reevaluate to ensure that all definitions accurately reflect the application requirements, and are 'clean,' that is, all processes relate to all data with which they should be encapsulated.

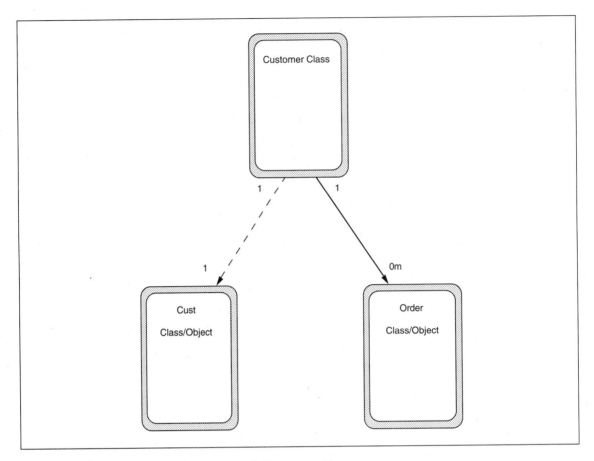

FIGURE 11-28   Order Entry Example of Customer Class

ABC Video Example Class Analysis

The class diagram for ABC rental processing is fairly simple (see Figure 11-33). First we draw the object classes: *Customer*, *VideoOnRental*, *Video-Inventory*, *BarCodeVideo*, and *TempTrans*.

Next, we evaluate the relationships between them. Referring back to the attribute list, we see that *VideoOnRental (VOR)* contains information from *Customer*, *BarCodedVideo*, and *VideoInventory*. The question is, Is this an inheritance relationship or a using relationship? In other words, are the data and processes also shared by *VOR* or does it simply use the data? The answer is found in the process descriptions. For all three class/objects, if the object

does not exist while rental processing is going on, the rental class/object is supposed to be able to add new customers and new videos. Therefore, the processes for adding and reading the information from all three class/objects are shared and should be inherited. If *VOR* simply used the data, the using relationship would have been more appropriate. *BarCodeVideo*, *Video-Inventory*, and *Customer* are drawn as classes because they will not actually store data. They manage the shared processes.

Next, we consider the relationship of *VideoOn-Rental (VOR)* to *TempTrans*. There is considerable overlap since VOR gets all new objects from *Temp-Trans*, and *TempTrans* gets all information about open rentals from *VOR*. In this example, neither can

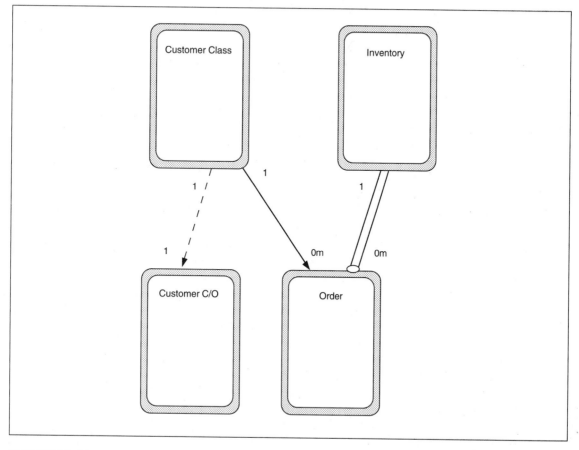

FIGURE 11-29   Example of Using Class

inherit the processes of the other. Since they both use each other's data, they have reciprocal using relationships which are expressed in the diagram (see Figure 11-33).

Then, we create new class/objects for attributes and processes not shared or inherited by *VOR* (see Figure 11-34).

Next, we consider the relationship between *BarCodedVideo* and *VideoInventory*. *VideoInventory* defines the characteristics of a group of inventory items. For instance, there will be one object with the value *Terminator 2* in the Video Name, but there might be many *BarCodedVideo* objects which refer to that name. That is, there are many copies of the movie, each with its own bar code. Therefore, the

characteristics of *VideoInventory* appear to be inherited by *BarCodedVideo*.

Next, we ask if the processes of *VideoInventory* also apply to *BarCodeVideo*. For instance, when we add a *BarCodeVideo*, do we need to know or do processing for *VideoInventory*? One attribute of *VideoInventory*, a count of the number of videos in stock, is created and updated every time *VOR* is created or used during rental processing. Therefore, a class for *VideoInventory* that includes the attribute(s) and processes that are shared is required. Now we have two classes dealing with *VideoInventory* and one class/object that will contain the data. The diagram reflecting these final data and processing requirements is shown in Figure 11-34.

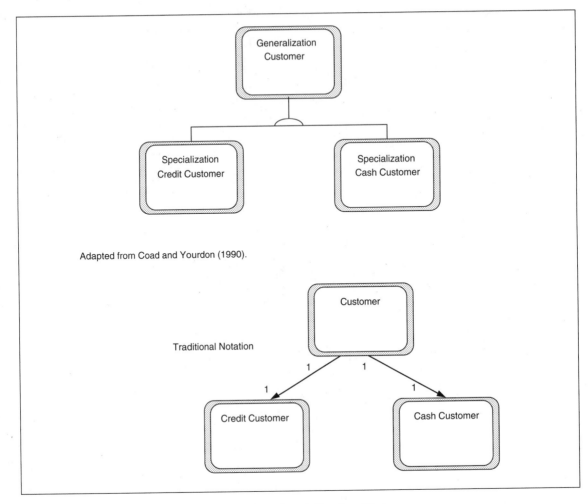

FIGURE 11-30 Example of Generalization-Specialization Classes

Draw State-Transition Diagram

Rules for Drawing a State-Transition Diagram

A **state-transition diagram** defines allowable changes for data objects. Specifically, for each change of data content for an object, we identify the initial state, the event that causes the change, the process by which the change occurs, and the resulting state. A **state** is a set of values an object can have

while a **transition** is an event causing a change to the set of values.

There are two subtly different types of state-transition diagrams known as the *Mealy model* and the *Moore model*. The **Mealy model** defines all state changes and associates each with an action; it is used in this text. The **Moore model** defines all actions and associates each with a state. Theoretically, both models lead to the same definitions, they take different perspectives. For novices, the Mealy model is simpler because it is easier to identify and verify state changes than it is to identify and verify that all actions are present.

The icons used in drawing a state transition diagram are shown in Figure 11-35 as a circle and directed line. The rules for developing a state-transition diagram are as follows:

1. Draw one diagram for each object/class and each class.
2. Identify the possible states the class/object can take.
3. Draw circles on a diagram labeling each with a state.

4. Connect the states to show transition from one state to another. Use directed arrow lines to show the direction of state change (i.e., from . . . to . . .). Each state should lead to one or a small number of other states.
5. Label the transition lines to identify the events that initiate the change. Write the event names above the lines.
6. Label the lines with the processes that manage the event. Write the process names under the lines.

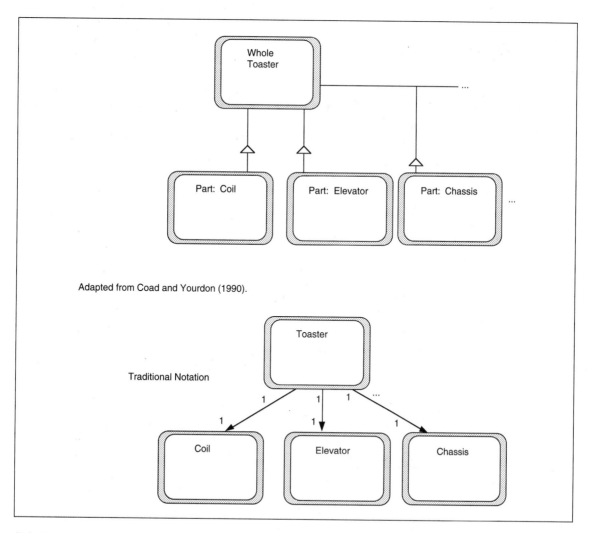

FIGURE 11-31   Example of Whole-Part Class

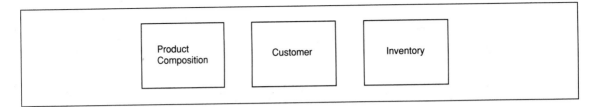

FIGURE 11-32   Example of Subject Diagram

7. Examine the diagram. If there are any recursive state changes, reanalyze that part of the diagram in more detail to remove the recursion or to specifically label the state and its processes as recursive.
8. Walk through the diagram with other team members until it is complete and accurate.

The circle identifies the states of the object. Directed lines signify transitions and lead to the resulting state. The *event* causing the transition is written on top of the directed line. The *process* that changes

the state is written under the directed line. The names of states should be unique, but the names of events and actions need not be unique if they, in fact, relate to more than one state. Events can spawn more than one process. Conversely, object states can require more than one event to be changed. If many events are required to initiate a state change, they are shown with separate lines leading to the state. If *any* of several events can initiate a state change, the lines converge into one line entering the state. Each *class* and *class/object* in an application has a state-transition diagram developed for it.

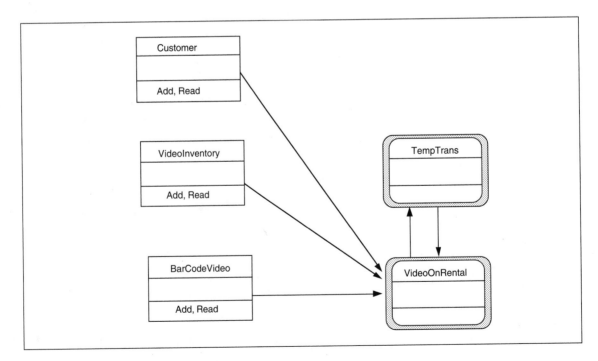

FIGURE 11-33   Class Diagram for VideoOnRental

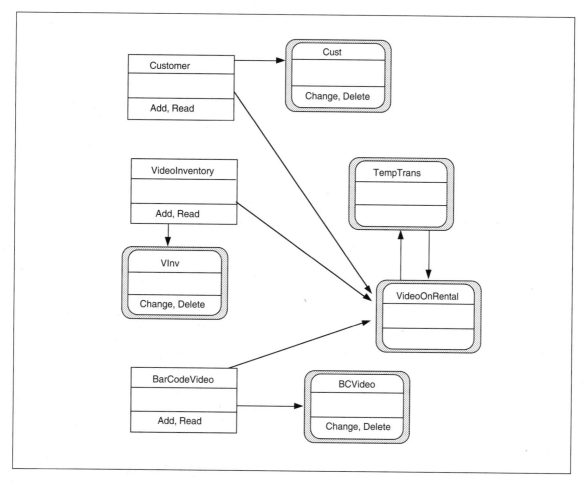

FIGURE 11-34   Class Diagram for ABC

State-transition diagrams are optional representations in object orientation. They are useful for diagramming the behavior of systems with

- multiple message types
- complex processes
- synchronization requirements.

Different diagrams, such as *fence diagrams*,[7] are often substituted for state transition diagrams when there are less than 20 states.

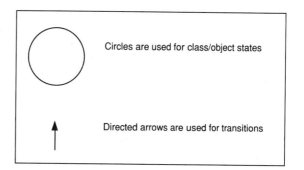

FIGURE 11-35   Icons Used in State Transition Diagrams

---

7 See Martin and McClure, 1985, for a further discussion of different substitute representations.

ABC Video Example of State-Transition Diagram

The steps to developing a state-transition diagram are to draw circles for each state that an object can take. Then connect the circles with lines showing which states lead to which next-states. Label the lines with the event triggering the change on top and the associated process from the application under the line. Rental *VOR* objects are the most complex in the ABC Video rental processing task, so they are discussed here. Development of state transition diagrams for the other objects is left as a student exercise.

In its most simple form, a rental is either open or closed (that is, no rental). So, the first iteration of the state transition diagram will begin with those two states. The high level diagram is in Figure 11-36. For each path between these two states, we ask ourselves the question, What causes the change? First, what causes the change from no rental to an open rental? Open rentals are created when a customer *requests a rental*; this is the event for the line from no rental to open rental. The process accompanying this event is to *create an open rental*.

Second, what causes the change from open rental to no rental? Return of the video(s) and payment of late fees can cause an open rental to be closed. There are two events in this statement, so now we ask ourselves about the events' timing. Are all returns and

payments performed at the same time? If not, what is different about them? From the description of the rental process, we know that returns can be made without any payment taking place. So, we separate these events.

Consider returns first. When a video return takes place, what process is performed? The answer is that we update the rental with the return date. The rental does not change from open to closed when a return is performed, however; so, we draw a recursive line from *open rental* to *open rental* and mark it with the event and process. *This recursive line identifies a need for another level of detail on rental states because each state should have its own circle for clarity of expression.*

Finally, we evaluate the other event, payment of rental fees. This event causes a rental to become closed. The directed line connects open rental to no/closed rental, the event is *pay late fees*, and the process is *close rental*.

We already know we have to create another level of detail to this diagram to be more specific about return date processing, but we also want to evaluate this diagram to see what else is required. Does this diagram account for *all* rental states? The answer is no. It does not account for situations when late fees are owed (in other words, if there is already an open rental), and it does not account for updates for fees paid. So, we redraw the diagram to include these states.

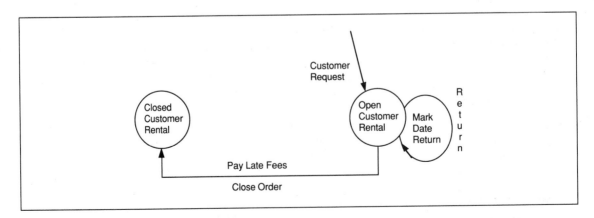

FIGURE 11-36   High-Level State-Transition Diagram for ABC Rental Processing

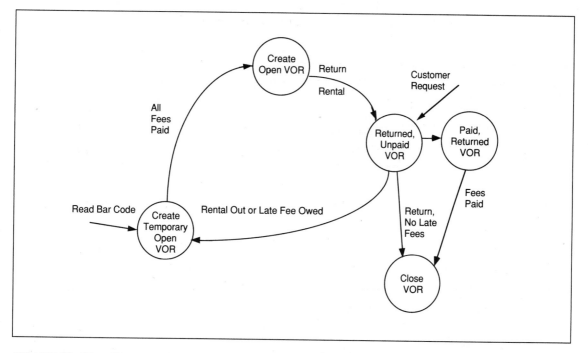

FIGURE 11-37   State-Transition Diagram for ABC Rental Processing

In the revised diagram (see Figure 11-37), we continue the thought process we used to draw the first diagram while accounting for the details we omitted from the first diagram. Now, we try to identify the states through which a rental proceeds from its opening to its closing. The states are:

- open
- temporary, new rental in memory, until fees paid
- unpaid, returned *VOR* may have late fees
- paid, returned VOR
- closed rental with return date and all fees paid

Next we draw the lines showing how each of these states comes to exist. Notice that a customer request triggers a search of open rental and will result in either the temporary rental status or the add-on rental status, depending on whether or not a rental for this client exists. The remaining events are *return-Rental* and all fees paid.

AUTOMATED SUPPORT TOOLS FOR OBJECT-ORIENTED ANALYSIS

Object orientation is less than five years old in its use in business. Yet the number and variety of support tools and environments available attests to its growing popularity and legitimacy. The tools presented here represent both partial and complete support for one or another method of developing object views of the world (see Table 11-1). Many tools include code generation capabilities which automatically generate C++ or other object-oriented code objects from the logical definitions provided in object analysis and design.

SUMMARY

Object orientation is a methodology that alternates evaluation between objects and processes to develop

TABLE 11-1 Automated Support Tools for Object-Oriented Analysis

Product	Company	Technique
DSEE, HP/Softbench	Apollo/Hewlett-Packard	Integrated CASE Product Supporting OO Analysis
Excelerator	Index Tech. Cambridge, MA	State-Transition Diagram Matrix Graph (RTS)
Object View	KnowledgeWare Atlanta, GA	Application Prototyping Software Using 4GL or SQL Code
Object Vision	Borland International	Visual Application Development System
OOA Tool	Object International, Inc. Austin, TX	Coad's Tool Supporting Object Analysis Using Coas & Yourdon Graphics
ProMod	Promod, Inc. Lake Forest, CA	Control Flow Diagram State-Transition Diagram Module Networks Function Networks
Software Backplane Cohesion	Atherton Technology/ Digital Equipment Corporation Maynard, MA	Integrated CASE Product Supporting OO Analysis
SW Thru Pictures	Interactive Dev. Env. San Francisco, CA	Control Flow State-Transition Diagram
Teamwork	CADRE Tech. Inc. Providence, RI	DFD Control Flow State-Transition Diagram Process Activation Table
Telon	Pansophic Systems, Inc. Lisle, IL	State-Transition Diagram
Visible Analyst	Visible Systems Corp. Newton, MA	State-Transition Diagram
vs Designer	Visual Software Inc Santa Clara, CA	Booch Diagram Visual RD Diagram Ward-Mellor Diagram

a complete view of an application. Objects are entities to be automated. They are encapsulated with processes which operate on them or which read them.

Encapsulated class/objects may be identified for creation of reusable, normal, or polymorphic modules. Reusable modules perform the same action on the same data type class/objects, but are called by more than one class/object. Normal modules perform one action on data from one object. Polymorphic modules perform one action on data from many objects of differing data types. Object-process capsules are evaluated to determine their interrelationships. The interrelationships usually describe a hierarchic network of relationships for which the lower-level capsules inherit both the data and processes of the higher capsules. Encapsulated class/objects with multiple relationships have multiple inheritance from related higher capsules.

The declarative steps performed to develop an object analysis include identification of class/objects, identification of processes, class and hierarchy definition, definition of attributes of operations, definition of interobject messages, and class/object state-transition definition. The procedural evaluations within each step consist of questions to be answered and actions to be taken based on the answers to the questions.

REFERENCES

Berrard, E. V., *An Object Oriented Design Handbook for Ada Software*. Frederick, MD: EVB Software Engineering, Inc., 1985.

Booch, G., *Object Oriented Design with Applications*. Redwood City, CA: Benjamin/Cummings Publishing Company, Inc., 1991.

Coad, P., and E. Yourdon, *Object-Oriented Analysis*. Englewood Cliffs, NJ: Prentice-Hall, 1990.

Coad, P., and E. Yourdon, *Object-Oriented Design*. Englewood Cliffs, NJ: Prentice-Hall, 1991.

Graham, Ian, *Object-Oriented Methods*. Reading, MA: Addison-Wesley, 1991.

Taylor, David, *Object Orientation and Information Systems: Planning and Implementation*. NY: John Wiley & Sons, 1992.

KEY TERMS

abstract data type (ADT)	meta-class
attribute	Moore model
class	multiple inheritance
class hierarchy	object
class/object	object-oriented analysis
client object	part class
encapsulation	polymorphism
generalization class	primary key
inheritance	private part (of a class/object)
instance	problem space
instantiate	process attribute
Mealy model	public part (of a
message	class/object)
solution space	superset class
specialization class	supplier object
state	transition
state-transition diagram	user object
subject class	whole class

EXERCISES

1. Complete the state-transition diagrams of the ABC Video rental processing application. Walk through the diagrams in class and discuss the difficulties and alternatives you found in developing the state transition diagrams.

2. Perform an object-oriented analysis on the Eagle Rock Golf League in the appendix. Develop all lists, tables, diagrams, and pictures required to document the requirements of the problem.

3. Split the class into three teams. Have each team develop a second-level analysis of ABC *CustomerOnVideo* maintenance using object-oriented analysis. Compare the resulting views of the application.

4. Debate this assertion: Object orientation is more likely than process or data methodologies to lead to well-defined modules which automatically deal with problem complexity by hiding information, being single-purpose, and having minimal coupling.

STUDY QUESTIONS

1. Define the following terms:

class	meta-class
class/object	multiple inheritance
encapsulation	object
inheritance	

2. Describe the sequence of events during analysis.

3. Compare the differences between the major forms of documentation in structured analysis and object-oriented analysis.

4. Compare the differences between the major forms of documentation in information engineering and object-oriented analysis.

5. Why is the summary paragraph in object-oriented analysis so important?

6. Compare and contrast the definitions of objects, processes, and encapsulated objects.
7. List the documents and graphics created in object-oriented analysis and describe how they are related to each other.
8. What are the decisions you must make in object-oriented definition of object hierarchies? Why are they important?
9. What rules in object-oriented analysis simplify quality control and review?
10. How do you determine that the allocation of objects to processes is correct? What are the questions asked, and why are they important?
11. What is polymorphism? What is its importance in object orientation?
12. What is the purpose of a state-transition diagram?
13. Describe the development of a state-transition diagram.
14. What is the relationship between a state-transition diagram and objects, processes, or encapsulated objects?
15. What is the purpose of a graphical class diagram?

EXTRA-CREDIT QUESTIONS

1. What are the rules for identifying objects? Can you think of others that might be useful?
2. The steps that use nouns and verbs to identify objects and processes, respectively, have been criticized as too simplistic. Can you think of a different approach to identifying objects and processes, perhaps borrowing from another methodology, that improves on the process?

OBJECT-
ORIENTED
DESIGN

INTRODUCTION

Object-oriented analysis defines classes and class/objects, processes, and the assignment of objects to processes, resulting in encapsulated objects. In object-oriented design (OOD), we continue this analysis of the problem domain to assign the encapsulated objects to one of the four subdomains, elaborate component definitions to include service processes, design module interactions, and define the required messages and their type.

CONCEPTUAL FOUNDATIONS

Encapsulation and inheritance are the basis for OOD, just as they were for object-oriented analysis. In addition, the scope of the thinking process is expanded. The design approach is holistic, designing people, hardware, software, and data as the four components of object-oriented systems.[1] As Figure 12-1 shows, the four components all relate to each other and can all communicate with each other. This design methodology makes a valuable contribution to methodological thinking by integrating the components, many of which are frequently ignored. As multiprocessor computing, such as in client/server, increases, this type of classification will be required of *any* methodology. Object method developers have led the thinking about multiprocessor applications because of the closeness between object-oriented applications and operating systems from which many concepts are borrowed.

OOD explicitly uses an iterative approach to detailed design that Booch calls **"round-trip gestalt"** [Booch, 1991, p. 188], meaning the incremental development of whole applications. Each prototype

---

1 This concept of four components is from Coad, Peter & Edward Yourdon, *Object-Oriented Design*. Englewood Cliffs, NJ: Prentice-Hall, 1992.

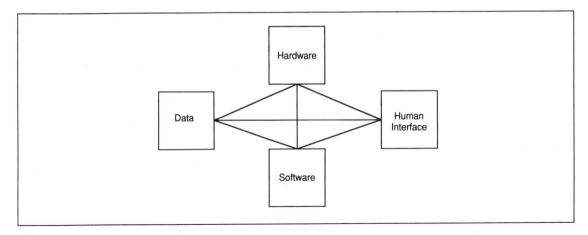

FIGURE 12-1   Object-Oriented Subdomains

is the entire application as currently defined. As the prototype is examined, further details of operation are explicated for incorporation in the next iteration of the prototype. Following the format of previous chapters, we first define terms used in the OOD process, then move on to developing guidelines for each step and an example of the step and thinking processes for ABC Video's rental application.

DEFINITION OF OBJECT-ORIENTED DESIGN TERMS

The seven steps to performing an object-oriented design are:

1. Allocate objects to four subdomains, including human, hardware, software, or data.
2. Develop time-event diagrams for each set of cooperating processes and their objects.
3. Determine service objects to be used.
4. Develop Booch diagrams.
5. Define message communications.
6. Develop process diagram.
7. Develop package (i.e., module) specifications and prototype the application.

In this section, we define the terms used in these steps, again integrating and extending the work of

Booch with that of Coad & Yourdon. Keep in mind that while the terms are fairly well-defined, the manner and order of implementing the steps is not. The documentation created by these steps is summarized in Table 12-1.

In the first step, problem domain objects are assigned to one of the human, hardware, software, or data subdomains. The **human subdomain** defines human-computer interaction in the form of dialogues, inputs, outputs, and screen formats. A **dialogue** is interactive communication that takes place between the user and the application, usually via a terminal, to accomplish some work. A dialogue defines actions of users and actions of the application and hardware. Inputs (i.e., data entry), outputs (e.g., reports), and screens are the three modes of communication used for a dialogue. The task being performed is usually a transaction relating to a business event (e.g., sale of goods), but could also relate to application-generated events, such as sensor readings in process control or a data request in a query application. A screen design alone is a static definition of field formats while the dialogue is a series of interactions that takes place via a dialogue.

The **hardware subdomain** defines object assignment to physical processors or firmware.[2] The hard-

---

2 Firmware refers to software that is permanently on a programmable chip and that processes significantly faster than
memory-resident software program code.

TABLE 12-1 Object-Oriented Design Documentation

Tables

Process Assignment to Object Table	Contains all solution space objects and, for each, the processes that act on the object
Subdomain Allocation Table	List of processes and subdomain assignments
Message Table	Contains, for each process, the calling object, the called object, the input message contents, the output message contents, and the object to which control is returned

Diagrams

Subdomain Allocation Diagram	Optional graphical depiction of process-subdomain assignments
Time-Ordered Event Diagram	Depicts required sequencing of processes
Booch Package Diagram	Depicts objects and message flow for the entire application. Lower-level Booch diagrams, one per processor, are created to show objects and processes with message flow.
Process Diagram	Shows hardware configuration and process assignment to processors

ware interface is significant as we develop applications using more firmware, mainframes augmented by local intelligent devices, and distributed processing. To support these types of processing, allocation of tasks to hardware must explicitly be part of the methodology.

The **software subdomain** defines service control and problem-domain objects. **Service control objects**, also known as **utility objects**, manage application operations. Depending on the complexity of the application, synchronizing, scheduling, or multitasking services to control object/process work might be required. **Problem-domain objects** are the class/objects and objects (hereafter, both are referred to as *objects*) defined during analysis and describing the application functions.

The last subdomain relates to **data**, which are the actual instances of the objects in the solution set. During the data design, data are normalized and redesigned to accommodate operational efficiencies. Depending on the 'purity' of the object implementation, the physical data storage may or may not implement encapsulated data and processes in the database. The most common variation of data storage is a template definition that uses physical address pointers to reference the physical data store for data and processes. The template is analogous to the *File* and Working-Storage *Sections* of a COBOL program, but includes a process template as well as a data template.

The second step for all processes, regardless of their subdomain assignment, is to develop time-event diagrams. **Time events** are the business, system, or application occurrences that cause processes to be activated. Time-event diagrams show sequences, concurrency, and nesting of processes across objects. The **time-event diagram**, then, shows the relationships between processes that are triggered by related events or have constraints on processing time. Process relationships are either sequential or concurrent, determining the types of service objects required in the application. Processes that are not concurrent are sequential and related only by data or parameters passed between the processes. **Concurrent processes** operate at the same time and can be dependent or independent. Dependent concurrent processes require synchronization of some sort.

Above, we defined service control objects as managers of application operations. The third OOD step is to determine which service objects are needed to control the application. There are three broad categories of service objects: synchronizing, scheduling, and multitasking.

Synchronizing is the coordination of simultaneous events. **Synchronizing objects** provide a rendezvous for two or more processes to come together after concurrent operation (see Figure 12-2).

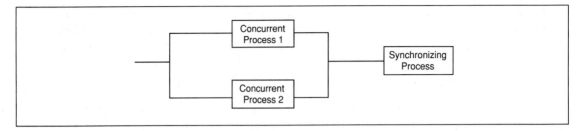

FIGURE 12-2   Diagram of Synchronizing Object Functions

Scheduling is the process of assigning execution times to a list of processes. **Scheduling objects** can be for sequential, concurrent-asynchronous (i.e., independent), or concurrent-synchronous (i.e., dependent) processes. In the terminology of COBOL, scheduling objects are analogous to a mainline routine (see Figure 12-3), but the scheduler performs many functions beyond those of a COBOL mainline.

Multitasking is the simultaneous execution of sets of processes (see Figure 12-4). Each set of concurrent processes is called a **thread of control**. These threads are initiated by the scheduling objects and controlled by multitasking objects. **Multitasking objects** track and control the execution of multiple threads of control and can be in both the problem domain and the service control domain. These three types of service control objects provide the structure within which problem domain objects execute.

Service object definition is based on time-event diagram analysis. If all objects are sequential and used one at a time, then only scheduling objects are required. If concurrent processing takes place, syn-chronizing and scheduling objects are used. If many users are supported concurrently, multitasking objects are added to the other types.

After service objects are identified, the next step is to begin to develop a Booch diagram. A **Booch diagram** depicts all objects and their processes in the application, including both service and problem domain objects. First, a draft diagram is created. Then, several message passing schemes are evaluated. After a message passing scheme is identified, message contents are defined.

The basic graphical forms used are rectangles and ovals (see Figure 12-5). Vertical rectangles signify a *whole* package. A **package** in OOD is a set of modules relating to an object that might be modularized for execution. Service packages are single purpose and do not usually have subparts that are visible to the rest of the application. Service objects have no visible data, that is, no oval identifying a data part to the object. Problem-domain packages have data identifiers for objects and processes. The object in the oval and the process names are each in their own horizontal rectangle (see Figure 12-5). In Figure 12-5, the lines connecting modules show allowable paths for messages.

Next, messages are defined. A message is the only legal means of communications between encapsulated objects. Messages are clear in their intention, but not clear in their implementation which is completely determined by the language. For instance, at the moment, Ada does not implement message communication. In this text, a **message** is the unit of communication between two objects. Messages contain an addressee (that is, the object providing the process, also called a service object), and some identification of the requested process.

Get object
Get memory location
Store object
Enqueue object
Dequeue object
Set time
Check time
Stop time

FIGURE 12-3   Scheduling Object Functions

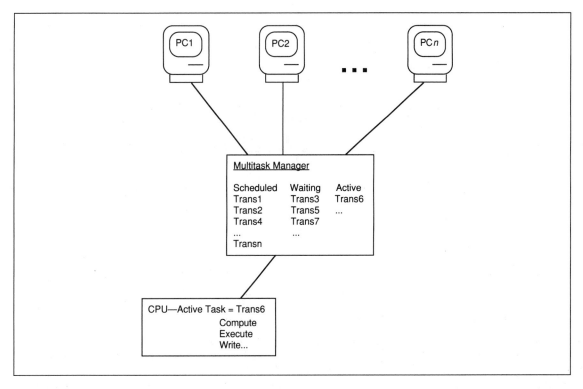

FIGURE 12-4   Multitasking Management of Multiple Threads

Messages may be unary, binary, or keyword (see Figure 12-6). **Unary messages** contain only an addressee and service identifier. **Binary messages** contain addressee, service identifier, and two arguments (that is, variable object names or addresses upon which the service is performed). **Keyword messages** contain addressee, service identifier, and one or more keywords, each with an argument

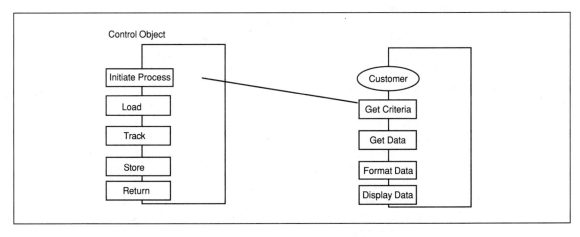

FIGURE 12-5   Sample Booch Diagram—Simple Inquiry Process

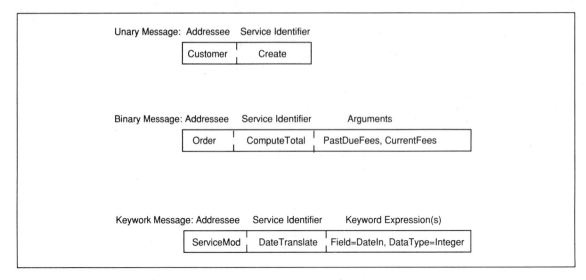

FIGURE 12-6   Example of Message Types

to show optional process selection. Message definitions probably will expand as languages capable of expressing and processing object-oriented designs develop.

The next step is to develop a **process diagram** that defines the hardware environment and shows process assignments to hardware. The first activity is to draw a hardware configuration showing processors (shadowed boxes in Figure 12-7) and devices (plain boxes in Figure 12-8). Lines connecting processors identify allowable message paths. At this summary level, multiple messages may travel each path.

When the process diagram is complete, the Booch diagram is divided and redrawn for each processor in the configuration. These subdiagrams show the extent of replication in the application and may identify new service object needs to control interprocessor communications. The message list is reexamined to ensure that all interprocessor messages are accommodated and complete. For multiprocessor applications, the timing of processes is reverified to ensure correct definition.

Using the information from the problem domain analysis and the OOD diagrams describing object interrelationships and timing, the next step is to develop package specifications and prototype the application. These are not the last steps in

the design, only the last steps in an iteration of the design process which may have several iterations. As a result of prototype development, other service objects might be recognized as needed. Iterating requires review of all design steps and redoing analysis as required to support development of a complete application prototype for each iteration.

Package specifications define the public interface for both data and processes for each object, and define the private implementations and language to be used. The **public interface** is that part of the data and process definitions visible to all objects in the application. The **private interface** describes the physical data structure and actual functions (i.e., data manipulations, calculations, or control processes) to be coded for the application. Multiple implementations of the same function that operate on different data types might be required. The function that has one name but multiple implementations is called polymorphic. **Polymorphism**, is the ability to have the same process, using one public name, take different forms when associated with different objects.

One item in a package specification is a definition of the language to be used. Process timing (i.e., sequential or concurrent) and a need for polymorphism determine the type of implementation language required. Some languages are more con-

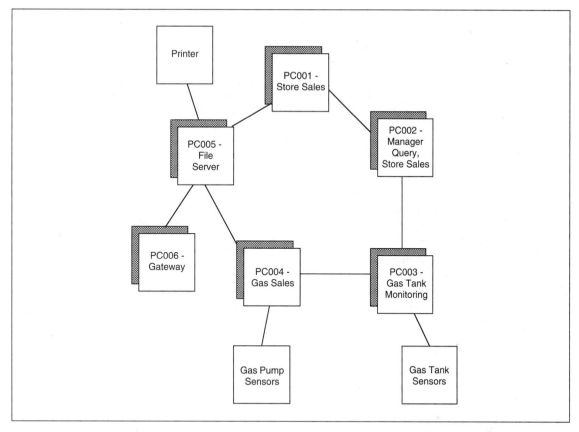

FIGURE 12-7   Process Diagram Example of Convenience Store/Gas Station Network

straining than others. To understand these language differences, binding and client/server relationships should be understood. **Binding** is the process of integrating the code of communicating objects. Binding of objects to operations may be **static** (fixed at compile time), **pseudo-dynamic** (parameter driven and decided at the beginning of a session), or **dynamic** (decided for each object while the system is executing, that is, at run time).

A major difference between object orientation and other methodologies is the shifting of responsibility for defining the data type of legal processes from server (or called) objects to client (or calling) objects. A **server object** is one that performs a requested process. A **client object** is one that requests a process from a supplier. For instance, you might need to translate a date from month-day-year format to year-month-day format. As a client object,

you request the translation of the supplier object and pass it the date to be translated. If the language supports dynamic binding, you also pass the data type of the date (for example, binary string or packed matrix). This shift, to client/server logic, plus the notions of inheritance and dynamic binding, support the use of polymorphism.

Let's return to the idea of binding and work our way through these ideas and how they work together. In most business applications, we think of processes as always operating on the same type of data. For example, items on an order have an order quantity (for example, 2), quantity type (for example, each or dozen), and price (for example, $1.20) that is expected to match the quantity type. To compute the line item total, we multiply quantity times price for a given quantity type. But what if the type quantity is not known beforehand and the formula must change based on the type? Then, we have three choices. First, we could write many routines that are all resident in the compiled code as static binding requires. This is the most common COBOL solution.

Second, we could write many routines that use information passed to the computation procedure to identify which routine to use for the session (for instance, only dozens will be processed in one session). This is called pseudo-dynamic binding (e.g., in Ada at the moment).

Third, we can write many routines and pass the quantity type to the computing object in the request message to dynamically bind and select the routine it needs to compute the total (as in Assembler, C++, or Smalltalk). Dynamic binding is done *on-the-fly* at run time. When the computation is complete, the quantity type code no longer is kept in the computer's memory.

Binding time is a function of the language used and the application's requirements. If the application is batch, single-thread, and sequential, there is no *need* for any but static binding. If the application is anything else (multithread, concurrent, real-time), dynamic binding is desirable, but many languages only support pseudo-binding. Then, the application requirements, in the form of business needs for response time or process time, should drive the language selection decision.

We no longer assume that a called object can do only one thing in only one way; instead, a called object can do only one thing but it can do it in many ways. This ability to do one thing many ways *is* polymorphism. Polymorphic processes take different forms when associated with different objects, but a process *always* takes the same form with a given object. Client-object message requests contain both the process and the form of the process. The polymorphic process then loads its correct process code to service the request via the *dynamic binding mechanism* of the implementation language. An example of pseudocode for polymorphic pairwise item comparison is shown in Figure 12-8.

This discussion summarized the major terms, diagrams, and procedural steps in object-oriented design. Next, we discuss the steps of OOD in detail, including allocation of objects to the subdomains, developing time-event diagrams, determining service objects, developing Booch diagrams, developing process diagrams, and developing module specifications. Prototyping is beyond the scope of this text.

```
Pairwise Compare—          Pairwise Compare—
Two Numbers                Two Matrices

If A = B                   Set sub = 1
    return-code = 1        Set return-code = 0.
else                       Perform compare
    return-code = 0.           varying sub by 1
Return return-code.            until sub = 1st-entry.
                           Return return-code.


                           Compare.
                           If A(sub) not = B(sub)
                               return-code =1.
                           Compare-exit.  Exit.
```

FIGURE 12-8   An Example of Polymorphic Descriptions for a Comparison Process

OBJECT-ORIENTED DESIGN ACTIVITIES

In ABC's rental application, we are using off-the-shelf software in an off-the-shelf hardware environment. In the environment, the operating system, network, database, and form of human interface are all given. Because of our choices—PCs, MS-DOS, Novell Netware, and a SQL DBMS—the application does not easily lend itself to object-oriented design that assumes none of the services and functions provided in our target environment. Because of the differences, we will discuss ABC at two levels: one for SQL DBMS which becomes unobject-like, and one for a Unix/C++ environment that stays object-like. First, we follow ABC through the process of design keeping in mind that the off-the-shelf software will be used. Think of this design as **object-based**, that is, based on object thinking, but decidedly *not* object-oriented in implementation. Object-based design is what is practiced by most novice object-designers, and is what most CASE tools being retrofitted for object orientation will be. In the chapter appendix, we present a second design for a Unix/

C++ environment that is completely object-oriented. Without both discussions, the view of object orientation that you would get is not complete, and some of the discussions would be inaccurately stated for object-oriented design.

Allocate Objects to Four Subdomains

Heuristics for Allocating Objects to Human, Hardware, Software, and Data Subdomains

The first step is to allocate the problem domain processes to one of the subdomains: hardware, software, data, and human interface. Each process and the data it requires from its object[3] are examined to determine whether they are best implemented as part of the human interface, hardware, software, or data subdomains. There is no particular order to the allocation process. It is recommended to allocate the software domain last, because it is the default for all processes not allocated elsewhere. Since these implementation alternatives are usually not broken apart by other methodologies, and since hardware is usually completely ignored, the consideration of these subdomains and explicit allocation of objects to them provides useful detail that is explicitly documented for maintenance. Also, since hardware options are becoming more numerous and common (e.g., automated teller machines have local intelligence and some of the application code for deposit and withdrawal processing), this mechanism accommodates hardware and firmware in design decisions.

We will discuss data first, because current guidelines demonstrate some of the shortcomings of current OOD writing. Booch suggests that standard database activities should be assumed to be under the control of the data domain, including create, retrieve, update, and delete processes (i.e., CRUD). All other data manipulations or computations are allocated 'somewhere else.' Coad & Yourdon, and most authors published after 1992, assume the use of

a DBMS and usually an object-oriented one that includes the properties of persistence, inheritance, and abstract object-oriented data definition. Some authors assume use of an SQL-compatible database with an equally unobject-like language, recommending that the data functions should be separated from the application which will maintain its object-like properties for all non-data operations.

Keep in mind that this is an inexact process that is highly dependent on the implementation language and the implementation environment. For example, if we were using Smalltalk, in which *everything* is an object, separation of data access and manipulation is usually more efficient than keeping the functions all together. Conversely, if an OODBMS, such as Gemstone, were used, the DBMS object performs the physical CRUD actions and the application objects usually control the logical CRUD functions that are grouped by object. The key idea is that judgment on allocation of functions is required and needs to be done with knowledge of the entire implementation environment.

If the application *needs* to use a nonOODBMS, then evaluating whether data integrity, security, and access controls can be adequately maintained by *not* using the DBMS language is required. If the application can both perform the functions faster, and provide for integrity and so forth, then there should be a real analysis of where the functions should be. The application requirements for execution and response time may force use of a programming language when constraints are tight, and default to use of the DBMS language when there are no constraints.

Table 12-2 summarizes this discussion, showing that allocation of physical and logical read, write, and delete actions and the control over security, integrity, and access be tied to constraints and the type of database environment used. If no DBMS is used, the alternatives are either to allocate DBMS functions to each object, or to design data control objects that perform DBMS functions, or to design a polymorphic reusable object that performs all DBMS functions.

We said before that DBMSs illustrate the problem of all authors in object-oriented design. For the most part, OO authors do not work in commercial business and do not build commercial applications; they

---

3 Superset objects, class/objects, and objects are all assumed in the use of the term *object*.

TABLE 12-2   Heuristics for Data Allocation Processes

Type Database	OO	OO	Non-OO	Non-OO	None
Functional or response time constraints	Y	N	Y	N	—
Allocate CRUD to DBMS	Phys.	All	*Phys.	Phys. *Log.	—
Allocate CRUD to Object or generic	Log.	—	*Phys. Log.	*Log.	All
Allocate security, integrity checking, access control to DBMS	—	All	—	*All	—
Allocate security, integrity checking, access control to Object or create generic objects	*All	—	All	*All	All

Legend:

Phys.	=	Physical functions (read, write)
Log.	=	Logical functions (edit)
*	=	Requires analysis and judgment
All	=	Physical and logical
Y	=	Yes
N	=	No

work in defense-related businesses and build real-time, embedded applications which function as part of some larger system. For instance, defense applications might include building a guidance system for a missile, a monitoring system for airplane radar, or a reporting system on the Hubble microscope. These applications all have *no persistent data*; rather, they work on sensor data and pass on the information they filter for processing or feedback by other systems.

The problem with applying embedded-system thinking to persistent object problems is that there is little overlap in designing for temporary and persistent data. Persistent data and, in particular, DBMS-stored persistent data, have entirely different thinking processes that the computer-scientist authors of most object-oriented methods do not recognize. Because of this lacking recognition, these heuristics on object allocation are more crude than those of, say, process methods which have been tried for the last 20 years.

A similar problem occurs in the hardware domain. Object-oriented authors most often are designing state-of-the-art hardware as part of their application design including customized operating systems and software. Most business applications use off-the-shelf hardware that is generalized in function and has many user features. The only custom development in most business applications is the application software itself. So, the design problem with hardware is opposite that of DBMSs. For hardware, the methodology authors do more detailed levels of development than is necessary in most business applications. You will see this problem again when we discuss service object definition.

Now let's consider allocation of functions to the other subdomains. The human interface is exactly what you think it is, the interactions with people, usually through a terminal device, that provides the essential inputs and outputs of the application. The human interface is discussed poorly in the OOD books that do exist (including all of those in the references of this chapter) because of the traditional lack of human users in object-oriented applications. Because of this lack, they are discussed in Chapter 14 as one of the 'forgotten activities' of systems analysis and design.

In general, the activities that provide human interface control, such as screen interactions, are recommended to be relegated to the human component of the application. Again, there are no *compelling* reasons for blindly making this decision, therefore it is subject to analysis. Activities that can be grouped across objects, such as line control, error message display, and screen reads and writes can all be abstracted out of the individual objects and placed in reusable, generic objects. The actual editing of data from screens should remain with the original object unless there are sufficient similarities across screens and data items to warrant abstracting them out as well, or unless the functions will be assigned to human interface hardware. To perform this abstraction requires listing all the detailed, primitive actions required of screen interactions for each object, identifying which actions are performed automatically by the DBMS or other application software and removing them from the list, and re-evaluating the remaining items to determine whether or not there are commonalities across objects.

This primitive level of detail may be deferred automatically when you relegate all *screen interactions* to the human interface. This deferral allows you to build the interface during prototyping even though you may not know all of the primitives during the first iterations. In other words, allocating screen interactions to the human interface is a means of deferring *detailed* design decisions until initial prototype development.

The more distributed devices and processors, the more likely that processing might be allocated to firmware embedded in otherwise unintelligent devices. For instance, automatic teller machines include some intelligence for editing magnetic strip information from the cards used for withdrawal and deposit of funds from banks. They can, for instance, tell what type of card, such as Visa, is being used, and whether or not the personal ID number (PIN) is a valid combination of digits. They cannot tell whether or not the PIN matches the card number

entered because that requires access to a database that is not stored locally. In addition, specific hardware functions, such as accepting a deposit envelope, are functions that would be allocated to hardware.

Allocation of processes to hardware/firmware is determined by the need for fast response time, minimum communication delay, and minimum processing time. Whenever any of these three constraints are present in an application's functional specification, hardware process allocation should be investigated. Some authors recommend that allocation to hardware can include functions to be performed by the resident operating system. When there is access to these functions and they can be used as generics, this is a useful, time-saving idea. So, for instance, in systems such as Unix and Smalltalk, where the environment, operating system, and application are essentially inseparable, thinking of operating systems and hardware as one simplifies design thinking.

Finally, we have allocation of processes to software. This allocation assumes that all problem-domain processes not already allocated elsewhere will be implemented in software in the software domain. This allocation includes remaining service and problem domain objects after the other allocations are complete. Now, let us turn to ABC Video to see what allocation means in this application.

ABC Video Example of Subdomain Allocation

ABC's rental application will be an interactive, multithread set of processes which will service up to six threads of control, with growth to some higher number. Therefore, the concurrent processing requirements of the application should be considered when allocating processes to subdomains to ensure that timing requirements will be met.

To refresh your memory, we had decided to use an SQL-compatible database to implement the application. We can interface the SQL language with other languages, but, as is typical of most DBMS software, all data accesses must go through the DBMS. This implies that the create, retrieval, update, and delete (CRUD) functions will all be allocated to the data subdomain as discussed above.

By doing this allocation, we explicitly are deciding what is and is not object-oriented. SQL is not object-oriented. Therefore, any functions performed in SQL are not object-oriented. The design can proceed in an object manner until the primitive level is reached, then the design is completed in SQL.

If we look at the output from the analysis where we allocated objects to processes, we can identify all those processes relating to these functions. Each object has simple CRUD functions as well as a need for CRUD functions on a user-view of the database that incorporates *Customer*, *Inventory*, and *VideoOnRental*. Eventually, for SQL implementation, we will collapse the superset objects back with the class/objects and will control the use of add and read functions by logic in the SQL DBMS application code. Any access control on superset objects is controlled by the DBMS.

Figure 11-20 processes are listed in Table 12-3 with their subdomain allocations. First, consider the data subdomain. From Table 12-2 we know that we *can* allocate the data functions based on application requirements. We are using a non-object DBMS and have no constraints on processing. Part of the attraction of the fourth generation database is its ease of use, therefore, anything that can be allocated to the DBMS should be. As Table 12-3 shows, all CRUD functions are allocated to the data function. Similarly, printing, which interfaces with external devices, is allocated to hardware. Print control is allocated to hardware because in a LAN, spooling and printing are network operating system functions that are not under application control.

All data entry functions are allocated to the human interface for design and control. Remaining processes are allocated to the software subdomain.

Draw Time-Order Event Diagram

Rules for Drawing a Time-Event Diagram

A time-event diagram graphically depicts the timing constraints and events that trigger related objects, showing sequences of processing, concurrent processes, and nesting of processes across objects. Time-ordered event diagrams show neither flow of control nor if-then-else logic. These diagrams are showing what *can* happen in time, including required timing. The time-order event diagram becomes the basis for decisions about concurrent processes and is helpful in identifying service-object needs of the application.

The diagram is a two-dimensional graphic with objects listed down the left axis and time, broken into segments corresponding to events in the application, along the horizontal axis. For processes that might run concurrently, multiple lists of the objects are shown. Synchronization of concurrent events is shown by the divergent lines returning to one event at some point (see Figure 12-9).

Two formats for time-event diagrams are used. One shows deviations from an otherwise horizontal line with events and critical times demarcated by vertical bars (see Figure 12-10). The other format shows rising steps to mark events and critical time slots within the main object (see Figure 12-11). If one diagram per transaction is created, the rising step method is preferred because it is easy to see the points of change. If one diagram per application is drawn, the information can be presented more compactly with the horizontal line method.

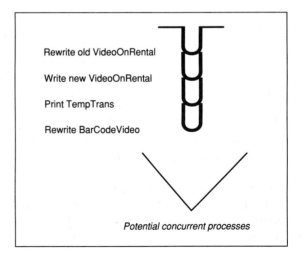

Rewrite old VideoOnRental

Write new VideoOnRental

Print TempTrans

Rewrite BarCodeVideo

Potential concurrent processes

FIGURE 12-9   Potentially Concurrent Processes

TABLE 12-3   Process Subdomain Assignments

Process Name	Data	Hardware	Process	Human
	Subdomain			
EnterCustPhone				X
ReadCust	X			
CreateTempTrans			X	
RetrieveVOR	X			
DisplayTempTrans				X
EnterBarCode				X
RetrieveInventory	X			
ComputeTempTransTotal			X	
EnterPayAmt				X
ComputeChange			X	
DisplayChange				X
UpdateInventory	X			
WriteVOR	X			
PrintTempTrans		X		
EnterBarCode				X
RetrieveVOR	X			
DisplayTempTrans				X
AddRetDateTempTransVOR			X	
Add1toVInv			X	
UpdateInventory	X			
ComputeLateFees			X	
WriteVOR	X			
EnterCustomer				X
CreateCustomer	X			
EnterVideoInventory				X
CreateVideoInventory	X			

Diagram segments are defined as event-driven or clock-driven. For time-constrained segments of the diagram, the allowable maximum time is labeled along the horizontal axis (see Figure 12-12). For event-driven segments, the event is identified on the horizontal axis. Actual drawing requires knowledge of the problem domain requirements for processing.

The steps to creating a time-event diagram are:

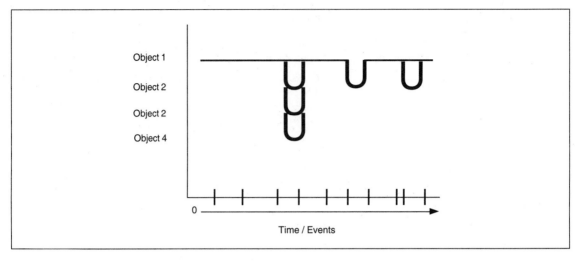

FIGURE 12-10   Horizontal Time-Event Diagram

1. Define all allowable transactions in the application.
2. Define the processing steps for each transaction.
3. For each transaction, design a time-event diagram reflecting the dependence or independence of processing steps.

ABC Video Example of a Time-Order Event Diagram

For ABC, Table 12-4 shows the transactions allowed in the application. The transactions should have no surprises by this stage of design, and should be closely related to the processes defined for each

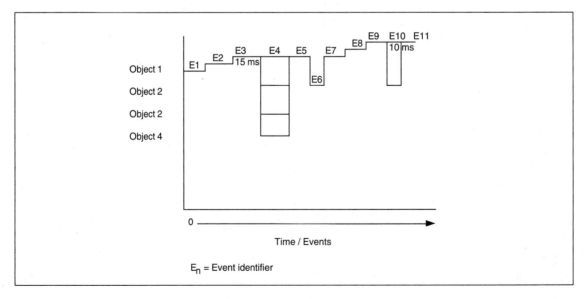

FIGURE 12-11   Rising Step Time-Event Diagram

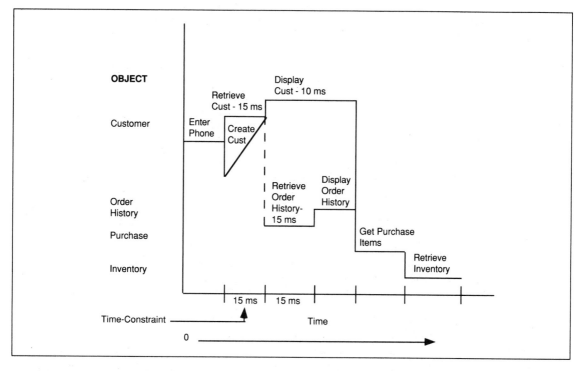

FIGURE 12-12   Diagram Segments Identified as Time-Driven or Event-Driven

object. Some objects, such as *TempTrans*, have processes that relate to more than one transaction, while other objects each have processes that reflect one transaction, such as for *Customer*.

Of the transactions shown, we will discuss two that are representative of the others: video inventory additions and rental processing.

First, we describe what happens for a *Video-Inventory* addition. This step requires detailed knowledge of the specific processing to be performed. This knowledge comes from user interviews, study of current procedures, and so on. Subprocess details should be based on the process-object assignment list (Figure 11-20). If there are discrepancies between the use of objects here and the list, the list should be revised to reflect this more detailed level of thought. The steps to adding inventory are:

1. Enter a new *VideoId* and remaining information for a particular film.

2. When the *NumberOfCopies* is entered, add the new video information to *VideoInventory*. Begin prompting for *BarCodeId* until the number of bar codes is equal to *NumberOfCopies*.

3. As each *BarCodeId* is entered, add the new *BarCodeVideo* entry to the database.

4. When the number of *BarCodeId*s entered is equal to *NumberOfCopies*, signal completion of the transaction to the clerk and end processing.

Figure 12-13 shows the time-event diagram for the processing steps about video inventory creation. Notice that two objects are involved: *VideoInventory* and *BarCodeVideo*. Even though *VideoInventory* is begun first, its processing is completed before *BarCodeVideo* processing takes place. The processes are related in that the *VideoId* is passed to the *BarCodeVideo* process, but they are otherwise

TABLE 12-4   ABC Transaction List

Object	Transactions
Customer	Create Retrieve Update Delete
VideoInventory	Create Retrieve Update Delete
BarCodeVideo	Create Retrieve Update Delete
VideoOnRental	Rental without Returns Rental with Returns Returns without Rental Returns with Rental
Video History	Create Retrieve
Customer History	Create Retrieve
EndOfDay	Create Retrieve Delete

independent. There is no necessary concurrency within the transaction.

The rental transaction shows that several processes might be concurrent. First the steps to completion of a rental process are:

1. Get the entry and determine its type (either *CustomerPhone* or *VideoId*).
2. If the entry is *CustomerId*, get all relevant customer information (e.g., name, address, and so on).
3. If the entry is *VideoId*, get the corresponding *VideoOnRental* and place it in memory.
    Use *CustomerId* to get all relevant customer information (e.g., name, address, and so on),

4. Get all current outstanding rentals (i.e., either unpaid late fees or unreturned rentals).
5. Compute *LateFees* on returned tapes.
6. Compute *TotalAmountDue*.
7. Display all information.
8. Process returns and redo steps 5–7 until no more returns.
9. Get *VideoId*s of new rentals until end of transaction is signaled. For each, get *VideoInventory* and *BarCodeVideo* information; format and display the relevant information; recompute and display *TotalAmountDue*.
10. At transaction end, process payment and make change until *TotalAmountDue* equals zero.
11. Write new *VideoOnRental* entries; update and rewrite old *VideoOnRental* entries; print *TempTrans*; update and rewrite *BarCodeVideo* as required; end transaction.

The first event, data entry, results in one of two possible processes being invoked. These are shown with dotted lines on the diagram to show that only one is running at a time. If the *VideoId* is entered, then we have a choice to either nest getting the customer or transfer control. If we transfer control, the video information must have been stored in memory for the first *VideoOnRental* to avoid passing unnecessary data. If we do not transfer control, and nest retrieval of customer information, then the customer information is unnecessarily passed through the retrieval process for *VideoOnRental*. The best object-oriented decision would be transfer control to maximize information hiding here, but we can treat these accesses as one if the DBMS supports a user view that links the relevant information. SQL DBMS does provide user views and we select that option. (Make sure you read the appendix for true object-oriented design of this information. It is significantly different.) Once *VideoOnRental* is accessed, then, the related information from *VideoInventory*, *BarCodeVideo*, and *Customer* are all present automatically (see Figure 12-14).

Eventually, we loop through getting all current outstanding rentals from *VideoOnRental*. This itera-

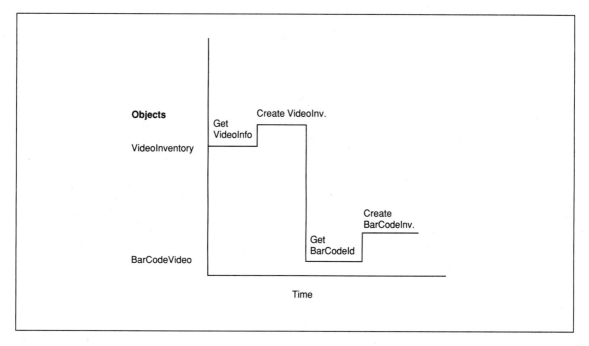

FIGURE 12-13   Time-Event Diagram for Inventory Creation Transaction

tion can be programmed to run until a return code indicating no more videos on rental are present. This return code, then, becomes the event to trigger the next step of the process.

Control is passed to compute Late Fees on returned tapes that will require a count of the number of *VideoOnRentals* in memory to be maintained and passed to control this process. Having processed late fees until this count is reached triggers the next step to compute *TotalAmountDue*. This is a one-time event at this point, and its completion leads to display of all current customer and rental information on the user screen.

At this point, if there are new rentals, the *BarCodeId*s are entered. This triggers obtaining *BarCodeInventory* and *VideoInventory* information. To simplify memory processing, we have a choice similar to that above for customer and *VideoOnRental* in step 3. In this case, the decision is between treating *BarCodeVideo* and *VideoInventory* as separate and independent or nested or the same. In order to treat them the same, we must be accessing a user view

that contains the relevant information. Again, SQL allows user views, and we use the user view that collapses this activity from two to one. As each video's information is displayed, the *TotalAmountDue* is recomputed and redisplayed.

Upon receiving the trigger that the rentals, or returns, are complete, payment processing takes place and continues until *TotalAmountDue* equals zero. At that time, all of the *VideoOnRentals*, *BarCodeVideo* locations, and video history counts (for returns) are updated. These are once again assumed to be in the same object as a result of having user view capabilities in SQL.

Determine Service Objects

Guidelines for Determining Service Objects

Service objects perform background scheduling, synchronizing, and multitasking control for the application. The activities performed by some service

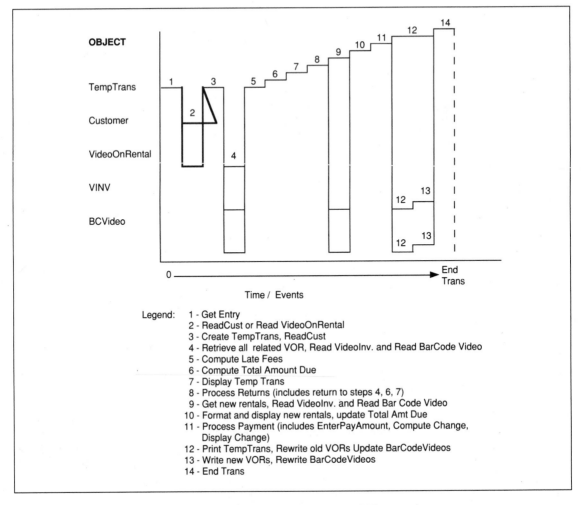

FIGURE 12-14   Time-Event Diagram for ABC Video Rental Transaction

objects are analogous to those of an operating system in a mainframe environment which provides job management, task management, memory management, I/O management, and data management. For that reason we will digress a minute to discuss these operating system functions, relating them to service objects.[4]

Job management routines initiate processing for individual applications. In multitasking applications, that means that the first scheduling tasks are loaded and turned over to the task management routines for execution. In mainframes, there are multiple jobs, sometimes as many as 50, executing concurrently. The job management routines keep track of all jobs active in the system.

The task manager monitors and tracks individual steps within a multistep set of sequential processes (i.e., a job). Task management is similar to monitor-

4 This discussion is necessarily short. For further information see Per Brinch Hansen, *The Architecture of Concurrent Programs*, Englewood Cliffs, NJ: Prentice-Hall, Inc., 1977.

ing done for multiple threads of control for concurrent processes. The work of job and task manager routines are similar and include:

- Load, schedule, execute
- End, abort
- Get/set process attributes
- Create/terminate process
- Wait for time
- Wait/signal event
- Get/set process attributes for jobs, files, or system data

Multiple-thread management requires both job and task management. Think of individual transactions as analogous to jobs to be managed, and of individual steps to completing a transaction as tasks, or processes in OOD terminology. The job management, transaction routines manage whole transactions, and task management routines manage atomic processes to perform the transaction.

Monitoring of individual processes (or transactions) and sequences of processes, one per thread, is accomplished either by stacks (sometimes called heaps) or queues, depending on the operating system software. The stack commands are *push* to add something to the stack and *pop* to take something off the stack. The queueing commands are *enqueue* and *dequeue*, to add and delete items, respectively. The stack (or que) items, in multithread control, include the name of the task, its current execution status (i.e., running, idle, or waiting), and the address of the next command to be executed. One set of stacks is managed for each transaction, and one set is managed for each process. Stacks operate on a last-in, first-out principle while queues are first-in, first-out.

Similarly, the I/O manager and data managers act together to perform physical inputting and outputting of information to central processing unit (CPU) memory. The I/O manager interacts with terminals, printers, and other devices that are moving information physically into and out of the computer. The data manager interacts with secondary storage devices, such as disks. The activities performed by these managers include file manipulation and device management. The key activities include:

File Manipulation:

- Create/delete file
- Open/close
- Read, write, reposition
- Get/set file attributes

Device Management:

- Request/release
- Read, write, reposition
- Get/set device attributes

These tasks are usually provided in primitive form by the operating system and in a more abstract form by a DBMS. The more sophisticated the software environment, like a DBMS, the more likely the services are provided by the environment.

Finally, memory management keeps track of the location of each item, in random access memory (RAM). Recall that all data and programs must be memory-resident to be executed. In dynamic applications in which modules and data are being moved into and out of memory constantly, memory management is a crucial function. The main functions provided by the memory manager include:

- Allocate/delete memory (can be dynamic or static)
- Track used and free memory location by task
- Track used and free memory within each task's allocation
- Garbage collection (identify and erase or write-over unused objects)

All operating system management is accomplished by cooperating processes that use event-driven interrupts to provide services in the system. Interrupts at the operating system level are called **supervisor calls** (SVCs). The implementation of SVCs differs across operating systems.[5]

---

5 For a more complete treatment of this information, see any operating systems text. Some good ones include A. J. van de Goor, *Computer Architecture and Design*, Reading, MA: Addison-Wesley Publishing Company, 1989; Anthony P. Sayers, *Operating Systems Survey*, NY: Auerbach, 1971; J. Peterson and A. Silbershatz, *Operating System Concepts*, Reading, MA: Addison-Wesley Publishing Company, 1983.

Now, let's relate this operating system information to applications. All of these functions are required for the three types of control provided by service objects. If you are working in a Unix or Smalltalk environment which already have been used for application development, many of these functions should already be available for reuse. If you have to write your own, you need to test and retest these functions *very thoroughly* to ensure proper application functioning. In any case, you need to decide which of the service object functions are needed and provide them for your application.

The steps to identifying the service objects are:

1. Examine the event diagram and identify each process as sequential or concurrent, and, if concurrent, as independent or cooperating.
2. Define the service needs for loading the object, processing the object, synchronizing the process to others, and sending any messages the object might generate.
3. Compare this list to one specific to the target operating environment that identifies reusable service objects that can be used by this application.
4. Enter the name, language, and any other information needed to identify the reusable object. For all service objects, make sure that the class, object, event, and/or process using the service object are identified.
5. When all reusable objects have been identified, the remaining service objects included in the remaining tasks are divided among the four subdomains as appropriate for module specification.

In general, all applications need scheduling objects (see Table 12-5). The need for synchronization and multitasking are determined by the time-event diagram and whether or not the objects are concurrent and multiuser. Table 12-5 shows that concurrent, single-user processes need synchronization while concurrent and multiuser objects need synchronizing and multitasking services. Multiuser, sequential processes, like ABC, require both scheduling and multitasking services.

TABLE 12-5 Decision Table for Service Object Type Requirements

Problem Domain Object Characteristics:				
Sequential	Y	Y	—	—
Concurrent	N	N	Y	Y
Multiuser	N	Y	N	Y
Service Objects Required:				
Scheduling	X	X	X	X
Synchronization	—	—	X	X
Multitasking	—	X	—	X

ABC Video Example of Service Objects

First, we examine the time-event diagram to identify each related process as sequential or concurrent, and independent or cooperating.

There are three possible sets of concurrent processes within one rental transaction shown on Figure 12-15 as circled and numbered sets. The other processes are sequential. Our decision on concurrency, then, is based on the implementation environment. Let's say that SQL supports multithread but not multitasked processing, therefore, we need to decide sequential ordering of the processes and how the processes will be performed in SQL.

Next, for each process, define the service needs for loading the object, processing the object, synchronizing the process to others, and sending any messages the object might generate. SQL supports user views. By creating user views to link *VideoInventory* to *BarCodeVideo*, and *VideoOnRental* to *Customer*, *VideoInventory*, and *BarCodeVideo*, the opportunity for most concurrency disappears in one database access that retrieves all the related information.[6]

---

6 See Chapter 12 appendix discussion of ABC in which the service object discussion results in a different outcome.

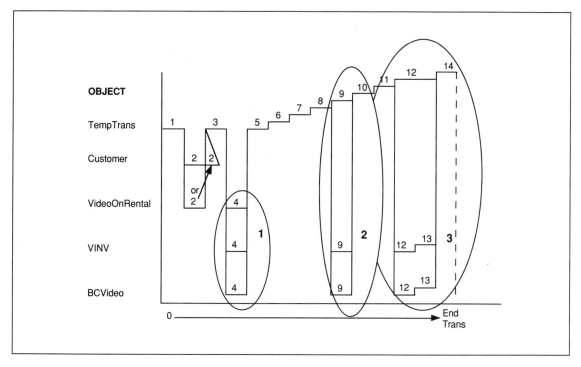

FIGURE 12-15   Potential Concurrent Sets of Processes

Even though we have removed concurrent object processing from the diagram, we still have both transaction level and process level service object requirements. Transactions and processes all need scheduling, including processes that load, store in memory, initiate, terminate, monitor events, and possibly provide message communications between objects.

This list is compared to our target operating environment: SQL on a PC LAN running Novell Netware.™ The services are all provided transparently by the operating environment and are not needed to be developed in primitive form for ABC's application. Even though the target environment is not object-oriented, the need for service objects disappears because these are all services provided in the operational environment.

The next step is to examine a current library of reusable objects for use as problem domain processes. Since ABC's environment is new, there is no

reusable library; therefore, any modules would need specification and development.

Develop Booch Diagram

Guidelines for Developing Booch Diagram

Booch diagrams, also called **module structure diagrams**, provide a graphical summary of the class and object information in the entire application. The icons for drawing the diagram are shown in Figure 12-16 with service objects in vertical rectangles with no other detail beyond their name, and problem domain objects in vertical rectangles with smaller ovals to identify the object and horizontal rectangles to identify the individual processes. One diagram connecting the domains as required is drawn; then one Booch diagram for each subdomain (or for the whole project if it is small) is developed.

The steps to drawing a Booch diagram are:

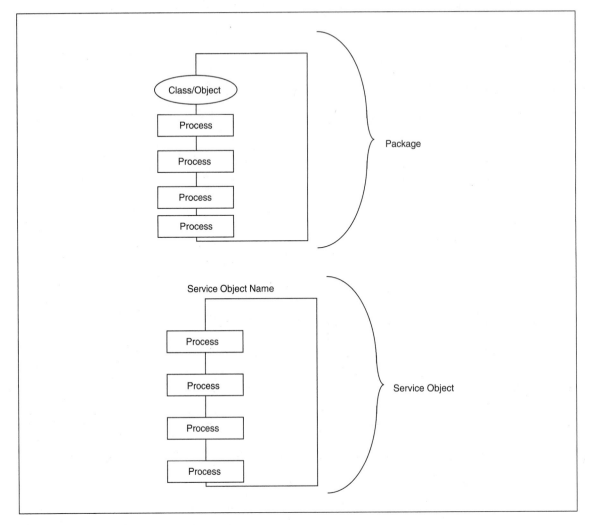

FIGURE 12-16   Booch Diagram Icons

1. Draw the Booch icons (see Figure 12-16) relating to service and problem domain objects.
2. Evaluate and choose a scheme for connecting the objects via messages.
3. Draw lines between objects to signify the legal message connections.
4. Define message processing scheme.

Service objects selected for controlling application operations are arranged by personal preference, but can be grouped by function performed: schedul-

ing, synchronizing, and multitasking within subdomain. The service objects described in the previous section are shown with subdomain grouping in Figure 12-17.

Problem-domain objects are obtained from the process-object assignment list developed during analysis. This table is now reversed with the information arranged by object for this diagram. During the reversal process, a reevaluation of process-object assignment should be made to ensure that the processes are associated correctly with their necessary objects. Subdomain groups may be maintained on

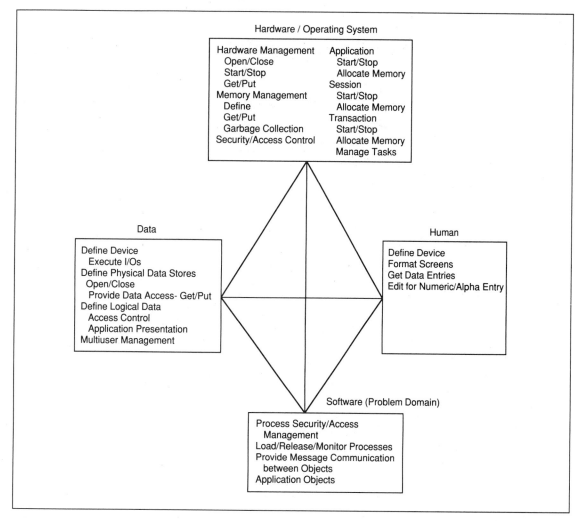

FIGURE 12-17   Service Objects by Subdomain

the diagram which means that we may have new superset objects to define the split between objects for subdomain processing.

Processes that are candidates for generic, reusable object development should be marked consistently in some way, for instance by **bold** or *italic* print to identify them visually. A quick glance at the diagram gives the viewer a sense of the extent to which reusable objects and processes are being leveraged in the application.

After the icons are drawn, they are *played with* to evaluate different message passing schemes.

There is no one *right* way to do message passing, but there are definitely some methods that are better than others. We will walk through a reasoning process for message passing definition in the ABC Video example. In general, the goal of messages are

1. To accomplish the application's tasks.
2. Pass minimal information and pass only to objects requiring information.
3. Minimize the potential for bottlenecks.
4. Maximize the potential for application throughput.

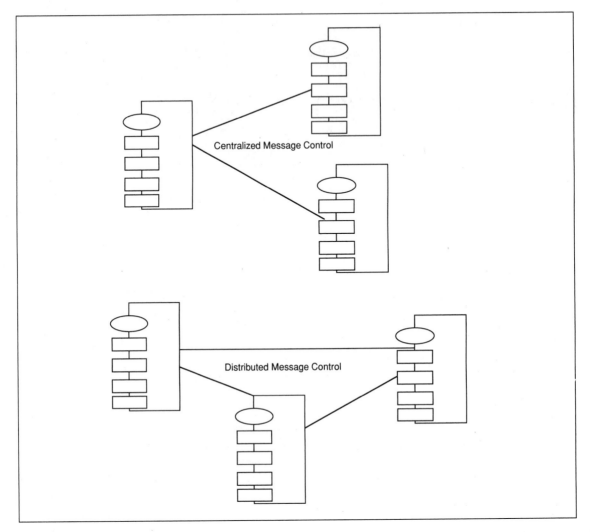

FIGURE 12-18 Sample Configurations of Object Message Passing

The evaluation of alternatives is to determine the best throughput scheme of message passing without creating bottlenecks, while accomplishing the first two goals. Booch suggests a **3x5 approach** to this evaluation in which, rather than drawing the diagram icons on paper, the information for each object is written on a 3" × 5" card. The cards are arranged spatially in different configurations on a large piece of paper with lines drawn to signify the required inter-object message communications. When a configuration is identified that might be useful, it is annotated for further analysis. Figure 12-18 shows two different configurations for a simple application. You can see how, if you have 20 or 30 objects, the 3" × 5" method simplifies evaluation of message passing schemes.

All further alternative configurations are evaluated to determine message traffic. **Message traffic** is the number and direction of messages in the system. Overall, the goal is to minimize the number of messages passed for any single transaction, while not overloading any single object with message traffic

related work.[7] The minimum number of messages is $n-1$, where n is the number of packages needing to communicate in the application. That is, once initiated, each package must communicate with at least one other package. The centralized message control scheme shown in Figure 12-18 shows an example of $n-1$ messages. The arrangement with the best message traffic configuration is selected for prototype development, and the design process continues.

ABC Booch Diagram

Before we can develop a Booch diagram, we need to digress and redefine some application needs to fit the SQL environment.[8] The drawing of packages normally assumes no consolidation of functions or data via user views, but we have collapsed our processing to take advantage of SQL features. Therefore, Table 12-6 shows the effects of user views on data domain processes: the 11 data processes are now eight consolidated processes. The remaining subdomains are not affected by the data changes.

First, we will draw the packages based on what we now know to be the design of the application (see Table 12-6). There are four data packages: *Customer*, *VideoInventory*, *UserView1* which includes VideoOnRental, VideoInventory, BarCodeVideo and Customer, and *UserView2* which includes Video-Inventory and BarCodeVideo (see Figure 12-19). The related processes for those data objects are placed in horizontal rectangles in their respective packages.

There is one scheduling service object (which we may not need because of the environment) that includes initiation and termination of the application, user sessions, and transactions. There is an interface service object to provide all display and input from personal computers (see Figure 12-19). The hardware service object contains only one process for printing TempTrans. Finally, the *TempTrans*

object contains the data and problem domain processes that are the core of rental processing.

Next, we try different configurations of the objects to develop a message passing scheme that will provide necessary processing and information to called objects, while minimizing the communications overhead in the application. Figure 12-20 shows one reasonable message passing scheme that follows the logic of processing. The scheduling object passes control to the interface object which has some choices. The interface object could pass, for instance, a *CustomerPhone* to either *TempTrans* or *Customer* to initiate rental processing. If the pass is to *Customer*, it could return and pass the customer information to *TempTrans*, or *Customer* could continue and initiate *TempTrans* directly. You see how the options can build and get complex. We will opt for a fairly traditional scheme in which the *Interface* will pass any rental transaction data to *TempTrans* which will determine what to do with it. This decision is reflected by the line connecting *HumanInterface* with *TempTrans*.

TempTrans then initiates one of three data retrievals: *Customer*, *UserView1*, or *UserView2*. The data is returned and *TempTrans* continues processing. This method of passing provides the most information hiding between objects, but could result in a bottleneck within *TempTrans* which is controlling all of the interobject communication for the problem (e.g., software), hardware, and data subdomains. This is a potential problem that would be checked during prototype development.

The *HumanInterface* object also communicates directly with *Customer* and *VideoInventory* for create processing which does not require *TempTrans*. All completed transactions, regardless of type, return to the *Scheduling* object to terminate the transaction.

Define Message Communications

Rules for Defining Messages

The next step after the Booch diagram is to actually define message contents to provide interobject interfaces for the application. A table is created to

---

7 This would cause a bottleneck.

8 Don't forget to read the Chapter 12 Appendix for a complete discussion of object-oriented design using an object-oriented development environment.

TABLE 12-6 Consolidated Process Subdomain Assignments for Oracle

Process Name	Subdomain			
	Data	Hardware	Process	Human
EnterCustPhone				X
ReadCust	X			
CreateTempTrans			X	
RetrieveVOR (includes VideoInventory, BarCodeVideo, and Customer)	X			
DisplayTempTrans				X
EnterBarCode				X
Retrieve BarCodeVideo (includes VideoInventory)	X			
DisplayInventory				X
ComputeTempTransTotal			X	
EnterPayAmt				X
ComputeChange			X	
DisplayChange				X
WriteVOR	X			
PrintTempTrans		X		
EnterBarCode				X
DisplayTempTrans				X
AddRetDateTempTransVOR			X	
Add1toVInv			X	
Rewrite VOR data	X			
ComputeLateFees			X	
WriteVOR data	X			
EnterCustomer				X
CreateCustomer	X			
EnterVideoInventory				X
CreateVideoInventory	X			

document the specific requirements of each message (see Table 12-7). The objects that act as clients are listed in the *Calling Object* column, service objects are in the *Called Object* column. This information should come from the Booch diagram coupled with the Process table generated during analysis that identifies objects with the processes that act on them. The *Input Message* column describes the data that is sent

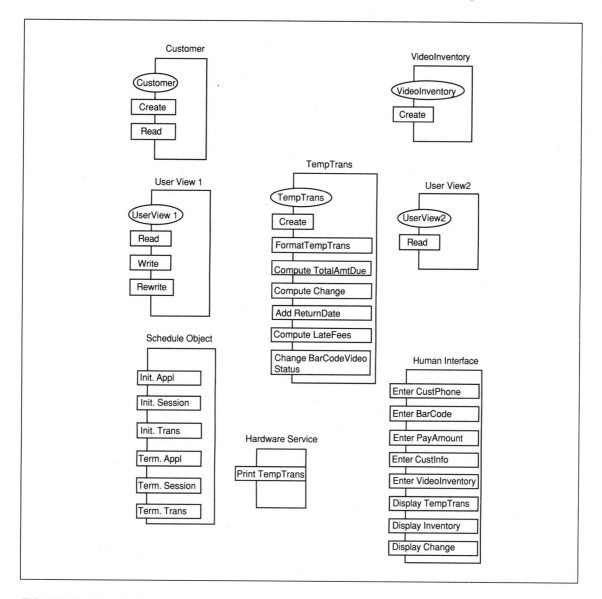

FIGURE 12-19   ABC Rental Booch Diagram Objects

as part of the calling object message to be processed. The output message is the result data that is sent on (or returned) by the called object after processing. The columns *Action Type* and *Return Object* are optional. The action type describes the process to be performed in terms of CRUD or other processing. The return object provides continuity of processing

logic when the called object does not return directly to the calling object.

For each process-object pair defined in the Process Definition List, we will have one input message to initiate processing and, if needed, an output message which reports the results of processing. The message list contains one column for each of the

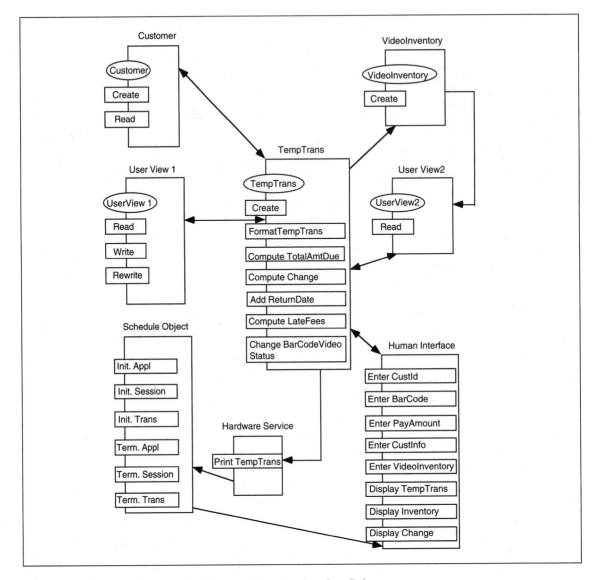

FIGURE 12-20   ABC Booch Diagram Message Passing Scheme

types of information shown in Table 12-7. The steps to creating the message list are:

1. Make a table with headings as listed in Table 12-7.
2. Refer to the list of all object-process combinations. The objects from that list are listed in the 'Called object' column. The processes from the process list are placed in the 'Input message' column.
3. Next, decide both the 'Calling object' and other 'Input message' entries.

These two definitions seem to go together because as we define the input message, we know the information required to perform the process. Once we know the information to perform the process, we

TABLE 12-7   Message List Contents

Header	Contents
Calling object	Identifies the client.
Called object	Identifies the server.
Input message	Identifies the process to be performed and any input parameter data needed to perform the process, for instance, the data type for polymorphic processes.
Output message	Defines the output to be passed, if any.
Action type	Defines the process as Read, Read/Write, Write, Display, or Print.
Return to	Identifies either the object to which the result is returned or a nested object for further processing, if any.

decide which object has that information to pass it on. This step determines much of the logical process flow from one encapsulated object-process to another. The **logical process flow** defines the sequence of processing in the application.

4. Define the 'Output messages' by determining what type of information is required next from each process as it completes. For data entry type processes, frequently the output message is only an acknowledgement of processing (ACK = successful, NACK = unsuccessful). For some processes, no response is required.
5. Complete the 'Action type' column.

The action type summarizes the type of processing for designers to determine possible implementation consolidation of activities, or to decide on further allocation of processing to hardware, software, or firmware.

6. Define the return object column.

This column usually refers to the calling object which is ordinarily the object to which control returns, but some nested subprocess might take place. When subprocessing occurs, the return object column identifies the next object entered to help other software engineers understand the logic flow.

Completeness and correctness review of the message list is done to ensure that each process-object pair has an associated message in the table and that the calling/return objects are correct.

ABC Video Example of Message List

First, we make a table with the above headings. Then, referring to the process list that we used to draw the Booch diagram, we list all object process combinations. The objects from that list are listed in the 'Called object' column. Make sure that all process-object pairs have one entry in the table.

Next, we decide both the 'Calling object' from the Booch diagram and the 'Input message' for each entry (Table 12-8 shows the completed list). Then the 'Output message' is completed for each entry. As the output message is complete, we complete each line with the 'Action' and 'Return Object' definitions.

Table 12-8 shows the message list for ABC's application. It reflects the consolidated data objects, the messages decided during the development of the Booch diagram, and the details of information that must be provided for each object-process. Notice that many processes are called from within an object itself. This localizing of processing is desirable to simplify interobject communication and ensure information hiding, but it also can encourage development of nonobject-oriented designs. Make sure that each message contains all, and only, the information required to perform the process. Make sure that each message returns only the information required by the client object.

Develop Process Diagram

Guidelines for Developing the Process Diagram

A process diagram depicts the hardware configuration and the allocation of processes to processor

TABLE 12-8 Message List for ABC Video Rental Processing

Calling Object	Called Object	Input Message	Output Message	Action Type	Return Object
Human Interface	Customer	Customer Information	CustomerPhone	Create	Human Interface
Human Interface	Video Inventory	Video Information	VideoId, # BarCode Videos Created	Create	Human Interface
Schedule	Schedule	Application Id	Queue Address	Execute Init Appl	Schedule
Schedule	Schedule	UserId	Memory Address or Logoff	Execute Init Session	Schedule
Schedule	Schedule	Session Id, Menu Selection for Rental	None or Quit Session	Execute Init Session	Human Interface
Human Interface	Human Interface	No data (Initiate Request)	Trans Request Data Memory Address	Enter Request	TempTrans
Human Interface	TempTrans	Trans Request data	Data access key	Create TempTrans	UserView1 or Customer
TempTrans	Customer	Data access key	Customer Info	Read	TempTrans
TempTrans	UserView1	Data access key	Customer, VideoOnRental, VideoInventory, BarCodeVideo	Read	TempTrans
Customer or UserView1	TempTrans	TempTrans Info	TempTrans	Format	TempTrans
TempTrans	TempTrans	Memory Location, VideoOnRental, Rent/Return Date	Ack	Compute Late Fees	TempTrans
TempTrans	TempTrans	Memory location (Amounts Due) and End of rentals/returns when present	Ack	Compute Total Amount Due	TempTrans
TempTrans	Human Interface	TempTrans Info and End of rentals/returns when present		Display	Human Interface

TABLE 12-8   Message List for ABC Video Rental Processing (*Continued*)

Calling Object	Called Object	Input Message	Output Message	Action Type	Return Object
Human Interface	Human Interface	No data (Execute Request)	Prompt BarCode or End of Rentals/ Returns	Prompt	TempTrans
Human Interface	TempTrans	BarCode (Rental) or End of rental	None	Format	UserView2 or TempTrans
Human Interface	TempTrans	BarCode (Return) or End of return	None	Format	TempTrans
Temp Trans	User View2	Bar Code (new rental)	Video Inventory, BarCodeVideo	Read	TempTrans
UserView2	TempTrans	TempTrans Info	TempTrans	Format	Human Interface TempTrans
Human Interface	Human Interface	End of Rentals/ Returns	Payment Amount	Data Entry	TempTrans
Human Interface	TempTrans	Payment Amount	Change or Payment Due	Compute Change	Human Interface
Temp Trans	Human Interface	Change or Payment Due	End of Trans	Display	TempTrans
Human Interface	Temp Trans	End of Trans	None	Change BarCode Status	User View1
Temp Trans	User View1	Video on Rental Information	Ack	Rewrite	TempTrans
Temp Trans	User View1	Video on Rental Information	Ack	Write	TempTrans
Temp Trans	Hardware Services	TempTrans	None	Print	Schedule
Hardware Services	Schedule	Trans Id		Terminate Trans	Schedule
Schedule	Schedule	Session Id		Terminate Session	Schedule
Schedule	Schedule	Appl Id		Terminate Appl.	System

platforms in a distributed environment. There are two types of icons used in the diagram: processor and device. A **processor** is any intelligent device that performs data, presentation (i.e., monitor display), or application work. A **device** is any dumb device that is part of the hardware configuration supporting application work. Processors are shown on the diagram as a shadowed cube; devices are shown as transparent cubes (see Figure 12-21). This diagram is a crude equivalent of a system flowchart used before process methods were developed. It is crude because devices and processors are all treated as the same, the only immediate visual knowledge the user gets is the configuration size and the extent to which intelligent processors are used.

The methodology assumes that hardware configuration decisions are not part of the SE task and that the hardware decisions are known. Similarly, there are no guidelines for allocating processes to processors. This is an artifact of the development of OO in a defense environment in which the application developers are working from specifications developed by government employees in another city. In the absence of guidelines from the methodology, we can borrow the distribution decision techniques from information engineering and apply them to this decision. In any case, the processes are listed in small print next to the processor in which they will operate.

One shadow cube is drawn for each processor. Individual processes are allocated to each processor. Lines are drawn to show communications capabilities between the *processes*, not between the processors (i.e., the processors are assumed to be

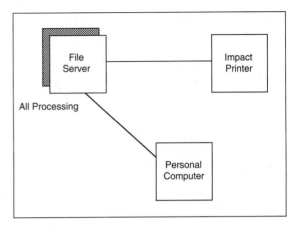

FIGURE 12-22   First-Cut ABC Process Diagram

networked whether or not the application processes communicate). Only one line per set of processors is drawn, since the details of messages are documented elsewhere. The lines only have directional pointers to show one-way communication.

Next, for each processor, draw the terminals, printers, disk drives, and other peripheral devices that are attached to it. If there are more than one disk drive in the configuration, a list of the classes, class/objects, and objects is made near each drive that will contain data used by the application.

Finally, the diagram is compared to the message list to ensure that all messages are accommodated in the diagram and accurately depict communications between processes. The Booch diagram or the message list can also be used to validate the accuracy and completeness of processes allocated to processors, and of the data allocated to storage devices.

ABC Video Process Diagram

The most simple form of ABC's process diagram shows the file server as the processor and the PCs and printers as terminal devices (see Figure 12-22). This allocation of work is a problem because it does not take advantage of PC intelligence and, therefore, is suboptimal in terms of benefits to be gained from using PCs. Having said this, the allocation is constrained by the software environment. If SQL sup-

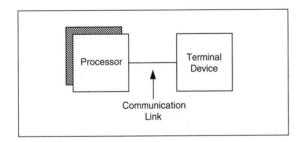

FIGURE 12-21   Process Diagram Icons

ports multilocation processing, then the comment stands. If SQL does not support multilocation processing, then the figure is complete. As it is currently, SQL does not support multilocation processing although it does support distribution of databases.

An alternative process distribution is shown in Figure 12-23. Even with SQL, we could distribute editing, the hardware management functions, payment and change processing, and printing of the rental copy to the local PCs. This is a more complex application because the multiple sites now require synchronization and intraprocessor scheduling in order to coordinate their work, but, if bottlenecks show up in a prototype of the first-cut process distribution, this is a likely candidate for the second iteration of design and prototyping. As it is, we select the simple design because it is significantly easier to implement and maintain, having no synchronization overhead. If it works and is robust to additional users, the first prototype will be completed and placed into production.

Develop Package Specifications and Prototype

Guidelines for Package Specifications and Prototyping

At this point in the design, the functions to be performed are translated into package specifications for translation into program code. A **package** is an encapsulated definition that contains both data and process specifications that define an execute unit. The data might be defined in the form of a class, class/object, or object, with specific attributes and identification. There may be one or more process in a package; they result in individual module specifications and are independently executed under the control of service objects.

Packages have both public and private parts which are specified. The **public package part** identifies the data and processes to the application without any indication of how they are physically implemented. The **private package part** defines the

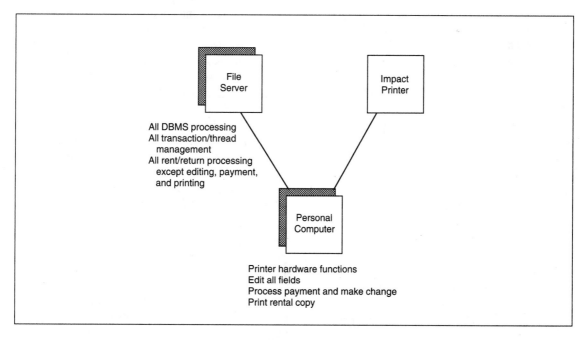

FIGURE 12-23   Alternative ABC Process Diagram

physical implementation. If there are polymorphic definitions of a function, each version of the function is defined separately, and the control mechanism for interpreting the message and activating the appropriate function is defined. Service objects should be used for this interpretation and activation if at all possible.

The steps to package specification are:

1. Review the diagram/list set.
2. Redraw a subset of Booch diagrams, one per processor in the process diagram, to depict objects and processes by processor.
3. Document packages.
4. Design physical database if not already designed.
5. Develop pseudocode specifications for all processes and messaging handling routines.

ABC Video package specifications are not created for this step as it is beyond the scope of this text.

What We Know and Don't Know from OOA and OOD

Object orientation, based on the contents of tables and diagrams, provides a detailed, reasonably complete view of an application. Exceptions to this view are human interface design and specific attention to database, input, and output design. Object-oriented design is distinguished by three characteristics: detail, all potential environments are accommodated, and the need for an object-oriented implementation environment to obtain the payoff from the exercise.

The extensive detail generated in object-oriented design leads directly to module specification which should be straightforward since the definition of process details, the class/object data, constraints, and message communications are all completely defined.

Object orientation, as seen by the exercise in the chapter, can accommodate even nonobject-oriented environments. The benefit of OOD's ability to accommodate any application environment is that, for on-line, object application environments, the

methodology *does* lead to information hiding, minimal coupling, and maximal cohesion by virtue of the thinking processes. Object orientation requires good understanding of operating system concepts, object thinking, and interactions between services and applications. The design process, as the chapter appendix shows, requires iteration and prototyping to get required levels of detail and to ensure efficient processing of message traffic. Most important, object thinking IS NOT the same as entity thinking or as process and data methodology thinking. Object orientation requires a paradigm shift to be done correctly.

Object orientation is not very object-oriented in an SQL implementation environment. The choice of SQL changes the entire design from what it would be in an object environment to be object-based. Like COBOL, the methodology can be made to do anything. Is this the *best* use of OOD? Not in my opinion. Unless an application is at least on-line and will be in an object-oriented environment, the work required for object-oriented design is not worth the effort. Especially with a fourth-generation DBMS, like SQL, the undesign that must be done wastes tremendous time and could result in a worse design than use of some other methodology. While this compromise is acceptable for a small, on-line application such as ABC, it would not be acceptable for applications with real-time or more complex processing requirements. Much of the effort to develop an object-oriented design is wasted when the implementation environment is not object-oriented. Therefore, the choice of methodology should be driven by the expected implementation environment.

Automated Support Tools for Object-Oriented Design

There are a vast number of object-oriented CASE tools that have all come on the market in the last few years. Some are more complete in life cycle coverage than others. Some environments, such as 001 Tool Suite, cover most of a development life cycle,

TABLE 12-9   Automated Support Tools for Object-Oriented Design

Product	Company	Technique
001 Tool Suite	Hamilton Technologies, Inc.	Full life cycle multiuser OOA, OOD, and code generation tool for C or Ada
Actor	Symantec Cupertino, CA	OOD environment for client/server applications. Links to C and SQL databases.
Aide-De-Camp	Software Maintenance and Development Systems Concord, MA	Configuration management software with support for OO languages.
BOCS	Berard Software Engineering, Inc.	Berard object and class specification
C/Spot/Run	Procase, Corp. Santa Clara, CA	Interactive, GUI environment for C language development on Sun, HP, and Apollo hardware
Design/1X0, Design/IDEF, Design/OA	Meta Software Corp.	Data and behavior modeling expressed in OO C-language tool
DSEE, HP/Softbench	Apollo/Hewlett-Packard Palo Alto, CA	Integrated CASE Product Supporting OO Analysis
Excelerator	Index Tech. Cambridge, MA	State-transition diagram Matrix graph (RTS)
IPSYS OOA/RD Tool Suite	IPSYS Software	Shlaer-Mellor OOA and Recursive Design
Object View	KnowledgeWare Atlanta, GA	Application prototyping software using 4GL or SQL code
Object Vision	Borland International Scotts Valley, CA	Visual application development system

(Table continues on next page)

in this case, from analysis through code generation. Some tools, such as ObjectView, are more object-based than object-oriented. Some, like Software Through Pictures, try to shield the user from code altogether by sophisticated graphics that generate objects for that environment. Their existence attests to the object revolution that is beginning to be felt in business organizations.

SUMMARY

Object-oriented design (OOD) requires detailed development of all required functionality in the operating system and how it interacts with an application. In this chapter we developed the seven steps to object-oriented design, linking them to the tables developed during object-oriented analysis. First, the

TABLE 12-9   Automated Support Tools for Object-Oriented Design (*Continued*)

Product	Company	Technique
ObjectMaker	Mark V Systems	Full life cycle structured analysis using Ward-Mellor extensions tool with code generation for Ada, C, and C++
OMTool, OMT/SQL	GE Advanced Concepts Center	OOA and OOD with schema compilation compatible with Oracle, Ingres, and Sybase
ProMod	Promod, Inc. Lake Forest, CA	Control flow diagram State-transition diagram Module networks Function networks
Smalltalk/V	Digitalk Los Angeles, CA	32-bit Smalltalk for OS/2 hardware
Software Backplane Cohesion	Atherton Technology/Digital Equipment Corporation Maynard, MA	Integrated CASE Product Supporting OO Analysis
Software Thru Pictures	Interactive Dev. Env. San Francisco, CA	Control flow State-transition diagram
Teamwork	CADRE Tech. Inc. Providence, RI	DFD Control flow State-transition diagram Process activation table
Telon	Pansophic Systems, Inc. Lisle, IL	State-transition diagram Code generation
Treed4C, Tree4Fortran, Tree4Pascal, TreeSoft1	1 Software Engineering Camarillo, CA	Program code reengineering products for Sun hardware
Visible Analyst	Visible Systems Corp. Newton, MA	State-transition diagram
vs Designer	Visual Software Inc. Santa Clara, CA	Booch diagram

objects are allocated to four subdomains: human, hardware, software, and data. The split of processing into these four areas accommodates the use of, for instance, firmware, distributed computing, DBMSs, and intelligent interfaces in what would otherwise be a monolithic development of an application.

The second step of OOD is the development of time-event diagrams for all processes and all objects.

The purpose of a time-event diagram is to allow the analysts to identify independent, sequential, concurrent, independent, and concurrent, dependent processes. Usually, several alternative ways of looking at the timing of processes emerge from this analysis, one of which is selected for development.

Once the types of process are defined, their service object needs are identified. Service objects closely parallel operations performed by an operating system (OS). OSs have five main functions to manage: memory, job, task, I/O, and secondary storage. The memory, I/O, and secondary storage management functions are directly translatable into object thinking. Job management functions are analogous to those performed at the control level for an entire application and/or user. Job management is more appropriately called session, or user, management in object terms. Similarly, tasks are individual steps of a job and are analogous to transaction-related modules when thinking in objects. Therefore, the term used here for task functions is transaction management. Each type of management function requires its own type of processing and the processes selected are particular to the application and implementation environment.

The fourth step of OOD is to develop a Booch diagram to summarize the objects—both application and service—and their interactions. Booch recommends a 3" x 5" approach for which each object and its processes are shown as a package on a 3" x 5" index card. The set of cards is moved into different configurations and message connections are drawn. The purpose of this exercise is to choose a message-passing scheme that minimizes the potential for bottlenecks and that provides information hiding and minimal coupling. The final configuration selected is documented for the application.

The message connections decided during design of the Booch diagram are elaborated in the next step, which is to define message communications. Each called object and its calling object, input message, output message, action type, and return object are identified.

At a higher level of abstraction, the next step is to develop a process diagram that shows the distribution of functionality and equipment for the application being developed. A process diagram depicts processors, for example, computers, and devices, that is, limited-intelligence equipment such as a disk drive. All equipment and their interconnections are identified. Multiprocessor interconnections show allowable message movement throughout a network, while the device connections show hardware configuration. The functions performed at each processor in a multiprocessor configuration are also on the diagram.

The last step of OOD is to develop package, or module, specifications for programming. The information from the various tables and graphics is rearranged to show the relevant information for each particular module. Also, details of each module's logic, if not already documented in a dictionary, are defined in the package specifications.

OOD CASE tools come in several varieties: object-oriented life-cycle development, object-oriented design without code support, object-oriented coding without design support, or object-based thinking through adaptation of existing methods.

REFERENCES

Booch, Grady, *Software Engineering with Ada*, second ed. Menlo Park, CA: Benjamin/Cummings Publishing Co., Inc., 1987.

Booch, Grady, *Object Oriented Design with Applications*. Redwood City, CA: Benjamin/Cummings Publishing Co., Inc., 1991.

Coad, Peter, and Edward Yourdon, *Object-Oriented Analysis*, second ed. Englewood Cliffs, NJ: Prentice-Hall, 1990.

Coad, Peter, and Edward Yourdon, *Object-Oriented Design*. Englewood Cliffs, NJ: Prentice-Hall, 1991.

Graham, Ian, *Object-Oriented Methods*. Reading, MA: Addison-Wesley Publishing Co., 1992.

LaFore, Robert, *Object-Oriented Programming in Turbo C++*. Emeryville, CA: The Waite Group Press, 1991.

Peterson, J., and A. Silbershatz, *Operating System Concepts*. Reading, MA: Addison-Wesley Publishing Company, 1983.

Rumbaugh, James, Michael Blaha, William Premerlani, Frederick Eddy, and William Lorensen, *Object-Oriented Modeling and Design*. Englewood Cliffs, NJ: Prentice-Hall, 1991.

KEY TERMS

3" x 5" approach	device
binary message	dialogue
binding	dynamic binding
Booch diagram	hardware subdomain
client object	human subdomain
concurrent processes	keyword message
data subdomain	logical process flow

message
message traffic
module
module structure diagram
multitasking
multitasking objects
object-based
package specification
package
polymorphism
private interface
private package part
problem-domain objects
process diagram
processor
pseudo-dynamic binding
public interface

public package part
round-trip gestalt
scheduling
scheduling objects
server object
service objects
software subdomain
static binding
supervisor call (SVC)
synchronizing
synchronizing objects
thread of control
time events
time-event diagram
unary message
utility objects

EXERCISES

1. Continue with the exercise begun in Chapter 11. Design the application for Eagle Rock Golf League.
2. Design all *Customer* processing for ABC's application. Why is it different from that of *VideoInventory*? If we add multiple members to a household, how does that change the design?
3. Compare the SQL and C++ designs for ABC rental processing. If there are bottlenecks in processing for the two designs, where are they likely to be? How might they be removed? Which design gives you better control over the computer and its resources?

STUDY QUESTIONS

1. Define the following terms:
   message   service objects
   object   synchronizing
   polymorphism   thread of control
   problem domain   time-event diagram
   round-trip gestalt
2. Define the four subdomains and the type of objects found in each.
3. What benefits accrue from the allocation of processes to hardware, software, database, and human subdomains?

4. Why are service objects needed? When are they needed and when not?
5. What is multitasking? Why is it important in application design?
6. What is the purpose of a Booch diagram?
7. List and compare three types of message formats.
8. What is the purpose of a process diagram?
9. Describe client/server computing and how it relates to object orientation.
10. What is binding? What types of binding are possible? How do you know what type is used in an application you are developing?
11. Describe an example of polymorphism.
12. What are some of the problems associated with allocation of processes to subdomains?
13. What does the configuration ⊔ on a time-event diagram mean?
14. Describe how to interpret a time-event diagram.
15. Describe how operating systems relate to service objects.
16. Describe the kinds of activities managed by the task manager.
17. What are the control levels in object orientation that are analogous to job and task management in an operating system? Distinguish between them and the tasks they manage.
18. What is memory management and why is it necessary?
19. List the steps to defining service objects. Describe some of the problems related to this activity.
20. What is the purpose of a Booch diagram?
21. Describe the steps to developing a Booch diagram. What information is shown on the diagram?
22. What is a package? What are its contents on a Booch diagram? What are its contents in a working application?
23. Booch recommends the use of 3" × 5" cards to create and 'play' with the Booch diagram contents. What is the playing for? Why are 3" × 5" cards helpful to that process?
24. List three design goals of messages. Create an example of message passing in an object-oriented application. Describe different types

of messages to illustrate good and poor message designs.

25. What information is placed in the message table to document message traffic in an application?
26. Why is message definition a difficult activity?
27. Describe the icons used in a process diagram and their purpose.
28. How many Booch and process diagrams are drawn for an application?
29. Describe the validation processes used throughout an object-oriented design process. Why is each validation step where it is in the process and what is the purpose of each validation?
30. Discuss the statement: "There is no such thing as a one-shot object-oriented design."
31. What information is provided for package specification documentation? How do you decide what is public and what is private information to an object?
32. What is the role of prototyping in object orientation?

★ EXTRA-CREDIT QUESTIONS

1. Research queue or stack management. Write a two-page paper to describe the functions of that type of management. Then, design the object-oriented class/objects and processing routines that would accomplish these functions.
2. Booch discusses primitive processes in detail and names several different types of primitive processes. Research these types of processes and discuss their importance to object-oriented design. How important is it to have a name for each type of *thing* in a design?

APPENDIX: UNIX/ C++ DESIGN OF ABC VIDEO

Although the Chapter 12 presentation of ABC Video's design began as object-oriented, it ended as a hybrid: part-object and part-not, because of the implementation environment. This appendix is the same design with a discussion of the decisions and alternatives from a purely object-oriented perspective. Chapter 12 presented a consistent discussion of the implementation throughout the text and shows what happens when you deobjectify the application to fit a particular language environment. This appendix, then, gives you a basis for contrasting what would happen if you designed a purely object-oriented application. Each stage of the process is presented with enough comment for you to see the differences between the hybrid and object designs. Package specifications and a prototype are still beyond the scope of this discussion, but we present a partial package specification so you can contrast the levels of detail for OOD to the other methodologies.

A few terminology differences exist with the Unix, C++ environment and we start with them. Class structure is similar in C++ to the discussion in the chapter. Data in C++ is defined by *structures*. A structure that contains both data and functions is called a *class*. Classes were defined in the chapter as having public and private parts. In C++ classes have public, private, and protected parts. The public part is that part accessible by the rest of the system. The private part is not directly accessible by any other classes. These two definitions have not changed from the chapter. A **protected** part specifies what may be inherited, that is, processes that are accessible by member processes in its own class or in any class derived from its own. A **derived class** is one that has multiple inheritance and is made up of its own, and its inherited, data and functions. Class inheritance is implemented by having processes that have a *protected* status. Thus, in C++, the manner of implementing inheritance is to provide the protected part of an object and to distinguish inheriting objects by calling them derived classes.

The term process refers to **function**s in C++. Functions can be part of a class (i.e., a member) and restricted in use, or they can be stand-alone entities that are independent of a class. At least one independent function, **main**(), is required to initiate processing of a program or application. Many functions are provided in a library of reusable functions that are link-edited to compiled code for execution. We will not spend much effort on functions since they are most evident at the code level.

Individual language operators are analogous to other languages. Polymorphism is termed operator **overloading** but the meaning is the same. **Virtual functions** are the method used to provide run-time binding for polymorphic functions. Other function types beyond the typical ones associated with classes include **friend functions**, that have *read only* access to the private data of a class, and **static functions**, that operate on the class level rather than at the object (i.e., instance) level. Borland's Turbo C++ provides an entire set of classes with functions and inheritance as the basis for developing applications. The 'container' classes, for instance, include several types of arrays, associations, hash tables, lists, stacks, and queues. The container classes are important because they provide a means for implementing service objects. Next, we discuss the object-oriented design (OOD) activities.

Allocate Objects to Subdomains

In object-oriented analysis (OOA), we defined classes, class/objects, and superset classes needed to properly define all of the interrelationships among objects in the application. This diagram and the table matching processes to their objects are the basis for this activity. The allocation in Table 12-3 has no change here (see Table 12-A1).

In allocating the data handling functions to the data subdomain in C++, we commit to designing generics to handle all files. This means that we need a new object for DB actions. Also, there will be no collapsing of data objects as in SQL. Object-access control will be implemented as a superset of functions to mirror the object relationships. To implement the generics, a fixed message type that accommodates all of the processing for all of the data objects is required. Such a message's minimal contents are: From-Object, To-Object, Action, Object, Return-code, Physical-Location-Key, Length-of-Data, and Data.

While the subdomain allocations do not change, the handling of them does. Once functions are allocated to a DBMS, all developers need to know all allowable interactions. Those interactions must be *defined* and *designed* manually when no DBMS is used. A partial list of functions required includes:

Locate Data (transform key to physical location)
Get Data (may include a prechange write to a log for recovery)
Rewrite (may include a postchange write to a log for recovery)
Write (may include a postchange write to a log for recovery)
Delete (may include a postchange write to a log for recovery)
Space Management
Queue Management (including service requests and service responses)
Backout Management
Commit Management
Lock Management
Access Control Management
Error processing for such problems as data not found, out of space, hardware error, or unsuccessful read, write, rewrite, or delete.

These functions can be defined and incorporated into documentation at subdomain allocation time or during service object definition.

The human interface definition is also going to be different. In the main text of this chapter we designed the system for a 4GL, in which a screen is *painted* and the programmer only needs to know the fields, their format, and desired characteristics. The 4GL software manages all of the formatting and setting of field attributes. In a lower level language, such as C++, screen format, line, starting position, length, field attributes (e.g., blink, reverse video, or color), and field contents are all managed by the programmer and, therefore, require design.

Another choice we make is to have full-screen, line-at-a-time, field-at-a-time, or character-at-a-time interactions. Selection of input method is application specific. In ABC's case, we decide that using a method that will not slow down users the least during peak periods is best. Since actual data entry is limited to *CustomerPhone*, *VideoBarCode*, and *money amounts*, for rental processing, and since rental processing is the most used function, we choose field-at-a-time entry. If the application had thousands of users and millions of transactions each day, we might have field-level entry for rent/return processing and screen entry for customer and video

TABLE 12-A1   Process Subdomain Assignments

Process Name	Subdomain			
	Data	Hardware	Process	Human
EnterCustPhone				X
ReadCust	X			
CreateTempTrans			X	
RetrieveVOR	X			
DisplayTempTrans				X
EnterBarCode				X
RetrieveInventory	X			
Display Inventory				X
ComputeTempTransTotal			X	
EnterPayAmt				X
ComputeChange			X	
DisplayChange				X
UpdateInventory	X			
WriteVOR	X			
PrintTempTrans		X		
EnterBarCode				X
RetrieveVOR	X			
DisplayTempTrans				X
AddRetDateTempTransVOR			X	
Add1toVInv			X	
UpdateInventory	X			
ComputeLateFees			X	
WriteVOR	X			
EnterCustomer				X
CreateCustomer	X			
EnterVideoInventory				X
CreateVideoInventory	X			

maintenance, because they are more data-entry intensive activities. Whichever input 'chunking' method is chosen, we must intercept start and stop characters from the keyboard and bar code reader to synchronize processing between the input devices and the computer.

With field-level input, we could choose field-level interactions, having local, PC-based intelligence simulating a 4GL that checks alphabetic/numeric contents and beeps on errors. This greatly complicates the application and is decided against. At some future date, if the number of users begins to tax the file server, we could revisit this decision to speed processing by off-loading work from the server.

Draw a Time-Event Diagram

The time-event diagram also does not change and is presented here as Figure 12-A1. Now we will pay more attention to the potential for concurrency, because we must be able to prove the processing and that implies monitoring of the success of all write, rewrite, and print actions.

The choices for concurrent processing all relate to data I/O, and the consequences of deciding for concurrency must be considered. First, consider consequences of concurrency if we opt for read/write concurrency. At the hardware level, the affected databases must be on separate buses (on a PC) or channels (on a mainframe) to ensure that the processes are not contending for the same hardware disk access time. Second, management and synchronizing modules to reunite multiprocesses within a thread and to verify processing are required. This implies a need for queues for each process and for each thread. For each process we need process ID, thread ID, and return code. For each thread, we need all concurrent processes' IDs and return codes from processing. Side effects of potential errors must be considered. For instance, if *WriteVideoOnRental*, *RewriteVideoOnRental*, *PrintReceipt*, and *WriteHistory* objects are all active at the same time, we need to decide acceptable combinations of successful/ unsuccessful processing *and* actions taken for each possible combination.

Concurrency decisions should be based on business constraints and needs for processing or response time. There should be some attempt to compute how long a transaction will take and to determine response time. For example, ABC rental transactions have an approximate processing time of 8.6 seconds (8566 ms; see Table 12-A2) during nonpeak time and about 11 seconds during peak processing times. From this table, which the SEs generate, we see that input and output from the terminal account for 8.1 seconds of the total and actual internal processing is about 506 ms or slightly over one-half second. If the internal time were over two seconds, we would opt for concurrency to minimize the internal strain on processing. With under a half-second processing time, we can continue thinking of sequential processing as we did with the SQL solution. The differences in using SQL versus an object-oriented language are not yet apparent. The major difference so far has been the level of detail of the reasoning process to make concurrency and data-related decisions. This level of detail is similarly lower for the other OOD reasoning processes as well.

Determine Service Objects

In this section, we list the required service object functionality to show the level of detail and complexity required of true object systems, but without much explanation. We will assume that the Unix/ C++ environment being developed for ABC will employ reusable code objects for many service functions. 'Free' code is one of the benefits of using consultants who come with their own implementation modules for many functions. We still need to determine which modules are needed, however. Referring back to Table 12-5, ABC is a sequential, multiuser application with needs for scheduling and multi-tasking management, in addition to I/O, user, transaction, thread of control, memory, startup/ shutdown, and data management. Table 12-A3 lists high level service objects required to support ABC's application.

Input/output is straightforward. There are four I/O functions to design: keyboard, bar code reader, display screen, and printer. We assume that all input interactions are from the keyboard or bar code reader, which read slightly differently. The keyboard is read one character at a time until a field is complete. The bar code reader reads the entire code, or field, at once. Thus, we can use polymorphic modules to *GetField* and possibly for other functions as well. Likewise, we assume all output interactions are to the display screen and printer. The basic actions for all four devices is to start, synchronize (abbreviated synch from now on), get/put, wait, or stop.

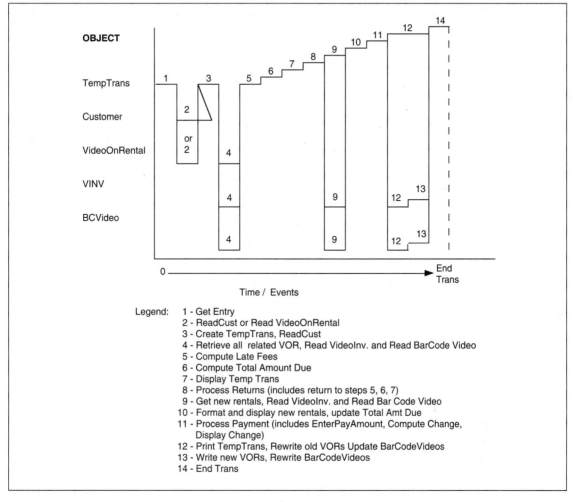

FIGURE 12-A1   ABC Time-Event Diagram

Waiting requires a queue to manage multiple waiting requests.

User routines initiate an application session and verify user access. The 'put' commands all interface to the screen I/O manager, handing off the message to be displayed. Similarly, the 'get' commands all interface with the keyboard or bar code routines of the I/O manager. The purpose of user logon routines is to identify physical terminal address (*TermID*) and user (*UserID*).

The transaction object and its routines manage individual transactions selected from menus. Information is directed to a specific device based on the *TermID* and *UserID* passed from the User routines. For instance, customer *Maintenance* has four transactions: create, delete, update, and retrieve. Job routines then display menus and alter menu contents based on user logon and access codes. As above, 'puts' interface with the screen or printer routines of the I/O manager objects and 'gets' interface with the keyboard or bar code reader routines. The information passed to the command object for use in process control includes *TermID*, *UserID*, and *TransCode*.

Thread of control is handled by a command object and routines which manage atomic processes,

TABLE 12-A2   Rent/Return Transaction Processing Time Estimate

Instruction	Input*	Internal Process	Output	Total
Get	1000			1000
Read (average 3) 30 ms each plus data transfer of 6 ms each		96		96
Compute late fees		30		30
Compute amount due		10		10
Display (average 20 lines, 150 ms/line)			3000	3000
Get Returns (30% of transactions)	1000			1000
Retrieve VOR (average 3)		96		96
Compute late fees and amount due (10 ms each)		30		30
Display 3 lines			450	450
Get Rental (assume one)	1000			1000
Retrieve 3 DBs		96		96
Compute amount due		10		10
Display rental line, amount due line			300	300
Process payment—enter amount	1000			1000
Compute change		10		10
Display new amount due, change			300	300
Print (assumes automating queuing and time to transfer queue address)			10	10
Rewrite (average 3)		96		96
Write (average one)		32		32
Subtotal (nonpeak time)	4000	506	4060	8566
Time in queue (average .33 trans waiting during peak times transaction time)				2855
Total peak processing time				11421

*All times are in milliseconds.

TABLE 12-A3   Service Objects Required for C++ ABC Application

I/O Manager			
Keyboard Processes	Get character until end of field		Put password prompt
	Ready to receive (Sync keyboard)		Get password
	Start keyboard entry		Verify password
	Reset keyboard		Put password error
	Send entry to screen formatter	Transaction	Put menu
Bar Code Reader	Start reader	object	Get selection
	Sync reader		Verify selection
	Get bar code		Get memory
	Send bar code to calling routine		Release memory
			Set up global user area
Display Screen	Identify screen location and type interaction		Release global user area
			Call defrag for user area
	Format screen protected lines		
	Format screen data lines	Thread of	Get memory address of data
	Put keyboard entry in field	control—	Get memory
	Set field attributes	Command	Set status
	Check allowable value	Object	Queue instructions for execution
	Get error message		(i.e., call object/process)
	Send entry to calling routine		Transfer control to TempTrans or
	Put screen		Data
	Put screen line		Enqueue transaction
			Dequeue transaction
Printer	Sync printer		Execute instruction
	Start print		Check status
	Put lines until end of print		Create status
	Stop printer		Delete status
	Get print lines until end of print		Release memory
	Wait to print		
	Store print lines for 60 seconds	Memory	Allocate memory
	Queue address, length of print information	Manager	Deallocate (free) memory
			Defrag memory (i.e., defragment)
			Queue memory request
User Object	Put logon prompt		Dequeue memory request
	Get logon		
	Verify logon		
	Put error		*(Table continues on next page)*

that is, they supervise execution of code modules. The object reads code into memory, passes one instruction at a time to the CPU for execution, and interfaces to the other manager routines to perform I/O, memory, and data management. The command object uses the fields passed from the transaction object and adds to it the task and task status.

Memory management is designed simply to allocate the maximum amount of space for a transaction to any request. The largest transaction is a rental/

return which is estimated to take 13,860 bytes as follows:

Design Element	Bytes
Screen 80 × 22	1,760
Max fields 100 bytes × 10 lines	1,000
Attribute bytes three/field	300
Miscellaneous data area	800
Code	10,000
Total	13,860

TABLE 12-A3   Service Objects Required for C++ ABC Application (*Continued*)

Start/shut Main()	Set up all memory	Read DB
	Initiate managers	Write DB
	Load application code	Rewrite DB
	Allocate transaction code locations	Position DB
	Store application code	Determine physical location
	Get DB indexes	Request Read
	Store DB indexes	Wait read
	Start DBs	Request Write/Rewrite
	Close DBs	Position Index
	Transfer to User	Read Index
Data Manager	Open DB (Open Index, Read Index into memory, Position Index, Open DB files)	Wait write/rewrite
		Check item locks
		Enqueue item lock
	Close DB (Write Index, Close Index, Release Locks, Backup DB, Backup Indexes, Close DB files)	Dequeue item lock
		Wait for item lock

While this over-allocates memory, the alternative, to size memory to each transaction, is more complex. If memory becomes scarce, the change to transaction size allocation can be made. To contrast the amount of memory required, a Customer Create transaction takes approximately 5K memory.

Startup and shutdown could be handled as part of the user object, but a cleaner implementation is to design them as separate. This start/shut object allocates memory, initiates application and DB processing, including bringing all transaction code and DB indexes into memory. In C++ implementation terms, the start/shut object will be the main() routine that initiates ABC processing.

Last, data management could be by file or by function. By file is simpler and easier for novices to maintain, but it also requires much more code and, therefore, more maintenance. Here we will define one set of generic CRUD functions for the data object with each requiring the specific DB name and data. If necessary, polymorphic processes for the CRUD functions can be customized for each database.

After the services objects are developed, they are allocated to the four subdomains of data hardware, software, and human interface as shown in Table 12-A4. Allocation of keyboard and bar code to hardware would be a possible choice. They are left with

TABLE 12-A4   Service Object Allocation

Data	Hardware	Process	Human
Data Manager	I/O—Print	User Manager	I/O—Keyboard, Display, and Bar code reader
		Memory Manager	
		Transaction Manager	
		Command Manager (Thread of Control)	

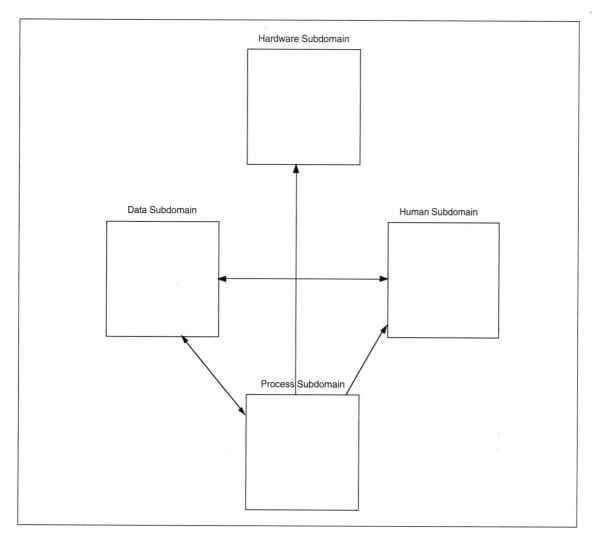

FIGURE 12-A2   Subdomain-Level Booch Diagram

the human interface because they are closely related to the display processes which mirror all of their input. Keeping these processes together reduces the object-switching overhead required to change from one object context to another.

Develop a Booch Diagram

The first Booch diagram in Figure 12-A2 shows the subdomain-level communication. To simplify the communications in the system, based on the subdo-main message interchanges, we will define a generic message for use in most communications. The second Booch diagram, shown in Figure 12-A3, is at the object level and is obviously more complex than the SQL solution.

There are several major differences between the SQL and C++ designs. First, the schedule in SQL is a mainline routine that determines the next code to execute and is a centralized controller of the application. That function is performed to some extent by the command manager objects in the C++ design,

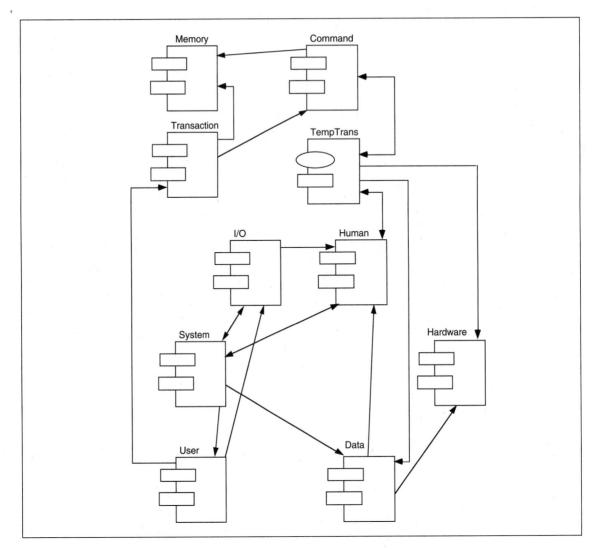

FIGURE 12-A3   Object-Level Booch Diagram

but the scheduler functions are at a lower level and spread over the service objects. At this level, the specific processes are not shown because the diagram would be more complex than necessary. Instead, we have shown the service and data objects only. To implement the application, we would complete that detail.

The design as shown in Figure 12-A3 is still incomplete for the data part of the processing. In Figure 12-A4 the next lower level of detail to show the complexity of the data objects is developed.

Based on this diagram, we might decide to denormalize the data to provide minimal accessing of databases during rental processing. For instance, we might replicate all *VideoInventory* information in each *BarCodeVideo* object to eliminate the need to access another object as part of rental processing. Similar denormalization might be done with *Customer* and *VideoOnRental*. Before a prototype could be built, a second design iteration on all objects and complete design of the details is required.

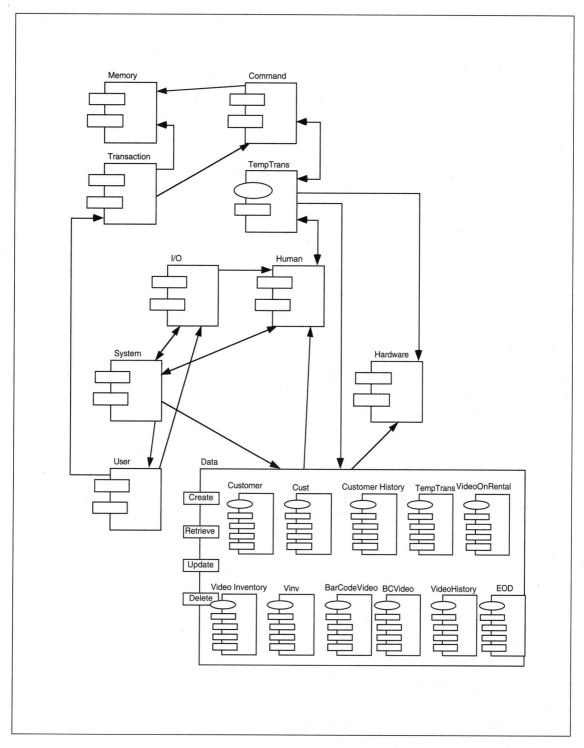

FIGURE 12-A4   Object-Level Booch Diagram with Data-Object Detail

Define Message Communications

The message list is shorter than that of the SQL solution if we use a generic message as described above. The generic message list for the C++ Booch diagram is shown as Table 12-A5. If we do not use a generic message, the number of connections increases from the SQL number of about 30 messages to over 170 messages for C++ as shown in Figure 12-A5, which depicts *all* connections in the Booch diagram, summarizing the processing for Command and I/O manager objects. In Figure 12-A5, the processes with no specific arrows have multiple calling routines and return to the caller. The other routines with arrows are chained as shown.

In the SQL design, the network operating system and SQL shielded the application programmer from most of the complex elements—the service objects. With C++, the increased number of connections also increases the application's complexity. If we cannot use DB user views, there are more data objects on the diagram. If we do not have a sophisticated operating system to monitor execution and physical I/O aspects of the application, the capability must be part of the application. By using generic messages, we reduce the complexity somewhat by reducing object abends for wrong message type and by allowing generic code for message reception and interpretation.

Develop Process Diagram

The process diagram has no changes from Figure 12-22, which is redrawn here as Figure 12-A6.

Develop Package Specifications and Prototype

Package specifications for SQL would be simple compared to those of C++. One package description/program specification is shown below for customer data. The specification identifies public and private parts, plus the processing to be performed. Following the specification is an example of a C++ code

module to read the customer file based on a location that is passed to the read module.

Customer Specification

Item:	Description
Name:	Customer
Documentation:	The customer database contains information about legal customers for ABC. All access is through the data manager routines. All data is passed to using routines.
Visibility:	Private
Cardinality:	400–600
Hierarchy:	
Superclass	Customer
Class	Cust
Metaclass	None
Generic parameters:	&custloc &custrec
Interface- Implementation:	
Public:	Only through passed parameters

Protected:	Uses:Customer class
	 Fields =
	     char custphon [10];
	     char custln [50];
	     char custfn [25];
	     char custadd1 [50];
	     char custadd2 [50];
	     char custcity [30];
	     char custstat [2];
	     char custzip [10];
	     char cctype [1];
	     char ccno [17];
	     date ccexp [8];
	     date entrydat [8];

Operations:	Add (put) Seek (read) Update (put) Delete
Persistence:	Static

TABLE 12-A5   C++ Design Message List for ABC Rental Processing

Calling Object	Called Object	Input Message	Output Message	Action Type	Return Object
Temp Trans Start/Shut	Data Manager	Task ID, Terminal ID, Thread ID, Database ID, Type Request, Data	Task ID, Terminal ID, Thread ID, Database ID, Type Request, Return Code, Data	CRUD, Open, Close	Caller
Print Term Trans	Hardware-Print	Data Address, Type Print	None	Print	None
Temp Trans, Start/Shut	I/O-Bar Code Reader, I/O-Keyboard	Task ID, Terminal ID, Thread ID, Database ID, Type Request	Task ID, Terminal ID, Thread ID, Database ID, Type Request, Return Code, Data	Input	Caller
Start/Shut, User Mgr, Trans Mgr, Human Interface, Data Mgr	I/O-Display	Task ID, Terminal ID, Thread ID, Database ID, Type Request, Data	ACK or Task ID, Terminal ID, Thread ID, Database ID, Type Request, Return Code	Display	Command
System	Start/Shut	Begin	Non until shut down	Process	User Mgr
Start/Shut	User Mgr	Term Id	I/O-Display— Logon screen request (no message return to caller)	Put Prompt	I/O-Display
Command	Temp Trans	Task ID, Terminal ID, Thread ID, Database ID, Type Request, Data	Depends on next called routine, either Task ID, Terminal ID, Thread ID, Database ID, Type Request, Data or Task ID, Terminal ID, Thread ID, Database ID, Type Request, Return Code, Data	Process	Either Command, Human Mgr, Data Mgr, HW-Printer I/O Mgr

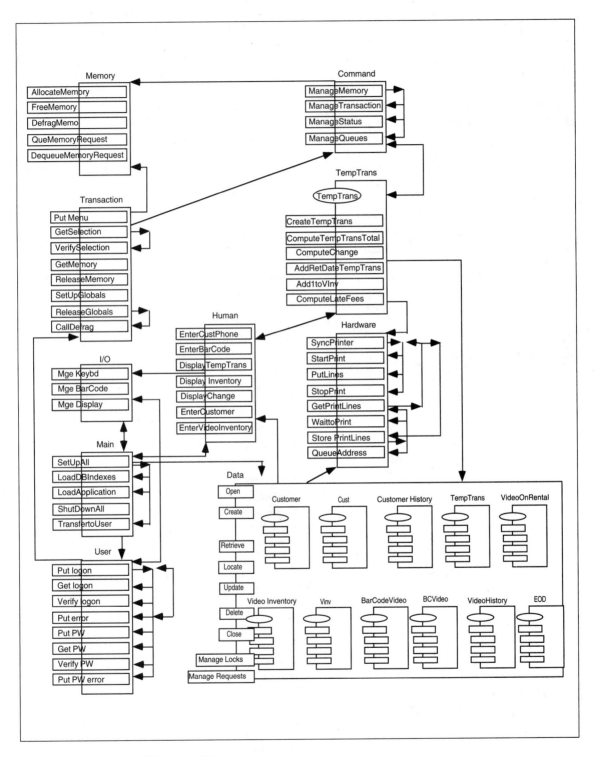

FIGURE 12-A5   ABC Process Diagram

Program fragment to read the customer data:

```
//seekc.cpp
//read particular customer using
passed customer location
#include <fstream.h>  //file stream
class customer
{
protected:
  char custphon [10];
  char custln [50];
  char custfn [25];
  char custadd1 [50];
  char custadd2  [50];
  char custcity [30];
  char custstat [2];
  char custzip [10];
  char cctype [1];
  char ccno [17];
  date ccexp [8];
  date entrydat [8];
public:
  void custdb();
};
void main(custloc& custloc)
  //customer location passed
{
person cust;
  // establish customer object
ifstream cust;
  // establish customer file
infile.seekg(0,ios:end);
  //go to 0 bytes from end
int endposition=cust.tellg();
  //find file position
int n=endposition/sizeof(cust);
  //number of customer on file
int position=(custloc-1) *
sizeof(cust);
  //relative location # * record
size locates individual record
cust.seekg(position);
cust.read((char*)&cust,sizeof
  (cust));
  // read customer information
}
```

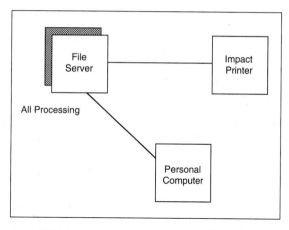

FIGURE 12-A6   ABC Process Diagram

## CHAPTER 13

SUMMARY AND FUTURE OF SYSTEMS ANALYSIS, DESIGN, AND METHODOLOGIES

INTRODUCTION

There are an unlimited number of ways in which the methodologies discussed in the preceding six chapters might be compared and analyzed. In addition, significant research is proceeding on individual methods as well as on integrating different methods. To confuse matters, new technologies introduced daily profoundly impact our ability to develop applications and will require equally profound changes in methodologies to be used efficiently and effectively. In this chapter, we first compare the three methodologies to get a fix on their completeness and ability to be used to analyze and design applications. Next, computer-aided software engineering tools (CASE) are critiqued and summarized. The deficiencies and usefulness of CASE are discussed and related both to development of current applications and to the future applications that companies now desire to build. Then, the changes in organizational and technological environments that

will require continuous evolution of methodologies are described and related to problems in application development.

COMPARISON OF METHODOLOGIES

In this section, we take two different approaches to summarizing the usefulness and sophistication of the three methodologies discussed in the preceding six chapters. In the first analysis, the phases, information developed, characteristics, and decisions made in the three classes of methodologies are traced following the work of Olle et al. [1988] and expanding the information analyzed for each of the methodologies. Then, Watts Humphrey's maturity framework is described and applied to the methodologies to describe which, if any, might be appropriate for use in a maturing IS organization. In the concluding remarks in this section, we summarize the findings and discuss the future of the methodology classes and, in particular, the three methodologies discussed in this text.

Information Systems Methodologies Framework for Understanding

In their classic work, Olle et al. [1988], developed the **information systems methodology framework** to compare methodologies, discuss the representation forms, and identify information supported in methodologies available for use in the mid-1980s, including the process methods and data methods analyzed in this text. Here, we summarize the framework to analyze activities and phases supported by the three representative methodologies. Then we extend the analysis to evaluate the phases in which information becomes known, the general capabilities of the methodologies, and the sophistication of resulting designs. Before the evaluation, please be cautioned that these analyses are not intending to condemn or otherwise pass a value judgment on the methodologies presented in this text. If they were not the best of their class, they would not have been selected in the first place. Rather, any shortcomings in the methodologies only point out that an organization must compensate for the lacking activities, phases, or decisions by providing its own guidelines and methods, or by hoping that their analysts have the requisite skills to perform these tasks on their own.

Activities and Phases

This section analyzes the phases of application development work that may begin at the organization level to develop information systems plans (ISPs) based on business objectives. An **ISP** is an analysis of both data and processes that includes manual or automated work to capture a snapshot of the work performed in an enterprise. The ISP is modified to provide the basis for organizational reengineering analysis as discussed in Chapter 5 (which is not part of Olle et al.'s work). Work proceeds according to the framework to include business process, entity and feasibility analysis for a given application. Analysis and design are discussed in terms of the orientation of the majority of tasks performed during those phases. Support for human interface design, allocation of work to hardware or firmware, and DBMS design are all included. Maintenance, the final phase of a project's life, is considered in the extent to which it is supported in the methodology.

Table 13-1 shows the ratings of the process, data, and object methodologies from Chapters 6–12 on these activity and phase criteria. The process method, including the work of DeMarco and Yourdon & Constantine, is most focused, including only analysis, design, and program development techniques and methods.

The information engineering (IE) data methodology is the most complete, covering all phases of the life cycle except maintenance explicitly, and covering all design items to some extent (see Table 13-1). The support for hardware/firmware design is limited to allocation of tasks and data to distributed environments. There are no decisions in IE for how to allocate work to hardware or firmware as in object orientation.

The enhanced Booch and Coad & Yourdon object-oriented (OO) approach ignores front-end tasks, including organization level, business analysis of entities and process, and feasibility analysis. Rather, it assumes that these tasks have been performed before object-oriented methods begin to be used. Object orientation is more specific in its approach to analysis and design than process orientation, and, for some items, than data orientation. OO examines and selects the objects and processes of interest in developing the application during the analysis process. These are then subsequently refined and further defined until design primitives are developed. Object design explicitly discusses the control structure of the application in the form of service objects which can support either batch, interactive, or real-time applications with any number of users, in addition to providing for distributed computing through the development of process diagrams. The other two methodologies do not specifically address design differences that relate to timing or number of users for an application.

TABLE 13-1   Methodology Comparison: Activities and Phases

Knowledge	Process	Data	Object
Business objectives as basis for applications	No	Yes	No
Organization Level Analysis	No	Yes—Information Systems Plan (ISP) or Organizational Reengineering	No
Business Process Analysis	No	Yes	No
Business Entity Analysis	No	Yes	No
Feasibility Study	No	Yes	No
Analysis	Process-Oriented	Balanced Data and process analysis	Objects incorporate both Data and Processes and are defined during Analysis
Design	Process-Oriented	Balanced Process data integration	Encapsulated Object-Oriented
Program Development	Program design has some heuristics but relies on personal expertise of SEs	Program design has some heuristics but assumes use of CASE which generates code	Iterative prototype development is an integral part of the methodology . . . some methods are oriented to specific languages
Human Interface Guidelines	No	Yes	No
Hardware/Firmware Attention	No	Distribution analysis	Yes
DBMS Design Attention	No	Yes—Assumes 3rd normal form relational DBs	No
Maintenance Support	No	No	Assumes independent modules which *should be* easily maintained

To summarize, information engineering (IE) covers more phases of the life cycle and more specific activities as identified by the Olle framework. Object orientation (OO) has more depth to the design phase by providing for design of problem domain, hardware, *and* service object activities. The guidance provided by IE for distributed computing decisions is significantly more detailed than the heuristics provided by object-oriented design for allocation of work to processors.

Where Information Becomes Known

Next, we evaluate the phases in which information becomes known by classifying data, processes, relationships, and module information at different levels of detail.

Table 13-2 shows that both data and object methodologies provide analysis of all the items but some items are completed in different phases. Major entities and processes can be known during the information systems planning (ISP) activity of IE, if it is conducted. In addition, the current automation state of the entities and processes is identified during ISP as well. The same items, using the term object for entity, are defined during object-oriented analysis and are subject to refinement during object-oriented design. There is no explicit identification of cur-rent automation status for any of the items in OO methods.

Business events and processing triggers are both identified in IE and object orientation. The timing of events, via event diagrams, is analyzed in more detail in object-oriented design, providing a basis for concurrent processing decisions. In IE, events are used to identify triggers for processing and to show where external data entry is performed in the application. Process methods identify necessary data flows into and out of the application, but they are not specifically tied to business events or triggers. The event/trigger distinction is important because it identifies necessary and sufficient inputs whereas data flow identification leads to continuation of past data interactions without consciously reflecting on their need.

The process method does not provide for data relationship analysis, nor is data structure analyzed at either the logical or physical levels. The process method explicitly ignores timing and interprocess relationships.[1] The lack of relationship analysis means that the resulting designs will be less likely to mirror the business requirements of the application. Even Yourdon's 1989[2] update to the

methodology fails to integrate data with process analysis.

Object orientation appears more complete for real-time and database applications in explicit analysis and decisions for system, database, or software-specific attributes and processes that might be required of the application. The event diagram more explicitly identifies opportunities and requirements for concurrency than the other methodologies. The reliance of both process and data methodologies (with or without extensions) on designer knowledge and experience leaves too much to chance and puts pressure on designers to remember these tasks (i.e., concurrency analysis and software-specific data design).

General Capabilities

In this section, the methodologies are compared according to the extent to which they support analysis and design of the application characteristics described in Chapter 1: inputs, data, outputs, and constraints. In addition, processes and management of different sources of complexity are analyzed to complete the general description of an application. Inputs include the extent to which information and events that trigger processing are included in the analysis and design of the application. Data are internal, computerized representations of facts about entities in the real work that are stored in the database for the application. Outputs are information that leaves the computer system either to a display or to paper or some other (e.g., image) media. Processes describe the activity being automated, for instance, transaction, decision, or inferential processing.

Constraints define restrictions on objects, entities, data, relationships, or processes within an application. Constraint types include prerequisites, temporal, inferential, structural, and control constraints.

Although not explicitly defined in Chapter 1, the ability of the methodology to facilitate management of problem complexity is a key concern to developers. **Complexity** stems from several sources, including management of the number of elements in the application; the degree and types of interactions, and the need to support novelty and ambiguity.

---

1 This explicit ignoring of process timing and relationships is in DeMarco and Yourdon & Constantine. In extensions of process methods for real-time systems, these are both analyzed explicitly. For a discussion of the real-time extensions, see Ward, P. T., and S. J. Mellor, *Structured Development of Real-Time Systems* (three volumes). NY: Yourdon Press, 1985.

2 See Yourdon, Edward, *Modern Structured Analysis*. Englewood Cliffs, NJ: Prentice-Hall, Inc., 1989.

TABLE 13-2   Methodology Comparison: General Capabilities

Knowledge	Process	Data	Object
Entities/Objects	Feasibility—Begun Design—Complete Terminology differs	During ISP if done Feasibility—High level fully known Analysis—Complete	Analysis—May be revised during iterations
Entity Attributes	Feasibility—Begun Design—Complete Terminology differs	Analysis Design—Complete	Analysis Design—Complete
Entity Identifiers	Design Terminology differs	Analysis	Analysis Design—Complete
Entity Class/Object Structure	NA	Design	Analysis, subject to change during Design
Data Relationships	No	Analysis—Entity Hierarchy	Analysis—Object Lattice Hierarchy
Specific attributes required of operating system, DBMS, or software	Design—Required knowledge of designers, not part of methodology	Design—Required knowledge of designers, not part of methodology	Design—Specifically part of the methodology
Physical Data Design	Design, Programming	Design, Programming	Design, Prototyping
General Processes	Feasibility—Begun Design—Complete	During ISP if done Feasibility—High level fully known Analysis—Complete	Analysis
Detail Process Logic	Feasibility—Begun Analysis—Complete	Analysis Design—Complete	Design
Data relationship to processes	Design	Analysis Design—Complete	Analysis Design—Complete
Events, Triggers	None—Analysis includes identification of external entity inputs only.	Design-Process Triggers on PDFD	Design-Event Diagrams State Transition Diagrams
Process relationships	No	Analysis Design—Complete	Process Timing defined in Analysis with State-Transition and in Design with Event/Triggers
Module Structure	Design	Design	Design
Module Specifications	Design	Design	Design

TABLE 13-3   Methodology Comparison: General Capabilities

Knowledge	Process	Data	Object
Inputs	None	Trigger Identification; Screen Design Heuristics	Event Analysis State Transition Analysis
Data	Minimal	Entity Relationship Diagram, DBMS, Normalization	Object Analysis Object Attribute Analysis
Output	None	Screen Design Heuristics	None
Prerequisite Constraints	None	Yes	Yes
Temporal Constraints	None	Limited	Yes
Inferential Constraints	None	None	None
Structural Constraints	None	Data only	Hierarchic inheritance for data and processes
Controls	None	Problem domain	Includes both problem and service domains
Complexity Management	Top-down perspective	Top-down perspective	Round-trip Gestalt perspective
	Relies on SE skill for proper manual decomposition	Relies on SE skill for proper manual decomposition	Allocate processes to hardware, software, DBMS, and human interface; treat as four separate elements
Management of Novelty	None	None	None
Management of Ambiguity	None	None	None

As Table 13-3 shows, none of the methodologies are complete in providing for analysis of all types of design criteria. None of the methodologies support design of inputs or outputs, even though both data and object methods identify the *need* for inputs via event/trigger identification.

None of the methodologies deal with inferential constraints (see Table 13-3). Remember, the fact that constraints might be missing from a methodology does not mean that they cannot be in the resulting application, only that they must be remembered and designed outside of the methodology and rely on designer skills. Process methods are the most limited

in providing no constraint identification and processing as part of the methodology. In contrast, object-oriented analysis specifically provides a step to identify and define the constraints on processing and structural constraints as they relate to both data and processes. IE and data methods are in the middle with prerequisite constraints shown on action diagrams, while structural constraints are limited to those expressed in a class hierarchy for data. Controls are explicitly provided for in both data and object methods and are absent from process methods.

Complexity management is similar in data and process methods since both take a top-down perspective and are controlled through SE skills. IE decomposition is somewhat easier when an ISP is performed, because the software decomposition follows from primitive business processes which translate into computer processes. The SE skills required, then, are for further decomposition of computer processes into modules and execution units that provide for desired software characteristics such as minimal coupling, maximal cohesion, and so on.

The OO design perspective of round-trip gestalt and explicit use of iterative prototype development supports complexity management to some extent by providing increasingly detailed abstractions of the application with each iteration. OO design also manages complexity through inheritance which minimizes the replication of both data and processes and by allocation of processes to hardware, software, DBMS, and human interface. Through the allocation of objects and processes to each subdomain, the subdomains can be considered independently, even by different design groups. The only need for intergroup coordination is for interprocess message definition.

For complexity management of ambiguous or novel requirements, none of the methodologies provides guidance.

None of the methodologies guide input/output design. Process and object methods are unlikely to be useful in identifying conversion requirements of an application, since they do not differentiate automated from manual data as IE does. Similarly, process and object methods are not likely to lead to well-defined databases since the methods do not provide guidelines for database design.[3] IE provides explicitly for normalization and logical database design while recognizing the need for physical design based on data usage requirements.

None of the methodologies are perfect at complexity management. Object orientation appears to facilitate complexity management more than the other methodologies through its support for inheritance and allocation of processes to subdomains.

Novelty and ambiguity of requirements are not addressed by any methodologies.

Sophistication in Explicit Design Decisions

Sophistication means "developed in form or technique,"[4] complex, or worldly. In this section, we rate the methodologies in their ability to guide the development of sophisticated modules, programs and applications to exhibit characteristics of reusability, modularization, information hiding, maximal cohesion, and minimal coupling. The issue is not can the methodologies use or result in modules with these characteristics—the answer is absolutely yes, they can. The issue is the extent to which the methodologies explicitly provide guidelines and validation heuristics for reaching designs that exhibit these characteristics.

Neither data nor process methodologies provide for information hiding, maximal cohesion, or minimal coupling beyond somewhat arbitrary heuristics. Only object orientation specifically can result in a clean design (see Table 13-4), but it can also be corrupted if the designers significantly change intraobject and class/object structures or relationships during design. By early encapsulation of objects and processes during analysis, object orientation automatically imbeds cohesion in the application. By only allowing communication via minimal messages, object orientation automatically provides minimal coupling and information hiding. When implemented using object-oriented DBMSs and languages, object designs should have these properties.

Problems and a loss of minimal coupling and information hiding *will* occur if nonobject languages or software are used to implement OO designs. For instance, COBOL is the antithesis of object orientation. COBOL assumes global data and cannot manage encapsulated objects because it assumes separation of data and process. Therefore, if COBOL is the target language, object orientation would not be a good choice of methodology, all other things considered.

3 Attempts by Booch (1991), for instance, to design databases into an OOD and by Yourdon (1989) to integrate entity-relationship and data analysis in *Modern Systems Analysis* are incomplete and cursory.

4 From *Webster's New World Dictionary*, pocket edition. NY: Popular Library, 1973, p. 544.

TABLE 13-4 Methodology Comparison: Explicit Design Decisions

Knowledge	Process	Data	Object
Extent of Information Hiding	NA	NA	Analysis—Begun Design—Complete
Extent of Modularization	Heuristics rely on SE skill	Uses Process-design heuristics and SE skill	Forces design until primitives, highly dependent on implementation language. Relies on SE skill and proto-typing.
Extent of Maximal Cohesion	Heuristics rely on SE skill	Heuristics rely on SE skill	Analysis—Begun Design—Complete
Extent of Minimal Coupling	Heuristics rely on SE skill	Heuristics rely on SE skill	Forced by the methodology but could be subverted by SE errors.
Supports reusable object design	No	No	Heuristics and procedure for identifying reusable objects
Supports reusable module/object use	Yes	Yes	Includes heuristics and limited procedure for identi-fying reusable objects
Extent of Reusability	Relies entirely on SE skill	Relies entirely on SE skill	Can be 80%+ Organization dependent

The other measure of sophistication is the extent to which the methodologies support reusability and reusable module/object design. Only object orientation provides for explicit identification of potential reusable processes and objects. Once the reusable items are identified, object orientation does not provide further guidance in how to actually design reusable modules; nor should it necessarily provide such guidelines.

IE covers the whole life cycle, something both process and OO methodologies need to provide for application development. The IE data methodology provides more human interface design guidance and is the only methodology that covers the complete life cycle of an application. IEs' disadvantage is that many activities rely on SE skill and experience to know the activity should be performed rather than incorporating the need for the activity in the methodology. When data is complex, nonobject software (either DBMS or language or both) are used, or if human interface design is paramount, information engineering would be the choice.

Structured analysis and design, the process methodology, is the least prescriptive in telling users how to perform the various activities, and it has the least activities in the methodology.

Overall, object-oriented methodologies would be expected to lead to a design that more closely resembles the functional requirements, if the functional requirements are adequately stated before OO analysis begins. The lack of front-end activities in OO hinders its usefulness in business. Keep in mind that just because object orientation is the most explicit methodology, it is weak in actual data design, human interface design, and must be used with object-oriented languages in order to realize the benefits from its use. Also, every author has a *different* OO methodology with *different* notation and *different* reasoning. As a result, the fledgling OO methodology will change and be refined over the next decade. Large-scale commitment to OO without attaining some consensus and stability of methods certainly adds risk to application development.

Humphrey's Maturity Framework

The **Humphrey's maturity framework**[5] was developed for the Department of Defense as a self-assessment framework that identifies levels of computing and application development *process* maturity. The goal of the framework is to provide a means of assessing and accelerating technology transfer from research to practice throughout the Department of Defense. According to Humphrey, the ideal software process is predictable, consistent, measurable, and monitored according to objective standards. The maturity levels are initial, repeatable, defined, managed, and optimizing (see Figure 13-1).

At the **initial level**, neither measures (i.e., statistical control) nor orderly progress are possible. This is the level at which organizations operating under no methodology and no life cycle operate. Managerial oversight for quality, productivity, and change control to provide some stability to project schedules are required organizational supports that must be present to even attain the initial level.

At the **repeatable level** the organization has introduced managerial controls in the form of project

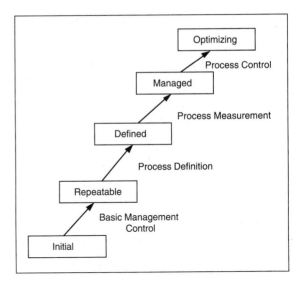

FIGURE 13-1   Humphrey's Five Levels of Maturity

management cost, schedule, and change controls. Project team members are expected to commit to their tasks and be measured against their commitments. While never actually saying the words, the repeatable level implies the recognition of *both* a life cycle and a methodology, that is, a repeated set of global level tasks with deliverable *products* that implicitly become the measures of schedule and cost performance and that are performed within a definable *process*. Humphrey's reason for having a life cycle/methodology is to provide a framework within which to address the risks to a development project from new tools, methods, and/or technologies. Organizational support in the form of providing for walk-throughs, formal design methodologies, configuration management for code, and application testing standards and methods are required at the repeatable level to continue to the next stage. Humphrey argues the need for a **process group** (i.e., a Standards group) which defines the steps to making orderly progress in project work and that provides a nucleus for transferring the process knowledge to the working groups.

The **defined level** requires the definition of the software development process, which defines the methodology in sufficient detail to guide the work

---

5 See Humphrey, Watts, *Managing the Software Process*. Reading, MA: Addison-Wesley Publishing, Inc., 1989.

process and define detailed subphase products that collectively become the phase deliverables needed to further manage the tasks. Each deliverable product has process and product measures of quality and productivity that are aggregated to the phase and project level for managerial oversight and assessment. At this stage, a quality assurance group that performs independent analysis of product and application quality is formed to report to management on a product-by-product basis. At the defined level, a *process database* is established and all SEs are trained in the use of the information to provide history for the organization on the use and productivity of each project and tool.

At the **managed level** the organization initiates "comprehensive process measurements, beyond those of cost and schedule" [Humphrey, 1988, p. 302]. The managed process requires analysis of the process database measures to ensure that comparable statistics are available and can be universally interpreted, and that project-specific data that highlight unique characteristics or aspects of application development projects are stored and interpreted properly. At the managed process level, the data for the process database should be gathered automatically and used to modify the process to "prevent problems and increase efficiency" [Humphrey, 1988, p. 306]. Humphrey takes pains to point out that the database should not be used to penalize either project teams or individuals, but that type of use by managers can be taken. One example of measures is function points.

The **optimizing level** is one at which the organization continues improvements begun at the managed level and starts development process optimization. The optimizing level, ideally, allows SEs to identify many types of errors in advance of their causing delays and problems on a current project by analyzing and identifying the patterns of mistakes from other projects based on information in the process database. In my opinion, this is truly an ideal at this point in time since our ability to detail the steps to what appear to be random incidences of Murphy's Laws is rudimentary, at best, and nonexistent, in practice.

While Humphrey's framework is useful for discussing key differences between methodologies,

it is not without problems. First, it is based on Humphrey's and others' experiences in the field but has never been subjected to empirical validation of its definitions. Humphrey asserts that the maturity framework "represents the actual ways in which software-development organizations improve" [Humphrey, 1988, p. 307]. The stages are presented as distinct and sequential, with the implicit understanding that to attain, for instance, the optimizing level, an organization must have moved through all previous levels. There is no basis for this supposition. In fact, the framework represents Humphrey's ways of attaining software development maturity without recognizing that it may not fit all situations. The second drawback to the framework in analyzing methodologies is that many of the requisite support activities are organizational, not methodological. For instance, walk-throughs, configuration management software, and testing standards are outside the scope of methodologies. We assume they are not an issue in this discussion.

Having said these criticisms, the framework is still useful for discussing problems with methodologies that relate to the extent to which they define development activities and support phase work.

Table 13-5 shows my subjective ratings of the methodologies with respect to Humphrey's framework. None of the methodologies has a uniformly high rating in all of the categories.

In general, process methods are the least predictable, consistent, measurable, or monitorable because they leave so many activities to SE skill and omit specific activities from the methods. At worst, process methods are at Humphrey's initial stage; at best, they are repeatable. Because the focus is on process, I would assume that consistency and measurability of processes should be medium, that is, different people should arrive at similar analyses. In fact, we think they are low to medium. Designs would be expected to vary most because the heuristics are vague. Data analysis, data design, and human interface design, which some authors add on as an afterthought, would all be expected to vary significantly across different SEs because they are not explicitly part of the methodology.

Measurability is low to medium. Assuming function point metrics, measurability is low because

TABLE 13-5   Methodology Comparison: Humphrey's Framework

Knowledge	Process	Data	Object
Predictable	Low	Medium-High	Medium
Consistent	Low-Medium	Medium-High	Low-Medium
Measurable	Low-Medium	Medium	Medium-High
Monitored	Low-Medium	Medium	Low-Medium

function points concentrate on externals (e.g., numbers of interfaces, files, I/Os, and so on) and not on processing complexity.

The ability to monitor the methodology-defined tasks is probably about medium. The ability to monitor process-oriented applications is low when only methodology-supported phases and tasks are monitored and would be inconsistent if monitored tasks were defined by project.

The data methodologies have slightly better overall ratings. In Humphrey's framework they are, at worst, repeatable and, for some activities, reach the defined level. IE is reasonably predictable in having a set of activities defined into phases for ISP, feasibility, analysis, design, and program design. If using, for instance, Texas Instruments' version of IE, there are many more tasks that are not all necessary for a given application; thus the activities are not completely predictable across projects. The activities should provide a level of consistency across SEs who should be expected to define the same entity-relationship diagram and the same activities even though details would probably differ. Therefore, consistency should range from medium to high. The extent to which IE analyses and designs are measurable is ranked as medium. If function point analysis is used and baselines for the company have been defined, the measurability is probably medium since IE analyzes the major function point items. The extent to which IE can be monitored is medium. IE defines more tasks and activities and follows more phases of the application life cycle; therefore, its ability to be monitored is greater than that of process and object methods. However, all projects are subject to unforeseen problems that require unplanned time, and monitoring cannot assist in

foreseeing those problems. Therefore, not all tasks and activities can be monitored to the extent that they eliminate problems during the development process. If a CASE tool, such as IEF, is used for development, monitorability is high because the entire life cycle has well-defined stages, products, and reports on status that can be tracked for all phases.

Object orientation, in the form of the enhanced and integrated Booch/Coad & Yourdon methodology is similar to IE in predictability and measurability. Consistency is lower and varies from low to medium because individual SE skill is required to define the calling sequences and ultimate operational structure of the application, even though the definition of the object *pieces* is fairly well described. The difference between a good calling sequence and message set and a bad one is difficult to define in abstract, procedural terms, but can only be noticed through prototyping and actual comparison of different schemes. Monitorability is less because of the ill-defined nature of service-object identification and of language-specific OO requirements. Moving targets, like OO, are hard to measure. OO is repeatable at best in Humphrey's framework.

The bottom line on methodologies and Humphrey's framework is that the methodologies alone do not offer enough guidance to support the *defined level* of application development management, let alone get to the optimizing level. For this reason, more work on methodologies, life cycle, and development activities are needed to accommodate the variety of work for different types of applications. Having said this, we also need to be realistic about just how much predefinition of decision processes can, in fact, be imbedded in methodologies. Two things seem obvious. One is that we *can* define some of the methodology-driven activities more completely. The other is that the engineering nature of the SE task is that each application *will* require unique characteristics and design that *cannot be codified!*

In summarizing this section, no single methodology appears to be complete and sufficient for all the tasks and activities performed during an application development. There is no *silver bullet* that will solve our application development problems or provide a complete cookbook for the development process. For these reasons, there will always be a need for SE expertise in application development. There is also a need for continued definition of tasks needed during application development and the continuous evolution of techniques that are integrated into the various methodologies to guide those tasks.

COMPARISON OF _____ AUTOMATED _____ SUPPORT _____ ENVIRONMENTS _____

There is a marked degree of consensus on many design features of the ideal CASE environment. Table 13-6 summarizes many features and functions that Pressman, Gane, Booch, Martin, and McClure recommend. The curiosity is that the vendors do not seem to listen. Take three general requirements as an example: integration, intelligence, multiuser support.

CASE integration is the absence of barriers between one graphical or text form and others. The experts agree that the most useful CASE should support all project life-cycle activities within an integrated environment. The rationale for this position is that tools that support only application development, even if they include project management, address only a small, possibly noncritical, portion of the SE discipline. Further, the integration should be **seamless**, that is, transparent to users. Transparent integration includes the automatic conversion of diagrams and design text into other forms of docu-

mentation or program code with little or no manual intervention. The integration should be both between tools and between life-cycle phases. This level of integration implies that some resolution of fundamental semantic and syntactic differences between phases is required. Specifically, differences between analysis and design should be eliminated through CASE use. To reach this sophisticated level of integration, the methodologies require some redesign to remove their own built-in lack of seamlessness between phases activities. For instance, in process methods, one major intellectual stumbling block is the transition from data flow diagram (DFD) in analysis to structure diagram in design. Many people ask, Why not develop a structure diagram in analysis instead? Or, conversely, Why not carry DFDs through to design?

Next, intelligence in tools is desirable. **Artificial intelligence (AI) in CASE** facilitates reusability and provides consistency and completeness checking within and between graphical and text forms. AI routines can be used to implement the concepts of reusable analysis, design, program specifications, and code. The routines can locate, retrieve, and select specifications matching design parameters and can identify specification fragments that do not match what is required. Other applications of AI are the analysis of completeness and consistency of requirements or code. Other checking is between phases to match logical design to physical design to code. This use of AI is technically feasible and not particularly difficult. What we don't know about AI for these uses is what to match, how to match it, and when the best time for matching occurs. New metalanguage descriptions of analysis and design requirements will be required to fully exploit AI in CASE. These meta-languages must also be consistent and no additional burden to the other integration and multiuser support requirements of CASE.

One consistently recurring theme in all CASE products and research is concern over the replacement of one sort of complexity with another sort of complexity. The solution to software development productivity, quality, and reliability problems is to build tools that, in hiding some complexities of the development process, are necessarily complex themselves. The hidden complexities require absolute

TABLE 13-6   Desired Computer-Aided Software Engineering Features and Functions

Project Management: Work breakdown Cost estimation Person/task scheduling Monitoring allocated vs. actual times Budget creation Monitoring budget vs. actual money spent	**Design** All analysis functions above First-cut of *next step graphical form* from analysis via automated functions Support for program definition language (PDL) with interface to code generators for several languages Bi-directional interface to analysis and code from design Sensitivity analysis on designs
Documentation for all Work Word processing editor functionality Integration of text and graphics Nesting of text, graphics, and so on with recall at all levels Document templates—predefined and customizable Query capabilities to all parts of the graphical and text definitions Version/release control support Change control support	**Code** All above plus Source code templates Source code syntax checking and comparison to requirements Automated code generation Automated third normal form database definition from repository data definitions Automated minimal test set definition . . . with generation of test data Integration to software configuration management tool
Analysis Graphical and text support for specific methodology Intelligent syntactic evaluation of completeness and correctness Repository (i.e., dictionary) support for all graphic and text information with nesting and linkage within and between levels Support for reusable component recognition, definition, use Human interface definition support Prototyping support Customizable reporting facility	**General** Consistent interface with function keys having identical uses across phases On-line documentation, suggestions for problems Adaptability to local conventions for methodology use Support on any operating system, hardware platform, DBMS generation, and if not, machine indepen- dence of designed application Interfaces to other tools and products

accuracy and reliability themselves to make their use worthwhile; the systems will have to reveal themselves upon request so users may understand internal processing. With AI routines, that, for instance, learn to predict what is required for code based on design specifications, these revelations are crucial to guaranteeing CASE's continued use.

The integration of phases and tools must also be multiuser. **Multiuser CASE** support implies some sort of centralized repository of information about the application that is accessible by any number of people concurrently. Warnings to users when a component is changed and automatic version control are desired features. Multiuser support extends to group

work collaboration, scheduling, tracking, sensitivity analysis, and electronic meeting support.

Now, let's first examine the extent to which the methodologies themselves exhibit the properties thought to be desired for CASE, then extrapolate from that to determine the level of support for these features we can realistically expect from CASE products.

First, integration across phases and graphical forms is important to building intelligence into CASE. If we examine the three methodologies described in this text, structure analysis and design (SA), information engineering (IE), and object orientation (OO), we would find the most integration in

OO with less in IE and even less in SA. OO begins with tables that are increasingly elaborate but whose contents can be traced from the beginning of analysis through to development of module specifications. There is no *shift* in thinking required once the data and processes become encapsulated, because they continue to be encapsulated throughout the remaining steps.

IE has less integration because there are two fairly distinct paths of thought in IE, one for data and one for processes. Within each path, the level of integration is consistent and high, but between paths, the integration is less consistent and there are few guidelines for integrating the two. One example of this lack of consistency is that, depending on the author, IE should not have data files or entities shown on action diagrams; action diagrams should remain a process sequencing and event trigger identifying graphical form. If this line of reasoning is followed, data and processes are integrated at the program specification level. Program specification work is micro-design that could then miss major global problems because of the lack of data-process integration.

SA is even less integrated than IE because data are not specifically addressed in the methodology. The analyst is supposed to know what 'data stores' are required and the appropriate contents of those data stores. Some authors[6] assert that a data store can refer to a group of related normalized relations, while others[7] assert a data store is a third normal form relation. When data analysis is not an official activity, by definition it cannot easily be integrated into the methodology. Similarly, there are numerous texts that describe how to use SA for developing real-time applications[8] and that provide a foundation for several of the graphical forms used in OO. But close analysis of the Ward & Mellor methodology, for instance, identifies a very different approach to developing applications from the original DeMarco and Yourdon & Constantine approaches.

Given the levels of integration as low for SA, medium for IE, and medium to high for OO, the greatest potential for CASE to provide *seamless*, complete integration of functions seems most likely for object orientation. Further, the higher the level of integration, the greater the intelligence that can be built into the software, once again, identifying OO as the most likely to provide extensive use of AI. Does that mean that AI cannot be used for the other methodologies? Absolutely no! It means that *sophisticated* AI that recognizes reusable analysis, design, or code fragments and that performs significant *semantic* analysis of the contents of diagrams and the interdiagram relationships is *most likely* in OO. Anyone using *any* CASE tool today knows that they provide fairly extensive syntactic evaluation intelligence that will tell you, for instance, if your connections on a data flow diagram (DFD) are all legal, or that the external entity interactions from the context diagram are all accounted for in the DFD.

From the discussion of the previous two issues, you should be able to figure out that multiuser support in products also lags behind the desire for its sophistication in industry . . . and it will continue to do so for at least five years. Multiuser support adds a level of underlying complexity because of the need for locking mechanisms, access security, and concurrent multiplatform hardware support that impedes vendor development. Since there are no competitive reasons for developing multiuser capabilities, that is, no other vendors have it either, vendors are not spending their resources on multiuser support. Current tools with a central repository allow segmenting of repository items, such as an ERD. When multiple users want to change the ERD, they check out segments and work on their respective segments individually. The completed checked-out segments are checked-in to a reconciliation procedure that frequently fails because of inconsistencies that are then manually reconciled. In a truly concurrent environment, locking mechanisms would support multiple concurrent users without segmenting and check-out processing, but with locking mechanisms similar to those used in DBMS software.

---

6 See Gane, Chris, *Computer-aided Software Engineering: The Methodologies, The Products, and The Future.* Englewood Cliffs, NJ: Prentice-Hall, Inc., 1990.

7 See Yourdon, 1989.

8 Ward, P. T., and S. J. Mellor, *Structured Development for Real-Time Systems* (three volumes). NY: Yourdon Press, 1985, is one of the most commonly used.

What does the state of integration and AI mean for CASE? CASE tools are necessarily limited in the number of processes, number of entities, number of attributes, complexity and detail of description, and so on. These limitations are higher candidates for removal by vendors than are these three more abstract concepts: integration, intelligence, and multiuser support. The CASE industry has entered a *push-pull* stage of product development. The *push* comes from the ever increasing desire of client companies to develop ever more complex and sophisticated applications, and their recognition that CASE *can* be used to deploy ITs to their competitive advantage. The *pull* comes from the products on the market and their growing sophistication. As soon as one vendor provides a feature or function, others feel obligated to offer it too, or risk losing market share. Many vendors try to support as many methodologies as they can, frequently without regard to underlying differences in mental thought processes required to comply with the methodologies. So, for instance, DeMarco's SA and IE analysis might both be advertised as supported by the same vendor. But DFDs are *not* action diagrams and vice versa, nor will they ever be. So, when vendors claim multimethodology support, beware of the claim.

RESEARCH RELATING TO ANALYSIS, DESIGN, AND METHODOLOGIES

There are two growing bodies of research[9] relating to methodologies and the application development process. The first research is attempting to reconcile the differences in methodologies to develop an improved hybrid. The second type of research studies the decision processes that occur in analysis and design activities. Both of these lines of research are described in this section and related to future changes that we might expect in methodologies and application development.

The methodology research consists of normative and descriptive writing on the procedures and application focus in analyzing application problems. From this body of work, we have over 60 identifiable methodologies with primary concentrations, such as SA, IE, and OO, described in this text. Unfortunately, the value of these methodologies has not been studied. There is no evidence that *any* of these methodologies is better than any other of these methodologies. Nor is there any evidence that *any* methodology is more appropriate for a particular problem domain than any other. Intuitively, they can't all be best in all situations. Current research is taking two directions to follow on this idea: First, one line of research attempts to integrate methods to create an improved hybrid; second, the other line of research is trying to determine when and which methodologies are appropriate for different types of problems.

Current research in building hybrid methodologies is primarily applied. All authors, so far, are seeking to integrate OO notions and notations with some other methodology, including structured analysis, Jackson systems design, information engineering, and others.[10] This research is purely prescriptive, of the form: "If I were going to put OO together with structured analysis, here's what I would do." While this research is promising, the lack of researcher attention to the differences in reasoning and thinking processes of the methods needs to be resolved. Also, these authors will need to offer evidence of the synergy they promise but for which they currently offer no evidence.

The second type of research discusses methodology learning by novices. Having learned COBOL or another procedural language, novice learning of structured analysis is easier and more accurate than learning of other methodologies.[11] Since there is less to learn, this is not surprising. In addition, this research notes that the thought processes of OO are decidedly different that those of SA and IE. We would conclude then that novices who learn Ada

---

9 See Adelson & Soloway, 1985; Guindon & Curtis, 1988; Guindon, Krasner, & Curtis 1987; Pennington, 1987; Vessey & Conger, 1993.

10 See for example, Sanden, 1989; and Ward, 1989.

11 See Vessey and Conger, 1993.

first, for example, would have an easier time learning OO than structured analysis, and their OO designs would be more accurate. This is a promising line of work that needs much more study, including analysis of real analysts doing real work before any results applicable to business use of methodologies can be expected.

The study did find that analysts' development of a mental model is crucial to complete solution of a task. The process followed by successful analysts includes development, expansion, and simulation of a mental model that uses personal problem-solving plans that are used to elaborate constraints, and notemaking as a means of deferring work until a later time. Many of these skills in Chapter 2 recommended for you to think of while studying the text were identified through this research.

Also, some comments about easy and hard features of methodologies can be developed. The easy features of OO are those that automatically lead to information hiding, minimal coupling and maximal cohesion, the traceability of information throughout the process, and the essential continuity of the method (i.e., building tables and progressively adding details to the information). The hard OO features are the extensive experience in operating systems required to determine service object requirements and the significant coupling between the implementation language and the application design.

The easy features of IE are entity analysis, full-life cycle approach including enterprise through maintenance phases, the methods for deciding distribution, and the balanced thinking given to both data and processes. The hard IE features are the mental shift required to move from design to program specification and from an action diagram to its components. The decisions about the size and content of components is left to the SE.

The easy feature of SA is the simplicity of the thought process which is easily grasped by most people. The hard SA features are the disjoint phase relationships moving from DFD to structure diagram and decomposing the structure diagram into modules. These actions, like similar ones of IE, are left to SE skills and have few guidelines.

To summarize the application development literature, we know that skills needed seem to vary by activity both across and within phases of a system development life cycle, that task domain facilitates the process of building a mental model of the problem solution, and that different types of domain knowledge exist, including methodology and task domains.

For SEs, this research has several implications. First, the entire field of methodology research is in its infancy. As it matures, both the methods and the way we use them should be expected to change. Second, hybrid methodology that attempts to integrate methodologies requiring different mental models of a problem, for instance, structured analysis and OO, are unlikely to be very productive. Rather, we need to identify which methodological orientation best fits different problem domains, concentrating on methodology improvement and use in the appropriate domains.

Last, since methodologies do not provide complete analysis of all aspects of problem domains, by definition, CASE tools based on the methodologies will also provide partial task coverage. The more complete the methodology, the more complete the CASE tool. Some vendors add completing tasks to support, for example, code generation; these CASE tools are even more complete than those that are only methodology-based. The most notable example of a more complete tool is Texas Instruments' Information Engineering Facility (IEF).

Applying Humphrey's framework to research in IS, methodologies are in either the initial stage or the defined stage. CASE tools help methodologies attain the defined stage, but sometimes impose such rigidity in doing so that usage is constrained and might not fit either the way SEs work or the work itself.

BUSINESS AND TECHNOLOGY TRENDS THAT IMPACT APPLICATION DEVELOPMENT

There are several trends in application management and development that will change dramatically the way business computing is performed in the next ten years. The trends are both technological and business related, including management of legacy systems and data, client/server computing, development of repositories and data warehouses, multimedia application development, and the business globalization. Each of these trends are briefly described with their impact on application development and software engineering.

Legacy Systems

Legacy means handed down as from an ancestor. **Legacy systems** are applications that are in a maintenance phase but are not ready for retirement. Legacy systems are most often mainframe, COBOL applications that were probably built using no methodology and no life cycle. Such applications are frequently referred to as 'held together with spit and glue' because they are **fragile**, that is, susceptible to introduction of errors caused by unrelated changes. In short, they are a liability. The reason these systems are not all rewritten and done away with is because of the tremendous investment in their development.

A related concept is **legacy data** which is data used by outdated applications that are required to be maintained for business records. Legacy data are as much as 50% incorrect and may be in an unusable form without considerable expenditures of time and money. In short, they are a liability. The reason legacy data are not reformatted in some new DBMSs that can optimize storage and access time is the inherent cost of correcting the data which could be ten times or more than the cost of reformatting.

The impact of legacy data and systems is to inhibit and slow the integration of data across organizations and applications, and to inhibit the integration of technologies for application use. Ultimately, companies with significant legacy problems will be forced, for competitive reasons, to spend the money to transform the systems and data into useful items or to abandon them and write off the expense.

The impact of legacy systems and data on SE is to continue to inhibit new application development by requiring attention. The new *pulls* from industry include need for reengineering data, methods, and

software that support data *scrubbing* to remove anomalies and errors. These are nontrivial needs that will divert some industry resources away from methodologies toward these very practical and real problems.

Repositories and Data Warehouses

A related issue is the notion that organizations no longer want to discard data. For instance, the maintenance of legacy data sometimes is mandated by the government. The means to store unlimited, continuously growing databases currently are called **data warehouses**.

Similarly, all of this data must have meta-data that defines each attribute and its related entities (or objects), the applications and software allowed to access the data, and the allowable using organizations. The meta-data definitions are in a **repository** which, in its most sophisticated form, is a data dictionary for data, processes, hardware, and software.

Repositories control and centralize management of data as an organizational resource. Distributed repositories will be developed in the future but are currently only available as one-user chunks of a centralized repository that must be reintegrated with the centralized, official data.

Both repositories and data warehouses have significant overhead (i.e., human) costs associated with managing and tracking all of the information actually managed by the software. Because of this overhead expense, companies must choose carefully those items they really want to maintain indefinitely. The luxury of being a 'data packrat' has currently unknown costs.

The impact of data warehouses will be felt in the need to design time-dependent databases[12] that have associative relationships and to migrate legacy data to the warehouse. **Associative data relationships** are irregular, dictated by data content rather than abstractions such as normalization. An example

---

12 Time-dependent databases are also referred to as temporal databases and have an entire body of research associated with their definition and use.

might be in an image document that describes an insurance policy. That policy needs to be related to the insured, the owner, the beneficiaries, and its value *over time* so that a complete reconstruction of its status at any single point in time can be determined. Existing database products can support temporal databases but are not specifically designed for temporal data. This implies the development of a specialized temporal database type, or the extension of existing database products to accommodate temporal data definitions.

Client/Server

Client/server computing describes a situation in which multiple processors share responsibility for managing pieces of an application. Currently, the pieces include data, presentation software for the human interface, and application. For a given processing request, one processor acts as a client requesting that a processing service be provided; the other processor is the server that executes the request. In this context, examples of a service request are to access data, perform a routine, or display data on a terminal screen. In a true client/server environment, any processor can be a client and any processor can be a server. The same processor might be a client for some actions and a processor for others. Therefore, the client/server environment, in its truest form, is describing a **peer-to-peer networking** scheme in which intelligent sharing of resources and data across multiple processors is taking place.

The state of client/server development changes almost daily, so by the time you read this, Figure 13-2 will be out-of-date. Don't worry, it is only to give an example of the alternatives and confusion in the client/server marketplace. The figure shows the alternative configurations of presentation software, data (and DBMS), and application software with traditional, centralized mainframe resource management on the upper left of the diagram. Moving down the diagonal to full distributed client/server processing, we have first presentation software that resides both on the mainframe and on a PC. The PC software interfaces to the mainframe presentation software and is translated for use by the application. At the next level of sophistication, the presentation soft-

ware is offloaded to the PC completely. Then data is partitioned (i.e., split by columns or rows or both), and accessible via DBMS in both places. Next, the data are moved fully to the distributed environment, possibly with replication (i.e., multiple data copies). At the next stage, some application functions are performed on a PC and others on a mainframe. In its most advanced state, all functions (or pieces of each) are stored both on mainframes and PCs and with access determined by the closest processor with available CPU time.

In client/server's most advanced form, for example, simple functions might be on a LAN and complex processing functions on a mainframe. The data might be anywhere. The application part closest to the request decides type of processing to be performed and ships the request off to be executed in the most efficient place. If that location is busy, its software might forward the processing request to another processor until idle CPU cycle time is found. The executing processor would obtain the nearest version of the data and perform the requested service. The result is sent back to the requesting processor.

Client/server processing is sometimes confused with downsizing. **Downsizing** is the shifting of processing and data from mainframes to some other, less expensive environment, usually to a multiuser mid-size machine, such as an IBM AS400, or to a LAN of PCs. Downsizing can occur with or without client/server computing. The reasons for buying mainframes are diminished with the availability of client/server computing, but the compelling argument for maintaining an existing mainframe environment is to obtain the most benefit from the tremendous start-up and maintenance costs associated with them. Downsized environments also have large start-up costs that sometimes are equivalent to mainframe start-up cost.

The impact of client/server computing on SE is here now. There is tremendous demand for SEs who know how to integrate data, applications, and presentation software over multiple processors and networks. The large accounting companies, such as Ernst & Young, who also do consulting, have found a niche in providing leading-edge services of this type. But the need is in every size of company, even

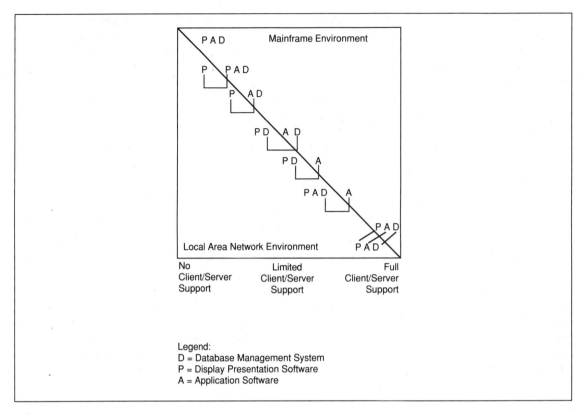

FIGURE 13-2   Client/Server Alternatives

those that cannot afford a large consulting company's fees. The pressure on SE professionals then is to develop the integration skills to develop and support these applications as fast as possible.

Multimedia

Multimedia is a term that describes the integration of object orientation, database, and storage technologies in one environment. By the 21st century, multimedia will transform both applications and the way we interact with them. New technologies must be able to be incorporated into traditional application processing to be useful in business organizations. By defining equipment as objects and storing the object definitions in a database repository, integrating new equipment and technologies in traditional applications becomes not just possible, but fairly easy.

SEs developing multimedia applications require new skills for authoring the contents of multimedia

systems, and for developing the applications that make the information accessible in a meaningful manner. For graphic design, video direction, and so on, one strategy has been to hire graphics artists or movie school graduates, for instance, to be multimedia authors rather than to teach an SE about video production. This splitting of duties still requires SEs to develop skills in integrating multimedia in applications. At present, the skills required include OO analysis and design, media knowledge, and human interface design incorporating moving and still-motion video, graphics, text, and data in the same interface.

Globalization

Globalization is the movement óf otherwise local businesses into world markets. In 50 short years, business organizations worldwide have evolved from national to multinational to global enterprises. As with all trends, there are forces that both ease and inhibit movement into global markets. In general, information technologies enable globalization; and, in general, cultural differences and history inhibit globalization. The technology enablers are application and communications technologies that remove the barriers of geography and time, while providing equal access to multimedia applications. The historical and cultural barriers inhibit cross-cultural exchange of ideas, technologies, and methods of work. Dealing successfully with both the technological and cultural issues is a challenge to information systems professionals and business managers. Preparing yourself for deploying globalizing technology is the challenge to SEs today.

There are three main social barriers to globalization of businesses: infrastructure differences, technology transfer differences, and political and cultural differences. **Infrastructure** usually refers to the installed base of equipment and services for communications, transportation, and services of a geographic entity (i.e., a country). Infrastructure relates to computers, telecommunications, and supporting software, including, for instance, database and networking software.

There are two infrastructure challenges to SEs. The first challenge is technical, learning both current and past technologies, and devising sometimes messy ways to integrate them. The second challenge is social, developing and presenting alternatives and trade-offs for imaginative, practical, cost-effective applications in developing countries.

Technology transfer is a large scale introduction of a new technology to some previously nontechnical environment. Transfers of computing and communications technologies to all developing countries in Eastern Europe, Asia, Latin America, and Africa are needed. History leaves me pessimistic about such transfers taking place easily, smoothly, or soon. Broadscale transfers for such disparate technologies as farming methods, birth control, building of dams, and water purification have failed simply because technologists fail to contend with cultural differences and resistance.[13] Technology transfer

suffers from the same bias that diffusion of innovation theory in general suffers: If the technology is not accepted, there is something wrong with the intended user, not the transfer agent or the technology. Naively, we think our way of implementing and using are the *right way* as if no other way is as good. The concept of **equifinality**—many paths lead to the same goal—eludes most Westerners. We fail to evaluate the technology *within the context* of the intended cultural structure. We assume stupidity on the part of the users and also assume this stupidity can be corrected by sufficient education. What we forget is that projects fail when planning is incomplete, potential difficulties are not assessed or are misassessed, and cultural impacts of projects are insufficiently analyzed. The challenge to SEs is not to oversimplify projects and circumstances of their implementation that inhibit technology transfer, but to attend to the cultural aspects of implementations.

In any technology transfer project, it is imperative that the sensitivity to local differences is maximal. Teaching and training in a different culture does not mean making the target audience the same as you. Equifinality must be allowed. SEs' roles change from doer to facilitator, with less control than usual over outcomes. Successful globalization of applications and technologies requires considerable breadth experience for SEs; for those who can develop and integrate the necessary business skills with their technical skills, the rewards will be huge.

Client/server and multimedia are technologies that enable globalization and require different ways of thinking in a global context. Most effective placement of data, database software, software, storage media, and computers is the main issue. Distribution of data and functionality will require new decision criteria. Before distributed applications, decisions were based on what the software and hardware could do. Constraints drove the decision process. Now we can have anything anywhere. The decision criteria shift from being technologically driven to being business driven. Why do we need data x for y PCs in location z if we can have a data for b PCs in location c? *What business requirements demand* this *placement of data, hardware, and so on?* The extent of distributed multimedia access and enabling of peoples in far-off locations that takes place will become a conscious business decision.

13 See Hirschman, A. O., *Development Projects Observed.* Washington, D.C.: The Brookings Institution, 1967.

Ethical, political, and practical issues inform distributed media placement decisions.

Multimedia applications, because they support data, graphics, photos, audio, and video images, also have a significant cultural component in a global application. Design of culture-free or culturally-rich applications becomes a decision. Is it truly possible to design culture-free applications? My feeling is no, all applications have cultural assumptions at least implicit in their design. Multimedia will make obvious our assumptions about appropriate words, pictures, and ideas for users. Biases that surface will relate to information system developers, user designers, and manager approvers. When applications go global, assumptions that survive in the United States, in all likelihood, will be inappropriate globally. The assumptions will require development of the same application with different media components to fit the using culture. SEs will need to learn how to surface cultural assumptions of application developers and how they carry over to the finished product. SEs will need to make assumptions explicit, then use the assumptions to design cultural diversity into applications.

In summary, business and technical trends are pointing toward breadth and depth of skill levels in SEs in many different areas. Methodologies do not support these trends today. Therefore, continued evolution and change to methodologies can be expected.

SUMMARY

Two methods of analyzing methodology classes were used in this chapter. The first, the information systems methodology framework, was extended to include the characteristics of applications from Chapter 1 and the desirable characteristics of applications. From the analysis we know that both information engineering (IE) and object orientation (OO) are more complete in describing applications than structured analysis (SA), but each addresses different phases of the life cycle. IE is more complete in coverage of organization level information systems planning and analysis, both of which precede design

and implementation. OO is more detail- and programming-oriented, resulting in a deeper level of design by the end of the design phase. SA is so process-oriented that data, input, output, and other detailed aspects of the application are left to SE skill and are not specifically addressed by the methodology.

The second analysis of methodologies used the Humphrey's maturity framework to discuss the maturity of methodologies. Humphrey discusses the initial, repeatable, defined, managed, and optimizing levels of maturity. The results of this analysis show that no methodologies are currently beyond the defined level and that SA is only at the initial level. There are too many activities that are not addressed by SA to reach the repeatable level for all requisite tasks. At the repeatable level different people would arrive at the same design. IE is at worst repeatable, and, when completed in a CASE tool, may reach the defined level. OO is at the repeatable level for many early activities, but is at the initial level for package and message communication design.

CASE tools were discussed in their ability to provide three key design objectives: integration, intelligence, and multiuser support. The ability of CASE is hampered by methodologies that are not themselves integratable because of shifts in thinking that must be made from one phase of work to another. In general, SA and IE characterize such shifts and have relative difficulty in CASE interphase integration of work. In contrast, OO is more consistent in the thinking and documentation forms both within and between phases, thus, the CASE tools supporting OO are more highly integrated and represent the ever more detailed thinking required in OOD, and do so within similar graphical and text forms throughout the CASE tools.

Next, business and technology trends that impact application development were discussed, including legacy systems, repositories and data warehouses, client/server computing, multimedia applications, and business globalization. Legacy systems and data are historical leftovers from premethodology days that may have errors and structural flaws that make their conversion to new environments costly and difficult. In particular, client/server, data warehouses, and repositories are three emerging technologies to which companies want to migrate the legacy systems and data. Client/server environments provide for storage and processing of data wherever it is most needed by the organization in a peer-to-peer network. Data warehouses are storage technologies that provide for massive amounts of historical data. Repositories are versatile means of storing information about data, applications, hardware, and software that provide the definitions of interchangeable technology components. Multimedia applications will use repositories to define the integration of object orientation, database, and storage technologies in one application environment.

Globalization is the movement of businesses into worldwide markets. Global application developers must deal with difficulties in development due to infrastructure differences and technology transfer difficulties. Technology transfer is the large-scale introduction of new technology to a new environment, usually a developing country. Problems in technology transfer relate to cultural and political differences more than to the new technology. SEs developing global applications will need to attend to the culture and politics to be successful. Client/server technology enables global applications. Multimedia was discussed as one type of application with a significant cultural component.

REFERENCES

Adelson, B., and E. Soloway, "The role of domain experience in software design," *IEEE Transactions on Software Engineering, SE-11*, Vol. 11, 1985, pp. 1351–1360.

Bergland, Gary D., "A guided tour of program design methodologies," *IEEE Computer*, October 1981, pp. 13–37.

Card, David N., Frank E. McGarry, and Gerald T. Page, "Evaluating software engineering technologies," *IEEE Transactions on Software Engineering*, Vol. SE-13, #7, July 1987, pp. 845–851.

Conger, S. A., "Teaching globalization in information systems courses," in *Global Information Technology Education: Issues and Trends* (M. Khosrowpour and K. D. Loch, eds.). Harrisburg, PA: Idea Group Publishing, December 1992, pp. 313–353.

Datamation, "The best in client/server computing," Special Issue, October 1, 1991, pp. 1–24.

Dunsmore, H. E., W. M. Zage, D. M. Zage, and G. Cabral, "Building an empirical case for CASE," Software Engineering Research Center Report SERC TR-8-P, Lafayette, Indiana, December 16, 1987.

Episkopou, D. M., and A. T. Wood-Harper, "Towards a framework to choose appropriate information systems approaches," *The Computer Journal*, Vol. 29, #3, 1986, pp. 222–228.

Gane, Chris, *Computer-Aided Software Engineering: The Methodologies, the Products, and the Future*. Englewood Cliffs, NJ: Prentice-Hall, 1990.

Guindon, R., and B. Curtis, "Control of cognitive processes during software design: What tools are needed," *CHI Proceedings*. ACM: 1988, pp. 263–268.

Guindon, R., H. Krasner, and B. Curtis, "Breakdowns and processes during the early activities of software design by professionals," in *Empirical Studies of Programmers—2nd Workshop* (G. Olson, E. Soloway, S. Sheppard, eds.). Norwood, NJ: Ablex Publishing Co., 1987, pp. 65–82.

Hirschman, A. O., *Development Projects Observed*. Washington, D.C.: The Brookings Institution, 1967.

Humphrey, Watts S., "Characterizing the software process: A maturity framework," reprinted in *Milestones in Software Evolution*, Paul W. Oman and Ted G. Lewis, eds. Washington, D.C.: IEEE Press, 1988, pp. 301–307.

Humphrey, Watts, *Managing the Software Process*. Reading, MA: Addison-Wesley Publishing, Inc., 1989.

Iivari, Juhani, "Levels of abstraction as a conceptual framework for an information system," *Proceedings of IFIPS WG 8.1: Information Systems Concepts: An In-Depth Analysis*, Belgium, October 18–20, 1989, pp. 122–151.

Kelly, John C., "A comparison of four design methods for real-time systems," *ACM SIGSOFT Software Engineering Notes*, Vol.12, 1987, pp. 238–251.

Keys, Paul, "A methodology for methodology choice," *Systems Research*, Vol. 5, #1, 1988, pp. 65–76.

McClure, Carma, *CASE Is Software Automation*. Englewood Cliffs, NJ: Prentice-Hall, 1989.

Olle, T. William, Jacques Hagelstein, Ian G. McDonald, Colette Rolland, Henk G. Sol, Frans J. M. Van Assche, and Alexander A. Verrign-Stuart, *Information Systems Methodologies: A Framework for Understanding*. Wokingham, England: Addison-Wesley Publishing Company, 1988.

Panzi, David J., "A method for evaluating software development techniques," *The Journal of Systems and Software*, Vol. 2, 1981, pp. 133–137.

Pennington, N., "Stimulus structures and mental representations in expert comprehension of computer programs," *Cognitive Psychology*, Vol. 19, 1987, pp. 295–341.

Pressman, Roger S., *Making Software Engineering Happen: A Guide for Instituting the Technology.* Englewood Cliffs, NJ: Prentice-Hall, 1988.

Sorenson, Paul G., Jean-Paul Tremblay, and Andrew J. McAllister, "The metaview system for many specification environments," *IEEE Software*, March 1988, pp. 30–38.

Wand, Yair, and Ron Weber, "On the deep structure of information systems," *Information Systems Research*, Vol. 4, #2, 1993, pp. 23–45.

Ward, P. T., and S. J. Mellor, *Structured Development for Real-Time Systems* (three volumes). NY: Yourdon Press, 1985.

Yourdon, Edward, *Modern Structured Analysis*. Englewood Cliffs, NJ: Prentice-Hall, 1989.

KEY TERMS

AI in CASE
associative data
  relationships
CASE integration
client/server
complexity
data warehouse
downsizing
equifinality
fragile applications
globalization
Humphrey's defined level
Humphrey's initial level
Humphrey's managed
  level
Humphrey's maturity
  framework
Humphrey's optimizing
  level

Humphrey's repeatable
  level
information systems
  methodology framework
information systems plan
  (ISP)
infrastructure
legacy
legacy data
legacy systems
multimedia
multiuser CASE
peer-to-peer network
process groups
repository
seamless CASE
technology transfer

EXERCISES

1. Write a three- to five-page paper describing some new technology—distributed database (e.g., Informix or Sybase), Multimedia, Simple Network Management Protocol (SNMP) (net-

working protocol), imaging. Predict how the technology will change in use in applications in the next five years. Predict IS and user organizational changes as well as design changes.

2. Discuss globalization of businesses and other changes to software engineering activities that might be required.

3. Compare the methodologies using your own technique. What are the important methodology issues to you? How easy or hard do you find the work involved in describing the ABC application in each methodology? How easy or hard is it to really learn each methodology? Which are you most likely to continue using? How likely do you think these methodologies are to be useful for the emerging technologies of client/server and multimedia? How would you change any or all of the methodologies to make them more usable? How might methodologies become less tied to technology? (Please send your responses to the author.)

STUDY QUESTIONS

1. Define the following terms:
   client/server   Humphrey's maturity
   downsizing   framework
   equifinality   legacy data
   globalization   repository

2. What phases of application development are in the Olle et al. information systems methodology framework?

3. Describe the features of the Olle et al. approach to comparing methodologies and identify the sophistication of the three methodologies on each feature.

4. Why do you think the ISP was left out of the process methods of Tom de Marco and Ed Yourdon? (You might refer back to Chapter 1's historical discussion for a hint.)

5. Object-oriented methodologies all ignore the front-end tasks of feasibility and data collection. Why? Can they continue to ignore those actions and still be useful in business applications? Why?

6. The Olle et al. framework was expanded to analyze the phases within each methodology where information is expected to become known. Describe this framework extension and identify, for data, processes, relationships, physical database model, and event triggers, where this information is known in each of the three methodologies.

7. What is the position of process methodologies with respect to data and data modeling? What is the significance of this position? How integrated is data to process description? What is the significance of this level of integration?

8. List three sources of application complexity. How does each source add to the complexity of an application?

9. Which methodology handles complexity the best and why? What is deficient about the other methodologies' handling of complexity?

10. To what extent do the three methodologies discussed guide input/output design? What is the significant of this?

11. Rate the three methodologies on desirable application characteristics: minimal coupling, maximal cohesion, and information hiding. Justify your ratings.

12. What is Humphrey's maturity framework? How is it used to assess IS organizations? How is it used to assess IS methodologies for application development?

13. What are three shortcomings of Humphrey's framework? How might they be eliminated?

14. List and describe the five levels of maturity in Humphrey's framework.

15. Do many organizations or methodologies reach the optimizing level of Humphrey's framework?

16. Describe the three methodologies in terms of Humphrey's framework.

17. If you have access to a CASE tool, use Table 13-6 to analyze the sophistication of your tool. List five ways in which the tool you use could be improved to contain more of the desired CASE features and functions.

18. Three issues in CASE are discussed: integration, intelligence, and multiuser support. How

does the author view current products on the market? How does a CASE tool you use rate on these three criteria? What changes might be made to the tool you use to improve its integration, intelligence, and multiuser support?

19. Describe the research that seeks to integrate the best of all methodologies into a new, improved hybrid. Critique the utility of such a methodology and identify three of the problems with this approach. What benefits might accrue from a hybrid methodology? Why is it such a popular topic of research?

20. Describe the research that studies novice analysis of problems and relate this research to that which seeks to integrate the best of all methodologies into a new, improved hybrid. How can the analyst research be used to improve methodologies? What effect will hybrids have on novice learning?

21. What impact do legacy systems and data have on the use of new methodologies and CASE tools?

22. Define and discuss the issues of legacy systems and data.

23. Define a data warehouse and why companies are moving toward implementation schemes of this concept.

24. What is an associative data relationship and why does it impact data storage techniques?

25. Define client/server computing and downsizing. Discuss how they relate.

26. What is multimedia and how does it relate to application development and methodologies?

27. Describe some of the cultural issues in global information systems development.

28. What are the main issues in deploying global applications?

★ EXTRA-CREDIT QUESTION

1. Change the scenario for ABC Video. Assume ABC is an international organization that not only rents videos but also sells concert tickets, CDs, and other related entertainment and musical merchandise. What cultural assumptions are

in the case description of ABC Video that need to be reexamined for an application to be used in locations all over the world? What other changes might be required for worldwide use of the rental application? Don't concentrate on merchandise; concentrate on the cultural and equipment differences. If each of 3,000 stores in 60 countries send information to a single site in, let's say, Los Angeles, once each day, what technology considerations might be required?

## CHAPTER 14

THE FORGOTTEN ANALYSIS AND DESIGN ACTIVITIES

INTRODUCTION

The forgotten activities of systems analysis are design of the human interface, conversion/implementation process, and user documentation. This chapter concentrates on human interface because the guidelines are not context specific and are based on research as well as practice. Rules of thumb for the other activities are discussed. Both the human interface and conversion are planned for ABC Video's rental processing application.

HUMAN INTERFACE DESIGN

The presentation of information for selection and data entry is the single most important design item in an application. The format, type, size, color, and content of the display all are important to a user locating, controlling, entering, or monitoring information. A badly designed screen makes a user tire faster, make more mistakes, and miss information that might have disastrous effects on decision making. Misrepresented data can have the same effects. The user's perception of the application and how it helps or hinders in performing his job is directly related to the human interface. If a user perceives the

application as helpful and facilitating productivity, the application will be used with a high degree of satisfaction. If a user perceives the application as difficult, obscure, or reducing productivity, the application will not be used voluntarily and user satisfaction will be low.

Interface design is one of the most intensely researched areas of computing, yet much of the research has not found its way to business application design. In this section, we try to remedy that situation. First, the conceptual foundations of interface design are reviewed briefly. Then the options and guidelines for each major activity during interface design are presented. Following each section, we discuss how to apply screen design guidelines to ABC rental processing.

Conceptual Foundations of Interface Design

A combination of research, theory, and practice blend to provide the guidelines for interface design. In general interface design needs to answer questions about when, what, and how to enter data into, and present data from, applications.

First, when to collect data has been resolved through long experience and research. The ideal data entry point is at the data source. There should be no creation and collection of paper from which data is then keyed into a machine. The more people who touch a transaction, the more errors it will have. Therefore, eliminate all middle men, enter data at its source, and errors are greatly reduced.

Second, which data to collect and display are also issues. The general answer, based on practice, is all data required for *business* reasons. Data may be expanded to include company specific requirements. Also, data items IS staff think might some day be necessary, but for which users have no current or future business need, *should not be collected or displayed.*

Last, and most complex, is how human–computer interactions should be structured and presented to ease learning, minimize errors, and facilitate use. Research and theory on physical and cognitive aspects of memory, information processing, pacing of work, color perception, icon perception, and key-stroke effectiveness all are used to determine guide-lines for interface design. The results of applying the research versus not applying the research are increased productivity and reduced errors. Since the research is so voluminous, it is presented in the con-text of the chapter.

With all the choices and research recommenda-tions, deciding how to actually design functional screens can be a confusing exercise. In the next sections, practical guidelines from research and practice are developed. Information from the analy-sis phase is used to define the display requirements of the human interface. The analysis information is used to define a task profile for the application. Then, a profile of users is developed to identify screen requirements that relate to users rather than to functions of the system. The task profile is matched to guidelines for the application type to define and select the general interface as menus, windows, or commands. Application type also sug-gests functional screens as forms oriented, ques-tions and answers, or direct manipulation. Once the general and functional interfaces have been defined, individual field presentation is defined and format-ted for the screen. Finally, extra field characteris-tics, such as color, are decided and added to the design. Each of these topics is summarized below and addressed in the following sections.

1. Define task profile.
2. Define user profile and application design response.
3. Choose option selection screen type.
4. Choose functional screen type.
5. Design option selection interface.
6. Design functional screen interface format.
7. Choose field format options for normal, abnormal, alert, and alarm data conditions.
8. Design on-line user documentation, error messages, and abnormal processing for all interfaces.
9. Design reports as required.

Develop a Task Profile

Guidelines for Developing a Task Profile

The first activity is to develop a **task profile** which summarizes work requirements of the application. The level of detail in developing a task profile depends on the type of application being developed. The first task, then, is to classify the application as either transaction, query, DSS, ESS, or process monitoring and control (a special type of TPS). Since transaction processing is the most frequent application type in businesses, they are discussed here. The level of detail and activities for task profile develop-ment are summarized in Table 14-1 for the above application types.

For each activity, a hierarchy of processes is defined. This is the basis for screen navigation design. The top activities identified become selection options on a menu. Upon selection, the entries at the second hierarchic level are presented, and so on until a functional work screen is presented. The level of detail for the hierarchy should match the level of processing detail for the application type.

Next, required and optional data are defined for each task (see Table 14-1). For business applications, following the methodologies discussed in Chapters 7–12, required and optional data for entities should have been defined and documented in the data dic-tionary. For most business applications, this infor-mation can be developed at the entity/relation level rather than the attribute/field level. The idea is to identify multivariate dependencies which, in real-

TABLE 14-1   Task Profile Development Activities

Activity	Transaction	Query	DSS	ESS	Process Control
Define Task Hierarchies	Process Level	Activity Level	Activity/ Process Level	Activity/ Process Level	Process Level
Define Required/ Optional Data	Transaction/ Field Level	Entity Level	Entity Level	Entity Level	By input source
Define Data Precision	Only if greater than 2 decimal places for numbers	Only if greater than 2 decimal places for numbers	Only if greater than 2 decimal places for numbers	Only if greater than 2 decimal places for numbers	For each field
Define Data Source	Process/ Transaction Level	Activity Level	Activity/ Process Level	Activity Level	Field Level
Define Purpose	Entity/ Transaction Level	Entity Level	Entity Level	Entity Level	Field Level
Define Accuracy	Only if it varies from 100%	Only if it varies from 100%	Only if it varies from 100%	Only if it varies from 100%	Field Level
Define Domain	Field Level	Field Level	Field Level	Field Level	Field Level
ID Specific Display Criteria	Field Level	Field Level	Field Level	Field Level	Field Level

time systems, may need to meet synchronization and timing constraints.

If not already defined, precision requirements should be specified, by field, for all numeric fields (Table 14-1). **Precision requirements** specify the number of decimal places and special display characters required for numeric information. Precision is very important in mathematical, statistical, and process control applications. Precision beyond two decimal places is frequent in business applications dealing with large financial transactions. Banking applications, for instance, frequently require precision to five decimal places for computing interest due and paid. Specific maximum field size, need for sign (e.g., +), and need for debit/credit indicators [e.g., CR or ( )] should all be defined. For text fields, the maximum length should be defined, if not already done. Possible edit characters for numeric

and text fields might be blanks, commas, or slashes. These definitions limit the number of data fields on a line while defining specific screen contents.

The source of data for each process should be identified next (see Table 14-1). Data source can be user-provided through data entry, measured data entry, or system-derived through computation. The key to identifying source, if it is unknown, is to determine where users go when they have a question about data on a screen. The answer might define a user, instrument type, or application as the information source. When user data entry is the source, training needs and help facilities are required to ensure proper entry. Edit checks for entry errors are required. When instrument measures are the source of data, the signal-to-noise ratio should be analyzed to determine the need for filtering devices or software. Fields for which the application is the source are called derived fields for which data entry is not allowed.

Next, the purpose of every entity or field should be defined, depending on the type of application. Possible choices for purpose are forms completion, information, alert, or alarm. Business applications data purposes are usually form completion and information. Rarely are data items used to alert or alarm the user. Because alarms are rare in business, entity level checking is sufficient for all but critical applications. For each entity, then, the task profile identifies needs to send alert or alarm signals to the user based on data changes or system process outcomes. For critical and process control applications, each data element should have its purpose defined since the task of process control is to monitor changes in a system and correct any abnormal or undesired processes. Alerts to changed conditions and alarms to abnormal conditions are an integral part of process control interface design.

The need for accuracy for each task and, if less than 100%, of the data processed should be assessed. In business applications, this definition should be provided only when it varies from 100%. Typically, variation in business is in query or ESS applications for which ballpark numbers are acceptable for many types of processing.

For instance, a marketing person may want to target a product to one or more specific demographic groups. If the target mailing is 1,000,000 pieces, the marketer needs to know how many groups he needs to meet this goal. A sample based on selection criteria (e.g., age, education level, and zip code) can be used to project the size of the population ±5%. In this case, a 0.1% sample might be sufficient. Rather than read a 20,000,000 record file, only 20,000 records are needed.

The last two pieces of task information—domain and display criteria—are defined if not already complete. The domain is the set of allowable values for each field. Special display criteria might include translations of data to text (or vice versa), or a special color for some field, and so on.

All of these task characteristics are used to determine the type of interface in system terms, and to determine training needs for users.

ABC Rental Application Task Profile

There is no special complexity in the ABC rental application, so completion of the task profile is relatively simple. We are using the Information Engineering analysis in Chapter 9 as the basis for this discussion. The first action is to create the task hierarchy. Using activity level as the top of each hierarchy, we rearrange the processes as the next level and their subprocesses as the third level, continuing until all processes are elementary (see Figure 14-1). This diagram is the basis for navigation between screens. Each leg of each level on the hierarchy is translated eventually into a menu selection list.

As of the analysis, all data were required for all entities (see Table 14-2). Precision for money fields is two decimal places. All other numeric fields are dates or integers. The source of *Customer*, *Video*, and *Copy* data is user data entry, so extensive edits will be needed in the entry programs to ensure that only correct data enters the system. *End of day*, *Video History*, and *Customer History* are all derived by the system and have no human interaction. The derived relations identify testing requirements for specific verification. The *Rental* relation is a combination of entered and derived data which identifies both edit and testing requirements.

The purpose of the entities is either forms completion or information with one *Rental* relation exception. The credit field will be used to deny rental privileges to customers who have a poor credit rating. Some special processing may be desired to highlight bad credit ratings. The possibility of highlighting bad credit rating information should be discussed with Vic and his approval obtained. No decision is made at this time.

Accuracy for all maintenance, rental, return, and query tasks is assumed to be 100% (see Table 14-2). If Vic, while performing ad hoc querying, chooses to sample the data rather than read the entire database, that is okay, but not of interest for this definition.

The domains of each field are in the data dictionary. No special display criteria are identified at this time.

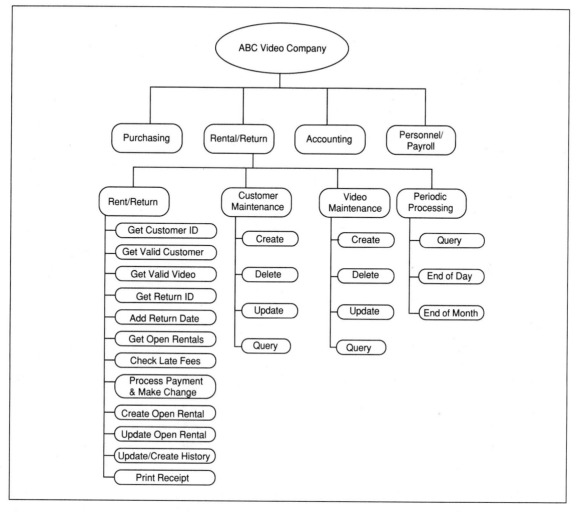

FIGURE 14-1   Process Hierarchy Chart for ABC Rental Application

Develop a User Profile

Guidelines for User Profile Development

A **user profile** is developed to determine the need for special interface design requirements that relate to the user rather than the task. User profile criteria include physical, educational, computer, and task capabilities (see Table 14-3). At the same time the user profile is developed, a matching profile for the application and how it will address the user needs is also developed.

Information in the user profile is obtained from users through interviews, questionnaires, or personnel file searches. If personnel file searches are performed, only average ratings of user skills should be computed unless each employee gives permission to use his or her information. Use of employee records for other than personnel purposes without permission is considered an unethical violation of privacy rights.

TABLE 14-2 ABC Rental Task Profile

Activity	Transaction	ABC Rental
Define Task Hierarchies	Process Level	See Figure 14-1
Define Required and Optional Data	Transaction/Field Level	All data required
Define Data Precision	Only if greater than 2 decimal places for numbers	None. Dollar amounts have 2 decimal places.
Define Data Source	Process/Transaction Level	User Entry and Derived, See Data Dictionary
Define Purpose	Entity/Transaction Level	Form Completion, Information
Define Accuracy	Only if it varies from 100%	100%
Define Domain	Field Level	See Data Dictionary
ID Specific Display Criteria	Field Level	() Required for Change field negative values. No other special requirements.

In critical applications with possible life threatening consequences, *each individual user* should be profiled and reviewed for proper skills, computer experience, and task expertise before being assigned to use the new application. Education can take care of some deficiencies in skill levels, but with some critical applications, people may be reassigned to other jobs when their knowledge does not match the application requirements. For noncritical applications, the profile can *average* user skills for each characteristic. User profile is used to determine sophistication of the interface and training needs.

Physical skills include color perception, typing skill, and physical disabilities that might be present in the user population. Color perception problems mean that reds and greens might not be perceived. If colors are used, users should be screened to ensure that they can recognize the selected colors. Also, color selection should relate to conventional meanings for each color used. For instance, red is the usual alarm-signaling color. In an application using red to signal an alarm condition, then, all users should be screened for their ability to perceive the color red.

Typing is the other typically used physical skill. If user typing skills are low, either the application must be designed not to require typing, or typing training should be provided to users.

Education and math profiles can be either individual or average analyses (see Table 14-3). Education level determines the level of writing required to explain errors. For math-intensive or numerical control applications, specific math skills might also be necessary of users. When this is the case, math skills needed are defined for each task (e.g., one task might need algebra, one might need the ability to interpret geometric drawings, and so on). Users whose profile does not match the required skill levels are trained or reassigned. Many companies, such as Texas Instruments, Chevron Oil, and others, retrain their employees in math skills needed to manage complex computerized manufacturing equipment.

When the average education and math levels are lower than high school-graduate level, the application interface must be designed as simply as possible. Instructions and text help must be written using sentences under 25 words and use words averaging less than three syllables. Different indexes can be

TABLE 14-3   User Profile and Application Response

User Characteristic	Description	Application Response
Physical Skills:		
Color Perception	Red/Green/Blue Color Perception	Either design application without the problem colors or reassign the users.
Typing	Ability in words/minute	Either design the application to fit the skill level or schedule typing training to increase skill level.
Disabilities	Sight, hearing, or physical impairment that might change application hardware, software, or interface design	Either design application to accommodate impairments or reassign the users.
Educational Skill:		
Education Level	Average or actual level of highest degree	For both education and math, design application help and training to ensure users can learn and use the application.
Math Proficiency	Average or actual level of math proficiency	
Language		
Native	All native languages not the same as intended implementation language	International applications should use language native to the region for the application interface.
Proficiency with application language	Average or actual level of proficiency	Training and text descriptions in application can be no more difficult than the average level of proficiency. Training should be provided to ensure that all users attain the average level (i.e., the average becomes the minimum).
Computer Proficiency		
Average Proficiency	Average or actual level of proficiency in years of experience	Design the application help, messages, and user documentation to ensure understanding of all functions, messages, and menu options.
Number of packages	Number and type of packages with which users are familiar	Define training method and requirements.
		Define level of supervision after training is complete.
Job Characteristics:		
Turnover	Average % new employees per year	Determine interface option selection type.
Experience	Average years task experience	Determine level of help and location (automated vs. manual and immediate screen message vs. requested help).

used to compute reading level of text. For instance, the software RightWriter©,[1] provides the Kincaid reading grade level (scale of 1–16), Flesch index of readability (scale of 1–10), and a fog index (ratio of nouns and verbs to total words in a sentence) as measures of text difficulty.

Information about native language is important to determining the language of the interface. As globalization of the economy and development of global organizations increases, the need to implement the same system worldwide will become commonplace. When applications are implemented in other countries, the native language should be used as much as possible. From research we know errors are reduced and some user satisfaction comes from working with applications in one's native tongue. Sometimes, this requirement is government imposed. For instance, in the early 1980s, the King of Saudi Arabia declared that as of 1990 all communications, documentation, and application interfaces used in the kingdom would be in Saudi language. This posed a tremendous challenge to every company doing business with Arabia because Arabic is read right to left, frequently omits vowels, and has as much as 50% of every sentence in a local dialect. At the time of the declaration, there was no one recognized Arabic dictionary for the Arab world. Rather, each country had its scholars map the language for their country. In general, the more critical the application for controlling some potentially catastrophic process, the more important native language processing becomes. I would not like to think of a person who barely speaks English as the controller of a nuclear power plant with all systems and manuals in English!

Next, computer experience is profiled. The average and range of number of years experience, number of software packages used, type of software (e.g., spreadsheet), and whether the individual develops his or her own software are all important to know. The level of computer experience, coupled with the skill level required of the application, determine the type of training that is most effective. For applications that are complex, critical, or have many vari-

able activities, classroom and hands-on training would be indicated. For applications that are simple and have few activities, classroom, computer-based training or on-the-job training are sufficient. Assignment of new staff on the job might require close supervision for a period of time to ensure that they possess the skills to use the system properly. Close supervision should be used for all critical applications regardless of complexity or method of training.

The level of task turnover in the next rating category determines which of the training methods is actually used. If turnover is low, classroom or computer lab training reach the most people at once and are the cheapest. If turnover is high, some method of individual training is required. Some alternatives for individual training are on-the-job, programmed instruction manuals, or computer-based programmed instruction. All can be effective means of training.

Finally, task experience is estimated. If the average user has a high level of task experience, the labels for fields can be more abbreviated, less text is needed to guide data entry, and an expert mode of operation might be preferred. If the average user has a low level of task experience, or experience is variable, novice and expert modes might both be needed.

Task experience and turnover information together determine the mode of interface as novice or expert, and the extent to which on-line help should be provided. Figure 14-2 shows that with low experience levels, novice-only modes are required. With a high experience level, either a mixed mode or an expert mode-only are required.

Figure 14-3 shows that the type of message and extent of on-line assistance also varies with experience and turnover. Low experience with low turnover suggests use of meaningful text error messages with on-line help to elaborate on the error messages. With high turnover, the on-line help should include information on menu options, fields to be completed, and error messages for data entry errors. With high experience levels, the on-line messages can be abbreviated (or eliminated with use of a beep instead of any text message), and with high turnover, supplemented with a paper manual documenting errors and error recovery.

Last, effective training for the application type, user education level, and experience level can be

---

1 RightWriter is a copy-protected product of RightSoft, Inc.

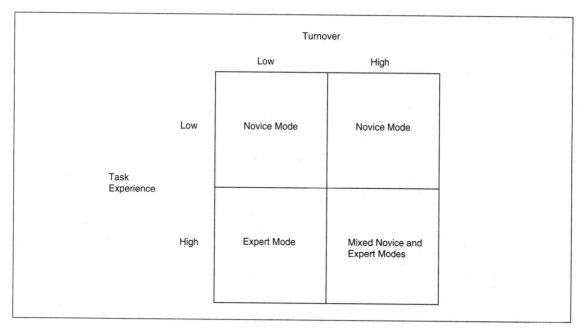

FIGURE 14-2   Turnover and Task Experience Determine Mode of Processing

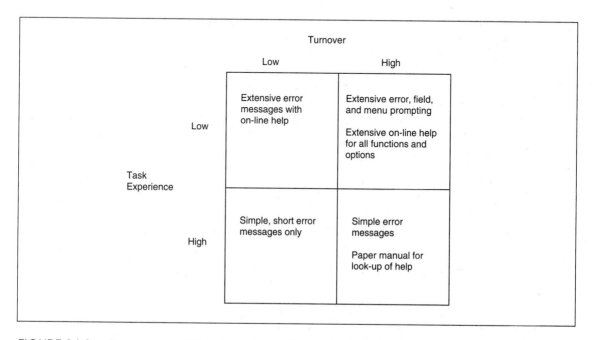

FIGURE 14-3   Turnover and Task Experience Determine Level of On-line Assistance

decided. Training choices include **classroom instruction**, **computer-based training (CBT)**, or **on-the-job training (OJT)**. Classroom training is the most cost-effective for groups of students. Students can ask questions and receive personalized training while a number of people are being trained simultaneously. The disadvantages of classroom training are high cost and the fact that training cannot be repeated without additional cost.

CBT is most effective for training one or a small number of people simultaneously and at different rates. CBT is self-paced, low pressure, and does not require a senior person to monitor the training. The major disadvantage of CBT is its cost, which is steadily dropping. Much training in business will be computer-based by the year 2000 because, by then, it will be cost-effective for most business uses.

On-the-job training is cheap but requires a senior person to teach trainees. The senior person is assumed to be a good teacher who can explain all necessary variations to someone else. These assumptions may not be valid. If OJT is used, some manager or senior staff person should monitor training and privately correct the teacher if a problem arises.

ABC Rental User Profile

Video stores hire younger people, who are frequently in high school. The turnover is high because it is part-time work with mostly evening hours (prime date time) and because the business is somewhat cyclical in video rental patterns. Since the specific users are not known, the average user is estimated based on the four current ABC employees. The analysis is summarized in Table 14-4.

In the ABC example, current employees have no physical impairments and none are anticipated. Typing skill is expected to be low. No particular prohibitions on color or special equipment will be needed except to compensate for the lack of typing skills.

The application will use a bar code reader, as suggested by Vic, to replace the need to type most information. The bar code reader minimizes the key strokes required of users. The reader will scan user IDs, if they are used, and video bar codes to enter the information to the computer. If user IDs are not used,

the phone (or other ID) number will be typed. Another typed entry is the total amount paid. This should not be too error prone because most people pay in even dollars, receiving change. If the need to enter a few numbers really worried Vic, user ID cards can replace the need to type user IDs, or, alternatively key pads are less error prone than typewriter keyboards and could be used.

The average education and math levels of employees is expected to be at the 10th-grade level. This means that algebra is the most abstract level of math skill. The system design criteria are KISS—keep it simple, stupid—so the 10th graders can do the work easily. The math level should be acceptable since the only skills required are to enter the amount paid and to make change.

The language of employees and the language of the application is expected to be English.

Task turnover is high and task experience varies from low to high. Vic has one employee who has worked there four years and two who have been there two months. The task experience of the longer employee is significantly greater than the other two. While the video rental business is not complex, the two newer employees cannot be expected to perform all functions. The system design criteria in response to high turnover and variable task experience is to provide a simple interface with message help on request for all selections, fields to be completed, and error messages.

Computer experience is also expected to be variable but generally low. Number of years' experience for the three employees ranges from zero to two years. Number of software packages ranges from zero to three. The software used is word processing by two people, and database and spreadsheet by one person. One person wrote his own software.

With little computer experience, high turnover, low task experience, low task complexity, and 10th-grade education, two alternatives are recommended. First, individual, self-paced, computer-based instruction (CBT) is recommended because the students can come in on their own time to train whenever it is convenient. When the store is not busy, they might continue their on-the-job training using the CBT. The method would be to give the person one each of the different transaction types. The

TABLE 14-4   ABC User Profile and Application Response

User Characteristic	Description	Application Response
Physical Skills:		
Color Perception	No Problems	None
Typing	Less than 15 WPM	Design to minimize data entry by using bar code reader for Video ID, Copy ID; data to be entered Customer Phone, Amount Paid
Disabilities	None	
Educational Skill:		
Education Level	10th Grade	On-line help
Math Proficiency	Algebra	Needs no special design. Users must be able to make change.
Language:		
Native	English/Spanish	None unless Vic wants to verify user ability to read all display text
Proficiency with application language	High	English will be the implementation language.
Computer Proficiency:		
Average Proficiency	Low, 0–3 yrs. Average = 1 Yr.	Training in basic computer skills, startup, shutdown, etc., required.
Number of packages	0–3, Lotus, WP	
Job Characteristics:		
Turnover	65% Yr.	Use extensive on-line help for all options, entry types, data types, forms fields. Provide expanded on-line help to supplement messages for errors.
Experience	Low to High, Average = Low	Provide extensive training in all transaction types, beginning with turning on the machine. Monitor performance for first week on the job to ensure that training was sufficient.

person would enter the information and the computer would automatically do all subsequent processing. Then, the person would do several of each type of transaction completely. The system would intercept their entries and prompt them for correction, displaying reasons for the correction when they made errors.

Second, if CBT is too costly, on-the-job training (OJT) with a senior person monitoring and assisting

the trainee should be sufficient. If this is the chosen alternative, the trainees should learn rental and return processing first. This can be followed with less important tasks after several days. If OJT is the preferred training method, Vic should monitor the trainer(s) and trainee(s) closely for several days to ensure that the trainers cover all alternatives, pace the instruction to fit the person, and make no assumptions about the trainees' skills.

Option Selection

Once the user profile is complete, the general form of the human interface is decided by mapping the user and task to the implementation environment. When this activity is complete, all interface recommendations are presented to the user for discussion and decision. Two choices are made from the mapping of user and task to implementation environment. Either or both of the choices may be constrained by particular hardware and software if these are already known. The choices are for general option selection screens and general functional screens. Each of these are summarized in Table 14-5. Each set of alternatives and guidelines is followed by a description of how to apply the information to screen design for ABC rental.

TABLE 14-5 Summary of Interface Choices

Interface Level	Alternatives
Option Selection	Menu
	Window
	Command Language
Functional Screen	Form
	Question & Answer
	Direct Manipulation
Data Presentation	Analog
	Binary
	Digital
	Bar Chart
	Column Chart
	Point Plot
	Pattern Display
	Mimic Display
	Text
	Text Form
Screen Item	Color
	Size
	Type Font
	Type Style
	Blink

Option Selection Alternatives

Choices for interface **option selection** design are menus, command languages, and windows for getting *to* some functional screen. **Menus** are lists of items from which a selection is made. **Command languages** are high-level programming languages that communicate with software to direct its execution. **Windows** are a form of direct manipulation environment that combine full screen, icon symbols, menus, and point-and-pick devices to simplify the human interface by making it represent a metaphorical desk environment.

In general, menus and windows are novice modes of operation, while command languages are expert modes. Windows are the interface design most recommended because they simulate an office desk and present the most familiar interface to users. The next section presents design guidelines for the selection level of processing. Details of design for menu and window design are presented in the following sections.

General Option Selection Guidelines

General design guidelines relate to the development of a consistent, standardized interface, consisting of a header, a body, and a footer (Figure 14-4). The screen may include error message lines and command entry lines as well. Many companies have standards for screen design, so much of the work is already complete.

The **header section** of the screen should contain an identifier of the application, function, date, time, screen ID, and program ID. An example is shown in Figure 14-5.

The **body of the screen** contains variable information (see Figure 14-4). In hierarchic menu processing applications, the body contains menu selection, forms for completion, graphics output, or graphical monitoring measures. The body of the screen is subject to many other guidelines which are discussed in the next section.

IBM standards also suggest a user message line and an error message line (see Figure 14-6). Defining user commands and error message lines as fixed may take too many lines away from the screen, so these are optional.

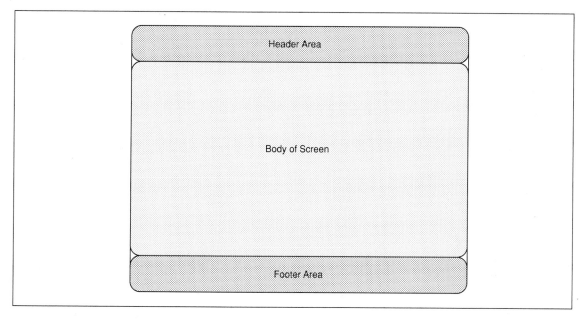

FIGURE 14-4   General Screen Design

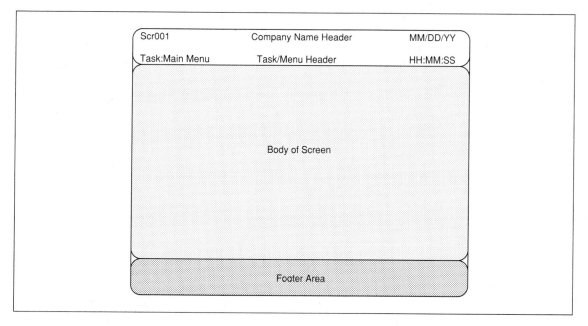

FIGURE 14-5   Screen Header Example

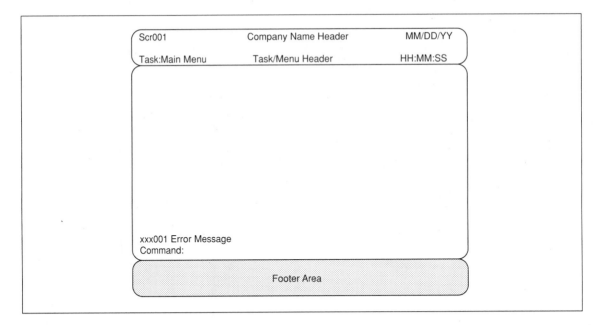

FIGURE 14-6   Command and Error Line Examples

The **footer screen section** contains indicators of navigation choices. Navigation choices should identify which key to select for each allowable movement option. Movement can be within a screen, between screens, or between menus and functional screens. Usually, screen navigation actions are taken by using special keys: escape (ESC), delete (DEL), or programmed function keys (PF or F keys). The allowable actions should be identified at the bottom of the screen in a manner similar to that shown in Figure 14-7. The identifiers should always contain a connector (such as colon) between the key label and the action label. The action labels should be concise, clear, and consistent across the entire application (see Figure 14-7). Ideally, only actions allowed from the current screen should be shown. Others might be blanked out or muted to indicate that they cannot be chosen here.

Menu Standards

The research on menu processing has given us guidelines for location and ordering of menu options. User/SE choices prevail for menu option names and option selection technique. First, based on the number of items on the menu, location is decided. If the number of options is less than 10, the items should be centered as a left-justified list of options. If numbers or letters are assigned to the options, they should be right-justified, followed by a period, and two spaces to the left of the corresponding choice (see Figure 14-8).

When the number of options is 10 or greater, you should experiment with different layouts to make the menu simple and easy to use. If the options are all independent, separating sequences of four or five options by blank lines enhances understandability (see Figure 14-9). If list options are interrelated, then experiment with segmenting the screen into different areas with each area containing an area ID and a centered, justified list of options for the area (see Figure 14-10).

The options for menu selection are entry of an option ID without cursor movement, point and pick, or entry of an option ID with cursor movement. Either of the first two are recommended and selection should be based on user preference (see Figure 14-11). The third option requires more key strokes

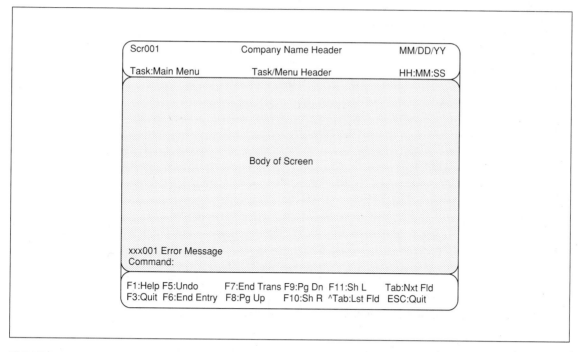

FIGURE 14-7   Screen Footer Example with Function Keys

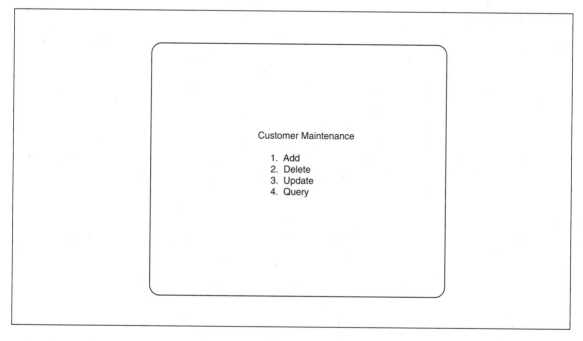

FIGURE 14-8   Numbered Menu Option List, Less than 10 Choices

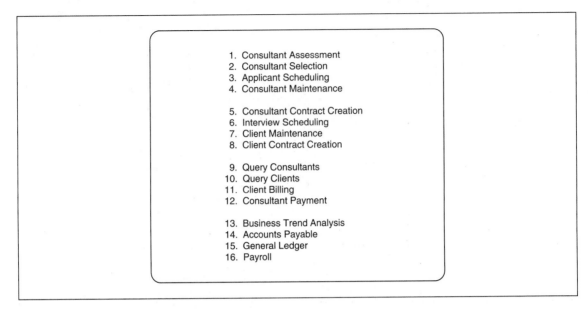

FIGURE 14-9   Menu Option List, More than 10 Independent Choices

and is more error prone; therefore, it is not recommended. Option IDs can be alphabetic or numeric; alphabetic options can be the first letter of the option or letters assigned from the alphabet in sequence. Again, there is no one right answer and user preference should prevail. If a point-and-pick

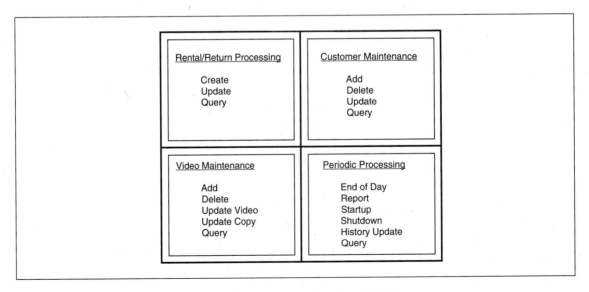

FIGURE 14-10   Menu Option List, More than 10 Interrelated Choices

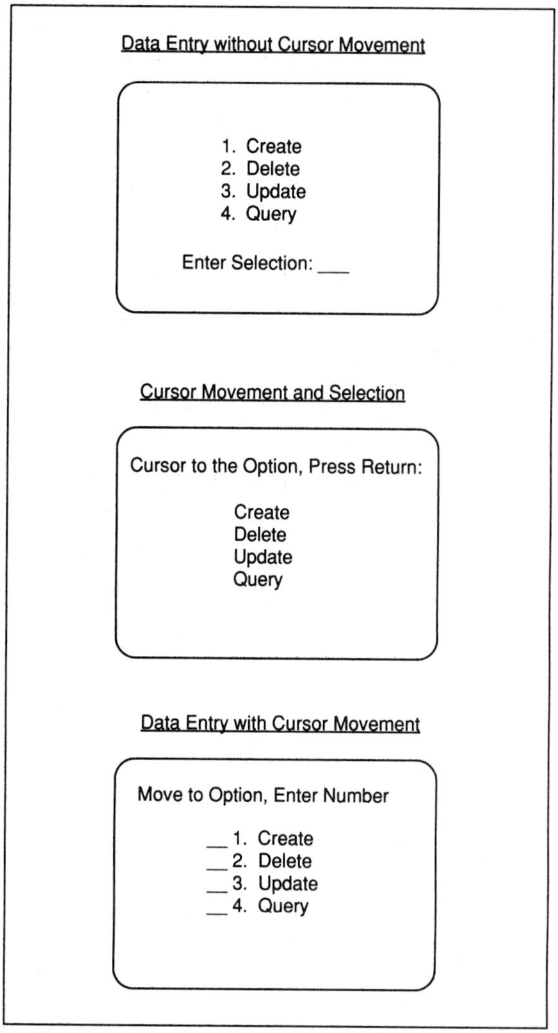

Data Entry without Cursor Movement

1. Create
2. Delete
3. Update
4. Query

Enter Selection: ___

Cursor Movement and Selection

Cursor to the Option, Press Return:

Create
Delete
Update
Query

Data Entry with Cursor Movement

Move to Option, Enter Number

___ 1. Create
___ 2. Delete
___ 3. Update
___ 4. Query

FIGURE 14-11   Menu Selection Options

device, such as a mouse, is used, no option IDs are required.

In all cases, when entry of a selection option is used, the message requesting the data entry should be centered on the screen, two lines under the last menu item, and should be in this location on all screens. This means that the location of the entry line should be two lines under the longest list in the entire

application, and that it is always displayed on that line.

The listing of options within the menu should be based on frequency of choice when point-and-pick selection is used, and should be based on alphabetic order of choices when entry of a selection ID is used. Frequency listing is used for point-and-pick selection because the cursor should be positioned automatically at the most frequent choice (see Figure 14-12). The positioning by frequency of use minimizes keystrokes when moving to other choices. Alphabetic sequence of choices is used when a selection ID is entered, because users can read and understand an alphabetic list faster than a random list (see Figure 14-13). Both alternatives assume a novice user who does not know the options from memory.

The last issue in menu design is option names. Some authors[2] recommend specific names even if it means repeating some information (see Figure 14-14). Other authors[3] recommend concise but meaningful names with no repetitive information (see Figure 14-15). Combining these guidelines, we can design screens that are easily understood and used. First, the option names should be listed to completely define the process and entity(s) (as in Figure 14-14). Then, any information repeating in *all* entries should be removed and placed in a header for the menu list (see Figure 14-16). The result is the concise list from Figure 14-15 with a short header providing the additional information from Figure 14-14.

To summarize, menu applications should be designed in the context of a standard screen format that is used throughout the application. Menu items should be centered, selection action should be obvious, and minimal information should be in the body of the screen.

Window Standards

Windows are rectangular screen areas used to display information. Window displays differ from

---

2 For instance, Banks & Weimer [1992].

3 For instance, Galitz [1981]; Thomas [1982].

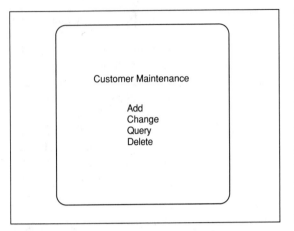

FIGURE 14-12   Menu Options Listed By Frequency

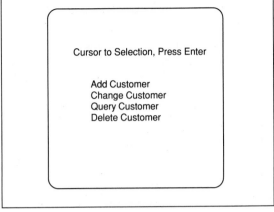

FIGURE 14-14   Complete Menu List

menu-driven full screen displays because users can view different, possibly unrelated information at the same time in different windows. For instance, in ABC's rental application, we might be looking for rental information for Sarah Cropley. We can begin a query function, then type, for example a '?' in the Customer Name field to indicate a look-up. A new window opens up and shows customer names. We select Sarah Cropley, the window closes, the name is moved to the first window, and we continue the query. Look-up and selection of information from a window is simpler than a menu system which uses the entire screen for one thing at a time. Because windows are different from menus, they have different guidelines and standards for their use.

A typical window can have the components shown in Figure 14-17. A **Close Box** stops processing and is similar to an F3 key use defined for a menu. The **Title Bar** names the window the same as the header line in the header portion of a menu. **Location ID** and **status indicator** identify where the user is in the window and whether or not processing

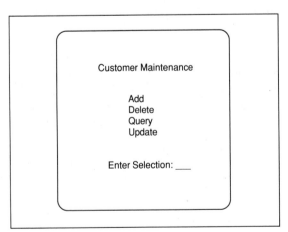

FIGURE 14-13   Menu Options Listed Alphabetically

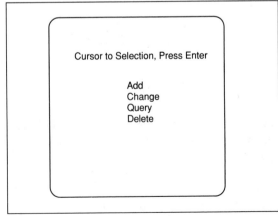

FIGURE 14-15   Concise Menu List

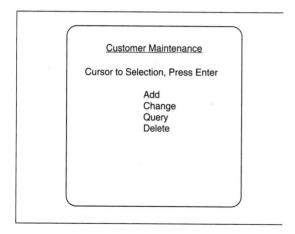

FIGURE 14-16   Combined Menu List

is normal. The **zoom box** and **resize box** both are used to change window shape. Zoom toggles between current size to full screen and back. Resize allows the user to customize the desired width and height to the window. **Scrolling elements**, arrows, bars, and boxes are used to move vertically and horizontally in the window, and are similar to function keys F8-F11 we defined for the menu system. A **scroll box** is dragged to move a variable distance, while a **scroll bar** pages up or down depending on where it is touched, and a **scroll arrow** moves one line at a time. Most window elements are available for use in a windowing application, such as Paradox, but usage is selected by the programmer. All are recommended if the application contains multiscreen forms completion. At least one type of scrolling element for each dimension should be provided.

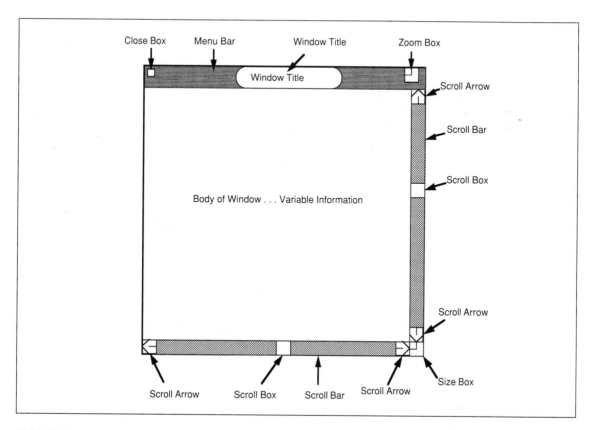

FIGURE 14-17   Window Components

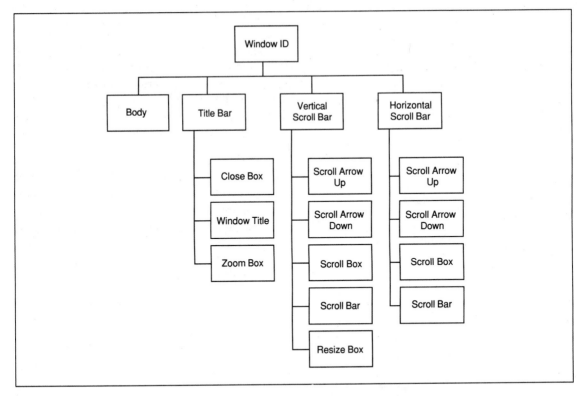

FIGURE 14-18   Window Component Hierarchy

Windows have two basic varieties: tiled and overlapping. **Tiled window systems** only create non-overlapping windows. These work best for process control and nondata intensive applications. When many functions and types of data may be active at once, overlapping windows might be desired. **Overlapping windows** layer windows as opened, one on another, until the application maximum. To move from one window to another, the user clicks on the edge of the desired window to bring it to the front of the stack.

Windows are defined as hierarchies of objects for management. Figure 14-18 shows the hierarchy for the window components in Figure 14-17. As new windows are opened, a new hierarchy is built. All of the window hierarchies are managed by a screen manager which links all hierarchies.

Windows should be set off from each other and from the background by thick, easily recognized borders. Tiled windows should provide blank space,

if it is available, between windows. In current windowed systems, the user has little choice about positioning of selected options for title bar and scroll bars, for example, but, if choice is allowed, the design should be consistent in all tasks. One of the best features of the Macintosh environment is that Apple Computer requires any software operating on the Mac to use exactly the same interface definition as the Apple operating system. All software seems familiar before it is even used. Finally, if no other features beyond a window space are used, scrolling to allow viewing of all window accessible information should be provided.

Window menu styles include horizontal pull-down, Lotus-style horizontal pop-up, and vertical pop-up. **Horizontal pull-down menus** show the top-level selection choice across the top of the screen, taking the least screen space of all menu options (see Figure 14-19). When a menu is activated, by having the cursor moved to its location, the

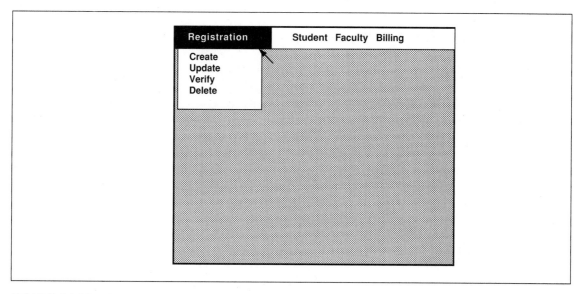

FIGURE 14-19   Horizontal Pull-Down Menu Example

second-level menu is *pulled-down* from the original entry. To make a selection, the cursor is moved to the desired option and activated. Activation is either through a return key or by pressing a mouse button.

Lotus-style horizontal pop-up menus present a second level of options shown as menu items (see Figure 14-20). The main difference is that pop-up selection continues to show between pull-down and pop-up menus the second level actions, whereas pull-down menus disappear as a selection is made.

Vertical pop-up menus are long lists that contain a portion of the list in a scrollable window (see

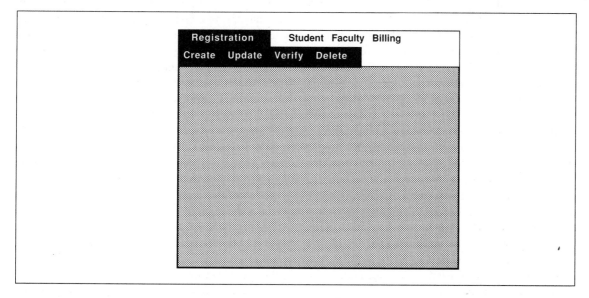

FIGURE 14-20   Lotus-Style Horizontal Pop-Up Menu Example

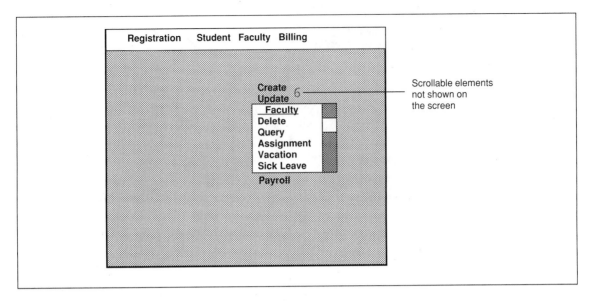

FIGURE 14-21   Vertical Pop-Up Menu Example

Figure 14-21). To select an action not currently showing, the menu is scrolled until the desired action is visible. Then it is activated. Vertical pop-up menus also disappear once an action is activated. In Figure 14-21, the items that would not be showing on the screen are in the gray area.

There is no research on the effectiveness of these three types of menus. In general, though, we know from past research that familiarity with the interface type leads to greater satisfaction with the software. Both horizontal pull-down and Lotus-style pop-up screens are familiar to most PC users. Vertical pop-ups remain useful for long lists.

Both pull-down and vertical pop-up menus offer a simple means for providing expert and novice modes of work. Command keys can be defined for specific functions and shown on a menu for optional use (see Figure 14-22). Novices can use the menu without paying attention to the commands, while experts can learn commands as they need them, becoming proficient in some areas and remaining a novice in others. This option, plus the office desk metaphor that people easily relate to, make windowed environments the preferred development screen style.

ABC Rental Option Selection

The ABC rental application is mostly transaction processing with some query processing. Both windows and menus are recommended for transaction systems, with windowed query development recommended for query applications. Both graphical and digital presentation are recommended. If hardware has not already been chosen, these recommendations imply math and graphic capabilities for the workstations. Standard displays should be sufficient unless Vic wants many graphics, in which case, one display should be high-resolution for graphical use.

The key screen design decision is between windows and full screen menus for selection. There is no one best choice in this decision. When software is chosen before screen design, software sometimes dictates the interface. For instance, mainframe software, for the most part, does not support windows as this text is written. The most advanced screens require a full-screen menu interface. Conversely, some PC software does not support anything but menu bars and windows. To use full-screen menus in this software is cumbersome and costly. User pref-

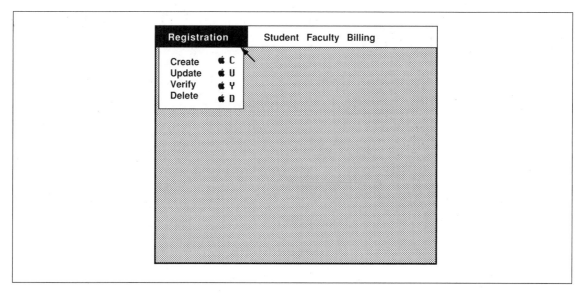

FIGURE 14-22   Function Keys on Pull-Down Menu for Expert Use

erence for selection tends to be strong and should be the deciding factor.

Assume no software is selected yet. To give Vic an informed choice we should sketch both window and menu screen and let Vic choose which he likes best. To do both, we have to design the interface to accommodate the application. For windows, the menu bar should include each major entity and/or process. The menu bars and subchoices for ABC rental processing are shown in Figure 14-23. This design might change with software selection, such as dBase IV, so a sample menu bar with subchoices for dBase is also shown as Figure 14-24. Next, a hierarchic menu system is defined for contrast (see Figure 14-25). The hierarchy menus mirror the task hierarchy defined above. One menu is present for each activity and for its successive levels of subactivities until the functional screens are reached.

The recommended design uses windows. Vic selects windows with the Figure 14-23 menus to be used. He dislikes the dBase menu because none of the functions relate to his applications. Finally, Vic requests a 'quick look' at the screens on the computer to confirm his choice.

Functional Screen Design

Functional Screen Design Alternatives

Once all navigation through menus or commands is complete, the functional level of screen is presented for the real work of the application. Functional level screen choices are direct manipulation, question and answer, and form filling. **Direct manipulation** interactions are those in which the user performs an action directly on some display object. CAD/CAM, CASE, and some computer-based training (CBT) systems have direct manipulation interfaces.

Question and answer (Q&A) interfaces are those in which progressively more focused dialogue takes place based on responses to preceding questions. Artificial intelligence applications and some CBT systems are the most common uses of the Q&A format.

Form-filling interfaces are most common in transaction processing applications but can be used for any application needing to collect discrete, single values for variables. **Form-filling** interfaces present the user with labels and indicators of where data is to be entered. Users are led through the form

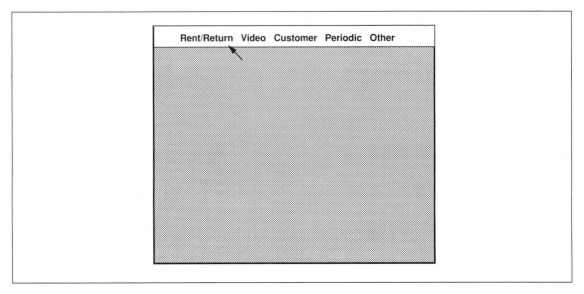

FIGURE 14-23   Menu Bar for ABC Rental Processing

completion process by cursor movement and messages from the software.

Functional Screen Design Guidelines

In general, the application type determines the most appropriate functional screen design. Recommended interface designs are shown in Table 14-6 for all application types. Windows are the preferred method of selection presentation because they can be layered to keep track of thinking processes during long selection sequences, and because their pop-up action matches the way people think more closely than menus. Command languages are not preferred for

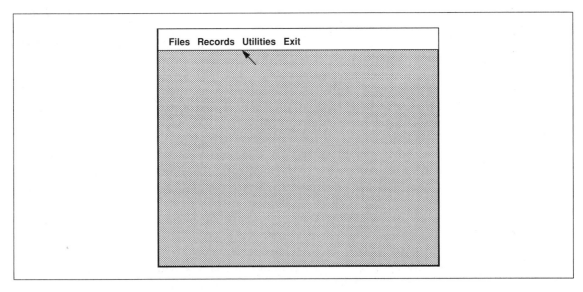

FIGURE 14-24   dBase IV Menu Bar for ABC Rental Processing

Option 1:   All Menu Choices on One Screen

	Customer Maintenance
Rent/Return	Create Update Delete Query
Video Maintenance Create Update Delete Query	Periodic Processing End of Day History Update Query Startup Shutdown

Option 2: Individual Menus for Each Level of Choice

```
SCR01     ABC Video       mmddyy

    Rental Processing Application
         Main Menu

Move the cursor to your choice,
Press Enter

       Rental Processing
       Customer Maintenance
       Video Maintenance
       Periodic Processing




F1:Hlp F3:End
```

```
SCR02     ABC Video       mmddyy

    Rental Processing Application
    Customer Maintenance Menu

Move the cursor to your choice,
Press Enter
              Create
              Update
              Delete
              Query




F1:Hlp F3:End F5: Main
```

```
SCR03     ABC Video       mmddyy

    Rental Processing Application
      Video Maintenance Menu

Move the cursor to your choice,
Press Enter
             Create
             Update
             Delete
             Query



F1:Hlp F3:End F5: Main
```

```
SCR04     ABC Video       mmddyy

    Rental Processing Application
      Periodic Processing Menu

Move the cursor to your choice,
Press Enter
             End of Day
             History
             Update
             Query
             Startup
             Shutdown

F1:Hlp F3:End F5: Main
```

FIGURE 14-25   Hierarchic Menu Set for ABC Rental Processing

TABLE 14-6   Interface Design by Application Type

Application Type	Selection	Function	Display
AI	Window Menu Command Language	Q&A Form	Text short answer is usual display; could also include graphic results.
DSS and ESS	Window Menu	Forms Windows	Graphical-bar column, point plot Digital Need help and cautionary comments for inappropriate output form use.
Process Monitor/Control	Window Menu Command Language	Analog display Mimic display for multivalued or multidimensional data Digital display for specific numbers with symbols, numbers or indicators (e.g., alert) Command Language Direct Manipulation	N/A
Query	Window Menu Command Language	Window Form Command Language	Graphical-bar column, or point plot Digital
Transaction Processing	Window Menu Command Language	Forms	Forms

DSS and ESS because the users of these applications are usually managers who should not be expected to know a command language. DSS and ESS may be used infrequently and the interface should *chauffeur* and lead the user as much as possible. Command languages are the third choice for all application types because they assume expert level knowledge both of the task and of the computer system doing the task. Ideally, a combination of windows with optional expert commands should be provided.

For transaction applications, forms completion screens are preferred for functional processing. Q&A is much less efficient for transaction applications (TPS) than forms because line-by-line entry takes longer and is fatiguing. Direct manipulation is inappropriate for TPS.

For query applications, all options can be used for selection *and* query generation. Query generation is the functional processing in a query application. For query generation, windows with query criteria are preferred. For experts, direct command language use is preferred. Query results can use graphical or digital styles of presentation.

DSS and ESS should use a consistent interface until data results are presented. Either window selection with window request formulation or menu selection with form request formulation are recommended. Results screens can combine any graphic and digital presentation styles, although warning messages for inappropriate display selections might be desirable.

Artificial language applications usually result in a Q&A format. Each AI language environment uses its own method. For instance, Turbo Prolog™[4] uses a combination of windows and command language to initiate processing. A text answer which may have an associated probability of correctness is the usual AI output. Some AI language environments also support limited graphical display.

Last, in process control applications, the functional display *is* the results display. Analog, mimic, and graphical display are all common in process control, sometimes on the same screen. The display usually has a command line at the bottom of the screen. Commands are limited to requesting additional information about a certain measurement or part of the system being monitored, or requesting a different display. The most flexibility and sophistication of design are required in process control applications because they are most likely to be critical in terms of having life-sustaining responsibility.

ABC Functional Screen Selection

ABC rental processing is a TPS and will use forms for the data entry functions. The forms screens for data entry include rental, return, customer maintenance, video maintenance, periodic, and query selection processing. These screens should not change regardless of which option selection inter-

face is selected. Therefore, they could be designed at the same time the general interface is being decided. In any case, the forms screens should be presented to Vic to get general comments and to correct any design he might dislike before a prototype is built.

Presentation Format Design

Once the general form of the interface is decided, details of display are decided. The first set of choices are for data presentation based on the type of data. The second set of choices are for specific field formats. Presentation format describes the method of displaying data on a screen.

Presentation Format Design Alternatives

The options for presentation format include analog, digital, binary graphic, bar chart, column chart, point plot, pattern display, mimic display, text, and text forms.

ANALOG.   **Analog displays** are for continuously variable data (see Figure 14-26) and are usually used in direct manipulation interfaces. Analog displays use a pointer of some kind to show a position that is *analogous* to a value the position represents. Analog displays all should have a scale, pointer, a **direction indicator** of increasing/decreasing measure, and an indicator of normal/abnormal measures (see Figure 14-26). For instance, analog display is effective for the pounds per square inch of pressure (psi) to show a measure of exerted force. Another example from manufacturing is the continuous flow of various densities of oil from a cracking plant which is effectively conveyed via analog display.

The **scale** is a numeric indicator of the item measures. A **pointer** indicates the current position on the scale. Pointers might be arrowheads or needles and may be fixed or moving. The indicator of increasing/decreasing direction is usually a combination of arrows and text to indicate the meaning of direction of pointer movement. **Normal and abnormal measures** can be indicated by a shaded section of the scale, different colors to scale numbers, a change in color of the pointer, a tone for abnormal measures, or

---

4 Turbo Prolog is a trademarked product of Borland International.

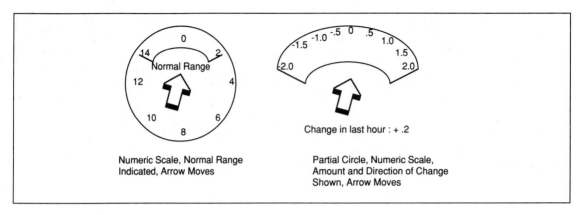

FIGURE 14-26   Examples of Analog Displays

some means of showing expected and unexpected numbers.

The guidelines for analog displays are summarized as follows:

Display Contents
    Scale to which the measure applies
    Pointer to indicate position on the scale
    Indicator of increasing/decreasing direction
    Normal/abnormal measures indicated
Display Design
    Use conventional user mental model of item
    Use moving points on fixed scales
    Use same analog design for all analog
        measures on display
    Use design method—circular scale or open,
        partial circle scale—to facilitate user
        recognition
Usage
    Rate of change
    Range of values for continuous data
    Determine acceptable operation

In general, the most effective displays fit the users' mental model of the measure, use moving pointers on fixed scales, and are consistently designed when more than one analog measure is used. If numeric analog values must be tracked, a semicircular open scale using a fixed pointer with a moving scale allows faster numeric recognition.

Analog displays are best used for monitoring rate of change, monitoring a range of analog values, or

for determining ranges of acceptable operation. Examples of rate of change are the flow of oils in a cracking plant or the voltage fluctuation in cables. A monitoring example is a speedometer for speed limit. Pressure gauges in a nuclear power plant or bond ratings selections that must fall within company guidelines are examples of ranges of operation.

DIGITAL.   A **digital display** is used to convey exact numerical information. Digital displays are most effective when used for variables that have one value at a time. Each value requires a label to identify the data value.

Guidelines for digital data and an example are shown in Table 14-7. In general, only that data of required precision for accuracy should be displayed. Field size should provide for the maximum and minimum values. If data displayed changes frequently, as in a stock trading application, the data should stay on the screen long enough for comprehension, about five seconds, before being changed. If the user is monitoring change, an arrow, plus/minus signs, or other indicator of direction of change might be shown.

BINARY.   **Binary** means having two parts. A **binary display** shows some graphic to indicate a two-value selection option. Usually, we think of binary items as having on-off, or yes-no, or zero-one values.

TABLE 14-7   Guidelines and Example of Digital and Binary Data

Display Contents:
a.   'Y' or 'N' or other character
b.   o or •
c.   'On' or 'Off'
d.   1 or 0 (One or zero) or other numerals
e.   √ or blank

Display Design
   If text form, use contents a, c, or d above
   If analog display, use b or e
   If in a menu list, use b or e

Usage
   To indicate an item that is 'turned on' or 'turned off'
   To indicate a two position setting

Example of digital time display

```
┌─────────────────┐
│                 │
│     07:15       │
│                 │
└─────────────────┘
```

Binary interface information can be presented using text or graphics in several ways (see Figure 14-27). The binary item can be displayed in text using the words yes-no or on-off, or with letters 'y', 'n'. A menu can list the option with a check mark to indicate an 'on' condition. A graphical button, or circle, can be used—when the button is empty, the item is not on; when the button is filled in, the item is on.

By itself, binary indicator selection may not be a major decision. It becomes important when used with other information on the screen at the same time. If used in a menu, a check mark, change of color intensity, or change of color can all be used to effectively indicate an 'on' condition without using any extra characters. If used within a line of text, text presentation (e.g., 'y' or 'n') is more effective.

BAR CHART.   A **bar chart** summarizes numeric data as one or more horizontal bars whose lengths correspond to the values of related variables (see Figure 14-28).

By convention, bar charts show increases in value as the chart is read left to right. Bar charts are effectively used to show task plans over time, percentage of task completion, comparisons of item values (i.e., *item 1* value vs. *item 2* value), and cyclic data (e.g., product sales over a fixed period). In business applications, bar charts are rarely used on screens with other graphic displays; they are generated by applications as summary output for managers, and can be easily generated on-line by many software packages.

COLUMN CHART.   A **column chart** is a bar chart using vertical bars rather than horizontal ones. Bar charts are most often used when time is a fixed period (or is not relevant). Column charts are most often used when time varies and is shown on the x-axis (across the bottom). For instance, cyclic data is most effective in a bar chart when comparing a fixed period (see Figure 14-29). When comparing cyclic data over periods, a column chart is more effective.

The general rule is to use column charts for multiple time periods, to compare different items on the same scale, or for consistency with cultural conventions which assume a vertical scale (e.g., plotting temperatures, times, revenues, sales).

POINT PLOT.   A **point plot** is a column chart that shows the x-y points on the diagram with or without a line connecting them (see Figure 14-30). Point plots might have trend lines generated to show the direction of change. A **band chart** is a special type of point plot that plots several variables on the same diagram. Band charts use shaded areas of the diagram to show variable participation. Bar charts are most effective for showing cumulative variable participation or percentage of participation of each variable (see Figure 14-31).

PATTERN DISPLAY.   Pattern recognition is a human strength. When designing displays that are monitored for change in complex systems, patterns

Example of Alphabetic Listing Using Y/N Indicators

Name	Sex	Married ?	Deceased?
Jones, Sandra	F	N	N
Andrews, Darcy	F	Y	Y
Lane, Bruce	M	Y	Y

Example of Menu List
Using • or Blank Indicators

Font

10 Pt.
12 Pt.
• 14 Pt.

Cairo
Helvetica
• New Century
Times Roman

FIGURE 14-27   Examples of Binary Indicators

are effective. **Pattern displays** repeat the same graphic several times with identical 'normal' displays (see Figure 14-32a). When a change to one portion of the pattern occurs (see Figure 14-32b), it is easily perceived by users. These are not very common in business applications.

MIMIC DISPLAY.   A **mimic display** shows a schematic or other replica of a system to allow the user to monitor its functioning (see Figure 14-33). Because mimic displays are usually symbolizing complex systems, the information presented should be kept to a minimum needed to control, monitor,

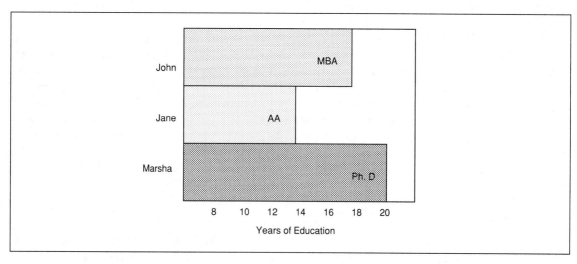

FIGURE 14-28   Example of Bar Chart

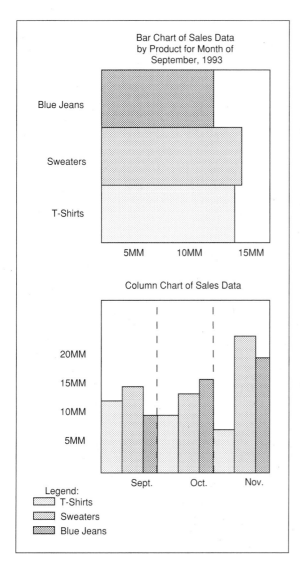

Bar Chart of Sales Data
by Product for Month of
September, 1993

Column Chart of Sales Data

Legend:
T-Shirts
Sweaters
Blue Jeans

FIGURE 14-29   Bar and Column Charts of
Sales Data

or obtain information needed. The symbols, spacing, and relative sizes of symbols used in the display should conform to business conventions to convey immediately meaningful information. For example, Figure 14-33 shows an electrical diagram, not a plumbing diagram; therefore, the users should be electricians or electrical engineers.

Mimic displays are best used when a monitoring application requires a view of the whole system. They provide understanding of system component relationships and can be more easily understood than other types of graphics for the same information. Colors can be used to highlight abnormal functioning of components. In business applications, mimic displays are effective for monitoring network components, telecommunication linkages between networks, and even for tracking problems in application interfaces.

NARRATIVE TEXT.   **Text** is verbiage in which words, rather than numbers or symbols, are used to describe the intended information. Text is hard to read, time consuming to understand, and requires a high skill level of the user. Ideally, text is minimized; but some applications require comments or special, noncodable instructions that must be in text format. Some guidelines for text usage are the following:

- Use no more than 60 characters per 80 character line.
- Wrap text as a word processor does. Do not require the user to change lines.
- Use abbreviations common to the work context, and use abbreviations sparingly.
- Allow users to scroll, change paragraphs, and control the text creation process.

TEXT FORMS.   One of the major uses of displays in business applications is for data entry that corresponds to a *form*. **Form screens** present a series of labeled fields of information for which some information is completed by the user and some information is generated by the application. Forms screens simulate paper forms that they replace or automate. Because forms automate information from paper, the format, sequence, spacing, and information to be completed should mirror that of the analogous paper form.

Forms screens should have standard header, instruction, body, and footer information that differs from the general screen format (see Figure 14-34). The different areas should be clearly delineated, grouping information that is related (e.g., the header) or that repeats. The header should contain an application identifier, function identifier, date, time, and a

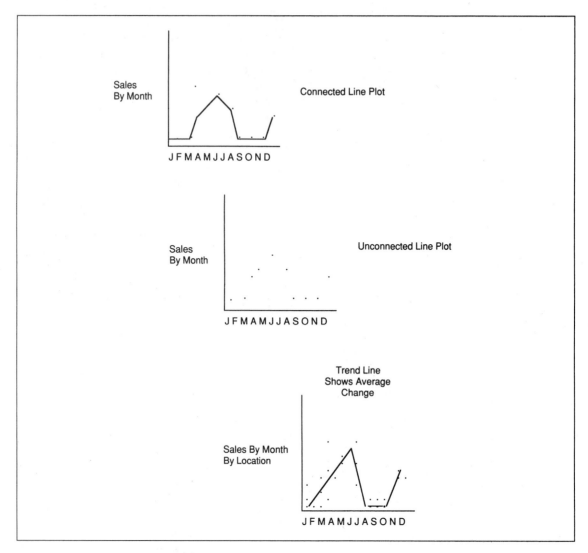

FIGURE 14-30   Example of Point Plots

screen/program ID as discussed above. The header may be the same as the general screen header.

The instructions can be in the form of screen text, help availability, or a short description of expected action. As much as possible, the screen should provide intuitive guidance. Instructions should lead the user to supply information to get to the next step.

The **body of a form** contains the labeled fields to be entered in an easily understood, contextually related format. The **footer** should provide screen summary totals or other summarizing informations. Footers and instructions are optional. The body, then, is the main focus of attention.

The body of the form should be partitioned or windowed to mirror sections of data to be entered (see Figure 14-35). The screen in Figure 14-35 shows a simple *Customer Add* screen for ABC Video. All information relates to the customer and there is no additional family member information in the application. If additional family members are

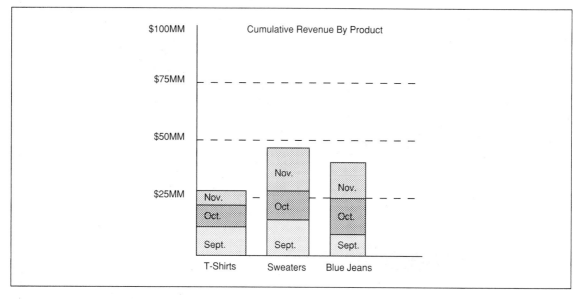

FIGURE 14-31   Example of Band Chart

added to the membership, the *Customer Add* screen might look like Figure 14-36 which shows two sections, one for general customer information and one for additional family members.

Each field or group of fields should be clearly labeled to identify the required information. Customer preferences are needed to design identification for some fields. For instance, three variations of name and address information are shown in Figure 14-37; all three conform to different, good design guidelines. The first variation shows each field labeled. The second shows major fields labeled and minor fields with understood labels. The third shows one heading for all fields; this heading minimizes the text on the screen. No one of these is preferred over the others. Rather, the customer should be allowed to choose the preferred design.

Labels, and any codes designed as well, should be designed to be familiar, less than five characters long, and include letters and numbers. For instance, Figure 14-38 shows four possible codes for a *Customer ID*. The first alternative, 913-8041, is a phone number. It is low in recognition for the clerks in the store, but the highest of any choice for the customer. Who doesn't know their own phone number? For that reason, high customer recognition, a phone number, is a good choice for *Customer ID*.

The second choice, CONG001, is a combination alpha and numeric code. The first four characters are the first four letters of a last name and the last three characters are a sequential number. This is also high in recognition for both customers and clerks. It is less recognizable than a phone number, but a good choice in any case. The next code, 03001 uses '03' to denote 'C' and a sequential number '001' to denote sequence within the Cs. The purely numeric code is

```
a. Normal Pattern Display for 100 Indicators

o o o o o    o o o o o    o o o o o    o o o o o    o o o o o
o o o o o    o o o o o    o o o o o    o o o o o    o o o o o
o o o o o    o o o o o    o o o o o    o o o o o    o o o o o
o o o o o    o o o o o    o o o o o    o o o o o    o o o o o


b. Abnormal Pattern Display for Several of 100 Indicators

o o o o o    o o o o o    o o o o o    o o o o o    o o o o o
o o o o ●    o o o o o    o o o o o    o o o o o    o o o o o
o o o o o    o o o o o    o o o o o    o o o o o    o o o o o
o o o o o    o o o o o    o o o o o    o o o o ●    o o o o o
```

FIGURE 14-32   Normal (a) and Abnormal (b) Pattern Displays

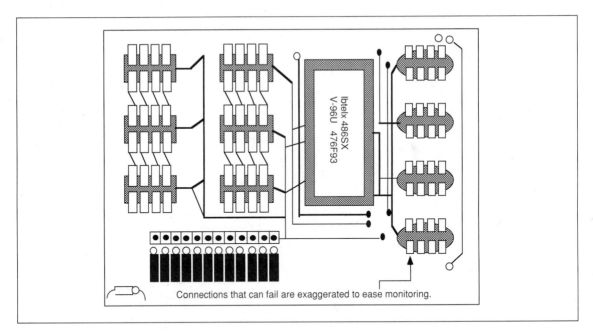

Connections that can fail are exaggerated to ease monitoring.

FIGURE 14-33   Mimic Display for Electrical Monitoring System

cryptic but short. It is less useful than the first two choices.

Text information, such as names, should always be left-justified. Ideally, they should be long enough to provide for the maximum length of the information. This is difficult with names, especially hyphenated names. Each application defines its own maximum; but, in general, over 90% of names in the United States are shorter than 35 characters. If disk storage space is tight, shortening fixed-length text fields is one way to conserve space; another is to define a variable length field that does not store unused spaces.

After the individual labels, fields, and field codes are defined, the next task is to position them on the screen. The design is context related and should group fields that logically go together. From cognitive psychology research we know human brain capacity is limited to holding 5–7 bits of information called 'chunks' in our short-term memories. **Short-term memory** (STM), also called 'active' memory, is what is in your head while you are thinking. STM is measured in nanoseconds of response time for processing and is analogous to the arithmetic/logic unit (ALU) on a computer where all processing takes place. In designing presentation formats, we try to group items to take advantage of the chunking phenomenon. For instance, in the *Customer Add* screen

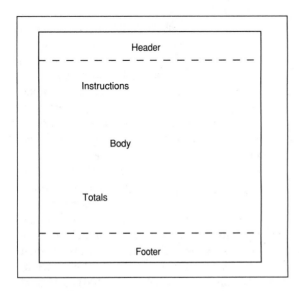

FIGURE 14-34   Sections of a Form Screen

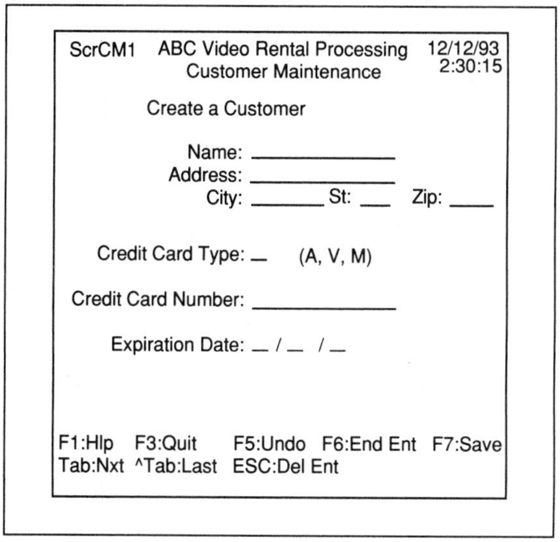

```
┌─────────────────────────────────────────────────┐
│  ScrCM1   ABC Video Rental Processing   12/12/93  │
│           Customer Maintenance          2:30:15   │
│                                                   │
│        Create a Customer                          │
│                                                   │
│           Name: _____                    │
│        Address: _____                    │
│           City: _____  St: ___   Zip: ____      │
│                                                   │
│    Credit Card Type: _     (A, V, M)              │
│                                                   │
│    Credit Card Number: _____              │
│                                                   │
│    Expiration Date: _ / _ / _                     │
│                                                   │
│                                                   │
│                                                   │
│  F1:Hlp  F3:Quit    F5:Undo  F6:End Ent  F7:Save  │
│  Tab:Nxt ^Tab:Last  ESC:Del Ent                   │
│                                                   │
└─────────────────────────────────────────────────┘
```

FIGURE 14-35   Customer Add Screen

in Figure 14-35 above, address and credit card information form two natural groupings of information that should be on the screen as a group. Another aspect of short-term memory chunking is to position required fields first, followed by optional fields. This placement should allow users to signal com-

```
┌─────────────────────────────────────────────────┐
│  ScrCM1   ABC Video Rental Processing   12/12/93  │
│           Customer Maintenance          2:30:15   │
│           Create a Customer                        │
│           Customer Number: aaa999                 │
│      Name: _____ , _____        │
│   Address: _____                         │
│      City: _____  St: ___   Zip: _____          │
│                                                   │
│   Credit Card Type: _     (A, V, M)               │
│                                                   │
│         Number: _____                     │
│                                                   │
│           Date: _ / _ / _                         │
│                        First Name  Last (if Different) │
│  Additional Members:   _____  _____     │
│                        _____  _____     │
│                        _____  _____     │
│                        _____  _____     │
│  F1:Hlp  F3:Quit    F5:Undo    F6:End Ent  F7:Save│
│  Tab:Nxt ^Tab:Last  ESC:Del Ent                   │
└─────────────────────────────────────────────────┘
```

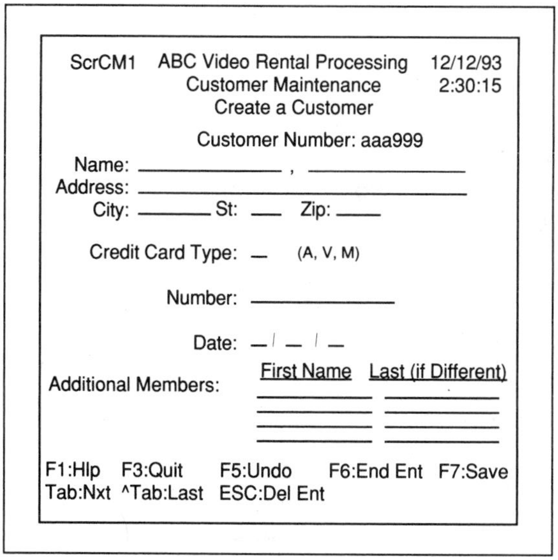

FIGURE 14-36   Customer Add Screen with Additional Family Members

pletion of data entry without having to tab through or touch unneeded fields.

We must also account for long-term memory processing in screen design. **Long-term memory** is what is stored in your brain, similar to disk storage for a computer. Retrieval of stored information uses a schema, or mental model, of what are effectively primary and secondary keys for retrieving information. Retrieval time is measured in 100s of milliseconds or slower. When chunking cannot be done, screen items should be spatially separated to allow users to switch contexts as they move their eyes from one section of the screen to another.

When positioning information on screens, you should also consider possible reusability for screens. For instance, the *Customer Add* screen above could also be used for delete verification, updating, and individual customer query.

When positioning is complete, each screen should be given a system name that is added to the task hierarchy to relate screens to tasks.

It used to be thought that the shortest possible terminal interaction time was desirable, but this is not true any more. Research shows that we need to pace work so that 'psychic overload' does not occur. Chunking items for data entry that logically go together is one way of pacing work. Another is in pacing the response time for different types of work. Long transactions can take a relatively long time, up to 20 seconds, while short transactions should take a short time, less than five seconds. Keystroke response is a simple, direct interaction and should have immediate response from the computer. A query, request to activate a function, and selection of a menu item are all examples of simple interactions. Examples of complex interactions are a database update, saving a word-processed document, or sending a facsimile transmission of several pages. Delays of up to 20 seconds are acceptable *if* the user is kept informed on the status of the processing. Some methods of telling the user the system is working are a message, '. . . *Working* . . .', a clock icon with hand movement synchronized to different percentages of completion, or a whirring sound from the equipment.

Other field definitions for forms relate to character entry and default values. Guidelines for

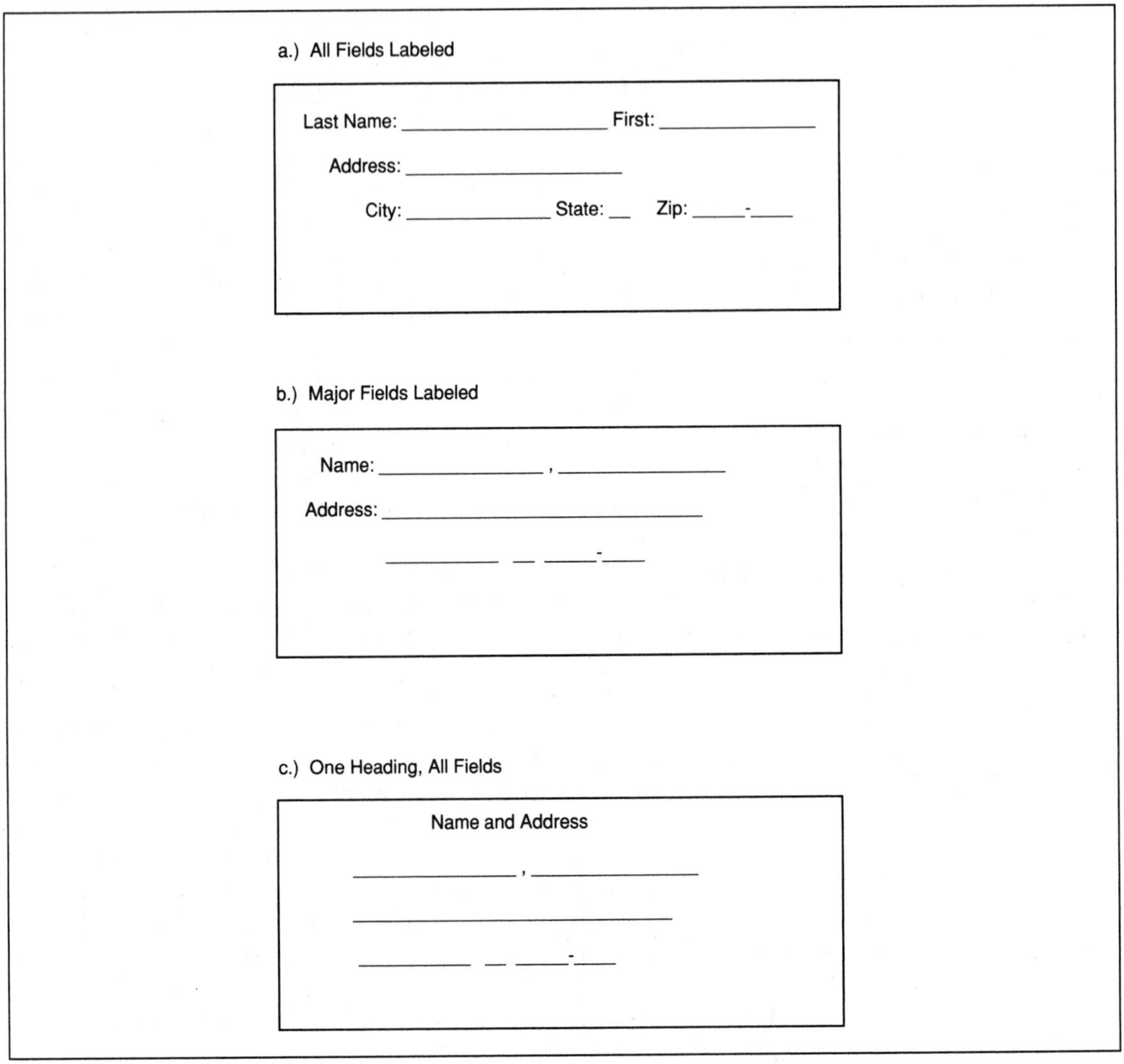

a.) All Fields Labeled

Last Name: _____ First: _____

Address: _____

City: _____ State: __ Zip: _____-____

b.) Major Fields Labeled

Name: _____ , _____

Address: _____

_____ __ _____-____

c.) One Heading, All Fields

Name and Address

_____ , _____

_____

_____ __ _____-____

FIGURE 14-37   Label Variations for Name and Address Information

character entry are listed below; examples of field guidelines are shown in Table 14-8.

- Always display keyed information.
- Never require delimiters to be keyed. For instance, in a social security number, provide dashes to split the numeric parts: xxx-xx-xxxx.
- Do not require entry of leading zeros for numeric fields or of following blanks for text fields.

- Make areas of the screen not used for input inaccessible to the user.

Guidelines for default values are:

- Display all defaults before any data entry begins.
- Confirm defaults by tabbing past the field.
- Default replacement should not alter current default value. For instance, if the default date is today's date, and the operator places yester-

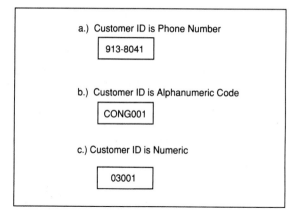

FIGURE 14-38   Variations for Customer ID Code

day's date in the field, the next transaction should still have the default of today's date.

ABC Rental Presentation Format

First, design the standard interface for all functional screens in the application. This should include header, date, time, screen ID, and program ID (see Figure 14-39).

Next, design the keys for navigation, error correction, and help and design the footer to identify them and their functions. The standard used here is fairly common. Program keys and their meanings are shown in Figure 14-40.

We need to know when a portion of processing is done, for instance, when returns are complete (F6), and we need to know when the transaction is complete for inputting the total amount paid (F6). The F8-F11 functions are used for retrieval and query processing to browse through multiscreen output (F8-F9) that is longer than 80 characters (F10-F11). The other keys are for changing actions during data entry.

The designations for F1, F3, and F8 through Escape (ESC) are IBM standards that have been followed by many PC applications. The remaining keys: F2, F4–F7 are open to definition. F2 and F4 are not used here and can be used for future changes. We could have assigned the End Entry type and End

Transaction functions to F2 and F4 as easily as to F6 and F7 (see Figure 14-40). F2 and F4 are not used to minimize the probability of hitting the wrong key and canceling a good transaction. If either of these keys is pressed accidentally, it should have no effect.

Finally, we design the detail form screen for rental/return processing. The periodic processing and customer and video maintenance screens are left as assignments at the end of the chapter. Rental/return processing includes chunks for *Customer* information, *Open Rental* information, *New Rental* information, and *Payment* information. Corresponding to the chunks of information, the screen can be thought of as having four sections. The middle two sections are identical except that *New Rentals* cannot have return dates, late fees, or other fees applied. So, we design three different sections. Each section is designed separately, keeping in mind that there are 20 usable lines on the screen and that we want about 75% blank space. For this screen design, we assume a screen size of 24 lines by 80 characters per line.

The sections of screen information should be prioritized for condensation and crowding if it becomes necessary. For ABC rental processing, the priorities are highest to lowest: rentals, payment information, returns, and customer. Since new rentals are generating the payment information, they are most important. Payment information is second because it must be accurate and easily understood for the clerk to handle money properly. Returns are a low priority here because 90% of returns are on time. Customer information is only important for the clerk to verify the customer name. If necessary, the remaining customer information could be condensed onto one line for display.

The first section of the screen is for *Customer* information. The information to be included is name, address, city, state, zip, phone number, and credit status.

The first issue to be decided is what type of field labels to use. For example, the options for *Customer* are individual field identifiers, only a *Customer* identifier, or some combination of the two (see Figure 14-41). To minimize information on the screen, we use only the word *Customer* (Option 2, Figure 14-41). This also makes sense since the *Customer ID* probably is to be scanned to minimize data

TABLE 14-8   Field Format Guidelines

Content	Poor Design	Better Design
Do not intersperse letters and numbers	A1B1C1	ABC001
Use alpha mnemonics that are meaningful, predictable, easy to remember, distinct	ZXCVB001	Video001
Try not to mix special characters with letters and numbers	User types: $123.45	Preformatted $_ _ _._ _ User types: 12345
Break long codes into groups of three and four digits	277426631	277-42-6639
Do not use frequently confused letters in codes	o and 0 1 and I	Use zero, 0, only Use one, 1, only
Identify maximum number of spaces for item data entry; replace space marker as data is entered.	Enter Vid-ID	Enter Vid-ID: _ _ _ _ _ after three char. Vid-ID:123_ _

Labels	Poor Design	Better Design
Use abbreviations and contractions	Video Identification	Video ID
Try to keep labels less than eight characters long	Customer name and and address	Customer:
Design abbreviations to be less than five characters	Ident	ID
Separate mnemonics by hyphens	VidID	Vid-ID
Place label to left of single occurrence field	Name: Sam Jones	Name: Sam Jones
Place label over column of repeating information	Name: Sam Gerry Leonard Jesus	Name: Sam Gerry Leonard Jesus

entry and the *Customer* information is displayed automatically.

The second issue is format of the information. The options in Figure 14-41 all follow a conventional post office address format. The address need not be formatted in that manner, but the high recognizability of addresses in this format is a strong inducement to keep it the same. Unless screen space is a major problem, the post office format will be kept.

Two fields remain: *Customer ID* and *Credit Status*. *Customer ID* is an important field as the identifier of the information and should be positioned in a way that highlights its presence. Conversely, *Credit*

TABLE 14-8   Field Format Guidelines (*Continued*)

Error Messages	Poor Design	Better Design
Use upper and lower case if possible	ALL UPPER CASE IS DIFFICULT TO READ	Mixed case is preferred to enhance readability.
Only use asterisks in extreme situations	*****This ***** is *****very ***** distracting *****.	*****ALERT***** The database may have been destroyed.
Error IDs should be in a consistent location	PF001 Error 001 Error 002 PF002	PF001 Error 001 PF002 Error 002
Should be brief	Numerics were expected by the application but you entered some nonnumeric information.	Numerics expected.
Should be positive	You entered an illegal date format.	Enter date format mm/dd/yy
Should be constructive	You idiot! This mistake should NEVER occur.	Reconstruct database and begin again.
Should be specific	Illegal entry or ?	Enter data format mm/dd/yy
Should be comprehensible	FAC DB 29081230123	Database error. Call the DBA at x3456.
Should allow the user to feel as if they control the system rather than the system controlling them.	?	To undo, press F5.
Provide levels of messages with less detail for error message and more detail for requested help.		

Status is only important when it is the cause of a canceled request. So, *Credit Status* needs some sort of 'alert' design but, otherwise, can be positioned to conserve space. Several alternatives for *Customer ID* and *Credit Status* formats are shown in Figure 14-42. All alternatives are acceptable; the third option is selected because it minimizes labels and has credit in an easy-to-spot location—the upper right corner of the screen.

The second section of the screen is for *Open Rentals* information. The information needed on the screen includes *Video ID*, *Copy ID*, *Description*, *Rental Prices*, *Rental Date*, *Return Date*, *Late Fees*, and *Other Fees*. By convention, a typical bill,

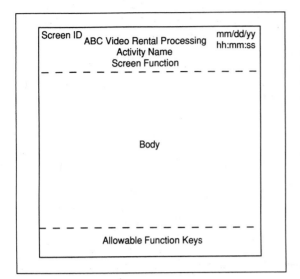

FIGURE 14-39   Standard for ABC Video Functional Screens

invoice, purchase order, or shipping papers list the item identifier followed by its description. We follow this convention for ABC. Two basic alternatives for fees and dates are shown in Figure 14-43. Since the same line design will be used for the *New Rentals* screen section, the alternatives as they would display for new rentals are also shown.

Key	Functions
F1	Help
F2	Not Used
F3	Quit/No Save
F4	Not Used
F5	Undo Last Entry
F6	End Entry
F7	End Trans/Save
F8	Page Forward
F9	Page Back
F10	Shift Page Right
F11	Shift Page Left
DEL	Delete Character
ESC	DEL/Cancel Field
TAB	Go to Next Field
Shift/Tab	Go To Last Field

FIGURE 14-40   Program Keys and Functions

The alternative which is easier to read and understand should be selected. If neither is obviously easier to read, the user should be consulted. The choice here is the first alternative. Keeping the dates together allows fast understanding of a tape's lateness, while keeping the rental information and return information separate allows fast understanding of rental fees owing. Vic has stated that no rentals are made without payment of rental fees, so the second option loses some appeal. The first option is selected then on the basis of keeping like things together—dates with dates and money with money. When returns are processed, the default of today's date should be placed in the *Return Date* field.

The third section of the screen is for *New Rentals* information. For this section, we use the *Open Rentals* line definitions and blank out the fields for return dates, late fees, and other fees (Figure 14-43a). A default of today's date should be placed in the *Rental Date* field. The only issue is how many tapes should a customer be allowed to rent at any one time. There are arguments for any number one can select and they all are determined by opinion. Therefore, Vic should select the number of allowable tapes out on rent at any one time.

When asked, Vic wants no restrictions at first. Then, he reconsiders. "If I allow unlimited tapes, someone could theoretically give me a stolen credit card as identification, rent many tapes, leave town, and I'm out the tapes. Maybe I should limit the number. But, one or two does not seem enough. What if they are short, like music videos? What if they want to watch movies all day? Why should I stop them? Hmmmm. I think someplace between 10 and 20 is probably okay because most people would never rent that many. My biggest customer is George Anderson and he takes out about six tapes at a time. So, I guess 10 is a reasonable limit."

With ten tapes as the limit, the screen needs no scrolling because all information will fit on one screen. Because this choice turns out to be an important design decision, Vic should be reconsulted and told that scrolling will not be available for rent/return processing. If he chooses to change the number, or asks for scrolling, it should be provided.

The fourth section of the screen is for *Payment* information. For payments, the fields are the *Total*

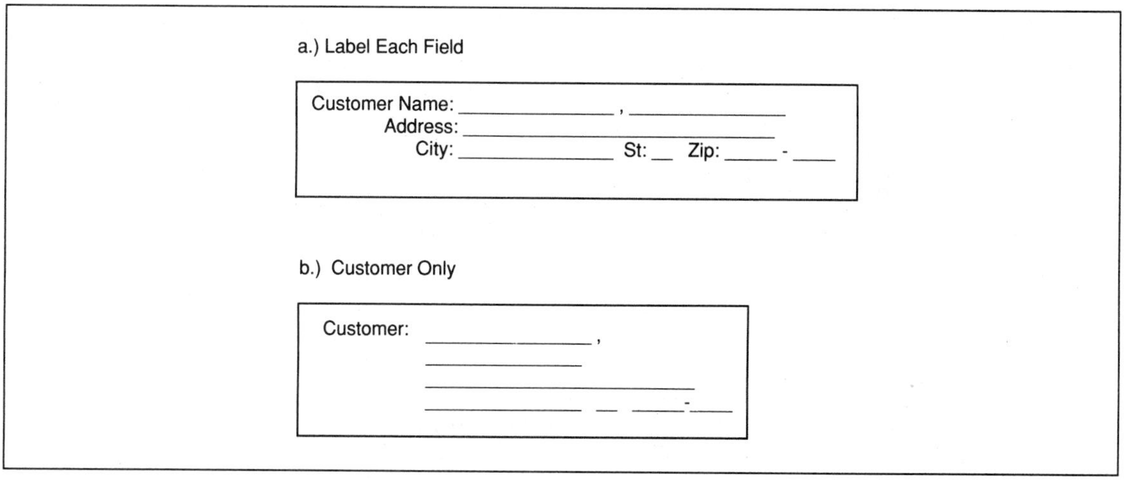

a.) Label Each Field

Customer Name: _____ , _____
        Address: _____
            City: _____ St: __ Zip: _____ - ____

b.) Customer Only

Customer: _____ ,
             _____
             _____
             _____ __ __ ___-___

FIGURE 14-41   Customer Name Screen Options

Amount Due, Total Amount Paid, and *Change.* These could be on one line, two lines, or three lines as shown in Figure 14-44.

The choices for payment should be first, readability and understandability, and second, space available. For ABC, all information can fit on the screen with three-line spacing and still have room left over. So, the last alternative (Figure 14-44c) is selected as most easily read. The money fields should be right-justified with one set of numbers on the rental/return lines. The title fields should be right-justified for the group of three lines.

Last, we consider placement of the entire screen in the blank area between the standard screen header and footer. So far we have 22 lines accounted for in the rental screen: two standard header, one screen header, two footer, four customer, ten rent/return, two rent/return header, and three total lines. There

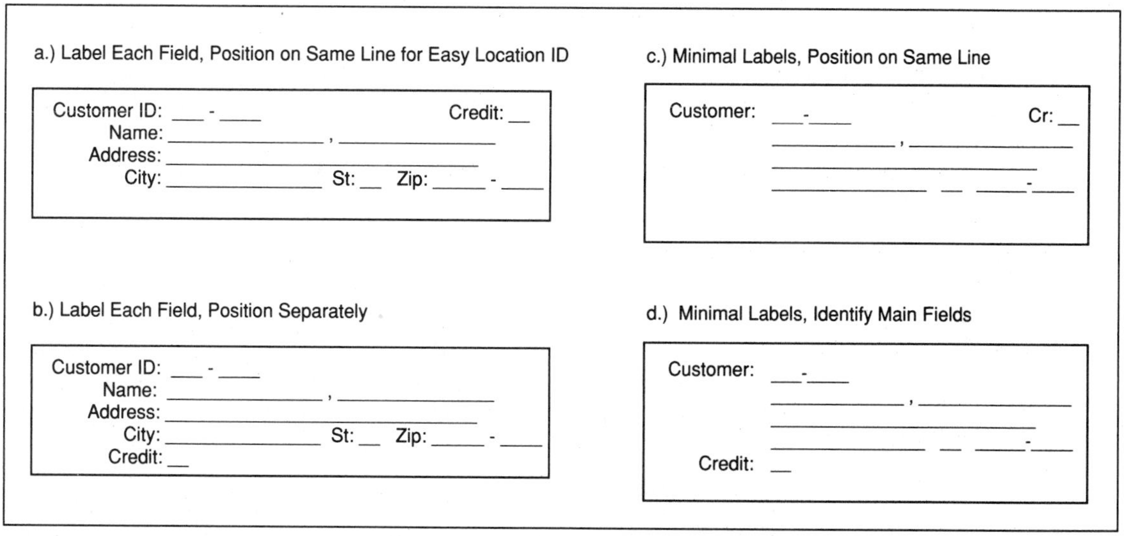

a.) Label Each Field, Position on Same Line for Easy Location ID

Customer ID: ___ - ____   Credit: __
      Name: _____ , _____
   Address: _____
       City: _____ St: __ Zip: _____ - ____

b.) Label Each Field, Position Separately

Customer ID: ___ - ____
      Name: _____ , _____
   Address: _____
       City: _____ St: __ Zip: _____ - ____
     Credit: __

c.) Minimal Labels, Position on Same Line

Customer: ___ - ____   Cr: __
             _____ , _____
             _____
             _____ __ __ ___-___

d.) Minimal Labels, Identify Main Fields

Customer: ___ - ____
             _____ , _____
             _____
             _____ __ __ ___-___
Credit: __

FIGURE 14-42   Alternatives for Customer ID and Credit Status

Alternative A. Dates First, Fees Second

Video ID	Copy #	Description	Rental Date	Return Date	Rent Fees	Late Fees	Other Fees
xxxxx	xx	xxxxxxxxxxxxxxxxxxxxxxxxxxxxx	99/99/99	99/99/99	99.99	99.99	99.99
xxxxx	xx	xxxxxxxxxxxxxxxxxxxxxxxxxxxxx	99/99/99		99.99		

Alternative B. Rental Information First, Return and Extra Fees Second

Video ID	Copy #	Description	Rental Date	Rent Fees	Return Date	Late Fees	Other Fees
xxxxx	xx	xxxxxxxxxxxxxxxxxxxxxxxxxxxxx	99/99/99	99.99	99/99/99	99.99	99.99
xxxxx	xx	xxxxxxxxxxxxxxxxxxxxxxxxxxxxx	99/99/99	99.99			

FIGURE 14-43   Alternatives for Dates and Fees

are no extra lines on the screen (see Figure 14-45). Ideally, one blank line should separate the header and footer from the body. Also, one blank line is desired to separate the rental/return information from customer information. To provide blank lines, we either delete a header line or change the arrangement of information on the screen. According to our priorities, customer information should be condensed onto fewer lines to gain the blank lines. The *Customer ID* can be added to the customer name line and given its own label to specifically identify it (Figure 14-46a). This makes reading the *Customer ID* somewhat more difficult but adds to the readability of the rental information. A better choice is to redesign the standard header and make it two lines, with the second line identifying the function, and only display function keys available and use one line. This screen (Figure 14-46b) is preferred and recommended. In the end, Vic should select *his* preferred screen and it should be the final design. Vic selected the recommended screen for the same reasons that informed its design.

A. One line

  Total Due 999.99 Total Paid 999.99 Change 999.99

B. Two lines

  Total Due 999.99 Total Paid 999.99
                        Change 999.99

C. Three lines

  Total Due   999.99
  Total Paid 999.99
  Change   999.99

FIGURE 14-44   Alternatives for Payment Information

Field Format Design

Field Format Alternatives

Field format design selects the characteristics of individual fields or values of fields on a screen. The alternatives for field format design include size, font, style, color, and blink for individual field values, and include coding options for field labels.

SIZE.   Size is an issue in field attribute definition when it is selectable. For many software platforms, the size, spacing, and selection of characters is fixed within the application. Size of characters is mea-

```
SCRR01                         ABC Video Rental Processing                    12/02/94
                                  Rent/Return Processing                       02:03:15
                                    Rentals and Returns

Customer: #xxx999                                          Cr: x
          xxxxxxxxxxxxx xxxxxxxxxxxxx
          xxxxxxxxxxxxxxxxxxxxxxxxxxx
          xxxxxxxxxxxxx, xx  99999

Video   Copy                            Rental      Return      Rent    Late    Other
ID      #      Description              Date        Date        Fees    Fees    Fees

xxxxx   xx     xxxxxxxxxxxxxxxxxxxxxxxxxxxxx    99/99/99    99/99/99    99.99   99.99   99.99
xxxxx   xx     xxxxxxxxxxxxxxxxxxxxxxxxxxxxx    99/99/99    99/99/99    99.99   99.99   99.99
xxxxx   xx     xxxxxxxxxxxxxxxxxxxxxxxxxxxxx    99/99/99    99/99/99    99.99   99.99   99.99
xxxxx   xx     xxxxxxxxxxxxxxxxxxxxxxxxxxxxx    99/99/99    99/99/99    99.99   99.99   99.99
xxxxx   xx     xxxxxxxxxxxxxxxxxxxxxxxxxxxxx    99/99/99    99/99/99    99.99   99.99   99.99
xxxxx   xx     xxxxxxxxxxxxxxxxxxxxxxxxxxxxx    99/99/99                99.99
xxxxx   xx     xxxxxxxxxxxxxxxxxxxxxxxxxxxxx    99/99/99                99.99
xxxxx   xx     xxxxxxxxxxxxxxxxxxxxxxxxxxxxx    99/99/99                99.99
xxxxx   xx     xxxxxxxxxxxxxxxxxxxxxxxxxxxxx    99/99/99                99.99
xxxxx   xx     xxxxxxxxxxxxxxxxxxxxxxxxxxxxx    99/99/99                99.99
                                            Total Due:  999.99
                                          Amount Paid:  999.99
                                               Change:  999.99

F1: Hlp   F3: Quit   F5: Undo   F6: End Ent   F7: End Trans   F8: Pg Up   F9: Pg Dn   F10: Sh R   F11: Sh L
Tab: Nxt Fld ^Tab: Lst Fld   ESC: Cncl
```

FIGURE 14-45   Alternative 1 for ABC Rental Screen

sured in points. A **point** is a measure of type that is approximately 1/72 of an inch (about 2.8 mm). In general, the size of characters should be no less than 10 points and no more than 14 points unless an alert or alarm situation is being shown. These sizes are in the range of normal printed point sizes for display processing. An example of the range of point sizes is shown in Figure 14-47.

The default in most applications is 12-point type. As you can see from Figure 14-47, the larger the point size, the fewer characters fit on a screen. At 18 inches, the minimum point size should be about 9 and a comfortable point size is 12. The further away from the screen the user is, the larger the point size should be. At 30 inches, the minimum point size should be 10 points and either 12 or 14 points print size are acceptable. At 10 feet, the size should be about 72 points, or one inch.

FONT.   Most software applications have a fixed default for type font as well as type size. Most applications default to a serif style such as that used in this text. A serif font has been proven easier to read and faster to comprehend than a sans-serif style such as this. If fonts are selectable, the rule of thumb is to select one or, at most, two fonts and use them consistently throughout the application for obvious distinctions. For instance, use one font for all field labels and another font for all information entered by the application user. Do not mix fonts for the same purposes or users will get confused and error rates will increase.

STYLE.   Type styles might include regular, **bold**, *italic*, outline, reverse video, SMALL CAPS, ALL CAPS, underline, or ~~strike through~~. While the options make for interesting reading, interchanging

a.) Customer ID on Customer Name Line

```
ID: xxx999  Customer: xxxxxxxxxxxxx xxxxxxxxxxxxx          Cr: x
                      xxxxxxxxxxxxxxxxxxxxxxxxxxxx
                      xxxxxxxxxxxxx, xx  99999-9999
```

b.) Recommended Screen Design

```
SCRR01                        ABC Video                        12/02/94
                         Rent/Return Processing                02:03:15

Customer: #xxx999                                    Cr: x
          xxxxxxxxxxxxx xxxxxxxxxxxxx
          xxxxxxxxxxxxxxxxxxxxxxxxxxxx
          xxxxxxxxxxxxx, xx  99999
```

Video ID	Copy #	Description	Rental Date	Return Date	Rent Fees	Late Fees	Other Fees
xxxxx	xx	xxxxxxxxxxxxxxxxxxxxxxxxxxxxx	99/99/99	99/99/99	99.99	99.99	99.99
xxxxx	xx	xxxxxxxxxxxxxxxxxxxxxxxxxxxxx	99/99/99	99/99/99	99.99	99.99	99.99
xxxxx	xx	xxxxxxxxxxxxxxxxxxxxxxxxxxxxx	99/99/99	99/99/99	99.99	99.99	99.99
xxxxx	xx	xxxxxxxxxxxxxxxxxxxxxxxxxxxxx	99/99/99	99/99/99	99.99	99.99	99.99
xxxxx	xx	xxxxxxxxxxxxxxxxxxxxxxxxxxxxx	99/99/99	99/99/99	99.99	99.99	99.99
xxxxx	xx	xxxxxxxxxxxxxxxxxxxxxxxxxxxxx	99/99/99		99.99		
xxxxx	xx	xxxxxxxxxxxxxxxxxxxxxxxxxxxxx	99/99/99		99.99		
xxxxx	xx	xxxxxxxxxxxxxxxxxxxxxxxxxxxxx	99/99/99		99.99		
xxxxx	xx	xxxxxxxxxxxxxxxxxxxxxxxxxxxxx	99/99/99		99.99		
xxxxx	xx	xxxxxxxxxxxxxxxxxxxxxxxxxxxxx	99/99/99		99.99		

```
                                        Total Due: 999.99
                                      Amount Paid: 999.99
                                           Change: 999.99

F1: Hlp   F3: Quit   F5: Undo   F6: End Ent   F7: End X   Tab: Nxt Fld   ^Tab: Lst Fld   ESC: Cncl
```

FIGURE 14-46   Alternative 2 for ABC Rental Screen

the styles on a form to be completed make it much harder to comprehend and will increase error rates. In general, regular print is acceptable in all applications for text display. For general purpose, noncritical text, regular print is recommended.

Bold print and reverse video are useful to call attention to a field if it is warranted. For instance, bold type style is effective for alert field values on a monochrome screen. A common use of reverse video is to show cursor position. The character at which the cursor is positioned is shown in reverse video and switches back to normal as soon as the cursor is moved.

Italics and outline are not generally used because they are harder to read and, therefore, increase comprehension time. Strike-through and underline are used mostly in word processing applications and can be effective in that context. For most forms-

This is 10 point type.

This is 12 point type.

This is 14 point type.

This is 18 point type.

This is 24 point type.

FIGURE 14-47   Sample Point Sizes

completion TPS applications, neither of these is recommended. Finally, research studies have shown that use of all capital letters increases comprehension time and they are not recommended.

COLOR.   Color can be an effective addition to screen design, or it can seriously detract from the understandability and readability of the information. For indicating binary or ternary conditions, color is faster and easier to comprehend than any other coding scheme.

Research provides clear guidance on appropriate and inappropriate uses of color for application displays. Color is most effectively used for search tasks in which the goal is to find one or two objects (of the same color) that differ from surrounding objects. This type of search does not occur often in business applications. Color coding also is effective for:

- unformatted display of information
- symbols which may be within a high density of information on the screen
- tasks in which the position of the item to be identified is not known but the color is
- screens for which color relates to the task
- user tasks involving search and recognition of differences in symbol color

Color is least effective for tasks in which a large number of colors are indiscriminately used, for which colors selected do not differ sufficiently to enable distinction, and for tasks in which the goal is to identify large numbers of objects (of the same color) when surrounded by a large number of objects of other colors. These ineffective color uses result in problems of discrimination. Research findings show that performance deteriorates with more than six colors on a screen. Many writers suggest using no more than four colors at any one time for business tasks.

Research on color selection recommends selection by wavelengths, ensuring sufficient contrast to speed comprehension. For instance, Figure 14-48 shows common colors on a spectrum by wavelength. Poor choices would be blue, blue-green, and green for different meanings on the same screen. Good choices would be red, yellow, and blue, because they are sufficiently different to facilitate understanding.

Because color blindness and other color perception problems are common, user profiles and user testing should be used to guarantee that all users can recognize all colors on a screen. Bold or odd colors of any type, for example, olive-green, should be avoided.

Common meanings ascribed to colors should be used in the application, and the common meanings which change by culture should be adapted. The government recommends using red only for alert conditions, yellow for warning, and green for normal

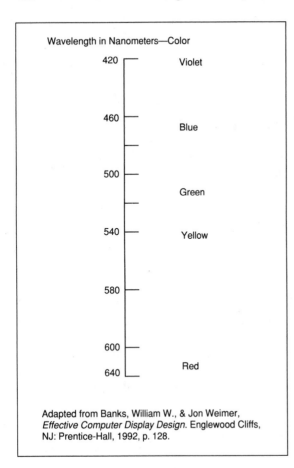

Wavelength in Nanometers—Color

Adapted from Banks, William W., & Jon Weimer,
Effective Computer Display Design. Englewood Cliffs,
NJ: Prentice-Hall, 1992, p. 128.

FIGURE 14-48   Color Spectrum

because that is the common, conventional use for these colors. The use of a flashing red signal should be limited to an emergency condition requiring immediate action.

BLINK.   Blinking characters or 'flashing' is a useful attention-getting device for monochrome or limited color displays. Blinking is considered more annoying than color codes by most users and should be limited to no more than one field at a time or one meaning at a time. An example of effective flashing would be to flash all data entry fields in error. As errors are corrected, flashing stops.

Blinking rates need to be monitored for the **flash rate** or speed of blinking. The optimal flash rate is

2–3 times per second with equally spaced intervals for on and off. Rates of 8–12 flashes, while discernable, can cause nausea and even seizures in people with photo-epilepsy. For those of us over age 30, a phenomenon called **flicker fusion** causes us to see constant light when the flash rate is very high, over 50 times per second.

Guidelines for Field Format Design

Assignment of field format characteristics is a judgmental activity based on SE experience and common sense. Follow the tenet 'less is more' in defining field formats that add formatting options. The use of these options diverts attention, causing a delay in the thinking process. If delay and attention shift are not desired, the result will increase error rates and reduce productivity.

Effective uses of color, blink, or audio sound for directing attention should be considered; however, user approval should be obtained before adding formatting changes to the screens.

ABC Field Format Design

One field on a rental screen, credit standing, might be worth highlighting. In addition, when processing takes place, several other items might be highlighted. In particular, data entry errors and insufficient payments, late tapes, and special fees should be considered for use of color, blinking, or bold type. These items are chosen because they represent all of the abnormal conditions that occur during rental processing.

A customer's credit standing is acceptable unless it is specifically changed by Vic during an update process. Since its change requires management action, a customer with a poor rating should probably be denied rental rights. This process has never been discussed with Vic and needs verifying. If he approves, the credit standing for poor ratings only could be displayed as a red or a blinking field to highlight credit status.

Data entry errors can also be highlighted. Since red is being used to signify denial of rental rights, a different color should be chosen. If data entry errors are highlighted, the recommended colors are either yellow or blue to make them distinct from the red used for credit standing.

Insufficient payment occurs when the *Change Amount* is a negative number. The current design calls for moving the cursor to the payment field which is updated with the new *Total Amount Due*. Since this is not an expected occurrence, clerks might miss the cursor movement and complete the transaction even though insufficient payment has been made. Some method of highlighting is also desirable to ensure against such mistakes. The recommendation is to blink all money fields and move the cursor to the new *Total Amount Due*.

Late tapes might cause a justifiable denial of rental rights, but this has also never been discussed with Vic. The number of days that constitutes significant lateness needs to be defined. If monitoring of lateness is desired, a red, blinking value in the rental date field could be used to represent significant lateness.

Last, special fees, which require management update, might also be highlighted and a cause for rental denial. The use of special fees is not well-defined to the project team at this point. Presumably Vic is using special fees for lost or damaged tape assessments. Perhaps if the fees are over a certain amount, to be defined, Vic would want the field highlighted and, unless paid, rentals would be denied. If Vic wants this highlighting, a red, blinking field, consistent with other rental denial fields, would be suggested.

A long conversation with Vic resolves all of these issues. The recommendations for errors, credit problems, and insufficient payments are all accepted. Vic likes the idea of denying rental rights when tapes are over 10 days late. He questioned the use of the same blinking red signal, however, thinking that white blinking might be more effective. The SE explained that if one signal, blinking red, is used for rental denial regardless of reason, it will be more easily learned by the clerks. Vic agrees with the recommendation. He does not want special fees highlighted, nor does he want rental denied. He is using special fees for the two purposes described, but he also is using it for tapes purchases with money still owing, a usage never before defined.

Design of Report Output

In many companies, formal reports are no longer produced from application systems. Instead, users are provided with a query language and told to develop ad hoc reports as they are needed. When formal reports are required, they usually are based on queries of the same information. The guidelines for reports, then, follow similar guidelines for screens.

1. Design a standard header and footer and be consistent in the general format on all reports.
2. Keep report body as close to query screens as possible.
3. If query screens are not present for the specified reports, follow the design guidelines for screens. Define clearly identifiable areas for grouping information that is related or that repeats. Follow reasoning for individual fields on a report that parallels the reasoning used for screen design.

The ABC rental receipt is shown in Figure 14-49 as an example of a report that follows the design of its related screen. Notice that while the receipt has a header, it is preprinted and differs from that of the screen. Preprinted information is most effective when it is printed in some unobtrusive color, such as turquoise, which users can ignore when they become familiar with the report format.

CONVERSION

Conversion of applications is a systems analysis and design in miniature. The activity is only concerned with transforming data from its current format and storage media into a new application's format and storage media. Conversion is usually concurrent with design and done as a side activity by a small group of one to three people who report to the PM

ABC Video Rental
5930 Preston Rd.
Atlanta, Ga. 30303

Customer Information: #xxx999   MM/DD/YY

xxxxxxxxxxxxx xxxxxxxxxxxxx
xxxxxxxxxxxxxxxxxxxxxxxxxxx
xxxxxxxxxxxxx, xx 99999

Video ID	Copy #	Description	Rental Date	Return Date	Rent Fees	Late Fees	Other Fees
99999-	999	xxxxxxxxxxxxxxxxxxxxxxxxxxxxx	mm/dd/yy	mm/dd/yy	99.99	99.99	99.99
99999-	999	xxxxxxxxxxxxxxxxxxxxxxxxxxxxx	mm/dd/yy	mm/dd/yy	99.99	99.99	99.99
99999-	999	xxxxxxxxxxxxxxxxxxxxxxxxxxxxx	mm/dd/yy	mm/dd/yy	99.99	99.99	99.99
99999-	999	xxxxxxxxxxxxxxxxxxxxxxxxxxxxx	mm/dd/yy	mm/dd/yy	99.99	99.99	99.99
99999-	999	xxxxxxxxxxxxxxxxxxxxxxxxxxxxx	mm/dd/yy	mm/dd/yy	99.99	99.99	99.99
99999-	999	xxxxxxxxxxxxxxxxxxxxxxxxxxxxx	mm/dd/yy	mm/dd/yy	99.99	99.99	99.99
99999-	999	xxxxxxxxxxxxxxxxxxxxxxxxxxxxx	mm/dd/yy	mm/dd/yy	99.99	99.99	99.99
99999-	999	xxxxxxxxxxxxxxxxxxxxxxxxxxxxx	mm/dd/yy		99.99		
99999-	999	xxxxxxxxxxxxxxxxxxxxxxxxxxxxx	mm/dd/yy		99.99		
99999-	999	xxxxxxxxxxxxxxxxxxxxxxxxxxxxx	mm/dd/yy		99.99		
99999-	999	xxxxxxxxxxxxxxxxxxxxxxxxxxxxx	mm/dd/yy		99.99		

Total Fees Due: 999.99
Total Paid: 999.99
Change: (99.99)

Accepted By: _____

FIGURE 14-49   ABC Rental Receipt

and work with the DBA to define and populate the new database environment. The activities of conversion are:

1. Identify current and future locations for all data items.
2. Define edit and validate criteria for all attributes.
3. Define data conversion activities.
4. Define options for data conversion.
5. Recommend and gain approval for data conversion strategy.
6. Develop a schedule for data conversion based on estimates of time to convert one data item.
7. Define options for application conversion and implementation.
8. Recommend and gain approval for implementation strategy.
9. Develop a schedule for application implementation.

Identify Current and Future Data Locations

The first task is to identify the data being converted. A matrix listing every relation with its attributes/fields is developed. Then, in one column, the present location of each attribute is identified. An automated data field entry has the current file, relative address in the logical record, length, type characters, and current data name. A manual field entry identifies the data source and person responsible for data accuracy.

A third column is created to identify specific conversion errors if they are known.

Define Attribute Edit and Validate Criteria

For attributes that are simply being moved from one location to a new location, the edit and validate criteria should already be defined in a data dictionary. If this information is not already defined, the conversion team defines and documents necessary edit and validate criteria.

When attributes are being encoded to use a shortened storage format, the encoding scheme must have been defined. If a coding scheme is not already defined, the conversion team works with the design team to define and document the encode-decode scheme.

Define Data Conversion Activities and Timing

Three major issues relate to data conversion. First, the automation status is either automated or manual; second, is data accuracy and reliability; third, is the ease of mapping from the old data storage technique to the new data storage technique (see Figure 14-50).

The extent to which data is already automated, clean, and has a simple mapping from the old to the new data storage technique, makes conversion simple. When data are manual, inaccurate, or not easily mapped, conversion is difficult. When data are all three—manual, inaccurate, and not easily mapped—conversion becomes a critical task that may define the critical path for the application development.

Manual data that must be automated require extensive edit and validation criteria in the data entry program to prevent bad data from getting into the database. Data that are not easily mapped may have no simple way for conversion staff to verify accuracy of processing, therefore, testing and test verification with user assistance become critical tasks in determining data conversion success.

Data that are inaccurate require two things. First, the conversion team must define what the possible correct data values are. Second, the conversion team and user must define the mapping from incorrect values to correct values. Then, any new values that might change the mapping from old to new storage technique must be reviewed with the systems design team to ensure that the application design is still valid. Third, an army of clerks must be hired to correct the errors. This means that special training for data correction is required. Fourth, training for the new application must address the data inaccuracies, the new values, and their interpretation for all current data users.

Data that have combinations of problems require multiple skills of conversion team members and complicate the conversion process. Data conversion planning should be complete early in the design stage. The planners should know which types of these problems are present and how the conversion team is planning to minimize their impact.

Select and Plan an Application Conversion Strategy

The methods of conversion are direct cutover and gradual conversion. Both methods may or may not be supplemented by continuing **parallel execution** of the old application to allow comparison of results and verification of processing.

Direct cutover means that on the set day, the old way of work is abandoned and the new way begins to be used. This is a risky method since few applications work perfectly the first time. There is no way to compare results and verify correctness of the new processing.

Gradual, or **incremental**, **cutover** is a conversion approach in which the new application is implemented in some piecemeal form. The implementations may be geographic, functional, iterative, or some combination of these. **Geographic** conversion is an approach in which the entire application is implemented in each location, one location at a time. The application that is used to account for pay telephones in the United States, COIN, has several different versions in operation across the country at a time. As a new version is implemented, one of the locations volunteers to be the first to use it. It is

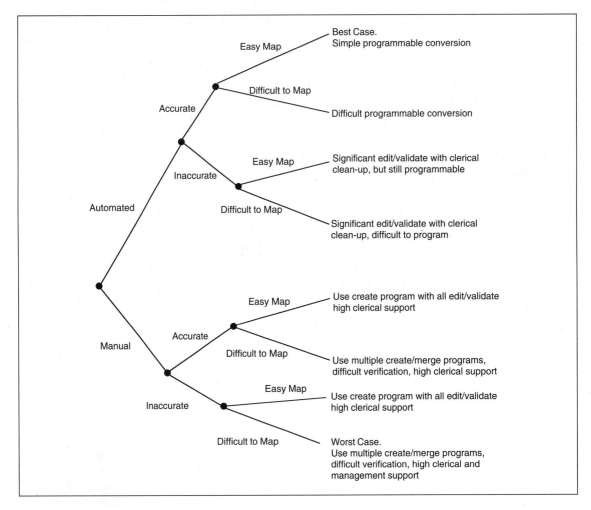

FIGURE 14-50   Decision Tree on Ease of Data Conversion

implemented in that one geographic location for six months. Then another location is added. After another six months, a third location is added. The timed geographic technique keeps the lives of the implementers relatively stable and allows the distributed companies using the software to choose their own implementation times.

Functional conversion has three variations. First, work functions can be cut over one at a time to the new application. This is a local version of the geographic conversion method. Second, **incremental software development** can place specific work functions into production use as soon as

they are tested. Third, small numbers of transactions or one type of transaction might be implemented first using **transaction conversion**. Then, as the users gain experience and the application stabilizes, more transactions are cut over until all are in production. In the first variation, the entire application is implemented in one department or group at a time. In the second, pieces of the application are implemented one at a time, and may be in production company-wide or by group. In the transaction variation, the whole application is complete, but it is implemented piecemeal by transaction type.

When a new application changes the old method of work, or when a specific problem is highlighted during feasibility or analysis for immediate implementation, some form of functional, incremental conversion is useful. Both of these circumstances occur in large business applications. Small applications may not have enough functionality to allow iterative conversion, requiring the complete application to be placed into production at one time.

Gradual conversions can not always be done. When the new application is automating a previously manual process, gradual conversion may be difficult unless unrelated transactions can be identified. When this occurs, the project team should develop a final test using live data that parallels daily production and can, therefore, be checked for accuracy.

Parallel conversion means that the new and old methods of work, including any applications work, are both done every day for some period, usually one or two cycles of processing. Parallel conversions only work if the new application produces the same outputs as the old application and has comparable formulae and processing on the data. In the parallel method, the people using the application would do their jobs in the new way and follow it by doing the work in the old way *with the same data*. That is, the same information is processed twice. If the formulae, processing, or outputs are very different, parallel processing might not work. Parallel conversion is also difficult when the number of people doing the work is insufficient for processing the double volume of work. Then, if parallel conversion is desired, some gradual method should be coupled with parallel execution.

ABC Conversion Strategy

Conversion in ABC is from a totally manual to a totally automated application. This means that the planning for conversion should follow the need for data. Each relation is examined individually to determine its criticality for processing on the first day of Rental/Return use (see Table 14-9).

Of the seven relations in the application, four (i.e., Rentals, Customer History, Video History, and End of Day) are derived from processing and need no conversion. The other three—Customer, Video,

TABLE 14-9   ABC Rental/Return Data Relations and Conversion

Relation	Status	Priority
Rental/Return	Derived from Processing	0
Customer	Manual/Clean	1
Video	Manual Clean if known	2
Copy	Manual Need a count	3
Customer History	Derived from Processing	0
Video History	Derived from Processing	0
End of Day	Derived from Processing	0

and Copy—are manual and needed the first day of operation. All could have the same priority because the application cannot be tested without all three relations. The customer relation is given the highest priority because it has accurate data from the card file, and therefore, should be more easily converted. Another reason for choosing the customer relation first is because if it turns out to be error-ridden, the other two files can be assumed to be as bad or worse. Customers tend to overestimate the quality of their data, and errors become known when the method of processing changes.

The strategy then is convert the customer file from the existing card files, followed by the video and copy information. The next issue is who is to do the data entry. The clerks might enter *Customer* information during nonbusy work hours or could be hired for extra hours of work. The estimate of conversion for customer information is approximately 70 hours (4 minutes * 1,000 customers / 60 minutes in an hour). This assumes four minutes of data entry time for each of 1,000 customers. The ideal solution is to hire clerks for extra work so their entire attention is only on conversion at the time. This speeds the process and minimizes errors that might occur from interruptions during the work day.

One alternative for doing the data conversion is to hire the current staff to work more hours. If three ABC clerks each worked two extra hours each day, and all work a five-day week, the customer conversion would take between ten days and two weeks. This alternative is attractive because the current clerks know the data. The disadvantage of this alternative is that the clerks don't type and the four minute estimate might be very low for them. Another disadvantage is that because the clerks' typing skills are low, name and address errors, which are very difficult to identify via computer, might get into the file.

A better alternative is to hire an experienced data entry person(s) from a temporary agency. The cost is not too high, $10–14/hour, and their accuracy will be greater. For an experienced typist, the four minutes is probably a high estimate.

The next relations to be converted are *Video* and *Copy*. One issue in this conversion is the high amount of time for bar coding each copy of a video. Assignment of bar codes affects database design. Alternatives are to use the bar code to identify each tape uniquely and duplicate video information in the copy relations, or identify each video with a portion of the bar code and identify each copy by a unique sequence number within bar code. The preferred solution from a data perspective is to generate one *Video ID* bar code that is the same for all copies of a tape. Database storage and typing time are minimized, and retrievals will be faster. This solution is recommended. The only advantage to the other alternative is that no sorting of the physical inventory is required. The disadvantage of the unique base code for each tape alternative is that video information is replicated a number of times thus increasing the time for data entry, error rates, and retrieval time.

The related issue in video-copy conversion is the physical inventory identification of all copies of each video for entry into the application. The scheme we chose of one *Video ID* bar code for all copies of the same tape makes data entry easy but makes the physical work more difficult. The people doing this work must sort all of the tapes by video, assign the *Video ID*, and generate and affix the bar codes to each copy. Last, each copy's bar code must be entered into the system. Since we chose one *Video ID* bar code

for all copies, we can enter the video information and a count of copies and have the application generate all *Copy* relations. Part of the change procedure for a video, then, must include changing the number of copies. Increasing the number poses no problems. Decreasing the number means that a check for outstanding or past rentals must be made and, if present for a number to be removed, the number may not be removed. These maintenance requirements should be discussed with the design team to ensure that they treat video processing in this way.

The last issue to decide about data conversion is who should do the video and copy conversion data entry. The estimated time for a complete physical inventory is about 28 hours. This number assumes six seconds of inspection time per tape for 10,000 tapes, plus four seconds overhead for extra movement of tapes to make room for the sorted ones (i.e., 10 * 10,000 / 60 seconds per minute / 60 minutes per hour = approximately 28 hours). This includes sorting the tapes by title alphabetically and keeping them in that order until the data are completely entered. Tapes out on loan must be included in each day's conversion process to ensure 100% conversion coverage. Once the tapes are in sequence, the clerks putting tapes back into inventory are assumed to alphabetize them automatically, adding no extra time to the conversion.

The data entry for each tape, because of the coding scheme defined, should take only about two minutes per tape for a total time of about 33 hours (i.e., 2 * 10,000 / 60). The total conversion time for the ABC rental/return application is about 120 hours, or about three weeks.

Again, the clerks, who know the inventory best, could be hired extra hours to work on conversion sorting and data entry, or Vic might hire outside workers to come in daily for 8–10 hours for several days.

If Vic wants to use his current clerical staff to use otherwise idle time, the amount of time for conversion is 120 hours divided by the number of idle hours per day. If the three clerks are idle a total of six hours per day, the conversion will take approximately 20 days. This is a long period of time and usually, the longer conversions continue, the greater the likelihood of errors. The recommended approach is to hire temporary data entry clerks to sort the tapes, assign bar codes, and enter the data into the system.

The alternatives and recommendations are presented to Vic for his approval. He chooses to hire two temporaries for two weeks to work full-time on converting all data. His rationale is that he really wants his clerks to concentrate on customers, and he decides they can help with the physical inventory sort in their spare time. The remainder of the time they should be working at helping customers. If videos are missed during the inventory sort, they will be found as they are rented and their information will be entered into the application then.

USER DOCUMENTATION

Mix of On-Line and Manual Documentation

User documentation is important because it is usually the first information about an application that new employees are given. Therefore, it should be developed and maintained to disclose accurate usage information about an application. User documentation is started after analysis and can be a parallel activity to design. Some researchers and practitioners recommend developing the user documentation before design begins. The application is then designed to meet the requirements of the user documentation.

Frequently, *users* develop the manual documentation and define what they would like for on-line help and messages. At the least, users should participate in developing user documentation. The arguments for having users develop their own documentation are:

- Users are less likely to assume knowledge that SEs take for granted (e.g., how to start an application).
- Users know what to do better than SEs.
- Users who develop their own documentation require less training because they already know how the system will work.

With complete novices who have never used a computer system, having them develop the user manuals is NOT a good idea.

Contents of the user documentation vary with each project and company. In general, the writing style should not be patronizing, but should take the users' general level of computer expertise into consideration. This means that documentation written for experts can be concise, use jargon, and have less explanatory information about how to get started. Documentation written for novices should begin at an elementary level, for example, "The button to turn on the machine is located. . . ."

An outline for general contents of user documentation is provided in Table 14-10. First, any document should contain a table of contents. A system overview describing the scope of processing is next. Assumed level of user and expected system-user interactions should be included in the overview. Diagrams should be frequent and 'understood by your mother.' Also in the overview, include information about whom to call for help and what kind of help they offer. For instance, Operations provides assistance if the terminal malfunctions, or the Information Center assists in developing ad hoc queries.

Describe the hardware, software, and at a very high level, how the equipment is connected. This is especially important when LANs, distributed applications, or PCs hooked to mainframes are being used and some functions are local and some remote. Be specific about what work is performed in what location and how to determine problems.

Next, describe the general formats for screens and functions. Begin the details of system operation with startup and shutdown, including security information, without documenting security codes! Describe all function keys and what they do.

Then, for each screen in the application, present the screen and the required/optional entries made by the operator. Be specific about the type of data to be provided. Present an example of a correct screen and of an incorrect screen with error messages. Sequence this information by logical groupings of activities. For instance, for ABC, there would be four functional description sections: rental/return, customer maintenance, video maintenance, and

TABLE 14-10   User Documentation Contents

Introduction
   Application Overview
   Special Features
   Format of Document
   Support Group Services, Contacts

General System Information
   Obtaining a User ID
   Starting the Machine
   Shutting the Machine Down

System Access Procedures
   Logon Procedures
   Logoff Procedures

General Data Entry Information
   Menus and Menu Selection with examples
     of all screens
   Data Entry Screen Format with one example screen
   Function Key Assignments

Rent/Return Procedures
Customer Maintenance
   Procedures
Video Maintenance Procedures
Periodic Processing Procedures
Backup/Recovery Procedures
Error Recovery Procedures
Error Messages

} For each section:
List screen(s)
  Required
   entries
  Optional
   entries
Procedure for
  screen
  completion

periodic processing. For each screen, describe normal, error, optional, and required processing.

Include backup and recovery information if the user is expected to perform those activities. Be specific about what actions are performed and the sequence of actions. If recovery must be activated from a specific terminal, for instance, begin the instructions with something like the following. "At Terminal 011, located on the 2nd floor of 235 West Covina in the southwest corner, and labeled 'MAIN OPERATOR TERMINAL,' enter the following."

In an appendix, provide a list of all error messages, by message ID with a detailed description of how to correct the error. Format the appendix to correspond to the sequence of functional sections in the body of the report.

AUTOMATED SUPPORT FOR FORGOTTEN ACTIVITIES

Many products are available to support the activities in this chapter. For screen design, screen 'painters' and application generators both provide screen design. **Screen painters** are forms-oriented design tools that allow fast prototyping and layout of screens that then generate coded descriptions of the screens. A user identifies that screen design is desired; if the relation is described in the tool, the fields can be listed to provide screen design guidance, and the user 'paints' the screen by placing labels and field names on the screen in the target location. When complete, the screen can be called up to allow printing and viewing of the screen as it would be presented to the data entry clerk. Screen painters can be stand-alone software packages but are more frequently a function of CASE environments.

A second type of software support for screen design is available in application generator software. The screens for menus are designed first with menu entries typed in by the software user. Then as functional screens are reached, the program code to generate the requisite screen interaction (e.g., SQL) is coded. If custom form design for data entry is required, some packages include that activity, too; others require the designer to generate the code within the package.

Conversion software support is mostly in the form of utility programs that allow easy reformatting of data to move from a current automated file to one or more new files. Merging of information from two sources to create new composite files is sometimes provided but requires more complex software coding.

Manual-to-automated data conversion ideally uses the application code for data creation to further test it and increase estimations of reliability. Several application generator packages, for example, Focus™,[5] provide automatic screen generation with no underlying edit or validation for 'quick and dirty' data entry. This is useful in prototyping and demonstrating prototypes, but should not be used for the production application. Focus generates the screen by sequentially listing the fields as defined in the database. As a line fills up with data, a new line is generated. This automatic screen utility only works on files with no repeating information and cannot join files for combined data entry.

Help packages are now plentiful in the marketplace. Help used to be totally manual and all messages had to be in the user documentation. As help has moved to become an on-line function, more messages are documented on-line than in manuals. The advantage of a Help package that is independent of specific software is that it, and its messages, can be used across applications and software environments. This cross-application use can help ensure that definitions are consistent throughout the company and can make data administration standards compliance easier to monitor.

The automated packages supporting the screen design, conversion, and help processing are summarized in Table 14-11.

the presentation format, each screen item's characteristics of size, type font, style, color, and blink rate are defined. In designing forms, decisions about the chunks of data to be presented and formatting of chunks on the screen are required.

Conversion alternatives are direct conversion or incremental conversion. Incremental conversion may be geographic or functional (by transaction, by department function, or by application function). Direct conversion has the highest risk of failure because the old method disappears at conversion; therefore, when an alternative is present, it is usually recommended. Incremental conversion type selected is determined by the context of the application.

Reports are designed following the same general guidelines as those of screens. Whenever a report is of displayed information, both screen and report should use the same format.

User documentation is an important introduction to an application for many new employees. As such, it should be easy to read, oriented toward the education and computer experience level of the reader, and should include all information for normal and abnormal processing of an application. Lists of contacts for different types of problems should be identified.

SUMMARY

In this chapter, human interface, conversion, and user documentation were discussed as three required activities during analysis and design that are omitted from many methodology discussions.

Human interface design focuses on screen interactions between users and the application. Using a task profile and user profile to guide the design process, first the option selection method is chosen. The alternatives for option selection are menus, windows, or command languages. Then, the presentation format(s) most effective for the data to be displayed are decided. Presentation formats include analog, digital, text, text form, bar chart, column chart, point plot, pattern, and mimic displays. Within

REFERENCES

Bailey, R. W., *Human Performance Engineering: Using Human Factors/Ergonomics to Achieve Computer System Usability*, 2nd ed. Englewood Cliffs, NJ: Prentice-Hall, 1989.

Banks, William W., Jr., and Jon Weimer, *Effective Computer Display Design*. Englewood Cliffs, NJ: Prentice-Hall, 1992.

Carter, R. C., "Visual search with color," *Journal of Experimental Psychology: Human Perception and Performance*, Vol. 8, 1982, pp. 127–136.

Christ, R. E., "Review and analysis of color coding research for visual displays," *Human Factors*, Vol. 17, 1975, pp. 542–570.

Cohen, Barbara F. G. (ed.), *Human Aspects in Office Automation*. New York: Elsevier, 1984.

Galitz, Wilbert O., *Human Factors in Office Automation*. Atlanta, GA: Life Office Management Association, Inc., 1980.

---

5 Focus is a product of Information Builders, Inc., New York.

TABLE 14-11 *Automated Support for Interface Design, Conversion, and On-Line Documentation*

Product	Company	Technique
APS Dev. Center	Sage SW Rockville, MD	Screen/Form/Report Painters
Deft	Deft Ontario, Canada	Form/Report Painter
Easytrieve	Ribek, Inc. Tacoma Park, MD	Data Conversion Utility
Focus	Information Builders, Inc. New York, NY	Prototyper Screen Generator Application Generator
Foundation	Arthur Anderson & Co. Chicago, IL	Prototype Generation Screen Design Version Control
IEF	Texas Instruments Dallas, TX	Dialog Flow Screen Design
IEW, ADW(PS/2 Version)	Knowledgeware Atlanta, GA	Screen Design
PacBase	CGI Systems, Inc. Pearl River, NY	Screen Flow
Teamwork	Cadre Technologies Inc Providence, RI	Screen Painter
Telon and other products	Pansophic Systems, Inc. Lisle, IL	Screen/Report Layout
Visible Analyst	Visible Systems Corp. Newton, MA	Screen Painter/Prototyper

Galitz, Wilbert O., *Handbook of Screen Format Design.* Wellesley, MA: QED Information Sciences, Inc., 1981.

Martin, James, *Design of Man-Computer Dialogues.* Englewood Cliffs, NJ: Prentice-Hall, 1973.

Mayhew, D. J., *Principles and Guidelines in Software User Interface Design.* Englewood Cliffs, NJ: Prentice-Hall, 1992.

Morland, D. Verne, "Human factors guidelines for terminal interface design," *Communications of the ACM*, Vol. 26, #7, July 1983, pp. 484–494.

Powell, James E., *Designing User Interfaces.* San Marcos, CA: Microtrend Books, 1990.

Olsen, Dan R., Jr., *User Interface Management Systems: Models and Algorithms.* San Mateo, CA: Morgan Kaufmann Publishers, 1992.

Schneiderman, Ben J., *Designing the User Interface: Strategies for Effective Human-Computer Interaction.* Reading, MA: Addison-Wesley, 1987.

Thomas, John C., "User interface design," *Proceedings of NYU Symposium on Human Factors*, New York, NY, May 1982.

Tullis, T. S., "Screen design," *Handbook of Human Computer Interaction*, Mark Helander (ed.). New York: Elsevier, 1988, pp. 377–411.

KEY TERMS

analog display	menu
band chart	mimic display
bar chart	normal/abnormal measures
binary	on-the-job training (OJT)
binary display	option selection
body of form	overlapping windows
body of screen	parallel conversion
classroom instruction	parallel execution
close box	pattern display
column chart	paint
command language	point
computer-based training	point plot
(CBT)	pointer
derived field	precision requirements
digital display	question & answer format
direct cutover	resize box
direct manipulation	scale
direction indicator	screen painter
field format	scroll arrow
flash rate	scroll bar
flicker fusion	scroll box
footer screen section	scrolling elements
form screen	short-term memory
functional conversion	status indicator
geographical conversion	task profile
gradual cutover	text
header screen section	tiled windows
horizontal pull-down menu	title bar
incremental cutover	transaction conversion
incremental software	user profile
development	vertical pop-up menu
location ID	window
long-term memory	zoom box
Lotus-style horizontal	
pop-up menu	

EXERCISES

1. Complete the screen design for *Customer* and *Video* data entry for ABC Video. For video data entry, keep in mind how conversion defines the add function to automatically provide for *Copy* relation creation. Specifically, identify reused portions of screens or whole screens for different functions. Discuss why complete reuse of *Create Video* screens is not possible for *Video Update* processing.

2. For the CCD Medicaid case described in Appendix A, design windowed menus for the application. Design the screen for Patient Information Creation. How much scrolling is necessary? What colors, type, style, font, and so forth, do you recommend for each field?

STUDY QUESTIONS

1. Define the following terms:

analog display	OJT
field format	scrolling elements
flash rate	user profile
form	task profile
horizontal pull-down	
menu	

2. Why is the data source the best location at which data should be entered into automated applications?

3. Why should screen design guidelines be followed?

4. Describe a task profile and how it is used in the application development screen design and conversion.

5. When should individual users be profiled and when can average user information be used?

6. Describe how novice/expert modes of operation should be determined.

7. Describe how extent and type of on-line messages and help are defined.

8. Describe the option selection choices and how you decide which to use.

9. Why is command language use by itself rare?

10. What is a screen window and why are they popular?

11. How many scrolling options are available? What is the minimum scrolling that should be provided in an application?

12. What are the differences between tiled and overlapped windows?

13. Why should function keys be consistent?

14. Describe general screen design contents.
15. What is direct manipulation interface?
16. What application types use forms as the most common functional screen design?
17. List and define five data presentation alternatives. For each alternative, describe one possible business application use.
18. When are bar and column chart use recommended?
19. How are fields positioned on a screen? On a line?
20. Why are short-term memory (STM) and long-term memory (LTM) important in screen design?
21. When is color effective in screen design? How many colors should be used on screens at any one time?
22. How can type font be varied for effective screen design?
23. What are three options for incremental conversion? How do you choose which to use?

24. Discuss issues in data conversion.
25. Why should users do user documentation? Why should application developers do user documentation?
26. Discuss how contents of user documentation can be varied to match user skills and computer expertise.

★ EXTRA-CREDIT QUESTION

1. Define a poorly designed menu and functional screens for ABC Customer Maintenance. Use at least 10 bad design elements. Then, fix the design problems and define effective screens for the same function. Describe the guidelines followed in defining each element of the good screens. Write a paragraph discussing the kind of errors that users might make from using the poorly designed screens.

IMPLEMENTATION AND MAINTENANCE

The five chapters in this section discuss implementation and maintenance issues. An application is never completed until it is retired. After analysis and design, we must be able to implement the design on computer hardware using computer software or our work is useless. The first three chapters in this section relate to implementation issues: selecting a computer language; evaluating and selecting hardware, software packages, or consulting services; and testing/quality assurance of the finished product.

Chapter 15 defines characteristics of languages, to allow us to distinguish between ten languages that are evaluated. Then, the languages are matched to the application types discussed in Chapter 1 and to the methodologies discussed in Chapters 7–12. Language selection, rather than code structure, is emphasized because of the increased use of computer-aided software engineering (CASE) tools to

generate code. The language selected must be able to support the application requirements. In Chapter 15, we first describe identifying characteristics of languages. Then, the implementation of each characteristic is described for ten languages. Based on the language characteristics, we define the types of applications for which each language is best suited.

Similarly, outsourcing and use of software packages are growing in all industries because it is frequently cheaper to *buy* rather than *build* an application and/or its environment. In Chapter 16, we discuss the evaluation process and highlight the types and alternatives for soliciting bids from vendors. Sections and contents of a request for proposal (RFP) are defined and developed for the ABC case to show what they look like. Hardware, software, and consulting services might all be contracted for in the same request, or could individually be the subject of RFPs. Examples of RFP expectation criteria for each type of work are provided to give a sense of the level of detail to which work is defined in an RFP. Then, vendor proposal evaluation alternatives are defined and discussed in relation to ABC Video's application.

Regardless of the development product—packaged software, generated CASE code, or manually programmed code—proving that the software works by testing it at various levels of detail and aggregation is required. Chapter 17 defines the different strategies for testing and types of testing performed. Test types are matched to strategies to develop an effective overall strategy for testing applications. For each level of testing, key issues in test case development are identified. Based on research on testing errors found, guidelines for deciding when to stop testing at each level are provided. The ABC case is then analyzed to demonstrate how the theories apply in practice.

The last two chapters relate to change. Chapter 18 discusses application change management that all take place throughout the life of a project. Change is a way of life in computing and application development is no exception. In Chapter 18, we first discuss how to design for reusability by using templates and reusable modules. Then, change management techniques that apply to documents, decisions, software, and application configurations are presented. The automated tools section includes software representative of each type of change management.

Documentation for project work can be thousands of pages long. Since errors in code usually begin to be traced through documentation, it is important to identify changes to facilitate the error tracing process. Also, users and maintenance personnel who might only infrequently review documentation should be directed to the new information rather than having to read entire documents each time. The techniques for identifying change easily are identified in Chapter 18.

Similarly, application decisions might provide a useful trace of the considerations and discarded ideas throughout a project's life. Few project teams keep such a decision trace because, historically, to do so meant maintenance of more thousands of pages of paper. With automated decision support and sophisticated word processing, keeping a record of decision history is now feasible and can be useful in organizations with rapidly changing management or on projects that support business functions that are subject to rapid industry change.

Software changes and application configuration management are the other major topics of Chapter 18. A recent buzzword identifies *software reengineering*, also called *reverse engineering*, as the backward design of undocumented programs and applications that were probably built without the team having followed a methodology to guide the work. Also called *spaghetti code*, such applications can be maintained beyond a useful life. In the chapter, we describe how to decide when to reverse engineer, reengineer, or retire applications and/or individual programs. Once the decision is made to maintain software, management of the software maintenance process is an important task in determining that the correct configuration of modules, functions, programs, and so on, is in production. The issue of configuration management is more complicated when multiple versions of software, such as a DOS and MVS versions, exist. Techniques and management practices for configuration management are described in the chapter.

Finally, your career is important and requires management by you for your working life. It is difficult to plan a career without having a sense of what opportunities and expectations are available. First, the typical job levels and types of jobs found in busi-

nesses are described. Then, one way to plan a career by thinking through your wants and requirements for technical, job, company, geography, and opportunities for advancement is developed. A method for defining your chances of job success is defined next. Trends of IS jobs over the last five years by geography, salary, and industry are discussed. Part of developing yourself into a professional and having a career is to maintain your professional status. Techniques for maintaining professional status and building on knowledge areas including education, professional association membership, accreditation, and reading are all defined, with suggested approaches to applying the information to your own situation.

CHOOSING AN IMPLEMENTATION LANGUAGE

INTRODUCTION

In this chapter, we discuss the selection of a language for implementing an application. **Programming** is the process of designing and describing an algorithm to solve a class of problems. As any programmer knows, any activity *can* be programmed in *any* language . . . just not necessarily as effectively or completely in each language. When working on an application, we do not always have a choice of the language we use. But with the selection of the wrong language, we constantly compromise the requirements to fit the constraints of the language. In this chapter, we discuss characteristics of languages and how to select a programming language based on requirements of an application so that, if there is a choice to be made, an appropriate language can be selected. The activity of programming is not discussed in this text because, with CASE environments and tools, much program code is automatically generated.

First, the characteristics of languages are defined. Then 10 computer languages—SQL, Focus, BASIC, COBOL, Fortran, C, Pascal, Ada, PROLOG, and Smalltalk—are evaluated according to the characteristics. These languages represent the major programming paradigms, including procedural (Fortran, COBOL, BASIC, Pascal), object orientation (Smalltalk, Ada), declarative processing (SQL,

PROLOG), fourth-generation languages (4GL, Focus), and expert systems (PROLOG). They also represent the most popular languages in use in business organizations today and in the years to come. Then, languages are matched to different types of applications and methodologies. Finally, automated support for programming is discussed. First, we develop the characteristics that distinguish between languages.

CHARACTERISTICS OF LANGUAGES

To differentiate languages, we must evaluate how each language deals with data definition and processing, mathematical and logical processing, control, conditional, array, input/output, and subprogram processing in addition to nontechnical assessment of each language's ease of use, portability, and maintainability. Finally, available automated development aids such as CASE and code generators are noted.

Data Types

Each language supports some data types. A **data type** is a language-fixed definition of data. All languages support variables and constants for numeric

Data Type	Example
Integers	1, 2, 3
Real	−1.01, 3.21
Character/String	Abc12;'.

FIGURE 15-1   Examples of Universal Data Types

and character data. The universally supported data types are integers, real numbers, and character strings. Example of each are shown in Figure 15-1. **Integers** are whole numbers such as one, two, or three. **Real numbers** include positive and negative continuous numbers, including all decimals. **Character strings** are any legal combination of alphanumeric characters.

Fewer languages support one or more of logical, Boolean, pointer, object, bit, date, or user-defined data types. **Logical data types** are notation providing for nonnumeric comparison including *and*, *or*, or *not* processing (see Figure 15-2 for example). Also, the comparison operators used in logical data

Data Type	Example
Logical	And, Or, Not, <, >, =, ≤, ≥, ≠
Boolean	True, False
Pointers	16F26 (where 16F26 is a valid memory address)
Object	Customer=12346, Add, Change, Delete, Inquire
Bit	0, 1
Date	02 28 93

FIGURE 15-2   Examples of Nonuniversal Data Types

types include all variations of equality and inequality operators (see Figure 15-2).

Boolean operators generate binary true/false indicators based on some logical comparison (see Figure 15-2). **Pointers** are addresses of other program or data constructs that are used for reference within a program.

Objects are programmed encapsulations of data with methods. The example in Figure 15-2 shows only the names and ID of an object with the names of the methods or program modules that can manipulate the data. In actuality, an object contains all of the data and all of the program code for the methods.

A **bit** is an individual binary digit (see Figure 15-2). Bit manipulation is highly desirable in programs using binary status indicators. In an eight-bit character set, use of one bit rather than eight to indicate a single value can save millions of characters of storage space.

Date data types define combinations of months, days, and years that support only legal date entries (see Figure 15-2). Rather than writing routines to validate dates, the language may have built-in validation processing.

Finally, **user-defined** data types are data definitions that become fixed within a program or application. User-defined data types can be for any application-specific combination of legal characters. A common user-defined data type is for a date construct when the language does not provide a date data type.

Data Type Checking

Data type checking refers to the extent to which a language enforces matching of specific data definitions in mathematical and logical operations. There are four levels of type checking, ranging from typeless to strong checking. Which level is required is dependent on the application type. In general, the more stringent the requirements for accuracy and consistency of processing, the more desirable strong type checking becomes. With object methodologies, strong checking is desirable because with polymorphism, the ability to have multiple modules processing the same function but on different data types,

```
01   COBOL-INFO.

     05    EXAMPLE-NUMBER      PIC 9(5).

01   TARGET-INFO.

     05    TARGET-NUMBER       PIC 9(5).

     ....

PROCEDURE DIVISION.

     Move 'A124X" to COBOL-INFO. *** Causes no
        errors ***

     Move COBOL-INFO to TARGET-INFO.
        *** Causes no errors ***

     Move EXAMPLE-NUMBER to TARGET-
        NUMBER. *** Abend—Illegal data in
        EXAMPLE-NUMBER ***
```

FIGURE 15-3   Cobol Typeless Checking

the probability of errors is reduced with strong type checking.

Typeless checking means that there is no explicit checking performed. In typeless languages, such as BASIC or COBOL, alphanumeric characters are allowed in an integer field, but might cause an abend if the field is referenced as an integer (See Figure 15-3). Operations using typeless fields are not guaranteed to execute successfully. Typeless field processing is not consistent across languages or compilers.

The next level provides **automatic type coercion** in which mixed data types are allowed, but conversion of incompatible types occurs when used together. Also called **mixed mode type checking**, different data types within a category (e.g., numeric) are converted to a single target type for mixed mode operations. In Fortran, for instance, mixing a real and integer number in a mathematical operation leads to unpredictable results because the target type is determined by the result field definition (see Figure 15-4). If the result field is defined as real, the process will yield a real number. In Fortran, the first character of a field determines its data type. Names beginning with A–H and O–Z are real; names beginning with I–N are integer. In Figure 15-4a, the result field begins with B; therefore, the result field is

a real number. If the result field is defined as integer, the process rounds the answer and the result is integer. In the example in Figure 15-4b, the answer is either zero or one depending on the computer system and how it rounds integers. Obviously, without detailed knowledge of the internal language processing, programming errors can result.

Pseudostrong type checking, the third level of data type checking, permits operations only on data objects of the same data type when they are defined in the same module. But, unlike strong type checking languages, there are language inconsistencies, or *undocumented features*, that allow programmers to mix data types. Pascal is a pseudostrong type checking language in that it supports strong typing *within* modules, but has no type checking *across* modules. So, data passed from one module to another for processing may be combined in the called module with another data type with no penalty.

At the highest level of data type checking, languages with **strong type checking** permit operations only on data objects of the same, prespecified data type whether in the same or other modules. If a module contains an illegal data type, the application would stop processing and issue an error message. Ada provides strong type checking.

Language Constructs

Language constructs determine what and how operations on data are carried out. They provide for sequencing, iteration, selection, and data structure

---

a. The formula is: I/A = B
                     5/10.0 = 0.50

The data are converted to real because B is a real name.

b. The formula is: I/A = J
                     5/10.0 = 1.0 *or* 0.0

Data are converted to integer and rounded.
Results vary depending on the computer system.

FIGURE 15-4   Mixed-Mode Data Type Checking

processing, and differ for each language classified. In general, the richer the language, the more these constructs will be present. However, with the richness comes a trade-off in language complexity that forces users to learn more language details to become proficient.

The need for rich language constructs depends somewhat on the language paradigm. For instance, **SQL** is a declarative, set processing language that does not need iteration because iteration is embedded in the language. In a declarative language, you code *what* you want to do, not *how*. With *set* processing, you identify the database and the language controls all file manipulation. The more procedural the language, the richer the language constructs need to be. The more detailed the application, the richer the language of the application should be.

Sequencing occurs between and within commands. Between-command sequencing is controlled by you as the programmer who defines the order of commands. Intracommand sequencing is part of language definition and is called operator precedence. **Operator precedence** is the prioritizing of symbols to manipulate data. All languages have at least four arithmetic symbols in common: + for add, − for subtraction, * for multiplication, and / for division. Most languages also have many other symbols and operations supporting unary and binary operations including relational processing (e.g., "less than," "less than or equal," etc.), logical processing (e.g., "and," "or," or "not"). A list of operators available in different languages is provided in Figure 15-5.

Control language constructs support iteration, sequential or selection processing via loops, exits, conditional statements, or case constructs. **Loops** provide iterative, repetitive processing and are usually supported through structured programming notations such as "do while . . ." or "do until. . . ." **Conditional statements** support "if . . . then . . . else" processing. Conditional statements are used in some languages to control iterative loop processing. Common loop notations are shown in Figure 15-6.

Case statements allow identification of code segments that combine to identify the "case," for example, in Focus file maintenance processing you can code screen processing cases for add, change, and delete cases. This simplifies the thought pro-

Operator	Symbol
Add	+
Subtract	−
Multiply	*
Divide	/, ÷
Exponent	**, ∧
And	AND
Or	OR
Not	¬
Equal	=
Less	<
Greater	>
Less or equal	≤, =<, <=
Greater or equal	≥, =>, >=

FIGURE 15-5   Language Operators

cesses involved in programming by "chunking" case contents.

Exits leave the current code module and return to the calling module or to some other named module. Exits can be simple returns to the calling module, such as *Return*, *Cut*, or *Exit* statements (see Figure 15-7); exits can indicate the nature of the end as in PROLOG's *Fail* exit, or exits can return to a named module in a *Goto* statement.

Arrays, or **tables**, are a third type of language construct that may or may not be supported by a language. Linear arrays, or lists, are one type of data that are relatively simple to support (see Figure 15-8). When higher dimension arrays are supported, the maximum number of dimensions are identified. Occasionally a language will support *n*-dimensional arrays, with a user-defined maximum.

Next there are four possible alternatives for **physical input and output (I/O)** of information to and from automated files or data entry fields. First, specific I/O statements (e.g., read/write) for externally stored data may be one of three types: record-oriented, set-oriented, or array-oriented. **Record-oriented I/O** reads (or writes) a physical record of

BEGIN . . . END

BLOCK

DO . . . ENDDO

FOR . . .

FOR . . . END FOR

ifFalse . . .

ifTrue . . .

INDEX . . .

LOOP . . . ENDLOOP

REPEAT . . .END

REPEAT . . .

WHILE . . .

WHILE . . . ENDWHILE

whileFalse . . .

whileTrue . . .

FIGURE 15-6   Loop Notations

Linear Array, List

1

2

3

4

5

Two Dimensional Array of Months and Days

January	31
February	28
March	31
April	30

Three Dimensional Array of Sales By Year By Month

Year	Month	Sales
1996	January	220,000
1996	February	250,000

Year	Month	Sales
1995	January	150,000
1995	February	170,000

Year	Month	Sales
1994	January	100,000
1994	February	100,000

FIGURE 15-8   Types of Arrays

information that may contain one or more logical records. Recall from database class that records (or tuples in relational terminology) are groupings of related fields. Record-oriented I/O requires opening and closing of files, reading or writing of records, and user management of all file processing, such as checks for end-of-file. COBOL, Fortran, Assembler languages, and Ada are record-oriented.

Exit Type	Processing
Return	Return to Calling Module
Cut	Return to Calling Module/Instruction
Exit	Return to Calling Module
Fail	Go to Calling Module/Instruction with Boolean indicating process failure
Goto	Go to Named Module

FIGURE 15-7   Exit Types

Set-oriented I/O assumes that all *records* (or tuples) are treated the same and that some selection criteria, when applied, identify the desired information. The language controls all file and read/write processing according to user-defined selection criteria. At the end of a procedure, the set of records (tuples) resulting from the procedure are stored in memory for printing or display. SQL is set-oriented.

Implicit I/O is similar to set-oriented I/O. Implicit I/O is used in 4GLs in which reading and writing of data is hidden from the user. The user specifies the type of process, for instance, TABLE FILE . . . , and the language infers the type of file processing required from the command. Set-oriented I/O is more rigorously defined and has provably correct contents based on mathematical set theory which underlies relationship processing. Implicit I/O, on the other hand, is in languages which predate relational theory and do not have provably correct results.

Array-oriented I/O reads and writes strings of fields that are assumed to be some sort of array. The user is responsible for defining and manipulating the nature and data type of array. The language simply reads or writes until the end of the array. Pascal is an array-oriented language.

List-directed I/O is a variant of array-oriented I/O. **List-directed I/O** is used in Fortran to define a list of variable names to which items are *directed* as they are read. The language reads until the list is full, then continues processing until the read is again executed. Data items are not specifically formatted, rather the format is implicit in the variable names.

The extent to which data formats and I/O processing can be defined and controlled distinguishes languages as I/O-oriented versus CPU-oriented in their processing. The more elaborate the I/O processing, the more I/O-oriented the language. The more primitive the I/O processing, the more CPU-oriented the language. Fortran is an example of a CPU-oriented language, while COBOL is an example of an I/O-oriented language.

Modularization and Memory Management

The extent to which modularization and memory management are supported is an indication of language sophistication. **Modularization** is the creation of subprograms or stored functions. Languages differ in the manner in which the subprogram and their data are supported. First, the ability to define subprograms or functions is important to attaining desirable program characteristics such as maximal cohesion. Not all languages allow subprograms. In particular, set-oriented languages (SQL) do not easily support subprograms.

Second, how data in modules is managed is important. Data can be local or global. **Local data** storage defines data variables and constants that are only used within a given module. **Global data** are accessible to any module in the application. The ability to have local data is important to attaining information hiding and minimal coupling. The extent to which global data is required limits the quality of resulting programs by limiting information hiding and cohesion.

Subprograms' activation is similar across languages. Called modules are referenced by module name. For instance, "CALL FACTORIAL, 5" might be a subprogram call that passes the value five for factorial computation. Modules must reside in a library that is linked to the calling module via control language (e.g., JCL). Options for call processing include passing of variable data either by name, by address, or directly, by value. Value passing requires local data definition while passing data by name or address is used with either local or global data.

Generally, when using subprograms, a main module calls the subprogram which performs its processing and returns to the calling module. The ability to support subprogram processing requires one or more entry and exit points. Exit and return processing are also important when passing control of processing between modules. In general, the more opportunities to enter and exit a given module, the more proficient the programmer needs to be to ensure proper processing. According to structured programming tenants, a well-designed module should have one entry and one exit point. Some languages, such as Smalltalk and Ada, enforce this idea by allowing only one entry and one exit per module. One entry–one exit modules are less error-prone than modules that allow many alternatives.

The next level of sophistication is the extent to which programmers have control over their own memory management. **Memory management** refers to the ability of a program to allocate more computer memory as required. This is an option frequently desired in variable list processing and real-time applications that manage multiuser resources. Memory in less sophisticated languages is **static**: The program is assigned a maximum at the time it is initiated for processing. If more memory than that allocated is needed, the program abends, more memory is requested manually via job control language, and the program is rerun.

With **dynamic memory management** capabilities, the program monitors its own use of storage and allocates more memory as needed. In sophisticated languages, the capability to dynamically allocate memory is present.

Exception Handling

Exception handling is the extent to which programs can be coded to intercept and handle program errors without abending a program. This capability adds to both the complexity and the range of usefulness of a language. This capability ranges from none to some. For instance, COBOL allows you to intercept data errors such as overflow or divide by zero, but not others, such as invalid data definition or read past end-of-file. In contrast, Smalltalk allows the interception of any error.

Multiuser Support

The extent to which language constructs for memory management, global/local variables, and subprogram management are available, determines the extent to which a language can support multiple users. There are three levels of support for multiple users that relate to program modules having the properties of reusability, recursion, and reentrancy. **Reusability**, also called serial reusability, is a property of a module such that many tasks, in sequence, can use the module without its having to be reloaded into memory for each use (see Figure 15-9). To accomplish this level of program, any changes to local variables must be reset to their original contents before the completion of processing and return to the calling module. The easiest way to develop reusable programs is to provide global variables that can change contents and local variables that either cannot change or are always reset after the module's use. Reusable programs can support sequential or interactive processing, but not multiuser or real-time processing.

Recursiveness is a property of modules such that they call themselves or call another module that, in turn, calls them. An example is factorial multiplication in which the same process is performed on a different number of variables a number of times (see

Reusable Pseudo-code

```
Factorial (N, Nfact)
End=0
If N=0 or 1
        go to exit.
Loop.
        If N=1
                go to exit
        else
                Nfact = N * (N-1)
                N = N-1
                go to Loop.
Exit. Exit.
```

Recursive Pseudo-code

```
Function FACT (N)
Begin
        If N =0
                Then Factout = 1
        Else Factout = N * FACT(N-1)
End {Function Fact};
```

FACT is a function that recurs continuously until N = 0.

Reentrant Pseudo-code

```
Load N, Nfact, First-Exec
If N = (0 or 1) and First-Exec = 0
        Then Nfact = 1
Else
        If N > 1
                Nfact = N * (N-1)
                N = N-1
                First-Exec =1
                Save N, Nfact, First-Exec.
```

FIGURE 15-9   Examples of Reusable, Recursive, and Reentrant Modules

Figure 15-9). Processing with recursion is explicitly outlawed in some languages, while it is considered a main strength of others, such as PROLOG. Recursion requires serial reusability of programs in addition to the ability to maintain a queue (or stack) of outstanding requests to be completed. This queueing support provides for multiple uses of the module by one user.

Reentrancy is a property of a module such that it can be shared by several tasks concurrently. There is a constant part and a variable part to each reentrant module. The constant part is loaded into memory once and it services tasks in a serially reusable manner until it is overwritten by another program. A copy of the variable part is activated for each task when it is initiated (see Figure 15-9). A queueing mechanism keeps track of the user's identification, the location of the variable part, program status word, and register contents for the task. This information is swapped into (or out of) the active area as the user becomes activated (or interrupted). Only one task is active at a time, but several tasks might be in various stages of task completion. Only the property of reentrancy allows true real-time processing and support for multiple concurrent users. Both serial reusability and recursiveness are required to achieve reentrancy in programs.

To summarize, programming languages differ in the extent to which they support alternatives for defining data types, input/output processing, mathematical, relational, logical, bit, control, array, subprogram, and memory processing. The less extensive the language constructs supported, the simpler the language, but the more restricted the domain of problems to which it is amenable. The more extensive the language constructs supported, the more complex the language, and the more extensive the domain of problems to which it is appropriate.

Nontechnical Language Characteristics

Nontechnical characteristics are at least as important as technical characteristics when selecting a language. The nontechnical characteristics evaluated here are uniformity, ambiguity, compactness, locality, linearity, ease of design to code translation, compiler efficiency, and portability. The availability of CASE tools, availability of code generators, and availability of testing aids also add to a language's attractiveness, and are discussed in a later section.

Uniformity is the use of consistent notation throughout the language. An example of nonuniformity in Focus is the use of single quotes for cus-

tomized report column titles and the use of double quotes for customized report page titles. This type of inconsistency hinders the learning of the language and almost guarantees that novices and infrequent users will make mistakes.

Ambiguity of a language refers to the extent to which humans and compilers will differ in their interpretation of a language statement. Ideally, humans' thinking should be identical to compiler interpretation, *and* that compiler interpretation should be intuitive to humans. Unfortunately, ambiguity may be inherent to some problems, such as artificial intelligence applications which reason through a process. As new rules and inferences are added to an AI application, interpretation of existing data and rules might also change, thus introducing ambiguity into a previously unambiguous application.

Compactness of a language is its brevity. The presence of structured program constructs, keywords and abbreviations, data defaults, and built-in functions all simplify learning and programming. Contrast SQL or Focus, both fourth-generation languages, with COBOL, a third-generation language. A report that takes three to five lines in 4GL procedure code requires 50–150 lines of COBOL code (see Figure 15-10). That learning time is considerably shorter for Focus than COBOL, partly due to the compactness of the language.

In turn, compactness implies **locality** in providing natural "chunks" of code that facilitate learning, mental visualization of problem parts, and simulation of solutions. Locality is provided through block, case, or other similar chunking mechanisms in languages. Chunks might be implemented via a performed section of code in COBOL, a case construct in Focus, or an object definition in Smalltalk. In all three of these examples, a user's attention is focused only on the chunk of the code present. By being able to ignore other parts of the code, learning of the chunk is simplified.

Linearity refers to the extent to which code is read sequentially. The more linear a language, the easier it is to mentally "chunk" and understand the code. Linearity facilitates understanding and maintainability. In Figure 15-10, the COBOL code chunks in paragraphs and performed sections; these

```
4GL—Focus
      TABLE FILE SALES
      HEADING CENTER 'SAMPLE SALES REPORT'
      SUM SALES
              BY REGION
              ACROSS MONTH
              BY YEAR
      ON YEAR SUMMARIZE
      ON YEAR PAGE-BREAK
      END


3GL—COBOL
...
      WORKING-STORAGE SECTION.
      01 CONTROL-TOTALS.
              05      LINE-COUNT          PIC 99          VALUE 55.
              05      END-OF-FILE         PIC 9           VALUE ZERO.
                      88      EOF                                     VALUE 1.
              05      CURRENT-REGION PIC 99 VALUE ZERO.
              05      SUM-SALES.
                      10      JAN-SUM     PIC 9(5)        VALUE ZEROS.
                      10      FEB-SUM     PIC 9(5)        VALUE ZEROS.
                      10      MAR-SUM     PIC 9(5)        VALUE ZEROS.
                      10      APR-SUM     PIC 9(5)        VALUE ZEROS.
                      10      MAY-SUM     PIC 9(5)        VALUE ZEROS.
                      10      JUN-SUM     PIC 9(5)        VALUE ZEROS.
                      10      JUL-SUM     PIC 9(5)        VALUE ZEROS.
                      10      AUG-SUM     PIC 9(5)        VALUE ZEROS.
                      10      SEP-SUM     PIC 9(5)        VALUE ZEROS.
                      10      OCT-SUM     PIC 9(5)        VALUE ZEROS.
                      10      NOV-SUM     PIC 9(5)        VALUE ZEROS.
                      10      DEC-SUM     PIC 9(5)        VALUE ZEROS.
      01      REPORT-HEADER.
              05      FILLER              PIC X(48)       VALUE SPACES.
              05      HD1                 PIC X(19)       VALUE
                      'SAMPLE SALES REPORT'.
      01      COL-HEADER1.
              05      FILLER              PIC X(132)      VALUE
                      'REGION      MONTH'.
      01      COL-HEADER 2.
              05      FILLER              PIC X(132)      VALUE
              '    JAN   FEB   MAR   APR   MAY
              JUNE   JULY  AUG   SEPT  OCT   NOV   DEC'.
      01      REPORT-DETAIL.
              05      FILLER              PIC XXX         VALUE SPACES.
              05      REGION              PIC XX          VALUE SPACES.
              05      FILLER              PIC X(10)       VALUE SPACES.
              05      SALES               PIC X(84)       VALUE ZEROS.
```

FIGURE 15-10   4GL versus 3GL Language Compactness

```
        05        SALES-NUMERICS REDEFINES SALES.
            10      JAN-SALES              PIC ZZZ,ZZZ      VALUE ZEROS.
            10      FEB-SALES              PIC ZZZ,ZZZ      VALUE ZEROS.
            10      MAR-SALES              PIC ZZZ,ZZZ      VALUE ZEROS.
            10      APR-SALES              PIC ZZZ,ZZZ      VALUE ZEROS.
            10      MAY-SALES              PIC ZZZ,ZZZ      VALUE ZEROS.
            10      JUN-SALES              PIC ZZZ,ZZZ      VALUE ZEROS.
            10      JUL-SALES              PIC ZZZ,ZZZ      VALUE ZEROS.
            10      AUG-SALES              PIC ZZZ,ZZZ      VALUE ZEROS.
            10      SEPT-SALES             PIC ZZZ,ZZZ      VALUE ZEROS.
            10      OCT-SALES              PIC ZZZ,ZZZ      VALUE ZEROS.
            10      NOV-SALES              PIC ZZZ,ZZZ      VALUE ZEROS.
            10      DEC-SALES              PIC ZZZ,ZZZ      VALUE ZEROS.
        ...
PROCEDURE DIVISION.
...


PERFORM SUMMARY-CONTROL THRU PRINT-REPORT-EXIT.
...



SUMMARY-CONTROL.
        IF REGION = CURRENT-REGION
                GO TO PAGE-CONTROL
        ELSE
                MOVE SUM-SALES TO SALES-NUMERICS
                MOVE YEAR TO REGION
                WRITE REPORT-DETAIL AFTER 3.
                ADD 3 TO LINE-COUNT.
PAGE-CONTROL.
        IF LINE-COUNT > 50 OR REGION NOT = CURRENT-REGION
                WRITE REPORT-HEADER AFTER PAGE
                WRITE COL-HEADER1 AFTER 2
                WRITE COL-HEADER2 AFTER 1
                MOVE 4 TO LINE-COUNT.
        MOVE REGION TO CURRENT-REGION.
PRINT-REPORT.
        MOVE CORRESPONDING INPUT-SALES-SUMMARY TO REPORT-DETAIL.
        WRITE REPORT-DETAIL AFTER 1.
        ADD 1 TO LINE-COUNT.
PRINT-REPORT-EXIT.
        EXIT.
```

FIGURE 15-10   4GL versus 3GL Language Compactness (*Continued*)

language features facilitate COBOL program understandability.

The ease with which program specifications are **translated** into code is also important in language selection. In general, more declarative languages, such as SQL, are considered easier to code than more procedural languages such as Fortran. However, PROLOG and other inferential languages, while declarative and simple in developing single rules, are *not* simple when trying to determine whether the rules aggregate to the proper knowledge structures.

Compiler efficiency is the extent to which a compiled language generates efficient assembler code. Compiler efficiency varies by vendor and by language. Compiled code efficiency is important especially when programming for small computer systems or for embedded applications that interact with other system components as part of a larger system.

Along with efficiency of executable code, portability of code is important. **Portability** is the ability to transplant the code without change to a different operating platform that might include hardware, different operating system, or different software environment. A hardware platform may be a single-user personal computer, a workstation, or a mainframe. Each of these might run the same operating system, for example Unix, or might use a different operating system. The more code that must be changed to accommodate a specific hardware or operating environment, the less portable the language. As global and distributed applications become more prevalent, the need for language portability will increase. Ideally, programs should be able to be developed anywhere for execution on any hardware or operating system platform.

In summary, when technical characteristics do not distinguish languages for application use, nontechnical characteristics of languages become important to their selection. The nontechnical characteristics evaluated here include uniformity, ambiguity, compactness, locality, linearity, ease of code development, compiler efficiency, portability, and availability of automated development tools. In the next section, we discuss ten popular programming languages and the extent to which they contain the language constructs above. Then we discuss application characteristics and how they map to the languages.

COMPARISON OF LANGUAGES

Ten languages are evaluated in this section to highlight the differences across paradigms and language generations for all of the characteristics defined above. The ten languages selected were chosen because of their current and expected future popularity either in academic circles (e.g., Pascal) or in industry. The languages include SQL, COBOL, Fortran, BASIC, Focus, C, Pascal, PROLOG, Ada, and Smalltalk. Each language is discussed briefly below to highlight the characteristics that make it popular and unique. Table 15-1 summarizes the 10 languages on all of the characteristics described above.

SQL

As the American National Standards Institute's standard for database query language, SQL has enjoyed a successful life. **SQL** pervades any database course taught in North America and is a query language front-end to virtually every database package on the market regardless of machine size, number of users supported, or complexity of the database. SQL's virtues are mostly nontechnical: ease of learning, compactness, uniformity, locality, linearity, portability, and availability of automated tools (see Table 15-1). The simplicity of the language is evident in the small number of hours of learning time it takes novices to begin using the language. A novice might begin writing queries in literally minutes. Proficiency, of course, takes longer, but time to become proficient is shorter than most database languages.

Many CASE environments that support analysis and design also support logical database design through the process of normalization. Those products also generate SQL database definitions as the logical DB design output. Many of the same

(Text continues on page 656)

TABLE 15-1   Comparison of Languages

	SQL	Focus	BASIC	COBOL	Fortran
Data Types					
Real	Yes	Yes	Yes	Yes	Yes
Integer	Yes	Yes	Yes	Yes	Yes
Character	Yes	Yes	Yes	Yes	Yes
String	No	No	No	Yes	No
Boolean	No	No	No	No	No
Date	No	Yes	No	No	No
User-Defined	No	No	No	No	No
Pointer	No	No	No	No	No
Bit Identification	No	No	No	No	No
String-Mask	No	No	No	No	No
Data Type Checking					
Typeless			X	X	
Automatic type coercion	X				
Mixed mode		X			X
Pseudostrong					
Strong					
Operator Precedence	0^ */±	0^ */±	0^ */±	0^ */±	0^ */±
Binary and Unary Operators	Yes	Yes	Yes	Yes	Yes
Arithmetic +,−,*,/	Yes	Yes	Yes	Yes	Yes
Relational <,=,>,≤,≥	Yes	Yes	Yes	Yes	Yes
Logical and,or,not	Yes	Yes	Yes	Yes	Yes
Bit	No	No	No	No	No
Type Conversion	No	Yes, Limited	No	Yes, Limited and Inconsistent	Yes, Limited and Inconsistent
Control					
Loops	No	No	FOR ... NEXT	PERFORM ... UNTIL	FOR ... CONTINUE
Exits	No	EXIT, GOTO	EXIT, GOTO	EXIT	EXIT, GOTO
Conditional Statements	WHERE	IF ... ELSE	IF ...	IF ...THEN ... ELSE	IF ...
Case Statements	No	Yes (not in query language)	No	COBOL 88 only	No
Arrays					
Linear Arrays	No	No	Yes	Yes	Yes
Multiple Dimensions	No	No	Up to 2	Up to 3	Up to 3

(Table continues on next page)

TABLE 15-1   Comparison of Languages (*Continued*)

	SQL	Focus	BASIC	COBOL	Fortran
Input/Output					
I/O of Records	No	No	Yes	Yes	Yes
I/O of Arrays	No	No	No	No	Yes
Implicit I/O	Yes	Yes	No	No	No
Format Control	Automatic or Programmed	Automatic or Programmed	Programmed only	Programmed only	Programmed only
Data-directed I/O	No	No	No	No	Yes
Subprograms					
Subroutines	Nested	Yes	Yes	Yes	Yes
Functions	Limited	Yes	Limited	Limited	Limited
Local/Global Storage	No	Yes	Limited	Programmed only	Yes
Static/Dynamic Storage	No	No	No	No	No
Entry Points	No	Yes	Yes	Yes	One
Pass Parameters	No	Yes	Yes	Yes	Yes
Call by Address	No	No	No	No	No
Call by Value	No	No	No	No	No
Call by Name	No	Yes	Yes	Yes	Yes
Reusability	No	Yes	Yes	Yes	Yes
Reentrancy	No	No	No	No	No
Recursion	No	No	No	No	No
Concurrency	Only when used with DB2	Yes	No	No	No
Exception Handling	No	Limited	Limited	Limited	Limited
Nontechnical					
Uniformity	High	Medium-High	Medium	Medium	Medium
Ambiguity	Low-Medium	Low-Medium	Medium	Medium	Medium
Compactness	High	High	Medium-High	Low	Medium-High
Locality	High	High	Programmed only	Programmed only	Programmed only
Linearity	High	High	Low-Medium	Low-Medium	Low-Medium
Ease of design to code	High	High	Low-Medium	Low-Medium	Low-Medium
Compiler Efficiency	Yes, when used as embedded language; otherwise SQL is interpreted	Medium, Mostly Interpreted	Medium, Mostly Interpreted	Medium-High	Medium-High
Source code portability	High	High	Medium	High	High

TABLE 15-1   Comparison of Languages (*Continued*)

	SQL	Focus	BASIC	COBOL	Fortran
Nontechnical, cont.					
Availability of					
CASE tools	Yes	Yes	No	Yes	No
Code generators	Yes	No	No	Yes	No
Testing aids	Yes	No	Yes	Yes	Yes
Maintainability	High	Medium-High	Low-Medium	Low-High	Low-Medium

	C	Pascal	PROLOG	Ada	Smalltalk
Data Types					
Real	Yes	Yes	Yes	Yes	Yes
Integer	Yes	Yes	Yes	Yes	Yes
Character	Yes	Yes	Yes	Yes	Yes
String	Yes	Yes, Limited	Yes	Yes	Yes
Boolean	No, but can be user defined	Yes	No	Yes	Yes
Date	No	No	No	No	No
User-Defined	Yes	Yes	No	Yes	Yes
Pointer	Yes	No	No	Yes	Yes
Bit Identification	Yes	No	No	Yes	Yes
String-Mask	No	Limited	Yes	No	No
Data Type Checking					
Typeless	X				
Automatic					
Mixed mode			X		
Pseudostrong		X			
Strong			TurboProlog	X	X
Operator Precedence	( ) [ ] –> + – (unary) ++ –– ! ~ * & size of (type) * / % + – << >> <= >= != == & ^ && || ?: = op=,	not */ div mod + and – or =<> < <= > >= <in |	( ) + – unary mod div * / + – binary relational operators	** not abs * / mod rem + – unary + – & binary relational logical short-circuit	unary binary keyword
	No exponent operator	No exponent operator	No exponent operator	No exponent operator	
Operators					
Binary and Unary	Yes	Yes	Yes	Yes	Yes

(Table continues on next page)

TABLE 15-1 Comparison of Languages (*Continued*)

	C	Pascal	PROLOG	Ada	Smalltalk
Operators, cont.					
Arithmetic +,−,*,/	Yes, also % for modulus	Yes	Yes	Yes	Yes
Relational <,=,>,≤,≥	Yes	Yes	Yes	Yes	Yes
Logical and,or,not	Yes	Yes	Yes	Yes	Yes
Bit	Yes	No	No	Yes	Yes
Type Conversion	No	No	No	No	No
Loops	DO	WHILE . . . FOR . . . REPEAT . . . END	Simulated via REPEAT . . . WHILE . . . INDEX . . .	BEGIN . . . END WHILE . . . FOR . . . BLOCK LOOP . . . END LOOP	ifTrue ifFalse whileTrue while False
Exits	RETURN	RETURN GOTO	FAIL CUT RETURN	EXIT GOTO	
Conditional Statements	IF . . . ELSE	IF THEN BEGIN . . . END . . . ELSE . . .;	None	IF . . .THEN . . . ELSE ELSEIF CASE	ifTrue ifFalse whileTrue whileFalse
Arrays					
Linear Arrays	Yes	Yes	Only as LIST	Yes	Yes
Higher Dimensional Arrays	No limit to number of dimensions	No limit to number of dimensions, Some dynamic allocation support	No	No limit to number of dimensions, Dynamic allocation support	No
Input/Output					
I/O Statements	Only using defined function	No	TurboProlog, else No	Yes	Yes
I/O of Arrays	Only using defined function	Yes	No	No	No
Implicit I/O	Only using defined function	No	TurboProlog, else No	No	No
Format Control	Only using defined function	Limited	Yes	Yes	Yes
Data-directed I/O	No	No	No	No	No

TABLE 15-1   Comparison of Languages (*Continued*)

	C	Pascal	PROLOG	Ada	Smalltalk
Subprograms					
Subprograms	Yes	Yes	TurboProlog, else No	Yes	Yes
Functions	Yes	Yes		Yes	Yes
Local/Global Storage	Both	Both	Both	Both	Both
Static/Dynamic Storage	Both	No control	Both	Both	Both
Entry Points	One per function	One per routine	One per program	One per routine	One per object
Parameters					
Call by Address	Yes	No	No	Yes	No
Call by Value	No	Yes	No	Yes	No
Call by Name	Yes	Yes	Clause name as subgoal	Yes	Yes
Reusability	Yes	Yes	Yes	Yes	Yes
Recursion	Yes	Yes	Yes	Yes	Yes
Reentrancy	No	Yes	No	Yes	Yes
Concurrency	No, unless C++	Concurrent Pascal only	Depends on version	Yes	Yes
Exception Handling	Yes	No	Yes	Yes	Yes
Nontechnical					
Uniformity	Low-High	Medium-High	Medium-High	Medium-High	Medium-High
Ambiguity	Low-Medium	Low-Medium	Medium-High	Low-Medium	Low-Medium
Compactness	Low-High	Medium-High	Low-High	Low-High	Low-High
Locality	Low-High	Low-High	Low-Medium	Low-High	Low-High
Linearity	Low-High	Low-High	Low-High	Low-High	Low-High
Ease of design to code	Medium-High	Medium-High	Medium	Medium-High	Medium-High
Compiler Efficiency	High	High	Usually interpreted	Medium-High	High
Source code portability	High	Medium-High	Low	Medium-High	Low
Availability of CASE tools	No	In academia, yes	No	Yes	Yes
Code generators	No	No	No	No	No
Testing Aids	Yes	Yes	No	Yes	Yes
Maintainability	Low-High	Low-High	Low-High	Medium-High	Medium-High

products also provide code generation of Cobol with embedded SQL providing DB access. Examples of CASE products are ADW™ and IEF™. These products have their own code generators and can interface to code generation software.

In terms of technical capabilities, SQL is limited. It is assumed that complex programming is done in some other language with SQL embedded as described above. SQL can define and modify databases, perform simple mathematical processing on fields for reporting, and generate default or customized reports.

Focus

As a fourth-generation language, **Focus** consists of a database engine with its own query language, SQL compatibility, a full-screen processor, and language subsets for graphical, statistical, file maintenance, and intelligent processing. Focus DB supports relational, hierarchic, and network files as well as providing an interface to many popular mainframe DBMSs, such as IMS, IDMS, Adabas, Model 204, and so on.

Like SQL, Focus' main strengths lie in the nontechnical characteristics of the language: compactness, locality, linearity, ease of code translation, portability, and availability of CASE tools for documenting analysis and design (see Table 15-1). Occasionally, Focus can be ambiguous in interpreting handling of data across a hierarchy or in multiple joined files.

Focus is a full-function database language. This means that files can be defined, maintained, validated, modified by transaction processing, and queried all in the same environment and the same language regardless of the hardware/software platform. This high level of portability and full-function nature of the processing make Focus a popular 4GL for rapid application development and user query processing.

A reentrant version of Focus is available to support multiuser processing. Application code in Focus is not reentrant. A compiler is available for file modify routines; otherwise, Focus is interpreted. Focus is a language of defaults that does not support user-defined or user-managed resources.

BASIC

BASIC is short for *Beginner's All-purpose Symbolic Interchange Code*. BASIC is present in this evaluation because of the number of applications written in it regardless of whether it were appropriate or not. BASIC is, well, basic. Nothing fancy is supported in this language, but all rudimentary processing is present (see Table 15-1). BASIC is fairly easy to learn and write, with reasonable levels of uniformity, compactness, and good automated testing aids. The remaining characteristics vary considerably from one version of BASIC to another. In particular, its portability is low-medium since the I/O commands usually must change to suit a particular environment.

BASIC does standard programming operations, supporting a limited, but standard number of data types, with no type checking. There are language constructs for loop, condition, and array processing. Files can be read and written.

BASIC is popular because a whole generation of college graduates was subjected to it as the basis for learning programming. Provided an application does not require any nonstandard processing, BASIC can perform adequately.

COBOL

COBOL stands for *COmmon Business Oriented Language*. It is the most frequently used language in computer history and continues to maintain that status even though its demise is regularly reported as imminent. COBOL can be likened to a bus. Buses are uncomfortable, take longer than most other modes of transportation, but are suited to many types of trips. Similarly, COBOL is uncomfortable to code, it takes a long time to develop code, but it is suited to many business problems. As an all-purpose language, COBOL does most everything, and it is written in a language that is close to English.

COBOL input/output processing is consistently superior in efficiency and range of data structures supported (see Table 15-1). COBOL is not good for real-time applications and cannot be used to code reentrant or recursive structures. It is teamed with multiuser software, such as CICS for telecommunication interface processing or IMS DB/DC for telecommunication interface and database manipulation, to build effective interactive, multiuser applications.

In the nontechnical areas, COBOL rates high on availability of CASE tools, code generators, and testing aids. As the most frequently used language, it was first on the list of languages for which automated support was developed. It is a highly portable language and is supported by many efficient compilers. In the other nontechnical areas, COBOL rates less desirable than SQL and Focus, but is comparable to or better than other procedural languages.

Fortran

Shorthand for *FOR*mula *TRAN*slation, **Fortran** gained popularity as a *number-cruncher* language in the 1960s and has maintained a dwindling, but steady, popularity ever since. Fortran's weakness is in the data and file structures it supports (see Table 15-1). It does not interface to DBMS software and is limited to sequential, indexed, and direct files. Also, input/output processing of most Fortran compilers is slow, character operations are awkward and not recommended, and data format control is more limited than other languages.

Fortran's strength is in the efficiency of algorithms generated to perform numeric processing. Fortran's compilers usually are accompanied by a subprogram library that includes many frequently used algorithms for sort, statistical, and mathematical processing. Subroutine and subprogram processing is facilitated through easily defined and accessed global and local variables. The mixed mode data typing in Fortran is an important language feature because numeric processing will have different results depending on the definitions of the fields being processed.

Reusable programs can be developed using Fortran, but no one would use Fortran to develop a complete on-line, interactive system. Rather, Fortran routines for numeric processing might be embedded in a system developed in some other language.

C

C is a *high*-level language developed to perform *low*-level processing.[1] Its generality and lack of constraints coupled with autonomy of data structure definition and a rich set of operators make it an effective language for many tasks, including interactive, reusable, and recursive applications (see Table 15-1). A C program is a series of functions that are invoked by embedding their names in code. Transfer of control is automatic as is return processing. System operators, called *escape sequences*, are embedded in the program and recognized by a preceding backslash '\'.

C is a concise, cryptic language that can be efficient in the hands of an experienced, skilled programmer and can be a mess in the hands of a novice or poor programmer. "The language imposes virtually no rules regarding design or structure of programs and enforces nothing at all. This is not a dummy-proof programming language, and it certainly is not for beginners" [Friedman, 1991, p. 398]. As such, the nontechnical aspects of the language all range from low to high because the rating depends on the skill of the programmer. For expert programmers who understand how to build reusable modules, C language provides the capabilities to build reusable libraries with applications built from them.

Pascal

Pascal is a language designed to be unambiguous for teaching students of computer science.[2] Programs in Pascal are free-format, but the language contains natural structuring syntax that can be indented to make the language easily readable.

ConcurrentPascal provides for real-time control over processing. Other versions of Pascal support development of reusable and recursive programs and

---

1 C was developed at Bell Labs by Kernighan & Ritchie, 1978.

2 For instance, Cooper & Clancy, 1985, is a frequently used Pascal text.

subprograms (see Table 15-1). However, standard Pascal cannot use subroutine libraries since it assumes all program modules are *instream*, that is, embedded within the code of a single program. There is little control over interrupt processing in the language, so abends cannot be intercepted and redirected. I/O processing is more limited than some languages in not supporting random access files and in very limited string processing.

Pascal is similar to C on the nontechnical characteristics in that the readability, ambiguity, locality, and so forth of the language are dependent on the author using indentation and separation of statements to ensure these characteristics. But, unlike C, the language constructs of Pascal support readability once the indentation is done. Pascal requires less technical knowledge of hardware or operating systems to be efficient.

Because Pascal was developed as a teaching tool, automated programming support environments are available at least in academic settings.[3] These environments require the student to enter the construct desired; the software then displays a template of options for which the student fills in the blanks of the selected subconstructs. There are also many automated testing aids such as visual execution environments available to support Pascal program testing.

PROLOG

PROLOG is short for *PRO*gramming in *LOG*ic. PROLOG is the only strictly artificial intelligence language included in this group. PROLOG was developed at the University of Marseilles in the early 1970s with the most common version in the United States that of David H. D. Warren. PROLOG is a goal-oriented, declarative language with constructs for facts and rules. **PROLOG facts** are pieces of concrete, factual information. A fact might be: "A part of a widget is a *wid*." Another fact might be:

"A *wid* weighs 1.25 pounds." **PROLOG rules** define how facts are assembled to make information. An example of a rule might be: "If a widget is overweight, check the weight and tolerance of each component."

PROLOG goals are data that match some selection criteria, for example, the probable cause of a manufacturing problem specified in the query: What could cause finished widgets to be 3.2 pounds overweight? **Subgoals**, which would be subprograms in the terminology of the other languages, are determined from the goal. In the example above, widget components, their weight, weight allowances, and how each is used in widget manufacturing might all be subgoal information to be determined to answer the query. Goals are satisfied/answered by satisfying all subgoals. When a subgoal fails, an alternative for arriving at similar information is found via logical backtracking through the rules. The subgoal might remain unsatisfied, leading to a low level of confidence in the deduced answer.

Although the constructs for PROLOG are similar in many ways to those of declarative, procedural, and object languages, there are many significant differences in both data and program processes (see Table 15-1). Data are facts that are normally stored *in* the program rather than as separate files. This is a limitation in using PROLOG for general purpose business processing.

Program control is maintained through the ordering of clauses for execution and through the use of verbs like *fail*, which initiates backtracking by failing a subgoal, or *cut*, which prevents any more backtracking when a subgoal is fulfilled. Subprograms are simulated via *call/return* processing to clauses. Iteration is performed via recursive processing of rules.

How one rates PROLOG on the nontechnical aspects of the language depends on the size of the problem being automated. For small problems, the language can be compact, local, and linear. For large problems, the language can be highly ambiguous, noncompact, difficult to follow in a linear manner, and without local references to facilitate understanding. Ironically, PROLOG is viewed as a good language for novices with little exposure to procedural

---

3 Thomas Reps, MIT, developed a Pascal programming environment for Cornell as part of his dissertation [Reps, 1984].

languages. It is easy to learn if one can think in the goal-oriented manner of the language.

Smalltalk

Smalltalk was developed as both operating environment and language during the 1970s at the Xerox Palo Alto Research Center by the Learning Research Group. It is an object-oriented language that treats everything as an object, even for instance, integers. Smalltalk is highly customizable and can, therefore, be used to design efficient applications.

Many important object-oriented concepts are embodied in the language, including abstraction, encapsulation, and some class processing (see Chapters 11 and 12). Abstraction is the definition of identifying characteristics of an object. Encapsulation is the term used to describe the packaging of data and allowable processing on that data together. Objects communicate with each other only by message passing. An individual object is an instance of a class. Classes describe objects that share common data and processes but that also may have data and processes that differ. For instance, the class employee might have subclasses manager, professional, and clerk. All subclasses are also employees and share that data and processing as well as their own. In addition, an individual might be a member of professional and manager classes at the same time.

Smalltalk is a full-function, unconstrained programming language that can literally be used to do anything (see Table 15-1). The major weakness of Smalltalk is that it does not specifically support **persistent objects**, also known as files. But if the file is an object, then it, too, can be processed in Smalltalk.

The strength of Smalltalk is in its use for event-driven processing as in process control, heating system monitoring, or just-in-time notification of manufacturing needs. These types of applications use nonpersistent messages from the external environment to drive the processing done by the application; these applications do not necessarily need files for processing. Similarly, message processing support in Smalltalk assumes point/pick devices, such as a mouse, for interactive, nonpersistent communication with the application user. The only major caveat on Smalltalk use is that object orientation, and therefore object-oriented programming, requires a different kind of thinking than procedural language programming such as COBOL.

Ada

Ada, the official language of the U.S. Department of Defense, with a user population in the hundreds of thousands, has had more thought about its implementation than any other language. Ada was named after Ada, Countess of Lovelace, who originated the idea for stored programs to drive the use of computing devices.

Ada's design by committee has not resulted in a perfect language, but in one that is better than most. Current versions of Ada are object based rather than object oriented. In object-based applications, programs are cooperative collections of objects, each of which represents an instance of some object type. All object types are members of a hierarchy of types which are linked through processing rather than through inheritance relationships. Classes, rather than types, are not formally recognized; there are no persistent objects such as files, and inheritance is not supported (see Table 15-1).

Ada files, as in Smalltalk, are defined as a type within the constructs of the language and all processing is on the type. Also, there is no real message processing in Ada, at least as of 1992. Rather, the system is fooled through function calls and parameter passing to simulate message processing. Like Smalltalk, Ada's strength is its ability to support event-driven processing, like missile guidance in embedded defense-related systems.

Future versions of Ada are expected to adapt multiclass inheritance structures and processing, dynamic binding of objects, real message processing, and persistent objects that provide a variety of data structures. With these extensions, Ada is suitable for virtually any application. The same warning about the difference in object-oriented thinking expressed about Smalltalk is also appropriate here: Object-oriented design and program development is different in kind than procedural development of applications via languages such as COBOL.

PROGRAMMING LANGUAGE EVALUATION

Two ways of matching program languages are considered in this section. The first is to match the programming language to the application type (from Chapter 1). The second is to match the language to the methodology used for developing the application (from Chapters 7–13).

Language Matched to Application Type

Few heuristics have been available to guide programmers in matching a programming language to application type. The lack of heuristics is due mostly to the newness of most languages and their restricted use in academia (e.g., Pascal and PROLOG). Part of the reason for a lack of heuristics is also because most businesses have developed only transaction processing applications until the late 1980s; one or two languages were sufficient for most computing in the organization. With the development of query languages, AI applications and object orientation, more languages have proliferated and heuristics have slowly developed. Keep in mind that as experience with emerging paradigms, such as object orientation and intelligent applications grow, the heuristics will be refined and changed from those presented here. For each application type discussed in Chapter 1, the normally relevant characteristics and language choices are discussed below and summarized in Table 15-2.

Transaction processing applications are divided for classification into batch, on-line, and real-time as the predominant form of processing. For batch applications, COBOL and Focus are best suited (see Table 15-2). For on-line applications, all languages except Fortran and PROLOG might be used. Fortran is excepted because of its poor I/O processing; PROLOG is not recommended because data are usually embedded in the code, precluding most TPS processing. Language actually chosen should be based on the transaction volume, with high volume

TPS moving away from the SQL and 4GL languages toward compiled, full-function languages. If there is a DBMS or other special data access software, the choices narrow to Focus or COBOL depending on the specific DBMS.

Some business systems are specialized because they are real-time and have stringent response time requirements in addition to being critical to at least one organization. Examples of real-time TPS include airline reservations, securities transaction processing, manufacturing process control, robotics control, or analog I/O applications. For such systems, the language recommendations are restricted to C, Pascal, Ada, and Smalltalk (see Table 15-2). Any of these languages can be used to develop reentrant, multiuser, real-time applications, although attention to a specific dialect (or vendor version) is required to choose a reentrant version of the language. An alternative is to develop such applications using assembler language as the reentrant base with one or more of the application languages used for individual modules.

Query processing is restricted to SQL, Focus, and PROLOG (see Table 15-2). SQL, Focus, and PRO-LOG support declarative statements of *what* is desired without having to anticipate the outcome in advance. As such, they are the only three languages of these ten to support query processing. PROLOG has the added feature that it can explain its reasoning process and provide probabilities of accuracy for its data. Both SQL and Focus assume they are working on complete information and there is only one answer to a given query. PROLOG can be programmed to develop confidence estimates in answers as well as to develop all possible answers to a query.

Data analysis applications are those in which statistical routines, trend analysis, or other mathematical manipulation of data is desired. Data analysis applications can be programmed or can use packages combined with programs. For such applications, Focus, Fortran, Pascal, PROLOG, Ada, and Smalltalk might be used (see Table 15-2). COBOL is conspicuously absent from this list because it is not as adept at data analysis as other languages. Focus provides statistical modeling, financial modeling, graphical processing, and query processing all

TABLE 15-2   Application Type Matched to Language

Application Type	SQL	Focus	BASIC	COBOL	Fortran	C	Pascal	PROLOG	Ada	Small-talk
TPS—Batch	X	X	X	X						
TPS—On-Line	X	X	X	X		X	X		X	X
TPS—Real-Time						X			X	X
Query	X	X								
DSS/Data Analysis	X	X			X	X	X	X	X	X
AI/Expert Systems								X		
EIS		X				X			X	X

within its one language. As such, it is the most full-function data analysis tool in this group. The other languages have the individual tools for a programmer to build a data analysis application, but the assumption is that some processing would be done by general purpose modeling languages (e.g., Statistical Analysis System—SAS.[4] If complex simultaneous equations are required, Focus is not the appropriate language. Then, choices are restricted to Fortran, Ada, or Smalltalk. Fortran does not actually provide simultaneous equation solutions, but it can be 'fooled' into performing as if it does. The other languages are better choices for simultaneous equation processing. Some dialects of C (i.e., Concurrent C) and Pascal (i.e., Object Pascal) might also be used for simultaneous equations.

ESS or DSS applications may have changing requirements that are not well understood due to the unstructured nature of the problem domain. For such applications, C, Pascal, PROLOG, Ada, or Smalltalk might be used (see Table 15-2). One or more of these languages might be combined with purchased soft-ware packages to provide all the functions of such applications.

GDSS applications almost always use packages to support group decision processes, but might use C, Pascal, PROLOG, Ada, or Smalltalk for part of the processing, depending on the environment (see Table 15-2).

Finally, artificial intelligence applications, specifically expert systems, might use PROLOG (see Table 15-2). Only PROLOG supports inference through logic programming. None of the other languages is appropriate to AI applications.

Language Matched to Methodology

The experience with methodologies is similar to that of languages in that few heuristics are known to guide methodology selection. Rather, at the present time, a company tends to adopt and learn one methodology and it is used for all applications, whether appropriate or not. The position taken here is that the methodology and language should match the application type. In this section, the ten

---

4 SAS is a registered trademark of the SAS Corporation, Cary, NC.

TABLE 15-3 Application Type Matched to Methodology

Methodology	SQL	Focus	BASIC	COBOL	Fortran	C	Pascal	PROLOG	Ada	Small-talk
Process	X	X	X	X	X	X	X		X	
Data	X	X		X		X			X	
Object						C++		X	X	X

languages are matched to methodologies which were discussed in Chapters 7–13.

Process methodologies which prevailed in business until the mid-1980s are most successfully used with SQL, Focus, BASIC, COBOL, Fortran, C, Pascal, and Ada (see Table 15-3). The other languages require too much attention to data or program design to lead to optimal language use with process methods. Also, the use of process methods should not be used with data-intensive applications because of the lack of specific attention given to data with such methods. The C-language is here because it is process oriented; if C++ were the language, it should only be used with object-oriented (OO) methods. Similarly, Ada *can* be used here but it is best used with OO methods.

Data methodologies balance the design of processes and data evenly and are useful with SQL, Focus, COBOL, C, and Ada applications (see Table 15-3). For interactive applications in which the programmer needs only limited control, SQL and Focus are useful. For more complex applications, COBOL, with a DBMS and telecommunications monitor, provides interactive processing capabilities. The process discussion on C and Ada applies here; both languages *can* be used with data methods but are recommended with OO methods.

Finally, for object methodologies, C++, PROLOG, Ada, and Smalltalk are most likely to lead to successful implementations (see Table 15-3). The languages omitted in the object category do not easily support one or more of the object tenets of polymorphism, message passing, class inheritance, or encapsulation.

AUTOMATED SUPPORT FOR PROGRAM DEVELOPMENT

In the age of the smart machine, the availability of developmental aids, CASE environments, code generators, and testing aids such as debuggers, incremental compilers, windowed execution environments, and so on, all speed development of working code. Any language which has such automated development aids is assumed to lead to increased programmer productivity over languages that do not have such aids (see Table 15-4).

CASE tools frequently have built-in code generators or have interfaces to other vendor's code generators, allowing you to mix and match the development environment and the language generated.

The automated support tools include code generation tools, incremental compilers, and program generation environments. All of these are loosely called *Lower CASE* or *Back-end CASE* tools.

SUMMARY

In this chapter, a number of distinguishing characteristics of languages were defined. These included: data type definitions supported, data type checking, operators supported, type of user processing supported, and processing for loops, conditional statements, arrays, I/O, and subprograms. In addition, nontechnical characteristics included uniformity,

TABLE 15-4   Automated Support Tools for Code Generation

Product	Company	Technique
ADW—Construction Workbench	Knowledgeware, Inc. Atlanta, CA	Builds Pseudocode for modulesthat can be used to Generate Code for MsDOS, MVS
C Development Environment, OOSD/C++	Environments (IDE) San Francisco, CA	Object-oriented C++ code development environment
Developer Assistant for Information Systems (DAISys), Secure user Programming by Refinement/DAISys	S/Cubed Inc. Stamford, CT	Generates COBOL for IBM mainframe, AS/400, OS/2 Generates C Code for MSDOS, OS/2
IEW	Texas Instruments Dallas, TX	Generates COBOL with Embedded SQL Generates C Code for MVS, MsDOS, OS/2 Interfaces to Telon and other Code Generators
NeXTStep 3.0	NeXT Computer Redwood City, CA	Object Oriented DB development environment
ObjectMaker	Mark V Systems	Generates C or C++ Code for MsDOS, VMS, Unix, AIX
Software Through Pictures	Integrated Development	Generates C or C++ Code for Unix, AIX
System Architect	Popkin Software & Systems Inc. New York, NY	Generates C Code for MsDOS, OS/2
Teamwork, Ensemble	Cadre Technologies Providence, RI	Generates C or C++ Code for for Unix, OS/2, AIX
Visible Analyst Workbench	Visible Systems Corp. Newton, MA	Generates C Code for MsDOS

ambiguity, compactness, locality, linearity, ease of code translation, portability, compiler efficiency, and availability of CASE, code generation, and testing tools. Each of ten languages were described according to the characteristics. Then the languages were defined as appropriate for supporting different application requirements and were discussed in terms of their support for development of transaction, query, data analysis, DSS, ESS, and ES applications.

REFERENCES

Ageloff, Roy, and Richard Mojena, *Applied Fortran 77 Featuring Structured Programming*. Belmont, CA: Wadsworth Publishing, 1981.

Alcock, B., *Illustrating Pascal*. New York: Cambridge University Press, 1987.

Barnes, J. G. P., *Programming in Ada*, 3rd ed., Reading, MA: Addison Wesley, 1989.

Barnett, Eugene H., *Programming Time-Shared Computers in Basic*. New York: John Wiley, 1972.

Bjorner, D., and C. B., Jones, *The Vienna Development Method: The Meta-Language*. New York: Springer-Verlag, 1978.

Booch, Grady, *Software Engineering with Ada*, 2nd ed., Menlo Park, CA: The Benjamin/Cummings Publishing Co., Inc., 1987.

Bordillo, Donald A., *Programmer's COBOL Reference Manual*. Englewood Cliffs, NJ: Prentice-Hall, 1978.

Clocksin, William, "A prolog primer," *Byte*, August, 1987, pp. 146–158.

Cooper, Doug, and Michael Clancy, *Oh! Pascal!*, 2nd ed., New York: W. W. Norton & Company, Inc., 1985.

Date, C. J., and Colin While, *A Guide to DB2*, 2nd ed., Reading, MA: Addison-Wesley, 1988.

Friedman, Linda Weiser, *Comparative Programming Languages: Generalizing the Programming Function*. Englewood Cliffs, NJ: Prentice-Hall, 1991.

Gear, C. W., *Programming and Languages*. Chicago: Science Research Associates, 1987.

Goldberg, Adele, *Smalltalk-80: The Interactive Programming Environment*. Reading, MA: Addison-Wesley Publishing Co., 1984.

Higman, B. A., *Comparative Study of Programming Languages*. New York: American Elsevier, 1967.

Information Builders, Inc., *Focus Users Manual*. New York: IBI, Inc., 1984.

Kernighan, Brian W., and Dennis M. Ritchie, *The C Programming Language*. Englewood Cliffs, NJ: Prentice-Hall, 1978.

Martin, J., *Fourth Generation Languages*, Vols. 1–2. Englewood Cliffs, NJ: Prentice-Hall, 1985.

S. Medema, C. H., P. Medema, and M. Boasson, *The Programming Languages: Pascal, Modula, Chill, and Ada*. Englewood Cliffs, NJ: Prentice-Hall, 1983.

Nagrin, Paul, and Henry Ledgard, *Basic with Style: Programming Proverbs*. Rochelle Park, NJ: Hayden Books, Inc., 1978.

Philippakis, A. S., and Leonard J. Kazmier, *Advanced COBOL Programming*, 2nd ed., New York: McGraw-Hill, 1983.

Reps, Thomas W., *Generating Language-Based Environments*. Boston, MA: MIT Press, 1984.

Stroustrup, Bjorn, "Data abstraction in C," *AT&T Bell Labs Technical Journal*, Vol. 63, October 8, 1984, pp. 1701–1732.

Warren, David, H. D., "The SRI model for Or-parallel execution of PROLOG—Abstract design and implementation issues," *Proceeding, 1987 International Symposium on Logic Programming*, August 31–September 4, San Francisco, CA, IEEE, pp. 92–102.

KEY TERMS

Ada
ambiguity
array
array-oriented I/O
automatic type coercion
BASIC
bit data type
Boolean
C
case statement
character string
COBOL
compactness
compiler efficiency
conditional statement
control language
  constructs
data type
data type checking
date data type
dynamic memory
  management
ease of code translation
exception handling
exit
Focus
Fortran
global data
input/output (I/O)
integer
language constructs
linearity
list-directed I/O
local data
locality
logical data type

loop
memory management
mixed mode type
  checking
modularization
object
operator precedence
Pascal
persistent object
physical I/O
pointer
portability
programming
PROLOG
PROLOG facts
PROLOG goals
PROLOG rules
PROLOG subgoals
pseudostrong type
  checking
reentrant
real number
record-oriented I/O
recursive
reusability
set-oriented I/O
Smalltalk
SQL
static memory
  management
strong type checking
table
typeless checking
uniformity
user-defined data type

EXERCISES

1. For any (or all) of the cases in the Appendix, define the application concept as batch, on-line, real-time, or a mix of these. For the applications you choose, select an implementation language and develop the reasons why the language you recommend is best. What specific features and characteristics of the language make it your preferred choice?

STUDY QUESTIONS

1. Define the following terms:

Boolean data type	reentrant
dynamic memory management	set-oriented I/O
	static memory
local data	management
modularization	type checking
operator precedence	user-defined data type
pointer	

2. Why should we concentrate on language selection rather than on programming?

3. In your opinion, is programming going to disappear as an activity? Justify your response.

4. What is a data type and why is it important in language selection?

5. When is strong type checking important?

6. Why do you think type checking is absent from a language like COBOL?

7. Why is type checking important in object-oriented programs?

8. Define three logic-related language constructs and discuss their differences.

9. What is operator precedence? Why, as a programmer, must you be aware of operator precedence in a language?

10. In an ideal program, how many exits should a module contain? Why?

11. Define the three types of arrays that are commonly supported in languages.

12. For SQL, COBOL, Fortran, Ada, C, and Pascal, define the type of I/O orientation as record-oriented, set-oriented, array-oriented, or list-directed. What difference does the I/O orientation make?

13. What are the differences between local and global data? How do they relate to properties of programs such as reusability, reentrancy, and recursion?

14. Contrast static and dynamic memory management.

15. Why is exception handling desirable in a language? Why don't all languages support exception handling?

16. What level of code sophistication is required to support multiple concurrent users? Why?

17. What is the relationship of recursion, reentrancy, and reusability of programs?

18. List three nontechnical language characteristics and describe why they are important in language selection.

19. Define language portability. Is this property of growing or decreasing interest to businesses, and why?

20. What is COBOL's appeal?

21. Why is C a potentially dangerous language?

22. Describe how and why PROLOG differs so much from the other nine languages in this chapter.

23. How does PROLOG handle databases?

24. What are the object-oriented languages? How do they differ from the other languages?

25. Even though SQL and Focus both use implicit I/O, they are different. What is the main difference in the way they treat data? Which language is 'cleaner' in guaranteeing the results of a query?

★ EXTRA-CREDIT QUESTIONS

1. PROLOG is not the only logic-oriented, artificial intelligence programming language. Lisp is also popular. Investigate the differences between the two programming languages using the characteristics discussed in this chapter.

2. Object orientation and artificial intelligence are two characteristics of applications that are of growing interest to businesses. Can a typical COBOL transaction processing application incorporate object and AI tenets? Will COBOL change or will other languages come to be used? Can other languages be 'grafted on' or interfaced to COBOL gracefully? Be sure to document your arguments.

CHAPTER **16**

PURCHASING HARDWARE AND SOFTWARE

INTRODUCTION

When PC software companies first created the end-user market in the early 1980s, the number of PCs in companies was about one per every 4,000 people. By 1986, the number of PCs was about one per every 100 people; companies had settled on standard, supported products for spreadsheets, databases, and word processing. In the intervening years, there was a mad scramble for market share during which vendors' claims were sometimes unfounded, the notion of *vaporware* was created, and major evaluations were done by buying companies. For every new market that develops, a similar set of activities takes place. In the 1990s, object-oriented languages, expert systems, imaging systems, multimedia, CASE products, and distributed databases are the new markets that will have developed recognized leaders by the end of the decade. At best, a company selects a product and vendor that will weather the storms of industry growth and emerge a leader. At worst, they purchase several products before settling on one that works for their company.

The purchasing process tries to minimize the guesswork and provide a rational, objective method of selecting hardware, software, or services. The techniques can be used on products of any type. There are two basic processes, one informal and one formal. There is a great deal of overlap in the activities. The major difference is that the formal process is usually conducted in a more open environment, frequently for legal compliance. All governmental contracting for goods and services, for instance, is subject to a formal procurement process that includes the solicitation of proposals from vendors.

In this chapter, we discuss how to evaluate and choose between alternatives for application use. The trade-off between building the item in-house or purchasing it elsewhere is commonly called a **make-buy decision**. This name is not always accurate, however, because you might be comparing development alternatives, for instance, having a consulting company build a customized application versus purchasing a software package. These alternatives all are considered in the make-buy decision process. RFPs can be used for deciding between vendors that have the same package but are selling turnkey products including all hardware and software in an 'environment,' or for hardware only, software only, services only, or some combination of those three.

In this chapter, we first discuss the formal procurement process, describing the steps performed in the purchasing decision process. The informal process is then described and compared with the formal process. Then, the contents of each RFP section are detailed. Next, we discuss the selection process and criteria that are important to it. Finally, automated support tools for RFP management and evaluation are presented. The ABC case is woven throughout the discussion, providing examples of the major points.

REQUEST FOR
PROPOSAL
PROCESS

A **request for proposal**, or **RFP**, is a formal, written request for bids on some product. In our context, an RFP might relate to hardware, firmware, software, or services such as programming or operations management. Also called **RFQ**, for **request for quotation**, an RFP provides formal requirements, ground rules for responses, and, usually, a standard format for the proposal responses. The basic stages of the request for proposal process, which are discussed in the ensuing sections, include the following:

1. Develop and prioritize requirements
2. Develop schedule and cost
3. Develop requests for proposal
4. Receive proposals
5. Evaluate proposals and select alternative

Develop and Prioritize Requirements

The initial step in all software engineering projects, regardless of whether it is going out for bids or not, is to determine the requirements. When proposals are solicited, the requirements define the problem and the features and functions of the solution that will constitute the work of the bidding companies. In general, the requirements provided in an RFP are identical to those developed during analysis. If a requirements specification is available, it should be appended to the RFP and referenced in the document. If no requirements specification has been developed, at a minimum, the topics summarized below should be provided.

1. General instructions
2. Statement of work

3. Technical specifications
4. Management approach
5. Financial requirements
6. Company information requirements
7. Vendor response guidelines
8. Standard contract terms and conditions

The level of detail and specificity of the requirements varies with the context, situation, and company. Some companies spell out every item in excruciating detail, leaving nothing to the vendors' imaginations. The advantage of such detail is that the proposals can be easily compared to the list of requirements to determine compliance with the basic request. Also, the likelihood of misunderstanding of requirements is lower when more detailed descriptions are used. The disadvantage of detailed requirements is that, in information systems work, the complex engineering nature of the work frequently requires creative design that might be stifled or overshadowed by too specific a requirements list. The creative aspects of systems design also provide for cost differentiation that might not otherwise surface. To overcome this problem, when creativity is desired, it can be specifically identified as a selection criteria in the RFP.

There are four types of requirements: technical, managerial, financial, and company. **Technical requirements** address the specific hardware, software, or services to be provided. **Managerial requirements** identify the level of detail at which schedule, staff plans, and staff management should be discussed in the proposal. **Financial requirements** list the type of bid desired and the expected format for the financial portion of the response. **Company requirements** list the type of vendor information to be supplied to assure the client of vendor ability to complete the work successfully. The details of each section are discussed in the RFP contents section.

Develop Schedule and Cost

The schedule and cost developed during an RFP process are neither as detailed nor as refined as if the item costs were developed in-house. If the in-house estimate is being compared to the vendors' estimates in a make-buy decision, a detailed schedule and cost should be developed. If the RFP is comparing only external purchase options, less detail and precision are required. In this case, the schedule provides an estimated end-date for the item to be used in comparing the proposals. The expected end-date might be omitted and left as a proposal item, or might be listed as either required or desired in the proposal.

Occasionally, a user manager will mandate the desired completion date for a project. In that case, the in-house estimates are developed to determine the realism of the mandated date. If the date is unlikely because it is very different from the estimate, the vendors can be asked in the proposal requirements how they deal with completion date problems and a tight schedule.

The planning process is the same as that followed in Chapter 6, with the level of precision adjusted to fit the situation. Requirements are converted into a task list. Each task's development time is estimated for the most likely outcome. Sophisticated estimates, including optimistic, average, and pessimistic times, may or may not be developed. During the proposal evaluation process, vendor time estimates are compared to the planned completion date.

A similar activity is done for personnel estimates. A rough estimate of the number of people and their skill levels should be developed, based on the tasks and times for each task. During proposal evaluation, the estimated project team skills are matched against the skills of the people to be assigned to the project by each vendor. The closeness of match indicates several things. First, the closer the match, the more confidence you can have that the vendor understands the problem. Second, the closer the match, the more likely the vendor's reasoning is consistent with your reasoning about the project's needs. Third, the less close the match, the more likely the vendor is staffing the project with people who are learning new skills and who, therefore, will not be fully knowledgeable about the technology or application area of your problem. This third case is not necessarily bad, but it does imply that there will be one, or possibly two, key person(s) on whom the success of the project rests. This places you, as the client, in a somewhat more vulnerable position because you must rely totally on the key person(s), ensuring that they remain on the project until it is operational.

Staffing estimates are used to develop personnel costs for the project. If the proposal includes hardware or software, each item should be priced at the best retail prices available. For instance, *MacWorld* and *PC* magazines include tear-out pages of advertising by discount vendors for both hardware and software. Professional data sources, such as *DataPro™*,[1] provide retail prices which can be used as a basis to which proposed costs might be evaluated.

Develop Request for Proposal

The steps in developing the RFP are first, to determine likely vendors; second, select from the likely vendors the few that best meet your requirements; and third, develop and send the proposal to the vendors.

Determine Likely Vendors

Several stages of information gathering precede the actual bidding process. First, potential vendors are identified. Vendor identification can be from a commercial information service, such as *DataPro™*, or from trade magazine advertisements, for instance, from *PC* Magazine, *Computerworld*, or *Network Week*. This process should identify ten or more vendors.

Narrow the Number of Vendors

When potential vendors are identified, they are contacted and requested to send information. Depending on the company and item, this can be an informal telephone call or can be a formal, written **request for information (RFI)**. Documentation on the products requested is reviewed to narrow the number of alternatives to a manageable few, usually between two and five.

The information review frequently identifies a need for more information to differentiate between products. Either requirements are refined or more information is obtained, or both. Another round of

---

1 DataPro is a trademarked name of DataPro, Inc., Delran, NJ.

information gathering might then take place. At this point, remaining vendors might be called in to present their product(s) and demonstrate how they work. Specific technical questions to provide missing information are asked.

The decisions after this round of information gathering depend on the nature and use of the product being purchased. If the number of users is small and the product is inexpensive (e.g., under $10,000), a selection might be made. The more users and the more expensive the product, the more extensive the evaluation. Other companies that use the product might be solicited for experience with the company and product, and perhaps, are visited for an on site demonstration. In these cases, when the field of vendors is narrowed to between two and five, an RFP is developed and proposals are requested.

Develop and Send the Proposal to Vendors

The RFP can be developed in parallel with vendor identification. There is some risk that doing so, however, will produce a biased requirements set that favors one particular vendor. The best approach, therefore, is to develop the requirements first, then search for vendors. When the vendor list has been narrowed to between two and five, the RFP is finalized, vendors are notified that they will receive the proposals, and the proposals are sent or delivered to each vendor. From this point, the requesting company begins to manage the proposal process.

Manage Proposal Process

The **proposal process** begins with release of an RFP to vendors and continues until the proposals are delivered and the selection process begins. The proposal process might include one or more formal meetings, informal meetings, inquiry sessions, or other methods of information exchange between the vendors and the requesting organization. The more money involved and the more complex the proposed work product, the more process management is needed to ensure equitable treatment of all vendors. Equitable treatment means ensuring that all vendors receive the same information. Firm compliance with

due dates and locations for delivery of proposals is maintained. Late or incorrectly delivered proposals are dropped from further consideration, providing equitable treatment of all vendors.

Assume a proposal is being let by the local police department for development of an application that would deploy computer terminals in each police car for interactive look-up of license plates, arrest warrants, and moving violations. The application requires both hardware and software to be developed for 14,000 police cars in a large metropolitan area with over 3,000,000 inhabitants and covering several jurisdictions. Examples might be Washington, D.C., Los Angeles, New York City, Houston, or Chicago. Hardware cost alone is over $2,000,000. The databases each will have millions of entries with issues to be resolved about how and when information is removed from the files. Interfaces to several other applications for license plate information and access to arrest warrants from multiple local and national databases are desired.

The proposed application has several sources of complexity, the least of which is that vendors probably know little about how a police officer spends his day. When New York City let a similar contract for its police force, they had a formal announcement of the proposal to vendors. Vendors were selected and invited to the presentation by mail based on previous contract work or reputation. Nonsolicited vendors were also welcome in response to announcements of the RFP that ran in the local newspaper for several days.

At the formal presentation, each vendor was invited to spend up to four hours traveling with an officer to view the tasks firsthand, for which the application would be built. A specific officer was identified as the liaison for these tours.

In addition, the liaison officer was available for questions at any time until proposals were submitted. If questions were asked by a vendor, the question and response were recorded and a list of all such queries was sent to all vendors attending the proposal announcement meeting. The purpose of providing all queries and responses to all vendors was to ensure that information inadvertently left out of the RFP that might alter the decision process could not be used by one vendor to the detriment of the others. By giving everyone all responses, every vendor had the same information.

Halfway through the two-month proposal process, another meeting was held for vendors to come ask more questions and to clarify the requirements from the document. That meeting was well attended but contained no real information. When one person was asked why he bothered attending, he replied, "To see what the competition asked."

Each vendor presented his or her proposal on the due date and left the written copy for NYC review. Each vendor, then, heard the other vendors' proposals and had some sense of the differences between them. Ironically, the company with the best solution lost because the company was too small. One shortcoming of the RFP was that it had not identified company size as a selection criterion; if it had, the vendor would not have wasted his time bidding.

Evaluate Proposals and Select Alternative

The sections of the proposal responses are each evaluated separately, then summarized together. The technical evaluation reviews that requirements are met and scores the proposal based on the priority criteria developed during the preparation of the RFP. A **benchmark**, or comparison test, might be used to identify differences between hardware or software packages.

The management approach is evaluated for the type, quality, and nature of staff and vendor company resources proposed for the work. A financial evaluation is developed to show the present value of the proposed amount(s). Other analysis, such as payback period, or average cost per vendor employee, might be developed for comparison purposes. Next, the vendor's prior experience with the firm, similar applications, and business reputation are ranked to evaluate the vendor's capability to do the proposed work. Finally, each section is weighted again for comparative section importance, creating a summary of the ratings and final weighted score for each vendor. Objectively, the vendor with the highest, overall weighted score is selected for the work. Each type evaluation is discussed in the evaluation

sections. After selection, a contract is negotiated and work begins.

INFORMAL PROCUREMENT

Most of the same information required for the RFP is required for the informal procurement process. The major difference is in the approach. In the informal process, few, if any, written documents are used for vendor-client communications. Rather, telephone calls, meetings, and document reviews are the major sources of information. The process of selection is similar to that of the RFP process, including trials and benchmarks for acceptance of the item being procured.

Negotiation is verbal and may go back and forth between the principals for several weeks. Vendors signify agreement with the negotiated terms via a memo. A memo proposal summarizes the main points of agreement, then lawyers are called in, as with an RFP, to add the legal terms.

CONTENTS OF RFP

RFP contents include a summary, information on the technical, managerial, company and financial aspects of the bid, a schedule of the process, selection criteria, vendor response requirements, and any standard contract terms (e.g., for EEO or OSHA compliance). Each RFP section is detailed below to identify optional and required information.

Vendor Summary

The Vendor Summary section provides a short, one-page summary of the work to be done (see Table 16-1). General terms and conditions of the proposal process are usually first to allow vendors to quickly decide whether or not they are interested in the engagement. The contents of the general instructions sections should include proposal instructions, location and date for proposal delivery, dates for bidders' conferences, and contacts for status reporting and inquiries.

TABLE 16-1   Detailed RFP Outline

1.0 General instructions

2.0 Statement of work
    2.1 Description of work to be performed
    2.2 Project milestones and deliverable products
    2.3 Criteria for vendor qualification

3.0 Technical specifications
    Technical outlines are in Tables 16-4, 16-5, and 16-7 for hardware, network, or operating system, and customer software or package, respectively.

4.0 Management approach
    4.1 Schedule and staffing
    4.2 Support requirements of vendor
    4.3 Reporting
    4.4 Staff reporting structure and problem management

5.0 Financial requirements

6.0 Company information

7.0 Vendor response guidelines

8.0 Standard contract terms and conditions

Required Information

The requirements list details the requirements of the work as described in the sections on hardware and software. The section can refer to an attached document that might have been developed in-house for functional requirements of the application, hardware, or software. In any case, requirements should be listed and identified as mandatory or optional. A set of prioritized weights for the requirements should also be developed for use in scoring, but weights should not be published in the RFP. There are four general classes of requirements: technical, management, corporate, and financial.

Technical Requirements

GENERAL REQUIREMENTS.   The requirements should place the company and problem in a context for the vendors. First, a brief overview of the industry, company, and work domain is appropriate. Then, a summary of the problem being automated is presented. The major complexity, such as geo-graphic dispersion across 16 states, should be identified. Then, the details of work to be provided are described.

DETAILED REQUIREMENTS.   The work might include hardware, software, programming services, or other IS services. The criteria for each item should be detailed as much as possible. In general, regardless of the type of procurement, the features and functions of the equipment should be described in sufficient detail to enable the vendor to design a solution. Functional requirements—*what*—the item is expected to do are described in detail. Volume of data, throughput, response times, and growth requirements are identified. The type, contents, timing, and format of interfaces also are provided. A hardware interface might list, for instance, a network interface connection to a fractional T-1 (cable) service for internetwork communication. A software interface might list, for instance, a DBMS interface connection to a SQL server. An application interface might list, for instance, electronic messages to be sent to an Accounts Receivable Application.

For services, the work description varies depending on the work. The two most common service RFPs request proposals for software development and for outsourcing of operations. For software services, the application requirements are the information provided. For outsourcing operations, the business functions included and any existing job descriptions relating to those functions should be provided to the vendors.

Diagrams, tables, and lists should be supplemented by text to provide clarification of incomplete, misleading, or ambiguous diagrams. For instance, a data flow diagram cannot describe timing of processes or process interrelationships that might be important. They also do not include constraints, need for simultaneous processes, and so on. Requirements for these items would be described in text as required.

AUDIT AND APPLICATION CONTROL REQUIREMENTS.   Recall from Chapter 10 that audit controls are frequently needed to prove processing. The audit and control section of the RFP identifies the minimum acceptable level of auditability required. If audit controls are in compliance with laws or other professional guidelines, the requisite laws and guidelines should be referenced.

Vendors' designs might assume human interventions to ensure accurate application processing. A requirement should be developed to surface such assumptions. For instance, controls might include data integrity, data and process access, exception management, and print control of prenumbered documents (e.g., checks). These examples usually require manual interventions supplemented with interactive processing to recover from failures or to fix hardware problems. For instance, a check might jam in a printer after it is printed. Both software and human procedures are required to reprint the check and to account for the damaged check. (See Chapter 10 for types of failures that should be planned.) Vendors should be required to identify and detail all such interventions as part of their proposal.

PERFORMANCE REQUIREMENTS.   Performance requirements include manual, hardware, and software performance. For instance, hardware performance might define acceptable limits for downtime, precision for mathematical computation, or cycle time.

CONVERSION REQUIREMENTS.   Recall that conversion requirements define the required changes from the current environment to the new automated environment (see Chapter 14 to review this discussion). The RFP typically identifies data for conversion, including the current format, current volume, and growth required. Conversion timing constraints should be identified if any exist. The vendors' designs should describe the target database for the data and a migration path for conversion. The vendors' conversion plans also should estimate conversion impacts on users, computer operations, and project staffing.

TRAINING.   Training to be provided as part of the contract should be listed as a required topic of the vendors. Training options can be left open to vendor proposal or be specified as requirements. Training might be provided for users, software maintenance staff, operations staff, or user support staff.

The type of training can be one-on-one, programmed, individually self-paced, classroom, computer-based training, or some variation of these. Training information provided might include the type, number of sessions, location, and audience for training. The qualifications of expected trainers should also be requested.

ACCEPTANCE.   **Acceptance criteria**, specifying the contents and timing of the acceptance test, should be identified so the vendor knows how work will be judged. Acceptance criteria might include type and amount of test data, length of time for parallel and pilot runs, phased cutover approach and speed desired (e.g., five locations per month for five months), and performance criteria for success (e.g., five consecutive days with all accounts in balance at the end of daily processing).

Hardware and software packages are usually benchmarked to verify that they perform as advertised. A benchmark is a comparison test between two or more configurations. The contents of the test are a suite of application programs that are representative of the expected work load of the production system. A benchmark test provides you the ability to compare throughput performance with the representative work load. In addition to the benchmark which precedes installation, hardware and software packages might also be run through a trial period similar to that described above for acceptance.

Management Approach

SCHEDULE AND STAFFING.   Vendors should be required to develop a schedule for the proposed work. Pert, critical path (CPM), Gantt charts, or other graphical schedules might be required. Milestones for the project and deliverable work products should be identified as specific requirements. The discussion of work should be required to include number, timing, and skills of the expected employees. For contract software development, vendors frequently attach resumes of the intended project manager(s) and project team members for client information. If the client wants the right of refusal on all employees, a representative set of contractor staff resumes should be provided for client review.

PROJECT MANAGEMENT.   Project management is an important issue in an RFP because it frequently identifies the one or two people the client will work with most closely. The requirements can include reporting structures, management of work, and problem resolution policies of the vendor firm. In general, vendors should identify an on-site manager and a more senior, vendor manager to oversee and guarantee the quality and quantity of vendor work. The resumes of one or both of those contacts should be required in the response to allow assessment of the qualifications of the managers for the proposed work.

PROJECT REPORTING.   Status reporting form, content, and timing should be requested of vendors. This can be left to the vendor to describe, or can be stated as a requirement for compliance by the vendor. Normally, status meetings are held as required or weekly, whichever is more often. A written status report should be required to identify work completed, progress against the schedule, problems needing resolution for project completion, and work assignments for the next period.

VENDOR ASSUMPTIONS.   Special vendor requirements should be identified. The idea behind this section is that there should be no surprises because of erroneous assumptions by a vendor after a selection is made. The vendor's assumptions are stated in the response to ensure that the client also shares the same assumptions. Any hardware, configuration, purchased software, or facilities alterations assumed by the vendor to be available for their use are solicited. For instance, when vendors build custom software, they normally assume that their employees work at the client site, use client computing equipment and software, and follow the client's employment practices.

The vendor's expectations and type of support required from the client should be identified. For instance, copying, clerical, and secretarial support might be expected. In addition, access to the users should be identified with estimates of the number and expected participants for data gathering meetings.

Further assumptions about how application information will be entered into the computer (e.g., keyboard entry by clerks, keyboard entry by programmers), the availability of computer resources for testing, and the frequency of tests for each vendor staff member should be identified.

Company Information

Information in this section should qualify the vendor as viable to perform the work. Standard company information required in an RFP includes the company history, ownership, growth, current size, previous contracts with the requesting company, and references for similar work. If the company performs a specialized service, such as LAN installation and service, it can be highlighted in this section.

Financial Information

The last of the requirements is for a cost estimate of the work. Cost estimates vary depending on whether the work is for hardware or software or services (see summary in Table 16-2). In general, the vendors' responses provide the opening for negotiation of the financial aspect of a procurement. Except for fixed-price bids defined below, the price quoted is rarely nonnegotiable.

For purchased hardware, the options are to lease, to lease with an option to buy, or to purchase the equipment. Under a **lease option**, equipment is on loan from the vendor and is paid under a monthly leasing arrangement. In general, the more equipment leased, the more flexible the vendor for lease negotiation.

The **lease with option to buy** provides a basic leasing arrangement with some percentage of the lease payment applied to purchase of the equipment. At the end of the lease period, the lessor has the option of returning the equipment to the vendor or of paying the vendor the **residual price** (i.e., the remaining value of the equipment) and purchasing the items.

A **purchase option** identifies the total current cost of the equipment and the payment terms that can be offered to entice a purchase. Frequently the purchase of very expensive equipment (e.g.,

TABLE 16-2 Financial Options

Item Being Acquired	Financial Options
Hardware	Lease Lease with Option to Buy Purchase
Software	Base License Fee Plus Monthly/Annual Maintenance Fees
Services	Time & Materials (T&M) Fixed Price T&M with Ceiling

$250,000+) can span several years and the variations between proposals can be great.

Software **package purchases** usually include a one-time **license fee** with a monthly maintenance fee, both of which are negotiable. The more sites and higher number of users, the lower the per copy price of software. As the number of sites and users increases, the average incremental cost per user decreases. The goal, then, of the licensing options is to have the vendor define available options from which a negotiation begins.

For services, the financial options are a fixed price, time and materials (T&M) estimate, or T&M with a ceiling (i.e., semifixed). A **fixed price bid** means that the work is contracted for a set price and neither side is expected to renegotiate the terms unless a major change in the contractual arrangements occurs. Fixed-price bids can be analyzed with no change.

Time and materials bids (T&M) sum the total cost of personnel time plus the cost of paper, secretarial, copy, computer, and any other vendor-supplied support in doing the work. T&M bids are frequently presented as a range of times and costs. Optimistic, realistic and pessimistic estimates might be provided. The formula for determining the cost to be used in the financial analysis develops a weighted average cost which favors realistic estimates (see Figure 16-1).

Bids that are **T&M with a ceiling** purport to provide the best risk sharing between vendor and client. Fixed-price bids put the risk of not completing the work as scheduled on the vendor who loses any moneys above the bid price. T&M bids place the risk on the client who pays for all work until it is done whether it is on schedule or not. T&M with a ceiling tries to share the risk by allowing T&M, assuming the work is on budget, or a ceiling with vendor risk if the schedule is not kept. Whether this notion works·or not in reality is subject to debate. In any case, the ceiling price is most commonly used in comparisons since most projects tend to end up at that price anyway.

Schedule of RFP Process

The schedule provides important dates throughout the RFP process, including all dates and periods of time for interaction between the vendors and requesting company, and the due date for the RFP. In addition, it should include the important dates for requesting company action, especially the decision date for the winning proposal.

Description of Selection Processes

The more vendors know about the selection process, the better able they are to determine if it is worth their effort to prepare a proposal. Specific require-

---

Weighted Average Cost = ((Optimistic + (2 * Realistic) + Pessimistic) / 4)

Example:

Total Optimistic Time	=	4.2 Person Years
Total Realistic Time	=	6.0 Person Years
Total Pessimistic Time	=	10 Person Years

WAC = ((4.2 + (2 * 6) + 10) / 4) = 26.2 / 4 = 6.55 Person Years

FIGURE 16-1   Weighted Average Cost Formula

ments that might alter a vendor's interest in bidding are especially important. For instance, if only companies for which the proposed work is less than 10% of net income will be considered, this should be made known.

Other information that might be provided is a brief description of the selection process in terms of required and mandatory functions, and the relative importance of the four major areas of information: technical, management, financial, and company. The individual weights should *never* be identified or the responses will be written to get a good score rather than to address the design issues.

Vendor Response Requirements

An optional part of an RFP is the format for the vendor's response. The argument for requiring a set response is that the comparison of multiple proposals is simplified when the responses all use the same format. The disadvantage of a fixed response is that some important area of consideration that might have been overlooked in the RFP or in the outline for the response, might never surface until after a vendor is selected. Some companies opt for requiring the financial data to be identical but allow discretion for the remainder of the vendors' responses.

The major advantage of a standardized vendor response is an easier comparison of responses. If there is no standard format, you must first find the answer to each piece of desired information in each proposal, then create a cross-reference document, or otherwise identify each item for easy reference. Having no standard format also requires you to be much more careful in reading every document to ensure that you have identified the requisite information.

The response outline should be tailored to fit the specific proposal and to ease response evaluation. In general, the sections follow the requirements above: Technical Response, Management Approach, Corporate Information, and Cost/Price. A full outline for a vendor response is provided in Table 16-3.

One of the most important standard response formats is for financial information. Each vendor usually provides his own information in his own format

TABLE 16-3   Vendor Response Outline

1.0 Technical response
    1.1 Overview of the system
    1.2 Diagram(s) of processes and data
    1.3 Configuration diagram(s)
    1.4 Performance data
    1.5 Detailed explanation of the system features
        and functions
    1.6 Compatibility (with other client equipment,
        applications, etc.)
    1.7 Degree of risk in using proposed hardware,
        software, or application
    1.8 Maintenance estimates
    1.9 Reliability
    1.10 Quality assurance and control
    1.11 Training
    1.12 Deliverable products

2.0 Management approach
    2.1 Organization
    2.2 Personnel and manpower controls
    2.3 Vendor/subcontractor and client relationship
    2.4 Delivery schedules and project plans
    2.5 Proposed staffing
    2.6 Consultants to the vendor (e.g., subcontractors)
        2.6.1 Subcontractor identification
        2.6.2 Subcontractor relationship and
            management structure
    2.7 Status reporting schedule and approach

3.0 Corporate information
    3.1 Company background—Ownership, size, age,
        experience, capabilities, products, services
    3.2 Vendor previous experience with the client
        company
    3.3 Vendor experience with similar projects

in such a way that his proposal is favorably presented. The risk is that information from several vendors will not contain information in such a way that it can be compared. The solution to this problem is to tell the vendors exactly how to present financial information. A simple format that summarizes all costs for easy use and analysis is best. Figure 16-2 provides a sample financial summary format that includes all information that you, as the requesting organization, might need to compare the proposals. In customizing the form for a

PRICE PROPOSAL FOR VENDOR _____

Application Name _____ Number _____

_____ Development _____ _____ Operating Expenses _____

Item:	Analysis	Design	Implement	Test	Parallel	Year1	Year2	Year3	Year4	Year5
I. Hardware										
1.										
2.										
3.										
4.										
TOTAL Hardware										
II. Software										
1.										
2.										
3.										
TOTAL Software										
III. Labor (by Type) Rates: Base and Overtime										
1.										
2.										
3.										
4.										
TOTAL Labor										
IV. Other										
1. Documentation										
2. Testing/Assurance										
3. Site Preparation										
4. Supplies										
5. Travel										
6. Maintenance										
7.										
8.										
9.										
10.										
TOTAL Other										

TOTAL Project Price (Operating + Development) $ __,___,___.__

FIGURE 16-2   Sample Financial Summary Form for Vendor Response

specific procurement, you omit sections not required. So, for software-only procurement, omit all hardware sections.

Standard Contract Terms

Finally, the RFP should include any standard contract terms and conditions that might be desired. For instance, penalties for nonperformance against the contract or conditions under which payments will be made or withheld are terms of an agreement for which companies frequently require standard contract clauses.

HARDWARE

Hardware might be described in detail, or more commonly, is described by its functionality. In this section we discuss the hardware criteria that are usually in an RFP. The main categories of hardware information in this section are functionality, operational environment, and performance. Training and acceptance criteria were discussed above and also apply to hardware.

Functionality

A technical requirements section outline for hardware is shown as Table 16-4. Keep in mind that the outline would be customized to fit the specific components desired. If hardware requirements are known, they should be specified in sufficient detail to exactly identify needs. In this case, the vendors are not selecting a solution to your problem; they are bidding on a hardware configuration. For this type of specification, if the configuration does not meet all of your needs, the vendor is not liable because you detailed specific hardware.

More often, you will not know the specific hardware, but you do know the functions to be performed by the hardware. In this case, the information provided is to detail the work environment closely enough that the solution will work. For hardware, this means that all work to be performed and the constraints for the work should be identified. The number of users, work profile for each user, timing of

TABLE 16-4 Technical Requirements Outline for Hardware

3.0 Technical Hardware Requirements
    3.1 CPU cycle time
    3.2 Number of processors
    3.3 Memory cycle time and processing
    3.4 Number and type of registers
    3.5 Number, type, and priority structure for interrupts
    3.6 Memory organization, maximum addressable memory
    3.7 Parallel operation capabilities
    3.8 Math/graphics co-processors
    3.9 Number, type, and transfer rate for data channels
    3.10 Channel control unit—type, maximum device assignment, effect on CPU
    3.11 Storage devices—number and type
    3.12 Tape drives—density, speed, transfer rate, tracks, size
    3.13 Disk—access time (seek + search), rotational delay, transfer rate, tracks and cylinders, capacity per unit
    3.14 Communications control capabilities—maximum remotes, lines, interfaces
    3.15 Ability to connect to I/O peripherals—bar code, microform, imaging, graphics, multimedia, and other special purpose equipment
    3.16 Expandability
    3.17 MTBF—mean time between failures
    3.18 MTTR—mean time to repair
    3.19 Support
    3.20 Software compatibility for operating systems and specific packages desired
    3.21 Site requirements—air-conditioning, electrical, heating, cooling, etc.
    3.22 Budget limitations
    3.23 Throughput requirements
    3.24 Delivery requirements

work, volume of inputs and printed outputs, types, volume and contents of files, and software are minimal requirements to specify.

More detailed requirements, such as CPU cycle time or response time to a type of query, are provided for any critical requirements. Critical requirements, here, mean those monitoring or relating to human life (e.g., EKG monitor or space rocket lift-off). Error processing, error recovery, security, types of human intervention, and so on are all specified if they are important considerations in the decision process.

Equipment *not* desired should also be identified. For instance, most configurations can alternate between minicomputers or local area networks. If minicomputers, for instance, are not desired as a solution, the requirements should be stated as: "This proposal is for a local area networking solution to support . . ." followed by a list of major application functions. ABC's RFP might finish that sentence: ". . . a rent/return processing application for a video store."

Operational Environment

The operational environment includes the geographic, building, and room specifications for the equipment. The extent of vendor responsibility and information should be defined as explicitly as possible. If the vendor is responsible for the installation, that information should also be included. If a location is known, but the site is not improved for the equipment yet, the vendor should be required to specify flooring, air, ventilation, electrical, plumbing, and other environmental requirements of the installation. If a site is already prepared for equipment, it should be described in sufficient detail for the vendor to know whether his configuration will tolerate the environment or if further alteration is required. Schematics of desk configurations should be provided for multiunit RFPs.

Performance

Performance requirements identify the tolerance limits for different types of problems. Hardware performance requirements might include any of the following:

- Acceptable limits of downtime
- Inquiry response time
- File update response time
- Maximum percentage of communication errors
- Recovery times for hardware failures

- Maintenance and reliability requirements
- Peak and average transaction time requirements
- Geographic or other environmental constraints on equipment

Frequently, in the absence of specific hardware design requirements, performance requirements are the basis for the RFP. A sample outline for operating system or network performance requirements is shown as Table 16-5. In the table, the list includes support for all desired functions of the environment. The implication is that hardware is less important than the functional support to be provided by the operating system. Table 16-6 shows an example of performance requirements that might be used to specify a local area network to support diverse work.

Vendor responses to hardware requests should be required to include all operating system, programming language, software, and interface requirements, growth capabilities, and limitations.

Software

The basic categories of software criteria are needs, resources, performance, flexibility, and operating

TABLE 16-5   Technical Requirements Outline for Operating System or Network Performance

---

3.0 Generic Operating System Requirements
    3.1 Instruction set and types of numeric processing
    3.2 Cache memory
    3.3 Hardware compatibility
    3.4 Software compatibility
    3.5 Virtual and real memory requirements
    3.6 Job, task, data management structure and function
    3.7 Multiprocessing capabilities
    3.8 Fixed system overhead
    3.9 Variable system overhead
    3.10 Control language
    3.11 Compilers supported
    3.12 Packaged software supported
    3.13 File access methods supported

TABLE 16-6   Example of LAN Performance Requirements

3.1 Software Requirements
Must support and run DB2 or SQL Server software.
Must support and run Quattro or Lotus spreadsheet.
Must support and run ADW or IEF PC-based CASE tools.
Must support and run Word Perfect.
 	
Must provide multiuser support for simultaneous users of all software with lockout at the record or data item level. File level locking should be a user-selectable option.
Must allow levels of security including at least three levels for department, group, and user; security assignment by software package, directory, or minidisk; and by function (e.g., read, write, or both).
Must support transaction logging either in the operating system or by other packages, e.g., the database server and CASE packages.
Must support roll-back processing or permit it by the software in the environment.
 	
3.2 Printing
Must support direct access to printers by all users.
Must provide printing of at least 100 pages per minute (ppm).
Printer(s) must accommodate:
  One-ply, preprinted forms,
  8½ × 11, 16-lb or 20-lb paper
	3.2 Printing, *continued*
	  8½ × 14, 16-lb or 20-lb paper
	  4 × 9 envelopes
	  7 × 10 envelopes
	  Transparencies for overheads
	  Graphics
	  Address labels
	
	3.3 Processing
	Interactive processing for up to 64 PCs at a time.
	Growth to 120 PCs at a time in five years.
	Able to accommodate Word Perfect—36 users, SQL processing (see above)—12 users, spreadsheet (see above)—10 users, and CASE tool processing—six users simultaneously.
	Able to accommodate doubling of users in all categories within five years.
	
	3.4 Benchmark Evaluation Criteria
	Current and past workload data.
	Current size and planned growth.
	Future fiscal policies that affect how computers are charged to users.
	Current and future manpower for operations support.

characteristics. These categories and the major requirements specified in an RFP are summarized in Table 16-7 and discussed below.

Needs

Needs identify context-specific requirements such as file processing, maximum number of simultaneous users, number of buffers, size of files and records that can be handled, or precision of numbers for mathematical computation.

In addition, environmental factors are extremely important. The operating system, programming language, and interfaces with other software determine whether the package can exist in your operational environment, even if your requirements are met.

Resources

Package resources identify the hardware configuration requirements for the software. The **working set** is the minimal, real memory usage when the software is running. All software is designed to have two components, a real memory component and a virtual memory component. The virtual component is swapped in and out of memory as it is accessed. When it is out of memory it is stored on some peripheral device, usually a disk. The real memory component is that minimal core of the software that maintains the beginning and ending addresses for buffers, queues, lists, arrays, and other memory the software manages, and the task management software to control the software's execution.

TABLE 16-7   Technical Requirements Outline for Customer Software or Package (Section 3.0 of Detailed RFP Outline Table 16-1.)

3.0 Technical Specifications
   3.1 Concept and overview
      3.1.1 Diagrams of processes, entities, configuration, etc. as appropriate
      3.1.2 Functional requirements classified as mandatory or optional
      3.1.3 Dictionary defining all terms, items, processes, entities, and relationships in the diagrams and above sections in detail sufficient to provide complete understanding of the nature of the work expected
   3.2 Audit and data integrity requirements
   3.3 Security and recoverability requirements
   3.4 Performance requirements
   3.5 Conversion requirements
   3.6 Interface requirements
   3.7 Special requirements, e.g., facilities alterations
   3.8 Training
   3.9 Acceptance criteria

In addition to the working set, the peak usage real memory component is important. When the maximum number of users are present on the system, maximum sizes of the working set and virtual memory requirements should be identified. If there is no change to the memory requirements, but there is an optimum size for real memory for efficient processing, that should be required information.

The third type of resource information required is the amount of disk space required to store the software on disk, and the average storage requirements for several standard sizes of files. An example of a standard file is a 10,000 record file with 50 fields of 8 characters each, and three multifield indexes.

Performance

The performance requirements should identify both total throughput and individual transaction response requirements if there are any.

Flexibility

Flexibility issues are of two types. First, the packages' interconnectivity to other packages might be of interest. Second, the potential for client modification and customization might also be of interest. For either type of flexibility, the ability of the package to change, expand functionality, and loosen restrictions (e.g., move from ten open files to 256 open files at once) are a good indicator of how fast the package can change to accommodate different business needs.

To assess the vendor's capabilities, you can require a list of packages with which the package under review is compatible. Also, you can require information about the type and frequency of new releases of the software. If the new releases only fix old bugs, the software is more risky than if the new releases enhance package functionality.

To assess the extent to which you might be able to customize the software, the requirements should specify this as necessary. In general, many software companies will not honor warranties on software if any code is changed. Several mainframe software vendors, for instance D&B-MSA™,[2] specifically design their software for client customization.

Operating Characteristics

The operating characteristics requirements should require identification of the hardware, operating systems, and compatible configurations of networks on which the software can run. If interplatform connections are desired, such compatibility should be identified as a requirement.

A second operating characteristic is the form of package code. Vendors typically supply a load module form of package that cannot be examined for errors. If package does not function, the vendor is the only recourse for help. In this case, clients usually request source code and have a contract clause that specifies that source code should be held in escrow and made available at such time that the vendor

---

2 D&B-MSA™ is a wholly owned subsidiary of Dun and Bradstreet, New Jersey.

company goes out of business or the software ceases to function. The same argument and requirements should be written for access to data stored under proprietary methods in a software package.

The type of installation work required and vendor assistance available are the other operating characteristics of interest. Some installations require little or no planning, with the installer simply running a program that actually does the installation. Other software installations require weeks of planning, including both logical and physical design, and decisions about how internal queues, buffers, and so on will be stored. The amount of work is important for operations planning, but the type and amount of vendor support during the installation are also important.

RFP EVALUATION

General Evaluation Guidelines

In general, the evaluation proceeds as follows. In each section, the required items are scored using a rating system previously decided. Vendor recommendations beyond the requirements are identified and evaluated. Through discussion and professional judgment, the contribution of enhancements to the quality of the finished work product is determined and scored. The weighted scores for the individual items are summed by vendor to yield a section score. For the financial section, formulae are applied to the bids and like numbers across proposals are compared and scored. The weighted scores for each section are summarized and summed to yield a single score for each vendor. The vendor with the highest overall score is selected.

If there is a tie or several vendors are very similar, the proposals are reevaluated for scoring method, weights, and relative importance of each type of information to eventually select a winner. The reevaluation is a form of sensitivity analysis that determines where the scoring method is most sensitive to between-vendor differences and if the method should be changed to remove the sensitivity, or if one vendor is clearly superior in some area.

Scoring Methods

The scoring for the technical evaluation requires assessment of the extent to which the vendor complies with requirements and addresses the required features and functions in the proposal. An implicit ranking of quality of proposed solution is included in the technical assessment.

There is no one right way to score a proposal. Rather, three methods are most common. One scoring method ranks each item according to its relative merit compared to the other vendors. If there are three vendors the items are all ranked on a scale of one to three. The second common method is to use a fixed scale, say zero to ten, and all items are evaluated and placed on that scale regardless of the number of proposals. The third scoring method is to simply list requirements of the application and simply score a *zero* if the requirement is not met and a *one* if the requirement is met. The chosen scale is then used for scoring technical requirements, management approach, and company history.

Figure 16-3 shows the effect of the three methods on the same set of requirements. The second method is most sensitive to qualitative differences but is also the most subjective. The binary scoring method is most objective but the least sensitive to qualitative differences. The first method is both objective and able to distinguish differences. Therefore, the first method is recommended for your use when you are given a choice.

In the remaining example, we use the ranking method for the four vendors evaluated. Each item is scored and entered on the list. When the list is complete, the item scores are multiplied by the weights to develop the weighted scores. The weighted scores are summed to give a section evaluation score for each vendor.

The flaws of the methods are seen in the example in Figure 16-3. According to the summary, we would select vendor 3 using the first two scoring methods and Vendor 2 with the binary method. However, let's say we disqualify Vendor 3 for noncompliance with the second requirement. Then, the first two methods give us different answers. This example highlights the need to do sensitivity analysis on

Requirements	Vendor 1 Ranking					
	Method 1 (Rank 1–3)		Method 2 (Rank 1–10)		Method 3 (Binary)	
Provide for at least 10 relational files to be open simultaneously	Weight 1	Rank 1	Weight .5	Rank 1	Weight .5	Rank 0
Provide at least three indexes per relation	Weight 2	Rank 3	Weight 1.5	Rank 10	Weight 1.5	Rank 1
Provide user views that join up to six relations	Weight 3	Rank 2	Weight 3	Rank 3	Weight 3	Rank 1
Summary Σ (Weight * Rank)	13		24.5		4.5	

Requirements	Vendor 2 Ranking					
	Method 1 (Rank 1–3)		Method 2 (Rank 1–10)		Method 3 (Binary)	
Provide for at least 10 relational files to be open simultaneously	Weight 1	Rank 2	Weight .5	Rank 9	Weight .5	Rank 1
Provide at least three indexes per relation	Weight 2	Rank 2	Weight 1.5	Rank 10	Weight 1.5	Rank 1
Provide user views that join up to six relations	Weight 3	Rank 1	Weight 3	Rank 4	Weight 3	Rank 1
Summary Σ (Weight * Rank)	9		31.5		5	

FIGURE 16-3   Example of Requirements Scoring Methods

the scale used in scoring to ensure balancing of weights and scores.

Technical Evaluation

In ABC's scoring example, the technical section evaluation shows one page of technical requirements that describe characteristics of a software environment without specifying the software (see Figure 16-4). This list might be an additional 8–10 pages longer when complete. To get the ranks for each item, the vendor responses are reviewed and the quality and completeness of each response is rated. The ranks are multiplied by the item weight and weighted scores are summed. The weighted score can then be normalized to account for between-section differences in the number of items ranked by dividing the weighted score by the number of items, in the example, eleven.

In both scoring systems, raw and normalized, Vendor 4's solution meets more criteria with a higher quality rating than the other vendors. Vendor 4 did not get the highest marks on all items, however. Vendors 1 and 2 have low scores for the technical section with more bottom ratings than the other vendors. These vendors would probably not be chosen and could be deleted from the remaining analysis if it were extensive.

None of the proposed language solutions has all required items with the highest rating. This means two things. First, the solution, whichever one is selected, should be reevaluated before a final deci-

Requirements	Vendor 3 Ranking					
	Method 1 (Rank 1–3)		Method 2 (Rank 1–10)		Method 3 (Binary)	
Provide for at least 10 relational files to be open simultaneously	Weight 1	Rank 3	Weight .5	Rank 10	Weight .5	Rank 1
Provide at least three indexes per relation	Weight 2	Rank 0	Weight 1.5	Rank 0	Weight 1.5	Rank 0
Provide user views that join up to six relations	Weight 3	Rank 3	Weight 3	Rank 10	Weight 3	Rank 1
Summary Σ (Weight * Rank)	12		35		3.5	

Method	Vendor 1	Vendor 2	Vendor 3
1	**13**	9	12
2	24.5	31.5	**35**
3	4.5	**5**	3.5

Selected Vendor is shown in bold for each method

FIGURE 16-3   Example of Requirements Scoring Methods (*Continued*)

sion to ensure that the application can be done without too many design compromises because of flaws in the proposed language. Second, more evaluation of possible languages for implementation can be done and a language recommendation might be made to the selected vendor. In other words, the language for implementation becomes a negotiating point for lowering the cost or for changing the proposed solution.

Management Approach Evaluation

The section of the proposal on the management approach includes all the information about how the vendor will manage the staff and the process to the satisfactory completion of the client. The schedule, staffing, management reporting, and problem resolution should be included. In addition, the vendor discusses expected resources of the client company for the work engagement.

There is no one right way to evaluate the management approach. Rather, this section is reviewed to determine the fit with client expectations and the realism of the approach. For instance, if there are more than one vendor staff, one of the staff should be designated the 'senior' person in charge of the work products and problems of the other person(s). Any personnel problems of vendor staff should not be dealt with by the client; the senior person has this responsibility. Also, a person from the vendor's management staff should be designated as responsible for guaranteeing the quality of work product by the company's staff. This person is usually the management contact for the client and is the ultimate manager for the vendor staff even though there may also be an on-site, working manager.

Proposals should be assessed in a manner consistent with that of the technical requirements. That is, either a zero/one grading system, or a ranking system, is used, depending on which is used for technical requirements. The management techniques requested in the RFP for the management approach should have been previously prioritized and weighted. The items are listed, scored, and

Technical Requirements	Weight	Vendor 1 Rank	Vendor 2 Rank	Vendor 3 Rank	Vendor 4 Rank
3 files with 2,000—200 character records, 40 fields	5	1	2	3	4
2 files with 50,000—40 character records, 10 fields	5	2	1	4	3
Process up to six simultaneous transactions	5	2	1	4	3
Up to six attributes in compound key	5	1	2	3	4
Max text field length of 300 characters	3	2	1	3	4
Max integer length 15 digits	3	2	1	3	4
Max decimal number 9.2	3	1	2	3	4
Provide for at least 10 relational files to be open simultaneously	4	3	1	2	4
Provide at least three indexes per relation	5	3	2	1	4
Provide user views that join up to six relations	5	2	1	3	4
Supports bar code reader	4	2	4	1	3
Summary Σ (Weight * Rank) for items shown	–	90	77	129	174
Normalized score	–	8.2	7	11.7	15.8

FIGURE 16-4   ABC Technical Scoring

weighted. Finally, a weighted average score for management approach is computed for each vendor and added to the financial summary sheet.

In the example shown in Figure 16-5, Vendor 1 omitted resumes of the proposed staff and lost several rating points as a result. Vendor 2 assumed many more client resources than the company was willing to commit and lost points as a result. Only Vendors 3 and 4 provided information that was complete. Their scores reflect their proposals' assessed quality differences.

Financial Evaluation

The next analysis evaluates the financial aspects of the proposals. The financial evaluation is independent from the technical evaluation and assumes that all required features are present. In fact, the technical and financial evaluations might be done by different people in different departments. The project manager and SEs usually perform the technical evaluation, while the project manager and/or a financial support group might do the financial evaluation.

Management Requirements	Weight	Vendor 1 Rank	Vendor 2 Rank	Vendor 3 Rank	Vendor 4 Rank
Schedule and staffing	5	1	2	3	4
Project management	5	2	1	4	3
Status reporting	5	2	1	4	3
Problem management	5	1	2	3	4
Summary Σ (Weight * Rank)	–	30	30	70	70
Normalized score*	–	7.5	7.5	17.5	17.5

*Normalized Score = Σ (Weight * Rank) / # Items

FIGURE 16-5   ABC Management Approach Scoring

Recall that for services such as custom software development, there are three types of financial proposals: fixed, time/materials (T&M), and T&M with a ceiling (semifixed). For hardware, there are three types of proposals: lease, lease with option to buy, and purchase. And for software packages, there is a basic license fee plus a maintenance fee. The first step in the financial analysis is to determine what set of numbers to compare. The proposal should specify the type(s) of financial bids solicited, but, if not, the three types need to be equated for proper comparison.

After deciding on which numbers to compare, a simple net present value (NPV) analysis may be developed (see Chapter 6). Recall that NPV computes the present value of multitime period expenditures, assuming a specific interest rate on money (see Figure 16-6). If all vendors' proposed expenditures are in the same time period, NPV is not necessary and a simple comparison is used. The final value of each project is entered on the summary evaluation sheet (see Figure 16-7). Other analyses might include payback period, cost per vendor employee, and so on, depending on company convention.

In Figure 16-7, the present value of all hardware options is listed and separated from the cost of labor. Then, rankings for hardware and software are applied based on the low cost. Both average and nor-

$$NPV = \sum_{t=0}^{n} \frac{B_t - C_t}{(1 + d)^t}$$

Where: d = Discount interest rate

n = Life of project in years

B_t = Value of benefits in period t

C_t = Value of costs in period t

For instance, assume the life of the project is five years, and the per period cost is $1,000,000 at .075 interest. The benefits of the project for the five years are zero, $100,000, $250,000, $450,000, and $2,000,000. The NPV is:

$NPV = (-1,000,000)/1.075$

$+ (100,000 - 1,000,000)/1.075^2$

$+ (250,000 - 1,000,000)/1.075^3$

$+ (700,000 - 1,000,000)/1.075^4$

$+ (2,000,000 - 1,000,000)/1.075^5$

$= -930,232 - 576,923 - 443,548$
$- 223,880 + 689,655$
$= -\$1,494,928$

FIGURE 16-6   Sample Net Present Value Computation

Financial Summary	Vendor 1	Vendor 2	Vendor 3	Vendor 4
Net Present Value Hardware Lease	$22,000	$30,000	$27,250	$22,300
NPV Hardware Lease with Option to Purchase	$30,000	$32,000	$31,750	$24,600
NPV Hardware Purchase	$45,000	$37,800	$37,500	$32,500
Total Cost T&M Labor	$17,500	$22,600	$28,400	$27,500

	Weight	Vendor 1 Rank	Vendor 2 Rank	Vendor 3 Rank	Vendor 4 Rank
Hardware Rank	4	4	1	2	3
Software Rank	6	4	1	2	3
Summary Σ (Weight * Rank)		40	10	20	30

FIGURE 16-7   ABC Financial Evaluation Summary

malized scores can be generated as we have shown. The normalized scores are used in the comparison with the scores of the other sections. In the rankings, the higher the score, the lower the cost. In this case, Vendor 1 receives the highest cost scores for both hardware and software. Vendor 4, the highest ranked vendor in the technical section, was third on both items, with a weighted score of 3. If hardware and software are equally important, we could have averaged the scores for each vendor. Using weights which are somewhat higher than the weights for the other score categories increases the importance of the financial evaluation relative to the technical and other evaluations.

Company Evaluation

One risk any client takes when contracting work to others is that the vendor might not meet the terms of the contract for some reason. The company evaluation is one way to define such risks and assign a score to each vendor company.

In general, the longer the company has been in business and the larger the size, the less likely the company is to go out of business. Similarly, the smaller a percentage of the total company's work this particular contract is, the less likely schedule problems, for fixed price work, for instance, are to severely hamper the vendor's ability to do business. The first score assessed, then, is one of risk that the vendor can do this work without straining his or her own organization.

The second type of evaluation gives credit for past work with the client company. The idea is to favor a company with successful past experience because their personnel are likely to know the client's way of doing business and need less introductory time than vendors without that experience. Other project managers who know the vendor should be asked about the quality and quantity of work of vendor employees, satisfaction with the vendor, and compliance with contract terms. A high ranking should be given for successful past projects and a low ranking (e.g., negative) for unsuccessful past work. Obviously, no ranking can be given for a company with no history at the client site. If this item is the decision criteria for a proposal, then the technical evaluation should be reevaluated to ensure that the best proposal is being selected.

A similar evaluation gives vendors who have developed similar work products credit for that knowledge. Vendors who are already familiar with the problem domain, and who need less start-up time to learn the domain, are favored over those without that knowledge.

Vendor Company Criteria	Weight	Vendor 1 Rank	Vendor 2 Rank	Vendor 3 Rank	Vendor 4 Rank
Age/Size	5	3	1	4	2
Similar work	5	3	1	2	4
Work with ABC	5	0	0	0	0
Reputation	5	3	1	4	2
Summary Σ (Weight * Rank)	–	45	15	50	40
Normalized score		9	3.7	12.5	10

FIGURE 16-8   ABC Vendor Company Rating

Vendors who claim similar experience should be checked by discussing the experience with reference clients. Unless another firm gives a positive recommendation, no credit for domain experience should be given. A neutral or negative recommendation does not necessarily mean a negative rating. Rather, a negative rating raises a flag that not all projects are perfect but should not cause a vendor to be disqualified. If all recommendations are negative, then the vendor might be given a negative rating.

The scores for company evaluation are entered in the summary sheet which is completed. The final scores in all areas are multiplied by the weight for the section and summed to develop a final weighted assessment. The company with the highest overall score is selected unless some extenuating circumstance is present.

In Figure 16-8, all four vendors scored zero in prior work with ABC, meaning that none have worked with ABC before. Vendor 4, the preferred vendor based on technical scores, ranks low in age/size and low in reputation. These numbers can be interpreted as identifying a small, fairly new company that has had some successes and some failures. This interpretation implies some risk in using Vendor 4.

If we look at Vendor 3, who was ranked second on the technical list, the age/size and reputation are the best of the four vendors. The problem here is that Vendor 3 has little experience with similar work, thus, also identifying a source of risk.

The summary form (see Figure 16-9) shows the proposals summarized on one page for a management overview. The weighted and normalized weighted scores should both be shown as an indicator of the sensitivity of the weighting system in selecting the proposal winner.

AUTOMATED SUPPORT TOOLS FOR VENDOR EVALUATION

There are no automated tools that are advertised as specifically for RFP use. Rather, there is general purpose software that can be used for different parts of the work. For instance, spreadsheets can be used for the financial analysis and for maintaining and monitoring the scores easily. Word processing and CASE tools might be used in the preparation of the RFP document, but are of less use in evaluating the vendor proposals. Table 16-8 shows the most popular spreadsheets on the market at this time. Any of these packages can be used in the RFP analysis.

SUMMARY

This chapter discusses the procurement of hardware, software, or services for an IS organization. The formal RFP process includes the development of work

Criteria	Weight	Vendor 1 Rank	Vendor 2 Rank	Vendor 3 Rank	Vendor 4 Rank
Technical	.4	90	77	129	174
Management approach	.2	30	30	70	70
Company	.1	45	15	50	40
Financial average rank	.3	40	10	20	30
Cost of cheapest alternative		$42,500	$42,600	$55,650	$49,800
		Vendor 1	Vendor 2	Vendor 3	Vendor 4
Total weighted score		58.5	41.3	76.6	96.6
Total weighted normalized score		14.6	10.3	19.2	24.2

FIGURE 16-9   ABC Vendor Summary Ratings

requirements, identification of vendors, development of a Request for Proposal (RFP), management of the RFP process, evaluations of the proposals, and selection of a vendor.

An RFP consists of a management summary, statement of requirements, proposal process description with important dates, and standard contract terms. Optional sections of the RFP include a definition of the vendor response.

Ranking RFP responses requires the definition of the ranking scheme and of weights signifying the relative importance of the ranked items. The least subjective, most informative of the three common ranking schemes is one that uses the number of vendors as the number of ranks. Other options are a binary system and a subjective ranking based on an arbitrary number of ranks, such as 10.

All response areas—technical, managerial, company, and financial—are ranked taking care to compare like things across the vendors. When complete, the weighted ranks are summed by section and for the whole RFP, and the vendor with the highest

TABLE 16-8   Automated Tools for Vendor Evaluation

Product	Company	Technique
COMNET, LANNET	CACI San Diego, CA	Simulation of network performance for different network operating systems
Excel, Multiplan	MicroSoft Redmond, WA	Spreadsheet for financial evaluation
Lotus 1-2-3	Lotus Development Corp.	Spreadsheet for financial evaluation
Quattro Pro	Borland Corp.	Spreadsheet for financial evaluation

score is selected. Do sensitivity analysis of the ranking scheme to minimize obvious bias.

REFERENCES

Joslin, Edward O., *Computer Selection*. Reading, MA: Addison-Wesley Publishing Co., Inc., 1968.

King, John L., and Edward L. Schrems, "Cost-benefit analysis in information systems development and operation," in *Computing Surveys*, Vol. 10, #1, March 1978, p. 25.

Lucas, Henry C., Jr., *The Analysis, Design and Implementation of Information Systems*, 4th ed., New York, Mitchell McGraw-Hill, 1992.

Stamper, David, *Business Data Communications*, 3rd ed., Redwood City, CA: The Benjamin/Cummings Publishing Company, Inc., 1991.

KEY TERMS

acceptance criteria
benchmark
company requirements
data communications
   network
financial requirements
fixed price bid
lease option bid
lease with option to buy bid
license fee
make-buy decision
management approach
management
   requirements

package purchase
proposal process
purchase bid
request for information
   (RFI)
request for proposal (RFP)
request for quotation (RFQ)
residual price
T&M with ceiling bid
technical requirements
time and materials bid
   (T&M)
working set

EXERCISES

1. Using the information provided for the ABC Case in Chapter 16, develop a different way of scoring the vendor responses that is plausible. Defend the use of your method.

2. Develop an analysis of two well-known packages, such as Lotus and Quattro spreadsheets. What features are the same? Which are different? How would you choose between them?

3. Develop a list of issues for deciding what PC software packages should be the standards for a company. Are the criteria software features organizational in nature? Why?

STUDY QUESTIONS

1. Define the following terms:

   benchmark   T&M
   fixed price bid   management approach
   make-buy decision   technical requirements
   RFI   working set

2. Is the process of selecting a product through the RFP completely objective? Why or why not?

3. What is the purpose of an RFP?

4. How does the RFP process differ from the informal procurement process?

5. List and describe the seven types of financial proposals.

6. Why are there so many types of financial proposals?

7. List five criteria to be provided in a hardware RFP.

8. List five criteria to be provided in a software package RFP.

9. List five criteria to be provided in a software development RFP.

10. What RFP criteria are provided for a network?

11. Describe the three types of scoring systems for vendor proposals, identifying the pros and cons of each.

12. Why is a standard for vendor responses a good idea?

13. What formula is applied to develop the financial analysis? When is it *not* needed?

14. What is the purpose of a benchmark? For which type(s) of procurement is benchmarking used?

15. How can you determine a company's reputation?

★ EXTRA-CREDIT QUESTION

1. Take some application that might be used at ABC Video—accounts payable, general ledger, payroll, rental order processing—and perform a software evaluation for two competing products. Try to be objective in the criteria and weights you assign. What are the deciding factors in the evaluation?

TESTING AND QUALITY ASSURANCE

INTRODUCTION

Testing is the process (and art) of finding errors; it is the ultimate review of specifications, design, and coding. The *purpose* of testing is to guarantee that all elements of an application mesh properly, function as expected, and meet performance criteria.

Testing is a difficult activity to accept mentally because we are deliberately analyzing our own work or that of our peers to find fault. Thus, after working in groups and becoming productive teams, we seek to find fault and uncover mistakes through testing. When the person conducting the test is not on the project as, for instance, acceptance testers, they are viewed as adversaries.

Testing is a difficult activity for management to accept because it is costly, time consuming, and rarely finds all errors. Frequently, resources are difficult to obtain and risks of not testing are inadequately analyzed. The result is that most applications are not tested enough and are delivered with 'bugs.'

Research studies show that software errors tend to cluster in modules. As errors are found in a tested unit, the probability that more errors are present increases. Because of this phenomenon, as severe errors are found, the lower the confidence in the overall quality and reliability of the tested unit should be.

In this chapter, we discuss useful strategies for testing and the strategies which are most applicable to each level of testing. Then, we discuss each level of testing and develop test plan examples for the ABC rental system. Finally, automated test support within CASE tools and independent test support tools are defined and examples listed. The next section defines testing terminology.

TESTING TERMINOLOGY

As above, **testing** is the process (and art) of finding errors. A good test has a high probability of finding undiscovered errors. A successful test is one that finds new errors; a poor test is one that never finds errors.

There are two types of errors in applications. A **Type 1 error** defines code that does not do what it is supposed to do; these are errors of omission. A **Type 2 error** defines code that does something it is not supposed to do; these are errors of commission. Type 1 errors are most prevalent in newly developed applications. Type 2 errors predominate in maintenance applications which have code 'turned off' rather than removed. Good tests identify both types of errors.

Testing takes place at different levels and is conducted by different individuals during the application development. In this chapter we discuss the testing performed by the project team and testing performed by outside agents for application acceptance. Project team tests are termed **developmental tests**. Developmental tests include unit, subsystem, integration, and system tests. Tests by outside agents are called quality assurance (QA) and acceptance tests. The relationship between testing levels and project life-cycle phases are summarized in Figure 17-1.

A **unit test** is performed for each of the smallest units of code. **Subsystem, integration** tests verify the logic and processing for suites of modules that perform some activity, verifying communications between them. **System tests** verify that the functional specifications are met, that the human interface operates as desired, and that the application works in the intended operational environment, within its constraints. During maintenance, testers use a technique called regression testing in addition to other types of tests. **Regression tests** are cus-

tomized to test that changes to an application have not caused it to *regress* to some state of unacceptable quality.

Finally, outside agents perform **quality assurance (QA) tests of acceptance** for the application. The outside agent is either the user or a user representative. The goal is to perform an objective, unbiased assessment of the application, and an outside agent is considered more objective than a team member. QA tests are similar to system tests in their makeup and objectives, but they differ in that they are beyond the control of the project team. QA test reports usually are sent to IS and user management in addition to the project manager. The QA tester plans his own strategy and conducts his own test to ensure that the application meets all functional requirements. QA testing is the last testing done before an application is placed into production status.

Each test level requires the definition of a strategy for testing. Strategies are either white box or black box, and either top-down or bottom-up. **Black-box strategies** use a 'toaster mentality': You plug it in,

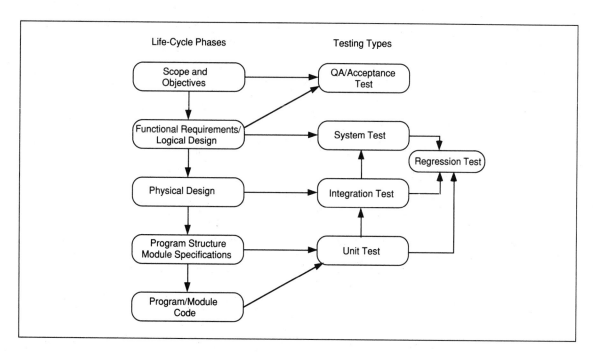

FIGURE 17-1   Correspondence between Project Life-Cycle Phases and Testing

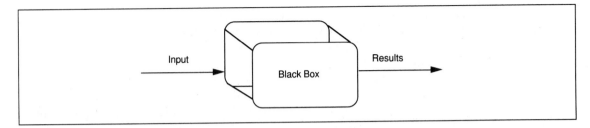

FIGURE 17-2   Black Box Data Testing Strategy

it is supposed to work (see Figure 17-2). Created input data is designed to generate variations of outputs without regard to how the logic actually functions. The results are predicted and compared to the actual results to determine the success of the test.

White-box strategies open up the 'box' and look at specific logic of the application to verify *how* it works (see Figure 17-3). Tests use logic specifications to generate variations of processing and to predict the resulting outputs. Intermediate and final output results can be predicted and validated using white-box tests.

The second type of testing strategy defines how the test and code development will proceed. **Top-down testing** assumes that critical control code and functions will be developed and tested first (see Figure 17-4). These are followed by secondary functions and supporting functions. The theory is that the more often critical modules are exercised, the higher the confidence in their reliability can be.

Bottom-up testing assumes that the lower the number of incremental changes in modules, the lower the error rate. Complete modules are coded

and unit tested (see Figure 17-5). Then the tested module is placed into integration testing.

The test strategies are not mutually exclusive; any of them can be used individually and collectively. The test strategy chosen constrains the type of errors that can be found, sometimes necessitating the use of more than one. Ideally, the test for the application combines several strategies to uncover the broadest range of errors.

After a strategy is defined, it is applied to the level of test to develop actual test cases. **Test cases** are individual transactions or data records that cause logic to be tested. For every test case, all results of processing are predicted. For on-line and real-time applications, **test scripts** document the interactive dialogue that takes place between user and application and the changes that result from the dialogue. A **test plan** documents the strategy, type, cases, and scripts for testing some component of an application. All the plans together comprise the test plan for the application.

Testing is iterative until no errors, or some acceptable number of errors, are found. In the first step

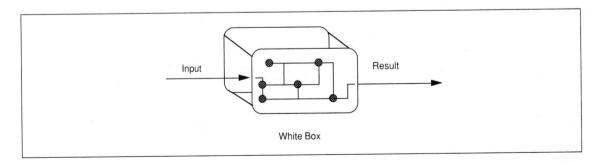

FIGURE 17-3   White Box Logic Testing Strategy

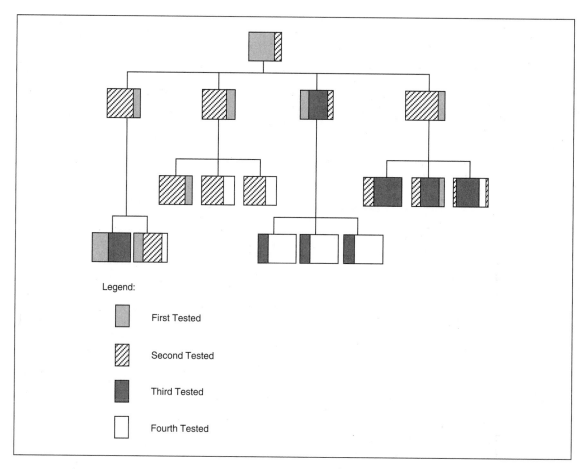

FIGURE 17-4   Top-Down Testing Strategy

of the testing process, test inputs, configuration, and application code are required to conduct the actual test. The second step is to compare the results of the test to predicted results and evaluate differences to find errors. The next step is to remove errors, or 'debug' the code. When recoding is complete, testing of changes ensures that each module works. The revised modules are then reentered into the testing cycle until a decision to end testing is made. This cycle of testing is depicted in Figure 17-6 for a top-down strategy.

The process of test development begins during design. The test coordinator assigned should be a capable programmer-analyst who understands the requirements of the application and knows how to conduct testing. The larger and more complex the application, the more senior and skilled the test coordinator should be. A test team may also be assigned to work with the coordinator on large, complex projects. The testing team uses the functional requirements from the analysis phase and the design and program specifications from the design phase as input to begin developing a strategy for testing the system. As a strategy evolves, walk-throughs are held to verify the strategy and communicate it to the entire test team. Duties for all levels of testing are assigned. Time estimates for test development and completion are developed. The test team works independently in parallel with the development team to do their work. They work with the DBA in developing a test database that can support all levels of testing. For unit testing, the test team verifies results

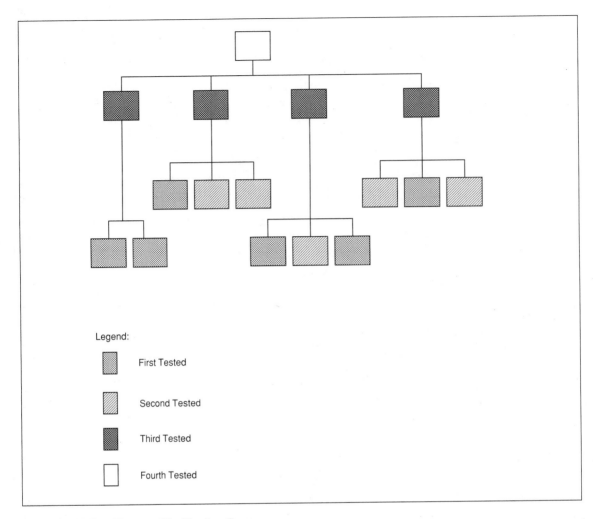

FIGURE 17-5   Bottom-Up Testing Strategy

and accepts modules and programs for integration testing. The test team conducts and evaluates integration and system tests.

TESTING _____
STRATEGIES _____

There are two kinds of testing strategies. The first type of strategy relates to how logic is tested in the application. Logic testing strategies are either black-box or white-box. Black-box testing strategies assume that module (or program or system) testing is concerned only that what goes in comes out correctly. The details of logic are hidden and not specifically analyzed. Black-box strategies are data-driven, which means that all test cases are based on analysis of data requirements for the test item.[1]

White-box approaches to testing assume that specific logic is important and to be tested. White-box tests evaluate some or all of the logic of a test item to verify correct functioning. White-box strategies are

_____
1 *Test item* is the term used through the remainder of the discussion to identify some *thing* being tested. A test item might be a module, group of modules, or the whole application.

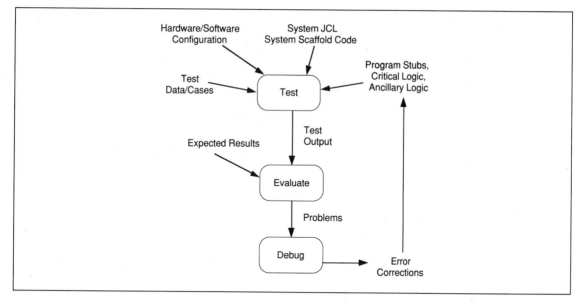

FIGURE 17-6   Testing Information Flow

logic-driven, which means that all test cases are based on analysis of expected functions of the test item.

The second type of testing strategy relates to how testing is conducted, regardless of logic testing strategy. These conduct, or process, strategies are top-down and bottom-up. Both top-down and bottom-up testing fit the project life-cycle phases in Figure 17-1; the difference is in the general approach. Top-down is incremental; bottom-up is 'all or nothing.'

Top-down testing assumes the main application logic is most important. Therefore, the main logic should be developed and tested first and continuously throughout development. Continuous successful testing raises confidence levels about code reliability. **Program stubs** that contain minimal functional logic are tested first with additional logic added as it is unit tested. Top-down testing frequently requires extra code, known as **scaffolding**, to support the stubs, partial modules, and other pieces of the application.

Bottom-up testing assumes that individual programs and modules are fully developed as standalone processes. These are tested individually, then combined for integration testing. Bottom-up testing treats test phases as somewhat discrete. Unit testing

leads to integration testing which leads to system testing. The next section discusses variations of black- and white-box testing strategies.

Black-Box Testing

Black-box testing attends to process results as evidenced by data. The test item is treated as a *black box* whose logic is unknown. The approach is effective for single function modules and for high-level system testing. Three commonly used methods of black box testing are:

- equivalence partitioning
- boundary value analysis
- error guessing

A fourth method that is less common in business, cause-effect graphing, is also used. Each of these methods are described in this section.

Equivalence Partitioning

The goals for equivalence partitioning are to minimize the number of test cases over other methods and design test cases to be representative of sets of data. For the given level of test, the test item data inputs are divided into **equivalent partitions** each representing some set of data. Then, test cases are designed using data from each representative, equivalent set. The theory is that by exhaustively testing one item from each set, we can assume that all other *equivalent* items are also exhaustively tested.

For instance, at the module level, field values identify equivalent sets. If the field domain is a range of values, then one set is allowable values and the other set is disallowed values. The analysis to define equivalent domain sets continues for each data item in the input.

Equivalence partitioning gains power when used at more abstract levels than fields, however. For instance, interactive programs, for integration tests, can be defined as equivalent sets at the screen, menu selection, or process levels. At the system test level, equivalence can be defined at the transaction, process, or activity level (from Information Engineering).

Test scripts for on-line applications can be black-box equivalence partitioning tools. A test script is an entry-by-entry description of interactive processing. A script identifies what the user enters, what the system displays in response, and what the user response to the system should be. *How* any of these entries, actions, and displays takes place is not tested.

Boundary Value Analysis

Boundary value analysis is a stricter form of equivalence partitioning that uses *boundary* values rather than *any* value in an equivalent set. A boundary value is *at the margin*. For example, the domain for a month of the year ranges from one to 12. The boundary values are one and 12 for valid values, and zero and 13 for the invalid values. All four boundary values should be used in test cases. Boundary value analysis is most often used at the module level to define specific data items for testing.

Error Guessing

Contrary to its name, error guessing is not a random guessing activity. Based on intuition and experience, it is easy for experts to test for many **error** conditions by **guessing** which are most likely to occur. For instance, dividing by zero, unless handled properly, causes abnormal ending of modules. If a module contains division, use a test that includes a zero divisor. Since it is based on intuition, error guessing is usually not effective in finding all errors, only the most common ones. If error guessing is used, it should always be used with some other strategy.

Cause-Effect Graphing

One shortcoming of equivalence and boundary testing is that compound field interactions are not identified. Cause-effect analysis compensates for this shortcoming. A **cause-effect graph** depicts specific transformations and outputs as effects and identifies the input data causing those effects. The graphical notation identifies iteration, selection, Boolean, and equality conditions (see Figure 17-7). A diagram of the effects works backward to determine and graph all causes. Each circle on the diagram represents a sequence of instructions with no decision or control points. Each line on the diagram represents an equivalent class of data and the condition of its usage. When the graph is done, at least one valid and one invalid value for each equivalent set of data on the graph is translated into test case data. This is considered a black-box approach because it is concerned not with logic, but with testing data value differences and their effect on processing. An example cause-effect graph for Customer Create processing is shown in Figure 17-8.

Cause-effect graphing is a systematic way to create efficient tests. The trade-off is in time to develop the set of graphs for an application versus the time consumed executing large numbers of less efficient, possibly less inclusive test cases. The technique is used more in aerospace than in general business.

Cause-effect graphs are more readily created from DFDs, PDFDs, and state-transition diagrams than from Booch diagrams even though it is particularly useful for real-time and embedded systems. Both types of systems use state-transition diagrams to show the causes and effects of processing. A cause-effect graph can be superimposed on a state-transition diagram or easily developed from the state-transition diagram. Cause-effect graphing can be used in place of white-box approaches whenever

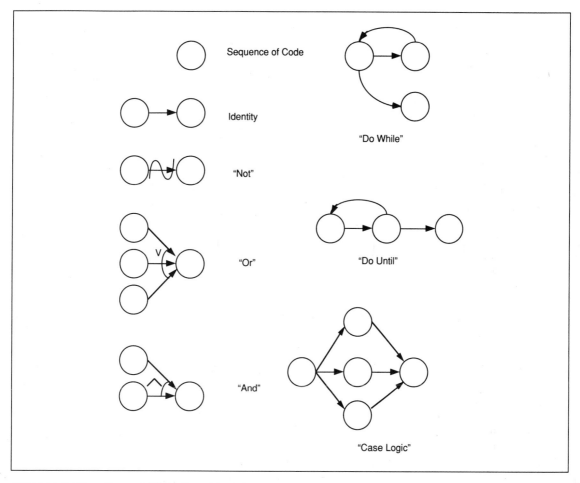

FIGURE 17-7   Cause-Effect Graphical Notation

specific logic cannot be realistically tested because of combinatorial effects of multiple logic conditions.

White-Box Testing

White-box testing evaluates specific execute item logic to guarantee its proper functioning. Three types of white-box techniques are discussed here: logic tests, mathematical proofs, and cleanroom testing. Logic coverage can be at the level of statements, decisions, conditions, or multiple conditions. In addition, for mathematically specified programs, such as predicate logic used in artificial intelligence applications, theorem proof tests can be conducted.

The newest development in white-box strategies is the 'clean room' approach developed by IBM.

Logic Tests

Logic tests can be detailed to the statement level. While execution of every statement is a laudable goal, it may not test all conditions through a program. For instance, an *if* statement tested once tests either success or failure of the *if*. At least two tests are required to test both conditions. Trying to test all conditions of all statements is simply not practical. In a small module with 10 iterations through a four-path loop, about 5.5 million test cases would

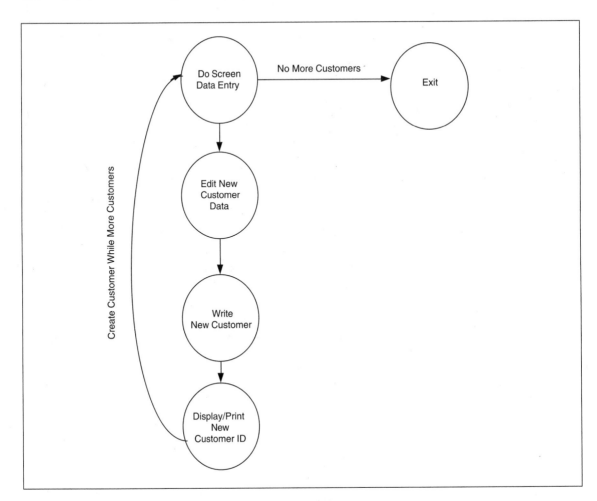

FIGURE 17-8   Cause-Effect Graph for Customer Create

be needed to try all possible combinations of paths (i.e., $4^{10} + 4^9 + 4^8 \ldots + 4^1$). Obviously, some other method of deciding test cases is needed. The other white-box logic testing strategies offer some alternatives.

Decision logic tests look at each decision in a module and generate test data to create all possible outcomes. The problem is that decisions are not always discrete and providing for compound decisions requires a different strategy. A problem with logic tests at this level is that they do not test module conformance to specifications. If the test is developed based on the specification, but the specification is interpreted differently by the programmer

(for better or worse), the test is sure to fail. The solution to this issue is to require program specifications to detail all logic. While this may be practical for first- and second-generation languages (i.e., machine and assembler languages), it defeats the purpose of higher level, declarative languages.

Condition logic tests are designed such that each condition that can result from a decision is exercised at least once. In addition, multiple entry conditions are tested. Thus, condition tests are more inclusive than decision logic tests. They still suffer from the problem of ignoring compound decision logic.

Multicondition tests generate each outcome of multiple decision criteria and multiple entry points to a module. These tests require analysis to define multicriteria decision boundaries. If the boundaries are incorrectly defined, the test is ineffective. When designed properly, multicondition logic tests can minimize the number of test cases while examining a large number of conditions in the case. The use of this technique requires practice and skill but can be mentally stimulating and even fun.

Mathematical Proof Tests

When evaluating logic, the goal is zero defects. One method of approaching zero defects is to apply mathematical reasoning to the logic requirements, proving the correctness of the program. This method requires specifications to be stated in a formal language such as the **Vienna Development Method (VDM)**. Formal languages require both mathematical and logic skills that are beyond the average business SE's ability at the present time. An example of a general process overview for a payroll system as specified in VDM is shown as Figure 17-9. While a detailed discussion of these methods is beyond the scope of this text, they deserve mention because they are the only known way for attaining zero defects and knowing it.

Cleanroom Tests

Cleanroom testing is an extension of mathematical proof that deserves some comment. Cleanroom testing is a manual verification technique used as a part of **cleanroom development**. The theory of cleanroom development is that by preventing errors from ever entering the process, costs are reduced, software reliability is increased, and the zero defect goal is attained. The process was introduced in IBM in the early 1980s by Mills, Dyer, and Linger, and applies hardware engineering techniques to software. Formal specifications are incrementally developed and *manually* verified by walk-through and inspections teams. Any program that is not easily read is rewritten. All program development is on paper until all verification is complete.

Cleanroom testing techniques are walk-throughs and formal mathematical verification. The goal is to decompose every module into functions and their linkages. Functional verification uses mathematical

techniques, and linkage verification uses set theory whenever possible to prove the application design and code.

After verification, an independent testing team compiles and executes the code. Test data is compiled by analysis of the functional specification and is designed to represent statistical proportions of data expected to be processed by the live system. In addition to normal data, every type of catastrophic error is produced to test that the application does degrade gracefully.

The success of cleanroom development and testing is such that more than 80% of reported projects have an average failure time of less than once every 500 software years. Software years are counted by number of sites times number of years of operation. For example, 100 sites for one year is 100 software years. This is an impressive statistic that, coupled with the 80-20 rule, can guide redevelopment of error-prone modules. The 80-20 rule says that 80% of errors are in 20% of modules. If those modules can be identified, they should be redesigned and rewritten. Modules for redevelopment are more easily identified using cleanroom techniques than other techniques. The disadvantages of cleanroom development are similar to those of mathematical proof. Skills required are beyond those of the average business SE, including math, statistics, logic, and formal specification language. We will say more about the 80-20 rule later.

Top-Down Testing

Top-down testing is driven by the principle that the main logic of an application needs more testing and verification than supporting logic. Top-down approaches allow comparison of the application to functional requirements earlier than a bottom-up approach. This means that serious design flaws should surface earlier in the implementation process than with bottom-up testing.

The major drawback to top-down testing is the need for extra code, known as scaffolding, to support the stubs, partial modules, and other pieces of the application for testing. The scaffolding usually begins with job control language and the main logic of the application. The main logic is scaffolded

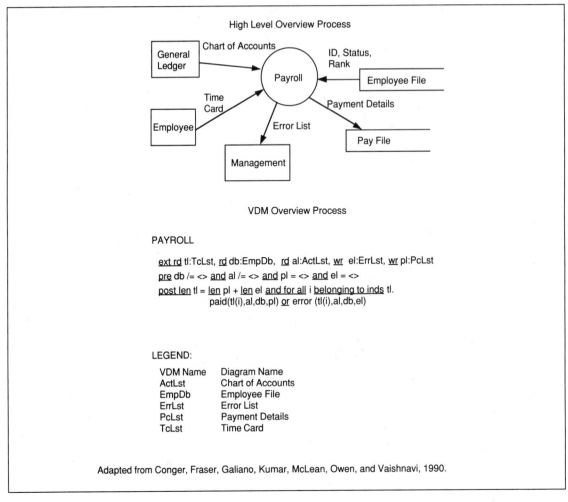

High Level Overview Process

VDM Overview Process

PAYROLL

ext rd tl:TcLst, rd db:EmpDb, rd al:ActLst, wr el:ErrLst, wr pl:PcLst

pre db /= <> and al /= <> and pl = <> and el = <>

post len tl = len pl + len el and for all i belonging to inds tl.
paid(tl(i),al,db,pl) or error (tl(i),al,db,el)

LEGEND:

VDM Name	Diagram Name
ActLst	Chart of Accounts
EmpDb	Employee File
ErrLst	Error List
PcLst	Payment Details
TcLst	Time Card

Adapted from Conger, Fraser, Galiano, Kumar, McLean, Owen, and Vaishnavi, 1990.

FIGURE 17-9   Vienna Development Method (VDM) Formal Specification Language Example

and tested hierarchically. First, only the critical procedures and control logic are tested.

For example, Figure 17-10 shows the mainline logic for *Customer Maintenance*. The mainline of logic is important because it will be executed every time a maintenance request is performed. Since customer creation is the most probable maintenance activity, it should be guaranteed as much as possible. Further, if creation works, it is easily modified to provide update and delete capabilities which are a subset of creation functionality. Figure 17-11 is an example of COBOL stub logic for *Create Customer*.

These two modules would be tested first, before any other logic is verified.

When critical procedures are working, the control language and main line code for less critical procedures are added. In the example above, the stubs for updating, deleting, and querying customers would be tested second. These are tested and retested throughout development as proof that the mainline of logic for all modules works.

After stubs, the most critical logic is coded, unit tested, and placed into integration testing upon completion. In our example, the code for *Create Cus-*

```
Procedure Division.
    Main-Line.
        Display Cust-Maint-menu.
        Accept Cust-Maint-Selection.
        If Cust-Maint-Selection =("A" or F6)
            Call Create-Customer

        else
        If Cust-Maint-Selection =("U" or F7)
            Call Update-Customer

        else
        If Cust-Maint-Selection =("D" or F8)
            Call Delete-Customer

        else
        If Cust-Maint-Selection =("R" or F9)
            Call Query-Customer

        else
        If Cust-Maint-Selection =("E" or F3)
            Go to Cust-Maint-Exit

        else
        Display Selection-Err
        Go To Main-Line.

    Cust-Maint-Exit. Exit.
```

FIGURE 17-10   Mainline Logic for Customer Maintenance

```
Identification Division.
    Program-ID.
        CreateCust.
Environment Division.
Configuration Section.
Source-Computer. IBM.
Object-Computer. IBM.
File Section.
FD   Customer-Screen
        ...
01   Customer-Screen-Record.
        ... screen description
FD   Customer-File
        ...
01   Customer-File-Record.
        ... customer record description
Data  Division.
Working-Storage Section.
01   Cust-Screen.
        ...
01   Customer-relation.
        ...
Procedure Division.
Main-Line.
    Perform Display-Cust-Screen.
    Perform Accept-Values.
    Perform Edit-Validate.
    Perform Write-Customer.
    Display Continue-Msg.
    Accept Cust-Response.
    If Cust-Resp = 'y'
            go to main-line
        else
            go to create-customer-exit.
Display-Cust-Screen.
    Write Cust-Screen from Customer-Screen-Record.
DCS-exit.  Exit.

Accept-Values.
AV-Exit. Exit.

Edit-Validate.
EV-Exit. Exit.

Write-Customer.
    Write Customer-Relation from Customer-File-Record
        on error perform Cust-Backout-Err.
WC-Exit. Exit.
Create-Customers-Exit. Exit.
```

FIGURE 17-11   COBOL Stub Program for Customer Create

tomer would be tested next. The 'critical' code includes screen data entry and writing to the file. Finally, ancillary logic, such as editing input fields, is completed and placed into testing. In our example, the less critical code is the actual edit and validation processing with error messages. Thus, in top-down testing, the entire application is developed in a skeletal form and tested. As pieces of the skeleton are *fleshed out*, they are added to the test application.

In theory, top-down testing should find critical design errors earlier in the testing process than other approaches. Also, in theory, top-down testing should result in significantly improved quality of delivered software because of the iterative nature of the tests. Unit and integration testing are continuous. There is no discrete integration testing, per se. When the unit/integrated test is complete, further system tests are conducted for volume and constraint tests.

Top-down easily supports testing of screen designs and human interface. In interactive applications, the first logic tested is usually screen navigation. This serves two purposes. First, the logic for interactive processing is exhaustively exercised by the time all code and testing is complete. Second, users can see, at an early stage, how the final application will look and feel. The users can test the navigation through screens and verify that it matches their work.

Top-down testing can also be used easily with prototyping and iterative development. Prototyping is iterative and follows the same logic for adding code as top-down testing. Presenting prototyping, iterative development, and top-down testing together for user concurrence helps ensure that prototypes actually get completed.

Bottom-Up Testing

Bottom-up testing takes an opposite approach based on the principle that any change to a module can affect its functioning. In bottom-up testing, the entire module should be the unit of test evaluation. All modules are coded and tested individually. A fourth level of testing is frequently added after unit testing to test the functioning of execute units. Then, execute units are turned over to the testing team for integration and systems testing.

The next section discusses the development of test cases to match whatever strategy is defined. Then, each level of testing is discussed in detail with ABC Video test examples to show how to design each test.

Test Cases

Test cases are input data created to demonstrate that both components and the total system satisfy all design requirements. Created data rather than 'live,' production data, is used for the following reasons:

1. Specially developed test data can incorporate all operational situations. This implies that each processing path may be tested at the appropriate level of testing (e.g., unit, integration, etc.).
2. Predetermined test case output should be predicted from created input. Predicting results is easier with created data because it is more orderly and usually has fewer cases.
3. Test case input and output are expanded to form a model database. The database should

statistically reflect the users' data in the amount and types of records processed while incorporating as many operational processing paths as possible. The database is then the basis for a regression test database in addition to its use for system testing. Production data is real, so finding statistically representative cases is more difficult than creating them.

Each test case should be developed to verify that specific design requirements, functional design, or code are satisfied. Test cases contain, in addition to test case input data, a forecast of test case output. Real or 'live' data should be used to reality test the modules after the tests using created data are successful.

Each component of an application (e.g., module, subroutine, program, utility, etc.) must be tested with *at least* two test cases: one that works and one that fails. All modules should be deliberately failed at least once to verify their 'graceful degradation.' For instance, if a database update fails, the application should give the user a message, roll back the processing to leave the database as it was before the transaction, and continue processing. If the application were to abend, or worse, continue processing with a corrupt database, the test would have caught an error.

Test cases can be used to test multiple design requirements. For example, a requirement might be that all screens are directly accessible from all other screens; a second requirement might be that each screen contain a standard format; a third requirement might be that all menus be pull-down selections from a menu bar. These three requirements can all be easily verified by a test case for navigation that also attends to format and menu selection method.

The development of test case input may be facilitated by the use of test data generators such as IEBDG (an IBM utility) or the test data generators within some case tools. The analysis and verification of processing may be facilitated by the use of language-specific or environment-specific testing supports (see Figure 17-12). These supports are discussed more completely in the section on automated supports.

COBOL Language Supports:
    Display
    Exhibit
    Ready Trace
    Interactive Trace
    Snap Dump

Focus Language Supports:
    Variable Display
    Transaction Counts
    Online Error Messages
    Online Help

FIGURE 17-12   Examples of Language Testing Supports

To insure that test cases are as comprehensive as possible, a methodical approach to the identification of logic paths or system components is indicated. Matrices, which relate system operation to the functional requirements of the system, are used for this purpose. For example, the matrix approach may be used in

- unit testing to identify the logic paths, logic conditions, data partitions or data boundaries to be tested based on the program specification.
- integration testing to identify the relationships and data requirements among interacting modules.
- system testing to identify the system and user requirements from functional requirements and acceptance criteria.

An example of the matrix approach for an integration test is illustrated as Figure 17-13. The example shows a matrix of program requirements to be met by a suite of modules for *Read Customer File* processing. The test verifies that each module functions independently, that communications between the modules (i.e., the message format, timing, and content) are correct, and verifies that all input and output are processed correctly and within any constraints.

The functional requirements of the *Read Customer File* module are related to test cases in the

	Good Cust-ID	Bad Cust-ID	Missing ID	Retrieve by Name (Good)	Retrieve by Name (Bad)	Good Credit	Bad Credit	Good Data	Bad Data	Call from GetValid Customer (Good)	Call from GetValid Customer (Bad)
1.	X	X	X	X	X					X	X
2.	X					X	X			X	X
3.	X	X	X					X	X	X	X
4.	X	X	X	X	X	X	X	X		X	X

Legend:

1. Read Customer

2. Check Credit

3. Create Customer

4. Display Customer

FIGURE 17-13   Read Customer File Requirements and Test Cases

matrix in Figure 17-13. The 11 requirements can be fully tested in *at most* seven test cases for the four functions.

Matching the Test Level to the Strategy

The goal of the testers is to find a balance between strategies that allows them to prove their application works while minimizing human and computer resource usage for the testing process. No one testing strategy is sufficient to test an application. To use only one testing strategy is dangerous. If only white-box testing is used, testing will consume many human and computer resources and may not identify data sensitive conditions or major logic flaws that transcend individual modules (see Table 17-1). If only black-box testing is used, specific logic problems may remain uncovered even when all specifications are tested; type 2 errors are difficult to uncover. Top-down testing by itself takes somewhat longer than a combined top-down, bottom-up approach. Bottom-up testing by itself does not find strategic errors until too late in the process to fix them without major delays.

In reality, we frequently combine all four strategies in testing an application. White-box testing is used most often for low-level tests—module, routine, subroutine, and program testing. Black-box testing is used most often for high-level tests—integration and system level testing. White-box tests find specific logic errors in code, while black-box tests find errors in the implementation of the functional business specifications. Similarly, top-down tests are conducted for the application with whole tested modules plugged into the control structure as they are ready, that is, after bottom-up development. Once modules are unit tested, they can be integration tested and, sometimes, even system tested with the same test cases.

Table 17-2 summarizes the uses of the box and live-data testing strategies for each level of test. Frequently black- and white-box techniques are combined at the unit level to uncover both data and logic errors. Black-box testing predominates as the level of test is more inclusive. Testing with created data at all levels can be supplemented by testing with live data. Operational, live-data tests ensure that the application can work in the real environment. Next, we examine the ABC rental application to design a strategy and each level of test.

TABLE 17-1 Test Strategy Objectives and Problems

Test Strategy	Method	Goal	Shortcomings
White-Box	Logic	Prove processing.	Functional flaws, data sensitive conditions, and errors across modules are all difficult to test with white-box methods.
Black-Box	Data	Prove results.	Type 2 errors and logic problems difficult to find.
Top-Down	Incremental	Exercise critical code extensively to improve confidence in reliability.	Scaffolding takes time and may be discarded. Constant change may introduce new errors in every test.
Bottom-up	All or nothing	Perfect parts. If parts work, whole should work.	Functional flaws found late and cause delays. Errors across modules may be difficult to trace and find.

TABLE 17-2   Test Level and Test Strategy

Level	General Strategy	Specific Strategy	Comments on Use
Unit	Black-Box	Equivalence Partitioning	Equivalence is difficult to estimate.
		Boundary Value Analysis	Should always be used in edit-validate modules.
		Cause-Effect Graphing	A formal method of boundary analysis that includes tests of compound logic conditions. Can be superimposed on already available graphics, such as state-transition or PDFD.
		Error Guessing	Not a great strategy, but can be useful in anticipating problems.
	Math Proof, Cleanroom	Logic and/or mathematical proof	The best strategies for life-sustaining, embedded, reusable, or other critical modules, but beyond most business SE skills.
	White-Box	Statement Logic	Exhaustive tests of individual statements. Not desirable unless life-sustaining or threatening consequences are possible, or if for reusable module. Useful for 'guessed' error testing that is specific to the operational environment.
		Decision Logic Test	A good alternative to statement logic. May be too detailed for many programs.
		Condition Logic	A good alternative providing all conditions can be documented.
		Multiple Condition Logic	*Desired alternative* for program testing when human resources can be expended.
	Live-Data	Reality Test	Can be useful for timing, performance, and other reality testing *after* other unit tests are successful.
Integration	Black-Box	Equivalence Partitioning	Useful for partitioning by module.
		Boundary Value Analysis	Useful for partitioning by module.
		Cause-Effect Graphing	Useful for application interfaces and partitioning by module.
		Error Guessing	Not the best strategy at this level.

(Table continues on next page)

TABLE 17-2   Test Level and Test Strategy (*Continued*)

Level	General Strategy	Specific Strategy	Comments on Use
Integration	Live-Data	Reality Test	Useful for interface and black-box tests *after* other integration tests are successful.
System/QA-Application Functional Requirements Test	Black-Box	Equivalence Partitioning	Most productive approach to system function testing.
		Boundary Value Analysis	Too detailed to be required at this level. May be used to test correct file usage, checkpoint/restart, or other data-related error recovery.
		Cause-Effect Graphing	Can be useful for intermodule testing and when combined with equivalence partitioning.
	White-Box	Statement Logic	Not a useful system test strategy.
		Decision Logic Test	May be used for critical logic.
		Condition Logic	May be used for critical logic.
		Multiple Condition Logic	May be used for critical logic.
System/QA-Human Interface	Black-Box	Equivalence Partitioning	Useful at the level for screen and associated process and for screen navigation.
		Boundary Value Analysis	Useful at screen level for associated process and screen navigation.
			Useful for QA testing.

TEST PLAN FOR ABC VIDEO ORDER PROCESSING

Test Strategy

Developing a Test Strategy

There are *no rules* for developing a test strategy. Rather, loose heuristics are provided. Testing, like everything else in software engineering, is a skill that comes with practice. Good testers are among the most highly skilled workers on a development team. A career can revolve around testing because skilled testers are in short supply.

As with all other testing projects, the strategy should be designed to prove the application works and that it is stable in its operational environment. While scheduling and time allotted are not most important, when the strategy is devised, one subgoal is to minimize the amount of time and resources (both human and computer) that are devoted to testing.

The first decision is whether and what to test top-down and bottom-up. There are no rules, or even

TABLE 17-2   Test Level and Test Strategy (*Continued*)

Level	General Strategy	Specific Strategy	Comments on Use
System/QA-Human Interface	White-Box	Condition Logic	May be used for critical logic.
		Multiple Condition Logic	May be used for critical logic.
System/QA-Constraints	Black-Box	Equivalence Partitioning	May be useful at the execute unit level.
		Boundary Value Analysis	Should not be required at this level but could be used.
		Cause-Effect Graphing	Might be useful for defining how to measure constraint compliance.
	White-Box	Multiple Condition Logic	Could be used but generally is too detailed at this level of test.
	Live-Data	Reality Test	Useful for black-box type tests of constraints *after* created data tests are successful.
System/QA-Peak Requirements	White-Box	Multiple Condition Logic	May be used for critical logic, but generally too detailed for this level of testing.
	Live-Data	Reality Test	Most useful for peak testing.

heuristics, for this decision. Commitment to top-down testing is as much cultural and philosophical as it is technical. To provide some heuristics, in general, the more critical, the larger, and the more complex an application, the more top-down benefits outweigh bottom-up benefits.

The heuristics of testing are dependent on the language, timing and operational environment of the application. *Significantly* different testing strategies are needed for third (e.g., COBOL, Pl/1), fourth (e.g., Focus, SQL), and semantic (e.g., Lisp, PRO-LOG) languages. Application timing (see Chapter 1) is either batch, on-line, or real-time. Operational environment includes hardware, software, and other co-resident applications. Heuristics for each of these are summarized in Table 17-3.

Package testing differs significantly from self-developed code. More often, when you purchase package software, you are not given the source code or the specifications. You are given user documen-

tation and an executable code. By definition, you have to treat the software as a black box. Further, top-down testing does not make sense because you are presented with a complete, supposedly working, application. Testing should be at the system level only, including functional, volume, intermodular communications, and data-related black-box tests. Next, we consider the ABC test strategy.

ABC Video Test Strategy

The ABC application will be developed using some SQL-based language. SQL is a fourth-generation language which simplifies the testing process and suggests certain testing strategies. The design from Chapter 10, Data-Oriented Design, is used as the basis for testing, although the arguments are the same for the other methodologies.

First, we need to decide the major questions: Who? What? Where? When? How?

TABLE 17-3   Test Strategy Design Heuristics

Condition

Critical	Y	Y	–	–	N	N	N	N	N	N
Large	Y	–	Y	–	N	N	N	N	N	N
Complex	Y	–	–	Y	N	N	N	N	N	N
Timing	–	–	–	–	BS	BE	BS	BE	BE	–
Language Generation	–	–	–	–	2	2	3/4	3	4	Rule

Test Strategy

Top-Down/ Bottom-Up, Both, or Either	Both	Both	Either	Either	Either	Either	Cont T Mod B	Either	Both	Cont T Mod B
Black/White/ Both/Either	Both	Both	Cont W Mod Bl	Cont W Mod Bl	Both	Either or Both	Either or Both	Both	Cont W Mod Bl	Bl

Legend:

Y	=	Yes
N	=	No
BS	=	Batch—stand-alone
BE	=	Batch—execute unit
Cont	=	Control Structure
Mod	=	Modules
T	=	Top-down
B	=	Bottom-up
W	=	White
Bl	=	Black

Who? The test coordinator should be a member of the team. Assume it is yourself. Put yourself into this role and think about the remaining questions and how *you* would answer them if you were testing this application.

What? All application functions, constraints, user acceptance criteria, human interface, peak performance, recoverability, and other possible tests must be performed to exercise the system and prove its functioning.

Where? The ABC application should be tested in its operational environment to also test the environment. This means that *all* hardware and software of the operational environment should be installed and tested. If Vic, or the responsible project team member, has not yet installed and tested the equipment, they are now delaying the conduct of application testing.

When? Since a 4GL is being used, we can begin testing as soon as code is ready. An iterative, top-down approach will be used. This approach allows Vic and his staff early access to familiarize themselves with the application. Testing at the system level needs to include the scaffold code to support top-down testing. The schedule for module coding should identify and schedule all critical modules for early coding. The tasks identified so far are:

1. Build scaffold code and test it.
2. Identify critical modules.
3. Schedule coding of critical modules first.
4. Test and validate modules as developed using the strategy developed.

How? Since a top-down strategy is being used, we should identify critical modules first. Since the application is completely on-line, the screen controls and navigation modules must be developed before anything else can be tested. Also, since the application is being developed specifically to perform rental/return processing, rental/return processing should be the second priority. Rental/return cannot be performed without a customer file and a video file, both of which try to access the respective *create* modules. Therefore, the creation modules for the two files have a high priority.

The priority definition of create and rental/return modules provides a prioritized list for development. The scaffolding should include the test screens, navigation, and stubs for all other processing. The last item, backup and recovery testing, can be parallel to the others.

Next, we want to separate the activities into parallel equivalent chunks for testing. By having parallel testing streams, we can work through the system tests for each parallel stream simultaneously, speeding the testing process. For ABC, *Customer Maintenance*, *Video Maintenance*, *Rental/Return*, and *Periodic* processing can all be treated as stand-alone processes. Notice that in Information Engineering (IE), this independence of processes is at the *activity* level. If we were testing object-oriented design (Chapters 11 and 12), we would look at *processes* from the *Booch diagram* as the independent and par-

allel test units. If we were testing process design (Chapters 7 and 8), we would use the structure charts to decide parallel sets of processes.

Of the ABC processes, *Rental/Return* is the most complex and is discussed in detail. *Rental/Return* assumes that all files are present, so the DBA must have files defined and populated with data before *Rental/Return* can be tested. Note that even though files must be present, it is neither important nor required that the file maintenance processes be present. For the two create processes that are called, program stubs that return only a new *Customer ID*, or *Video ID /Copy ID*, are sufficient for testing.

In addition to parallel streams of testing, we might also want to further divide *Rental/Return* into several streams of testing by level of complexity, by transaction type, or by equivalent processes to further subdivide the code generation and testing processes. We choose such a division so that the same person can write all of the code but testing can proceed without all variations completed. For example, we will divide *Rental/Return* by transaction type as we did in IE. The four transaction types are rentals with and without returns, and returns with and without rentals. This particular work breakdown allows us to test all major variations of all inputs and outputs, and allows us to proceed from simple to complex as well. In the next sections, we will discuss from bottom-up how testing at each level is designed and conducted using *Rental/Return* as the ABC example.

Next, we define the integration test strategy. The IE design resulted in small modules that are called for execution, some of which are used in more than one process. At the integration level, we define inputs and predict outputs of each module, using a black-box approach. Because SQL calls do not pass data, predicting SQL set output is more important than creating input. An important consideration with the number of modules is that intermodular errors that are created in one module but not evidenced until they are used in another module. The top-down approach should help focus attention on critical modules for this problem.

Because SQL is a declarative language, black-box testing at the unit level is also appropriate. The SQL code that provides the control structure is logic and becomes an important test item. White-box tests are most appropriate to testing the control logic. Therefore, a mix of black- and white-box testing will be done at the unit level.

To summarize, the top-down strategy for testing the application includes:

1. Test screen design and navigation, including validation of security and access controls.
2. Test the call structure for all modules.
3. Test rental/return processing.
4. Test create processing for customers and videos.
5. Test remaining individual processes and file contents as parallel streams.
6. Test multiple processes and file manipulations together, including validation of response time and peak system performance. The test will use many users doing the same and different processes, simultaneously.
7. Test backup and recovery strategies.

Now, we develop and try a unit test to test the strategy. If a small test of the strategy works, we implement the strategy.

Unit Testing

Guidelines for Developing a Unit Test

Unit tests verify that a specific program, module, or routine (all referred to as 'module' in the remaining discussion) fulfills its requirements as stated in related program and design specifications. The two primary goals of unit testing are conformance to specifications and processing accuracy.

For conformance, unit tests determine the extent to which processing logic satisfies the functions assigned to the module. The logical and operational requirements of each module are taken from the program specifications. Test cases are designed to verify that the module meets the requirements. *The test is designed from the specification, not the code.*

Processing accuracy has three components: input, process, and output. First, each module must process all allowable types of input data in a stable, predictable, and accurate manner. Second, all possible errors should be found and treated according to the

specifications. Third, all output should be consistent with results predicted from the specification. Outputs might include hard copy, terminal displays, electronic transmissions, or file contents; all are tested.

There is no one strategy for unit testing. For input/output bound applications, black-box strategies are normally used. For process logic, either or both strategies can be used. In general, the more critical to the organization or the more damaging the possible errors, the more detailed and extensively white-box testing is used. For example, organizationally critical processes might be defined as any process that affects the financial books of the organization, meets legal requirements, or deals with client relationships. Examples of application damage might include life-threatening situations such as in nuclear power plant support systems, life-support systems in hospitals, or test systems for car or plane parts.

Since most business applications combine approaches, an example combining black- and white-box strategies is described here. Using a white-box approach, each program specification is analyzed to identify the distinct logic paths which serve as the basis for unit test design. This analysis is simplified by the use of tables, lists, matrices, diagrams, or decision tables to document the logic paths of the program. Then, the logic paths most critical in performing the functions are selected for white-box testing. Next, to verify that all logic paths not white-box tested are functioning at an acceptable level of accuracy, black-box testing of input and output is designed. This is a common approach that we will apply to ABC Video.

When top-down unit testing is used, control structure logic paths are tested first. When each path is successfully tested, combinations of paths may be tested in increasingly complex relationships until all possible processing combinations are satisfactorily tested. This process of simple-to-complex testing ensures that all logic paths in a module are performing both individually and collectively as intended.

Similarly, unit testing of multiuser applications also uses the simple-to-complex approach. Each program is tested first for single users. Then multiuser tests of the single functions follow. Finally, multiuser tests of multiple functions are performed.

Unit tests of relatively large, complex programs may be facilitated by reducing them to smaller, more manageable equivalent components such as

- transaction type:
  e.g., Debit/Credit, Edit/Update/Report/Error
- functional component activity
  e.g., Preparing, Sending, Receiving, Processing
- decision option
  e.g., If true . . . If false . . .

When the general process of reduction is accomplished, both black-box and white-box approaches are applied to the process of actually defining test cases and their corresponding output. The black-box approach should provide both good and bad data inputs and examine the outputs for correctness of processing. In addition, at least one white-box strategy should be used to test specific critical logic of the tested item.

Test cases should be both exhaustive and minimal. This means that test cases should test every condition or data domain possible but that no extra tests are necessary. For example, the most common errors in data inputs are for edit/validate criteria. Boundary conditions of fields should be tested. Using equivalence partitioning of the sets of allowable values for each field we develop the test for a date formatted YYYYMMDD (that is, 4-digit year, 2-digit month, and 2-digit day). A good year test will test last year, this year, next year, change of century, all zeros, and all nines. A good month test will test zeros, 1, 2, 4 (representative of months with 30 days), 12, and 13. Only 1 and 12 are required for the boundary month test, but the other months are required to test day boundaries. A good day test will test zeros, 1, 28, 29, 30, 31, and 32, depending on the final day of each month. Only one test for zero and one are required, based on the assumption that if one month processes correctly, all months will. Leap year and nonleap years should also be tested. An example of test cases for these date criteria is presented. Figure 17-14 shows the equivalent sets of data for each domain. Table 17-4 lists exhaustive test

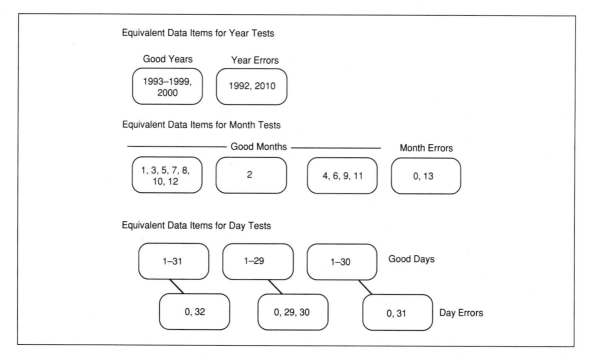

FIGURE 17-14   Unit Test Equivalent Sets for a Date

TABLE 17-4 Exhaustive Set of Unit Test Cases for a Date

Test Case	YYYY	MM	DD	Comments
1	aaaa	aa	aa	Tests actions against garbage input
2	1992*	0	0	Tests all incorrect lower bounds
3	2010	13	32	Tests all incorrect upper bounds
4	1993	1	31	Tests correct upper day bound
4a	1994	12	31	Not required . . . could be optional test of upper month/day bound. Assumption is that if month = 1 works, all valid, equivalent months will work.
5	1995	1	1	Tests correct lower day bound
6	1996	12	1	Not required . . . could be optional test of upper month/lower day bound. Assumption is that if month = 1 works, all valid, equivalent months will work.
7	1997	1	32	Tests upper day bound error
8	1998	12	32	Not required . . . could be optional test of upper month/upper day bound error. Assumption is that if month = 1 works, all valid, equivalent months will work.
9	1999	12	0	Retests lower bound day error with otherwise valid data . . . Not strictly necessary but could be used.
10	2000	2	1	Tests lower bound . . . not strictly necessary
11	2000	2	29	Tests leap year upper bound
12	2000	2	30	Tests leap year upper bound error
13	1999	2	28	Tests nonleap year upper bound
14	1999	2	29	Tests nonleap year upper bound error
15	1999	2	0	Tests lower bound error . . . not strictly necessary
16	2001	4	30	Tests upper bound
17	2001	4	31	Tests upper bound error
18	2002	4	1	Tests lower bound . . . not strictly necessary
19	2003	4	0	Tests lower bound error . . . not strictly necessary

*Valid dates are between 1/1/93 and 12/31/2009.

TABLE 17-5   Minimal Set of Unit Test Cases for a Date

Test Case	YYYY	MM	DD	Comments
1	aaaa	aa	aa	Tests actions against garbage input
2	1992	0	0	Tests all incorrect lower bounds
3	2010	13	32	Tests all incorrect upper bounds
4	1993	1	31	Tests correct upper day bound
5	1995	1	1	Tests correct lower day bound
6	1997	1	32	Tests upper day bound error
7(9)	2000	2	29	Tests leap year upper bound
8(10)	2000	2	30	Tests leap year upper bound error
9(11)	1999	2	28	Tests nonleap year upper bound
10(12)	1999	2	29	Tests nonleap year upper bound error
11(14)	2001	4	30	Tests upper bound
12(15)	2001	4	31	Tests upper bound error

cases for each set in the figure. Table 17-5 lists the reduced set after extra tests are removed.

Other frequently executed tests are for character, field, batch, and control field checks. Table 17-6 lists a sampling of errors found during unit tests. Character checks include tests for blanks, signs, length, and data types (e.g., numeric, alpha, or other). Field checks include sequence, reasonableness, consistency, range of values, or specific contents. Control fields are most common in batch applications and are used to verify that the file being used is the correct one and that all records have been processed. Usually the control field includes the last execution date and file name which are both checked for accuracy. Record counts are only necessary when not using a declarative language.

Once all test cases are defined, tests are run and results are compared to the predictions. Any result that does not *exactly match* the prediction must be reconciled. The only possible choices are that the tested item is in error or the prediction is in error. If the tested item is in error, it is fixed and retested. Retests should follow the approach used in the first tests. If the prediction is in error, the prediction is researched and corrected so that specifications are accurate and documentation shows the correct predictions.

Unit tests are conducted and reviewed by the author of the code item being tested, with final test results approved by the project test coordinator.

How do you know when to stop unit testing? While there is no simple answer to this question, there are practical guidelines. When testing, each tester should keep track of the number of errors found (and resolved) in each test. The errors should be plotted by test shot to show the pattern. A typical module test curve is skewed left with a decreasing number of errors found in each test (see Figure 17-15). When the number of errors found approaches zero, or when the slope is negative and approaching zero, the module can be moved forward to the next level of testing. If the number of errors found stays constant or increases, you should seek help either in interpreting the specifications or in testing the program.

ABC Video Unit Test

Above, we said we would use a combination of black- and white-box testing for ABC unit tests. The

TABLE 17-6   Sample Unit Test Errors

Edit/Validate
> Transaction rejected when valid
> Error accepted as valid
> Incorrect validation criteria applied

Screen
> Navigation faulty
> Faulty screen layout
> Spelling errors on screen
> Inability to call screen

Data Integrity
> Transaction processed when inconsistent with
>   other information
> Interfile matching not correct
> File sequence checking not correct

File Processing
> File, segment, relation of field not correctly
>   processed
> Read/write data format error
> Syntax incorrect but processed by interpreter

Report
> Format not correct
> Totals do not add/crossfoot
> Wrong field(s) printed
> Wrong heading, footing or other cosmetic error
> Data processing incorrect

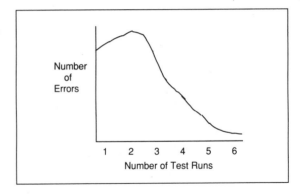

FIGURE 17-15   Unit Test Errors Found Over Test Shots

application is being implemented using a SQL software package. Therefore, all code is assumed to be in SQL. The control logic and non*SELECT* code is subject to white-box tests, while the *SELECT* modules will be subject to black-box tests.

In Chapter 10, we defined *Rent/Return* processing as an execute unit with many independent code units. Figure 17-16 shows partial SQL code from two *Rent/Return* modules. Notice that most of the code is defining data and establishing screen addressability. As soon as two or three modules that have such strikingly similar characteristics are built, the need to further consolidate the design to accommodate the implementation language should be obvious. With the current design, more code is spent in overhead tasks than in application tasks. Overhead code means that users will have long wait times while the system changes modules. The current

design also means that debugging the individual modules would require considerable work to verify that the modules performs collectively as expected. Memory locations would need to be printed many times in such testing.

To restructure the code, we examine what all of the *Rent/Return* modules have in common—*Open Rentals* data. We can redefine the data in terms of *Open Rentals* with a single-user view used for all *Rent/Return* processing. This simplifies the data part of the processing but increases the vulnerability of the data to integrity problems. Problems might increase because the global view of data violates the principle of information hiding. The risk must be taken, however, to accommodate reasonable user response time.

The common format of the restructured SQL code is shown in Figure 17-17. In the restructured version, data is defined once at the beginning of *Rent/Return* processing. The cursor name is declared once and the data is retrieved into memory based on the data entered through the *Get Request* module. The remaining *Rent/Return* modules are called in sequence. The modules have a similar structure for handling memory addressing. The problems with many prints of memory are reduced because once the data is brought into memory, no more retrievals are necessary until updates take place at the end of the transaction. Processing is simplified by unifying the application's view of the data.

```
UPDATE OPEN RENTAL FILE  (BOLDFACE CODE IS REDUNDANT)
        DCL       INPUT_VIDEO_ID          CHAR(8);
        DCL       INPUT_COPY_ID           CHAR(2);
        DCL       INPUT_CUST_ID           CHAR (9);
        DCL       AMT_PAID                DECIMAL (4,2);
        DCL       CUST_ID                 CHAR(9);
        ...
          CONTINUE UNTIL ALL FIELDS USED ON THE SCREEN OR USED TO
        CONTROL SCREEN PROCESSING ARE DECLARED ...
        DCL       TOTAL_AMT_DUE           DECIMAL(5,2);
        DCL       CHANGE                  DECIMAL(4,2);
        DCL       MORE_OPEN_RENTALS       BIT(1);
        DCL       MORE_NEW_RENTALS        BIT(1);
        EXEC SQL INCLUDE SQLCA: /*COMMUNICATION AREA*/
        EXEC SQL DECLARE CUSTOMER TABLE
              (FIELD DEFINITIONS FOR CUSTOMER RELATION);
        EXEC SQL DECLARE VIDEO TABLE
              (FIELD DEFINITIONS FOR VIDEO RELATION);
        EXEC SQL DECLARE COPY TABLE
              (FIELD DEFINITIONS FOR COPY RELATION);
        EXEC SQL DECLARE OPENRENTAL TABLE
              (FIELD DEFINITIONS FOR OPENRENTAL RELATION);
EXEC SQL DECLARE SCREEN_CURSOR CURSOR FOR UPDATE OF
              ORVIDEOID
              ORCOPYID
              ORCUSTID
              ORRENTALDATE;
ORDER BY ORCUSTID, ORVIDEOID, ORCOPYID;
EXEC SQL OPEN SCREEN, CURSOR;
GOTOLABEL
EXEC SQL FETCH SCREEN CURSOR INTO TARGET
              :CUSTID
              :VIDEOID
              :COPYID
              :RENTALDATE
IF SQLCODE = 100  GOTO GOTOEXIT;
EXEC SQL UPDATE OPENRENTAL
              SET ORCUSTID = CUSTID
              SET ORVIDEOID = VIDEOID
              SET ORCOPYID = COPYID
              SET ORRENTALDATE = TODAYSDATE
WHERE CURRENT OF SCREEN_CURSOR;
GOTO GOTOLABEL;
GOTOEXIT;
EXEC SQL CLOSE SCREEN_CURSOR;
```

(Figure continues on next page)

FIGURE 17-16   Two Modules Sample Code

```
ADD RETURN DATE (Boldface code is redundant)
        DCL      INPUT_VIDEO_ID           CHAR(8);
        DCL      INPUT_COPY_ID            CHAR(2);
        DCL      INPUT_CUST_ID            CHAR (9);
        DCL      AMT_PAID                 DECIMAL (4,2);
        DCL      CUST_ID                  CHAR(9);

        ...
        CONTINUE UNTIL ALL FIELDS USED ON THE SCREEN OR USED TO
        CONTROL SCREEN PROCESSING ARE DECLARED ...
        DCL      TOTAL_AMT_DUE            DECIMAL(5,2);
        DCL      CHANGE                   DECIMAL(4,2);
        DCL      MORE_OPEN_RENTALS        BIT(1);
        DCL      MORE_NEW_RENTALS         BIT(1);
        EXEC SQL INCLUDE SQLCA: /*COMMUNICATION AREA*/
        EXEC SQL DECLARE CUSTOMER TABLE
                (FIELD DEFINITIONS FOR CUSTOMER RELATION);
        EXEC SQL DECLARE VIDEO TABLE
                (FIELD DEFINITIONS FOR VIDEO RELATION);
        EXEC SQL DECLARE COPY TABLE
                (FIELD DEFINITIONS FOR COPY RELATION);
        EXEC SQL DECLARE OPENRENTAL TABLE
                (FIELD DEFINITIONS FOR OPENRENTAL RELATION);
        EXEC SQL DECLARE SCREEN_CURSOR CURSOR FOR
                SELECT * FROM OPEN_RENTAL
                        WHERE VIDEOID = ORVIDEOID
                        AND COPYID = ORCOPYID;
        EXEC SQL OPEN SCREEN_CURSOR
        GOTOLABEL
        EXEC SQL FETCH SCREEN CURSOR INTO TARGET
                :CUSTID
                :VIDEOID
                :COPYID
                :RENTALDATE
        IF SQLCODE = 100  GOTO GOTOEXIT;
        EXEC SQL SET :RETURNDATE = TODAYS_DATE
                WHERE CURRENT OF SCREEN_CURSOR;
        EXEC SQL UPDATE OPEN_RENTAL
                SET ORRETURNDATE = TODAYS_DATE
                WHERE CURRENT OF SCREEN_CURSOR;
        GOTO GOTOLABEL;
        GOTOEXIT;
        EXEC SQL CLOSE SCREEN_CURSOR;
```

FIGURE 17-16   Two Modules Sample Code (*Continued*)

The restructuring now requires a change to the testing strategy for *Rent/Return*. A strictly top-down approach cannot work because the *Rent/Return* modules are no longer independent. Rather, a combined top-down and bottom-up approach is warranted. A sequential bottom-up approach is more effective for the functional *Rent/Return* processing. Top-down, black-box tests of the *SELECT* code are done before being embedded in the execute unit. Black-box testing for the *SELECT* is used because SQL controls all data input and output. Complete *SELECT* statements are the test unit.

```
DCL       INPUT_VIDEO_ID          CHAR(8);
DCL       INPUT_COPY_ID           CHAR(2);
DCL       INPUT_CUST_ID           CHAR (9);
DCL       AMT_PAID                DECIMAL (4,2);
DCL       CUST_ID                 CHAR(9);
   ...
   continue until all fields used on the screen or used to control screen processing are
declared ...



DCL       TOTAL_AMT_DUE           DECIMAL(5,2);
DCL       CHANGE                  DECIMAL(4,2);
DCL       MORE_OPEN_RENTALS       BIT(1);
DCL       MORE_NEW_RENTALS        BIT(1);
EXEC SQL INCLUDE SQLCA: /*COMMUNICATION AREA*/
EXEC SQL DECLARE  RENTRETURN TABLE
(field definitions for user view including all fields from customer, video, copy,
open rental, and customer history relations);


EXEC SQL DECLARE SCREEN_CURSOR CURSOR FOR
        SELECT * from rentreturn
        where (:videoid = orvideo_id  and :copyid = orcopyid)
        or :custid = orcustid)
EXEC SQL OPEN SCREEN_CURSOR
EXEC SQL FETCH SCREEN_CURSOR INTO TARGET
        :Request
If :request eq "C?" set :custid = :request
else      set :videoid = :request1
          set :copyid = :request2;



          (At this point the memory contains the related relation data
          and the remaining rent/return processing can be done.)

All the other modules are called and contain the following common format:

GOTOLABEL
EXEC SQL FETCH SCREEN_CURSOR INTO TARGET
:screen fields


IF SQLCODE = 0  next step;   (return code of zero means no errors)
IF SQLCODE = 100 (not found condition) CREATE DATA or CALL END PROCESS;
IF SQLCODE < 0 CALL ERROR_PROCESS, ERROR-TYPE;
Set screen variables (which displays new data)
Prompt next action


GOTO GOTOLABEL;
GOTOEXIT;
EXEC SQL CLOSE SCREEN_CURSOR;
```

FIGURE 17-17   Restructured SQL Code—Common Format

Test	Type
1. Test SQL SELECT statement	Black Box
2. Verify SQL cursor and data addressability	White Box
3. Test *Get Request*	White Box
4. Test *Get Valid Customer, Get Open Rentals*	Black Box for embedded SELECT statement, White Box for other logic
5. Test *Get Valid Video*	White Box for logic, Black Box for embedded SELECT statement
6. Test *Process Payment and Make Change*	White Box
7. Test *Update Open Rental*	Black Box for Update, White Box for other logic
8. Test *Create Open Rental*	Black Box for Update, White Box for other logic
9. Test *Update Item*	Black Box for Update, White Box for other logic
10. Test *Update/Create Customer History*	Black Box for Update, White Box for other logic
11. Test *Print Receipt*	Black Box for Update, White Box for other logic

FIGURE 17-18   Unit Test Strategy

The screen interaction and module logic can be tested as either white box or black box. At the unit level, white-box testing will be used to test inter-module control logic. A combination of white-box and black-box testing should be used to test intra-module control and process logic.

The strategy for unit testing, then, is to test data retrievals first, to verify screen processing, including SQL cursor and data addressability second, and to sequentially test all remaining code last (see Figure 17-18).

Because all processing in the ABC application is on-line, an interactive dialogue *test script* is developed. All file interactions predict data retrieved and written, as appropriate. The individual unit test scripts begin processing at the execute unit boundary. This means that menus are not necessarily tested. A test script has three columns of information developed. The first column shows the computer messages or prompts displayed on the screen. The second column shows data entered by the user. The third column shows comments or explanations of the interactions taking place.

A partial test script for Rent/Return processing is shown in Figure 17-19. The example shows the script for a return with rental transaction. Notice that the test begins at the *Rent/Return* screen and that both error and correct data are entered for each field. After all errors are detected and dispatched properly, only correct data is required. This script shows one of the four types of transactions. It shows only one return and one rental, however, and should be expanded in another transaction to do several rentals and several returns; returns should include on-time and late videos and should not include all tapes checked out. This type of transaction represents the requisite variety to test returns with rentals. Of course, other test scripts for the other three types of transactions should also be developed. This is left as an extra-credit activity.

Subsystem or Integration Testing

Guidelines for Integration Testing

The purpose of integration testing is to verify that groups of interacting modules that comprise an execute unit perform in a stable, predictable, and accu-

System Prompt	User Action	Explanation
Menu	Press mouse, move to Rent/Return, and release	Select Rent/Return from menu
Rent/Return screen, cursor at request field	Scan customer bar code 1234567	Dummy bar code
Error Message 1: Illegal Customer or Video Code, Type Request	Enter: 1234567 <cr>	Dummy bar code
Customer Data Entry Screen with message: Illegal Customer ID, enter new customer	<cr>	Carriage return entered to end Create Customer process
Rent/Return screen, cursor at request field	Scan customer bar code 2221234	Legal customer ID. System should return customer and rental information for M. A. Jones, Video 12312312, Copy 3, Terminator 2, Rental date 1/23/94, not returned.
Cursor at request field	Scan 123123123	Cursor moves to rented video line
Cursor at return date field	Enter yesterday's date	Error message: Return date must be today's date.
Cursor at return date field	Enter today's date	Late fee computed and displayed . . . should be $4.00.
Cursor at request field	Scan new tape ID— 123412345	New tape entered and displayed. Video #12341234, Copy 5, Mary Poppins, Rental date 1/25/94, Charge $2.00.
Cursor at request field	Press <cr>	System computes and displays *Total Amount Due* . . . should be $6.00.
Cursor at Total Amount Paid field	Enter <cr>	Error Message: Amount paid must be numeric and equal or greater than *Total Amount Due.*
Cursor at Total Amount Paid field	Enter 10 <cr>	System computes and displays *Change Due* . . . should be $4.00. Cash drawer should open.
Cursor at Request field	Enter <cr>	Error Message: You must enter P or F5 to request print.
Cursor at Request field	Enter P <cr>	System prints transaction

Go to SQL Query and verify Open Rental and Copy contents

Open Rental tuple for Video 123123123 contents should be:

    222123412312312301239402000125940400000000000000

Open Rental tuple for Video 123412345 should be:

    222123412341234501259402000000000000000000000000

Copy tuple for Video 12312312, Copy 3 should be:

    12312312311019200103

Copy tuple for Video 12341234, Copy 5 should be:

    12341234511319010000

Verify the contents of the receipt.

FIGURE 17-19   ABC Video Unit Test Example—Rent/Return

rate manner that is consistent with all related program and systems design specifications.

Integration tests are considered distinct from unit tests. That is, as unit tests are successful, integration testing for the tested units can begin. The two primary goals of integration testing are compatibility and intermodule processing accuracy.

Compatibility relates to calling of modules an operational environment. The test verifies first that all modules are called correctly, and, even with errors, do not cause abends. Intermodule tests check that data transfers between modules operate as intended within constraints of CPU time, memory, and response time. Data transfers tested include sorted and extracted data provided by utility programs, as well as data provided by other application modules.

Test cases developed for integration testing should be sufficiently exhaustive to test all possible interactions and may include a subset of unit test cases as well as special test cases used only in this test. The integration test does *not* test logic paths within the modules as the unit test does. Instead, it tests interactions between modules only. Thus, a black-box strategy works well in integration testing.

If modules are called in a sequence, checking of inputs and outputs to each module simplifies the identification of computational and data transfer errors. Special care must be taken to identify the source of errors, not just the location of bad data. Frequently, in complex applications, errors may not be apparent until several modules have touched the data and the true source of problems can be difficult to locate. Representative integration test errors are listed in Table 17-7.

Integration testing can begin as soon as two or more modules are successfully unit tested. When to end integration tests is more subjective. When exceptions are detected, the results of all other test processing become suspect. Depending on the severity and criticality of the errors to overall process integrity, all previous levels of testing might be reexecuted to reverify processing. Changes in one module may cause tests of other modules to become invalid. Therefore, integration tests should be considered successful only when the entire group of modules in an execute unit are run *individually and*

TABLE 17-7   Sample Integration Test Errors

Intermodule communication

    Called module cannot be invoked

    Calling module does not invoke all expected modules

    Message passed to module contains extraneous information

    Message passed to module does not contain correct information

    Message passed contains wrong (or inconsistent) data type

    Return of processing from called module is to the wrong place

    Module has no return

    Multiple entry points in a single module

    Multiple exit points in a single module

Process errors

    Input errors not properly disposed

    Abend on bad data instead of graceful degradation

    Output does not match predicted results

    Processing of called module produces unexpected results does not match prediction

    Time constrained process is over the limit

    Module causes time-out in some other part of the application

collectively without error. Integration test curves usually start low, increase and peak, then decrease (see Figure 17-20). If there is pressure to terminate integration testing before all errors are found, the rule of thumb is to continue testing until fewer errors are found on several successive test runs.

ABC Video Integration Test

Because of the redesign of execute units for more efficient SQL processing, integration testing can be concurrent with unit code and test work, and should

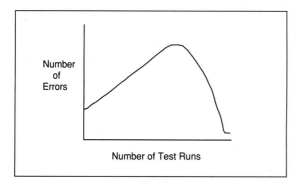

FIGURE 17-20   Integration Test Errors Found Over Test Shots

integrate and test the unit functions as they are complete. The application control structure for screen processing and for calling modules is the focus of the test.

Black-box, top-down testing is used for the integration test. Because SQL does not pass data as input, we predict the sets that SQL will generate during *SELECT* processing. The output sets are then passed to the control code and used for screen processing, both of which have been unit tested and should work. To verify the unit tests at the integration level, we should:

1. Ensure that the screen control structure works and that execute units are invoked as intended.
2. Ensure that screens contain expected data from *SELECT* processing.
3. Ensure that files contain all updates and created records as expected.
4. Ensure that printed output contains expected information in the correct format.

First, we want to define equivalent sets of processes and the sets' equivalent sets of data inputs. For instance, the high level processes from IE analysis constitute approximately equivalent sets. These were translated into modules during design and, with the exception of integrating data access and use across modules, have not changed. These processes include *Rent/Return*, *Customer Maintenance*, *Video Maintenance*, and *Other* processing. If the personnel are available, four people could be assigned to

develop one script each for these equivalent sets of processing. Since we named *Rent/Return* as the highest priority for development, its test should be developed first. The others can follow in any order, although the start-up and shutdown scripts should be developed soon after *Rent/Return* to allow many tests of the entire interface.

First, we test screen process control, then individual screens. Since security and access control are embedded in the screen access structure, this test should be white box and test every possible access path, including invalid ones. Each type of access rights and screen processing should be tested. For the individual screens, spelling, positioning, color, highlighting, message placement, consistency of design, and accuracy of information are all validated (see Figure 17-21).

The integration test example in Figure 17-22 is the script for testing the start-up procedure and security access control for the application. This script would be repeated for each valid and invalid user including the other clerks and accountant. The start-up should only work for Vic, the temporary test account, and the chief clerk. The account numbers that work should *not* be documented in the test

---

1. Define equivalent sets of processes and data inputs.
2. Define the priorities of equivalent sets for testing.
3. Develop test scrips for *Rent/Return*, *Other* processing, *Customer Maintenance*, *Video Maintenance*.
4. For each of the above scripts, the testing will proceed as follows:
   a. Test screen control, including security of access to the *Rent/Return* application.
   b. Evaluate accuracy of spelling, format, and consistency of each individual screen.
   c. Test access rights and screen access controls.
   d. Test information retrieval and display.
   e. For each transaction, test processing sequence, dialogue, error messages, and error processing.
   f. Review all reports and file contents for accuracy of processing, consistency, format, and spelling.

FIGURE 17-21   ABC Integration Test Plan

Test Startup Security

System Prompt	User Action	Explanation
C:>	StRent<cr>	StRent is Exec to startup the Rental/Return Processing application
Enter password	<cr>	Error
Password must be alphanumeric and six characters.		
Enter Password	123456<cr>	Error—illegal password
Password illegal, try again.		
Enter Password.	Abcdefg	Error—illegal password
Three illegal attempts at password. System shutdown		
C:>	StRent<cr>	Error—3 illegal attempts requires special start-up.
Illegal start-up attempt		
System begins to beep continuously until stopped by system administrator. No further prompts.		

Single User Sign-on		
C:>	StRent<cr>	StRent is Exec to startup the Rental/Return Processing application
Enter Password:	<cr>	Error
Password illegal, try again.		
Enter Password:	VAC5283	Temporary legal entry
User Sign-on menu		
Enter Initials:	<cr>	Error
You must enter your initials.		
Enter Initials:	VAV	Error
Initials not authorized, try again.		
Enter Initials:	VAC	Legal entry (VAC is Vic)
Main Menu with all Options	Begin Main Menu Test.	

FIGURE 17-22 ABC Video Integration Test Script

script. Rather, a note should refer the reader to the person responsible for maintaining passwords.

In the integration portion of the test, multiuser processing might take place, but it is not necessarily fully tested at this point. File contents are verified after each transaction is entered to ensure that file updates and additions are correct. If the integration test is approached as iteratively adding modules for testing, the final run-through of the test script should include all functions of the application, including start-up, shutdown, generation and printing of all reports, queries on all files, all file maintenance, and all transaction types. At least several days and one monthly cycle of processing should be simulated for ABC's test to ensure that end-of-day and end-of-month processing work.

Next, we discuss system testing and continue the example from ABC with a functional test that is equally appropriate at the integration, system, or QA levels.

System and Quality Assurance Testing

Guidelines for Developing System and Quality Assurance Tests

The system test is used to demonstrate an application's ability to operate satisfactorily in a simulated production environment using its intended hardware and software configuration. The quality assurance test (QA) is both a system test and a documentation test. Both tests also verify that all of the system's interacting modules do the following:

1. Fulfill the user's functional requirements as contained in the business system design specifications and as translated into design requirements in the design spec and any documents controlling interfaces to other systems.
2. The human interface works as intended. Screen design, navigation, and work interruptability are the test objects for human interface testing. All words on screens should be spelled properly. All screens should share a common format that is presented consistently throughout the application. This format includes the assignment of program function keys as well as the physical screen format. Navigation is the movement between screens. All menu selections should bring up the correct next screen. All screens should return to a location designated somewhere on the screen. If direct navigation from one screen to any other is provided, the syntax for that movement should be consistent and correct.

If transactions are to be interruptible, the manner of saving partial transactions and calling them back should be the same for all screens. System level testing should test all of these capabilities.

3. All processing is within constraints. General constraints can relate to prerequisites, postrequisites, time, structure, control and inferences (see Chapter 1). Constraints can be internally controlled by the application or can be externally determined with the application simply meeting the constraint. Internally controlled constraints are tested through test cases specifically designed for that purpose. For instance, if response time limits have been stated, the longest possible transaction with the most possible errors or other delays should be designed to test response. If response time for a certain number of users is limited, then the test must have all users doing the most complex of actions to prove the response time constraint is met. Externally controlled constraints are those that the application either meets or does not. If the constraints are not met, then some redesign is probably required.
4. All modules are compatible and, in event of failures, degrade gracefully. System tests of compatibility prove that all system components are capable of operating together as designed. System components include programs, modules, utilities, hardware, database, network, and other specialized software.
5. Has sufficient procedures and code to provide disaster, restart, and application error recovery in both the designed and host software (e.g., DB2)
6. All operations procedures for the system are useful and complete. Operations procedures include start-up, shutdown, normal processing, exception processing, special operator interventions, periodic processing, system specific errors, and the three types of recovery.

In addition, the QA test evaluates the accuracy, consistency, format, and content of application documentation, including technical, user, on-line, and operations documentation. Ideally, the individual performing the QA test does not work on the project team but can deal with them effectively in the adversarial role of QA. Quality assurance in some companies is called the acceptance test and is performed by the user. In other companies, QA is performed within the IS department and precedes the user acceptance test.

The system test is the final developmental test under the control of the project team and is considered distinct from integration tests. That is, the successful completion of integration testing of successively larger groups of programs eventually leads to a test of the entire system. The system test is conducted by the project team and is analogous to the quality assurance acceptance test which is conducted by the user (or an agent of the user). Sample system test errors are shown in Table 17-8.

Test cases used in both QA and system testing should include as many normal operating conditions as possible. System test cases may include subsets of all previous test cases created for unit and integration tests as well as global test cases for system level requirements. The combined effect of test data used should be to verify all major logic paths (for both normal and exception processing), protection mechanisms, and audit trails.

QA tests are developed completely from analysis and design documentation. The goal of the test is to verify that the system does what the documentation describes and that all documents, screens, and processing are consistent. Therefore, QA tests go beyond system testing by specifically evaluating application information consistency across environments in addition to testing functional software accuracy. QA tests find a broader range of errors than system tests; a sampling of QA errors is in Table 17-9.

System testing affords the first opportunity to observe the system's hardware components operating as they would in a production mode. This enables the project's test coordinator to verify that response time and performance requirements are satisfied.

Since system testing is used to check the entire system, any errors detected and corrected may

TABLE 17-8   Sample System Test Errors

Functional

Application does not perform a function in the functional specification

Application does not meet all functional acceptance criteria

Human Interface

Screen format, spelling, content errors

Navigation does not meet user requirements

Interruption of transaction processing does not meet user requirements

Constraints

Prerequisites treated as sequential and should be parallel . . . must all be checked by (x) module

Prerequisite not checked

Response Time/Peak Performance

Response time not within requirements for file updates, start-up, shutdown, query, etc.

Volume of transactions expected cannot be processed within the specified run-time intervals

Batch processing cannot be completed in the time allotted

Expected number of peak users cannot be accommodated

Restart/Recovery

Program—Interrupted printout fails to restart at the point of failure (necessary for check processing and some confidential/financial reporting)

Software—Checkpoint/restart routine is not called properly

Hardware—Printer cannot be accessed from main terminal

Switches incorrectly set

System re-IPL called for in procedures cannot be done without impacting other users not of this application

Expected hardware configuration has incompatible components

TABLE 17-9   Sample QA/Acceptance Test Errors

Documentation

>   Two or more documents inconsistent
>
>   Document does not accurately reflect system feature

Edit/Validate

>   Invalid transaction accepted
>   Valid transaction rejected

Screen

>   Navigation, format, content, processing inconsistent with functional specification

Data Integrity

>   Multifile, multitransaction, multimatches are incorrect

File

>   File create, update, delete, query not present or not working
>
>   Sequence, data, or other criteria for processing not checked

Report specification

>   Navigation, format, content, processing inconsistent with functional

Recovery

>   Printer, storage, memory, software, or application recovery not correct

Performance

>   Process, response, user, peak, or other performance criteria not met

User Procedures

>   Do not match processing
>
>   Incomplete, inconsistent, incomprehensible
>
>   On-line help differs from paper documents

Operations Procedures

>   Do not match processing
>
>   Incomplete, inconsistent, incomprehensible

require retesting of previously tested items. The system test, therefore, is considered successful only when the entire system runs without error for all test types.

The test design should include all possible legal and illegal transactions, good and bad data in transactions, and enough volume to measure response time and peak transaction processing performance. As the test proceeds, each person notes on the test script whether an item worked or not. If a tested interaction had unexpected results, the result obtained is marked in the margin and noted for review.

The first step is to list all actions, functions, and transactions to be tested. The information for this list is developed from the analysis document for all required functions in the application and from the design document for security, audit, backup, and interface designs.

The second step is to design transactions to test all actions, functions and transactions. Third, the transactions are developed into a test script for a single user as a general test of system functioning. This test proves that the system works for one user and all transactions. Fourth, the transactions are interleaved across the participating number of users for multiuser testing. In general, the required transactions are only a subset of the total transactions included in the multiuser test. Required transactions test the variations of processing and should be specifically designed to provide for exhaustive transaction coverage. The other transactions can be a mix of simple and complex transactions at the designer's discretion. If wanted, the same transaction with variations to allow multiple use can be used. Fifth, test scripts for each user are then developed. Last, the test is conducted. These steps in developing system/QA tests are summarized as follows:

1. List all actions, functions, and transactions to be tested.
2. Design transactions to test all actions, functions, and transactions.
3. Develop a single-user test script for above.
4. Interleave the tests across the users participating in the test to fully test multiuser functioning of the application.
5. Develop test scripts for each user.

6. Conduct the test.
7. Review test results and reconcile anomalous findings.

Designing multiuser test scripts is a tedious and lengthy process. Doing multiuser tests is equally time-consuming. Batch test simulator (BTS) software is an on-line test aid available in mainframe environments. BTSs generate data transactions based on designer-specified attribute domain characteristics. Some BTSs can read data dictionaries and can directly generate transactions. The simulation portion of the software executes the interactive programs using the automatically generated transactions and can, in seconds, perform a test that might take people several hours. BTSs are not generally available on PCs or LANs yet, but they should be in the future.

Finally, after the system and QA tests are successful, the minimal set of transactions to test the application are compiled into test scripts for a regression test package. A **regression test package** is a set of tests that is executed every time a change is made to the application. The purpose of the regression test is to ensure that the changes do not cause the application to *regress* to a nonfunctional state, that is, that the changes do not introduce errors into the processing.

Deciding when to stop system testing is as subjective as the same decision for other tests. Unlike module and integration tests, system tests might have several peaks in the number of errors found over time (see Figure 17-23). Each peak might represent new modules or subsystems introduced for testing or might demonstrate application regression due to fixes of old errors that cause new errors. Because of this multipeak phenomenon, system testing is the most difficult to decide to end. If a decreasing number of errors have not begun to be found, that is, the curve is still rising, do not stop testing. If all modules have been through the system test at least once, and the curve is moving toward zero, then testing can be stopped if the absolute number of errors is acceptable. Testing should continue with a high number of errors regardless of the slope of the line. What constitutes an acceptable number of errors, however, is decided by the project manager, user, and IS managers; there is no right number.

QA testing is considered complete when the errors do not interfere with application functioning. A complete list of errors to be fixed is developed and given to the project manager and his or her manager to track. In addition, a QA test report is developed to summarize the severity and types of errors found over the testing cycle. Errors that are corrected before the QA test completes are noted as such in the report.

The QA report is useful for several purposes. The report gives feedback to the project manager about the efficacy of the team-testing effort and can identify weaknesses that need correcting. The reports are useful for management to gain confidence (or lose it) in project managers and testing groups. Projects that reach the QA stage and are then stalled for several months because of errors identify training needs that might not otherwise surface.

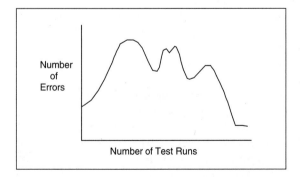

FIGURE 17-23   System Test Errors Found Over Test Shots

ABC Video System Test

Because ABC's application is completely on-line, the system test is essentially a repeat of the integration test for much of the functional testing. The system test, in addition, evaluates response time, audit, recovery, security, and multiuser processing. The functional tests do not duplicate the integration test exactly, however. The first user might use the integration test scripts. Other user(s) dialogues are designed to try to corrupt processing of the first user data and processes and to do other

Trans #	Rents	Returns	Late Fees	Payment	Receipt
T111	2	0	–	Exact	Automatic
T112	1	0	–	Over	Automatic
T113	1	1 (Total)	No	Over	Automatic
T121	10	0	–	Over	Automatic
T122	0	2 (From T121)	No	–	No
T141	0	2 (From T121)	2, 4 days	Over	Automatic
T151	4	2 (From T121)	2, 5 days	Over	Automatic
T211	1	1 (Total)	1 day	Exact	Automatic
T212	0	1 (Total)	No	–	No
T213	0	1 (Total)	No	–	Requested
T214	0	1 (Total)	2 days	Under, then exact	Automatic
T221	2	0	–	Under—abort	No
T222—Wait required	0	2 (From T121)	No	–	Requested
T311	0	1 (Total)	10 days	Over	Automatic
T312	1 (with other open rentals)	0	–	Over	Automatic
T313	6 (with other open rentals), error then rent 5	1	0	Exact	Automatic
T411=T311 Err	0	1 (Total)	10 days	Over	Automatic
T412=T312 Err	1 (with other open rentals)	0	–	Over	Automatic
T413=T313 Err	6 (with other open rentals), error then rent 5	1	0	Exact	Automatic
T331	0	2 (From T121)	2, 2 days	Exact	Automatic
T332	2	0	–	Under—abort	No
T511	5 (with other open rentals)	2	1 tape, 3 days	Over	Automatic

NOTE: Txyz Transaction ID: x = User, x = Day, z = Transaction number

FIGURE 17-24   ABC Video System Test Overview—Rent/Return Transactions

independent processing. If the total number of expected system users is six people simultaneously, then the system test should be designed for six simultaneous users.

The first step is to list all actions, functions, and transactions to be tested. For example, Figure 17-24 lists required transactions to test multiple days and all transaction types for each major file and process-

User 1	User 2	User 3	User 4	User 5	User 6
Start-up—success	Start-up—Err	Start-up—Err	Password—Err	Logon—Err	
Logon	Logon	Logon	Logon	Logon	Logon
Rent—T111 Errs + Good data	Rent—T211 Errs + Good data	Cust Add Errs + Good data	Cust Change—Err, Abort	Video Add Errs + Good data	Shutdown—Err
Rent—T112	Rent—T111 Err, abort	Rent—T311	Cust—Change	Copy Change—Errs + Good data	Try to crash system with bad trans
Rent—T113	Rent—T212—Err	Rent—T312	Rent—T411	Rent—T511	Delete Cust—Errs + Good data
Rent—T14	Rent—T213	Rent—T313	Rent—T412	Rent—any trans	Delete Video Errs
Rent—any trans	Rent—any trans	Rent—any trans	Rent—any trans	Rent—any trans	Delete Copy—Errs + Good data
END OF DAY, SHUT-DOWN, and STARTUP					
Rent—T121	Rent—T221	Rent—any trans	Rent—any trans	Rent—any trans	Rent—any trans
Rent—T122	Rent—T111	Rent—any trans	Rent—any trans	Rent—any trans	Rent—any trans
END OF DAY, SHUT-DOWN, and STARTUP					
Cust Add Errs + Good data	Cust Change—Err, Abort	Rent—T331	Copy Change—Errs + Good data	Try to crash system with bad trans	Rent—any trans
Delete Cust—Errs + Good data	Delete Video Errs	Rent—T332	Cust—Change	Video Add	Rent—any trans
END OF DAY, SHUT-DOWN, and STARTUP					
END OF MONTH					
NOTE: Txyz Transaction ID: x = User, x = Day, z = Transaction number					

FIGURE 17-25   ABC Video System Test Overview—Test Schedule

ing activity for *Rent/Return*. These transactions would be developed into a test script for a single user test of the application.

Then, the transactions are interleaved with other erroneous and legal transactions for the other ABC processes as planned in Figure 17-25. Notice that the required transactions are only a subset of the total transactions included in the test. The required transactions provide for exhaustive transaction coverage. The other transactions in Figure 17-25 are a mix of simple and complex transactions. Test scripts to follow the plan for each user are then developed; this is left as a student exercise.

Last, the test is conducted. During each shutdown procedure, the end-of-day reports are generated and reset. The data may or may not be checked after the first day to verify that they are correct. If errors are suspected, the files and report should be checked to verify accuracy. When one whole day is run through without errors, the entire set of test scripts can be executed. After an entire execution of each test script completes, the test team convenes and reviews all test scripts together to discuss unexpected results. All data from the files are verified for their predicted *final* contents. That is, unless a problem is suspected, intermediate intraday results are not verified during system testing. Errors that are found are reconciled and fixed as required. The test scripts are run through repeatedly until no errors are generated. Then, the test team should take real transactions for several days of activity and do the same type of test all over again. These transactions should also have file and report contents predicted. This 'live-data' test should be successful if system testing has been successful. If it is not, the errors found should be corrected and transactions to cause the same errors should be added to the system test. After the test is complete, the regression test package is developed for use during application maintenance.

AUTOMATED SUPPORT TOOLS FOR TESTING

Many CASE tools now support the automatic generation of test data for the specifications in their design products. There are also hundreds of different types of automated testing support tools that are not related to CASE. Some of the functions of these tools include

- static code analyzers
- dynamic code analyzers
- assertion generators and processors
- test data generators
- test driver
- output comparators

In Table 17-10, several examples of CASE testing tools are presented. Many other types of testing support tools are available for use outside of a CASE environment. The most common test support tools are summarized below and sample products are listed in Table 17-11.

A code analyzer can range from simple to complex. In general, **static code analyzers** evaluate the syntax and executability of code without ever executing the code. They cross-reference all references to a line of code. Analyzers can determine code that is never executed, infinite loops, files that are only read once, data type errors, global, common, or parameter errors, and other common problems. Another output of some static analyzers is a cross-reference of all variables and the lines of code on which they are referenced. They are a useful tool, but they cannot determine the worth or reliability of the code which are desired functions.

A special type of code analyzer *audits* code for compliance to standards and structured programming (or other) guidelines. Auditors can be customized by each using company to check their conventions for code structure.

A more complex type of code analyzer is a dynamic tool. **Dynamic code analyzers** run while the program is executing, hence the term dynamic. They can determine one or more of: coverage, tracing, tuning, timing, resource use, symbolic execution, and assertion checking. **Coverage analysis** of test data determines how much of the program is exercised by the set of test data. **Tracing** shows the execution path by statement of code. Some tools list values of key variables identified by the programmer. Languages on PCs usually have dynamic tracers as an execute option. **Tuning analyzers** identify the parts of the program executed most frequently, thus identifying code for tuning should a timing problem occur. **Timing analysis** reports CPU

TABLE 17-10 CASE Test Tools

Tool Name	Vendor	Features and Functions
Teamwork	Cadre Technologies, Inc. Providence, RI	Testing Software
Telon and other products	Pansophic Systems, Inc. Lisle, IL	Code Generation, Test Management

time used by a module or program. **Resource usage** software reports physical I/Os, CPU time, number of database transactions, and other hardware and software utilization. **Symbolic executors** run with symbolic, rather than real data, to identify the logic paths and computations for programmer-specified levels of coverage.

An **assertion** is a statement of fact about the state of some entity. An **assertion generator** makes facts about the state the data in a program should be in, based on test data supplied by the programmer. If the assertions fail based on program performance, an error is generated. Assertion generators are useful testing tools for artificial intelligence programs and any program language with which a generator can work. **Assertion checkers** evaluate the truth of programmer-coded assertions within code. For instance, the statement *'Assert make-buy = 0.'*, might be evaluated as true or false.

A **test data generator (TDG)** is a program that can generate any volume of data records based on programmer specifications. There are four kinds of

TABLE 17-11 Other Testing Support Tools

Tool Name	Vendor	Features and Functions
Assist		Coverage analysis, logic flow tracing, tracing, symbolic execution
Attest	University of Massachusetts Amherst, MA	Coverage analysis, test data generation, data flow analysis, automatic path selection, constraint analysis
Automatic Test Data Generator (ATDG)	TRW Systems, Inc. Redondo Beach, CA	Test data generation, path analysis, anomaly detection, variable analysis, constraint evaluation
Autoretest	TRW, Defense Systems Dept. Redondo Beach, CA	Comparator, test driver, test data management, automated comparison of test parameters
C/Spot/Run	Procase Corp. Santa Clara, CA	Syntax analysis, dependency analysis, source code filtering, source code navigation, graphical representation of function calls, error filtering

TABLE 17-11   Other Testing Support Tools (*Continued*)

Tool Name	Vendor	Features and Functions
COBOL Optimizer Instrumentor	Softool Corp. Goleta, CA	COBOL testing, path flow tracing, tracing, tuning
Cotune		Coverage analysis, timing
Datamacs	Management & Computer Services, Inc. Valley Forge, PA	Test file generation, I/O specification analysis, file structure testing
DAVE	Leon Osterweil University of Colorado Boulder, CO	Static analyzer, diagnostics, data flow analysis, interface analysis, cross-reference, standards enforcer, documentation aid
DIFF	Software Consulting Services Allentown, PA	File comparison
FACOM and Fadebug	Fujitsu, Ltd.	Output comparator, anomaly detector
Fortran Optimizer Instrumentor	Softool Corp. Goleta, CA	Coverage analysis Fortran testing, path flow tracing, tracing, tuning
McCabe Tools	M. McCabe & Associates Columbia, MD	Specification analysis, visual path testing generates conditions for untested paths computes metrics
MicroFocus Cobol Workbench	MicroFocus Palo Alto, CA	Source navigation, interactive dynamic debugging, structure analysis, regression testing, tuning
Softool 80	Softool Corp. Goleta, CA	Coverage analysis, tuning, timing, tracing
UX-Metric	Quality Tools for Software Craftsmen Mulino, OR	Static analyzer, syntax checking, path analysis, tuning, volume testing, cyclic tests

test data generators: static, pathwise, data specification, and random. A **static TDG** requires programmer specification for the type, number, and data contents of each field. A simple static TDG, the IEBDG utility from IBM, generates letters or numbers in any number of fields with some specified number of records output. It is useful for generating volumes of test data for timing tests as long as the records contain mostly zeros and ones. Unless the test data generator is easy to use, it quickly becomes more cumbersome than self-made test data.

Pathwise TDGs use input domain definitions to exercise specific paths in a program. These TDGs read the program code, create a representation of the control flow, select domain data to create representative input for a programmer-specified type of test, and execute the test. The possible programmer choices for test type include all feasible paths, statement coverage, or branch coverage. Since these are white-box techniques, unless a programmer is careful, a test can run for excessively long times.

Test drivers are software that simulate the execution of module tests. The tester writes code in the test driver language to provide for other module stubs, test data input, input/output parameters, files, messages, and global variable areas. The driver uses the test data input to execute the module. The other tester-defined items are used during the test to execute pieces of code without needing physical interfaces to any of the items. The major benefits of test drivers are the ease of developing regression test packages from the individual tests, and the forced standardization of test cases. The main problem with drivers is the need to learn another language to use the driver software.

On-line test drivers are of several types. **Batch simulators** generate transactions in batch-mode processing to simulate multi-user, on-line processing. **Transaction simulators** copy a test script as entered in single-user mode for later re-execution with other copied test scripts to simulate multi-user interactions.

Output comparators compare two files and identify differences. This makes checking of databases and large files less time-consuming than it would otherwise be.

SUMMARY

Testing is the process of finding errors in an application's code and documentation. Testing is a difficult activity because it is a high-cost, time-consuming activity for which the returns diminish upon success. As such, it is frequently difficult for managers to understand the importance of testing in application development.

The levels of developmental testing include unit, integration, and system. In addition, an agent, who is not a project team member, performs quality assurance testing to validate the documentation and pro-

cessing for the user. Code tests are on subroutines, modules, and programs to verify that individual code units work as expected. Integration tests verify the logic and processing for suites of modules, verifying intermodular communications. Systems tests verify that the application operates in its intended environment and meets requirements for constraints, response time, peak processing, backup and recovery, and security, access, and audit controls.

Strategies of testing are either white-box, black-box, top-down, or bottom-up. White-box tests verify that specific logic of the application works as intended. White-box strategies include logic tests, mathematical proof tests, and cleanroom tests. Black-box strategies include equivalence partitioning, boundary value analysis, and error guessing. Heuristics for matching the test level to the strategy were provided.

REFERENCES

Curritt, P. A., M. Dyer, and H. D. Mills, "Certifying the reliability of software," *IEEE Transactions of Software Engineering*, Vol. SE-12, 1986, pp. 3–11.

Dunn, Robert H., *Software Quality: Concepts and Plans*. Englewood Cliffs, NJ: Prentice-Hall, Inc., 1990.

Mills, H. D., M. Dyer, and R. Linger, "Cleanroom software engineering," *Software*, Vol. 4, #5, 1987, pp. 19–25.

Musa, J. D., and A. F. Ackerman, "Quantifying software validation: When to stop testing?" *Software*, Vol. 6, #3, May, 1989, pp. 19–27.

Myers, Glenford J., *The Art of Software Testing*. NY: John Wiley & Sons, 1979.

Selby, R. W., V. R. Basili, and F. T. Baker, "Cleanroom software development: An empirical evaluation," *IEEE Transactions of Software Engineering*, Vol. SE-13, 1987 pp. 1027–1037.

BIBLIOGRAPHY

De Millo, Richard A., W. Michael McCracken, R. J. Martin, and John F. Passafiume, *Software Testing and Evaluation*. Reading MA.: Benjamin Cummings Publishing Co., 1987.
This text describes testing and evaluation for military contracts and compliance with Department of Defense standards such as 2167a which describes the phases

and documents required of all government sponsored software development projects. It includes a rich description of different types of testing, in particular formal verification.

Dyer, M., *Cleanroom Software Development Method.* IBM Federal Systems Division, Bethesda, MD, October 14, 1982.

This monograph is a detailed description of the cleanroom development method.

Mills, H. D., M. Dyer, and R. Linger, "Cleanroom software engineering," *Software*, Vol. 4, #5, 1987, pp. 19–25.

This is a brief description of the methodology of cleanroom development which includes a description of testing.

Musa, John D., Anthony Iannino, and Kazuhira Okumoto, *Software Reliability: Measurement, Prediction, and Application.* NY: McGraw-Hill Book Co., 1987.

This text takes a quantitative approach to proving program correctness.

Musa, J. D., and A. F. Ackerman, "Quantifying software validation: When to stop testing?" *Software*, Vol. 6, #3, May, 1989, pp. 19–27.

Musa and Ackerman's article discusses the trajectory of error finding over test shots and when the risk of stopping begins to diminish.

Myers, Glenford J., *The Art of Software Testing.* NY: John Wiley & Sons, 1979.

This is the best book I have ever read on testing. It is short, clear, and easy to follow. The only drawback is that real-time systems were not prevalent enough to have been included in the book.

Selby, R. W., V. R. Basili, and F. T. Baker, "Cleanroom software development: An empirical evaluation," *IEEE Transactions of Software Engineering*, Vol. SE-13, 1987 pp. 1027–1037.

This article reviews cleanroom projects and develops statistics about reliability of the software.

KEY TERMS

acceptance test
assertion
assertion checker
assertion generator
batch simulator
black-box strategy
bottom-up testing
boundary value analysis

cause-effect graphing
cleanroom development
coverage analysis
developmental test
dynamic code analyzer
equivalence partitioning
error guessing
integration test

output comparator
pathwise test data generator
program stub
quality assurance (QA) test
regression test
regression test package
resource usage
scaffolding
static code analyzer
static test data generator
subsystem test
symbolic executor
system test
test case
test data generator (TDG)

test driver
test plan
test script
test strategy
testing
timing analyzer
top-down testing
tracing
transaction simulator
tuning analyzer
type 1 error
type 2 errors
unit test
Vienna Development Method (VDM)
white-box strategy

EXERCISES

1. Describe the process of test development for an application. What are the roles, activities, documentation, and procedures followed by participants to testing?
2. Develop a test script for user 1 for the system test.

STUDY QUESTIONS

1. Define the following terms:
   scaffolding   test strategy
   white box testing   test case
   black box testing   test plan
   integration test
2. What is testing and why is it important?
3. How do you know when a test result is right?
4. Why do managers shorten the time allotted to testing?
5. Why do SEs and programmers sometimes resent testing?
6. What is the purpose of predicting results? Do the results have to be exact or can they be approximated? Why?
7. What is the purpose of a unit test? How is it met through test strategy selection?
8. When is it appropriate *not* to test all program logic? How do you decide what *to* test?

9. What are the different test strategies? Define each and discuss how they differ.

10. How many test cases does a program need?

11. What is the purpose of an integration test? What test strategy(s) are usually used in integration testing? Why?

12. What is the purpose of a systems test and how does it differ from the other test types: unit and integration?

13. Why is top-down testing *by itself* not a good idea at the system level?

14. Why is top-down testing a good idea at the system level?

15. At which test levels are bottom-up and top-down most appropriate? How do the top-down and bottom-up pieces get integrated?

16. At which level of testing does the human interface get tested?

17. How does prototyping fit with testing? Does prototyping also require a testing strategy? Why or why not?

18. What is the role of users during testing? Can users conduct the systems test? the integration tests? the unit tests? For each, why or why not?

19. For each level of testing, when can you end testing?

★ EXTRA-CREDIT QUESTIONS

1. Develop the test plan for Customer Maintenance in the ABC rental application.

2. Develop test scripts to unit test the other three transaction types for ABC Video. Use the screen design from Chapter 14 to help you visualize the data and processing requirements. The three transaction types are rentals without returns, returns without rentals, rentals with returns (i.e., *Customer ID* is entered first rather than *Video ID*).

3. Develop a test strategy for testing the entire application for a case in the appendix. Keep in mind that testing that involves users should minimize their time commitment while obtaining essential information from their involvement. Specifically define roles, responsibilities, timing, and test strategy for each level of testing.

4. Develop a presentation to senior user and IS managers to justify the time and resources required to do application testing. Present the discussion to your class.

## CHAPTER 18

CHANGE
MANAGEMENT

INTRODUCTION

Nothing is rarer in information systems development than an application without changes. Users forget requirements and remember them late in the design. The business changes. Bugs get fixed and require documentation. Change occurs in all phases and all levels of application development. Procedures to manage change, therefore, are necessary to maintain sanity and order on the project team.

The three major types of change in an application's life cycle—requirements, software, and documentation—are discussed in this chapter. For each, the importance of the change management techniques is discussed. Then, for each, techniques for managing changes are developed. At the end of the chapter, automated tools are identified for collaborative work, documentation, reverse engineering, and code management. First, we discuss the importance of designing for maintenance, regardless of the environment, architecture, or item being developed.

DESIGNING FOR MAINTENANCE

Applications are usually in production for an average of eight years. Many applications are much older, having been patched and modified regularly

for 10 or even 20 years. Applications that are flexible enough to withstand years of modification are designed with change in mind. That is, regardless of the methodology, independent modules with local effects are developed.

Programs with 10,000 lines of, for instance, COBOL procedure code, rarely are modified easily. Usually, they are such spaghetti, that if they ever work, it is due to good luck. Frequently, change is precarious and likely to cause problems in untouched parts of the program.

In this section, we discuss the techniques used in designing for maintenance. The first, reusable libraries, have been used widely in the aerospace industry. Because cost savings can now be demonstrated from reusable libraries, they are moving into other industry segments. Reusable modules are complete programs that perform some complete function. The next section relates methodology to maintenance effort and discusses how each methodology attempts to provide for maintenance. Finally, CASE tools are related to maintenance and change.

Reusability

Reusability is a property of a code module such that the module can be used, as is, by several applications. In designing for reuse, the goal is to identify modules for potential reuse. The two most popular methods of implementing code reuse are program templates and reusable modules.

Program templates consist of standard code that performs a simple function. For instance, there are three basic types of business programs: report, edit/validate, and file update. For a report, there are standard sections for reading file data, formatting the data, and writing the report (see Figure 18-1). Reading and writing can be standardized regardless of the data definition for input. The formatting of data must be customized. In writing the report, there are sections of code for beginning-of-page, body-of-page, and end-of-page. There may be sections for beginning-of-report and end-of-report, too. The report program might or might not have an internal sort routine that changes the sequence of the input file.

Templates can be developed to describe the 12 or so most common variants of the three basic types of programs. For instance, a report program is developed with and without sorts. COBOL or some other procedural language is used to define the standard versions and the only items left to the application programmer are procedures specific to the application.

The templates are stored as **read only** modules in a library. When a new use is defined, the module to be used is copied and given a new name. The newly named module is then modified and customized for its current use.

The advantage of a template is that a finite number of variations are developed and then are modified as needed for a specific use. There is little or no maintenance on the templates once they are developed, and only a few new templates per year would ever be developed. The number of support staff could be close to zero.

A template is a partial program that is completed for a particular application. A **reusable module** is a small, single function, well-defined, and standardized program module that can be used as a called routine, or as a *copy book* in COBOL. For instance, a date edit routine might be developed as a reusable module (see Figure 18-2).

When a reusable module is desired, a **library of reusable modules** is studied to determine which ones fit the application's needs. For reusable modules that do fit an application, the individual module code is examined to verify that it performs as required. Then the module is called at the appropriate place in the application's processing.

Each application team determines which modules it might have that could be reused in its own or in other applications. Then the modules are singled out for special development as independent routines. The finished module is quality assurance tested by the librarians to ensure that it performs as documented. The **librarian** is an expert in reusable standards, quality assurance testing, and code management techniques. Eventually, the code is stored in a reusable library whose contents are published for application developers' use.

Publication of reusable library contents can be awkward. Paper might be too voluminous to be useful or cost-effective. Electronic publication requires indices to assist users in identifying potential modules for their use. The indices might include keywords to describe function, language, date of development, type of input, and so on. If indices are not coded to capture the essential characteristics of the modules, they are useless.

The amount of organizational support required to maintain reusable libraries has been the major impediment to reusable library adoption in most industries. Librarians test, store, and maintain references to the modules in the reusable library. A large number of modules, for instance over 1,000, makes maintenance of the library integrity and accuracy a major task. Locating modules for use is also a major task. Librarians become specialized in performing these functions. Without proper organizational support, reusable libraries soon become unused and useless.

The arguments for reuse are substantial. As much as 75% of all code on a typical business application is redundant, and therefore, a candidate for reuse. Database descriptions, program procedure templates, and individual modules are all candidates for reuse that can save companies time and money in application development. The more reused code, the less extensive the custom code developed, the less extensive the testing required, and the less the cost of the application.

```
Identification Division.
Program-ID.  ABCVIDADD.
Environment Division.
Configuration Section.
Source-Computer.  IBM-3080.
Object-Computer.  IBM-3080.
File Section.
   Select Input-File from UR-D0001 as RPTIN.
   Select Report-File from UR-P001 as RPTOUT.
File Division.
Input Section.
FD        Input-File
   Block contains 100 records.
   Record contains 400 characters.
01        Input-File-Record          Pic x(400).
FD        Report-File
   Block contains 1 record.
   Record contains 132 characters.
01        Report-File-Record         Pic x(132).
Working-Storage Division.
01        Miscellaneous-counters.
          05    Page-Count           Pic 99          value zero.
          05    Line-Count           Pic 99          value zero.
          05    Input-record-count   Pic 9(7)        value zero.
          05    Output-record-count  Pic 9(7)        value zero.
          05    End-of-file-marker   Pic 9           value zero.
                88    End-of-file                    value 1.
                88    Not-end-of-file                value 0.
********
01        Copy Input-File-Description statement goes here.
********
01        Report-Headers.
          05    Header-01.
                10    Filler      pic x(45)       Value spaces.
                10    H1          pic x(23)       value
                      'Company Standard Header'.
                10    Filler      pic x(15)       value spaces.
                10    Date        pic x(8)        value spaces.
          05    Header-2.
                10    Filler      pic x(45)       Value spaces.
                10    H1          pic x(23)       value
                      'Report Standard Header'.
                10    Filler      pic x(15)       value spaces.
                10    Time
                      15    Hour    pic xx        value spaces.
                      15    Filler  pic x         value ':'.
                      15    Hour    pic xx        value spaces.
                      15    Filler  pic x         value ':'.
                      15    Hour    pic xx        value spaces.
```

FIGURE 18-1   Partial COBOL Program Template for a Report

```
              Linkage Section.
              01        In-Date.
                        05        In-Date-Month              pic xx.
                        05        In-Date-Day                pic xx.
                        05        In-Date-Year               pic xx.
              01        Errors.
                        05        Err-table   occurs x times.
                                  10 Err                     pic 9 comp.
              Procedure Division.
              Link.
                        Enter linkage.
                        Entry Link-date-edit using in-date, errors.
                        Enter COBOL.
              Initialize.
                        Move zeros to Errs.
              Check-Numerics.
                        If In-Date-Mo         not numeric move 1 to err(1).
                        If In-Date-Day        not numeric move 1 to err(2).
                        If In-Date-Year       not numeric move 1 to err(3).
                        If err(1) = 1 or err(2) = 1 or err (3) = 1 go to End-Test.
              Check-values.
                        If In-Date-Day > 0
                                  continue
                        else
                                  move 1 to err(4).
                        If In-Date-Year > 1992
                                  and In-Date-Year < 2015
                                  continue
```

FIGURE 18-2   Reusable COBOL Module for Date Edit

Methodology Design Effects

In this section, we discuss the suitability of reusable libraries and program templates to the three classes of methodologies. Because of the encapsulation of data and function in object orientation, object methods are best suited to the large scale development of reusable modules. The other methodologies, process and data, can use program templates and reusable modules, but such modules are not identified as naturally as with objects.

Object methods are best suited to reusable components because the design method results in small, single function modules automatically. The method assumes that only data needed for a function will be available to it when it is called. Thus, the entire method assumes and strives for modules that are potentially reusable. When a module is identified in object analysis as being invoked from multiple calling objects, it is automatically targeted as potentially reusable. Further analysis determines if the functionality is identical for all users. If the functionality is the same, the module becomes locally reusable.

The step from local reuse to organizational reuse is small, with the criteria being the number of other applications needing the function. Here too, object methods are more amenable to identifying reusable functionality at the analysis stage than the other methodologies. Think back to Chapter 11, in which we developed the table of actions (or functions) and the objects to which they were attached (see Table 18-1). It is at this stage that reuse is identified. When an action has more than one object attached, they are examined to determine whether the same action is performed for each. If both objects use the action identically, they are labeled potentially reusable.

```
                    else
                            move 1 to err(5).
             If In-Date-Month = 2
                     If In-Date-Year = (1992 or 1996 or 2000 or 2004 or 2008 or 2012)
                             If In-Date-Day < 30
                                     go to End-Test
                             else move 1 to err(6)
                     else
                     If In-Date-Day < 29
                             go to End-Test
                     else move 1 to err(7)
             else
             If In-Date-Month = (4 or 6 or 9 or 11)
                     If In-Date-Day < 31
                             go to End-Test
                     else move 1 to err(8)
             else
             If In-Date-Month = (1 or 3 or 5 or 7 or 10 or 12)
                     If In-Date-Day < 32
                             go to End-Test
                     else move 1 to err(9)
             else
                     move 1 to err(10).
     End-Test.
             Enter linkage.
             Return.
             Enter COBOL.
```

FIGURE 18-2   Reusable COBOL Module for Date Edit (*Continued*)

Then, the potentially reusable actions are used to search the reusable library to see if similar actions in reusable form already exist. When a match is found, the reusable module code is examined to determine its fit to the current need. Based on the closeness of fit, the designers choose to design their own module or use the reusable module. The reusable module can be used as it exists or can be customized to exactly fit the application. The point is that the analysis action is matched to a reusable action at the *logical* level. Only when the logical actions match, the physical implementation is then examined for its appropriateness. When many such logical level matches are found, the time savings in analysis, design, and implementation can be considerable.

It has long been held that structured and modular design reduces maintenance effort by facilitating the definition of understandable *chunks* of analysis and designs. Modular design, in turn, is then applied to program modules. The designer uses his or her experience, applying the principles of information hiding, minimal coupling and maximal cohesion, to develop single function modules. In this manner, the nonobject methodologies are more *brute force* methods of developing modules with object-like properties. While the nonobject methodologies rely on personal designer knowledge, such knowledge also is more important in object methods than is commonly recognized at present. The results in nonobject methodologies, though, are less uniform and less likely to cause ready recognition of reusable components than object methods. Therefore, reusable component libraries are most likely to be effective and widely used in object-oriented environments.

TABLE 18-1   Sample Actions with Related Objects

Verb from Paragraph	Space	Process Name	Objects–Action*
is entered	S	EnterCustPhone	Customer, Data entry (DE)
to create	S	CreateOrder	Order (R)
are displayed	S	DisplayOrderVOO	Order, VOO (D)
are entered	S	EnterBarCode	VOO (DE)
are retrieved	S	RetrieveInventory	VideoInventory (R)
are displayed	S	DisplayInventory	VideoInventory (D)
computes	S	ComputeOrderTotal	Order (Process)
is entered	S	EnterPayAmt	Order (DE)
is computed	S	ComputeChange	Order (P)

*Actions are (R)ead, (W)rite, Data Entry (DE), (D)isplay (P)rocess in memory, (PR)int

The opposite situation is true of program templates. The nonobject methods, because they are used mostly for COBOL applications, can take advantage of program template libraries easily and effectively. As much as 60–80% of all COBOL code is **boilerplate**, that is, code which does not vary from one program to another. The boilerplate can be standardized and provided as program templates.

With object methods, the boilerplate in an object package is minimal but still can be standardized. The remaining code is either reused or customized. The types of COBOL template programs, for instance, a report with a sort, do not exist in the same form as objects. There might be a report object and there might be a sort object, and both might be reusable, but the code for *using* either object is most likely provided by custom developed code.

Role of CASE

Computer Aided Software Engineering (CASE) tools are critical to maintaining applications at the functional level rather than at the code level. The argument for CASE runs something like this. The 40-20-40 rule applies to software engineering application development. The rule states that 40% of the work is performed during feasibility, analysis, and design; 20% is during coding; and the remaining 40% is during testing (see Figure 18-3).

The 80-20 rule also applies (see Figure 18-3). According to this rule, 20% of the development work is performed during the original application development. The other 80% is performed during maintenance. This ratio holds because maintenance is a much longer period of an application's life.

Putting these two rules together, to gain substantive productivity increases we need to reduce time spent on coding, testing, and maintenance *more* than we need to reduce the time spent on analysis and design. CASE that covers analysis and design only reduces the time spent on documentation and maintenance of documents. CASE that includes database schema generation and code generation further reduces the coding, testing, and maintenance activities. Fully integrated CASE tools, I-CASE (see Chapter 3 and Automated Tools section of this chapter), that interface with code generators, support all of these productivity improvements. With I-CASE tools, maintenance changes are reflected in the requirements for an application. The requirements are, in turn, used to regenerate the database schemas and code for the application. Thus, the changes take place at the logical level and are *automatically generated* by the CASE tool at the physical level. The capability to do all application maintenance in this way is not here yet but should be before the new century.

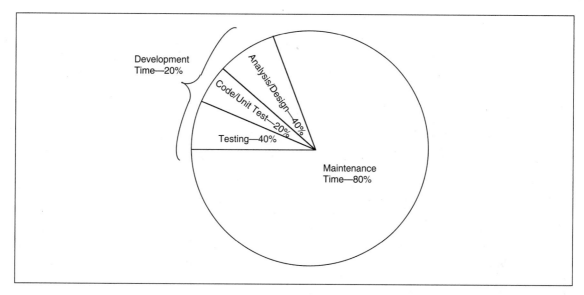

FIGURE 18-3   Application Life Cycle Time Distribution

A more futuristic feature of CASE tools will be the ability of the tool to recognize *reusable analysis and design fragments*, rather than relying on humans to recognize reusable *code fragments*. Purchasable options of the CASE tools will include intelligent options to detect feature and function similarities across applications. The fragments would then be imported from the original library to the using application library (or repository). Very intelligent CASE will be able to recognize a design fragment, logically link to the base definition of the reused item, and use already operational code modules. This level of intelligent CASE that could manage the use of reusable code may surface in our lifetimes, but not soon.

APPLICATION
CHANGE
MANAGEMENT

Importance

Applications frequently undergo redesign. Three typical conditions for redesign are assignment of a new management team, a project that is chronically over budget, late, and full of bugs, and the loss of the user-owner confidence that the SEs understand their needs. Even without drastic redesign, reviews (e.g., for user agreement or quality assurance) frequently turn up items that were originally compromised or rethought several times before final version agreement. The history of decisions and the reasoning about decisions is rarely kept as part of project notes. But, any project manager and SE can tell you that they frequently rehash the same arguments and reasonings over and over, even reaching the same conclusions.

In a paper-based work environment, keeping track of the history of decisions is not practical; so much paper would be generated that finding anything becomes impossible. In a CASE environment, or in an imaging environment, maintaining the history of application decisions electronically becomes a manageable, and sometimes desirable, activity. The ability to recall reasoning through a decision, whether it is logical or political, can save time and provide continuity between managers.

Finally, changes in the business, legal requirements, or stakeholders in the application can all necessitate legitimate changes to application designs. Knowing the history of decisions sometimes makes them more palatable and easier to convey to staff. For instance, being able to relate a change of design to a developing business situation helps those who must cope with the change appreciate the business of the application. If the change is to keep a valued customer or increase competitiveness in a new area, the systems developers are more likely to be enthusiastic about shifting design.

Changes can be to requirements, designs, programs, interfaces, hardware, or purchased software. Most changes are initiated from within the organization developing the application, but might be motivated by some outside event, such as a change in laws. Using change controls protects the development team from user whims while allowing for action on legitimate requests. The idea that a specification is **frozen**, meaning not changeable after it is accepted as complete, motivates users to be as complete in their thinking as possible.

Designs do not stay frozen forever. Usually, once an application begins coding, no changes are implemented until the application becomes operational. Then the project manager, SE, and user review the backlog of requests to develop priorities and plan the changes. Some changes may be so critical that the design is unfrozen to add the crucial functionality, regardless of the phase of development.

Change Management Procedures

Change control management is in effect from the time the work product is accepted as complete until the project is retired. First, baseline work products that are to be managed are identified. A **baseline** work product is a product that is considered complete and that is the basis for other, current work by the project development team. A baseline document would be, for instance, the functional requirements specification after it is accepted by the user.

A history of change request file actions for a functional specification are listed here as an example.

1. Create Open Request
2. File Impact Statement
3. File Approval of Schedule and Cost signed by User/Owner

4. Complete Project Manager's Check List for the Change
5. File Documentation relating to changes. If documentation or programs changed, identify date and items updates completed. If procedures or training changed, identify dates at which revisions were operationalized.
6. File Close Request Form Approved by User/Owner
7. Summarize Dates, Durations, and Costs

First, the baseline document is frozen, then change requests are added, but no action is taken. The fourth request, for example, might be urgent and receive immediate attention. When the functional specification is updated to accommodate the change, it is again frozen and the work continues. The three previous requests might have been added to the application if they did not significantly alter it. They may just as likely be ignored until after the application is implemented.

Changes can be classified in several ways. First, they can be classified by type as eliminating defects, improving performance, or changing functionality. Second, changes can be classified as required or optional. Third, change can be classified by priority as emergency, mandatory with a required end date, mandatory with an open end date, or low priority. Usually, eliminating defects is a required emergency, while changing functionality is required mandatory maintenance, and improving performance is optional and might have any priority.

Knowing the change request classification determines whether it is subject to change control or not. Emergency changes usually circumvent the change control procedures in that the activities might all be followed but they are documented after the change is complete. All other change types should be required to comply with change controls.

For example, changes to functional requirements can occur at any time, but once the functional requirements specification is approved, it is frozen until the application is operational. Changes are subject to change control: they are added to a change request list for future consideration unless given an emergency designation.

Project # _____

Project Name _____

<u>CHANGE CONTROL REQUEST</u>

Inittiator _____   Date _____

Department _____   Request # _____

<u>Reason for Request</u>

<u>Description of Change</u>

<u>Documents Affected:</u>		<u>Category of Change</u>	
Func. Spec.	_____	A. Reqts.	_____
Interface	_____	B. Design	_____
Design	_____	C. Code	_____
Mod. Spec.	_____	D. Interface	_____
Code	_____	E. Hardware	_____
Operations	_____	F. Other	_____
User Doc.	_____		

<u>Class of Change</u>

Emergency	_____
Mandated	_____
Enhancement	_____
Other	_____

Initiator	Date		
Owner	Date	Prroject Manager	Date

FIGURE 18-4   Sample Change Request Form

A procedure for change control (listed below) requires that a formal request for a change is submitted by the user to the project manager (PM).

1. User sends the project manager and owner (if different person) a Change Request form (see Figure 18-4).

2. Project manager and SE develop an impact statement. At this time, the project manager's Check List is used to identify all work actions and changes relating to the request.

3. The Change Request is discussed with the User/Owner to establish priority, schedule, and cost changes.

4. Agreement is formalized and User/Owner approval of schedule and cost changes is obtained.

5. Using the impact statement, application and all related documentation are changed. Implement the change. As tasks are complete, check off the task on the project manager's Check List.

6. User/Owner approval to close the request is obtained and the request is closed.

The PM and SE define the schedule and cost impacts of the change (see Figure 18-5). The changes are then discussed with the user. Based on the negotiation with the user, the change is assigned a priority for action, and the cost and schedule are changed.

The request, expected date of action, schedule change, and cost increments are added to a project history file. The changes may be monitored by a **Change Control Clerk**, a person charged with maintaining project history and change control records, and with issuing a monthly change control report. A **Change Control File** contains all requests, correspondence, and documentation about changes. An **Open Change Request** is created when the request is made and a change number is assigned. The open change request stays on file until the request is completed, closed, and reported.

As the change is made, affected items are updated, including the appropriate documentation, code, training, and so forth (see Figure 18-6). A project manager's check list is used to check off required actions. The new documentation is filed with the Change Control Clerk who distributes it to all interested parties.

The completion date for the change is entered in the Change Control File. The change is identified as closed in the next status report and the open request is removed from the Change Control File.

Depending on the organization, the IS executive might want to track change requests for projects to identify success in meeting requests. Overall costs of changes for a year are used as one indicator that an application is a candidate for either retirement or reengineering. In such cases, both costs and volumes of change requests are tracked through the change control process. Summary reports by project of the changes over a given period, or comparing periods (e.g., a current period compared to the same period last year) can be developed. Three such reports are shown as Figures 18-7 through 18-9 for total cost by type, cost and schedule impacts, and change requests, respectively.

Historical Decision Logging

At the beginning of the project, the project manager and SE decide to use tools to store the decision process. This means that either electronic group meetings are used or that a written version of meetings and decisions is maintained and stored in word processed form. With electronic meetings, the electronic transcripts are maintained. With manual recording, the old version is updated and renamed when a document changes. For instance, functional specifications for ABC might be named *ABCFS-mmddyy*, where *ABC* is the company, *FS* abbreviates Functional Specification, and *mmddyy* is the date. The date portion of the name would change for every major change of the document. The change management procedure in the next section would be followed.

Documentation Change Management

Documentation changes should be identified by a change table of contents at the beginning of each document. The change table of contents includes the effective date, affected sections of the document, and a summary of the change (see Figure 18-10). The purpose of the change table of contents is to summarize all changes for the reader.

Changes should be redlined in the text to identify the changed portion. If the old information is important, it may be moved to a footnote, dated, and labeled as a previous version. An example of this type of documentation change is shown in Figure 18-11. Keep in mind that you also keep the old version of the document for history.

(Text continues on page 749)

Project # _____

Project Name _____

CHANGE CONTROL IMPACT ASSESSMENT

Date _____

Request # _____

Impact of Change Request:

Impact

Type	Cost	Person Days	Business Days	Budget Control	
A.	_____	_____	_____	Initiation Date	_____
B.	_____	_____	_____	Request #	_____
C.	_____	_____	_____	Amount	_____
D.	_____	_____	_____	Approval Date	_____
E.	_____	_____	_____		
F.	_____	_____	_____		
Total	_____	_____	_____		

STATUS	Scheduled Completion	Actual Completion
Initiated Date	_____	_____
Analysis Date	_____	_____
Development Date	_____	_____
Testing Date	_____	_____
Implementation Date	_____	_____

Comments:

Initiator	Date		
Owner	Date	Prroject Manager	Date

FIGURE 18-5   Sample Change Request Impact Form

Project # _____   Date _____

Project Name _____   Request # _____

PROJECT MANAGER CHANGE CONTROL CHECK LIST

DEVELOPMENT

	Required	Completion Date
1. QA/Documentation Review	_____	_____
2. Update Source Document(s)	_____	_____
3. Update Baseline Document(s)	_____	_____
4. Update Program Specifications	_____	_____
5. Revise Code	_____	_____
6. Update User Documentation	_____	_____
7. Update Operations Documentation	_____	_____
8. Other: _____	_____	_____

_____

IMPLEMENTATION

	Required	Completion Date
1. Baseline Documents Update	_____	_____
2. Requirement Change	_____	_____
3. Design Changes	_____	_____
4. Programming Changes	_____	_____
Pgm #'s ____, ____, ____	_____	_____
____, ____, ____	_____	_____
5. Unit Testing	_____	_____
6. System/Regression Testing	_____	_____
7. Interface Changes	_____	_____
8. Operations Changes	_____	_____
9. Other: _____	_____	_____

_____

Comments:

_____
Initiator   Date

_____
Owner   Date   Prroject Manager   Date

FIGURE 18-6   Project Manager's Change Check List

CHANGE CONTROL ANALYSIS BY TYPE

Month of: May, 1994

PROJECT-TO-DATE

Number and Cost of Change by Type

Application Name:	A #	A Cost	B #	B Cost	C #	C Cost	D #	D Cost	E #	E Cost	F #	F Cost	G #	G Cost	Total #	Total Cost
1. Branch Pilot	60	$45.6	1	$ 2.6	–	–	–	–	3	$40.7	–	–	–	–	64	$ 88.9
2. Securities Transfer	17	–	–	–	2	–	–	–	–	–	–	–	–	–	19	–
3. Settlements	16	36.0	11	18.6	–	–	–	–	–	–	2	.5	–	–	29	55.1
4. Float Allocation	–	–	3	6.0	16	$11.0	–	–	3	.4	1	$10.0	–	–	23	27.4
Total	93	$81.6	15	$27.2	18	$11.0	–	–	6	$41.1	3	$10.5	–	–	135	$171.4

Change Type Legend

A. Requirements/Design
B. Application Programs/Testing
C. Documentation
D. Hardware
E. Purchased Software
F. Interfaces
G. Application Support

Notes: Costs in thousands
Changes with no cost are planned maintenance.

FIGURE 18-7   Summary Report of Change Costs

CHANGE CONTROL COST/SCHEDULE IMPACT*					Month of May, 1994	
	Current Month		Year-to-Date		Project-to-Date	
Application	Cost	Schedule	Cost	Schedule	Cost	Schedule
1. Branch Pilot	–	–	$ 48.8	24	$ 88.9	39
2. Securities Transfer	$ 15.0	8	15.0	8	25.0	14
3. Settlements	111.0	64	111.0	64	225.0	140
Total	$126.0	72	$174.8	96	$338.9	193

*All data based on change Submission Date

Cost in thousands

Schedule in business days

FIGURE 18-8   Summary Report of Cost and Schedule Impacts

CHANGE CONTROL ACTIVITY													Month of May, 1994					
	Current Month						Year-to-Date						Project-to-Date					
Project Name	S	P	A	D	O	C	S	P	A	D	O	C	S	P	A	D	O	C
1. Branch Pilot	–	–	–	–	–	–	6	1	4	1	1	3	64	1	51	12	25	26
2. Securities Transfer	3	1	2	–	1	1	22	1	18	3	6	12	22	1	18	3	6	12
3. Settlements	16	9	7	–	3	4	16	9	7	–	3	4	16	9	7	–	3	4
Total	19	10	9	–	4	5	42	11	29	4	10	19	102	11	76	15	34	42

LEGEND:

S   Submitted
P   Pending
A   Approved
D   Disapproved/Cancelled
O   Open
C   Completed

FIGURE 18-9   Summary of Change Requests

CHANGE PAGE		
Page No.	Reason for/description of change	Date
1–48	Original issue	11/4/93
All	Audit review and Revisions	1/3/94
1–2, 22	Corrections and revisions to reflect organization changes	2/6/94
6, 9, 37–44	Describe imaging interface	6/3/94

FIGURE 18-10   Sample Document Change Table of Contents

SOFTWARE MANAGEMENT

Introduction

Two of the roles of the SE in software management are to recommend what type of maintenance should be performed and to select code maintenance software. These are discussed in this section.

Types of Maintenance

The types of maintenance are minor modifications, restructuring, reengineering, or rebuilding.[1] **Minor**

modifications are changes to existing code and can be any of the project manager classifications discussed above. **Restructuring** is the redevelopment of a portion of an application with a bridge to the old application. **Reengineering** is the reverse analysis of an old application to conform to a new methodology, usually Information Engineering or object orientation. Reengineering is also known as **reverse engineering**. **Rebuilding** is the retirement and redevelopment of an application.

To select the appropriate type of maintenance, several questions are asked (see Figure 18-12). First, ask if the software works. If the answer is no, you retire the old application. Then you reengineer and rebuild it using a methodology. If the answer is yes, you continue to the next question: Does the

---

1 This discussion is based on Martin, 1990.

Functional Specification Settlements

1/15/94
Page 22

...

The settlements system uses relational database design techniques and fully normalized data entities.[1] The database design is fully documented in Figure 2-1. The diagram shows the 17 entities used in settlements processing and the relationships between them. Each entity and its descriptive attributes are fully described in the data dictionary attached as Appendix 1; they are also available on-line through both IEF, the CASE tool being used for the application, and Project-Notes, the on-line help tool.

...

---

1 Prior to January, 1994, a nonnormalized, relational approach to the data was used. This resulted in a loss of data integrity that necessitated strict enforcement of relational theory to comply with audit requirements for the application.

FIGURE 18-11   Sample Documentation Change with Old Contents

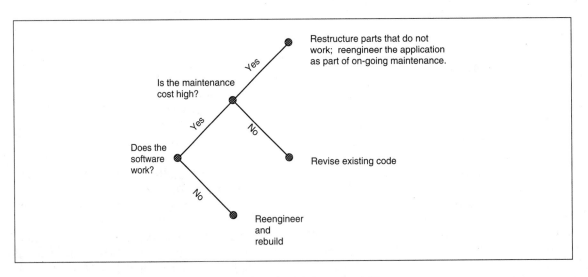

FIGURE 18-12   Decision Tree for Selecting the Maintenance Type

application have a high maintenance cost? If the maintenance cost is low, the answer is no; then do a simple revision. If the answer is yes, immediately restructure the parts that do not work, and reengineer the entire application as part of on-going work.

Reengineering

Reengineering is the analysis and design of an existing application to bring it into conformance with a methodology. When the application conforms to a methodology, it is rebuilt. To reengineer program code, the code first must be structured. Code restructuring can be done by automated tools. The restructured code from all programs in an application is entered into a CASE tool with reverse engineering capabilities.

Code restructuring also can be done manually. If no CASE products are used, the code is analyzed and the underlying data and process structures are mapped into a methodology. If Information Engineering is used, for instance, an entity relationship diagram (ERD) and a process data flow diagram (PDFD) are first developed for each program. Then, the diagrams are consolidated across programs to develop application ERDs and PDFDs. A data dictionary to document diagram contents is developed. The ERD is normalized and compared to the automated data to determine the extent of deviation from the normalized state. If the denormalized state was for performance purposes (this is an example of the importance of a historical file of design decisions), then problems with data integrity resulting from the denormalization should be noted for correction. Finally, the detailed process diagrams are used to develop a process hierarchy diagram. The hierarchy diagram is matched to the real organizational functions to determine the extent of application function redesign required.

If the methodology is object-oriented, the code modules are classified by object type and function. If multiple objects call a function, it is classified as reusable and set aside for further analysis. After module classification, the extent to which the code matches a true object design is determined. Reusable modules are evaluated to ensure that they perform single functions, hide information, and use minimal coupling techniques. For minor deviation from the object method, individual modules or object types are reengineered to bring them into conformance with object tenets. For major deviation, the application is reengineered and redeveloped using object techniques.

CONFIGURATION _____
MANAGEMENT _____

Introduction

In the mainframe world, one disk storage device can hold 10,000 or more different data files; large projects develop hundreds of program modules every year; and programmers may manage several different versions of code modules at one time. To support multiple users across different platforms might require multiple operational versions and variations of code modules, and they all have to be maintained. **Configuration management** is the identification, organization, and control of modifications to software built by a programming team. **Code library** management software provides a means to identify and manage the baseline for program code modules. The **baseline** is the *official* version of a code module that is in production use at any time. Two types of code libraries and the application types they support are discussed in this section. Derivations, which identify each module's history, are included in the discussion.

Configuration management addresses problems originally present in large COBOL applications but are equally useful for the more complex environments of object and distributed software. A programmer might keep several copies of a program and personally track which is in production at any one time. The problem with individual programmers maintaining their own copies is that eventually their multiple copies will diverge and knowing which is the most current can be a problem. Trusting individuals to be good librarians is asking for errors.

Assume next that one *official* version of programs exists. If several people are performing maintenance tasks on the one version of a program, a high probability exists that the changes of one person will interfere with the changes of the other person. Either the changes of one will be cancelled by being overwritten by the other, or one person will have to wait while the other makes the changes. Both situations lead to delays and are error prone.

In the complex world of distributed systems and multiple hardware/software platforms, different versions of the same software might be present. The only differences might be to accommodate platform idiosyncrasies, but such differences imply multiple versions of software that can cause maintenance problems. When a general change is made, somehow it must be verified as being made to all versions for all platforms. Specific changes for each platform must also be accommodated to allow fixing of bugs or changes that only affect one type of hardware.

Configuration management that consists primarily of code library management software plus manual procedures supports both single and multiple versions of programs to control for different platforms, evolving functionality, and debugging of software changes.

Types of Code Management

The most common code management procedure is the creation of derivations. The two code management types are for versions and variations. They can all be supported in the same software library or can be in separate libraries. Each type serves a different purpose.

Derivation

A **derivation** is a list that identifies the specific versions of multiple modules that were linked to create a load module or joint memory resident work unit. The purpose of a derivation is to allow tracing of errors that might be due to vendor software. All software used to create a load unit are specifically identified with vendor, version, and last installation date. The sample shown in Figure 18-13 identifies specific platform, operating system, compiler, for creation of a work unit, and the dates of the creation of each stage. If a problem were found, for example, a

rounding error occurs in computing interest, the error is traced backward through the development software to find the problem. The program is checked first, then the compiler, then the operating system, and so on. Let's say, for instance, that a new version of the compiler was installed one week before this module's creation, and that, upon inspection, the rounding algorithm used only allowed four decimal places to real numbers. If more than four places are needed, a new compiler would be required.

The difference between a load module and joint memory resident work unit is in the dynamism of the processes. A **load module** is a compiled version of one or more source code modules that have been compiled and link-edited together, forming the load module. **Compilation** translates a module from source code to object (assembler) code. **Linkage editing** resolves references to other modules by replacing *Call* references with relative memory addresses, thus joining related modules for processing as a single work unit (see Figure 18-14).

A joint **memory resident work unit** is a series of load modules that work together in a dynamic, real-time environment. Linkage editing creates static modules that are fixed until the next linkage edit process. In real-time application environments, one goal of the procedures is to relieve the need to freeze specific module references until they are needed in operation. This liberates programmers from the linkage editing process but can create chaos when an error occurs and must be traced. Both situations require maintenance of derivations.

Recording of derivations requires precise identification of the software, option, code inputs, responsible person, and date that a load module was created (see Figure 18-15). The level of detail for derivations should match each process a module undergoes from source code to load unit. This means that if the translation is from source code to load unit, there are two derivations. If the translations are from source to object to load unit, there are three derivations. *All* software used in creating the derivation is recorded, including the compiler, linkage-editor, and so on, and their versions. Derivation maintenance provides an audit trail for software and is the only way that errors can be guaranteed to be traceable.

Work Unit Name: _____
Creation Date: _____

Date	Time	Software	Options	Code Module	Person
2/1/93	2:53a	Cob 88, 2.1	Defaults	STL1001	A. Bryon
2/1/93	2:54a	Cob 88, 2.1	Defaults	STL1002	A. Bryon
2/1/93	2:56a	Cob 88, 2.1	Defaults	STL1003	A. Bryon
2/1/93	2:58a	Cob 88, 2.1	Defaults	STL1004	A. Bryon
2/1/93	2:59a	Cob 88, 2.1	Defaults	STL1005	A. Bryon
2/1/93	3:00a	LinkEdit 88, 3.7	Defaults	STL1001, STL1002, STL1003, STL1004, STL1005 object	A. Bryon

Comments:

FIGURE 18-13   Sample Derivation

Delta Version

Delta means *difference*. A **delta file** is a file of *differences* between versions of a program. **Versions** are multiple copies of a single program that represent incremental changes.

When a delta version is kept, the main program logic is maintained once. Then, the delta version is applied to the main logic, with specific lines of code being replaced to derive the delta (see Figure 18-16). The advantage of using a delta strategy is that changes in functionality affect only the original

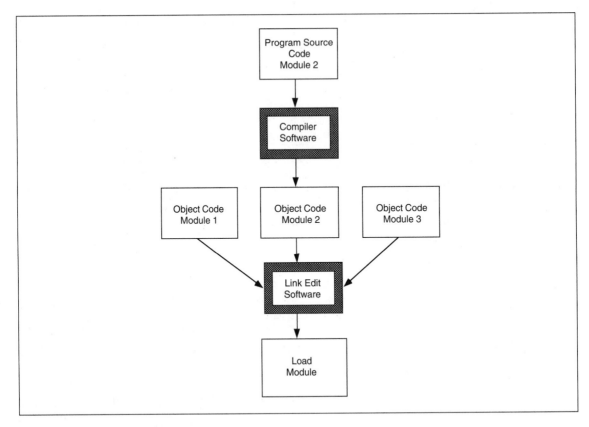

FIGURE 18-14   Compile and Link Edit

code. The disadvantages are that loss or corruption of the original also affects all deltas, and that delta references based on code line numbers can lead to errors when the original changes.

Many software librarians and operating system editors work on the delta version principle. For instance, the Unix editor maintains delta versions of changes to text files, which includes program code. Using line numbers as the reference point, the original is stored. As changes are made, changed lines are kept plus new line numbers are appended in a delta file. When the file is referenced, the original is loaded into memory, then the deltas are applied until the memory version reflects all changes.

When using a delta version, then, it is important to create a new file periodically to save storage and processing time for delta overlays. This minimizes the extent to which you are making changes to

changes. To create the new file, you save the old file with a new name. Renaming modules is necessary to create a permanent version of the program with deltas incorporated into the saved version. Maintaining many renamed versions can cause errors in remembering the most current version, too.

Variation Storage

Variations are alternative, interchangeable program modules created for multiple environments or purposes. For instance, you might create an IBM PS/2 version of a program and a Novell Netware 386 version of a program. The functionality is the same, but specific modules are different to support the specific hardware/software platform.

Variations in a COBOL environment, for instance, might have a different interface for users in

Item	Definition
Date	Date when the derivation was created
Time	Time of day when the derivation was created
Software	Specific software used to create the derivation
Options	Software options selected or defaults
Code Module	Name of input module(s)
Person	Person executing the derivation create
Hardware	Machine ID if there are multiple machines
Installation	Location or other installation ID when there are multiples

FIGURE 18-15   List of Requirements for Recording Derivations

1. File baseline code module.
2. Allow checkout for read-only purposes to individuals needing access. For instance, test team needs access for testing.
3. Allow chargeout for update to authorized programmers.
4. Monitor that chargeout items are returned.
5. Notify testers of chargein items for testing.
6. Verify that the text preamble to code identifies the change, date, programmer, and lines of code affected.
7. Chargein the item, refiling the module.
8. If derivations are used, file the derivation with project documentation.

When a project is in the code and unit test stage, the project librarian establishes an application library. As each module is unit tested and moves into subsystem and integration testing, the programmer's final version is given to the project librarian for addition to the library.

Error fixes, changes during testing, and maintenance changes are all managed the same way. The programmer tells the librarian she or he is checking the module out for update, and the librarian keeps track of this fact. The code is copied out of the library and into the programmer's own workspace. The changes are made and unit tested. Upon completion of the unit test, the programmer gives the module and documentation to the librarian for reentry to the library.

The librarian checks that no other changes have been made during the time the programmer has the module out for update. If not, the module is rewritten into the library.

Depending on the library software used, additional features allow the librarian to issue a charge-out against a module. A **charge-out** causes a lock to be placed on the module such that no other chargeouts for update may be performed until the lock is removed. When the changed version of the code module is reentered into the library, a **charge-in** occurs. A charge-in is the updating of a charge-out module to remove the lock. The more intelligent the software, the more actions taken during charge-in. For instance, some library software packages initiate a regression test when a chargein action is taken.

the United States and users in South America. Variations in an Ada environment, as another example, might be for performing the same process using integers or using real numbers.

Variations are named rather than numbered because there is no meaningful relationship between variations (see Figure 18-17). The name of each variation should reflect what makes it different. For instance, the names *PS2SORT* (for PS/2 sort routine) and *N386SORT* (for Netware 386 sort routine), would be good variation names because they identify both the platform and the function of the variation.

Configuration Management Procedures

Strict configuration management requires that one person (or group) on each development and maintenance project be assigned as the project librarian. The **project librarian** is the only person authorized to write into the baseline library for the project. The procedure is summarized below.

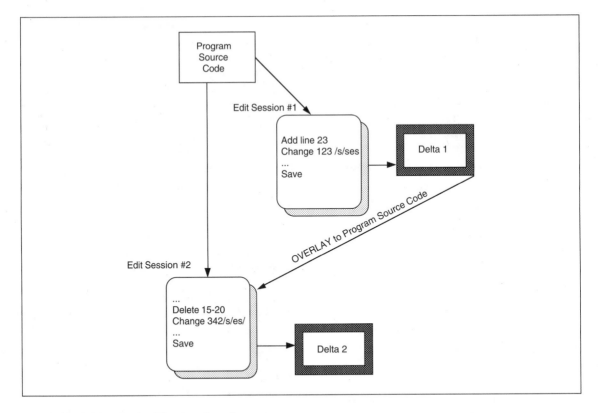

FIGURE 18-16   Delta Version Development

The disadvantage to having a formal project librarian is that the librarian becomes indispensable. The risk is that the librarian might become a bottleneck to updating the production library. For instance, if one person is the librarian, he or she might be called for jury duty and be out of work for several weeks. During that time, unless another librarian is named, no updates can be performed.

AUTOMATED TOOLS FOR CHANGE MANAGEMENT

There are different classes of automated tools for each type of change management. Each class of tools is discussed separately in this section.

Collaborative Work Tools

Collaborative work tools support group decision making and facilitate the development and historical maintenance of project decisions. Collaborative tools have developed out of research programs in group decision making at the Universities of Arizona and Minnesota in collaboration with IBM. Relatively primitive software of the 1980s for facilitating meetings has blossomed into a new industry for facilitating group work. Xerox Palo Alto Research Center (PARC) is a major contributor of new technology to this industry.

The specific technologies involved range from the relatively familiar, like electronic mail, or e-mail, to the exotic, for instance, *media space* clear boards that change our concepts of *being there* (see Table 18-2). Many of the technologies are emerging, but the emergence is at such a rapid

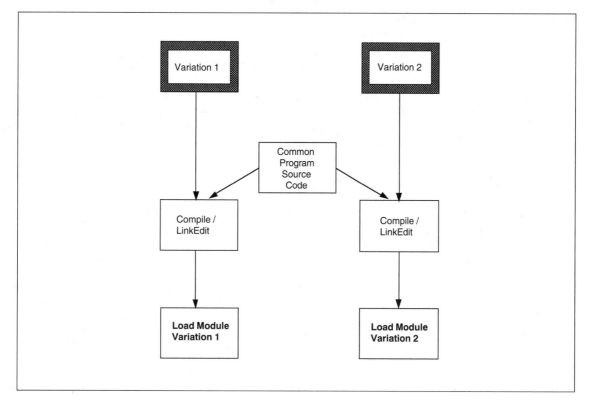

FIGURE 18-17   Variation Development

rate that by the new century we will routinely use many of these technologies at work, if not at our homes.

Media space technology allows several participants to sit on opposite sides of a *clear* glass *board* display that has electronics imbedded in it. The board can display computer images, text, and graphics as well as reflect hand-drawn notes and graphics of the meeting participants. The most effective use at the moment is between two people who both have clear access to the board. Clear boards allow people to see both the work and the co-worker, minimizing attention shift time. At the moment, the technology requires the people to be co-located, that is, in the same room; but the intention is to provide video conferencing capabilities using clear boards that are mirror images, thus *simulating* the face-to-face experience with the added electronic board interface. Thus, the user sees both the face of the other participant(s) and the contents of the board simultaneously. By removing the limitations of both time and geography our concept of *being there* is altered. By removing these limitations, clear board technology facilitates group work. This technology was developed, in this country, at Xerox PARC.

A different type of product provides a text-based communication environment that supports group passing of messages with storage of reader comments. Such a product, Notes,[2] provides an e-mail feature with the capability of user-built discussion *forums* and other data-sharing features. These products allow the development of decisions, history of the process, and easy sharing of information within and between work groups.

---

2 Notes® is a product of Lotus Development Corp.

TABLE 18-2   Collaborative Work Tools

Tool	Vendor	Functions
Cruiser®™	Bellcore Morristown, NJ	A video windowing system that allows the user to *cruise* offices visually and, perhaps, initiate a visit. Uses telephone and video technologies.
Greyboard	NeXT Computer Mountain View, CA	Multiuser drawing program
Groupkit	Dept. of Computer Science University of Calgary Calgary, Alberta, Canada	Real-Time Conferencing Toolkit; requires Interviews Software, Unix running X-Windows
Notes	Lotus Development Corp. MA	E-mail, group bulletin board, data sharing
Oracle Mail, Alert, Toolkit, and Glue	Oracle Corp. Redwood City, CA	E-mail, application development, and application programming interfaces for LANs
Timbuktu™	Farallon Computing, Inc. Berkeley, CA	Sharing of single-user software among several users
Video Whiteboard	ACM SIGCHI Proceedings '91, pp. 315–322	Wall-mounted whiteboard that portrays shadow of the other user
VideoDraw	ACM SIGCHI Proceedings '90, pp. 313–320	Multiuser drawing program
Windows for Workgroups	Microsoft, Inc. Belleview, WA	LAN-based windows sharing

Documentation Tools

Word processing tools, such as WordPerfect, are rapidly being replaced with more sophisticated and intelligent products for document development and maintenance (see Table 18-3).

In the old days of the 1980s, word processors became sophisticated enough to support such functions as **redlining**, the identification of changes in documents by means of a vertical line drawn in the margin of the change area. Typical word processors that merely automate the document preparation, such as redlining, still require significant text manipulation and creation of multiple documents with redundant information. Newer tools are beginning to emerge in the workplace that will eventually become as important as word processing has been.

One drawback of serial, word-processed text is that ideas that interrelate to many different topics either have to be replicated or cross-referenced in some way. **Hypertext** software eliminates that need by allowing any number of associative relationships to be defined for a given text item. **Hypermedia** extend hypertext to support audio, video, image, graphics, text, and data. In hypermedia, these multiple technologies may all be interrelated and co-resident in one environment. In addition, because these tools do not restrict the number of connections an item may have, and because they use mainstream computer technology, application documentation remains on-line and interactively available to all users. Of course, interactive availability also implies a need for hyperlibrary management to control changes to library contents.

TABLE 18-3   Documentation Maintenance Tools

Tool	Vendor	Functions
Folio Views	Folio Provo, UT	Works with Word Perfect to provide multimedia support, highlighting and post-it type document annotation.
Hypertext™	Apple Computer Cupertino, CA	Associative management of text and graphics
MS/Word	Microsoft, Inc. Belleview, WA	Word processing
Word Perfect and Word Perfect Mac with Grammatik	Word Perfect Corp. Orem, UT	Word processing plus grammar checking
Words and Beyond	Lundeen and Associates Alameda, CA	Documentation production including text and graphics

Tools for Reverse Engineering of Software

Reverse engineering tools are rapidly becoming sophisticated enough that the needs for human intervention and extensive training to understand them are diminishing. Several CASE products support reverse engineering through the analysis of code to determine data and process structures that underlie the code (see Table 18-4). Individual programs are analyzed at this point. By the next century, whole applications will be able to be analyzed with intelligent functions pointing out inconsistencies and errors across the old 'spaghetti' code. All tools represented in this section are available in the market and are rated as usefully working products.

Tools for Configuration Management

Configuration management tools, commonly called software libraries or code libraries, have been around since the early 1970s (see Table 18-5). The more sophisticated, newer models make version and variation management simpler by supporting complex functions, such as conditional compilation.

SUMMARY

To increase productivity in the application life cycle and reduce time spent in the code, test and maintenance phases are important. To reduce the effort in these phases, applications should use change control, design for maintenance, use reusable libraries, and use code templates. Object methods are best suited to reusable libraries; nonobject methods are best suited to program templates.

I-CASE is critical in reducing coding and testing through automatic code generation. I-CASE is also required to build intelligence to support reusable designs.

If managing application change, change control procedures and management are critical. Requirements, designs, programs, interfaces, hardware, or purchased software are all subject to change. Change management procedures track requests from initiation through implementation and allow management reporting of cost, types, and impacts of changes.

Logging and management of historical decisions can be useful in volatile environments in which applications are subject to redevelopment. A historical decision log keeps track of arguments, reasoning, and rationales for decisions as they are made.

After an application enters operation, documentation is still subject to change to reflect the current

TABLE 18-4   Reverse Engineering Tools

Tool	Vendor	Functions
ADW/Maintenance Workstation	KnowledgeWare, Inc. Atlanta, GA	Reverse engineering for information engineering: Entity-relationship diagrams Process data flow diagrams
Bachman Series	Bachman Information Systems, Inc. Burlington, MA	Reverse engineering of data structures
Design Recovery	Intersolv, Inc.	Reverse engineering of program structure
Ensemble	Cadre Technologies, Inc. Providence, RI	Reverse engineering charts, metrics, and design
Hindsight	Advanced Software Automation, Inc. Santa Clara, CA	Reverse engineering of C-language code: documentation, structure charts, complexity analysis
RE for IE	Texas Instruments, Inc. with Price Waterhouse Dallas, TX	Reverse engineering for information engineering: Entity-relationship diagrams Process data flow diagrams
Smartsystem	Procase Corp. Santa Clara, CA	Reverse engineering of C-language code: function call graphing, syntax and consistency checking
Via/Renaissance	Viasoft, Inc. Phoenix, AZ	Reverse engineering of data structures

TABLE 18-5   Software Configuration Management Tools

Tool	Vendor	Functions
Copylib	IBM Armonk, NY	Software code library for IBM and compatible mainframes
Data Expeditor	Data Administration, Inc.	Data management software—Allows viewing of file definitions from Librarian, Panvalet, and Copylibs, to locate occurrences and variations of data.
Librarian	Pansophic Systems Lisle, IL	Software code library for IBM and compatible mainframes
Panvalet	Pansophic Systems, Inc. Lisle, IL	Software code library for IBM and compatible mainframes

state of the application. A document table of contents summarizes all changes and the parts of the document affected by each change. Similarly, software documentation is kept in derivations to summarize the actual software and steps used to develop a load module or work unit. Configuration management is the use of software code libraries to manage the official, operational code modules of an application. Delta version and variation management are the principle techniques.

REFERENCES

Babich, Wayne A., *Software Configuration Management: Coordination for Team Productivity*. Reading, MA: 1986.

Baecker, Ronald M., ed., *Groupware and Computer-Supported Cooperative Work: Assisting Human-Human Collaboration*. San Mateo, CA: Morgan Kaufmann Publishers, Inc., 1993.

Collofello, James S., and Jeffrey J. Buck, "Software quality assurance for maintenance," *IEEE Software*, September, 1987, pp. 46–51.

Figlar Consulting, Inc., "Automating the reengineering process," presented to New York City Data Administration Management Association (DAMA), May 21, 1992.

Ingram, Ray, "Application reengineering for productivity, performance, and cost effectiveness," Course Handout, Multi-Soft, December 10, 1991.

Lientz, B. P. and E. B. Swanson, *Software Maintenance Management: A Study of Maintenance of Computer Application Software in 487 Data Processing Organizations*. Reading, MA: Addison-Wesley, 1980.

Martin, James, *Information Engineering, Vol. 3: Design and Construction*. Englewood Cliffs, NJ: Prentice-Hall, 1990.

Nash, Kim S., "Whipping worn-out code into new shape," *Computerworld*, August 17, 1992, p. 69.

BIBLIOGRAPHY

Babich, Wayne A., *Software Configuration Management: Coordination for Team Productivity*. Reading, MA: 1986.
Babich is a recognized authority on the use of different types of libraries for configuration management.

Baecker, Ronald M., ed., *Groupware and Computer-Supported Cooperative Work: Assisting Human-Human Collaboration*. San Mateo, CA: Morgan Kaufmann Publishers, Inc., 1993.
This book reprints groupware articles from periodicals, proceedings, and edited texts that might not otherwise be accessible to a reader.

Lientz, B. P. and E. B. Swanson, *Software Maintenance Management: A Study of Maintenance of Computer Application Software in 487 Data Processing Organizations*. Reading, MA: Addison-Wesley, 1980.
Identifies the applicability of the 80-20 rule in the application life cycle with this study of software maintenance in business organizations.

Mantei, Marilyn, and Ronald M. Baecker, eds., *Proceedings of CSCW '92: Sharing Perspectives*. NY: Association for Computing Machinery, 1992.
This annual conference discusses trends and research in computer-supported cooperative work (CSCW). The proceedings of the most recent conference identify many emerging technologies that will alter the way we work.

KEY TERMS

baseline	load module
boilerplate	media space technology
change control clerk	memory resident
change control file	work unit
changes	minor modifications
charge-in	open change request
charge-out	program template
code library	project librarian
compile	read only module
configuration	rebuilding
management	redlining
delta	reengineering
delta file	restructuring
derivation	reusability
frozen specification	reusable module library
hypermedia	reusable module
hypertext	reverse engineering
librarian	variations
linkage edit	version

EXERCISES

1. Delta Insurance Company has a policyholder subsystem that is causing them fits. Over the

years, the application evolved from using fixed length, multirecord type files to using a hierarchic database to using relational database. The programs did not change much, but the data structures changed radically. Program code was patched to provide for the new data structure. The amount of people-time allocated to policyholder maintenance grew 15% per year over the last five years and is now costing as much per year as it did in 1980 to develop the original application. No one ever considered reevaluating the subsystem for redevelopment, but they would like to now. Upon inspection, the documentation was found to be up-to-date and includes flow charts and data flow diagrams. There are no current diagrams of the data structure. There are also no historical files of decisions or of changes. What should the company do to get this application in order? What type(s) of maintenance should they consider for the next set of changes?

2. Discuss the ethics of group work tools. If a history is kept, does it violate anyone's privacy? What issues are involved in privacy versus open access to information in group work? Is there a *right* solution to these issues?

3. Discuss the implications of group work tools for global organizations. If you consider cultural differences in, for instance, comfortable distance between acquaintances, how might cultural differences impact the use of group tools? How might companies and cultures need to change to avoid misunderstandings with new tools?

STUDY QUESTIONS _____

1. Define the following terms:

delta	restructuring
derivation	rebuilding
frozen specification	variation
reengineering	version
reverse engineering	

2. Why is designing for maintenance important?

3. Describe how determining reusability of a module works.

4. How can program templates reduce code created?

5. Which methodologies are best suited for reusable libraries and program templates? Why?

6. What is the significance of I-CASE product recognition of design fragments?

7. Discuss the change management procedure recommended for applications undergoing development.

8. Why is it important to have a baseline product? What happens to a baseline when the product changes?

9. Write a job description for a Change Control Clerk.

10. Describe the life cycle of a change request.

11. What types of reports are useful to managers in tracking maintenance requests?

12. What is the purpose of renaming documents when major changes take place?

13. List the four types of maintenance actions that can be taken. Discuss the reasoning process for deciding which action to take.

14. How is reengineering done in a manual environment?

15. What is a code library? What are the variations in how a code library works?

16. When a delta management system is used, why do you periodically need to create a renamed copy of the code?

17. Describe the contents of a derivation. Why is each item necessary?

18. Compare code versions to variations.

19. What is chargeout and why is it important?

20. What is the purpose of collaborative work tools?

★ EXTRA-CREDIT QUESTIONS

1. Research collaborative work tools and develop a 15-minute presentation to the class about tools on the market, or tools that should be available in the next five years.

2. Get a sample demonstration copy of some emerging software that can be used for configu-

ration management, group work, decision history tracking, and so on. Show the demonstration to the class and spend some time brainstorming about how the product might change work practices.

3. Develop the pros and cons of keeping a decision history. What legal or governmental requirements might impact the decision to keep a historical log? What political and organizational issues impact the decision?

SOFTWARE ENGINEERING AS A CAREER

INTRODUCTION

In every student's path lies a career they will pursue. Nowhere are there as many varied opportunities as in information technology related professions. This chapter examines possible career paths for achieving software engineer status, maintaining job skills, and planning for your next job. After you have identified your own job requirements, we show one way to determine the likelihood of your job search success and a way to determine when you need to broaden your job requirements.

EMERGING CAREER PATHS

Software engineering used to be thought of as the province of computer scientists. Over the years, computer scientists tended to migrate into scientific and defense programming, operating systems support, and software package development. In those areas, they applied engineering methods to designing and developing efficient and effective software. In contrast, business organizations used the term *systems analyst* to describe the person who applied computer skills to the development of business transaction processing applications. Computer sci-

entists tended to build one-of, real-time applications while information systems (IS) specialists tended to build batch business transaction applications. As IS moved to on-line applications, the technology gap that somewhat fueled the split between the disciplines got smaller.

Computer science (CS) SEs increasingly study the same topics as IS SEs. The term *systems analyst* is giving way to the term *software engineer* as engineering techniques increasingly are used in business application development. The differences between the two groups are mainly in the emphasis on *technology* for CS and on *application* of technology in *business* for IS. The CS majors still tend to work in the traditional CS industries—defense, scientific organizations, and software development firms. The IS majors still tend to work in finance, manufacturing, government, and retail.

As teaching emphasis moves away from the 'one right way' approach to an ever growing set of theories from which we choose the most appropriate, CS and IS will converge even more. The two groups probably will not be melded completely, however. There is a need for both types of training that will continue to grow throughout the 20th century. The goal of both programs is to teach theories and approaches to problem solving with ways to apply them that prepare you for continuous change in the IS body of knowledge.

For the last decade, the radical changes in applications development coupled with changes in the types of applications businesses build are resulting in a split of duties in the development environment. The first type of career is more technical. This SE will build ever more complex state-of-the-art applications using new technologies. The second type of career is less technical. These SEs work as liaisons to user departments and act as *chauffeurs* for computer usage to assist users who are not inclined to become computer literate themselves. Within a generation, most business people will be computer literate, and these jobs will evolve to developing and managing DSS and EIS for managerial staff.

The issue over whether to get a degree in CS or IS is not too important from an employability perspective. There are careers for both types. Both types are useful and valuable to adding to our store of knowledge about how to build applications. In this chapter, first job levels and types of jobs available are defined. Then, an approach to defining a first job (or next job if you are already employed) is developed. Finally, means to maintaining your competence in the ever-changing world of IS and information technologies are presented.

CAREERS IN INFORMATION SYSTEMS

Job opportunities in information systems can be classified by level and job type. Job levels are generally classified as junior, intermediate, senior, lead, technical specialist, and manager. Each level is defined in terms of how much supervision is provided at the level and how much information and expertise the individual is expected to possess. Job type identifies the nature of the work performed.

Level of Experience

In this section, we discuss the job levels to which you might aspire. The levels are junior, intermediate, senior, lead, technical specialist, and manager. When times in a level and starting years of experience are

mentioned in each section, they imply years of different, changing experiences. Many people simply do the same thing over and over; this is not gaining experience.

Junior

A **junior** staff member is directly supervised, but is expected to work on his or her own on some aspects of a job. This is an entry-level position. Juniors are expected to have basic skills and ability to find information to enhance skills. They are in a learning mode most of the time. The time you might expect to perform in a junior-level position is about two years.

Intermediate

An **intermediate** staff member works independently most of the time, requiring direction on some activities. A mid-level person possesses a range of skills and experience but is still in a learning mode much of the time. Starting intermediate people have two to four years of experience. The average time at the intermediate level is from two to five years.

Senior

Seniors work unsupervised most of the time; they possess a wide range of both job and technical experience that is used to train and aid others. Senior-level staff supervise others, depending on the size and complexity of the project. Frequently, senior-level jobs are generally a prerequisite to lead or specialist titles.

A starting senior-level staff member has from five to seven years of experience. Expect to stay at this level at least three years. Many people end their careers at this level and stay on related projects throughout, becoming expert in both a technology and an application type.

Lead

A **lead** person works on his or her own, performing all levels of supervision. A lead person might also be called a *project leader*. Project leaders are a step above seniors and aspire to managerial positions. The lead skill levels are similar to seniors, but a lead person has more managerial/supervisory responsibility.

A lead person might end a career at this level, becoming totally responsible for small projects but never reaching a managerial level in charge of multiple projects.

Technical Specialist

A **technical specialist** is a person who has extensive experience in a number of different areas. The integration skills needed to develop distributed database networked applications exemplify the expertise of such a person; the skills of an integration specialist include application development, networking, database, and operating systems. The specialist is at the same level as a manager, having many of the same duties and capabilities without the personnel and budget responsibilities of a project manager. Specialists typically have been in IS positions for 10 years or more and might remain at the specialist level until retirement.

Manager

Managers work independently, performing personnel evaluation, budgeting, progress reporting, and managing projects. Managers may or may not be technical in orientation; they have a wide range of job experience and mostly managerial responsibility. For technical managers the distinguishing features of their jobs are the planning, budgeting, monitoring, personnel management, and liaison activities discussed in Chapter 3.

The levels are shown with logical career moves from junior through manager in Figure 19-1. As the figure shows, there is little choice in level movement for junior through senior positions. Once someone is fully knowledgeable about several types of jobs, they can choose to remain technical and become a technical specialist, or to move into management, usually becoming a project leader, then manager. Keep in mind that this career ladder identifies only level of expertise, not area. Movement between job types is possible at all levels and often is required to

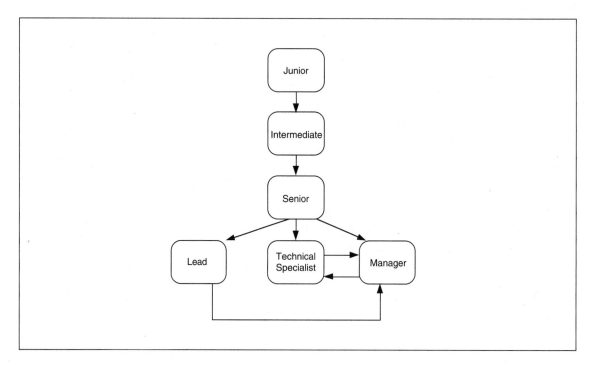

FIGURE 19-1   Career Path for Different Levels of Jobs

```
Application Development
        Programmer
        Software Engineer (Includes Analyst
            and Designer)
        Knowledge Engineer

Application Support
        Application Specialist
        Data Admininstrator
        Database Administrator
        AI Engineer
        Consultant

Technical Specialist
        Communications Analyst
        Communications Engineer
        LAN Specialist
        Systems Programmer
        Software Support Specialist

Staff
        Security Specialist
        EDP Auditor
        Trainer
        Standards Developer
        Technical Writing
        Quality Assurance Specialist
        Technology Planner

Other
        Product Support
        Product Marketing
        End User Specialist
```

FIGURE 19-2   Summary of IS Jobs

move to specialist and lead positions. Job type definitions are in the next section.

Job Type

Within a given level of experience, job type identifies the job content and nature. Job types are discussed in terms of the areas of specialization: application development, application support, technical specialties, staff positions, and others. The jobs are summarized in Figure 19-2. Keep in mind that these are representative of the specialities in large organizations; the smaller the organization, the more likely multiple skills are required of individual staff members.

Application Development

The main application development jobs are programmer, software engineer, and knowledge engineer. Keep in mind that there are entry-level positions all the way through technical specialist positions in many of these jobs. There is great variety across development jobs depending on the hardware and software environments. Hardware platforms include personal computers, workstations, and mainframes as well as equipment for communications, robotics, process control, office automation, imaging, and microforms. In addition, application environments are increasingly diverse. The software environment might include database, communications, programming language, hypermedia management, computer-aided software engineering (CASE), fourth generation languages, and expert system shells, just to name a few. With this diversity in mind, we discuss application development jobs.

PROGRAMMER.   **Programmers** translate design specifications into code modules that they design and unit test themselves. Programmers might rotate duties between development and maintenance applications.

Senior programmers perform other duties besides programming. For instance, they participate in analysis, design, or testing activities for the entire application.

Beginning programmers specialize in one language, while more senior programmers are conversant and experienced in multiple languages. The main generations of languages that apply here include

2GL—Assembler
3GL—COBOL, Fortran, Pascal, Ada, C, C++
4GL—Focus, Lotus, Paradox, dBase, Oracle,
    SQL
5GL—Lisp, PROLOG.

SOFTWARE ENGINEER.   An **SE** performs the functions of analysts, designers, and programmers. **Analysts** define and document functional requirements of applications. Senior analysts also participate in organizational-level IS planning and feasibility studies. **Designers** translate functional requirements into physical requirements of applications. These traditional titles still exist and frequently are combined in the title *analyst*. Programmers develop and test code modules as discussed above. SEs may do all three—analysis, design, and programming—as well as acting as project leader or project manager, as needed. The differences are in job emphases. A junior SE would spend most of the time programming, while a senior SE would concentrate more on planning, feasibility, analysis, and design.

KNOWLEDGE ENGINEER.   **Knowledge engineers** elicit thinking patterns from experts for building expert and artificial intelligence systems. Knowledge engineers are similar in status to SEs, but have specialized skills applying to AI problems. Developing models and programs of knowledge structures requires observation, protocol analysis, in-depth interviewing skills, the ability to abstract in areas that are not areas of personal expertise to make sense of reasoning and information needs, and the capability to develop uncertainty predictions about the information and its accuracy with experts.

Application Support

Application developers require expertise from a number of different specialties in developing even the most routine applications. The jobs that most often support application development include application specialist, data administration, database administrator, artificial intelligence engineer, and consultant. These jobs are not all distinct and may overlap with each other in many organizations; the areas of overlap are most noticeable for consultants who may do all of these specialties. This overlap is ignored for the moment for purposes of defining the essential skills of these support functions.

APPLICATION SPECIALIST.   **Application specialists** have the problem domain expertise that allows them to consult to project teams for specific types of applications. For instance, a senior analyst in real-time money transfer might split time between domestic and international money transfer projects, overseeing compliance with all the rules and regulations of the Federal Reserve Bank as well as the various money transfer organizations, (e.g., Bank-Wire, Swift, NYCHA, etc.)

Frequently applications specialists are members of external standards setting organizations. In this capacity, the specialist is a liaison between his or her company and other companies in the industry. Standards are set by consensus development of what should be done and how to do it. The standards get highly detailed, for instance, specifying the number of characters in a header of a bank wire message and the meaning of each character. The major skills needed for this type job are communications-oriented diplomacy, technical application, and problem domain knowledge.

DATA ADMINISTRATION.   **Data administrators (DA)** manage information as a corporate resource. In this capacity, data administrators help users define all data used in the company, identifying the data that are critical to the company's functioning. DAs establish and maintain standards and dictionaries for corporate data. These on-line dictionaries, or repositories, are used by on-line 'help' software to provide users with data definitions as they are using a computer.

Once data are defined, a DA works to define and structure subject databases for use by applications. They also track application use of data. For new project development, DAs work with the application developers to locate data that is already automated, and with DBA staff to provide the application group easy access to automated databases.

DATABASE ADMINISTRATOR.   **Database administrators** (DBA) manage the physical data environment of an organization. DBAs analyze, design, build, and maintain databases and the software database environment. Working with DA definitions of data, DBAs define physical databases and load actual information into them.

A DBA works with application development teams to provide access to already automated data, and to define the specific database needs for information to be automated.

ARTIFICIAL INTELLIGENCE ENGINEER. **Artificial Intelligence (AI) engineers** work as consultants to project teams to define, design, and implement intelligence in applications. At present, AI is in its infancy and its use in applications is sparse. Most AI work takes place as part of an expert system development. AI engineers work with knowledge engineers to translate and test problem domain data and reasoning information in a specific AI language, such as Lisp. As AI matures and its use increases, this position may move from a support location to application development location in organizations.

AI engineers have attained a higher level of expertise than KEs. As AI experts, they participate in software and hardware surveillance, evaluation, planning, and implementation on a company-wide basis. As experts, they are usually involved in hiring decisions for other AI experts and KEs.

CONSULTANT. **Consultants** are jacks-of-all-trades and practitioners of all. The higher the number of years experience, the greater the knowledge is expected to be. The areas of expertise would likely include several of the job types discussed in this section.

Consultants are hired most often to supplement staff or to provide exotic skills not available in-house. When hired because of exotic skills, they frequently train the in-house staff during the work engagement. Consultants are expected to have specifically identified skills when they are hired, and to apply those skills in performing the consulting engagement.

Consultants are sometimes preferred to permanent hires because they get no benefits and do not require raises from the hiring organization; they already have the desired skills and need no career path planning; they have their own managers and require less personnel-type management. Consultants are easier to hire and fire than full-time staff, too.

Technical Specialists

Other technical specialties are common in organizations but do not always interact with application developers on a regular basis. Some of these specialties include communications analysts and engineers, LAN specialists, systems programmers, and software support specialists.

COMMUNICATIONS ANALYSTS AND ENGINEERS. **Communications analysts and engineers** analyze, design, negotiate, and/or install communications-related equipment and software. They are required to be fully conversant with communications technologies and may work on mainframe or PC-based communication networks.

Integration of voice, data, graphic, and video signals via telecommunications networks is growing in importance to every organization. Certainly, integration of data and voice is commonplace. As the integration levels of information delivery increase, this specialty becomes crucial to organizational success.

To start in communications at an entry-level position, educational background might be in electronics, engineering, applications, computer science, or telecommunications. To transfer into a communications-related position requires intelligent positioning and career planning once you are within the company.

LAN SPECIALISTS. **Local Area Network (LAN) specialists** plan, oversee installation, manage, and maintain local area network capabilities. There is no essential difference between a LAN specialist and a communications specialist except *scale*. A communications specialist works with multiple networks including mainframes; a LAN specialist works on geographically limited networks that are comprised of personal computers (PCs).

The educational background can be in IS or CS with a concentration in telecommunications. In addition, many LAN specialists have certification by a vendor, such as Novell, which certifies its engineers as having basic knowledge as a *Certified Novell Engineer* (CNE).[1]

LAN administrator is an entry-level position in many companies. A LAN administrator creates new

---

2 Certified Novell Engineer™ is a trademark of the Novell Corporation, Provo, Utah.

users, implements or changes security levels and codes, installs new versions of the LAN operating software, installs new versions of database or other LAN-based software, oversees the resources provided through the LAN, provides backup and recovery capabilities to the LAN, and manages the LAN configuration. Troubleshooting the LAN when problems arise is a valuable skill that frequently qualifies the individual for increasing responsibility beyond an entry level position.

SYSTEMS PROGRAMMER. **Systems programmers** install and maintain operating system and application support software used in mainframe installations. For instance, an IBM 309x class mainframe machine contains several million lines of code in its operating system (OS). At any given time, 50–100 'bugs' might be outstanding and need to be fixed. 'Fixes' are 'patched' into the operating system software until a new level of the operating system is released. If no problems occur in your installation, the fixes are not needed. Evaluating the new features and whether they are necessary at the time is a skill system programmers develop. Monitoring all of the hundreds of applications to determine whether their problems relate to OS problems is a major task. In addition, applying a fix might cause another problem, so the systems programmer needs to be fully conversant with normal operations to determine any ripple effects.

SOFTWARE SUPPORT SPECIALIST. Application software support is a similar, but different, type of system programming. **Software support specialists** install and maintain software packages used by both applications developers and by users. Database, query language, backup and recovery, spreadsheet, disk space management, telecommunications interface, and any other nonoperating system software are in this category.

Application software support programmers and specialists work with application developers and with technology surveillance staff to define the needs of the organization. Then, they work with vendors to obtain and install the product. Finally, they maintain the product on an on-going basis, providing the application development staff with usage support for the product.

System software support (SSS) programmers and specialists work with systems programmers to maintain the software provided as a shared resource for others in the company to use. For instance, in a LAN environment, an SQL Server might be used. The SQL Server software is supported by an SSS person, while the network operating system (NOS) is supported by a systems programmer.

Staff Positions

Most organizations have one or more persons performing these functions, even if they do not have a title to go along with the duties. The tasks that are most often given titles include security specialist, EDP audit, training, standards and technical writing, quality assurance, and technology planning.

SECURITY SPECIALIST. A **security specialist** is responsible for security and for disaster recovery readiness. For security, a specialist establishes standards for data security, assists project teams in determining their security requirements, and establishes standards for data center security. Similarly, for disaster recovery, the security specialist assists managers and project teams in identifying critical data needs of the organization. Then, the specialist assists data centers and project teams in developing and testing disaster recovery plans. This is a valuable specialization that is most often found in large organizations but is needed in all companies.

Research by IBM and others has shown that companies without any backup and recovery plan *will* go out of business in event of a disaster. The studies looked at different geographic areas, different types of disasters, and spanned several years. The result was always the same. If a company could not recreate the data critical to its continuing in business, it could not survive a disaster.

Most disasters are from weather (tornados, hurricanes, and earthquakes), but they can also include acts of terrorism, fires, and other nonweather means of losing a data center. In addition to loss of a data center, security specialists plan for less severe losses, such as loss of disk drives or malicious tampering with data.

EDP AUDIT.   **EDP auditors** perform accountability audits on application designs. Any application that maintains legal obligations, fiduciary responsibilities, or books of the company, *must* be able to recreate any transaction and trace its processing. EDP auditors ensure that company exposure to losses or law suits is minimized through good application design. The design aspects evaluated by auditors are audit trails, recoverability, and security.

TRAINING.   A **technical trainer** learns new technologies, vendor products, new language features, and so on, then teaches their use to others in the organization. Training might be done within a company, or in a specialized training company, or as a consultant in a short-term assignment.

Training is often considered a temporary or rotational assignment for people whose career path or job assignments allow them to perform a staff function for some period. The thinking is that training is more easily related to current job assignments in an organization when it is done by someone who is holding, or has recently held, such an assignment. Teaching forces the trainer to organize thoughts, make presentations, answer questions, and develop good communication skills. Therefore, training assignments are one way to allow someone who is a valued employee, but who lacks good communication skills, to develop and practice those skills in a work setting that is not too threatening.

STANDARDS AND TECHNICAL WRITER. **Standards developers** work with managers to define what aspects of work they want to standardize, and to formalize the requirements into standard policies and procedures for the organization. The most important skills for standards developers are verbal and written communications.

Company standards vary in level of detail and breadth of activities covered. Some companies standardize their complete methodology, providing minute detail on all of the steps to developing a project, guidelines on the tasks performed, required signatures and approvals for project work, detailed lists of liaison departments that must be consulted, and so on. Other companies provide loose guidelines with checklists to be consulted to ensure that all needed tasks are considered for inclusion in the project's work plan. Both types require the ability to run meetings, obtain the standards' requirements, negotiate between managers, and write accurate descriptions of desired rules.

Standards development and technical writing are related activities. A **technical writer** takes information about software products, applications, or other information technology products and develops documentation to describe their features, functions, and use. A technical writer needs to have good technical and nontechnical communication skills. The writer uses the technical communication skills in talking with and developing an understanding of the product being documented. He or she uses the nontechnical communication skills in writing about the products for a user audience.

QUALITY ASSURANCE.   **Quality assurance** is an IS function that performs quality audits on application feasibility, analyses, designs, programs, test plans, documentation, and implementations. QA is usually functionally separate from the development groups it is auditing; however, in a small company, QA may be an analyst's, or SE's, temporary assignment.

The form of the audit differs by the product being reviewed. A QA analyst is assigned to a development project as it is initiated. He or she has little involvement until the first work products from the development team are available. Then, as documents become available, the QA analyst reviews them for consistency, completeness, accuracy, and feasibility. Any problems found during the review are documented in a memo to the project manager. The problems must be responded to by either explaining why the issue is not a problem or by correcting the erroneous item.

As you can see from the description of this task, QA is a natural adversary to application developers since the QA analyst's job is to find fault with the work of the project team. QA work is usually assigned to senior staff who are respected enough to be listened to and tactful enough not to cause revolts by the project teams. QA analysts need senior technical, communication, and problem domain skills to perform a quality review. They need experience in all aspects of project development in order to know how it should be done and where problems might arise. At the same time, tact and skill at identifying only critical issues is important. No one likes to be told publicly they have made a mistake, even though they might know intellectually that the project work will benefit from the criticism. The QA analyst needs to be sensitive to both the politics and the problems identified.

TECHNOLOGY PLANNING. **Technology surveillance specialists** monitor technology developments to identify trends, select technologies that are appropriate for experimentation in their organization and, eventually, champion the implementation of new technologies in the organization. These senior staff are liaisons to the outside world and vendor community for the company. Junior-level staff in technology planning might work with a senior person who guides the work, while the junior person does some coordination and technology monitoring.

Other

Numerous other positions relating to ITs and IS development are available for students of IS. Some of these include product support, product marketing, and end-user specialist.

PRODUCT SUPPORT. **Product support staff** work for an end-user group or vendor to provide product-related technical expertise or other "hotline" support. In addition to technical knowledge about the product(s) supported, the individuals in this job require excellent phone skills and must be able to talk nonjargon language to users with problems.

PRODUCT MARKETING. **Marketing support staff** work for vendors to provide technical information to sales representatives in marketing situations. This type of job requires excellent communication and people skills, with some knowledge of marketing tactics, such as narrowing focus of conversation and closing techniques, to effectively work with a sales representative. All software, hardware, and consulting companies have people to perform these functions. Usually, this job is for senior-level people, but if you have a particular area of expertise and support in that area is needed, then you might qualify for such a job without being a senior staff person.

END-USER SPECIALIST. **End-user specialists** translate user requirements into technical language for developers to use. In some companies this is the function of the systems analyst or SE. In other companies, there are end-user liaisons in the user departments to perform this function.

In summary, every company needs many different combinations of job characteristics in all departments of the organization. The challenge to graduates is to decide which aspect of the work fascinates you most. The career is there for the making. To further your chances of a successful entry into the job market, your undergraduate courses should concentrate on *core knowledge* of application development, programming, database, and telecommunications. Then concentrate elective courses in one or more specialties from the above array of jobs.

PLANNING A CAREER

Defining your next job is the first step to determining what to ask for when you talk to personnel recruiters. You must have a goal that is fairly well defined yet realistic for the job market you wish to enter. Once you begin work, you need to know how to plan the next job, and so on. Also, one degree and job in IS does not qualify as a 'career.' Rather, continued growth and development in depth and in breadth of knowledge is required. In this section, we discuss how to plan your first job and extrapolate from that to plan your career. In the next section, we discuss how you keep current to continue to grow as a professional SE. As you read through this section, assess your job wants. The more honest you are about your skills and desires, the more useful you will find this exercise.

Decide on Your Objective

The first activity is to decide on an objective or goal. Where do you want to be in five years? Try to be as specific as possible. Do you want to be making $60,000 a year? Do you want to have a title of Project Manager? Do you want to be a specialist in software engineering? Your objective might be money-related, title-related, or job content-related, or all three, or something else.

Make sure your objective relates to job criteria. For instance, if your objective is to own a house, decide how much you anticipate spending, then translate that into a salary. Once you have identified an objective, use the following sections to determine the company and job characteristics that are most likely to help you meet your goal. Try to translate the money into a position and title, working backward to identify a starting job. If your goal is title- or job-related, use the following sections to identify the most likely tasks, job characteristics, and companies to help you meet your goal.

Define Duties You Like to Perform

Once you have a tentative goal, begin to think about how to reach that goal through one or more jobs during the five-year period. What are likely starting jobs? How do those starting jobs relate to you? In performing this evaluation, you need to do an honest assessment of duties you like to perform. Evaluate the list below, making your own list of tasks and placing a percentage next to each item you are interested in doing in your next job. Make sure that all of the percentages add to 100%.

- Programming (i.e., new development and maintenance)
- Analysis
- Testing, Quality Assurance
- Technology Surveillance
- Consulting
- User or Technical Training
- User, Help Line, or Product Support
- Standards Development
- Technical Writing
- DBA or other specialized technical position, and so on

Keep in mind that, while this exercise is to find your ideal next job, the work tasks should also be realistic. About 50–70% of newly minted undergraduates begin as programmers. Another 10–15% begin as LAN managers, with an equal percentage beginning as programmer-analysts or SEs. A few begin as technical writers, help line support, and trainers.

Define Features of the Job

After job tasks are identified, evaluate the external features of jobs you prefer. There are two types of job features you should define: technical and non-technical. The technical features are what this text is all about. Choose from the following list those characteristics that appeal to you.

Project type—Maintenance, development, or a mix

Technology type—Mature, or state of the art, or experimental, leading edge

Type position—Project, staff, operations, sales, support, or other

Phases of project work—Planning, feasibility analysis, design, maintenance, programming, or all

Methodology—Process, data, object, semantic

Hardware platform—Mainframe, micro, workstation

Technologies—DBMS, language(s), package(s), CASE tools, LAN

Be as specific as you can in defining each of these job components. This information is used to select target-specific jobs for your job search. Be equally specific about job functions you do *not* want to learn, if there are any. The nice thing about defining the ideal job for yourself is that there is no wrong answer, only ones that fit you better than others.

Next, assess the type of duties you want to perform. Do you want narrowly-defined, specific assignments, or broadly-scoped and less well-defined assignments? In general, the larger the company, the more esoteric and specific your requirements *can* be, but there is no standard. Also, in general, the smaller the company, the more casual and broader the assignments. This means that a person defined as a programmer might have entirely different time allocations depending on the size of the company. In a large company, a programmer will spend 40–60% of his or her time coding and unit testing program specifications developed by an SE or designer. Remaining time is spent in nonproject work such as reading manuals, attending meetings, learning, and communicating about the work. In a small company, a programmer is likely to spend 20–40% of his or her time developing the specifications with the analyst or SE, 20–40% programming and unit testing, and the remaining time in other activities. Which scenario do you prefer? The larger the company, the more specialized and the narrower the job. Also, the larger the company, the more likely you will be paired with a senior *mentor* who is responsible for monitoring your progress.

Think about how you like to learn new things. Do you like to be given a book and an assignment for completion? Or do you prefer to attend classes and have someone to answer your questions? The first learning approach is one used most by consulting and smaller companies. The classroom approach is used more by large companies.

Next, evaluate nontechnical features of a job, including title, salary, working hours, autonomy, and travel. Title is a more important issue in some industries than others. For instance, in manufacturing institutions, being an 'officer' of the company is significant. But in a bank, about 25% of the staff will be officers. Of this 25%, 60% will be assistant treasurers, or the lowest level officer; 25% will be second vice presidents; 10% will be some level of vice president; and the remaining 5% are executive vice presidents or higher. The titles are more for external prestige and to compensate for low pay than anything else. If title is important, then, financial services and consulting are the most status-conscious of the industries listed. In contrast, a private consulting company might have two to five *principals* and 200–300 *consultants*, and those are the only two titles.

What salary would you like to be making in five years? Target the five-year time frame because your first salary is relatively inelastic if you are not already working in IS. By inelastic, we mean that the salary range for new, inexperienced hires is relatively narrow: $28,000–$34,000 for undergraduate IS degrees, and $30,000–$38,000 for graduate IS degrees, in 1994; and the salaries are relatively invariant across industries.

Take the midpoint of the range that describes your situation and assess the ideal raises you might receive to derive your salary in five years. If you expect to double your salary in five years, you need a compounded growth of about 15% annually to meet that goal. You might get 15% raises in consulting, but it is unlikely anywhere else. Realistically, companies give regular raises that keep a third of all salaries even with inflation. If you are in the top third, you might qualify for merit increases which might be 2–4% over the inflation rate. If you want a six-figure income within five years, then you are either thinking of your own company, or are a genius, or are unrealistic. It is nice to dream, but thinking of salaries requires hard reality.

The next nontechnical issue is the number of hours you want to work. This is an ideal that you might never actually reach, but each industry has different intrinsic demands about hours of work that should be considered. The normal work week is 40 hours in the United States. This time is spent from Monday to Friday with few organizations requiring weekend work.

In addition to the number of hours, *which* hours might also be important. There are two issues here: flextime and shift work. Can you get up and maintain a schedule that requires you to be in an office at a fixed time every day? What if the hours are 7 A.M. to 4 P.M.? How about 9 A.M. to 6 P.M.? If a company has flextime, you choose the time of your arrival, within limits, and work a regular seven- to eight-hour day once you are at work. Most companies in large metropolitan areas use flextime to cope with the vagaries of traffic and transportation problems.

You might consider a job in an industry that works at night. Do you mind shift work? Can you cope with a schedule that requires you to sleep during the day? Keep in mind that you might be a night owl at college, but all of your friends will probably get day jobs. Will night work shut you off from your social life? How important is that to you?

The last time issue is overtime. Do you mind overtime? How often is overtime acceptable? Could you work for a company that expected a 60-hour week even though the advertised required number of hours is 40? Can you deal with midnight phone calls when you are 'on call' for application problems? Some companies will tell you that you are expected to work until the job is done, and if that means overtime, then you work overtime. Can you live with such an agreement? If not, what are your time requirements for work? If you cannot deal with any overtime, you need to search for a low pressure, staff job or a maintenance job that requires little or no overtime. If you can deal with overtime, then all jobs are open for you. The longest hours are usually in consulting, but most development projects in most companies end up requiring some overtime work.

Next, consider the extent to which you want to work autonomously. As an entry-level person, you most likely will be coupled with a senior person who would be responsible for helping you with problems, bugs, or other issues you are not sure how to deal with. But each company has its own levels of autonomy that its employees are allowed. Do you want leeway in figuring out your own answers or do you want close supervision, at least for a while? In general, the smaller the company, the more autonomy you will be given, and the greater the breadth of the jobs you will be assigned. If you like working alone, then select a smaller company.

Finally, consider the amount of travel you want as part of your job. Be realistic. Travel is demanding, rewarding, and wearing. It requires extreme organization because once the plane leaves you cannot return to the office for that forgotten piece of paper. It also demands family and personal sacrifices because you are frequently on a plane during birthdays and holidays. You may find that you want to travel for awhile and cut back after a few years. After all, someone else *is* paying the bills. That is also an acceptable scenario, just be prepared for the action when it arises. Several industries, especially consulting, require significant travel and frequent temporary relocation for project work. You might

need to leave for months at one or two days' notice in this environment. The rewards are commensurate with the sacrifices: The pay in consulting is the highest after successful entrepreneurship.

Define Features of the Organization

Even though this section is for defining features of the organization, you are still assessing your needs in a job. In this section, you assess how 'hard' you want to work, how 'smart' you want to work, and how much ambiguity and stress you can cope with. To some extent you have already answered some of these questions; they have not been phrased in just this way.

When you define how many hours a week, and what type of work you desire, you are, to some extent, answering the 'hard' and 'smart' questions. Several different hierarchies of organizations can be developed for you to position yourself in different industries and different company types. The first hierarchy is based on industry. Based on several different salary surveys over the last 10 years, a hierarchy of industries in average salary order is shown in Figure 19-3. This hierarchy shows that you are most likely to make the most money owning your own company, and are most likely to make the least money working in academia or nonprofit organizations. This hierarchy also translates into a 'hard' work hierarchy. The amount of time and personal sacrifice expected of employees is directly proportional to the amount of money paid. That is, the companies that pay the best expect the most. If you cannot stand stress and long work days, then remove ownership and consulting from your list. If you want the least possible stress and least possible work, target your search in nonprofit, retail, government, and academic organizations.

Keep in mind that these are general rules of thumb at work here. All companies have positions of all types. The generalizations drawn here identify the majority of positions.

A second hierarchy can be developed based on the position of a given company within its industry. Figure 19-4 shows one industry, soft drink

Highest-to-Lowest Salary Industries**	Example
Your own company	
Consulting	
Big 4 Accounting Firm	Ernst & Young, Arthur Anderson
Large IS Consulting	Cap Gemini (CGA)
Internal Consulting in Large Company	
Private Consulting Company	
Vendors	Novell, Microsoft, ATT, Pacific Bell, Bell Labs
Conglomerate Headquarters	Boeing, Mobil
Financial Services and Insurance	American Express, Citibank, Prudential
Government, Transportation, Utilities	U.S. Department of Agriculture, American Airlines, Brooklyn Union Gas
Manufacturing	Whirlpool, Babcock & Wilcox
Retail, Publishing, Medical	Macy's, Any large metropolitan hospital
Nonprofit, Small business of any type	United Way
Education	School Districts, High Schools, Colleges, Universities

**Based on numerous articles in *Computerworld*, *Datamation*, *Wall Street Journal*, *Dallas Morning News* and *The New York Times*.

FIGURE 19-3   Salary-Based Hierarchy of Industries

Largest to Smallest Industry Position:

Coca-Cola
PepsiCo
Dr. Pepper/7-Up
Shasta
Snapple
Others

FIGURE 19-4   Industry Position for Soft Drink Companies

acterization for the industry and how it fits your personality.

Next, try to match your personality to the company style. Do you want to work for the leading company and be the one to beat? Or do you want to work harder at #2 which is trying to become #1? Or are you more comfortable being at some other level company with less stress? There is nothing wrong with working at any of the levels. The idea is to choose the one that fits you best.

Keep in mind that all of these statements about companies are generalizations. Many companies are not even close to the top of their industries but are in a turnaround position that requires maximum effort from everyone. Such turnaround companies are sometimes the best of places to work and sometimes are the worst of places to work. Similarly, a large, longtime company that is first in its industry might be ready to take a fall. IBM, in 1990–1994 was not a fun place to work.

We identify industry leaders because they are generally more innovative than other companies and have more money to spend (and spend it) on new technologies. Not all is positive for large industry leaders. In some cases, the larger and more leading the company, the slower to promote people to new positions and the more likely to be results-oriented without being people-oriented. Also, not all companies, regardless of industry position, recognize the importance of information technologies to meeting their mission. Ideally, you want to find a company that has a culture that is compatible with your personality, that is as people-oriented as you need, that recognizes the importance of information technolo-

manufacturing, with the major contenders. As the figure shows, Coca-Cola is closely followed by PepsiCo, Dr. Pepper/7-Up, and all others. This industry is fiercely competitive and marketing driven. To be in this industry is to be competitive. Therefore, when you select an industry, try to think of a char-

gies, and that will help you reach your personal goals.

Finally, if you have prior experience in some industry, try to leverage that knowledge. Problem domain expertise takes two to four years to learn. If you already have experience and can target IS jobs in your old field, your starting salary should be 5–10% higher than new employees in the same industry.

Define Geographic Location

Next, consider the ideal geographic location for you. You may want to stay near where you are from. That is perfectly reasonable. If you want to live somewhere else because of weather, life-style, or some other criteria, now is the time to choose where you want to live and work.

In the United States, there has been a 30-year migration toward the southern half of the country, but the jobs have not always followed. According to salary surveys covering 1992–1993, the best paying and highest number of jobs are in Alaska. Both New York City and California, traditionally high growth, high-income areas, follow Alaska. Other large, diversified-industry, metropolitan areas also top the list (see Figure 19-5).

The lowest paying and lowest number of positions are in the South and Southeast, particularly Florida.[2] The center of the country has not faired so well either. In 1992, St. Louis and Philadelphia graced the bottom of the salary list.[3]

Define Future-Oriented Job Components

The last job-related components relate to job security, benefits, and speed of advancement. You won't use these until you are interviewing, but it is a good idea to have some goals in mind for these job components when selecting companies and industries. Also, if you are looking for security in a volatile

---

2 Based on Robert Half *1992 Salary Guide*, and *1993 Salary Guide*, San Francisco, CA: Robert Half International, Inc.

3 *Computerworld* publishes an "Industry Snapshot" highlighting hiring trends in a specific industry in each weekly issue.

Highest Salary Locations:

  Alaska, New York metro area, California,
  Dallas–Fort Worth, Minneapolis–St. Paul
  Chicago, Denver
  Boston

Lowest Salary Locations:

  St. Louis
  Last: Southeast and South

Based on Robert Half, International 1992 and 1993 Salary guides and articles in *Datamation*, *Computerworld* and *The New York Times*

FIGURE 19-5   IS Salary by Location in the United States

industry, like stock brokerage finance, then you need to reassess your requirements to align more closely with reality.

Security relates to the stability of the industry. For over 50 years, the United States had relative stability in industry, with only companies that had fallen on hard times resorting to layoffs. Many companies (e.g., Chase Manhattan Bank and IBM) used to brag that they had never had a layoff in the company's history. The late 1980s and early 1990s changed all that. The recession during the early 1990s was deeper and longer than many since the Great Depression of 1929, and had the added problem of being worldwide in scope. Virtually every company over $100 million in sales went through some reassessment of company structure and size, laying off and eliminating millions of jobs. As we slowly recover from that period, stability is an issue on which we all share concern.

Financial success is one indicator of likely stability. Companies that have higher percentages of net income and profits compared to competitors are more likely to be stable. But, at the moment, there are no guarantees. If security is very important to you, target companies that are successful relative to their competition, regardless of the industry, and target companies in relatively inflation-proof industries, such as office products.

Benefits include vacation, retirement, medical support, dental support, child support, aging parent support, and so on. The average starting benefits include two weeks' vacation after one year, with some medical and dental support. Retirement benefits are in a state of flux. In 1993, most large companies still offer retirement benefits, but the vesting period (that is, the time at which the money becomes legally yours), varies considerably. If you plan to stay with a company a long time, vesting periods are moot. If you foresee some movement between companies in your future, the vesting period becomes important to your consideration of how long you might be tied to a specific company.

The more progressive and larger the company, the more likely they are to also have programs providing some type of support for child or parent care. Decide how important these benefits are to you and keep this information in mind when you are evaluating companies. When you begin interviewing, use your ideal benefits and security needs as one criteria to separate the companies you are interested in from those you are not.

Speed of advancement may be an important factor to you. Do you expect to be promoted every year, assuming that you have exceeded all job requirements? Some companies have average time in grade figures that they might share with you during the interviewing process. In general, consulting companies have the most career mobility; they are also organizations in which you either succeed or you are out. Following this generalization, the industries that pay more, expect more and reward more.

Search for Companies That Fit Your Profile

The next step in targeting companies for jobs is to map the geographic, job, and salary requirements with your intended market area. For the target city or location, map your industry and company characteristics with those of specific organizations in the area. This step requires library searching of business reference guides, *Business Week, Forbes, Fortune, Money* and other business magazines that publish annual reviews of companies by industry.

Look for the geographic region that matches yours, then research the industries in that region. All of this can be done at a global level in an encyclopedia. Next, look at an annual review (e.g., *Fortune*'s '500'), and locate companies in your industry(s) and geographic area. If the headquarters are not in the area, you will need further research. Read company annual reports to locate subsidiaries and their locations. Research companies and industries in each of your target states and metropolitan areas by contacting Better Business Bureaus or Chambers of Commerce. Read reference materials from trade associations and the government to find target companies.

The major warning in this search is to be realistic. If you target, for instance, the chemical and pharmaceutical industries to take advantage of your summer jobs in a small chemical company, the ideal geographic area is the state of New Jersey. Every major pharmaceutical company *in the world* maintains some sort of facility in New Jersey or New York City. At least four major pharmaceutical companies have regional or worldwide headquarters in the area (i.e., Merck, Pfizer, Hoffman-LaRoche, Warner-Lambert). If you target that industry and begin looking in, for instance, Mississippi and Louisiana, you will find only small companies and less than a handful of large ones.

Assess the Reality of Your Ideal Job and Adjust

When you have found the population of companies from which you expect to have a job, evaluate how realistic your chances are. The realism of your probable job is a function of industry turnover and the number of jobs of the type you want in the area in which you want to live. The IS profession has, on average, 15% turnover per year. This means that 15% of the people in IS professions change jobs every year.

In addition, software engineering is the hottest growing job classification in the 1990s.[4] In the same book, Krantz rates computer systems analyst as sec-

---

4 The growth of software engineering is documented in Les Krantz' *The Jobs Rated Almanac*, 2nd ed., NY: Pharos Publishing, 1992.

ond; computer service technician as fifth; computer programmer as 25th; and technical writer as 147th [Krantz, 1992, p. 218].

If you are choosing an analyst, programmer, or SE position, and you are targeting a geographic area with a large number of target companies, you probably do not need to go through this exercise. If you choose any nonmainstream job, or a limited geographical area, then this exercise might help you assess the reality of your goals. The steps to assessing the reality of your ideal job are:

1. Estimate the number of entry-level jobs available.
2. Estimate the number of people competing for the jobs.
3. Assess the ratio of available jobs to job applicants and adjust your expectations as needed.

Estimate Number of Entry-Level Jobs

First, in assessing the number of potentially available positions, the items of interest are the number of people in IS jobs in an area, the percent of jobs of the type that you want, the average turnover in IS positions, and the percent of entry-level positions. The number of people in IS jobs is one which you must unearth through library and other research. Figure 19-6 shows the major IS job types and estimated percentages of people with that title. Average IS turnover is historically between 15% and 18%. The average number of entry-level positions varies from 2% to 5% per year. When in doubt, use the conservative numbers for your calculations.

The formula for computing the number of likely jobs is as follows:

Number of IS jobs in area
× Percent jobs for your ideal
× Average IS turnover
× Percent of entry level positions
    = Number of available jobs

Let's look at an example. If you target the pharmaceutical industry in the New Jersey/New York area, there are approximately 8000 IS jobs. Using the target jobs of programmer or DBA, the total number of likely jobs is 2000 (i.e., (.20 × 8000)

Position	Estimated Percentage of Staff
Administration	1% per company
Application Programmer	15–20%
Technical Support, Systems Programming, System Software Support	3–5%
Data Base Administrator	3–5%
Analysts/Designers/ Software Engineers	10–15%
Project Managers	5–10%
Operations	25–35%
EDP Audit	3–5%
Consulting	3–5%
PC/User Support, Help Desk, Information Center	3–5%
Telecommunications	8–10%
Data Administration	3–5%
Other	3–5%

FIGURE 19-6   Estimated Percentage of Major IS Jobs

+ (.05 × 8000)). Multiply this by the 2% to 5% entry-level positions, and you have approximately 40 to 100 programmer and DBA entry-level positions in the pharmaceutical industry in the New Jersey–New York area available in any one year.

Estimate the Number of Competitors

Next, evaluate your competition. The competition is all graduating IS majors from local colleges and universities. The number of people moving into and out of the area are not considered here. According to *Computerworld*, the average number of computer-related majors is approximately 2.5% of entering freshman classes.[5] For our purpose, we will use this

---

5 See *Computerworld*, Vol. 27, #17, April 26, 1993, p. 105.

percentage to extrapolate to graduates. The formula used is:

Total number of graduates from four-year
  institutions
× Percent of IS graduates
= Number of competitors for IS jobs

For our example, the average number of graduates per year in the New Jersey–New York area is about 16,000. Multiply this by .025 and you find there are about 400 other entry level people against whom you will compete. Since pharmaceuticals employs less than 30% of the IS people in the metropolitan area, your competition should be (400 × .3) or about 120.

Assess Ratio

After computing the number of likely jobs and likely competition, compare the two. If the ratio of jobs to applicants is high, begin your job search. If the ratio of jobs to applicants is low (i.e., less than 1:10), you need to reassess the realism of your goals. In the example, there are 40 to 100 jobs in the industry and job desired. There are about 400 total competitors for all jobs and, on average, about 120 competitors for the same jobs desired. In a growing economy, there is a reasonable likelihood (about 83% probability) of your getting the job you defined. In a weak or falling economy, fewer jobs will be available and the probability of success would be less.

Adjust your Expectations for an Unfavorable Ratio

If you reassess, decide how realistic *this* job is. You might broaden the geographic area or job description you are searching to greatly increase your likelihood of success. If the absolute number of jobs is very low (i.e., under ten per year), then you may need to broaden your view of jobs you are willing to perform. If you want a really specialized job, such as computer game designer, then there might not be many full-time opportunities, but there may be other alternatives and issues to assess. For instance, what is the likelihood of part-time work? What are hiring practices in this industry? Are they different

in any way that you can exploit to your advantage? How willing are you to look until you find exactly *this* job?

If there are only a few jobs, but you have your heart set on one of them, plan your job campaign carefully. Why should a company hire you? List the skills and attributes that make you one of the top two candidates out of a field of hundreds. What unique skills or personality characteristics do you possess that you could exploit in this position? Make sure your resume highlights all of your attributes and succinctly summarizes all of your capabilities enough to make a personnel representative want to bring you in for interviews.

Keep in mind that companies are looking for professionals who know how to work, team players who can get along in groups, and self-motivated, domain specialists who know how to find information when they need it.[6] What sells you to a company is your potential and attitude about work. If you present a professional demeanor and appear competent, your probability of success increases.

This section summarizes an approach to locating the ideal job by defining your ideal, then matching it to realistic estimates of the number of likely jobs available in your target geographic area. Keep in mind that the percentages of industry representation for jobs is constantly in a state of change and that you need to do some research to have accurate figures. Fifteen years ago there were no PC-support groups, PC software developers, or LAN managers. Now, those and related jobs are the fastest growing segments of IS professions, just as software engineering is the largest growth position in IS.

MAINTAINING _____
PROFESSIONAL _____
STATUS _____

Above we mentioned that continuous learning is a requirement for a career in IS. With over 1,000 prod-

---

6 These traits have been discussed numerous times in *The New York Times*, *Computerworld*, *Datamation*, and other trade periodicals over the last ten years.

uct announcements and introductions a week, the field is everchanging and is changing at an ever-increasing rate. Change is a way of life. You, as a professional SE, must also change and grow to continue to be a valued employee of a company. In this section, we discuss how to develop as a professional through educational, professional, and other types of organizations. Eventually, you need to develop a 'spiral' approach to your knowledge in which you are constantly building on what you have already learned to both reinforce and fix old knowledge more strongly in your mind, and to add nuances and new information that broaden the scope of your knowledge.

Education

As a novice in IS, an undergraduate degree is sufficient for most entry-level positions. If you aspire to managerial or technical specialist positions, however, you should consider obtaining an MS or MBA in either computer science or IS, depending on how technical you wish to be.

The undergraduate degree gives you basic knowledge about the field and a quick survey of theory in developing applications and programs. The emphasis in undergraduate programs is on providing both a skill set to get you a job and a theoretical basis for continued learning in the field. The graduate program emphasizes decision making, problem analysis and solution, and theory of information systems more. The entry-level positions of people with advanced degrees is somewhat higher than that of entry-level undergraduates. The normal masters entry-level position is at an analyst or a first line manager level.

Graduation from a degree program is not sufficient to maintain your growth in the ever-changing field of information systems work. New technologies, new ways of working, new methodologies, and new organizations all demand that you maintain some currency in the field. Many politicians and educators are calling for a *learning-for-life* approach. Using this approach, you take formal degrees and supplement them with continuous education throughout your life. The learning-for-life approach is appropriate to any job in information

systems, especially jobs of software engineers. You are the expert in the deployment of new technologies for your company. As the expert, you must learn where and how to find information about any subject required. As the expert, you must try to develop some level of expertise in many fields that are not your specialization. In short, you should try to become a jack-of-all-trades *and* an expert of several.

Professional Organizations

One method to provide you continuous learning experiences while having fun at the same time is to participate in professional organizations. Every organization has conferences or conventions at least annually if not more often. Every specialty has its own organizations or special interest groups (SIGs) as part of a larger, general group. You should seek to be on panels, present papers, or simply participate in at least one conference or convention each year. Many companies pay for their employees to attend such conventions because it is in their interest to have you remain current, too.

Professional organizations are good for a variety of personal goals: keeping current, knowing what other companies are doing, and developing a network of friends for future job possibilities. It is not necessary to belong to every organization; rather, you should pick the one that maps to your goals most closely, provides the literature you most want to keep current with, and is most active in your geographic area. Each organization is discussed in terms of their membership profiles, types of professional activities sponsored, and chances for involvement of industry professionals. Some of these organizations are profiled in this section.

General Technical Organizations

There are many worthy professional organizations in which SEs can participate. Two of the oldest and largest are featured here: ACM and IEEE Computer Society. The addresses for these and other organizations are included in Figure 19-7 for your convenience in contacting them for membership information.

ACM
New York, NY

American Society for Information Science (ASIS)
Washington, DC

Association for Systems Management (ASM)
Cleveland, OH

Computing Professionals for Social Responsibility
(CPSR)
Washington, D.C.

Data Processing Management Association (DPMA)
Park Ridge, IL

Graphic Communications Computer Association
(GCCA)
Arlington, VA

IEEE
Washington, DC

The Institute for Management Sciences (TIMS)
Providence, RI

Society for Information Management (SIM)
Chicago, IL

Women in Computing (WIC)
New York, NY

FIGURE 19-7   Professional IS Organizations

The Association for Computing Machinery (ACM) is the oldest and largest organization specifically for IS professionals. The ACM was founded in 1947 and has grown to over 81,000 members. The membership ranges from beginning IS students to experienced professionals in industry, education, government, and research. ACM publishes 12 major periodicals with *Communications of the ACM (CACM)* included in the price of membership. *CACM* is generally recognized by academic researchers as *the* premier journal in computing.

Over 30 special interest groups (SIGs) whose specialties span the computing field also have their own newsletters, conferences, and symposia. The SIGs are active organizations that are constantly looking for infusions of new ideas, welcoming new members. Many of the conferences represent both industry and academic members with hundreds of active participants. A representative sample of SIGs includes SIGCHI—computer and human interaction, SIGOIS—office information systems, SIGMOD—management of data, SIGSOFT—software engineering, SIGPLAN—programming languages, SIGGRAPH—graphics, SIGBIT—business information technology, and SIGCAS—computers and society.

Opportunities for involvement include initiating local chapters of SIGs or ACM, participating in one or more of the 30–50 conferences sponsored by ACM each year, participating in any of the SIGs' or ACM's management. Almost all of the work done for ACM is voluntary and requires a time commitment, but the professional recognition and personal benefits are worth the effort.

Another organization, the Institute of Electrical and Electronics Engineers (IEEE), is a 300,000 member organization, of which about one third are members of the Computer Society. The original organization, the American Institute of Electrical Engineers, was founded in 1884 by Thomas A. Edison, Alexander Graham Bell, and Charles P. Steinmetz to foster the development of the engineering profession. Over the years the organization's name changed several times before becoming the IEEE in 1963. In the 1940s, the IEEE established a Committee on Computing Devices that evolved into the Computer Society.

The IEEE is active in all phases of engineering and computing for new and established technologies. Over 30 conferences each year are sponsored by the organization. IEEE Computer Society is known for its quality publications which include tutorials on every major technological development in recent years. The tutorials are compilations of articles exploring the issues, research directions, and likely market outcomes for new technologies and techniques (e.g., object orientation).

IEEE publications are both technically and nontechnically oriented. IEEE *Computer* and *Software* are specifically oriented to professionals working in industry who are trying to maintain current knowledge in the field. Other more technical publications are special interest publications with two of special interest to SEs: *IEEE Transactions on Software Engineering (TSE)* and *IEEE Transactions on Knowledge and Data Engineering (KDE)*. The *TSE* provides basic research papers on specification, design, development, maintenance, measurement, and documentation of applications. *TSE* is one of the best publications for early discussion of emerging techniques. Its research orientation may make it 'too technical' for some readers. *KDE* is a similar publication aimed at applications' methodologies, storage techniques, AI modeling, and development.

IEEE is subdivided into technical committees (TCs) which participate in industry standards development, conferences, and publications. There are over 20 hardware, software, and interdisciplinary TCs. The software TCs, for instance, include software engineering, computer languages, data engineering, operating systems, real-time systems, and security and privacy.

Conferences are a major TC activity with each group sponsoring one or more major conferences each year. The TC on software engineering coordinates the International Conference on Software Engineering (ICSE), which attracts about 1,500 worldwide participants annually. The major topic areas of ICSE include design, modeling, analysis, and application of software and software systems. The conference usually includes a 'tools fair' which provides vendors an opportunity to feature prototyping languages, CASE environments, language generators, and other software development support tools.

IEEE is more actively involved in standards development than most other organizations. For instance, the 802 committee is the sponsor of many LAN standards in this country. Subcommittees define, for example, the 802.3 ethernet standard. Participants in the technical standards committees are volunteers who are sponsored by their business organizations to participate in the intensive and time-consuming, but personally rewarding, standards definition activities.

Like all of the professional organizations, IEEE strives to involve all of its members in activities. Almost all of the work is voluntary and might include local chapter participation, or participation in national conferences, publications, or organizations.

There are many other equally rewarding organizations listed in Figure 19-7 that are too numerous to

detail here. There is significant overlap between the interests of *all* of the organizations, and there is room for you in one or more of them. Keep in mind that it is not necessary to join all of the organizations, but one or two help you maintain current knowledge of IS developments.

User Organizations

In addition to industry organizations, there are many professional user organizations that are sponsored by vendors for their users, or by interested individuals who share common interests.

Hardware User Organizations

Hardware user organizations are vendor-sponsored groups that are convened for users to share their use of the hardware, develop solutions to problems, and to provide guidance and requests to the vendors for future services or capabilities. The organizations are all very active and use volunteers from using organizations whose participation is sponsored by their companies. All major vendors sponsor user groups, including IBM, DEC, Unisys, CDC, Honeywell, AT&T, Sun, Apple, and so on.

IBM, for instance, has two such user organizations: GUIDE and SHARE. GUIDE is an organization of several thousand business and government installations whose use of computers is primarily for business applications, such as transaction processing or decision support applications. SHARE was founded by scientific businesses to support their special needs. Over the years, the missions of the two organizations have come to be similar, but the two organizations remain distinct. Each organization sponsors conferences and workshops several times each year. The conventions are like any professional convention, composed of general sessions in which presentations on topics of interest are made, and working sessions where commitments to work on projects or to present at future meetings are made. The working groups are completely voluntary and first time participants are recommended to attend the meetings of many working groups to get a feel for what they do.

Working group areas include hardware, operating systems, telecommunications, applications, CASE, database, data management, language (e.g., COBOL), security, audit control, and disaster recovery, to name a few.

Software User Organizations

Similar to hardware vendors, major software vendors provide user group support for their users. All user participation is voluntary and at the expense of the user's company. Software vendors include, for instance, Information Builders, Inc. for its 4GL FOCUS, Novell for its network operating system, and all major database vendors, such as Software AG for its Adabas. Each vendor schedules an annual meeting of its user group, providing the facility. Presentations by users center around using the product in their organizations and discussing innovative product use or problems and how they are overcome. The vendors also make presentations at these meetings, including tutorials about using their product and new feature announcements.

Birds-of-a-Feather Groups

Birds-of-a-feather groups are semiformal groups of IS and nonIS professionals who share an interest in some area. The topic matter might be technically specific. For instance, the Data Administration Management Association (DAMA) is a support group for people who are interested in or perform the functions of data administration in business organizations. Similar groups exist for the insurance industry, sponsored through the Life Operations Management Association (LOMA).

For some groups, the topic matter is less specific. For instance, the Boston PC Users Group which number about 15,000 members, is interested in supporting and networking PC users in the Boston metro area. Every metro area has its own user groups that are loosely organized by the type of computer or operating software they own—PC, Macintosh, Pick operating system, Unix operating system, and so on.

Professional Educational Organizations

Another approach to keeping current is to attend seminars that are organized and presented through professional education organizations. There are many noted speakers who reach their audiences in this way, for instance, James Martin, Carma McClure, and Grady Booch, just to name a few. Most such training is company sponsored because of the expense. Expect to pay $600+ per day for these courses.

When attending professionally sponsored training, several important issues should be monitored. Only choose seminars that specifically address your concerns. If you choose, for instance, object-oriented analysis, hoping to hear information about object-oriented languages, you might be disappointed.

Also, beware of the instructor. Review the entire outline of a multiday seminar to make sure that the 'name' person who is to speak actually speaks for a good portion of the time. Review the credentials of all speakers and instructors to ensure that they are qualified to teach the course. If you cannot tell from the brochure, call for more information about the person and the class.

Review outlines of courses for content to ensure that you are attending the course you think you are attending. Sometimes the names and the content are not congruous. Stay away from courses that are programming without any hands-on. If hands-on sessions are planned, assistants (or the instructor) should be present during the session, each student should have a PC, and there should be additional time available at night.

Finally, ask questions about seminar size and maximum number of participants to get a sense of your ability to interact with the instructor. Avoid sessions that have no maximum or minimum or that have maximums over 30 participants except for high-level topic introductions. You know from your own classes that class sizes over 30 are presented differently and have less intimacy between instructor and class. Similarly, less than ten people is not conducive to sharing either. In small groups, it is easier for one individual to monopolize discussion times, making the instructor's job one of personality management rather than class interaction.

Research and Academic Organizations

The last type of organization in which you might participate focuses on research and teaching of IS-related subjects. Academics have their own conventions that may serve as a forum for debate and presentation of the latest techniques and research on emerging areas of interest. They also provide an outlet for research presentations on a wide variety of topics.

The largest such conference is the International Conference on Information Systems (ICIS) which is held annually in early December. The location of the conference rotates around the world with the majority of conferences currently held in North America. The conference locations for the next several years include Vancouver, British Columbia—1994; The Netherlands—1995; Cleveland, Ohio—1996; and Atlanta, GA—1997.

Topics of interest at recent ICIS conferences include globalization of IS, object orientation, ethics and IS professionals, use of ITs in business organizations, CASE, and computer-supported diversity of organizations. Although about 90% of attendees at ICIS are academics, the remaining 10% of professionals is increasing. Panel sessions frequently include practitioners from industry. Key note addresses are mostly by local CEOs or CIOs who discuss the future of IS from their perspective.

ICIS is not a conference that all practitioners need to attend regularly. Rather, if the theme of the conference matches an interest in your organization, ICIS is a good place to hear about the latest research in the area, and to meet the people doing the research. Occasional attendance at a conference such as ICIS once every three to five years is probably enough to maintain contact with academia.

Accreditation

Professional organizations help you keep current in the field with new developments in new areas and with updates on areas you already know. Accreditation is one method to prove to the world that you indeed are expert in some area. You take an exam which is given once or twice each year, and, if you pass, you obtain a certificate that you know a particular technical area. The major proponents of general IS accreditation are professional organizations, such as DPMA, which sponsors the exams for Certified Data Processor (CDP), Certified Systems Professional (CSP) and others.

A different type of accreditation is managed and provided through vendors to certify the knowledge base of people who support their products. Novell's Certified Netware Engineer (CNE), for instance, requires the passing of an exam that follows completion of a networking and telecommunications course. The courses may be intensive one to two week events that are sponsored by the vendor, or they may be offered through a continuing education program at a local university and span several months of part-time study.

The motivation for accreditation is simple: Many people profess to be IS professionals, few really are. Those few should be rewarded by having the recognition of their knowledge and expertise. Then, when, for instance, consultants advertise their ability to perform a job, the credentials they offer have *some* instant credibility when they include accreditation ratings. The word *some* is emphasized here because passing an exam is still not the same as performing on a job. The point of accreditation is to separate those who have detailed knowledge about the field from those who do not. Having accreditation is no guarantee of work performance.

Read the Literature

Reading *is* fundamental to maintaining currency in methodologies, technologies, and industry with changes that take place as rapidly as in the information systems field. When selecting periodicals, newspapers, and/or books for keeping current, you should have a clear idea of why you are spending your hard-earned money on each purchase. For each type of literature, this section discusses what you should try to keep current on, why you should be current, the general tone and content of articles and/or chapters for the type of literature, and what you should get from reading this type of writing. The three general types of literature discussed are practitioner journals and newspapers, books, and academic research journals.

Practitioner journals/papers allow you to maintain awareness of the market place and vendors. When reading journals and newspapers, always keep in mind how applicable the products might be to your organization. These periodicals are good for finding out the latest announcements and about products that are already on the market. They provide the following:

- product introductions
- product comparisons
- case studies or descriptions of other organizations' product use

Some periodicals that are in this category include *Computerworld, Datamation, CIO, CASE Trends, PC Week, PC World, MacUser, MacWorld, Info-World, Byte, PC, LAN, LAN Week*, and so on.

Books are the next type of reading material you should maintain and read. Books provide summaries of what is currently known on a subject. Read books to increase your knowledge, learn new techniques, find out about a new area, or get ideas to try in your own company. Begin to build a library of reference materials you can use throughout your career. To do this requires careful selection of topics and authors. Seek books that provide information on the following topics as well as others of your interest and *read them!*

- New methodologies (e.g., object orientation such as Peter Coad & Ed Yourdon, *Object Oriented Analysis*, second edition)
- New techniques (e.g., normalization or entity-relationship diagramming such as Peter Chen, *Entity Modeling Techniques*)
- Intellectual development of one person's research (e.g., artificial intelligence such as Roger Schank, *Tell Me a Story*)
- Interesting approaches to solving a problem (e.g., a 37¢ mistake in a Unix LAN billing report led to a spy ring in Germany in Clifford Stoll's, *The Cuckoo's Egg*)

- New ways of combining disparate technologies that will change future ways of computing (e.g., how to combine database, object orientation, and artificial intelligence in Parsaye et al.'s, *Intelligent Database Systems*)
- Well-written and comprehensive text books on all IS topics (e.g., costing, estimating, and CoCoMo use by Barry W. Boehm *Software Engineering Economics*)
- Classics that describe the intellectual growth of IS professions (e.g., Ed Yourdon, *Writings from the Revolution*, or ACM, *Turing Award Lectures 1966–1985*)

Finally, research journals discuss the latest theories about technology use and how it impacts organizations. Many studies are empirical, that is, using a large enough sample to apply statistical techniques in analyzing the theorized behavior. You may not understand all of the statistics in such research, but you should be able to evaluate the quality of the research and assess its applicability to your organization.

Sample journals you might read periodically include *IEEE Transactions on Software Engineering, Computer, Software, Communication of the ACM, TOOIS, MIS Quarterly, Information Systems Research*, and the *IBM Systems Journal*.

AUTOMATED SUPPORT TOOLS FOR JOB SEARCH

Two types of automated tools for job search are available and growing in use. First, universities are going on-line in their support of jobs databases that are accessible to students. Gone are the days of leafing through volumes and volumes of randomly organized paper job notices. Instead, the jobs are categorized by seniority, location, salary, job classification, and other demographics. You use a query system to narrow the search and find leads for jobs in which you are interested.

Second, computer bulletin boards for jobs are available in a number of local markets and on the

TABLE 19-1   Automated and Other Support Tools for IS Career Definition

Title	Author/Source	Content
Looking for Work: An Interactive Guide to Marketing Yourself	Frank L. Greenagel, InterDigital Inc. 25 Water St. Lebanon, NJ 08833 (908) 832-2463	Under $30, provides worksheets and tips to finding the right job for you.
No Specific Shareware Title	Software Labs 100 Corporate Point Suite 195 Culver City, CA 90231 (800) 569-7900	Many diskettes available at under $4 each that offer tips on IS jobs.
Bootstrappin' Entrepreneur: The Newsletter for Individuals With Great Ideas and a Little Bit of Cash	Kimberly Stansell Suite B261 8726 S. Sepulveda Blvd. Los Angeles, CA 90045	A free booklet of tips for beginner entrepreneurs.

Internet. Internet is a network of networks that links academic, government, and business organizations worldwide. At last count, there were over one million nodes on the network and many millions of users. Internet and local bulletin boards provide local, almost free access to information about a wide range of subjects. Those relating to job search offer applicants seeking to work in small companies a means to find a company with minor effort. The use of bulletin boards, automated search systems, and other freely available information (e.g., via Internet) will grow considerably in the future.

In addition to automated advertising, tools and booklets are available to help you set your job search course. Several recent publications are listed in Table 19-1.

SUMMARY

In this chapter we discussed emerging career paths for software engineers. Computer science and information systems education are converging due to increasing overlap on areas of emphasis to both groups. While IS SEs will still predominate in business enterprises, and CS SEs will continue to be more technically oriented, both will apply systematic engineering skills and methods to the development of applications.

Next, careers in IS are classified by level and type. The levels of experience are junior, intermediate, senior, lead, technical specialist, and manager. Job types differ depending on area of specialization, including application development, application support, technical specialization, staff positions, and other positions.

Application development includes programmer, software engineer, and knowledge engineer. Application support positions include application specialists, data administration, database administration, artificial intelligence engineering, and consulting. Technical specializations are communications, LANs, systems programming, and software support. Staff positions include security, EDP audit, training, standards and technical writing, quality assurance, and technology planning. The other positions include product support, marketing, and end-user specialists.

Next, one approach to career planning was described. The steps in obtaining your next job are to decide your objective, search companies that fit your profile, assess the likelihood of your attaining the ideal job and, if necessary, adjust your expectations.

Keeping current is important to continued growth as an IS professional. Several methods of maintaining currency were discussed. First, continuous education is important to IS which undergoes continuous change. Professional organization membership and active participation are also useful to maintaining current knowledge of IS developments. Establishing your credentials through accreditation can help you attain credibility with potential employers. Continuous reading of books, periodicals, and research journals can help you continue to grow as a professional software engineer.

REFERENCES

"Computerworld 1992 salary survey," *Computerworld*, Vol. 26, May, 1992.

Kennedy, Joyce Lain, "Getting a fair share: Shareware that can help you find a job," *Dallas Morning News*, Sunday, April 18, 1993, Section D, page 1.

Krantz, Les, *The Jobs Rated Almanac*, 2nd ed. NY: Pharos Publishing, 1992.

Robert Half International, Inc., *1992 Salary Guide*. San Francisco, CA: Robert Half International, Inc., 1991.

Robert Half International, Inc., *1993 Salary Guide*. San Francisco, CA: Robert Half International, Inc., 1992.

KEY TERMS

analyst
application specialist
artificial intelligence (AI) engineer
communications analyst
consultant
data administrator (DA)
database administrator (DBA)
designer
EDP auditor
end-user specialist
junior staff member
intermediate staff member
knowledge engineer
lead staff member
local area network (LAN) specialist
manager
marketing support staff
product support staff
programmers
quality assurance
security specialist
senior staff member
software engineer (SE)
software support specialist
standards developer
system software support specialist
systems programmer
technical specialist
technical trainer
technical writer
technology surveillance specialist

EXERCISES

1. Plan your job search. Identify the type of job, the kind of company, location, and benefits you want. Do research to locate specific companies and to determine your competition. Then, compute the likelihood of getting your ideal job. Discuss your plan with the class or in small groups to assess how realistic your plan is.
2. Research the professional and user organizations that you might join and define a rationale for yourself to choose one or two in which you are interested. Join those organizations.
3. Select one or two periodicals that are of interest to you and further your professional goals. Subscribe to them if you do not already.
4. When you have decided your career goal, go to the library and perform a book search to identify potential books for your personal library. Scan five of the books, then share your information with the class, identifying the one or two of the books you intend to buy. Go buy the books and begin to build your library.
5. Choose four technologies for which you would like to become expert. Map a strategy for jobs, reading, and professional group involvement that will help you become an expert within five to ten years. Discuss your strategy in class or in small groups to assess how realistic it is and to obtain suggestions for other ways to reach your goal.

STUDY QUESTIONS

1. Define the following terms:
   analyst
   DA
   DBA
   programmer
   software engineer
   technology surveillance specialist
2. How do computer science majors and information systems majors differ in the approaches

taken by their academic programs? How do they complement each other?

3. What are the levels of experience generally used in titles to separate different levels of expertise?

4. How do the duties of a lead person differ from those of a manager?

5. How do the duties of a lead person differ from those of a technical specialist?

6. In application development, the job types are programmer, software engineer, and knowledge engineer. Define each job and describe how their job content differs.

7. How do the functions of a DA and DBA differ? How do they complement each other?

8. Why and how do companies use consultants? What are companies' expectations of consultants' knowledge?

9. How does an AI specialist differ from a knowledge engineer?

10. What are the duties of a systems programmer?

11. Why are security specialists needed in organizations?

12. Why is quality assurance in an adversarial role with application development project teams?

13. In what types of companies do product and market support people work?

14. Define the steps to planning a career.

15. Why is it important to have an objective when looking for a job?

16. How do you compute your chances of getting the job you desire in the type of company you want?

17. What are the types of organizations you might join to continue growth as an SE professional? Which type appeals the most to you?

18. Why is continued growth of both knowledge and experience important to a professional SE? What happens if you do not continue to learn?

CASES FOR ASSIGNMENTS

ABACUS PRINTING COMPANY

This case describes a currently manual process. Your job is to automate the order processing, scheduling, and customer service functions. Make sure you list any assumption you make during analysis and design.

Abacus Printing Company is a $20-million business owned and operated by three longtime friends. They are automating their order processing for the first time. Abacus Printing is located in Atlanta, Georgia and employs 20 people full-time.

The owners are the sales force. The company is set up so that each owner sells for a different, wholly-owned subsidiary (A Sub, B Sub, and C Sub) to separate commissions and expenses for tax purposes. Below is a description of the work to be automated.

Three clerks do order entry and customer service. An order is given to one of the three clerks to be entered into the order entry part of the system. Orders are batched by subsidiary for processing in the system. There is at least one batch per clerk per day. When a batch is complete, orders are printed. After orders are printed, the system should maintain individual orders for processing (i.e., the integrity of the batch is no longer needed).

Orders are printed and become internal job tickets which are used to schedule and monitor work progress. All order/job tickets go to the scheduler who sorts and prioritizes them to develop a production schedule. Each Monday, he gives the first person in the work chain (there are three possible sequences of processing) the job tickets for completion that week. As the week progresses, he adds to or changes the schedule by altering the order and adding new tickets to the stack of each person beginning a work chain. Each job goes through the same basic steps:

Step 1. Perform requested manufacturing (i.e., the engraving or printing work) according to the job ticket instructions.

Step 2. Verify quality of printed items and count output, that is, actual printed sheets of paper or envelopes. Write the actual count of items to be shipped on the job ticket.

Step 3. Update the order/job ticket with actual shipment information; print shipping papers and invoices which reflect actual shipments.

Step 4. Bundle, wrap, and ship the order.

The updating of the order with actual shipment information may be done by either the shipping clerk or by the same person who entered the order. The second printing 'closes' the order from any other changes and results in a multipart form being printed. Two of the parts are copies of the invoices, showing all prices and other charges with a total amount due. One invoice copy is sent to the customer; the other is filed for further processing by accounts receivable. The third part of the set of forms is the bill of lading, or shipping papers, that shows all information except money amounts. The fourth part of the form is filed numerically by invoice number in a sequential history file. The fifth part is filed in a customer file which is kept in alphabetic sequence.

The system must allow order numbering by subsidiary company, and must be able to print different subsidiary name headers on the forms. The clerks batch orders so that only orders from one subsidiary are in each batch. Order types include recurring orders, blanket orders (which cover the year with shipments spaced out over the period), and orders with multiple ship-to addresses that differ from the sold-to addresses.

When customers call to change or determine the status of an order, the clerk taking the call first checks the customer file to see if the order is complete. Then, he or she checks with the scheduler to see if the order is in the current day's manufacturing mix. If the order is not complete or scheduled, he or she manually searches current orders to find the paperwork. About 15% of customer calls are answered while the customer is on the phone. About 80% require research and are answered with a call back within 30 minutes. The remaining 5% require tracking, which results in identifying an order taken verbally by a partner and never written down. Customers have been complaining of the lost orders and threatening to go elsewhere with their business.

The current computer system is a smart typewriter and storage facility. The owner wants to provide personal computer access via a local area network for the three partners, three clerks, two shipping staff, and one scheduler. He would like to eliminate the numerical and alphabetical paper filing systems but wants to maintain the information on-line indefinitely for customer service queries.

The managers want ad hoc reporting access to the information at all times. The senior clerk is also the accounting manager and, along with the owner, should be allowed access to an override function to correct errors in the system. The other clerks should be allowed to perform data entry for order processing and actual goods shipped, and to print invoices/shipping papers. The shipping clerk should be allowed to perform order updates with actual goods shipped and to generate shipping papers with a final invoice. The scheduler should be allowed access to all outstanding orders to alter and schedule work for the manufacturing processes. No one else in the company should be allowed access to the system or to the data.

AOS Tracking System

The AOS case is a logical description of a desired application that also includes manual problems to be corrected.

The manager of Administrative Office Services (AOS) wants to develop an automated application to track work through its departments. The departments and services provided include: word processing and proofing, graphic design, copying, and mailing. Work can come into any of the departments, and any number of services might be combined. For instance, word processing and proofing can be the only service. Word processing, proofing, and graphic design might be combined. Another job might include all of the services.

The current situation is difficult because each manager has some knowledge of the work in his or her own area, but not where work is once it leaves their area. Overall coordination for completing jobs using multiple services requires the AOS manager to give each department a deadline. Then, the AOS manager must track the jobs to ensure that they are completed and moved along properly.

The basic work in each department is to receive a job, check staff availability based on work load and skills, assign staff, priority, and due date, and update job information (for instance, if the work is reassigned). Jobs are identified by a unique control number that is assigned to each job. Other job information maintained includes: requestor name, requestor phone, requestor budget code, manner of receipt (either fax, paper, or phone dictation), manner of delivery (either fax, paper, or phone dictation), and dates and times work is received, due, completed, canceled, notified, and returned to requestor.

A job consists of requests for one or more types of service. For each type of service, information must also be kept. Services include word processing and proofing, copying, graphic design, and mailing.

Information kept for word processing and proofing services includes a description of the job, type of request (letter, memo, statistics, legal document, special project, chart, manual, labels, etc.), other services included with this request (i.e., copying, graphic design, mailing), software to be used (Word-Perfect, Harvard Graphics, Lotus, Bar Coding, Other), type of paper (logo, plain bond, user provided, envelope, other), color of paper (white, pink, blue, green, buff, yellow, other), paper size (8.5" × 11", 8.5" × 14", other), special characteristics (2-hole punch, 3-hole punch, other), type of envelope (letter, legal, letter window, legal window, bill, kraft 9" × 12", kraft 10" × 13", supplied by requestor, other), number of copies requested, user control number, dates/times required, started, completed, reassigned, proof started, proof completed, revisions started, and revisions completed.

Information kept for copying includes the above except software and dates/times relating to proofing and revisions. In addition, keep requirements for collating, stapling, one-side or two-side, special formats (e.g., reduced 60% and put side-by-side in book format).

Information kept for graphic design and mailing includes that for word processing, except type of envelope. The code schemes for type of request, paper, software, and special characteristics are different from those used for word processing. For instance, paper for graphics refers to type of output media which might actually include slide, transparency, paper, envelope, video still, photograph, moving video, and so on. The type of request must be expanded to include the number of colors, specific color selections, intended usage (intracompany, external, advertising, public relations, other) and level of creativity (i.e., user provides graphic and this department automates the design; user provides

concept and this department provides several alternative designs, etc.).

Information kept for mailing includes requested completion date, and the dates and times requests were received, completed, and acknowledged back to requestor as complete. Other information includes whether or not address labels were provided, mailing list to be used (choice of four), number of pieces, method of mailing (e.g., zip+four, carrier route code, bar code, bulk, regular, special delivery, etc.), machinery required (e.g., mail inserter, mail sorter, etc.), and source of mailing (e.g. word processing in AOS, user, other).

As a department's staff gets an incoming job, it should be logged into the system, assigned a log number, and the job information should be entered into the system. In addition, the receiving department completes their service-specific information (e.g., typing) and identifies the sequence of departments which will work on the job. As the individual departments get their task information, they complete the service-specific fields.

Each department manager assigns a person to the task based on skills and availability. First, information matching service requests to staff skills should be done. Then, the staff with required skills should be ordered by their earliest availability date for assignment to the task. The system should allow tracking (and retrieval) of a task by job, department/task, person doing the work, date of receipt, due date, or user.

The manager of AOS would like to receive a monthly listing of all comments received (usually they are complaints) and be able to query details of the job history to determine the need for remedial action. Comments should be linked to a job, service, user, and staff member.

THE CENTER FOR CHILD DEVELOPMENT

This case describes a currently manual process. The analysis and design task is to develop a new work

TABLE 1   Client Card File Information

Last Name
First Name
Middle Initial

Fiscal Year
Medicaid Number
    Family Identifier
    Line/Person Identifier
    Sex
    Year of Birth
    Diagnosis Code (NA)
    Issue Date
Dates of Visits
Fees per Week
Amount Paid
Balance Due (Updated Monthly)

flow and automated system for as much of the Medicaid payment process as possible.

The Center for Child Development (CCD) is a not-for-profit agency that provides psychiatric counseling to children, serving approximately 600 clients per year. Each client has at least one visit to CCD per week when they are in therapy. Most often, the client has multiple visits to the center and to other agencies in one day (e.g., to CCD and, say, to a hospital). Medicaid reimburses expenses for only one such visit per day. This means that multiple appointments at CCD for a given day will have one appointment reimbursed; multiple claims on the same Medicaid number for the same day are paid on a first-in, first-paid basis by Medicaid. The current claims processing takes place monthly; for CCD to remain competitive, Medicaid processing must be done daily. To provide daily Medicaid processing, automation of the process is required. The Medicaid Administration has arranged with personal computer owners to take claims in automated form on diskettes, provided that they conform to the information and format requirements of paper forms.

To develop Medicaid claims, the business office clerk reviews the client card file to obtain Medicaid number and visit information for each client (see Table 1 for Client Card File Information and Table 2 for Visit Card File Information recorded). Based on the card file information, Medicaid forms are completed: one per client with up to four visits listed on each form (see Table 3 for Medicaid information required). Most clients have multiple forms produced because they have more than four visits to the center per month. Each form must be completed in its entirety (i.e., top and bottom) for Medicaid to process them (the forms cannot be batched by client with only variable visit information supplied).

One copy of each form is kept and filed in a Medicaid–Pending Claims File. The other copies of the forms (or disks) are mailed to Medicaid for processing.

About four to six weeks after submission of claims, Medicaid sends an initial determination report on each claim. The response media is either diskette or paper. Reconciliation of all paid amounts is done by manually matching the Medicaid report information with that from the original claim. If automated, report entries are in subscriber (i.e., CCD client) sequence. The paid claims are then filed in a Medicaid–Paid Claims File.

Claims that are disputed by Medicaid (almost 90% are pending on the initial report; of pending claims, 10–20% are ultimately denied) are researched and followed up with more information as required. Electronic reconciliation in other companies reduces the 90%-pending to as few as 10%, thus speeding the reimbursement process. CCD has a contact at Medicaid with whom they work closely to resolve any problems.

TABLE 2   Visit Information

Day
Date
Type Appointment (i.e., Intake, Regular)
Client Name
Time of Appointment
Single/Group Visit
Amount Paid
Amount Owed
Insurance Company
Medicaid (Y/N)
Last Date Seen
Therapist

TABLE 3 Medicaid Claim Form Information

Permanently Assigned Fields	Information Completed by CCD
Company Name (CCD)	Billing Date (must be within 90 days of service)
Invoice Number (Assigned by Medicaid, preprinted on the forms)	Recipient ID Number (Client Medicaid Number)
	Year of Birth
Group ID Number (Not Applicable, i.e., NA)	Sex
Location Code (03)	Recipient (Client) Name
Clinic (827)	Social Worker License Number
Category (0160)	Name of Social Worker
Number of Attachments (NA)	Primary/secondary diagnosis (Table look-up, 120 entries)
Office Number (NA)	Date of Service
Place of Service (NA)	Procedure Code (This is a two-line entry to identify first the treatment payment on the first line and the treatment code on the second line.)
Social Worker Type (NA)	
Coding Method (6)	
Emergency (N, i.e., No)	Procedure Description
Handicapped (N)	Times Performed
Disability (N)	Amount
Family Planning (N)	Name of person completing the form
Accident Code (0)	Date
Patient Status (0)	
Referral Code (0)	
Abort/Sterile Code (0)	
Prior Approval Number (NA)	
Ignore Dental Insurance (Y)	

(Information in parentheses is the permanent value of that field for CCD)

COURSE REGISTRATION SYSTEM

This case is a logical description of the desired application. Your task is to analyze and design the data and processes to develop an automated application to perform course registration.

A student completes a registration request form and mails or delivers it to the registrar's office. A clerk enters the request into the system. First, the Accounts Receivable subsystem is checked to ensure that no fees are owed from the previous quarter. Next, for each course, the student transcript is checked to ensure that the course prerequisites are completed. Then, class position availability is checked. If all checks are successful, the student's social security number is added to the class list.

The acknowledgment back to the student shows the result of registration processing as follows: If fees are owing, a bill is sent to the student; no registration is done and the acknowledgment contains the amount due. If prerequisites for a course are not filled, the acknowledgment lists prerequisites not met and that course is not registered. If the class is full, the student acknowledgment is marked with 'course closed.' If a student is accepted into a class, the day, time, and room are printed next to the course number. Total tuition owed is computed and printed on the acknowledgment. Student fee information is interfaced to the Accounts Receivable subsystem.

Course enrollment reports are prepared for the instructors.

Dr. Patel's Dental Practice System

The dental practice uses a manual patient and billing system to serve approximately 1,100 patients. The primary components of the manual system are scheduling patient appointments, maintaining patient dental records, and recording financial information. Due to increased competitive pressure, Dr. Patel desires to automate his customer records and billing.

New patients must complete the patient history form. The data elements are listed in Table 1. Then, at the first visit, the dentist evaluates the patient and completes the second half of the patient history information with standard dental codes (there are 2,000 codes) to record recommended treatments. The data elements completed by the dentist are listed as Table 2. The patient history form is filed in a manila folder, with the name of the patient as identification, along with any other documents from subsequent visits.

A calendar of appointments is kept by the secretary, who schedules follow-up visits before the patient leaves the office. The calendar data elements are shown as Table 3. Also, before the patient leaves, any bills, insurance forms, and amounts due are computed. The client may pay at that time, or may opt for a monthly summary bill. The secretary maintains bill, insurance, and payment information with the patient history. Financial data elements are shown in Table 4. Every week, the secretary types mailing labels that are attached to appointment

reminder cards and mailed. Once per month, the secretary types and sends bills to clients with outstanding balances.

TABLE 1   Patient History Information

Patient name
  Address
  City
  State
  Zip
  Home telephone
  Date of birth
  Sex
  Parent's name (if under 21) or emergency contact
    Address
    City, state, zip
    Telephone number
  Known dental problems (room for 1–3)
  Known physical problems (room for 1–3)
  Known drug/medication allergies (room for 1–3)

Place of work name
  Address
  City
  State
  Zip
  Telephone number

Insurance carrier
  City, state, zip
  Policy number

Last dentist name
  Address
  City, state, zip

Physician name
  City, state, zip

TABLE 2   Dentist Prognosis Information

Dentist performing evluation
  Date of evaluation
  Time of evaluation
  Recommended treatment (room for 1–10 diagnoses and treatments)
  Procedure code
  Date performed (completed when performed)
  Fee (completed when performed)

TABLE 3   Appointment Calendar

Patient name
    Home telephone number
    Work telephone number
    Date of last service
    Date of appointment
    Time of appointment
    Type of treatment planned

TABLE 4   Patient Financial Information

Patient name
    Address
    City, state, zip
    Home telephone number
    Work telephone number
    Date of service
    Fee
    Payment received
    Date of payment
    Adjustment
    Date of adjustment
    Outstanding balance
    Date bill sent
    Date overdue notice sent

THE EAGLE ROCK GOLF LEAGUE

This is a logical description of a desired application. The task is to analyze and design the data and processes required to track golfers and rounds of golf, including computation of match rankings.

The members of the Eagle Rock Golf League regularly compete in matches to determine their comparative ability. A match is played between two golfers; each match either has a winner and a loser, or is declared a tie. Each match consists of a round of 18 holes with a score kept for each hole. The person with the lowest gross score (gross score = sum of all hole scores) is declared the winner. If not a tie, the outcome of a match is used to update the ranking of players in the league: The winner is declared better than the loser and any golfers previously beaten by the loser. Other comparative rankings are left unchanged.

The application should keep the following information about each golfer: name, club ID, address, home phone, work phone, handicap, date of last golf round, date of last golf match, and current match ranking.

Each round of golf should also be tracked including golfer's club ID, name, scores for all 18 holes, total for the round, match indicator (i.e., Yes/No), match opponent ID (if indicator = Y), winner of the match, and date of the match. The application should allow golfers to input their own scores and allow any legal user to query any information in the system. Only the system should be allowed to change rankings. Errors in data entry for winters or losers should be corrected only by a club employee.

GEORGIA BANK AUTOMATED TELLER MACHINE SYSTEM

Georgia Bank describes an application to be developed. The functional requirements are described at a high level of abstraction and the task is to do more detailed analysis or to begin design.

The Georgia Bank is automating an automated teller machine (ATM) network to maintain its competitive position in the market. The bank currently processes all deposit and withdrawal transactions manually and has no capability to give up-to-the-minute balance information. The bank has 200,000 demand-deposit account (DDA, e.g., checking account) customers and 100,000 time deposit (e.g., savings account) customers. All customers have the same account prefix with a two-digit account type identifier as the suffix.

The ATM system should provide for up to three transactions per customer. Transactions may be processed via ATM machines to be installed in each of the 50 branches and via the AVAIL™ network of

Georgia banks. The system should accept an ATM identification card and read the ATM card number. The ATM card number is used to retrieve account information including a personal ID number (PIN) and balances for each DDA and time account. The system should prompt for entry of the PIN and verify its correctness. Then the system should prompt for type of transaction and verify its correctness.

For DDA transactions, the system prompts for amount of money to be withdrawn. The amount is verified as available, and if valid, the system instructs the machine to dispense the proper amount which is deducted from the account balance. If the machine responds that the quantity of money required is not available, the transaction is aborted. A transaction acknowledgment (customer receipt) is created. If the amount is not available or is over the allowable limit of $250 per day per account, an error message is sent back to the machine with instructions to reenter the amount or to cancel the transaction.

For time deposit transactions, the system prompts for amount of money to be deposited and accepts an envelope containing the transaction. The amount is added to the account balance in transit. A transaction acknowledgment is created.

For account balances, the system prompts for type of account—DDA or time—and creates a report of the amount. At the end of all transactions, or at the end of the third transaction, the system prints the transaction acknowledgment at the ATM and creates an entry in a transaction log for all transactions. All other processing of account transactions will remain the same as that used in the current DDA and time deposit systems.

The customer file entries currently include customer ID, name(s), address, social security number, day phone, and for each account: account ID, date opened, current balance, link to transaction file (record of most recent transaction). The transaction file contains: account ID, date, transaction type, amount, source of transaction (i.e., ATM, teller initials) and link to next most recent transaction record. The customer file must be modified to include the ATM ID and password. The transaction log file contains ATM ID, account ID, date, time, location, transaction type, account type, and amount.

SUMMER'S INC. _____
SALES TRACKING _____
SYSTEM _____

This case describes a manual system for sales tracking. Your design should include work procedures and responsibilities for all affected users.

Summer's Inc. is a family-owned, retail office-product store in Ohio. Recently, the matriarch of the family sold her interest to her youngest son who is automating as much of their processing as possible. Since accounting and inventory management were automated two years ago, the next area of major paper reduction is to automate retail sales to floor processing.

The sales floor has four salespersons who together serve an average of 100 customers per day. There are over 15,000 items for sale, each available from as many as four vendors. The system should keep track of all sales, decrease inventory for each item sold, and provide an interface to the A/R system for credit sales.

A sale proceeds as follows. A customer selects items from those on display and may request ordering of items that are not currently available. For those items currently selected, a sales slip is created containing at least the item name, manufacturer's item number (this is not the same as the vendor's number), retail unit price, number of units, type of units (e.g. each, dozen, gross, ream, etc.), extended price, sales tax (or sales exemption number), and sale total. For credit customers, the customer name, ID number, and purchaser signature are also included. The sales total is entered into a cash register for cash sales and the money is placed into the register. A copy of the sales slip is given to the customer as a receipt, and a copy is kept for Summer's records. For orders or credit sales, the information kept includes customer name, ID number, sale date, salesman initials, and all details of each sales slip. For credit sales, a copy of credit sale information should be in an electronic interface to the accounting system where invoices are created.

In the automated system, both cash and credit sales must be accommodated, including the provision of paper copy receipts for the client and for

Summer's. The inventory database should be updated by subtracting quantity sold from units on hand for that unit type, and the total sales amount for the year-to-date sales of the item should be increased by the amount of the sale. The contents of the inventory database are shown in Table 1.

TABLE 1 Summer's Inc. Inventory Database

General Item Information

Item Name (e.g. Flair Marker, Fine-Point Blue; Flair Marker, Wide-Point Blue, etc.)
Item Manufacturer
Date began carrying item
  Units information*
  Unit type (e.g., each, dozen, gross, etc.)
  Retail unit cost
  Units on order
  Units on hand
  Total units sold in 1993

  Vendor-Item Information*
  Vendor ID
  Vendor item ID
    Vendor-units information*
    Unit type (e.g., each, dozen, gross, etc.)
    Last order date
    Discount schedule
    Wholesale unit cost

Vendor General Information

Vendor ID
Vendor name
Vendor address
Terms
Ship method
Delivery lead time
  Item-Information
  Vendor item ID
  Unit type (e.g., each, dozen, gross, etc.)
  Last order date
  Discount schedule
  Wholesale unit cost

(Note: Primary keys are underlined; repeating groups are identified with a boldface name and an asterisk.)

TECHNICAL CONTRACTING, INC.

Technical Contracting, Inc. (TCI) describes a manual process to be automated. The data and processes are approximately equally complex; both require some analysis and design before the automated application can be designed. First, decide what information in the problem description is relevant to an automated application for client-contractor matching, then proceed with the assignment.

TCI is a rapidly expanding business that contracts IS personnel to organizations that require specific technical skills in Dallas, TX. Since this business is becoming more competitive, Dave Lopez, the owner, wants to automate the processing of personnel placement and resume maintenance.

The files of applicant resumes and skills are coded according to a predefined set of skills. About 10 new applicant resumes arrive each week. A clerk checks the suitability of the resume for the services TCI provides and returns unsuitable resumes with a letter to the applicant. The applicant is invited to reapply when they have acquired skills that are in high demand, several of which are listed in the letter. High-demand jobs are determined by counting the type of requests that have been received in the last month. Resumes of applicants are added to the file with skills coded from a table. There are currently 200 resumes on file that are updated every six months with address, phone, skills, and project experience for the latest period. Most of the resume information is coded. There is one section per project for a text description. This section is free-form text and allows up to 2,500 characters of description.

Client companies send their requests for specialized personnel to TCI either by mail, phone, or personal delivery. For new clients, one of TCI's clerks records client details such as name, ID, address, phone, and billing information. For each requirement, the details of the job are recorded, including skill requirements (e.g., operating system, language, analysis skills, design skills, knowledge of file structures, knowledge of DBMS, teleprocessing knowledge, etc.), duration of the task, supervisor name, supervisor level, decision authority name, level of difficulty, level of supervision required, and hourly rate. For established clients, changes are made as required.

Once a day, applicant skills are matched to client requirements. Then Dave reviews the resumes and, based on his knowledge of the personalities involved, selects applicants for interviewing by the client company. When Dave selects an applicant, the resume is printed and sent with a cover letter. Dave follows up the letter with a phone call three days later. If the client decides to interview the applicant(s), Dave first prepares them with a sample interview, then they are interviewed by the client.

Upon acceptance of an applicant, two sets of contracts are drawn up. A contract between TCI and the client company is developed to describe the terms of the engagement. These contracts can be complicated because they might include descriptions of discounts in billings that apply when multiple people are placed on the contract, or might include longevity discounts when contractors are engaged over a negotiated period of time. A contract between TCI and the applicant is developed to describe the terms of participation in the engagement. Basically, the applicant becomes an employee of Dave's organization for the duration of the contract.

TCI keeps information on demand for each type of skill, whether they provide people with the skill or not. Dave also monitors TCI performance in filling requests for each skill and evaluating lost contracts due to nonavailability of applicants (to raise his fees for those services, and to advertise for those skills). TCI advertises for applicants with specific skills when client demand for new skills reaches three requests in any one month, or when demand for skills already on file increases to such an extent that the company is losing more than three jobs per month.

XY UNIVERSITY MEDICAL TRACKING SYSTEM

The XY University case is a brief logical description of a simple tracking system with a complex data structure. The key to a good design is to analyze and define the data and services properly.

XY University student medical center serves a student population of 60,000 students and faculty in a large metropolitan area. Over 300 patients receive one or more medical services each day. The university has a new president who wishes to overhaul the existing medical support structure and modernize the facilities to improve the services. In order to plan for these changes, more information on which services are in fact used is required. The university wishes to develop a patient tracking system that traces each patient throughout their stay in school for each visit to the facility.

Students and faculty are identified by their identification numbers. They should be logged into the system (i.e., date, time, and ID) when they enter the facility. They may or may not have appointments. Then, some means of recording and entering information into the computer system must be provided for each of the following: station visited, medical contact person, type of contact (i.e., consultation, treatment, follow-up check, routine checkup, emergency, etc.), length of contact, diagnosis, treatment, medicine prescribed (i.e., name, brand, amount, dosage), and follow-up advised (yes/no). All information must be available for query processing and all queries must be displayed either at terminals or on printers.

GLOSSARY

abstract data type   In object orientation, the user-defined data type that encapsulates definitions of object data plus legal processes for that data.

action diagram   In information engineering, a graphical representation of procedural structure and processing details suitable for automated code generation.

activity   In information engineering, some procedure within a business function that can be identified by its input data and output data which differ.

afferent flows   In structured design, the input-oriented processes which read data and prepare it for processing.

affinity   Attraction or closeness.

affinity analysis   In information engineering, a clustering of business processes by the closeness of their functions on data entities they share in common.

analysis   The act of defining what an application will do.

application   The set of programs that automate some business task.

application characteristic   Descriptive information that is common to all applications and includes data, processes, constraints, and interfaces.

application complexity   Fundamental application difficulty which comes from several sources, including management of the number of elements in the application, the degree and types of interactions, support, novelty, and ambiguity.

application type   The business orientation of the application as transactional, query, decision, or intelligent.

architecture   A snapshot of some aspect of an organization, e.g., data, business processes, technology, or communications network.

associative data relationships   Irregular entity relationships, dictated by data content rather than abstractions such as normalization.

atomic process   A system process that cannot be further decomposed without losing its system-like qualities.

attribute   In object orientation, a named field or property that describes a class/object or a process.

audit control   Application design components that prove transaction processing in compliance with legal, fiduciary, or stakeholder responsibilities.

backup   The process of making extra copies of data to ensure recoverability.

baseline   A product that is considered complete and which is the basis for other current work by the project development team.

batch applications   Computer applications in which transactions are processed in groups.

benchmark   A comparison test used to identify differences between hardware or software products.

benefit   Some improvement in the work product or process that results from a specific alternative.

bid   The financial response to an RFP. Bid types for hardware are lease, lease with option to buy, or purchase. For software, bid types are time and materials (T&M), T&M with a ceiling, or fixed price.

binding   In object orientation, the process of integrating the code of communicating objects. Binding of objects to operations may be static, pseudo-dynamic, or dynamic.

black box   A testing strategy that determines correctness of functioning by creating input data is designed to generate variations of outputs without regard as to how the logic actually functions. Black-box strategies include equivalence partitioning, boundary value analysis, and error guessing.

body of screen   The large middle part of a screen containing application-specific variable information.

boilerplate   Code that is invariant from one program to another, regardless of program function.

Booch diagram   In object orientation, a graphical representation of all objects and their processes in the application, including both service and problem domain objects.

bottom-up testing   A testing strategy that tests complete modules, assuming that the lower the number of incremental changes in modules, the lower the error rate.

bracket   In information engineering, a graphical structure on an action diagram.

business activity   In information engineering, some high level set of procedures within a business function.

business area analysis   In information engineering, a tabular clustering of processes which share data creation authority for an entity.

business function   In information engineering, a group of activities that accomplish some complete job that is within the mission of the enterprise.

business process   Details of an activity, fully defining the steps taken to accomplish the activity.

cardinality The number of an entity relationship; can be one-to-one, one-to-many, or many-to-many.

CASE integration The absence of barriers between one graphical or text form and others.

central transform In structured design, processes having as their major function the change of information from its incoming state to some other state.

champion A manager who actively supports and sells the goals of the application to others in the organization.

change control Project management techniques for dealing with changes to specifications, application functions, documentation, etc.

class In object orientation, like objects that have exactly the same properties, attributes, and processes.

class hierarchy In object orientation, the basic hierarchy of relationships between classes of objects that also accommodates lattice-like network relationships.

class/object In object orientation, a set of items which share the same attributes and processes, and manage the instances of the collection.

client object In object orientation, an object that requests a process from a supplier object.

code The low-level program elements of the software product created from design documentation; procedural computer instructions.

code generator A program that reads specifications and creates code in some target language, such as Cobol or C.

coding The stage of application development during which computer code is generated.

cohesion A measure of internal strength of a module with the notion that maximal or functional cohesion is the goal.

command language High-level programming languages that communicate with software to direct its execution.

composite cost model (CoCoMo) A combination of estimating techniques based on thousands of delivered source instructions.

compromise of requirements A change to application functions to rescope, manipulate, drop, or otherwise change them to fit the environment's limitations.

computer-aided software engineering (CASE) A computer application that automates the development of graphics and documentation of application design. CASE can be intelligent and include verification capabilities to ensure syntactic correctness of information entered.

concurrent processes In object orientation, processes that operate at the same time and can be dependent or independent.

configuration management Management of software code libraries.

constraint Limitations on the behavior and/or processing of entities, including prerequisite, postrequisite, time, structure, control, or inferential.

context A setting or environment.

context diagram A graphic developed during structured analysis to define the interactions of the application with the external world.

contingency planning The identification of tasks designed to prevent risky events and tasks to deal with the events if they should occur.

control point A location (logical or physical) in a procedure (automated or manual) where the possibility of errors exists.

controlled redundancy The deliberate duplication of data for control purposes.

conversion The placing of a computer application into production use; includes direct cutover, functional, geographic methods.

cost The amount of money or other payment for obtaining some benefit.

cost/benefit analysis The comparison of the financial gains and payments that would result from selection of some alternative.

coupling A measure of intermodule connection with minimal coupling of the goal (i.e., less is best).

critical path The sequence of interrelated tasks during application development that takes the most time to develop.

critical success factor Some business activity or function that is crucial to the organization's success.

CRUD matrix *See* entity/process matrix.

cutover A method of conversion such that, on a set day, the old way of work is abandoned and the new way begins to be used.

data The elements in raw material—numbers and letters—that relate to each other to form fields (or attributes) which define entities.

data administration (DA) The management of data to support and foster data sharing across multiple divisions, and to facilitate the development of database applications.

data characteristics Descriptive information about data including ambiguity, completeness, semantics, structure, time-orientation, and volume.

data collection techniques Methods of obtaining information and application requirements, including interviews, meeting, observation, questionnaires, temporary job assignment, document review, and external source review.

data dictionary   In structured analysis, a compilation of detailed definitions for each element in a DFD.

data distribution choices   In data distribution analysis, possible designs include data centralizing, replicating, vertical partitioning, subset partitioning, or federating.

data flow diagram   In structured analysis, a graphic representation of the application's component parts.

data methodology   Those development methods that begin defining functional requirements by first evaluating data and their relationships to determine the underlying data architecture.

data model   A conceptual description of the major data entities of interest in an organization for reengineering, or in an application for subject area database definition.

data self-sufficiency   A property of application target organizations such that 70% (or more) of data used in performing the business functions originates within the subject organizations.

data type   A language-fixed definition of data, e.g., integers.

data warehouse   The means to store unlimited, continuously growing databases.

data-oriented methodology   Approaches to developing applications that assume data are fundamentally more stable than processes and should, therefore, be the focus of activities.

database administration (DBA)   An organization created to maintain and monitor DBMS use, including responsibility for physical DB design, disk space allocation, and day-to-day operations support for the actual database.

denormalization   The process of designing storage items of data to achieve performance efficiency.

decision support applications (DSS)   Applications whose purpose is to seek to identify and solve problems.

depth of hierarchy   In structured design, the number of levels in the diagram.

derived field   Fields/attributes for which the application is the source, i.e., computed fields.

design   The act of defining how the requirements defined during analysis will be implemented in a specific hardware/software environment.

developmental tests   Testing conducted by the project development team, including unit, subsystem, integration, and system tests.

dialogue   In object orientation and information engineering, interactive communication that takes place between the user and the application, usually via a terminal, to accomplish some work.

dialogue flow diagram   In information engineering, a diagram summarizing allowable movement between entries on a menu structure diagram.

direct manipulation   Screen interactions during which the user performs an action directly on some display object.

display   The screen portion of a computer.

distributed computing   A situation in which multiple processors share responsibility for managing pieces of an application.

divide and conquer   The principle in structured analysis by which a complex application problem is divided into its parts for individual analysis. A technique to simplify management of application complexity.

document   A general analysis and design task that is performed to create useful documents from graphics and supporting text either manually or with computer-based tools.

domain   A conceptual area of interest. In organizational reengineering the domains are data, process, network, and technology; in database, a domain is the set of allowable values for an individual attribute.

downsizing   The shifting of processing and data from mainframes to some other, less expensive environment, usually to a multiuser midsize machine, such as an IBM AS400, or to a LAN of PCs.

efferent flows   In structured design, the output-oriented processes which write, display, and print data.

elaboration   A general analysis and design task that is performed to define the details of each thing identified.

elementary process   *See* atomic process.

encapsulation   In object orientation, a property of programs that describes the complete integration of data with legal processes relating to the data.

entity   In information engineering, some person, object, concept, application, or event from the real world about which we want to maintain data; includes attributive, associative, and fundamental entity types.

entity relationship diagram   In information engineering, a graphical representation of the normalized data environment and data scope of the application.

entity/process matrix (CRUD)   A two-dimensional table of entities and business processes that identifies the functions each process is allowed to perform on data, including create, retrieve, update and delete (e.g., CRUD).

equifinality   Many paths lead to the same goal.

estimating   Use of expertise to define project work effort, including use of algorithms, models, delphi techniques, expert opinion, function points, top-down, and bottom-up techniques.

ethical dilemma Any situation in which a decision results in unpleasant consequences requiring moral reasoning.

ethics The branch of philosophy that studies moral judgment and reasoning.

exception handling The extent to which programs can be coded to intercept and handle program errors without abending a program.

executable units In structured design for non-real-time languages an execute unit is a link-edited load module. For real-time languages, an execute unit identifies modules that can reside in memory at the same time and are related, usually by mutual communication.

executive information system (EIS) A spinoff from DSS. EIS applications support executive decision making and provide automated environmental scanning capabilities.

expert systems (ES) application Computer applications that automate the knowledge and reasoning capabilities of one or more experts in a specific domain.

external entity In structured analysis, a person, place or thing with which the application interacts.

facilitator A specially trained individual who runs JAD, fast-track, JRP, or walk-through sessions.

factoring In structured design, the process during which net outputs from a DFD are used to determine the initial structure of the structure chart.

fast track A different name for JAD.

feasibility The analysis of risks, costs, and benefits relating to technology, economics, and using organizations.

field format The characteristics of individual fields or values of fields on a screen display, including size, font, style, color, and blink for individual field values, and coding options for field labels.

flash rate Blinking speed for a screen display item.

flicker fusion A physical phenomenon that causes us to see constant light when the flash rate is very high.

footer The lower portion of a screen.

form follows function A principle from architecture which, when applied to structured analysis, defines application functions that transform data as the defining characteristic of applications.

frozen specification A specification that cannot be changed without specific user/sponsor approval with accompanying modification of budget and cost.

function A small program that is self-contained and performs a well-defined, limited procedure.

function key A programmable computer keyboard key used to provide a shortcut command.

function point analysis A method of defining the com-

plexity of an application by systematic definition of global application characteristics.

functional decomposition The division of processes into modules.

functional screen A screen at which the application processes are performed.

generalization class In object orientation, defines a group of similar objects.

global data Data variables and constants that are accessible to any module in the application.

globalization The movement of otherwise local businesses into world markets.

goals of software engineering To build a quality product through a quality process.

group decision support systems (GDSS) A special type of DSS applications. GDSS provide an historical memory of the decision process in support of groups of decision makers who might be geographically dispersed.

hardware installation plan A plan identifying work required, environmental changes (e.g., air conditioning), work responsibilities, timing of materials and labor, and scheduling of tasks as they relate to the installation of computer and other information technology equipment.

hierarchical structure chart In structured design, a graphical input-process-output view of the application that reflects the DFD partitioning.

human interface The means by which an application communicates to its human users.

Humphrey's maturity framework A framework adapted to compare methodologies as having reached initial, repeatable, managed, defined, or optimizing levels of sophistication.

hypermedia Software that allows any number of associative relationships to be defined for a given item; supports audio, video, image, graphics, text and data.

I/O bound In structured design, a structure chart in which the skew is equally balanced between input and output, but processing is a small part of the application.

identification A general analysis and design task that is performed to find the focal things that belong in analysis and how logical requirements will work in the target computer environment in design.

implementation The period of time during which a software product is integrated into its operational environment and is phased into production use. Implementation includes the completion of data conversion, installation, and training.

information engineering (IE) A data-oriented methodology that borrows from both practice and theoretical research to support the development of enterprise level plans through to individual project developments. IE concentrates on business understanding, assumes user involvement, and covers more phases of the SPLC than most other methodologies.

information hiding   A program design principle by which only data needed to perform a function is made available to that function.

information systems architecture framework (ISA)   Zachman's method of defining distinct architectures relating business context to application context at progressively more detailed levels.

information systems methodology framework   A standard for comparing methodologies based on their representation forms and types of information supported.

information systems plan (ISP)   An enterprise level analysis of data, processes, and technology that includes manual or automated work to capture a snapshot of the enterprise in order to define and prioritize applications for development.

inheritance   In object orientation, a property that allows the generic description of objects which are then reused by related objects.

input-bound   In structured design, a structure chart in which the skew is on the input side.

instance   In information engineering, a specific occurrence of an entity, e.g., entity = customer, instance = Sam Jones.

integration test   Tests that verify the logic and processing for suites of modules that perform some activity, verifying communications between them.

interdependence   A way of describing the interrelationships between organizations; includes pooled, sequential, and reciprocal relationships.

interface   Some person, application, or organization with which an application must communicate.

iterative project life cycle   A cyclic repetition of analysis, design, and implementation activities.

joint application development/design (JAD)   A special form of structured meeting during which user representatives, application developers, and a facilitator meet continuously over several days to define the functional requirements of an application.

language constructs   Features of computer languages that determine what and how operations on data are carried out.

learn-as-you-go project life cycle   An approach to the development life cycle that assumes every project is so unique that it has no prior precedent upon which to base activities.

legacy data   Data used by outdated applications that are required to be maintained for business records.

legacy systems   Applications that are in a maintenance phase but are not ready for retirement.

leveled set of DFDs   Verified balanced set of entities, data flows and processes within a hierarchic DFD diagram set.

leverage point   Some business or application activity from which a competitive advantage can be gained.

librarian   A person working with an application development or maintenance team to provide librarian services relating to maintenance of documentation, code objects, reusable modules, etc.

local data   Data variables and constants that are used only within a given module.

logical data model   An abstract definition of data in an organization that describes the way a user views data

maintenance   The changes made to the logic of the system and programs to fix errors (perfective), provide for business changes (adaptive), or make the software more efficient.

make/buy decision   The tradeoff between building the item in-house or purchasing it elsewhere.

memory management   The ability of a program to allocate more computer random-access memory (RAM) as required.

menu   Lists of options on a screen from which a selection is made.

menu structure   In information engineering, a diagram translating process alternatives into a hierarchy of menu selection options for an application.

message   In object orientation, the unit of communication between two objects.

meta-class   In object orientation, classes whose instances are other classes.

meta-data   Data about data that gives meaning to data and is information about data, e.g., data type= integer.

meta-meta-data   Information about the meta-data that describes its allowable use to the application, e.g., type=hardware.

methodology   Procedures, policies, and processes used to direct the activities of each phase of a software life cycle, including process, data, object, semantic, or none.

model   A conceptual definition of something, e.g., logical data, physical data, business processes, etc.

modularity   The structured design principle that calls for design of small, self-contained units that should lead to maintainability.

module   *See* program package.

morphology   Form or shape. In structured design, morphology refers to the shape of a structure chart.

multimedia   A term that describes the integration of object orientation, data base, and storage technologies in one environment.

multitasking   In object orientation, the simultaneous execution of sets of processes.

multitasking objects   In object orientation, objects that track and control the execution of multiple threads of control.

multiple inheritance   In object orientation, the ability to share attributes and processes from multiple class/ objects.

net present value (NPV)   A mathematical method of comparing multiperiod projects that equalizes the cost estimates by accounting for the time value of money.

normalization   The refinement of data relationships to remove repeating information, partial key dependencies, and nonkey dependencies.

object   In object orientation, an instance of the class definition.

object-based   A design that is based on object thinking, but is not object-oriented in its implementation.

object-oriented analysis   A methodology for analyzing data objects and their allowable processes as encapsulated and having inheritable properties.

object-oriented methodology   An approach to system life cycle development that takes a top-down, encapsulated view of data objects, their allowable actions, and the underlying communication requirement to define an application architecture.

off-site storage   A location usually 200+ miles away from the main computing site used to store backup copies of databases, software, etc.

on-line application   Applications that provide interactive processing to the user with or without immediate file update.

operations   The daily processing of a computer application.

option selection   The choice for application navigation from among menus, command languages, and windows used to get to a functional screen.

organizational reengineering   An evaluation of an organization's data, processes, technologies, and communications needs to ensure that its goals as stated in its mission statement are met.

out-of-the-box thinking   Examining a problem or issue without respect to the current context to determine novel approaches to resolving the issue.

output-bound   In structured design, a structure chart in which the skew is on the output side.

package specification   In object orientation, defines the public interface for both data and processes for each object, and the private implementations and language to be used. Similar to a program specification in non-object methodologies.

packages   In object orientation, a set of modules relating to an object which might be modularized for execution.

part class   In object orientation, defines a component of a whole class.

partitioning   The basic activity of dividing processes into modules.

peer-to-peer networking   A computer communications network in which intelligent sharing of resources and data across multiple processors is taking place.

persistent object   An object that is maintained over time, a database item.

physical data model   The physical definition of data, describing its layout for a particular hardware device.

physical database design   The actions required to map a logical database to storage devices in a specific DBMS implementation environment.

physical input and output   The movement of data between external computer (e.g., disk) storage and random-access memory (RAM). I/O statements (e.g., read/write) may be record-oriented, set-oriented, or array-oriented.

polymorphism   In object orientation, the ability to have the same process take different forms when associated with different objects.

presentation format   The method chosen for summarizing information for screen display, including analog, digital, binary graphic, bar chart, column chart, point plot, pattern display, mimic display, text, and text forms.

primary key   A unique set of values comprised of one or more attributes identifying an entity, an object, or a database item, depending on the context.

private part (of a class/object)   In object orientation, defines local, object-only data and the specific procedures each action takes.

problem space   In object orientation, identifies objects/ processes that are required to describe the problem, but are not required to describe the solution.

problem-domain objects   In object orientation, the class/objects and objects defined during analysis and describing the application functions.

process   The sequence of instructions or conjunction of events that operate on data.

process data flow diagram (PDFD)   In information engineering, a graphical representation of processes and the data and event triggers that initiate processing. The PDFD is the basis for action diagrams in IE design.

process dependency diagram   In information engineering, a graphical representation of the sequence and types of relationships among processes.

process diagram   In object orientation, graphical representation of the hardware environment showing process assignments to hardware.

process model   A conceptual description of the business processes of an organization.

process-oriented analysis   A method of analyzing application transformation processing as the defining characteristic of applications.

process-oriented methodology   Methodologies that take a structured, top-down approach to evaluating problem processes and the data flows with which they are connected.

process/location matrix   In data distribution analysis, a table containing processes and, for each location under analysis, the major and minor involvement in performing each process.

program package   In structured design, one or more called modules, and functions, and in-line code that will be an execute unit to perform some atomic process. Also called a program unit.

program specification   A description of a program's purpose, process requirements, the logical and physical data definitions, input and output formats, screen layouts, constraints, and special processing considerations that might complicate the program.

program template   Standard code that performs a simple function.

program unit   *See* program package.

programming   The process of designing and describing an algorithm to solve a class of problems.

project life cycle   The breakdown of work for initiation, development, maintenance, and retirement of an application.

project manager (PM)   The person with primary responsibility for organization liaison, project staff management, and project monitoring and control. The PM also performs activities with the SE including project planning, assigning staff to tasks, and selecting from among application approaches.

project plan   A summary of the project planning effort that identifies the work breakdown tasks, their interrelationships, and the estimated time to complete each task.

prototyping   The building of a subset of an application to assist in requirements definition, to test a proof of concept, or to provide a partial solution to a particular problem.

pseudo-code   Specification of processing using the syntax from a programming language in abbreviated form for easy translation.

public part (of a class/object)   In object orientation, defines what data are available in the object and the allowable actions of the object.

quality assurance (QA)   Any review of an application development work product by a person who is not a member of the project team to determine whether or not the analysis requirements are satisfied.

quality assurance (QA) test   A test by an outside agent to determine that functional requirements are satisfied. The outside agent can be a user or a user representative.

query application   Another term for data analysis applications.

question   Words phrasing an asking sentence that can be open-ended, without a specific answer, or closed-ended and requesting a yes/no or very short specific answer.

reentrant   A property of a module that allows it to be shared by several tasks concurrently.

real-time application   Applications that process transactions and/or events during the actual time that the related physical (real-world) process takes place.

recovery   The process of restoring a previous version of data (or software) from a backup copy to active use following some damage to, or loss of, the previously active copy.

recursive   A property of modules such that they call themselves or call another module that, in turn, calls them.

regression test   Customized tests to check that changes to an application have not caused it to regress to some state of unacceptable quality.

relationship   In entity-relationship diagrams, mutual association between two or more entities. It is shown as a line connecting the entities; includes one-to-one, one-to-many, and many-to-many relationship cardinalities.

repository   A data dictionary in a CASE environment that contains not only data, file, process, entity, and data flow definitions, but also contains definitions of all graphical forms, their contents, and allowable definitions (e.g., entity-relationship diagram, process decomposition, etc.)

request for information (RFI)   A formal request for information on some product that usually precedes the RFP process.

request for proposal (RFP)   A written request for bids on some product, providing formal requirements, ground rules for responses, and, usually, a standard format for the proposal responses. ,

request for quotation (RFQ)   *See* request for proposal.

responsiveness   The underlying time orientation of the application as batch, on-line, or real-time.

retirement   The period of time in the software life cycle during which support for a software product is terminated.

reusability   Also called serial reusability, a property of a module such that many tasks, in sequence, can use the module without its having to be reloaded into memory for each use.

reusable components   Programs, functions, or program fragments that are specially designed for use in more than one program.

reusable module   A small, single function, well-defined, and standardized program module that can be used as a called routine or as a copy book in COBOL.

reverse engineering   *See* software reengineering.

review   A general analysis and design task that is to analyze quality of the reviewed product.

risk   Events that would prevent the completion of, in this case, an application development alternative in the manner or time desired.

risk assessment   A method of determining possible sources of events that might jeopardize completion of the application.

round-trip gestalt   In object orientation, an iterative approach to detailed design in which prototypes are built in an incremental development life cycle.

scaffolding   Extra code to support the stubs, partial modules, and other pieces of the application, usually created to support top-down testing.

scheduling   In object orientation, the process of assigning execution times to a list of processes.

scheduling objects   In object orientation, objects that define sequential, concurrent-asynchronous (i.e., independent), or concurrent-synchronous (i.e., dependent) processes.

scope   Definition of the boundaries of the project: what is in the project and what is outside of the project.

scope of effect   In structured design, the collection of modules that are conditionally processed based on decisions by the module under review.

screen formats   The general layout of a screen display including definition of the menu/selection format, the presentation format, and individual field formats.

security plan   A plan identifying the physical, data, and application means used to protect corporate information and technology assets.

semantic methodology   Methodologies used in the automation of artificial intelligence (AI) applications, including recognizing, reasoning, and learning applications.

sequential development life cycle (SDLC)   A subcycle of the SPLC, including phases for analysis, conceptual design, design, implementation, testing, installation and checkout, and ending with delivery of an operational application.

sequential project life cycle (SPLC)   The period of time from inception to retirement of a computer application. Phases in SPLC include: initiation, problem definition, feasibility, requirements analysis, conceptual design, design, code/unit test, testing, installation/checkout, operations and maintenance, and retirement.

server object   In object orientation, an object that performs a requested process (i.e., client/server processing).

service objects   In object orientation, manage application operations, including synchronizing, scheduling or multitasking objects, as required.

skew   In structured design, a term to describe the lopsidedness of a program structure chart.

social methodology   An approach to SDLC that attends to social and job-related needs of individuals who supply or receive or use data from the application being built.

software engineer   Skilled professionals who have a variety of skills that they apply using engineering-like techniques to the definition, design, and implementation of computer applications.

software engineering   Systematic development, operation, maintenance, and retirement of software.

software reengineering   The reverse analysis of an old application to conform to a new methodology, usually information engineering or object orientation.

solution space   In object orientation, identifies objects/processes that are required both to describe the problem, and to develop a solution.

specialization class   In object orientation, a subclass that reflects an *is-a* relationship, defining a more detailed description of the gen class.

sponsor   A manager who pays for the project and acts as its champion.

stakeholders   People and organizations affected by an application.

state   In object orientation, a specific configuration of attribute values of an object.

state transition diagram   In object orientation, defines allowable changes for data objects.

structure chart   In structured design, a hierarchic, input-process-output view of the application that reflects the DFD partitioning.

structured decomposition   A technique for coping with

application complexity through the principle of "divide and conquer."

structured design   The art of designing system components and the interrelationships among those components in the best possible way to solve some well-specified problem.

structured English   Language-independent specification of processing using a restricted subset of English.

structured systems analysis   A process-oriented analysis methodology that defines a top-down method of defining and graphically documenting procedural aspects of applications.

subsystem design   Subphase of the design phase during which the application is divided into relatively independent chunks for detailed specification.

subsystem test   *See* integration test.

subdomain   In object orientation, application design is seen as taking place in four distinct domains: human, hardware, software, and data. Encapsulated class/objects (or a subset of them) are assigned to one of the subdomains during design.

subject area data base   In information engineering, a database that supports one or more business functions.

supplier object   In object orientation, an object that performs a requested process.

synchronizing   The coordination of simultaneous events.

synchronizing objects   In object orientation, objects that provide a rendezvous for two or more processes to come together after concurrent operations.

synthesis   A general analysis and design task that is performed to build a unified view of the application, reconciling any parts that do not fit, and representing requirements in graphic form.

system test   A test to verify that the functional specifications are met, that the human interface operates as desired, and that the application works in the intended operational environment within its constraints.

systems theory   A theory defining inputs as fed into processes to produce outputs with feedback providing a check on the process.

task profile   A description of the job(s) to be performed using a computer application.

technology transfer   The large-scale introduction of a new technology to some previously nontechnical environment.

test case   Individual transactions or data records that cause logic to be tested.

test plan   Documents the strategy, type, cases, and scripts for testing some component of an application. All of the plans together comprise the test plan for the application.

test script   Documents the interactive dialogue that takes place between user and application, and the changes that result from the dialogue for on-line and real-time applications.

test strategy   The overall approach to testing at some level, used to guide the tester in developing test cases. Test strategies are white-box, black-box, bottom-up or top-down. They are not mutually exclusive and are usually used in combination.

testing   A phase of the SDLC during which the application is exercised for the purpose of finding errors.

thread of control   In object orientation, a set of potentially concurrent processes. Usually, a single thread of control relates to a single user or a single application-level transaction.

time events   In object orientation, the business, system, or application occurrences that cause processes to be activated.

time-event diagram   In object orientation, a diagram depicting the relationships among processes that are triggered by related events or have constraints on processing time.

top-down   A perspective that begins the activity (e.g., analysis or design) at an abstract level and proceeds to more detailed sublevels.

top-down development   A way of thinking about problems that begins at a high level of abstraction and works through successively more detailed levels.

top-down testing   A testing strategy that assumes that critical control code and functions will be developed and tested first and followed by secondary functions and supporting functions.

transaction analysis   In structured design, a method of analyzing generic activities by transaction type to develop structure charts of processing.

transaction processing application (TPA)   Applications that support the day-to-day operations of a business, e.g., order processing.

transaction volume matrix   In data distribution analysis, a table summarizing volume of transaction traffic by location.

transform analysis   In structured design, a method of identifying the central transform through analysis of afferent and efferent flows.

trigger   In information engineering, some data or event that causes a business process to execute.

type 1 error   Defines code that does not do what it is supposed to do; errors of omission.

type 2 errors   Defines code that does something it is not supposed to do; errors of commission.

type checking   The extent to which a language enforces matching of specific data definitions in mathematical and logical operations; includes typeless, mixed-mode, pseudo-strong, and strong.

unit test   Tests performed by the author on each of the code units.

user-managed application development   The overall management of application development by the user/sponsor of the project to foster a business partner relationship with IS staff and to improve the quality of the finished product.

user profile   A description of the user(s) of a computer application.

utility object   *See* service object.

validation   A review to establish the fitness or quality of a software product for its operational purpose.

vendor response   A proposal in response to an RFP.

verification   A review to establish the correctness of correspondence between a software product and its specification.

walk-through   A formal, structured meeting held to review work products and find problems.

white box   A testing strategy that uses logic specifications to generate variations of processing and to predict the resulting outputs. White-box strategies look at specific logic to verify how it works, including various levels of logic tests, mathematical proofs, and cleanroom testing.

whole class   In object orientation, defines a composed object type.

windows   A form of direct manipulation of the environment that combines full screen, icon symbols, menus, and point-and-pick devices to simplify the human interface by making it represent a metaphorical desk environment.

work around   A rethinking of an application design caused by limitations of the language, package, or target environment.

working set   The minimal, real random-access memory (RAM) required by software when it is running.

INDEX